TEACHER'S EDITION

Thinking About Psychology

The Science of Mind and Behavior

TEACHER'S EDITION

The Science of Mind and Behavior

Charles T. Blair-Broeker
Cedar Falls High School, Iowa

Randal M. Ernst
Lincoln High School, Nebraska

Special Consultant:
David G. Myers
Hope College, Michigan

Teacher's Edition written by
Amy C. Fineburg
Homewood High School, Alabama

With additional materials by
Kristin H. Whitlock
Viewmont High School, Utah

Worth Publishers

Publisher: Catherine Woods
Sponsoring Editor: Graig Donini
Development Editor: Elaine Epstein
Senior Marketing Manager: Renée Altier
Associate Managing Editor: Tracey Kuehn
Production Editor: Danielle Pucci
Production Manager: Barbara Anne Seixas
Art Director: Barbara Reingold
Cover and Text Designer: Lissi Sigillo
Cover art: Marie Bertrand (*Untitled,* 2002)
Composition: TSI Graphics
Printing and Binding: R. R. Donnelley and Sons Company

ISBN: 0-7167-5525-4

Printed in the United States of America
First printing, 2003

Worth Publishers
41 Madison Avenue
New York, New York 10010
www.worthpublishers.com

Preface

Resources for *Thinking About Psychology*: A Roadmap for Instruction

Active learning is at the heart of any successful psychology course. Psychology is the scientific study of what it means to be human; it gives students an opportunity to delve into the intricacies of their own lives. The sheer volume of activity opportunities provides teachers with a smorgasbord of lesson ideas designed to engage students in the high-level critical thinking, analytical, and evaluative skills desired by parents, teachers, and the community at large. Although the variety and volume of activities offer great freedom and flexibility, they can also seem overwhelming to manage. What activities suit your students' specific learning needs? Which ones offer variety of instruction? How much preparation will you need to present a particular activity? All these questions (and more) were fundamental to our development of the teacher's resource package for *Thinking About Psychology*. This *Teacher's Edition* is designed to be a roadmap to teaching a high school psychology course using the resources that accompany this text. It is our hope that this *Teacher's Edition* will be a useful, user-friendly tool for planning, preparing, and presenting the concepts in *Thinking About Psychology*.

National Standards: A Tool for Promoting Excellence

In August, 2000, the American Psychological Association approved the adoption of the *National Standards for the Teaching of High School Psychology*, a document that outlines the fundamentals of the teaching of psychology as a scientific discipline (**http://www.apa.org/ed/hscontents.html**). These standards, authored by a committee of outstanding high school teachers (including the two authors of this textbook – Charlie Blair-Broeker and Randy Ernst), outline the areas in psychology that should be addressed in high school classrooms, ensuring that each student who takes a standards-based course will get an accurate picture of this scientific, vibrant discipline. The National Standards are divided into five main content areas called domains. These domains are further divided into "Standard Areas," that reflect major units of psychological inquiry, and "Content Standards" that describe what students should comprehend after completing a particular unit. "Performance Standards" indicate what the student should be able to do within a specific Content Standard. *Thinking About Psychology* was written to align with these national standards by organizing the text into the same 5 domains as the national standards: methods, biopsychological, cognitive, developmental, and sociocultural. The chapters of the text reflect the Standard Areas, while each module within the chapter encompasses the Content and Performance Standards. Information presented in this *Teacher's Edition* ties the Standard Areas, Content Standards, and Performance Standards to the textbook.

A common problem faced by many high school psychology instructors is figuring out what units to teach in a standards-based psychology course. Realizing that it is virtually impossible to cover all of the Standard Areas, the task force recommended that teachers select one or two units from each of the five domain areas. When choosing units, teachers should consider

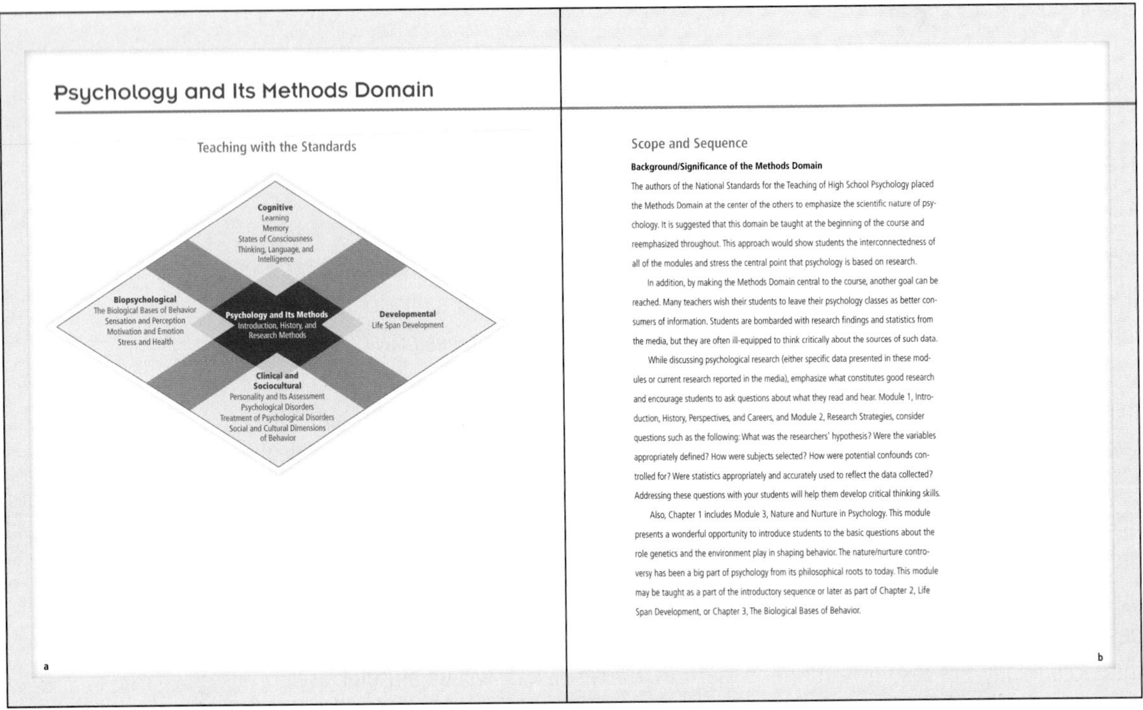

Psychology and Its Methods Domain

Teaching with the Standards

a

Scope and Sequence

Background/Significance of the Methods Domain

The authors of the National Standards for the Teaching of High School Psychology placed the Methods Domain at the center of the others to emphasize the scientific nature of psychology. It is suggested that this domain be taught at the beginning of the course and reemphasized throughout. This approach would show students the interconnectedness of all of the modules and stress the central point that psychology is based on research.

In addition, by making the Methods Domain central to the course, another goal can be reached. Many teachers wish their students to leave their psychology classes as better consumers of information. Students are bombarded with research findings and statistics from the media, but they are often ill-equipped to think critically about the sources of such data.

While discussing psychological research (either specific data presented in these modules or current research reported in the media), emphasize what constitutes good research and encourage students to ask questions about what they read and hear. Module 1, Introduction, History, Perspectives, and Careers, and Module 2, Research Strategies, consider questions such as the following: What was the researchers' hypothesis? Were the variables appropriately defined? How were subjects selected? How were potential confounds controlled for? Were statistics appropriately and accurately used to reflect the data collected? Addressing these questions with your students will help them develop critical thinking skills.

Also, Chapter 1 includes Module 3, Nature and Nurture in Psychology. This module presents a wonderful opportunity to introduce students to the basic questions about the role genetics and the environment play in shaping behavior. The nature/nurture controversy has been a big part of psychology from its philosophical roots to today. This module may be taught as a part of the introductory sequence or later as part of Chapter 2, Life Span Development, or Chapter 3, The Biological Bases of Behavior.

b

Domain Opener, pp. a–b

the length of their course, the needs of their students, and their own strengths. The national standards are not meant to be a rigid set of guidelines, but rather a guide for teachers to help them design courses that present a balanced picture of the field of psychology.

Each domain opens with a description of how that particular domain fits into the framework of the national standards (see above). This section offers scope and sequence suggestions that provide guidance about what to teach and when to teach it. By using the suggestions on these pages, teachers can be sure they are covering the concepts that are central to an understanding of psychology.

Each chapter is preceded by a detailed outline called **Teaching with the Standards**. The Standard Areas and Content Standards covered in each module of the chapter, as well as the pages where the material appears, are listed here. In addition, **Scope and Sequence** charts provide suggestions for pacing content in specific modules, and list the standards achieved in each lesson.

Finally each module is preceded by a detailed list of the **Performance Standards** that are covered in the module. Performance indicators highlight how students might demonstrate their knowledge of the standards. These indicators can help guide teachers to choose activities and assessments that will effectively demonstrate knowledge and mastery of the objectives for the course.

Note that the Content Standards and Performance Standards in each Standard Area are numbered consecutively starting with the number 1. Be aware that there are many Content and Performance Standards numbered 1, 2, 3, or 4. We have tried to include the appropriate domain or Standard Area at the top of each page that lists Content and Performance Standards to help you reference the appropriate section of the standards.

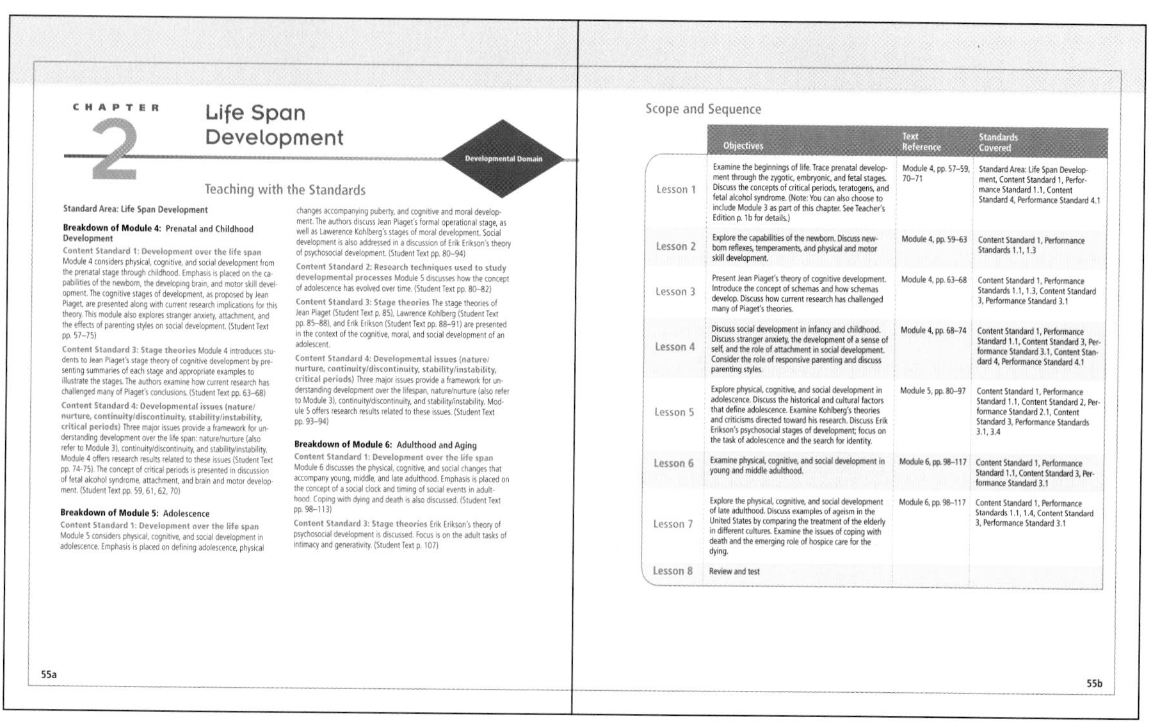
CHAPTER 2

Life Span Development

Developmental Domain

Teaching with the Standards

Standard Area: Life Span Development

Breakdown of Module 4: Prenatal and Childhood Development

Content Standard 1: Development over the life span Module 4 considers physical, cognitive, and social development from the prenatal stage through childhood. Emphasis is placed on the capabilities of the newborn, the developing brain, and motor skill development. The cognitive stages of development, as proposed by Jean Piaget, are presented along with current research implications for this theory. This module also explores stranger anxiety, attachment, and the effects of parenting styles on social development. (Student Text pp. 57–75)

Content Standard 3: Stage theories Module 4 introduces students to Jean Piaget's stage theory of cognitive development by presenting summaries of each stage and appropriate examples to illustrate the stages. The authors examine how current research has challenged many of Piaget's conclusions. (Student Text pp. 63–68)

Content Standard 4: Developmental issues (nature/nurture, continuity/discontinuity, stability/instability, critical periods) Three major issues provide a framework for understanding development over the life span: nature/nurture (also refer to Module 3), continuity/discontinuity, and stability/instability. Module 4 offers research results related to these issues (Student Text pp. 74-75). The concept of critical periods is presented in discussion of fetal alcohol syndrome, attachment, and brain and motor development. (Student Text pp. 59, 61, 62, 70)

Breakdown of Module 5: Adolescence

Content Standard 1: Development over the life span Module 5 considers physical, cognitive, and social development in adolescence. Emphasis is placed on defining adolescence, physical changes accompanying puberty, and cognitive and moral development. The authors discuss Jean Piaget's formal operational stage, as well as Lawerence Kohlberg's stages of moral development. Social development is also addressed in a discussion of Erik Erikson's theory of psychosocial development. (Student Text pp. 80–94)

Content Standard 2: Research techniques used to study developmental processes Module 5 discusses how the concept of adolescence has evolved over time. (Student Text pp. 80–82)

Content Standard 3: Stage theories The stage theories of Jean Piaget (Student Text p. 85), Lawrence Kohlberg (Student Text pp. 85–88), and Erik Erikson (Student Text pp. 88–91) are presented in the context of the cognitive, moral, and social development of an adolescent.

Content Standard 4: Developmental issues (nature/nurture, continuity/discontinuity, stability/instability, critical periods) Three major issues provide a framework for understanding development over the lifespan, nature/nurture (also refer to Module 3), continuity/discontinuity, and stability/instability. Module 5 offers research results related to these issues. (Student Text pp. 93–94)

Breakdown of Module 6: Adulthood and Aging

Content Standard 1: Development over the life span Module 6 discusses the physical, cognitive, and social changes that accompany young, middle, and late adulthood. Emphasis is placed on the concept of a social clock and timing of social events in adulthood. Coping with dying and death is also discussed. (Student Text pp. 98–113)

Content Standard 3: Stage theories Erik Erikson's theory of psychosocial development is discussed. Focus is on the adult tasks of intimacy and generativity. (Student Text p. 107)

55a

Scope and Sequence

	Objectives	Text Reference	Standards Covered
Lesson 1	Examine the beginnings of life. Trace prenatal development through the zygotic, embryonic, and fetal stages. Discuss the concepts of critical periods, teratogens, and fetal alcohol syndrome. (Note: You can also choose to include Module 3 as part of this chapter. See Teacher's Edition p. 1b for details.)	Module 4, pp. 57–59, 70–71	Standard Area: Life Span Development, Content Standard 1, Performance Standard 1.1, Content Standard 4, Performance Standard 4.1
Lesson 2	Explore the capabilities of the newborn. Discuss newborn reflexes, temperaments, and physical and motor skill development.	Module 4, pp. 59–63	Content Standard 1, Performance Standards 1.1, 1.3
Lesson 3	Present Jean Piaget's theory of cognitive development. Introduce the concept of schemas and how schemas develop. Discuss how current research has challenged many of Piaget's theories.	Module 4, pp. 63–68	Content Standard 1, Performance Standards 1.1, 1.3, Content Standard 3, Performance Standard 3.1
Lesson 4	Discuss social development in infancy and childhood. Discuss stranger anxiety, the development of a sense of self, and the role of attachment in social development. Consider the role of responsive parenting and discuss parenting styles.	Module 4, pp. 68–74	Content Standard 1, Performance Standard 1.1, Content Standard 3, Performance Standard 3.1, Content Standard 4, Performance Standard 4.1
Lesson 5	Explore physical, cognitive, and social development in adolescence. Discuss the historical and cultural factors that define adolescence. Examine Kohlberg's theories and criticisms directed toward his research. Discuss Erik Erikson's psychosocial stages of development; focus on the task of adolescence and the search for identity.	Module 5, pp. 80–97	Content Standard 1, Performance Standard 1.1, Content Standard 2, Performance Standard 2.1, Content Standard 3, Performance Standards 3.1, 3.4
Lesson 6	Examine physical, cognitive, and social development in young and middle adulthood.	Module 6, pp. 98–117	Content Standard 1, Performance Standard 1.1, Content Standard 3, Performance Standard 3.1
Lesson 7	Explore the physical, cognitive, and social development of late adulthood. Discuss examples of ageism in the United States by comparing the treatment of the elderly in different cultures. Examine the issues of coping with death and the emerging role of hospice care for the dying.	Module 6, pp. 98–117	Content Standard 1, Performance Standards 1.1, 1.4, Content Standard 3, Performance Standard 3.1
Lesson 8	Review and test		

55b

Chapter Opener, pp. 55a–55b

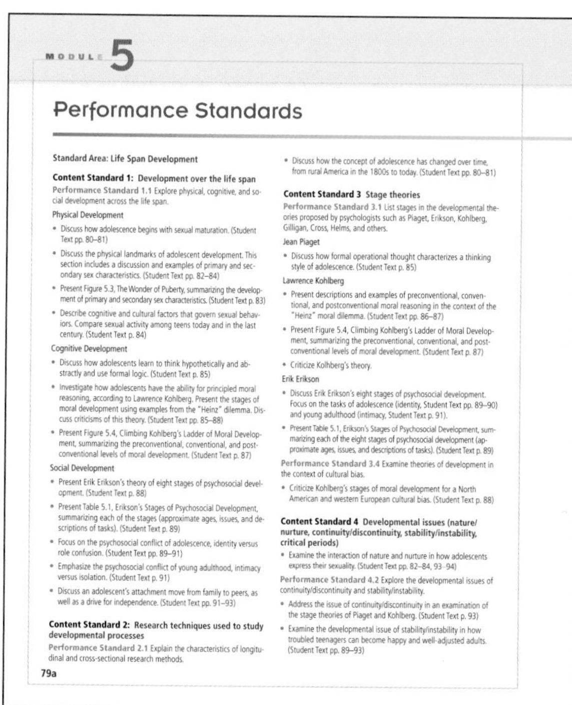
MODULE 5

Performance Standards

Standard Area: Life Span Development

Content Standard 1: Development over the life span

Performance Standard 1.1 Explore physical, cognitive, and social development across the life span.

Physical Development

- Discuss how adolescence begins with sexual maturation. (Student Text pp. 80–81)
- Discuss the physical landmarks of adolescent development. This section includes a discussion and examples of primary and secondary sex characteristics. (Student Text pp. 82–84)
- Present Figure 5.3, The Wonder of Puberty, summarizing the development of primary and secondary sex characteristics. (Student Text p. 83)
- Describe cognitive and cultural factors that govern sexual behaviors. Compare sexual activity among teens today and in the last century. (Student Text p. 84)

Cognitive Development

- Discuss how adolescents learn to think hypothetically and abstractly and use formal logic. (Student Text p. 85)
- Investigate how adolescents have the ability for principled moral reasoning, according to Lawrence Kohlberg. Present the stages of moral development using examples from the "Heinz" dilemma. Discuss criticisms of this theory. (Student Text pp. 85–88)
- Present Figure 5.4, Climbing Kohlberg's Ladder of Moral Development, summarizing the preconventional, conventional, and postconventional levels of moral development. (Student Text p. 87)

Social Development

- Present Erik Erikson's theory of eight stages of psychosocial development. (Student Text p. 88)
- Present Table 5.1, Erikson's Stages of Psychosocial Development, summarizing each of the stages (approximate ages, issues, and descriptions of tasks). (Student Text p. 89)
- Focus on the psychosocial conflict of adolescence, identity versus role confusion. (Student Text pp. 89–91)
- Emphasize the psychosocial conflict of young adulthood, intimacy versus isolation. (Student Text p. 91)
- Discuss an adolescent's attachment move from family to peers, as well as a drive for independence. (Student Text pp. 91–93)

Content Standard 2: Research techniques used to study developmental processes

Performance Standard 2.1 Explain the characteristics of longitudinal and cross-sectional research methods.

- Discuss how the concept of adolescence has changed over time, from rural America in the 1800s to today. (Student Text pp. 80–81)

Content Standard 3 Stage theories

Performance Standard 3.1 List stages in the developmental theories proposed by psychologists such as Piaget, Erikson, Kohlberg, Gilligan, Cross, Helms, and others.

Jean Piaget

- Discuss how formal operational thought characterizes a thinking style of adolescence. (Student Text p. 85)

Lawrence Kohlberg

- Present descriptions and examples of preconventional, conventional, and postconventional moral reasoning in the context of the "Heinz" moral dilemma. (Student Text pp. 86–87)
- Present Figure 5.4, Climbing Kohlberg's Ladder of Moral Development, summarizing the preconventional, conventional, and postconventional levels of moral development. (Student Text p. 87)
- Criticize Kolhberg's theory.

Erik Erikson

- Discuss Erik Erikson's eight stages of psychosocial development. Focus on the tasks of adolescence (identity, Student Text pp. 89–90) and young adulthood (intimacy, Student Text p. 91).
- Present Table 5.1, Erikson's Stages of Psychosocial Development, summarizing each of the eight stages of psychosocial development (approximate ages, issues, and descriptions of tasks). (Student Text p. 89)

Performance Standard 3.4 Examine theories of development in the context of cultural bias.

- Criticize Kohlberg's stages of moral development for a North American and western European cultural bias. (Student Text p. 88)

Content Standard 4 Developmental issues (nature/nurture, continuity/discontinuity, stability/instability, critical periods)

- Examine the interaction of nature and nurture in how adolescents express their sexuality. (Student Text pp. 82–84, 93–94)

Performance Standard 4.2 Explore the developmental issues of continuity/discontinuity and stability/instability.

- Address the issue of continuity/discontinuity in an examination of the stage theories of Piaget and Kohlberg. (Student Text p. 93)
- Examine the developmental issue of stability/instability in how troubled teenagers can become happy and well-adjusted adults. (Student Text pp. 89–93)

79a

Module Performance Standards, p. 79a

Using *The National Standards for the Teaching of High School Psychology* will help take the guesswork out of creating an excellent course that meets the needs of high school psychology students.

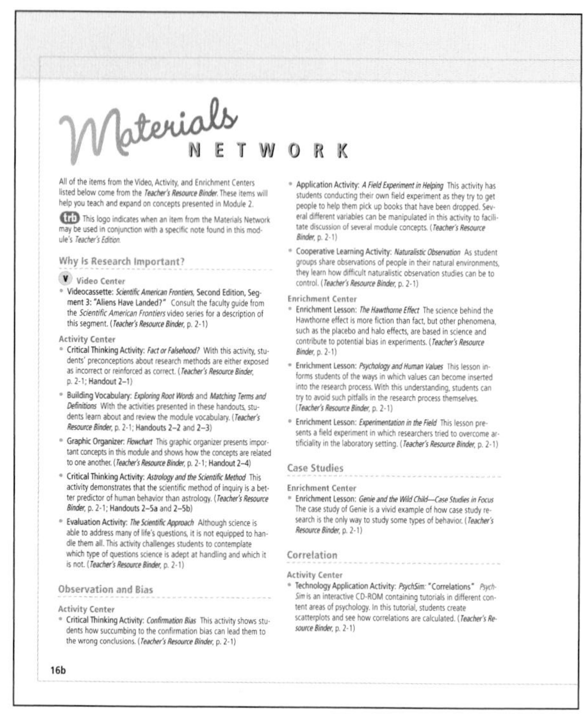

Materials NETWORK

All of the items from the Video, Activity, and Enrichment Centers listed below come from the *Teacher's Resource Binder*. These items will help you teach and expand on concepts presented in Module 2.

trb This logo indicates when an item from the Materials Network may be used in conjunction with a specific note found in this module's *Teacher's Edition*.

Why Is Research Important?

V Video Center

- **Videocassette:** *Scientific American Frontiers*, **Second Edition, Segment 3: "Aliens Have Landed?"** Consult the faculty guide from the *Scientific American Frontiers* video series for a description of this segment. (*Teacher's Resource Binder*, p. 2-1)

Activity Center

- **Critical Thinking Activity:** *Fact or Falsehood?* With this activity, students' preconceptions about research methods are either exposed as incorrect or reinforced as correct. (*Teacher's Resource Binder*, p. 2-1; **Handout 2–1**)
- **Building Vocabulary:** *Exploring Root Words* and *Matching Terms and Definitions* With the activities presented in these handouts, students learn about and review the module vocabulary. (*Teacher's Resource Binder*, p. 2-1; **Handouts 2–2** and **2–3**)
- **Graphic Organizer:** *Flowchart* This graphic organizer presents important concepts in this module and shows how the concepts are related to one another. (*Teacher's Resource Binder*, p. 2-1; **Handout 2–4**)
- **Critical Thinking Activity:** *Astrology and the Scientific Method* This activity demonstrates that the scientific method of inquiry is a better predictor of human behavior than astrology. (*Teacher's Resource Binder*, p. 2-1; **Handouts 2–5a** and **2–5b**)
- **Evaluation Activity:** *The Scientific Approach* Although science is able to address many of life's questions, it is not equipped to handle them all. This activity challenges students to contemplate which type of questions science is adept at handling and which it is not. (*Teacher's Resource Binder*, p. 2-1)

Observation and Bias

Activity Center

- **Critical Thinking Activity:** *Confirmation Bias* This activity shows students how succumbing to the confirmation bias can lead them to the wrong conclusions. (*Teacher's Resource Binder*, p. 2-1)
- **Application Activity:** *A Field Experiment in Helping* This activity has students conducting their own field experiment as they try to get people to help them pick up books that have been dropped. Several different variables can be manipulated in this activity to facilitate discussion of several module concepts. (*Teacher's Resource Binder*, p. 2-1)
- **Cooperative Learning Activity:** *Naturalistic Observation* As student groups share observations of people in their natural environments, they learn how difficult naturalistic observation studies can be to control. (*Teacher's Resource Binder*, p. 2-1)

Enrichment Center

- **Enrichment Lesson:** *The Hawthorne Effect* The science behind the Hawthorne effect is more fiction than fact, but other phenomena, such as the placebo and halo effects, are based in science and contribute to potential bias in experiments. (*Teacher's Resource Binder*, p. 2-1)
- **Enrichment Lesson:** *Psychology and Human Values* This lesson informs students of the ways in which values can become inserted into the research process. With this understanding, students can try to avoid such pitfalls in the research process themselves. (*Teacher's Resource Binder*, p. 2-1)
- **Enrichment Lesson:** *Experimentation in the Field* This lesson presents a field experiment in which researchers tried to overcome artificiality in the laboratory setting. (*Teacher's Resource Binder*, p. 2-1)

Case Studies

Enrichment Center

- **Enrichment Lesson:** *Genie and the Wild Child—Case Studies in Focus* The case study of Genie is a vivid example of how case study research is the only way to study some types of behavior. (*Teacher's Resource Binder*, p. 2-1)

Correlation

Activity Center

- **Technology Application Activity:** *PsychSim*: **"Correlations"** *PsychSim* is an interactive CD-ROM containing tutorials in different content areas of psychology. In this tutorial, students create scatterplots and see how correlations are calculated. (*Teacher's Resource Binder*, p. 2-1)

16b

Materials Network, p. 16b

Materials Network: A Guide to Incorporating Active Learning

Have you ever had a great resource, and then forgetten to incorporate it into your plans? Do you remember a time when you wondered where a particular resource fit in the overall scheme of the unit? The *Teacher's Resource Binder* that accompanies this text contains an extensive collection of ideas that you can incorporate into your lessons, making them deeper and more active. But with so many ideas, where do they all fit? To make lesson-planning easier, we've added a **Materials Network** to each module. The Materials Network is a listing of the video, activity, and enrichment resources found in the *Teacher's Resource Binder*. Having the list of resources from the *Teacher's Resource Binder* handy in the *Teacher's Edition* will make referencing the different ideas you can use in your lessons easier. Throughout the module, the Materials Network is referenced to correspond with a particular idea or tip found in the sidebars and bottom of each page so you can remember to use the resources at the correct time to optimize the learning experience.

You will find reference logos throughout this *Teacher's Edition* to help you quickly locate materials that are available as additional resources from Worth Publishers.

trb Items preceded by this logo indicate that the resource, or a description of the video or multimedia resource, is available in the *Teacher's Resource Binder*.

V The video logo indicates that a clip from one of Worth Publisher's many video resources is appropriate to further discussion of the text materials.

tr The transparency logo indicates that a piece of art or a table is available as either a black-line master in the *Teacher's Resource Binder* or as a four-color overhead transparency. The transparency set of more than 100 images is sold separately.

web Items preceded by the web logo indicate activities or resources available online. This would include specific Web sites, as well as general activities that can be enhanced by using the Internet.

tb This logo indicates that materials from the Test Bank can be used to further assess students' progress in the course.

The Teacher's Edition: The Focal Point of Lesson Planning

Teacher's editions are usually too cluttered or simplistic for practical use in the classroom. Many teachers use their teacher's edition only as a copy of the textbook and not as an integral tool for lesson planning. This *Teacher's Edition* was developed with this problem in mind. We didn't create notes just to avoid "white space" – we were comfortable leaving blank spaces if there were no activities or ideas relevant to the topics in that section. We refined our list of headings so they would be pertinent, helpful, and accessible to a teacher going through a daily and weekly lesson plan. Our philosophy for this *Teacher's Edition* centered on providing tools that teachers would really use. We didn't want to fill a book with clutter – we wanted to create a focal point of lesson planning.

Introducing the Module

Every module begins with an **Introducing the Module** section. Objectives, activities, and teaching tips will make sure you get your students into the topic quickly and effectively.

What's the Point: Making Content Relevant Throughout the student text, the authors incorporated **What's the Point?** questions to help students see what the learning objectives are for each section. Students can use these questions as they study, using SQ3R (Scan, Question, Read, Recite, Review), a study system that actively engages students in the material. The first step in this study technique involves scanning the headings and bold print of the text for main ideas. Second, students are to formulate pertinent questions that they have about the material. This step helps students anticipate what material to look for as they move toward the final three R's—Read, Recite, and Review. Each module of the *Teacher's Edition* starts with a list called **The Point: Module Objectives** so you can keep in mind what main ideas students should be gleaning from reading the text. You can use these objectives as main points for each day's lesson, guiding students in their reading and comprehension of the material.

Building Vocabulary: Building a Foundation The Module Objectives are followed by a **Building Vocabulary** activity that focuses on key terminology. Handouts and activities from the *Teacher's Resource Binder* provide the student with opportunities to memorize vocabulary, learn about the origins of biological and psychological terms, and to organize the key concepts visually.

Getting Started The bottom of each module-opening page contains a **Getting Started** section. An activity or series of activities are suggested to help you and your students on your journey into the materials presented in each module.

Teaching the Points

After introducing the module, the **Teaching the Points** section takes you through the meat of the lesson. A multitude of teaching aids, handouts, visual resources, as well as demonstrations and connections to everyday life are presented along the side and bottom of each student page.

Teaching Tips: Planning with Experience Whether it's your first time teaching psychology or your twentieth, some concepts are easier to teach to students than others. That's where our **Teaching Tips** come in handy. Teaching Tips are designed to give teachers an extra resource for introducing and explaining difficult concepts and provide suggestions for online resources to use as you plan your lessons. Additionally, Teaching Tips offer insight into why concepts may be confusing and how experienced teachers have handled teaching them to students.

Journal Writing: Writing Across the Curriculum Research has consistently shown that writing about information is integral to understanding it more deeply. **Journal Writing** prompts provide students with the opportunity to apply psychological concepts to their lives. Journal Writing also encourages writing across the curriculum which is something that education professionals agree is important for stimulating critical thinking and problem solving in all disciplines. The Journal Writing prompts can be used in several ways to engage students:

1. Start off each class period with a 5- to 10-minute journal writing exercise to prime their thinking about the day's lesson.
2. Assign Journal Writing prompts periodically throughout the unit and have students compile their best entries in a portfolio.
3. Use Journal Writing prompts as a formative assessment tool to check if students understand the material as the unit progresses.

Regardless of how you choose to use Journal Writing, students will benefit from reflecting on psychology and applying it to their lives.

FYI: Broadening Knowledge of Psychology Impress your students with your wealth of knowledge about psychology by using our helpful **FYI** notations. These notations were designed to expand on the information in the text. Ever wonder what happened to John Watson after he left psychology for good? Or maybe your students have wondered if new wrinkles form in the brain when we learn something new? FYI notes will enlighten you and your students and dispel the myths we all cling to about psychology.

Looking at the Issues and Applying the Points: Going Beyond the Classroom Psychologists study phenomena in all areas of life: politics, business and industry, diplomacy, and medicine, just to name a few. Taking a course in psychology is beneficial to all walks of life, so help students see how the discipline applies to the walk of life they will choose by using the tips found in the **Looking at the Issues** and **Applying the Points** headings. Looking at the Issues explores how psychology can help students understand current issues like cloning, standardized testing, and school start times. Applying the Points suggests ways students can participate in service-learning opportunities related to a particular module's concepts or guest speaker options you can use to bring a change of pace to the daily classroom routine. Both of these headings take psychology beyond the classroom and into students' lives.

Multicultural Connections: Connecting Psychology to the World Traditions in American psychology have evolved both similarly and differently than psychology in other parts of the world. Encourage students to explore how other cultures view psychology with the **Multicultural Connections** heading. How do the Russian people view Pavlov: as a physiologist or psychologist? Do people in India encode information differently from people in the United States? With the Internet's creation of a global community, students can delve into these questions and even interact with psychology students from across the globe.

Multicultural Connections also helps students in your class from other cultures engage in the material. This heading provides tips on how they can explore concepts within the framework of their own cultures and how you can support their learning if they are still trying to learn the English language, in addition to mastering psychology. In our ever-shrinking world, connecting psychology to the world is important to help students see beyond their own borders and understand human behavior in a global context.

Checking for Understanding: Assessing During Learning Periodically throughout each module we offer **Checking for Understanding** suggestions for quizzing your students on what they've learned up to that point. Some quizzing can be reflective as you get students to write on how the concepts apply to their lives or certain situations. You can lead them through a series of review-oriented questions that hit the main points of the module. You can also create quick quizzes using the Test Bank that comes with these resources.

Meeting Individual Needs and Enriching: Differentiating Instruction Mainstreaming. Least restrictive environment. Multiple intelligences and learning modalities. These are a few of the terms today's teachers must know to educate the diversity of students who pass through their classrooms. Different types of students with different types of needs are given the opportunity to experience a quality education, posing interesting and complicated challenges for the typical classroom teacher. Psychology teachers have the unique opportunity to explore questions of development, intelligence, and learning with students of all backgrounds and abilities. Reaching these students takes creativity – and teamwork. Use the tips found in this *Teacher's Edition* under the headings **Meeting Individual Needs** and **Enriching** for adapting your instruction to help students with diverse needs. The tips in Meeting Individual Needs detail how students with special learning needs can be successfully engaged in the material; the Enriching sections provide suggestions for students who need to go deeper into the subject matter to challenge themselves intellectually and academically.

In addition, **Graphic Organizers,** available for each module and found in the *Teacher's Resource Binder*, address the needs of visual learners and assist in developing proper note-taking skills. Use the Graphic Organizers as lecture guides, reading comprehension strategy, or tutoring guides so advanced students can help others in learning the material.

Suggested Readings: Enhancing Comprehension Through Reading To further challenge eager students, use any of the **Suggested Readings** found in each module. Students can read a recommended book for their own interest, for an extra credit assignment, or for example, to write a review to add to a portfolio of work produced throughout the unit or course.

Cooperative Learning and Demonstrating: Encouraging Active Learning All students do not learn exclusively by listening to lectures. By encoding information in multiple ways, students are more likely to recall what they learn at the appropriate time. So teaching in a variety of formats is key to successful teaching and learning. **Cooperative Learning** and **Demonstrating** activities suggest ways everyone can actively engage in the content. With Cooperative Learning, students can work in mixed-ability groups to tutor each other and develop presentations to teach the rest of the class. Demonstrating suggests teacher-led activities that provide hands-on application of the module's contents. Both types of lesson ideas will make psychology a memorable course that students will be clamoring to take!

Cross-Curricular Connections: Building Bridges In Module 1, students study history. In Module 2, they explore the fundamentals of scientific thinking. Modules 4, 5, and 6 explore the biology of development. And don't forget Modules 7 and 8 where students uncover the fascinating world of neuroscience where chemistry, biology, and anatomy are explored. What other discipline encompasses so many others? The study of human behavior blends naturally with the curricula taught by other teachers in your school. Using the tips in **Cross-Curricular Connections** will increase students' critical thinking skills as they transfer their knowledge to other areas. Use these tips to build your own knowledge base in other subject areas or to plan lessons with colleagues as you build bridges across the school. If students can see how psychology extends to other areas of their studies, they may also see how relevant all areas of school are to their lives.

Reteaching: Solidifying the Knowledge Base After all is said and done, what if the students still don't get it? Do you have to go over everything again? Who has got time for that? Not every student will understand everything you teach, but you can help them along with **Reteaching** tips. These tips outline quick strategies for reviewing the module's concepts one more time –hopefully, the one more time your students need to master the material.

Close: Wrapping Up the Points

After leading your students through the materials in the module, it is often difficult to tie everything together in a practical way that also reinforces what they have learned. The **Close** section appears before the summary and suggests activities and discussion that focus on practical applications of the materials the students have just studied.

Checking the Points

This *Teacher's Edition* also contains several assessment strategies that will help you determine how well students have learned the material in each module.

Just as diversity in instruction is important to student learning, so is diversity of assessment to measuring student performance. Led by researchers Howard Gardner and Carol Ann Tomlinson, the call has grown steadily louder for teachers to employ a variety of assessment strategies to ensure students are given ample opportunity to demonstrate their knowledge. We've developed several options you can use to assess your students' progress both traditionally and alternatively.

Using the Test Bank Writing your own quality questions is time-consuming. Even after questions are written, are you really assessing multiple-levels of knowledge and exposing your students to challenging questions? Rob McEntarffer, a teacher from Lincoln Southeast High School in Nebraska and a table leader at the readings for the College Board's Advanced Placement Program in psychology, has compiled a thorough catalogue of assessment questions based on Bloom's taxonomy of knowledge. Using these questions to build your formative and summative assessment tools will ensure that you are tapping into the different levels of knowledge your students possess and exposing them to questions that mirror those they would see on tests outside your own classroom.

Self-Tests At the end of each module of the *Student Edition*, the authors have provided multiple-choice, matching, and short-answer questions that students can use to evaluate their own understanding of the material. In the *Teacher's Edition*, we've provided answers to these questions so you can help your students correctly assess their knowledge. Use these assessments as independent assignments students can complete on their own, guided practice to be completed during class, or as remediation lessons for students needing extra help.

Alternative Assessment Portfolio assessments are the hottest thing in education today. Educators realize that alternative assessment options are key to ensuring students can demonstrate their multiple intelligences. We've included suggestions for alternative assessments for students to create portfolios they can submit for evaluation. Rubrics and further instructions for most alternative assessment activities can be found in the *Teacher's Resource Binder* that accompanies this text.

Multimedia Resources: Tools for the 21st Century

Technology dominates the lives of our students, and using technology in the classroom is essential to reaching this generation of students who become savvier with each passing month. We've compiled a plethora of resources that will help you incorporate technology into your lessons. References to videos, Internet links, and transparencies you can use to teach each lesson are included within the modules to give you guidance in how to use these tools for lesson planning, student engagement, remediation, and enrichment. Some of the resources obtainable through Worth Publishers to complete your resources for *Thinking About Psychology* include the following:

The Brain Teaching Modules, Second Edition Edited by Frank J. Vattano, Thomas L. Bennet, and Michelle Butler, all of Colorado State University. Created with Annenberg/CPB Multimedia, this collection of short clips provides vivid examples for myriad topics in introductory psychology. Individual segments range from 4 to12 minutes in length, providing flexibility in highlighting specific topics. Available in VHS and DVD. Faculty Guide available separately.

The Mind Teaching Modules, Second Edition Edited by Frank J. Vattano, Colorado State University, with the consultation of Charles Brewer, Furman University, and David Myers, in association with WNET. This collection of 34 short clips contains updated segments on language processing, infant cognitive development, heredity factors in alcoholism, and living without memory. Available in VHS and DVD. Faculty Guide available separately.

Scientific American Frontiers, Second Edition Hosted by Alan Alda, these are 8- to 12-minute teaching modules from the highly praised Scientific American, Inc. The collection contains more than thirty video modules. The Scientific American Frontiers Videos are an excellent way to show students how psychological research is actually conducted. Available in VHS and DVD. Faculty Guide available separately.

***Psychology: The Human Experience* Teaching Modules** This new series includes more than three hours of footage from the new Introductory Psychology telecourse, "Psychology: The Human Experience," produced by Coast Learning Systems in collaboration with Worth Publishers. These brief clips are ideal for lecture openers and include footage of noted scholars, the latest research in psychology, and beautiful animations. Available in VHS and DVD. Faculty Guide available separately.

Worth Publishers' Digital Media Archive: Psychology This Instructor's Presentation CD-ROM, compatible with both Windows and Macintosh computers, contains a rich collection of more than 40 digitized video clips of classic experiments and research. Footage includes Albert Bandura's "Bobo" doll experiment, Harold Takoshian's bystander studies, Piaget's conservation experiment, electrical brain stimulation footage, Harlow's monkey experiments, Milgram's obedience experiments, and Ulric Neisser's selective-attention studies. The Digital Media Archive clips are available in QuickTime and MPEG formats, and are compatible with Microsoft PowerPoint software. Also available in VHS and DVD. Faculty Guide available separately.

Teacher's Presentation CD-ROM The easy-to-operate *Teacher's Presentation CD-ROM* allows teachers to build classroom presentations. With the presentation CD-ROM, teachers can:

- Integrate video clips into presentations
- Preview slides; build and run a presentation
- Import custom graphics files and Web sources
- Use and edit pre-built PowerPoint slides featuring all module art and illustrations

Student and Instructor Web Site Kent Korek of Germantown High School in Wisconsin has developed the Web-based resources that accompany *Thinking About*

Psychology. This student and instructor resource can be found at **www.worthpublishers.com/thinkingaboutpsych**. Student resources include:

- **Detailed Module Overviews,** which provide students with a snapshot of module materials, and highlight key concepts to remember
- **Critical Thinking Exercises** that probe relevant module topics and include links to psychology-related Web sites
- **Online Module Quizzes**
- **Interactive Flashcards** that tutor students on all module/text terminology and allow them to quiz themselves on the terms
- **Interactive Animations and "Drag-and-Drop" Quizzing Exercises**, allowing students to learn key anatomy and biological processes. These range from physiological animations to interactive sensation and perception activities.
- **Annotated Web Links**

The Web site also includes a **password-protected Instructor Site** that offers a full array of teaching tools, such as text-specific PowerPoint slides, an online gradebook, and links to various resources including Worth's **Image and Lecture Gallery**. Using the Image and Lecture Gallery, teachers can browse, search, and download all module art, illustrations, outlines, and pre-built PowerPoint presentation files for all Worth titles. Users can also create personal folders for easy organization of the materials.

Student Research: A Guide to Creating Scientific Learners

Psychology Fairs: A Showcase for Student Achievement

Two additional resources are available as appendices in the *Teacher's Resource Binder* that will help you incorporate student research and presentations into your lesson planning. Allyson Weseley, EdD, of Roslyn High School in New York, has written a step-by-step guide to leading students as they conduct research. Dr. Weseley is the director of social science research at her school, and her students have won national awards and recognition for their research. Her expertise and suggestions for getting students to use psychology in an active way will be a valuable addition to any psychology classroom.

Additionally, Carol Dean, EdD, a veteran high-school teacher from Illinois, has written a guide to conducting a psychology fair. Dr. Dean, a past chairperson for Teachers of Psychology in Secondary Schools, is a pioneer in developing and sharing ideas about holding a psychology fair that both highlights student work and markets psychology to the general public. Conducting your own psychology fair will be easier by utilizing the years of expertise Dr. Dean shares in this appendix.

About the Authors

Amy C. Fineburg

Amy C. Fineburg has been teaching psychology and English since 1995 in Birmingham, Alabama. She received her BA in psychology, English, and education in 1994 and her MA in educational administration in 2000, both from Samford University, and is currently pursuing a PhD in Educational Psychology from the University of Alabama. She has served on the Teachers of Psychology in Secondary Schools (TOPSS) Executive Board since 2002. She has directed two workshops for high school psychology teachers in Alabama and presented at regional and national conferences such as the Southeastern Psychological Association conference, the National Institute for the Teaching of Psychology, the Measuring Up: Best Practices in Assessment Conference, Kansas-—Teachers of Psychology in Secondary Schools workshop, Southeastern Teaching of Psychology Conference, the 1999 NKU/NSF Teaching the SCIENCE of Psychology Institute, and two Positive Psychology Summits. She has developed a unit plan for positive psychology (published in 2003 by TOPSS) and created Web-based resources with Martin Seligman, PhD, and Randy Ernst as co-chair of the Positive Psychology Teaching Task Force. She also serves as a curriculum-design consultant for a US Department of Education research project based in Philadelphia, Pennsylvania, investigating the impact of a positive humanities curriculum for ninth-grade students. She received a citation for Excellence in Teaching from TOPSS in 2002. She has been involved in the College Board's Advanced Placement Program in psychology as a reader for the exam since 2000 and is the author of the 2003 edition of the Teacher's Guide for Advanced Placement Psychology. She is married to a wonderfully supportive husband and is the mother of one son, Micah Samuel.

Kristin Habashi Whitlock

Kristin H. Whitlock has been teaching Advanced Placement Psychology at Viewmont High School in Bountiful, Utah, for eleven years. She is a current member of the American Psychological Association's Task Force for the Development of the National High School Psychology Standards. She also serves as a member of the Test Development Committee for the Advanced Placement Psychology exam and as a table leader at the readings. She served as Member-at-Large for Teachers of Psychology in Secondary Schools (TOPSS) and co-founded Utah Teachers of Psychology in Secondary Schools. She was the recipient of the TOPSS 2002 Excellence in Teaching Award presented by the American Psychological Association.

Thinking About Psychology

The Science of Mind and Behavior

Thinking About Psychology

The Science of Mind and Behavior

Charles T. Blair-Broeker
Cedar Falls High School, Iowa

Randal M. Ernst
Lincoln High School, Nebraska

Special Consultant:
David G. Myers
Hope College, Michigan

Worth Publishers

To our families
Lynn, Carl, and Eric
Sherri, Emily, Meredith, and Jocelyn

Publisher: Catherine Woods
Associate Sponsoring Editor: Graig Donini
Development Editors: Christine Brune, Nancy Fleming
Marketing Manager: Renée Altier
Associate Managing Editor: Tracey Kuehn
Art Director: Babs Reingold
Cover and Text Designer: Lissi Sigillo
Layout Designer: Lee Ann Mahler
Cover Art: Marie Bertrand (*Untitled,* 2002)
Illustrations: David Chen, TSI Graphics
Caricatures: Ray Alma
Illustration Coordinator: Bill Page
Photo Editor: Meg Kuhta
Photo Researchers: Deborah Goodsite, Nigel Assam
Production Manager: Barbara Anne Seixas
Composition: TSI Graphics
Printing and Binding: R. R. Donnelley and Sons

Library of Congress Cataloging-in-Publication Data has been applied for.
ISBN: 0-7167-5467-3

Printed in the United States of America

First printing 2003

Worth Publishers
41 Madison Avenue
New York, NY 10010
www.worthpublishers.com

About the Authors

Charlie Blair-Broeker has taught psychology at Cedar Falls High School (Iowa) since 1978. He has been involved in a number of APA initiatives, serving as a member of the Task Force that authored the *National Standards for High School Psychology,* as chair of the Executive Board of Teachers of Psychology in Secondary Schools (TOPSS), and as co-editor of the fourth volume of the *APA Activities Handbook for the Teaching of Psychology.* For three years, Charlie co-directed Teaching the Science of Psychology, a summer institute for high school psychology teachers supported by the National Science Foundation and the Northern Kentucky University Foundation. He has been a table leader or reader for Advanced Placement Psychology Examinations since the test was first administered in 1992, completed a three-year term on the AP Psychology Test Development Committee, and led many conferences on AP Psychology. He is currently serving on the Positive Psychology Teaching Task Force. Among his teaching awards are the Grinnell College Outstanding Iowa Teacher Award, the University of Iowa Distinguished Teacher Award, and the APA Division 2 Teaching Excellence Award.

Randy Ernst's main career in psychology has been teaching high school psychology at Lincoln (Nebraska) High School. In addition to that responsibility he also is a co-author of the National Standards for the Teaching of High School Psychology, co-editor of the fourth volume of the APA Activities Handbook for the Teaching of Psychology, and author of the College Board's Guide for Advanced Placement Psychology. Randy has served as Chair of the Teachers of Psychology in Secondary Schools (TOPSS) Executive Board, as a member of the College Board's Advanced Placement Psychology Test Development Committee, and is a Question Leader at the annual Advanced Placement Psychology Reading. He is an author or co-author of several TOPSS unit plans, and is co-chair of the Positive Psychology Curriculum Task Force. He has presented at workshops and summer teaching institutes in over twenty states and provinces, and is a recipient of the APA's Division 2 Teaching Excellence Award, the University of Nebraska's Distinguished Educator Award, and Time-Warner's "Crystal Apple" National Teacher Award.

...and special consultant

David Myers received his Ph.D. in psychology from the University of Iowa. He has spent his entire 30-year professional teaching career at Hope College, Michigan, where he is the John Dirk Werkman Professor of Psychology. He has taught dozens of introductory psychology sections. Hope College students have invited him to be their commencement speaker and voted him "outstanding professor." His scientific articles have appeared in over two dozen scientific periodicals, including *Science, American Scientist,* and *American Psychologist,* and he has served on the editorial boards of the *Journal of Experimental Social Psychology* and the *Journal of Personality and Social Psychology.* In addition to his scholarly writing and his textbooks, *Psychology, Psychology in Modules, Exploring Psychology, Exploring Psychology in Modules,* and *Social Psychology,* he has also written about psychological science for general readers. His writings have appeared in more than two dozen magazines, from *Today's Education* to *Scientific American.* He has also published numerous trade books on subjects ranging from happiness to hearing loss.

Brief Contents

Contents

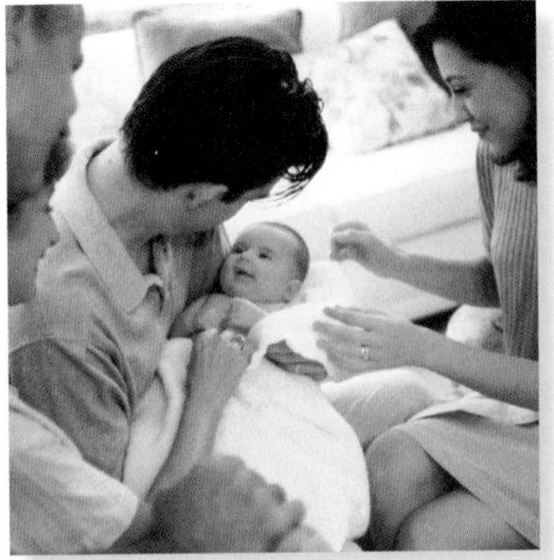

HEX

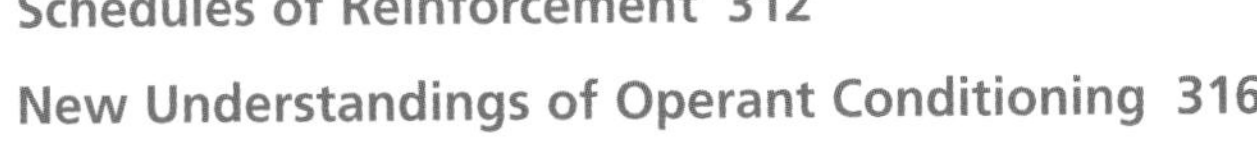

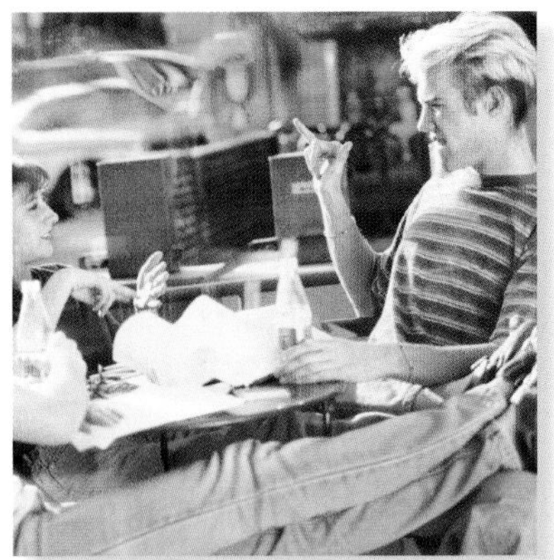

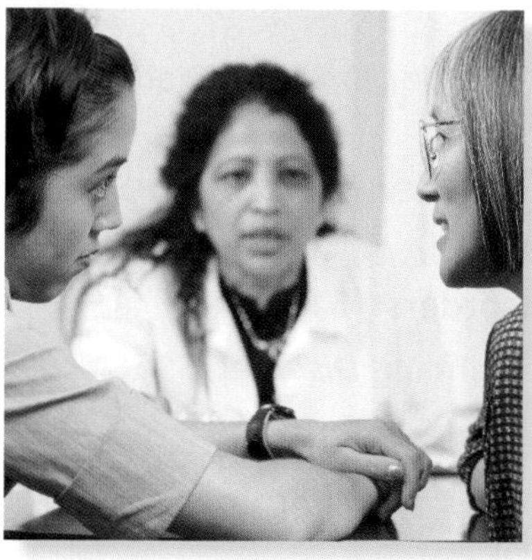

Preface

Psychology is a young field that's still inventing itself. This makes teaching and learning about psychology a wonderful adventure. The field rests on a foundation of critical thinking, so not only do students master meaningful content, but they also learn thinking skills that help them navigate all sorts of real-life problems. This book will be an ally for teachers striving to ignite a passion in their students for psychology's many relevant findings, and for students wanting to satisfy a growing curiosity about themselves, their families, their friends, and the world of people around them.

We were teachers long before we were authors. We know that worthwhile textbooks have to be much more than a compilation of factual information. Complex concepts must be clearly explained in straightforward language and illustrated with engaging examples students can relate to. Our goal has been to provide a foundation upon which teachers can build a successful course within any school's schedule. With tremendous support from colleagues and Worth Publishers, we think we have succeeded. Here is what we have to offer.

A Modular Approach

Thinking About Psychology has 14 traditional chapters, but they have been divided into 34 modules written to stand independently from one another. Chunking the material into these shorter modules helps sustain student understanding and interest, and provides more flexibility for structuring your course. You may cover the whole book, or you may select the modules you'd like to cover, and then use them in any order that works for you. Student understanding of later modules does not depend upon reading the content of preceding modules.

The National Standards for the Teaching of High School Psychology

Both of us served on the American Psychological Association Task Force that authored the *National Standards*, so we thoroughly understand the content of the standards and the philosophy behind them. This book is

xvii

structured to allow easy incorporation of the *Standards* in two ways. First, the text covers every Standard Area *and* provides support for the Content Standards in each area. Second, this book's 34 modules are organized into the same five domains as the *Standards*:

- Psychology and Its Methods
- Developmental
- Biopsychological
- Cognitive
- Clinical and Sociocultural

The *Standards* strongly recommend that every course teach content from all five domains; our book's independent modules easily facilitate this recommendation. No matter how long your psychology course, there will not be enough time to teach everything you want to teach. By covering material from each domain, however, you can be sure that you are accurately representing the breadth of the field. Even if your students never take another psychology course, they will be aware of the fascinating variety of topics that fall within its reach. If you don't have a copy of the *Standards,* we strongly encourage you to download them at: http://www.apa.org/ed/natlstandards.html

The Voice of Experienced High School Teachers

If you've looked at other high school psychology texts, you know that the authors are usually college professors. Some of our best friends are college professors, but they don't spend their days with high school students. This book was created specifically *for* high school students *by* high school teachers. We've worked hard to stay "real" for our readers, even to the extent of introducing each module with a cartoon caricature so students will know which of the two authors is speaking to them.

It was daunting to even think of writing a textbook, but we have had experiences that prepared us well for the task. In addition to our intensive involvement with the *National Standards* and the Advanced Placement program in psychology, we have had two other key opportunities.

1. We have been co-directors of month-long National Science Foundation summer institutes for high school psychology teachers, as well as leaders of numerous shorter workshops.
2. We served on the American Psychological Association (APA) planning committee that led to the formation of Teachers of

Psychology in Secondary Schools (TOPSS) in 1992. Each of us has been elected to chair the TOPSS Executive Board and has represented TOPSS on the appropriate subcommittee of APA's Board of Educational Affairs.

The Counsel of David G. Myers

Dave Myers is a psychology professor at Hope College in Holland, Michigan, and author of several bestselling college-level psychology textbooks. He has been our primary consultant on this project, reviewing every page of text and helping us create an accurate, up-to-date introduction to the field of psychology for high school students. His friendship and expertise have guided us from step one to the end. We are fortunate indeed to learn from a master writer and teacher.

Innovative Features

As classroom teachers, we know the kinds of features that elevate a text from a compendium of facts to an effective teaching tool. We have also taken the time to listen to dozens of other teachers by way of focus groups, surveys, and manuscript reviews. Teacher input has helped us create an effective set of features.

- To enhance student reading skills, each major section begins with a "What's the point?" question. These questions are repeated and answered in paragraph form in the end-of-module review.
- A marginal glossary defines key terms and summarizes the contributions of key people on the page where the term or the person is first introduced. For easy review, end-of-module lists of key terms and key people are referenced to the page on which the term or person was introduced. End-of-book English and Spanish glossaries include an alphabetized list with definitions/summaries of all the book's key terms and key people.
- Boxed essays throughout the text provide expanded coverage and encourage scientific reasoning.

  Critical Thinking boxes challenge students to evaluate research findings thoughtfully.

  Psychology Is a Science boxes show how scientific methods are applied to psychological topics.

  Up Close boxes allow students to examine interesting topics in greater depth.

- End-of module Self-Tests help assess student comprehension. Answers to these multiple-choice, fill-in-the-blank, matching, and short answer/essay questions are provided in the Teacher's Edition.

Print and Media Supplements

Worth Publishers has assembled a truly impressive package of supplements to accompany our book. We insisted from the start that the focus be on quality and not quantity, because we had seen too many book packages where publishers seemed intent on overwhelming already overwhelmed classroom teachers with an endless series of weak pamphlets and other marginal-quality materials. Imagine our delight when Worth presented a package with both quality *and* quantity. We know you'll want the Teacher's Edition, Teacher's Resource Binder, and Test Bank. We know your students will appreciate the companion Web site. Beyond that, there is a vast smorgasbord from which you can choose those resources that will help meet your individual needs.

- Amy Fineburg (Homewood High School, Alabama), with assistance from Kristin Whitlock (Viewmont High School, Utah), prepared the wraparound **Teacher's Edition.** It is designed to supplement the text and serve as a road map to other ancillaries.
- Amy also prepared the **Teacher's Resource Binder.** Amy adapted many of these resources from Martin Bolt's (Calvin College, Michigan) renowned Instructor's Resources for David Myers' texts. You will find activities, lecture topics, demonstrations, handouts, graphic organizers, and video suggestions, among other things, all "under one roof." The three-ring binder format allows you to snap out materials by module and take home only what you need for immediate planning purposes. Additional resources for the Binder were contributed by Carol Dean (recently retired from Lake Park High School, Illinois), Marissa Sarabando (Memorial High School, Texas) and Allyson Weseley (Roslyn High School, New York).
- The **Test Bank** by Rob McEntarffer (Southeast High School, Nebraska) is available in both print and computerized versions. Rob's questions are all keyed to specific topics in the text and page referenced. Each question is also categorized as knowledge/comprehension, application/analysis, or synthesis/evaluation to help you assess your learning objectives appropriately.

- Kent Korek (Germantown High School, Wisconsin) developed a free **Companion Web Site** (www.worthpublishers.com/thinkingaboutpsych). Student resources include module overviews, critical thinking exercises, demonstrations, interactive animations, quizzes, interactive flashcards, and Web links for more information on specific topics. Password-protected teacher resources include PowerPoint slides and an online quiz gradebook.
- Our **Teacher's Presentation CD-ROM** will help you build classroom presentations around a variety of still and moving images—from *Thinking About Psychology,* from your own sources, or from the World Wide Web. With the Presentation CD-ROM, you can integrate video clips into presentations, preview slides, build and run a presentation, and import custom graphics files and Web sources. The Presentation CD-ROM also includes customizable PowerPoint slide sets that have been pre-built for each module—featuring module outlines and all module art and illustrations.
- Additional presentation resources for teachers include **overhead transparencies,** a CD-based **Digital Media Archive** with video clips of classic experiments, and an on-line **Image and Lecture Gallery** that offers numerous additional illustrations for all key topics covered in the book.
- A wealth of Video/DVD resources includes ***Psychology: The Human Experience Video Teaching Modules, Scientific American Frontiers Video Collection for Introductory Psychology, The Brain*** and ***The Mind Video Teaching Modules,*** and Frank Vattano's (Colorado State University, Fort Collins, Colorado) newest video titled ***The Many Faces of Psychology.***

Acknowledgments

There were times we thought we'd never reach the point of working on this Preface, the last writing task for *Thinking About Psychology*. Sometimes, the light at the end of the tunnel appeared to be attached to a speeding locomotive. We never would have made it, either, without an amazing level of support from an amazing number of people. Books truly are a cooperative effort, and we are fortunate to be a part of such a skilled, dedicated group of individuals. From the FedEx delivery person who always showed up with both a package and a dog biscuit (for the dog!) to the personal support and encouragement of Catherine Woods, Worth's publisher, every member of our team performed his or her duties with good cheer, competence, and efficiency.

xxi

At a dinner soon after we had agreed to write this book, we met a new Worth editor. Although she was not to be involved in our project, it was interesting to hear her compare Worth with the publisher she had worked for previously. The biggest difference, she said, was that the folks at Worth actually liked books! Amused at first, we quickly came to see that she was right. A passion for quality work and products is a thread common to every Worth employee we have met. At the risk of sounding like an Academy Award acceptance speech, we are going to thank a few of them here. The book you are holding would not exist without their efforts.

Christine Brune has both led and pushed us from beginning to end with wisdom, broad vision, and a sense of unwavering purpose. Multiple daily e-mails and numerous conference calls have made her a part of our lives and families. We are richer for the experience. So are you, for her mark can be felt in every sentence and illustration of this book. Nancy Fleming can work magic with a page of text by moving a word here and changing a punctuation mark there. Her sharp pencil helped our writing come alive. Graig Donini, Associate Sponsoring Editor, ably coordinated the supplements described earlier and provided additional guidance throughout the writing process. Other people from Worth who played key roles include Associate Managing Editor Tracey Kuehn, Art Director Babs Reingold, Layout Designer Lee Mahler, Editorial Assistant Andrea Musick, Production Manager Barbara Seixas, Photo Editor Meg Kuhta, and Photo Researcher Debbie Goodsite. Mike Saltzman, Director of Sales and Marketing, and his sales team and Renée Altier, Senior Psychology Marketing Manager, have been contagiously enthusiastic about our book! They are doing a wonderful job sharing the news.

Finally, we need to express our appreciation for outstanding teachers who mentored us long before this book was even a dream. These teachers include Don Davis, Mary Kay Reed, Cliff Fawl, and Perilou Goddard. Both of us owe a deep debt of gratitude to Ludy T. "Ben" Benjamin, Jr., who brought us together for the first time at a Texas A&M summer teaching institute. Ben's support of high school psychology teachers is unmatched, and he opened countless doors of opportunity for the two of us. We also recognize the efforts of our colleagues, who share the joys and frustrations of our daily efforts to teach psychology. Several of you have taken the time to review our manuscript and help us make it better, and we are grateful for your insights and suggestions:

xxii

Karl C. Berndlmaier
Damien Memorial High School (HI)

Pamela Bowman
Woodrow Wilson High School (NJ)

Jan Breehl
Brockport High School (NY)

Stacy Brosier
Belvidere High School (IL)

Deborah Chaddick
Quartz Hill High School (CA)

Margaret J. Davidson
L. V. Berkner High School (TX)

Carol Dean
Lake Park High School (IL)

Carol Farber
Miami Killian High School (FL)

Amy Fineburg
Homewood High School (AL)

Nancy Grayson
McLeman Community College (TX)

A.J. Johnson
Kingfisher High School (OK)

B. Dale Kinney
Ralston High School (NE)

Donald Kober
St. Francis De Sales High School (OH)

Riki Koenigsberg
Yeshiva University High School for Girls (NY)

Cindy Kremer
Beloit Memorial High School (WI)

Cherie Jantzen
Gabriel Richard High School (MI)

Dave Johnston
Southeast Polk High School (IA)

Kenneth D. Keith
University of San Diego (CA)

Donna Kotting
Sherwood High School (MD)

Barbara L. Loverich
Hobart High School (IN)

Laura Maitland
W. C. Mepham High School (NY)

Ruth Martin
James Madison Memorial High School (WI)

Jamie Martindale
Pike High School (IN)

Maureen A. McCarthy
Austin Peay State University (TN)

Rob McEntarffer
Lincoln Southeast High School
Nebraska Wesleyan University (NE)

Kay Miller
Nemitz High School (TX)

Katherine Minter
Westwood High School (TX)

David G. Myers
Hope College (MI)

Joyce Nelson
Pella Community High School (IA)

Debra Park
West Deptford High School (NJ)

Steve Ricard
Benson Public School (MN)

Sandee Rindone
Hilltop High School (CA)

Peg Rinkenberger
Morris Area High School (MN)

Carol Rutenbeck
Burlington Community High School (IA)

Chuck Schallhorn
San Benito High School (CA)

Stefanie S. Scher
Ft. Lauderdale High School (FL)

Kristin Habashi Whitlock
Viewmont High School (UT)

Jenny Wilmetti
Rock Springs High School (WY)

James Yohe
Blairsville High School (PA)

We especially appreciate the efforts of David G. Myers and Amy Fineburg, who reviewed every page of our manuscript.

Your two authors have been friends for more than 10 years. We have accomplished many things together, but none more satisfying than this book. We hope it helps spread interest in psychology among both teachers and students, and we welcome any and all feedback.

Charlie Blair-Broeker Randy Ernst

www.worthpublishers.com/thinkingaboutpsych

xxiv

Thinking About

Psychology

The Science of Mind and Behavior

Psychology and Its Methods Domain

Teaching with the Standards

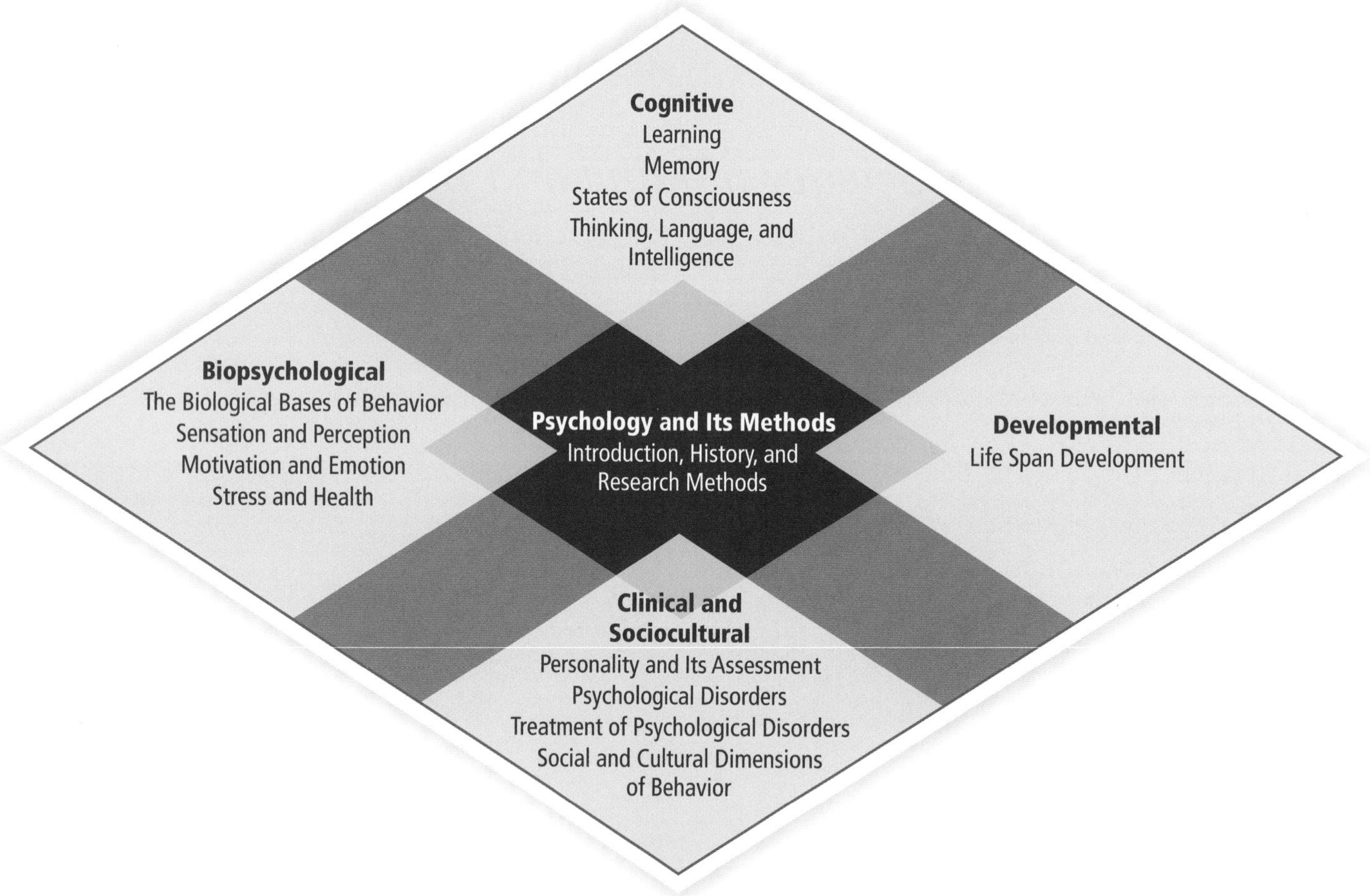

Cognitive
Learning
Memory
States of Consciousness
Thinking, Language, and Intelligence

Biopsychological
The Biological Bases of Behavior
Sensation and Perception
Motivation and Emotion
Stress and Health

Psychology and Its Methods
Introduction, History, and Research Methods

Developmental
Life Span Development

Clinical and Sociocultural
Personality and Its Assessment
Psychological Disorders
Treatment of Psychological Disorders
Social and Cultural Dimensions of Behavior

Scope and Sequence

Background/Significance of the Methods Domain

The authors of the National Standards for the Teaching of High School Psychology placed the Methods Domain at the center of the others to emphasize the scientific nature of psychology. It is suggested that this domain be taught at the beginning of the course and reemphasized throughout. This approach would show students the interconnectedness of all of the modules and stress the central point that psychology is based on research.

In addition, by making the Methods Domain central to the course, another goal can be reached. Many teachers wish their students to leave their psychology classes as better consumers of information. Students are bombarded with research findings and statistics from the media, but they are often ill-equipped to think critically about the sources of such data.

While discussing psychological research (either specific data presented in these modules or current research reported in the media), emphasize what constitutes good research and encourage students to ask questions about what they read and hear. Module 1, Introduction, History, Perspectives, and Careers, and Module 2, Research Strategies, consider questions such as the following: What was the researchers' hypothesis? Were the variables appropriately defined? How were subjects selected? How were potential confounds controlled for? Were statistics appropriately and accurately used to reflect the data collected? Addressing these questions with your students will help them develop critical thinking skills.

Also, Chapter 1 includes Module 3, Nature and Nurture in Psychology. This module presents a wonderful opportunity to introduce students to the basic questions about the role genetics and the environment play in shaping behavior. The nature/nurture controversy has been a big part of psychology from its philosophical roots to today. This module may be taught as a part of the introductory sequence or later as part of Chapter 2, Life Span Development, or Chapter 3, The Biological Bases of Behavior.

Psychology and Its Methods Domain

Introducing the Domain

The Points: Domain Objectives

- Define psychology and describe its scientific nature.
- Trace the historical development of psychology including contributions from researchers from diverse backgrounds.
- Briefly describe the different perspectives from which psychologists examine behavior and mental processes, understanding that each perspective provides a significant contribution to psychology.
- Describe the variety of career options to individuals pursuing a psychology degree.
- Differentiate among the different types of research methodologies psychologists have at their disposal to study human behavior.
- Understand the impact of genetic predisposition on behavior.
- Determine in what aspects of a child's life parental and peer influences have the most importance.
- Understand the influence of culture on a person's behavior.

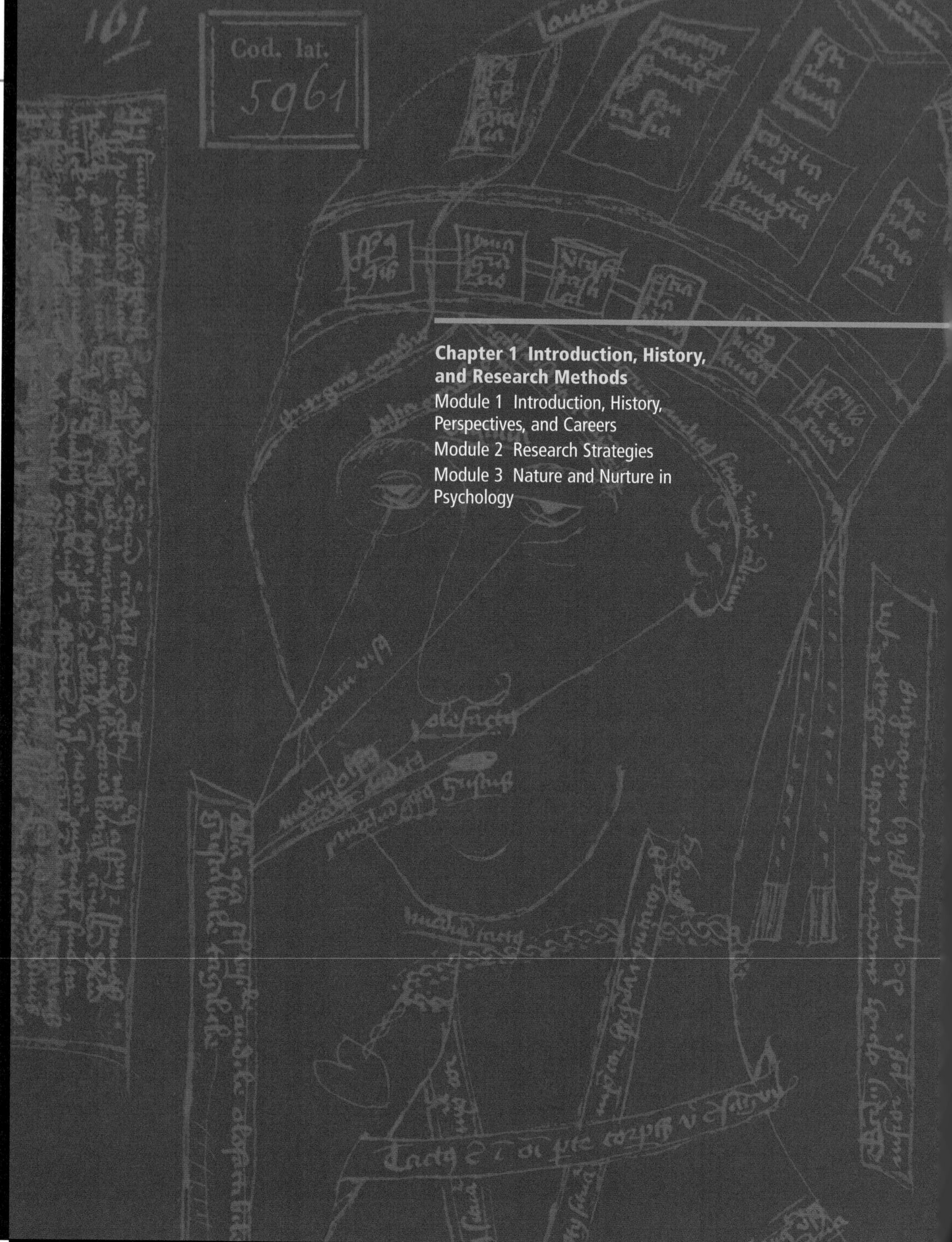

Enriching

You may want to use **Critical Thinking Activity:** *The Science/Art Continuum* (*Teacher's Resource Binder*, p. 1-1; **Handout 1–7**) to get students thinking about psychology as a science. Ask them whether they view psychology as a scientific discipline like chemistry or biology, or if they view it as a discipline more like philosophy. Have them discuss what constitutes a science, highlighting how psychology fulfills these requirements.

Psychology and Its Methods Domain

In this textbook, we have divided all the ideas, notions, and facts making up the science of psychology into five broad conceptual domains. The domains are like themes in a novel, but in this text they help us understand what psychology is all about. Within each domain, modules, grouped into chapters, examine specific aspects of each domain in greater detail.

The first domain, which has one chapter containing three modules, is central to understanding the science of psychology and its emphasis on scientific research methods. You see, psychologists differ in their interests, but they use the same methods to explore behavior and mental processes. All the modules, from 1 through 34, contain citations to many different studies, all of which used sound scientific research.

In addition to identifying the methods by which psychologists examine behavior and mental processes, this first domain defines *psychology,* discusses its history, and looks at some of the paths open to you if you decide to make psychology your career.

Cross-Curricular Connections

Have students bring their biology, chemistry, or physics textbooks to class and explore how the different disciplines relate their concepts to human behavior.

- What human behaviors are studied and explored in each discipline?
- What fundamental concepts in each discipline help people understand themselves and others?

CHAPTER 1 Introduction, History, and Research Methods

Psychology and Its Methods Domain

Teaching with the Standards

Standard Area: Introduction and Research Methods

Breakdown of Module 1: Introduction, History, Perspectives, and Careers

Content Standard 1: Modern psychological perspectives The text discusses the cognitive, biological, social-cultural, behavioral, humanistic, and psychodynamic approaches to explaining behavior. Using the example of helping another person pick up dropped groceries, the author compares these different schools of thought. New areas of interest, such as behavior genetics and evolutionary and positive psychology, are also introduced. (Student Text pp. 9–12)

Content Standard 2: Careers and subfields in psychology The text provides a comparison of applied and basic research, as well as a discussion of different subfields in psychology. The following subfields are highlighted: biological, social, developmental, and cognitive. Emphasis is placed on the questions the psychologists in these fields attempt to answer. Organizational psychologists, human-factors psychologists, psychometricians, and educational psychologists are also introduced. (Student Text pp. 12–14)

Content Standard 6: The roots of scientific psychology The text presents a brief survey of the history of psychology, from Wilhelm Wundt, E. B. Titchener, Gestalt psychologists, William James, Sigmund Freud, and Ivan Pavlov to modern psychologists such as Carl Rogers, Roger Sperry, and Judith Rodin. The text focuses on the shift in focus from philosophy to empirical science and uses salient examples to help students understand the roots of this science. There is a discussion of the historical ethnic and gender disparity in the field, as well as current trends toward greater diversity. (Student Text pp. 4–8)

Breakdown of Module 2: Research Strategies

Content Standard 3: Research tools used by psychologists to answer psychological questions The text introduces the use of naturalistic observation, surveys, case studies, longitudinal and cross-sectional studies, and experiments to explore human behavior and mental processes. Each method is presented in the context of a hypothetical research question that examines the effectiveness of listening to music using headphones during study hall. The text addresses the issues of bias and the need for control and replication. (Student Text pp. 17–20, 22–30, 31)

Content Standard 4: Use of statistics to analyze and understand psychological research In the context of the hypothetical research question of listening to music while studying, the text addresses the use of correlation and inferential statistics to interpret collected data. (Student Text pp. 21–22, 30)

Content Standard 5: Ethical considerations in research with human participants and animals The ethical guidelines of the American Psychological Association are presented to help students understand the principles that guide all research using human participants. The text also presents reasons for the use of other animals in psychological research and the regulations that protect these animals from abuse. (Student Text pp. 31–33)

Breakdown of Module 3: Nature and Nurture in Psychology

Standard Area: Biological Bases of Behavior

Content Standard 1: Neural functioning Module 3 considers the role of experience on brain development in a brief review of current research, including that of Mark Rosenzweig and David Krech on rats raised in enriched or impoverished environments. (Student Text pp. 46–47)

Content Standard 7: The interaction of nature and nurture to influence behavior Module 3 examines such biological concepts as chromosomes, DNA, and genes; it considers the concept of predisposition to explain the development of certain traits. The text also presents evidence from twin and adoptive children studies to examine the effects of genetics and environment on behavior. (Student Text pp. 39–46)

Content Standard 8: Evolutionary influences on psychological properties The text considers how individuals from many cultures demonstrate similar behaviors. (Student Text pp. 41–42)

Standard Area: Life Span Development

Content Standard 3: Developmental theories Module 3 explores how culture influences the behaviors we exhibit. Specifically, the text explores collectivist and individualistic cultures and resulting behavioral differences. (Student Text pp. 48–49)

Content Standard 4: Nature and nurture issues in development Module 3 considers a fundamental question of development, "How much are we affected by our heredity and our environment?" This module considers cultural and biological factors that influence our psychological development. (Student Text pp. 39–49)

Scope and Sequence

	Objectives	Text Reference	Standards Covered
Lesson 1	Define *psychology*. Present a brief history of psychology by comparing its philosophical roots to modern science. Present early researchers and their findings, and discuss the lack of ethnic diversity and gender among early psychologists. Also, discuss current trends.	Module 1, pp. 3–8	Standard Area: Introduction and Research Methods, Content Standard 6, Performance Standards 6.1, 6.2, 6.3, 6.4
Lesson 2	Introduce the modern perspectives. Introduce key psychologists known for each perspective. Tie these psychologists to philosophical roots discussed in Lesson 1. Use an example of human behavior to illustrate each perspective.	Module 1, pp. 4–11	Content Standard 1, Performance Standard 1.1, Content Standard 6, Performance Standards 6.1, 6.2, 6.3
Lesson 3	Discuss the major subfields and possible careers in psychology. Introduce new areas of interest such as behavior genetics and evolutionary and positive psychology.	Module 1, pp. 11–14	Content Standard 2, Performance Standard 2.1
Lesson 4	Introduce psychological research. Compare advantages and disadvantages of naturalistic observations, case studies, surveys, and longitudinal and cross-sectional studies. Introduce experimentation.	Module 2, pp. 17–20, 22–24	Content Standard 3, Performance Standards 3.1, 3.3
Lesson 5	Discuss setting up an experiment. Use an example hypothesis, and design a hypothetical experiment by discussing independent and dependent variables, subject selection, control, and replication.	Module 2, pp. 24–30, 31	Content Standard 3, Performance Standards 3.1, 3.2, 3.3
Lesson 6	Discuss the use and importance of statistics. Apply the hypothetical experiment designed in Lesson 5 to illustrate use of correlation, measures of central tendency, variation, and statistical significance.	Module 2, pp. 21–22, 30; Psychology's Statistics, pp. A-1–A-17	Content Standard 4, Performance Standards 4.1, 4.2, 4.3, 4.4
Lesson 7	Discuss ethical considerations in psychological research for both human participants and for animals.	Module 2, pp. 31–33	Content Standard 5, Performance Standard 5.1
Lesson 8	Examine the role of genetics and the environment in determining intelligence and personality. Consider evidence gathered in twin and adoption studies. (Note: This lesson may act as an introduction for Chapter 2. You might consider testing students on Modules 1 and 2 and including coverage of Module 3 with Chapter 2.)	Module 3, pp. 39–53	Standard Area: Biological Bases of Behavior, Content Standard 1, Performance Standard 1.3, Content Standard 7, Performance Standard 7.1, Content Standard 8, Performance Standard 8.1 Standard Area: Life Span Development, Content Standard 3, Performance Standard 3.4, Content Standard 4

CHAPTER 1

Introduction, History, and Research Methods

Introducing the Chapter

The Points: Chapter Objectives

- Define *psychology* and describe its scientific nature.
- Trace the historical development of psychology, including contributions from researchers from diverse backgrounds.
- Briefly describe the different perspectives from which psychologists examine behavior and mental processes, understanding that each perspective provides a significant contribution to psychology.
- Describe the variety of career options to individuals pursuing a psychology degree.
- Discuss the advantage of the scientific research method over other ways of knowing.
- Identify ways bias influences research outcomes.
- Discuss the advantages and disadvantages of the case study method.
- Understand the difference between causation and correlation.
- Identify the advantages and disadvantages of the survey method.
- Evaluate the importance of the experimental method on behavioral research.
- Evaluate the importance of statistics in the research process.
- Summarize the ethical principles for working with humans in research.
- Determine why animals are important to psychological research, and discuss the ethical considerations for working with animals.
- Understand the impact of genetic predisposition on behavior.
- Determine what traits are more likely to be passed from one generation to the next.
- Understand the influence of culture on a person's behavior.

CHAPTER 1

Introduction, History, and Research Methods

Have you ever seen headlines similar to these in a newspaper or on a news-oriented Web site: Local Water Pollution Levels Rise; International Conflict Continues, More Violence Predicted; Energy Conservation a Concern as Winter Approaches; More Single Parents as Divorce Rate Increases.

Do you notice a thread or two tying these headlines together? First and most obvious, all these headlines focus on some sort of problem. Second, and more interesting from a psychological perspective, all these problems involve behaviors (pollution, conflict, conservation, divorce), which means their solutions will include the work of those who study behavior for a living: psychologists.

Psychology's success in helping solve these and other problems will depend in part on whether you, your friends, and your family understand some of psychology's fundamental beliefs. For example, we all should know that behavior has multiple causes, and that knowledge of psychological methods or practices makes behavioral change more likely.

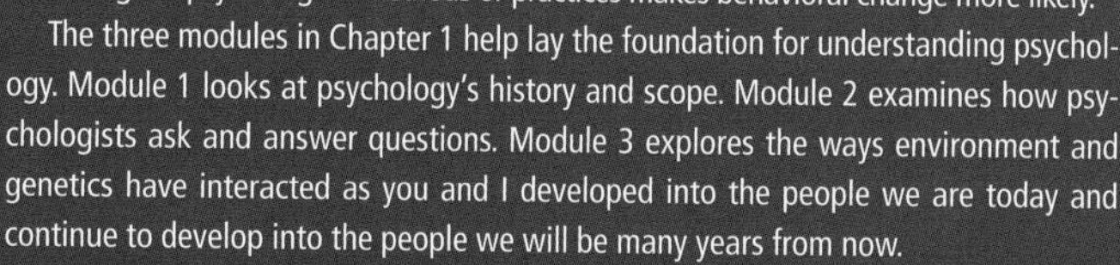

The three modules in Chapter 1 help lay the foundation for understanding psychology. Module 1 looks at psychology's history and scope. Module 2 examines how psychologists ask and answer questions. Module 3 explores the ways environment and genetics have interacted as you and I developed into the people we are today and continue to develop into the people we will be many years from now.

Performance Standards

Standard Area: Introduction and Research Methods

Content Standard 1: Modern psychological perspectives

Performance Standard 1.1 Examine the biological, behavioral, cognitive, and social-cultural perspectives.

- Discuss the theories of the twentieth century and examine the roots of the modern perspectives. (Student Text pp. 4–8)
- Discuss how each of the six contemporary perspectives—cognitive, biological, social-cultural, behavioral, humanistic, and psychodynamic—explain helping behavior. (Student Text pp. 9–11)
- Introduce the "new" perspectives—behavior genetics, evolutionary psychology, and positive psychology—and use them to explain helping behavior. (Student Text pp. 11–12)

Content Standard 2: Careers and subfields in psychology

Performance Standard 2.1 Name and understand the major subfields of psychology.

- Define *clinical psychologist*. (Student Text pp. 12–13)
- Present Figure 1.3, Specialty Areas in Psychology, and Where Do APA Psychologists Work? (Student Text p. 13)
- Discuss basic research and four examples of academic psychologists—biological, social, developmental, and cognitive psychologists. (Student Text p. 13)
- Discuss applied research and four examples of such researchers—organizational psychologists, human-factors psychologists, psychometricians, and educational psychologists. (Student Text pp. 13–14)

Content Standard 6: The roots of scientific psychology

Performance Standard 6.1 Explore the philosophical roots of psychology.

- Discuss the difference between modern psychology and its philosophical predecessor. (Student Text p. 4)

Performance Standard 6.2 Describe the development of empirical psychology.

- Discuss the early research by Wilhelm Wundt, E. B. Titchener, Gestalt psychologists, William James, Ivan Pavlov, and John B. Watson. (Student Text pp. 4–6)

Performance Standard 6.3 Examine psychological theories in the twentieth century.

- Discuss Gestalt psychology. (Student Text p. 6)
- Discuss Sigmund Freud's psychoanalysis and development of psychodynamic theory. (Student Text pp. 5–6)
- Present the behaviorism of Ivan Pavlov, John B. Watson, B. F. Skinner, and Albert Bandura. (Student Text p. 6)
- Introduce the humanistic theories of Abraham Maslow and Carl Rogers. (Student Text p. 6)
- Present Jean Piaget's study of children's cognitive abilities. (Student Text p. 6)
- Present Figure 1.1, a comprehensive chart detailing major historical events from 1879 to 1977. (Student Text p. 7)

Performance Standard 6.4 Understanding psychology's increasing ethnic and gender diversity.

- Discuss the lack of ethnic and gender diversity in early psychology. (Student Text p. 8)
- Present men and women who were psychological pioneers—G. Stanley Hall, Mary Whiton Calkins, Margaret Floy Washburn, Francis Cecil Sumner, and Inez Beverly Prosser. (Student Text p. 8)
- Present Figure 1.1, a comprehensive chart detailing major historical events from 1879 to 1977. (Student Text p. 7)
- Discuss current statistics revealing changes in ethnic and gender diversity among current psychologists. (Student Text p. 8)

Materials NETWORK

All of the items from the Video, Activity, and Enrichment Centers listed below come from the *Teacher's Resource Binder.* These items will help you teach and expand on concepts presented in Module 1.

trb This logo indicates when an item from the **Materials Network** may be used in conjunction with a specific note found in this module's *Teacher's Edition.*

Modern Psychology's Roots

Activity Center

- **Critical Thinking Activity:** *Fact or Falsehood?* Students' preconceptions about psychology are either exposed as incorrect or reinforced as correct. (*Teacher's Resource Binder*, p. 1-1; **Handout 1–1**)
- **Critical Thinking Activity:** *Psychology as Science (PAS) Scale* Students' understanding and attitude toward the study of psychology is gauged with this questionnaire. (*Teacher's Resource Binder*, p. 1-1; **Handout 1–2**)
- **Building Vocabulary:** *Crossword Puzzle* and *Matching Terms and Definitions* Students learn module terms and names. (*Teacher's Resource Binder*, p. 1-1; **Handouts 1–3** and **1–4**)
- **Graphic Organizer:** *Charts* As students fill in these charts, they become acquainted with famous names in psychology and psychological perspectives. (*Teacher's Resource Binder*, p. 1-1; **Handouts 1–5** and **1–6**)
- **Technology Application Activity:** *Applying Psychology Through Study Skills* With this Web-based activity, students discover a direct relationship between psychology and their lives. (*Teacher's Resource Binder*, p. 1-1; **Handout 1–7**)
- **Critical Thinking Activity:** *Describing Psychologists as Scientists* A brainstorming activity helps students explore preconceptions about the professions of psychologist and scientist. (*Teacher's Resource Binder*, p. 1-1)
- **Critical Thinking Activity:** *Science/Art Continuum: Where Does Psychology Fit?* Using a visual continuum, students explore their thoughts of where the study of psychology belongs. (*Teacher's Resource Binder*, p. 1-1; **Handout 1–8**)
- **Technology Application Activity:** *What Happened on Your Birthday?* This Internet activity helps students connect their birthdays with dates of important psychological events. (*Teacher's Resource Binder*, p. 1-1)
- **Cooperative Learning Activity:** *Read All About It! Wundt Opens a Psychology Lab: A Newspaper Assignment for the History of Psychology* Working in groups, students create newspapers that detail psychological and world events for specific years. (*Teacher's Resource Binder*, p. 1-1)
- **Cooperative Learning Activity:** *Diversity in Textbooks* This activity helps students explore the prevalence of minorities and women in both current and past psychology texts. (*Teacher's Resource Binder*, p. 1-1)

Enrichment Center

- **Enrichment Lesson:** *Philosophical Roots of Psychology* This is a quick discussion of the history of Western philosophy as it relates to human behavior. (*Teacher's Resource Binder*, p. 1-1)
- **Enrichment Lesson:** *Psychology's First Experiments* Students will find Morton Hunt's account of history's first recorded psychology experiment interesting, even amusing. (*Teacher's Resource Binder*, p. 1-1)

Six Contemporary Perspectives

Activity Center

- **Cooperative Learning Activity:** *What Perspective Is Dominant in Scientific Psychology?* This activity helps students appreciate each perspective. (*Teacher's Resource Binder*, p. 1-1)

Enrichment Center

- **Enrichment Lesson:** *History of Psychology* Advanced students will appreciate some clarification about psychological schools. (*Teacher's Resource Binder*, p. 1-1)

Psychology's Horizon

Activity Center

- **Application Activity:** *A Beautiful Day* Positive psychology will seem less abstract when students seek to create and live out their ideal "beautiful day." (*Teacher's Resource Binder*, p. 1-1)

Enrichment Center

- **Enrichment Lesson:** *Positive Psychology in Focus* The emerging field of positive psychology is an area where timeless ideas are being given new emphasis. (*Teacher's Resource Binder*, p. 1-1)

Careers in Psychology

Activity Center

- **Technology Application Activity:** *Careers in Psychology* With this activity, students explore Web sites that tell about the array of careers in psychology. (*Teacher's Resource Binder*, p. 1-1)
- **Technology Application Activity:** *Introducing APA and APS on the World Wide Web* This activity will introduce students to two organizations that have profoundly affected psychology since its founding. (*Teacher's Resource Binder*, p. 1-1; **Handout 1–9**)

Enrichment Center

- **Enrichment Lesson:** *Psychology's Subfields* Students learn about many of psychology's subspecialties that provide for diverse career choices and opportunities. (*Teacher's Resource Binder*, p. 1-1)

MODULE 1

Introduction, History, Perspectives, and Careers

What's the point? 1. What is psychology?

A crush of students collects outside my classroom during the six-minute passing time between class periods. They are standing on tiptoe, craning their necks side-to-side, attempting to gain better views of the struggle not far from my door. Echoing through the hall, the tardy bell does little to disperse them.

Predictably, the observing crowd swells in number, making it nearly impossible to identify the two combatants at the center of this undeserved attention. An assistant principal intervenes, and as quickly as it started, the skirmish ends. Both students receive three-day, "in-house" suspensions.

Fortunately, disruptions such as this are rare in my high school. And with talk of "the fight" buzzing from desk to desk, we start discussing some of the questions *psychologists* might pose about the incident we've just witnessed.

- Are some of us born more aggressive than others?
- How are levels of aggression affected by what we learn from our parents, peers, and cultural groups?
- What are the biological influences on aggression?
- What motivates some people to settle their differences physically while others talk them out?
- Are young adults more likely than middle-aged adults to take part in physical confrontations?
- How could this situation have been avoided or defused?
- Why were students so much more likely to watch this conflict (and be late to class!) than to break it up?

This psychology course will help you answer these and many other interesting questions.

MODULE 1

Introduction, History, Perspectives, and Careers

Introducing the Module

The Points: Module Objectives

- Define psychology.
- Trace when and where modern psychology began.
- Determine if any one psychological perspective can answer all of psychology's questions.
- Identify new areas of interest that psychologists are exploring today.
- Describe what psychologists do.

trb Building Vocabulary

Give students the opportunity to interact with the module terminology with **Building Vocabulary:** *Crossword Puzzle* and *Matching Terms and Definitions* (*Teacher's Resource Binder,* p. 1-1; **Handouts 1–3** and **1–4**). The crossword puzzle deals with schools of thought, while the matching exercise deals with famous names from psychology's history.

■ JOURNAL WRITING

Invite students to use the following questions and writing prompts as springboards for entries in their psychology journals:

- Describe what you think a psychologist does.
- How do psychologists affect your life?
- How are science and intuition different from one another?
- What are some psychological questions you always wanted to know the answers to?

Getting Started

Before students begin reading, you might have them write down the first five words that come to mind when they hear the word *psychology.* Suggest they look at their list from time to time to compare and contrast these initial responses with concepts about psychology they discover while reading this module.

trb The following activities will help identify misconceptions about psychology and guide students toward an understanding of psychology as a science: **Critical Thinking Activity:** *Fact or Falsehood?* (*Teacher's Resource Binder,* p. 1-1; **Handout 1–1**) and **Critical Thinking Activity:** *Psychology as Science (PAS) Scale* (*Teacher's Resource Binder,* p. 1-1; **Handout 1–2**).

MODULE 1

Teaching the Points

■ TEACHING TIPS

web (1) You can log on as an instructor to the book companion site for *Thinking About Psychology* at **www.worthpublishers.com/thinkingaboutpsych.** It contains teacher resources for class presentations as well as review and assessment of module concepts and terms.

(2) Because this module deals so much with history, help students connect their inherent curiosity about human behavior to famous people from the past who had the same drive to understand themselves and the world around them. Having students gather their thoughts on psychology as a science along with their questions about human behavior will help facilitate this connection.

trb At this point, you may wish to use **Enrichment Lesson:** *Philosophical Roots of Psychology* (*Teacher's Resource Binder*, p. 1-1).

trb (3) To help students make connections between science and psychology, you may wish to use **Critical Thinking Activity:** *Describing Psychologists as Scientists* (*Teacher's Resource Binder*, p. 1-1) and **Critical Thinking Activity:** *Science/Art Continuum: Where Does Psychology Fit?* (*Teacher's Resource Binder*, p. 1-1).

■ MULTICULTURAL CONNECTIONS

trb (1) Important historical and psychological events from other cultures and countries may be researched by using the following activities: **Technology Application Activity:** *What Happened on Your Birthday?* (*Teacher's Resource Binder*, p. 1-1) and **Cooperative Learning Activity:** *Read All About It! Wundt Opens a Psychology Lab: A Newspaper Assignment for the History of Psychology* (*Teacher's Resource Binder*, p. 1-1).

(2) Invite nonnative English speakers to make presentations to the class about psychology in their native culture. This will not only provide a forum for these students to use their English-language skills, but it will also help listeners appreciate a culture's effect on psychology.

What Makes Us Smile? Psychologists use scientific methods to study topics such as happiness, love, and friendship.

Psychology is a science. More specifically, psychology is the *science of behavior and mental processes*. Before going any further, let's make sure we understand the three parts of this definition.

When we say that psychology is a *science*, we mean that psychologists rely on scientific research methods in their attempts to unravel answers to questions like, "Why do some people offer help when, under the same circumstances, others do not?" Psychologists systematically collect their research data and use mathematical formulas to analyze the results. Scientific methods are an essential key to unlocking human behavior's secrets.

The last two parts of our definition, *behavior* and *mental processes*, establish the incredibly broad range of interesting topics that psychologists study. Any directly observable thing you do, from laughing to turning the pages of this book, is a behavior that psychologists could study. But psychologists also study the unobservable—our mental processes, which include thoughts, feelings, and dreams.

Modern Psychology's Roots

2. When and where did modern psychology begin?

We have probably been curious about ourselves and how we interact with the world around us for as long as humans have been around. A basic "study" of psychology can be found in the world's earliest philosophical and biological writings. But the history of *modern* psychology, as we know it today, represents only about the last 125 years. Most of the other sciences are much older than psychology.

Psychology's earliest pioneers shared a keen interest in understanding mental processes and, later, behavior. One of these early pioneers, German philosopher/physiologist **Wilhelm Wundt** (pronounced, *Voont*), is often called the "father" of psychology. Psychology was "born" in 1879, when Wundt opened a laboratory devoted exclusively to psychological experiments.

Wundt's student, **E. B. Titchener,** introduced **structuralism,** the first prominent system for organizing psychological beliefs, to the United States. Just as a chemist tries to understand the different elements in chemical compounds, structuralists tried to understand the *structure* of conscious experience by analyzing the intensity, clarity, and quality of its basic parts. For example, picture a blade of grass. A structuralist might have lingered over the intensity of the green color of the blade of grass, the clarity of its texture, and the roughly rectangular shape of the blade. For Titchener and his students, successful descriptions

► **psychology** The scientific study of behavior and mental processes.

► **Wilhelm Wundt** (1832–1920) Founder of modern psychology.

► **E. B. Titchener** (1867–1927) Founder of structuralism.

► **structuralism** Theory that analyzed the basic elements of thoughts and sensations to determine the structure of conscious experience.

Suggested Readings

Use the following works as teacher-preparation tools or as enrichment for advanced students:

Hunt, M. (1993). *The story of psychology.* New York: Doubleday.

Kimble, G. A., & Wertheimer, M. (Eds.). (2000). *Portraits of pioneers in psychology* (Vols. 1–4). Washington, DC: American Psychological Association.

Pickren, W. E., & Dewsbury, D. A. (Eds.). (2002). *Evolving perspectives in the history of psychology.* Washington, DC: American Psychological Association.

Seligman, M. E. P., & Csikszentmihalyi, M. (2000). Positive psychology: An introduction. *American Psychologist, 55,* 5–14.

Street, W. R. (1994). *A chronology of noteworthy events in American psychology.* Washington, DC: American Psychological Association.

of such aspects were the building blocks of consciousness. Perhaps the greatest contribution structuralism made to psychology, though, is that it provided a theory to disprove, giving rise to other psychological systems.

Gestalt (a German word that means "configuration" and is pronounced gih–SHTALT) **psychology** offered one of these alternative systems. Opposed to merely analyzing the elements of consciousness, Gestalt psychologists protested that adding the individual elements of an experience together creates something new and different—that *the whole is different from the sum of its parts*. For example, think of the notes to your favorite song. Individually, each note doesn't mean much, but put them together and you have a tune. Combining the elements creates something that did not exist before. Most of the prominent Gestalt psychologists fled Nazi Germany in the 1930s, but their work resurfaced in subsequent psychological theories later in the century.

Another psychologist who disagreed with the structuralist approach was Harvard professor **William James.** James, the first American psychologist, once noted that the first psychology lecture he ever heard was his own. He went on to write the first psychology textbook, published in 1890. His textbook—which took him 12 years to write—stimulated thought and influenced thousands of students over the next several decades. For James, the goal of psychology was to study the *functions* of consciousness, or the ways consciousness helps people adapt to their environment, a view that became known as **functionalism.**

Few outside of psychology have heard of structuralism and functionalism, but almost everyone has heard of **Sigmund Freud.** Have you seen the stereotypic therapist, complete with beard and note pad, talking to a patient reclining on a couch? The cartoon below is patterned after Freud. In 1900, this Austrian physician introduced the first complete theory of personality, which he called *psychoanalysis*. Freud's **psychoanalytic perspective** differed from other perspectives in two key ways:

- It focused on abnormal behavior, which Freud attributed to unconscious drives and conflicts, often stemming from childhood.
- It relied on personal observation and reflection instead of controlled laboratory experimentation as its means of discovery.

Freud claimed his work was scientific, but because he relied on self-reported reflections rather than scientific methods to gather information, it really wasn't.

Freud died in 1939, and many of his ideas are out of date or have since been disproved. But, elements of Freud's original theory are still very much a part of our

"Sure, I'm Alfred the Great now, but in high school I couldn't get a date."

▶ **Gestalt psychology** Psychological perspective that emphasized our tendency to integrate pieces of information into meaningful wholes.

▶ **William James** (1842–1910) First American psychologist and author of the first psychology textbook.

▶ **functionalism** Theory that emphasized the functions of consciousness and the ways consciousness helps people adapt to their environment.

▶ **Sigmund Freud** (1856–1939) Founder of psychoanalysis.

▶ **psychoanalytic perspective** School of thought that focuses on how behavior springs from unconscious drives and conflicts; contemporary version is called *psychodynamic perspective*.

■ TEACHING TIPS

(1) Help students with the various schools of thought, which might at first seem confusing and abstract. Here are some issues that might benefit through clarification:

- *Structuralism versus functionalism* Make sure students understand that the name of each school helps define the school's focus.
- *Gestalt psychology* This school is often considered the most abstract. Along with the music note analogy cited in the text, you may also use examples with letters and words that follow the same logic.
- *Misconceptions about psychoanalysis* To most students, this is psychology. Be sure to emphasize the drawbacks of Freud's methodology while acknowledging his contributions.
- *The strict rules of behaviorism* Be sure students understand that, for behaviorists, if a behavior couldn't be observed, it wasn't considered in the realm of psychology.
- *The "third force" moniker for humanistic psychology* The two predominant "forces" in psychology prior to 1960 were psychoanalysis and behaviorism. Humanistic psychology's title of "third force" refers to its break from these two schools.

(2) Because students often want to know which perspective is "right," be sure to emphasize that psychology is a diverse field that subscribes to an eclectic approach—that is, using multiple theories to explain human behavior.

trb At this point, you may wish to use **Cooperative Learning Activity:** *What Perspective Is Dominant in Scientific Psychology?* (*Teacher's Resource Binder*, p. 1-1).

Meeting Individual Needs

trb GRAPHIC ORGANIZERS Provide learning opportunities for all levels of learners with one of the following options for using **Graphic Organizer:** *Charts* (*Teacher's Resource Binder*, p. 1-1; **Handouts 1–5** and **1–6**):

- **Independent Learners** Students can fill out the organizers on their own or follow along in class during discussion and lecture.
- **Cooperative Learners** Students may use the textbook as a resource and work in groups to find the answers that fit in the blanks.
- **Exceptional Learners** Graphic organizers can fill a special education need to provide notes for exceptional students. These students can fill in the blanks independently, with a student or teacher/tutor, or along with class discussion and lecture.

MODULE 1

■ **JOURNAL WRITING**

Invite students to use the following questions as springboards for entries in their psychology journals:

- Why might it be difficult to explain human behavior using only one perspective?
- How is each of the schools of thought limited in explaining human behavior?
- How might psychologists encourage men and women of all cultural and social backgrounds to pursue psychology?

trb At this point, you may wish to use **Cooperative Learning Activity:** *What Perspective Is Dominant in Scientific Psychology?* (*Teacher's Resource Binder*, p. 1-1).

■ **CHECKING FOR UNDERSTANDING**

Here are several ways to assess comprehension at this point in the module:

- Assign any or all of the journal questions or prompts for an in-class writing assessment.
- Divide the students into groups or pairs and give each group or pair a journal question prompt. As student groups or pairs present their answers to the class, correct any misconceptions that may arise.

▶ **Ivan Pavlov** (1849–1936) Russian physiologist who showed that animals learn some things through association.

▶ **John B. Watson** (1878–1958) Founder of behaviorism.

▶ **behaviorist perspective** School of thought that focuses on how we learn observable responses.

▶ **B. F. Skinner** (1904–1990) American psychologist whose brand of behaviorism focused on the role of responses in learning.

▶ **humanistic psychology** School of thought that focuses on the study of conscious experience, the individual's freedom to choose, and capacity for personal growth.

▶ **Abraham Maslow** (1908–1970) Leader in the humanistic psychology movement.

▶ **Carl Rogers** (1902–1987) Leader in the humanistic movement.

▶ **Jean Piaget** (1896–1980) Developmental and cognitive psychologist known for his studies of children's thought processes.

pop culture today. A "Freudian slip," for example, is a misstatement reflective of something you'd *like* to say. "Do you want to study for tomorrow's kizz?" a boy might stammer to the girl of his dreams. The phrase "anal-retentive" comes from one of Freud's developmental stages and refers to someone who is excessively neat, clean, and compulsive (stuck in the "anal stage," where one supposedly comes to terms with bodily functions). Freud's greater legacy, however, was his novel approach to understanding behavior, and some of these ideas have been incorporated into *psychodynamic theory*, which is a modernized version of Freud's original theories. Psychologists influenced by psychodynamic theory still assume, as Freud did, that our unconscious thoughts, inner conflicts, and childhood experiences significantly affect our personality and behaviors.

Russian physiologist **Ivan Pavlov's** classic studies of animal learning in 1906 fueled a move in psychology toward interest in *observable* behaviors and away from the self-examination of inner ideas and experiences. Seven years later, in the United States, the following words appeared in *Psychological Review* and struck a nerve in the world of psychology:

> Psychology as the behaviorist views it is a purely objective experimental branch of natural science. Its theoretical goal is the prediction and control of human behavior.

With these words, **John B. Watson** launched *behaviorism*, the most dominant perspective of the twentieth century. Watson's **behaviorist perspective** studied only observable and objectively describable acts. For Watson, studying the unconscious, or anything you cannot see, was of little value. Watson's work made psychology more objective and scientific in its methods, though most behaviorists today recognize the significance of studying mental processes *as well as* behaviors. In the past 40 years, this school of thought has been modified somewhat by other behaviorists, such as **B. F. Skinner** and Albert Bandura. Today behaviorism focuses on learning through rewards and observation.

Behaviorism and psychoanalysis maintained their hold on the field into the 1960s, when **humanistic psychology** became the "third force" in psychology (Schultz & Schultz, 1996). In contrast to supporters of the other two perspectives, humanistic psychologists such as **Abraham Maslow** and **Carl Rogers** emphasized *conscious experience* as the proper focus of psychology. They also believed that humans have free will in their decision making, and that healthy people strive to reach their full potential. They rejected the idea that humans are controlled by a series of rewards and reinforcements.

Swiss biologist/psychologist **Jean Piaget** (pronounced pee-ah-ZHAY) is another pioneer, best known for his work on how children develop their thinking abilities. His interest began in 1920, and his work continued for 50 years!

Psychology's origins can be traced to various countries and academic fields (Figure 1.1).

Cross-Curricular Connection

trb **HISTORY** You may wish to work with a history teacher to connect psychology's past with past world events, using one of the following suggestions:

- Team-teach so that all students can learn about the history of the world and the relevant psychological implications of historical events.
- History teachers can enhance students' understanding of world events after students complete **Cooperative Learning Activity:** *Read All About It! Wundt Opens a Psychology Lab: A Newspaper Assignment for the History of Psychology* (*Teacher's Resource Binder*, p. 1-1) and **Technology Application Activity:** *What Happened on Your Birthday?* (*Teacher's Resource Binder*, p. 1-1).

Wilhelm Wundt (1832–1920)

William James (1842–1910)

Sigmund Freud (1856–1939)

Mary Whiton Calkins (1863–1930)

Margaret Floy Washburn (1871–1930)

John B. Watson (1878–1958)

Inez Beverly Prosser (1897–1934)

B. F. Skinner (1904–1990)

Eric Erikson (1902–1994)

Abraham Maslow (1908–1970)

Roger Sperry (1913–1994)

Eleanor Maccoby (1917–)

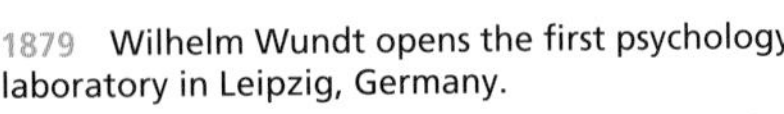

1879 Wilhelm Wundt opens the first psychology laboratory in Leipzig, Germany.

1890 William James publishes the first psychology textbook, *Principles of Psychology.*

1892 G. Stanley Hall founds the American Psychological Association (APA). E. B. Titchener introduces structuralism.

1900 Sigmund Freud publishes his psychoanalytic views in *The Interpretation of Dreams.*

1905 Mary Whiton Calkins becomes the first woman to be president of the APA. Alfred Binet develops the first intelligence test.

1906 Ivan Pavlov publishes his results on learning by association.

1908 Margaret Floy Washburn becomes the first woman to receive a doctoral degree (Ph.D.) in psychology.

1913 John B. Watson publishes "Psychology as the Behaviorist Views It."

1920 Francis Cecil Sumner becomes the first African-American to earn a doctoral degree in psychology.

1926 Jean Piaget publishes *The Language and Thought of the Child.*

1933 Inez Beverly Prosser becomes the first African-American woman to earn a doctoral degree in psychology.

1938 B. F. Skinner promotes behaviorism, publishing *The Behavior of Organisms.*

1939 Kenneth Clark and Mamie Phipps Clark begin work that will be cited by the U.S. Supreme Court 1954 decision ending racial segregation in public schools.

1945 Karen Horney challenges the male bias in Freud's psychoanalytic theory and proposes a social-cultural approach.

1950 Erik Erikson publishes *Childhood and Society,* outlining stages of psychosocial development.

1954 Abraham Maslow presents the humanistic perspective. Gordon Allport publishes *The Nature of Prejudice.*

1961 Albert Bandura stresses the importance of imitation in learning, proposing a social-learning theory.

1964 Roger Sperry demonstrates the importance of the brain in behavior with split-brain research.

1969 John Berry calls attention to the importance of cross-cultural research in psychology.

1974 Eleanor Maccoby and Carol Jacklin publish *The Psychology of Sex Differences.* Sandra Bem and Janet Spence develop tests assessing and promoting female competence.

1977 Judith Rodin shows the importance of perceived control.

E. B. Titchener (1867–1927)

G. Stanley Hall (1844–1924)

Alfred Binet (1857–1911)

Ivan Pavlov (1849–1936)

Francis Cecil Sumner (1895–1954)

Jean Piaget (1896–1980)

Mamie Phipps Clark (1917–1983)

Karen Horney (1885–1952)

Gordon Allport (1897–1967)

Albert Bandura (1925–)

Sandra Bem (1944–)

Judith Rodin (1944–)

Figure 1.1 Important People in the History of Psychology

■ TEACHING TIP

Students should be able to see from this timeline that psychology has been influenced by a wide diversity of people. Women and people of color have been influential since psychology's early days even though society was not always open to their involvement and input.

trb At this point, you may wish to use **Cooperative Learning Activity:** ***Diversity in Textbooks*** (*Teacher's Resource Binder,* p. 1-1).

F • Y • I

Two Nobel Prize winners are included in this chart of psychology's important people.

- **Ivan Pavlov** won the prize in medicine and physiology in 1904 for his work in digestion in dogs. Through this work, he discovered the principles of *classical conditioning,* a fundamental theory of learning supported by the behaviorists. Pavlov was a profound influence on John B. Watson.
- **Roger Sperry** won the prize in medicine and physiology in 1981 for his work with split-brain patients. Sperry's work established that there was a difference between the left and right hemispheres of the brain.

Reteaching

trb Reinforce students' knowledge of the famous names in psychology by using **Graphic Organizer:** ***Charts*** (*Teacher's Resource Binder,* p. 1-1; **Handout 1–5**). Students can fill in the information on each famous name, connecting these people with the contributions they made to further our knowledge of human behavior.

MODULE 1

■ **LOOKING AT THE ISSUES**

The dominance of white males in academia in the early part of the twentieth century led to a skew in the availability and interpretation of data collected in studies during that time. Have students consider the following questions:

- What were some common assumptions about the behavior of women and minorities at this time in history?
- How might confirmation bias (only looking for results that confirm your expectations) have influenced the interpretation of data from this time period?
- What aspects of the behavior of women and minorities might have been ignored by white males at this time?

■ **APPLYING THE POINTS**

If possible, have students contact the admissions offices at universities in your area to inquire about the number of women and minorities admitted to undergraduate and graduate programs. The following questions can guide research and subsequent discussion of students' findings:

- Are the number of women and minorities attending that college reflective of the general population? Why or why not?
- How does the university encourage more women and minority applicants? What advice would the admissions officer give to women or members of minority groups considering that particular university?

■ **MULTICULTURAL CONNECTIONS**

Have students explore how psychology has evolved and influenced other cultures around the world. The following questions can guide research and subsequent discussion of students' findings:

- Psychology flourished in Europe and North America during the late nineteenth and early twentieth centuries, but how was it viewed in other parts of the world?
- Is psychology a universally studied discipline? Why or why not?

trb At this point, you may wish to use Cooperative Learning Activity: *Diversity in Textbooks* (*Teacher's Resource Binder*, p. 1-1).

Up Close

Psychology's American Groundbreakers

Like other academic fields, early psychology lacked the ethnic and gender diversity it has today. Though difficult to imagine by today's standards, women and minority students were often discouraged from attending colleges and universities at the time of psychology's birth, and for decades after. If this seems shocking, remember that women were not allowed to vote in the United States until 1920. The spirit of the times in North America and in Europe (where psychology flourished) favored the advancement of white men at the expense of women and people of color. These racial and gender barriers meant white males dominated psychology (and all sciences), because other people rarely had the opportunity to gain the education, knowledge, and training necessary to become a psychologist.

Several of America's groundbreakers in psychology excelled in, and in spite of, the cultural climate.

G. Stanley Hall was a student of Wundt's who achieved a number of psychological firsts. Hall was the first American to receive a doctoral degree (Ph.D.) in psychology. He also opened the first psychology laboratory in the United States (at Johns Hopkins University), and he was the first American Psychological Association (APA) president, elected in 1892.

As we have seen, John Watson's belief that only observable behavior (and not mental processes) should be studied dominated psychology's focus for half a century.

Working with William James, **Mary Whiton Calkins** had to overcome discrimination and prejudice against women to become the first woman to complete the requirements for a Ph.D. in psychology in 1895. Harvard at that time did not admit women and so would not award her a degree. Years later, Harvard offered to give her a degree from Radcliffe College (established by Harvard to educate women). Calkins refused the offer, stating that she had completed her work *at Harvard*, not Radcliffe. Calkins was elected president of the APA in 1905.

Margaret Floy Washburn was E. B. Titchener's first graduate student at Cornell University, and she was the first woman to receive a Ph.D. in psychology. In 1908, Washburn wrote the first textbook on comparative psychology, which examined animal behavior.

Francis Cecil Sumner, in 1920, became the first African-American to receive a Ph.D. in psychology. Sumner wrote many articles on racial prejudice, education for African-Americans, and nature-nurture issues. Sumner also established the psychology department at Howard University.

Inez Beverly Prosser, the first African-American woman to earn a Ph.D. in psychology, completed the requirements in 1933 at the University of Cincinnati. She studied the development of African-American children in segregated and integrated schools.

Today, half of all psychology doctorates are awarded to women, and two-thirds of all psychology graduate students (those who already have a bachelor's degree) are women (Martin, 1995). But, while roughly 33 percent of the U.S. population currently consists of minorities, the proportion of minority students in graduate programs is far from one in three. We can only hope that this gap will continue to close as university psychology departments across the country work to recruit the best and brightest students from all backgrounds. To meet the demands of our increasingly multicultural and ethnically diverse population, psychology will need to continue evolving.

Enriching

Have students do a research paper or presentation on the lives of the people mentioned on this page, in addition to any other influential figures from psychology's history. Students' work should address the following questions:

- What type of childhood did these people have? Did it seem remarkable or predictive of their future success in psychology? Why or why not?
- What type of schooling did they receive?
- What interests outside psychology did they pursue? Did those pursuits impact their research?
- What interesting facts helped to make these people more real to you?

Six Contemporary Psychological Perspectives

3. Can any one psychological perspective answer all of psychology's questions?

We can view behavior from many different viewpoints. **Psychological perspectives,** *schools of thought*, and *psychological approaches* are all synonyms for ways psychologists classify collections of ideas. Put another way, the psychologist who believes in a particular collection of ideas is said to view behavior from that particular perspective.

Psychology has seen perspectives come and go (Figure 1.2 on page 10). Most of the earlier, historical perspectives were forerunners to one or more modern perspectives.

To understand the contemporary perspectives, let's apply each to the same real-life possibility: whether a person helps a stranger pick up a spilled sack of groceries when given the opportunity. Why do some people help when others don't? Each perspective has an explanation.

With structuralism, functionalism, and Gestalt psychology as its forerunners, the **cognitive perspective** has grown dramatically more popular since the 1960s. Cognitive psychologists focus on how people think—how they take in, process, store, and retrieve information. Remembering something you've learned, for example, is a cognitive activity. From this perspective, helping could be a function of how we think about or interpret a situation. We may choose to help the shopper who drops a bag of groceries because we *think* it will make us look good to others. If we think helping will cause us to look silly, we leave the groceries on the ground.

The **biological perspective** attempts to understand behavior by studying the biological structures and substances underlying a given behavior, thought, or emotion. Biological psychologists might, for example, remind us that levels of a naturally occurring "feel-good" chemical found in the brain could affect helping behavior. Those lacking normal amounts of this brain chemical may be depressed, and depression could keep the person from wanting to help pick up the spilled groceries.

The **social-cultural perspective** focuses on how thinking and behavior change depending on the *setting* or *situation*. Social-cultural psychologists might tell us that helping is more likely to occur if you're with a couple of friends and 50 feet from your front door, and less likely if you're in a crowded, big-city movie theater lobby where few faces are familiar.

Three of the historically significant perspectives—the *behavioral*, *humanistic*, and *psychodynamic* (the modern version of the psychoanalytic perspective)—discussed earlier in this module also qualify as contemporary perspectives.

► **G. Stanley Hall** (1844–1924) First American man to earn a Ph.D. in psychology; opened first psychology lab in the United States; founded, and was the first president of, the American Psychological Association (APA).

► **Mary Whiton Calkins** (1863–1930) First woman to complete the requirements for a Ph.D. in psychology; first woman to be elected president of the American Psychological Association.

► **Margaret Floy Washburn** (1871–1930) First woman to receive a Ph.D. in psychology.

► **Francis Cecil Sumner** (1895–1954) First African-American man to receive a Ph.D. in psychology.

► **Inez Beverly Prosser** (1897–1934) First African-American woman to receive a Ph.D. in psychology.

► **psychological perspective** A particular view of behavior and/or mental processes that has grown into a movement.

► **cognitive perspective** School of thought that focuses on how we take in, process, store, and retrieve information.

► **biological perspective** School of thought that focuses on the physical structures and substances underlying a particular behavior, thought, or emotion.

► **social-cultural perspective** School of thought that focuses on how thinking or behavior changes in different contexts or situations.

■ LOOKING AT THE ISSUES

Technology has helped psychology develop as a science throughout the years. Some schools that were prominent in the early years of psychological history faded away as technology showed the limitations of a particular viewpoint. Other schools were born and reinforced as technology became available to lend insight into human behavior. Ask students to consider the following:

- What schools would have been phased out as technology became available? *(Structuralism and functionalism experienced a gradual fading as technology gave insight into the workings of the brain, learning, and body functions. Psychoanalysis also became less attractive as technology revealed the workings of the brain.)*
- What schools have thrived with the advent of new technologies?
- What schools may be unaffected by technology as we currently know it?

■ JOURNAL WRITING

Invite students to use the following questions as springboards for entries in their psychology journals:

- Which school of psychology appeals most to you? Which one appeals the least? Explain your answers.

Reteaching

Create a concept web that links the modern schools of thought with the historical perspectives. You can show how the three historical perspectives that are still flourishing today have influenced other schools.

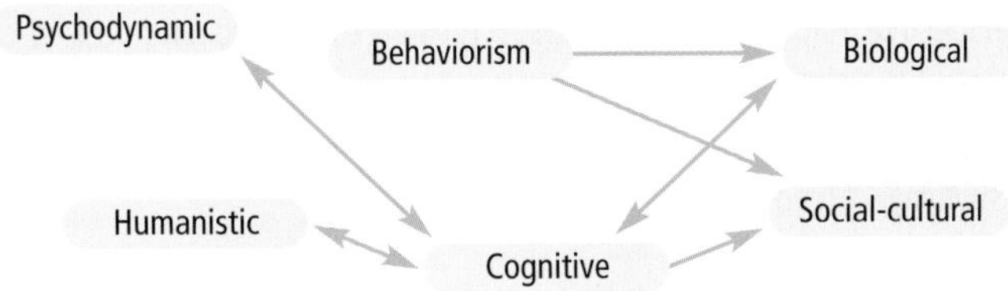

MODULE 1

■ TEACHING TIP

Link the following concepts with the three modern schools of thought that have thrived to modern times:

- *Behavioral*— classical and operant conditioning, learned helplessness and optimism, systematic desensitization
- *Humanistic*— positive psychology, self-actualization, hierarchy of needs, unconditional positive regard, client-centered therapy
- *Psychodynamic*— psychoanalysis, id, ego, superego, psychosexual development

tr A four-color transparency of Figure 1.2, Historical Development of Psychology's Main Schools of Thought, is available in the **Overhead Transparencies Set.**

■ CHECKING FOR UNDERSTANDING

Project the timeline from Figure 1.2 on an overhead with the key perspectives covered up. Have students identify the perspectives along the timeline to be sure they have the big picture of how psychology has evolved.

trb At this point, you may wish to use **Graphic Organizer:** *Psychological Perspectives* (*Teacher's Resource Binder*, p. 1-1; Handout 1–6).

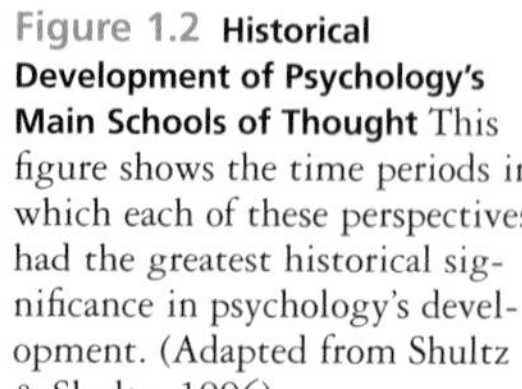
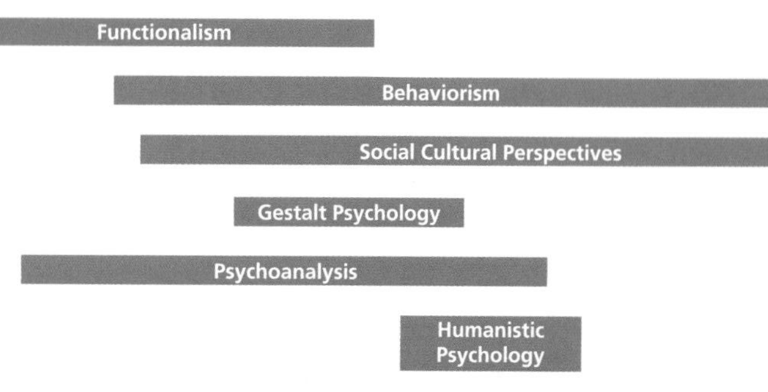

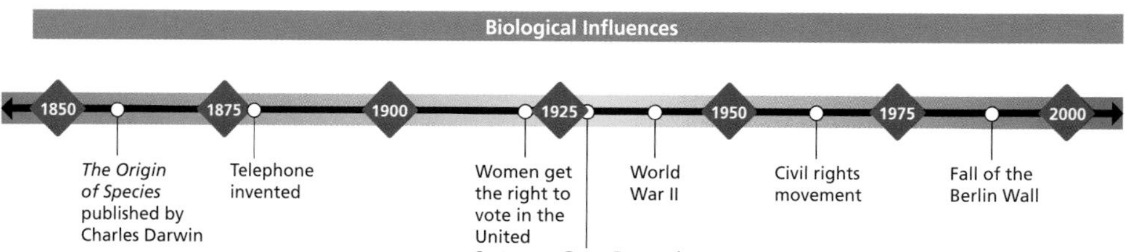

Figure 1.2 **Historical Development of Psychology's Main Schools of Thought** This figure shows the time periods in which each of these perspectives had the greatest historical significance in psychology's development. (Adapted from Shultz & Shultz, 1996)

Psychologists working from the *behavioral* perspective believe we learn certain responses through rewards, punishments, and observation. A behaviorist might suggest that a person who helps has previously observed someone being rewarded for helpful behavior. Learning that rewards come to those who help others fosters helping behavior.

Humanistic psychologists consider how healthy people strive to reach their full potential. A humanistic psychologist might suggest that a person who has met his or her safety and physiological needs (hunger, thirst, shelter) would be able to reach out socially and help another person in need.

Psychologists working from the *psychodynamic* perspective will consider how our helping behavior springs from unconscious drives and conflicts. A psychologist influenced by this perspective might suggest, for example, that helpful behavior results from an unfulfilled childhood wish to have one's mother accept one's offer to help.

As you can see, no one perspective lays claim to having all the answers to the question, "What makes us tick?" But now look at these six perspectives collectively. Can you see why most psychologists today subscribe to more than one perspective? The perspectives complement one another, and we draw from them all in our attempts to understand behavior and mental processes. Sometimes, we even look beyond these six—to developments on psychology's horizon—in our efforts to understand.

Cooperative Learning

Divide students into six groups, assigning to each group a particular perspective. Ask all groups to consider the same behavior—for example, why students fight with their parents or why they don't study for tests. Have group members discuss and then come to a consensus on the behavior from their assigned perspective. Allow time for groups to present their ideas and answer any questions from you or the rest of the class.

trb At this point, you may wish to use **Cooperative Learning Activity:** *What Perspective Is Dominant in Scientific Psychology?* (*Teacher's Resource Binder*, p. 1-1).

TABLE 1.1 SIX PERSPECTIVES ON PSYCHOLOGY

PERSPECTIVE	EXPLANATION OF THE HELPING BEHAVIOR
Cognitive How we process information	Our individual interpretations of an event affect how we respond.
Biological How our biological structures and substances underlie a given behavior, thought, or emotion	Brain chemistry controls the emotions and thoughts that eventually produce helping behavior
Social-Cultural How thinking and behavior change depending on the setting or situation	If we come from a cultural background that values helping, we're more likely to help. We're also more likely to help if we are in a comfortable situation, such as with a good friend, than if we are in a large, unfamiliar crowd.
Behavioral How we learn through rewards, punishments, and observation	If we have witnessed or been rewarded for helping behavior, we are more likely to help.
Humanistic How healthy people strive to reach their full potential	If our needs for nourishment and safety have been met, we are more likely to feel we can reach out and help others.
Psychodynamic How we are affected by unconscious drives and conflicts	Unresolved inner conflicts can affect whether we help others.

Psychology's Horizon

4. What new areas of interest are psychologists exploring today?

Psychology continues to grow. Three particularly strong developing areas in psychology are behavior genetics, evolutionary psychology, and positive psychology.

Those studying **behavior genetics** focus on the relative effects of our genes and environment on our behavior. Does this sound like a combination of biology and behaviorism? You bet. Let's apply the behavior genetics view to our helping example. A psychologist interested in behavior genetics might ask two questions: Is there a helpfulness trait? If so, is it triggered into action by growing up in a family that promotes and values helping those in need? If the answer to both questions is "yes," and if you possess the helping trait and the helpful family, you'll be bending down, picking up the oranges and the loaf of bread off the floor. Helping behavior is the product of learning *and* inherited genetic traits.

▶ **behavior genetics** School of thought that focuses on how much our genes and our environment influence our individual differences.

Enriching

Have students informally debate how nature and nurture influence behavior by eliciting responses to the following questions:

- Is behavior determined more by genes or by environment?
- How can scientists study which has more influence?
- How much of your own personality is determined by your genes? By your environment? Explain your answers.

■ CHECKING FOR UNDERSTANDING

Use the black-line master for Table 1.1, Six Perspectives of Psychology, available in the **Black-Line Masters Appendix** in the *Teacher's Resource Binder.* Blank out key spaces on the table before handing copies of the master to students. Then have students fill in the blanks with the correct concepts to see if they can identify and distinguish among the different perspectives on psychology.

■ TEACHING TIP

The three schools of thought mentioned in the Psychology's Horizon section have names that describe what areas they focus on.

- **Behavior genetics** studies the relationship between human behavior and the nature-nurture issue.
- **Evolutionary psychology** studies what qualities have evolved through natural selection that have helped humans adapt through the years.
- **Positive psychology** looks at what makes life good, fulfilling, and, well, positive.

trb At this point, you may wish to use **Enrichment Lesson:** *Psychology's Subfields* (*Teacher's Resource Binder*, p. 1-1).

■ APPLYING THE POINTS

Have students research universities that offer graduate study in behavior genetics or related fields in neuropsychology. In particular, have students search for answers to the following questions:

- How many programs are there? Are any of these programs in your area?
- What job opportunities are available to people who earn a degree in behavior genetics?

trb At this point, you may wish to use **Enrichment Lesson:** *Psychology's Subfields* (*Teacher's Resource Binder*, p. 1-1).

MODULE 1

■ TEACHING TIP

Discussion of the theory of evolution is controversial in some areas. Be sensitive to your students' feelings about evolution while educating them about how the theory has been applied to an explanation of human behavior.

■ APPLYING THE POINTS

Have students consider how the following behaviors might be explained from an evolutionary viewpoint:

- dating and marriage
- getting an education
- working at a stable job

■ LOOKING AT THE ISSUES

Positive psychologists feel that studying the positive aspects of human behavior is important because being happy is not just the absence of being sad or ill. Have students meet in small groups to discuss the following questions about positive psychology as a legitimate way to study behavior:

- Is being happy more than just not being sad or ill? Why or why not?
- How is the study of positive traits similar to the study of negative qualities? How is it different?
- Should the government fund positive psychology as it funds negative psychology? Why or why not?

trb At this point, you may wish to use Enrichment Lesson: *Positive Psychology in Focus* (*Teacher's Resource Binder*, p. 1-1).

▶ **positive psychology** Movement that focuses on the study of optimal human functioning and the factors that allow individuals and communities to thrive.

▶ **basic research** Pure science that aims to increase the scientific knowledge base.

▶ **applied research** Scientific study that aims to solve practical problems.

Some psychologists study behaviors that helped our ancestors survive. These psychologists hope to gain insight into behavior using the *evolutionary psychology* approach. This approach combines biological, psychological, and social aspects of human behavior. Is it possible to explain helping from an evolutionary psychology perspective? Well, helping may have been a behavior generally seen as favorable, and helping could have occurred in the past because it made us more desirable to others. Those who were well liked in the community had good odds for surviving and successfully producing offspring.

The **positive psychology** movement started with Martin E. P. Seligman's 1998 American Psychological Association presidential address. In that address, Seligman reminded psychologists of the field's three distinct missions in the years before World War II:

1. Curing mental illness
2. Making life more productive and fulfilling
3. Identifying and nurturing high talent

According to Seligman, by the end of the twentieth century, psychology had lost track of the second and third missions.

Seligman and many others have called for a return to the other two "distinct missions" of psychology. He suggests moving away from a preoccupation with *repairing* the worst things in life to *building* on positive qualities. Seligman writes (Seligman & Csikszentmihalyi, 2000):

> The field of positive psychology...is about positive individual traits: the capacity for love and vocation, courage, interpersonal skill, perseverance, forgiveness, originality, future mindedness, spirituality, high talent, and wisdom. At the group level, it is about civic virtues and the institutions that move individuals toward better citizenship: responsibility, nurturance, altruism, moderation, tolerance, and work ethic.

Some say the topics addressed by positive psychologists resemble the topics humanistic psychologists discussed 40 years ago. A major difference between the two is that Seligman sees *research* as positive psychology's "protector and shield," guarding against the unscientific self-help techniques that grew out of humanistic psychology's great promise.

Careers in Psychology

5. What do psychologists do?

Contrary to popular belief, not all psychologists make a living analyzing personalities or talking others through problems. True, those who diagnose and treat patients for psychological problems, the *clinical psycholo-*

Cooperative Learning

Divide students into three groups. Assign to each group a pillar of positive psychology and have all the groups explore how their pillar is present in their own lives and community:

- *Positive character*—individuals and groups who represent paragons of virtue and strength
- *Positive emotions*—happiness, optimism, flow, hope, etc.
- *Positive institutions*—those that foster development of virtues and strengths

trb At this point, you may wish to use Enrichment Lesson: *Positive Psychology in Focus* (*Teacher's Resource Binder*, p. 1-1).

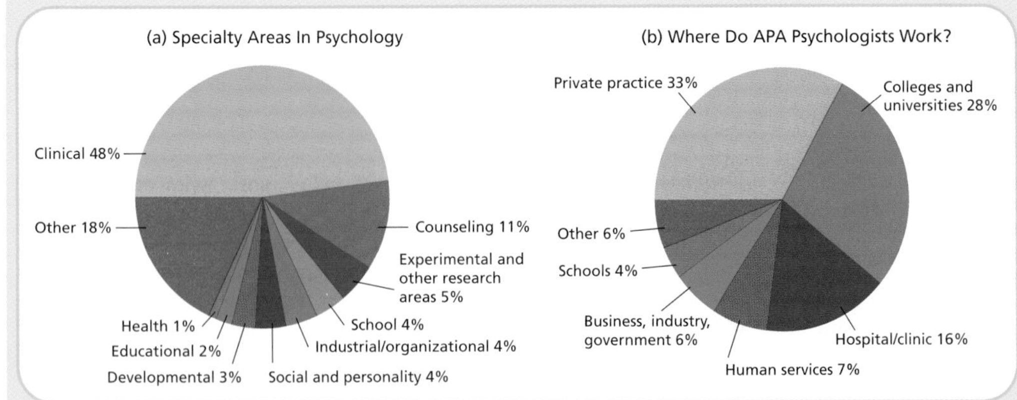

Figure 1.3 **Psychologists at Work** These data are based on membership in the American Psychological Association (APA), which tends to have a higher percentage of clinical psychologists registered than some other psychology organizations. Nonetheless, it conveys a general idea of (a) psychologists' specialty areas, and (b) the places that psychologists work (APA, 1998).

gists, do represent the largest number of professional psychologists. But if you look at Figure 1.3, you'll see that the field of psychology has a wide range of occupations and specialties.

Many of those earning a doctorate in psychology become *academic psychologists*. These psychologists work in colleges and universities conducting **basic research** in a number of subfields. To appreciate some of their interests, consider these four examples of academic psychologists and a question they might attempt to answer:

- *Biological psychologists* explore the physiological roots and results of our behaviors. A biological psychologist might ask, "Do repetitive behaviors, such as piano playing, produce changes in the brain?
- *Social psychologists* explore the influence others have on behavior. A social psychologist might ask, "Under what circumstances do young adults conform to the wishes of their peers?"
- *Developmental psychologists* study the growth or development that takes place from womb to tomb. A developmental psychologist might ask, "How do the friendships of 6-year-olds differ from the friendships of 10-year-olds?"
- *Cognitive psychologists* study thought processes. A cognitive psychologist might ask, "How does the memory of an old home phone number affect the memory of a new home phone number?"

Other psychologists are more interested in **applied research**—in solving specific, practical problems rather than expanding the scientific knowledge base of psychology. *Organizational psychologists* use psychological concepts to help entire businesses and organizations operate better and more efficiently. *Human-factors psychologists* explore how people and machines interact at home and in the workplace to minimize frustration

■ TEACHING TIP

Because students often want to enter psychology as a career to "help people," assist these students in finding areas of psychology that capitalize on their interests. Also, help students realistically calculate how long it takes to earn a professional degree.

trb At this point, you may wish to use Technology Application Activity: *Careers in Psychology* (*Teacher's Resource Binder*, p. 1-1).

F • Y • I

Professional psychology is encouraged through organizations that sponsor and promote research and practice in the field. Two major organizations fund research, publish journals, and establish ethical and practical guidelines for professionals to follow.

- American Psychological Association (APA) was founded in 1892. It is the primary publisher of scholarly journals in the field. It promotes research and practice through funding initiatives and conferences.
- American Psychological Society (APS) was founded in 1988 to promote the development of scientific psychology. While the APA focuses on both research and practice, APS strictly promotes research, application, and teaching of scientific psychology.

trb At this point, you may wish to use Technology Application Activity: *Introducing APA and APS on the World Wide Web* (*Teacher's Resource Binder*, p. 1-1; **Handout 1–9**).

CLOSE

trb Have students complete **Critical Thinking Activity:** *Science/Art Continuum: Where Does Psychology Fit?* (*Teacher's Resource Binder*, p. 1-1; **Handout 1–8**) as a way to determine their knowledge of the scientific nature of psychology. If students created a continuum earlier in the module, have them compare how they gauged psychology as a study before reading the full module with their thoughts on the study of psychology now that they have read the text. Moreover, help students see that as psychology matures as a discipline, it becomes less artistic and more scientific.

MODULE 1

Checking the Points

■ TEACHING TIPS

web (1) The book companion site for *Thinking About Psychology* at www.worthpublishers.com/thinkingaboutpsych contains a module quiz, flashcards of key terms and people, as well as other student activities and resources for this module. You will also find PowerPoint lectures, a quiz grade book, and other teaching resources by logging on as an instructor.

trb (2) At this point, you may wish to review and confirm concepts about psychology with **Critical Thinking Activity:** *Fact or Falsehood?* (*Teacher's Resource Binder*, p. 1-1; **Handout 1–1**). Suggest that students work in groups. Members can take turns reading items aloud, and the group as a whole can then discuss whether the item is true or false. Encourage groups to check and review their responses against the information in their texts.

Group Therapy Many psychologists do work in clinical positions, such as the therapist shown here. However, the available careers for psychologists extend well beyond the clinical fields.

and maximize safety and productivity. *Psychometricians* create and evaluate the standardized tests you've been taking since elementary school. *Educational psychologists* apply psychological principles to the classroom and to curriculum development.

There are many more types of psychologists working in the field, but you get the idea. While many psychologists help people work through depression, overcome fears, or analyze character, the range of other available roles is wide.

REVIEW

Module 1: Introduction, History, Perspectives, and Careers

What's the Point?

1. *What is psychology?*

   Psychology is the science of behavior and mental processes. Psychologists use scientific methods to study observable behaviors and unobservable mental processes, including thoughts, feelings, and dreams.

Modern Psychology's Roots

2. *When and where did modern psychology begin?*

   The history of modern psychology began with the laboratory that Wilhelm Wundt opened in Europe in 1879. In 1890, William James, the first American psychologist, wrote the first psychology textbook. In the more than 100 years that have passed since that time, men and women from many countries and many academic fields have contributed to the science of psychology as we know it today. Few women or people of color appear in the early history of psychology. Today, however, both genders and members of many different ethnic groups make important contributions to the expanded vision of contemporary psychology.

Six Contemporary Psychological Perspectives

3. *Can any one psychological perspective answer all of psychology's questions?*

   No one school of thought or approach within psychology can answer all the questions that psychology addresses. Each of the six perspectives—cognitive, biological, social-cultural, behavioral, humanistic, and psychodynamic—examines human behavior and mental processes from a different viewpoint. Most psychologists today choose to view behavior from more than one perspective because they know that this choice will increase their chances of understanding the topics that interest them.

Reteaching

Use a concept web to clarify concepts in this module. Start with the term that might confuse students in the center. Have students generate qualities of that term gleaned from their notes or textbook. Some examples appear in the web that follows:

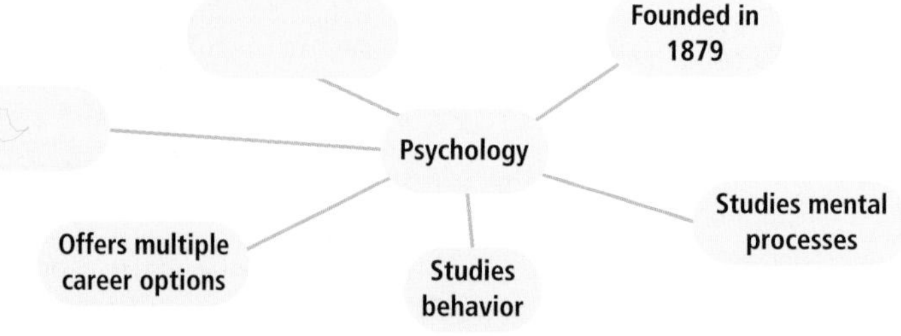

Psychology's Horizon

4. *What new areas of interest are psychologists exploring today?*
   Three new areas in today's psychology are behavior genetics, evolutionary psychology, and positive psychology. Behavior genetics explores the relative effects of genes and environment on behavior. Evolutionary psychology studies how biological, psychological, and social aspects of human behavior helped our ancestors survive and produce offspring. Positive psychology applies scientific research to the study of positive individual traits.

Careers in Psychology

5. *What do psychologists do?*
   The largest number of professional psychologists diagnose and treat people with psychological problems, but more than half of all psychologists are employed in other areas. Psychologists in colleges and universities conduct basic research that increases our understanding of basic biological, social, developmental, and cognitive processes. Other psychologists apply the findings of psychological research, practicing in schools, hospitals, clinics, businesses, testing offices, and other locations where they help people live better lives.

Key Terms and Concepts

psychology, p. 4
structuralism, p. 4
Gestalt psychology, p. 5
functionalism, p. 5
psychoanalytic perspective, p. 5
behaviorist perspective, p. 6
humanistic psychology, p. 6
psychological perspective, p. 9
cognitive perspective, p. 9
biological perspective, p. 9
social-cultural perspective, p. 10
behavior genetics, p. 11
positive psychology, p. 12
basic research, p. 13
applied research, p. 13

Key People

Wilhelm Wundt, p. 4
E. B. Titchener, p. 4
William James, p. 5
Sigmund Freud, p. 5
Ivan Pavlov, p. 6
John B. Watson, p. 6
B. F. Skinner, p. 6
Abraham Maslow, p. 6
Carl Rogers, p. 6
Jean Piaget, p. 6
G. Stanley Hall, p. 8
Mary Whiton Calkins, p. 8
Margaret Floy Washburn, p. 8
Francis Cecil Sumner, p. 8
Inez Beverly Prosser, p. 8

Self-Test

Multiple-Choice Questions

Choose the *best* answer for each of the following questions.

1. The ________________ perspective is especially interested in how we take in, process, store, and retrieve information.
   a. cognitive
   b. behavioral
   c. psychodynamic
   d. humanistic

2. The ________________ perspective is especially interested in how we learn observable responses.
   a. humanistic
   b. behavioral
   c. biological
   d. social-cultural

MODULE 1

trb ■ TEACHING TIP

You may also wish to provide students with **Graphic Organizer:** ***Flowcharts*** (*Teacher's Resource Binder*, p. 1-1; **Handouts 1–4** and **1–5**). Have students fill out the organizer as a tool for reviewing concepts related to research. Encourage students to fill in the graphic organizer without referring to the text or copies of the organizer they may have filled out earlier in the module. Next, have students work in small groups to complete their organizers and, when necessary, look up information in the text to clarify confusing concepts.

tb Using the Test Bank

The *Test Bank* that accompanies this textbook offers a wide variety of questions in different formats and levels of complexity. Use the software to construct whole tests or to integrate standardized questions into teacher-made tests.

Self-Test Answers

Multiple-Choice Questions

1. a, 2. b

Alternative Assessment/Portfolio Project

trb EXPLORING PSYCHOLOGY In their portfolios, students may include:

- **Technology Application Activity:** *Applying Psychology Through Study Skills* (*Teacher's Resource Binder*, p. 1-1; **Handout 1–7**)
- **Technology Application Activity:** *What Happened on Your Birthday?* (*Teacher's Resource Binder*, p. 1-1)
- **Technology Application Activity:** *Careers in Psychology* (*Teacher's Resource Binder*, p. 1-1)
- **Technology Application Activity:** *Introducing APA and APS on the World Wide Web* (*Teacher's Resource Binder*, p. 1-1; **Handout 1–9**)

For further details and a general rubric, see **Alternative Assessment/Portfolio Project:** *Exploring Psychology* (*Teacher's Resource Binder*, p. 1-1; **Handout 1–10**).

MODULE 1

Self-Test Answers

Multiple-Choice Questions (continued)

3. c, 4. c, 5. c, 6. d

Matching Terms and Definitions

7. a. (3), b. (7), c. (4), d. (1), e. (6), f. (9), g. (10), h. (5)

Fill-in-the-Blank Questions

8. Gestalt, 9. Behavior genetics, 10. basic; applied

Brief Essay Question

11. Be sure students understand that psychologists study both behavior that can be observed and measured and mental processes that must be studied indirectly or through biological techniques like brain imaging. Psychologists have come to understand that behavior and mental processes are different yet related, so each must be studied separately and in context of each other.

3. The _______________ perspective is especially interested in how thinking or behavior changes in different contexts or situations.
   a. cognitive   b. biological
   c. social-cultural   d. humanistic

4. The _______________ perspective is especially interested in how healthy people strive to reach their full potential.
   a. psychodynamic
   b. behavioral
   c. humanistic
   d. social-cultural

5. The _______________ perspective is especially interested in the physical structures and substances underlying a given behavior, thought, or emotion.
   a. cognitive
   b. humanistic
   c. biological
   d. social-cultural

6. The _______________ perspective is especially interested in how our unconscious drives and conflicts affect our behavior.
   a. behavior genetics
   b. behavioral
   c. biological
   d. psychodynamic

Matching People and Achievements

7. For each achievement, choose the *best* matching person from the list that follows.

Achievements

a. author of first psychology textbook
b. American behaviorist who focused on the role of responses in learning
c. founder of psychoanalysis
d. "father" of modern psychology
e. founder of behaviorism
f. founder of the American Psychological Association and its first president
g. famous for studying children's thought processes
h. Russian physiologist and famous learning theorist

People

(1) Wilhelm Wundt
(2) E. B. Titchener
(3) William James
(4) Sigmund Freud
(5) Ivan Pavlov
(6) John B. Watson
(7) B. F. Skinner
(8) Abraham Maslow
(9) G. Stanley Hall
(10) Jean Piaget

Fill-in-the-Blank Questions

8. The _______________ psychologists believed that the whole is greater than the sum of its parts.

9. _______________, one of the new schools of thought in psychology, focuses on the extent to which genes and the environment influence our individual differences.

10. Psychologists interested in increasing psychology's scientific knowledge base are doing _______________ research; psychologists interested in applying psychology's findings are doing _______________ research.

Brief Essay Question

11. What do we mean when we say that "psychology is the science of behavior and mental processes"? In four to five sentences, break down the two parts of this definition.

Performance Standards

Standard Area: Introduction and Research Methods

Content Standard 3: Research tools used by psychologists to answer psychological questions

Performance Standard 3.1 Designing an experiment.

- Discuss how an experiment is the only method used to determine cause and effect. (Student Text p. 24)
- Design a hypothetical experiment around the hypothesis that students assigned to wearing headphones each day in study hall will have higher grade point averages at the end of the quarter. (Student Text pp. 24–25)
- Present Figure 2.5, a chart detailing experimental design in the context of wearing headphones and studying. (Student Text p. 27)
- Discuss operational definitions and their importance. (Student Text pp. 24–25)
- Identify independent and dependent variables. (Student Text pp. 25–26)
- Discuss the use of experimental and control groups. (Student Text p. 26)
- Discuss the importance of random assignment. (Student Text p. 26)
- Discuss the need for control of confounding variables. (Student Text pp. 26–27)
- Present Figure 2.6, a chart outlining the challenges of confounding variables in experimentation. (Student Text p. 28)
- Present the use of double-blind procedures as a control. (Student Text pp. 28–29)
- Explore the use of placebos as a control for potential confounds. (Student Text p. 29)
- Discuss the importance of replication. (Student Text p. 31)
- Present Table 2.2, Experiments Step by Step, illustrating experimental design from developing a hypothesis to analyzing collected data. (Student Text p. 30)

Performance Standard 3.2 Understand the significance of random sampling in research.

- Discuss population and random sampling, tied to the hypothetical study of students listening to music over headphones. (Student Text pp. 22–23)

Performance Standard 3.3 Compare quantitative and qualitative research strategies.

- Present the research question "Does listening to music using headphones affect studying?" Identify suitability of different methods for studying this hypothesis, that is, naturalistic observation, case study, correlation, survey, longitudinal and cross-sectional studies, and experiments. (Student Text pp. 17–20, 22–30)

Content Standard 4: Understand the use of statistics to analyze and understand psychological research

Performance Standard 4.3 Describe correlation and understand how it used in psychological research.

- Discuss the concept of correlation, both positive and negative relationships. (Student Text p. 21).
- Present Figure 2.2, a chart containing scatterplots that indicate positive and negative correlations. (Student Text p. 21)
- Discuss how correlations do not prove a cause-and-effect relationship. (Student Text p. 22)
- Present Figure 2.3, a chart illustrating three variables that may lead to correlations reinforcing the idea that an experiment is the only method that can be used to identify cause and effect relationships. (Student Text p. 22)
- Discuss how correlations are useful for making predictions. (Student Text p. 22)

Performance Standard 4.4 The use of inferential statistics in psychological research.

- Define statistical significance and its application to a hypothetical study of listening to headphones. (Student Text p. 30)

Content Standard 5: Ethical considerations in research with human participants and animals

Performance Standard 5.1 Recognize ethical issues in psychological research.

- Discuss ethical issues in psychological research, with an example given of studying corporal punishment versus other punishments and why it would be unethical to conduct such an experiment. (Student Text p. 31)
- Discuss the four basic principles in the ethical guidelines from the American Psychological Association for working with human participants and animals. (Student Text pp. 31–32)
- Discuss reasons for using animals in psychological research and the protections that are available. (Student Text pp. 32–33)

Materials NETWORK

All of the items from the Video, Activity, and Enrichment Centers listed below come from the *Teacher's Resource Binder.* These items will help you teach and expand on concepts presented in Module 2.

trb This logo indicates when an item from the Materials Network may be used in conjunction with a specific note found in this module's *Teacher's Edition.*

Why Is Research Important?

V Video Center

- **Videocassette:** *Scientific American Frontiers,* **Second Edition, Segment 3: "Aliens Have Landed?"** Consult the faculty guide from the *Scientific American Frontiers* video series for a description of this segment. (*Teacher's Resource Binder,* p. 2-1)

Activity Center

- **Critical Thinking Activity:** *Fact or Falsehood?* With this activity, students' preconceptions about research methods are either exposed as incorrect or reinforced as correct. (*Teacher's Resource Binder,* p. 2-1; **Handout 2–1**)
- **Building Vocabulary:** *Exploring Root Words* and *Matching Terms and Definitions* With the activities presented in these handouts, students learn about and review the module vocabulary. (*Teacher's Resource Binder,* p. 2-1; **Handouts 2–2** and **2–3**)
- **Graphic Organizer:** *Flowchart* This graphic organizer presents important concepts in this module and shows how the concepts are related to one another. (*Teacher's Resource Binder,* p. 2-1; **Handout 2–4**)
- **Critical Thinking Activity:** *Astrology and the Scientific Method* This activity demonstrates that the scientific method of inquiry is a better predictor of human behavior than astrology. (*Teacher's Resource Binder,* p. 2-1; **Handouts 2–5a** and **2–5b**)
- **Evaluation Activity:** *The Scientific Approach* Although science is able to address many of life's questions, it is not equipped to handle them all. This activity challenges students to contemplate which type of questions science is adept at handling and which it is not. (*Teacher's Resource Binder,* p. 2-1)

Observation and Bias

Activity Center

- **Critical Thinking Activity:** *Confirmation Bias* This activity shows students how succumbing to the confirmation bias can lead them to the wrong conclusions. (*Teacher's Resource Binder,* p. 2-1)
- **Application Activity:** *A Field Experiment in Helping* This activity has students conducting their own field experiment as they try to get people to help them pick up books that have been dropped. Several different variables can be manipulated in this activity to facilitate discussion of several module concepts. (*Teacher's Resource Binder,* p. 2-1)
- **Cooperative Learning Activity:** *Naturalistic Observation* As student groups share observations of people in their natural environments, they learn how difficult naturalistic observation studies can be to control. (*Teacher's Resource Binder,* p. 2-1)

Enrichment Center

- **Enrichment Lesson:** *The Hawthorne Effect* The science behind the Hawthorne effect is more fiction than fact, but other phenomena, such as the placebo and halo effects, are based in science and contribute to potential bias in experiments. (*Teacher's Resource Binder,* p. 2-1)
- **Enrichment Lesson:** *Psychology and Human Values* This lesson informs students of the ways in which values can become inserted into the research process. With this understanding, students can try to avoid such pitfalls in the research process themselves. (*Teacher's Resource Binder,* p. 2-1)
- **Enrichment Lesson:** *Experimentation in the Field* This lesson presents a field experiment in which researchers tried to overcome artificiality in the laboratory setting. (*Teacher's Resource Binder,* p. 2-1)

Case Studies

Enrichment Center

- **Enrichment Lesson:** *Genie and the Wild Child—Case Studies in Focus* The case study of Genie is a vivid example of how case study research is the only way to study some types of behavior. (*Teacher's Resource Binder,* p. 2-1)

Correlation

Activity Center

- **Technology Application Activity:** *PsychSim:* **"Correlations"** *PsychSim* is an interactive CD-ROM containing tutorials in different content areas of psychology. In this tutorial, students create scatterplots and see how correlations are calculated. (*Teacher's Resource Binder,* p. 2-1)

- Critical Thinking Activity: *Correlating Test-Taking Time and Performance* Show the impact of correlations with this activity by having students collect data from a previous test they have taken and correlate the data to their grades. (*Teacher's Resource Binder*, p. 2-1)
- Application Activity: *Creating Scatterplots* With this activity, students discover that scatterplots are an easy, visual way to show the relationship between variables. (*Teacher's Resource Binder*, p. 2-1; Handout 2–6)
- Critical Thinking Activity: *Evaluating Media Reports of Research* Most people get information about science from the media, even though what the media report might not be accurate. This activity includes an article that implies a cause-and-effect relationship when the variables are actually correlated. (*Teacher's Resource Binder*, p. 2-1; Handout 2–7)
- Application Activity: *Correlation and the* Challenger *Disaster* The disaster of the *Challenger* explosion is one of our country's most vivid tragedies. This lesson offers insight into the decision to launch the shuttle and how scientists can be misled if they don't look at all the relevant data. (*Teacher's Resource Binder*, p. 2-1; Transparency Masters 2–1a and 2–1b)

Enrichment Center

- Enrichment Lesson: *Understanding Correlations* This lesson offers several examples of correlational data that is misrepresented in interesting ways. (*Teacher's Resource Binder*, p. 2-1)
- Enrichment Lesson: *Misinterpreting Correlations* Two fundamental problems come up when interpreting correlations – the directionality problem and the third variable problem. Advanced students may benefit from learning about how these problems have affected people in the past. (*Teacher's Resource Binder*, p. 2-1)

Surveys

Activity Center

- Critical Thinking Activity: *The Wording of Survey Questions* This activity demonstrates quickly how bias in survey questions can change the answers to a question. (*Teacher's Resource Binder*, p. 2-1; Handout 2–8)
- Cooperative Learning Activity: *Designing and Distributing Surveys* Surveys provide an easy way to apply research methods to real life. In this activity, students work in groups to develop and distribute a survey for their peers. (*Teacher's Resource Binder*, p. 2-1)

Enrichment Center

- Enrichment Lesson: *Bias in Surveys* This lesson highlights examples of how different surveys have been affected by problems with vocabulary, respondents, questions, response options, and question and response order. (*Teacher's Resource Binder*, p. 2-1)
- Enrichment Lesson: *Survey Research and Random Samples* This lesson relates several examples of survey results that are questionable because the sample wasn't chosen randomly or didn't represent the population. (*Teacher's Resource Binder*, p. 2-1)
- Enrichment Lesson: *Types of Survey Questions* In addition to multiple-choice questions, Likert scales, yes/no/maybe questions, rank order questions, and open-ended questions can all be used to measure the attitudes of subjects. (*Teacher's Resource Binder*, p. 2-1)

Longitudinal and Cross-Sectional Studies

Video Center

- Videocassette: *Scientific American Frontiers,* Second Edition, Segment 4: "Return to the Wild" Consult the faculty guide from the *Scientific American Frontiers* video series for a description of this segment. (*Teacher's Resource Binder*, p. 2-1)

Enrichment Center

- Enrichment Lesson: *The Nun Study* Starting in the 1920s, researchers followed a group of nuns and measured their physical and psychological health. The results of this longitudinal study point to the value of a person's healthy lifestyle and an active mental life. (*Teacher's Resource Binder*, p. 2-1; Handout 2–9)

Experiments

Video Center

- Videocassette: *Scientific American Frontiers,* Second Edition, Segment 1: "Tackling a Killer Disease" Consult the faculty guide from the *Scientific American Frontiers* video series for a description of this segment. (*Teacher's Resource Binder*, p. 2-1)

Activity Center

- Critical Thinking Activity: *Demonstrating Experimental Design Logic* Guide students through a mock experiment by proposing the hypothesis "Chocolate-glazed doughnuts improve memory." (*Teacher's Resource Binder*, p. 2-1)
- Critical Thinking Activity: *Finding Meaning in the Method* Create an experimental situation where personal bias influences the outcome of research. This activity shows how easy it would be for researchers to bias the results to their own personal views. (*Teacher's Resource Binder*, p. 2-1; Handout 2–10)
- Application Activity: *Writing an Experimental Hypothesis* Give students experience in formulating hypotheses from experimental descriptions. (*Teacher's Resource Binder*, p. 2-1; Handout 2–11)
- Application Activity: *Writing an Operational Definition* Give students practice writing operational definitions. In the activity handout, students learn about words that need to be defined more concretely for experimental purposes. (*Teacher's Resource Binder*, p. 2-1; Handout 2–12)
- Application Activity: *Identifying Independent and Dependent Variables* In this activity, students choose independent and dependent variables from a hypothesis presented in the activity handout. (*Teacher's Resource Binder*, p. 2-1; Handout 2-13)

- Cooperative Learning Activity: *A Tasty Sample(r): Teaching About Sampling Using M&Ms* This enjoyable activity allows students to use M&M plain candies to study concepts such as sampling and quality control. (*Teacher's Resource Binder*, p. 2-1; Handout 2–14)
- Application Activity: *Selecting Appropriate Research Methods* This activity helps students apply knowledge of the different research methods to different research descriptions. (*Teacher's Resource Binder*, p. 2-1)
- Application Activity: *Organizing and Interpreting Data* This activity uses the ages of the U.S. presidents when they took office to give students practice calculating descriptive statistics. (*Teacher's Resource Binder*, p. 2-1; Handout 2–15)
- Application Activity: *Describing Data* Using data the students supply about themselves through this short survey can be an effective tool for understanding what descriptive statistics tell us. (*Teacher's Resource Binder*, p. 2-1; Handout 2–16)
- Technology Application Activity: *PsychSim*: "Descriptive Statistics" *PsychSim* is an interactive CD-ROM containing tutorials in different content areas of psychology. In this tutorial, students calculate measures of central tendency and variation while working with graphs. (*Teacher's Resource Binder*, p. 2-1)
- Evaluation Activity: *More Cases Are Better Than Fewer* "The more subjects in a study, the better" is a guiding principle in research. The focus of this activity is evaluating situations where conclusions based on a small population may be misleading. (*Teacher's Resource Binder*, p. 2-1; Handout 2–17)
- Critical Thinking Activity: *Sample Size* If Tiger Woods were to challenge you to a game of golf, would you have a better shot beating him in 2 holes or 18? This question kicks off an activity that reinforces the idea that larger sample sizes are better than smaller ones. (*Teacher's Resource Binder*, p. 2-1; Handout 2–18)
- Application Activity: *When Is a Difference Significant?* Significant differences are the gold standard of research outcomes. Demonstrate the importance of significant differences with this activity that measures the number of times pennies placed on their sides fall and reveal heads. (*Teacher's Resource Binder*, p. 2-1)

Enrichment Center

- Enrichment Lesson: *Understanding Hypotheses* Hypotheses are classified by the way they are written. One-tailed, two-tailed, and null hypotheses are described in this lesson. (*Teacher's Resource Binder*, p. 2-1)
- Enrichment Lesson: *The Power of Vivid Cases* This lesson relates the interesting findings of two studies by Richard Nesbitt that show how people rely on vivid information rather than hard facts. (*Teacher's Resource Binder*, p. 2-1)
- Enrichment Lesson: *Differences Between Groups* Three important points should be noted when teaching about data analysis: comparison groups are very important; statistics suggest the probability of an outcome, not the likelihood; and statistical significance is not the same as practical significance. (*Teacher's Resource Binder*, p. 2-1)

Ethics

Activity Center

- Application Activity: *Ethics in Research* This activity presents four situations that might violate ethical research guidelines. Students use their knowledge of ethical standards to determine whether the research should be allowed and what could be done to make the study ethical if it is not. (*Teacher's Resource Binder*, p. 2-1; Handout 2–19)
- Role-Playing Activity: *Animal Care and Use Committee* Students can use their knowledge of the ethics of animal research by pretending to be on an Animal Care and Use Committee to determine whether a series of experiments should be allowed to go forward. (*Teacher's Resource Binder*, p. 2-1; Handout 2–20)

Enrichment Center

- Enrichment Lesson: *Research Ethics* Ethical research boils down to the question of whether the results of the study outweigh the potential risk to subjects. This summary of a debate between Diana Baumrind and Robert Baron highlights the two sides of the cost-benefit debate in the research community. (*Teacher's Resource Binder*, p. 2-1)
- Enrichment Lesson: *Do Animals Have Rights?* This lesson provides two of the major arguments against animal research presented by animal rights advocates that would facilitate a class discussion of this hotly contested issue. (*Teacher's Resource Binder*, p. 2-1)

MODULE 2
Research Strategies

How do you know what you know? There are many ways, of course. You can know something because a friend told you, or because you read it. You can also know something because it "seems obvious," in other words, through common sense. All of these ways of knowing may be right. But they may also be wrong. Psychologists rely on knowledge gained by using the **scientific method,** because it is more likely to answer certain kinds of questions correctly. In this module, we explore some of the research tools available to scientists seeking knowledge. It is because psychologists use these tools that psychology is considered a science.

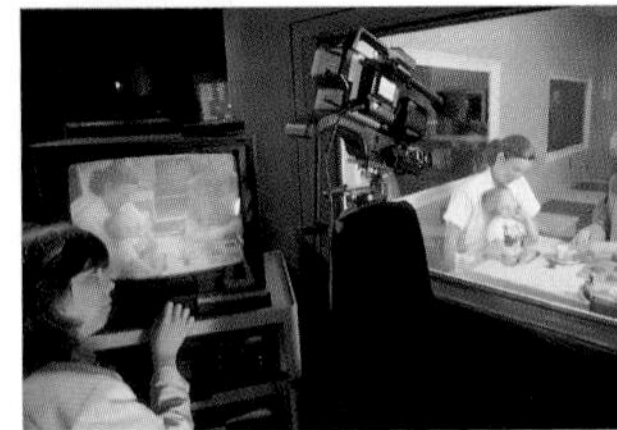

The Scientific Method at Work What do these individuals have in common? They are researchers who rely on the scientific method to learn about their chosen area of study. By using the tools of science and critical thinking, they can help us understand how the world operates.

Why Is Research Important?

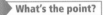

1. What advantage does research have over other ways of knowing things?

Many students sign up for their first psychology class hoping to cover the "good stuff" associated with the psychology they've seen on TV and in popular magazines. How do I analyze my dreams? Does my friend

▶ **scientific method** A method of learning about the world through the application of critical thinking and tools such as observation, experimentation, and statistical analysis.

Getting Started

Ask volunteers to describe any psychology-related research they may have heard or read about from television programs, radio, books, newspapers, or magazines.

trb Use **Critical Thinking Activity:** *Fact or Falsehood?* (*Teacher's Resource Binder*, p. 2-1; **Handout 2–1**) as a prereading strategy to find out what students already know about research methods. This will prime them to note terms and concepts that confirm or dispel their preconceptions.

MODULE 2

Research Strategies

Introducing the Module

The Points: Module Objectives

- Discuss the advantage of research over other ways of knowing.
- Identify ways in which bias can influence research.
- Discuss advantages and disadvantages of case studies.
- Understand why we cannot conclude cause-and-effect relationships from correlational data.
- Understand why we should be wary of data obtained from surveys.
- Discuss advantages and disadvantages of longitudinal and cross-sectional studies.
- Understand what it means to operationalize variables.
- Distinguish between an independent and dependent variable in an experiment.
- Identify possible confounds in research and some ways to control them.
- Evaluate how the double-blind procedure and placebos help control for confounding variables.
- Understand the role of statistics in the experimental method.
- Analyze the importance of replication of experiment results.
- Summarize four ethical principles that must guide human research.
- Understand why researchers sometimes use animals in their research.

trb Building Vocabulary

With two handouts available in this module, students can learn about roots in scientific jargon as well as practice vocabulary with a matching game (*Teacher's Resource Binder*, p. 2-1; **Handouts 2–2** and **2–3**).

MODULE 2

Teaching the Points

■ **TEACHING TIPS**

web (1) You can log on as an instructor to the book companion site for *Thinking About Psychology* at www.worthpublishers.com/thinkingaboutpsych. It contains teacher resources for class presentations as well as review and assessment of module concepts and terms.

(2) As students read the section "Why Is Research Important?" emphasize that research methodology contains terms and concepts that underlie the entire study of psychology as a science. Challenge students to use the terms they learn about research during class discussions.

trb At this point, you may wish to use **Critical Thinking Activity:** *Astrology and the Scientific Method* (*Teacher's Resource Binder*, p. 2-1; **Handouts 2–5a** and **2–5b**) and **Evaluation Activity:** *The Scientific Method* (*Teacher's Resource Binder*, p. 2-1).

■ **JOURNAL WRITING**

Invite students to use the following questions and writing prompts as springboards for entries in their psychology journals:

- Why should people rely on the scientific method as a way of understanding human behavior? Come up with at least two different reasons and explain them.
- What are some questions you have about human behavior that psychology might address?
- When have you used common sense? Did it help or hinder you? How?

trb At this point, you may wish to use **Evaluation Activity:** *The Scientific Method* (*Teacher's Resource Binder*, p. 2-1).

V You may wish to show **Videocassette:** *Scientific American Frontiers*, **Second Edition, Segment 3: "The Aliens Have Landed"** (*Teacher's Resource Binder*, p. 2-1).

Figure 2.1 **How Do You Know What to Believe?**

have an eating disorder? What makes the opposite sex tick? Without research, there would be no reliable, systematic way to consider these questions, or thousands more.

And if you don't believe you're interested in research, please give it a chance! Do you like solving problems and figuring out the answers to puzzles? If so, research should be right up your alley, because research is not just a series of experiments. It's a set of methods, a way of asking questions about the world and drawing logical, supported conclusions. These are important life skills for everyone. Headlines daily trumpet the latest findings about caffeine, and news anchors are forever introducing segments on new ways to treat depression. If you don't know enough about research to decide when conclusions are reasonable and when they're not, you leave yourself at the mercy of the media (Figure 2.1). We surely won't all conduct research, but we will all be called on to evaluate its relevance. Just as modern civilization requires people to be computer literate to function well, it requires people to be research literate to make informed decisions.

Listen Up!
Does listening to music through headphones affect studying? Science can provide answers to questions like this.

In this module, you will learn more about research by considering an example. Let's say your school is about to institute a new policy banning the use of headphones for listening to music in study halls. How might we predict the effect of this new policy?

One way is to use common sense. Perhaps the school administrators were using common sense when they designed the new policy. Their common sense told them that students would be able to concentrate more effectively if they were not distracted by music. But wait! *Your* common sense might well lead you to the opposite conclusion. Maybe you feel that the music would allow you to block out distracting noises and focus more effectively on your homework. That's the trouble with common sense; too often it can lead you to whatever conclusion you want (Table 2.1)! Scientific methods can help you to evaluate the competing hunches.

TABLE 2.1 THE LIMITS OF COMMON SENSE

Common sense leaves us unsure of the truth, but research helps us apply principles appropriately in different situations.

COMMON SENSE SAYS . . .		
Opposites attract.	and	Birds of a feather flock together.
Out of sight, out of mind.	and	Absence makes the heart grow fonder.
Nothing ventured, nothing gained.	and	A penny saved is a penny earned.

Suggested Readings

Use the following books as teacher-preparation tools or as enrichment for advanced students:

Bell, J. (1999). *Evaluating psychological information: Sharpening your critical thinking skills* (3rd ed.). Boston: Allyn & Bacon.

Huck, S. W., & Sandler, H. M. (1979). *Rival hypotheses.* New York: HarperCollins.

Levy, D. A. (1997). *Tools of critical thinking: Metathoughts for psychology.* Boston: Allyn & Bacon.

McBurney, D. H. (1996). *How to think like a psychologist: Critical thinking in psychology.* Upper Saddle River, NJ: Prentice Hall.

Meltzoff, J. (1998). *Critical thinking about research: Psychology and related fields.* Washington, DC: American Psychological Association.

Smith, R. A. (1995). *Challenging your preconceptions: Thinking critically about psychology.* Pacific Grove, CA: Brooks/Cole.

Observation and Bias

2. What are some ways that bias can influence research?

Confirmation Bias
Both the administrator and a student tend to notice examples that support their points of view.

The simplest scientific technique is *observation*. In our example, you might watch students wearing headphones and compare them with students not wearing headphones. Which students look more focused, more intent on their work? This technique, however, also presents a problem: Your observations may be influenced by what you want to discover. This tendency is one of many kinds of **researcher bias.** Bias occurs when any factor unfairly increases the likelihood that the researcher will reach a particular conclusion. As you might imagine, researchers try to avoid bias as they would the plague. In this case, you and an administrator might observe students wearing headphones while studying and come to completely opposite conclusions, because each of you would tend to notice only those behaviors that support your own ideas. You want the research to demonstrate that headphones are helpful, so you may be especially sensitive to behaviors that support this conclusion. An administrator may be more likely to miss the behaviors you notice and may pay closer attention to actions that seem to indicate headphones are distracting. Both you and the administrator are being influenced by your biases.

There are many ways to reduce researcher bias, and the best method depends on the particular study. In this case, we might try to make the observations more *objective* (that is, less biased) by finding ways to rely less on the observer's opinion. For example, we could compare the grades of students who wear headphones while studying with the grades of students who don't. Or, perhaps we could have the observers count specific behaviors, like how many times in a 10-minute period a student has conversations with others, or how many pages a student reads in 10 minutes. If you're thinking these methods could have flaws as well (just because students are turning pages doesn't mean they are learning anything), congratulations! You're beginning to get the hang of the kind of **critical thinking** that psychologists and other scientists value!

The point is, there is no perfect way to eliminate bias. The goal is to minimize it and maximize the probability of obtaining a reliable, meaningful result.

Researchers must also watch for **participant bias,** which can affect results. For example, maybe the students will act differently because they know someone is observing them. If so, they might study harder because the administrator is in the room, but the administrator might

▶ **researcher bias** A tendency for researchers to engage in behaviors and selectively notice evidence that supports their hypotheses or expectations.

▶ **critical thinking** Thinking that does not blindly accept arguments and conclusions. Rather, it examines assumptions, discerns hidden values, evaluates evidence, and assesses conclusions.

▶ **participant bias** A tendency for reseach participants to respond in a certain way because they know they are being observed or they believe they know what the researcher wants.

MODULE 2

■ **TEACHING TIP**

Help students understand the following scientific principles inherent in observational research techniques:

- *Laboratory research can be artificial.* People might not behave naturally in a lab setting. Naturalistic observation and field experiments that are conducted with controls in place offer insight into human behavior that lab settings might not.
- *Even in natural settings, controlling for extraneous variables is of the utmost importance.* Scientists who do research in natural settings follow several guidelines to place controls on their studies. One such guideline involves operationally defining the behaviors they are looking for so others can replicate their work.

trb At this point, you may wish to use **Enrichment Lesson:** *The Hawthorne Effect* (*Teacher's Resource Binder*, p. 2-1) and **Cooperative Learning Experience:** *Naturalistic Observation* (*Teacher's Resource Binder*, p. 2-1).

F • Y • I

When researchers look for information that confirms their expectations, their approach is called **confirmation bias.** Confirmation bias can be detrimental to the outcome of a study. If researchers look only for answers that will confirm the hypothesis, they can easily overlook glaring evidence that disproves the hypothesis.

trb At this point, you may wish to use **Critical Thinking Activity:** *Confirmation Bias* (*Teacher's Resource Binder*, p. 2-1).

Meeting Individual Needs

trb **GRAPHIC ORGANIZERS** Provide learning opportunities for all levels of learners. Along with **Graphic Orgainzer:** *Flowchart* (*Teacher's Resource Binder*, p. 2-1; **Handout 2–4**), use one of the following options:

- **Independent Learners** Students can fill out the organizer on their own or follow along in class during discussion and lecture.
- **Cooperative Learners** Students may use the textbook as a resource and work in groups to find the answers that fit in the blanks.
- **Exceptional Learners** The graphic organizer can fill a special education need to provide notes for exceptional students. These students can fill in the blanks independently, with a student or teacher/tutor, or along with class discussion and lecture.

MODULE 2

F • Y • I

Some of the most famous psychological phenomena are based on case study research.

- **Psychoanalysis** Sigmund Freud developed much of his theory of human personality through case studies of his female patients. His protégé, Carl Jung, based many of his theories of the unconscious on case studies of clients.
- **Behaviorism** John Watson and Rosalie Rayner conducted an intensive experiment involving one person to demonstrate classically conditioned emotions. The subject, Little Albert, was trained to fear white, furry objects by associating those objects with a loud noise. Whether Albert was deconditioned of his fear is one of psychology's most infamous mysteries.
- **Neuroscience** Broca's area was discovered in the late 1800s by Paul Broca, who studied the brain of one of his patients named "Tan." The patient could only utter one syllable, "tan." Upon Tan's death, Broca studied Tan's brain, hypothesizing that the damaged area was where our ability to speak lies. (Technology in the twentieth century confirmed his hypothesis.)

trb At this point, you may wish to use **Enrichment Lesson:** *Genie and the Wild Child—Case Studies in Focus* (*Teacher's Resource Binder*, p. 2-1).

■ APPLYING THE POINTS

Some disciplines like anthropology, sociology, and zoology rely heavily on case studies and observational research. Have students contact working researchers in these fields to assess how they use these techniques to increase basic knowledge in their fields. Students may also explore the lives and work of some famous researchers like Jane Goodall and Dian Fossey who used observational field research extensively.

Naturalistic Confirmation Under which circumstances do your think the principal's observations are more accurate? Naturalistic observation requires that the behavior not be unduly influenced by the observer. Can you see that this might sometimes produce ethical concerns?

conclude that these students are studying effectively because they aren't distracted by headphones. To minimize participant bias, psychologists often use **naturalistic observation,** a technique in which the observer makes no attempt to manipulate or control the situation. To avoid influencing participants' behavior simply because of their presence, observers in a lab setting may use hidden cameras or one way-mirrors. This type of research design can raise ethical issues. More on that later.

Case Studies

3. What are the advantages and disadvantages of case studies?

Researchers who study single individuals in depth in the hope of revealing universal principles are using the **case study** method. It is important to keep in mind that this method is prone to bias, and it may not be possible to extend the results of one case study to other situations. For example, an in-depth study of just one headphone-wearing student in study hall could provide some very unrepresentative results.

Sometimes, however, a case study is all that is ethically possible. Child abuse, for example, is usually researched with case studies. It would be unethical for researchers to abuse a sample of children, so they must wait until authorities discover a case of abuse and then attempt to study the effects of that abuse. "Genie" was the subject of just such a study. She was discovered in California in 1970, a 13-year-old victim who had spent her life in such isolation that she had not even learned to speak. Since 1970, psychologists have intensively studied Genie's behavior and progress to learn about the development of language, social, and other skills. Researchers who study cases such as Genie's hope that they can glean important knowledge from these tragic situations.

Since no two cases of abuse are exactly alike, there is always some doubt as to the real effects. But, as similar case studies accumulate, researchers gain increasing confidence in the accuracy of their conclusions.

► **naturalistic observation** Observing and recording behavior in naturally occurring situations without trying to manipulate and control the situation.

► **case study** A research technique in which one person is studied in depth in the hope of revealing universal principles.

Cooperative Learning

Have students collect case studies from the newspaper and professional journals about different types of psychological phenomena for which it would be unethical to conduct experiments. Have students compile a list of behaviors that all the case studies have in common to see if they can draw any conclusions about the phenomena. Some phenomena that students might explore include the following:

- child or elder abuse
- brain disorders (strokes, tumors, and so on)
- impact of criminal behavior on perpetrators or victims

trb At this point, you may wish to use **Enrichment Lesson:** *Genie and the Wild Child—Case Studies in Focus* (*Teacher's Resource Binder*, p. 2-1).

Correlation

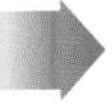

4. Why can't we conclude cause-and-effect relationships from correlational data?

Think of how many times it's useful to know the extent to which two variables are related. Is there a relationship between diet and health? Between communication style and divorce? Between training techniques and success in the Olympics? The research technique that answers such questions is the **correlational study.** In the question we are examining, the two variables are

1. whether or not a student wears headphones, and
2. studying effectiveness.

If effectiveness of studying increases when students wear headphones and decreases when students do not wear headphones, we can say that the two variables are *positively correlated*. That is, both variables increase (or decrease) together. But if studying effectiveness decreases when students wear headphones, and increases when they do not wear headphones, the variables are *negatively correlated*—one variable increases while the other decreases (Figure 2.2).

▶ **correlational study** A research project designed to discover the degree to which two variables are related to each other.

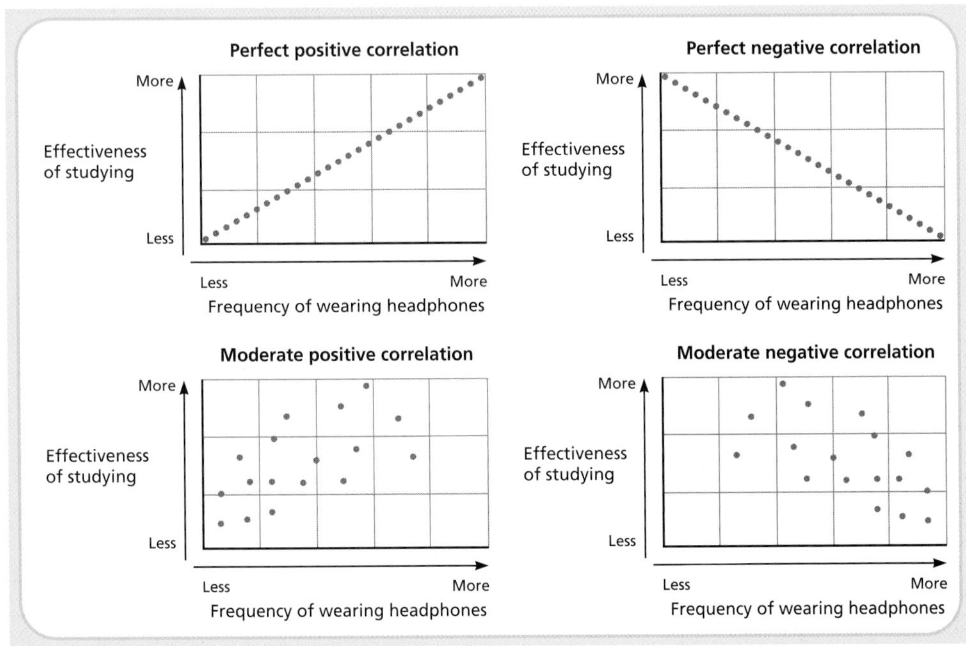

Figure 2.2 **Positive and Negative Correlations** The two top graphs show what perfect positive and negative correlations would look like for headphone usage and studying effectiveness. In the positive correlation, as headphone use increases, so does effectiveness of studying. In the negative correlation, effectiveness of studying decreases as headphone use increases. Actual data would surely look more like the two bottom graphs.

MODULE 2

■ **TEACHING TIP**

Emphasize to students that the term *correlation* does not mean "causation." Remind them that **correlation** tells you that certain variables are related but not why they are related.

As students learn the details about the experimental method, their ability to distinguish correlation from causation becomes very important, in particular when they need to act as critical thinkers about research reports in the media.

tr A four-color transparency of Figure 2.2, Positive and Negative Correlations, is available in the **Overhead Transparencies Set.**

trb At this point, you may wish to use **Enrichment Lesson:** ***Understanding Correlations*** (*Teacher's Resource Binder*, p. 2-1) and **Application Activity:** ***Correlation and the*** **Challenger** ***Disaster*** (*Teacher's Resource Binder*, p. 2-1; **Transparency Masters 2–1a** and **2–1b**).

■ **JOURNAL WRITING**

Invite students to use the following questions as springboards for entries in their psychology journals:

- Many health-related studies published in media reports seem to have a causal link when they actually have a correlational link. What is the impact of these reports on the general public?
- What can the media do to better educate the public about the difference between correlation and causation?

trb At this point, you may wish to use **Critical Thinking Activity:** ***Evaluating Media Reports of Research*** (*Teacher's Resource Binder*, p. 2-1; **Handout 2–7**).

trb At this point, you may wish to use **Technology Application Activity:** ***PsychSim: "Correlations"*** (*Teacher's Resource Binder*, p. 2-1).

Reteaching

trb You may wish to use **Application Activity:** ***Creating Scatterplots*** (*Teacher's Resource Binder*, p. 2-1; **Handout 2–6**) to reinforce students' knowledge of correlation. With this activity, students discover that scatterplots are an easy, visual way to show the relationship between variables.

trb tr ■ TEACHING TIP

A black-line master of Figure 2.3, Correlation Is Not Causation, is available in the **Black-Line Masters Appendix** of the *Teacher's Resource Binder.* Students can work with partners to better understand correlation by reviewing the circumstances provided in Figure 2.3 and explaining to one another why these three pieces of information do not provide causes but do provide correlations.

tb ■ CHECKING FOR UNDERSTANDING

Here are several ways to assess students' comprehension:

- Assign any or all of the journal questions or prompts for an in-class writing assessment.
- Divide the students into groups or pairs and give each group or pair a journal question prompt. Have groups or pairs present their answers to the class, and correct any misconceptions that may arise.
- Use questions from the *Test Bank* or the **Building Vocabulary** worksheets to do a quick assessment of their knowledge of the concepts.

■ LOOKING AT THE ISSUES

Psychological studies are reported in the popular press on an almost daily basis. Often these studies are reported as "experiments" when they actually are correlations. Have students collect reports of studies from newspapers and magazines and evaluate whether the reports represent the appropriate interpretations of the conclusions of the studies.

- Does the report represent a correlational study as an experimental study? Why or why not?
- What are the variables that the study evaluates? What outcome does the article suggest be drawn from this study?
- Are the primary researchers interviewed for the story? If so, do they caution people to interpret a correlational study appropriately? Why or why not?

trb At this point, you may wish to use **Enrichment Lesson:** *Misinterpreting Correlations* (*Teacher's Resource Binder*, p. 2-1).

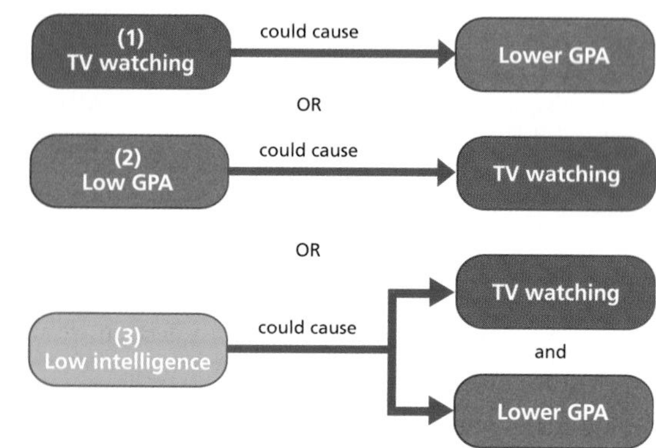

Figure 2.3 **Correlation Is Not Causation**
The discovery of a negative correlation between TV watching and grade point average would not provide us with any information about what caused the correlation. Here are three equally plausible explanations.

It is very important to remember that the discovery of a correlation *does not prove that a cause-and-effect relationship exists*. Correlational research results can tell you that certain variables are related, but not *why* they are related. For example, let's say a researcher discovered a negative correlation between TV watching and grade point average: students who watched more TV had lower GPAs. Based on this alone, can we conclude anything about whether TV watching causes grades to suffer? The answer is no. It is indeed possible that watching TV causes one's grades to decline. But can you imagine other possibilities? It is also possible that having low grades causes one to watch TV. It is even possible that some other variable, say low intelligence, could cause both a lot of TV watching and low grades. Correlation does not tell us which of these explanations is correct (Figure 2.3).

Although correlations cannot establish cause-and-effect relationships, they are very useful for making predictions. If you know there is a strong negative correlation between TV watching and grades, and if you know a student watches several hours of TV each day, you can predict that the student will have a relatively low GPA. This is true even if TV watching does not directly cause the low grades. The stronger the correlation, the more accurate your prediction will be.

▶ **survey method** A research technique designed to discover the self-reported attitudes or behaviors of a sample of people through the use of questionnaires or interviews.

▶ **population** All the cases in a group, from which samples may be drawn for a study.

▶ **random sample** A sample that fairly represents a population because each member has an equal chance of inclusion.

▶ **longitudinal study** A research technique that studies the same group of individuals over a long period of time.

Surveys

5. Why should we be cautious of data obtained from surveys?

Returning to our headphone example, how would you go about collecting data to establish a correlation? One way would be to use the **survey method**, perhaps by having students fill out a short questionnaire about the effect of headphone use in study hall. Surveys allow researchers to collect large amounts of data efficiently through the use of questionnaires and interviews.

There is no doubt about the efficiency of surveys, or about the value of being able to collect data from large numbers of people relatively inexpensively. The problem is that surveys are almost seductively efficient. It seems so simple to create a survey that people often don't consider how easy it is to allow bias into the wording of the questions. "Do you like flowers?" for example, will not get the same response as the question, "Do you like horticulture?" Surveys also raise the problem of *social desirability*. People may try to please the researcher by answering the way they think they should.

"How would you like me to answer that question? As a member of my ethnic group, educational class, income group, or religious category?"

But assume you have carefully designed your questions to avoid bias. You still must be sure your survey results will be relevant to the large group, known as a **population,** that interests you. To do this, you must draw a **random sample** of an adequate number of individuals (Figure 2.4).

In a random sample, every member of the population has an equal chance of being selected. If the population you wish to study is the students in study halls at your school, you could, for example, draw a random sample by selecting every tenth name from a list of students registered for study halls. How big a number is adequate? Researchers answer that question with mathematical formulas, but, in general, larger samples are better—if they're *random*. If the sample is not random, it is said to be biased.

Figure 2.4 **Sample and Population**
The larger jar contains a population, in this case, a mixture of two colors of marbles. You can efficiently learn the percentage of each color in this larger group of marbles by randomly removing a sample (represented by the marbles in the smaller jar) and counting the two colors.

Longitudinal and Cross-Sectional Studies

6. What are the advantages and disadvantages of longitudinal and cross-sectional studies?

Longitudinal and cross-sectional studies are techniques of particular use to *developmental psychologists*, who study how individuals change throughout the life span. **Longitudinal studies** follow the same group of individuals for many years. In 1921, psychologist Lewis Terman began a famous longitudinal study of a group of highly intelligent California children. He, and later other researchers, studied these individuals for 70 years to discover what happens to bright children as they

Cooperative Learning

trb You may wish to use **Cooperative Learning Activity:** *Designing and Distributing Surveys* (*Teacher's Resource Binder*, p. 2-1) in teaching students to apply the principles of survey research. Surveys provide an easy way to apply research methods to real life. In this activity, students work in groups to develop and distribute a survey for their peers.

trb You may also wish to use **Critical Thinking Activity:** *The Wording of Survey Questions* (*Teacher's Resource Binder*, p. 2-1; **Handout 2–8**) to help students as they construct their surveys. This activity demonstrates quickly how bias in survey questions can change the answers to a question.

■ LOOKING AT THE ISSUES

Surveys are so widespread that we take them for granted. Good surveys require careful attention to detail and the proper selection of subjects.

- Emphasize the importance of critical thinking. Explain that by developing their critical thinking about surveys, students are also helping themselves become better consumers.
- Guide students to choose appropriate issues for surveys they distribute to peers. Help them avoid surveys based on issues that invoke strong emotions from participants and that might be considered objectionable for minors by parents and administrators.

trb There are several activities you may wish to use related to guiding students through survey research projects.

- **Critical Thinking Activity:** *The Wording of Survey Questions* (*Teacher's Resource Binder*, p. 2-1; **Handout 2–8**)
- **Cooperative Learning Activity:** *Designing and Distributing Surveys* (*Teacher's Resource Binder*, p. 2-1)
- **Enrichment Lesson:** *Bias in Surveys* (*Teacher's Resource Binder*, p. 2-1)
- **Enrichment Lesson:** *Survey Research and Random Samples* (*Teacher's Resource Binder*, p. 2-1)
- **Enrichment Lesson:** *Types of Survey Questions* (*Teacher's Resource Binder*, p. 2-1)

■ JOURNAL WRITING

Invite students to use the following questions as a springboard for an entry in their psychology journals:

- How might culture pose problems for research, especially surveys? In what ways can researchers avoid cultural bias?

trb You may wish to use **Enrichment Lesson:** *Bias in Surveys* (*Teacher's Resource Binder*, p. 2-1) before or after students write in their journals.

MODULE 2

■ TEACHING TIPS

(1) Help students distinguish between longitudinal and cross-sectional studies by having them list the benefits and drawbacks of each type. Afterward, students can study the completed lists, which will focus on characteristics of each kind of study.

(2) Explain to students that operational definitions do not have to include every possible behavior to be accurate. Students should come up with a few behaviors that can be observed to create a good definition. Replication of experiments allows for definitions to be refined or changed.

web (3) Have students participate in research on line by visiting **http://psych.hanover.edu/research/exponnet.html**. Have students choose a study, obtain parental consent to participate (if minors are called for as subjects), and then participate. Have them keep a written journal of their experience, which, if you wish, may constitute extra credit. Their journal entries should address the following questions:

- What was the purpose of the study?
- Can they tell whether it was descriptive, correlational, or experimental?
- What is it like to be an on-line participant?
- What might be the benefits and limits of conducting research on the Internet?
- Did the researchers employ the proper ethical considerations?

trb ■ **JOURNAL WRITING**

You may wish to have students read the article in **Enrichment Lesson:** ***Nun Study*** (*Teacher's Resource Binder*, p. 2-1) before they answer the following questions in their journals:

- In what ways are nuns particularly good research subjects?
- In what ways may generalizations be formed from results in the nun study? If generalizations may not be formed from results in the study, why not?
- Which results from the nun study may be regarded as correlational? Which results, if any, may be regarded as causal?
- What experimental hypotheses can be proposed from looking at the nun study?

▶ **cross-sectional study** A research technique that compares individuals from different age groups at one time.

▶ **experiment** A research method in which the researcher manipulates one or more factors (independent variables) to observe the effect on another variable (dependent variable) while controlling for confounding variables.

▶ **hypothesis** An investigator's testable prediction about the outcome of research.

▶ **operational definition** A specification of the exact procedures used to make a variable specific and measurable for research purposes.

grow up. In general, these gifted people had very successful careers. Longitudinal studies provide a rich source of data as time passes, but they are quite expensive and difficult to conduct. As a result, they tend to be pretty rare. Imagine the challenges of keeping track of a group of study hall students throughout their lifetimes to determine the long-term effects of wearing (or not wearing) headphones!

It is more common to conduct **cross-sectional studies,** which compare people of different ages at one time. A psychologist interested in how creativity changes over the life span could gather a random sample of people from different age groups and administer a test of creativity to all of them. Cross-sectional studies have the advantage of being much more efficient than longitudinal studies, but they have their own problems. If the test showed that the older groups were less creative than the younger groups, that *could* mean that creativity declines as people age. But this difference could also be explained by other factors, such as changes over time in the educational system, or the introduction of computers (or headphones!).

Experiments

Observation, case studies, correlational studies, surveys, longitudinal studies, and cross-sectional studies are all important research techniques. Psychologists often use these techniques in combination—for example, using naturalistic observations to do a case study, or doing surveys to establish correlations. But for establishing *cause and effect*, there is only one game in town, and researchers prefer it above all others. The **experiment** is the *only* method that allows us to draw conclusions about cause-and-effect relationships. Because experiments require researchers to control the variables in a study, the chances of isolating the variable causing a particular effect are much greater.

Let's design an experiment to find out if banning headphones in study halls would affect grades.

Hypotheses and Operational Definitions

7. What does it mean to operationalize variables?

In designing our experiment, the first thing we would do is to generate a **hypothesis**—a testable prediction of the experiment's outcome. Researchers often start with general expectations ("Headphones influence concentration in study halls"), but then put their variables in a more specific form that allows them to be precisely measured. In the language of research, they provide **operational definitions** of the variables. One way to operationalize our hypothesis is to put it in this form: "Students assigned to wear headphones in study hall will have higher average

Enriching

In the book *Rival Hypotheses* (listed in Suggested Readings on *Teacher's Edition* page 18), Schuyler Huck and Howard Sandler provide 100 short summaries of research studies and the conclusions drawn from the data. In each case, Huck and Sandler believe there is some problem with design, methodology, or analysis that makes it possible to account for the findings through one or more rival hypotheses. The student's task is to detect the plausible alternative explanation. Solutions at the back of the book provide logical hypotheses that might invalidate the original claim.

grades at the end of the quarter than students banned from wearing headphones." Notice that we could have operationalized the hypothesis in many other ways as well. We could have said, "Students who are banned from wearing headphones each day in study hall will read fewer pages each day than students who aren't banned from wearing headphones," or "Students who may wear headphones each day in study hall will have fewer conversations with other students than students who are not allowed to wear headphones." Each of these versions has slightly different implications. Researchers must settle on one they believe does the best job of accurately reflecting the general hypothesis.

This is a very important point to understand, even if you never conduct an experiment of your own. When you are evaluating the research done by others, you should consider whether the operational definitions are appropriate or inappropriate. For example, every year *Money* magazine publishes an article about the "best places" to live in the United States. How do these researchers operationalize "best"? You have to read the article to learn that they use a complex formula to score each considered community on a variety of variables, including climate, unemployment rate, cultural opportunities, crime, and so on. If you don't agree with these criteria, you won't find the conclusions acceptable, either. If you like snowstorms, already have a steady job, and don't care much for theater and the ballet, you may end up seriously disappointed in a highly rated community!

Independent and Dependent Variables

8. What is the difference between the independent variable and the dependent variable in an experiment?

Back to our experiment. Let's assume we have agreed on this hypothesis: "Students assigned to wear headphones each day in study hall will have higher average grades at the end of the quarter than students banned from wearing headphones." To discuss this hypothesis and understand research design in general, you should know a little more about how variables are labeled. Trying to discuss experiments without knowing these terms is like trying to discuss skateboarding without knowing the names of the tricks. It may be possible to describe a "kickflip backside tailslide" without knowing the phrase, but it sure is awkward.

You already know that the purpose of an experiment is to establish a cause-and-effect relationship. Every experimental hypothesis reflects this cause-and-effect pattern, and when you read a hypothesis, you should be able to identify two variables:

- The variable that should *cause* something to happen is the **independent variable (IV).**
- The variable that should show the *effect* of the IV (or the outcome) is the **dependent variable (DV).**

▶ **independent variable (IV)** The research variable that a researcher actively manipulates, and if the hypothesis is correct, will cause a change in the dependent variable.

▶ **dependent variable (DV)** The research variable that is influenced by the independent variable. In psychology, the behavior or mental process where the impact of the independent variable is measured.

MODULE 2

F • Y • I

Technically speaking, researchers actually try to disprove the null hypothesis in experiments. The **null hypothesis** states that no relationship exists between the variables being studied. The **alternative hypothesis** is the one nonprofessionals are most familiar with. It states the relationship between the variables that the researcher hopes to prove.

trb At this point, you may wish to use **Critical Thinking Activity:** *Demonstrating Experimental Design Logic* (*Teacher's Resource Binder*, p. 2-1) and **Enrichment Lesson:** *Understanding Hypotheses* (*Teacher's Resource Binder*, p. 2-1).

■ **TEACHING TIP**

Students often mix up *independent* and *dependent variables.* To help them keep the terms straight, have them remember the following:

- The **dependent variable** is the behavior that researchers are looking for. Students should look for the behavior that is occurring in the experiment to identify this variable.
- The **independent variable** is what causes the behavior to happen. After finding the dependent variable, students should ask themselves, "What caused this behavior?" To answer this question, they have to find the independent variable.
- The dependent variable "depends" on the independent variable for its existence. Researchers hope that if they introduce the independent variable, the behavior that is the dependent variable will happen as a result.

trb At this point, you may wish to use **Application Activity:** *Identifying Independent and Dependent Variables* (*Teacher's Resource Binder*, p. 2-1; **Handout 2–13**).

Reteaching

trb You may wish to use **Application Activity:** *Identifying Independent and Dependent Variables* (*Teacher's Resource Binder*, p. 2-1; **Handout 2–13**) to solidify students' knowledge of these important concepts. In this activity, students choose independent and dependent variables from a hypothesis presented in the activity handout.

MODULE 2

■ TEACHING TIP

Help students understand distinctions among the concepts *random sample, representative sample,* and *population.*

- **Random sample** Randomization helps make a sample representative.
- **Representative sample** When a group is chosen randomly and every person in that population of people has an opportunity to be picked, the sample represents the population.
- **Population** Results gained from studying the sample can be generalized to the population at large.

trb At this point, you may wish to use **Cooperative Learning Activity:** ***A Tasty Sample(r): Teaching About Sampling Using M&Ms*** (*Teacher's Resource Binder*, p. 2-1; Handout 2–14).

F•Y•I

Simple experiments have only two groups—the experimental group and the control group. Experiments can have more than one experimental group, however. Subjects can be difficult to obtain (how many of you would volunteer your time to participate in a psychological experiment?), so researchers often try to gather as much data as possible with a group of subjects. They may test different but related variables or different levels of the same variable.

trb At this point, you may wish to use **Enrichment Lesson:** ***Differences Between Groups*** (*Teacher's Resource Binder*, p. 2-1).

Whenever you are thinking about an experiment, a good first step is to identify the IV and the DV. If you are unable to figure this out, you will almost certainly not understand the point of the experiment.

What is the IV—the "cause variable"—for our example? In our hypothesis, the variable that we predict will make a difference—our IV—is the presence or absence of headphones. The DV, or variable that shows the effect of headphones, is the participants' average end-of-quarter grades.

Groups, Random Assignment, and Confounding Variables

9. What are confounding variables? What are some ways to control for these variables?

The way we make the independent variable vary (take on different values) is to set up groups of participants. Typical experiments have at least two groups, an **experimental group** and a **control group** (sometimes referred to as the experimental and control *conditions*). In our case, the experimental group will comprise all students assigned to wear headphones, and the control group will comprise all students who are not allowed to wear headphones. These two groups will permit us to compare the effect of headphones on two groups of similar students.

The number of participants assigned to each group depends on some complicated statistical factors, but often there are at least 20 participants per group. Therefore, we will need to select 40 students for the experiment. We need to draw these students randomly from the entire population of 400 study hall students (for example, selecting every tenth name from a complete list of study hall students). If the selection is not random, the sample may be biased, and we would not be able to apply our results to the whole study hall population.

Now comes one of the most important steps: How do we decide which 20 students in our pool of participants should be in the experimental group and which 20 should be in the control group? An absolutely critical feature of experimental design is that the participants are placed in groups by **random assignment.** (You could use a computer program to do the random assignment, or a low-tech method of drawing names out of a box.) Since chance alone determines the assignment, we can assume that individual differences among the participants will be equally distributed between the two groups. Figure 2.5 summarizes the various components of our design.

These individual differences among participants are the largest category of a special kind of variable known as **confounding variables.** Confounding (from a Latin word that means "to pour together, or to confuse") variables are variables other than the IV that could produce a change in the DV. An experiment that does not adequately

▶ **experimental group** The participants in an experiment who are exposed to the treatment, that is, the independent variable.

▶ **control group** The participants in an experiment who are not exposed to the independent variable. These individuals function as a comparison for the experimental group participants.

▶ **random assignment** Assigning participants to experimental and control groups by chance, thus minimizing preexisting differences among those assigned to different groups.

▶ **confounding variable** In an experiment, a variable, other than the independent variable, that could influence the dependent variable. To draw cause-and-effect conclusions from an experiment, researchers must control for confounding variables.

Reteaching

Use the following diagram to reinforce the concepts of *randomization, representative sample,* and *population:*

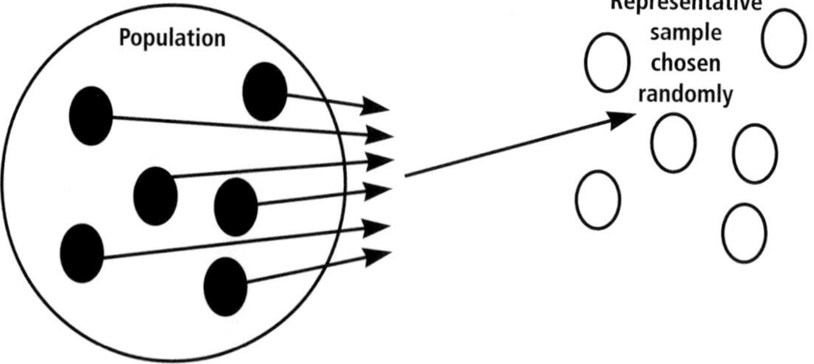

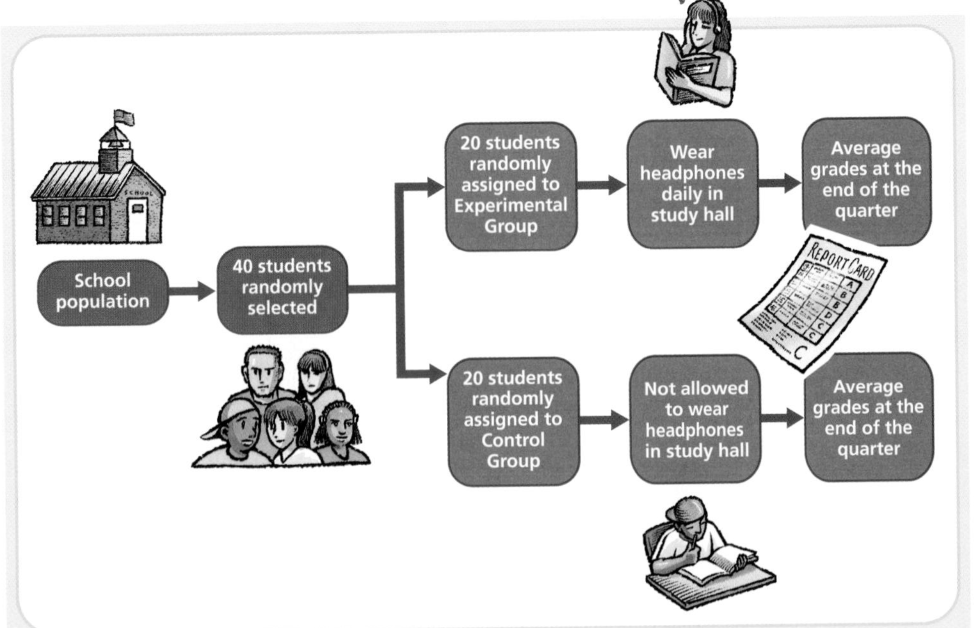

Figure 2.5 Experimental Design
Hypothesis: Students assigned to wear headphones in study hall will have higher average grades at the end of the quarter than students banned from wearing headphones.

control for confounding variables cannot achieve its purpose of showing a cause-and-effect relationship between the IV and the DV. To see how this works, imagine for a moment that the students in our experimental group (those assigned to wear headphones) are also healthier than students in the control group (those banned from wearing headphones). If the experimental group does have higher average grades at the end of the quarter, how would we know what caused this? The cause could have been the IV—wearing headphones—but it could also have been the higher general level of health in the experimental group. We really don't know, because the health variable *confounds* the headphone variable.

If we're not careful about how we set up our groups, we might not be able to eliminate a variety of confounding variables that could influence our experimental group's performance. Potential confounding variables include the amount of sleep participants get, the number of personal problems they're experiencing, and the quality of the teachers they have. This is why random assignment of participants to groups is so critical: It enables the researcher to assume that these factors will balance almost evenly across the two groups, just as 40 coin flips will usually balance fairly evenly between heads and tails. (Go ahead. Try it!) Without random assignment, there is a much greater likelihood that a confounding variable will bias the results of the research. So, if you have

Demonstrating

RANDOM ASSIGNMENT Gather data from students that would be skewed without randomly assigning students to groups. Some examples of such data are GPA or standardized test scores, height or weight, and shoe size.

Begin the demonstration by selectively dividing the students into groups. Try placing boys in one group and girls in another or purposely selecting certain students to put into groups that might reflect a skewed difference. Gather the data and discuss with the students the results. Then randomly divide the students into groups and collect the data again. Compare the results from the first groups to see if a difference arose. Emphasize to students how random assignment helps to limit the effect of individual differences.

F • Y • I

Groups in an experiment can be compared in several different ways.

- **Within-groups** comparisons occur when the group of subjects is compared to itself. In this case, the group of subjects serves as both the experimental and control group.
- **Between-groups** comparisons occur when two different groups of subjects are compared to each other. One group is the control group and the other is the experimental group. This is the more traditional group comparison, and it works well when there is a large group of subjects.
- **Matched-subjects** group comparisons use the between-subjects comparison with a twist. To control for individual differences, each subject in the control group has a "twin" in the experimental group that matches him or her in ways that would otherwise confound the study. For example, each group may have the same number of men and women or people of color or people from a particular religious or socioeconomic background, depending on what the IV or DV is.

trb At this point, you may wish to use **Enrichment Lesson:** ***Differences Between Groups*** (*Teacher's Resource Binder*, p. 2-1).

■ TEACHING TIP

tr A four-color transparency of Figure 2.5, Experimental Design, is available in the **Overhead Transparencies Set.**

Using this transparency, have students supply different hypotheses and populations. Guide students through how an experiment testing those hypotheses would look. You may even challenge your students to go through the process of conducting an actual experiment with one of their proposed hypotheses. Set up an in-house Institutional Review Board to go over the projects in order to ensure that ethical standards are kept.

trb At this point, you may wish to use **Application Activity:** ***Selecting Appropriate Research Methods*** (*Teacher's Resource Binder*, p. 2-1).

MODULE 2

■ TEACHING TIP

(tr) A four-color transparency of Figure 2.6, The Challenge of Confounding Variables, is available in the **Overhead Transparencies Set.** Using this transparency, lead students through other hypotheses and variables, brainstorming about what confounding variables might surface as explanations for a particular study's results. If students are pursuing their own experimental design projects, have them do this activity with their own hypotheses so that they can avoid confounding variables.

(trb) At this point, you may wish to use **Critical Thinking Activity:** *Finding Meaning in the Method* (*Teacher's Resource Binder*, p. 2-1; **Handout 2–10**).

■ LOOKING AT THE ISSUES

Environmental factors can have a big impact on how a person behaves. Some students do better in morning classes while others thrive later in the day. Some individualized education plans (IEPs) for exceptional learners call for specialized scheduling to compensate for highs and lows that occur during a school day. Have students consider the following:

- If you could create your ideal class schedule (assuming you had to take a class each period), how would you structure your day? Would academic classes fall in the morning or afternoon? Would you plan classes at night? Why or why not?
- What types of learning challenges might call for specialized scheduling?

not randomly assigned participants to groups, you have not conducted a true experiment and you cannot be sure you've identified a cause-and-effect relationship between the IV and the DV.

Control for Other Confounding Variables

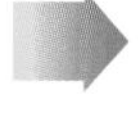

10. How can the double-blind procedure and placebos help control for confounding variables?

In addition to controlling for individual differences, a good research design must control for two other types of confounding variables: environmental differences and expectation effects (Figure 2.6). To control for environmental differences, you would want to make sure that all participants were in a study hall with the same temperature, lighting, and noise conditions.

Researchers take special care to control for expectation effects. They begin by making sure that participants are not aware of the hypothesis of the experiment. If they were, their expectations could influence the

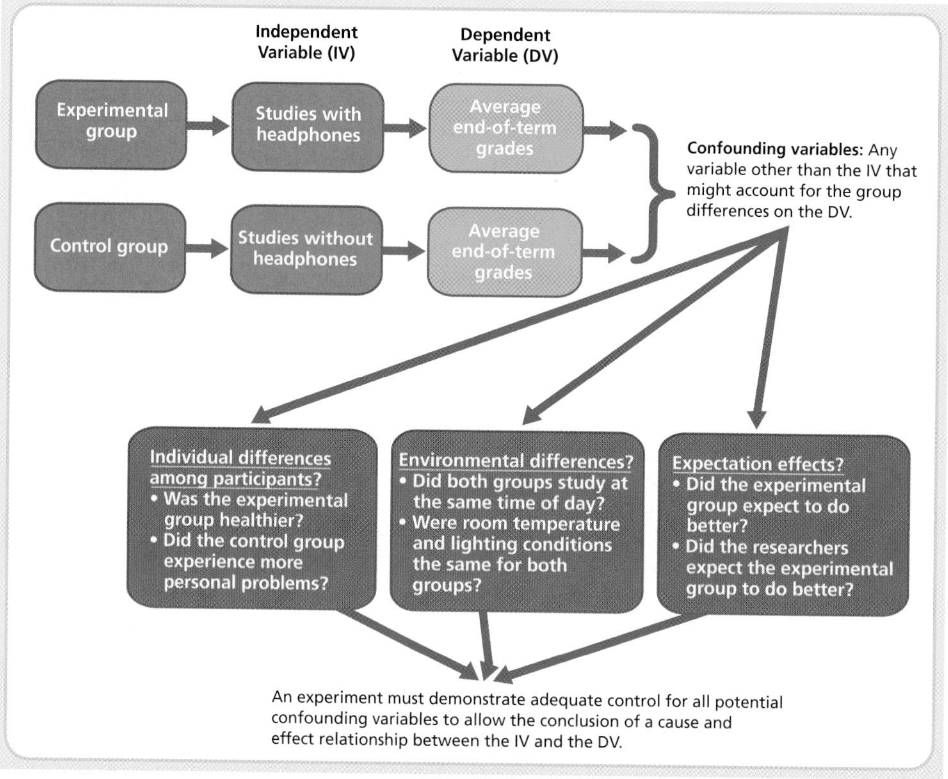

Figure 2.6 The Challenge of Confounding Variables Experimenters use a variety of techniques to minimize the disruptive effects of confounding variables. There are really two challenges involved: anticipating what the confounding variables are, and then deciding on the best method to deal with each of them.

outcome. In our example, students in the experimental group might do better because their knowledge of the hypothesis raised their confidence. To control for such effects, experimenters often use a *blind* (or masked) procedure, which means that they don't tell participants what the hypothesis is until after the data are collected. Sometimes even the people collecting the data don't know the expected outcome of the research or which participants are in which group. This is known as a **double-blind procedure,** and it is particularly important when those collecting data are asked to make judgments about the dependent variable. Otherwise, they might be influenced by their own expectations.

Experimenters use a special kind of control, a **placebo,** to deal with expectations in some experiments, including all drug studies. Imagine that you want to test the effectiveness of a new drug that may enhance memory. To set up this experiment, you would form an experimental group and a control group to manipulate whether participants would receive the drug, the IV. You would measure the impact of the drug by comparing the two groups' performance on a memory task, the DV. However, if the experimental group receives a pill, and the control group does not, you will not be able to successfully interpret better performance by the experimental group. Why? Because our expectations have a profound and well-documented effect on our responses. People receiving a pill of any sort will expect to experience change, and they will work harder to achieve the expected results. Given this extra work, you would not know whether the drug caused the enhanced memory in the experimental group, or whether the expectations created by taking that drug enhanced people's memory (Kirsch & Saperstein, 1998). You could control for this, however, by giving a placebo pill, containing no active substances, to the control group. Now, since all participants in both groups receive a pill and neither group knows whether the pill contains active or inactive substances, you could be sure that the expectations produced by getting a pill did not account for any improvement in memory.

Let's return to our original example, and review what we've accomplished so far. We are conducting an experiment to test the hypothesis, "Students assigned to wear headphones each day in study hall will have higher average grades at the end of the quarter than students banned from wearing headphones." We have identified the IV as the presence or absence of headphones and created this variable by establishing an experimental group and a control group. We have randomly selected the participants for the experiment from the entire study hall population, so we can be sure that our sample is not biased and our results will apply to all study hall students. We randomly assigned the participants to the two groups to control for any individual differences among them, and we controlled for other confounding variables by making sure the environmental conditions and expectation effects for the two groups are as similar as possible. The only thing we want to differ between the two groups is the IV—whether or not

▶ **double-blind procedure** An experimental procedure in which both the research participants and the research staff are ignorant (blind) as to the expected outcome of the research. This procedure is used to control for the effects of expectation as a confounding variable.

▶ **placebo** A nonactive substance or condition that may be administered instead of a drug or active agent to see if the drug has an effect beyond the expectations produced by taking it.

■ TEACHING TIP

Placebos are easiest to understand when discussing drug research, but the placebo effect can occur with any type of treatment. Studies have shown that even when people just decide to seek therapy, their problems seem to dissipate whether or not they actually complete the therapy. So researchers must take care to have all patients in a study participate in some sort of "treatment," even if the control treatment is just an exercise in futility.

■ LOOKING AT THE ISSUES

The use of placebos is standard practice for medical and psychological efficacy studies. In fact, most funding of pharmaceutical research requires the use of a placebo group to ensure that the effects of the drug are not due to the patient's expectations. Have students consider the following questions about placebos:

- If a drug shows effectiveness during a research study, what ethical responsibility do the researchers have to provide the benefits to all patients in the study? *(If a drug shows significant promise during study, then the study is halted and all patients are provided an opportunity to receive the treatment.)*
- How might patients feel if their doctors outside a research setting gave them a placebo instead of medicine? Is this practice ethical? Why or why not?

V At this point, you may wish to show **Videocassette:** ***Scientific American Frontiers,*** **Second Edition, Segment 1: "Tackling a Killer Disease"** (*Teacher's Resource Binder,* p. 2-1).

Meeting Individual Needs

Help students understand how the word *blind* can be used in this context.

- Obviously, when one is blind, one cannot see the world. In a **blind experiment,** the subjects are unaware of which group they are in—in essence, they cannot see their true place in the experiment.
- In a **double-blind experiment,** two different groups of people—the experimenters and the subjects—are unaware of what group the subjects are in.

MODULE 2

■ TEACHING TIPS

tr **trb** A black-line master for Table 2.2, Experiments Step by Step, is available in the **Black-Line Masters Appendix** in the *Teacher's Resource Binder.*

F • Y • I

Introduce the following measures of central tendency:

- **Mean** = sum of the responses divided by the total responses. The mean (average) is perhaps the most useful measure of central tendency but can be skewed by extremely high or low numbers in the data set.
- **Median** = the number that falls in the exact middle of a group of numbers arranged in numerical order. Note that the median of a group of even numbers is calculated by taking the average (mean) of the two numbers in the middle. The median in a number set that is balanced can reflect what the typical piece of data looks like.
- **Mode** = the number that occurs most often in the number set. The mode shows the most frequent response, which is sometimes a more accurate representation of the results than the mean.
- **Variance** = the difference between the highest and the lowest numbers in a set. The variance shows how different the two most extreme scores are.
- **Standard deviation** = the standard deviation shows how much each piece of data differs from the others. The higher the standard deviation, the more different the data are. Larger data sets typically yield lower standard deviations.

trb At this point, you may wish to use **Application Activity:** *Organizing and Interpreting Data* (*Teacher's Resource Binder,* p. 2-1; **Handout 2–15**).

students wear headphones—because we want to be able to conclude that there is a cause-and-effect relationship between wearing headphones and end-of-quarter grades.

Data Analysis

11. What role do statistics play in the experimental method?

Now we run the experiment and collect the data. Then we analyze the numbers, using statistics, to find out if the hypothesis is supported.

Let's say the average end-of-quarter grade for the experimental group is a B, and for the control group is a C. Is this enough of a difference to conclude that there is a cause-and-effect relationship? Maybe. But what if the difference was between a B and a B−? How different must the values of the DV be for the two groups? Perhaps you've heard the phrase *statistically significant*. In the United States, most researchers have agreed that we can consider a result statistically significant if the possibility that the difference between groups would occur by chance alone is no more than 5 percent. To determine this likelihood, we must consider three questions:

1. How big is the difference between the groups?
2. How uniform are the results within each group?
3. How many participants are in each group?

If we find a big difference *between* two large groups of students, and small variations in results *within* each group (for example, mostly A's and B's in one group and mostly C's and D's in the other), we can be confident that our results are statistically significant.

The steps of the experimental method are summarized for you in Table 2.2.

TABLE 2.2 EXPERIMENTS STEP BY STEP

1. Develop the *hypothesis*.
2. Create *operational definitions* for the *independent and dependent variables*.
3. *Randomly select* a sample of participants from the population.
4. *Randomly assign* the participants to the *experimental and control groups*.
5. Expose the experimental group, but not the control group, to the IV. If necessary, use a *placebo* with the control group to balance expectations.
6. Control for other *confounding variables* by using a *double-blind procedure* and treating both groups the same except for exposure to the IV.
7. Learn the impact of the IV by measuring the DV for both groups.
8. Use *statistical analysis* to discover whether the difference in the DV between the two groups is likely to have been caused by the manipulation of the IV.

Cross-Curricular Connections

MATH AND STATISTICS Try some of the following collaborative lessons with a colleague:

- Since many statistical measures can be done by calculator, invite a math teacher to lead a tutorial in how to use the statistical functions on the students' calculators.
- If the schedule permits (or an after-school session is feasible), team teach a lesson in basic statistics with a math colleague. While the math teacher can offer the calculation instruction, you can offer instruction in the practical use of statistics in psychological research, using some of the examples provided in the *Teacher's Resource Binder* that accompanies this text.

Replication

12. What do we mean when we say that experimental results must be replicable, and why is this important?

There is one other safeguard required for an experiment. Psychological scientists need to ask: "Can the results of this experiment be **replicated,** or reliably repeated?" If an experimental result can be obtained only once, we must conclude that it was caused by some chance variable and not by the IV. This means there is no apparent cause-and-effect relationship between the IV and the DV. In our study hall experiment, replication studies might involve repeating the experiment at different schools or under slightly different conditions. Replication helps us to know that our results apply in a variety of situations, and it underlines the importance of clear operational definitions for all our variables. It is no accident that our topic in this module is research—not search. You have got to be able to demonstrate your findings again and again and again!

▶ **replication** Repeating a research study to see whether the results can be reliably reproduced. Unless a study can be replicated, the results are likely to be a fluke occurrence.

Ethics

Human Research

13. What four ethical principles must guide research on humans?

There are ethical considerations with all research, especially when the participants are humans. These issues extend well beyond the methodological issues we have been discussing so far. For moral reasons, many hypotheses cannot be tested experimentally, even though we could design sound experiments that would provide good answers. For example, suppose that you have a hypothesis that children who are disciplined by being whipped with a belt will not behave as well as children disciplined without corporal punishment. This experiment would be quite simple to set up. The IV would be exposure to whippings and the DV would be some measure of behavior, such as number of broken rules. You would then choose a sample of participants and randomly assign them to two groups. Those in the experimental group would be whipped by their parents, and those in the control group would be disciplined by their parents in other ways. Here we have a straightforward experimental design, but you can see why it would be unethical to conduct this experiment. You would be exposing your experimental group participants to a procedure that you believe would harm them.

Most research takes place on university campuses, where ethics committees screen all research proposals in advance. The committee checks

F•Y•I

One of the goals of research is to be able to generalize the findings to the public at large. A study has little value if the findings apply only to a specific group of people. The more a study is replicated, the more likely the findings can be applied to the general public.

trb At this point, you may wish to use **Evaluation Activity:** *More Cases Are Better Than Fewer* (*Teacher's Resource Binder*, p. 2-1; **Handout 2–17**).

■ TEACHING TIPS

(1) Emphasize to students that experiments are more likely to be replicated effectively if clear operational definitions are used. Operational definitions attempt to clearly define the behaviors that researchers are looking for. If the operational definitions are clear enough, then others can more easily and accurately replicate the study.

trb At this point, you may wish to use **Application Activity:** *Writing an Operational Definition* (*Teacher's Resource Binder*, p. 2-1; **Handout 2–12**).

(2) Some famous studies in social psychology have spurred a tightening of ethical standards. Stanley Milgram's obedience study and Philip Zimbardo's prison guard study forced researchers to consider the long-term psychological effects on subjects who may commit acts they didn't realize they were capable of. You may want to highlight these two studies and discuss how different they might look if conducted today.

trb At this point, you may wish to use **Application Activity:** *Ethics in Research* (*Teacher's Resource Binder*, p. 2-1; **Handout 2–19**).

- If your schedule does not permit you to team teach a lesson in basic statistics, videotape a collaborative lesson delivered by yourself and a math colleague. Each of you can use the video or video clips to enhance the lessons provided in your own classrooms.

trb At this point, you may wish to use **Application Activity:** *Organizing and Interpreting Data* (*Teacher's Resource Binder*, p. 2-1; **Handout 2–15**), **Application Activity:** *Describing Data* (*Teacher's Resource Binder*, p. 2-1; **Handout 2–16**), **Technology Application Activity:** *PsychSim:* **"Describing Statistics"** (*Teacher's Resource Binder*, p. 2-1), and **Enrichment Lesson:** *Differences Between Groups* (*Teacher's Resource Binder*, p. 2-1).

MODULE 2

■ LOOKING AT THE ISSUES

Have students discuss any other ethical considerations that might be necessary for conducting experiments on human and animal subjects. Challenge students to develop an ethics code for conducting their own experiments. They should address the following questions:

- What considerations might need to be enhanced?
- What additional ethical considerations must be followed when working with minors?
- How does the use of deception affect the ethics of a study?

trb At this point, you may wish to use **Application Activity:** *Ethics in Research* (*Teacher's Resource Binder*, p. 2-1; **Handout 2–19**).

■ TEACHING TIP

web Have students go to the APA's Web site and examine the APA Ethics Code in detail (www.apa.org/ethics). They can see what specific considerations researchers must follow when conducting experiments with both human and animal subjects.

trb At this point, you may wish to use **Application Activity:** *Ethics in Research* (*Teacher's Resource Binder*, p. 2-1; **Handout 2–19**) and **Enrichment Lesson:** *Research Ethics* (*Teacher's Resource Binder*, p. 2-1).

■ APPLYING THE POINTS

Contact a local university or medical school to see what types of animal research are conducted at the institution. Use the following questions as a guide for an informal interview as well as for class presentation:

- What are the goals of the research studies being conducted on animals? Is it to learn more about animal or human behavior?
- How does the institution ensure that animals are treated ethically?
- Has the institution had trouble with animal rights protests? Why or why not?

trb At this point, you may wish to use **Enrichment Lesson:** *Do Animals Have Rights?* (*Teacher's Resource Binder*, p. 2-1).

that the research will comply with the strict ethical guidelines for research with human participants set by the American Psychological Association (1993). There are four basic principles:

- ***Informed consent*** Researchers must inform potential participants in advance about the general nature of the research and any potential risks involved. Participants must understand that they have a right to refuse to participate or to withdraw at any time.
- ***The right to be protected from harm and discomfort*** Researchers may conduct studies that involve harm and discomfort only under certain circumstances and only with the participants' informed consent.
- ***The right to confidentiality*** Researchers must never release data about individual participants, and members of the research team may not gossip or spread information about the participants.
- ***The right to debriefing*** Participants must receive a full explanation of the research when their involvement is done. This is especially important if the research has included deception.

Animal Research

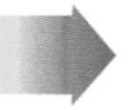

14. Why do researchers sometimes use animals for their research?

The ethical principles we've discussed help protect the rights of human research participants, but what about animals? We often hear media reports of research that seems to subject animals to unwarranted cruelty, pain, and suffering. Why are animals used in research? What is done to protect them?

Psychologists use animals in research for several reasons:

- Many psychologists are simply interested in animal behavior. It is a fascinating and legitimate field of study.
- There are biological and behavioral similarities between animals and humans. Therefore, by studying animals we can learn things that also apply to humans.
- Since many species of animals develop more rapidly and therefore have shorter life spans than humans do, we can study genetic effects over generations much more rapidly in animals than in humans.

Cooperative Learning

trb The APA Ethics Code requires institutions that conduct animal experimentation to establish an Animal Care and Use Committee to review whether the studies done on animals follow ethical standards. Divide students into groups and, using **Role-Playing Activity:** *Animal Care and Use Committee* (*Teacher's Resource Binder*, p. 2-1; **Handout 2–20**), have group members use their knowledge of the ethics of animal research by pretending to be on an Animal Care and Use Committee. As members of this committee, students in each group should determine whether a series of experiments should be allowed to go forward.

- It is often possible to exercise more control over experiments with animals than is the case with humans. For example, researchers can observe animals 24 hours a day and control their diet completely. Humans usually won't agree to such conditions.
- Procedures that are not ethical to perform on humans may be considered acceptable when performed on animals. My sister-in-law once had a job in a medical laboratory, where she performed surgery on dogs that had been slated to be killed at a local animal shelter. She tied off an artery and created heart attacks in these dogs, so that researchers could run controlled tests of experimental drugs designed for human heart attack patients. Is it right to place the needs of humans above those of animals? We live in a society where some animals (cows, chickens) are raised for food and others (rats, insects) are exterminated to reduce the threat of disease. Defenders of animal research argue that it's permissible to use or even sacrifice animals for the good of humans.

What is done to protect animals from abuses? Federal legislation has been passed to protect animals used in research. This legislation, which has the support of most researchers (Johnson, 1990), provides that animals must have clean housing, adequate ventilation, and appropriate food, and that they must be otherwise well-cared for. The media accounts portraying animals in psychological research as "victims of extreme pain and stress, inflicted upon them out of idle curiosity" appear to be untrue. One study (Coile & Miller, 1984) checked every animal study published in all of the American Psychological Association's journals for five years. That study was unable to identify a single instance of inappropriate abuse.

Just as every marathon runner is also an athlete, and every pianist is also a musician, every psychologist is a scientist. This means psychologists use a particular set of methods to learn about behavior and mental processes. All the factual information you will read in this book was gathered using these methods. Your knowledge of these methods will deepen your understanding of psychology and help prepare you to think critically in a world where research can (and should) drive many decisions. Now, what will you say when your school administrators announce that new headphone policy?

■ APPLYING THE POINTS

Have students explore what specific federal regulations exist for ensuring that animals are treated well in experimental laboratories by addressing the following questions:

- How big do living quarters need to be for different types of animals? Why are there differences?
- What is "adequate ventilation"?
- Should there be more stringent measures in place to protect animal rights? Why or why not?

trb At this point, you may wish to use Enrichment Lesson: *Do Animals Have Rights?* (*Teacher's Resource Binder*, p. 2-1).

Close

Emphasize to students that research methodology underlies the entire discipline of psychology. Scientific principles of control, integrity, and ethics are at the heart of all the findings studied in this text. What we know about human behavior relies on how well scientific studies follow these principles. When you learn or hear about studies in the classroom or media, remember the concepts presented in this module to help you be a better thinker and consumer.

MODULE 2

Checking the Points

■ TEACHING TIPS

web (1) The book companion site for *Thinking About Psychology* at www.worthpublishers.com/thinkingaboutpsych contains a module quiz, flashcards of key terms and people, and other student activities and resources for this module. You will also find PowerPoint lectures, a quiz grade book, and other teaching resources by logging on as an instructor.

trb (2) At this point, you may wish to review and confirm concepts about research methods with **Critical Thinking Activity:** *Fact or Falsehood?* (*Teacher's Resource Binder*, p. 2-1; **Handout 2–1**). Suggest that students complete the handout individually without referring to the copy of the handout they may have completed earlier in the module. In small groups, students can review confusing concepts and confirm the correct answers with passages in the text.

REVIEW

Module 2: Research Strategies

What's the Point?

This module has focused on the ways that psychologists gather information about our behaviors and mental processes. Psychologists gain their knowledge by using the scientific method—the application of critical thinking and research tools such as observation, experimentation, and statistical analysis.

Why Is Research Important?

1. *What advantage does research have over other ways of knowing things?*

   Research leads to logical, supported conclusions that allow us to make informed decisions. Well-designed research produces more reliable answers than do conclusions based on common sense, which tend to vary from one person to another.

Observation and Bias

2. *What are some ways that bias can influence research?*

   Bias is any influence that unfairly increases the possibility that we will reach a particular conclusion. Psychologists are human, too, and they may unknowingly pay more attention to behaviors that support their ideas, and less attention to those that offer no support. Research participants can influence results by behaving in ways that they think are appropriate or expected.

Case Studies

3. *What are the advantages and disadvantages of case studies?*

   Case studies offer two advantages: (1) They focus on one person in depth, giving a detailed view of a particular condition or set of behaviors, and (2) they may be possible when other types of research are unacceptable or unethical, as in the study of child abuse. The disadvantage of case studies is that they will tell us little about human beings in general if the person studied is not typical of the wider population.

Correlation

4. *Why can't we conclude cause-and-effect relationships from correlational data?*

   If we know that two things are correlated, we know that they are consistently associated with each other. If the correlation is positive, one thing tends to increase when the other increases, or decrease when the other decreases (skiing and snow, for example). If the correlation is negative, one thing tends to decrease when the other increases, or to increase when the other decreases (baseball and snow, for example). But correlations do not tell us *why* the two things are associated; so we cannot say that one (skiing) causes the other (snow). We can, however, use our knowledge of the consistent relationship to make predictions—when it snows, many people will ski; when it snows, few people will play baseball.

Surveys

5. *Why should we be cautious of data obtained from surveys?*

   Psychologists use surveys to collect large amounts of data from many people, so surveys are efficient research tools. But survey results will be unreliable if the wording of the questions leads people to make certain responses, or if the survey sample does not represent the population being studied.

Longitudinal and Cross-Sectional Studies

6. *What are the advantages and disadvantages of longitudinal and cross-sectional studies?*

   Developmental psychologists often use longitudinal and cross-sectional studies to see how individuals change through the life span. Longitudinal studies follow the same group for many years. These studies yield a wealth of data but are expensive. Cross-sectional studies compare people of different ages at one time. They are more efficient than longitudinal studies, but the results may be confusing because each age group may have different life experiences.

Experiments

Experiments are the only research method that allows us to conclude that one thing causes another. For that reason, the experimental method is often the tool of choice in psychological research.

7. *What does it mean to operationalize variables?*

   For the results of an experiment to be meaningful, a psychologist must state a hypothesis and give a specific description, or operational definition, of each variable in the hypothesis. These specific descriptions allow precise measurement of variables.

8. *What is the difference between the independent variable and the dependent variable in an experiment?*

   A hypothesis identifies two different variables: The independent variable (IV or "cause" variable) is the part of the experiment that the researcher will deliberately manipulate in some way, so that it takes on different values. The dependent variable (DV or "effect" variable) is the part of the experiment that will respond, or change, as the IV is manipulated—assuming the hypothesis is correct.

9. *What are confounding variables? What are some ways to control for these variables?*

   Confounding variables are variables other than the IV that can produce changes in dependent variables. Confounding variables may consist of individual differences, environmental differences, or expectation effects. To eliminate confounding variables, researchers set up a control group (or control condition) in addition to the experimental group, and they randomly assign participants to the two groups. Random assignment controls for individual differences.

10. *How can the double-blind procedure and placebos help control for confounding variables?*

    In a double-blind procedure, the participants do not know the hypothesis being tested, and the people collecting the data do not know which group is the control group or the experimental group. This design helps reduce chances that participants' expectations and experimenters' expectations will influence the results of the experiment. Placebos are inert or neutral substances administered to the control group so that these participants feel they have received some sort of treatment and develop the same sort of expectations as the experimental group. Without placebos, an experimental group would be more likely to expect (and therefore experience) change, because only they would be receiving a treatment, such as a pill. Placebos help control for the confounding effects of expectation.

11. *What role do statistics play in the experimental method?*

    Statistics help us analyze the results of an experiment and know when results are meaningful. Psychologists generally agree that results of a well-designed experiment are statistically significant when the possibility of the result occurring by chance alone is no greater than 5 percent.

MODULE 2

trb **tr** ■ TEACHING TIP

At this point, students may benefit from completing the handouts **Building Vocabulary:** *Exploring Root Words* and *Matching Terms and Definitions* (*Teacher's Resource Binder*, p. 2-1; **Handouts 2–2** and **2–3**) without referring to copies of the handouts they may have completed earlier in the module. Working with partners, students can use the text to confirm correct answers. You can project transparencies of **Handouts 2–2** and **2–3** (with answers inserted) so that students can check their work.

tb **Using the Test Bank**

The *Test Bank* that accompanies the textbook offers a wide variety of questions in different formats and levels of complexity. Use the software to construct whole tests or to integrate standardized questions into teacher-made tests.

Self-Test Answers

Multiple-Choice Questions

1. c, 2. a

12. *What do we mean when we say that experimental results must be replicable, and why is this important?*

    An experiment is replicable if another person can reliably perform the same procedures, using the same variables, under the same conditions, and get the same results. If this is not possible, the result was probably a chance occurrence, not a true cause-and-effect relationship.

Ethics

13. *What four ethical principles must guide research on humans?*

    To protect research participants, members of the American Psychological Association (APA) have agreed that researchers must (1) inform participants about the general nature of the research and its risks and secure their informed consent to participate, (2) protect participants from harm and discomfort during the research, (3) ensure that participants' privacy will be protected and that all personal information will remain confidential, and (4) provide participants with a full explanation of the research when it is completed.

14. *Why do researchers sometimes use animals for their research?*

    Some researchers use animals in research to learn more about animal behavior. Others conduct controlled studies on animals that they could not conduct on humans because of ethical concerns or practical problems, such as the relatively long human life span or the problems of running long-term controlled studies over several generations.

Key Terms

scientific method p. 17
researcher bias p. 19
critical thinking p. 19
participant bias p. 19
naturalistic observation p. 20
case study p. 20
correlational study p. 20
survey method p. 22
population p. 23
random sample p. 23
longitudinal study p. 23
cross-sectional study p. 24
experiment p. 24
hypothesis p. 24
operational definition p. 24
independent variable (IV) p. 25
dependent variable (DV) p. 25
experimental group p. 26
control group p. 26
random assignment p. 26
confounding variable p. 26
double-blind procedure p. 27
placebo p. 27
replication p. 31

Self-Test

Multiple-Choice Questions

Choose the *best* answer for each of the following questions.

1. If you are using ____________, you will examine assumptions, seach for hidden values, evaluate evidence, and assess conclusions when you hear an argument or conclusion.
   a. random assignment
   b. replication
   c. critical thinking
   d. naturalistic observation

2. Lee wants to know how many of her 100 classmates will vote for her if she runs for class president. Her best chance of getting this information would be to
   a. conduct a survey, contacting every fifth person on an alphabetical list of her classmates.

Alternative Assessment/Portfolio Project

trb CONDUCTING STUDENT-LED RESEARCH/RUNNING A PSYCHOLOGY FAIR Leading students through a research experiment of their own provides a valuable critical thinking and learning experience. Using the **Research Guide** by Allyson Weseley, Ed.D., and the **Psychology Fair Guide** by Carol Dean, Ed.D., both found in the *Teacher's Resource Binder*, you can help students explore the research process and encourage them to showcase their work in a science/psychology fair. Some guidelines to consider include the following:

- Encourage students to choose topics that have a rich background of research. This research will provide a solid foundation for formulating research plans and experimental conditions.

b. do a case study of last year's winner and try to figure out what characteristics are important for a class president.
c. do an experiment, dividing her friends into an experimental group and a control group, and have them click "yes" or "no" buttons to questions presented on a computer monitor.
d. conduct a longitudinal study of the 100 people in her class, tracking their social and political views.

3. Tony has to design a research study, and he is running late. To save time, he wants to design a study using the simplest research technique. He would be best advised to do a (an)
   a. observation study.
   b. replication study.
   c. case study.
   d. correlational study.

4. The American Psychological Association has outlined four basic principles to guide research on humans. Which of the following is NOT one of those principles?
   a. Informed consent
   b. A right to debriefing
   c. A right to confidentiality
   d. A right to fair compensation

5. Psychologists tend to agree that a finding is statistically significant if
   a. it is the result of an experiment.
   b. it can be replicated.
   c. the possibility of its happening by chance is no greater than 5 percent.
   d. the possibility of its happening by chance is no greater than 50 percent.

6. The tendency to notice evidence that supports one's hypothesis is known as
   a. participant bias.
   b. informed consent.
   c. researcher bias.
   d. critical thinking.

7. Confounding variables, which can influence the results of an experiment, may consist of
   a. the independent variable, the dependent variable, and environmental conditions.
   b. individual differences among participants, environmental differences, and expectation effects.
   c. control groups, the double-blind procedure, and placebos.
   d. negative correlations, positive correlations, and associations.

8. Marcia thinks she would like to do a case study for her psychology class assignment. She should be aware that the biggest disadvantage of doing a case study is that
   a. she will violate ethical guidelines for research.
   b. she may not be comfortable studying one person in such detail.
   c. her results may not be statistically significant.
   d. her findings may not apply to most people.

Matching Terms and Definitions

9. For each definition, choose the *best* matching term from the list that follows.

Definitions

a. _____ An investigator's testable prediction about the outcome of research.
b. _____ A specification of the exact procedures used to make a variable specific and measurable for research purposes.
c. _____ The variable that the researcher will actively manipulate and, if the hypothesis is correct, will cause a change in the other major variable in the experiment.
d. _____ The research variable that will be influenced by the manipulated variable.

Self-Test Answers

Multiple-Choice Questions (continued)

3. a, 4. d, 5. c, 6. c, 7. b, 8. d

Matching Terms and Definitions

9. a. (7), b. (1), c. (10), d. (9)

- Have students work in cooperative learning groups (to decrease the number of studies you will have to monitor) and provide students with lessons in teamwork.
- Reinforce students' critical thinking abilities as well as their sense of academic integrity by emphasizing scientific principles.
- Insist on following ethical guidelines. No research should be conducted without obtaining informed consent from the subjects.
- Create a rubric that places emphasis on critical thinking, good research skills, and ethics.

Self-Test Answers

Matching Terms and Definitions (continued)

e. (2), f. (4), g. (12)

Fill-in-the-Blank Questions

10. Confounding variables, 11. sample; random, 12. scientific method, 13. naturalistic observation

Brief Essay Question

14. The primary difference between experiments and correlations is that experiments seek to determine a cause-and-effect relationship while correlations do not. In both, variables are compared, yet the conclusions that can be drawn from each one are different. Be sure students understand that correlations describe a relationship between variables and experiments manipulate one variable to coax another variable to occur.

e. _____ The participants in an experiment who are exposed to the treatment.

f. _____ The participants in an experiment who are not exposed to the treatment.

g. _____ Repeating the essence of a research study to see whether the results can be reliably reproduced.

Terms

(1) operational definition
(2) experimental group
(3) random assignment
(4) control group
(5) double-blind procedure
(6) experiment
(7) hypothesis
(8) confounding variable
(9) dependent variable
(10) independent variable
(11) placebo
(12) replication

Fill-in-the-Blank Questions

10. _______________ occurs when any factor unfairly increases the likelihood that a particular conclusion will be reached.

11. To be reasonably sure that your observations will apply to the group you are studying, you should select a _______________ from the population and ensure that the selection is_______________.

12. The _______ _________ is a method of learning about the world through the application of critical thinking and tools such as observation, experimentation, and statistical analysis.

13. A researcher who is using the technique of ________ ________ would observe and record behavior in naturally occurring situations without trying to manipulate and control the situation.

Brief Essay Question

14. Experiments and correlational studies are two popular research methods used in psychology. In two short paragraphs (or about 10 sentences), explain how these two types of studies differ from each other, and why only one of them can reveal cause-and-effect relationships.

Performance Standards

Standard Area: Biological Bases of Behavior

Content Standard 1: Neural functioning

Performance Standard 1.3 Neurological functioning can be changed by environment and heredity.

- Discuss evidence that rats housed in an enriched environment had brain weight increases. (Student Text p. 46)
- Explore how premature infants demonstrate more rapid physical and neurological development when massaged. (Student Text p. 46)
- Discuss how sixth-graders from impoverished environments, when raised in enriched environments as infants, had higher intelligence test scores. (Student Text p. 46)
- Present research by Rosenzweig and Krech on neural development in rats raised in enriched environments versus impoverished environments. (Student Text p. 47)

Content Standard 7: The interaction of nature and nurture to influence behavior

Performance Standard 7.1 Measure the effects of nature and nurture on behavior.

- Identify the roles of chromosomes, DNA, and genes. (Student Text pp. 40–41)
- Examine twin and adoption studies to measure the role of heredity and environment on intelligence, personality, divorce rates, attitudes, and other belief systems. (Student Text pp. 42–45)

Content Standard 8: Evolutionary influences on psychological properties

Performance Standard 8.1 Examine the interaction of how evolved behavioral inclinations interact with an individual's current cultural environment to influence behavior.

- Discuss that some human behaviors, such as feeling disappointment when someone breaks a promise, are similar in all people, regardless of environment. Discuss how evolutionary psychologists believe that these similarities exist because certain behaviors allowed our genetic ancestors to survive. (Student Text pp. 41–42)

Standard Area: Life Span Development

Content Standard 3: Developmental theories

Performance Standard 3.4 Examine the relationship of developmental theories to cultural influences.

- Explore how development differs between individuals raised in collectivist versus individualist cultures. Present research by Atkinson (1988) that illustrates how Japanese teenagers, raised in a collectivist culture, are more likely to be concerned than Americans by the statement, "My parents will be disappointed in me." (Student Text pp. 48–49)

Materials NETWORK

All of the items from the Video, Activity, and Enrichment Centers listed below come from the *Teacher's Resource Binder.* These items will help you teach and expand on concepts presented in Module 3.

trb This logo indicates when an item from the Materials Network may be used in conjunction with a specific note found in this module's *Teacher's Edition.*

Genetics in Brief

V Video Center

Consult the faculty guide from *The Brain* and *Scientific American Frontiers* video series for descriptions of these modules or segments.

- Videocassette: *The Brain,* Second Edition, Module 12: "Huntington's Disease" (*Teacher's Resource Binder*, p. 3-1)
- Videocassette: *Scientific American Frontiers,* Second Edition, Segment 22: "Bypass Genes" (*Teacher's Resource Binder*, p. 3-1)

Activity Center

- Critical Thinking Activity: *Fact or Falsehood?* With this activity, students' preconceptions about nature versus nurture are either exposed as incorrect or reinforced as correct. (*Teacher's Resource Binder*, p. 3-1; Handout 3–1)
- Building Vocabulary: Graphic Organizer: *Concept Web* The graphic organizer provided for this module combines a vocabulary practice exercise with a visual representation in the form of a concept web. It shows how terms from biology are applied to psychology. (*Teacher's Resource Binder*, p. 3-1; Handout 3–2)
- Application Activity: *Self-Assessment of Psychology's Big Issues* With this activity, students can assess their own opinions about the issues that are central to psychology. The issues in focus within this activity are the following: stability versus change, rationality versus irrationality, and nature versus nurture. (*Teacher's Resource Binder*, p. 3-1; Handout 3–3)
- Technology Application Activity: *Human Genome Project* Genetic research has exploded in recent years. This activity will expose students to the fascinating, cutting-edge advances in mapping the human genome. The interactive Web site offers an education kit that contains a short video and accessible articles ideal for sparking students' interest in doing further research in the social, ethical, and legal implications of genetic research. (*Teacher's Resource Binder*, p. 3-1; Handout 3–4)
- Technology Application Activity: *Mendel, the Game* Students may have learned about Gregory Mendel and his experiments in genetics. In this interactive game, students log on to a Web site and try to create new breeds of pea plants using Mendelian laws of genetics. As the site states, the game "is easy to learn, easy to play, but difficult to master." (*Teacher's Resource Binder*, p. 3-1)
- Analysis Activity: *Genetics—An Informal Debate* Genetic testing is fast becoming one of the top hot-button issues of our time. In this activity, students can become informed participants in the debate over genetic testing. (*Teacher's Resource Binder*, p. 3-1; Handout 3–5)

Enrichment Center

- Enrichment Lesson: *Designer Babies?* With recent research development, gene therapy has new potential. The question of parents choosing the traits of their future children is one, among others, that fuels the controversy over genetic testing and stem cell research. (*Teacher's Resource Binder*, p. 3-1)
- Enrichment Lesson: *Human Cloning* Dolly, the result of the first successful cloning of an adult mammal, startled the scientific community. If the scientific community can clone animals, can they clone humans? And if they can, should they? (*Teacher's Resource Binder*, p. 3-1)
- Enrichment Lesson: *The Genetic Revolution* Genetic testing may offer insight into illnesses one might develop later in life. But this knowledge can also lead to discrimination by employers and insurers. (*Teacher's Resource Binder*, p. 3-1)

Nature and Similarity

Activity Center

- Technology Application Activity: *Evolutionary Psychology* Research in behavior genetics that reveals the impact of genes on our behavior has made evolutionary psychology a popular area of study. The Web sites in this activity provide students with the opportunity to explore how psychology uses evolutionary theory to explain human behavior. (*Teacher's Resource Binder*, p. 3-1; Handout 3–6)

Enrichment Center

- Enrichment Lesson: *Evolutionary Psychology* Peter Gray of Boston College notes that students often have misconceptions about evolution. What is evolutionary psychology? How did it start and how closely does it relate to Darwin's theories? This lesson will help students understand this growing perspective in psychology. (*Teacher's Resource Binder*, p. 3-1)

- Enrichment Lesson: *Misunderstanding Evolutionary Theory and Psychology* Evolution is a controversial theory that has been blasted in some circles. This lesson will provide students with the popular misconceptions about evolutionary theory and how psychology has integrated relevant principles of evolution into its explanation of human behavior. (*Teacher's Resource Binder*, p. 3-1)

Nature and Individual Differences

 **Video Center**

Consult the faculty guide from *The Mind* and *Scientific American Frontiers* video series for descriptions of these modules or segments.

- Videocassette: *The Mind,* Second Edition, Module 16: "The Effect of Aging on Cognitive Function: Nature/Nurture" (*Teacher's Resource Binder*, p. 3-1)
- Videocassette: *Scientific American Frontiers,* Second Edition, Segment 23: "Bringing Up Monkey" (*Teacher's Resource Binder*, p. 3-1)

Activity Center

- Critical Thinking Activity: *Striking Similarities* Stories abound of twins separated at birth who are eerily similar to one another. Use this activity to challenge this assumption; the activity is designed to show how two random people could have some striking similarities with each other. (*Teacher's Resource Binder*, p. 3-1; Handout 3–7)

Enrichment Center

- Enrichment Lesson: *The Minnesota Twin Study* The most comprehensive study of twins in the world is the Minnesota Twin Study. The first part of the study began in 1979. The second part of the study continued over a ten-year period. This study does both cross-sectional and longitudinal research on twins reared together and apart. The findings over the years have provided valuable insight into the interplay of nature and nurture in the developing person. (*Teacher's Resource Binder*, p. 3-1)

Environment Matters

 **Video Center**

- Videocassette: *The Brain,* Second Edition, Module 2: "Effect of Hormones and Environment on Brain Development" Consult the faculty guide from *The Brain* video series for a description of this module. (*Teacher's Resource Binder*, p. 3-1)

Activity Center

- Technology Analysis Activity: *The Most Important Influence in One's Life* A question similar to this one was asked of a 20-member teen panel by *USA Today*. This activity will help students make an informed decision about the role of environment in their own lives. (*Teacher's Resource Binder*, p. 3-1)

Enrichment Center

- Enrichment Lesson: *Do Parents Really Matter?* Despite the current emphasis on the role of heredity and environmental influences other than parenting in influencing characteristics, Annie Murphy Paul shows how parents still play an important role. Students may find this question humorous, but this lesson will challenge students to examine the role their parents have had in making them who they are now. (*Teacher's Resource Binder*, p. 3-1)
- Enrichment Lesson: *"Mom Always Liked You Best!"* Developmental psychology's biggest puzzle may be the question "Why are children in the same family so different?" Do parents treat siblings differently depending on gender, birth order, or relative age? (*Teacher's Resource Binder*, p. 3-1)

Nature and Nuture: The Future

Activity Center

- Analysis Activity: *Intercultural Learning Activities* This activity exposes students to situations in which one's culture affects behavior. It highlights how cultural norms or rules for accepted and excepted behavior often become known to outsiders only when the norms or rules are violated. Learning the impact of culture on behavior teaches students tolerance and perspective. (*Teacher's Resource Binder*, p. 3-1; Handout 3–8)
- Critical Thinking Activity: *Cross-Cultural Dialogues* With this activity, students discover situations in which the value judgments that are clear in one culture may not be so clear if looked at from another culture's perspective. (*Teacher's Resource Binder*, p. 3-1; Transparency Master 3–1)
- Critical Thinking Activity: *Independent and Interdependent Selves* Collectivist cultures encourage the development of the interdependent self while individualist countries promote the independent self. This activity explores whether students value a more collectivist or individualistic perspective. (*Teacher's Resource Binder*, p. 3-1; Handout 3–9)

- **Critical Thinking Activity:** *A Matter of Context* This intricate card game helps students discover how difficult it can be to adjust to a new culture. (*Teacher's Resource Binder,* p. 3-1; **Handouts 3–10a** through **3–10g**)

Enrichment Center

- **Enrichment Lesson:** *Differences in Cultural Norms* This lesson will help students explore the subject of cultural diversity. What may fascinate students the most are the examples of cultural norms from a variety of cultures around the world. (*Teacher's Resource Binder,* p. 3-1)

MODULE 3

Nature and Nurture in Psychology

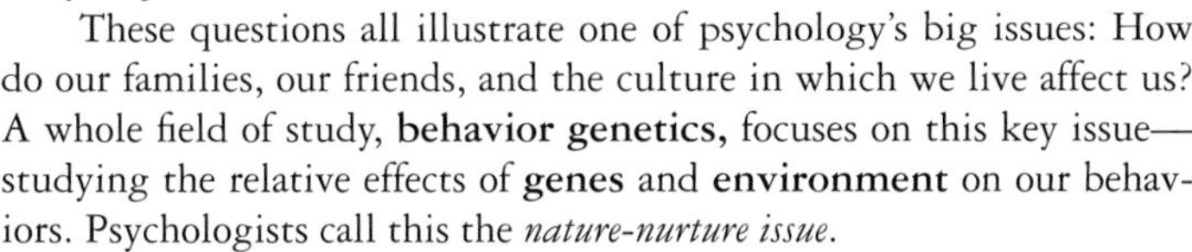

Imagine for a moment that your adoring parents, who believe you are perfect, decide to clone you, creating a perfect genetic replica of you. Would the new baby, your identical twin, grow up to be exactly like you? What if the baby were exposed to a different prenatal environment—one polluted (or not) by drugs or viruses? What if your parents had to give this baby up for adoption, or decided to move to a different part of the world? And how would this child be affected by growing up as a part of a different generation? (Remember that 17 years from now, when this new person is in high school, Britney Spears will be in her forties and the "golden oldies" radio stations will be playing music by N'Sync, Ja Rule and Pink!)

What Makes You *You*?

These questions all illustrate one of psychology's big issues: How do our families, our friends, and the culture in which we live affect us? A whole field of study, **behavior genetics,** focuses on this key issue—studying the relative effects of **genes** and **environment** on our behaviors. Psychologists call this the *nature-nurture issue*.

The influence of "nature" consists of the *genetic code* passed along by your parents the moment you were conceived. The influence of "nurture" comes from all the environmental factors that affect us from conception to death. Possible environmental factors are so numerous that it is impossible to keep them all in mind. Here are a few examples:

- Being exposed to placental abnormalities, viruses, drugs, or no ill effects in the womb
- Consuming wholesome food and clean water or lower-quality food and contaminated water
- Growing up in a household with smokers or nonsmokers
- Being raised bilingually or monolingually

▶ **behavior genetics** The study of the relative power and limits of genetic and environmental influences on behavior.

▶ **genes** The biochemical units of heredity that make up the chromosomes; a segment of DNA.

▶ **environment** Every nongenetic influence, from prenatal nutrition to the people and things around us.

MODULE 3

Nature and Nurture in Psychology

Introducing the Module

The Points: Module Objectives

- Define *predisposition*.
- Determine what traits are most likely to be passed from one generation to the next.
- Appreciate how twin and adoption studies help us understand nature and individual differences.
- Identify some of the key environmental influences on development.

trb Building Vocabulary

Graphic Organizer: *Concept Web* (*Teacher's Resource Binder*, p. 3-1; Handout 3–2) combines a vocabulary practice exercise with a concept web to help students make the connection between terms from biology and their application to psychology.

Teaching the Points

web ■ TEACHING TIP

You can log on as an instructor to the book companion site for *Thinking About Psychology* at www.worthpublishers.com/thinkingaboutpsych. It contains teacher resources for class presentations as well as review and assessment of module concepts and terms.

Getting Started

Before students begin reading, ask, "What makes you who you are?" Write factors that students mention in the discussion on the chalkboard. From time to time, have students refer to the list and either confirm or revise the factors based on what they read in this module.

trb Critical Thinking Activity: *Fact or Falsehood?* (*Teacher's Resource Binder*, p. 3-1; Handout 3–1) may be used as a prereading strategy to evaluate what students already know about the nature–nurture issue and to prime students to look out for information that could prove or disprove their preconceptions.

MODULE 3

■ TEACHING TIPS

tr (1) A four-color transparency of Figure 3.1, Genes: Their Location and Composition, is available in the **Overhead Transparencies Set.**

(2) Inspire critical thinking in your students by playing devil's advocate for both sides of the debate of nature vs. nurture. When you do this, students convinced of a particular side will see the interaction of both nature and nurture in determining human behavior.

trb At this point, you may wish to use **Analysis Activity:** ***Genetics—An Informal Debate*** **(*****Teacher's Resource Binder*****, p. 3-1; Handout 3–5).**

■ JOURNAL WRITING

Invite students to use the following questions as springboards for entries in their psychology journals:

- How much impact have your genes had on making you who you are? What about your environment? Explain your answer.
- What might be the potential benefits or drawbacks of genetic testing? Which side of this issue would you argue in a debate?

▶ **chromosomes** Threadlike structures made of DNA molecules that contain the genes.

▶ **DNA (deoxyribonucleic acid)** A complex molecule containing the genetic information that makes up the chromosomes.

- Identifying with a particular cultural, ethnic, or religious group
- Learning how your culture expects boys or girls to think and act
- Making countless life choices, such as one's career or partner, and deciding to live in an urban, suburban, or rural location

What roles do you think nature and nurture have played in making you who you are?

Genetics in Brief

What's the point? 1. What is a predisposition?

You (and every creature on this planet) have your very own genetic code, a biological blueprint that is found in every cell nucleus and that contains the master plan for your entire body (Figure 3.1). Inside each nucleus are 46 **chromosomes,** 23 each from your mother and father, paired together at the moment of conception. Your chromosomes are composed of molecules called **DNA (deoxyribonucleic acid).** The smaller sections of DNA strands, the stairs on DNA's staircase, store your genetic code, your *genes.* Our genes not only set up our physical beings—making us humans, or dogs, or artichokes—but also influence our behaviors in many ways.

Genes are distinguished from one another using four-letter codes. Each letter in the code (A, T, C, or G) is called a *nucleotide.* Your largest chromosome has about 250 million nucleotides, and even the smallest has 50 million (Wade, 1999). Consider that all 46 chromosomes can be found in every cell nucleus you have: How many nucleotides must there be in every nucleus? Billions.

Figure 3.1 **Genes: Their Location and Composition**

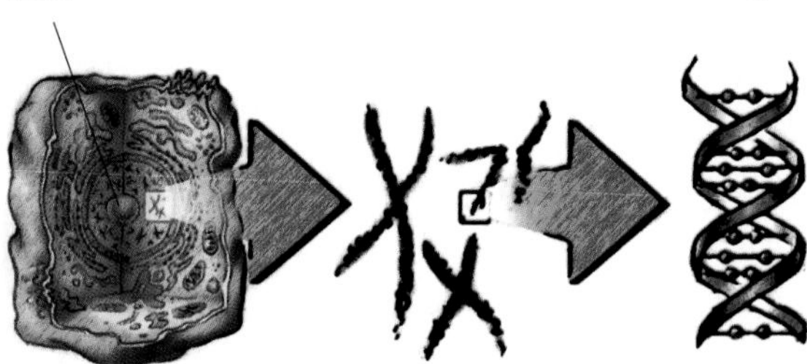

Suggested Readings

Use the following books as teacher-preparation tools or as enrichment for advanced students:

Buss, D. M. (1999). *Evolutionary psychology: The new science of the mind.* Needham Heights, MA: Allyn & Bacon.

Harris, J. R. (1998). *The nurture assumption.* New York: Free Press.

Miller, T. (1995). *How to want what you have.* New York: Avon Books.

Storti, C. (1994). *Cross-cultural dialogues.* Yarmouth, ME: Intercultural Press.

The fruit fly, with a circumference half that of an apple stem, has about 15,000 genes. So how many genes do you have? A million? A billion? Imagine the astonishment of those mapping the human **genome** when they learned that humans have only about 30,000 genes (Davies, 2001)! You may be surprised to learn that 99.9 percent of your four-letter DNA sequences match that of every other human (Plomin & Crabbe, 2000). Genetically speaking, you are nearly identical to everyone else in the world. Does this mean you should look or act like everyone else in the world? No. Genes are responsible for *predisposing* our appearance and behavior, not for concretely determining either.

We are far more similar than we are different, but we do vary from one another, too. Scientists have found *snips,* or sites, throughout our DNA that naturally differ between two unrelated individuals. And other variations exist where they shouldn't. These DNA **mutations** are random errors in the replication of a parent's genes that lead to changes in the offspring's genetic code. Some mutations are desirable—most of us would appreciate a mutation leading to superior eyesight, for example. Other mutations, like those that *predispose* one to cancer, are undesirable and feared. Predispositions are then passed along through the DNA to future generations.

Predisposition is an important concept, so let's look at this idea in a bit more detail. The presence of a predisposition for colon or breast cancer or some other disease does not necessarily doom one to getting the disease. Predisposition merely means that the *possibility* of developing a disease exists. Whether that possibility will become reality often depends on environmental factors (poor diet, polluted air, stress). To choose a simple example, I may be predisposed to sunburn very easily, but if I limit my exposure to the sun's rays, I won't have to put up with the pain of burned skin. Perhaps you can see why we refer to the nature *and* nurture issue, rather than nature *versus* nurture.

▶ **genome** The complete instructions for making an organism, consisting of all the genetic material in its chromosomes.

▶ **mutation** Random errors in gene replication that lead to a change in the individual's genetic code; the source of all genetic diversity.

Nature and Similarity

2. What traits are most likely to be passed from one generation to the next?

Our differences may attract the most attention, but our human similarities also deserve explanation. Perhaps it is not surprising, with so much identical genetic make-up, that people from all countries exhibit similar behaviors. Worldwide, we enjoy greeting loved ones whom we've missed. In countries around the globe, three-month old babies smile, which tends to elicit smiling, cooing, and cuddling from adults. And no matter where we live, we experience happiness when we make someone feel better and disappointment when someone breaks a promise.

■ APPLYING THE POINTS

Students can research a particular topic related to the Human Genome Project (HGP) and write a research paper. Possible topics are cloning, genetic testing of adults for predispositions of disorders, prenatal genetic testing, and insurance issues related to genetic testing.

trb At this point, you may wish to use **Technology Application Activity:** ***Human Genome Project*** (*Teacher's Resource Binder,* p. 3-1; **Handout 3–4**).

■ TEACHING TIP

Students may not appreciate the importance of the concept of predisposition. While a person's gene code determines many physical and personal qualities like eye color, hair color, height, weight, and extraversion/introversion, these qualities interact with the environment to influence things like popularity, interests, and dating choices. Even identical twins, who share 100% of the same genes, can differ in many ways depending on even slightly different environmental influences.

■ CHECKING FOR UNDERSTANDING

To check their understanding of genetics and behavior, have students write a one-page response paper to the following question:

- If a person has the gene for Alzheimer's disease, is that person certain to get the disease? Why or why not?

Look for answers that reflect the idea that a predisposition for a disease does not mean that one will certainly get it later in life. Be willing to discuss this concept briefly during the next class meeting if students seem to misunderstand this important concept.

Demonstrating

GENETICS: QUICK AND SIMPLE Use these quick demonstrations to show that many traits and behaviors are inherited:

- Have students draw a straight horizontal line on a sheet of paper. When the tip of their ring finger is placed on the line, does the tip of the forefinger also reach the line? *(Research indicates that short forefingers are determined by a recessive trait in females, whereas in males it is dominant.)*
- When interlocking their fingers, do students place the left or right thumb on top? *(Particular characteristics are genetically controlled. Practice or experience has no effect.)*

trb At this point, you may wish to use **Technology Application Activity:** ***Mendel, the Game*** (*Teacher's Resource Binder,* p. 3-1).

MODULE 3

■ **TEACHING TIP**

Evolution is a controversial subject in many parts of the country. Some communities view the theory of evolution as a direct contradiction of religious teaching. Be aware of your community's views regarding evolution so that you can address students' questions in a thoughtful, sensitive way.

trb At this point, you may wish to use **Enrichment Lesson:** *Evolutionary Psychology* (*Teacher's Resource Binder*, p. 3-1) and **Enrichment Lesson:** *Misunderstanding Evolutionary Theory and Psychology* (*Teacher's Resource Binder*, p. 3-1).

■ **APPLYING THE POINTS**

With their permission, have twins or adopted students in your class volunteer to share unique aspects of their situations and experiences. Have these students convey one or two experiences based on that situation in their lives.

trb At this point, you may wish to use **Enrichment Lesson:** *The Minnesota Twin Study* (*Teacher's Resource Binder*, p. 3-1).

■ **LOOKING AT THE ISSUES**

Some of the controversy surrounding cloning involves whether or not parents could choose different traits for their unborn children. Critics of cloning fear that parents could engineer "the perfect child," creating a child with only desirable qualities who is resistant to disease and the ill effects of aging. Have students ponder the following questions:

- Should parents be allowed to craft their ideal child? Why or why not?
- What qualities would you consider to be ideal? Do others share your ideas? Why or why not?
- How would culture affect genetic engineering of children?
- What if parents chose traits that actually affected their child adversely from an evolutionary standpoint?

trb At this point, you may wish to use **Enrichment Lesson:** *Human Cloning* (*Teacher's Resource Binder*, p. 3-1).

▶ **evolutionary psychology** The study of the evolution of behavior and the mind, using principles of natural selection.

▶ **natural selection** The principle that, among the range of inherited trait variations, those contributing to survival will most likely be passed on to succeeding generations.

▶ **identical twins** Twins who develop from a single fertilized egg that splits in two, creating two genetically identical organisms.

▶ **fraternal twins** Twins who develop from separate eggs. They are genetically no closer than any other brothers and sisters, but they share a fetal environment.

▶ **heritability** The proportion of variation among individuals that we can attribute to genes.

Why are we alike in so many ways? **Evolutionary psychologists** maintain that some of our shared similarities stem from mutated genes that provided an adaptive advantage to our ancestors, helping them face and conquer problems. These helpful genetic mutations were subsequently passed from generation to generation, because people who carried them would be more likely to stay in the gene pool than people who carried less helpful mutated genes. The concept of **natural selection** maintains that among the traits we inherit, those contributing to survival are most likely to be passed to succeeding generations. You can see how this would work if you consider our earliest ancestors, who had to discover through trial and error which foods kept them healthy and which foods made them sick. Any helpful genes that emerged and increased the capacity to remember which foods were toxic would have been an asset. Early humans who could remember which foods were deadly stood a better chance of living long enough to have their own children, thus passing their set of genes to another. We all carry the genetic legacy of those who came before us.

Nature and Individual Differences

3. How do twin and adoption studies help us understand nature and individual differences?

Intertwined from the moment of conception until death, nature and nurture are the two parts of the complex equation that is you. Our genetic similarity is amazing, but there is still that fraction of a percent that, when combined with innumerable environmental factors, can make each of us enormously different from all others. Why do some people seem "smarter" than others? Why are some always slower at getting a joke? Why can some sing beautifully, while there are others whose mouths we'd prefer stayed shut? *Behavior geneticists* study such questions using twin studies and adoption studies.

Identical Twins These teens developed from a single fertilized egg that divided into two identical copies.

Twin Studies

Only in Hollywood movies do you find cloned human beings living their lives in a genetically engineered environment so that some mad scientist can study what makes them tick. But nature has provided its own potential genetics lab participants in the form of human twins. **Identical twins** are nature's human clones; they are genetically the same, beginning life from the same fertilized egg. **Fraternal twins** develop

Cross-Curricular Connection

BIOLOGY, GOVERNMENT Team with teachers in other disciplines to develop the following lessons:

- With a biology teacher, develop an integrated lesson on genetics that provides instruction on biological details as well as wider implications of our genetic heritage on behavior.

trb At this point, you may wish to use **Technology Application Activities:** *The Human Genome Project* and *Mendel, the Game* (*Teacher's Resource Binder*, p. 3-1).

- With a social studies teacher, create a lesson in which students research laws related to genetics and prepare a presentation about the impact of these laws on daily life.

trb At this point, you may wish to use **Enrichment Lesson:** *The Genetic Revolution* (*Teacher's Resource Binder*, p. 3-1).

from two different fertilized eggs and are no more similar than any other two siblings (Figure 3.2). So, do the genetically identical twins behave more similarly than their fraternal twin counterparts? This is a question that intrigues behavior geneticists, who study the **heritability** of various traits, or the degree to which our traits are inherited

Here's a simplified example of how a behavior geneticist might set up a study of identical and fraternal twins to investigate the heritability of intelligence.

Fraternal (non-identical) Twins These teens are also twins, but they developed from two different eggs, each fertilized by a different sperm cell.

1. Collect and compare data on the intelligence levels of *identical twins* raised in the same home.
2. Collect and compare data on the intelligence levels of *fraternal twins* raised in the same home.
3. Compare the similarity in intelligence levels of the identical twins with the similarity in intelligence levels of the fraternal twins.

If the intelligence levels of the identical twins are significantly more similar than the intelligence levels of the fraternal twins, we can infer that genetics, or nature, is at work. And researchers have indeed found a greater similarity in intelligence among identical twins (Lykken, 1999).

Genetic influences on personality traits appear to follow the same pattern. Studies in Sweden and Finland, using thousands of twin pairs, reveal that if one identical twin is outgoing, the other is much more likely to be outgoing than is the case between fraternal twins. The same increased similarity can be found in the emotional stability of identical versus fraternal twins.

The findings of one study (McGue & Lykken, 1992) that looked at middle-age twin divorce rates even seem to indicate that genes influence divorce risk! The results showed that if one identical twin was divorced, the odds of the other identical twin divorcing went up 5.5 times. However, if a fraternal twin divorced his or her spouse, the other fraternal twin was only 1.6 times more likely to wind up divorced.

But wait a minute! How can divorce be heritable? It's not even an option in some cultures, which forbid it. What we must remember is that *the behavior itself*, in this case divorce, *is not inherited.* What *is* inherited is the genetic predispositions that may lead to the behavior. For instance, those with a greater predisposition to anger or conflict may be more likely to divorce than those who are not so predisposed.

As you can see, twin studies have helped us learn about the heritability of certain traits. Equally important, though, they have

Figure 3.2 **Conception of Identical Versus Fraternal Twins** Identical twins develop from a single fertilized egg that divides into two identical copies. Fraternal twins develop from two different eggs, each fertilized by a different sperm cell.

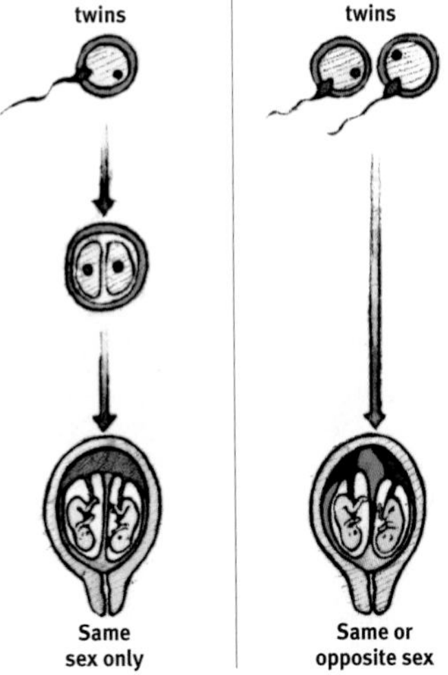

Meeting Individual Needs

Students may have some difficulty understanding the concept of *heritability*. The word itself is not commonly used, so students who have difficulty processing language may feel overwhelmed by it. Help them break down the word into its component parts.

- *Herit-* comes from the word *inherit*. To inherit means to possess something that someone else has given you. For example, we inherit our traits and qualities from our parents.
- *-ability* as a suffix means "capability." A trait that is genetically passed on from one generation to the next is a trait that is capable of showing up in the children of people who possess that quality.
- Help students see that a **heritable** trait is one that is capable of being passed down from parent to child.

■ APPLYING THE POINTS

With permission, invite sets of twins, triplets, or other multiples and their parents to class to have them discuss what it is like to be a multiple. You may guide an informal interview and discussion with the following questions:

- Are the multiples fraternal or identical? If they are identical, how can people tell them apart?
- How much are the siblings alike? Different? If possible, provide examples.
- What challenges have siblings faced being a multiple? What advantages exist?
- How do the siblings strive to be individuals? What do their parents do to encourage individuality?

trb At this point, you may wish to use **Critical Thinking Activity:** ***Striking Similarities*** (*Teacher's Resource Binder*, p. 3-1; **Handout 3–7**) and **Enrichment Lesson:** ***"Mom Always Liked You Best!"*** (*Teacher's Resource Binder*, p. 3-1).

F • Y • I

- Identical twins are also referred to as **monozygotic** twins. They come from one zygote that split during early pregnancy.
- Fraternal twins are also referred to as **dizygotic** twins. They come from two different fertilized eggs. The mother produced two eggs during the same menstrual cycle, both of which were fertilized, producing twins.

tr A four-color transparency of Figure 3.2, Conception of Identical Versus Fraternal Twins, is available in the **Overhead Transparencies Set.**

trb At this point, you may wish to use **Enrichment Lesson:** ***The Minnesota Twin Study*** (*Teacher's Resource Binder*, p. 3-1).

MODULE 3

F • Y • I

Identical twins are unique in that they share 100% of the same genes. Interestingly, identical twins, while sharing the same genotype, can have different phenotypes. Some identical twins are mirror-images of each other (for example, one being left-handed, the other right; one having a mole on the left side of the face while the other has one on the right). Others may have different personalities and interests, showing that heritability of a trait doesn't mean that it will occur even in two people who share the same genes. Fraternal twins, even though they may look alike and act alike, are only as similar to one another as any sibling combination.

trb At this point, you may wish to use **Critical Thinking Activity:** *Striking Similarities* (*Teacher's Resource Binder*, p. 3-1; **Handout 3–7**).

■ LOOKING AT THE ISSUES

Many states do not allow adoptees to learn information about their biological parents in order to protect the privacy of people who put up children for adoption. Have students consider the following questions:

- What would be the benefits of confidentiality laws that favor biological parents? What are the disadvantages?
- Should adoptees be allowed to find out all information about their biological parents? Why or why not?
- What compromise could you propose that would enable adoptees to learn about their biological heritage and protect the privacy of biological parents?

taught us much about the influence of environment. Studies of reunited twins, those separated at birth and raised apart from each other, have helped demonstrate that *no* trait is completely inherited and that the behaviors of identical twins are not identical. Yet these genetic replicas, who sometimes grew up in dramatically different environments, have exhibited startling similarities in tastes and habits. Take identical twins Oskar Stohr and Jack Yufe, one raised by his grandmother in Germany as a Catholic and a Nazi, the other raised in the Caribbean as a Jew. Despite the obvious differences in their environments, both enjoy spicy foods, are domineering toward women, and report flushing the toilet before using it. The similarities between the two did not stop there, but perhaps you're wondering the same thing critics of the separated twin studies wonder: Couldn't two strangers sit down at a table, and over the course of a couple of hours discover many bizarre, but coincidental similarities? Enter science.

Using scientific measuring equipment, psychologists have studied separated identical twins and have found remarkable similarities in heart rates, brain waves, and intelligence levels (Holden, 1980a, 1980b; Wright, 1998). Other studies have found statistically significant similarities in personalities, abilities, attitudes, and fears (Bouchard & others, 1990; DiLalla & others, 1996; Segal, 1999). If a soccer match were held to determine whether nature or nurture has a bigger impact on development, clearly the evidence from genetics and twin studies would be a goal scored for the nature team. But before we announce the winner, let's consider adoption studies.

Adoption Studies

Another way to assess the effects of nature and nurture is through adoption studies. Here the biological parents are providing the nature, and the adoptive parents are providing the nurture. By the time an adopted, one-week-old girl reaches the age of 10, will her personality more closely resemble her biological parents' personalities or the personalities of the parents who actually raised her? What's your guess?

Nature and Nurture
In adoption studies, biological parents supply the nature, and adoptive parents supply the nurture.

Study after study has yielded the same surprising result: Adopted children share more personality trait similarities with their biological parents than with their adoptive parents (Plomin & Daniels, 1987). Score one more goal for nature.

But the match is far from over. While our personality seems to be something we're mostly born with, there are many other powerful areas in which parenting can influence a child. What

Enriching

Have students research other stories of identical twins separated at birth and report their findings to the class in oral presentations.

- What similarities did the twins share? How were they different?
- How did each twin feel growing up—did the twins sense that they had a twin or did they not feel a connection to the other sibling?
- How did they feel when they reunited with their twin?

trb At this point, you may wish to use **Critical Thinking Activity:** *Striking Similarities* (*Teacher's Resource Binder*, p. 3-1; **Handout 3–7**) and **Enrichment Lesson:** *The Minnesota Twin Study* (*Teacher's Resource Binder*, p. 3-1).

about values, attitudes, and manners? What about political and religious beliefs? For all of these areas, nurture scores a goal. Several adoption studies show that parenting plays a major role in belief system development and the development of behaviors important to functioning as a good citizen in our diverse societies (Brodzinsky & Schechter, 1990; Kelley & DeGraaf, 1997; Rohan & Zanna, 1996). Adopted children score higher on intelligence tests and are more likely to be involved in charitable activities than their biological parents (Sharma & others, 1998). Good parenting remains important. Nurture is back in the game.

Environment Matters

4. What are some of the key environmental influences on development?

One of the more celebrated separated-twin cases illustrates how easy it is to lay credit or blame at the feet of a child's parents for any given behavior. In this case, two identical twin boys, separated at birth and raised apart, were reunited in their thirties. Both could be considered "neat freaks" in the way they kept their homes, dressed, and scrubbed their "hands regularly to a raw, red color." When asked to explain the origin of their neatness, the first twin credited his mother and growing up in an extremely ordered environment, where he learned to appreciate that everything should be kept in its proper place. The second twin also credited his mother, though for different reasons. Why the perfectionism? "The reason is quite simple. I'm reacting to my mother, who was an absolute slob" (Neubauer & Neubauer, 1990).

Parents are an important part of most people's early environment, and with genetic influences accounting for roughly half the variation in our personality traits, parenting is a likely source to turn toward in accounting for the other 50 percent of those traits. But how much credit do parents really deserve for the child who wins a debate tournament, dances the role of Clara in the *Nutcracker Suite* ballet, or is elected president of the student council? How much blame should we heap on parents for the teenager who always shows up late at practice or rehearsal, takes up smoking, or has frequent scrapes with the law? If we listen to "pop" psychology, we hear all kinds of unfounded claims:

- Overprotective/overbearing parenting permanently underprepares a child for the real world.
- Parents who spank leave irreparable scars on a child's personality.
- Lenient parents who do not punish children severely create irresponsible children who will become troublemakers.

■ JOURNAL WRITING

Invite students to use the following questions as springboards for entries in their psychology journals:

- What is the most obvious trait you've inherited from your parents? What is the most obvious thing you've learned from them?
- At this point in your life, which has more influence over your morals and values: parents or peers? Why? Which has more influence over your personality? Why?

■ MULTICULTURAL CONNECTIONS

With permission, have students who are immigrants or whose parents are immigrants to the United States share their unique experiences in moving from one culture to another. Conduct an informal interview that includes the following questions:

- How is life in the United States different from life in your native culture?
- How much of the culture in the United States have you adopted as your own, and what native cultural traditions have you kept? How do other family members balance the two cultures?

trb At this point, you may wish to use **Critical Thinking Activity:** ***A Matter of Context*** (*Teacher's Resource Binder*, p. 3-1; **Handouts 3–10a** through **3–10g**).

Cross-Curricular Connections

GOVERNMENT Have students research and discuss adoption laws in your state:

- What do biological parents have to do to put up a child for adoption? Does your state require both father and mother to relinquish parental rights? Why or why not?
- How do adoptive parents apply for adoption? What restrictions exist to qualify as an adoptive parent?
- How long do biological parents have to reconsider their decision? What might happen if a biological father didn't know of the birth of the child? Could he contest the adoption days, months, weeks, or even years later? Why or why not?
- When can adoptees learn of the details of their adoption? Can they know the identities of their biological parents? Why or why not?
- Does your state have "safe haven" laws? How do these laws affect adoptions?

MODULE 3

■ **TEACHING TIP**

You may have students who are adoptees. Be sensitive to them as you discuss research concerning the impact of nature and nurture on their development. Some adoptees may know that their biological parents had substance abuse problems or other psychological issues, and this knowledge may cause them concern over whether they will turn out like their biological parents. Help those students see that while a trait may be heritable, it doesn't necessarily mean that the trait will manifest itself.

■ **LOOKING AT THE ISSUES**

Author Judith Rich Harris, in the book *The Nurture Assumption,* proposed that parents do not have as much influence on the development of their children as society believes. In his book *The Blank Slate: The Modern Denial of Human Nature*, Steven Pinker also argues that infants are born not blank but with a structure that influences how they behave and think. Have students consider the following questions:

- How much of your behavior would you attribute to biology? How much to environment? Why?
- How would you feel knowing that your behavior was mostly determined by your genes? Why?
- Why might people in Western societies feel more comfortable with the idea that environment is the major influence on behavior?

trb At this point, you may wish to use **Enrichment Lesson:** *Do Parents Really Matter?* (*Teacher's Resource Binder*, p. 3-1).

Parents Matter The nurturing of parents and guardians plays an important role in the development of a child.

Is the mother or father who, even with the best intentions, occasionally pulls too hard in parenting's tug-of-war really inflicting permanent psychological damage? Should we blame our parents for our failures in life, and subsequently, blame ourselves when our children fail?

For answers to such questions, many researchers look to comparisons of nonidentical siblings raised together. Behavior geneticist Robert Plomin has found that "Two children in the same family [are on average] as different from one another as are pairs of children selected randomly from the population" (Plomin & Daniels, 1987). Another well-respected researcher, Sandra Scarr, believes parents should receive less blame for kids who don't turn out as hoped or expected, and less credit for children who do (1993).

Certainly, environment matters, but growing up in the same household accounts for only a small portion (around 10 percent) of our personality differences. What other environmental factors might account for nurture's role in personality development? Let's look at three possible answers: early learning experiences, peer influence, and culture.

Early Learning and Brain Development

You've heard the phrase, "Use it or lose it." Nowhere is this truer than with your brain, where experience nurtures nature. We do not remember everything we learn, but the brain processes we used in early learning do pave the way for later learning of more complex information. Consider the following neurological evidence:

- Rats housed for 60 days in an enriched (fun, stimulating) environment had brain weight increases of 7 to 10 percent more than rats housed in an impoverished (boring) environment (Rosenzweig, Bennett & Diamond, 1972). The same study also found a dramatic 20 percent increase in communication connections in the brain (Figure 3.3).
- Premature babies who receive special handling (touch, massage) grow more rapidly physically and neurologically than preemies who do not receive the same treatment (Drummond, 1998).
- Sixth-graders from impoverished environments who were given stimulating care as infants had higher intelligence test scores than their classmates who did not receive such care (Ramey & Ramey, 1992).

Enriching

Have students collect books and magazines that give parents advice on rearing children. They can find several pieces of advice and investigate whether each claim is backed up by psychological research.

trb At this point, you may wish to use **Enrichment Lesson:** *Do Parents Really Matter?* (*Teacher's Resource Binder*, p. 3-1) and **Enrichment Lesson:** *"Mom Always Liked You Best!"* (*Teacher's Resource Binder*, p. 3-1).

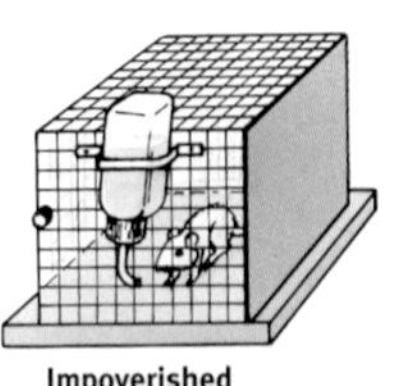

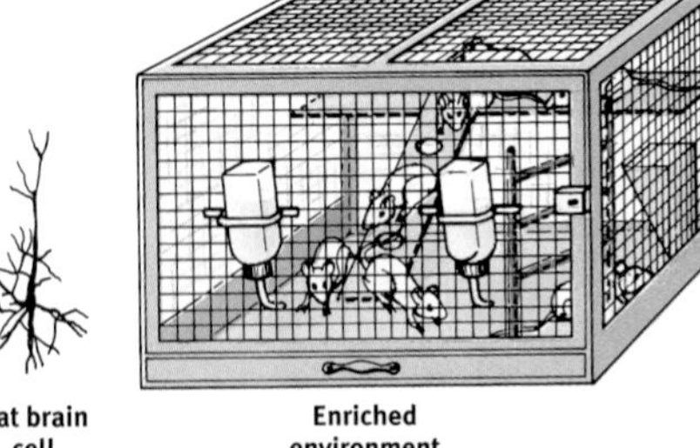

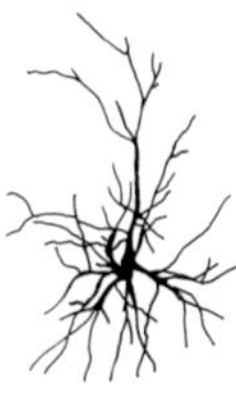

Figure 3.3
Experience Affects Brain Development Mark Rosenzweig and David Krech reared rats either alone in an environment without playthings or with others in an environment enriched with playthings that were changed daily. In 14 of 16 repetitions of this basic experiment, the rats placed in the enriched environment developed significantly more cerebral cortex (relative to the rest of the brain's tissue) than did those in the impoverished environment. (From "Brain changes in response to experience" by M. R. Rosenzweig, E. L. Bennett, and M. C. Diamond. Copyright © 1972 Scientific American, Inc. All rights reserved.)

For our brains to meet their developmental potential, early experience is critical. The child born with perfect pitch will never have a chance to develop this gift if prevented from hearing music in early life. A child raised in abusive isolation will never learn to read, write, or speak like a normal adult.

As you get older, your brain's tissue will continue to change. The brain's pathways maintained through practice or experience will remain strong, while neglected pathways will fade with disuse. I recently found this out the hard way. Although I had learned to roller skate in sixth grade and had skated periodically after that, I had to relearn this skill after seven years without putting on my roller blades. Similarly, you may find that the theorems and proofs you learned in geometry will seem foreign to you later in life, unless you pursue a mathematically oriented career. The examples are endless, but one thing is clear: Use those brain pathways, created by nurture and nature, or lose them.

Peer and Parent Influence

The tango danced by nature and nurture continues from childhood into adolescence, where peer influence becomes powerfully real and tangible. One of the most reliable predictors of dropout rate and failure in school is social rejection by one's peer group (Rubin & others, 1999). Why, despite all the anti-smoking commercials, posters, and warnings on the cigarette packages, has smoking among teenagers recently increased? Those inclined to pin blame on smoking parents are surprised to learn parental concern over smoking is less of a factor than researchers originally believed. Rather, teens in peer groups where members smoke are far more at risk to start this life-endangering habit than are those with nonsmoking peers (Rose & others, 1999).

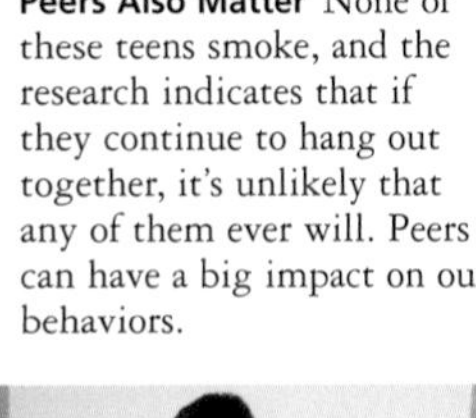

Peers Also Matter None of these teens smoke, and the research indicates that if they continue to hang out together, it's unlikely that any of them ever will. Peers can have a big impact on our behaviors.

tr ■ **TEACHING TIP**

A four-color transparency for Figure 3.3, Experience Affects Brain Development, is available in the **Overhead Transparencies Set.**

■ **JOURNAL WRITING**

Invite students to use the following questions as springboards for entries in their psychology journals:

- How different or similar are you to your brothers and/or sisters?
- Do you blame or credit your parents for your failures or successes? Explain.
- What skills from childhood have you lost the ability to use as a teen?

V At this point, you may wish to use **Technology Application Activity:** ***The Most Important Influence in One's Life*** (*Teacher's Resource Binder*, p. 3-1).

■ **APPLYING THE POINTS**

Have students contact a local neonatal intensive care unit to see whether they employ massage therapy in caring for premature infants. The following questions can guide an informal interview and discussion of students' findings:

- How does the facility deliver the treatment? Do parents or volunteers (or both) massage the babies?
- What results has the facility seen with this type of treatment?
- What other types of stimulation do they give the babies?

V At this point, you may want to show **Videocassette:** ***The Brain,*** **Second Edition, Module 2: "Effect of Hormones and Environment on the Brain"** (*Teacher's Resource Binder*, p. 3-1).

tb ■ **CHECKING FOR UNDERSTANDING**

Here are several ways to assess students' comprehension:

- Assign any journal questions or prompts for an in-class writing assessment.
- Assign student pairs or small groups a journal prompt. As students respond, correct any misconceptions that may arise.
- Use questions from the *Test Bank* to do a quick assessment of their knowledge of the concepts.

MODULE 3

■ APPLYING THE POINTS

Have students browse the infant section of a major store and observe the types of toys available for infants—especially those that stimulate infant brain development.

- What qualities in common do toys that stimulate infant brain development have?
- Are these toys expensive? Why or why not?

■ TEACHING TIP

Link *early learning* and *brain development* with *brain plasticity*. **Plasticity** refers to the brain's ability to adapt to changes and recover from damage. The younger one is, the more likely the brain is to recover lost function due to brain illness or damage.

F•Y•I

The brain's pathways develop as a result of learning through a process called *long-term potentiation*. The more a neural pathway is used, the quicker the response of the neurons in that pathway will be the next time it is used. This process seems to be the biological component of learning.

V At this point, you may wish to show **Videocassette:** ***The Brain,*** **Second Edition, Module 2: "Effect of Hormones and Environment on the Brain"** (*Teacher's Resource Binder*, p. 3-1).

▶ **culture** The shared attitudes, beliefs, norms, and behaviors of a group communicated from one generation to the next.

▶ **norms** Understood rules for accepted and expected behavior; norms prescribe "proper" behavior.

▶ **individualism** Giving priority to one's own goals over group goals, and defining one's identity in terms of personal attributes rather than group identification.

▶ **collectivism** Giving priority to the goals of one's group (often one's extended family or work group) and defining one's identity accordingly.

Peer groups with smokers (a) offer easy access to cigarettes, (b) model pleasure from smoking, and (c) present the message that fitting in includes lighting up. Regardless of parental protests, thousands of American teens start their smoking addiction each day.

Peer group influence has been demonstrated in younger peer groups, too. Preschoolers who won't eat a particular food at home are much more likely to eat that food when seated at a table with peers who like it (Harris, 1998). Immigrant children living in an environment filled with nonimmigrant peers will quickly adopt the culture of the peer group, sometimes at the expense of the culture they share with their parents. Psychologist Howard Gardner (1998) clearly sees the importance of peer group *and* parents in raising children:

> Parents are more important when it comes to education, discipline, responsibility, orderliness, charitableness, and ways of interacting with authority figures. Peers are more important for learning cooperation, for finding the road to popularity, and for inventing styles of interaction among people of the same age. Youngsters may find their peers more interesting, but they will look to their parents when contemplating their own futures. Moreover, parents choose the neighborhoods and schools that supply the peers.

Cultural Influences

Culture is an elusive, invisible, abstract concept that forms the basis for much of our understanding of life (Ernst & others, 2000). **Culture** is the shared attitudes, beliefs, norms, and behaviors of a group communicated from one generation to the next. **Norms** are understood rules for accepted and expected behavior within a group. Researcher David Matsumoto (1996) calls culture the "software of our minds." Culture influences our food selection, religious choices, family activities, and much more.

Because of the cultural rules we all possess, we develop a set of expectations about the kinds of behaviors others should exhibit. If others behave according to expectation, we may think, "This person is good." When others behave in a way we do not consider "normal" or socially appropriate, we have negative reactions, such as frustration and anger. In such cases, we may think, "This person is bad." or "This person is stupid." Sadly, we tend to make these snap judgments without a second thought, often toward people from cultures that differ from our own.

One meaningful dimension of cultural differences is **individualism** versus **collectivism**. Individualists see people as separate and independent, with personal needs and goals taking precedence over the needs of others. Collectivists see people as connected to others; individual needs

Cooperative Learning

Have students brainstorm about different tasks that they have not participated in since childhood. You may suggest to students that they might not play certain video games, ride a bicycle, jump rope, or play certain games like four-square any more. Set up centers where students can attempt to try these activities in class. Have them time each other to see how long it takes to complete each task. Have them try to do the task several times to see if they get better with practice.

Cultural Effects Our cultural backgrounds are a big part of the "nurture" that influences our behavior and attitudes.

are sacrificed for the good of the group (Matsumoto, 1997). Asians and Africans typically raise their children in a collectivist environment. Europeans and North Americans are usually raised as individualists.

These different cultural viewpoints manifest themselves in a number of ways. One interesting study asked teenagers whether the phrase, "My parents will be disappointed in me" is ever a concern. Japanese teens were three times more likely than their American counterparts to express this as a concern (Atkinson, 1988).

We tend to believe that *our* culture's way of raising children is the *best* way. Be careful: Successful child rearing has been accomplished using many different methods. There is tremendous diversity worldwide in the way children are brought up, and leaders and heroes have emerged from both collectivist and individualist cultures.

So, how exactly do nature and nurture work together to make us who we are? We don't yet know the answer to that question. Behavior genetics is still in its infancy. The ethical implications of genetic engineering and cloning are just beginning to emerge, and much reflection on the meaning of this research lies ahead.

■ MULTICULTURAL CONNECTIONS

Have students reflect on how culture has affected their development.

- Does your behavior reflect the culture of the region of the United States where you live? Why or why not?
- Do you have a cultural heritage different from the predominant one in the region where you live? If so, how does it affect your life?

trb At this point, you may wish to use **Analysis Activity:** *Intercultural Learning Activities* (*Teacher's Resource Binder*, p. 3-1; **Handout 3–8**).

Close

Designate one corner of the room as "Nature" and an opposite corner as "Nurture." Mark a line on the floor between the two points with masking tape. Ask students to stand at the point on the line they feel is the level of influence between nature and nurture in determining people's behavior.

Discuss with the class why individuals stood where they did, guiding students toward embracing the goal of this module—balancing both sides of the controversy in shaping individual behavior.

MODULE 3

Checking the Points

■ TEACHING TIPS

web (1) The book companion site for *Thinking About Psychology* at www.worthpublishers.com/thinkingaboutpsych contains a module quiz, flashcards of key terms and people, as well as other student activities and resources for this module. You will also find PowerPoint lectures, a quiz grade book, and other teaching resources by logging on as an instructor.

trb (2) At this point, you may wish to review and confirm concepts about nature and nurture with **Critical Thinking Activity:** *Fact or Falsehood?* (*Teacher's Resource Binder*, p. 3-1; **Handout 3–1**). If students filled in a handout earlier in the module, ask them not to refer to that version. Suggest that students complete the handout individually, taking the time to look up information in the text to respond correctly to questions. Have students then meet in small groups to review their responses and discuss concepts that may be confusing or difficult. Groups should use the text as a source with which to clarify and check responses.

REVIEW

Module 3: Nature and Nurture in Psychology

What's the Point?

The relative effects of genes and environment on behavior is sometimes called the nature-nurture issue. Behavior genetics is the field of study that focuses on this key issue.

Genetics in Brief

1. *What is a predisposition?*

   From the viewpoint of genetics, all humans are nearly identical, since we share 99.9 percent of our DNA sequences with everyone else. But we also differ from one another. Some of these differences result from mutations, random errors in the replication of parents' genes. And some of these mutations make us especially vulnerable to particular diseases. These predispositions mean that the possibility for a disease exists, if environmental factors pull the trigger and set the disease process in motion.

Nature and Similarity

2. *What traits are most likely to be passed from one generation to the next?*

   Our ancestors, by definition, lived to have offspring, although some other early humans surely did not. The difference may have been particular genetic mutations that contributed to our ancestors' survival. Evolutionary psychologists believe that such traits had a good chance of being passed on to future generations. This is known as the principle of natural selection.

Nature and Individual Differences

3. *How do twin and adoption studies help us understand nature and individual differences?*

   Studies of identical twins allow researchers to watch the effect of different environments on genetically identical individuals, something that would be unethical in a laboratory setting. Studies of fraternal twins, who are no more similar genetically than any other siblings, allow researchers to consider the effects of similar environments on genetically different individuals. Adoption studies allow us to see the effect of genetic influences (nature) by comparing similarities between an adopted child and his biological parents, and to see the effect of environmental influences (nurture) by comparing similarities between that child and his adopted parents.

Environment Matters

4. *What are some of the key environmental influences on development?*

   Parents influence such areas as education, discipline, responsibility, orderliness, charitableness, and attitude toward authority figures. In other areas, however, peers exert an important influence, especially in patterning "normal" behaviors and interactions with other people of the same age. Other important environmental factors are the influence of early learning on brain development, and the effect of the culture one experiences while growing up.

Reteaching

Create a chart on the chalkboard or overhead projector with three columns—the first column labeled "Nature," the second column labeled "Nature and Nurture," and the third column labeled "Nurture." Have students brainstorm for evidence of human behavior that might fall into each category, using their textbooks as a source for details that support each category.

Key Terms

behavior genetics p. 39
genes p. 39
environment p. 39
chromosomes p. 40
DNA (deoxyribonucleic acid) p. 40
genome p. 41
mutation p. 41
evolutionary psychology p. 42
natural selection p. 42
identical twins p. 42
fraternal twins p. 42
heritability p. 43
culture p. 48
norms p. 48
individualism p. 48
collectivism p. 48

Self-Test

Multiple-Choice Questions

Choose the *best* answer for each of the following questions.

1. Sal is one of four children in a family with a predisposition to develop diabetes, a disease in which the body produces too little insulin to use blood sugar efficiently. This means that Sal
   a. will definitely get diabetes because it is in his genetic program.
   b. probably will not get diabetes because he could develop a helpful mutation that would overcome this predisposition.
   c. will definitely not get diabetes because it is not in his personal genetic program.
   d. may not get diabetes if he educates himself about all the environmental factors that trigger the disease and eliminates those risks from his life-style.

2. The principle of natural selection maintains that
   a. the genes that are most likely to be passed on to future generations are those that contribute to survival.
   b. we all share 99.9 percent of our genetic makeup.
   c. the extent to which variation exists among individuals is a function of their genes.
   d. it is unethical to clone human beings, but not to select particularly valuable work animals and clone them.

3. Dr. Frothingale is interested in whether intelligence is inherited in our genes. She will probably ask members of three of the following four groups to be participants in her research study. Which group is LEAST likely to be included?
   a. Adopted children and their biological parents
   b. Identical twins separated at birth
   c. Fraternal twins raised together
   d. People who get the highest scores on their SATs

MODULE 3

trb ■ TEACHING TIP

You may also wish to provide students with **Building Vocabulary: Graphic Organizer:** *Concept Web* (*Teacher's Resource Binder*, p. 3-1; **Handout 3–2**). Have students work with partners to fill out this organizer as a tool for reviewing concepts related to nature and nurture. Encourage pairs to fill in the graphic organizer individually, at first without referring to the text or copies of the organizer they may have filled out earlier in the module. Next, allow time for students to use their texts to review information and fill in concepts they had difficulty with.

tb Using the Test Bank

The *Test Bank* that accompanies this textbook offers a wide variety of questions in different formats and levels of complexity. Use the software to construct whole tests or to integrate standardized questions into teacher-made tests.

Self-Test Answers

Multiple-Choice Questions

1. d, 2. a, 3. d

Alternative Assessment/Portfolio Project

trb NATURE VS. NURTURE Ask students to choose a few of their best entries from the following module activities. For detailed instructions regarding this portfolio assessment, see **Alternative Assessment/Portfolio Project:** *Nature vs. Nurture* (*Teacher's Resource Binder*, p. 3-1; **Handout 3–11**).

- **Technology Application Activity:** *Human Genome Project* (*Teacher's Resource Binder*, p. 3-1; **Handout 3–4**)
- **Technology Application Activity:** *The Most Important Influence in One's Life* (*Teacher's Resource Binder*, p. 3-1)
- **Critical Thinking Activity:** *A Matter of Context* (*Teacher's Resource Binder*, p. 3-1; **Handouts 3–10a through 3–10g**)
- Any entries in students' psychology journals made during the study of this module.

MODULE 3

Self-Test Answers

Multiple-Choice Questions

4. d, 5. c

Matching Terms and Definitions

6. a. (6), b. (4), c. (5), d. (2), e. (1), f. (11), g. (8), h. (9)

4. Mrs. Chang is worried that her 12-year-old son will start smoking cigarettes, like other boys in his friendship group. Her friends tell her she should not worry, because neither Mr. Chang nor Mrs. Chang smokes. The best advice you could give her is that
   a. her worries are not justified, because parents have great influence over the behavior of their children.
   b. her worries are not justified, because federal law prevents retailers from selling cigarettes to minors.
   c. her worries are realistic, because most 12-year-old boys do smoke cigarettes.
   d. her worries are realistic, because peers who smoke cigarettes influence a child's behavior by modeling smoking, by making cigarettes available, and by defining what's popular.

5. Research shows that early learning
   a. is not as important as the kind of learning we experience during our school years.
   b. is not important because we are too young to remember what we learn as very young children.
   c. is important because it lays down pathways in our brain—pathways that we use for later learning.
   d. is important because it is an indicator of the extent to which our families care about us, and therefore whether they will help us to learn what we need to learn.

Matching Terms and Definitions

6. For each definition, choose the *best* matching term from the list that follows.

Definition

a. A scientist who studies the relative power and limits of genetic and environmental influences on behavior.
b. Random errors in gene replication that lead to a change in the sequence of nucleotides.
c. A complex molecule containing the genetic information that makes up the chromosomes.
d. A scientist who studies behavior and the mind, using principles of natural selection.
e. A threadlike structure made of DNA molecules that contain the genes.
f. The complete instructions for making an organism, consisting of all the genetic material in its chromosomes.
g. An understood rule for accepted and expected behavior.
h. The biochemical units of heredity that make up the chromosomes.

Term

(1) chromosome
(2) evolutionary psychologist
(3) individualists
(4) mutation
(5) DNA
(6) behavior geneticist
(7) collectivists
(8) norm
(9) gene
(10) culture
(11) genome

Fill-in-the-Blank Questions

7. A person who gives priority to the goals of the group and defines her identity in terms of those goals probably lives in a(n) _______________ culture. A person who gives priorities to his own goals over the goals of the group and defines his identity in terms of his own attributes probably lives in a(n) _______________ culture.

8. The proportion of variation among individuals that we can attribute to genes is known as _______________.

9. _______________ is the shared attitudes, beliefs, norms, and behaviors of a group communicated from one generation to the next.

Brief Essay Question

10. What are "nature" and "nurture?" In two short paragraphs (about 5 sentences each), describe nature and nurture, and explain what researchers mean when they say that the two work together to make us who we are.

Self-Test Answers

Fill-in-the-Blank Questions

7. collectivist; individualistic, 8. heritability, 9. culture

Brief Essay Question

10. Students should identify nature as our genetic heritage passed on to us from our parents. Nurture should be identified as the environmental influences that shape behavior and cognition. Students should understand that while we inherit traits from our parents through our genes, we are not guaranteed to display the qualities those traits imply. Environmental influences can negate a predisposition, leading to different behavior from an individual.

Developmental Domain

Teaching with the Standards

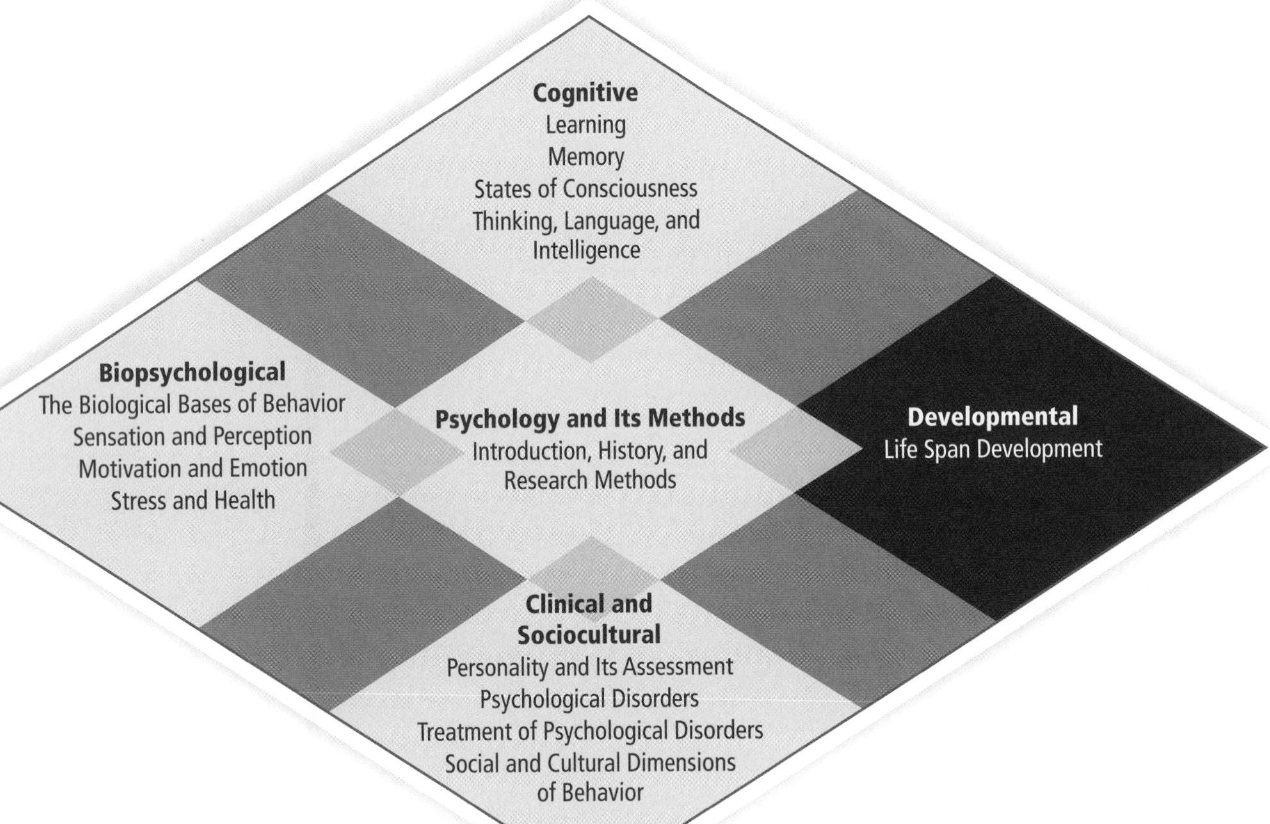

Cognitive
Learning
Memory
States of Consciousness
Thinking, Language, and Intelligence
Biopsychological
The Biological Bases of Behavior
Sensation and Perception
Motivation and Emotion
Stress and Health
Psychology and Its Methods
Introduction, History, and Research Methods
Developmental
Life Span Development
Clinical and Sociocultural
Personality and Its Assessment
Psychological Disorders
Treatment of Psychological Disorders
Social and Cultural Dimensions of Behavior

Scope and Sequence

Background/Significance of the Developmental Domain

Historically, psychologists were primarily interested in understanding the developmental milestones of childhood. Development in early, middle, and late adulthood was virtually ignored, possibly because of the belief that little change occurred after childhood. However, in the past few decades, psychologists have expanded their interest in development beyond childhood to the entire life span. Modern research reveals life as much more dynamic than previously viewed. There are not only obvious physical changes associated with aging, but interesting social and cognitive changes, as well.

The authors of the American Psychological Association's National Standards for High School Psychology wanted students to be exposed to the physiological and environmental influences on development from conception to death. They believed that studying development through the life span allows students to better understand how all people are similar and different. The authors believed that such an understanding is crucial for developing an appreciation of our multicultural society. In addition, they believed that teaching this domain will result in helping students develop methods for adapting to change in their own lives.

Chapter 2, including Module 4, Prenatal and Childhood Development, Module 5, Adolescence, and Module 6, Adulthood and Aging, presents this modern view of development. You may wish to include Module 3 (from Chapter 1, Nature and Nurture in Psychology) to address the physiological and environmental forces that influence development. In the modules of Chapter 2, students investigate physical, social, and cognitive changes across the life span. In doing so, they develop a better understanding of their own and others' development.

Developmental Domain

Introducing the Domain

The Points: Domain Objectives

- Differentiate among the zygote, embryo, and fetus stages of prenatal development.
- Analyze how maturation affects behavior in infancy and whether environmental factors affect maturation.
- Identify Jean Piaget, his theory of childhood cognitive development, and recent research that has changed our understanding of cognitive development.
- Determine how attachment develops, and then explore the effects of attachment between infant and parent.
- Define adolescence and evaluate how adolescence has changed over the last century.
- Summarize the physical changes that occur during adolescence.
- Analyze how the reasoning ability of adolescents differs from that of younger children.
- Describe how moral reasoning changes over time, according to Lawrence Kohlberg.
- Identify evidence of Erik Erikson's idea of identity-seeking behaviors in adolescence.
- Evaluate how adolescence relates to developmental psychology's three major issues.
- Describe the effects of physical changes in middle and late adulthood.
- Analyze the effect of aging on memory and intelligence.
- Identify the factors that affect social well-being as adults age.

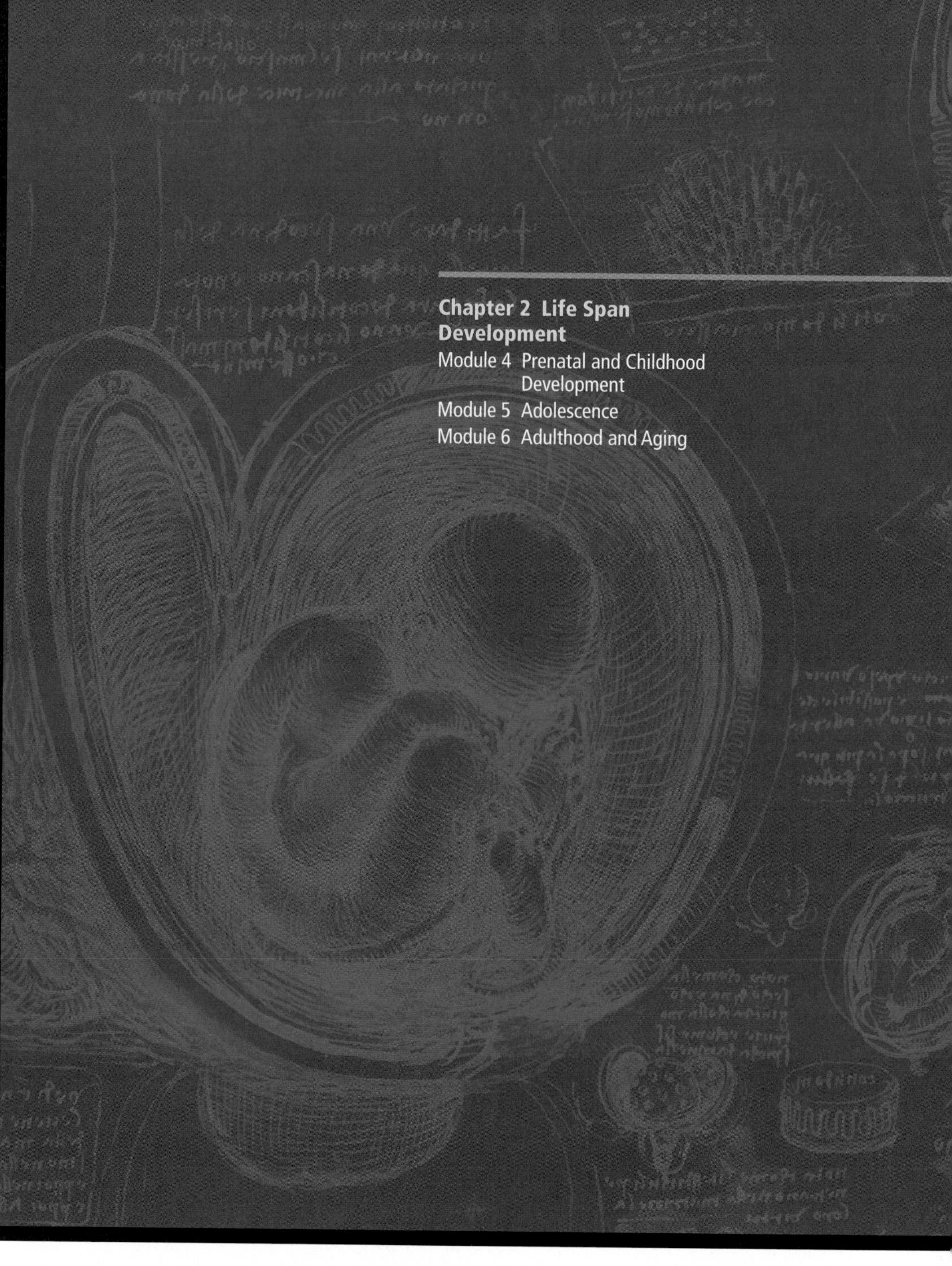

Enriching

Have students construct a lifeline of their own lives up to this point, highlighting the key developmental milestones they've experienced.

- What milestones do they remember from their early childhood? Do they remember learning new words or how to read? What was that like?
- What milestones were most important for them to conquer during elementary school? What were their goals for life during that time?
- What impact did physical maturity (puberty) have on their lives?
- Have them extend the lifeline to project the milestones they want to reach after high school. Would this lifeline look different if they lived during their parents' generation? Why or why not?

Developmental Domain

Our second domain, developmental, consists of one chapter containing three modules. The developmental domain explores, as Shakespeare did in the soliloquy below, growth processes occurring throughout the life span. From womb to tomb, we'll see how our individual development is different from and similar to one another.

All the world's a stage,
And all the men and women merely players;
They have their exits and their entrances,
And one man in time plays many parts,
His acts begin seven ages. At first the infant,
Mewling [crying] and puking in the nurse's arms.
Then the whining schoolboy, with his satchel [backpack]
And shining morning face, creeping like a snail
Unwilling to school. And then the lover
Sighing like a furnace, with a woeful ballad
Made to his mistress' eyebrow. Then a soldier,
Full of strange oaths . . . and then the justice,
In fair round belly

. . . The last scene of all
That ends this strange eventful history
Is second childishness, and mere oblivion
Sans teeth, sans eyes, sans taste, sans every thing.

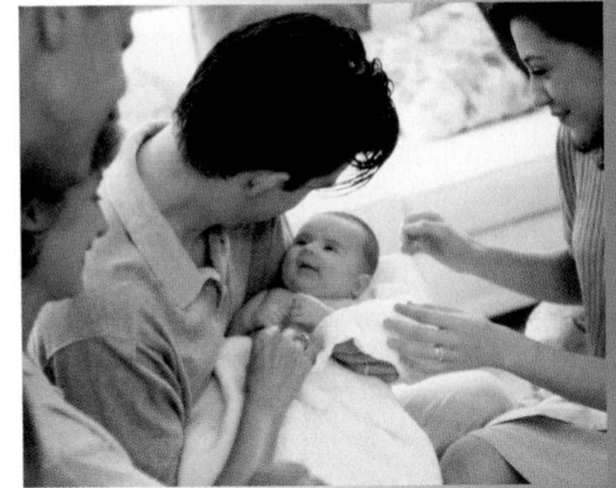

Adapted from William Shakespeare's *As You Like It*

If all the world is a stage, it's time to get the developmental show on the road.

CHAPTER 2

Life Span Development

Developmental Domain

Teaching with the Standards

Standard Area: Life Span Development

Breakdown of Module 4: Prenatal and Childhood Development

Content Standard 1: Development over the life span Module 4 considers physical, cognitive, and social development from the prenatal stage through childhood. Emphasis is placed on the capabilities of the newborn, the developing brain, and motor skill development. The cognitive stages of development, as proposed by Jean Piaget, are presented along with current research implications for this theory. This module also explores stranger anxiety, attachment, and the effects of parenting styles on social development. (Student Text pp. 57–75)

Content Standard 3: Stage theories Module 4 introduces students to Jean Piaget's stage theory of cognitive development by presenting summaries of each stage and appropriate examples to illustrate the stages. The authors examine how current research has challenged many of Piaget's conclusions. (Student Text pp. 63–68)

Content Standard 4: Developmental issues (nature/nurture, continuity/discontinuity, stability/instability, critical periods) Three major issues provide a framework for understanding development over the life span: nature/nurture (also refer to Module 3), continuity/discontinuity, and stability/instability. Module 4 offers research results related to these issues (Student Text pp. 74-75). The concept of critical periods is presented in discussion of fetal alcohol syndrome, attachment, and brain and motor development. (Student Text pp. 59, 61, 62, 70)

Breakdown of Module 5: Adolescence

Content Standard 1: Development over the life span Module 5 considers physical, cognitive, and social development in adolescence. Emphasis is placed on defining adolescence, physical changes accompanying puberty, and cognitive and moral development. The authors discuss Jean Piaget's formal operational stage, as well as Lawerence Kohlberg's stages of moral development. Social development is also addressed in a discussion of Erik Erikson's theory of psychosocial development. (Student Text pp. 80–94)

Content Standard 2: Research techniques used to study developmental processes Module 5 discusses how the concept of adolescence has evolved over time. (Student Text pp. 80–82)

Content Standard 3: Stage theories The stage theories of Jean Piaget (Student Text p. 85), Lawrence Kohlberg (Student Text pp. 85–88), and Erik Erikson (Student Text pp. 88–91) are presented in the context of the cognitive, moral, and social development of an adolescent.

Content Standard 4: Developmental issues (nature/nurture, continuity/discontinuity, stability/instability, critical periods) Three major issues provide a framework for understanding development over the lifespan, nature/nurture (also refer to Module 3), continuity/discontinuity, and stability/instability. Module 5 offers research results related to these issues. (Student Text pp. 93–94)

Breakdown of Module 6: Adulthood and Aging

Content Standard 1: Development over the life span Module 6 discusses the physical, cognitive, and social changes that accompany young, middle, and late adulthood. Emphasis is placed on the concept of a social clock and timing of social events in adulthood. Coping with dying and death is also discussed. (Student Text pp. 98–113)

Content Standard 3: Stage theories Erik Erikson's theory of psychosocial development is discussed. Focus is on the adult tasks of intimacy and generativity. (Student Text p. 107)

Scope and Sequence

	Objectives	Text Reference	Standards Covered
Lesson 1	Examine the beginnings of life. Trace prenatal development through the zygotic, embryonic, and fetal stages. Discuss the concepts of critical periods, teratogens, and fetal alcohol syndrome. (Note: You can also choose to include Module 3 as part of this chapter. See Teacher's Edition p. 1b for details.)	Module 4, pp. 57–59, 70–71	Standard Area: Life Span Development, Content Standard 1, Performance Standard 1.1, Content Standard 4, Performance Standard 4.1
Lesson 2	Explore the capabilities of the newborn. Discuss newborn reflexes, temperaments, and physical and motor skill development.	Module 4, pp. 59–63	Content Standard 1, Performance Standards 1.1, 1.3
Lesson 3	Present Jean Piaget's theory of cognitive development. Introduce the concept of schemas and how schemas develop. Discuss how current research has challenged many of Piaget's theories.	Module 4, pp. 63–68	Content Standard 1, Performance Standards 1.1, 1.3, Content Standard 3, Performance Standard 3.1
Lesson 4	Discuss social development in infancy and childhood. Discuss stranger anxiety, the development of a sense of self, and the role of attachment in social development. Consider the role of responsive parenting and discuss parenting styles.	Module 4, pp. 68–74	Content Standard 1, Performance Standard 1.1, Content Standard 3, Performance Standard 3.1, Content Standard 4, Performance Standard 4.1
Lesson 5	Explore physical, cognitive, and social development in adolescence. Discuss the historical and cultural factors that define adolescence. Examine Kohlberg's theories and criticisms directed toward his research. Discuss Erik Erikson's psychosocial stages of development; focus on the task of adolescence and the search for identity.	Module 5, pp. 80–97	Content Standard 1, Performance Standard 1.1, Content Standard 2, Performance Standard 2.1, Content Standard 3, Performance Standards 3.1, 3.4
Lesson 6	Examine physical, cognitive, and social development in young and middle adulthood.	Module 6, pp. 98–117	Content Standard 1, Performance Standard 1.1, Content Standard 3, Performance Standard 3.1
Lesson 7	Explore the physical, cognitive, and social development of late adulthood. Discuss examples of ageism in the United States by comparing the treatment of the elderly in different cultures. Examine the issues of coping with death and the emerging role of hospice care for the dying.	Module 6, pp. 98–117	Content Standard 1, Performance Standards 1.1, 1.4, Content Standard 3, Performance Standard 3.1
Lesson 8	Review and test		

CHAPTER 2

Life Span Development

Introducing the Chapter

The Points: Chapter Objectives

- Differentiate among the zygote, embryo, and fetus stages of prenatal development.
- Analyze how maturation affects behavior in infancy and whether environmental factors affect maturation.
- Identify Jean Piaget, his theory of childhood cognitive development, and recent research that has changed our understanding of cognitive development.
- Determine how attachment develops, and discuss the effects of attachment between infant and parent.
- Define adolescence and evaluate how adolescence has changed over the last century.
- Summarize the physical changes that occur during adolescence.
- Analyze how the reasoning ability of adolescents differs from that of younger children.
- Describe how moral reasoning changes over time, according to Lawrence Kohlberg.
- Identify evidence of Erik Erikson's idea of identity-seeking behaviors in adolescence.
- Evaluate how adolescence relates to developmental psychology's three major issues.
- Describe the social clock, and discuss the things that affect how it is set.
- Describe the effects of physical changes in middle and late adulthood.
- Analyze the effect of aging on memory and intelligence.
- Identify the factors that affect social well-being as adults age.

CHAPTER 2

Life Span Development

You are very different physically than you were five or six years ago. If you compare a sixth-grade photo to a current photo, you might even find the differences startling! These changes are obvious because you can see them. But you also differ in ways that are not obvious to the eye. You think differently than you did in grade school, and your emotions are more developed. Psychologists interested in these changes are found in *developmental psychology,* a branch of the field that studies physical, cognitive, emotional, and social changes throughout the life span.

The modules in this chapter explore three different periods of development, but they share a common theme. The research presented in all three modules focuses on three fundamental developmental issues:

1. *Nature and Nurture:* How much of our development is a result of genetics (our nature) and how much is a result of environment (the nurturing we receive)? (Module 3 explored this question in depth.)
2. *Continuity and Stages:* Is development a gradual continuous process, like a ski lift moving up a mountain, or is it a series of distinctly different stages, like stair steps?
3. *Stability and Change:* Will the person you think of as the "real" you still be there in 2050, or will that person change dramatically as you move through adulthood?

We will search for answers to these questions in the next three modules, as we look at prenatal and childhood development, adolescence, and adulthood.

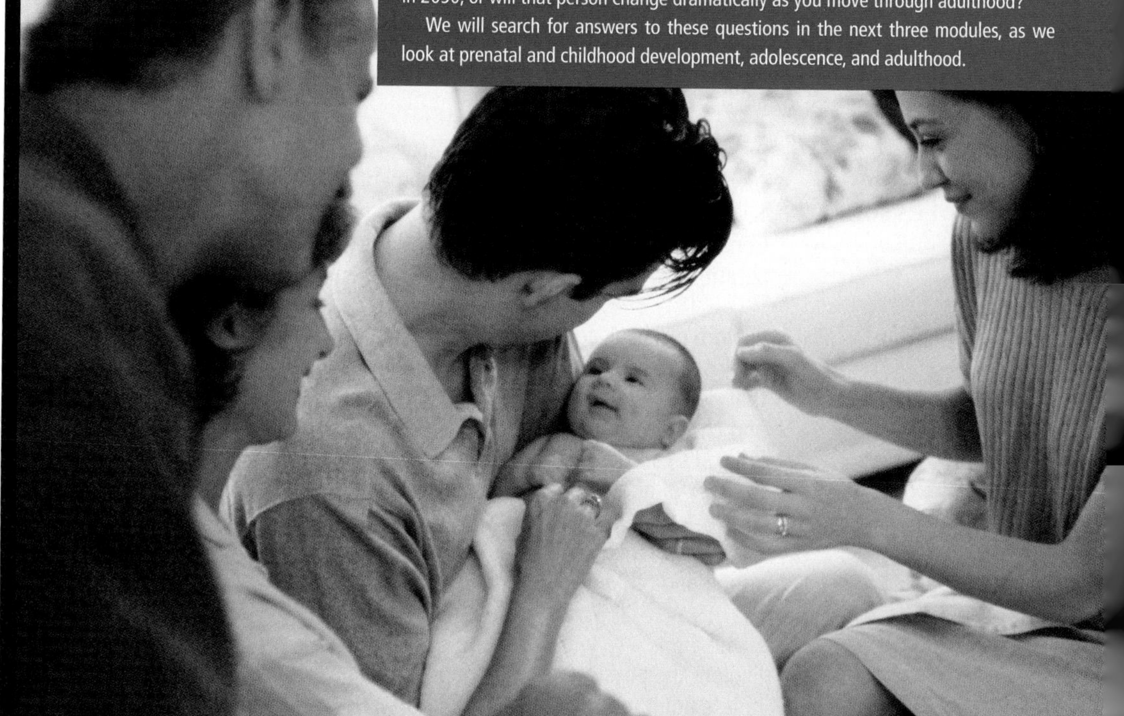

Performance Standards

Standard Area: Life Span Development

Content Standard 1: Development over the life span

Performance Standard 1.1 Describe physical, cognitive, and social development across the life span.

Physical Development

- Explore the milestones of prenatal development. (Student Text pp. 57–58)
- Discuss newborn abilities. (Student Text p. 59)
- Discuss temperament. (Student Text p. 60)
- Present the concept of maturation with examples of motor skill development. (Student Text pp. 61–62)
- Present Figure 4.2, a chart illustrating motor development for each skill. (Student Text p. 62)
- Trace brain development through childhood. (Student Text p. 61)

Cognitive Development

- Present Jean Piaget's theory of cognitive development. (Student Text pp. 63–68)
- Present Table 4.1, Piaget's Stages of Cognitive Development, which summarizes this theory. (Student Text p. 65)

Social Development

- Present the concept of stranger anxiety as an introduction to attachment. (Student Text pp. 68–69)
- Discuss Harry Harlow's research on the role of contact comfort in attachment. (Student Text pp. 69–70)
- Discuss critical periods in relation to attachment and Konrad Lorenz' research on imprinting. (Student Text pp. 70–71)
- Investigate Mary Ainsworth's research on attachment. (Student Text p. 71)
- Discuss characteristics of different parenting styles with implications on a child's social development. Address cultural differences. (Student Text pp. 72–74)

Performance Standard 1.3 Identify the cognitive capabilities of infants and children.

- Compare memory ability in newborns, 3-year-olds, and 10-year-olds. (Student Text p. 61)
- Explore Piaget's theories of cognitive development. (Student Text pp. 63–67)
- Discuss the impact of current research on Piaget's theory. (Student Text pp. 63–68)

Content Standard 3: Stage theories

Performance Standard 3.1 List stages in the developmental theories proposed by psychologists such as Piaget, Erikson, Kohlberg, Gilligan, Cross, Helms, and others.

- Explore Jean Piaget's stages of cognitive development. (Student Text pp. 64–68)
- Present the concept of schemas and how they develop through assimilation and accommodation. (Student Text pp. 63–64)
- Discuss object permanence, egocentrism, and conservation. (Student Text pp. 65–67)

Content Standard 4: Developmental issues (nature/nurture, continuity/discontinuity, stability/instability, critical periods)

- Present research on the effects of nature and nurture on development. (Student Text pp. 74–75)

Performance Standard 4.1 Understand the concept of critical periods and the relationship to development.

- Discuss teratogens and their effects on the fetus. (Student Text pp. 58–59)
- Discuss maturation and how experience—for example, abuse—can hinder development. (Student Text p. 61)
- Investigate motor skill development. (Student Text p. 62)
- Define *critical period*, with connection to attachment. (Student Text pp. 70–72)

Performance Standard 4.2 Explore the developmental issues of continuity/discontinuity and stability/instability.

- Cognitive skills and attachment develop more continuously than motor skills. (Student Text p. 74)
- Temperament is relatively stable through development, but change is possible. (Student Text p. 74)

Materials NETWORK

All of the items from the Video, Activity, and Enrichment Centers listed below come from the *Teacher's Resource Binder.* These items will help you teach and expand on concepts presented in Module 4.

trb This logo indicates when an item from the Materials Network may be used in conjunction with a specific note found in this module's *Teacher's Edition.*

The Beginnings of Life

V Video Center

Consult the faculty guide from *The Mind* video series for descriptions of these modules.

- Videocassette: *The Mind,* Second Edition, Module 12: "Teratogens and Their Effects on the Developing Brain and Mind" (*Teacher's Resource Binder*, p. 4-1)
- Videocassette: *The Mind,* Second Edition, Module 13: "Capabilities of the Newborn" (*Teacher's Resource Binder*, p. 4-1)

Activity Center

- Critical Thinking Activity: *Fact or Falsehood?* With this activity, students' preconceptions about development are either exposed as incorrect or reinforced as correct. (*Teacher's Resource Binder*, p. 4-1; Handout 4–1)
- Building Vocabulary: Graphic Organizer: *Development Charts* The charts in the graphic organizer allow students to review module vocabulary words and relate vocabulary to key concepts about development. (*Teacher's Resource Binder*, p. 4-1; Handouts 4–2a and 4–2b)
- Application Activity: *EAS Temperament Survey* This survey measures temperament on four different scales. It measures scores for sociability, emotionality, distress, and fearfulness. (*Teacher's Resource Binder*, p. 4-1; Handout 4–3)
- Technology Application Activity: *Temperament on the Web* The Preventative Ounce nonprofit organization has a Web site that explores the impact of temperament on human behavior. This site was founded in 1984 by two psychologists who wanted to help parents understand how their children's temperaments may be related to a variety of developmental problems. (*Teacher's Resource Binder*, p. 4-1)

Enrichment Center

- Enrichment Lesson: *Prenatal Sensory Development* This lesson details the different developmental milestones that take place during pregnancy, starting in the second month, when a fetus may show reflexes that seems to involve the senses. (*Teacher's Resource Binder*, p. 4-1)

Physical Development in Infancy and Childhood

V Video Center

- Videocassette: *Scientific American Frontiers,* Second Edition, Segment 24: "Baby Body Sense" Consult the faculty guide from the *Scientific American Frontiers* video series for a description of this segment. (*Teacher's Resource Binder*, p. 4-1)

Activity Center

- Cooperative Learning Activity: *Identifying Developmental Landmarks* Capture students' attention about infancy and childhood with this activity. Students can work in groups to determine what they believe to be the ages at which several developmental milestones occur in early childhood. (*Teacher's Resource Binder*, p. 4-1; Handout 4–4)
- Application Activity: *Physical Development* With this activity students interact with a child (with parental consent) between the ages of 3 and 6 to evaluate physical development. (*Teacher's Resource Binder*, p. 4-1; Handout 4–5; Transparency Masters 4–1a through 4–2b)

Enrichment Center

- Enrichment Lesson: *"Normal" Height and Weight* What does it mean for a child to be of "normal" weight and height? Parents often wonder what "normal" height and weight are as they rear their children. This lesson helps students realize that "normal" varies widely, depending on gender and ethnicity. (*Teacher's Resource Binder*, p. 4-1)

Cognitive Development in Infancy and Childhood

V Video Center

Consult the faculty guides from *The Mind* and the *Scientific American Frontiers* video series for descriptions of these modules or segments.

- Videocassette: *The Mind,* Second Edition, Module 14: "Infant Cognitive Development " (*Teacher's Resource Binder,* p. 4-1)
- Videocassette: *Scientific American Frontiers,* Second Edition, Segment 25: "The Magic Years" (*Teacher's Resource Binder,* p. 4-1)
- Videocassette: *Scientific American Frontiers,* Second Edition, Segment 27: "A Change of Mind" (*Teacher's Resource Binder,* p. 4-1)

Activity Center

- Application Activity: *Musk LifeSavers* Students can experience assimilating information into a new schema by tasting musk-flavored LifeSavers, a favorite flavor in Australia. This is a delightful way for students to be introduced to the concept of *schemas.* (*Teacher's Resource Binder,* p. 4-1)
- Application Activity: *Lollipops and Gloquex* What is a *gloquex?* Students can use their imaginations as they experience a completely novel stimulus, just as young children do with everyday things. This activity will help students understand some basic Piagetian terms. At the same time, it will help them better appreciate how infants and children face developmental tasks. (*Teacher's Resource Binder,* p. 4-1)
- Critical Thinking Activity: *Demonstrating Preoperational Thought* Students can better understand preoperational thought with this critical thinking activity that challenges their ability to understand conservation of volume. This amusing demonstration that is strikingly similar to a classical Piagetian task has challenged many a college student! (*Teacher's Resource Binder,* p. 4-1)
- Critical Thinking Activity: *Conservation and Jelly Beans* Some students may be fooled by this activity, which demonstrates conservation of number. It also presents the principles of *centration* and *irreversibility,* which are Piagetian concepts. (*Teacher's Resource Binder,* p. 4-1)
- Technology Application Activity: *PsychSim:* "Cognitive Development" *PsychSim* is a CD-ROM containing tutorials in different content areas of psychology. With this tutorial of cognitive development, students experience Piagetian cognitive tasks, including various tests of conservation. (*Teacher's Resource Binder,* p. 4-1)
- Application Activity: *Intellectual Development* Students interact with a child (with parental consent) between the ages of 3 and 6. With this activity, they observe the children firsthand in order to evaluate cognitive development. (*Teacher's Resource Binder,* p. 4-1; Handout 4–6)
- Critical Thinking Activity: *The Water-Level Task* This test of preoperational thought often tricks college and graduate students! See how well your students do on this classic Piagetian task. (*Teacher's Resource Binder,* p. 4-1; Handout 4–7)

Enrichment Center

- Enrichment Lesson: *Preoperational Thought and Moral Development* According to Piaget, children pass through two stages of morality: *morality of strength* and *morality of cooperation.* As this lesson discusses, preoperational thought influences the cognitive processes behind moral reasoning in young children. (*Teacher's Resource Binder,* p. 4-1)

Social Development in Infancy and Childhood

Video Center

- Videocassette: *The Mind,* Second Edition, Module 15: "Social Development in Infancy" Consult the faculty guide from *The Mind* video series for a description of this module. (*Teacher's Resource Binder,* p. 4-1)

Activity Center

- Application Activity: *Parental Authority Questionnaire* What kind of parenting style have your students been reared with—*permissive* style, *authoritarian* style, or *authoritative* style? This survey will get their perspectives on their parents' style. (*Teacher's Resource Binder,* p. 4-1; Handout 4–8)
- Application Activity: *Social Development* Students interact with a child (with parental consent) between the ages of 3 and 6. With this activity, they interact with the children in order to evaluate social development. (*Teacher's Resource Binder,* p. 4-1; Handout 4–9)

Enrichment Center

- Enrichment Lesson: *Attachment Types* This lesson explores the three types of attachment infants develop with their parents: *secure, anxious/ambivalent,* and *avoidant.* (***Teacher's Resource Binder***, p. 4-1)

- Enrichment Lesson: *Spanking* To spank or not to spank? That is a question parents have been wrestling with for years. This lesson gives some insight into the effectiveness of spanking as a punishment. (***Teacher's Resource Binder***, p. 4-1)

MODULE 4

Prenatal and Childhood Development

You are a genetic and environmental marvel, who in only about nine months grew from the size of the dot on this *i* to a full-size newborn baby. From the moment the egg from your mother and the sperm cell from your father united, until the minute you were born, the cells that became you progressed through a delicate, predictable, and fantastic sequence of events. This sequence is virtually the same for all of us.

The Beginnings of Life

If you are a young woman, you were born with all the egg cells you'll ever have, though of course they were immature when you were just a baby. Approximately one in 5000 of these cells will mature and be released from an ovary. If you are a young man, you did not begin producing sperm cells until you reached puberty. You'll keep producing them until you die. Though the rate slows with age, you will produce more than 1.5 million sperm cells in the 30 minutes you take today for lunch, a rate of about 1000 per second.

Prenatal Development

1. How do the zygote, embryo, and fetus differ from one another?

Prenatal means literally before (*pre-*) birth (*-natal*). The prenatal stage of development starts at conception and ends at birth.

Getting Started

trb You may wish to use **Critical Thinking Activity:** ***Fact or Falsehood?*** (*Teacher's Resource Binder*, p. 4-1; **Handout 4–1**) as a prereading strategy to find out what students already know about early development. The activity will prime students to note terms and concepts in the text that confirm or dispel their preconceptions about this subject.

trb You may also wish to use **Application Activity:** ***Writing Letters to Parents and Children*** (*Teacher's Resource Binder*, p. 6-1; **Handout 6–4**). This activity works as an introduction to concepts in Modules 4–6 as well as a conclusion to the concepts about development learned in these three modules.

MODULE 4

Prenatal and Childhood Development

Introducing the Module

The Points: Module Objectives

- Differentiate among the zygote, embryo, and fetus.
- Evaluate if humans are completely helpless at birth.
- Identify maturation, and analyze how it affects memory and physical skills in infancy and childhood.
- Identify Jean Piaget, and explain what he contributed to our understanding of how children's thought processes develop.
- Determine if recent research has changed the way we view cognitive development.
- Understand when and why infants develop stranger anxiety.
- Determine how attachment develops and how it affects the relationship between infant and parent.
- Describe the three different parenting styles, and evaluate which one tends to have the best outcomes.

trb Building Vocabulary

Using the Key Terms on page 77 of their books, have students work with partners to define vocabulary words and relate each vocabulary word to the category under which it is presented in **Building Vocabulary: Graphic Organizer:** ***Development Charts*** (*Teacher's Resource Binder*, p. 4-1; **Handouts 4–2a** and **4–2b**).

Teaching the Points

web ■ **TEACHING TIP**

You can log on as an instructor to the book companion site for *Thinking About Psychology* at **www.worthpublishers.com/thinkingaboutpsych**. It contains teacher resources for class presentations as well as review and assessment of module concepts and terms.

MODULE 4

F • Y • I

According to the National Center for Health Statistics (2001), about 50 more males than females are born per 1000 births each year. More babies are born in August than any other month, and more babies are born on Tuesdays, regardless of race.

Source: Ventura, S.J., Martin, J. A., Curtin, S. C., Menacker, F., & Hamilton, B. E. (2001, April 17). Births: Final data for 1999. *National Vital Statistics Report, 49*(1). Hyattsville MD: National Center for Health Statistics.

■ MULTICULTURAL CONNECTIONS

Births of twins (and triplets, quads, etc.) are viewed as blessings, curses, and/or omens in different cultures. Have students explore how different cultures regard the births of multiples.

■ LOOKING AT THE ISSUES

(1) Fertility technologies increase the likelihood of multiple fetuses developing in one pregnancy, resulting in births of multiples, including the famous McCaughey septuplets of Iowa and the Harris sextuplets of Alabama. Invite interested students to research the following:

- What advances in technology make it more likely that multiples can survive?
- What developmental problems can parents of multiples expect?
- What kind of community responses do parents of multiples receive?
- What ethical dilemmas do doctors and parents face with multiple fetuses developing in one pregnancy?

(2) Explore these ethical issues about fertility by asking the following questions:

- What are the pros and cons of having children later in life? What societal implications will this practice produce?
- Should human cloning be allowed? Why or why not?

"Of all the joys that brighten suffering earth, what joy is welcomed like a newborn child?" Caroline Norton (1808–1877), author.

A newly fertilized egg is called a **zygote.** Not even one in two zygotes makes it past the first 14 days (Grobstein, 1979). Luckily, you and I survived that risky period. A lot happens during those two weeks. First, the single-cell zygote begins to divide into identical cells; one cell becomes two, and two become four. In the first week, after dividing about seven times, the cells start to *differentiate,* to specialize in function. Our **genes** direct this process, leading some cells, for example, to develop into a brain and others to develop into lungs or a heart.

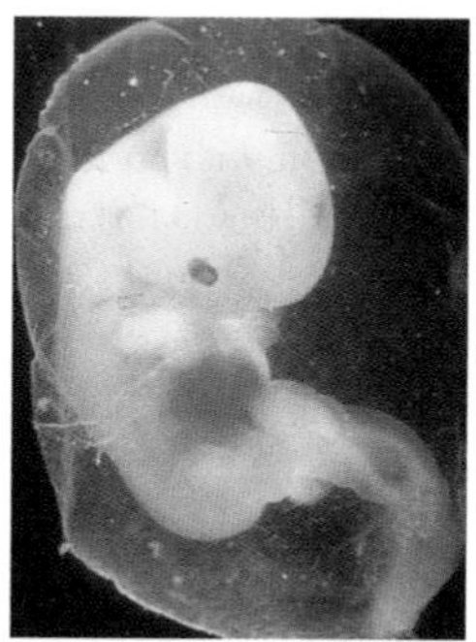

Eight Weeks After Conception Facial features, hands, and feet are visible at this time.

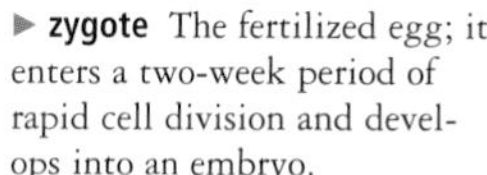

► **zygote** The fertilized egg; it enters a two-week period of rapid cell division and develops into an embryo.

► **genes** The biochemical units of heredity that direct how our cells become specialized for various functions (for example, creating brain, lungs, heart, hair) during prenatal development.

► **embryo** The developing human organism from about two weeks after fertilization through the end of the eighth week.

► **fetus** The developing human organism from nine weeks after conception to birth.

► **teratogens** Substances that cross the placental barrier and prevent the fetus from developing normally.

Around the tenth day, the zygote attaches to the mother's uterine wall, where it will stay for about 37 weeks. But when the developing human organism passes the 14-day milestone, it is no longer known as a *zygote*; it is now an **embryo.** It has a noticeable heartbeat and red blood cells produced by its own liver. This embryonic stage, which starts at two weeks, will last until eight weeks, and at the end of that time, most of the body's major organs will have formed.

At nine weeks, the developing organism enters the fetal period. A **fetus** is unmistakably human in form. Fetuses born prematurely at the end of six months have organs that are well enough developed to provide a chance at survival.

But let's not hurry things. While still in the mother's body, the fetus receives oxygen and nutrients from the *placenta,* a cushion of cells that also serves to screen out some of the substances that could harm the fetus. Unfortunately, the placenta is not a perfect screen, and some viruses, toxins, and drugs do slip through. **Teratogens** are substances that cross the placental barrier and prevent the fetus from developing normally.

Suggested Readings

Use the following books as teacher-preparation tools or as enrichment for advanced students:

Cohen, D. B. (1999). *Stranger in the nest: Do parents really shape their child's personality, intelligence, or character?* New York: Wiley.

Erikson, E. (1978). *Childhood and society.* New York: Norton. (Original work published 1950)

Halpern, D. (1996). *Thought and knowledge: An introduction to critical thinking* (3rd ed). Hillsdale, NJ: Erlbaum.

Inhelder, B., & Piaget, J. (1959). *The growth of logical thinking from childhood to adolescence.* New York: Basic Books.

Kagan, J. (1994). *Galen's prophecy: Temperament in human nature.* New York: Basic Books.

Piaget, J. (1965). *The moral judgment of the child.* New York: Free Press.

Teratogens take many forms. Radiation, toxic chemicals in the water or air, or viruses like German measles can harm a fetus, as can some prescription and over-the-counter drugs. Other teratogens include nicotine, alcohol, and the viruses associated with sexually transmitted diseases (STDs). Women who smoke during pregnancy increase the risk of abnormal fetal heartbeat, premature birth and its related complications, and miscarriage (Slotkin, 1998). The effects of alcohol on a fetus can be even more dramatic. There is no known "safe" quantity of alcohol to consume while pregnant, and even moderate drinking can damage a fetus's brain (Braun, 1996). Children whose mothers drink heavily during pregnancy may be born with **fetal alcohol syndrome (FAS),** marked by both physical and mental abnormalities. Mothers may also transmit STDs to their unborn children. Pregnant women with STDs are more likely than other women to have babies with mental retardation and blindness (Bee, 1997).

Fetal Alcohol Syndrome If his mother had stayed free of alcohol during her pregnancy, this child would not have been born with FAS.

Frightening as teratogens are, however, most fetuses do survive their nine months in the womb and enter the world as healthy newborns.

The Newborn

2. Are humans completely helpless at birth?

Do you think of newborn babies as helpless? Certainly, if left to fend for themselves shortly after birth, infants would not survive. However, newborns are not passive little bundles who don't notice the world around them.

Within the first half hour of life, infants will turn their heads to watch a picture or drawing of a human face, but they will not turn their heads to view an indistinguishable jumble of images (Johnson & others, 1991; Mondloch & others, 1999). Newborns also turn their heads toward human voices, and they have definite taste preferences. Sugar water and mother's milk? Yes, please! Milk with a spoiled taste or smell to it? No thanks!

Newborns don't have to learn sucking, swallowing, or grasping. These *reflexes* (automatic, unlearned responses) are survival behaviors, and nearly every baby comes equipped with them. To help find the breast or bottle that supplies nourishment, newborns have a **rooting reflex:** Touch them on the cheek or corner of the mouth, and they will turn their faces toward the touch, mouths open, looking for something to suck.

▸ **fetal alcohol syndrome (FAS)** A series of physical and cognitive abnormalities that appear in children whose mothers consumed large amounts of alcohol while pregnant. Symptoms may include noticeable facial misproportions.

▸ **rooting reflex** A baby's tendency, when touched on the cheek, to open the mouth and search for the nipple; this is an automatic, unlearned response.

Enriching

Students may be interested in learning about the APGAR test. It is a quick physical test given to every newborn at birth. Scores are given at 1 and 5 minutes after birth. If problems exist, then another test is given at 10 minutes after birth. A score of 7 to 10 is considered normal. Infants scoring 4–6 might need resuscitation, while scores under 3 usually require immediate resuscitation. APGAR is an acronym for the following tests:

A = activity or muscle tone. How active muscle movement is right after birth is measured.
P = pulse. Ideally, babies have a heart rate of higher than 100 beats per minute
G = grimace or reflex irritability. Active babies sneeze and cough during suctioning of the mucus in their noses and mouths.
A = appearance. Doctors look for normal skin color. Blue-gray or pale skin color is not a good sign.
R = respiration. Babies should be crying and breathing regularly.

■ **LOOKING AT THE ISSUES**

Some states can terminate parental rights if evidence of substance abuse exists during pregnancy. Guide a class discussion with the following questions:

- How do you think the criminal justice system should deal with mothers who abuse drugs during pregnancy? What effect do these decisions have on society in general?

V At this point, you may wish to show **Videocassette: *The Mind,* Second Edition, Module 12: "Teratogens and Their Effects on the Developing Brain and Mind"** (*Teacher's Resource Binder,* p. 4-1).

F • Y • I

Infants have many reflexes. In **Babinski's reflex**, the toes flair out and then curl back in when the bottom of the foot is stroked. In the **moro reflex**, the arms are thrust out and the back is arched in response to surprise or a sudden noise or movement. In the **plantar reflex**, the toes curl in when the ball of the foot is pressed. In the **swimming reflex**, for a short period of time, babies hold their breath and move their arms and legs as if they are swimming while submerged in water. In the **stepping reflex**, babies move their feet up and down as if they are walking if they are held up over a flat surface.

V At this point, you may wish to show **Videocassette: *The Mind,* Second Edition, Module 13: "Capabilities of the Newborn"** (*Teacher's Resource Binder,* p. 4-1).

■ **TEACHING TIP**

Make a link to sensation by reminding students that our sense of taste is part of our evolutionary adaptation. Sweet and salty tastes signal safe foods to eat, bitter tastes signal poison, while sour tastes alert us to spoiled or rotten food. (For more information, see **Module 9.**)

MODULE 4

■ JOURNAL WRITING

Invite students to use the following questions as a springboard for entries in their psychology journals:

- Since early childhood, has your temperament remained consistent or has it changed over time? Explain why you feel the way you do.

trb At this point, you may wish to use Application Activity: *EAS Temperament Survey* (*Teacher's Resource Binder*, p. 4-1; Handout 4–3).

F • Y • I

Parents of babies with "difficult" temperaments often feel guilty about their children's behavior and reactions to events. The Center for Effective Parenting suggests that parents of difficult babies protect their children from new and stressful situations by establishing a consistent environment and setting a tight schedule for feeding and sleeping. Experts from the center say that behaviors associated with difficult temperaments often diminish by one year of age.

Source: Zolten, K., & Long, N. (1997). *Infant temperament.* Retrieved March 11, 2003, from www.parenting-ed.org/handout3/General%20Parenting%20Information/infant%20temperament.htm

Reflexes The grasping reflex allows this newborn to support its own weight. This reflex disappears by the baby's first birthday. At right, stroking this baby's cheek initiates the rooting reflex, as the baby searches for something to suck.

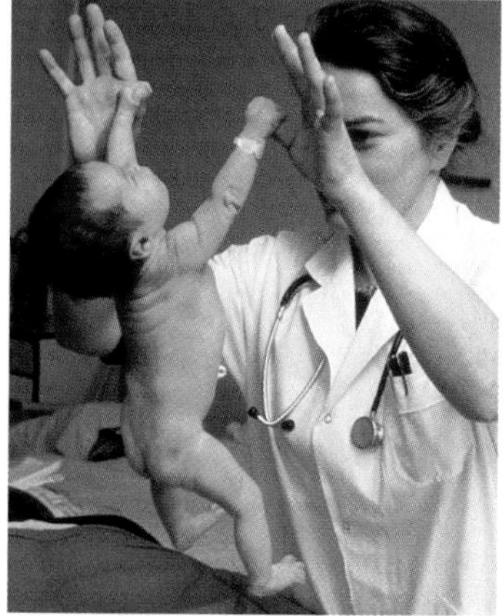

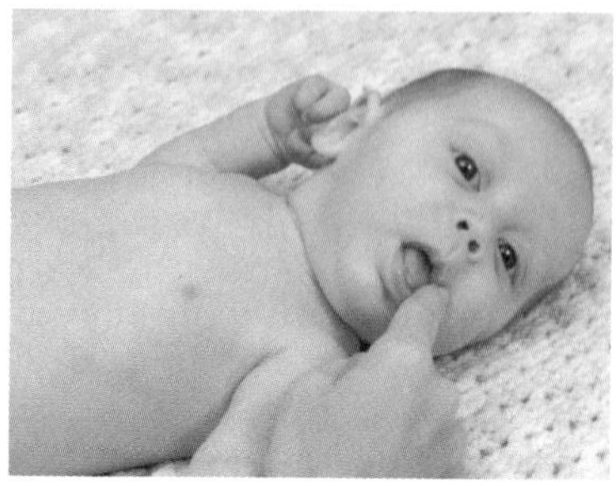

But newborns don't just roll off the assembly line, interchangeable with each other. Even in the first few hours of life, a baby's **temperament**—his or her characteristic emotional excitability—is evident. In the weeks following birth, an "easy" baby displays predictable sleeping and eating patterns, appears relaxed, and is cheerful. During these same weeks, a "difficult" baby is unpredictable, intense, and irritable. And the "slow-to-warm-up" baby will avoid new situations, have relatively low activity levels, and take more time to adapt to something new (Chess & Thomas, 1987).

Temperament is a relatively stable personality aspect. The most intense preschoolers grow up to be intense young adults (Larson & Diener, 1987). Inhibited, fearful 2-year-olds generally become shy second-graders (Kagan & others, 1994).

Physical Development in Infancy and Childhood

3. What is maturation, and how does it affect memory and physical skills in infancy and childhood?

Infancy is the first year of a child's life. From about 1 year to 3 years of age, a child is a toddler. Childhood includes the span between toddler and teenager.

Throughout infancy and childhood, we develop at an amazing pace on many different fronts—physically, cognitively (in our thought processes), emotionally, and socially. Let's look first at physical development during this early part of life.

▶ **temperament** A person's characteristic emotional reactivity and intensity.

Enriching

web Preventive Ounce's Web site (www.preventiveoz.org) has a temperament questionnaire that provides a profile of a child's temperament. Students may complete the questionnaire for a specific child they know—a sibling or perhaps a child for whom they regularly provide care. The Web site provides an immediate profile, indicates specific behavioral issues often associated with the profile, and outlines possible strategies for managing the highs and lows of the child's temperament.

trb At this point, you may wish to use Technology Application Activity: *Temperament on the Web* (*Teacher's Resource Binder*, p. 4-1).

The Developing Brain

During prenatal development, your body was making nerve cells at the rate of 4000 per *second.* With your first breath of air, your brain cells were where they needed to be, but your nervous system was still very immature. You could not walk, talk, or remember as you now do because your brain had not yet formed the neural networks that would let you perform these behaviors. In part, these networks, which continue developing even in adolescence, were a result of **maturation**—the biological growth processes that are programmed into your genes and that enable orderly changes in behavior (Figure 4.1). Experience has little effect on maturation. You rolled over, crawled, walked, and learned to run based largely on your genetic blueprint, and no amount of experience will change your blueprint. However, experience does affect *development.* Parents who talk and read to their children foster neural connections that help reading skills develop. Those who abuse and neglect their children also deprive them of these complex neural connections and hinder development.

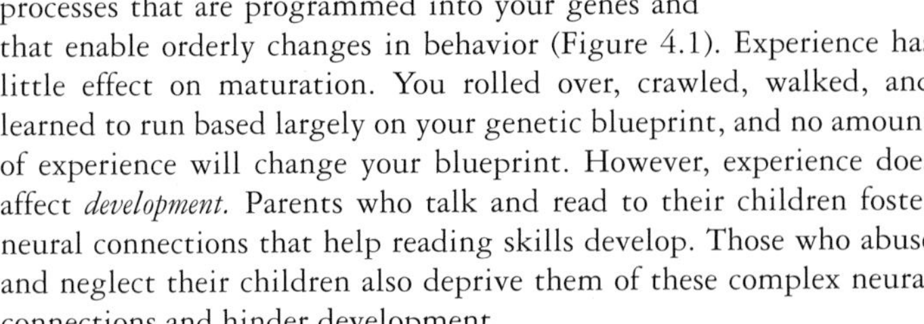

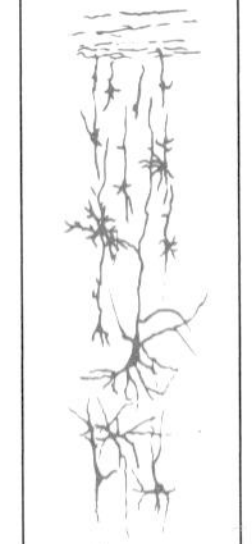

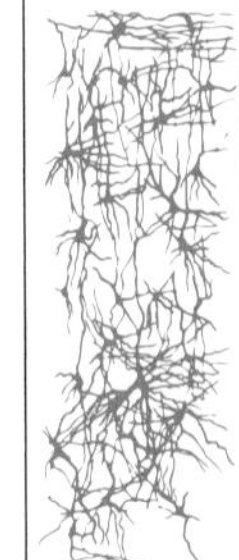

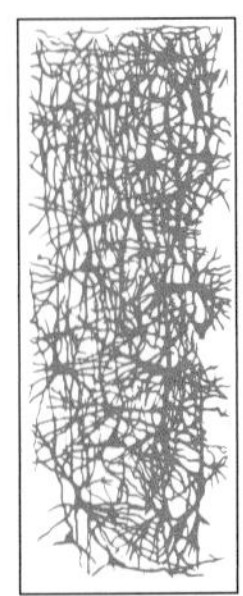

Figure 4.1 Neural Development These drawings show how the brain's neural networks grow increasingly more complex as a child matures.

To see how maturation affects memory, try to remember anything about your first birthday party, or try to remember wearing diapers. Any luck? If you're like most of us, the answer is no. We are not able to remember much before about the age of 3, and we remember very little that happened during ages 3 through 5, because we did not have the neural connections in our brains that allow us to remember. Memory researcher Elizabeth Loftus (1996) says that trying to remember things that happened before age 5 is like trying to read documents formatted by an older version of a computer operating system. So, do our memories function at all when we are very young? Yes, but in different ways.

- One-year-olds will imitate the making of a rattle (putting a button in a box) three months after observing this act (Mandler & McDonough, 1995).
- Three-year-olds recognize an out-of-focus picture more quickly if they saw a clear version of the picture three months earlier (Drummey & Newcombe, 1995).
- Most 10-year-olds say they recognize only 1 in 5 of the classmates they have not seen since preschool. But their physiological responses (measured as skin perspiration) are greater to former classmates, even to those they claim they don't recognize. The nervous system remembers what the conscious mind does not (Newcombe & Fox, 1994).

► **maturation** Biological growth processes that enable orderly changes in behavior, relatively uninfluenced by experience.

MODULE 4

trb tr ■ **TEACHING TIP**

A black-line master for Figure 4.1, Neural Development, is available in the **Black-Line Masters Appendix** of the *Teacher's Resource Binder.*

F • Y • I

For several years, many parents believed that exposing their babies to classical music would increase intelligence later in life. This was known as the Mozart effect, and the practice seemed to be the key to making smart babies. Unfortunately, the Mozart effect was based on one study; subsequent studies have shown that the effect does not have the impact on intellectual development that proponents claimed it had.

■ **JOURNAL WRITING**

Invite students to use the following questions as springboards for entries in their psychology journals:

- What is your earliest memory of learning how to do something (for example, tying your shoes or riding a bike)? Describe the memory, including the method used to teach you the task.
- How would you describe the development of your physical self-image from childhood to now?

■ **MULTICULTURAL CONNECTIONS**

Study of certain tribes in Africa has shown that maturational milestones can occur on different schedules. Using library or Internet resources, have students explore timelines these tribes develop on; then compare and contrast findings. Students will likely note that while the timing of events may differ from culture to culture, the order of development does not differ.

trb At this point, you may wish to use **Cooperative Learning Activity:** ***Identifying Developmental Landmarks*** (*Teacher's Resource Binder*, p. 4-1; **Handout 4–4**).

Cooperative Learning

Have students work in groups, and distribute to each group several parenting magazines and books. Ask groups to look through the books and magazines in order to learn what these publications say about developmental milestones. You could assign a specific milestone for each group to focus on, such as infancy, toddlerhood, or early childhood. Have each group report on what their publications say about that period of time in a child's life by responding to the following questions:

- What are some key milestones children in this stage should accomplish?
- What are the age ranges for different milestones?
- What advice do these publications give if a child doesn't reach a milestone at the appropriate time?

■ TEACHING TIP

Students should understand that the timing for developmental milestones isn't etched in stone. Parents who don't understand these time ranges may endure unnecessary worry and heartache as they wait for their child to develop "on time."

tr A four-color transparency of Figure 4.2, Motor Development, is available in the **Overhead Transparencies Set.**

trb At this point, you may wish to use **Cooperative Learning Activity:** *Identifying Developmental Landmarks* (*Teacher's Resource Binder*, p. 4-1; **Handout 4–4**) and **Enrichment Lesson:** *"Normal" Height and Weight* (*Teacher's Resource Binder*, p. 4-1).

■ LOOKING AT THE ISSUES

Some researchers believe that critical periods exist for certain aspects of development. Have students do research about the story of Genie, the girl from California who was severely abused by her father and kept isolated in a room for 13 years. (Information about Genie can be found in Module 3.)

- Is there a critical period for learning how to walk and talk? What evidence supports your views?
- What should parents do to encourage their children's development? What preventative measures can parents take to combat developmental delays?

V At this point, you may wish to show **Videocassette:** *Scientific American Frontiers,* **Second Edition, Segment 25: "The Magic Years"** (*Teacher's Resource Binder*, p. 4-1).

trb At this point, you may wish to use **Application Activity:** *Physical Development* (*Teacher's Resource Binder*, p. 4-1; **Handout 4–5** and **Transparency Masters 4–1a** through **4–2b**) and **Enrichment Lesson:** *"Normal" Height and Weight* (*Teacher's Resource Binder*, p. 4-1).

Motor Development

Physical skills and muscular coordination are products of the developing brain. The neural pathways and muscles necessary for crawling (or scooting on your bottom) mature before the pathways and muscles for walking. We all walk before we run because we are developmentally ready to walk before we are ready to run (Figure 4.2).

Unfortunately, those developmental charts that show "normal" ages for crawling, standing, and walking haunt some new parents. I've seen parents trying to force their child to crawl, ignoring the baby's tearful protests, as a "deadline for normal behavior" approached. Here's some good advice you can give if you see a parent prodding a child to "catch up": Relax! Developmental charts provide age *ranges.* In this country, 25 percent of the babies walk at 11 months. Within a week of their first birthday, 50 percent are walking, and almost all of the remaining 50 percent will walk sometime shortly thereafter. The child's brain creates the readiness for crawling or

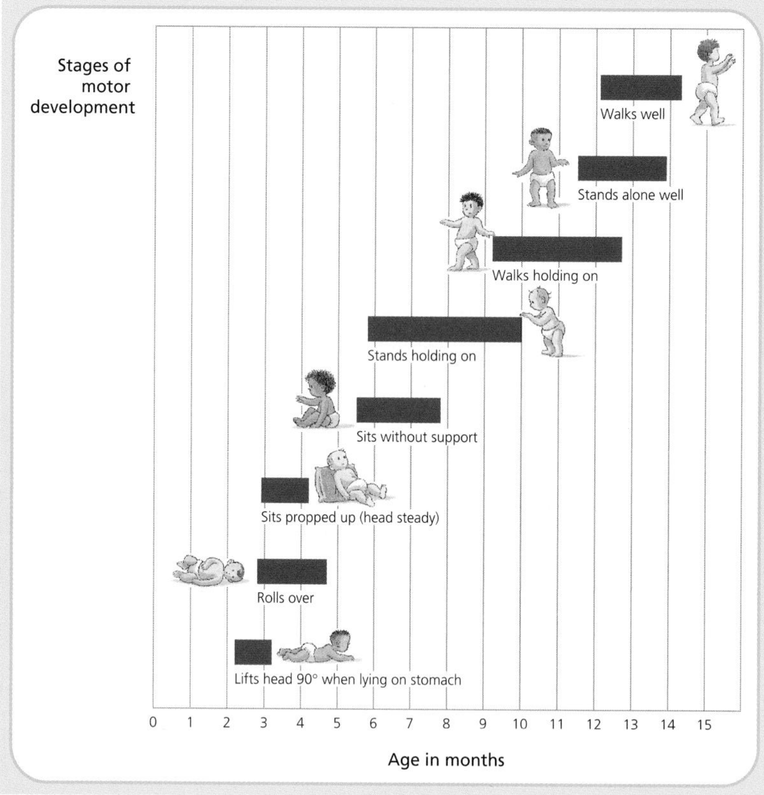

Figure 4.2 **Motor Development** Some infants reach each milestone ahead of others, but the order of the stages is the same for all infants. The colored bars show developmental norms—the ages at which infants master the motor skill. The left end of the bar indicates the age by which 50 percent have mastered the movement. The right end of the bar indicates the age by which 90 percent have mastered the movement.

Cross-Curricular Connections

FAMILY AND CONSUMER SCIENCE Team up with the family and consumer science teacher in your school to develop a lesson on child development. The following ideas may be incorporated into the lesson:

- Have students work in groups, and provide each group with a baby profile (include the baby's age, general health, etc.). Within groups, have students discuss what they might do to care for their baby. Ask each group to develop a journal of their caregiving experience, detailing what they did to care for their baby in terms of feedings, diaper changing, and so on. Some groups might approach child care as single caregivers while others might approach it as caregiving couples.
- Have students develop a budget for taking care of a baby during the first year of life. Have them design a nursery, find potential child care, and price baby products (diapers, strollers, and so on).

walking, not the parent's prodding. The same holds true for all physical skills, including bladder and bowel control. Before a baby achieves the needed neural and muscular maturation, no amount of begging, bribing, or scolding will accomplish toilet training. Knowledge of this fact helped my wife and me potty-train our daughters (when they were ready, not when we were ready) in a few days instead of a prolonged period of several months.

Cognitive Development in Infancy and Childhood

Piaget's Cognitive Stages

4. Who was Jean Piaget, and what did he contribute to our understanding of how children's thought processes develop?

Few people have had a greater impact on developmental psychology than Swiss psychologist **Jean Piaget** (pronounced pee-ah-ZHAY). In 1920, Piaget was working on intelligence tests and determining the age at which children were likely to answer questions correctly. However, Piaget became very interested in the *incorrect* responses children gave, cleverly realizing there was a lot to learn from wrong answers. Children at a given age were making remarkably similar mistakes.

Over the next 50 years, Piaget advanced the belief that the way children think and solve problems depends on their stage of cognitive development. **Cognition** refers to all the mental activities associated with thinking, knowing, and remembering. Children know less than you and I know, but they also think *differently.* Trying to explain to a 3-year-old how you exchange pretend money for property gets you nowhere. Tell an 8-year-old that Boardwalk costs $400, and you're playing Monopoly. But given your more advanced reasoning skills, that same 8-year-old will not stand much of a chance against you if you're playing a game of strategy.

Piaget wrote that all people, even as infants, constantly face and adapt to environmental challenges. We do so by developing **schemas** (sometimes called *schemes*), which are concepts or mental frameworks that organize and interpret information. As a toddler, for example, your schema for getting food may have been to pull on the pant leg of the nearest adult, or to start to cry. By now you have countless schemas, from how to start the car to how to go about asking someone to watch a movie with you. How did you develop all of these helpful mental plans? Piaget's answer would be that you used two different experiences:

- **Assimilation**—interpreting your new experiences in terms of your existing schemas.
- **Accommodation**—adapting your current schemas to incorporate new information.

▶ **Jean Piaget** (1896–1980) Pioneer in the study of developmental psychology who introduced a stage theory of cognitive development that led to a better understanding of children's thought processes.

▶ **cognition** All the mental activities associated with thinking, knowing, and remembering.

▶ **schemas** Concepts or mental frameworks that organize and interpret information.

▶ **assimilation** Interpreting one's new experience in terms of one's existing schemas.

▶ **accommodation** Adapting one's current understandings (schemas) to incorporate new information.

tb ■ CHECKING FOR UNDERSTANDING

Here are several ways to assess students' comprehension:

- Assign any or all of the journal questions or prompts for an in-class writing assessment.
- Assign to a group or pair a journal question or prompt for an oral response. Correct any misconceptions that may arise during the presentation.
- Use questions from the *Test Bank* for a quick assessment of students' knowledge of the concepts.

■ MULTICULTURAL CONNECTIONS

Are the stages of cognitive development as described by Piaget true for children of different cultures? Encourage students to do research on whether Piaget's theory describes cognitive development of children in non-Western cultures.

trb At this point, you may wish to use Application Activity: *Musk LifeSavers* (*Teacher's Resource Binder*, p. 4-1).

F • Y • I

Jean Piaget was a child prodigy who excelled in many areas, including zoology (in which he obtained his PhD), cognitive psychology, and education. His impact on education and psychology was so influential that he was named one of *Time* magazine's 100 Most Important People of the Twentieth Century.

MODULE 4

■ **TEACHING TIP**

Another example of simple schemas comes from the Disney movie *Bambi.* When the young Bambi is sniffing the flowers with his rabbit friend Thumper, a little skunk pokes his head up through the flowers to say hello. Bambi, having just learned the word *flower,* immediately calls the skunk "Flower," mistaking the skunk for what he was smelling.

tr A four-color transparency of Figure 4.3, Assimilation and Accommodation, is available in the **Overhead Transparencies Set.**

trb At this point, you may wish to use **Application Activity:** *Lollipops and Gloquex* (*Teacher's Resource Binder,* p. 4-1).

■ **JOURNAL WRITING**

Invite students to use the following questions and prompts as springboards for entries in their psychology journals:

- Recall a time when your schema about a situation or person was wrong. How did you assimilate new information? Did you accommodate your schema to adapt to the new information?
- Have you recently accommodated a schema? Describe your experience, explaining why you had to change your previous schema.

Two-year-old Jocelyn has learned the schema for "dog" from her picture books.

Jocelyn sees a cat and calls it a "dog." She is trying to assimilate this new animal into an existing schema. Her mother tells her, "No, it's a cat."

Jocelyn accommodates her schema for 4-legged animals and continues to modify that schema to include different kinds of dogs and cats in the neighborhood.

Figure 4.3 **Assimilation and Accommodation**

Children assimilate and accommodate all the time. Consider a 2-year-old, whose simple schema for *dog* is *four-legged animal.* This concept works wonderfully for all the dogs in the neighborhood, but not for the cats. The toddler must accommodate or modify her schema to account for four-legged animals that are not doggies (Figure 4.3).

Now consider another example, using a relatively familiar behavior: inviting someone to a movie. You may have learned how to ask someone to a movie by observing older siblings, watching actors on TV, or listening to friends, but at some point, you developed your own ask-to-a-movie schema. Asking someone you've just met is a new experience, which you must *assimilate* into your existing schema. But wait! What if that schema doesn't work as it has in the past? What if the person turns you down? Simple. You *accommodate* your existing schema, incorporating this new information into your existing mental plan. So, if part of your movie-asking schema was "Call Friday for a Saturday night show" and the person you called said, "I already have plans," perhaps you accommodate by calling earlier in the week the next time around.

In addition to explaining how we form plans to organize and interpret information, Piaget proposed that we all pass through four separate stages of cognitive development on our journey from childhood to adulthood. Table 4.1 describes Piaget's sensorimotor, preoperational, concrete operational, and formal operational stages.

▶ **sensorimotor stage** In Piaget's theory, the stage (from birth to about 2 years of age) during which infants know the world mostly in terms of their sensory impressions and motor activities.

▶ **object permanence** The awareness that things continue to exist even when you cannot see or hear them.

Sensorimotor Stage (Birth to About Age 2)

According to Piaget, during the **sensorimotor stage** you learned about the world by mouthing, grasping, looking, hearing, and touching. These sensory and motor interactions with objects provided you with information and helped you develop schemas.

You focused on things you could perceive through your senses. At first, things that you couldn't see or hear did not exist. Once you devel-

Meeting Individual Needs

trb GRAPHIC ORGANIZER Provide learning opportunities for all levels of learners with one of the following options for using **Building Vocabulary: Graphic Organizer:** *Development Charts* (*Teacher's Resource Binder,* p. 4-1; **Handouts 4–2a** and **4–2b**).

- **Independent Learners** Students may fill out the organizers on their own or follow along in class during discussion and lecture.
- **Cooperative Learners** Students may use the textbook as a resource and work in groups to find the answers that fit in the blanks.
- **Exceptional Learners** The graphic organizer can fill a special education need to provide notes for exceptional students. These students may fill in the blanks independently, with a student or teacher/tutor, or along with class discussion and lecture.

TYPICAL AGE RANGE	DESCRIPTION OF STAGE	KEY DEVELOPMENTAL EVENTS
Birth to nearly 2 years	*Sensorimotor* Experiencing the world through senses and actions (looking, touching, mouthing, and grasping)	• Object permanence
About 2 to 6 or 7 years	*Preoperational* Representing things with words and images but lacking logical reasoning	• Pretend play • Egocentrism • Language development
About 7 to 11 years	*Concrete operational* Thinking logically about concrete events; grasping concrete analogies and performing arithmetical operations	• Conservation • Mathematical transformations
About 12 through adulthood	*Formal operational* Abstract reasoning	• Abstract logic • Potential for mature moral reasoning

TABLE 4.1 PIAGET'S STAGES OF COGNITIVE DEVELOPMENT

Jean Piaget

oped **object permanence,** you became aware that things continue to exist even when you cannot see or hear them. You can test this idea yourself if you know a child who is about 8 months old. Hide one of the child's favorite toys behind your back and watch what happens. If the baby crawls around you to get the toy, you're witnessing object permanence. If the child simply sits and looks away, this little person has probably not yet developed object permanence.

Object permanence is a sensorimotor milestone because it is evidence of a working memory. Piaget assumed object permanence was not possible until around 8 months of age, but research indicates that he underestimated a young child's abilities. Piaget did not think children could think or deal with abstract ideas, but other researchers have produced evidence of early logical thinking. Consider the following:

- One-month-old babies were allowed to suck on one of two pacifiers without looking at either (Figure 4.4). Later, when the infants were shown the same two pacifiers, they looked primarily at the pacifier they had *felt* in their mouth, indicating the memory necessary for object permanence (Meltzoff & Borton, 1979). This study was later repeated with babies just 12 hours old, with similar results (Kaye & Bower, 1994).
- At 5 months of age, babies stare longer or do "double takes" at impossible situations (Wynn, 1992). The

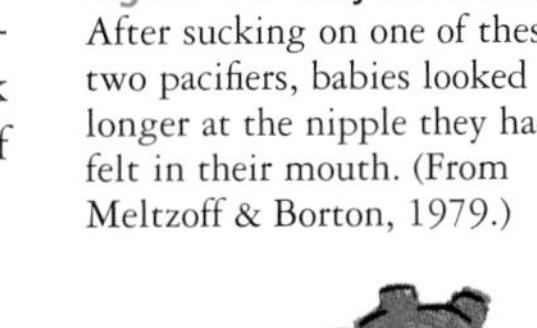

Figure 4.4 Early Memories After sucking on one of these two pacifiers, babies looked longer at the nipple they had felt in their mouth. (From Meltzoff & Borton, 1979.)

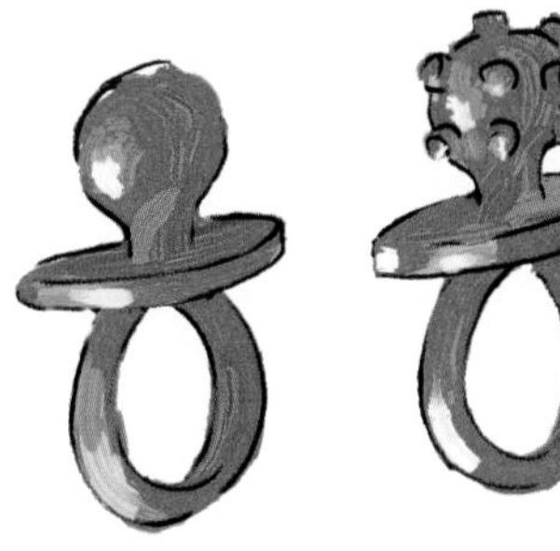

Enriching

Students may be interested in learning more about the sensorimotor stage. It can be broken down into three different substages:

- **Primary circular reactions** involve babies interacting and experimenting with their own bodies. They enjoy sucking, moving their arms and legs, and making noises with their mouths.
- **Secondary circular reactions** occur when babies respond to other people or objects. They learn that their actions elicit responses from others, so they will repeat actions over and over to get the desired response (such as a smile from mommy).
- **Tertiary circular reactions** take babies even further as they explore the outside world. Usually they will accidentally cause an event to occur, like kicking a ball. Then they will devise new activities with that object to make it do other things, like bouncing the ball or putting it in a box and taking it out over and over again.

■ TEACHING TIP

Help students remember the definition of the sensorimotor stage by breaking down the word itself into *sensory* and *motor.* Remind students that babies are sensory beings—that is, they put objects in their mouths, look intently at stimuli that interest them, and listen to their mother's voice or soothing sounds. Babies are also constantly moving, even before they crawl and walk—that is, they move their bodies, often by accident, to discover what they are capable of and what objects within their reach can do.

trb tr A black-line master for Table 4.1, Piaget's Stages of Cognitive Development, is available in the **Black-Line Masters Appendix** of the *Teacher's Resource Binder.*

trb At this point, you may wish to use **Technology Application Activity:** ***PsychSim:* "Cognitive Development"** (*Teacher's Resource Binder,* p. 4-1).

■ LOOKING AT THE ISSUES

Parents eager to expose their children to many learning opportunities start the children in various lessons (swimming, musical instruments, dance, reading, and so on) as early as the first year of life. Have students discuss some pros and cons of starting very young children in educational opportunities. Ask students how they think parents use knowledge about the cognitive development of children to help their children succeed and avoid anxiety when attempting new skills.

trb At this point, you may wish to use **Cooperative Learning Activity:** ***Identifying Developmental Landmarks*** (*Teacher's Resource Binder,* p. 4-1; **Handout 4–4**).

F • Y • I

After infants have mastered *object permanence,* they engage in something called *directed groping,* in which they will move in different ways to achieve a goal. They may use sticks or other objects to help get objects they want.

MODULE 4

F • Y • I

Children move through two stages of language development in the preoperational stage.

- **Holographic speech** appears around 1 year of age and involves using single words to stand for a whole sentence of meaning. For example, a child may say the word *ball* with varying inflections to mean anything from "I want the ball" to "Where is the ball?"
- **Telegraphic speech** appears around 2 years of age and involves two-word phrases that communicate more meaning. For example, children may differentiate desires by saying "want ball" and "where ball?" instead of just saying "ball."

TEACHING TIPS

tr (1) A four-color transparency of Figure 4.5, Early Object Permanence?, is available in the **Overhead Transparencies Set**.

(2) Understanding of conservation depends on understanding of reversibility. If children were able to think about situations both forward and backward, they would not have trouble with conservation.

trb **tr** A black-line master for Figure 4.6, Conservation Problem, is available in the **Black-Line Masters Appendix** of the *Teacher's Resource Binder*.

trb At this point, you may wish to use **Critical Thinking Activity:** *Demonstrating Preoperational Thought* (*Teacher's Resource Binder*, p. 4-1) or **Critical Thinking Activity:** *Conservation and Jelly Beans* (*Teacher's Resource Binder*, p. 4-1).

1. Objects placed in case.
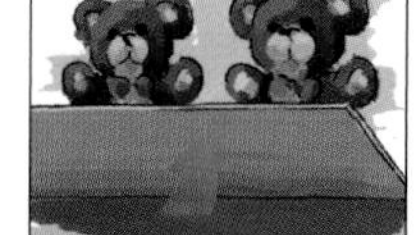
2. Screen comes up.

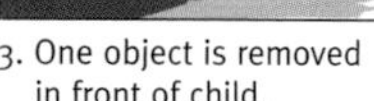
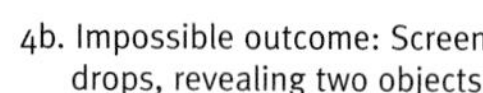
3. One object is removed in front of child.

4a. Possible outcome: Screen drops, revealing one object

4b. Impossible outcome: Screen drops, revealing two objects.

Figure 4.5 Early Object Permanence? Shown a numerically impossible outcome, 5-month-old infants stare longer, a finding that supports the development of object permanence far earlier than Piaget assumed. (From Wynn, 1992.)

example in Figure 4.5 shows how researchers observed this behavior. Infants also show surprise when a puppet that usually jumps three times jumps only twice (Wynn, 1998). Piaget would not have predicted that such young children could show either cognitive awareness of change or numerical thinking skills.

Preoperational Stage (Age 2 to About 6 or 7)

Piaget defined the **preoperational stage** as a time when children can use language but are not yet able to think logically. Show 5-year-olds two identical, clear glass beakers, each with 1000 milliliters of blue liquid in them, and they'll know the beakers hold the same amount. However, if you then pour the contents of one beaker into a taller, narrower beaker, causing the water line to move up, the children will probably tell you the new beaker now holds more liquid. Though the different-sized beakers hold the same amount of liquid, 5-year-olds typically focus only on the height dimension. These children lack **conservation,** an understanding that properties such as mass and volume remain the same even if you change an object's form. Without this understanding, 5-year-olds do not have the cognitive skills to mentally pour the tall beaker's contents back into the regular beaker (Figure 4.6).

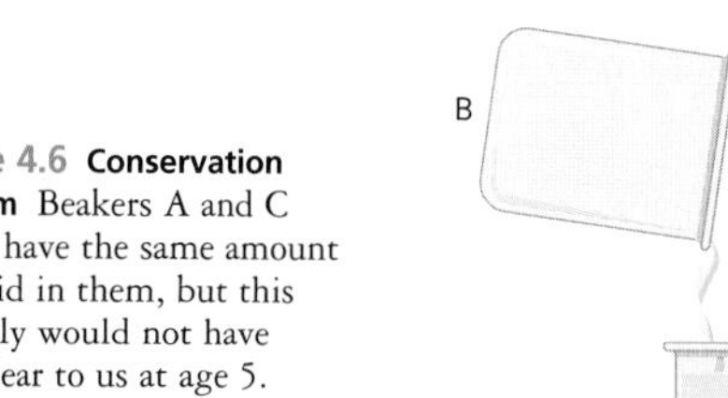

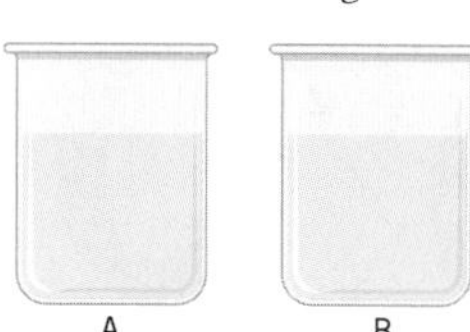

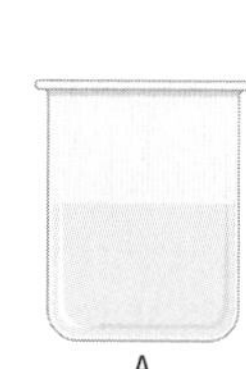

Figure 4.6 Conservation Problem Beakers A and C clearly have the same amount of liquid in them, but this probably would not have been clear to us at age 5.

Enriching

Children misunderstand conservation in several ways:

- **Volume** As described in the text, children believe that different-shaped containers hold different amounts of liquid.
- **Length** Children believe that an object's shape changes its mass. Taking a ball of Play-Doh and making a snake out of it will lead a child to believe that some of the Play-Doh is missing.
- **Area** Children believe that rearranging parts of an object changes it fundamentally.

If your students have access to young children, invite them to test these concepts and report their findings at the next class meeting.

Preoperational children develop language skills but their communication is often egocentric. **Egocentrism** is the inability to take another's point of view. Thus, preoperational children are likely to say whatever is on their minds without taking into account what others have said. Egocentrism shows up in the actions and statements of young children. Many years ago, my oldest daughter used to close her eyes when she didn't "want anybody to see" her. Ask a 4-year-old why the sun shines in the morning and you might hear the answer, "To wake me up."

We've learned that taking another's viewpoint, a form of symbolic thinking, appears earlier in the preoperational mind than Piaget thought. In one study, 3-year-olds were able to use a scale model of a real room to locate a hidden stuffed animal. If "little Snoopy" was hidden under a pillow in the scale model, 3-year-olds knew to look under the pillow in the real room 80 percent of the time. However, only 30 percent of $2\frac{1}{2}$ year-olds knew where to look for little Snoopy in the real room (DeLoache, 1987). Piaget did not see stage transitions as abrupt, and he probably would have been surprised that six months made such a difference in children's ability to use the scale model of a room as a symbol.

Concrete Operational Stage (Age 7 to About 11)

Piaget believed that in the **concrete operational stage,** children think logically and comprehend that mass and volume stay the same despite changes in the forms of objects (a sign of *conservation*). They understand that change in shape does not affect quantity. Whether you roll a batch of dough into one big loaf of bread or divide it into two dozen rolls, a child at this stage will know you're still cooking with the same amount of dough.

Children in the concrete operational stage, Piaget said, can comprehend mathematical transformations. They enjoy math-based jokes that used to be over their heads, like this joke:

> A king asked his baker to bring him a pie. When the baker brought a pie cut in six pieces, the king yelled at the baker, "Why didn't you bring me a pie cut in two pieces? I could never eat six."

Formal Operational Stage (Age 12 and Over)

Concrete reasoning requires actual experience. Thinkers in the **formal operational stage** can reason systematically and use imagined symbols and realities to think abstractly about things they may not have experienced. The ability to create and use the strategies necessary to play Monopoly or chess is a sign of formal operational thought. Think of the abstract reasoning necessary to understand algebra and geometry. Concrete thinkers would struggle in these classes. Young adolescents, said Piaget, become capable of solving hypothetical problems.

► **preoperational stage** In Piaget's theory, the stage (from about 2 to 6 or 7 years of age) during which a child learns to use language but does not yet comprehend the mental operations of concrete logic.

► **conservation** The principle (which Piaget believed to be a part of concrete operational reasoning) that properties such as mass, volume, and number remain the same despite changes in the forms of objects.

► **egocentrism** In Piaget's theory, the inability of the preoperational child to take another's point of view.

► **concrete operational stage** In Piaget's theory, the stage of cognitive development (from about 6 or 7 to 11 years of age) during which children gain the mental skills that let them think logically about concrete events.

► **formal operational stage** In Piaget's theory, the stage of cognitive development (normally beginning about age 12) during which people begin to think logically about abstract concepts and form strategies.

Enriching

Students may be interested in several ways that *egocentrism* manifests itself in children.

- Preoperational children playing together often engage in **collective monologues**—they will appear to be talking to each other in a dialogue, but they are really talking about two completely different subjects.
- In **animism,** children believe that nature is alive and controllable by them or their parents. To them, trees have feelings and the world is created just for them.
- **Artificialism** results when children believe natural phenomena are created by people—for example, children may believe that mountains were created by someone piling up a bunch of dirt.

trb At this point, you may wish to use **Enrichment Lesson:** *Preoperational Thought and Moral Development* (*Teacher's Resource Binder,* p. 4-1).

■ APPLYING THE POINTS

Develop a partnership with an elementary school or preschool in your area so that your students can interact with young children and learn how young children interact socially and intellectually, as well as how children process information as they try to solve problems in reading or math. Encourage students to write a narrative about their experiences as tutors and/or pen pals.

trb At this point, you may wish to use **Application Activity:** *Intellectual Development* (*Teacher's Resource Binder,* p. 4-1; **Handout 4–6**).

■ TEACHING TIP

Concrete operational thinking differs from *preoperational thinking* only in that concrete operational thinkers can understand the concepts preoperational children cannot. When conservation makes sense to concrete operational children, they become less egocentric.

trb At this point, you may wish to use **Critical Thinking Activity:** *Demonstrating Preoperational Thought* (*Teacher's Resource Binder,* p. 4-1).

trb ■ APPLYING THE POINTS

Invite a group of preoperational children to class (or visit their school) and conduct Piagetian tasks with them. Warn students that the younger children, who are solidly preoperational, will be pleased at their great performance on the tasks. Older children, who are moving toward concrete operations, may wonder if they are being tricked or if your students are a little dim themselves!

Overall, your students should encourage the children, regardless of their responses. If the children get the wrong answers, that does not reflect on intelligence.

trb At this point, you may wish to use **Critical Thinking Activity:** *Demonstrating Preoperational Thought* (*Teacher's Resource Binder,* p. 4-1), **Application Activity:** *Intellectual Development* (*Teacher's Resource Binder,* p. 4-1; **Handout 4–6**), and **Critical Thinking Activity:** *The Water-Level Task* (*Teacher's Resource Binder,* p. 4-1; **Handout 4–7**).

■ **TEACHING TIP**

Remind students that formal operational thought is a stage that might not be the be-all and end-all of cognitive thinking. Some studies have shown that even college students have trouble with some of Piaget's formal operational problems, while young children have solved some of the same problems. Piaget himself admitted that some people do not reach this stage. Others have suggested that even more stages exist beyond formal operations.

■ **MULTICULTURAL CONNECTIONS**

Are the language difficulties of Aborigines in Australia the only example of the cultural limitations of Piaget's theory? Using library or Internet resources, have students explore how well Piaget's cognitive tasks extend beyond developed Western cultures.

They can figure out the answer to "*If* this, *then* what" questions, such as the following:

> Whenever Emily goes to school, Meredith also goes to school. Emily went to school. What can you say about Meredith?

Every formal operational thinker answers this question with ease—but so do most 7-year-olds (Suppes, 1982), who do not fit Piaget's expected age range for this stage. Once again, recent research differs from Piaget's expectations; the mental skills that form the basis for Piaget's stages appear earlier than he predicted.

Assessing Piaget

5. Has recent research changed the way we view cognitive development?

We've seen that Piaget underestimated children's abilities in virtually every stage of his theory. Further, most developmental psychologists now believe development is fairly *continuous,* rather than divided into the discrete stages Piaget proposed. And Piaget's work did not reflect the effects of culture on cognitive development. For example, if you were raised an Aborigine in Australia, your language would have number words only up to five; all numbers or quantities after that are simply called "many." This language difference appears to delay the development of quantity conservation (Dasen, 1994).

Nevertheless, Piaget's identification of cognitive milestones broke new ground. Stimulated by his work, thousands of researchers ran experiments on how the mind develops and wrote countless articles on children. Piaget taught us that we learn best when the lesson builds on what we already know. He showed that new reasoning abilities require the stepping stones of previous abilities. Further, he taught us that children cannot reason using adult logic, and that it is unrealistic to expect a 3-year-old to reason like a 7-year-old. Piaget provided a wonderful base on which other researchers could build our current understanding of cognitive development.

Social Development in Infancy and Childhood

6. When and why do infants develop stranger anxiety?

Friends of ours recently called my wife and me to come over and watch their 9-month-old son take some wobbly steps as he was learning to walk. The excitement in their voices was clear: Baby Ethan was

Reteaching

Set up a lab practicum in which students must identify different Piagetian tasks and which concept each task measures.

trb At this point, you may wish to use **Application Activity:** *Intellectual Development* (*Teacher's Resource Binder*, p. 4-1; **Handout 4–6**).

taking his first steps! When we arrived, Ethan's father was changing his son's diaper, so we sat for a moment waiting for the baby's grand entrance. His dad brought Ethan in, placed him in a standing position, and encouraged him to walk. However, much to the dismay of his parents, Ethan took one look at us and started crying loudly enough to make the dog get up and leave the room. The child then started grabbing at his father's legs, frantically trying to climb up to safety.

Stranger Anxiety!

Now, I don't exactly think of myself as scary looking, but the fact is Ethan was frightened by what he saw. His reaction to me was normal for his age and was a classic sign of **stranger anxiety.** Around the age of 8 months, children have established schemas for familiar faces and often greet strangers with crying and distress. Ethan had not assimilated my face into any of his existing schemas.

Ethan's reaction shows how physical, cognitive, and social-emotional behaviors develop simultaneously. A few months later, we thought we'd give Ethan another try. We invited Ethan's family to our house, and he was fine when he came in. Then, my wife made the mistake of reaching out her arms and asking, "May I hold you?" Ethan immediately tightened his grip on his mother, and started saying "No!" with plenty of volume. This time, Ethan was showing *attachment* to his mother. Let's take a closer look at attachment and its effects on development.

Attachment

7. How does attachment develop, and how does it affect the relationship between infant and parent?

Attachment is an emotional tie with another person, shown by seeking closeness on a regular basis and distress on separation. At least three elements contribute to the infant-parent bond that forms during attachment. They are body contact, familiarity, and responsiveness.

Body Contact

Which is more important to fostering attachment: being fed or being held? Are you more likely to become attached to the person who nourishes you or to the person who provides you *contact comfort?* For years, developmental psychologists thought this question was a no-brainer. Surely, providing nourishment is the way to an infant's heart. Then in the 1950s, psychologist **Harry Harlow** tested this idea, using infant monkeys to assess whether food or the contact comfort of something cuddly is more important for attachment.

▶ **stranger anxiety** The fear of strangers that infants commonly display, beginning by about 8 months of age.

▶ **attachment** An emotional tie with another person; young children demonstrate attachment by seeking closeness to the caregiver and showing distress on separation.

▶ **Harry Harlow** (1906–1981) Psychologist who researched the relationship of body contact and nourishment to attachment, using infant monkeys and artificial mothers.

Enriching

Have students brainstorm about different childhood experiences that might produce more anxiety for children than others, such as the circus, big birthday parties, and theme parks—events that tend to be big, loud, and full of larger-than-life characters that may produce anxiety in a child. Conduct a discussion about these experiences by posing the following questions:

- How could parents make such situations less stressful for their children?
- Should parents expose only children of a certain age to these events? Why or why not?

F•Y•I

Provide students with the following advice about approaching a child with stranger anxiety:

- *Get permission from the child's parent before approaching.* If the parent greets you in a positive way, the child will be more likely to view you as friendly.
- *Approach the child on his or her level.* Crouch down to the child's eye level so he or she doesn't feel intimidated by your height.
- *Ask him or her to interact with you in a casual way.* For example, ask the child to give you "five" or to tell you what kittens say. Children are more likely to respond to these simple requests than to questions like "How are you doing today?"
- *If the child is very shy or nervous around you, back off and play with his or her toys.* The child will soon get over his or her inhibitions and play with you.

V At this point, you may wish to show Videocassette: *The Mind,* Second Edition, Module 15: "Social Development in Infancy" (*Teacher's Resource Binder,* p. 4-1).

■ **MULTICULTURAL CONNECTIONS**

International adoptions have been on the rise in recent years, and concerns about the quality of care in orphanages in foreign countries have increased as adoptive parents must overcome the neglect and ill treatment suffered by their new children. Using library or Internet resources, students may explore the policies for international adoptions and the quality of child care in orphanages in different countries around the world. You may wish to have interested students write a report on their findings for extra credit.

MODULE 4

F • Y • I

Harry Harlow's work on parental love was done during a time when psychologists and physicians believed that isolating children would protect them from disease. By showing that human contact and affection were important to survival, Harlow went against the establishment in psychology that centered around a behavioristic view—that is, if it can't be seen, it shouldn't be studied.

■ LOOKING AT THE ISSUES

Harry Harlow went further in his research by studying the effects of abuse and neglect on infants. After he subjected his monkeys to isolation, neglect, and even abuse to see if they adapted, he observed their responses. Have students explore these issues by considering the following questions:

- Should the same ethical constraints be imposed on animal research that exist for human subjects? Why or why not?
- Do Harlow's studies imply that women should be the primary caregivers for infants? Why or why not?

■ TEACHING TIP

Make a link between *familiarity* and *social psychology* by reminding students that the concept relates to the principle of the mere exposure effect. This effect demonstrates that being around an object long enough will cause one to develop an affection for the object. We tend to find objects, people, and places appealing and comfortable because we are around these things for extended periods of time.

Figure 4.7 **Out to Lunch** Harry Harlow's monkeys much preferred the soft, comfortable "mother" to the bare wire, wooden-headed "mother," even though the wire model provided nourishment. This discovery surprised many psychologists.

Harlow's infant monkeys could choose between two artificial mothers. One was foam rubber covered with soft terry cloth, and the other was a bare-wire cylinder. It was no surprise that if both "mothers" had a bottle attached for feeding, the baby monkeys preferred the soft, cuddly mother. But what if only the wire mother had the bottle? Which mother would the baby cling to when alarmed, or spend most of its time with? Harlow surprised psychologists (and parents) when he revealed that the infant monkeys preferred contact with the cuddly mother, even while feeding from the wire mother (Figure 4.7).

Attachment is not primarily a function of who provides the food. Human infants become attached to warm, soft parents who cuddle, rock, *and* feed.

Attachment provides an infant with a secure base from which to set out for wobbly explorations of the environment. Ethan needed the closeness of his mother, especially when he was stressed by the presence of someone he did not know. We still seek to maintain a secure base as we mature, though that base tends to become peers and partners (Cassidy & Shaver, 1999). As social creatures, we appear to have a greater chance of reaching our potential when we know a trusted friend or loved one will stand behind us, no matter what.

Familiarity

Body contact is one piece of the attachment puzzle; *familiarity* is another. My wife and I were unfamiliar faces to Ethan, so he pulled back to the safety of his parents. For some species, the attachment bond forms during a **critical period**—an optimal period shortly after birth when an organism's exposure to certain experiences produces proper development. **Konrad Lorenz** (1937) found that a newborn duckling, chick, or gosling will follow the first moving object it sees, which typically would be the little creature's mother. This process, known as **imprinting,** is a very adaptive response: Following and staying close to Mom provides safety and nourishment for these birds. Lorenz showed, however, that due to the critical period for attachment in baby birds, fledglings would imprint on black boots with yellow stripes, or on bouncing balls, if either of those objects were the first thing they saw (Johnson, 1992)! Ducklings that imprinted on the boots would follow those boots wherever they went, regardless of who was wearing them. Attachment in these animals is very hard to reverse once established.

THE FAR SIDE

When imprinting studies go awry . . .

Cross-Curricular Connections

BIOLOGY Have students explore the relationship between premature birth and parental contact. Have them interview a local obstetrician, pediatrician, or neonatal physician about the health-care procedures for infants born prematurely, both from the past and today. In their interviews, students should elicit answers to the following questions:

- To what illnesses are premature infants prone?
- How may human contact affect a newborn's health? What biological processes does human contact seem to impact?

Have students work individually or with partners to conduct their interviews. They may report their findings to the rest of the class.

Do humans have a similar critical period for attachment? No. Humans do not imprint, and babies who are adopted days, weeks, or even months after birth can become every bit as attached to their new caregiver as any child does to its birth parents. Familiarity fosters contentment, but human attachment develops gradually.

Responsiveness

The third element of the attachment bond is *responsiveness.* Responsive parents are very aware of what their children are doing, and they respond appropriately. Unresponsive parents often ignore their babies, helping them only when they feel like it. Mary Ainsworth (1979) found that responsiveness appears to affect whether a child is *securely* or *insecurely attached.* Securely attached children happily explore their environment when their primary caregiver is around. If that caregiver leaves, they appear distressed, and they go to their caregiver as soon as he or she returns. Insecurely attached children are often "clingy" and are less likely to explore and learn about the environment. When their caregiver leaves, they either cry loudly or show indifference to the caregiver's departure and return.

Dutch researcher Dymphna van den Boom (1990) designed a study to assess the role of the environment in attachment. She took 100 temperamentally difficult infants and randomly assigned half to a group in which their mothers received training on how to be a responsive caregiver, and half to a group where the mothers received no training. When the children reached their first birthday, van den Boom assessed their attachment to their mothers. A whopping 68 percent of the children whose mothers received training were deemed securely attached. Only 28 percent of the children in the other group were securely attached. Responsiveness matters.

Effects of Attachment

Does what we learn in the cradle last to the grave? Said differently, does secure or insecure attachment have long-term effects, or do these terms simply describe some bonds and behaviors limited to our early childhood? Consider the following:

- ***Secure attachment predicts social competence.*** Children identified as securely attached between the ages of 12 and 18 months were more outgoing, more confident, and more persistent in solving challenging tasks when restudied as 2- and 3-year-olds (Sroufe & others, 1983).
- ***Deprivation of attachment is linked to negative outcomes.*** Babies who grow up in institutions without a caregiver's regular stimulation and attention do not form normal attachments and often appear withdrawn and frightened (Carson, 1995). Physical

▶ **critical period** An optimal period shortly after birth when an organism's exposure to certain stimuli or experiences produces proper development.

▶ **Konrad Lorenz** (1903-1989) Researcher who focused on critical attachment periods in baby birds, a concept he called *imprinting.*

▶ **imprinting** The process by which certain animals form attachments during a critical period very early in life.

Enriching

The following procedure identifies the level of attachment in children.

Parent and infant enter an experimental room alone. The parent does not participate as the child explores. A stranger comes in the room, converses with the parent, and then approaches the child. The parent leaves the room inconspicuously.

In the *first separation episode,* the stranger's behavior is geared to that of the infant. In the *first reunion episode,* the parent greets and comforts the infant, then leaves again. In the *second separation episode,* the infant is alone. In the *continuation of the second separation episode,* the stranger enters and gears her behavior to that of the infant. In the *second reunion episode,* the parent enters, greets the infant, and picks up the infant. The stranger leaves the room inconspicuously.

Source: Ainsworth, M. D. S., Blehar, M. C., Waters, E., & Wall, S. (1978). *Patterns of attachment: A psychological study of the Strange Situation.* Hillsdale, NJ: Erlbaum.

F • Y • I

Mary Ainsworth worked for much of her career with John Bowlby, another leading figure in developmental psychology. It was Bowlby who developed the idea of separation anxiety. He believed this feeling was different from fear, which resulted from environmental cues, and anger or hostility, which resulted from being rejected by parents and family.

■ TEACHING TIP

It is important to remind students that children are usually distressed when their parents leave them. How infants behave when their parents are absent and how they react when their parents return indicate the level of attachment.

trb At this point, you may wish to use Enrichment Lesson: *Attachment Types* (*Teacher's Resource Binder,* p. 4-1).

■ LOOKING AT THE ISSUES

Parents who are slow or inconsistent in their responses to their children can foster insecure attachments. Using available resources, including the Internet, have students explore advice available to new parents about attachment.

- How can parents balance response to needs and a concern with spoiling their babies?
- Do babies cry in different ways to express different needs? How can parents know when their child is crying because of a need or crying for attention?
- How can parents foster an easy transition to child care?

Suggest that, for extra credit, interested students present their findings in a poster.

■ **LOOKING AT THE ISSUES**

Spanking has become a controversial issue in parenting today. Have students use library or Internet resources to research and discuss the following questions related to spanking:

- Should parents spank their children? When, why, and under what conditions? Why not?
- Do states have laws making a distinction between spanking and abuse? What are the distinctions?

trb At this point, you may wish to use Enrichment Lesson: *Spanking* (*Teacher's Resource Binder*, p. 4-1).

■ **JOURNAL WRITING**

Invite students to use the following questions and writing prompts as springboards for entries in their psychology journals. For these entries, tell students, "Imagine that you are the parent of a child who is very much the way you remember yourself at 5 or 6 years old."

- What would you give your child that you most wanted from your parents at a young age? Reflect on any difference between how you as a child felt about what you wanted and how you as a parent would feel about giving or not giving your child something that he or she most desires.
- Would you spank your child? Why or why not? How do you think this form of punishment would affect the child?
- What type of parenting style did your parents use in rearing you? Would you use the same style with your children? Why or why not?

trb At this point, you may wish to use Enrichment Lesson: *Spanking* (*Teacher's Resource Binder*, p. 4-1).

▶ **authoritarian parenting** Style of parenting marked by imposing rules and expecting obedience.

▶ **permissive parenting** Style of parenting marked by submitting to children's desires, making few demands, and using little punishment.

▶ **authoritative parenting** A style of parenting marked by making demands on the child, being responsive, setting and enforcing rules, and discussing the reasons behind the rules.

and emotional abuse often disrupts attachment as well. While most abused children show great resilience and do not grow up to be violent criminals or abusive parents, most abusive parents were, in fact, battered or emotionally abused as children (Kempe & Kempe, 1978).

- ***A responsive environment helps most infants recover from attachment disruption.*** Children who have been neglected but who are later adopted between the ages of 6 and 16 months at first have trouble sleeping, eating, and relating to their new parents (Yarrow & others, 1973). However, by age 10, this same group of adopted children showed virtually no adverse effects from the early neglect.

The evidence is consistent and clear. Children who have a warm relationship with familiar, responsive caregivers reap the benefits of secure attachment. Most often, attachment is a direct result of the parenting children receive. As long as parents are responsive, does their parenting *style* matter? Let's take a look.

Parenting Patterns

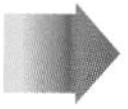

8. What are the three different parenting styles, and which one tends to have the best outcomes?

Roughly 9 in 10 people your age eventually wind up raising a child. Assume for a moment that you are the parent of a 2-year-old. What kind of parent are you? Do you spank? Try to talk everything out? Are you strict? Permissive? How will your parenting style affect your child's development?

Diana Baumrind (1971, 1996) was the first to describe the three main parenting styles and their characteristics (see Figure 4.8):

- **Authoritarian parenting:** These parents are low in warmth, and their version of discipline is strict and often physical. Communication is high from parent to child, but low from child to parent. Maturity expectations are high.

Which Style? Is this parent more likely to be authoritative or authoritarian?

Cooperative Learning

Divide students into groups and have members discuss any or all of the following prompts:

- Discuss your childhood nicknames or how you were referred to as children. Recall your feelings in response to these names.
- Introduce yourself to the members of your group as you might have been introduced by your parents when you were 5 years old, 10 years old, and currently. In addition, introduce yourself as you would have preferred your parents introduce you at any time in the past or in the present.

Source: Young, D. M., & Keppes, S. Y. (1988, August). *Techniques for exploring self-concept and self-esteem in the undergraduate classroom.* Paper presented at the 96th Annual Convention of the American Psychological Association, Atlanta, GA.

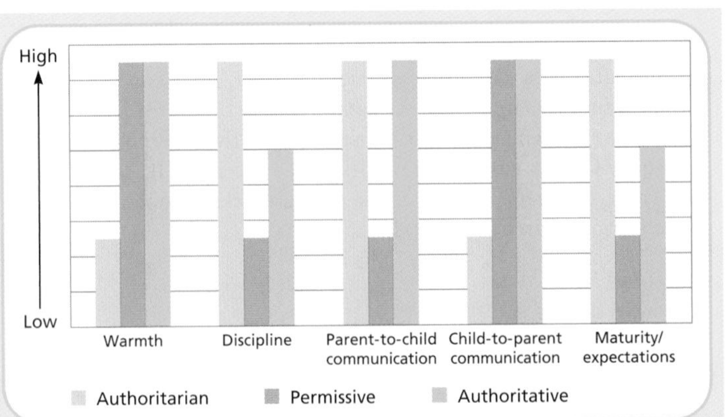

Figure 4.8 **Parenting Styles**

- **Permissive parenting:** These parents are high in warmth, but they rarely discipline their children. Communication is low from parent to child, but high from child to parent. Expectations of maturity are low.
- **Authoritative parenting:** These parents are high in warmth, and their version of discipline is moderate, with lots of talking and negotiating. These parents exert control by setting rules and enforcing them and by explaining the reasons behind the rules. Communication is high from parent to child *and* from child to parent. Maturity expectations are moderate.

Don't you realize, Jason, that when you throw furniture out the window and tie your sister to a tree, you make Mommy and Daddy very sad?

Does one form of parenting have a clear advantage over the other two? According to Baumrind and others, authoritative parents often produce children high in self-esteem, self-reliance, and social competence (Buri & others, 1988). These children are usually more successful, happy, and generous with others. What accounts for these findings? One factor may be that authoritative parents allow their children to develop a *sense of control* over their lives. People who believe they have some control over their destiny tend to be motivated and self-confident. Those without a sense of control are more likely to feel incompetent and helpless (Rohner, 1994).

Parenting style is not, however, a "one-size-fits-all" proposition. Bolder children often need more restrictive parenting, whereas fearful children often respond better to gentler parenting (Bates & others, 1998; Kochanska & Thompson, 1997). Cultural differences and expectations also influence parenting style (Wachs, 1999). For example, parents in cultures that emphasize respect for elders are more likely to use the authoritarian style.

■ TEACHING TIP

Emphasize that correlational evidence linking parenting style with certain childhood outcomes need not reveal cause and effect. For example, children's traits might influence parenting more than vice versa. Even when assuming a causal connection in which style shapes a child's traits, the style adopted depends in large part on what particular traits are prized.

tr A four-color transparency of Figure 4.8, Parenting Styles, is available in the **Overhead Transparencies Set.**

trb At this point, you may wish to use **Enrichment Lesson:** ***Attachment Types*** (*Teacher's Resource Binder*, p. 4-1).

■ MULTICULTURAL CONNECTIONS

Have students gain permission then interview students from different cultures about the way they were reared. Have students compare and contrast child-rearing practices in cultures other than the United States with those in the United States. Have students respond to the following questions:

- Do you think the child-rearing practices you learned exist in another culture are generally better or worse than those practiced in the United States? Give an example to support your response.
- What practices would you adopt for your own future children? Which would you reject? Why?

Reteaching

Help students remember the different types of parenting styles by associating each with a famous historical figure.

- *Authoritarian* can be associated with any oppressive dictator, from Hitler to Hussein.
- *Permissive* can be associated with the "laissez-faire" type of government that Thomas Jefferson advocated.
- *Authoritative* can be associated with the U.S. president, who is a symbol of democracy, where individuals are expected to be rational and law-abiding.

trb At this point, you may wish to use **Application Activity:** ***Parental Authority Questionnaire*** (*Teacher's Resource Binder*, p. 4-1; **Handout 4–8**).

MODULE 4

■ TEACHING TIP

You may have students in your class who are parents already. Encourage these students to discuss their child-rearing practices along with the pros and cons of being a teen parent. Discussion of these circumstances, hopefully, will help these students learn to be the best parents they can be by using psychological research as their guides.

Parenting is a challenging, full-time job. Anyone can make a baby, but it takes a lot of character to make a good parent. Few gifts are more important than a parent's investment of time, love, and warm responsiveness to their children. I am more likely to regret the time not spent with my children than the time spent with them. Perhaps Jacqueline Kennedy Onassis summed it up best when she said, "If you bungle raising your children, I don't think whatever else you do matters very much" (quoted in Lewis, 2002).

Three Key Developmental Issues

9. What are the three major issues in the study of developmental psychology?

We have looked at some of the important research on physical, cognitive, and social-emotional development during infancy and childhood. We can view this research, and other important work on development across the life span, in terms of three important issues that provide an organizing framework: *continuity and stages, stability and change, nature and nurture.* Here are some research results related to these issues in infancy and childhood.

Continuity and Stages

How is our development continuous, and how do we develop in stages? In some areas, such as attachment, development is a continuous process. Cognitive development is also more continuous than stagelike. But in other areas, such as motor development, we clearly pass through stages.

Stability and Change

What remains stable across our development, and how do we change? Temperament is relatively stable throughout the life span. But we can be thankful that change is possible for infants from neglectful backgrounds who move into more nurturing homes.

Nature and Nurture

How does the interaction of nature and nurture affect development? The interaction of both heredity and environment shapes a child's development. In the area of physical development, for example, environmental factors combine with a child's genetic tendencies to shape the fetus until the moment of birth. Two different outcomes stemming from this interaction are evident in the relative health of a child whose mother avoided alcohol and nicotine during pregnancy, and in the illnesses of children with FAS. In the area of cognitive development, children learn new behaviors based on developmental readiness, but also on whether they are raised in a stimulating or nonstimulating environment. And in the area of social development, children's interactions are influenced by both their inborn temperaments and the supportive or neglectful environments in which they are raised.

We have evidence for both continuity and stages in a child's growth. We see that children's lives have both stability and the capacity for change. And neither nature nor nurture has cornered the market on what makes us who we are.

Hi, Dad! Heredity plays a role in our development, but parenting and cultural effects matter more than this cartoon suggests.

R E V I E W

Review Module 4: Prenatal and Childhood Development

What's the Point?

The Beginnings of Life

1. *How do the zygote, embryo, and fetus differ from one another?*

   Zygote is a term applied to the developing human organism during the first two weeks of life. A zygote is a fertilized egg undergoing a period of rapid cell division. During this time, cells begin to have specialized functions. The stage of the embryo begins at about two weeks and ends at about eight weeks. By the end of the embryonic period, facial features, hands, feet, and most of the body's major organs have formed. The fetal period lasts from about eight weeks until birth. Teratogens—dangerous viruses, bacteria, or other substances that cross the placental barrier between mother and child—can harm the fetus, causing deformities or other problems related to abnormal development.

2. *Are humans completely helpless at birth?*

   Newborns are not helpless. They have a number of reflexes (automatic, unlearned responses), including the sucking, swallowing, and grasping reflexes. They also can turn toward familiar voices, and they prefer some tastes over others. Newborns demand more or less attention, depending on their temperament, a relatively stable personality characteristic that is present at birth.

■ **TEACHING TIP**

Structure a debate about the impact of nature and/or nurture in child-rearing. Since evidence exists for both, the debate should be lively. The resolutions students debate could include the following:

- People born with learning disabilities can expect only a certain level of achievement in school.
- Children in day care are more likely to be behavior problems at home and at school.
- Children born in poverty are more likely to be poor learners.

Close

Pose the three key questions in the study of development. Have students cite evidence above and beyond the text to support both sides of each question. The questions, again:

- Is development continuous or do we develop in stages?
- As we develop, is personality stable or does it change?
- How is development affected by the interaction of nature and nurture?

Checking the Points

■ **TEACHING TIPS**

web (1) The book companion site for *Thinking About Psychology* at www.worthpublishers.com/thinkingaboutpsych contains a module quiz, flashcards of key terms and people, as well as other student activities and resources for this module. You will also find PowerPoint lectures, a quiz grade book, and other teaching resources by logging on as an instructor.

trb (2) At this point, you may wish to review and confirm concepts about prenatal and childhood development with the **Critical Thinking Activity:** *Fact or Falsehood* (*Teacher's Resource Binder*, p. 4-10; **Handout 4–1**). If students worked with this handout earlier in the module, ask them not to refer to that version. Suggest that students complete the handout with partners, taking the time to look up information in the text to respond correctly to questions.

Physical Development in Infancy and Childhood

3. *What is maturation, and how does it affect memory and physical skills in infancy and childhood?*

   Maturation is a series of biological growth processes that result in predictable changes in behavior, such as crawling before walking, and walking before running. Experience has little effect on the sequence of changes that take place during maturation, but attentive care or extreme neglect can enrich or inhibit the behaviors a child engages in at any particular stage. Maturation is an important contributor to memory formation, because the brain of a toddler is not equipped to organize memories as an adult brain does.

Cognitive Development in Infancy and Childhood

4. *Who was Jean Piaget, and what did he contribute to our understanding of how children's thought processes develop?*

   Piaget proposed that we all move through a series of cognitive stages: the sensorimotor (birth to 2 years old), preoperational (from 2 to 6 or 7 years old), concrete operational (about 6 or 7 to about 11 years old), and formal operational (beginning at about age 12). At all ages, we organize and interpret information into schemas (concepts or mental frameworks). The way we do this is by assimilating new information, or incorporating it into our existing schemas, and by accommodating our schemas, or adapting them to include the new information. Perhaps Piaget's greatest contribution was to point out that the *way* children think differs from the way adults think. Piaget believed that in the earliest sensorimotor stage, children do not have object permanence—they do not know that objects exist when the objects are out of sight. In the preoperational stage, children are egocentric, or unable to take another person's viewpoint. In the concrete operational stage, children think logically but not abstractly, a quality they attain in the formal operational stage.

5. *Has recent research changed the way we view cognitive development?*

   Since Piaget's work, researchers have demonstrated that children's abilities are more continuous than Piaget believed—that their thinking abilities tend to resemble an inclined plane more than a set of stairs. Research also has shown that Piaget's theory underestimates children's abilities at each of his stages, and that it fails to accommodate the thinking patterns of children from cultures outside of western Europe or North America. But psychologists still respect Piaget's work for stimulating interest in how the mind develops, for showing that we learn by building on our previous experiences, and for showing that children cannot use adult logic to understand the world around them.

Social Development in Infancy and Childhood

6. *When and why do infants develop stranger anxiety?*

   Children begin to fear strangers at about 8 months. By this age, infants have established schemas for familiar faces, and the approach of strangers who don't fit those schemas elicits crying and distress responses.

7. *How does attachment develop, and how does it affect the relationship between infant and parent?*

   The attachment bond seems to have three separate strands: body contact, familiarity, and responsiveness. Harlow's studies of infant monkeys and artificial mothers showed that they chose the soft, cuddly "mother" as their secure base, not the hard, wire "mother" that provided food. Human babies do not imprint, as some birds do, but they do become attached to caregivers who are familiar figures—those who care for them on a regular basis. The degree to which a caregiver responds to a child tends to affect the quality of the attachment bond, which can range from insecure to secure attachment. There is some indication that this quality of attachment continues into adulthood and affects an individual's adult social relationships.

8. *What are the three different parenting styles, and which one tends to have the best outcomes?*
   Parents using an authoritarian parenting style tend to maintain an emotional distance from their children, impose strict rules, and enforce their authority with strict, often physical, discipline. Those using a permissive style behave very warmly toward their children, make few demands on them, submit to children's demands, and discipline rarely. Parents with an authoritative parenting style make demands on their children, are responsive to their needs, set and enforce rules, and discuss the reasons behind the rules. Studies indicate that parents who use an authoritative parenting style tend to have children who score high on self-esteem, self-reliance, and social competence.

Three Key Developmental Issues

9. *What are the three major issues in the study of developmental psychology?*
   The three key issues in developmental psychology are: continuity and stages, stability and change, nature and nurture. As infants and children, we tend to accumulate skills and knowledge in a somewhat continuous pattern, but we do mature in stages in some areas, as in motor development. We are to some extent stable (our temperament tends not to change), but we are capable of adapting to a new environment. And in the area of development, as in so many other areas, our heredity and our environment interact to make us who we are.

Key Terms

zygote, p. 58
genes, p. 58
embryo, p. 58
fetus, p. 58
teratogens, p. 58
fetal alcohol syndrome (FAS), p. 59
rooting reflex, p. 59
temperament, p. 60
maturation, p. 61
cognition, p. 63
schemas, p. 63
assimilation, p. 63
accommodation, p. 63
sensorimotor stage, p. 64
object permanence, p. 65
preoperational stage, p. 66
conservation, p. 66
egocentrism, p. 67
concrete operational stage, p. 67
formal operational stage, p. 67
stranger anxiety, p. 69
attachment, p. 69
critical period, p. 70
imprinting, p. 70
authoritarian parenting, p. 72
permissive parenting, p. 73
authoritative parenting, p. 73

Key People

Jean Piaget, p. 63
Harry Harlow, p. 69
Konrad Lorenz, p. 70

trb tr ■ **TEACHING TIP**

At this point, you may wish to provide students with **Building Vocabulary: Graphic Organizer:** ***Development Charts*** (***Teacher's Resource Binder***, p. 4-10; **Handouts 4–2a** and **4–2b**). Have students fill out this organizer as a tool for reviewing module vocabulary words and relating vocabulary to key concepts about development. Encourage students to fill in the graphic organizers individually, without referring to the text or copies of the organizer they may have filled out earlier in the module. Next, allow time for students to go over the charts with partners. Student pairs may now use the text to clarify confusing concepts and confirm responses.

You may also wish to use the handout as a transparency, insert answers in the charts, and project the completed charts for students to check their work.

MODULE 4

tb Using the Test Bank

The *Test Bank* that accompanies this textbook offers a wide variety of questions in different formats and levels of complexity. Use the software to construct whole tests or to integrate standardized questions into teacher-made tests.

Self-Test Answers

Multiple-Choice Questions

1. b, 2. a, 3. d, 4. c, 5. c, 6. a, 7. c

Self-Test

Multiple-Choice Questions

Choose the *best* answer for each of the following questions.

1. Monique is nine weeks into her pregnancy, and she had an appointment with her doctor today. She is very happy and excited because for the first time, she was able to hear her baby's heartbeat. Monique's baby is in the ______________ stage.
   a. preoperational c. embryonic
   b. fetal d. zygote

2. Zach and Annie are newborn twins, but they behave very differently. Annie responds very quickly to noises, cries frequently, and seems hungry all the time. Zach seems relaxed and happy, eats every four hours, and sleeps much of the time between meals. Zach and Annie seem to have different
   a. temperaments.
   b. levels of maturation.
   c. degrees of attachment.
   d. schemas.

3. Ashok's grandparents have come all the way from India to see their 8-month-old grandson for the first time. They are very sad, though, because Ashok cries and turns away when they go near him. Someone should tell Ashok's grandparents that his behavior is typical of babies at that age and is known as
   a. the rooting reflex.
   b. accommodation.
   c. conservation.
   d. stranger anxiety.

4. Laura's parents believe in the ______________ style of parenting. They have rules and make demands on Laura, and they enforce their rules with discipline. But they are careful to discuss their reasons for setting the rules, and they listen carefully to what Laura has to say.
   a. authoritarian c. authoritative
   b. permissive d. egocentric

5. At lunch today, Mark, who is 5 years old, complained that his milk glass had jelly on it and was making his fingers sticky. When Mark's mother poured his remaining milk into a taller, skinnier glass, Mark began to cry, saying that she had given him too much milk and he couldn't finish it. Mark apparently lacks an understanding of
   a. object permanence.
   b. accommodation.
   c. the principle of conservation.
   d. assimilation.

6. Rosa believes that she can remember being born in a taxi that was taking her mother to the hospital. Rosa's mother says that Rosa is unintentionally creating this memory from stories she has heard about the event. According to the evidence presented in this module,
   a. Rosa's mother is right, because children don't have enough of the right kind of neural connections in their brains to consciously remember things that happen before age 3.
   b. Rosa's mother is right, because children do not have object permanence before age 5, and Rosa could not therefore remember the taxi.
   c. Rosa is right, because research shows that we have vivid memories of events immediately surrounding our birth.
   d. Rosa is right, because research shows that children's memories may be slightly out of focus, but they are nevertheless valid memories.

7. After an atomic bomb was dropped on Hiroshima, Japan, during the Second

Alternative Assessment/Portfolio Project

trb CHILD STUDY Several projects in this module address different types of development in children ages 3 to 6. Include the following activities from the *Teacher's Resource Binder* as a part of a portfolio project.

- **tr** Application Activity: *Physical Development* (*Teacher's Resource Binder*, p. 4-1; Handout 4–5; Transparency Masters 4–1a through 4–2b)
- Application Activity: *Intellectual Development* (*Teacher's Resource Binder*, p. 4-1; Handout 4–6)
- Application Activity: *Social Development* (*Teacher's Resource Binder*, p. 4-1; Handout 4–9)

For more detailed instructions regarding this portfolio assessment, see *Teacher's Resource Binder*, p. 4-1; Handout 4–10. Modify the general rubric to suit your needs.

World War, many pregnant women exposed to the radiation gave birth to babies with severe deformities. The *radiation* was an example of

a. a critical period. c. a teratogen.
b. a schema. d. egocentrism.

Matching Terms and Definitions

8. For each definition, choose the *best* matching term from the list that follows.

Definition

a. Physical abnormalities (often including poorly proportioned facial features) and cognitive abnormalities in a child whose mother repeatedly drank large quantities of alcohol while pregnant.
b. Adapting one's current schemas to incorporate new information.
c. Interpreting one's new experience in terms of one's existing schemas.
d. In Piaget's theory, the stage of cognitive development (normally beginning about age 12) during which people begin to think logically about abstract concepts and to form strategies.
e. The awareness that things continue to exist even when you cannot see or hear them.
f. The fertilized egg, which undergoes a two-week period of rapid cell division.
g. An optimal period shortly after birth when an organism's exposure to certain stimuli or experiences produces proper development.
h. In Piaget's theory, the stage of cognitive development (from about 6 or 7 to 11 years of age) during which children gain the mental skills that let them think logically about concrete events.
i. A person's characteristic emotional reactivity and intensity.
j. All the mental activities associated with thinking, knowing, and remembering.

Term

(1) zygote
(2) fetus
(3) embryo
(4) fetal alcohol syndrome (FAS)
(5) cognition
(6) temperament
(7) assimilation
(8) accommodation
(9) object permanence
(10) sensorimotor stage
(11) preoperational stage
(12) concrete operational stage
(13) formal operational stage
(14) critical period
(15) attachment

Fill-in-the-Blank Questions

9. Konrad Lorenz's work on ____________ showed that newborn ducklings, chicks, and goslings would follow the first moving thing they saw after emerging from their eggs. This optimal period shortly after birth is an example of a _______ _______.

10. Jean Piaget's theory of ________________ ________________ proposed that children proceed through the following four stages as their thinking develops: sensorimotor, preoperational, concrete operational, and formal operational.

11. Harry Harlow studied the behavior of infant monkeys and artificial mothers to determine whether food or contact comfort was more important in the formation of ________________ in the monkeys.

Brief Essay Question

12. The three key issues in the study of developmental psychology are: continuity and stages, stability and change, nature and nurture. In three short paragraphs of about two or three sentences each, describe aspects of infant or child development that demonstrate both sides of each of these three issues.

Self-Test Answers (continued)

Matching Terms and Definitions

8. a. (4), b. (8), c. (7), d. (13), e. (9), f. (1), g. (14), h. (12), i. (6), j. (5)

Fill-in-the-Blank Questions

9. imprinting, 10. cognitive development, 11. attachment

Brief Essay Question

12. Students should cite evidence from physical, cognitive, and social development to address this question. Physical development seems to work in stages, be governed by change, and rely more heavily on nature. Cognitive development seems to support a more continuous developmental pattern, with reliance on stability and nurture. Finally, social development progresses continuously, seeks stability, and shows evidence supporting both nature and nurture.

MODULE 5

Performance Standards

Standard Area: Life Span Development

Content Standard 1: Development over the life span

Performance Standard 1.1 Explore physical, cognitive, and social development across the life span.

Physical Development

- Discuss how adolescence begins with sexual maturation. (Student Text pp. 80–81)
- Discuss the physical landmarks of adolescent development. This section includes a discussion and examples of primary and secondary sex characteristics. (Student Text pp. 82–84)
- Present Figure 5.3, The Wonder of Puberty, summarizing the development of primary and secondary sex characteristics. (Student Text p. 83)
- Describe cognitive and cultural factors that govern sexual behaviors. Compare sexual activity among teens today and in the last century. (Student Text p. 84)

Cognitive Development

- Discuss how adolescents learn to think hypothetically and abstractly and use formal logic. (Student Text p. 85)
- Investigate how adolescents have the ability for principled moral reasoning, according to Lawrence Kohlberg. Present the stages of moral development using examples from the "Heinz" dilemma. Discuss criticisms of this theory. (Student Text pp. 85–88)
- Present Figure 5.4, Climbing Kohlberg's Ladder of Moral Development, summarizing the preconventional, conventional, and postconventional levels of moral development. (Student Text p. 87)

Social Development

- Present Erik Erikson's theory of eight stages of psychosocial development. (Student Text p. 88)
- Present Table 5.1, Erikson's Stages of Psychosocial Development, summarizing each of the stages (approximate ages, issues, and descriptions of tasks). (Student Text p. 89)
- Focus on the psychosocial conflict of adolescence, identity versus role confusion. (Student Text pp. 89–91)
- Emphasize the psychosocial conflict of young adulthood, intimacy versus isolation. (Student Text p. 91)
- Discuss an adolescent's attachment move from family to peers, as well as a drive for independence. (Student Text pp. 91–93)

Content Standard 2: Research techniques used to study developmental processes

Performance Standard 2.1 Explain the characteristics of longitudinal and cross-sectional research methods.

- Discuss how the concept of adolescence has changed over time, from rural America in the 1800s to today. (Student Text pp. 80–81)

Content Standard 3 Stage theories

Performance Standard 3.1 List stages in the developmental theories proposed by psychologists such as Piaget, Erikson, Kohlberg, Gilligan, Cross, Helms, and others.

Jean Piaget

- Discuss how formal operational thought characterizes a thinking style of adolescence. (Student Text p. 85)

Lawrence Kohlberg

- Present descriptions and examples of preconventional, conventional, and postconventional moral reasoning in the context of the "Heinz" moral dilemma. (Student Text pp. 86–87)
- Present Figure 5.4, Climbing Kohlberg's Ladder of Moral Development, summarizing the preconventional, conventional, and postconventional levels of moral development. (Student Text p. 87)
- Criticize Kolhberg's theory.

Erik Erikson

- Discuss Erik Erikson's eight stages of psychosocial development. Focus on the tasks of adolescence (identity, Student Text pp. 89–90) and young adulthood (intimacy, Student Text p. 91).
- Present Table 5.1, Erikson's Stages of Psychosocial Development, summarizing each of the eight stages of psychosocial development (approximate ages, issues, and descriptions of tasks). (Student Text p. 89)

Performance Standard 3.4 Examine theories of development in the context of cultural bias.

- Criticize Kohlberg's stages of moral development for a North American and western European cultural bias. (Student Text p. 88)

Content Standard 4 Developmental issues (nature/nurture, continuity/discontinuity, stability/instability, critical periods)

- Examine the interaction of nature and nurture in how adolescents express their sexuality. (Student Text pp. 82–84, 93–94)

Performance Standard 4.2 Explore the developmental issues of continuity/discontinuity and stability/instability.

- Address the issue of continuity/discontinuity in an examination of the stage theories of Piaget and Kohlberg. (Student Text p. 93)
- Examine the developmental issue of stability/instability in how troubled teenagers can become happy and well-adjusted adults. (Student Text pp. 89–93)

Materials NETWORK

All of the items from the Video, Activity, and Enrichment Centers listed below come from the *Teacher's Resource Binder*. These items will help you teach and expand on concepts presented in Module 5.

trb This logo indicates when an item from the Materials Network may be used in conjunction with a specific note found in this module's *Teacher's Edition*.

What Is Adolescence?

Activity Center

- Critical Thinking Activity: *Fact or Falsehood?* With this activity, students' preconceptions about adolescence are either exposed as incorrect or reinforced as correct. (*Teacher's Resource Binder*, p. 5-1; Handout 5–1)
- Building Vocabulary: Graphic Organizer: *Charting Developmental Issues* The chart in the graphic organizer allows students to review module vocabulary words and terms in relationship to issues of adolescent development. (*Teacher's Resource Binder*, p. 5-1; Handout 5–2)
- Critical Thinking Activity: *Introducing Adolescent Development* In this activity students share their memories and reflect on their own adolescent experience. (*Teacher's Resource Binder*, p. 5-1; Handout 5–3)

Enrichment Center

- Enrichment Lesson: *What Is Adolescence?* This history lesson on the development of adolescence outlines the laws and events that created a time of adolescence in Western society. (*Teacher's Resource Binder*, p. 5-1)

Physical Development in Adolescence

Activity Center

- Critical Thinking Activity: *Writing About Puberty* This activity gets students to think about how they would discuss puberty with their future children. (*Teacher's Resource Binder*, p. 5-1)

Cognitive Development in Adolescence

Activity Center

- Critical Thinking Activity: *Formal Operational Thought* The critical thinking problems in this activity will test your students' level of cognition and spark discussion about the existence of Piaget's ultimate cognitive stage of formal operational thought. (*Teacher's Resource Binder*, p. 5-1; Handout 5–4)
- Critical Thinking Activity: *Explaining Morality Using Kohlberg* Use this activity to find out in what stage of moral development your students fall. It poses a classic moral dilemma, asking students to come up with explanations for behavior by using Kohlberg's stage theory as a guide. (*Teacher's Resource Binder*, p. 5-1)

Enrichment Center

- Enrichment Lesson: *Kohlberg's Theory of Moral Development* Kohlberg's theory of moral development actually has six substages, two for each overall category described in the text. (*Teacher's Resource Binder*, p. 5-1)

Social Development in Adolescence

Activity Center

- Analysis Activity: *Objective Measure of Ego Identity Status (OM-EIS)* With this activity, students discover into which of four categories they fall as they develop a sense of identity. (*Teacher's Resource Binder*, p. 5-1; Handout 5–5)
- Cooperative Learning Activity: *A Generation Gap?* Is there a generation gap? Students discuss this and other questions in this activity. (*Teacher's Resource Binder*, p. 5-1)

Enrichment Center

- Enrichment Lesson: *Adolescents' Friendships* This lesson explores the research surrounding how adolescents develop and view their close friendships. (*Teacher's Resource Binder*, p. 5-1)

MODULE 5

Adolescence

Introducing the Module

The Points: Module Objectives

- Define *adolescence* and evaluate how adolescence has changed over the last century.
- Summarize the major physical changes that occur during adolescence.
- Analyze how the reasoning ability of adolescents differs from that of younger children.
- Describe how moral reasoning changes over time, according to Lawrence Kohlberg.
- Identify evidence to support Erik Erikson's idea that a sense of identity is the primary challenge of adolescence.
- Define *intimacy*, according to Erik Erikson.
- Describe the road to independence from family.
- Evaluate how developmental psychology's three major issues apply to adolescence.

trb tr Building Vocabulary

Working in small groups, have students use the list of Key Terms and Key People on page 96 of their books to complete **Graphic Organizer:** *Charting Developmental Issues* (*Teacher's Resource Binder*, p. 5-1; **Handout 5–2**). When the groups have finished their work, they may check their responses against a completed chart that you show as a transparency.

MODULE 5

Adolescence

Just for a minute, think of yourself in the fourth grade. Think of your physical self, the things you liked to do, the sorts of thoughts that occupied your mental life, the activities you engaged in, and the friends you had. How have you changed between then and now? You may even be chuckling, very glad that you've left your former self behind. The changes that occur during adolescence are probably the most dramatic changes you'll ever go through, with the possible exception of the rapid changes that occurred very early in your life.

In a sense, everything about an introductory psychology course relates to you. Pick any module and you will find relevant material that helps you understand yourself and your world better. Yet, no module is more relevant to you than this one. Adolescence is where you're at! The physical, cognitive, and social aspects we'll discuss are psychology's best and most current efforts to explain this time of your life.

What Is Adolescence?

What's the point? 1. What is adolescence? How has it changed in the last century?

Imagine living in a hunting, gathering society that celebrated your thirteenth birthday with a ceremony proclaiming you an "adult." Shortly thereafter, you would marry, start your family, and settle in to your adult life-style. Your occupational choices would be quite limited.

Getting Started

Begin a discussion of adolescence by asking volunteers to name an adolescent character from a movie, television series, or novel they admire and to explain the reason for their choices.

trb You may wish to use **Critical Thinking Activity:** *Fact or Falsehood?* (*Teacher's Resource Binder*, p. 5-1) as a prereading strategy to find out what students already know about adolescence. The activity will prime students to note terms and concepts in the text that confirm or dispel their preconceptions about adolescence.

If you're female, you would devote yourself to child-rearing and domestic tasks. If you're male, your "occupation" would be hunting. Societies like this have existed, and, in some parts of the world, they still do. Had you been born into one, your experience of the developmental stage of **adolescence**—the period between childhood and adulthood—would be brief and very different from what you are most likely experiencing now as an American teen. Even in the more rural America of the 1800s, your transition from childhood to adult life would have happened more quickly. At that time, formal education for many young people ended with eighth grade, and young couples married, began farming, and started a family before they turned 20! Now, adolescence is becoming increasingly long and complex.

Adolescence begins with sexual maturation, which is happening about two years earlier than it did a hundred years ago (Figure 5.1). Adolescence is being extended on the other end, too. As more and more students extend their formal education to college and beyond, independent adult status is delayed longer and longer. Young Americans are also waiting longer to marry and start families. Children may remain at least partially dependent on their parents for financial support well into their twenties, and sometimes longer.

The fact that most teenagers reach physical maturity long before they are able to assume adult roles can—and does—create some tension and frustration, which you have most likely experienced. One day you may be eager to sample a more adult activity, say a road trip to another town to visit friends, only to have your parents deny permission because they feel you're not quite ready for that much independence. Next thing you know, your harmless but exuberant roughhousing with a sibling or friend is interrupted with a parental admonishment to "grow up and act

▶ **adolescence** The transition period from childhood to adulthood, extending from puberty to independence.

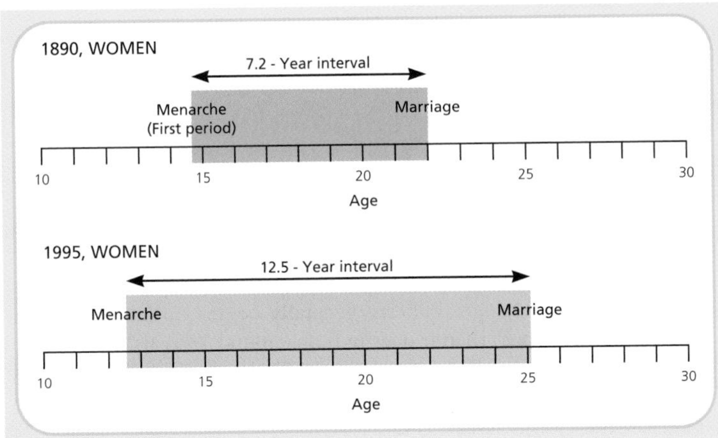

Figure 5.1 Adolescence Is Getting Longer Puberty is happening earlier, and marriage, financial independence, and the end of formal education are happening later. These events are stretching adolescence on both ends (Guttmacher, 2000).

MODULE 5

Teaching the Points

■ TEACHING TIPS

web (1) You can log on as an instructor to the book companion site for *Thinking About Psychology* at www.worthpublishers.com/thinkingaboutpsych. It contains teacher resources for class presentations, as well as review and assessment of module concepts and terms.

tr (2) A four-color transparency of Figure 5.1, Adolescence Is Getting Longer, is available in the **Overhead Transparencies Set.**

F • Y • I

Adolescence as we know it today did not evolve until the early twentieth century, when child-labor laws and compulsory education delayed the social onset of adulthood. *Adolescence* was a term coined by G. Stanley Hall, the father of American psychology. He called it "a time of storm and stress."

trb At this point, you may wish to use **Enrichment Lesson:** *What Is Adolescence?* (*Teacher's Resource Binder*, p. 5-1).

■ MULTICULTURAL CONNECTIONS

Have students research coming-of-age rituals (rites of passage) and how adolescence is viewed in cultures that are Native American, tribal African, African-American, Muslim, Hispanic, Indian, Eastern European, Western European, or Asian. Encourage students to present their findings to the class as a written paper, oral presentation, or poster.

trb At this point, you may wish to use **Enrichment Lesson:** *What Is Adolescence?* (*Teacher's Resource Binder*, p. 5-1).

■ LOOKING AT THE ISSUES

Students may be curious about why physical maturity is occurring earlier in modern youth. Explain to students that better health care and longer lives contribute to earlier physical development. Then ask students the following questions:

- What impact has early sexual development had on society?
- Are there cultures where sexual maturity happens later than in the United States? Earlier? Why are those cultures different?

Suggested Readings

Use the following books as teacher-preparation tools or as enrichment for advanced students:

Brown, L. M. (1998). *Raising their voices: The politics of girls' anger.* Cambridge, MA: Harvard University Press.

Colby, A., & Kohlberg, L. (1987). *The measurement of moral judgment* (Vols. I and II). Cambridge: Cambridge University Press.

Csikszentimihalyi, M., Rathunde, K., & Whalen, S. (1993). *Talented teenagers: The roots of success and failure.* Cambridge: Cambridge University Press.

Elkind, D. (1984). *All grown up and no place to go: Teenagers in crisis.* Reading, MA: Addison-Wesley.

Erikson, E. (1994). *Identity: Youth in crisis.* New York: Norton. (Original work published 1968.)

Inhelder, B., & Piaget, J. (1959). *The growth of logical thinking from childhood to adolescence.* New York: Basic Books.

■ APPLYING THE POINTS

Have students write down ten different answers to the question "Who am I?" listing only those things that, if lost, would make a real difference in their sense of identity—for instance, their roles or responsibilities, groups they belong to, beliefs, personality traits, needs, feelings, or behavior patterns.

When they have finished, ask them to imagine what life would be like if the items they listed were no longer true—for instance, what would the loss of a parent mean to those who wrote down "son" or "daughter"? After students have reviewed items in this way, ask them to rank-order their lists in terms of importance.

Source: Bugen, L. A. (1979). *Death and dying: Theory, research, practice.* Dubuque, IA: Wm. C. Brown.

trb At this point, you may wish to use Analysis Activity: *Objective Measure of Ego Identity Status (OM-EIS)* (*Teacher's Resource Binder*, p. 5-1; Handout 5–5).

■ JOURNAL WRITING

Invite students to use the following questions and writing prompts as springboards for entries in their psychology journals:

- Has your adolescence been stormy? Why or why not?
- Do you think adolescence is necessary? How long a transition period between childhood and adulthood do you think most people need? Why?
- Do you think society forces adolescents to grow up too soon? Explain your response.
- Describe a time when you and your parents disagreed on what your rights and responsibilities were. How did you feel about your parents? How did they feel about you? What resolutions did you reach with them?

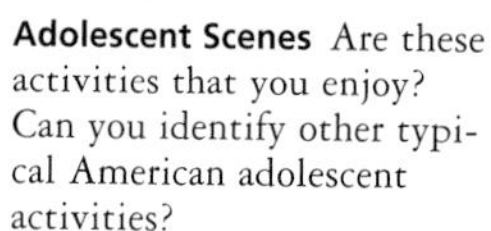

Adolescent Scenes Are these activities that you enjoy? Can you identify other typical American adolescent activities?

your age." When you want to be an adult, the message is often to be patient and wait. When you want to act childlike, you hear that it's important to be responsible and mature.

This is not to imply that adolescence must be a time of stormy rebellion and confusion. Teenagers display tremendous accomplishments—excelling in school, on the job, as volunteers, at sports, and in other creative endeavors. The transition from child to adult is jarring for some families, who struggle mightily with issues surrounding the amount of independence and responsibility teenagers should have. But others seem to navigate these waters with a minimum of disturbance and disruption. And for most families, the gradual growth in maturity and responsibility on the part of the teen is matched by a growing confidence on the part of the parents.

For the majority of teenagers, the experience of adolescence is an exciting opportunity to explore the possibilities of adult life. Ninety percent of high school seniors have reported that they are generally satisfied with themselves (*Public Opinion*, 1987).

► **puberty** The period of sexual maturation, during which a person becomes capable of reproducing.

► **primary sex characteristics** The body structures (ovaries, testes, and external genitalia) that make sexual reproduction possible.

► **secondary sex characteristics** Nonreproductive sexual characteristics, such as female breasts and hips, male voice quality, and body hair.

Physical Development in Adolescence

2. What major physical changes occur during adolescence?

The most important physical landmark of adolescent development is **puberty**, the time when a person matures sexually. A flood of hormones, which lead to physical and emotional changes, triggers this amazing time of change. Puberty generally begins earlier in girls (at about 11 years of age) than it does in boys (around 13 years). One of the most obvious changes is a growth spurt. Sixth- or seventh-grade girls often tower over their male classmates, but soon the boys catch up and outgrow the average female (Figure 5.2).

Enriching

Have students survey a sample of students in each grade to see whether those students view adolescence as a stressful, rebellious time or a smooth, growing experience. Have your students compare whether older students who take the survey have a more positive attitude about adolescence than younger students. Be sure to have any survey reviewed by an Institutional Review Board and to obtain informed consent from all participants in order to comply with ethical standards. Students can present their findings to the class or write about the survey experience in their psychology journals.

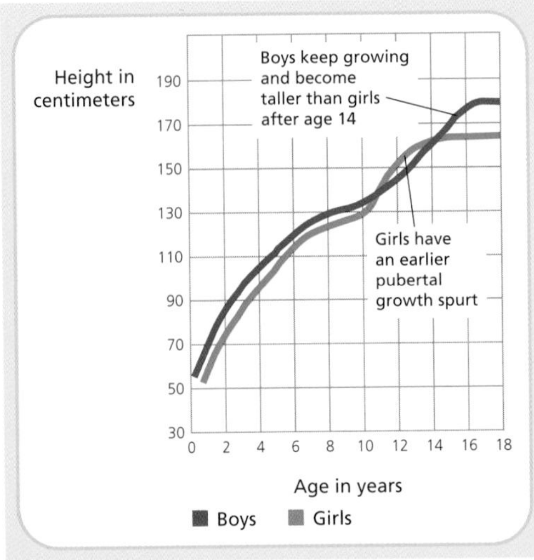

Figure 5.2 The Growth Spurt Girls start the growth spurt earlier, but once boys catch up at about age 14 they tend to grow taller than the girls. (Data from Tanner, 1978.)

Puberty involves sexual maturation, so a person passing this milestone is capable of reproduction. During the growth spurt, both primary and secondary sex characteristics develop (Figure 5.3). The **primary sex characteristics** are the reproductive organs (the *testes* in males and the *ovaries* in females). The **secondary sex characteristics,** such as breast development in girls and facial hair in boys, are less directly related to reproduction.

Figure 5.3 The Wonder of Puberty The release of hormones during puberty triggers amazing changes in the body. Some of those changes are illustrated here.

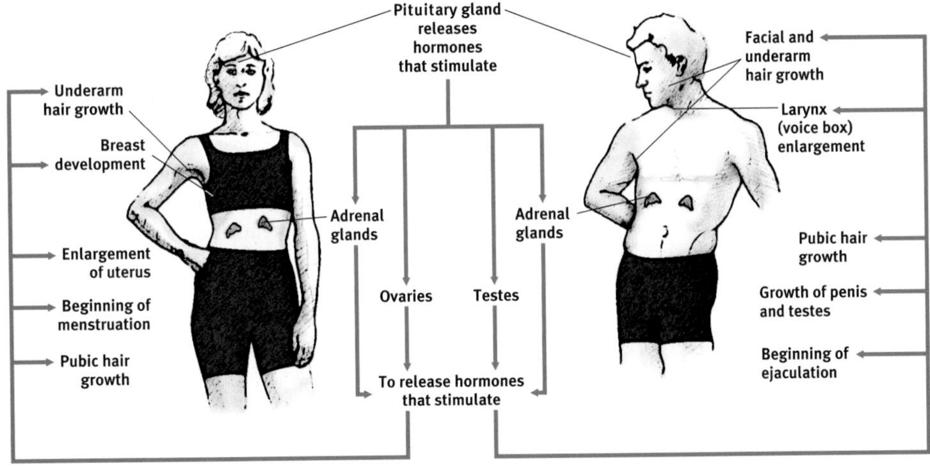

MODULE 5

■ TEACHING TIPS

tr (1) Four-color transparencies of Figure 5.2, The Growth Spurt, and Figure 5.3, The Wonder of Puberty, are available in the **Overhead Transparencies Set.**

(2) Since puberty may be an uncomfortable topic of discussion for some teens, be sensitive to this discomfort while still encouraging your students to talk about their feelings. You might enlist the help of a teacher of the opposite sex to help lead discussions about issues affecting both girls and boys. In this way, all students can feel comfortable talking about this sensitive time.

trb At this point, you may wish to use Critical Thinking Activity: *Writing About Puberty* (*Teacher's Resource Binder*, p. 5-1).

■ LOOKING AT THE ISSUES

Teen pregnancy is a controversial issue in many parts of the country. Have students work in small groups to research the following questions related to this issue:

- What are the health risks of having a baby in the teen years?
- What social factors contribute to teen pregnancy?
- What policies does your school have about pregnant teens? How do other students in school view these students?
- Should teen couples who are pregnant get married? Why or why not?

To clarify issues and hear student responses, visit with each of the groups as they respond to the questions.

Cross-Curricular Connections

BIOLOGY AND HEALTH Team up with a biology or health teacher to develop lessons that relate the physical development of adolescents to any of the following topics:

- reasons why the age of onset for puberty has become younger in the last century
- normal physical changes that occur in puberty
- sexually transmitted diseases

MODULE 5

F • Y • I

Physical development falls into two broad categories: early blooming or late blooming. Early blooming tends to be socially advantageous for boys since girls usually mature early anyway and find boys who are on their developmental level attractive. For girls, it is not advantageous to be early or late in blooming. If girls develop earlier than their peers, they may be attractive to boys, but other girls may find these early bloomers threatening. Late blooming for girls and boys may lead to feelings of awkwardness around peers who are ahead of them.

JOURNAL WRITING

Invite students to use the following questions and writing prompts as springboards for entries in their psychology journals:

- How did you feel about yourself when you started to develop physically? Were you an early or late bloomer?
- Did you feel prepared for sexual maturation? Why or why not? Did that affect your views about it?

LOOKING AT THE ISSUES

Sexually transmitted diseases (STDs) are a problem in U.S. society. Many students are unaware of the pervasiveness of and the dangers associated with STDs. Using library and Internet resources, have students work in small groups to do research on any of the following STDs: chlamydia, syphilis, AIDS, gonorrhea, pelvic inflammatory disease and cervical cancer, and herpes.

Groups should attempt to learn facts about the disease's symptoms and treatments as well as the number of people infected each year and the general prognosis for those infected with the STD. Each group should present its findings in an oral report or a graphic presentation about STDs and adolescents.

TEACHING TIP

Some of your students may be dealing with issues concerning sexuality, both heterosexual and homosexual. Discussions of homosexuality may be sensitive. Determine how you can promote informed tolerance for individual people who may be dealing with questions in this area.

Two of the more obvious events of puberty are the beginning of menstruation (known as *menarche*) for females and the beginning of ejaculation for boys (which often happens during sleep as a *nocturnal emission*). Each is a memorable event that produces a variety of emotions in the young woman or young man. Teens who have been prepared to expect these events are much more likely to view them as positive, rather than frightening or negative, experiences (Fuller & Downs, 1990; Greif & Ulman, 1982; Woods & others, 1983).

Sexuality is certainly a *biological* event, but *cognitive* and *cultural* factors also govern sexual behaviors. Our culture is saturated with sexual imagery. A typical hour of prime-time network television contains over a dozen sexual references, most of which ignore the risks of unwanted pregnancy and sexually transmitted diseases (Sapolsky & Tabarlet, 1991). Add to this the sexual content of popular music, print media, and the Internet, and mix in the increased sex drive triggered by the hormones released during puberty, and you have a recipe for the dramatic increase in teen sexual activity in the United States over the course of the last century (Smith, 1988). Teens receive a decidedly mixed message calling not only for abstinence but also for "safe" sex, protected by condom use. Rarely discussed are the tremendous emotional risks of committing oneself sexually to another person. Is it any wonder that making decisions is sometimes so difficult, especially when teens are still working to complete their development of decision-making skills (as we will see in the next section)?

Another source of conflict, anxiety, and misunderstanding is **sexual orientation,** one's attraction toward people of a particular gender. Heterosexuals ("straights") are attracted to members of the opposite sex, whereas homosexuals (gay men and lesbian women) are attracted to members of the same sex. A number of scientific studies indicate that 3 to 4 percent of men and 1 to 2 percent of women are exclusively homosexual (Laumann & others, 1994; National Center for Health Statistics, 1991; Smith, 1998). The vast majority of the remaining men and women are exclusively heterosexual, with perhaps 1 percent bisexual (attracted to members of both sexes).

► **sexual orientation** An enduring sexual attraction toward members of either the other gender (heterosexual orientation) or one's own gender (homosexual orientation).

► **Jean Piaget** (1896–1980) Pioneer in the study of developmental psychology who introduced a stage theory of cognitive development that led to a better understanding of children's thought processes.

► **Lawrence Kohlberg** (1927–1987) Created a three-stage theory of moral development.

We do not know what determines sexual orientation, but research has made some possibilities unlikely. Studies have not been able to establish that homosexuality is related to parenting styles, a person's hatred or fear of the opposite sex, or a childhood history of being raised or exploited by homosexual adults (Bailey & others, 1995; Golombok & Tasker, 1996; Storms, 1983). There have been studies that suggest a variety of biological factors may impact sexual orientation. Areas receiving attention include brain structure (LeVay, 1991), genetics (Hershberger, 1997; Whitam & others, 1993), and the level of hormones during the mother's pregnancy (Dorner, 1976).

Cross-Curricular Connections

GOVERNMENT Have students work in small groups to research laws and policies concerning sex education in your state. Before students begin their research, discuss the general purpose of sex education programs in your state and how, from community to community, these kinds of programs may vary. Students should focus their research on responding to the following questions:

- Do the policies differ from school system to school system?
- Why were policies adopted in certain communities?
- What does psychological research say about the effectiveness of different types of sex education programs?

Cognitive Development in Adolescence

Reasoning

3. How does the reasoning ability of adolescents differ from that of younger children?

As we move through our childhood, we progress through a sequence of increasingly sophisticated cognitive abilities. By the time adolescence begins, we are approaching what developmental psychologist **Jean Piaget** called the *formal operational stage,* when we may develop adult thinking and reasoning. Formal logic, abstract thinking, and hypothetical reasoning are now possible, and these changes represent a *qualitative* change—adolescents with these skills don't just think more, they think differently. Trying to teach typical six-year-old children geometry or calculus would be futile because children at this age simply can't "get it." Introducing these courses in the secondary curriculum is a different story, because most young people will have the mental tools to take on these abstract concepts.

Of course, not all adolescents think with perfect clarity and logic all the time. This is an age when one tends to focus on the self, often imagining that one's own feelings are particularly unique (Elkind, 1978). Falling in love for the first time often leads to the feeling that this experience is unlike anything anyone else has ever felt. And a first breakup can be so intense that it is nearly impossible to believe that others (even parents!) have had similar experiences.

In spite of this focus on self, people of your age are fully capable of idealistic thinking and can quickly recognize and condemn the hypocrisy you now so easily detect in the world around you. You and your age mates tend to work hard for causes in which you believe. Your newfound formal operational skills may lead you to examine your own and others' religious beliefs on a much deeper level than your childhood understandings allowed (Elkind, 1970; Worthington, 1989).

Growing Cognitive Capabilities Teenagers are often eager to exercise the reasoning skills that mark their entry into Piaget's formal operational stage. For some, this takes the form of involving themselves in society's important ethical debates.

Morality

4. According to Kohlberg, how does moral reasoning change over time?

One special aspect of cognitive development is morality—one's sense of right and wrong. Psychologist **Lawrence Kohlberg** (1981, 1984) authored a theory of moral reasoning to demonstrate how our way of thinking about moral situations changes with our level of development.

F • Y • I

Adolescents experience egocentrism, but in a different way from children. With adolescent egocentrism, teens experience the **imaginary audience phenomenon** in which they believe others are always paying attention to them, especially their flaws. Also, they feel that no one else has experienced life exactly like they have, referred to as the **nobody understands me phenomenon.**

■ **JOURNAL WRITING**

Invite students to use the following questions and writing prompts as springboards for entries in their psychology journals:

- Looking back, was puberty an overall positive or negative experience for you? Explain.
- Have you ever felt as though everyone in a room was focusing on you in terms of a particular flaw (that is, a new pimple or awkwardly fitting clothes)? Describe this feeling.
- Have you developed a sense of excitement or commitment for a certain cause or issue lately? If so, what is it? How have you demonstrated your enthusiasm?

Enriching

Have students break into groups and use available resources, including the Internet, to study youth-led activism—for example, the protests against the Vietnam War and in support of the French Revolution. Have them discuss the findings from the research by responding to the following questions:

- How did young people influence these movements? What impact have young people had on other revolutionary movements, like the American Revolution and the Civil War?
- How do current activist groups best utilize the energy and enthusiasm of youth to forward their agendas? How does government attempt to involve young people in its workings?

trb At this point, you may wish to use **Critical Thinking Activity:** ***Formal Operational Thought*** (*Teacher's Resource Binder,* p. 5-1; **Handout 5–4**).

MODULE 5

■ LOOKING AT THE ISSUES

Because teens often grapple with what is moral, pose the following questions to the entire class in order to help them focus on their definitions of *morality*:

- What does it mean to be a moral person?
- What stage of morality (based on Kohlberg) would you say you and your friends are in most of the time?
- Does the definition of *morality* change with a situation or does it remain the same all the time?

trb At this point, you may wish to use Critical Thinking Activity: *Explaining Morality Using Kohlberg* (*Teacher's Resource Binder*, p. 5-1).

F•Y•I

Kohlberg used the term *conventional* in his theory to describe the type of morality commonly found in society. Conventional morality was the stage he found most prevalent among people in general society. Therefore, preconventional morality existed before people would join society as relative adults, and postconventional morality was seen in a segment of the population that didn't seem to reflect the attitudes of the majority of adults. In fact, Kohlberg believed that a type of postconventional morality existed, but he was unable to find enough people who reflected this perspective to study over a long period of time to validate this idea.

trb At this point, you may want to use Enrichment Lesson: *Kohlberg's Theory of Moral Development* (*Teacher's Resource Binder*, p. 5-1).

■ TEACHING TIP

Kohlberg didn't believe that people could skip stages of moral development. He, like Piaget, believed that each stage built on the one before it, so skipping stages was not likely to occur. His theory fits into a "continuity versus stages" argument in favor of a stage theory of development.

He did this by posing moral dilemmas to the participants in his experiments. Here is one such dilemma Kohlberg used:

> In Europe, a woman was near death from a very bad disease, a special kind of cancer. There was one drug that the doctors thought might save her. It was a form of radium that a druggist in the same town had recently discovered. The drug was expensive to make, but the druggist was charging 10 times what the drug cost him to make. He paid $200 for the radium and charged $2000 for a small dose of the drug. The sick woman's husband, Heinz, went to everyone he knew to borrow the money, but he could get together only about $1000, which was half of what it cost. He told the druggist that his wife was dying and asked him to sell it cheaper or let him pay later. But the druggist said, "No, I discovered the drug and I'm going to make money from it." Heinz got desperate and broke into the man's store to steal the drug for his wife.

This story has a somewhat dated feel to it now, but it continues to draw out people's thought processes, which was Kohlberg's intent. He was not interested so much in whether a person thought Heinz was right or wrong. Rather, he wanted to record the reasoning individuals used to make their decisions about this and other scenarios. From the answers he received, he developed a theory that organized moral development into three levels, in which the focus shifts from concern with self, to concern with fitting in, to concern with broader ethical principles. We can think of these levels as three rungs on a moral ladder (Figure 5.4).

- ***Preconventional moral reasoning*** This most primitive level is characterized by a desire to avoid punishment or gain reward. Most children under the age of 9 show this type of reasoning, and some adults never progress beyond this level. Examples of statements that indicate preconventional reasoning include, "Heinz was wrong to steal the drug because he might be put in jail," or "Heinz was right to steal the drug because he would then have the companionship of his wife longer."
- ***Conventional moral reasoning*** The primary concern of conventional moral reasoning is to fit in and play one's role as a good citizen. People at this level have a strong desire to follow the rules and laws of society. Conventional moral reasoning is typical of most adults, according to Kohlberg. It is generally apparent by early adolescence, when Piaget's formal operational thought kicks in. Examples of statements indicating this type of moral reasoning include, "Heinz was wrong to steal because stealing breaks the law," or "Heinz was right to take the drug because most people would do what they must to protect a family member."

Demonstrating

A HEINZ DILEMMA ANALYSIS Conduct some active research with your students by having them present the Heinz dilemma (or an updated version) to their classmates. Subjects should write out a paragraph explaining how they would respond to the dilemma. Analyze the results to evaluate into which level of moral development each subject seemed to fit. Be sure to keep the following in mind:

- Have students obtain informed consent. This is an important ethical consideration that should be used for any research done, no matter how simple.
- Code the paragraphs to ensure anonymity of the subjects.

Figure 5.4 **Climbing Kohlberg's Ladder of Moral Development** As moral reasoning progresses, the focus changes from concern with self (preconventional) to concern with fitting in (conventional) to concern with broader ethical principles (postconventional).

- ***Postconventional moral reasoning*** Most people do not reach this third level, which is characterized by references to universal ethical principles that represent the rights or obligations of all people. Individuals at the postconventional level might say, "Heinz was justified because everyone has a right to live, and he was simply trying to help his wife stay alive," or "Heinz was wrong because everyone must respect the property of others, even the property of a selfish and greedy druggist."

F • Y • I

Kohlberg believed that social interaction encouraged moral growth. He felt that formal education offered the best opportunities for moral development. He also believed that subjects presented with moral dilemmas similar to the ones described in the text would see how reasonable the higher stages of morality were, encouraging subjects to aspire to deeper moral development.

trb At this point, you may wish to use **Critical Thinking Activity:** *Explaining Morality Using Kohlberg* (*Teacher's Resource Binder*, p. 5-1) and **Enrichment Lesson:** *Kohlberg's Theory of Moral Development* (*Teacher's Resource Binder*, p. 5-1).

■ **TEACHING TIP**

How would your students respond to the Heinz dilemma? Whether they have read the explanation of the dilemma or not, they can discuss what their responses would be to the situation, determining what stage of moral development they would fall into themselves.

tr A four-color transparency of Figure 5.4, Climbing Kohlberg's Ladder of Moral Development, is available in the **Overhead Transparencies Set.**

- Create a rubric for analyzing the paragraphs. What words or phrases will indicate each level of moral development?
- Have several students analyze each paragraph.
- Compare their evaluations to ensure reliability.
- Designate students to write up the research like a scholarly paper.
- Consider submitting your findings to a student journal.

MODULE 5

tb ■ **CHECKING FOR UNDERSTANDING**

Here are several ways to assess students' comprehension:

- Assign any or all of the journal questions or prompts for an in-class writing assessment.
- Use questions from the *Test Bank* to do a quick assessment of students' knowledge of the concepts.

■ **MULTICULTURAL CONNECTIONS**

With their permission, ask female students and students with different cultural backgrounds if they feel that Kohlberg's postconventional morality is a product of white male mentality. Have them respond to the following in a class forum:

- Are women more communal than men? Why or why not?
- Of the cultures represented in this classroom, are any of them more communal than typical U.S. society? If so, why—and how is their communal culture enacted? How has Americanization affected the moral beliefs of people in the United States from different cultural traditions?

■ **TEACHING TIP**

Erik Erikson was a student of Sigmund Freud, which explains why his theory looks similar to his mentor's psychosexual stages of development. Erikson believed that social influences were more important to development than sexual impulses, so he crafted his theory to highlight different influences than those supported by his teacher.

Has Kohlberg's theory survived the test of time and the scrutiny of other researchers? As is often the case, some evidence supports his theory and some doesn't fit quite so well. Follow-up studies support the idea of a progression from preconventional to conventional thought in childhood (Edwards, 1981, 1982; Snarey, 1985, 1987). The postconventional stage is not so well supported. The evidence indicates that this stage is largely a product of the white male population Kohlberg sampled (Eckensberger, 1994; Miller & Bersoff, 1995). This sample came mostly from groups that value *individualism.* In North America and western European countries, for example, individual goals tend to take precedence over group objectives (children are taught to "stand on your own two feet" and "think for yourself"). And in these countries, there is evidence of a progression to postconventional thinking. But in more *communal* cultures, with a greater emphasis on shared group goals (children are taught to put the needs of the family and community ahead of the self), the notion that postconventional morality is superior to conventional morality receives less support. Similarly, North American women, who tend to be more communal than their male counterparts, also show less of Kohlberg's postconventional reasoning.

Social Development in Adolescence

To be human is to be social. Even the shyest among us experiences *some* social interaction as a part of normal development. Social interaction lies at the heart of all communication, from daily negotiations between siblings to the gestures exchanged by drivers squabbling over who has the right of way at an intersection. Your friendships and romances, decisions about conformity and nonconformity, and concerns about popularity and separation from family all relate to *social development.*

Erik Erikson (1963) constructed a theory of social development that illustrates how certain issues peak during different periods of life, including adolescence. He divided the life span into eight stages, ranging from infancy to late adulthood (Table 5.1). Each stage has its own *psychosocial* developmental task. This task is a challenge, and the way the individual handles the task will lead to a more desirable or less desirable outcome. For example, in healthy situations, infants will develop more trust than mistrust, toddlers will develop more autonomy than shame or doubt, and preschoolers will show more initiative than guilt about their attempts to be independent. Let's take a closer look at what Erikson had to say about adolescence and young adulthood, the two stages you are closest to.

▶ **Erik Erikson** (1902–1994) Created an eight-stage theory of social development.

▶ **identity** One's sense of self; according to Erikson, the adolescent's task is to solidify a sense of self by testing and integrating various roles.

Enriching

Erikson saw the importance of adolescent identity seeking when he worked with the Oglala Lakota Indians. In their culture, young men would go off on their own to have an identity-determining dream that would guide the courses of their lives. When the U.S. government tried to assimilate the Lakota into American society, the tribe lost this rite of passage, and consequently the young men of the culture lost a time-honored way to find an identity.

Explore rites of passage with your students:

- What rites of passage do American youths go through to achieve adulthood?
- Do these rites help form a sense of identity? Why or why not?

TABLE 5.1 ERIKSON'S STAGES OF PSYCHOSOCIAL DEVELOPMENT

IDENTITY STAGE (APPROXIMATE AGE)	ISSUES	DESCRIPTION OF TASK
Infancy (to 1 year)	*Trust vs. mistrust*	If needs are dependably met, infants develop a sense of basic trust.
Toddlerhood (1 to 2 years)	*Autonomy vs. shame and doubt*	Toddlers learn to exercise will and do things for themselves, or they doubt their abilities.
Preschooler (3 to 5 years)	*Initiative vs. guilt*	Preschoolers learn to initiate tasks and carry out plans, or they feel guilty about efforts to be independent.
Elementary school (6 years to puberty)	*Competence vs. inferiority*	Children learn the pleasure of applying themselves to tasks, or they feel inferior.
Adolescence (teen years into 20s)	*Identity vs. role confusion*	Teenagers work at refining a sense of self by testing roles and then integrating them to form a single identity, or they become confused about who they are.
Young adulthood (20s to early 40s)	*Intimacy vs. isolation*	Young adults struggle to form close relationships and to gain the capacity for intimate love, or they feel socially isolated.
Middle adulthood (40s to 60s)	*Generativity vs. stagnation*	The middle-aged discover a sense of contributing to the world, usually through family and work, or they may feel a lack of purpose.
Late adulthood (late 60s and up)	*Integrity vs. despair*	When reflecting on his or her life, the older adult may feel a sense of satisfaction or failure.

Developing Identity

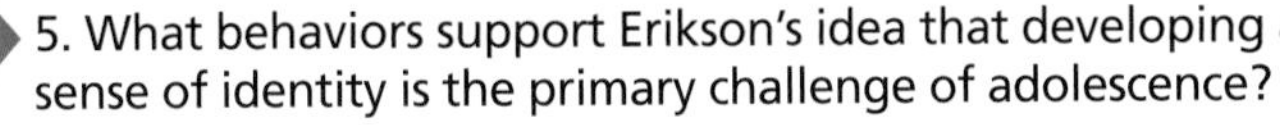

5. What behaviors support Erikson's idea that developing a sense of identity is the primary challenge of adolescence?

During adolescence and into the early twenties, your primary task is to develop an **identity,** a strong, consistent sense of who and what you are. As you try on different ways of thinking and behaving (Why did I act that way? What do I value in life? What are my priorities?) your goal is to generate a stronger and stronger sense of self.

The search for identity during adolescence has several characteristics:

- ***Experimentation*** Adolescents often experiment in healthy ways, exploring and taking advantage of a variety of school op-

■ TEACHING TIP

While outlining Erikson's theory in class, you might ask students to include in their notes the name of a person they know who fits each stage. The theory is likely to become less abstract and more meaningful as they check the stages against the reality of living examples.

trb tr A black-line master for Table 5.1, Erikson's Stages of Psychosocial Development, is available in the **Black-Line Masters Appendix** of the *Teacher's Resource Binder.*

trb At this point, you may wish to use **Analysis Activity:** ***Objective Measure of Ego Identity Status (OM-EIS)*** (*Teacher's Resource Binder,* p. 5-1; **Handout 5–5**).

Cooperative Learning

Divide students into groups to think about their plans for after high school graduation. Present the following questions as a starting point for discussion:

- Where do you see yourself one year from now? 5 years? 10 years? 20 years?
- What is your attitude about going to college? Why do you feel you have this attitude?
- What are your career/work plans?
- Do you feel your plans for the next few years are solid or do you hope your purpose in life will reveal itself soon?

trb At this point, you may wish to use **Analysis Activity:** ***Objective Measure of Ego Identity Status (OM-EIS)*** (*Teacher's Resource Binder,* p. 5-1; **Handout 5–5**).

MODULE 5

■ JOURNAL WRITING

Invite students to use the following questions or writing prompts as springboards for entries in their psychology journals:

- How can you tell that someone is your friend?
- Describe a time when you rebelled against authority. What feelings did you have when this happened? What were the consequences of your action?
- What are your feelings about leaving home one day?

■ LOOKING AT THE ISSUES

Studies show that adolescent students usually choose values and moral beliefs their parents taught them rather than those their friends may employ. Pose the following dilemma to your students to see how much they would or would not follow friends who were breaking rules:

> You and your friends find a sheet of paper that your teacher probably has lost. On the paper are the questions and answers for a test that you are going to have tomorrow. Your friends all plan to study from this sheet, and they want you to go along with them. You don't think you should, but they tell you to do it anyway. What would you really do: study from the sheet or not study from it?

trb At this point, you may wish to use Enrichment Lesson: *Adolescents' Friendships* (*Teacher's Resource Binder*, p. 5-1).

Who Am I? As adolescents search for a strong sense of identity, they may experiment with a variety of different looks.

portunities, observing various adult role models, or imagining life in a variety of careers. (What would it be like to be a physician? An artist? Yes, even an astronaut or a firefighter?) But as adolescents sort out what is appealing and what isn't, the experimentation can be less healthy and productive, involving drug use or promiscuous sexual behavior.

- ***Rebellion*** Healthy development includes building some independence. Most parents have an image of what their children should become, and most children do maintain the same core values as their parents. Nevertheless, the search for identity during adolescence may involve testing the limits parents set, or adopting styles of fashion and grooming that adults may not accept or understand. But the drive for independence becomes unhealthy when rebelling against society's standards takes the form of criminal or self-destructive behavior. Healthy adolescents exercise their independence in ways that do not harm themselves or others.
- ***"Self"-ishness*** Relationships during adolescence tend to be "self"-ish. Teens moving in and out of friendship cliques and romances learn more and more about their unique *self.* Each new relationship is a chance to try out different ways of interacting. Teen friendships are genuine and important, but they tend to be temporary. Some people do maintain lifelong friendships with high school friends, but most young adults find that these friendships become fond memories as they settle into career and family patterns a few years later. Of course, if you'd told me this when I was a teenager, I would have said you were nuts! My friends were the center of my life in high school. But as I finished my education and moved on to my career, most of these friendships gradually and naturally gave way to others that have lasted longer.
- ***Optimism and Energy*** Most teenagers, armed with their new and more powerful cognitive skills, view the world with a fresh (and refreshing) perspective. They have trouble understanding why some children go to bed hungry and why adults tolerate

Reteaching

Create a chart with four columns, labeling them with the four subheadings under "Developing Identity." Under each heading, have students brainstorm about situations in which adolescents demonstrate healthy experimentation, rebellion, "self"-ishness, and optimism. Although students may snicker about the unhealthy ways to demonstrate these identity-seeking arenas, encourage them to think critically about ways adolescents can achieve an identity without causing harm to themselves and others.

pollution, or discrimination, racism, or a thousand other injustices. Many adolescents are willing to tackle serious issues related to human rights, environmental concerns, political campaigns, and other causes. This willingness to contribute time and effort not only helps to make the world a better place but also helps teens to develop a strong sense of their own priorities.

Some adolescents realize a strong sense of identity with little or no struggle. A few may remain confused throughout their lives. Meeting the challenge is especially difficult for those individuals who have struggled with the tasks of previous stages. As you might imagine, achieving a sense of who you are is a lot easier if you're already trusting, autonomous, full of initiative, and competent. Erikson felt that adolescents who had not achieved the developmental goals of their younger years could experience profound confusion about their place in the world. But even if developmental goals do not come easily, they are always within reach. Most of us hit some rough patches before the pieces settle into place in the late teens or twenties.

▶ **intimacy** In Erikson's theory, the ability to form close, loving, open relationships; a primary task in early adulthood.

Developing Intimacy

6. What did Erikson mean by intimacy?

According to Erikson, young adults strive to achieve **intimacy**—a close, sharing, emotional, and honest relationship with other people. Many people have their most intense, intimate relationship with a spouse, but not all marriages achieve this type of closeness. Intimacy is not necessarily sexual by nature, and it often occurs outside of marriage with close, trusted friends and family members.

Intimacy Young adults are striving to develop intimate relationships based on open, honest communication.

As noted earlier, Erikson realized that "baggage" from previous stages would accumulate as we move from one stage to the next and would affect our ability to negotiate current developmental challenges. Young adults facing the challenge of *intimacy versus isolation* cannot share themselves honestly and openly if they are still confused about their own sense of self.

Independence from Family

7. What road does a typical American adolescent travel toward independence from family?

Separating from family is a journey that begins in childhood but picks up speed in adolescence. Children move from a primary attachment to parents to a primary attachment to peers. You can observe this in any

■ **APPLYING THE POINTS**

Have students interview their parents or other adults from their parent's generation, using the following questions as a guide:

- What is fundamentally different about this generation of teens from teens of your generation? What, if anything, is the same?
- Do you feel teens today are better off than teens of your generation? If so, how? If not, why not?

Have students write a paper in which they present their findings on whether a gap exists between them and their parents' generation.

trb At this point, you may wish to use **Cooperative Learning Activity:** *A Generation Gap?* (*Teacher's Resource Binder*, p. 5-1).

■ **LOOKING AT THE ISSUES**

More and more young adults are returning home after college to live with parents and postponing marriage to focus on career opportunities. Discuss the following questions with your students related to this phenomenon:

- Why would a young adult return home after college to live with parents? Would you? Under what circumstances?
- Why is marriage being postponed? Is career advancement the only reason? Explain your response.

Enriching

trb James Marcia expanded on Erikson's theory of identity formation—see **Analysis Activity:** *Objective Measure of Ego-Identity Status* (*Teacher's Resource Binder*, p. 5-1; **Handout 5–5**). He established four distinct ways adolescents express identity formation:

With **identity achievement**, adolescents arrive at a sense of identity on their own after considering their options. With **identity diffusion,** adolescents lack commitment to any goal. With **moratorium,** adolescents are still in a crisis period searching for an identity but not yet coming to a conclusion. With **foreclosure,** adolescents make a commitment to an identity without experiencing a crisis. Usually, adolescents will make an identity decision according to the expectations of others rather than their own choices.

Working in small groups, have students discuss the identity formations and provide an example for each one, based on a fictional adolescent that could be a student in your school.

■ TEACHING TIP

Ask students to describe their relationships with their parents before and after they entered adolescence. Ask them if at times they feel like the young man in the cartoon. Have them reflect on why adolescents may not express as much warmth and closeness toward their parents as younger children. This conversation may lead to students understanding their relationship with their parents better.

■ LOOKING AT THE ISSUES

Becoming an adult is the key developmental task during adolescence. Have students ponder the following questions:

- What steps has your family taken to encourage your development as an adult? To discourage your development?
- What adult responsibilities do you wish you had now? Why?
- What responsibilities do you want to put off as long as possible? Why?

trb At this point, you may wish to use Analysis Activity: *Objective Measure of Ego Identity Status (OM-EIS)* (*Teacher's Resource Binder*, p. 5-1; Handout 5–5).

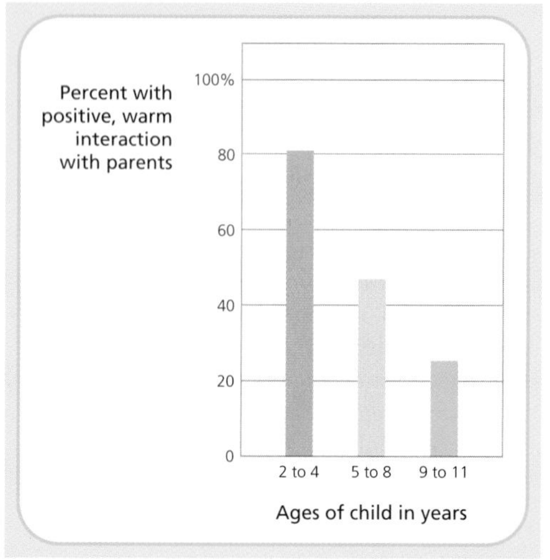

Figure 5.5 Changes in Parent-Child Relationships Over Time A large survey of Canadian families shows that there is less warmth, and presumably more distance, in parent-child interactions as children grow older. (Data from Statistics Canada, 1999.)

mall if you watch parents interacting with their preschool-age children and then watch parents interacting with teenage children. Your first observation will probably be that not as many teenagers go to the mall with their parents! When they are there together, parents and adolescents will probably display less warmth and emotional closeness than you'll see in families with younger children. Figure 5.5 shows how this progression develops over time. As children become adolescents, arguments with parents tend to become both more frequent (Tesser & others, 1989) and more intense (Laursen & others, 1998).

Independence Most adolescents achieve independence with relatively little friction in the family. Sometimes, however, things can get tense!

Doonesbury

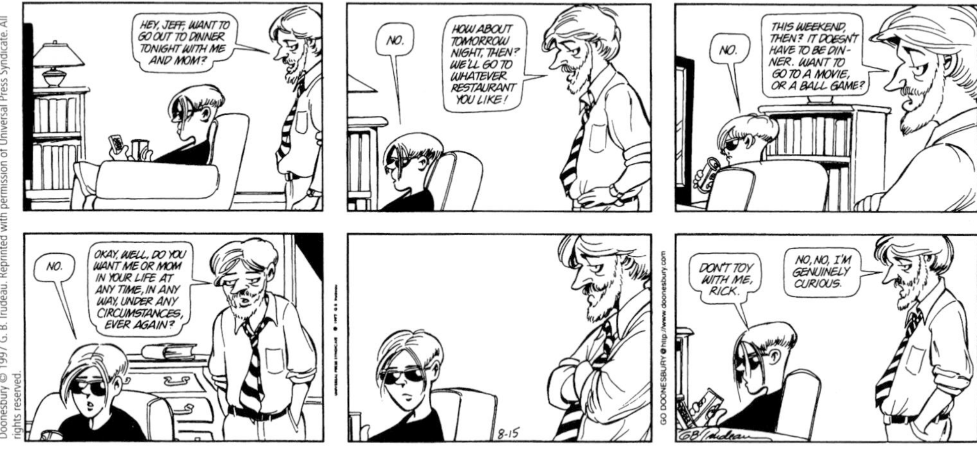

Cross-Curricular Connections

GUIDANCE COUNSELING Have your school's senior or college guidance counselor visit your classes to discuss the life options students might have available to them after leaving high school. Have the counselor present various options, including college, work, military service, and trade school. Request that the counselor also supply students with resources for financial aid, finding an apartment, and applying for jobs and college.

Some families suffer greatly as this move toward independence separates parents and children, but a much greater number adjust with a minimum of turmoil. Most of the time, parents and teenagers get along quite well, with 97 percent of American teenagers reporting that they get along either "fairly" or "very" well with their parents (Gallup International Institute, 1996). In another study, over half of all middle-class teenagers in a worldwide survey said that family relationships were the "most important" guiding principle in their lives. Eighty percent rated family relationships as "important" (Stepp, 1996).

Three Key Developmental Issues

8. How do developmental psychology's three major issues apply to adolescence?

Let's take a quick look at the three major developmental issues as we prepare to leave adolescence behind.

Continuity and Stages

Are we more like the stage development of a tadpole turning into a frog, or more like the continuous, gradual development of a sapling imperceptibly changing over many years into a towering oak tree? There is support for both positions. The theorists who have played such a prominent role in developmental psychology have focused on the abrupt changes as individuals move through stages. Piaget identified these jumps for cognitive development, Kohlberg was concerned with changes in moral development, and Erikson examined transitions in social development. Other researchers turn their attention to the more gradual growth that occurs *within* stages. Development relies on both continuity *and* stages.

Stability and Change

The period of adolescence is affected by both stability *and* change. Temperament and values are most likely to stay constant; relationships and certain behaviors are more likely to change. Many successful and happy adults were troubled people at your age.

Nature and Nurture

This pervasive issue is as important in adolescence as in other developmental periods. We can see the role of nature in the genetically determined sequence of changes that spark sexual feelings and interests. But

■ JOURNAL WRITING

Invite students to use the following questions or writing prompts as springboards for entries in their psychology journals:

- How are you getting along with your parents now? How has the relationship changed, if at all, from when you were a younger teenager? Why or why not?
- Are you excited about the prospect of moving away from home after high school? Why or why not?

■ APPLYING THE POINTS

To learn a parental perspective on how their adolescence as gone, have students interview their parents with the following questions:

- Has my adolescence been an enjoyable experience for you as a parent? Why or why not?
- What has been the best and most difficult part about my growing up?
- In hindsight, what would you do differently now in rearing an adolescent? If you have younger children, are you doing anything different? Why or why not?

■ TEACHING TIP

Have students debate which of the following factors have been most influential to their own development as an adolescent:

- *Continuity* or *stages*—Has their development progressed smoothly or in distinct stages?
- *Stability* or *change*—What has remained constant and what has changed?
- *Nature* or *nurture*—Are they more like their biological family or the people in their environment?

MODULE 5

Close

Ask your students if their adolescent experience has been a pleasant journey or a bumpy road. Then ask if they would rather go back to a time in history before adolescence was necessary, like the late 1800s, when people their age were expected to work on farms or in factories and get married. Encourage them to cite reasons why life is better for teens today than it was in the past.

Checking the Points

■ **TEACHING TIPS**

web (1) The book companion site for *Thinking About Psychology* at **www.worthpublishers.com/thinkingaboutpsych**. contains a module quiz, flashcards of key terms and people, and other student activities and resources for this module. You will also find PowerPoint lectures, a quiz grade book, and other reaching resources by logging on as an instructor.

trb (2) At this point, you may wish to review and confirm concepts about the adolescence systems with **Critical Thinking Activity:** *Fact or Falsehood?* (*Teacher's Resource Binder*, p. 5-1; **Handout 5–1**). Suggest that students complete the handout in small groups without referring to earlier versions of the handout they may have completed and taking the time to look up information in the text to respond correctly to questions. Have all the groups meet to review the handout, again asking students to use the text to support their responses.

nurture's hand is also evident: Adolescents learn to make decisions about expressing sexuality from their families and society. The expression of sexuality is determined by a complex interaction of both nature *and* nurture.

The opportunities and challenges of modern American adolescence are a reflection of a complex world. Life was simpler in the nineteenth century when educational and career opportunities were more limited, but few would choose to return to those more limiting times. Navigating adolescence successfully can be difficult, and most who travel this road will hit a few potholes along the way. It can also be an exciting adventure as one earns new freedoms and masters new skills.

REVIEW

Module 5: Adolescence

What's the Point?

What Is Adolescence?

1. *What is adolescence? How has it changed in the last century?*

   Adolescence is the transition period between childhood and adulthood. This period begins with a physical landmark, puberty—the time when a person becomes sexually mature and can reproduce. The end of adolescence is more variable, since people become adults at different times, depending on how their society defines "adulthood." In the last century, American adolescence has lengthened, as boys and girls reach sexual maturity at an earlier age, and men and women extend their education and wait longer to leave home.

Physical Development in Adolescence

2. *What major physical changes occur during adolescence?*

   A flood of hormones triggers the amazing changes that occur during puberty. Adolescents experience a major growth spurt, and they develop two kinds of sex characteristics. Primary sex characteristics—the reproductive organs—mature, enabling reproduction. Secondary sex characteristics—not essential to reproduction, but normal features of an adult body (such as breasts on girls and facial hair on boys)—also appear. During puberty, girls begin to have menstrual periods, and boys begin to ejaculate. Although the onset of sexuality is a biological event, cognitive and cultural factors influence our ideas about appropriate sexual behavior.

Cognitive Development in Adolescence

3. *How does the reasoning ability of adolescents differ from that of younger children?*

   Adolescents are able to think abstractly, use formal logic, and reason about hypothetical situations, skills that younger children lack. These abilities often lead to idealistic thoughts and behaviors. Teens also tend to focus on the self, particularly when thinking about social situations.

4. *According to Kohlberg, how does moral reasoning change over time?*

   Kohlberg viewed moral development as a series of stages that occur one after the other. In the preconventional stage, moral reasoning focuses on a desire to avoid punishment or gain reward. In the conventional stage, the primary focus is on fitting in and on being a good citizen. In the postconventional stage, the focus is on behaving in ways that reflect universal ethical principles. Later theorists have affirmed that these three stages occur among white males in the United States, the group Kohlberg tended to use in his experiments. But American women and people from other cultures may not follow the progression Kohlberg described.

Social Development in Adolescence

5. *What behaviors support Erikson's idea that developing a sense of identity is the primary challenge of adolescence?*

   Adolescence is a time when young people experiment, sometimes wisely and sometime not so wisely, with their personal appearance and with ways to act around other people. The attempt to build independence may include a degree of rebellion against rules or customs that suddenly feel too restrictive. Teens tend to view new relationships in terms of how they enhance the teens' self-image. The optimism and energy that teens bring to their daily life often let them view the world with a fresh, new perspective. All of these behaviors are part of building one's sense of identity—an idea of who one is and how one should behave.

6. *What did Erikson mean by intimacy?*

   To be intimate is to have a close, sharing, emotionally honest relationship with another person. Intimacy versus isolation is the challenge of young adulthood. Successfully mastering this challenge is much easier if you have achieved a strong sense of self during adolescence and have mastered the challenges of other earlier stages, according to Erikson.

7. *What road does a typical American adolescent travel toward independence from family?*

   We begin to establish our independence from family early in childhood (the terrible twos are all about "doing it myself"), but the pace of separating accelerates dramatically in adolescence. A primary bond of attachment to parents yields to a primary attachment to peers, and interactions with parents tend to decrease. Underlying this movement toward independence, however, is a strong network of family ties that in most cases will survive the changing parent-child relationship.

Three Key Developmental Issues

8. *How do developmental psychology's three major issues apply to adolescence?*

   Developmental psychologists explore three major issues as they do their research on the different periods of the life span. Each issue considers the relative importance of two contrasting concepts:

   - Continuity and stages: Adolescence is a time when we experience abrupt physical change (stages). Yet it is also a time when we gradually morph from a lesser version of ourselves into a more

MODULE 5

trb ■ TEACHING TIP

At this point, you may wish to provide students with **Building Vocabulary: Graphic Organizer:** *Charting Developmental Issues* (*Teacher's Resource Binder*, p. 5-1; **Handout 5–2**). Using the chart in this graphic organizer, students can review module vocabulary words and terms in relation to issues of adolescent development. Suggest that students fill out organizers individually, without referring to the text or copies of the organizer they may have filled out earlier in the module. Next, allow time for students to exchange organizers with partners to check their responses.

tb Using the Test Bank

The *Test Bank* that accompanies this textbook offers a wide variety of questions in different formats and levels of complexity. Use the software to construct whole tests or to integrate standardized questions into teacher-made tests.

Self-Test Answers

Multiple-Choice Questions

1. c, 2. b, 3. a, 4. d

developed version of that same self (continuity).

- Stability and change: While our personality traits and values remain impressively constant throughout adolescence (stability), many of our behaviors and relationships do adjust themselves in response to our changing environments (change).
- Nature and nurture: Adolescence represents a thorough interaction of our biological selves (nature) and our experiences with family, friends, and society at large (nurture).

Key Terms

adolescence, p. 81
puberty, p. 82
primary sex characteristics, p. 83
secondary sex characteristics, p. 83
sexual orientation, p. 84
identity, p. 89
intimacy, p. 91

Key People

Jean Piaget, p. 85
Lawrence Kohlberg, p. 85
Erik Erikson, p. 88

Self-Test

Multiple-Choice Questions

Choose the *best* answer for each of the following questions.

1. This is "Take Your Daughter to Work Day," and Mr. DiCastro has invited his seven-year-old daughter Naomi to observe him teaching his high school geometry class. This may be a bad idea because Naomi
   a. will see her father through the students' eyes.
   b. may be exposed to rude teenagers.
   c. is not old enough to have acquired formal operational thinking, which is necessary to understand geometry and other forms of abstract mathematics.
   d. has not yet reached the stage of postconventional reasoning.
2. Your adolescence probably started ______________ and will end ______________ than President George Washington's adolescence.
   a. sooner; sooner c. later; sooner
   b. sooner; later d. later; later
3. Justin, who is 15, dyes his hair orange, plays basketball and chess, dates three different girls, and volunteers to tutor special needs kids on Saturday mornings. Erikson would say that Justin appears to be a(n)
   a. typical adolescent searching for his identity.
   b. disturbed child who needs counseling.
   c. outcast in need of social development.
   d. rebellious kid stuck in the preconventional stage of adolescence.
4. Tom is 25, and he can easily get dates with young women who enjoy his company. But after dating Tom a while, these same women often break off the relationship, saying that Tom is too mixed up—that he doesn't really know who he is or what he wants out of life. Erikson might say that Tom failed to resolve the primary task of

Alternative Assessment/Portfolio Project

trb INTERVIEWING ADOLESCENTS Alternative assessment tools are designed to enable students to demonstrate understanding of concepts outside of traditional pen-and-paper assessments.

Have students conduct interviews of a person older than 55 years, teens older and younger than themselves, and teens their own age. **Handouts 5–6, 5–7,** and **5–8** from the *Teacher's Resource Binder* provide questions students can use in their interviews.

Students may then write a report or make an oral class presentation about how adolescence has changed over time and how teens of different ages view this time in their lives.

Use the general rubric provided by **Handout 5–9** in the *Teacher's Resource Binder* to evaluate the portfolios. Adapt the rubric to suit your needs.

the ________________ stage, which is to develop an identity.
a. infancy
b. toddlerhood
c. preschool
d. adolescence

5. Developmental psychologists are interested in three key issues when they do research on the various parts of the life span. Which of the following is NOT one of those three key issues?
a. Nature and nurture
b. Stability and change
c. Morality and cognition
d. Continuity and stages

Matching Terms and Definitions

6. For each definition, choose the *best* matching term from the list that follows.

Definition

a. The ability to form close, loving, open relationships; in Erikson's theory, a primary task in early adulthood.
b. One's sense of self; in Erikson's theory, the primary task of adolescence.
c. Moral reasoning characterized by a desire to abide by universal ethical principles that represent the rights and obligations of all people.
d. Moral reasoning characterized by a desire to fit in and play one's role as a good citizen.
e. The period of sexual maturation, during which a person becomes capable of reproducing.
f. Moral reasoning characterized by the desire to avoid punishment or gain a reward.
g. The ability to use formal logic, abstract thought, and hypothetical reasoning.
h. An enduring sexual attraction toward members of either the other sex or one's own sex.

Term

(1) individualism
(2) puberty
(3) menarche
(4) communalism
(5) formal operational stage
(6) sexual orientation
(7) intimacy
(8) identity
(9) conventional moral reasoning
(10) postconventional moral reasoning
(11) preconventional moral reasoning

Fill-in-the-Blank Questions

7. Puberty is the time when people mature sexually. A girl's menarche is an example of the development of a ________________ sex characteristic; a boy's facial hair is an example of the development of a ________________ sex characteristic.

8. Jean Piaget developed a theory of how the quality of our ________________ changes as we move through a series of stages, beginning at birth and ending in adolescence, when we achieve the formal operational stage.

9. Lawrence Kohlberg developed a theory of how our ________________ changes over time, beginning with the preconventional stage, usually found in children who are 9 years old or younger.

Brief Essay Question

10. In what ways do nature and nurture interact to create the period we know as "adolescence"? In your answer, use two paragraphs of two or three sentences each to describe some of the nature (biological) and nurture (environmental) aspects of adolescence.

Self-Test Answers

Multiple-Choice Questions (continued)

5. c

Matching Terms and Definitions

6. a. (7), b. (8), c. (10), d. (9), e. (2), f. (11), g. (5), h. (6)

Fill-in-the-Blank Questions

7. primary; secondary, 8. cognition, 9. morality

Brief Essay Question

10. Students should discuss the physical aspects of adolescent development, including those events involved in puberty. In addition, students should discuss parental relationships, peer relationships, and identity formation activities, also important for a complete answer.

MODULE 6

Performance Standards

Standard Area: Life Span Development

Content Standard 1 Development over the life span

Performance Standard 1.1 Explore physical, cognitive, and social development across the life span.

Physical Development

- Discuss physical changes that accompany middle adulthood (35- to 64-year-olds). Address female menopause. (Student Text pp. 100–101)
- Compare views of aging in the American culture and other cultures. (Student Text p. 101)
- Explore physical development in later adulthood (65–death). Discuss vision, smell, and hearing, as well as changes in the immune system and the brain. (Student Text pp. 101–102)
- Present Figure 6.1, Declining Senses, summarizing the decline in our sensory abilities as we age. (Student Text p. 102)
- Discuss diseases such as Alzheimer's and senile dementia. (Student Text pp. 103–104)

Cognitive Changes

- Review current research on memory ability as we age. Discuss how memory ability on recognition tasks remains stable between ages 20 and 60, but performance on recall tasks declines with age. (Student Text p. 104)
- Present Figure 6.3, Better at Recognition, which reveals how the ability to recognize words does not decrease as rapidly as the ability to recall. (Student Text p. 105)
- Discuss the contrast between fluid and crystallized intelligence. Discuss how, as we age, our fluid intelligence as well as our ability to reason abstractly decreases. (Student Text pp. 105–106)
- Present Figure 6.4, Age and Intelligence Test Scores, which reveals how verbal intelligence scores remain steady with age. (Student Text p. 106)

Social Development

- Define the concept of a social clock. Discuss cultural differences in social events like marriage. (Student Text pp. 98–100)
- Present Erik Erikson's psychosocial tasks of adulthood, intimacy, and generativity. (Student Text p. 107)
- Discuss the relationship of work to self-concept. (Student Text p. 107)
- Examine the role and importance of loving relationships in adulthood. (Student Text pp. 108–109)
- Discuss how the empty-nest syndrome is a myth. (Student Text p. 109)
- Discuss how ageism is an unfortunate part of American culture. (Student Text p. 110)
- Present that older adults report happiness and satisfaction with their lives. (Student Text pp. 110–111)
- Investigate how coping with death varies from culture to culture. (Student Text p. 112)
- Discuss the emerging role of hospice care in the United States. (Student Text pp. 112–113)
- Examine the need to mourn the loss of a loved one. (Student Text p. 113)

Performance Standard 1.4 Apply life span concepts to personal experience.

- Discuss Alzheimer's disease; asks students if they would want to take a genetic test to determine the likelihood that they will develop this disease. (Student Text p. 103)
- As an introduction to the concept of ageism, ask students to consider their perception of older adults. (Student Text p. 110)

Content Standard 3 Stage theories

Performance Standard 3.1 List stages in the developmental theories proposed by psychologists such as Piaget, Erikson, Kohlberg, Gilligan, Cross, Helms, and others.

- Discuss Erik Erikson's psychosocial tasks of adulthood, intimacy, and generativity. (Student Text p. 107)

Materials NETWORK

All of the items from the Video, Activity, and Enrichment Centers listed below come from the *Teacher's Resource Binder*. These items will help you teach and expand on concepts presented in Module 6.

trb This logo indicates when an item from the Materials Network may be used in conjunction with a specific note found in this module's *Teacher's Edition*.

Early Adulthood Transitions and the Social Clock

Activity Center

- Critical Thinking Activity: *Fact or Falsehood?* With this activity, students' preconceptions about adulthood and aging are either exposed as incorrect or reinforced as correct. (*Teacher's Resource Binder*, p. 6-1; Handout 6–1)
- Building Vocabulary: Graphic Organizer: *Adulthood and Aging* The idea web in this module's graphic organizer contains concepts about adulthood and aging that include module vocabulary for which students must provide definitions. (*Teacher's Resource Binder*, p. 6-1; Handout 6–2)
- Critical Thinking Activity: *Life Span Development* What preconceived notions do students hold about people at varying ages in the life span? With this activity, students reveal their attitudes toward people of different ages—from infancy and childhood through adolescence and early adulthood into the middle and late adult years. (*Teacher's Resource Binder*, p. 6-1; Handout 6–3)
- Cooperative Learning Activity: *Your Lot in Life* Life can throw many curve balls; some we hit and others we don't. This activity encourages students to relate the literature on developmental psychology to the everyday experiences of children and their parents. Students consider how they might handle different lots in life—both positive and negative. (*Teacher's Resource Binder*, p. 6-1)
- Analysis Activity: *Birthday Cards and Aging* Do greeting cards reveal how we as Americans view age? At first students might not consider birthday cards as a tool for analyzing attitudes toward aging. As they review a variety of commercial cards and uncover connotations these cards reflect, they begin to gain insights into attitudes about aging. (*Teacher's Resource Binder*, p. 6-1)

Physical Changes and Transitions

V Video Center

Consult the faculty guides from *The Mind* and *The Brain* video series for descriptions of these modules.

- Videocassette: *The Brain,* Second Edition, Module 19: "Alzheimer's Disease" (*Teacher's Resource Binder*, p. 6-1)
- Videocassette: *The Brain,* Second Edition, Module 31: "Brain Transplants in Parkinson's Patients" (*Teacher's Resource Binder*, p. 6-1)
- Videocassette: *The Mind,* Second Edition, Module 17: "Aging and Memory" (*Teacher's Resource Binder*, p. 6-1)
- Videocassette: *The Mind,* Second Edition, Module 18: "Effects of Memory and Physical Activity on the Brain/Mind" (*Teacher's Resource Binder*, p. 6-1)
- Videocassette: *The Mind,* Second Edition, Module 19: "Understanding Alzheimer's Disease" (*Teacher's Resource Binder*, p. 6-1)

Activity Center

- Application Activity: *Growing Old* What does it feel like to have arthritis, poor eyesight, or poor mobility? By interacting with one another while using earplugs, elastic bandages and medical tape, and eyeglasses with slight prescriptions, students experience some of the problems of aging. (*Teacher's Resource Binder*, p. 6-1)
- Evaluation Activity: *Perceptions of Old Age* In this unusual activity, students ask a peer and an older individual to draw a picture of a typical scene in the life of an elderly person. As students compare and contrast the drawings they have gathered, they gain insight into differences and misconceptions people their age often have about the elderly and the experience of growing old. (*Teacher's Resource Binder*, p. 6-1)
- Critical Thinking Activity: *Alzheimer's Quiz* This quiz may help students better understand Alzheimer's disease, a condition students may experience in their grandparents or people they know of their grandparents' generation. The quiz was originally taken by a cross-section of 1500 people in the United States older than 45. The quiz not only introduces the students to facts about Alzheimer's, it also helps students compare their preconceptions or misconceptions about this disease to those held by older Americans. (*Teacher's Resource Binder*, p. 6-1; Handout 6–4)

Cognitive Changes and Transitions

Enrichment Center

- Enrichment Lesson: *Achievement in Later Life* While cross-sectional studies suggest a decline, longitudinal studies indicate an intellectual stability in people after early adulthood. Other research shows that fluid intelligence declines while crystallized intelligence does not in later life. Old age doesn't signal the end of life as we know it. With this lesson, students learn about great accomplishments by people over the age of 60. (*Teacher's Resource Binder*, p. 6-1)
- Enrichment Lesson: *Living to 100* Only one in four Americans surveyed by the American Association of Retired Persons hoped to reach 100 years old. On average, Americans preferred to call it quits at 91. The number of centenarians in our society has grown; so, it is interesting for students to find out how this increasing segment of the population feels about their life at this point in the life span. Even though surveys show that most people would not want to live to be 100 years old, studies of centenarians show that they live full, rich lives. (*Teacher's Resource Binder*, p. 6-1)

Social Changes and Transitions

Activity Center

- Application Activity: *Writing Letters to Parents and Children* To help students gain perspective on the emotions and motivations behind parenting, they write two letters: one to a future child on his or her 18th birthday, and one to their parents as students approach their own 18th birthdays. These letters provide students with the opportunity to discuss developmental issues from a personal, concrete perspective. (*Teacher's Resource Binder*, p. 6-1; Handout 6–5)

Enrichment Center

- Enrichment Lesson: *Friendship in Marriage* John Gottman, a psychologist at the University of Washington, recently published results of his study of 650 couples that he tracked for 14 years. According to Gottman's study, what makes a marriage last? Not attraction but friendship, mutual respect, and interest in one another's lives. (*Teacher's Resource Binder*, p. 6-1)

A Lifetime of Well-Being

Activity Center

- Application Activity: *Writing a Biography* When students write a biography of an elderly person, they may form a bond with that person. The interview process makes students increasingly familiar with the major challenges and joys of their subject's lifetime. Information learned from the interview in addition to the interaction of members of different generations helps students appreciate their subject and his or her life achievements. (*Teacher's Resource Binder*, p. 6-1; Handout 6–6)
- Evaluation Activity: *Attitudes Toward the Elderly* How do students feel about the elderly? Word associations can help students discover their individual attitudes as well as those shared by other members of their generation. This quick activity measures positive and negative words students use to describe "old people." (*Teacher's Resource Binder*, p. 6-1)
- Evaluation Activity: *Life/Values/Goals Inventory* Challenge students to think about life beyond today with this inventory. Students are asked questions ranging from what they would like to have said about them if they were to die today, to what goals are important to them as they plan their lives, to what obstacles might keep them from achieving what they want from life. (*Teacher's Resource Binder*, p. 6-1; Handout 6–7)
- Critical Thinking Activity: *The Medical Directive* Each year, tens of thousands of people die of lingering terminal illnesses. The most overwhelming of these illnesses is cancer. To introduce a discussion of an experience that some people will face in their lives, students can complete this medical directive. In it they consider what they would want done if they had a terminal illness. For instance, would they want heroic measures taken to prolong their lives? This medical directive provides perspective on the decisions people sometimes face in tragic circumstances. (*Teacher's Resource Binder*, p. 6-1; Handout 6–8)
- Critical Thinking Activity: *Thinking About Death* One way in which students can begin to consider their thoughts and feelings toward death is to complete the measure presented in the handout. In it, students complete ideas such as "When I die, I would like to have at my bedside...." This activity will help students ponder the state of their lives and, in turn, discover their views on death and dying. (*Teacher's Resource Binder*, p. 6-1; Handout 6–9)

Enrichment Center

- Enrichment Lesson: *Negative Stereotypes of the Elderly* Mark Snyder and Peter Miene examined reasons that young people of college age harbor negative stereotypes of the elderly, as well as ways of changing these views. Undergraduates were assigned to one of three conditions in which they read different stories, each condition reflecting a different theory of why people stereotype others. All the stories described the experiences of a young person who reluctantly volunteers to spend time with a range of older adults from nursing homes and other settings. This lesson shows how three different psychological approaches explain our aversion to growing old. (*Teacher's Resource Binder*, p. 6-1)

- Enrichment Lesson: *Euthanasia and the Law* Although three-fifths of adult Americans say that doctors should be allowed to help terminally ill people in severe pain take their own lives, only the state of Oregon has a statute permitting doctor-assisted suicide. In 1997, the Supreme Court ruled that there is no constitutional right to physician-assisted suicide and thus left states to decide. Views on this topic vary from one state to another and from one individual to another. This lesson explores the ethical and legal questions related to euthanasia. (*Teacher's Resource Binder*, p. 6-1)

MODULE 6

Adulthood and Aging

Introducing the Module

The Points: Module Objectives

- Describe the social clock and the sorts of things that affect how it is set.
- Describe the effects of physical changes in middle and later adulthood.
- Analyze whether memory and level of intelligence normally increase, decrease, or stay the same as people grow older.
- Identify two kinds of events that most affect our social well-being during early and middle adulthood.
- Evalute if most older, retired people are happy and satisfied with their lives.
- Determine how we can cope with the death of our loved ones.

trb tr Building Vocabulary

The concepts in the idea web presented in **Building Vocabulary: Graphic Organizer:** *Adulthood and Aging* (*Teacher's Resource Binder*, p. 6-1; **Handout 6–2**) reflect the module vocabulary, as well as basic concepts related to adulthood and aging. You might first use the handout as a transparency to project for the class to see and ask questions about. Students may then complete the organizers on their own. Encourage students to combine their study of these terms with the terms from Modules 4 and 5, which are also related to development.

Teaching the Points

web ■ TEACHING TIP

You can log on as an instructor to the book companion site for *Thinking About Psychology* at **www.worthpublishers.com/thinkingaboutpsych**. It contains teacher resources for class presentations as well as review and assessment of module concepts and terms.

MODULE 6

Adulthood and Aging

Early Adulthood Transitions and the Social Clock

Physical Changes and Transitions

Cognitive Changes and Transitions

Social Changes and Transitions

A Lifetime of Well-Being

Dying and Death

How many times have you been asked, "What are you going to do after you graduate?" You've given this some thought, right? Will you go to college or enter the work force? No doubt, you're receiving all kinds of advice. Perhaps you've even been told what type of job to take, or where to go to college and what your major should be, or how you would benefit from "sitting out a year" just to take a break from learning. Making decisions about life after high school is a milestone in your continuing transition from adolescence and being dependent on your parents, to early adulthood and being dependent on yourself. In this module, we'll look at some of the other transitions that we all make as we move from early to middle to late adulthood (Table 6.1).

TABLE 6.1 PERIODS OF ADULTHOOD

PERIOD	APPROXIMATE AGE BRACKETS
Early adulthood	20 to 35
Middle adulthood	36 to 64
Late adulthood	65 and over

Early Adulthood Transitions and the Social Clock

1. What is the social clock, and what sorts of things affect how it is set?

► **social clock** The culturally preferred timing of social events such as marriage, parenthood, and retirement.

As you continue your journey from adolescence to adulthood, you'll face lots of other important questions: When will you move out of your parents' house? Where will you live? Will you marry? If so, when? How

Getting Started

trb You may wish to use **Critical Thinking:** *Fact or Falsehood?* (*Teacher's Resource Binder*, p. 6-1; **Handout 6–1**) as a prereading strategy to find out what students already know about adulthood and aging. The activity will prime students to note terms and concepts in the text that confirm or dispel their preconceptions about adulthood and aging.

You might also wish to ask students to identify an adult they admire outside of their immediate families and describe some of that person's admirable character traits. Ask students how they think the character traits of the person they described might be related to the aging process.

trb At this point, you may also wish to use **Evaluation Activity:** *Perceptions of Old Age* (*Teacher's Resource Binder*, p. 6-1).

Culture Affects the Social Clock In developed countries such as ours, even great-grandmothers go for their diplomas, as did this 87-year-old Smith College graduate, and teenagers are discouraged from marriage and parenting. Grandmothers don't go to college in developing nations, such as Indonesia, and teenagers, such as this Javanese girl, often marry and have children.

many children will you raise? Your answers to these questions may be influenced by the **social clock,** society's shared judgment about the "best" timing of certain life events. For example, if you got your driver's license shortly after you turned 16 or 18 (depending on your state), you were "on time." However, if you are 34 and still don't have your driver's license, you're "off time," and people are likely to ask, "What's wrong with you?" These social events or transitions can cause anxiety for those who feel they're not keeping up with their peers.

Social clocks have different settings in different cultures. For instance, in Jordan, 40 percent of all brides are in their teens, but in Hong Kong, only 3 percent of brides are this young (United Nations, 1992). And the settings of a social clock can change within a culture, too. In the changing U.S. culture, the "normal" time span for many life events, including marriage, has altered. Both men and women are marrying later in life than they did even 10 years ago.

The transitions in early adulthood are often stressful because we make so many of them at once. Where you are two years from now will be very different from where you were as a ninth-grader. Yet, your transition to adulthood will probably be less abrupt than it would have been a generation ago. Developmental psychologists have noticed that adolescents are easing ever more slowly into the self-sufficiency of true adulthood. In fact, a new developmental stage called *emerging adulthood* is getting a lot of attention from researchers. Consider Ken and Mary, who are 27 years old and married. In changing careers and moving from one state to another, Ken and Mary made an eight-month "stopover" at his parents' home to prepare for their new jobs and to save money for rent in their new city. Ken and Mary would like to have children some day, but they don't yet feel "settled" enough to be parents. Ken and Mary aren't unique. Amos, another friend of ours, is 30 and has a good job, but he still brings laundry to

■ LOOKING AT THE ISSUES

Brainstorm with students what factors may have led people in U.S. society to evaluate their conception of adulthood. For example, why did the federal government choose the age of 65 to grant people Social Security? Why didn't they choose either a younger or an older age?

trb At this point, you may wish to use Critical Thinking Activity: *Life Span Development* (*Teacher's Resource Binder*, p. 6-1, Handout 6–3).

■ JOURNAL WRITING

Invite students to use the following questions as a springboard for entries in their psychology journals:

- How do you feel about the challenges and responsibilities that come with entering early adulthood? What are they?

trb At this point, you may wish to use Cooperative Learning Activity: *Your Lot in Life* (*Teacher's Resource Binder*, p. 6-1) and/or Analysis Activity: *Birthday Cards and Aging* (*Teacher's Resource Binder*, p. 6-1).

■ MULTICULTURAL CONNECTIONS

Have students work with partners to explore other cultural differences in the social clock of human beings.

- Are all Islamic/Arabic countries similar to Jordan in terms of teenage marriages? Are all Asian cultures similar to Hong Kong in terms of later marriages? Why or why not?
- How do other cultures (including Hispanic/Latin, European, African, etc.) view the timing of marriage and childrearing? Do immigrants from these cultures adopt the U.S. social clock or do they keep their own cultural traditions?

Suggested Readings

Use the following books as teacher-preparation tools or as enrichment for advanced students:

Albom, M. (1997). *Tuesdays with Morrie.* New York: Doubleday.

Bugen, L. A. (1979). *Death and dying: Theory, research, practice.* Dubuque, IA: Wm. C. Brown.

Gottman, J. (1999). *The seven principles for making marriage work.* New York: Crown.

Greenberg, J. (1999). *Comprehensive stress management* (6th ed.). Boston: McGraw-Hill.

Kübler-Ross, E. (1978). *On death and dying.* New York: Macmillian. (Original work published 1969)

Myers, D. G. (1995). *The pursuit of happiness.* New York: Avon.

Stevens-Long, J., & Commons, M. (1992). *Adult life: Developmental processes* (4th ed.). Mountain View, CA: Mayfield.

MODULE 6

■ TEACHING TIP

Some students may have older siblings who fit nicely into the *emerging adulthood* stage of development. Discuss with them why their siblings have made certain choices, as well as whether—and how—their parents are supportive of these choices. Perhaps relying on family for support is a move by Western society back to a more traditional social structure.

■ JOURNAL WRITING

Invite students to use the following questions and writing prompts as springboards for entries in their psychology journals:

- Do you feel you are at your physical peak? Why or why not?
- An old adage states, "Youth is wasted on the young." Do you feel this statement is true? Why or why not?

■ LOOKING AT THE ISSUES

Although there are no 43-year-old wide receivers in the Super Bowl, there are older athletes who still perform well in their forties. Invite interested students to research who these athletes are, how their statistics have changed over the years, and why.

V At this point, you may wish to show **Videocassette: *The Mind,* Second Edition, Module 18: "Effects of Memory and Physical Activity on the Brain/Mind"** (*Teacher's Resource Binder*, p. 6-1).

tb ■ CHECKING FOR UNDERSTANDING

To assess students' comprehension:

- Divide the students into groups or pairs and give each group a journal question prompt. Have them present their answers to the class, correcting any misconceptions that may arise.
- Use questions from the *Test Bank* to do a quick assessment of their knowledge of the concepts.

Doonesbury **By Garry Trudeau**

Time to Grow Up? Some emerging adults stretch out the transition time from adolescence to adulthood.

his parents' home on the weekends. He also relies on their financial assistance periodically to make ends meet. Ken, Mary, and Amos are increasingly common examples of the changing social clock in Western cultures. They aren't adolescents, but they have not quite made the transition into adulthood, either.

Physical Changes and Transitions

2. How do physical changes affect us in middle and later adulthood?

You're not there yet, but you are less than a decade away from reaching your performance peak for reaction time, sensory awareness, and cardiac output. Most of these physical abilities will top out sometime during your twenties. If you're a world-class sprinter or swimmer, you'll notice your times slowing down after you reach your physical peak, and you'll know your body is changing. For the rest of us, the early signs of physical decline are harder to detect.

Middle Adulthood's Physical Changes

The midlife years, from around age 36 to 64, are a time of more noticeable physical changes, and these changes bring their own transitions. Twenty years ago, I was always told to "go long" during my family's annual Thanksgiving Day touch football game. Sprinting down the field, I would look over my shoulder for a high, arching pass that would bring a touchdown if I managed to catch it. Now, my nieces, nephews, and daughters are the touchdown threats, while I hike the ball and block for the quarterback. This phenomenon is not unique to touch football games. How many 43-year-old wide receivers will you see in the Super Bowl? None.

Demonstrating

ESSAY EXCHANGE Identify a group—elementary or secondary school students or even older adults in a retirement home—and have your class suggest questions that would help them better understand the interests, concerns, behaviors, motivations, and desires of the identified group. When the class has agreed on a set of questions, have each student also predict likely responses.

With permission, have the teacher or leader of the identified group obtain answers to the questions. Also, request that the interviewed group, in turn, ask questions of your students. After you report the results back to the class, have your students write an essay. The essay should cover responses to the following questions:

- How did the target group's answers help you to understand them better?

Some cultures welcome the outward signs of getting older, believing that those who achieve advanced age deserve status and respect. Not so in the United States, where cheating the aging process is a billion-dollar business that just keeps growing. I can remember sitting in large gatherings as a child, trying to figure out how many people around me dyed their hair. If I played this game now, the count would be much higher. Fewer middle-aged adults, male or female, carry the heads of gray I saw as a child. And the camouflage doesn't stop with hair color. Some try to hide wrinkles with cream; others stretch their skin surgically with a face lift to appear younger. But nature will win this contest as the lines continue to appear and the youthful body forms of the teen years—male and female—change shape.

A very noticeable sign of aging in women is **menopause,** when the menstrual cycle ends, usually between the ages of 45 and 55. Contrary to popular belief, menopause *does not* make most women depressed or irrational. Some women do experience "hot flashes" as their bodies adjust to the decreased amount of estrogen in their hormonal systems, but study after study has found that menopausal women are no more or no less depressed than women who are not experiencing this change (Busch & others, 1994; Matthews, 1992; McKinlay & others, 1987). Most women express "only relief" once their periods stop, with a mere 2 percent expressing "only regret" (MacArthur Foundation, 1999).

There is no male reproductive event equal to menopause. Men's testosterone levels drop, but not at the sharp rate of estrogen decrease in women. Though sperm counts decline, men do not lose their fertility. And for men as for women, the notion of a "midlife crisis" is far more Hollywood than reality. Midlife crises are the exception, not the norm, and usually coincide with a traumatic event, such as the death of a spouse or a close friend your age.

Is This Middle Age? Midlife identity crises are the exception, not the norm.

Later Adulthood's Physical Changes

When I was a young boy, my grandmother would turn on every light in the room when she saw me reading. I'd tell her there was plenty of light; she'd tell me it was too dark. I know now that we were both correct: The light was fine for me, but not for her. How could this be so? The answer lies in the physical changes that affect our senses and our health as we age.

▶ **menopause** The time of natural cessation of menstruation; also refers to the biological changes a woman experiences as her ability to reproduce declines.

■ JOURNAL WRITING

Invite students to use the following questions and writing prompts as springboards for entries in their psychology journals:

- How do you feel about growing old?
- What changes have you observed in adults you know well as they have grown older? How have these adults dealt with the changes you've observed?

trb At this point, you may wish to use **Application Activity:** ***Writing Letters to Parents and Children*** (*Teacher's Resource Binder,* p. 6-1; **Handout 6–5**).

■ LOOKING AT THE ISSUES

The business of appearance has become a multibillion-dollar industry for the baby boom generation (people born between 1946 and 1964).

Have small groups of students use library or Internet resources to research this topic. To focus their research, pose the following questions:

- Exactly how much in revenue does this industry make in a year? (Break down the figures into categories of cosmetic companies, plastic surgeons, and fashion/beauty magazines.)
- What impact does this business have on people in the baby boom generation as well as young people?

trb At this point, you may wish to use **Evaluation Activity:** ***Perceptions of Old Age*** (*Teacher's Resource Binder,* p. 6-1).

■ APPLYING THE POINTS

Using available resources, have students research the affects of older fathers on childhood development. Do children of older fathers deal with different developmental issues than children of younger parents? Why or why not?

- How did what you learned from their answers supplement or make clearer what you have learned in this unit?
- Were you surprised by some of the group's answers? Which specific responses surprised you the most? Why? What had you predicted?
- What are your answers to the questions posed to your class.

trb At this point, you may wish to use **Evaluation Activity:** ***Perceptions of Old Age*** (*Teacher's Resource Binder,* p. 6-1) and **Enrichment Lesson:** ***Negative Stereotypes of the Elderly*** (*Teacher's Resource Binder,* p. 6-1).

Source: **Katz, L.** (1996). Essay exchange with children: An exercise for the child development class. *Teaching of Psychology, 23,* 112–115.

MODULE 6

■ **MULTICULTURAL CONNECTIONS**
Using available resources, have students research how growing old is viewed in cultures that are Native American, tribal African, African-American, Muslim, Hispanic, Indian, Eastern European, Western European, or Asian. Encourage students to present their findings to the class as an oral report.

trb At this point, you may wish to use **Application Activity:** *Growing Old* (*Teacher's Resource Binder*, p. 6-1).

■ **APPLYING THE POINTS**
Invite a geriatric doctor and/or psychologist to discuss the physical and psychological challenges of growing older. If possible, ask the guest speaker to address the following questions and issues:

- Do older people experience sickness more than younger people? Why or why not?
- What are some ways people can decrease the likelihood of developing physical and mental illness later in life?
- How can people be more sensitive to the needs of older people in their families and communities?

trb At this point, you may wish to use **Evaluation Activity:** *Perceptions of Old Age* (*Teacher's Resource Binder*, p. 6-1) and/or **Application Activity:** *Growing Old* (*Teacher's Resource Binder*, p. 6-1).

■ **TEACHING TIP**
Some students may have grandparents or parents who are dealing with the effects of growing older. Help these students discuss their experiences, and guide them toward more sensitive ways to interacting with older people in their lives.

trb **tr** A black-line master for Figure 6.1, Declining Senses, is available in the **Black-Line Masters Appendix** of the *Teacher's Resource Binder.*

trb At this point, you may wish to use **Application Activity:** *Growing Old* (*Teacher's Resource Binder*, p. 6-1).

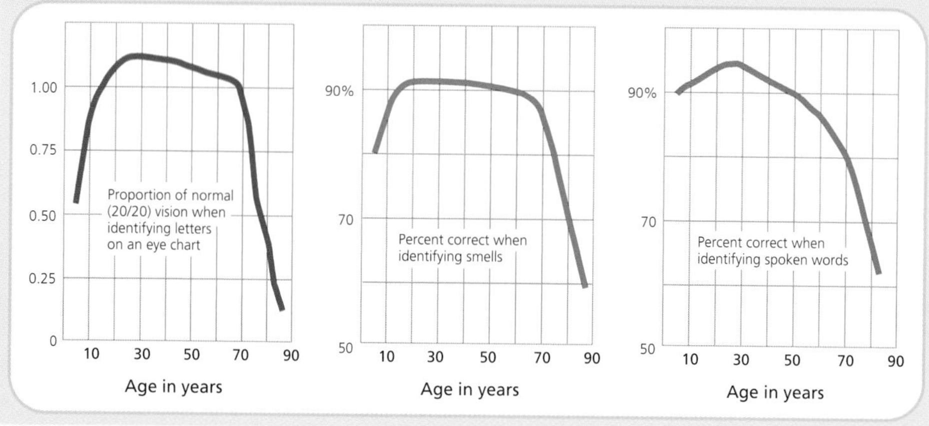

Figure 6.1 Declining Senses Our ability to see, smell, and hear declines with age. (From Doty & others, 1984.)

Our sight, smell, and hearing usually begin a steep decline once we hit age 65 (Figure 6.1). That decline began in early adulthood, but most people fail to notice the loss of small increments of sensory abilities. Muscle strength and stamina also diminish in late adulthood, and our bodies take longer to heal after injury.

So why did Grandma turn on all the lights? Her 68-year-old corneas and lenses had become less transparent, letting in only about 30 percent of the light that entered my young eyes. To experience the same level of illumination I was experiencing, Grandma needed lights three times brighter.

Does health automatically take a downhill turn as you become advanced in years? The answer is yes, and no. Your immune system will weaken as you age, increasing your susceptibility to disease. However, by the time you hit 65, you'll have built up antibodies to all the viruses you've ever had, making you less likely to catch a common cold. Come to think of it, I don't remember grandma ever having a cold.

Aging also slows down travel on our neural pathways. Older people require more time to react, remember names, and solve puzzles (Bashore & others, 1997; Verhaeghen & Salthouse, 1997). Portions of the brain start to atrophy, or waste away (Schacter, 1996). If you live to be 80, your brain will weigh 5 percent less than it does now. Cell loss in the memory regions of the brain is particularly detrimental.

You can compensate for lost brain cells and neural connections by remaining physically and mentally active (Jarvik, 1975; Pfeiffer, 1977). Exercise appears to foster brain cell development while helping prevent heart disease and obesity (Kempermann & Gage, 1999). Exercise may not be the fountain of youth, but it is usually a fountain of health.

▶ **Alzheimer's disease** A progressive and irreversible brain disorder characterized by gradual deterioration of memory, reasoning, language, and, finally, physical functioning.

▶ **senile dementia** The mental disintegration that accompanies alcoholism, tumor, stroke, aging, and most often, Alzheimer's disease.

Demonstrating

trb TO BE OLD What is it like to age physically? Students may get frustrated with older people who move more slowly than teens or have difficulty with other senses. Have students experience what it is like to have arthritis, lowered visual acuity, and lower auditory thresholds by simulating these ailments using tape, gloves, modified glasses, and earplugs. While students experience physical impairment, have them try to do simple tasks like write a check, read a distant sign or the small writing on a menu or in a newspaper article, and hear announced instructions. For more details on this assignment, see **Application Activity:** *Growing Old* (*Teacher's Resource Binder*, p. 6-1).

Fountain of Youth? Exercise is important throughout the life span.

Diseases Related to Aging

Our fortieth President, Ronald Reagan, wrote a letter to the American people in 1992, stating, "I now begin the journey that will lead me into the sunset of my life." At age 81, President Reagan was telling the world he had **Alzheimer's disease,** a brain disorder that 3 percent of the world's population develops by age 75. Alzheimer's is characterized by progressive and irreversible destruction of brain cells, resulting in a gradual deterioration of memory, reasoning, language, and, ultimately, physical functioning. Deteriorating neurons include those that produce a vital brain chemical (acetylcholine). Without this chemical, thinking and memory are greatly impaired.

Senile dementia is another type of mental disintegration (Figure 6.2). Dementia can be caused by alcoholism, tumor, strokes, or anything else that results in a substantial loss of brain cells.

Certain drugs slow down Alzheimer's progression, but there is no known cure. Several gene abnormalities have been linked to Alzheimer's disease, and a simple blood test can now be used to at least partially determine the likelihood of developing Alzheimer's. Would you want older relatives to take such a test? Would you take the test?

Not every older adult who forgets song titles or the location of that misplaced address book has Alzheimer's disease. Some memory loss is a normal part of aging. And the news about cognitive functioning isn't all bad, either. Let's look next at what happens to our thinking processes as we age.

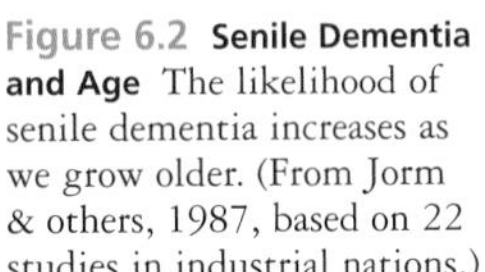

Figure 6.2 **Senile Dementia and Age** The likelihood of senile dementia increases as we grow older. (From Jorm & others, 1987, based on 22 studies in industrial nations.)

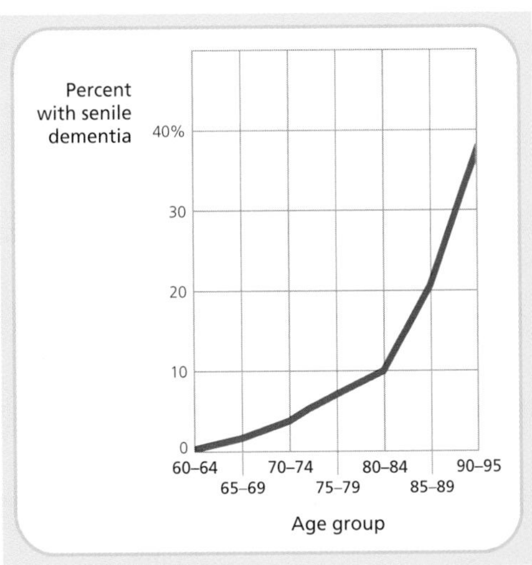

trb tr ■ **TEACHING TIP**

A black-line master for Figure 6.2, Senile Dementia and Age, is available in the **Black-Line Masters Appendix** of the *Teacher's Resource Binder.*

■ **LOOKING AT THE ISSUES**

Using available resources, have students learn more about Alzheimer's disease and senile dementia. Discuss findings in a class discussion, focused on the following questions:

- What are the causes, symptoms, and treatments for Alzheimer's and senile dementia?
- How can doctors make a definitive diagnosis for either or both conditions? Are either or both conditions often misdiagnosed?
- What are some early warning signs for each?
- What percentage of older people get either Alzheimer's or senile dementia?

V At this point, you may wish to show **Videocassette:** ***The Mind,*** **Second Edition, Module 19: "Understanding Alzheimer's Disease"** (*Teacher's Resource Binder,* p. 6-1).

trb At this point, you may wish to use **Critical Thinking Activity:** ***Alzheimer's Quiz*** (*Teacher's Resource Binder,* p. 6-1; **Handout 6–4**).

■ **APPLYING THE POINTS**

Students can contact a local support group for families of people suffering from Alzheimer's disease or senile dementia. Invite the group representative(s) to class to discuss what resources are available for families who must care for loved ones, either at home or in assisted living facilities.

V At this point, you may wish to show **Videocassette:** ***The Brain,*** **Second Edition, Module 19: "Alzheimer's Disease"** (*Teacher's Resource Binder,* p. 6-1).

Cross-Curricular Connections

GOVERNMENT Using available resources, have student pairs conduct research about laws related to health care of older people in the United States. Present the following questions to help focus research and guide a discussion of students' findings:

- When are older people eligible for Medicare? What benefits does Medicare offer compared with private insurance?
- What benefits are available to care for people with Alzheimer's disease or senile dementia? Are nursing homes the only alternative for people with these conditions?
- Once people are diagnosed with a degenerative neurological disorder, do they lose any privileges as citizens, such as driving or voting? What government body makes this decision? What are the reasons for some of these decisions?

MODULE 

■ **JOURNAL WRITING**

Invite students to use the following questions and writing prompts as springboards for entries in their psychology journals:

- What do you think will be your most vivid memory of high school when you are 50, based on your experiences to date? Why will this memory stand out for you?
- Are you better at taking recall tests (essay, fill-in-the-blank) or recognition tests (multiple-choice, matching)? Why?

■ **TEACHING TIP**

Point out that even teenagers have a more difficult time learning new things, like foreign languages, than younger children. Ask students if they had an easier time learning a new video game when they were in middle school than they do now. Although learning new tricks seems to be easiest for the young adult, being even younger than a teenager seems to be advantageous to learning some types of tricks.

V At this point, you may wish to show **Videocassette:** ***The Mind,*** **Second Edition, Module 17: "Aging and Memory"** (*Teacher's Resource Binder*, p. 6-1).

Cognitive Changes and Transitions

3. Do memory and level of intelligence normally increase, decrease, or stay the same as we grow older?

Obviously, 65-year-olds cannot run as fast as 20-year-olds; do thinking skills slow down just as much as physical skills? What do you think: "Can't teach an old dog new tricks" or "Never too late to learn"? Researchers have been taking a close look at this question, and the findings show that the answer depends in part on how we define *memory* and *intelligence.*

"My advice is to learn all the tricks you can while you're young."

Memory

When you're 50, what will you remember about your high school days? Will it be getting your driver's license? Your first job? The first time you voted? Graduation? When asked to remember the most important events in their lives, people in their fifties and older usually recall events from their teens or early twenties (Pillemer, 1998; Schuman & Scott, 1989). This is an important time of life!

People your age tend to do better than people in virtually any other age group on *recall* memory tasks—tasks that give us no clues to jog our memories. One study found that young adults recalled people's names significantly better than did people in their seventies (Crook & West, 1990). Another study asked British people to tell about where they were, whom they were with, and what they were doing when a popular prime minister resigned from office. Participants had to tell the story twice: once within hours of the resignation, and the second time 11 months later. Among participants in their twenties, 90 percent told the same story they had related 11 months earlier. Interestingly, only 42 percent of those 50 and over told stories with the same details (Cohen & others, 1994). In the older group, recall of the event changed over time.

Research reveals a clear tendency for younger adults to have better recall, but what does it tell us about other kinds of memory? One study revealed that *recognition* remains stable from age 20 to 60 (Schonfield & Robertson, 1966). Older adults had difficulty *recalling* a list of words, but they could *recognize* them in multiple-choice questions just as easily as people 40 years younger did (Figure 6.3). Older adults maintain the ability to remember *meaningful* materials, while losing the skills necessary to remember meaningless information (Graf, 1990; Labouvie-Vief & Schell, 1982; Perlmutter, 1983). Habitual tasks like taking medicine every day, and

Cooperative Learning

Divide students into two groups. Assign one group the adage "You can't teach an old dog new tricks"; assign the other group the adage "It's never too late to learn." Have each group come up with evidence and examples supporting their statement and then share the lists with the class as a whole. Revisit the lists after reading the section "Cognitive Changes and Transitions" to see what the evidence seems to support.

trb At this point, you may wish to use **Enrichment Lesson:** ***Achievement in Later Life*** (*Teacher's Resource Binder*, p. 6-1).

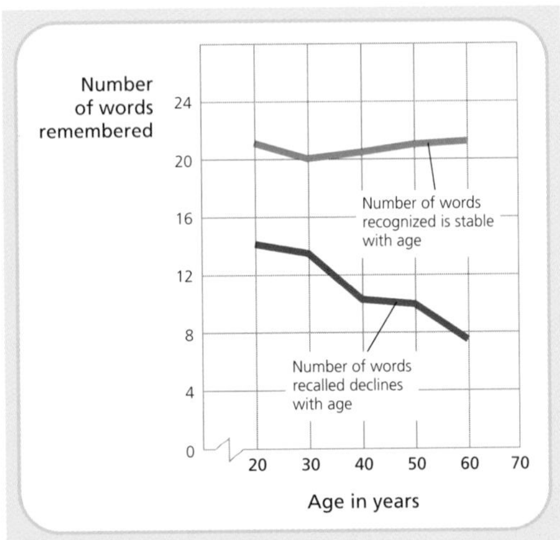

Figure 6.3 **Better at Recognition** In late adulthood, the ability to recognize words does not decrease as rapidly as the ability to recall words. (From Schonfield & Robertson, 1966.)

time-oriented tasks like appointments, are also more challenging for older adults (Einstein & McDaniels, 1990; Einstein & others, 1995, 1998).

It's important to note that in all of these studies, we are only talking about average tendencies. I know people in their seventies who have incredible memories for historical facts and events. And, I have teenaged students who forget to sign their names on an essay test, even when I tell them that their names will count for a point on their grade! Some 60-year-old retirees outperform most college students on a memory test; others will not outremember even middle school students. These individual differences also show up in measures of intelligence.

Intelligence

Does intelligence normally increase, decrease, or remain stable with age? As with memory, the answer depends on the kind of intelligence you're considering.

Fluid intelligence is our ability to reason speedily and abstractly, and we use it to solve novel logic problems. This kind of intelligence does tend to *decrease* during late adulthood. **Crystallized intelligence,** our accumulated knowledge and verbal skills, tends to *increase* with age (Cattell, 1963; Horn, 1982). Intelligence test scores show this difference. On one commonly used test, the Wechsler Adult Intelligence Scale (WAIS), verbal intelligence scores—a measure of crystallized intelligence—remain stable with age. Nonverbal intelligence scores (for example, the time it takes to put a puzzle together) reflect fluid intelligence and decline over time (Figure 6.4, page 106).

▶ **fluid intelligence** One's ability to reason speedily and abstractly; tends to decrease during late adulthood.

▶ **crystallized intelligence** One's accumulated knowledge and verbal skills; tends to increase with age.

■ APPLYING THE POINTS

Contact a local nursing home facility and interview the caregivers about the memory abilities of their patients. If possible, ask the guest speaker to address the following questions and issues and incorporate your findings into classroom lecture and discussion:

- Are there planned activities for patients to exercise their memories and intelligences? Describe them.
- Are the patients, on average, good at remembering to take their medication on schedule? Why or why not?

V At this point, you may wish to show **Videocassette:** ***The Mind,*** **Second Edition, Module 17: "Aging and Memory"** (*Teacher's Resource Binder,* p. 6-1).

■ TEACHING TIPS

tr (1) A four-color transparency of Figure 6.3, Better at Recognition, is available in the **Overhead Transparencies Set.**

(2) Have students share instances in which they forgot to do something simple. Also have them relate stories of older people who seem to have good memories. Compare the types of memory lapses that seem to occur with teens with those that seem to occur with older adults.

F • Y • I

Crystallized intelligence is the type of intelligence involved in learning skills, like riding a bike or ice-skating. Once you learn, you can still perform the skill after many years of no practice. Although the skill may not be very polished after a long period of inactivity, the task can still be performed.

Demonstrating

TESTS FOR INTELLIGENCE Contact your school's psychologist or special education testing coordinator to obtain a copy of an intelligence test used to measure IQ. The most commonly used test is the WISC (Weschler Intelligence Scale for Children). Show your students items from this test to demonstrate the types of questions that measure fluid and crystallized intelligence.

 ■ TEACHING TIP

A four-color transparency of Figure 6.4, Age and Intelligence Test Scores, is available in the **Overhead Transparencies Set.**

■ LOOKING AT THE ISSUES

Some states have been considering legislation that would put an age ceiling on driving. In small groups, have students discuss the following questions:

- Should people not be allowed to drive because of their age? Explain your answer and, if possible, provide examples to support your answer.
- What regulations would you implement to regulate the age of drivers?

trb At this point, you may wish to use **Application Activity:** *Growing Old* (*Teacher's Resource Binder*, p. 6-1) and/or **Enrichment Lesson:** *Negative Stereotypes of the Elderly* (*Teacher's Resource Binder*, p. 6-1).

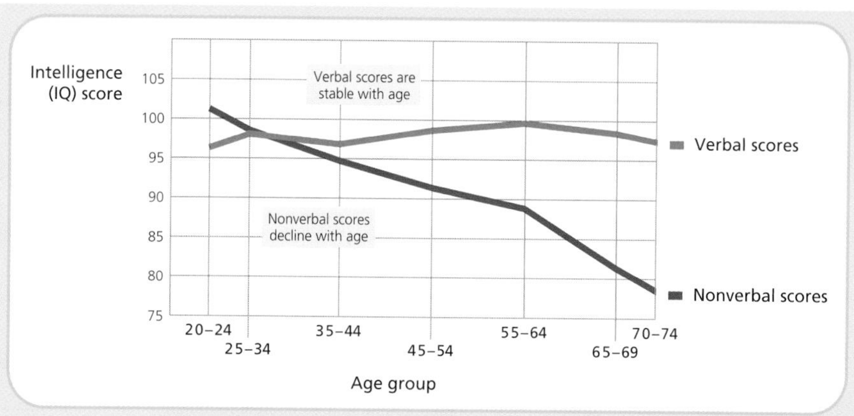

Figure 6.4 Age and Intelligence Test Scores Even after adjusting for educational background, verbal intelligence test scores (a measure of crystallized intelligence), remain steady with age. (Adapted from Kaufman & others, 1989.)

Perhaps increased crystallized intelligence is one of the reasons most chief executive officers of companies and international leaders are in the latter half of their life span. Similarly, literature, like Shakespeare's *Julius Caesar,* often depicts sages as older people who dole out advice for everyone to follow. Professions that favor one type of intelligence over another also differ in their patterns of creativity. Novelists, historians, and philosophers tend to produce their best work in their forties, fifties, sixties, and later, whereas mathematicians and scientists often do their most creative work in their twenties and thirties (Simonton, 1988, 1990).

Social Changes and Transitions

4. What two kinds of events most affect our social well-being during early and middle adulthood?

Many transitions of adulthood hinge on significant *life events,* rather than physical or cognitive changes. Family and work-related events often bring major lifestyle alterations. For instance, marriage brings

Cross-Curricular Connections

LITERATURE, SCIENCE, AND MATHEMATICS Have a group of students research and list famous American and international novelists, including winners of the Nobel Prize, Pulitzer Prize, and National Book Award. Have another group list winners of top math and science prizes, including the Nobel Prizes for Chemistry, Physics, and Economics, and the Fields medals. Note the age of each listed person when an accomplishment was achieved. Have students present the list and ask:

- Are more "great" novels written by older people? Do more book prizes go to younger or older writers?
- In the citations for these awards, how old was the recipient when he or she was engaging in the work that earned the prize?

Compare the ages of people successful in literature with those successful in math and science. Does age seem to be a factor, as the text suggests? Why or why not?

both the happiness of a close relationship and the challenge of blending two lives together. Starting a new job creates new friends, expectations, and demands. The birth of a child starts a series of new responsibilities that last a lifetime. All of these life events have the common thread of commitment running through them.

▶ **Erik Erikson** (1902–1994) Author of the psychosocial developmental stage theory.

▶ **Sigmund Freud** (1856–1939) Founder of psychoanalysis and the psychosexual stages of development.

Life's Commitments

Erik Erikson called them *generativity* (being productive and supporting future generations) and *intimacy* (forming close relationships). Synonyms for them include *achievement* and *affiliation, productivity* and *attachment,* and *competence* and *commitment.* Perhaps **Sigmund Freud** (1935) said it best, though, when he wrote that the healthy adult is one who can *work* and *love.*

Work

Deciding on a first career is an important and difficult decision. You may have a twinge of envy for a classmate who already knows she is going to be an engineer and will declare a major the first month of college. But you can take heart in knowing that your classmate is the exception, not the rule. Most first- or second-year college students

1. change their initial major field of study.
2. cannot accurately predict the careers they will have later in life.
3. change careers after entering the work force.

Post-college employment is often unrelated to college major (Rothstein, 1980).

Still, the questions you've been getting about what you'll do after graduation are just the first of many you'll be asked that will require you to explain what you do for a living. Many people tend to think a certain type of career will either make it possible or impossible for a person to feel self-fulfilled and satisfied with life. But if happiness is our target, must we hit it with the arrow labeled "occupation" in order to feel good about ourselves?

One study addressing the work-happiness connection compared women who (by choice) were employed and not employed. The researchers concluded that it's the quality of the experience, whether as a paid worker or a stay-at-home mother, that matters (Baruch & Barnett, 1986). Whether for pay or as a volunteer, you will work at many different productive activities during your adult life. And at the end of the day, work that is challenging, provides a sense of accomplishment, and fits your interests is most likely to hit the happiness target.

Enriching

Ask students to survey their parents and older siblings to see whether they fit what the research says about college students.

- Did they change their majors while in college? How many times?
- Did they change careers after entering the work force? Did they have to go back to school to accomplish the change?
- Have they been employed in a job unrelated to their college major?

Students might want to write a narrative that applies their research to concepts presented in this module for extra credit.

trb At this point, you may wish to use **Application Activity:** *Writing a Biography* (*Teacher's Resource Binder,* p. 6-1; **Handout 6–6**).

■ TEACHING TIP

In outlining Erikson's theory in class, you might ask students to include in their notes for each stage the name of a person they know. The theory is likely to become less abstract and more meaningful as students check the stages against the reality of living examples.

trb At this point, you may wish to use **Evaluation Activity:** *Life/Values/Goals Inventory* (*Teacher's Resource Binder,* p. 6-1; **Handout 6–7**).

F • Y • I

(1) Market Facts asked more than 1000 adults, "What is the ideal age?" Most respondents, regardless of their actual age, said they felt and acted as if they were in their mid-thirties. Both men and women wanted to be about 32 years old. The sexes differed, however, on the age they considered "old." Men thought old age occurred in the late sixties, and women said being old began in one's seventies. "Psychological age," suggested the pollsters, "may be just as important as real age when trying to understand people's behavior and such things as their buying decisions."

trb At this point, you may wish to use **Enrichment Lesson:** *Living to 100* (*Teacher's Resource Binder,* p. 6-1).

(2) Amy Wrzesniewski of New York University studies whether people view their occupations as jobs, careers, or callings. In one study of hospital janitors, she found that all of them fell into one of these three categories. Janitors who viewed their work as a job would not work overtime unless extra pay was involved. Janitors who viewed work as a career would work for advancement and recognition from superiors. Finally, those who viewed being a hospital janitor as a calling would go so far as to participate in patient care, talking with patients, and helping them get things they needed. So it seems that one's attitude about an occupation can determine how positively one views that work.

Source: Wrzesniewski, A. (2002). Discussion for Akumal V Positive Psychology Conference, Akumal, Mexico.

■ JOURNAL WRITING

Invite students to use the following questions as springboards for entries in their psychology journals:

- What do you consider the most important aspects of a relationship with someone you might date? Do you think these are the same aspects married people value? Why or why not?
- What is your view of divorce? How did you develop this view?
- Do teenage relationships possess the same qualities mentioned in the text as those that mark a love relationship? Why or why not?

trb At this point, you may wish to use Enrichment Lesson: *Friendship in Marriage* (*Teacher's Resource Binder*, p. 6-1).

■ TEACHING TIP

Many of your students may be children of divorced parents. Although the research shows that divorce is common today, many students may feel alone and confused when their parents split. Encourage healthy discussion of how to handle being a child of divorce so students know they are part of a growing segment of society that knows what divorce is like first-hand.

■ APPLYING THE POINTS

(1) Ask students what significant life events their families have experienced since they were born. Have they moved? Changed jobs, either voluntarily or involuntarily? Added family members, either through birth, adoption, or caregiving? What effect have these life events had on the lives of their parents and their relationship with their parents?

(2) Have students develop a pamphlet or presentation for younger children about how to handle being a child of divorce. Encourage your students to contact local psychologists who specialize in counseling children and families dealing with divorce for research-based tips they can offer others. This type of activity can help students deal with feelings they may have about their experiences with divorce.

Love

Do opposites really attract? Yes, but only if we're talking about magnets. Let's make sure we don't confuse magnetism with love. Love, by any name you call it—commitment, devotion, intimacy, attachment—is vital to a happy adulthood. Love lasts longer and is most satisfying when marked by

- intimate self-disclosure.
- shared emotional and material support.
- similar interests and values.

For many, love translates into marriage: Ninety percent of our population gets married at least once. Those marriages are more likely to last if both members are over 20, have a stable income from good employment, dated a long time before getting married, and are well educated (Myers, 2000). The divorce rate in the United States hovers around 50 percent. Three out of four who divorce will marry a second time (Vemer & others, 1989). Does this high divorce rate mean that people are jumping into marriage too quickly? Would it be better to "test drive" a relationship by living together first? According to 10 different studies, the answer is no. The divorce rate for those who lived together prior to marriage is higher than for couples who did not live together (Myers, 2000).

Despite the divorce epidemic, the monogamous bond of marriage remains a popular living arrangement, just as it has in various human societies through the centuries. One reason the institution of marriage endures is because of the well-being it brings to the couple. Married men and married women report greater happiness than unmarried, sep-

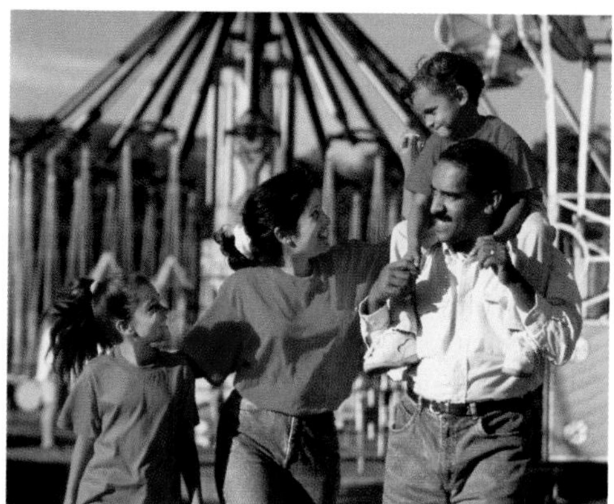

A Happy Union Married men and women report greater happiness than unmarried, separated, or divorced individuals.

Cross-Curricular Connections

GOVERNMENT AND CIVICS Develop a joint project with your school's government or civics teacher in which students research the laws concerning divorce and child custody in your state, as well as other states in which students might be interested. Individuals, partners, or small groups may take part in the research. After research findings are presented, lead a full-class discussion on the following questions:

- Do these laws seem to encourage or discourage divorce?
- What seem to be the biases the justice system has concerning divorce?

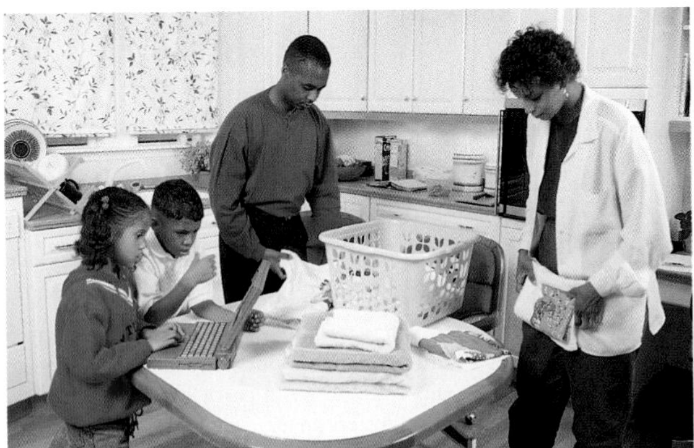

Sharing the Load Balancing household duties leads to a more satisfying marriage and better relationships with children.

arated, or divorced individuals (Inglehart, 1990). Lesbians in committed relationships also report greater well-being than individuals who remain alone (Wayment & Peplau, 1995).

Must a marriage be conflict-free to last? Very few marriages avoid conflict completely, but one indicator of marital success is the way couples interact. Stable marriages have a five-to-one ratio of positive to negative interactions. Marriages last when each partner compliments, hugs, and smiles five times more than he or she insults or criticizes (Gottman, 1994).

Love and marriage often result in the birth of children, an event that is usually met with great happiness. However, raising a child requires a serious investment of time, money, and emotion, which can exact a heavy toll on a couple's satisfaction with each other. As couples make the transition to being parents, they may disagree about the division of labor in the new family structure. Many women who work outside the home still carry the lion's share of the child-raising and housekeeping load (Belsky & others, 1986; Hackel & Ruble, 1992). Those who make the effort to spread the workload more evenly can anticipate a double reward: a more satisfying and successful marriage, and better parent-child relationships for both parents (Erel & Burman, 1995).

The "emptying of the nest" when children move out of the house is also a significant event. Yet, you may be surprised to hear that the empty-nest phenomenon brings more happiness than sadness (Adelmann & others, 1989; Glenn, 1975). Middle-aged women with children at home report lower levels of happiness and less marital satisfaction than those with an empty nest. If the relationship with the children moving out is positive and close, parents are likely to experience a "postlaunch honeymoon" (White & Edwards, 1990).

Cooperative Learning

LOVE AND WORK Divide students into groups to discuss their views on love and work.

- What kind of person would you look for as a marriage partner? Why are these particular qualities important in a partner?
- What kind of career do you aspire to have? Why this particular career?

trb At this point, you may wish to use **Enrichment Lesson:** *Friendship in Marriage* (*Teacher's Resource Binder*, p. 6-1).

■ APPLYING THE POINTS

To help students understand some of the challenges of parenting, ask them to imagine a child they might have one day. Then, ask students to imagine the challenges they and their child might face if the child had a developmental disorder. For extra credit, students may investigate (on the Internet or by telephone interview) community resources relevant to parenting a child with a developmental disorder. The findings could be presented as a written research paper or community service poster.

trb At this point, you may wish to use **Cooperative Learning Activity:** *Your Lot in Life* (*Teacher's Resource Binder*, p. 6-1).

■ TEACHING TIPS

(1) In a group discussion, have students share what the division of labor is among their own family members.

- Who does the most chores? Why?
- Who does the least chores? Why?
- How did the agreement about the divisions of labor occur in their families? Do they think those divisions are satisfactory? Why or why not?

(2) In small groups or with the entire class, have students share observations of parents who have experienced the empty nest syndrome with the departure of an older child.

■ CHECKING FOR UNDERSTANDING

Pose this question: "What is the ideal age?" Ask students why they believe the age they selected is ideal. You might also ask them, "What is the worst age to be, and why?"

Students' answers to this question will naturally lead to a recognition of the text's most fundamental point: development is lifelong, and at each age we are faced with different issues and challenges.

trb At this point, you may wish to use **Critical Thinking Activity:** *Life Span Development* (*Teacher's Resource Binder*, p. 6-1; **Handout 6–3**).

■ **APPLYING THE POINTS**
Invite any of the following people as a guest speaker to discuss ageism:

- gerontologist
- nursing home/assisted living administrator
- geriatric doctor
- geriatric psychologist
- lawyer specializing in ageism

trb At this point, you may wish to use Evaluation Activity: *Attitudes Toward the Elderly* (*Teacher's Resource Binder*, p. 6-1).

■ **LOOKING AT THE ISSUES**
Collect some magazines that cater to different demographic groups, from teens to the elderly. Compare how the different magazines portray older people.

- How often are older people featured in different magazines? Are the portrayals positive or negative?
- In each magazine, what activities are older adults engaged in?
- How vigorous are older people in the different magazines?

trb At this point, you may wish to use Evaluation Activity: *Attitudes Toward the Elderly* (*Teacher's Resource Binder*, p. 6-1) and/or Enrichment Lesson: *Negative Stereotypes of the Elderly* (*Teacher's Resource Binder*, p. 6-1).

■ **MULTICULTURAL CONNECTIONS**
Is ageism a problem in other cultures? Have students use available research resources to find out how older people are treated in other cultures. Students may even interview students from other cultures to learn how older people in those cultures are viewed.

■ **JOURNAL WRITING**
Invite students to use the following question as a springboard for entries in their psychology journals:

- Have you or has someone you know been subject to ageism? Describe the experience.

Up Close

Ageism

Common beliefs about the aging process result in negative stereotypes—oversimplified and biased views of what people are like. . . . The stereotype would have us believe that old people are tired, cranky, passive, without energy, weak, and dependent on others. (Schaie & Willis, 1996).

Does the above quote reflect your beliefs about elderly people? If so, your thoughts also reflect *ageism,* the tendency to categorize and judge people on the basis of their chronological age (Berger, 2001). Just as racism works against those who are not of the race in power, ageism prevents elderly people from being as productive as they could be, blocks happiness, and works against self-esteem. Ageism does not allow its targets to live their lives the way they want (Butler & others, 1991).

Does ageism affect only older adults? Absolutely not. Where I live I can go outside and walk around after 11:00 P.M., but my under-18 child cannot because of our local curfew. If we walk into a retail store together to buy tennis shoes, I will be waited on before my daughter. Ageism affects people of all ages.

Still, ageism does most of its damage to older adults. Not only does it reduce their self-esteem and their ability to participate in society, this prejudice fosters an attitude that accepts ageist policies. However, the tide seems to be turning. As baby-boomers age and swell the numbers of retired Americans, stereotyping the elderly will become more difficult. The image of the rocking chair Grandma is being replaced by mountain-climbing, marathon-running older people living life to the fullest.

As the number of retirees increases, society is finding it more difficult to ignore the needs of this segment of the population. The politician who endorses legislation that negatively affects the over-65 set stands to lose a sizable number of votes from a group that regularly makes its opinion known at the polls. Finally, advances by *gerontologists,* those who scientifically study old age, may help change the perception of elderly people as "tired, cranky, and passive." This change in perception may also help all of us identify with older people as our future selves instead of elderly others (Blaikie, 1999).

A Lifetime of Well-Being

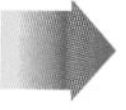

5. Are most older, retired people happy and satisfied with their lives?

For most of us, growing older beats the alternative we discuss in the next section. Yet age often brings a shrinking income, a deteriorating body, less energy, and the loss of friends to death. Would you guess that

Cross-Curricular Connections

GOVERNMENT Have students use available resources to explore existing laws that prohibit ageism.

- Have citizens been given the same protections against ageism as against racism? Why or why not?
- Is ageism more or less prohibited than sex discrimination? Why or why not?
- Do analysts predict that ageism will be given greater emphasis with the aging of the baby boom generation? Why or why not?
- Do laws concerning ageism protect both the old and young alike? Why or why not?

a sense of well-being, that life is good, is rare among older, retired adults? If so, you would be wrong.

Ronald Inglehart (1990) collected interview data from almost 170,000 people in 16 nations and found that, on average, older people are every bit as happy and satisfied with life as younger folks are (Figure 6.5). Another study showed that young people around the age of 25 are far more likely to report feeling worthless, sad, or nervous than are those in their seventies (Mroczek & Kolarz, 1998). Is it any wonder that, with some of the biggest stressors of life behind them, like choosing a career and a partner for marriage, the older set is "satisfied" with life as a whole? We can all take comfort in these findings as we look forward with hope to our own aging future.

We also tend to mellow as we age (Costa & others, 1987; Diener & others, 1986). Emotions later in life are less extreme and more enduring. Instead of letting the downers in life drag us down or the good things make us overly happy, we tend to chart a more even course. Not only are we less likely to feel on top of the world, but we are also less likely to feel depressed. This middle way appears to offer contentment, even if intense joy is lacking.

As an older adult, well-being may also depend on how you reflect on your past. Will you be satisfied with what you've done, or will you look back with regret? Interestingly, most of the regrets retirees express run along the lines of, "I wish I had hiked up Pike's Peak" or "I'm sorry I didn't tell my father more often that I loved him." Most regrets seem to focus on things the person *didn't* do rather than on mistakes made while actively pursuing a goal (Gilovich & Medvec, 1995).

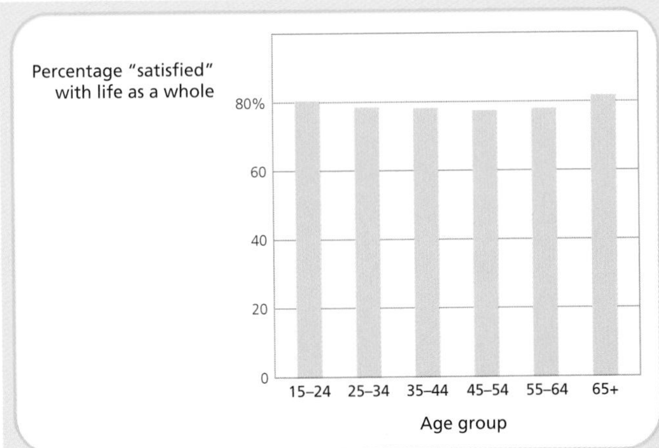

Figure 6.5 Satisfaction Remains High This multinational survey shows that age does not matter much when it comes to being satisfied with your life. (From Inglehart, 1992.)

MODULE 6

trb tr ■ **TEACHING TIP**

A black-line master for Figure 6.5, Satisfaction Remains High, is available in the **Black-Line Masters Appendix** of the *Teacher's Resource Binder.*

■ **LOOKING AT THE ISSUES**

Research findings have suggested that a higher perceived purpose in life is associated with less fear of death. Help students explore the issue of death with these questions:

- What are the different socially acceptable ways people feel about death?
- Did American poet Jesse Stuart speak truthfully when, in recovering from a near-fatal heart attack, he said, "No man really begins to live until he has come close to dying"?
- Do you think acceptance of the inevitability of death is what gives meaning to life? Explain your answer.

trb At this point, you may wish to use **Critical Thinking Activity:** ***The Medical Directive*** (*Teacher's Resource Binder,* p. 6-1; **Handout 6–8**) and **Critical Thinking Activity:** ***Thinking About Death*** (*Teacher's Resource Binder,* p. 6-1; **Handout 6–9**).

■ **JOURNAL WRITING**

Invite students to use the following question as a springboard for entries in their psychology journals:

- If you were 90 years old, what would be one thing in life that you would regret not having done by that point? Why?

trb At this point, you may wish to use **Enrichment Lesson:** ***Living to 100*** (*Teacher's Resource Binder,* p. 6-1).

F•Y•I

(1) Life and death are hot topics for humor. Humorist Woody Allen has said that he doesn't mind dying—he just doesn't want to be there when it happens. Moreover, he'd rather achieve immortality by not dying than by his works living on.

trb At this point, you may wish to use **Critical Thinking Activity:** *Thinking About Death* (*Teacher's Resource Binder*, p. 6-1; **Handout 6–9**).

(2) Chicago inventors have created the Timisis LifeClock to remind us of our mortality. Owners of the $100 clock program their age and sex, and the clock counts down the hours, minutes, and seconds left in one's lifetime—that is, assuming men live 75 years and women 80 years. Every minute, the clock also flashes one of 160 motivational messages designed to inspire productivity and creativity. Orders can be placed by calling 1-800-846-4747.

trb At this point, you may wish to use **Application Activity:** *Writing a Biography* (*Teacher's Resource Binder*, p. 6-1; **Handout 6–6**).

■ TEACHING TIP

Dying and death may be uncomfortable subjects for some students to discuss. Be prepared to work with students for whom death seems to be a sensitive subject. Encourage these students to share their feelings openly about death with those they trust or with the class.

trb At this point, you may wish to use **Critical Thinking Activity:** *Thinking About Death* (*Teacher's Resource Binder*, p. 6-1; **Handout 6–9**).

Dying and Death

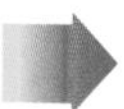

6. How can we cope with the death of our loved ones?

Few escape the sadness of having to cope with the death of relatives or friends. Invariably, one spouse outlives the other, a grief suffered five times more often by women than by men. When the death is sudden and unexpected, grief and subsequent depression can be particularly hard to handle and may continue for years (Lehman & others, 1987).

Reactions to death vary from culture to culture. In some parts of Africa, death brings status to an elder, who joins the ancestors in watching over those still living in the village (Opoku, 1989). Some cultures encourage a "stiff upper lip" and the hiding of grief; others, including many Muslim nations, expect outward and obvious expressions of grief by both men and women (Nobles & Sciarra, 2000). It's worth noting that in any culture there are individuals who grieve significantly more or less than others.

Here in the United States, attitudes toward death appear to be changing, with a greater openness toward the inevitability of death and facing it with dignity. Rejecting an impersonal and lingering hospital death, many patients with terminal illnesses are choosing *hospice care* instead. They receive comforting medical attention (often in their own home), but avoid death-defying interventions. Hospice care strives to make the dying person's remaining days as pleasant as possible, while also keeping family and friends informed and encouraging them to visit. Part of the hospice philosophy is helping the dying prepare for death while maintaining human dignity.

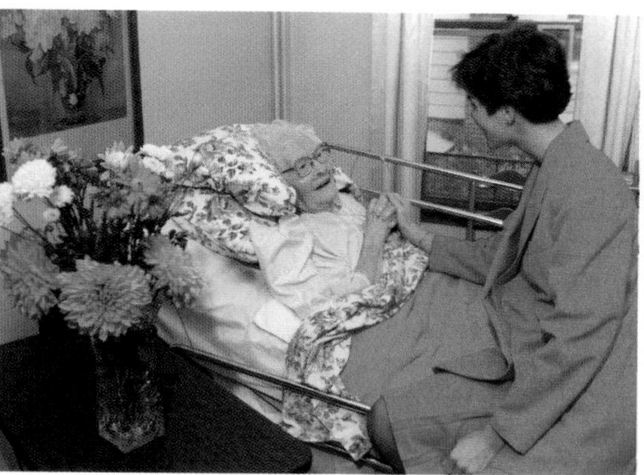

Hospice Care This volunteer holds the hand of a 92-year-old with a terminal disease. The fresh flowers and colorful bed sheets used in this hospice create a more pleasant atmosphere than that of a typical hospital.

Enriching

Have students write their own obituaries, modeling the format and style on obituaries in newspapers. Students should write what they want people to remember about them, reflecting on what they anticipate will be contained in the life's accomplishments and experiences within their speculated life spans.

trb At this point, you may wish to use **Evaluation Activity:** *Life/Values/Goals Inventory* (*Teacher's Resource Binder*, p. 6-1; **Handout 6–7**).

Although we know that everyone eventually dies, dealing with the death of our own loved ones can be very difficult. One popular misconception about grieving is that those who express strong grief immediately get rid of their grief more quickly. This simply is not true (Wortman & Silver, 1989). Nor is there any evidence to support the idea that we progress through predictable stages, like anger, denial, and acceptance (Nolen-Hoeksema & Larson, 1999). Some grieve briefly while others, given similar losses, grieve for months or years. Kathleen Berger reminds us of the value of grief (2001, page 720):

> No matter what method is used to work through emotions of grief, the experience may give the living a deeper appreciation of themselves as well as of the value of human relationships. . . . We all need to learn the lessons that mourners can teach.

What are the lessons from mourners? Can we learn from the grieving who say, "I should have told him how much I loved him"? Evaluating and tending to our important human relationships, resolving differences, and expressing appreciation to those we love may help us avoid devastating regret later.

REVIEW

Module 6: Adulthood and Aging

What's the Point?

Early Adulthood Transitions and the Social Clock

1. *What is the social clock, and what sorts of things affect how it is set?*

   The *social clock* is a term referring to the cultural definitions of the "right" time for certain social events, such as leaving home, marrying, having children, or retiring. The "settings" of social clocks vary from culture to culture and from one historical period to another within the same culture.

Physical Changes and Transitions

2. *How do physical changes affect us in middle and later adulthood?*

   Your reaction times, sensory awareness, and cardiac output will peak in your twenties, but even more significant changes will happen in middle adulthood (around age 36 to 64). Women go through menopause, usually in their mid-40s to mid-50s, a time many women greet with feelings of great relief. Men remain fertile, though their testosterone levels do drop. Sight, smell, and hearing begin to be less

Close

Have students draw a "lifeline" across a piece of notebook paper. They should label their birth date on the far left, project their death date on the far right, and show today's date at the appropriate place along this continuum. Students should note important events from their childhood and adolescence to the left and some possible future life events to the right of today's date.

Encourage students to compare and contrast events on their lifelines with a classmate. Finally, allow volunteers to tell the class what they learned from the exercise and how it relates to concepts about adulthood and aging that they read about in this module.

Source: Brick, Peggy. (1981). The life cycle. In L. T. Benjamin & K. D. Lowman (Eds.), *Activities handbook for the teaching of psychology* (pp. 128–130). Washington, DC: American Psychological Association.

Checking the Points

web ■ TEACHING TIP

The companion site for *Thinking About Psychology* at www.worthpublishers.com/thinkingaboutpsych contains a module quiz flashcards of key terms and people, as well as other student activities and resources for this module. You will also find PowerPoint lectures, a quiz grade book and other teaching resources by logging on as an instructor.

trb ■ TEACHING TIP

At this point, you may wish to review and confirm concepts about adulthood and aging with **Critical Thinking Activity:** *Fact or Falsehood?* (*Teacher's Resource Binder*, p. 6-1; **Handout 6–1**). If students filled in a copy of this handout earlier, have them set that version aside. Suggest that students take turns reading items from the handout with partners, with the responder answering either "true" or "false." Together, student pairs can check responses against information presented in the text.

acute in early adulthood and hit a sharp decline by about age 65. As we age, healing takes longer, we have less strength and stamina, our neural systems slow down, and our immune systems weaken. But by age 65, we've built up antibodies to many viruses. Exercising regularly and remaining physically and mentally active promote a healthy mind in a healthy body. Alzheimer's disease is a progressive and incurable disorder in which portions of the brain are destroyed, producing irreversible loss of memory, reasoning, language, and, in its final stages, physical functioning. Senile dementia is a form of mental disintegration that is most often caused by Alzheimer's.

Cognitive Changes and Transitions

3. *Do memory and level of intelligence normally increase, decrease, or stay the same as we grow older?*

Some kinds of memory do decrease as we age, but others seem to remain the same. Our ability to recall information or events decreases in late adulthood, but our ability to recognize materials seems to remain stable. Older adults also seem to have trouble remembering habit-based tasks (taking medicine each day) or time-based tasks (keeping appointments). But they can remember information that is meaningful to them, even though meaningless information may slip away.

Similarly, intelligence decreases in some areas and actually increases in others. Age affects our two types of intelligence differently. Fluid intelligence, our ability to reason swiftly and abstractly, tends to decrease with age. Crystallized intelligence, our accumulated knowledge and verbal skills, tends to increase as we grow older.

Social Changes and Transitions

4. *What two kinds of events most affect our social well-being during early and middle adulthood?*

Work and love are the two kinds of events that are intimate parts of who we are as adults. Whether we volunteer our time or work for pay, most of us find that the quality of the work experience—the challenges, the sense of accomplishment over performing the work, and the match to our own interests—determines the satisfaction we get from our work. People who attend college will probably change majors and jobs several times as they search for a longer-term career.

Love gives most satisfaction when the partners share intimate information about themselves, emotional and material support, and interests and values. Research indicates that married people tend to be happier than those who are not currently married. About 9 out of 10 people marry, but one half of them will divorce, and three quarters of those who divorce will remarry. A couple's interactions are a mirror that reflects the state of their marriage: In stable marriages, positive interactions outnumber negative interactions by a ratio of five to one. Couples with children will have happier marriages and better relationships with their children if they share the work of raising those children. But as much as parents enjoy being with their children, most empty nests are happy nests.

A Lifetime of Well-Being

5. *Are most older, retired people happy and satisfied with their lives?*

Most people in late adulthood are very happy and satisfied with their lives. They not only have resolved their issues with work and love, but also have become more mellow in their outlook. At this stage, most regrets focus on things people wanted to do but never got around to doing, rather than on poorly chosen actions or paths.

Dying and Death

6. *How can we cope with the death of our loved ones?*
   Our reactions to death depend in part on our culture, and what it teaches us about the appropriate way to mourn our loved ones. In the United States, we are becoming more accepting of death and more open in discussing and preparing for it. Hospices offer an alternative to hospitals for people with terminal conditions who wish to be as free of pain as possible and have no desire for desperate last-minute procedures.

Key Terms

social clock, p. 99
menopause, p. 101
Alzheimer's disease, p. 103
senile dementia, p. 103
fluid intelligence, p. 105
crystallized intelligence, p. 105

Key People

Erik Erikson, p. 107
Sigmund Freud, p. 107

Self-Test

Multiple-Choice Questions

Choose the *best* answer for each of the following questions.

1. Gina is 37 and loves swimming. She has always dreamed of winning a Gold Medal for a swimming event in the Olympics, and she is looking for a coach who will help her achieve this dream. The problem with Gina's dream is that
   a. most world-class swimmers reach their performance peak in their teens, so she probably will not be able to compete with younger athletes.
   b. most world-class swimmers reach their performance peak in their twenties, so she probably will not be able to compete with younger athletes.
   c. most world-class swimmers reach their performance peak in their forties, so she probably will not be able to compete with older athletes.
   d. There is nothing wrong with her dream. Most world-class swimmers reach their performance peak in their mid-thirties, so she has a good chance of winning an event in the Olympics.
2. Dan and Maureen are married and have two children, ages 7 and 12. Dan coaches Little League, and Maureen drives the kids to soccer practice. Dan works as a middle manager in a high-tech firm, and Maureen is a successful architect. They own their own house, two cars, and a boat. By the settings of the social clock used in the United States, a safe bet is that Dan and Maureen are in their
   a. early adult years.
   b. middle adult years.
   c. late adult years.
   d. either b or c could be correct.

MODULE 6

trb tr ■ TEACHING TIP

You may wish to provide students with **Building Vocabulary: Graphic Organizer:** *Adulthood and Aging* (*Teacher's Resource Binder*, p. 6-1; **Handout 6–2**). The idea web in this graphic organizer contains concepts that include module vocabulary. Have students fill out the organizer in small groups, first without referring to the text or versions of the same organizer that they might have filled out earlier in the module. Then, you may use the organizer as a transparency (with answers inserted) to project so all of the groups can confirm or revise their work.

tb Using the Test Bank

The *Test Bank* that accompanies this textbook offers a wide variety of questions in different formats and levels of complexity. Use the software to construct whole tests or to integrate standardized questions into teacher-made tests.

Self-Test Answers

Multiple-Choice Questions
1. a, 2. d

Alternative Assessment/Portfolio Project

trb ADULT DEVELOPMENT Several activities in this module allow students to learn about adulthood and aging through interaction with adults. The results of these interactions may become part of an alternative assessment/portfolio.

You may also use the following activities as part of a portfolio project on adult development. For more detailed instructions regarding this portfolio assessment, see **Alternate Assessment/Portfolio Project:** *Adulthood and Aging* (*Teacher's Resource Binder*, p. 6-1; **Handout 6–10**).

- Application Activity: *Growing Old* (*Teacher's Resource Binder*, p. 6-1)
- Evaluation Activity: *Perceptions of Old Age* (*Teacher's Resource Binder*, p. 6-1)
- Application Activity: *Writing Letters to Parents and Children* (*Teacher's Resource Binder*, p. 6-1; Handout 6–5)
- Application Activity: *Writing a Biography* (*Teacher's Resource Binder*, p. 6-1; Handout 6–6)

MODULE 6

Self-Test Answers

Multiple-Choice Questions (continued)

3. b, 4. c, 5. c

Matching Terms and Definitions

6. a. (7), b. (9), c. (1), d. (3), e. (10), f. (6), g. (12), h. (2)

3. Lisa and Manny got married last June, and their friends have noticed a change in their behavior this year. Although the couple seemed very much in love at first, they now criticize and insult each other constantly and rarely smile or hug. Lisa and Manny should
   a. consider having a child so that they would have a common interest.
   b. seek counseling; their recent behavior fits the profile for a marriage that won't last.
   c. relax; their recent behavior is perfectly normal for the second year of a marriage, when "the honeymoon is over."
   d. separate; single people tend to be happier than married people.

4. On Monday morning, students at Everyone's Regional High School learned that a very well-loved classmate had died in a traffic accident over the weekend. Miss Ruiz, the assistant principal, wants to hold a special assembly to encourage all students to scream and cry and express their grief openly and immediately. Mr. Shapiro, the guidance counselor, says that this approach will not help students get rid of their grief more quickly. Which of these two school officials is better informed?
   a. Miss Ruiz, because those who express strong grief get rid of their grief more quickly.
   b. Miss Ruiz, because she knows that students must move through the first two predictable stages of grieving—anger and denial—before reaching the final stage of acceptance.
   c. Mr. Shapiro, because he knows that there is no evidence for the popular idea that strong expressions of grief help people to get rid of their grief more quickly.
   d. Mr. Shapiro, because his field is counseling and he must know more than Miss Ruiz, whose specialty is administration.

5. Jamal, who is 25, works full time and attends college in the evenings. At present, he can't pay his tuition and also pay rent, so he is living at home with his mother and father until he graduates from college. A developmental psychologist might say that Jamal is a good example of the stage of
   a. delayed adolescence; he still depends on his parents to survive.
   b. early adulthood; he is one of three adults in his parents' home.
   c. emerging adulthood; he is not an adolescent, but he has not quite made the transition into adulthood.
   d. middle adulthood; his full-time job and his age qualify him for middle adulthood.

Matching Terms and Definitions

6. For each definition, choose the *best* matching term from the list that follows.

Definition

a. A progressive and irreversible brain disorder characterized by gradual deterioration of memory, reasoning, language, and finally, physical functioning.
b. The ability to remember things if we can see or hear a clue to jog our memory.
c. The culturally preferred timing of social events such as marriage, parenthood, and retirement.
d. Roughly, the period between age 36 to 64.
e. The tendency to categorize or judge people because of their age.
f. The time of natural cessation of menstruation; also refers to biological changes a woman experiences as her ability to reproduce declines.
g. A type of care given to people who are near death and do not want to die in a sterile hospital environment.
h. Roughly, the period between age 20 and 35.

Term
(1) social clock
(2) early adulthood
(3) middle adulthood
(4) late adulthood
(5) emerging adulthood
(6) menopause
(7) Alzheimer's disease
(8) recall
(9) recognition
(10) ageism
(11) senile dementia
(12) hospice care

Fill-in-the-Blank Questions

8. _______________ intelligence, one's accumulated knowledge and verbal skills, tends to increase with age. _______________ intelligence, the ability to reason speedily and abstractly, tends to decrease in late adulthood.

9. When President Ronald Reagan wrote that he was beginning "a journey that would lead me into the sunset of my life," he was telling the world that he had _______________ _______________, an irreversible brain disorder.

Brief Essay Question

10. In two paragraphs of two or three sentences each, discuss some of the characteristics of work and love as significant events that affect our social well-being during adulthood.

Self-Test Answers

Fill-in-the-Blank Questions

8. Crystallized; fluid, 9. Alzheimer's disease

Brief Essay Question

10. Students should discuss how work and love are significant events in adulthood by citing evidence from the text. Answers will vary.

Biopsychological Domain

Teaching with the Standards

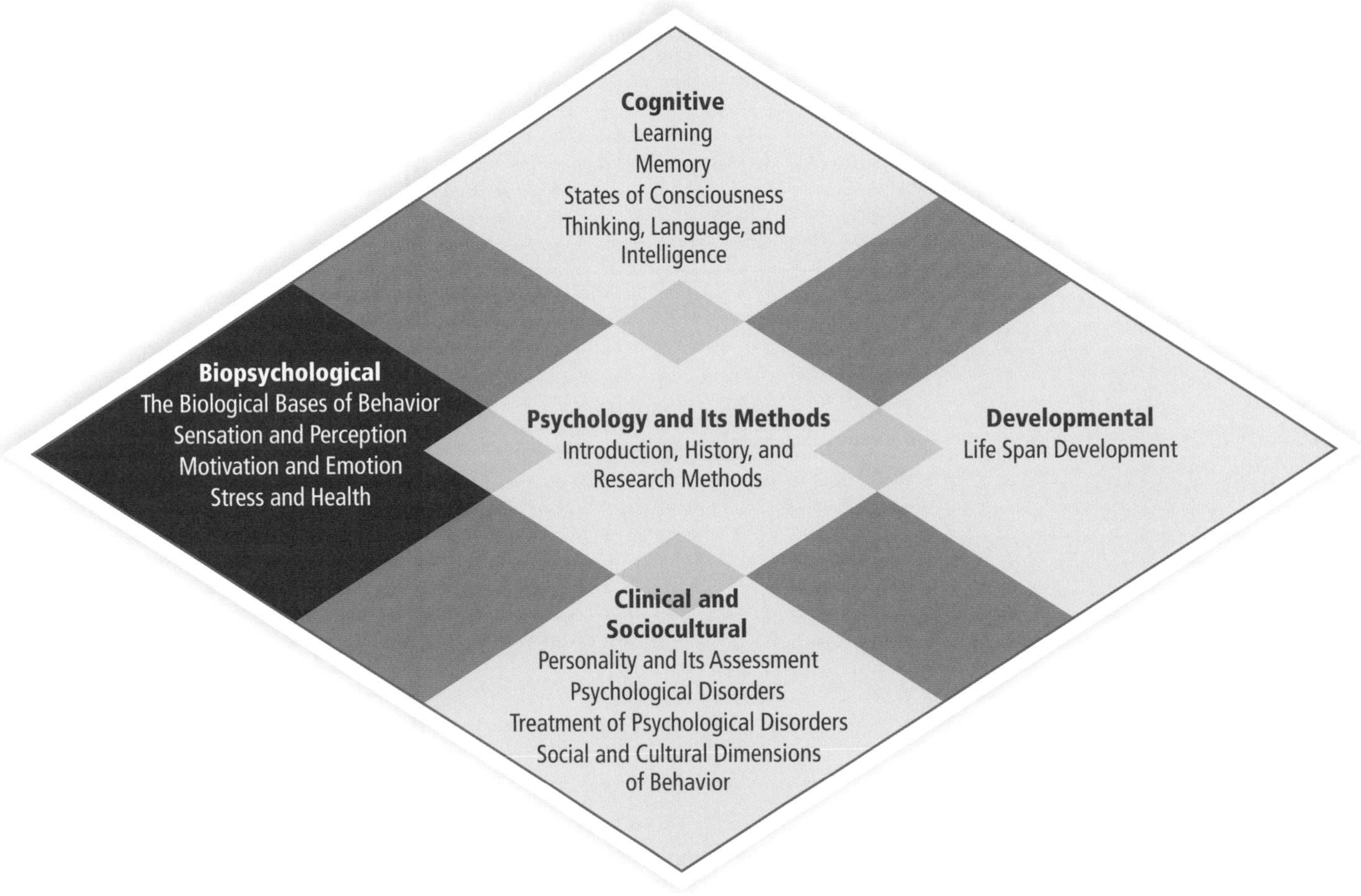

Cognitive
Learning
Memory
States of Consciousness
Thinking, Language, and Intelligence

Biopsychological
The Biological Bases of Behavior
Sensation and Perception
Motivation and Emotion
Stress and Health

Psychology and Its Methods
Introduction, History, and Research Methods

Developmental
Life Span Development

Clinical and Sociocultural
Personality and Its Assessment
Psychological Disorders
Treatment of Psychological Disorders
Social and Cultural Dimensions of Behavior

Scope and Sequence

Background/Significance for the Biopsychological Domain

Many psychologists believe that to truly understand human behavior one must have an understanding of the biological processes that underlie our actions. Although this viewpoint has increasingly dominated the psychological field, students sometimes neglect this important connection. They seem to separate the psychological from the biological.

The National High School Psychology Standards, developed by the American Psychological Association, emphasize the importance of helping students understand the underlying biological processes that shape behavior. In fact, it is suggested that emphasis be placed on teaching units devoted to these processes, such as Module 7, Neural and Hormonal Systems, and Module 8, The Brain. Such units reveal the internal workings of the brain and how our body adapts to external conditions.

In addition, the National Standards also suggest the inclusion of other units that will further highlight the important connection between physiological processes and behavior. Thus, teachers may wish to include Module 9, Sensation, and Module 10, Perception. These modules focus on how our brains interpret environmental sensations.

Module 11, Motivation, and Module 12, Emotion, may also be helpful additions. The focus of these units is on the physical drives that shape behavior and the full-body responses that ultimately lead to human emotion. Module 13, Effects of Stress, and Module 14, Promoting Wellness, explore how stress affects our abilities and the healthy choices we can make to improve our lives.

Emphasizing modules that illustrate these issues will help students understand the critical connection between the biological and psychological forces on their everyday behavior.

Biopsychological Domain

Introducing the Domain

The Points: Domain Objectives

- Explain the process of neural communication in terms of the resting potential, action potential, and refractory period.
- Explain the role of neurotransmitters in neural communication.
- Delineate the different steps of the neural chain.
- Identify the part and function of the various components of the nervous system.
- Analyze the difference between the endocrine and nervous systems.
- Identify the parts of the brainstem and the function of each.
- Determine the significance of signal detection theory in modern psychology.
- Identify the major components of the visual system and the function of each.
- Define the nature of sound.
- Identify the major components of the auditory system and the function of each.
- Identify the four basic tastes, and determine the tastes to which people are naturally more attracted, as well as those that people naturally avoid.
- Discuss the differences among the senses of taste, smell, and flavor.
- Identify the four basic touch sensations, and outline effective ways to control pain using the gate control theory.
- Identify the two body senses, and contrast one with the other.
- Determine figure and ground, and understand the importance of this concept.
- Describe the principles of similarity, proximity, closure, and continuity.
- Understand depth perception and its effect on our lives.
- Describe the two major binocular depth cues.

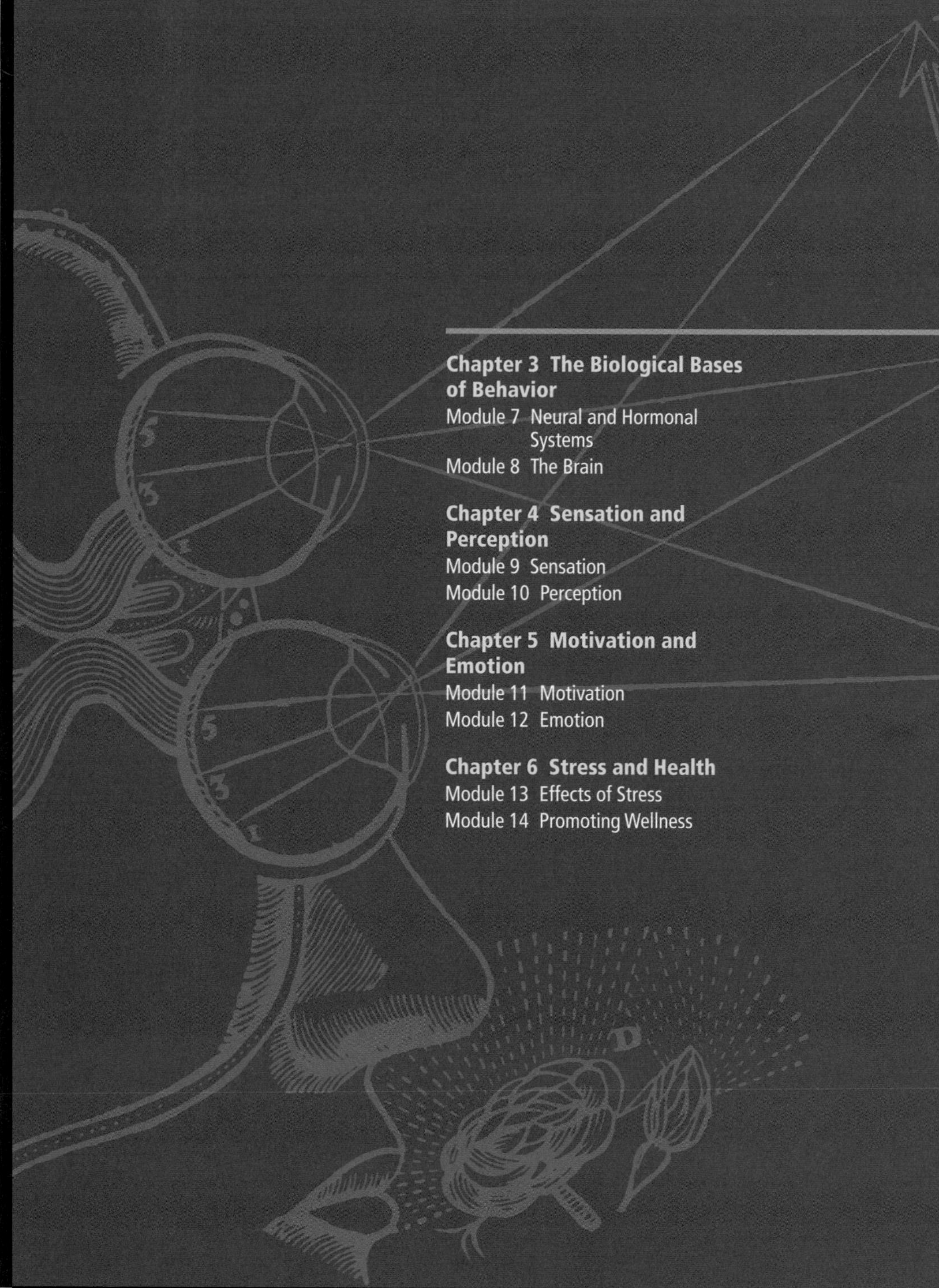

Enriching

Have students contemplate what it would be like if brain transplants were possible.

- Would they go through with a brain transplant if their life was threatened? Why or why not?
- Does the brain contain the "soul" or essence of who you are? Why or why not?

Biopsychological Domain

If you wanted to learn about cooking, one way to start would be to learn about kitchens. If you wanted to learn about transportation, one way to start would be to learn about cars. Likewise, to learn about the mind and behavior, one way to start is to learn about the body. Our biology both *enables* and *limits* our ability to behave, think, and feel.

The chapters and modules in this domain are the "nuts and bolts" of psychology. Our topics—the nervous and endocrine systems, sensation, perception, motivation, emotion, stress, and health—all attempt to reduce important aspects of functioning to the "machine" that makes them possible. Just as we can partially understand transportation by studying the car, we can partially understand mind and behavior by studying the body.

In the eight modules in this domain (and in other modules in later domains), we will frequently use two words. The first is *stimulus,* which is anything you can respond to—the sight of an object, the smell of cooking food, the sound of a friend's voice, and countless other bits and pieces of your world. The second word is *response,* which simply means any action or behavior resulting from a stimulus. Your next stimulus is Chapter 3. We hope you respond positively!

Now buckle up and enjoy the ride as we learn about the relationship between biology and psychology.

- Understand how monocular depth cues work.
- Identify the circumstances under which motion may be perceived when it is not really there.
- Appreciate the value of perceptual constancy in our lives.
- Analyze the effect of perceptual set on everyday sensory experiences.
- Appreciate the effect of context on perception.
- Discuss the similarities of instinct and drive theories.
- Discuss the difference between drive theory and homeostasis.
- Explain the reasons why intrinsic motivation is more beneficial than extrinsic motivation.
- Analyze the role our physiological and emotional needs play in reaching potential.
- Differentiate between historical and modern cognitive theories on emotion.
- Determine criteria for assessing gender differences in emotional expression.
- Define stress.
- Analyze what we know about the link between stress and heart problems.
- Explain how exercise contributes to wellness.
- Evaluate how social support makes a difference in our health and well-being.
- Describe the "faith factor" and how it relates to wellness.
- Analyze how "flow," happiness, and optimism contribute to our well-being.

Cross-Curricular Connections

BIOLOGY Have students explore how biology textbooks treat the study of the brain.

- How is the coverage of the brain in the biology textbook different from the coverage it gets in the psychology textbook?
- What key concepts are covered in both books? Does the psychology textbook cover the concepts in a different way than the biology book? If so, how?
- How can biology benefit from psychology? How can psychology benefit from biology?

CHAPTER 3

The Biological Bases of Behavior

Biopsychological Domain

Teaching with the Standards

Standard Area: Biological Bases of Behavior

Breakdown of Module 7: Neural and Hormonal Systems

Content Standard 1: Neural structure and functioning Module 7 explores the primary parts of the neuron and how these structures function. Emphasis is on how neurons communicate with one another. The roles of specific neurotransmitters are examined to illustrate how these chemicals affect behavior. (Student Text pp.121–130)

Content Standard 2: The structure of the nervous system The divisions of the nervous system are presented along with examples of how these divisions control various types of human behavior. The role of the sensory neurons, motor neurons, and interneurons are also explained. (Student Text pp.130–132)

Content Standard 6: The endocrine system The structures and function of the endocrine system are examined. Emphasis is on the connection between the glandular and neural systems. Also, the text focuses on specific glands, (for example, the adrenal gland) and the effect they have on the body. (Student Text pp.133–134)

Breakdown of Module 8: The Brain

Content Standard 3: Organization and function of the structures of the brain Module 8 introduces students to the parts of the brain and their functions. The brain is divided into lower-level brain structures and the cerebral cortex. Each structure is identified. Emphasis is placed on how each structure controls specific behaviors. The authors use the Greek and Latin roots of the words to help students understand how each brain structure functions. (Student Text pp.140–148)

Content Standard 4: Methods for analyzing the brain The text identifies several techniques that allow researchers to analyze brain structures and neural activity. Case studies can illuminate how brain functioning is altered because of injury. The fascinating case of Phineas Gage is presented as an example of this type of research. Also, the authors explain how modern technology has allowed researchers to investigate the living brain. (Student Text pp.142–143)

Content Standard 5: Hemispheric differences Module 8 investigates how the left and right hemispheres influence brain functioning. Emphasis is on language areas in the left hemisphere and spatial abilities in the right. Split-brain research is also presented, as well as the concept of brain "plasticity." (Student Text pp.148–151)

Scope and Sequence

	Objectives	Text Reference	Standards Covered
Lesson 1	Introduce the structure and function of the neuron. Introduce how a neural impulse travels down the axon and what occurs when the impulse reaches the axon terminals.	Module 7, pp. 121–124	Standard Area: Biological Bases of Behavior, Content Standard 1, Performance Standards 1.1,1.2
Lesson 2	Discuss neural communication. Focus on the role of neurotransmitters and how neurons communicate with one another. Introduce the "neural chain" by discussing the sensory, motor, and interneurons. Explore the effects of drugs, such as Prozac, on neural communication.	Module 7, pp. 125–130	Content Standard 1, Performance Standards 1.1,1.2, 1.3
Lesson 3	Explore the various divisions of the nervous system. Explain the function of each of the subsystems. Discuss how the brain is connected to the endocrine system. Focus on specific glands and how hormones affect behavior.	Module 7, pp. 130–134	Content Standard 2, Performance Standards 2.1, 2.2, Content Standard 6, Performance Standard 6.1
Lesson 4	Discuss the brain structures and their functions. Focus on "lower-level" brain structures, such as the medulla, reticular formation, thalamus, cerebellum, and the limbic system.	Module 8, pp. 140–145	Content Standard 3, Performance Standard 3.1
Lesson 5	Discuss different techniques used by researchers to study the brain. Introduce the case study of Phineas Gage. Discuss the use of CT, MRIs, PET scans, and EEGs. Emphasize how some methods are used to study brain structure and others to study brain activity.	Module 8, pp. 142–143	Content Standard 5, Performance Standard 5.1
Lesson 6	Discuss the brain structures and their functions. Focus on the cerebral cortex and the functions of the frontal, parietal, occipital, and temporal lobes. Introduce the location of the longitudinal fissure and the role of the corpus callosum.	Module 8, pp. 145–148	Content Standard 3, Performance Standard 3.2, Content Standard 5, Performance Standard 5.1
Lesson 7	Focus on how the left and right hemispheres influence brain functioning. Emphasize the language areas (Broca's and Wernicke's areas) in the left hemisphere and spatial abilities in the right. Present Sperry's and Gazzaniga's split-brain research and the concept of brain "plasticity."	Module 8, pp. 148–151	Content Standard 5, Performance Standard 5.1
Lesson 8	Review and Test		

CHAPTER 3

The Biological Bases of Behavior

Introducing the Chapter

The Points: Chapter Objectives

- Explain the process of neural communication in terms of the resting potential, action potential, and refractory period.
- Identify the role of neurotransmitters in neural communication.
- Understand the different steps of the neural chain.
- Identify the various components of the nervous system, as well as the function of each.
- Distinguish between the endocrine and nervous systems.
- Identify the parts of the brainstem and the function of each.
- Identify the two specialized language areas of the left hemisphere, and describe the right hemisphere's special function.
- Understand the concept of brain plasticity.

CHAPTER 3

The Biological Bases of Behavior

Perhaps you're wondering what this chapter is doing here. After all, you signed up for a course in *psychology,* not *biology!* In the next two modules, we'll be covering material that looks suspiciously as though it belongs in a biology textbook. What's going on?

Think of it this way. If your biological being suddenly disappeared, there would be nothing left. Without a body, there could be no behavior, and without a brain, there could be no mental processes. You couldn't play a sport or a musical instrument. You couldn't enjoy the taste of a ripe melon or a freshly baked chocolate chip cookie. You couldn't solve a problem or fantasize about the upcoming weekend. You could neither laugh at a joke (a behavior) nor understand the humor behind it (a mental process). You couldn't feel anxiety about an upcoming test or fall in love. In a nutshell, if biology disappeared, so would the stuff of psychology.

It's possible to study behavior and mental processes from a number of perspectives, including the cognitive perspective, the behavioral perspective, and the social-cultural perspective, and we will do that in other chapters of this book. But now it's biology's turn for the spotlight, and you may be surprised at the insight it provides.

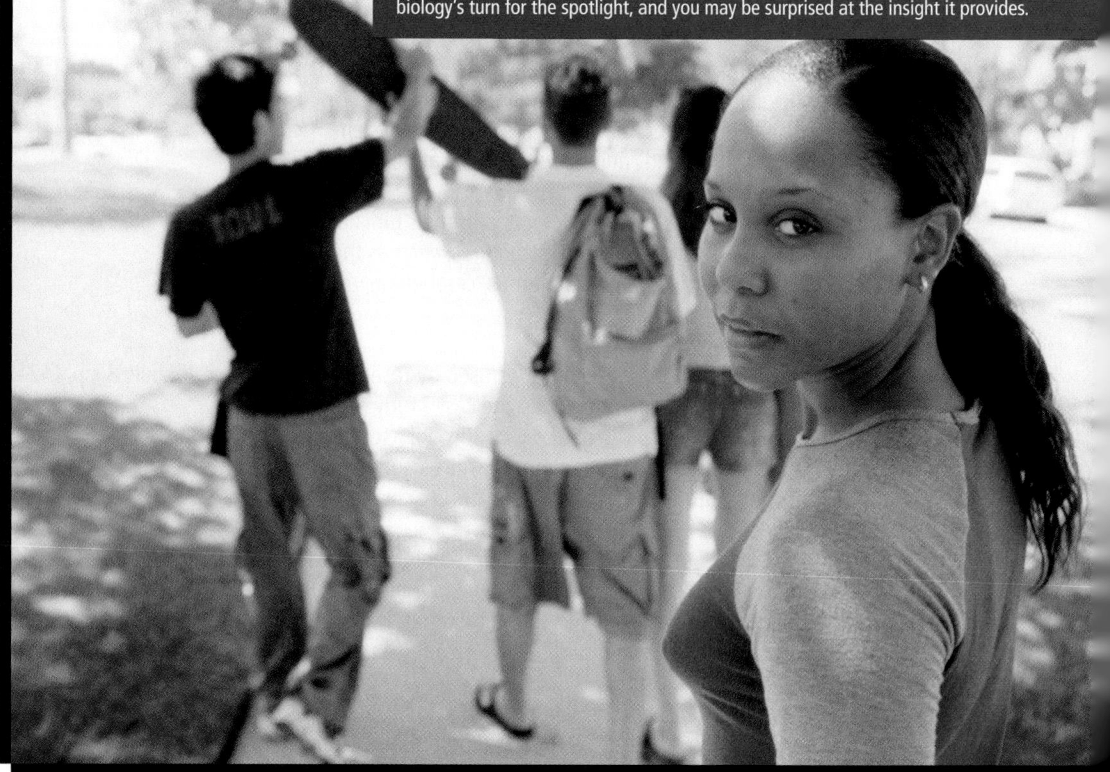

Performance Standards

Standard Area: Biological Bases of Behavior

Content Standard 1 Neural structure and functioning

Performance Standard 1.1 Identify the neuron as the basis for neural communication.

- Explain the basic tasks of a typical neuron: receiving information, carrying information, and passing information to the next neurons. The authors use the example of a computer to illustrate how a neuron works. (Student Text pp.121–122)
- Identify parts and functions of the neuron (dendrites, soma, axon, and axon terminals). (Student Text pp.122–123)
- Figure 7.1, "A Typical Motor Neuron," illustrates the parts and functions of a neuron. (Student Text p. 123)
- Explain the roles of the action potential, refractory period, and resting potential in generating a neural impulse. (Student Text pp. 123–124)
- Table 7.1, "Three Phases of Communication Within a Neuron," summarizes the role of the action potential, refractory period, and resting potential. (Student Text p. 124)

Performance Standard 1.2 Explain how neural information is transmitted.

- Examine the role of neurotransmitters in neural communication. (Student Text p. 125)
- Figure 7.2, "Communication Between Neurons," illustrates how neural information is shared between neurons. (Student Text p. 125)
- Explain inhibitory and excitatory connections. (Student Text p. 126)
- Explore the role of specific neurotransmitters. Explain the role of antagonists and agonists. (Student Text pp. 128–129)

Performance Standard 1.3 Explain how neural transmission can be altered by heredity and environment.

- Compare the effects of curare and black widow spider venom with the effects of neurotransmitters in relation to synaptic transmission. (Student Text pp.128–129)
- Discuss the role of neurotransmitters in schizophrenia. (Student Text pp.128–129)

Content Standard 2 The structure of the nervous system

Performance Standard 2.1 Identify the major divisions and subdivisions of the nervous system.

- Identify the central, peripheral, somatic, and autonomic nervous systems and explain the role they play in behavior. (Student Text pp. 130–131)
- Figure 7.5, "Divisions of the Nervous System," illustrates how the nervous system is divided. (Student Text p. 131)

Performance Standard 2.2 Divide the roles of the different subdivisions of the nervous system.

- Compare the roles of the sympathetic and parasympathetic nervous systems. (Student Text p. 132)
- Figure 7.6, "The Sympathetic and Parasympathetic Divisions of the Autonomic Nervous System," shows the division of responsibilities between these two systems for affecting change in the body. (Student Text p. 132)

Content Standard 6 The endocrine system

Performance Standard 6.1 Explain how the endocrine and nervous systems are connected.

- Explain the structures and function of the endocrine system. (Student Text pp. 133–134)
- Explore the connection between the hypothalamus and the pituitary gland. Emphasize how this relationship affects the body. (Student Text pp. 133–134)
- Discuss how specific hormones (for example, epinephrine and norepinephrine) are linked to specific behaviors. (Student Text p. 134)
- Figure 7.7, "Major Glands of the Endocrine System," illustrates the major glands in the body and their specific roles. (Student Text p. 133)

Materials NETWORK

All of the items from the Video, Activity, and Enrichment Centers listed below come from the *Teacher's Resource Binder.* These items will help you teach and expand on concepts presented in Module 7.

trb This logo indicates when an item from the Materials Network may be used in conjunction with a specific note found in this module's *Teacher's Edition.*

Neurons: The Building Blocks of the Nervous System

Activity Center

- Critical Thinking Activity: *Fact or Falsehood?* With this activity, students' preconceptions about the neural and hormonal systems are either exposed as incorrect or reinforced as correct. (*Teacher's Resource Binder*, p. 7-1; Handout 7–1)
- Building Vocabulary/Graphic Organizer: *The Neuron* With the graphic organizer, students identify the parts of the neuron and the function of each. (*Teacher's Resource Binder*, p. 7-1; Handout 7–2)
- Technology Application Activity: *Neuroscience and Behavior on the Internet* Several scholarly Web sites offer up-to-date information about advances in neuroscience. (*Teacher's Resource Binder*, p. 7-1; Handout 7–3)

Enrichment Center

- Enrichment Lesson: *Types of Neurons* This lesson describes oligodendroglia and astrocytes, two cells other than neurons found in the nervous system. (*Teacher's Resource Binder*, p. 7-1)

Neural Communication

V Video Center

Consult the faculty guides from *The Brain* and *The Mind* video series for descriptions of these modules.

- Videocassette: *The Brain,* Second Edition, Module 30: "Understanding the Brain Through Epilepsy" (*Teacher's Resource Binder*, p. 7-1)
- Videocassette: *The Mind,* Second Edition, Module 5: "Endorphins: The Brain's Natural Morphine" (*Teacher's Resource Binder*, p. 7-1)

Activity Center

- Technology Application Activity: *PsychSim:* "Neural Messages" *PsychSim* is an interactive CD-ROM containing tutorials in different content areas of psychology. This tutorial helps students understand the process of the action potential in detail. (*Teacher's Resource Binder*, p. 7-1)
- Application Activity: *Neural Transmission* Students engage in this interactive activity in which they create a life-size neuron model that uses Hershey's Kisses as neurotransmitters. (*Teacher's Resource Binder*, p. 7-1)
- Application Activity: *Using Dominoes to Illustrate the Action Potential* With this activity the seemingly complicated processes that make up the action potential can be easily explained using dominoes. (*Teacher's Resource Binder*, p. 7-1)

Enrichment Center

- Enrichment Lesson: *Multiple Sclerosis and Guillain-Barré Syndrome* This lesson tells about multiple sclerosis and Guillain-Barré syndrome, diseases of the neural system.
- Enrichment Lesson: *Endorphins* This lesson helps students understand the role of endorphins, our body's natural painkillers. (*Teacher's Resource Binder*, p. 7-1)
- Enrichment Lesson: *Parkinson's Disease and* Awakenings This lesson informs students about this debilitating disease and explains the science behind the film *Awakenings.* (*Teacher's Resource Binder*, p. 7-1)
- Enrichment Lesson: *The Reflex Arc* This lesson explores the reflex arc, a fundamental process that governs all human behavior. (*Teacher's Resource Binder*, p. 7-1)

The Structure of the Nervous System

Enrichment Center

- Enrichment Lesson: *Spinal Cord Repair* This lesson describes studies that seek to answer the question "Can a damaged spinal cord be repaired?" (*Teacher's Resource Binder*, p. 7-1)

The Endocrine System

Video Center

- Videocassette: *The Brain,* Second Edition, Module 2: "The Effects of Hormones and Environment on Brain Development" Consult the faculty guide from *The Brain* video series for a description of this module. (*Teacher's Resource Binder*, p. 7-1)

Enrichment Center

- Enrichment Lesson: *The Endocrine System* This lesson identifies many of the hormones in the endocrine system. (*Teacher's Resource Binder*, p. 7-1)

MODULE 7

Neural and Hormonal Systems

Your body is an incredible organization of functioning systems. Your skeletal system supports your body, your digestive system extracts nutrients from food, your immune system wards off disease, your respiratory system allows you to take in oxygen and rid your cells of carbon dioxide, and so on. But the systems that psychologists focus on are the nervous and endocrine (hormonal) systems, which enable communication and information processing within our bodies.

Neurons: The Building Blocks of the Nervous System

What's the point? 1. What are the primary parts of a typical neuron, and what functions do those parts perform?

The nervous system is your body's *electrochemical communication system.* Through it, your brain tells your body parts to move, your face to express emotion, and your internal organs to go about their business. Your nervous system, in partnership with your sensory systems, also gathers information so your brain can respond appropriately to stubbed toes, fire alarms, and the smell of popcorn. Like every other system in your body, your nervous system is built of cells, and taking a look at those cells is a good starting point for understanding the system as a whole.

Getting Started

Before students read the module, ask them to list familiar expressions that include the word *nerve.* (For example: "My nerves are on end," "Do you have the nerve to succeed?" "What nerve!") Suggest that the inclusion of the word *nerve* in these expressions points to the importance of nerves, whose functions this module will explain.

trb You may wish to use **Critical Thinking Activity:** *Fact or Falsehood?* (*Teacher's Resource Binder,* p. 7-1; **Handout 7–1**) as a prereading strategy to evaluate what students already know about the neural and hormonal systems. This activity will prime students to look out for information that could prove or disprove their preconceptions about these biological systems.

MODULE 7

Neural and Hormonal Systems

Introducing the Module

The Points: Module Objectives

- Define the primary parts of a typical neuron and the functions of each.
- Explain the roles of the action potential, refractory period, and resting potential in generating a neural impulse.
- Identify the role of neurotransmitters in neural communication.
- Understand the steps of the neural chain.
- Identify the various divisions of the nervous system, as well as the function of each of those subsystems.
- Distinguish between the way the endocrine system communicates and the way the nervous system communicates.

trb Building Vocabulary

By visually studying a diagram of the neuron in this module's graphic organizer, students can practice the module vocabulary by identifying the parts of the neuron, as well as the function of each (*Teacher's Resource Binder,* p. 7-1; **Handout 7–2**).

■ TEACHING TIP

Students often wonder why studying biology is important to psychology. As Charlie points out, without biology we have no behavior. To drive this point home, have students ponder this question: "If you could have a brain transplant, whose brain would you choose?" After some lively discussion of who has a brain worth having, it should be clear that having a different brain means being a different person. Without our own brains, we aren't ourselves.

trb At this point, you may wish to use **Technology Application Activity:** *Neuroscience and Behavior on the Internet* (*Teacher's Resource Binder,* p. 7-1; **Handout 7–3**).

MODULE 7

Teaching the Points

web ■ **TEACHING TIP**

You can log on as an instructor to the book companion site for *Thinking About Psychology* at **www.worthpublishers.com/thinkingaboutpsych.** It contains teacher resources for class presentations as well as review and assessment concepts and terms.

F•Y•I

The terms *nerve* and *neuron* are not interchangeable.

- A **neuron** is a single cell.
- A **nerve** is a bundle of neurons.

■ **LOOKING AT THE ISSUES**

People in the public eye afflicted with neurological disorders that affect neurons and the nervous system have helped raise awareness about these disorders. Suggest that students work individually or with partners to research the following neurological disorders: multiple sclerosis, Guillian-Barre syndrome, Parkinson's disease, and Lou Gehrig's disease (ALS). Have pairs make brief oral presentations to the class on their findings.

trb To accompany this research, you may wish to use **Enrichment Activity:** ***Multiple Sclerosis and Guillian-Barré Syndrome*** (*Teacher's Resource Binder*, p. 7-1).

■ **APPLYING THE POINTS**

Encourage students to find a local organization that offers support for sufferers of neurological disorders. Students can explore volunteer opportunities such as clerical tasks, visiting patients at local hospitals, or raising money for research.

V At this point, you may wish to show **Videocassette:** ***The Brain,*** **Second Edition, Module 30: "Understanding the Brain Through Epilepsy"** (*Teacher's Resource Binder*, p. 7-1).

Your brain, spinal cord, and nerves are formed from neurons, **neurons,** the highly specialized and unique cells of the nervous system. A neuron exists only to perform three tasks:

- To receive information (in the form of electrochemical impulses) from the neurons that feed into it
- To carry this information down its length
- To pass the information on to the next neurons in line

Every behavior, thought, and emotion you've ever experienced depends on the neuron's remarkable ability to move and process information.

The wonder of it all is that neurons are so limited in function—their main capability is transmitting an impulse, or "firing." In some ways, the guts of modern powerful computers operate similarly. Computers are binary—each electronic switch (or bit) in a central processor can be either on or off, set to represent either a 1 or a 0. All of a computer's extraordinary capabilities—its communication functions, elaborate games, "number crunching," mind-dazzling graphics, and sound—are ultimately accomplished by setting switches in the proper on-or-off pattern.

The Computer and the Brain. Both have amazing capabilities and get their power from millions of "switches" (electronic bits in the computer, neurons in the brain) that can either be on or off.

Neurons work in a similar way: They can "fire" (that is, send an impulse down their length) or not "fire." That's it. The beautiful colors you see in a sunset, the intense emotions you experienced during your first crush, the memory of your first day of kindergarten, the taste of pepperoni pizza, the thrill you feel when riding a roller coaster, and the devastating depression so many thousands suffer from—all emerge from a certain sequence of neurons either firing or not firing.

Neurons, like trees and dogs, come in a tremendous variety of shapes and sizes, but all neurons have similar important structures. Take a minute now to look at Figure 7.1, which shows, these structures in a *motor neuron,* a nerve cell that carries messages to muscles and glands. In this discussion, we will examine neuron parts following the order in which information travels.

A neuron has endings known as **dendrites,** which receive information. Dendrites look like branches, and in fact the word *dendrite* comes from the Greek word for "tree." The neuron's thickest part is the **soma,** or cell body. The soma is not responsible for transmitting information; rather, it contains the cell nucleus and other parts that keep the cell healthy and functioning properly. Perhaps the most interesting part of the neuron is the **axon,** an extension that adds length to the cell. The neuron's purpose is to move information from point A

▶ **neuron** A nerve cell; the basic building block of the nervous system.

▶ **dendrite** The bushy, branching extensions of a neuron that receive messages and conduct impulses toward the cell body (soma).

▶ **soma** The cell body of a neuron, which contains the nucleus and other parts that keep the cell healthy.

▶ **axon** The extension of a neuron through which neural impulses are sent.

Suggested Readings

Use the following books as teacher-preparation tools or as enrichment for advanced students:

Ramachandran, V. S., & Blakeslee, S. (1998). *Phantoms in the brain: Probing the mysteries of the human mind.* New York: William Morrow.

Restack, R. M. (1993). *Receptors.* New York: Bantam Books.

Sacks, O. (1973). *Awakenings.* New York: HarperCollins.

Carey, J. (Ed.). (1993). *Brain facts: A primer on the brain and nervous system.* Washington, DC: Society for Neuroscience.

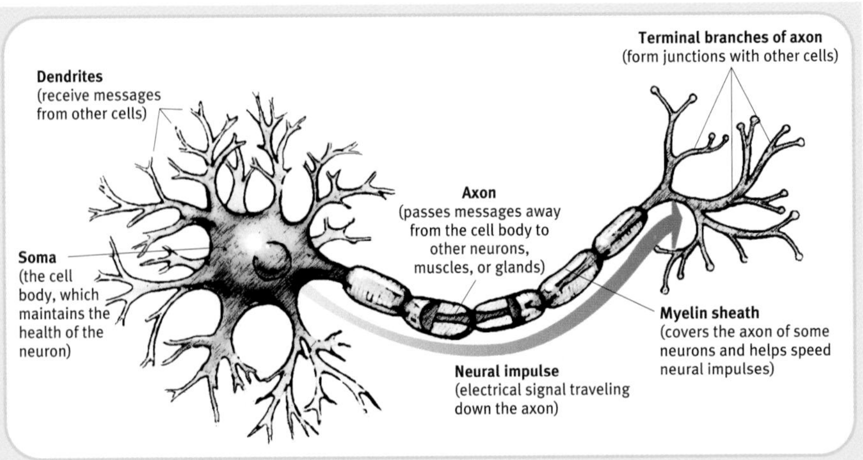

Figure 7.1 **A Typical Motor Neuron**

to point B, and the axon creates distance between these points. Axons of neurons in the brain may be very short, because information doesn't have to travel very far between the cells. But in some neurons in the leg, axons extend more than a meter, making these giant redwoods of the nervous system the longest cells in your body! Finally, the neuron ends with the **axon terminals,** which, as you will see, are the points of departure for information making its way to the dendrites of the next neurons in the sequence. Let's look more closely at what happens when a neuron "fires."

Neural Communication

The Neural Impulse

2. What roles do the action potential, refractory period, and resting potential play in generating a neural impulse?

When a neuron "fires," a tiny electrical charge, called an **action potential,** works its way from the dendrites to the axon terminals, much as a bite of swallowed food makes its way from your mouth to your stomach. This action potential represents the "on" condition of the neuron. Each action potential is followed by a brief recharging phase known as the **refractory period** (think of a camera flash that has to recharge before it can be used again). After the refractory period, the neuron is capable of another action potential when it is stimulated. When the cell is recharged and ready to fire again, a **resting potential** exists. Table 7.1 (page 124) illustrates these steps.

▶ **axon terminal** The endpoint of a neuron, where neurotransmitters are stored.

▶ **action potential** A neural impulse; a brief electrical charge that travels down the axon of a neuron.

▶ **refractory period** The "recharging phase" when a neuron, after firing, cannot generate another action potential.

▶ **resting potential** The state of a neuron when it is at rest and capable of generating an action potential.

■ TEACHING TIP

An explanation of the following concepts from other science courses may help students better understand the concept of the action potential:

- **Ions** have a charge, either positive or negative. When these particles move, they create electricity, which is what the action potential is.
- The natural tendency for matter is to move from a more crowded situation to a less crowded situation. The neuron is packed with negatively charged ions; the positively charged ions are positioned on the outside of the cell.
- The neuron's membrane is normally impermeable, but neurotransmitters weaken it, allowing the ions to move according to the principle above.

trb At this point, you may wish to use Application Activity: *Neural Transmission* (*Teacher's Resource Binder,* p. 7-1).

tr A four-color transparency of Figure 7.1, A Typical Neuron, is available in the **Overhead Transparencies Set.**

F • Y • I

Neurons can have an unlimited number of dendrites, making connections with several other different neurons at once. Most neurons are limited to one axon, however.

Meeting Individual Needs

trb GRAPHIC ORGANIZERS Provide learning opportunities for all levels of learners with one of the following options for using the graphic organizer (*Teacher's Resource Binder,* p. 7-1; Handout 7–2):

- **Independent Learners** Students can fill out the organizer on their own or follow along in class during discussion and lecture.
- **Cooperative Learners** Students may use the textbook as a resource and work in groups to find the answers that fit in the blanks.
- **Exceptional Learners** Graphic organizers can fill a special education need to provide notes for exceptional students. These students can fill in the blanks independently, with a student or teacher/tutor, or along with class discussion and lecture.

MODULE 7

F • Y • I

The charge of the neuron at rest is –70 millivolts. This cell is said to be polarized at this point. When activated by excitatory neurotransmitters, the cell becomes more positively charged (depolarized), creating the action potential.

■ TEACHING TIPS

trb tr (1) A black-line master of Table 7.1, Three Phases of Communication with a Neuron, is available in the **Black-Line Masters Appendix** of the *Teacher's Resource Binder.*

web (2) If you search the collection of general biopsychology animations and tutorials at **http://psychlab1.hanover.edu/Classes/Neuro/**, you will find links to biopsychology-related PowerPoint demonstrations and illustrations that may be helpful in class presentations.

web (3) John H. Krantz's Web site—**http://psych.hanover.edu/Krantz/neurotut.html**—provides a very good tutorial on both basic neural processes and the human brain. Included are separate sections on the neuron and the brain, factors involved in the action potential, and the normal brain structure atlas with images drawn from the *Whole Brain Atlas.* Mastery self-tests are associated with each section.

(4) Another way to state the all-or-none principle is "There is no such thing as a weak action potential." Neurotransmitters must reach a threshold before firing will occur, and then the charge that results looks no different from any other charge that cell would make. Action potentials are the same every time.

trb At this point, you may wish to use **Application Activity:** *Using Dominoes to Illustrate the Action Potential* (*Teacher's Resource Binder,* p. 7-1).

TABLE 7.1 THREE PHASES OF COMMUNICATION WITHIN A NEURON

Phase	Illustration	Description
Action potential		The neural impulse created when a neuron "fires." The impulse travels from the dendrites down the axon to the terminal branches.
Refractory period		The brief instant when a new action potential cannot be generated because the neuron is "recharging" after the previous action potential.
Resting potential		The state of a neuron when it is "charged" but waiting for the next action potential to be generated.

An interesting fact about how a neuron fires is called the **all-or-none principle,** which states that a neuron always fires with the same intensity. It doesn't matter if there is strong stimulation or weak stimulation at the cell's dendrites. As long as there is enough energy to trigger the cell, it will fire with the same intensity.

One of the best analogies to a neuron and how it fires is, perhaps unfortunately, a toilet. Stop for a moment and think of how a toilet is similar to a neuron. Here are some similarities (perhaps you will be able to think of more!):

- Like a neuron, a toilet has an action potential. When you flush, an "impulse" is sent down the sewer pipe.
- Like a neuron, a toilet has a refractory period. There is a short delay after flushing when the toilet cannot be flushed again because the tank is being refilled.
- Like a neuron, a toilet has a resting potential. The toilet is "charged" when there is water in the tank and it is capable of being flushed again.
- Like a neuron, a toilet operates on the all-or-none principle—it always flushes with the same intensity, no matter how much force you apply to the handle (providing, of course, you provide enough force to trigger the mechanism).

▶ **all-or-none principle** The principle stating that if a neuron fires, it always fires at the same intensity; all action potentials are the same strength.

▶ **synapse** The tiny, fluid-filled gap between the axon terminal of one neuron and the dendrite of another.

▶ **neurotransmitter** A chemical messenger that travels across the synapse from one neuron to the next and influences whether a neuron will generate an action potential (impulse).

Demonstrating

A FLUSH EXAMPLE For a fun in-house field trip, take students to a school restroom (making sure it is clear of visitors!) and demonstrate how the toilet and action potential are similar. It makes for quite a vivid understanding of the action potential!

Communication Between Neurons

3. What role do neurotransmitters play in neural communication?

So far, we have been discussing how information passes down the length of a single neuron. But how do messages travel from one neuron to the next? Amazingly, despite their large numbers, this happens without any two neurons actually coming in contact with one another! At every place where an axon terminal of one neuron and the dendrite of an adjacent neuron meet (and there may be thousands of such places on any single neuron), there is a very small, fluid-filled gap called a **synapse** that action potentials cannot jump. At this point, chemical messengers known as **neurotransmitters** continue the job and carry the information across the gap. When an action potential works its way to the end of a neuron, it causes the release of neurotransmitters from the axon terminals. The neurotransmitter molecules, which have a distinctive chemical shape, rapidly cross the synapse and fit into receptor sites on the dendrite of the next neuron (Figure 7.2).

Figure 7.2
Communication Between Neurons

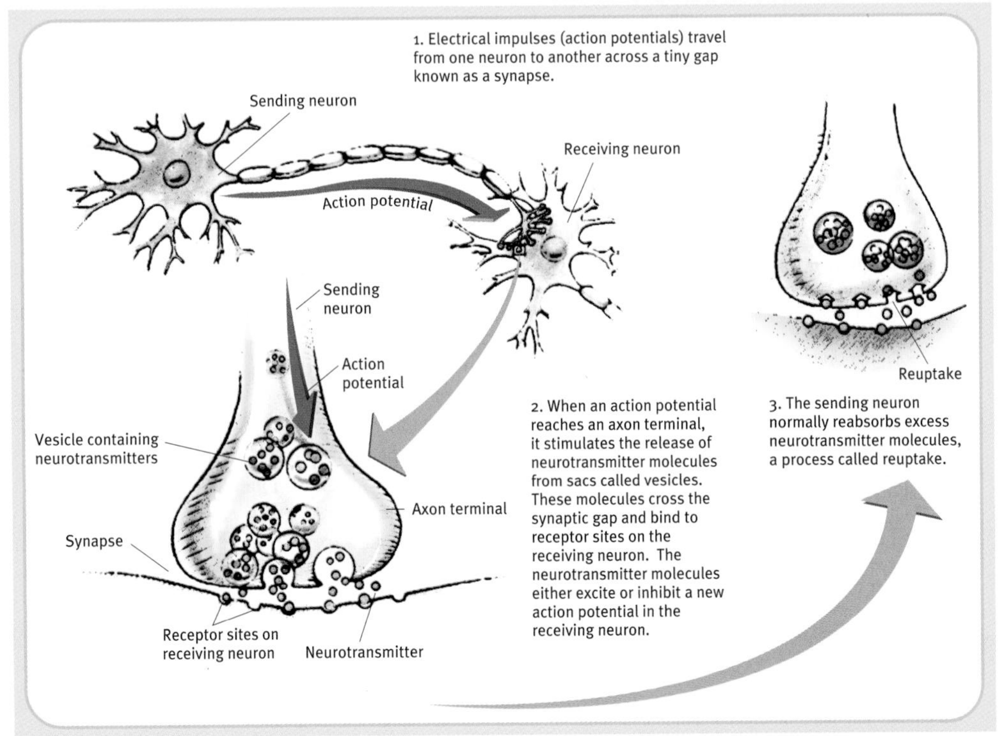

1. Electrical impulses (action potentials) travel from one neuron to another across a tiny gap known as a synapse.
Sending neuron
Receiving neuron
Action potential
Sending neuron
Action potential
Vesicle containing neurotransmitters
Axon terminal
Synapse
Receptor sites on receiving neuron
Neurotransmitter
2. When an action potential reaches an axon terminal, it stimulates the release of neurotransmitter molecules from sacs called vesicles. These molecules cross the synaptic gap and bind to receptor sites on the receiving neuron. The neurotransmitter molecules either excite or inhibit a new action potential in the receiving neuron.
Reuptake
3. The sending neuron normally reabsorbs excess neurotransmitter molecules, a process called reuptake.

F•Y•I

The **sodium-potassium pump** is the mechanism by which ions are allowed to pass through the membrane of the neural cell. Named for the two primary elements present in the ion exchange, this pump brings positively charged ions into the cell and then pumps them back out when the action potential is over.

trb At this point, you may wish to use Technology Application Activity: *PsychSim:* "Neural Messages" (*Teacher's Resource Binder*, p. 7-1).

■ TEACHING TIP

Explain that "reuptake" is the body's way of recycling neurotransmitters for later use. Drugs like Prozac block the reuptake of the neurotransmitter serotonin so it will remain in the synapse longer, elevating the mood that serotonin controls.

tr A four-color transparency of Figure 7.2, Communication Between Neurons, is available in the **Overhead Transparencies Set**.

■ CHECKING FOR UNDERSTANDING

Have students write a one-paragraph summary of the process of the action potential, using the terms from the text. This will help you evaluate whether students understand this complicated but fundamental concept in neuroscience. *(Students' answers should explain how the neuron at its resting potential is negatively charged. Neurotransmitters from other cells travel across the synapse, bind to a cell, and open up channels that exchange ions, which creates the electrical charge known as the action potential. Once the neuron has fired, it must repolarize during a refractory period before it can fire again. Enough neurotransmitters must be present for an action potential to take place, demonstrating the all-or-none principle.)*

Demonstrating

BODY MAGIC AND NEURAL COMMUNICATION Hold a dollar bill vertically between the middle finger and thumb of your dominant hand. At the same time, place the index finger and thumb of your other hand on either side of the note at its center, as close as possible without actually touching it. Release the bill, and you will have no problem catching it.

Hold the note as before, but instruct a second person to position his or her own finger and thumb as you did earlier for the catching. Emphasize that he or she must not move until you release the bill. Drop it and, surprisingly, his or her fingers will close on thin air. (Slightly more time is necessary for the other person to process both the visual information and the reaction, showing how neural communication and behavior are related.)

Fisher, J. (1979). *Body magic.* New York: Stein & Day.

MODULE 7

■ LOOKING AT THE ISSUES

When enough excitatory neurotransmitters attach to a neuron, an action potential occurs. If inhibitory neurotransmitters are more abundant, an action potential will not occur. Because drugs mimic or block neurotransmitters, they can affect proper functioning of the body. Have students discuss the following questions about drug use and neurotransmitters:

- How might the body respond if it is getting neurotransmitters from an outside source instead of producing them itself?
- What might be some possible behaviors that would result if excitatory neurotransmitters were mimicked or inhibited?
- What would happen if inhibitory neurotransmitters were mimicked or inhibited?
- How do you think knowledge of how neurotransmitters work might advance the ability to treat neurological disorders?

The neurotransmitter molecules can come to rest only in receptor sites designed to fit their shape, just as a key can open locks only with a certain configuration. Once in the receptor site, neurotransmitters can serve two broad functions. Under some circumstances, they have an **excitatory effect.** This means their arrival makes the receiving neuron more likely to fire. Other times, neurotransmitters have an **inhibitory effect,** which means their arrival makes a neuron less likely to generate an action potential. The excitatory role is like a green light. It shouts, "Just do it!" The inhibitory role is like a red light. Its message is "Just say no!"

There are dozens of neurotransmitters, though so far researchers have learned the specific functions of only a few. Neurotransmitters serve different functions, depending not only on the type of receptor site each locks into, but also on the place where they are released in the brain. (See Psychology Is a Science: Neurotransmitters and Drugs, page 128).

The Neural Chain

4. What are the steps of the neural chain?

The neural chain describes the path information follows as it is processed by the nervous system. To understand it, consider the example of playing your favorite radio station through your stereo system. What is necessary for this task? First, information must be available from the station. Whenever the station is broadcasting, its radio waves are present in the room, but people are not equipped to intercept and interpret these waves directly. That's why we need the stereo system! The stereo's antenna picks up the radio waves and sends them as an electronic message along a wire to the radio receiver. The receiver must process this information by amplifying and filtering it. Then the information is sent to the speakers, again via a wire. Finally, the speakers vibrate to create the sound of your favorite new hit. The stereo goes through this process of receiving, processing, and outputting information continuously.

Your nervous system also specializes in receiving and processing information, and it contains functional components similar to those that make up your stereo system. First, you need to gather information from your environment. Your "antennae" are the **receptor cells** of your various sensory systems. These amazing cells have the ability to take other kinds of energy and put them in the form of neural impulses your brain can understand. Your eyes, for example, have receptor cells that take light energy and turn it into nerve impulses. Your ears have similar cells

▶ **excitatory effect** A neurotransmitter effect that makes it more likely that the receiving neuron will generate an action potential (impulse).

▶ **inhibitory effect** A neurotransmitter effect that makes it less likely that a receiving neuron will generate an action potential (impulse).

▶ **receptor cells** Specialized cells in the sensory systems of the body that can turn other kinds of energy into action potentials (impulses) that the nervous system can process.

Cross-Curricular Connections

COMPUTER SCIENCE Arrange for someone knowledgeable in computer programming to make a presentation to the class about binary systems and how they can work. The presenter may be a computer teacher, a computer-literate student, or an outside computer programmer familiar with binary systems. Request that the presentation conclude with students attempting to program a computer to perform a simple task using binary code. This activity should help students see that complex behaviors can come from simple patterns.

that process sound energy, and elsewhere in your body other such cells process smells, tastes, and touch into nerve impulses. Without these receptor cells, your brain would be helpless. By itself, your brain cannot detect light, or sound, or smell. Just as you need your stereo to turn radio waves into something meaningful, your brain needs your senses and their receptor cells to gather and transform information into a form your brain can understand.

The sense organs are not actually located in the brain, so your nervous system must literally move the information your receptor cells pull in. This movement occurs as billions of neurotransmitter molecules pass messages among millions of neurons—from your fingertips, your eyeballs, your ears, your nose, and your mouth to the proper area of the brain for processing. As a stereo uses metal wires, your body uses living wires known as nerves, which are bundles of individual neurons. Those that connect the sense organs to the brain and spinal cord are **sensory nerves.** Without them, your brain would be no more effective than your stereo receiver would be if somebody cut the wire bringing information from the antenna.

The brain, like a stereo receiver, is the real powerhouse of the system, processing the constant, massive barrage of sensory data flowing in from the sensory nerves. Your brain must process information about what you see, hear, taste, smell, and feel throughout your body, if only to ignore much of the information as probably insignificant. It is the brain's responsibility to deal with it all and make appropriate decisions, just as your stereo receiver properly filters and amplifies an incoming radio signal. The billions of neurons that do this processing in your brain and spinal cord are called **interneurons.**

Many times, your brain determines that some action is necessary to deal with incoming information. If your brain detects a ball moving toward your head, you need to either catch the ball or duck to avoid getting hit. If your brain detects a question asked by your teacher, you need to decide on an appropriate answer and say it. If your brain detects that you're overheating, you need to begin sweating. The point is that while the brain can *determine* a course of action on its own (such as speaking or sweating), it cannot actually *do* these things. To trigger actions the brain must get word to the body's muscles and glands, just as your stereo system has to convey the processed sound signal from the receiver to the speakers. Your stereo uses more wires for this purpose. Similarly, your nervous system uses **motor nerves** to carry information away from your brain to the parts of the body that can take action. Without motor nerves and the muscles and glands they attach to, your brain could not accomplish anything. (Your stereo wouldn't be much good without speakers, would it?)

▶ **sensory nerves** Nerves that carry information from the sense receptors to the central nervous system.

▶ **interneurons** Nerve cells in the brain and spinal cord responsible for processing information related to sensory input and motor output.

▶ **motor nerves** Nerves that carry information to the muscles and glands from the central nervous system.

F•Y•I

Have you ever jerked away from a hot surface only to feel the burn after a delay? **Interneurons** make reflexes happen. These cells in the spinal cord process motor responses quickly to protect the body from harm. Without interneurons, you would experience severe burns if you left your hand on that hot surface long enough to process both the heat and the pain before jerking away!

trb At this point, you may wish to use **Enrichment Lesson:** *The Reflex Arc* (*Teacher's Resource Binder,* p. 7-1).

■ TEACHING TIP

Sensory and motor neurons are also known as **afferent** and **efferent neurons.** One way to remember these names is with the acronym SAME—*Sensory Afferent, Motor Efferent.*

Reteaching

The neural chain, also known as the **reflex arc,** can be described graphically if students need more instruction to understand how it works.

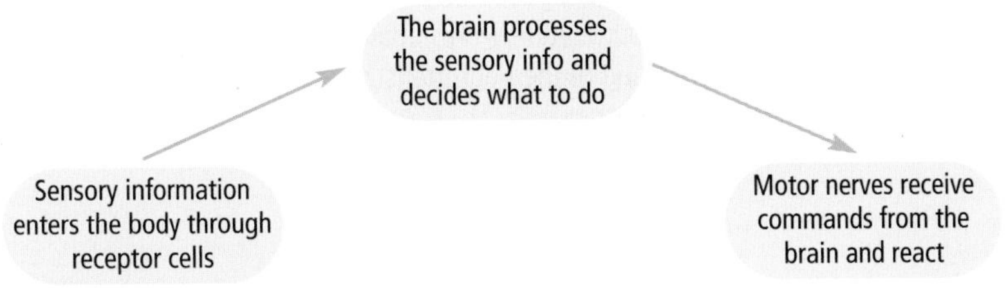

Sensory information enters the body through receptor cells

→ The brain processes the sensory info and decides what to do

→ Motor nerves receive commands from the brain and react

MODULE 7

F • Y • I

The body naturally produces substances that are similar to many of the drugs that affect it. When we introduce drugs into our bodies, we are either increasing the amount of these substances in the body or blocking those substances that are supposed to work in a specific way.

■ APPLYING THE POINTS

Have students research **myasthenia gravis**—a neurological disorder resulting from the depletion of acetylcholine (ACh). Without ACh, the muscles do not move properly. People with this disorder experience extreme fatigue since it takes enormous effort to move muscles at all.

■ TEACHING TIP

Students may find other neurotransmitters interesting to know about.

- **Substance P** is the body's pain neurotransmitter.
- **Endorphins**, or endogenous morphines, are the body's natural painkillers, inhibiting substance P. These are chemically similar to opiates, such as heroin, codeine, and morphine.
- **Norepinephrine** is adrenaline found in the central nervous system.

trb v At this point, you may wish to use **Enrichment Lesson:** ***Endorphins*** (*Teacher's Resource Binder*, p. 7-1) or show **Videocassette:** ***The Mind***, **Second Edition, Module 5: "Endorphins: The Brain's Natural Morphine"** (*Teacher's Resource Binder*, p. 7-1).

trb tr A black-line master of Table 7.2, Examples of Neurotransmitter Functions, is available in the **Black-Line Masters Appendix** of the *Teacher's Resource Binder.*

Psychology is a Science

Neurotransmitters and Drugs

The synapse is where it's at when it comes to the effects of many drugs. Let's take a look at the roles of three key neurotransmitters (Table 7.2), and see what happens when outside chemicals are added to the mix.

One neurotransmitter, **acetylcholine** (ACh), enables both memory and movement. ACh is present in every synapse of motor nerves. Chemical substances can disrupt the normal effects of ACh, however. Some native tribes in South America use such a substance, a poison called curare, to coat the tips of the darts they use in their blowguns. When these darts strike an animal, the result is paralysis. Why? Because the curare molecules fill the receptor sites on dendrites that normally receive ACh, but the curare molecules do not stimulate an action potential in the receiving neuron the way ACh would. Thus, since ACh is effectively blocked from doing its job, movement ceases. Substances such as curare that block the effects of a neurotransmitter are called **antagonists.**

Black widow spider venom also interacts with ACh, but not in the same way curare does. The venom fills the ACh receptor sites, but its chemical structure is so similar to ACh that it mimics ACh's effect on the receiving neuron. So now two substances, ACh and spider venom, are doing the same thing. The result is excessive and uncontrollable movement, in the form of convulsions. The spider venom is called an **agonist** because it enhances the effect of a neurotransmitter. Figure 7.3 illustrates how antagonists and agonists interact with neurotransmitters.

► **acetylcholine** [ah-seat-el-KO-leen] A neurotransmitter that triggers muscle contraction and affects learning and memory.

► **antagonist** A drug that blocks the effect of a neurotransmitter.

► **agonist** A drug that boosts the effect of a neurotransmitter.

► **dopamine** [DO-pa-mean] A neurotransmitter that affects learning, attention, and emotion; excess dopamine activity is associated with schizophrenia.

► **serotonin** [sare-oh-TON-in] A neurotransmitter that affects hunger, sleep, arousal, and mood; serotonin appears in lower than normal levels in depressed persons.

TABLE 7.2 EXAMPLES OF NEUROTRANSMITTER FUNCTIONS

Neurotransmitter	Functions
Acetylcholine (ACh)	• Muscle action • Learning • Memory • ACh-producing neurons have deteriorated in people with Alzheimer's disease.
Dopamine	• Learning • Attention • Emotion • Excess dopamine activity is associated with schizophrenia.
Serotonin	• Hunger • Sleep • Arousal • Mood • Low levels of dopamine are associated with depression.

Cross-Curricular Connections

LITERATURE *Antagonist* is a word used in literature to identify a character who is fighting against the main character or hero. Have students use this knowledge to enhance their recall of this term in psychology. The antagonist molecule works against the neurotransmitter by keeping the neuron from firing, much like the antagonist in literature works against the hero, blocking his or her actions. The agonist molecule is like a clone of the neurotransmitter, acting just enough like it to make the neuron fire.

Another neurotransmitter with interesting effects is **dopamine.** Schizophrenia, a serious illness that disrupts a person's sense of reality, is associated with high levels of dopamine. Drugs commonly prescribed for this illness alleviate some of the symptoms of schizophrenia by blocking the action of dopamine at the synapse. These drugs are dopamine antagonists. Another disorder, depression, is associated with low levels of the neurotransmitter **serotonin.** Some medications, the most famous of which is Prozac, work to reduce depression by enhancing the availability of serotonin at the synapse. Prozac, therefore, is a serotonin agonist.

Prescribed medications are not the only substances that exert their effects at the synapse. All mind-altering chemicals, ranging from caffeine to cocaine, operate by influencing neurotransmission. A single drug, such as alcohol, might influence several different neurotransmitters in different ways. Research on neurotransmitters is always in progress and brings fascinating and important results.

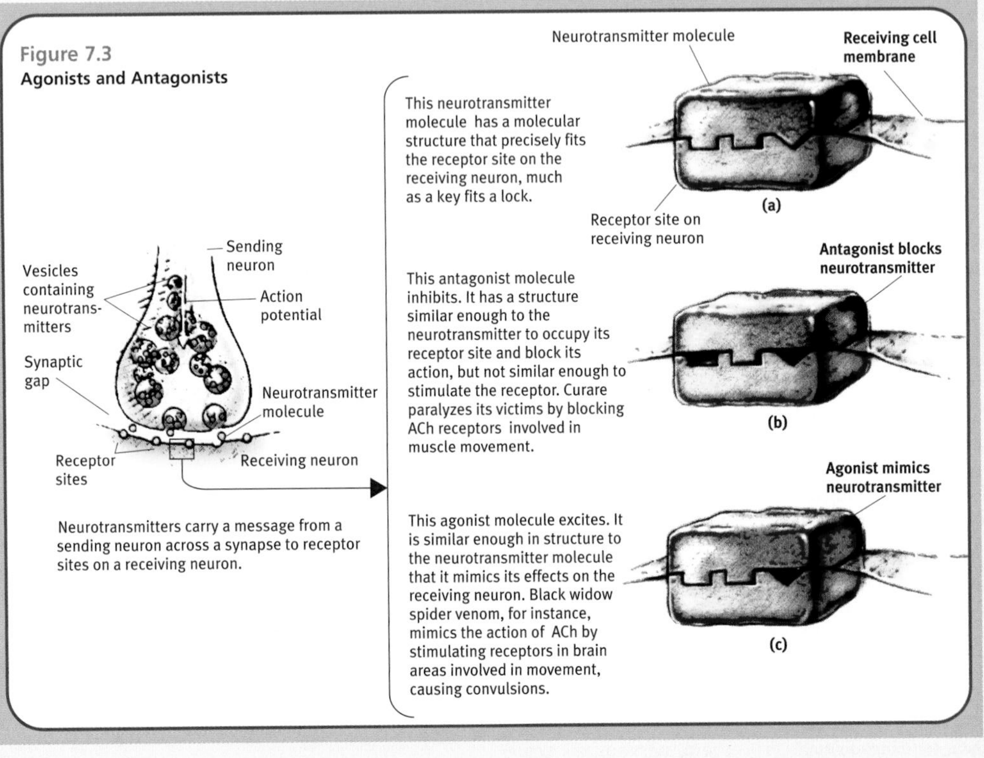

Sending neuron
Vesicles containing neurotrans-mitters
Action potential
Synaptic gap
Neurotransmitter molecule
Receptor sites
Receiving neuron
Neurotransmitters carry a message from a sending neuron across a synapse to receptor sites on a receiving neuron.
Neurotransmitter molecule
Receiving cell membrane
This neurotransmitter molecule has a molecular structure that precisely fits the receptor site on the receiving neuron, much as a key fits a lock.
Receptor site on receiving neuron
(a)
Antagonist blocks neurotransmitter
This antagonist molecule inhibits. It has a structure similar enough to the neurotransmitter to occupy its receptor site and block its action, but not similar enough to stimulate the receptor. Curare paralyzes its victims by blocking ACh receptors involved in muscle movement.
(b)
Agonist mimics neurotransmitter
This agonist molecule excites. It is similar enough in structure to the neurotransmitter molecule that it mimics its effects on the receiving neuron. Black widow spider venom, for instance, mimics the action of ACh by stimulating receptors in brain areas involved in movement, causing convulsions.
(c)

Figure 7.3
Agonists and Antagonists

F • Y • I

Patients who take dopamine inhibitors to treat schizophrenia often experience a side effect called **tardive dyskinesia.** Tardive dyskinesia involves symptoms similar to those of people with Parkinson's disease—shaking, twitching, and repetitive movements. Because of this effect and other related results of research studies, scientists learned that schizophrenia and Parkinson's disease are both related to dopamine levels in the brain.

trb tr ■ **TEACHING TIP**

A black-line master of Table 7.3, Agonists and Antagonists, is available in the **Black-Line Masters Appendix** of the *Teacher's Resource Binder.*

Reteaching

Help students remember each neurotransmitter's function by linking each one with a common substance that acts the same chemically.

- **Acetylcholine** = black widow spider venom. While the presence of spider venom causes uncontrollable movements, absence of acetylcholine causes the inability to move.
- **Dopamine** = antipsychotic drugs. Dopamine is linked to schizophrenia, a psychotic illness.
- **Serotonin** = Prozac. Prozac, the antidepressant, acts like serotonin to help alleviate depression.

MODULE 7

■ TEACHING TIPS

 (1) As a resource on spinal research, you might visit the Web site www.spinal-research.org. This site provides updates on the most recent research on spinal cord repair.

tr (2) A four-color transparency of Figure 7.4, A Neural Chain, is available in the Overhead Transparencies Set.

F • Y • I

Sensory neurons connect to the spinal cord dorsally (in the back). Motor neurons connect in the anterior of the spinal cord (in the front). Therefore, it is possible to lose feeling in lower portions of the body after a spinal cord injury but retain the ability to move if the spinal cord is not completely severed.

trb At this point, you may wish to use Enrichment Lesson: *Spinal Cord Repair* (*Teacher's Resource Binder*, p. 7-1).

■ CHECKING FOR UNDERSTANDING

Have students brainstorm different stimuli that would produce reflexive responses. Have them explain why the reflexive response is important to protect the body. Then, have them describe additional feelings about the situation that would require deeper processing by the brain. This activity will help you see if students understand the process of reflexes and the neural chain. *(Examples might include responses to heat, cold, pressure, or loud noise. Having quick reflexes in each of these situations would protect the body from burns, frostbite, insect bites, ear damage, or other dangers. Deeper processing could produce feelings of fear of the stimulus, relief for avoiding more danger, or more complex feelings of pain.)*

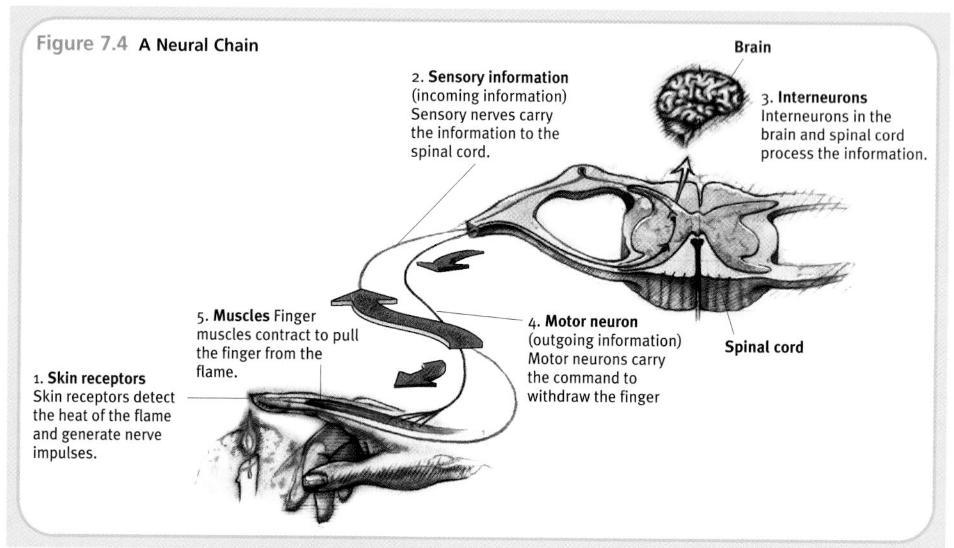
Brain
2. Sensory information (incoming information) Sensory nerves carry the information to the spinal cord.
3. Interneurons Interneurons in the brain and spinal cord process the information.
5. Muscles Finger muscles contract to pull the finger from the flame.
4. Motor neuron (outgoing information) Motor neurons carry the command to withdraw the finger
Spinal cord
1. Skin receptors Skin receptors detect the heat of the flame and generate nerve impulses.

Figure 7.4 A Neural Chain

Figure 7.4 shows a neural chain so basic that the initial action is determined by the spinal cord without the involvement of the brain. In this case, the response to the heat from the flame is a *simple reflex.* To react quickly to a dangerous situation, an interneuron in the spinal cord sends the command to withdraw the finger even before other interneurons relay the information to your brain!

▸ **central nervous system (CNS)** The brain and the spinal cord.

▸ **peripheral nervous system (PNS)** The sensory and motor nerves that connect the central nervous system to the rest of the body.

▸ **somatic nervous system** The division of the peripheral nervous system that controls the body's skeletal muscles.

▸ **autonomic** [aw-tuh-NAHM-ik] **nervous system** The division of the peripheral nervous system that controls the glands and muscles of the internal organs. Its subdivisions are the sympathetic (arousing) division and the parasympathetic (calming) division.

The Structure of the Nervous System

5. What are the various divisions of the nervous system, and what is the function of each of these subsystems?

So far we've examined the nervous system by zooming in on its smaller pieces, sensory and motor nerves made up of tiny neurons sending their neurotransmitters to one another. Now it's time to take a step back for a broader view of the whole communication system in which these pieces function.

One good way to understand the nervous system is to study its major divisions, which you can see in Figure 7.5. The nervous system has two major components, the central nervous system and the peripheral nervous system.

Reteaching

Help students understand the simple reflex by drawing the following flowchart:

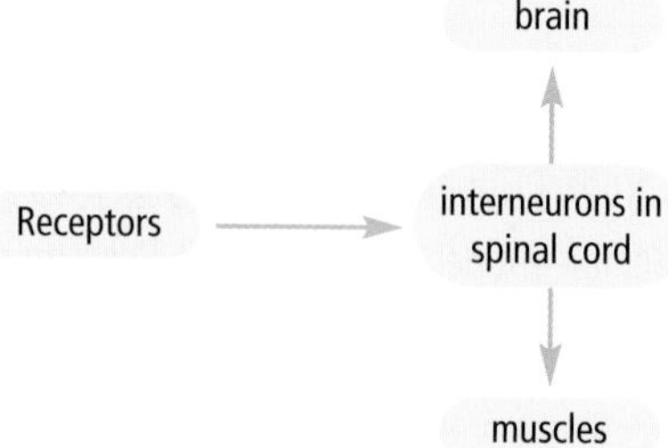
brain
Receptors
interneurons in spinal cord
muscles

The **central nervous system (CNS)** includes the brain and the spinal cord, so important to the nervous system that they are both encased in bone for protection. The brain is the location where most information processing takes place, and the spinal cord is the main pathway information follows as it enters and leaves the brain. In shape, the spinal cord tapers from about the thickness of a broomstick where it joins the brain to the diameter of a pencil at the base of the back. The interneurons that make up the CNS are responsible for processing information.

The **peripheral nervous system (PNS)** contains all the nerves that feed into and branch out from the brain and the spinal cord. The word *peripheral* means "outer region" (perhaps you've heard the phrase "peripheral vision," which refers to your ability to see things that are on the outer regions of your visual field). The PNS divides into two subsystems:

- The **somatic nervous system** contains the motor nerves you use to activate muscles voluntarily. You develop the idea to walk across a room using your central nervous system, but you rely on the motor and sensory nerves of your somatic nervous system to carry the CNS's commands to the muscles of your legs and to get feedback about what your legs are actually doing.
- The second component of the PNS is the **autonomic nervous system,** which monitors the automatic functions of your body. Your autonomic nervous system controls your breathing, blood pressure, and digestive processes.

Did you notice this is the second time in this module we have a word built from the Greek soma, *which means "body"?*

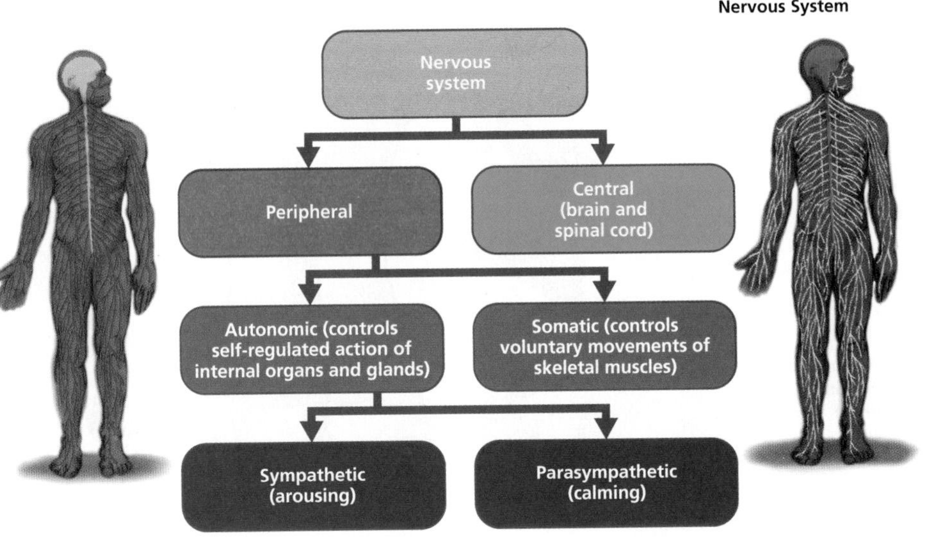

Figure 7.5 **Divisions of the Nervous System**

MODULE 7

tr ■ **TEACHING TIP**

A four-color transparency of Figure 7.5, Divisions of the Nervous System, is available in the **Overhead Transparencies Set.**

F • Y • I

Unlike central nerves, peripheral nerves—which extend out to the body's extremities—can regenerate when damaged.

trb At this point, you may wish to use **Enrichment Lesson:** ***Types of Neurons*** (*Teacher's Resource Binder*, p. 7-1) to discuss the mechanism in the peripheral nervous system that allows for regeneration of neurons.

■ **JOURNAL WRITING**

Invite students to use the following questions as springboards for entries in their psychology journals:

- If you had to choose between losing feeling or losing the ability to move, which would you choose, and why?
- For experimental purposes, animals' spinal cords are damaged so that scientists may see the results and determine if regeneration of nerve tissue is possible. Do you think the potential benefits of this type of research outweigh the harm to the animals? Why or why not?

trb At this point, you may wish to use **Enrichment Lesson:** ***Spinal Cord Repair*** (*Teacher's Resource Binder*, p. 7-1) to educate students about research in spinal cord injuries.

Reteaching

Help students remember the difference among nervous systems with these mnemonics:

- **Central nervous system** The brain and spinal cord are located in the *center* of the body.
- **Peripheral nervous system** Fingers and toes lie in the outermost areas of the body from the center—the *periphery* of the body.
- **Somatic nervous system** Volunteer work is done by choice, so the body's (or *soma*'s) voluntary actions are controlled by this nervous system.
- **Autonomic nervous system** *Autonomic* sounds like the word *automatic*, and the body's automatic actions (breathing, heartbeat, and so forth) are controlled by this nervous system.

MODULE 7

■ TEACHING TIP
Many of the body's functions are controlled by opponent processes, like the one described in the parasympathetic and sympathetic nervous systems. These processes work opposite each other to create a balance, or **homeostasis,** in the body.

tr A four-color transparency of Figure 7.6, The Sympathetic and Parasympathetic Divisions of the Autonomic Nervous System, is available in the **Overhead Transparencies Set.**

■ APPLYING THE POINTS
People have been known to lift cars or tractors in attempts to save others from harm. Stories like these show how the body can override its own usual limitations to accomplish what the mind sets out to do. Have students research stories of people who have accomplished superhuman feats of strength when under intense pressure or stress.

► **sympathetic division** The part of the autonomic nervous system that arouses the body to deal with perceived threats.

► **parasympathetic division** The part of the autonomic nervous system that calms the body.

A final split is within the autonomic nervous system, which has both a *sympathetic division* and a *parasympathetic division* (Figure 7.6). These two divisions work together in a masterful example of checks and balances—it's not just our government that relies on this principle! The **sympathetic division** is in charge of arousal; it controls a number of responses, collectively referred to as the *fight-or-flight response,* that prepare you to deal with threats or challenges. If you hear footsteps closing in behind you late at night on a deserted sidewalk, if a teacher announces a pop quiz at the beginning of class, if you're about to make a nervous call to a potential dating partner you've never phoned before, your sympathetic nervous system will kick in.

The **parasympathetic division** of the autonomic nervous system opposes the sympathetic division and generates responses that calm you down. The sympathetic division may send your blood pressure higher when your parent catches you coming in after your curfew; your parasympathetic division brings your blood pressure back down to normal when your parent responds calmly to your explanation of car trouble.

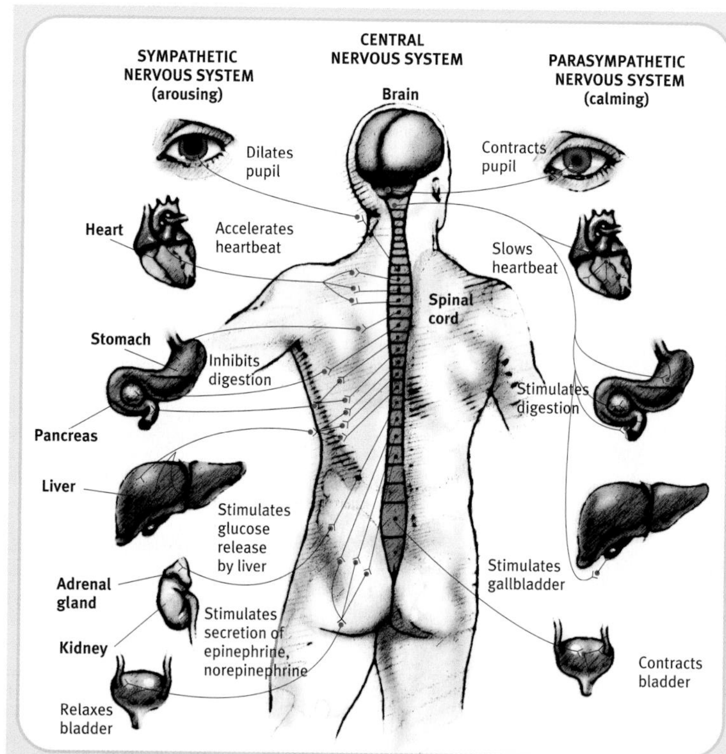

Figure 7.6 **The Sympathetic and Parasympathetic Divisions of the Autonomic Nervous System** The sympathetic division arouses us and expends energy. The parasympathetic division calms us and conserves energy.

Reteaching

Remember what the sympathetic nervous system does by thinking about what we do when we feel sympathy—we try to actively help by comforting and consoling others. When we act to help others, the sympathetic nervous system kicks in, giving us the energy we need to accomplish our goals.

The Endocrine System

6. How does the way the endocrine system communicates differ from the way the nervous system communicates?

Your body has another system for communicating information. This system, slower to awaken and slower to shut down than the nervous system, is the **endocrine system.** It is made up of the endocrine glands, which produce **hormones,** chemical substances that circulate throughout the body in the blood. Hormones and neurotransmitters are similar in function: Both carry messages, and both communicate by locking into receptor sites.

Figure 7.7 illustrates the major endocrine glands. The most important is the **pituitary gland,** so crucial it is sometimes referred to as the "master gland." The pea-sized pituitary is located at the base of the brain, and it actually connects to a brain part called the *hypothalamus* through tissue that is part glandular and part neural. This connection illustrates the close relationship between the nervous and

► **endocrine** [EN-duh-krin] **system** One of the body's two communication systems; a set of glands that produce hormones, chemical messengers that circulate in the blood.

► **hormone** Chemical messengers produced by the endocrine glands and circulated in the blood.

► **pituitary gland** The endocrine system's highly influential "master gland" that, in conjunction with the brain, controls the other endocrine glands.

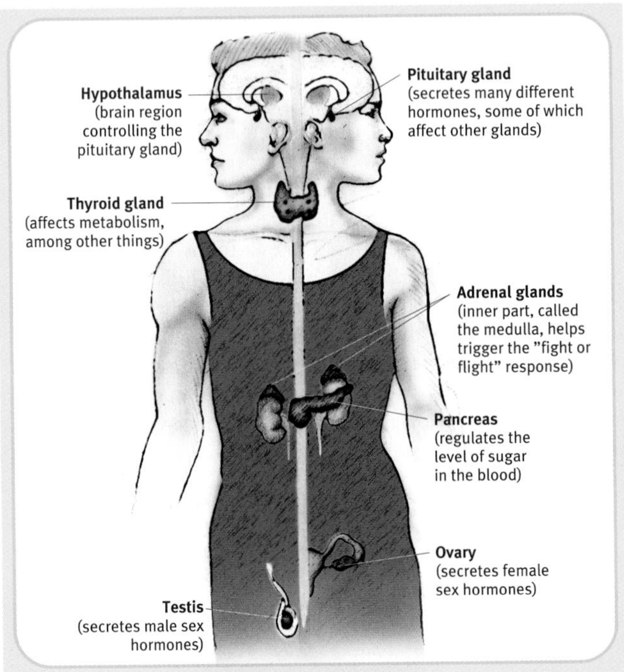

Figure 7.7 **Major Glands of the Endocrine System**

■ **TEACHING TIPS**

tr (1) A four-color transparency of Figure 7.7, Major Glands of the Endocrine System, is available in the **Overhead Transparencies Set.**

V (2) At this point, you may wish to show **Videocassette:** *The Brain,* **Second Edition, Module 2: "The Effects of Hormones and Environment on Brain Development."** (*Teacher's Resource Binder,* p. 7-1).

■ **APPLYING THE POINTS**

Have students research disorders of the endocrine system, including diabetes, abnormal growth, and hypo- and hyperthyroidism. Focus on the following questions:

- What physical problems do these disorders cause?
- What emotional problems do these disorders cause?
- What treatments are available for these disorders?

trb To go deeper into the workings of the human endocrine system, you may wish to use **Enrichment Lesson:** *The Endocrine System* (*Teacher's Resource Binder,* p 7-1).

Cross-Curricular Connections

BIOLOGY Team-teach a lesson with your school's biology teacher about how hormones influence both physical and emotional behavior.

MODULE 7

Close

Because of advances in neuroscience, Congress declared the 1990s the "Decade of the Brain." With the class, discuss the following questions to wrap up their study of the neuron and nervous systems:

- How can our understanding of neural communication enhance our understanding of behavior?
- What therapeutic and preventive advances do you think might be possible in the future, based on our current understanding of neural communication?

Encourage students to use information from the text and the *Teacher's Resource Binder* videos, activities, and lessons to help them develop thoughtful answers to these questions.

► **thyroid gland** Endocrine gland that helps regulate energy level in the body.

► **adrenal glands** Endocrine glands that help to arouse the body in times of stress.

endocrine systems. The brain may call on the pituitary to release hormones that stimulate or inhibit the release of other hormones from other endocrine glands. Can you see why the pituitary is called the master gland?

It is also true that the brain monitors the levels of hormones circulating in the blood, and may be influenced by their levels. Hunger, for example, is a response to a complex interaction of the neural and endocrine systems. The hypothalamus and pituitary work together to monitor and control the levels of glucose (blood sugar that your cells use for fuel) and insulin (a hormone the pancreas gland secretes, which allows the cells to use the available glucose) and thus determine, after considering a host of other factors, how hungry you are at any given moment. The important pituitary also releases hormones related to physical growth and pregnancy.

Other endocrine glands include the thyroid, the adrenals, and the sex glands (or gonads). The **thyroid gland,** located in the neck, helps to regulate energy level. The **adrenal glands,** which perch atop the kidneys, release *epinephrine* and *norepinephrine* (also called *adrenaline* and *noradrenaline*). These substances enhance strength and endurance in emergency situations. The sex glands—*ovaries* in females and *testes* in males—release hormones that influence emotion and physical development. The primary male hormone is *testosterone* and the primary female hormone is *estrogen,* but both males and females have each hormone present in their systems.

I'm seated at my desk right now, working on a computer that will process e-mail, connect to the Internet, and fax with a click of the mouse. It does this through a cable modem, which is also the source of the television programming I can access with the remote control that sits next to the telephone I used to talk to my son, 90 miles away, a few minutes ago. Also on the desk is a stack of bills, delivered via the U.S. Postal Service. Later this afternoon I will pay them—electronically—by using the computer to send instructions to my credit union. I depend on these methods of communication to function effectively in the world, just like my body depends on the nervous and endocrine systems for its communication needs. These systems are our personal information highways.

REVIEW

Module 7: Neural and Hormonal Systems

What's the Point?

Neurons: The Building Blocks of the Nervous System

1. *What are the primary parts of a typical neuron, and what functions do those parts perform?*

   Neurons are cells that are unique to the nervous system. Their primary parts are the dendrites, soma, axon, and axon terminals. Dendrites are bushy endings that receive information from other cells. The soma is the cell body, which contains the nucleus and other parts that maintain the cell's health. The axon ends in a number of axon terminals, which are the points at which messages leave the neuron for transmission to dendrites on other cells.

Neural Communication

2. *What roles do the action potential, refractory period, and resting potential play in generating a neural impulse?*

   Neurons, like guns, can either fire or not fire, and they always fire with the same intensity. When a neuron fires, the action potential—a tiny electrical charge—works its way down the axon to the axon terminals. Following this firing, the neuron requires a brief period of recharging—the refractory period. A neuron that has recharged but has not yet fired again is in a state known as the resting potential.

3. *What role do neurotransmitters play in neural communication?*

   The transfer of messages from one neuron to another is an electrochemical process. Within a neuron, most of the action is electrical. But when messages pass from one neuron to another, they take the form of chemical substances that travel across the synapse, the tiny gap between two neurons. These substances are called neurotransmitters, and they have unique shapes that fit like keys into sites on the dendrites of the cells receiving the messages. Once in place in the site, neurotransmitters either encourage the receiving cell to fire (excitatory effect), or they help to repress firing in the receiving cell (inhibitory effect).

4. *What are the steps of the neural chain?*

   A neural chain is the sequence of events that takes place when your nervous system gathers information, translates it into a form your brain can process, moves it to the brain for processing, and enables your body to take any necessary actions. In the first step, receptor cells in your sensory systems gather information and turn it into nerve impulses. In the second step, neurons and neurotransmitters move the impulses along sensory nerves to appropriate areas of your brain. In the third step, interneurons in your brain and spinal cord process the information and determine whether an action is necessary. In the fourth and final step, the brain uses motor nerves to transmit information to parts of your body that can react appropriately.

Checking the Points

■ **TEACHING TIPS**

web (1) The book companion site for *Thinking About Psychology* at **www.worthpublihsers.com/thinkingaboutpsych** contains a module quiz, flashcards of key terms and people, and other student activities and resources for this module. You will also find PowerPoint lectures, a quiz gradebook, and other teaching resources by logging on as an instructor.

trb (2) At this point, you may wish to review and confirm concepts about the neural and hormonal systems with **Critical Thinking Activity:** ***Fact or Falsehood?*** (*Teacher's Resource Binder*, p. 7-1; **Handout 7–1**). Suggest that students complete the handout in small groups, taking the time to look up information in the text to respond correctly to questions. Have all the groups meet to review the handout, again asking students to use the text to support their responses.

MODULE 7

trb **tr** ■ TEACHING TIP

At this point, you may wish to provide students with **Building Vocabulary: Graphic Organizer:** *The Neuron* (*Teacher's Resource Binder*, p. 7-1; **Handout 7–2**). Have students fill out this organizer as a tool for reviewing the parts of the neuron and the function of each. Encourage students to fill in the graphic organizer individually, at first without referring to the text or copies of the organizer they may have filled out earlier in the module. Next, allow time for students to work in small groups to complete and review their organizer, using the text to clarify confusing concepts. The handout may also be used as a transparency and projected for a full-class review of the neuron.

The Structure of the Nervous System

5. *What are the divisions of the nervous system, and what is the function of each of these subsystems?*

   The two major divisions of the nervous system are the central nervous system (CNS) and the peripheral nervous system (PNS). The CNS consists of the brain, where most information processing takes place, and the spinal cord, the main pathway information follows into and out of the brain. The PNS contains all nerves that connect the CNS to the rest of the body. The PNS is further divided into the somatic nervous system (which controls voluntary movements of the body's skeletal muscles) and the autonomic nervous system (which controls the self-regulated action of internal organs and glands). The autonomic nervous system in turn has two more subdivisions: the sympathetic division, which arouses us and expends energy, and the parasympathetic division, which calms us and conserves energy.

The Endocrine System

6. *How does the way the endocrine system communicates differ from the way the nervous system communicates?*

   The endocrine system comprises all the glands that produce hormones. The major endocrine glands are the pituitary, thyroid, adrenals, pancreas, and sex glands (ovaries in females and testes in males). Although both the nervous system and the endocrine system carry messages and communicate by locking chemicals into receptor sites, the endocrine system communicates more slowly than the nervous system. Another difference is that the nervous system's chemical messengers are neurotransmitters, which transmit information along nerves, whereas the endocrine system's chemical messengers are hormones, which travel through the bloodstream.

Key Terms

neuron, p. 122
dendrite, p. 122
soma, p. 122
axon, p. 122
axon terminal, p. 123
action potential, p. 123
refractory period, p. 123
resting potential, p. 123
all-or-none principle, p. 124
synapse, p. 125
neurotransmitter, p. 125
excitatory effect, p. 126
inhibitory effect, p. 126
receptor cells, p. 126
sensory nerves, p. 127
interneurons, p. 127
motor nerves, p. 127
acetylcholine, p. 128
antagonist, p. 128
agonist, p. 128
dopamine, p. 129
serotonin, p. 129
central nervous system (CNS), p. 131
peripheral nervous system (PNS), p. 131
somatic nervous system, p. 131
autonomic nervous system, p. 131
sympathetic division, p. 132
parasympathetic division, p. 132
endocrine system, p. 133
hormone, p. 133
pituitary gland, p. 133
thyroid gland, p. 134
adrenal gland, p. 134

Reteaching

Using the chalkboard or poster-size paper, present the following graphic of how the peripheral nervous system is organized into related sections:

Peripheral Nervous System

Somatic Nervous System
Controls voluntary movements

Autonomic Nervous System
Controls involuntary movements

Sympathetic Nervous System
Arouses the body in response to stress

Parasympathetic Nervous System
Brings the body back to homeostasis after stress

Self-Test

Multiple-Choice Questions

Choose the *best* answer for each of the following questions.

1. The nervous system is
   a. an electrical communication system.
   b. a chemical communication system.
   c. a hormonal communication system.
   d. an electrochemical communication system.

2. The all-or-none principle states that
   a. a neuron always fires with the same intensity; neurons either fire or they don't fire.
   b. neurotransmitters are found in all neural chains but not in the hormonal system.
   c. all live humans have firing neurons, but no dead humans have firing neurons.
   d. all the brain can do is determine a course of action; none of our behaviors are performed directly by the brain.

3. The brief recharging period when a neuron cannot fire is known as the
   a. action potential.
   b. refractory period.
   c. resting potential.
   d. neural impulse.

4. The chemical messengers in the neural system are
   a. neurotransmitters.
   b. hormones.
   c. agonists.
   d. antagonists.

5. In the nervous system, ______ ______ pick up information (about images, smells, tastes, and so on) from the world around us and transform that information into neural impulses that your brain can understand.
   a. the dendrites c. receptor cells
   b. axon terminals d. the interneurons

6. The two major components of the nervous system are
   a. the somatic nervous system and the autonomic nervous system.
   b. the central nervous system and the peripheral nervous system.
   c. the sympathetic nervous system and the parasympathetic nervous system.
   d. the hormonal system and the endocrine system.

7. The __________ gland is called the "master gland" because it has a close connection with the brain and helps to monitor and control other glands.
   a. adrenal c. thyroid
   b. hypothalamus d. pituitary

Matching Terms and Definitions

8. For each definition, choose the *best* matching term from the list that follows.

   Definition
   a. The tiny, fluid-filled gap between the axon terminal of one neuron and the dendrite of another.
   b. The part of the autonomic nervous system that arouses the body to deal with perceived threats.
   c. Nerves that carry information TO the central nervous system.
   d. The division of the peripheral nervous system that controls the body's skeletal muscles.
   e. Bushy, branching extensions of a neuron that receive messages and conduct impulses toward the cell body.
   f. The part of the autonomic nervous system that calms the body.
   g. The division of the peripheral nervous system that controls the glands and muscles of the internal organs.

tb Using the Test Bank

The *Test Bank* that accompanies this textbook offers a wide variety of questions in different formats and levels of complexity. Use the software to construct whole tests or to integrate standardized questions into teacher-made tests.

Self-Test Answers

Multiple-Choice Questions

1. d, 2. a, 3. b, 4. a, 5. c, 6. b, 7. d

Matching Terms and Definitions

8. a. (5), b. (11), c. (6), d. (9), e. (1), f. (12), g. (10)

MODULE 7

Self-Test Answers

Matching Terms and Definitions (continued)

h. (7), i. (2), j. (5)

Fill-in-the-Blank Questions

9. Neurons, 10. action potential, 11. excitatory; inhibitory

Brief Essay Question

12. Student answers should include discussions of the dendrites, cell membrane, cell body, axon, axon terminals, synaptic vesicles, and neurotransmitters. In addressing the synapse, students should discuss how the neurotransmitters from the previous cell are released and then bind to the receptor cells on the receiving neuron, causing the membrane to become permeable when enough of the neurotransmitter is attached to the cell (ruled by the all-or-none principle). If extra neurotransmitters are found in the synapse, they are recycled into the sending neuron in a process called reuptake.

h. Nerves that carry information FROM the central nervous system.
i. The cell body of a neuron, which contains the nucleus and other parts that keep the cell healthy.
j. The state of a neuron when it has recharged and is able to fire.

Term

(1) dendrites
(2) soma
(3) resting potential
(4) refractory period
(5) synapse
(6) sensory nerves
(7) motor nerves
(8) interneurons
(9) somatic nervous system
(10) autonomic nervous system
(11) sympathetic division
(12) parasympathetic division

Fill-in-the-Blank Questions

9. __________ are specialized cells found in the brain, spinal cord, and nerves.

10. The __________ __________ is a brief electrical charge that travels down the axon of a neuron.

11. A neurotransmitter that exerts an __________ effect makes the receiving neuron MORE likely to fire; a neurotransmitter that exerts an __________ effect makes the receiving neuron LESS likely to fire.

Brief Essay Question

12. How exactly would a neural message travel from one neuron to the next in its path through the body? Name the parts of the neuron that the message would travel through, and be sure to follow the correct order. Then discuss what happens at the synapse. Respond to this question in two paragraphs of 4 to 5 sentences each.

Performance Standards

Standard Area: Biological Bases of Behavior

Content Standard 3 Organization and function of the structures of the brain

Performance Standard 3.1 The structures of major brain regions and their functions.

- Identify the structures of the brainstem (medulla, reticular formation) and describe their functions. (Student Text pp.140–141)
- Discuss the location and function of the thalamus. (Student Text p. 141)
- Figure 8.2, "The Brainstem and the Thalamus," identifies the location of these brain structures. (Student Text p. 141)
- Present the location and function of the cerebellum. (Student Text pp.141–144)
- Figure 8.5, "The Cerebellum," displays the location of the medulla, spinal cord, and cerebellum. (Student Text p. 144)
- Identify the parts of the limbic system, the hypothalamus, hippocampus, and the amygdala, and describe their functions. (Student Text pp.144–145)
- Figure 8.6, "The Limbic System," identifies the location of the hypothalamus, amygdala, and the hippocampus. (Student Text p. 145)

Performance Standard 3.2 Functions of the lobes of the cerebral cortex.

- Identify the major regions of the cerebral cortex (frontal, parietal, occipital, and temporal) along with the longitudinal fissure and corpus callosum. Identify the association areas and explain the functions of the motor and somatosensory cortex. (Student Text pp.145–148)

Content Standard 4 Methods for analyzing the brain

Performance Standard 4.1 Recognize how technology has allowed researchers to investigate the brain.

- Discuss the methods and usage of each brain imaging technique (CT, MRIs, PET scans, and EEGs). (Student Text p.143)
- Figure 8.4, "Modern Scanning Techniques," provides a picture of each technique, specifically what the scanners and the scan look like. (Student Text p. 143)

Content Standard 5 Hemispheric differences

Performance Standard 5.1 Explore how the left and right hemispheres influence brain functioning.

- Explain the role of the corpus callosum in communication between the left and right hemispheres. (Student Text p.148)
- Discuss how language areas are focused in the left hemisphere and spatial abilities in the right. Emphasis is on Broca's and Wernicke's area in the left hemisphere. (Student Text pp. 148–149)
- Present Roger Sperry's and Michael Gazzaniga's research on split-brain patients. Emphasize what this research has taught us about hemispheric specialization. (Student Text pp. 150–151)
- Present the concept of "brain plasticity." (Student Text p. 149)

Materials NETWORK

All of the items from the Video, Activity, and Enrichment Centers listed below come from the *Teacher's Resource Binder.* These items will help you teach and expand on concepts presented in Module 8.

trb This logo indicates when an item from the Materials Network may be used in conjunction with a specific note found in this module's *Teacher's Edition.*

Lower-Level Brain Structures

V Video Center

Consult the faculty guides from *The Brain* and *The Mind* video series for descriptions of these modules.

- Videocassette: *The Mind,* Second Edition, Module 10: "Life Without Memory: The Case of Clive Wearing" (*Teacher's Resource Binder,* p. 8-1)
- Videocassette: *The Mind,* Second Edition, Module 11: "Clive Wearing, Part 2: Living Without Memory" (*Teacher's Resource Binder,* p. 8-1)
- Videocassette: *The Brain,* Second Edition, Module 1: "Organization and Evaluation of Brain Function" (*Teacher's Resource Binder,* p. 8-1)
- Videocassette: *The Mind,* Second Edition, Module 6: "Brain Mechanisms of Pleasure and Addiction" (*Teacher's Resource Binder,* p. 8-1)

Activity Center

- Critical Thinking Activity: *Fact or Falsehood?* With this activity, students' preconceptions about the brain are either exposed as incorrect or reinforced as correct. (*Teacher's Resource Binder,* p. 8-1; Handout 8–1)
- Building Vocabulary: *Greek and Latin Roots* Students use the text to find meanings for brain part names that contain Latin or Greek roots. (*Teacher's Resource Binder,* p. 8-1; Handout 8–3)
- Application Activity: *A Portable Brain Model* This activity uses students' hands as a three-dimensional model of the human brain. It is a model students can take with them into a test! (*Teacher's Resource Binder,* p. 8-1)
- Graphic Organizer: *The Brain* With this diagram of the brain, students can practice module vocabulary. They can also review the location and function of brain parts. (*Teacher's Resource Binder,* p. 8-1; Handout 8–2)

Enrichment Center

- Enrichment Lesson: *Brain Puzzles, Models, and Molds* Students may benefit from using any of these suggestions for brain puzzles, models, and molds. All the puzzles, models, and molds suggested in this lesson may be ordered through a catalog. (*Teacher's Resource Binder,* p. 8-1)
- Enrichment Lesson: *Why Can't We Tickle Ourselves?* It is very difficult to fool the brain! This lesson details a study in which researchers showed that the brain turns off its tickle centers when we try to tickle ourselves. (*Teacher's Resource Binder,* p. 8-1)

The Cerebral Cortex

V Video Center

Consult the faculty guides from *The Mind* and the *Scientific American Frontiers* video series for descriptions of these modules or segments.

- Videocassette: *Scientific American Frontiers,* Second Edition, Segment 8: "Old Brain, New Tricks" (*Teacher's Resource Binder,* p. 8-1)
- Videocassette: *The Mind,* Second Edition, Module 7: "The Frontal Lobes: Cognition and Awareness" (*Teacher's Resource Binder,* p. 8-1)
- Videocassette: *The Mind,* Second Edition, Module 18: "Effects of Mental and Physical Activity on Brain/Mind" (*Teacher's Resource Binder,* p. 8-1)

Activity Center

- Application Activity: *The Sensory Homunculus* With this memorable demonstration, students learn that the brain doesn't allocate much cortex to the sensitivity even of a human's toes. (*Teacher's Resource Binder,* p. 8-1)

Enrichment Center

- Enrichment Lesson: *Einstein's Brain and Genius* Albert Einstein, perhaps the most intelligent person ever to have lived, donated his brain to science. Study of his brain has shed light and posed questions about what we know about genius. At first, according to the psychologist who took charge of Einstein's brain for scientific research, the organ seemed to be "normal." Further study of the brain pointed to unique features. (*Teacher's Resource Binder,* p. 8-1)

- Enrichment Lesson: *Lobotomies* The disastrous and dramatic story of the use of the prefrontal lobotomy to treat schizophrenia in the 1930s through the 1950s is the focus of this lesson that highlights the importance of scientific testing and strict ethical guidelines in the use of this therapy on humans. (*Teacher's Resource Binder*, p. 8-1)

Hemispheric Differences

Video Center

Consult the faculty guides from *The Brain, The Mind,* and the *Scientific American Frontiers* video series for descriptions of these modules or segments.

- Videocassette: *The Brain,* Second Edition, Module 6: "Language and Speech: Broca and Wernicke's Areas" (*Teacher's Resource Binder*, p. 8-1)
- Videocassette: *The Mind,* Second Edition, Module 8: "Language Processing in the Brain" (*Teacher's Resource Binder*, p. 8-1)
- Videocassette: *Scientific American Frontiers,* Second Edition, Segment 7: "Severed Corpus Callosum" (*Teacher's Resource Binder*, p. 8-1)
- Videocassette: *The Brain,* Second Edition, Module 5: "The Divided Brain" (*Teacher's Resource Binder*, p. 8-1)

Activity Center

- Technology Application Activity: *PsychSim:* "Hemispheric Specialization" *PsychSim* is an interactive CD-ROM containing tutorials in different content areas of psychology. This tutorial walks students through the complexities of hemispheric lateralization. Its focus is on demonstrating the crossing over of functioning from left hemisphere to right hemisphere and vice versa. (*Teacher's Resource Binder*, p. 8-1)
- Application Activity: *Behavioral Effects of the Split-Brain Operation* Patients who have undergone split-brain surgery to treat epilepsy experience some confusion when the two sides of their brain don't communicate. This activity allows students to experience what it may be like to have a split brain—it's almost like being two people in one body! (*Teacher's Resource Binder*, p. 8-1)
- Critical Thinking Activity: *The Wagner Preference Inventory* Are you right-brain dominant or left-brain dominant? This inventory will show students the side of their brain that is more dominant, a circumstance typically related to handedness. (*Teacher's Resource Binder*, p. 8-1; Handout 8–4)
- Cooperative Learning Activity: *Hemispheric Specialization* With this activity, students demonstrate their own knowledge of the experimental method. Simultaneously, the activity tests how much language interferes with the ability to balance a wooden dowel in both the right and left hands. (*Teacher's Resource Binder*, p. 8-1)
- Application Activity: *Hand Usage Questionnaire* Handedness preference can be a signal to whether one has a dominant hemisphere. This survey will help students see if they are right-handed, left-handed, or ambidextrous. (*Teacher's Resource Binder*, p. 8-1; Handout 8–5)

Enrichment Center

- Enrichment Lesson: *Language on Two Sides of the Brain?* This lesson relates the story of V.J., a patient of researcher Michael Gazzaniga. V.J. demonstrated the ability to use language in the right hemisphere of the brain. The ability to use language in the right hemisphere is contrary to popular conceptions of hemispheric specialization. (*Teacher's Resource Binder*, p. 8-1)
- Enrichment Lesson: *The Right Brain Movement* In recent years, brain-based education has promoted the idea that both sides of the brain need to be educated. Brain-based educators seek out "right-brained" classroom activities that involve more hands-on and creative activities. But this brain-based education movement may not be as rooted in the hard facts of brain research as many educators and the general public believe it to be. (*Teacher's Resource Binder*, p. 8-1)

Brain Plasticity

V Video Center

Consult the faculty guides from *The Brain* and the *Scientific American Frontiers* video series for descriptions of these modules or segments.

- Videocassette: *The Brain,* Second Edition, Module 7: "Brain Anomaly and Plasticity: Hydrocephalus" (*Teacher's Resource Binder*, p. 8-1)
- Videocassette: *The Brain,* Second Edition, Module 32: "Neurorehabilitation" (*Teacher's Resource Binder*, p. 8-1)
- Videocassette: *The Brain,* Second Edition, Module 25: "The Frontal Lobes and Behavior: The Story of Phineas Gage" (*Teacher's Resource Binder*, p. 8-1)
- Videocassette: *Scientific American Frontiers,* Second Edition, Segment 5: "Mind Reading" (*Teacher's Resource Binder*, p. 8-1)

- Videocassette: *Scientific American Frontiers,* Second Edition, Segment 6: "Image-Guided Surgery" (*Teacher's Resource Binder,* p. 8-1)

Enrichment Center

- Enrichment Lesson: *New Brain Cells* It has long been believed that the cells in the central nervous system cannot regenerate. The belief was based on the notion that the brain lacked the stem cells that would allow for neuronal regeneration, also known as *neurogenesis.* Amazing new research hints that this may not be true after all. (*Teacher's Resource Binder,* p. 8-1)
- Enrichment Lesson: *Hemispherectomy* This lesson highlights the stories of several patients who have received hemispherectomies, in which one hemisphere of the brain is removed to treat some debilitating or fatal brain disorder. Although these patients do experience problems, such as paralysis and partial blindness, their brains demonstrate amazing plasticity and recover some vital functions that were thought to have been lost completely. (*Teacher's Resource Binder,* p. 8-1)

MODULE 8
The Brain

Lower-Level Brain Structures

The Cerebral Cortex

Hemispheric Differences

Brain Plasticity

What is the most amazing thing in the universe? The answer is a matter of opinion, no doubt, but surely one of the leading candidates must be the brain. Think about it—oops, I guess that's already impossible without your brain! All of the art, music, and literature ever created began in a brain. The world's great (and not so great) architecture started in a brain. The principles of democracy, mathematics, and science began in a brain. You name it, if humans (or other animals) were behind it, the brain is what allowed it to happen. A brain can even think of itself in an effort to understand itself. Your liver can't do that!

A Universe of Brains One indication of our endless fascination with brains is the number of products that use the shape of a human brain to attract attention. How many brains do you have in your house, other than the ones your family members are carrying around in their heads?

The brain's complexity is, well, mind-boggling, but our discussion will be limited to the basics. Vocabulary is the key. If you can master the words (most of which would already make perfect sense to you if you spoke Greek and Latin!), you will be well on your way toward understanding your brain.

Think of the brain as the most successful sports franchise of all time. Every player on the team has a role to play, and each must do it well to ensure the team's success. The team also needs support personnel—trainers, assistants, and equipment managers. Successful teams also have good coaches, coordinators, and talent scouts. And every good team has an efficient front office dealing with everything from media contacts to contract negotiations to ticket sales. Your brain is similar, but far more complex. Every *neuron* (nerve cell) plays a role as it combines with other neurons to form the various structures and substructures of the brain. Only one team can win the championship, but brains make everyone a winner. For the vast major-

Getting Started

trb You may wish to use **Critical Thinking Activity:** *Fact or Falsehood?* (*Teacher's Resource Binder,* p. 8-1; **Handout 8–1**) as a prereading strategy to find out what students already know about the brain. The activity handout will prime students to note terms and concepts in the text that confirm or dispel their preconceptions about the brain.

trb At the beginning of the module, you may also wish to distribute **Graphic Organizer:** *The Brain* for students to preview this module's focus (*Teacher's Resource Binder,* p. 8-1; **Handout 8–2**).

MODULE 8

The Brain

Introducing the Module

The Points: Module Objectives

- Identify the parts of the brainstem and the functions of each.
- Understand the function of the thalamus.
- Understand the function of the cerebellum.
- Identify the parts of the limbic system and the functions of each.
- Identify the major regions of the cerebral cortex.
- Identify and delineate the two specialized language areas of the left hemisphere, and describe the right hemisphere's special function.
- Understand the concept of brain plasticity.

trb Building Vocabulary

Have students work with partners to find and review Greek and Latin roots (cited throughout the module) of terms related to the brain. Then have pairs complete the handout (*Teacher's Resource Binder,* p. 8-1; **Handout 8–3**). This activity focuses on reading comprehension skills, in addition to module vocabulary.

■ TEACHING TIP

Discussion of the brain can become very surreal. Since students are maturing into more advanced levels of cognitive thinking, allow them to explore the following questions related to the importance of our complex brains to our species:

- Can other forms of life contemplate their existences like humans can? Why or why not? How do we know?
- What function does language have in understanding the world and ourselves?

MODULE 8

Teaching the Points

■ **TEACHING TIPS**

web (1) You can log on as an instructor to the book companion site for *Thinking About Psychology* at www.worthpublishers.com/thinkingaboutpsych. It contains teacher resources for class presentations as well as review and assessment of module concepts and terms.

(2) Help students marvel at the importance of each part of the brain as it works within the whole. Have them imagine what life would be like without each part. Remind students that most of what everyone does each day would be impossible without the brain.

V At this point, you may wish to show **Videocassette:** *The Brain,* **Second Edition, Module 1: "Organization and Evaluation of Brain Function"** (*Teacher's Resource Binder*, p. 8-1).

(3) Have students find Greek and Latin roots for other parts of the brain not defined in the text, such as the *medulla, reticular formation, corpus callosum, longitudinal fissure, frontal lobes, parietal lobes, occipital lobes,* and *temporal lobes.*

trb At this point, you may wish to use **Application Activity:** *A Portable Brain Model* (*Teacher's Resource Binder*, p. 8-1) in conjunction with **Building Vocabulary:** *Greek and Latin Roots* (*Teacher's Resource Binder*, p. 8-1; **Handout 8–3**).

■ **LOOKING AT THE ISSUES**

Have students contemplate the following questions:

- What parts of the brain do humans and other mammals share?
- What physical functions seem to be shared among mammals? What functions seem to be unique to humans?

V You may wish to show **Videocassette:** *Scientific American Frontiers,* **Second Edition, Segment 8: "Old Brain, New Tricks"** (*Teacher's Resource Binder*, p. 8-1).

tr A four-color transparency of Figure 8.1, Brain Similarities in Different Mammals, is available in the **Overhead Transparencies Set.**

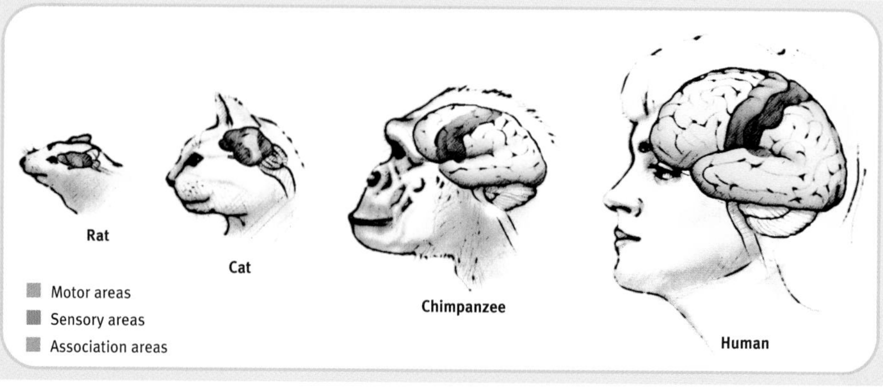

Figure 8.1 **Brain Similarities in Different Mammals** Every mammal has a brain that can engage in similar functions, such as the ones noted here. The core areas of mammal brains are even more similar than the outer surfaces depicted here.

ity of us, our brain takes care of all our required tasks with championship performance, even though we barely give these tasks a second thought.

The brains of most animals and all mammals share certain similarities (Figure 8.1). Mammal brains, for example, have similar components because all mammals also share certain functions, such as digestion and respiration. The more complex the organism, the more complex and highly developed its brain must be. The basic components that complex organisms share with less-complex life forms developed first, and these parts tend to be in the inside, lower regions of the brain. The parts of the brain that control uniquely human functions—things like judgment and sense of humor—are layered around and on top of these lower and more basic regions. In isolation, no one part would be capable of anything, but functioning together, the parts of the brain form an integrated whole with remarkable abilities. We begin our discussion with the lower structures and then progress to those that truly make humans special. (To see how we know what we know about brains, see Psychology Is a Science: Studying the Brain, pages 142–143.)

Lower-Level Brain Structures

The innermost structures of your brain are similar to the brains of all mammals. They are at the core because they evolved first. The newer regions are layered on top, much as paint builds up on the walls of houses.

The Brainstem

What's the point? 1. What are the parts of the brainstem, and what are their major functions?

The **brainstem** is the oldest, most basic part of the brain, the region where the spinal cord swells and becomes the brain (Figure 8.2). No structural

Suggested Readings

Use the following books as teacher-preparation tools or as enrichment for advanced students:

Carey, J. (Ed.). (1993). *Brain facts: A primer on the brain and nervous system.* Washington, DC: Society for Neuroscience.

Damasio, A. (1994). *Descartes' error: Emotion, reason, and the human brain.* New York: Putnam.

Gazzaniga, M. (1998). *The mind's past.* Sacramento: University of California Press.

Ramachandran, V. S., & Blakeslee, S. (1998). *Phantoms in the brain: Probing the mysteries of the human mind.* New York: William Morrow.

Sacks, O. (1985). *The man who mistook his wife for a hat.* New York: Summit Books.

Springer, S., & Deutsch, G. (1998). *Left brain, right brain* (5th ed.). New York: W. H. Freeman.

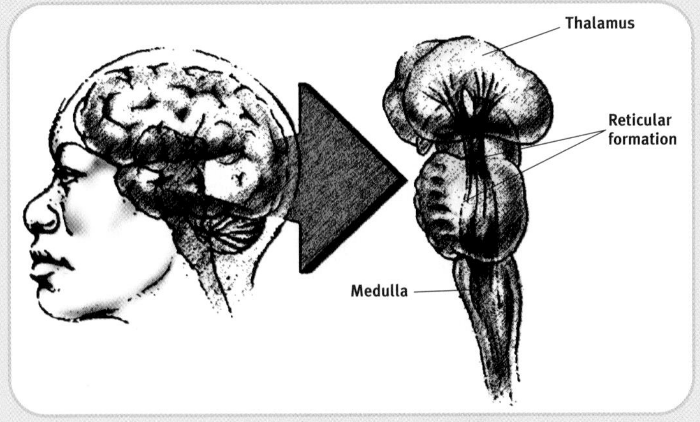

Figure 8.2 The Brainstem and the Thalamus The brainstem is a swelling at the top of the spinal cord. The medulla and reticular formation support fundamental processes like breathing and wakefulness. The thalamus, perched on top, routes sensory information to the proper regions of the brain.

point marks this junction of the brain and the spinal cord. You can either think of the brain as a rose that has blossomed on top of a stem, or think of the spinal cord as a tail that extends down from the brain. Your choice!

As you move up the spinal cord toward the brain, the area where the cord first swells marks one of the most important parts of the brainstem—the **medulla.** The medulla is in charge of basic life-support functions, such as breathing, circulation, and swallowing. Don't hurt yours! Damage in this region would almost certainly lead to death.

Another part of the brainstem is the **reticular formation,** a nerve network that extends up and down the back of the spinal cord as it rises into the brain. The reticular formation controls an organism's overall level of alertness. Damage to this region would cause a coma.

The Thalamus

2. What is the function of the thalamus?

The **thalamus,** Greek for "inner chamber," sits atop the brainstem in the very middle of things. Have you seen photographs of old-fashioned telephone switchboards, with an operator plugging in cords to route calls to the proper phone? Such is the role of the thalamus. It is the brain's sensory switchboard. The incoming fibers of all your senses except smell funnel into the thalamus, which then distributes the information to the proper regions of the brain for processing.

The Cerebellum

3. What is the function of the cerebellum?

The **cerebellum,** extending from the back of the brain, is one of the most strikingly apparent brain structures. The word *cerebellum* is Latin

▶ **brainstem** The oldest part and central core of the brain, beginning where the spinal cord swells as it enters the skull; the brainstem is responsible for automatic survival functions.

▶ **medulla** [muh-DUL-uh] The base of the brainstem; controls life-support functions like heartbeat and breathing.

▶ **reticular formation** A nerve network in the brainstem that plays an important role in controlling wakefulness and arousal.

▶ **thalamus** [THAL-uh-muss] The brain's sensory switchboard, located on top of the brainstem; it directs messages to the sensory receiving areas in the cortex.

▶ **cerebellum** [sehr-uh-BELL-um] The "little brain" attached to the rear of the brainstem; it helps coordinate voluntary movements and balance.

■ LOOKING AT THE ISSUES

Have students explore statistics regarding survival and recovery rates of spinal cord injuries.

- Do the rates of mortality and recovery differ as the injury moves closer to the brainstem?
- How do people with spinal cord injuries feel about life and their injuries?
- How have recent advances in spinal cord research changed the prognosis of people with spinal cord injuries?

F • Y • I

Studies in cats showed that stimulating the reticular formation caused them to perk up their ears like they had heard something. When the area was lesioned, the cats lapsed into an unrecoverable coma. Studies like this indicate that the reticular formation helps us pay attention to novel stimuli in the environment.

■ TEACHING TIP

All sensory information—except for smell—is routed through the thalamus, which sends the information to the appropriate cortex for processing. Smell, an "old" sense on the evolutionary scale, travels to the olfactory cortex and then to the thalamus for processing. It seems that our brains adapted other senses after smell, causing those senses to be processed differently.

tr A four-color transparency of Figure 8.2, The Brain Stem and the Thalamus, is available in the **Overhead Transparencies Set.**

■ JOURNAL WRITING

Invite students to use the following questions and writing prompts as springboards for entries in their psychology journals:

- From an evolutionary standpoint, the lower-level brain regions are considered to be the oldest part of the brain. How do you think the functions of these parts of the brain led researchers to believe this?
- Why do you think people take their brains for granted? What can you do to be more appreciative of what your brain can do for you?

Meeting Individual Needs

trb GRAPHIC ORGANIZERS Provide learning opportunities for all levels of learners with one of the following options for using the graphic organizer (*Teacher's Resource Binder*, p. 8-1; **Handout 8–2**):

- **Independent Learners** Students can fill out the organizer on their own or follow along in class during discussion and lecture.
- **Cooperative Learners** Students may use the textbook as a resource and work in groups to find the answers that fit in the blanks.
- **Exceptional Learners** Graphic organizers can fill a special education need to provide notes for exceptional students. These students can fill in the blanks independently, with a student or teacher/tutor, or along with class discussion and lecture.

MODULE 8

V ■ TEACHING TIP

For a vivid reenactment of Phineas Gage's accident, show **Videocassette:** ***The Brain,*** **Second Edition, Module 25: "The Frontal Lobes and Behavior: The Story of Phineas Gage"** (*Teacher's Resource Binder,* p. 8-1).

Psychology is a Science

Studying the Brain

Case Studies

A **case study** is a study of a single person or situation. One of the most famous case studies in the history of psychology is that of Phineas Gage. Gage, a young man in his twenties, was working for the railroad in 1848, when he suffered a devastating brain injury. An explosion blew a pointed, 4-foot-long rod through Gage's cheek, just behind his eye, and straight out through the top of his skull (Figure 8.3). Despite severe damage to his frontal lobe, Gage survived—he never even lost consciousness! The disruptive changes in his personality, however, have fascinated people ever since. He went from a responsible worker to an unreliable, irritable, dishonest man who could not hold his previous job. Despite living many more years, he was, in the words of a friend, "no longer Gage." Gage's injury, and the annals of many other brain injuries over the years, have allowed psychologists to speculate on the functions of the parts of the brain destroyed by the accidents.

Case studies have always been an important way to study the brain, but they are limited in the kind of information they provide because accidents are haphazard. Since case studies are based on a sample size of one, conclusions will almost certainly be biased. How do we know everyone would respond as Gage did to similar circumstances? Only *experiments* allow us to draw solid cause-and-effect conclusions. From a *scientific* point of view, our conclusions would be much more sound if we could systematically damage specific brain regions in experiments on humans. You are probably already considering the ethical difficulties with this—at the very least it would be difficult to secure volunteers! So, given the practical and ethical limits to gathering solid, experimental evidence on the brain, case studies can provide a wealth of important information. Luckily, however, new technology gives us another line of evidence.

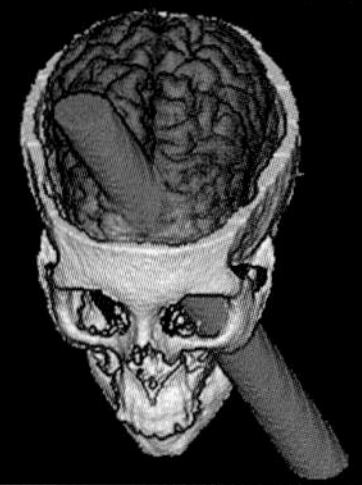

Figure 8.3 Phineas Gage This computer-generated image shows the probable path of the rod that passed through Gage's brain. This case study is so compelling it's still being researched more than 150 years after Gage's accident (Damasio and others, 1994).

▶ **case study** An observation technique in which one person is studied in depth in the hope of revealing universal principles.

▶ **computerized axial tomography (CT or CAT) scan** A series of x-ray photographs taken from different angles and combined by computer into a composite representation of a slice through the body.

▶ **magnetic resonance imaging (MRI)** A technique that uses magnetic fields and radio waves to produce computer-generated images that distinguish among different types of soft tissue; allows us to see structures within the brain.

▶ **electroencephalogram (EEG)** An amplified recording of the waves of electrical activity that sweep across the brain's surface. These waves, measured by electrodes placed on the scalp, are helpful in evaluating brain function.

▶ **positron emission tomography (PET) scan** A visual display of brain activity that detects where a radioactive form of glucose (blood sugar) goes while the brain performs a given task.

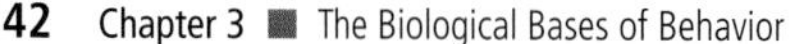

Cross-Curricular Connections

RESEARCH METHODS How do other fields of science use case studies when ethically or realistically experiments are not possible? Have students gather some research articles from other fields of science that have used case studies to see what conclusions they draw from the studies about their fields.

■ **APPLYING THE POINTS**

Invite a radiologist to class to discuss the different brain scans. Hopefully, he or she can bring examples of the brain scans and describe how the scans are administered, as well as how they are interpreted.

Scanning Techniques

Thanks to remarkable technological advances we can now study the brain without actually "going in." Various scanning techniques provide a window through which researchers can study healthy, functioning brains in living people. These techniques truly have revolutionized both brain research and the diagnosis and treatment of brain problems. Brain scans provide information in two different categories: *brain structure* and *brain function*, (Figure 8.4).

The most well-known *structural* scans are **computerized axial tomography** (usually referred to as CT or CAT scans) and **magnetic resonance imaging** (MRI). These scans are ideal for examining specific aspects of brain structure. For example, they can find a tumor or locate brain damage following a stroke.

The other scanning techniques provide information about brain *function*. The best known of these are the **electroencephalogram** (EEG), the **positron emission tomography (PET) scan,** and a new technology based on magnetic resonance imaging called *functional MRI (fMRI)*. These techniques allow researchers to see what the brain is doing at a given point in time. EEGs are often the tool of choice for diagnosing sleep disorders and seizure disorders. PET and fMRI scans are helpful in identifying which parts of the brain are active during a particular task. Such scans have taught us, for example, that the occipital lobe is responsible for visual processing, and that facial recognition occurs in the temporal lobe.

Phineas Gage remains famous for his tragic contribution to psychological knowledge. We are fortunate that new techniques have made it possible to learn more with less suffering. Consider what new "windows to the brain" will open up during your lifetime! Perhaps you will help develop one of them.

Figure 8.4 Modern Scanning Techniques The machines look scary, but they provide a window to the brain for both research and treatment of disorders.

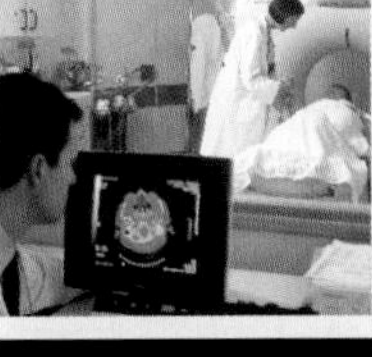
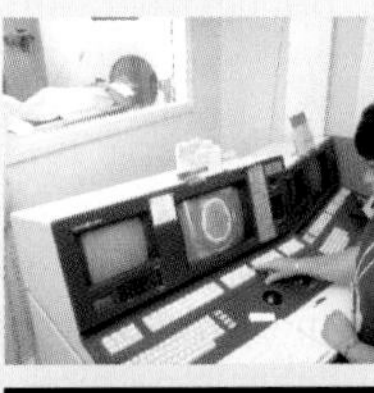
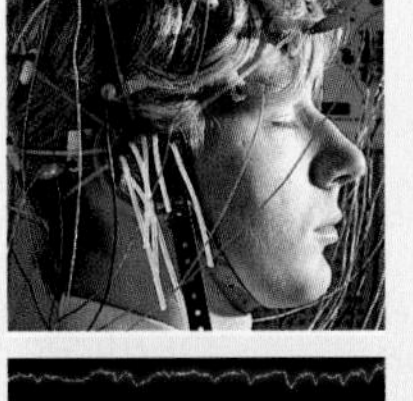
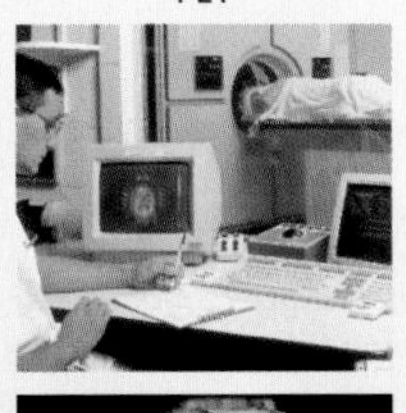
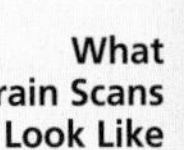
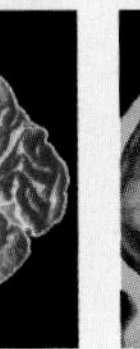
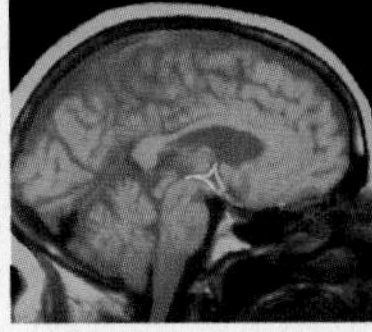
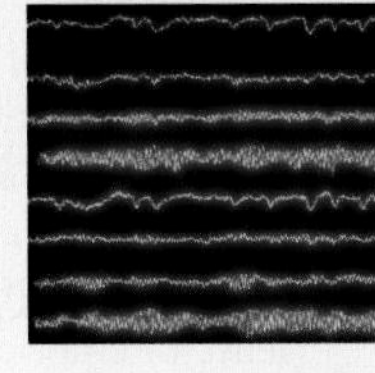
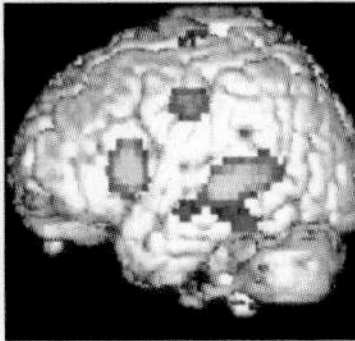

Meeting Individual Needs

Help students relate to brain imaging techniques by having them share their experiences if they've had any of the scans described. Although most scans are done on body parts other than the brain, hearing about a medical scanning experience can be enlightening for all students.

MODULE 8

F•Y•I

Studies in rats have shown that the *hypothalamus* can be divided into two sections: the **lateral side (LH)**, which controls hunger, and the **ventromedial side (VMH)**, which controls satiety. In these studies, stimulation to the LH produced behaviors that led to seeking out food while lesions to the VMH caused rats to overeat to the point of becoming obese.

trb You may wish to use **Application Activity:** *A Portable Brain Model* (*Teacher's Resource Binder*, p. 8-1) and **Enrichment Lesson:** *Brain Puzzles, Models, and Molds* (*Teacher's Resource Binder*, p. 8-1) to point out the location of the hypothalamus.

■ **TEACHING TIP**

Help students remember the functioning of the hypothalamus by reminding them that it controls the function of the pituitary gland, studied in Module 7. The pituitary gland, being the "master gland," directs the hormonal system in its functioning. If our hormones regulate everything from hunger to stress reactions to sex, then the hypothalamus really does control the body!

tr A four-color transparency of Figure 8.5, The Cerebellum, is available in the **Overhead Transparencies Set.**

trb ■ **CHECKING FOR UNDERSTANDING**

Using **Graphic Organizer:** *The Brain* (*Teacher's Resource Binder*, p. 8-1; **Handout 8–2**), have students label each brain part and describe its function.

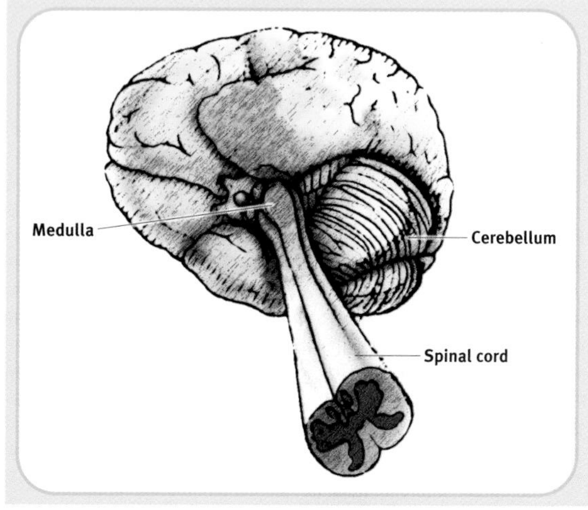

Figure 8.5 The Cerebellum The cerebellum is very obvious as it juts out from the bottom rear of the brain. Its primary role is coordination and balance. Lance Armstrong would be unable to ride his bicycle, much less ride with his hands in the air, if his cerebellum weren't working properly.

for "little brain," and indeed this structure does almost look as if it were some sort of extra mini-brain added at the last minute (Figure 8.5). In conjunction with other brain regions, your cerebellum controls balance, muscle coordination, and memories for knowing how to use your body for things like walking or playing the guitar. The cerebellum makes it possible to smoothly engage in tasks such as running or writing. If your cerebellum were damaged, you could still decide to move your feet, but you would lose much of the coordination and balance required for dancing well. You could move your hands, but you would lose the intricacy required to play the guitar.

The Limbic System

4. What are the parts of the limbic system, and what are their functions?

In the area around the thalamus is a final lower brain area, the **limbic system** (Figure 8.6), which derives its name from the Latin word for "border." This ring of structures forms the border between the older core regions and the more recently developed surface regions.

Of the many different structures in the limbic system, perhaps the most important is the **hypothalamus.** This small region tucks directly under the front of the thalamus (*hypo* means "beneath"). The hypothalamus helps regulate many of your body's most important functions, including hunger and thirst, the "fight or flight" reaction to stress, and body temperature. The hypothalamus also plays a large role in the experience of emotion, pleasure, and sexual function. Cell for cell, it would be hard to identify a more crucial brain part.

Ever notice how easily smell triggers memories? Smell information bypasses the thalamus and is routed directly to memory and emotion centers in the brain. This may be why the smell of your grandparents' house or a hospital can unleash a flood of emotions, sometimes positive and sometimes negative.

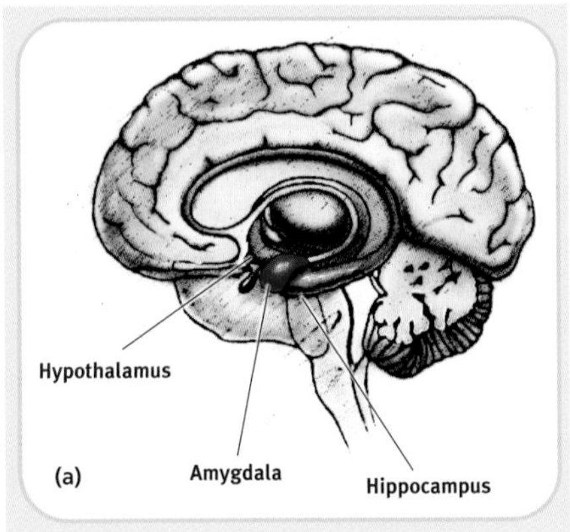

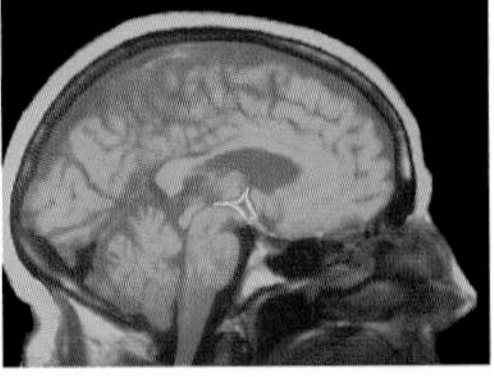

(b)

Figure 8.6 **The Limbic System** (a) The limbic system is a ring of structures surrounding the thalamus and forming a border between the older core regions and the more recently developed surface regions. (b) The hypothalamus is tiny, but it plays a huge role. The hypothalamus is the red-colored region in this MRI brain scan. It helps regulate responses ranging from thirst to pleasure.

Two other vital limbic structures are the **hippocampus** and the **amygdala**. The hippocampus, which looks something like a seahorse (you guessed it—*hippo* is Greek for "horse"), wraps around the back of the thalamus and plays an important role in processing new memories. *Amygdala* is Greek for "almond," and this structure in your brain does resemble two almonds. The amygdala controls many of your emotional responses, especially emotions like fear and anger.

▶ **limbic system** A ring of structures at the border of the brainstem and cerebral cortex; it helps regulate important functions such as memory, fear, aggression, hunger, and thirst. Includes the hypothalamus, hippocampus, and amygdala.

▶ **hypothalamus** [hi-po-THAL-uh-muss] A neural structure lying below the thalamus; it directs maintenance activities such as eating, drinking, and body temperature and is linked to emotion.

▶ **hippocampus** A neural center located in the limbic system; it helps process new memories for permanent storage.

▶ **amygdala** [ah-MIG-dah-la] Two almond-shaped neural clusters in the limbic system that are linked to emotions, such as fear and anger.

▶ **cerebral** [seh-REE-bruhl] **cortex** The intricate fabric of interconnected neural cells that form the cerebral hemispheres; the body's ultimate control and information-processing center.

▶ **longitudinal fissure** The long crack running all the way from the front to the back of the cerebral cortex, separating the left and right hemispheres.

The Cerebral Cortex

5. What are the major regions of the cerebral cortex?

Close your eyes and conjure up an image of a brain. What did you see? Probably not the lower-level structures we have been discussing, right? More likely, you thought of the brain's wrinkled outer surface—the **cerebral cortex** (Figure 8.7, page 146), which is the body's ultimate control and information-processing center. The cortex covers the brain's lower-level structures, just as a glove covers your hand. The word *cortex* derives from the Latin word for "bark," an appropriate name, given the barklike appearance of the brain's outer surface. The convolutions or wrinkles of the cortex allow more brain tissue to be packed into a confined space, like a sleeping bag in its stuff sack. Thanks to this efficient use of space, an estimated 30 billion nerve cells can exist in a tissue layer only one-eighth of an inch thick (Travis, 1994)!

The most dramatic feature of the cortex is the **longitudinal fissure,** the crevice that divides the brain into two halves called *hemispheres* (Figure 8.7a). If you were to poke your pencil down this fissure (not that you should try this, mind you), you would eventually meet resistance at the point where a large band of neural tissue connects the

F • Y • I

The hippocampus is the only known brain structure that can be completely removed without causing any physical problems. But while physical functioning is not lost, patients whose hippocampi are damaged or removed lack the ability to form new memories, leaving them constantly in the present. Like the main character in the movie *Memento,* these people cannot remember anything beyond a few minutes of time. Imagine what the world would be like if people had only a short-term memory!

■ **TEACHING TIP**

V Show **Videocassette:** ***The Brain,*** **Second Edition, Module 25: "The Frontal Lobes and Behavior: The Story of Phineas Gage"** (*Teacher's Resource Binder,* p. 8-1) to reinforce the relationship of the *amygdala* and the *limbic system* with the *cerebral cortex* and the *frontal lobe.* Without communication between these two brain regions, we would be like Phineas Gage, lacking the judgment to control our emotional reactions.

tr A four-color transparency of Figure 8.6, The Limbic System, is available in the **Overhead Transparencies Set.**

F • Y • I

The idea that we only use 10 percent of our brains is a myth that was developed in the last century. As brain research techniques have evolved, scientists have found that most of the brain is active at any given moment. Those areas that were thought to be unused were probably the association areas described in the text.

trb At this point, you may wish to use **Enrichment Lesson:** ***Einstein's Brain and Genius*** (*Teacher's Resource Binder,* p. 8-1).

Demonstrating

THE WRINKLY CORTEX Explain to students that the deeply convoluted surface of the brain is most strongly linked to intelligence. Because of its wrinkled appearance in humans, only approximately one-third of it is visible on the surface. Illustrate the surface area of the cortex by taping together two 11.5" × 17" sheets of paper (large-size copy paper). Before crumpling the paper into a ball, say: "This sheet represents the approximate surface area of that thin sheet of neural tissue that we call the cerebral cortex. How can we fit it inside a skull small enough, along with the rest of the fetus, to be delivered through the mother's birth canal?" *(Nature's answer is to crumple it up.)*

MODULE 8

tr ■ TEACHING TIP
A four-color transparency of Figure 8.7, Basic Landmarks of the Cerebral Cortex, is available in the **Overhead Transparencies Set.**

F • Y • I

Two major fissures on the sides of the brain outline the boundaries of different lobes.

- The **lateral fissure** marks the upper limits of the temporal lobes and the bottom limits of the frontal lobes.
- The **central fissure** marks the boundary between the frontal and parietal lobes. On the frontal lobe side of the central fissure lies the motor cortex. On the parietal side of the fissure lies the sensory cortex.

■ APPLYING THE POINTS
Consider these possibilities for students' hands-on experience related to brain research:

- Invite a neurologist from a local medical school or hospital to be a guest speaker.
- Visit a neuroscience research lab at a university or medical center.
- Inquire about and/or arrange a "shadowing" program or internship in neuroscience for interested students.
- Invite a forensic psychologist or medical examiner to speak to your class about how they use the brain to determine causes of death.

trb At this point, you may wish to use **Enrichment Lesson:** ***Einstein's Brain and Genius*** (*Teacher's Resource Binder*, p. 8-1) and **Enrichment Lesson:** ***Lobotomies*** (*Teacher's Resource Binder*, p. 8-1) to inspire curiosity in the applications of brain research.

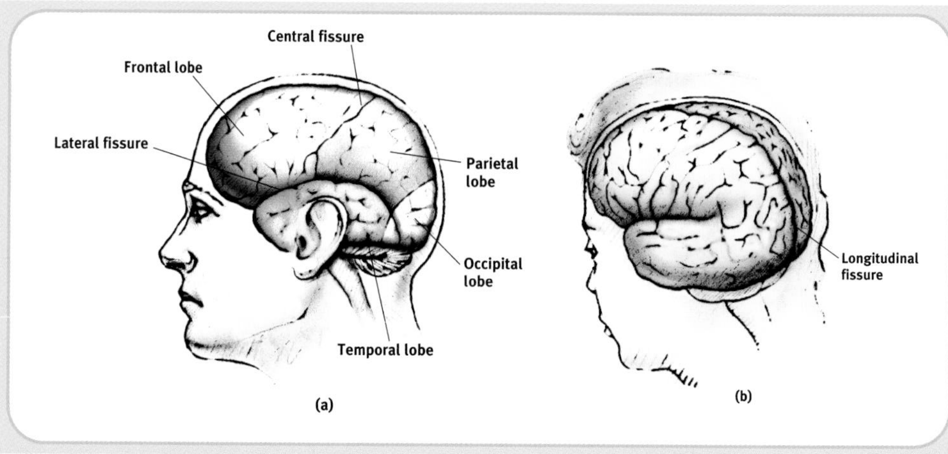

Figure 8.7 **Basic Landmarks of the Cerebral Cortex**

two hemispheres and allows them to communicate with each other. This band of neural tissue, called the **corpus callosum,** is clearly visible in the photo below.

If you look at Figure 8.7b (and use your imagination) you may note that the brain resembles a side view of a boxing glove. If you follow your way around the boxing glove, you can see that additional fissures create major divisions of tissue on each side. These divisions are brain lobes. The **frontal lobes** enable your most advanced cognitive (thinking) abilities, such as judgment and planning. The frontal lobes' rational abilities literally lie atop, and connect with, the more primitive limbic region where the roots of emotion are found. Behind the frontal lobes are the **parietal lobes,** which are largely designated as *association areas*—regions available for general processing, including much mathe-

▶ **corpus callosum** [KOR-pus kah-LOW-sum] The large band of neural fibers that connects the two brain hemispheres and carries messages between them.

▶ **frontal lobes** The portion of the cerebral cortex lying just behind the forehead; includes the motor cortex; is involved in making plans and judgments.

▶ **parietal** [puh-RYE-uh-tuhl] **lobes** The portion of the cerebral cortex lying at the top of the head and toward the rear; includes the somatosensory cortex and general association areas used for processing information.

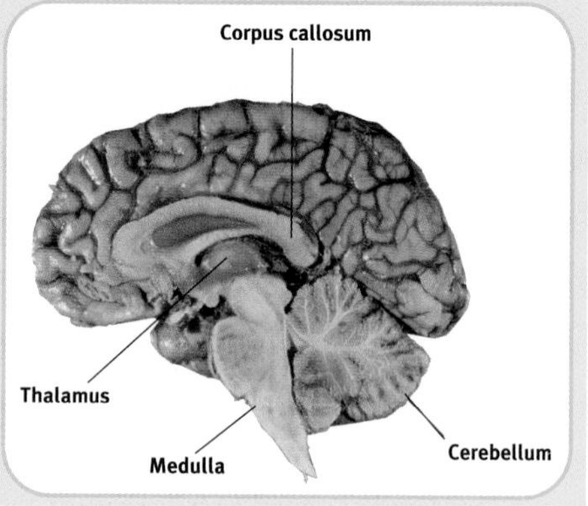

The Corpus Callosum The corpus callosum is clearly visible in this view of the brain, made by cutting straight down through the longitudinal fissure. You can also see other structures we have discussed: the thalamus, the medulla, and the cerebellum.

Cross-Curricular Connections

ANATOMY AND PHYSIOLOGY Team with your school's anatomy and physiology teacher to create a lesson on brain parts and functions. Feel free to explore parts of the brain that aren't included in the text. The anatomy teacher can present lessons about the specific parts and functions, and you can offer lessons that explore how these parts affect behavior.
If possible, have students review what they have learned with the following book:

Pinel, J. P. J., & Edwards, M. E. (1998). *A colorful introduction to the anatomy of the brain: A brain and psychology coloring book.* Needham Heights, MA: Allyn & Bacon.

trb You may wish to use **Graphic Organizer:** ***The Brain*** (*Teacher's Resource Binder*, p. 8-1; **Handout 8–2**) in this cross-curricular team teaching approach.

matical reasoning. At the rear of the cerebral cortex are the **occipital lobes,** the primary visual processing areas of the brain. You may not have eyes in the back of your head, but you do see with the back of your brain! Finally, the thumb region of the boxing glove holds the **temporal lobes.** This area includes the auditory cortex, where sound information is processed.

Have you ever wondered how your brain tells your body parts to move? What happens in your brain to let you walk, raise your hand, or wiggle your ears? Is there a specific spot where these things happen? The answer is yes. The **motor cortex,** a strip of tissue along the back edge of the frontal lobe, is in charge of the movement of your body parts (Figure 8.8). Different points on the motor cortex control different parts of your body, but in a curious cross-wired pattern. Thus the motor cortex in your right hemisphere takes care of movement on the *left* side of your body, and the motor cortex in your left hemisphere controls movement on the *right* side of your body.

Another odd thing is that the bigger parts of your body don't have the largest area on the motor cortex. Instead, the parts of the body that are capable of more intricate movements, like the hands and the face, demand more brain tissue than body parts where intricate movement is not possible. If you were to draw a body along the motor cortex, such that the body parts were proportionate to the amount of brain tissue, you would have a distorted drawing indeed, as is the case in Figure 8.8!

▸ **occipital** [ahk-SIP-uh-tuhl] **lobes** The portion of the cerebral cortex lying at the back of the head; includes the visual processing areas.

▸ **temporal lobes** The portion of the cerebral cortex lying roughly above the ears; includes the auditory (hearing) areas.

▸ **motor cortex** A brain area at the rear of the frontal lobes that controls voluntary movements.

Figure 8.8 **The Motor Cortex and the Somatosensory Cortex** On either side of the central fissure, two strips of brain tissue handle information flowing in from your senses and out to your body parts. The motor cortex is part of the frontal lobe, and the somatosensory cortex is part of the parietal lobe. The figure drawn on the expanded version of each strip represents the amount of tissue devoted to particular body parts.

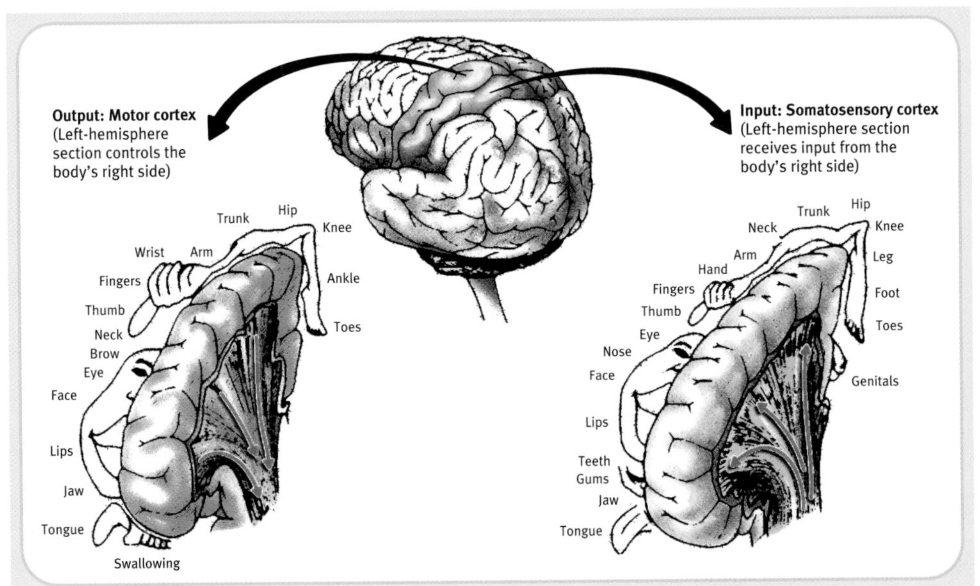

Enriching

BRAINY STORIES Tap into your students' creativity by having them write short stories using different parts of the brain as characters. Each story character should be a brain part whose function relates to the character's actions, feelings, or motives. Check for understanding by using the stories to make sure that the characters accurately reflect the brain part they represent. Request that volunteers read their work aloud or make the stories available for other students to read.

trb As students create or share their stories, encourage them to use **Graphic Organizer:** ***The Brain*** (*Teacher's Resource Binder,* p. 8-1; **Handout 8–2**).

■ LOOKING AT THE ISSUES

Frontal lobotomies were first performed in the 1940s to treat aggressive schizophrenics. In the most common procedure—the ice pick lobotomy—a surgeon would sweep a pick back and forth, severing the connections of the prefrontal cortex with the rest of the brain. Pose the following questions regarding lobotomies:

- Based on your knowledge of the brain, why did this surgery seem to work?
- Why do you think this surgery was used on hard-to-handle patients?
- What ethical guidelines today would prevent the use of lobotomies?

trb At this point, you may wish to use **Enrichment Lesson:** ***Lobotomies*** (*Teacher's Resource Binder,* p. 8-1).

■ TEACHING TIP

Students can remember the different lobes by associating function with placement.

- Since the **frontal lobe** controls thinking and judgment, have students tap their foreheads as if they were thinking through a difficult decision.
- Since the **temporal lobe** controls hearing, it is located just beside the ears.
- Since the **occipital lobe** controls vision, have students recall a time when they've gotten hit in the back of the head. Typically when this happens, people "see stars" since their visual system is momentarily impaired.
- Since the **parietal lobe** controls touch and sensory processing, have students scratch the tops of their heads like they are washing their hair. This will help them remember that touch is controlled by that part of the brain.

tr A four-color transparency of Figure 8.8, The Motor Cortex and the Somatosensory Cortex, is available in the **Overhead Transparencies Set.**

MODULE 8

V ■ TEACHING TIP

A wide array of videos from the series *The Brain* and *The Mind* touch on subjects related to hemispheric differences. At this point, you may wish to show one or more of the following videos:

- Videocassette: *The Brain,* Second Edition, Module 6: "Language and Speech: Broca and Wernicke's Areas" (*Teacher's Resource Binder*, p. 8-1)
- Videocassette: *The Mind,* Second Edition, Module 8: "Language Processing in the Brain" (*Teacher's Resource Binder*, p. 8-1)

■ LOOKING AT THE ISSUES

Have students research programs that claim to educate people on "both sides of the brain."

- What techniques do these programs use to accomplish their goals?
- How have these programs used scientific research well? How have they misinterpreted the research?
- What concerns about contemporary education do these programs try to address?

trb At this point, you may wish to use **Enrichment Lesson:** *The Right Brain Movement* (*Teacher's Resource Binder*, p. 8-1).

■ TEACHING TIP

Help students remember what Broca's area is responsible for by relating the story of the area's discovery. Paul Broca was a French doctor in the late eighteenth century. In working with a patient named Tan (named for the only sound the patient could utter), Broca theorized that the damaged region in the frontal left hemisphere was responsible for spoken language, which was confirmed approximately 100 years later when computed tomography scans of Tan's brain revealed the damaged area.

trb At this point, you may wish to use Enrichment Lesson: *Language on Two Sides of the Brain?* (*Teacher's Resource Binder*, p. 8-1).

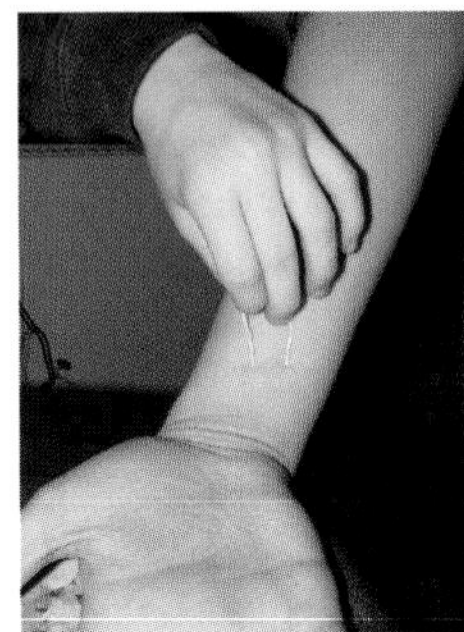

When Does One Point Become Two? Your sensitivity to touch increases as you move down the inside of your forearm toward your wrist and the palm of your hand. To test this yourself, unfold a paper clip so the two tips are about a quarter of an inch apart. Then drag the two-pointed clip slowly and very gently down a friend's arm while he has his eyes closed. If all goes well, your friend will report that the two points feel like one point higher on his arm, but that there is a spot lower on the arm where the clip begins to feel like two points. This happens because the wrist and hand have more sensitivity, and thus more area, on the somatosensory cortex than does the upper arm.

Just behind the motor cortex a similar strip of tissue stretches along the front edge of the parietal lobe. This is the **somatosensory cortex.** This term sounds more difficult than it really is. If you can remember that *soma* is Greek for "body," you'll remember that this strip of cortex is where your body senses register. For example, when you feel a tickle or the pain of a stubbed toe, your brain will register that stimulation in this area. Similar to the motor cortex, the somatosensory cortex allots more brain tissue to parts of your body that are more sensitive to touch (like your fingertips) than to those that are less sensitive (like your arms).

Hemispheric Differences

Have you ever heard people speak of the "right brain" and the "left brain," or even describe someone as being "left-brained" or "right-brained"? Like many popular ideas, this pop psychology idea is partly right and partly wrong. In truth, you have only one brain, not two. Yes, your single brain *is* divided into two hemispheres, and some functions differ significantly between the two halves. But the two sides of your brain are allies, not enemies. They communicate constantly via the corpus callosum, and to accomplish most tasks you must use both halves.

Language and Spatial Abilities

6. What are the left hemisphere's two specialized language areas, and how do they differ? What special functions does the right hemisphere handle?

Language is the best example of a clear-cut difference in function between your brain's two hemispheres. In most people, language functions are located mostly in the left hemisphere. A small percentage of the population seems to be "wired" in the opposite direction, and nobody is quite sure why.

Two particularly important language regions of the left hemisphere are *Broca's area* and *Wernicke's area* (Figure 8.9).

- **Broca's area,** located in the left frontal lobe, is involved with *expressive language*. Damage to this area (which often happens to victims of strokes), results in difficulty with spoken language because Broca's area directs the muscle movements we use in speech. The patient is able to form ideas but cannot turn those ideas into coherent speech.

► **somatosensory cortex** A brain area at the front of the parietal lobes that registers and processes body sensations.

► **Broca's area** A brain area of the frontal lobe, usually in the left hemisphere, that directs the muscle movements involved in speech.

Demonstrating

trb HANDEDNESS AND HEMISPHERE DOMINANCE Students will enjoy finding out if hand preference and hemisphere dominance are related. Using **Critical Thinking Activity:** *The Wagner Preference Inventory* (*Teacher's Resource Binder*, p. 8-1; **Handout 8–4**) and **Application Activity:** *Hand Usage Questionnaire* (*Teacher's Resource Binder*, p. 8-1; **Handout 8–5**), students can determine which hand they prefer and which hemisphere is dominant. Then they can relate the two pieces of information. Discuss with students why they may or may not have seen a relationship and what their results say about the workings of the brain.

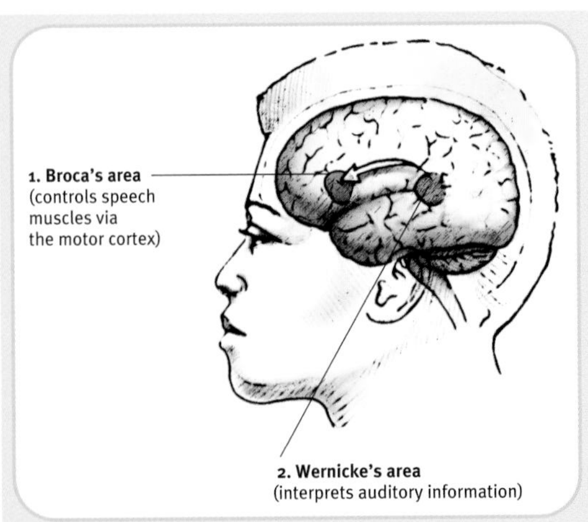

Figure 8.9 **Broca's Area and Wernicke's Area** These two language areas are found only in the left hemisphere in most people.

- **Wernicke's area,** located in the temporal lobe, helps control *receptive language*—your ability to understand what someone else says.

The right hemisphere, however, is not just a bystander. It houses most of your brain's spatial abilities. The word *spatial* relates to your ability to perceive or organize things in a given space, such as judging distance, understanding geometric objects, packing a car's trunk, and so on. The right hemisphere also provides the insight to help us make connections between words. What word goes with painting, ring, and nail? Our right hemisphere finds the answer: *finger.* For a small handful of people with surgically severed corpus callosums, however, the differing roles of the two hemispheres are much more dramatic (See Up Close: The Split Brain, pages 150–151).

Brain Plasticity

 7. What is brain plasticity?

Plasticity is the ability of brain tissue to take on new functions, just as soft plastic has the ability to be molded into new shapes. Plasticity is greatest in childhood. The older you are, the more difficult it is for your brain tissue to assume new functions. Note, however, that your brain never loses all of its capacity to do this.

Some of the most dramatic examples of brain plasticity have occurred when large areas of the brain have been removed because of disease. Even if an entire hemisphere is removed in a young child, there may be remarkably little change in the child's development.

▶ **Wernicke's** [VER-nik-ees] **area** A brain area involved in language comprehension and expression; usually in the left temporal lobe.

▶ **plasticity** The brain's capacity for modification, as evident in brain reorganization following damage (especially in children).

MODULE 8

(tr) ■ TEACHING TIP

A four-color transparency of Figure 8.9, Broca's Area and Wernicke's Area, is available in the **Overhead Transparencies Set.**

■ MULTICULTURAL CONNECTIONS

Ethical practices in medicine vary among countries. Assign small groups of students to research ethical guidelines for brain research on human subjects in one of the following regions or countries: The European Union, Russia, China, Japan, Mexico, Central and South America, South Africa, India, or Australia.

Have students focus on making comparisons between ethical guidelines in the part of the world they researched and the United States. Have groups present their findings to the class, emphasizing responses to the following questions:

- How are these policies similar and different from U.S. policy?
- Have the policies of this country or region positively or negatively affected patient health?

(trb) At this point, you may wish to use **Enrichment Lesson:** ***Lobotomies*** (*Teacher's Resource Binder,* p. 8-1).

■ JOURNAL WRITING

Invite students to use the following questions as springboards for entries in their psychology journals:

- Have you ever had a teacher try to gear his or her class toward educating the "whole brain"? If so, relate the experience.
- Why do you think brain research related to the right-brain movement could have misconstrued the research on split-brain patients?

Enriching

Have students research stories of **hemispherectomies**—procedures in which entire hemispheres of the brain are removed.

- Why would such a drastic procedure take place? What did doctors expect would be the result?
- What amazing recovery stories resulted from these procedures? Were there differences in recoveries of patients? Why were their differences?

(V) At this point, you may wish to show **Videocassette:** ***The Brain,*** **Second Edition, Module 7: "Brain Anomoly and Plasticity"** (*Teacher's Resource Binder,* p. 8-1) or **Videocassette:** ***The Brain,*** **Second Edition, Module 32: "Neurorehabilitation"** (*Teacher's Resource Binder,* p. 8-1).

(trb) At this point, you may wish to use **Enrichment Lesson:** ***Hemispherectomy*** (*Teacher's Resource Binder,* p. 8-1).

MODULE 8

■ TEACHING TIPS

(tr) (1) A four-color transparency of Figure 8.10, The Flow of Visual Information, is available in the **Overhead Transparencies Set.**

(2) Because the optic chiasm is not severed in the surgery, help students understand that split-brain patients do not experience problems in daily life. The **optic chiasm** is the place where the nerves connecting the eyes and the brain cross, leading to cross-hemispheric processing. Split-brain patients do receive visual information from both visual fields, so the abnormalities are only noticeable in specialized laboratory conditions.

(trb) At this point, you may wish to use **Application Activity:** ***Behavioral Effects of the Split-Brain Operation*** (*Teacher's Resource Binder*, p. 8-1).

F • Y • I

Roger Sperry won the Nobel Prize in Medicine and Physiology in 1981 for his work on split-brain research. Starting out his academic career with an English degree from Oberlin College, he quickly moved to PhD work in zoology and postdoctoral work at the Yerkes Primate Laboratory under Karl Lashley. Dr. Sperry died in 1994.

Up Close

The Split Brain

What would happen if the two halves of your brain were separated? Could you still function and come across to others as a normal person? Why would anyone even consider such a dramatic procedure?

The last question is the easiest to answer. In the 1960s, scientists were working on ways to treat severe epilepsy, a brain disorder in which a person has uncontrollable seizures. In an attempt to prevent these seizures from spreading from one side of the brain to the other, surgeons performed a "split-brain" operation in which they cut the corpus callosum. The operation was successful—seizures no longer plagued the patients whose brains were split.

But what about side effects? Cutting the corpus callosum prevents the two hemispheres of the brain from communicating with one another. Wouldn't this have a significant effect on the behavior, intellect, and personality of the individuals who experienced the surgery? Psychologists Roger Sperry and Michael Gazzaniga (1983, 1988) found that the surgery left patients' personality and intellect unchanged, but it altered perception—and corresponding behaviors—in some very interesting ways. To understand why these changes occurred, we need to take a closer look at the roles of the two hemispheres.

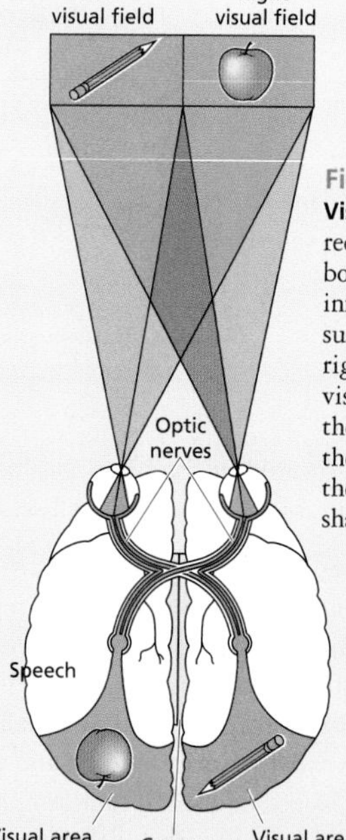

Figure 8.10 The Flow of Visual Information Both eyes receive information from both visual fields, but all the information from the left visual field ends up in the right hemisphere. The right visual field is processed in the left hemisphere. When the corpus callosum is cut, the two hemispheres cannot share information.

As you can see in Figure 8.10, we normally route visual information efficiently from the eyes to the brain. The important thing to notice is that information from your left visual field (the area to the left of your nose) falls on the right side of the retina at the back of each of your two eyes. In an intact brain, this design includes distributing the information across the corpus callosum so the visual information will be available to both hemispheres.

Sperry and Gazzaniga's clever experiments (Gazzaniga, 1983) identified just what happens when the information is not shared between the hemispheres. They asked split-brain patients to focus on a spot at the center of a screen while researchers projected images to either the left or right visual field. The results demonstrated some interesting gaps in perception among people whose corpus callosum had been severed. Here are two examples:

- When the picture of an item was projected to the *left visual field,* the patient was unable to identify the object verbally. Why? Because information from the left visual field is processed in the right hemisphere, but the speech center is located in the left hemisphere. There is no way to move the information from the right to the left hemisphere if the corpus callosum has been cut.
- Look at the situation in Figure 8.11. In this case, the split-brain patient focuses on the dot while the HE is projected to the left visual field and ART is projected to the right visual field. The results are perfectly predictable, based on

Reteaching

Remind students that visual information directed to each side of the brain comes from visual fields, not from each eye. The left eye doesn't send information to the right hemisphere and vice versa—the right halves of each eye send information to the right hemisphere and vice versa.

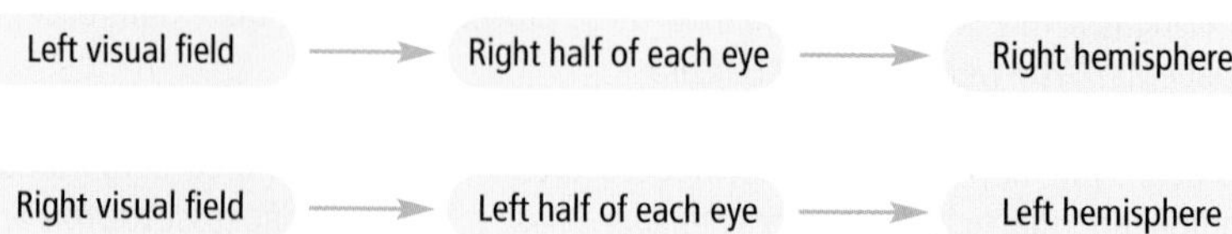

our understanding of the way the brain is organized. The patient will respond ART when asked what was seen, but will point to the word HE when asked to use her left hand to identify what she saw. What would the person do if asked to use her right hand to select the word she saw? That's right—she would point to ART. And, of course, a person with an intact corpus callosum would see the whole word HEART.

These results are pretty strange, a bizarre but literal case of the left hand not knowing what the right hand is doing. Why, then, did the researchers conclude that the side effects of the surgery were minimal? Remember that to find these results, Sperry and Gazzaniga set up a procedure that required participants to focus on a dot at the center of the visual field. In real life these people would be constantly moving their heads and eyes from side to side. Both visual fields would continually detect significant amounts of information and would make that information available to both brain hemispheres, despite the severed corpus callosum.

This is not to say the split-brain procedure has no lingering aftereffects. People who have had this surgery know that the left and right sides of the body seem at times to be under the command of different masters (because they are!). When there is a conflict between the two hemispheres, the left brain usually tries to make sense of it all (Gazzaniga, 1988). Thus, if the right hemisphere of the brain implements a behavior, like walking, the left hemisphere will try to explain the reason ("I'm going to get a Coke"). It must be unnerving to have one's brain at odds with itself, but these strange events would not significantly reduce a person's ability to function, and they usually would not be obvious to other people.

This unique attempt to control epilepsy yielded important information about the role of the brain's two hemispheres. The information has since been verified with modern brain-scanning techniques that were not available in the 1960s.

Figure 8.11 Wonders of the Split Brain This split-brain patient *says* she sees only the word ART because the speech center can receive information only from the left hemisphere, which processes the right visual field. Her left hand *points* to HE because it's controlled by the right hemisphere. The right hemisphere can process information only from the left visual field.

"Look at the dot."

Two words separated by a dot are momentarily projected.

"What word did you see?"

or

"Point with your left hand to the word you saw."

■ TEACHING TIPS

tr (1) A four-color transparency of Figure 8.11, Wonders of the Split Brain, is available in the **Overhead Transparencies Set.**

V (2) Reinforce the descriptions of Michael Gazzaniga's experiments with split-brain patients by showing **Videocassette: *Scientific American Frontiers*, Second Edition, Segment 7: "Severed Corpus Callosum"** (*Teacher's Resource Binder*, p. 8-1) and **Videocassette: *The Brain*, Second Edition, Module 5: "The Divided Brain"** (*Teacher's Resource Binder*, p. 8-1).

■ APPLYING THE POINTS

Invite a neurosurgeon who performs split-brain surgeries to class to discuss the medical uses of this procedure and the effects on epileptic patients. Have students ask the following questions:

- Why would this procedure be used?
- What side effects are at first noticeable in these patients? Do those side effects wear off over time?
- What are the long-term effects of this surgery on patients?

Close

Why do many young people seem to take their brains for granted, considering teenagers' reputation for engaging in reckless behavior (drug use, fast driving, drinking, smoking, and so forth)? Involve students in discussing this question. Guide the discussion toward the potential impact of unintentional brain damage on physical, mental, and social health.

Demonstrating

trb Using **Cooperative Learning Activity:** *Hemispheric Specialization* (*Teacher's Resource Binder*, p. 8-1), students can show how language can interfere with their ability to balance a dowel in either hand. *(Language tends to interfere with the left more than the right hemisphere, showing specialization of the left for language, which reinforces the research by Sperry and Gazzaniga.)*

MODULE 8

Checking the Points

■ TEACHING TIPS

web (1) The book companion site for *Thinking About Psychology* at **www.worthpublishers.com/thinkingaboutpsych** contains a module quiz, flashcards of key terms and people, and other student activities and resources for this module. You will also find PowerPoint lectures, a quiz grade book, and other teaching resources by logging on as an instructor.

trb (2) At this point, you may wish to review and confirm concepts about the brain with **Critical Thinking Activity:** *Fact or Falsehood?* (*Teacher's Resource Binder*, p. 8-1; **Handout 8–1**). Suggest that students take turns reading items from **Handout 8–1** and answering either "true" or "false." Together, student pairs can check responses with information in the text.

REVIEW

Module 8: The Brain

What's the Point?

Lower-Level Brain Structures

Many animals and all mammals share similar brain structures, reflecting shared functions, such as digesting food and breathing. Lower-level brain structures are the oldest and most basic parts of the brain. Although case studies provide useful information about the brain, researchers also gather information about the function and structure of the brain using brain-scanning tools—such as CT scans, MRIs, EEGs, and PET scans. These tools can study the intact brain in healthy people, without invading the person's body.

1. *What are the parts of the brainstem, and what are their major functions?*

   Moving from the spinal cord to the brain, the first part of the brainstem is the medulla, which regulates basic life-support functions, such as breathing, circulation, and swallowing. Next is the reticular formation, a network of fibers that controls wakefulness and arousal.

2. *What is the function of the thalamus?*

   The thalamus, which rests on top of the brainstem, receives messages from your senses and directs those messages to brain regions that can process them.

3. *What is the function of the cerebellum?*

   Your cerebellum, which looks like a mini-brain and extends down from the back of the rest of your brain, controls balance, muscle coordination, and your memories of physical skills, like walking and writing.

4. *What are the parts of the limbic system, and what are their functions?*

   The limbic system includes the hypothalamus, the hippocampus, and the amygdala. The hypothalamus regulates many body functions, including hunger, thirst, the experience of pleasure and sexual function, and reactions to stress. The hippocampus helps process memories for permanent storage. The amygdala controls emotional responses, such as fear and anger.

The Cerebral Cortex

5. *What are the major regions of the cerebral cortex?*

   The cerebral cortex, which controls our uniquely human functions, is a wrinkled layer of neural cells covering the brain's surface. The cortex is divided into two halves called *hemispheres*. Each hemisphere is divided into four regions, or lobes. The frontal lobes, located behind your forehead, are the seat of judgment and planning, and they also contain the motor cortex. The parietal lobes are at the top-rear of your head; the parietal lobes are home to the somatosensory cortex and to many association areas that handle general information processing. The occipital lobes are at the back of your head, and they contain visual processing areas. The temporal lobes lie roughly above your ears, and they contain the centers for processing sounds.

Hemispheric Differences

6. *What are the left hemisphere's two specialized language areas, and how do they differ? What special functions does the right hemisphere handle?*

In most people, the left hemisphere of the brain contains the regions that let us speak to other people and understand what they say to us. Broca's area, in the frontal lobe of the brain, directs the muscle movements we use in speech. Wernicke's area, in the temporal lobe, helps us decipher spoken language.

Your right hemisphere is specialized for spatial abilities—perceiving and organizing things in space. Your right hemisphere also gives you insights into connections between ideas and names of things.

Much of what we know about the functions of the left and right hemispheres comes from studies of people with damage or disease in parts of their brains. Studies of split-brain patients—those whose corpus callosums have been severed—have been especially helpful.

Brain Plasticity

7. *What is brain plasticity?*

Brain plasticity, which is greatest in childhood, refers to the brain's ability to modify itself after damage from injury or disease. Much of what we know about plasticity comes from case studies, in-depth studies of one person's experience.

Key Terms

brainstem, p. 140
medulla, p. 141
reticular formation, p. 141
thalamus, p. 141
cerebellum, p. 141
case study, p. 142
computerized axial tomography (CT or CAT) scan, p. 143
magnetic resonance imaging (MRI), p. 143
electroencephalogram (EEG), p. 143
positron emission tomography (PET) scan, p. 143
limbic system, p. 144
hypothalamus, p. 144
hippocampus, p. 145
amygdala, p. 145
cerebral cortex, p. 145
longitudinal fissure, p. 145
corpus callosum, p. 146
frontal lobes, p. 146
parietal lobes, p. 146
occipital lobes, p. 147
temporal lobes, p. 147
motor cortex, p. 147
somatosensory cortex, p. 148
Broca's area, p. 148
Wernicke's area, p. 149
plasticity, p. 149

trb tr ■ **TEACHING TIP**

You may also wish to provide students with **Graphic Organizer:** ***The Brain*** (*Teacher's Resource Binder*, p. 8-1; **Handout 8–2**). Have students fill out this organizer as a full-class activity. Call on volunteers to name brain parts and describe the function of each. If some items remain confusing for students, have them use their texts to check for the correct response. You may wish to use **Handout 8–2** as a transparency, insert correct labels, and project it for students to check and confirm the answers.

Alternative Assessment: Portfolio Project

UNDERSTANDING NEUROSCIENCE AND THE BRAIN Ask students to create a portfolio of activities and writing based on Modules 7 and 8 that include the following:

trb • **Technology Application Activity:** *Neuroscience and Behavior on the Internet* (*Teacher's Resource Binder*, p. 7-1; **Handout 7–3**)

- a research paper on a topic you review and okay; a poster presentation about the brain, the nervous system, or the hormonal system (students may work individually or in pairs)
- a public awareness campaign for peers created by small, cooperative groups of students
- an experimental project in which students work with local university professors or clinicians who specialize in brain research or neuroscience

trb You may wish to use **Handout 8–6** as a general rubric for evaluating portfolio projects.

MODULE 8

(tb) Using the Test Bank

The *Test Bank* that accompanies this textbook offers a wide variety of questions in different formats and levels of complexity. Use the software to construct whole tests or to integrate standardized questions into teacher-made tests.

Self-Test Answers

Multiple-Choice Questions

1. d, 2. b, 3. a, 4. c, 5. d, 6. a, 7. d

Self-Test

Multiple-Choice Questions

Choose the *best* answer for each of the following questions.

1. Joshua hit a stone wall while skateboarding, and he was not wearing a helmet. He is now in a coma, and his doctors think he may have damaged his
   a. cerebellum.
   b. hypothalamus.
   c. thalamus.
   d. reticular formation.

2. Nita was an exceptional dancer, and all of her friends loved watching her perform on the dance floor. After a bad fall in which she hit the back of her head, Nita was able to move her legs but she could no longer dance gracefully. She probably damaged her
   a. reticular formation.
   b. cerebellum.
   c. cerebral cortex.
   d. longitudinal fissure.

3. Paul's grandmother is unable to store new memories of what happened during her day. She probably has something wrong with her
   a. hippocampus.
   b. amygdala.
   c. hypothalamus.
   d. medulla.

4. Alicia hands out daily newspapers to patients at a local hospital. When she offers papers to some of the patients who have had strokes, something curious happens—they hear and understand what she says to them and they nod their heads, but they cannot form the word "yes." These patients may have suffered damage to ________________ in their left hemisphere.
   a. the visual cortex
   b. the auditory cortex
   c. Broca's area
   d. Wernicke's area

5. If your Wernicke's area in your left hemisphere was severely damaged, you would be unable to
   a. form ideas to communicate to others.
   b. turn your ideas into coherent speech.
   c. hear the sounds when a person speaks to you.
   d. understand the words a person speaks to you.

6. Studies of patients who had undergone split-brain surgery to cure symptoms of severe epilepsy were especially important in demonstrating the role of the two hemispheres and the way that
   a. the corpus callosum transfers information from one hemisphere to the other.
   b. the corpus callosum blocks information that would otherwise travel from one hemisphere to the other.
   c. either hemisphere can take over the functions of the other hemisphere if damage occurs.
   d. people can function with only two of the four lobes of the brain intact.

7. ________________ refers to the brain's ability to reorganize after damage, especially in young children.
   a. Brain scanning
   b. Cross wiring
   c. "Fight or flight" reaction
   d. Plasticity

Matching Terms and Definitions

8. For each definition, choose the *best* matching term from the list that follows.

Definition

a. portion of the cerebral cortex involved in making plans and judgments.
b. area at the rear of the frontal lobes that controls voluntary movements.
c. portion of the cerebral cortex where visual processing takes place.
d. part of the limbic system linked to fear and anger; shaped like two almonds.
e. portion of the cerebral cortex where auditory (hearing) processing takes place.
f. long crack separating the left and right hemispheres.
g. portion of the cerebral cortex that includes the somatosensory cortex.
h. the brain's sensory switchboard.

Term

(1) amygdala
(2) thalamus
(3) hypothalamus
(4) frontal lobes
(5) parietal lobes
(6) occipital lobes
(7) temporal lobes
(8) longitudinal fissure
(9) motor cortex
(10) somatosensory cortex
(11) case study

Fill-in-the-Blank Questions

9. The ________ ________ is a ring of structures that forms the border between the lower brain structures and the cerebral cortex.

10. The band of neural fibers that connects your left hemisphere with your right hemisphere and lets messages pass between those hemispheres is the _______ _______.

11. Damage to the ________________, which controls your heartbeat and breathing, would almost certainly lead to death.

12. To study normal brain function in healthy people, researchers can use one or more of the following four scanning techniques: ________________, ________________, ________________, and ________________.

13. Your right hemisphere controls movement on the ________________ side of your body; your left hemisphere controls movement on the ________________ side of your body.

Brief Essay Question

14. Psychologists often say that the cerebral cortex is the part of the brain that makes us uniquely human. What are some of the functions of the cerebral cortex that would justify this statement? (*Hint*: Think about how the lower-level brain structures differ from the cortex.) Answer this question in 4 to 5 sentences.

Self-Test Answers

Matching Terms and Definitions

8. a (4), b. (1), c. (6), d. (1), e. (7), f. (8), g. (5), h. (2)

Fill-in-the-Blank Questions

9. limbic system, 10. corpus callosum, 11. medulla, 12. CT scans; PET scans; MRI; EEG, 13. left; right

Brief Essay Question

14. Students should identify that thinking, judgment, and language are controlled by the cortex, which differs from the systems in other mammals. Lower brain regions control more basic functions like heartbeat, breathing, and muscle coordination. Even emotions that are not uniquely human are processed by lower brain regions. Interpretation of these phenomena is different in humans because our cortex takes care of higher-order processing.

CHAPTER 4 Sensation and Perception

Biopsychological Domain

Teaching with the Standards

Standard Area: Sensation and Perception

Breakdown of Module 9: Sensation

Content Standard 1: Basic concepts illustrating the functioning of the different sensory systems Module 9 begins with an explanation of "top-down" and "bottom-up" processing to illustrate the differences between sensation and perception. The concept of thresholds and sensory adaptation are also introduced as basic principles to understanding our sensory systems. The structures and functioning of the visual and auditory senses are discussed in detail. The senses of taste, smell, touch, kinesthetic, and vestibular are also presented. (Student Text pp. 157–176)

Content Standard 3: Attentional processes The concept of selective attention is discussed and applied to effective study skills. Signal detection theory is presented in a historical context and illustrated with current nonmilitary applications. (Student Text pp. 159–160, 161)

Breakdown of Module 10: Perception

Content Standard 1: Basic concepts illustrating the functions of the different sensory systems Perceptual constancy, size, shape, and lightness, are explained. Their value in our lives is examined through everyday examples. (Student Text pp. 194–195)

Content Standard 2: The influence of the individual and the environment on perception Module 10 explains Gestalt concepts and principles. Emphasis is on figure-ground, similarity, proximity, closure, and continuity. Principles of depth perception, including monocular and binocular depth cues, are also explained. The causes of perceiving motion are also explored. The influence of perceptual set and context on perception is discussed. This module also discusses basic perceptual principles that help create illusions. (Student Text pp. 183–193, 195–201)

Scope and Sequence

	Objectives	Text Reference	Standards Covered
Lesson 1	Illustrate the differences between sensation and perception by explaining the difference between bottom-up and top-down processing. Examine the following properties that our senses share: thresholds, adaptation, and selective attention.	Module 9, pp. 157–161	Standard Area: Sensation and Perception, Content Standard 1, Performance Standard 1.1, Content Standard 3, Performance Standard 3.1
Lesson 2	Discuss the visual system. Explore light by discussing the electromagnetic spectrum and our human limitations. Trace light through the structures of the eye from the cornea to the optic nerve. Examine the theories of color vision.	Module 9, pp. 162–169	Content Standard 1, Performance Standards 1.2, 1.3
Lesson 3	Discuss the auditory system. Explore the properties of sound and sound localization. Trace sound waves through the auditory systems from the auditory canal to the auditory nerve.	Module 9, pp. 169–173	Content Standard 1, Performance Standards 1.2, 1.3
Lesson 4	Discuss the other senses, including smell, taste, touch, and the body senses. Examine sensory interaction between our senses of taste and smell.	Module 9, pp. 173–177	Content Standard 1, Performance Standard 1.2
Lesson 5	Define *gestalt,* and examine the Gestalt principles of figure-ground, similarity, proximity, closure, and continuity.	Module 10, pp. 183–186	Content Standard 2, Performance Standard 2.1
Lesson 6	Explain depth perception. Discuss the development of depth perception. Discuss and illustrate binocular and monocular depth cues. Examine our ability to perceive motion.	Module 10, pp. 186–193	Content Standard 2, Performance Standard 2.2
Lesson 7	Discuss the principles of size, shape, and lightness constancy. Examine the role of perceptual set and context to our perceptions of the world around us. Use illusions to demonstrate and review the perceptual principles at work.	Module 10, pp. 194–201	Content Standard 1, Performance Standard 1.1, Content Standard 2, Performance Standard 2.3
Lesson 8	Review and test.		

CHAPTER 4

Sensation and Perception

Introducing the Chapter

The Points: Chapter Objectives

- Determine the significance of signal detection theory in modern psychology.
- Define the nature of light.
- Identify the major components of the visual system and the function of each.
- Identify the two theories of color vision, and understand why one is considered correct.
- Define the nature of sound.
- Identify the major components of the auditory system and the function of each.
- Identify the four basic tastes, and determine tastes to which people are naturally more attracted and those that people naturally avoid.
- Discuss the differences among the senses of taste, smell, and flavor.
- Identify the four basic touch sensations, and outline effective ways to control pain using the gate control theory.
- Identify the two body senses, and contrast one with the other.
- Differentiate the views of Gestalt psychologists from those of Wilhelm Wundt.
- Understand depth perception and its effect on our lives.
- Identify the circumstances under which motion may be perceived when it is not really there.
- Appreciate the value of perceptual constancy in our lives.
- Analyze the effect of perceptual set on everyday sensory experiences.
- Appreciate the effect of context on perception.
- Determine how we should evaluate claims of ESP.

CHAPTER 4

Sensation and Perception

Without sensation and perception, you could not read this book, find food, communicate with others, or experience any of the joys (or challenges) of life on planet Earth. No vision, no hearing, no taste, no smell, no touch, no movement—in a nutshell, no way to make "sense" of the world outside your body.

Sensation and perception are parts of the same process, but for the purpose of understanding, we can view *sensation* as the process of being *aware* and *perception* as the process of *interpretation*. Through your vision, hearing, and other senses, sensation processes information *bottom up*—providing raw material for your connections to the world. But what meaning do you assign to all this sensory information? That's where perception comes in. Your memories, emotions, and experiences all affect how you perceive, or interpret, the world around you through *top-down processing*. Attending a volleyball match with a friend, you may be sensing all the same sights and sounds, but you may have very different *perceptions*, especially if you are cheering for different teams.

Now it's time to sense and perceive the material in Module 9. Happy processing!

Performance Standards

Standard Area: Sensation and Perception

Content Standard 1: Basic concepts illustrating the functioning of the different sensory systems

Performance Standard 1.1 Discuss the principles of thresholds, adaptation, and constancy.

- Define absolute threshold and illustrate with everyday examples. (Student Text p. 158)
- Discuss the concept of a difference threshold, or just noticeable difference. (Student Text p. 159)
- Discuss sensory adaptation in the context of how it makes our lives easier. (Student Text pp. 160-161)

Performance Standard 1.2 Describe the functioning of our sensory systems.

- Explore the structures and functions of the visual system. The path of a single trace of light is followed from the cornea to the optic nerve. (Student Text pp. 163–166)
- Figure 9.5, "The Eye," summarizes the major structures of the eye. (Student Text p. 163)
- Figure 9.6, "Nearsightedness and Farsightedness," shows how problems with the lens lead to visual impairment. (Student Text p. 164)
- Figure 9.7, "The Retina," summarizes how light enters the retina and is absorbed by the rods and cones then a neural signal travels through the middle layer of bipolar cells to the outer layer of ganglion cells. (Student Text p. 165)
- Table 9.1, "Differences between the cone and rod receptors in the human eye," compares the differences between these photoreceptor cells. (Student Text p. 166)
- Figure 9.8, "A Blind Spot Detector," helps students find the point where the optic nerve leaves their eyes. (Student Text p. 166).
- Discuss the trichromatic and opponent process theories of color. (Student Text pp.167–169)
- Figure 9.10, "Color Afterimages," allows students to experience this effect. (Student Text p. 168)
- Discuss the major components and functions of the auditory system. Focus on how sound waves are traced from the auditory canal to the auditory nerve. (Student Text pp.170–172)
- Figure 9.12, "The Amazing Journey of a Sound," summarizes the major structures of the auditory system. (Student Text p. 171)
- Present the methods by which we locate sounds. (Student Text pp.172–173)
- Figure 19.3, "How Do You Know Where a Sound is Coming From?" illustrates the process of sound localization. (Student Text p. 172)
- Discuss the four basic tastes. Investigate research on "supertasters" and "nontasters." (Student Text pp.173–174)
- Present the olfactory system. Discuss the interaction between smell and taste. (Student Text pp.174–175)
- Figure 9.14, "The Sense of Smell," illustrates how the olfactory systems operates. (Student Text p. 175)
- Discuss the four basic skin senses of pain, warmth, cold, and pressure. (Student Text pp.175–176)
- Discuss the kinesthetic and vestibular senses. (Student Text pp.176–177)

Performance Standard 1.3 List forms of energy that our sensory systems do and do not have receptors to process.

- Present the electromagnetic spectrum along with the idea that humans can see a small portion of this range. (Student Text pp. 162–163)
- Figure 9.3, "Light and the Electromagnetic Spectrum," displays the portion of the spectrum visible to humans. (Student Text p. 162)
- Figure 9.4, "The Physics of Waves," presents a diagram to help students understand frequency and amplitude in relation to the dimension of the sound wave. (Student Text p. 163)
- Discuss the nature of sound waves. Emphasize the human range of hearing from 20 Hz to 20,000 Hz. (Student Text pp. 169–170)
- Discuss how sound is measured in decibels. Discuss how hearing loss is due to exposure to very loud sounds. (Student Text pp. 169–170)
- Figure 9.11, "How Loud Is Loud?" shows how decibels are measured and compares certain levels to common sounds. (Student Text p. 170)

Content Standard 3: Attentional processes

Performance Standard 3.1 Explain the concept of attention.

- Discuss the process of selective attention. Illustrate how this process is at work in our everyday lives. (Student Text p. 161)
- Present signal detection theory in a historical context and illustrated with current nonmilitary applications. (Student Text pp. 159–160)

Materials NETWORK

All of the items from the Video, Activity, and Enrichment Centers listed below come from the *Teacher's Resource Binder*. These items will help you teach and expand on concepts presented in Module 9.

trb This logo indicates when an item from the Materials Network may be used in conjunction with a specific note found in this module's *Teacher's Edition*.

Thresholds

V Video Center

- **Videocassette:** *The Mind,* **Second Edition, Module 9: "Studying the Effects of Subliminal Stimulation on the Mind"** Consult the faculty guide from *The Mind* video series for a description of this segment. (*Teacher's Resource Binder*, p. 9-1)

Activity Center

- **Critical Thinking Activity:** *Fact or Falsehood?* With this activity, students' preconceptions about sensation are either exposed as incorrect or reinforced as correct. (*Teacher's Resource Binder*, p. 9-1; **Handout 9–1**)
- **Building Vocabulary: Graphic Organizer:** *Parts of the Eye* Students can label the parts of the eye as they learn about each part's function. (*Teacher's Resource Binder*, p. 9-1; **Handout 9–2**)
- **Building Vocabulary: Graphic Organizer:** *Parts of the Ear* Students can label the parts of the ear as they learn about each part's function. (*Teacher's Resource Binder*, p. 9-1; **Handout 9–3**)
- **Building Vocabulary: Graphic Organizer:** *Parts of the Tongue* Students can label the parts of the tongue as they learn about each part's function. (*Teacher's Resource Binder*, p. 9-1; **Handout 9–4**)
- **Building Vocabulary: Graphic Organizer:** *Parts of the Skin* Students can label the parts of the skin as they learn about each part's function. (*Teacher's Resource Binder*, p. 9-1; **Handout 9–5**)
- **Building Vocabulary:** *Flashcards* Students make their own interactive flashcards to learn and review the vocabulary in this module. (*Teacher's Resource Binder*, p. 9-1)
- **Demonstration Activity:** *Backmasking – A Tape for the Classroom* Can backward messages in song lyrics influence behavior? This lesson explores how the power of suggestion is really at work in so-called backmasking of music. (*Teacher's Resource Binder*, p. 9-1)
- **Cooperative Learning Activity:** *Understanding Weber's Law* Weber's law expands on the textbook's description of the just noticeable difference, which students can witness for themselves with this activity. (*Teacher's Resource Binder*, p. 9-1)
- **Technology Application Activity:** *On-Line Signal Detection Theory Experiment* Signal detection theory can be applied by using this on-line experiment that tests students' ability to detect signals and avoid false positives. (*Teacher's Resource Binder*, p. 9-1)

Enrichment Center

- **Enrichment Lesson:** *Gustav Fechner and Psychophysics* Gustav Fechner was a pioneer in the study of the relationship between the psychological and the physical. Learn more about this fascinating scientist in this lesson. (*Teacher's Resource Binder*, p. 9-1)
- **Enrichment Lesson:** *Subliminal Persuasion* Discussion of thresholds leads to the question: Can we detect sensory signals unconsciously? This lesson on subliminal persuasion sheds some light on that question. (*Teacher's Resource Binder*, p. 9-1)
- **Enrichment Lesson:** *Applying Weber's Law* This lesson presents more about Weber's law as it applies to sales and purchases. (*Teacher's Resource Binder*, p. 9-1)

Sensory Adaptation

Activity Center

- **Demonstration Activity:** *Adaptation and the Taste of Water* Adaptation to the taste of one substance can affect the taste of another, either decreasing or increasing our sensitivity to taste, as this activity demonstrates. (*Teacher's Resource Binder*, p. 9-1)
- **Application Activity:** *Eye Movements* Our eyes are always moving, quivering just enough to guarantee that the retinal image continually changes. The figures in this activity will vividly demonstrate these eye movements, as well as their importance in maintaining vision. (*Teacher's Resource Binder*, p. 9-1; **Handout 9–6**)

Selective Attention

Activity Center

- **Demonstration Activity:** *Human Earphones* Dichotic listening activities demonstrate how difficult it is to pay attention to two different stimuli at the same time. This activity creates a human dichotic listening experiment by using students as earphones. (*Teacher's Resource Binder*, p. 9-1)
- **Technology Application Activity:** *The Stroop Effect On Line* The Stroop Effect is a powerful demonstration of selective attention. This on-line experiment, sponsored by the University of Mississippi, challenges students to overcome this effect. (*Teacher's Resource Binder*, p. 9-1)

The Visual System

Video Center

Consult the faculty guides from the *Scientific American Frontiers* and *The Brain* video series for descriptions of these segments or modules.

- Videocassette: *Scientific American Frontiers,* Second Edition, Segment 9: "Smart Glasses" (*Teacher's Resource Binder*, p. 9-1)
- Videocassette: *The Brain,* Second Edition, Module 8: "Visual Information Processing: Elementary Concepts" (*Teacher's Resource Binder*, p. 9-1)
- Videocassette: *The Brain,* Second Edition, Module 9: "Visual Information Processing: Perception" (*Teacher's Resource Binder*, p. 9-1)
- Videocassette: *The Brain,* Second Edition, Module 10: "Perception: Inverted Vision" (*Teacher's Resource Binder*, p. 9-1)

Activity Center

- Application Activity: *Locating the Retinal Blood Vessels* Students may be unaware that they look through blood vessels every day. With this activity, students will locate these "invisible" vessels. (*Teacher's Resource Binder*, p. 9-1)
- Application Activity: *The Hermann Grid* Why do people see small gray dots in a grid of black boxes? This activity demonstrates this phenomenon and explains why it happens. (*Teacher's Resource Binder*, p. 9-1; Handout 9–7)
- Demonstration Activity: *Movement Aftereffects* Afterimages occur not only with color but also with movement. Students won't forget this amazing activity! (*Teacher's Resource Binder*, p. 9-1; Handout 9–8)
- Analysis Activity: *The Color Vision Screening Inventory and Color Blindness* Students can test whether they are colorblind with this activity. (*Teacher's Resource Binder*, p. 9-1; Handout 9–9)
- Application Activity: *Subjective Colors* Sometimes our visual system creates color where none exists. This activity demonstrates this ability, using the Fechner-Benham disc. (*Teacher's Resource Binder*, p. 9-1; Handout 9–10)
- Application Activity: *Displacement Goggles* Our visual system has an amazing ability to adjust to the sensory input it receives. Using homemade displacement goggles, students discover how readily our eyes adapt. (*Teacher's Resource Binder*, p. 9-1)

Enrichment Center

- Enrichment Lesson: *Blind Spots* Why do we have blind spots? Why don't we see black dots in our field of vision? These questions are addressed in this lesson. (*Teacher's Resource Binder*, p. 9-1)
- Enrichment Lesson: *Blindsight* It is possible to be blind but have functioning eyes. These cases of blindsight show how important processing is to vision. (*Teacher's Resource Binder*, p. 9-1)
- Enrichment Lesson: *Functional Blindness* People who have experienced intense trauma may develop functional blindness, as discussed in this lesson about a group of Cambodian women. (*Teacher's Resource Binder*, p. 9-1)

Hearing

Activity Center

- Technology Application Activity: *PsychSim:* "The Auditory System" *PsychSim* is an interactive CD-ROM containing tutorials in different content areas of psychology. In this tutorial, two-dimensional drawings from the text come to life. (*Teacher's Resource Binder*, p. 9-1)
- Demonstration Activity: *Locating Sounds* Ears are positioned so that we can easily detect where sound is located—to an extent. Exactly what extent is demonstrated by this activity. (*Teacher's Resource Binder*, p. 9-1)

Enrichment Center

- Enrichment Lesson: *Recognizing Our Own Voices* When listening to our own voices, we often feel they sound tinny and nasal. This lesson explains why our voices have a different quality than we think they do. (*Teacher's Resource Binder*, p. 9-1)
- Enrichment Lesson: *Hearing Loss* Two types of hearing loss and the causes of both are described in this lesson. (*Teacher's Resource Binder*, p. 9-1)

Other Senses

TASTE

Video Center

- Videocassette: *Scientific American Frontiers,* Second Edition, Segment 12: "Tasters and Supertasters" Consult the faculty guide from the *Scientific American Frontiers* video series for a description of this segment. (*Teacher's Resource Binder*, p. 9-1)

Activity Center

- Application Activity: *Tasting Salt and Sugar* Genetic differences in taste can be demonstrated using simple household items—salt and sugar substitutes. (*Teacher's Resource Binder*, p. 9-1)
- Demonstration Activity: *Taste: The Four Basic Tastes* *Gymnemia sylvestre*—a taste modifier that selectively abolishes the sensation of sweet and leaves all the other taste modalities unchanged—can demonstrate our sensitivity to different tastes. (*Teacher's Resource Binder*, p. 9-1)
- Demonstration Activity: *Vision and Taste—Related Senses* With this activity, students discover that the color of food can determine our perception of its taste. (*Teacher's Resource Binder*, p. 9-1)
- Demonstration Activity: *Taste and Smell—Related Senses* Using different foods with similar textures, students discover that their sense of smell can impact their perception of tastes. (*Teacher's Resource Binder*, p. 9-1)
- Demonstration Activity: *Temperature and Taste* How warm a glass of sugar water is can affect how sweet the water tastes. (*Teacher's Resource Binder*, p. 9-1)

Enrichment Center

- Enrichment Lesson: *Taste Preferences* People tend to dislike food that is unfamiliar. This lesson explains why people avoid food that is novel. (*Teacher's Resource Binder*, p. 9-1)

SMELL

Activity Center

- Demonstration Activity: *Identifying Odors* People have an amazingly hard time identifying most odors. Demonstrate this phenomenon with this activity. (*Teacher's Resource Binder*, p. 9-1)

Enrichment Center

- Enrichment Lesson: *Gender-Related Odors* Can females detect certain odors better than men and vice versa? This lesson sheds some light on this question related to gender and smell. (*Teacher's Resource Binder*, p. 9-1)
- Enrichment Lesson: *Pheromones* Pheromones are important in the animal world, but how important are they in ours? Use this lesson to answer this question. (*Teacher's Resource Binder*, p. 9-1)
- Enrichment Lesson: *Fragrance Effects* What is the effect of certain odors on behavior? Pleasant odors elicit more cooperation and feelings of happiness than unpleasant odors. (*Teacher's Resource Binder*, p. 9-1)

TOUCH

V Video Center

- Videocassettes: *The Mind,* Second Edition, Module 20: "Phantom Limb Pain" and Module 21: "Treating Chronic Pain" Consult the faculty guide from *The Mind* video series for descriptions of these modules. (*Teacher's Resource Binder*, p. 9-1)

Activity Center

- Cooperative Learning Activity: *Two-Point Thresholds* The body's sensitivity to touch varies, depending on where the touch occurs on the body. Use this activity to demonstrate how different parts of the body have different levels of sensitivity. (*Teacher's Resource Binder*, p. 9-1)
- Cooperative Learning Activity: *Warm Plus Cold Equals Hot* The sensation of hot is actually a combination of warm and cold receptors being activated. This activity demonstrates how warm + cold = hot. (*Teacher's Resource Binder*, p. 9-1)
- Application Activity: *Touch Localization* Explore how touch is processed with this activity about touch localization. (*Teacher's Resource Binder*, p. 9-1)

Enrichment Center

- Enrichment Lesson: *Cultural Differences in Pain* How do culture and gender affect the detection of and sensitivity to pain? This lesson explores this question, citing examples from sports and culture to back up the point. (*Teacher's Resource Binder*, p. 9-1)
- Enrichment Lesson: *Pain Control* Treatment for chronic pain depends on how one typically copes with pain. This lesson examines the different ways people cope with pain and the treatments that work for them. (*Teacher's Resource Binder*, p. 9-1)

BODY SENSE

V Video Center

- Videocassette: *The Brain,* Second Edition, Module 11: "Sensory-Motor Integration" Consult the faculty guide from *The Brain* video series for a description of this module. (*Teacher's Resource Binder*, p. 9-1)

Activity Center

- Demonstration Activity: *Nystagmus* Nystagmus occurs when the eyes shift back and forth after a person becomes dizzy. Demonstrate this phenomenon with this activity. (*Teacher's Resource Binder*, p. 9-1)
- Application Activity: *Vision and Balance* With this activity, demonstrate how balance can be dependent on vision. (*Teacher's Resource Binder*, p. 9-1)

Enrichment Center

- Enrichment Lesson: *The Remarkable Case of Ian Waterman* Ian Waterman lost his *proprioception,* the ability to sense one's body. With this lesson, students learn how he overcame the deficit. (*Teacher's Resource Binder*, p. 9-1)

MODULE 9

Sensation

Stop for a moment and consider the amazing volume of information you're gathering right now. Begin by checking out the visual richness of your present environment. What kinds of shapes are present? Are people or things moving? How many colors can you detect? And vision is but one of your sensory systems. What sounds are you listening to? What can you feel? The texture of your clothing? Pressure from the chair you're sitting on? And what about tastes or odors? This *awareness* of the world around you is **sensation.** Your nervous system sorts through all of this incoming information by means of **bottom-up processing,** a form of information processing that analyzes the stimuli entering through your many sensory systems.

The analysis that takes place during bottom-up processing is part of **perception,** which is our *interpretation* of the incoming sensory information. *Sensation* allows you to know that an object is a red sphere, that it has a cool, hard surface, and that it fits comfortably in your hand. The object has a pleasant aroma when you smell it, and a satisfying crunch when you bite into it. When chewed, it produces a taste both sweet and tart. Analysis of this bottom-up stream of data leads to the *perception* that you're eating an apple.

Perception is also influenced by **top-down processing,** which draws on our experiences and expectations to interpret incoming sensations. Do you expect caramel-covered apples to taste great? I do, but I approach them with far more caution than most people because a friend of mine once tricked me into biting into a caramel-covered onion. It looked (and crunched!) just like a caramel-covered apple, but it sure

▶ **sensation** The process by which our sensory systems (eyes, ears, and other sensory organs) and nervous system receive stimuli from our environment.

▶ **bottom-up processing** Information processing that focuses on the raw material entering through our eyes, ears, and other organs of sensation.

▶ **perception** The process of organizing and interpreting sensory information.

▶ **top-down processing** Information processing that focuses on our expectations and experiences in interpreting incoming sensory information.

Getting Started

To introduce sensation, you might ask volunteers to identify what they think is the most important sense in their lives and explain their choices.

trb You may wish to use **Critical Thinking:** *Fact or Falsehood?* (*Teacher's Resource Binder*, p. 9-1; **Handout 9–1**) as a prereading strategy to find out what students already know about sensation. The activity will prime students to note terms and concepts in the text that confirm or dispel their preconceptions about sensation.

MODULE 9

Sensation

Introducing the Module

The Points: Module Objectives

- Identify absolute thresholds and difference thresholds and determine how they differ.
- Identify signal detection theory, and describe its significance in modern psychology.
- Analyze how sensory adaptation makes your life easier.
- Understand how selective attention relates to effective study skills.
- Define light.
- Identify the major parts of the visual system and the roles the parts play in our ability to see.
- Identify the two theories of color vision, and determine which one offers the better explanation of how we see colors.
- Define sound.
- Identify the major components of the auditory system and the function of each.
- Describe how you identify where sound is coming from.
- Identify the four basic tastes, and determine which tastes we are naturally attracted to and why we naturally avoid others.
- Differentiate among taste, smell, and flavor.
- Identify the four basic touch sensations, and outline effective ways to control pain according to the gate-control theory.
- Identify the two body senses and determine how they differ.

trb Building Vocabulary

Five activities offer students opportunities to improve their understanding of the module terms in the Building Vocabulary items in the *Teachers Resource Binder*. (*Teacher's Resource Binder*, p. 9-1; **Handouts 9–2** through **9–5**)

MODULE 9

Teaching the Points

web ■ TEACHING TIPS

(1) You can log on as an instructor to the book companion site for *Thinking About Psychology* at **www.worthpublishers.com/thinkingaboutpsych.** It contains teacher resources for class presentations as well as review and assessment of module concepts and terms.

(2) Use any or all of the following Internet sites to prepare for this module:

- Hugh Foley's page at **www.skidmore.edu/~hfoley/perception.htm**
- Psychology Tutorials at **http://psych.hanover.edu/Krantz/tutor.html**
- The Internet Psychology Lab (IPL) at **http://kahuna.psych.uiuc.edu/ipl/index.html**
- Interactive Eye at **www.iknow.net/iknow_pages/humanvision.html**

F • Y • I

As long ago as 1888, psychologist Joseph Jastrow speculated that lapses of attention, slight fatigue, and other psychological changes could cause fluctuations in the absolute threshold.

■ LOOKING AT THE ISSUES

Discussion of absolute thresholds may lead students to question whether subliminal signals are detected on some level. Although there is little to no scientific evidence to support subliminal persuasion, the belief in it abounds. Have students discuss what might be the appeal of believing that subliminal messages can influence behavior.

trb At this point, you may wish to use **Demonstration Activity:** *Backmasking—A Tape for the Classroom* (*Teacher's Resource Binder*, p. 9-1) and **Enrichment Lesson:** *Subliminal Persuasion* (*Teacher's Resource Binder*, p. 9-1).

V At this point, you may wish to show **Videocassette:** ***The Mind,* Second Edition, Module 9: "Studying the Effects of Subliminal Stimulation on the Mind"** (*Teacher's Resource Binder*, p. 9-1).

My. phone number 15 area code 555, 8761569. Please call!

Figure 9.1 Sensation and Perception Read this sentence carefully and you will note some odd things about it. The marks you interpreted as the word *is* in the top line are exactly the same marks you interpreted as *15* in the phone number. Can you find the other examples of the same marks being interpreted two ways? Here is where sensation and perception come together. Sensation involves moving the image from the book to your brain, a bottom-up process of gathering environmental information through the senses. Perception involves knowing what to make of the individual marks in the sentence. This top-down interpretation relies on your experiences with, and expectations about, language.

didn't taste like one! My perception of caramel-covered apples as a potential prank is an example of top-down processing produced by my experiences. For another example of top-down processing, see Figure 9.1.

Sensation and perception are two sides of the same coin. In reality, they can't be separated, because these processes blend together in our everyday experiences. In an effort to keep the information simple and organized, however, we will consider the sensation side of the coin in this module, and save the perception side for the next.

Thresholds

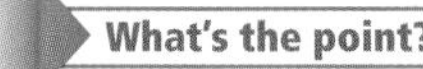

1. What are absolute thresholds and difference thresholds, and how do they differ?

A *threshold* is an edge, a boundary. One of the thresholds that interests psychologists is the **absolute threshold,** the minimum amount of stimulation a person can normally detect. For example, the dimmest visible star in the sky would be right at the absolute threshold for vision. Likewise, the least amount of basil you can taste in the spaghetti sauce would be at the absolute threshold for taste. Human beings have absolute thresholds that are low enough to detect most of the significant events that occur in our environment. According to one estimate, a person with normal vision in total darkness can detect the light of a single candle 30 miles away (Galanter, 1962)! If your hearing had a lower absolute threshold, you might constantly be distracted by the sound of blood pulsing near your ears! We have sensitive senses.

Making a Living on the Just Noticeable Difference People who have an unusual ability to detect very small differences between stimuli can often make very high salaries as a result. This perfume tester in Paris can identify subtle aromas that will make perfumes more pleasing.

Suggested Readings

Use the following books as teacher-preparation tools or as enrichment for advanced students:

Albrecht, K. (1980). *Brain power.* Englewood Cliffs, NJ: Prentice Hall.

Cialdini, R. B. (1993). *Influence: Science and practice* (3rd ed.). New York: HarperCollins.

Coren, S., Ward, L. M., & Enns, J. T. (1999). *Sensation and perception* (5th ed.). Fort Worth, TX: Harcourt Brace.

Fisher, J. (1979). *Body magic.* New York: Stein & Day.

Goldstein, B. (1999). *Sensation and perception* (5th ed.). Pacific Grove, CA: Brooks/Cole.

Goleman, D. (1985). *Vital lies, simple truths.* New York: Simon & Schuster.

Matlin, M., & Foley, H. (1997). *Sensation and perception* (4th ed.). Boston: Allyn & Bacon.

Melzack, R., & Wall, P. D. (1983). *The challenge of pain.* New York: Basic Books.

Schiffman, H. R. (1996). *Sensation and perception* (4th ed.). New York: Wiley.

Another threshold is the **difference threshold,** sometimes referred to as the *just noticeable difference (jnd).* As you might expect, the difference threshold represents an edge, too—this time, the ability to detect the changing levels of a stimulus. How much does the volume have to increase before you can tell that your stereo has gotten louder? How much do the laces on your hiking boots need to be loosened so that they feel slightly less tight? These are examples of the difference threshold—the smallest detectable change in a stimulus.

Signal Detection Theory

2. What is signal detection theory, and why is it a significant accomplishment for modern psychology?

Is that image on the monitor an innocent portable CD player in an airline passenger's luggage, or is it an explosive device? Is that shadow on the x-ray harmless scar tissue, or is it a life-threatening tumor just beginning to grow? Knowing that thresholds can have profound life-or-death implications, researchers have devised sophisticated mathematical formulas to understand how we detect these faint signals. **Signal detection theory** grew out of the Cold War in the 1950s and 1960s as a way of improving our ability to detect incoming nuclear warheads in time to respond appropriately. The idea was for the person monitoring the radar to score "hits"—to recognize missiles on a radar screen for what they were, and, equally important, to avoid mistakes. These mistakes were either "false alarms," where the missile later turned out to be a commercial aircraft or a flock of birds, or "misses," where the observer failed to detect a real missile blip on the screen, perhaps through exhaustion or distraction. National security depends on accurate signal detection.

▶ **absolute threshold** The minimum stimulation needed to detect a particular stimulus.

▶ **difference threshold** (just noticeable difference) The minimum difference that a person can detect between two stimuli.

▶ **signal detection theory** Set of formulas and principles that predict when we will detect the presence of a faint stimulus ("signal") amid background stimulation ("noise"). Detection depends on qualities of the stimulus, the environment, and the person who is detecting.

What Is That? Signal detection theory helps us understand how quickly we can notice and correctly interpret a blip on a radar screen. The researcher would consider the nature of the screen itself (how bright are the blips?), the surrounding environment (how much "noise" or distraction is there?), and the person doing the detecting (is he trained, motivated, healthy, and alert?).

■ APPLYING THE POINTS

Have students contact a local radiology department of a hospital or medical school to ask about the accuracy of their readings of lab results. Students can ask the radiologists about their knowledge of signal detection theory and techniques they might use to increase the likelihood of accurate readings while decreasing false positive readings.

trb At this point, you may wish to use **Technology Application Activity:** *On-Line Signal Detection Theory Experiment* (*Teacher's Resource Binder,* p. 9-1).

■ LOOKING AT THE ISSUES

With federal takeover of airport screening as a result of the events of September 11, 2001, accurate signal detection by Transportation Safety Administration (TSA) employees is an important concern. Contact a nearby TSA office or air traffic control office and interview a supervisor about the issues in signal detection. The following questions may be used to gather information and develop a class presentation of your findings:

- What policies do you have in place that increases accurate signal detection?
- What training programs do you use to equip screeners and help them make accurate calls about stimuli?
- Do you offer incentives based on accurate performance? Why or why not?
- Does your office engage in periodic checks of accurate signal detection? What methods do you use to study this area?

Demonstrating

ABSOLUTE THRESHOLDS Students can experience the variability of the absolute threshold for sound by placing an alarm clock (or wristwatch) on a table in an otherwise quiet room. They should move away so that they can no longer hear the ticking and then gradually move toward the clock until they begin to hear the sound. This is their "momentary" threshold. If they remain where they are, they will notice that occasionally they won't be able to hear the sound and will need to step forward to reach threshold. At other times, the sound will get louder and they will be able to step back. This changing sensitivity indicates that the "absolute threshold" is anything but absolute. Our sensitivity changes from moment to moment and from measurement to measurement.

Source: Coren, S., Ward, L. M., & Enns, J. T. (1999). *Sensation and perception* (5th ed.). Fort Worth, TX: Harcourt Brace.

MODULE 9

■ TEACHING TIP

A fun way to demonstrate the importance of sensory adaptation is to ask students what a day would be like if they could feel the different items they wore on a daily basis as they were wearing them—things like a wristwatch, glasses, underwear, socks, and so forth. Be descriptive as you ask students about these items they are wearing. Use questions like "Do you feel your socks gripping your ankles? Do you feel your watch squeezing your wrist?" Students become squirmy as they "feel" these items rather intensely!

trb At this point, you may wish to use Demonstration Activity: *Adaptation and the Taste of Water* (*Teacher's Resource Binder*, p. 9-1).

web ■ APPLYING THE POINTS

The University of Mississippi maintains an excellent Web site containing on-line experiments in all areas of psychology, especially sensation and perception, that students can participate in and download results from for analysis. Using a computer lab, students can participate in several different experiments or participate in experiments you choose by accessing **http://psychexps.olemiss.edu**.

■ LOOKING AT THE ISSUES

Have students research recent events where signal detection played an important role. Students can identify what role accurate signal detection played and what was done before and after the event to ensure accurate detection in the future. Some events you might explore through Internet research include the following:

- airplane crashes
- September 11, 2001
- outbreaks of disease
- weapons inspections

The signal detection formulas consider three kinds of variables:

- *Stimulus variables*—how bright is the blip on the radar screen?
- *Environmental variables*—how much distracting noise is there in the room with the radar equipment?
- *Organismic variables*—is the operator properly trained and motivated?

Signal detection theory is now used in a variety of nonmilitary applications, ranging from understanding how physicians can more accurately detect tumors in time for successful treatment, to improving air traffic controllers' ability to track aircraft and identify planes flying dangerously close to one another.

Sensory Adaptation

3. How does sensory adaptation make your life easier?

Living organisms are, if nothing else, adaptive, changing to meet the demands of their environment. This means we pay more attention to new stimuli, which are most likely to be significant. If nothing has changed in your visual field, you are probably okay. But if you sense movement off to one side, you'd best pay attention. That moving object could be an out-of-control car or something falling off a shelf; in either case, you're at risk.

Our adaptive nature means we are programmed to filter out the nonchanging aspects of our environments, a process known as **sensory adaptation.** When stimulation is constant and unchanging, you eventually fail to respond because you usually don't need to. One example of sensory adaptation occurs when you get into a swimming pool filled with cold water. At first, the water seems frigid, but if you stay in for a while you'll eventually "get used to it." In other words, you'll adapt to the constant stimulation of the cold water. You can also adapt to hot water, of course, or an odor, or the feel of an article of cloth-

Sensory Adaptation: What Smell? Inside the bucket is raw garbage that is to be fed to earthworms as part of a recycling demonstration. Notice that the young visitors have not yet adapted to the smell of garbage and so are holding their noses against the stench. The recyclers, on the other hand, have adapted to the smell and have probably filtered it out completely.

Demonstrating

WEBER'S LAW **Weber's law** states that the intensity of the just noticeable difference depends on how large the stimulus is. To apply this law, students need three quarters, two envelopes, and a pair of shoes. Have them place one quarter in one envelope and the remaining two quarters in the other. Lifting each envelope, they can easily determine which is heavier. Now have them put each envelope in a shoe. When they lift the shoes, one at a time, the weight difference will be imperceptible. **Weber's principle:** Difference thresholds grow with the magnitude of the stimulus.

Source: Coren, S., Ward, L. M., & Enns, J. T. (1999). *Sensation and perception* (5th ed.). Fort Worth, TX: Harcourt Brace College Publishers.

trb At this point, you may wish to use **Cooperative Learning Activity:** *Understanding Weber's Law* (*Teacher's Resource Binder*, p. 9-1) and **Enrichment Lesson:** *Applying Weber's Law* (*Teacher's Resource Binder*, p. 9-1).

ing, or a constant noise. I even adapted once to the feel and sight of my eyeglasses. I had been wearing them so long that they, in a sense, "disappeared." I spent several minutes looking for them before my wife started laughing and pointed out they were right on my face where they usually are. Sometimes sensory adaptation can make you feel like an idiot!

▶ **sensory adaptation** Diminished sensitivity as a result of constant stimulation.

▶ **selective attention** Focusing conscious awareness on a particular stimulus to the exclusion of others.

Selective Attention

4. How does selective attention relate to effective study skills?

Literally hundreds of millions of stimuli in your environment compete for your attention at any one time. Every page of this textbook is a stimulus, as is every paragraph, sentence, word, syllable, letter, and part of a letter. Every sound within your hearing range is a stimulus, as is every taste in your mouth. (Is your last meal still there?) Because you live in such a sensory-rich environment, you must select certain stimuli to attend to and ignore the rest. This ability to focus on one stimulus at a time is known as **selective attention.**

A good example of selective attention can be seen in E. G. Boring's famous old woman–young woman drawing (Figure 9.2). You can look at the drawing and see the old woman, *or* you can see the young woman. With practice, you can switch back and forth very quickly, but you can focus your attention on only one of these faces at a time.

Your ability to selectively pay attention to a small number of stimuli lets you function in a busy, noisy world. Right now, you are effectively blocking out a variety of stimuli in your environment—the feel of the clothes you are wearing, the temperature of the air around you, the noises outside the room you are in, and so on. Perhaps you have had the experience of being so caught up in a book or TV show that you entirely missed somebody walking into the room or saying something to you. Perhaps you can also identify times when you were trying to study and were much too easily distracted by stimuli in your environment. Selective attention (or lack of it!) plays an important role in our lives.

Figure 9.2 **Selective Attention: What Do You See?** You can perceive this famous drawing in one of two ways: as an old woman (her chin is tucked down against her chest, thin lips, and a big nose) or as a young woman (she's looking back over her right shoulder and wearing a black necklace, with her jaw line and left ear clearly visible). You can attend to one *or* the other, and even learn to switch back and forth quickly, but you can't see both at once.

MODULE 9

F • Y • I

People with attention-deficit-hyperactivity disorder (ADHD) seem to lack the ability to be selectively attentive. Instead of filtering out unimportant stimuli to focus on important ones, they attend to all stimuli in the environment, making it difficult, if not impossible, to process information correctly.

trb At this point, you may wish to use Demonstration Activity: *Human Earphones* (*Teacher's Resource Binder*, p. 9-1) and Technology Application Activity: *The Stroop Effect Online* (*Teacher's Resource Binder*, p. 9-1).

■ APPLYING THE POINTS

Extend the text's discussion of selective attention by having a volunteer in each of few small groups complete a simple task, such as a crossword puzzle or word find. Have the other group members test different types of noise interference on the person's ability to complete the task and then record the results. Afterwards, in a class discussion, consider the following questions:

- Did noise with words (reading a story) interfere more than noise without words (static or yelling "blah, blah")?
- Did music with words interfere more than music without words?
- How loud did the noise have to be before it became distracting?

■ TEACHING TIP

Link selective attention to perception by identifying the E.G. Boring "old woman–young woman" illusion as a *reversible image.* These images will be explored in more detail in Module 10.

trb **tr** A black-line master for Figure 9.2, Selective Attention: What Do You See?, is available in the **Black-Line Masters Appendix** of the *Teacher's Resource Binder.*

Meeting Individual Needs

Apply selective attention to students' lives by having volunteers share experiences in which they were either so caught up in an activity that they missed something obvious in the environment or in which the environment was so distracting that they couldn't concentrate.

By hearing these stories, students with attention difficulties may be reassured that others—especially their peers—are frequently unable to concentrate and that most people have times when their own intense concentration makes them miss things.

MODULE 9

■ TEACHING TIP

tr (1) A four-color transparency of Figure 9.3, Light and the Electromagnetic Spectrum, is available in the **Overhead Transparencies Set.**

web (2) Use the following Web sites to enhance students' understanding of our visual system:

- Vision Science at **www.visionscience.com/VisionScience.html**
- *The Joy of Visual Perception: A Web Book* at **www.yorku.ca/eye**

■ APPLYING THE POINTS

Have students use library or Internet resources to research animals that can detect different types of light. In particular, have them find answers to the following questions:

- Can certain animals detect infrared while others can detect x-rays? If so, which can detect infrared and which can detect x-rays?
- For what adaptive reasons have certain animals developed the skill to detect these types of light? Cite a specific animal as an example.

V At this point, you may wish to show **Videocassette:** ***The Brain,*** **Second Edition, Module 8: "Visual Information Processing: Elementary Concepts"** (*Teacher's Resource Binder,* p. 9-1).

■ LOOKING AT THE ISSUES

How do astrophysicists use the properties of light to determine the age of the universe? Contact the astronomy department at a local university and talk with an astrophysicist about how these scientists explore the universe by using their understanding of how light works. If possible, have a university representative (either a student or teacher) meet with your class to discuss the answer to this question. If a guest appearance is impossible to arrange, include what you learn from this interview in your lesson on our visual system.

▸ **electromagnetic energy** An energy spectrum that includes X-rays, radar, and radio waves, among other things. A small portion of this spectrum includes visible light energy, which can be detected by the eye.

▸ **hue** The color of light; determined by the wavelength of light energy.

The Visual System

The Nature of Light

5. What is light?

No light? No sight! Even nocturnal creatures depend on the low level of light available to their eyes at night. Light enters the eye as waves of **electromagnetic energy,** part of a broad, ever-present spectrum of electromagnetic radiation in our environment (Figure 9.3). Electromagnetic energy ranges all the way from gamma waves, with very short *wavelength,* to long-wave radio waves. The visible spectrum, the tiny part that produces the light we humans can see, is just a small portion of this range.

Two characteristics of waves determines what we see in the visual spectrum. The length of the wave determines the light's color, or **hue** (Figure 9.4a). Have you ever learned the memory trick "ROY G BIV" for remembering the colors of the rainbow (red, orange, yellow, green,

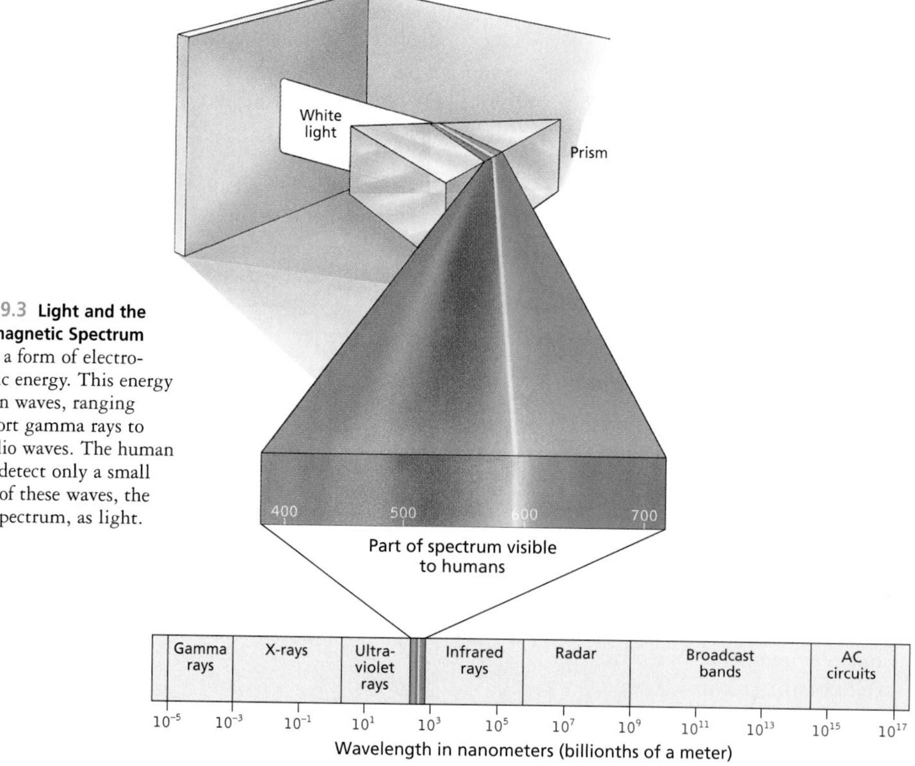

Figure 9.3 **Light and the Electromagnetic Spectrum** Light is a form of electromagnetic energy. This energy travels in waves, ranging from short gamma rays to long radio waves. The human eye can detect only a small portion of these waves, the visible spectrum, as light.

Cross-Curricular Connections

PHYSICS Team with your school's physics instructor to teach a lesson on the physics of light. Touch on these aspects of light:

- Light is an interesting phenomenon that behaves like both waves and particles.
- Our ability to see color depends on the wave properties of light.
- Objects reflect the wavelength of their colors back to the eye and absorb all other wavelengths of light.

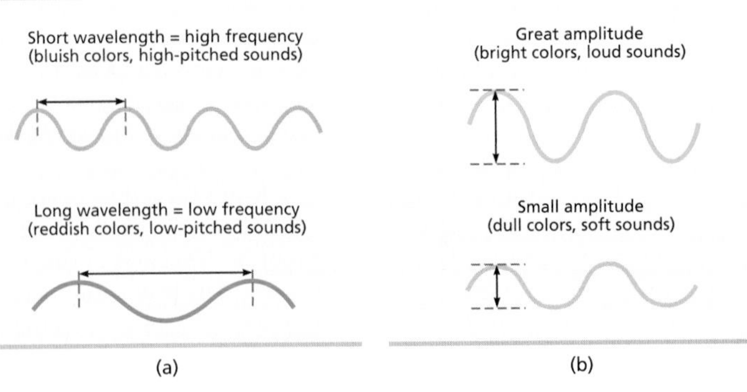

Figure 9.4 **The Physics of Waves** (a) One dimension of waves is *wavelength*, the distance from peak to peak. The shorter the wavelength, the more peaks reach you in a unit of time (frequency). For light waves, the length of the wave determines hue, or color. For sound waves, the length of the wave determines pitch. (b) The other dimension of waves is *amplitude*, the height of a wave. Amplitude determines brightness for light waves and loudness for sound waves.

blue, indigo, and violet) in order? These colors are produced as the wavelength of light shortens—red light, with a distance between peaks of about 700 billionths of a meter, has almost twice the wavelength of violet light, at about 400 billionths of a meter.

The second characteristic of waves—the *amplitude* or height of the wave—determines brightness (Figure 9.4b). Taller waves of the same wavelength produce brighter levels of the same color.

The Structure of the Visual System

6. What are the major parts of the visual system, and what roles do these parts play in our ability to see?

Let's trace the path of a single light ray as it enters the eye. As we take our little trip, follow along on Figure 9.5. The light first strikes the

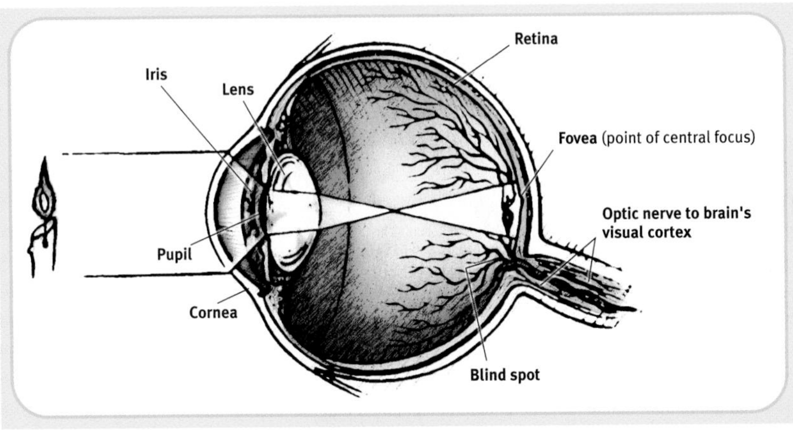

Figure 9.5 **The Eye** When you view an object, light rays travel through the cornea, the pupil, and the lens at the front of the eye. These structures work together to focus the image on the retina at the back of the eye. The retinal image is upside down and reversed, but your brain, of course, makes sure you perceive the world in its correct orientation.

■ **APPLYING THE POINTS**

Have students use crayons to show what the different wavelengths of light would look like. For instance, a bright red color would have a long wavelength with a great (tall) amplitude, while a dull blue color would have a short wavelength with a small (short) amplitude.

Suggest that students consult a physics textbook or search on line for help with different colors in between bright red and dull blue.

trb tr A black-line master for Figure 9.4, The Physics of Waves, is available in the **Black-Line Masters Appendix** of the *Teacher's Resource Binder.*

trb At this point, you may wish to use **Application Activity:** *Subjective Colors* (*Teacher's Resource Binder*, p. 9-1; **Handout 9–10**).

tr ■ **TEACHING TIP**

A four-color transparency of Figure 9.5, The Eye, is available in the **Overhead Transparencies Set.**

■ **JOURNAL WRITING**

Invite students to use the following questions as springboards and writing prompts for entries in their psychology journals.

- How is your vision? Describe how your visual ability helps or hurts you in a typical day.
- Imagine that you lost your vision. How would you feel? How would you adapt to your new condition?

Meeting Individual Needs

trb **GRAPHIC ORGANIZER: PARTS OF THE EYE** Provide learning opportunities for all levels of learners with **Building Vocabulary: Graphic Organizer:** *Parts of the Eye* (*Teacher's Resource Binder*, p. 9-1; **Handout 9–2**) by using one of the following options:

- **Independent Learners** Students may fill out the organizer on their own or follow along in class during discussion and lecture.
- **Cooperative Learners** Students may use the textbook as a resource and work in groups to find the answers that fit in the blanks.
- **Exceptional Learners** The graphic organizer can fill a special education need to provide notes for exceptional students. These students may fill in the blanks independently, with a student or teacher/tutor, or along with class discussion and lecture.

MODULE 9

■ TEACHING TIP

Nearsightedness occurs when the lens focuses objects in front of the retina. **Farsightedness** occurs when the lens focuses objects behind the retina.

Using an overhead projector, have students imagine the screen is the retina. When the projector is blurred in either direction, you have to move the projector or the screen to focus it.

tr A four-color transparency of Figure 9.6, Nearsightedness and Farsightedness, is available in the **Overhead Transparencies Set.**

■ LOOKING AT THE ISSUES

Corrective surgery for nearsightedness and farsightedness is very popular, especially with advances in laser technology. Have students use Internet or library sources to research the pros and cons of corrective eye surgery by focusing on learning answers to the following question:

- What different types of surgery are available? What are the risks and benefits of each?
- How expensive are the different types of surgery?
- What should patients look for in a doctor?
- What type of coverage does insurance offer for this type of surgery?

F•Y•I

web Blindsight occurs when people experience damage to the visual cortex of the brain. Their eyes are fully functioning, but they report they cannot see even when they demonstrate that they can. For an interesting demonstration of blindsight, as well as additional description of the phenomenon, have students visit **http://serendip.brynmawr.edu/bb/blindsight.html**.

trb At this point, you may wish to use **Enrichment Lesson:** *Blindsight* (*Teacher's Resource Binder*, p. 9-1).

▶ **cornea** The clear bulge on the front of the eyeball. The curvature of the cornea begins bending the light rays, a process the lens continues in order to produce a focused image on the retina.

▶ **iris** A ring of muscle tissue that forms the colored portion of the eye; regulates the size of the pupil, a hole in the center of the iris, to admit the proper amount of light to the eye.

▶ **pupil** The adjustable opening in the center of the iris; controls the amount of light entering the eye.

▶ **lens** A transparent structure behind the pupil in the eye; the thickness of the lens changes to focus images on the retina.

cornea, the clear curved bulge on the front of the eye. You can see the cornea move under the eyelid when someone looks back and forth with eyes closed. The cornea performs two tasks: It begins to focus the light by bending it toward a central focal point, and it also protects the eye. The cornea is rich in nerve endings, which you know if you've ever had the misfortune of scratching it!

Because the cornea is clear, we can see behind it a disk of colored tissue, the **iris.** It is the iris we are describing when we talk about the color of someone's eyes. The tiny black spot in the center of the iris is the **pupil,** which is literally a hole in the iris. The pupil admits light into the inner portion of the eye; it appears to be black because no light is emitted *from* the eye. It's similar to looking at the opening of a dark cave.

The iris and pupil work together to regulate the amount of light that enters the eye. When exposed to bright light, the iris expands inward, making the pupil smaller and letting less light enter the eye. When exposed to dim light, the iris draws back and the pupil enlarges to admit more light. You can actually watch this process if you wake up in the night and stumble your way to the bathroom mirror. Turn on the light, and you will see the pupil shrink before (and within!) your eyes. It is rapidly working to restrict the incoming light that you find much too bright.

Continuing our journey into the eye, we next encounter the **lens,** which finishes the focusing job begun by the cornea. The lens is a transparent structure surrounded by tiny muscles that stretch this clear tissue so it becomes thinner, or relax it so it becomes thicker. The thickness of the lens determines how much an entering light wave will be bent. The thickness adjusts automatically and without conscious awareness as you try to focus on things at various distances. Some of us have lenses that do not focus the light effectively (Figure 9.6). Lucky for us, help is available in the form of glasses or contact lenses. These wonderful inventions "correct" our vision (I, for one, would be lost without them) by helping the lens effectively focus light reflected from the objects we are viewing.

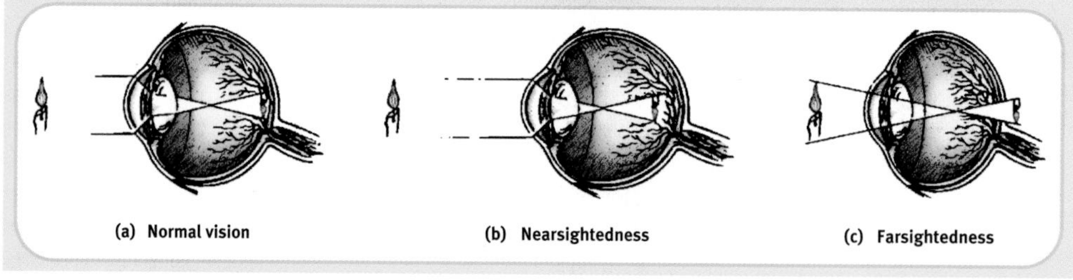

Figure 9.6 **Nearsightedness and Farsightedness** With normal vision (a), the lens changes in thickness to cause the light rays from a viewed object to converge at the retina. The result is a clear, focused image. In a nearsighted person's eye (b), the lens causes light rays from distant objects to converge in front of the retina, which blurs the image. If a person is farsighted (c), the lens causes light rays from close objects to converge behind the retina. Corrective lenses, either in eyeglasses or contact lenses, help the eye's own lens focus the image correctly.

Cross-Curricular Connections

PHOTOGRAPHY Invite your school's art/photography teacher to teach the students about how a camera is similar to the eye. Cameras use the eye as a model for how much light to let in to create a correct photograph of a given image or scene. Ask the guest teacher to cover the following concepts in his or her presentation:

- why certain film is important to use for different situations and images
- why a flash is important to use and when it should be used
- creative ways photographers use the camera's features to take interesting pictures

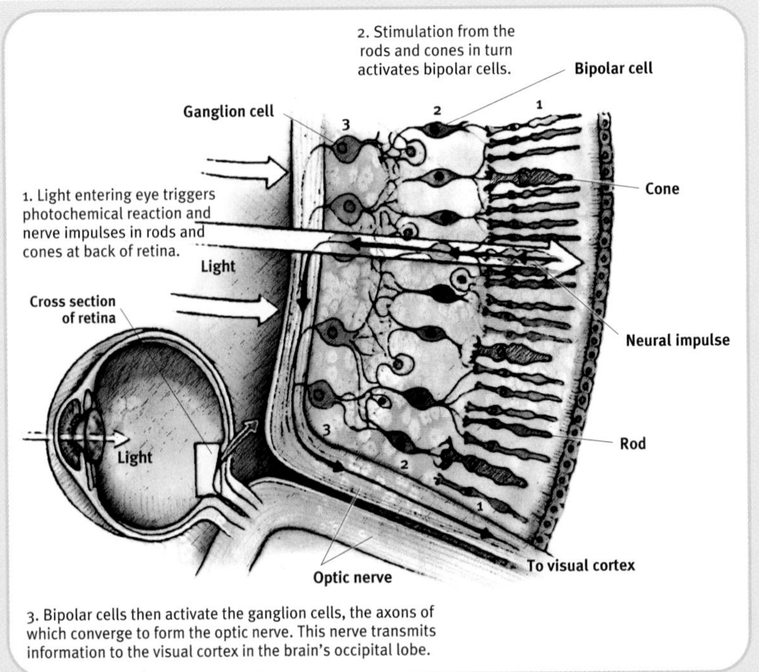
2. Stimulation from the rods and cones in turn activates bipolar cells.
Bipolar cell
Ganglion cell
3
2
1
Cone
1. Light entering eye triggers photochemical reaction and nerve impulses in rods and cones at back of retina.
Light
Cross section of retina
Neural impulse
Light
3
2
Rod
1
Optic nerve
To visual cortex
3. Bipolar cells then activate the ganglion cells, the axons of which converge to form the optic nerve. This nerve transmits information to the visual cortex in the brain's occipital lobe.

Figure 9.7 **The Retina** Light rays filter to the innermost layer of the retina before the rods and cones convert the visual information to neural impulses. The information then travels through the retina's middle layer (made of bipolar cells) and outer layer (made of ganglion cells). The long axon fibers from the ganglion cells come together to form the optic nerve, which exits the eye at the blind spot and carries the information to the brain for further processing.

Until now, these structures in the eye have been doing the equivalent of directing traffic, moving visual information to the **retina,** the important processing center on the back surface of the eye. This surface, like film in a camera, is sensitive to light. The retina is made up of three layers of special and interesting cells (Figure 9.7). We'll begin with the deepest layer, composed of **receptor cells,** which have the ability to change light energy into nerve impulses that the brain can interpret. Every sensory system has receptor cells that convert various forms of energy into such impulses; without these cells, the brain would be completely isolated from information in the outside world.

Your visual system has two different types of receptor cells: *rods* and *cones,* and they differ in both appearance and in function (Table 9.1, page 166). **Rods** can detect only black, white, and shades of gray. Also, rods have a lower absolute threshold than cone cells do. So under dim light conditions, only rods respond and you see the world in shades of gray. The less numerous **cones** detect sharp details and colors, but color becomes apparent only if there is enough light. The detail-oriented cones cluster at the center of the retina; this spot, known as the **fovea,** is the area where your vision is best.

▶ **retina** The light-sensitive surface at the back of the eyeball; contains rod and cone cells that convert light energy to nerve impulses.

▶ **receptor cells** Cells present in every sensory system to change some other form of energy into neural impulses that the brain can process.

▶ **rods** Visual receptor cells located in the retina. Rods detect only black, white, and gray, but they respond in less light than the color-detecting cone cells.

▶ **cones** Visual receptor cells located in the retina. Cones detect sharp details and color, but they require more light than rods.

▶ **fovea** The central focal point of the retina, the spot where vision is best.

F • Y • I

What is **red eye,** that annoying red dot that appears in people's eyes in pictures, and why does it occur? Usually, red eye occurs in pictures where the surrounding illumination is dim, so the flash from the camera must be used to take an accurate picture. The flash is so quick that the iris doesn't have time to contract, making the pupil big enough to see right through to the red retina! Cameras with so-called "red eye reduction" features provide a series of quick flashes that warn the eye that a picture is about to be taken. The iris reacts to the light and shrinks the pupil down so the retina is protected from the bright flash.

tr A four-color transparency of Figure 9.7, The Retina, is available in the **Overhead Transparencies Set.**

trb At this point, you may wish to use **Application Activity:** ***Locating the Retinal Blood Vessels*** *(Teacher's Resource Binder,* p. 9-1).

■ **APPLYING THE POINTS**

As a homework project, have students test their foveal vision in the dark. Ask them to go in to their backyards at night or into a dark room and try to focus their central vision on an image. They should reflect on how detailed the image appears. Then, have them look at the image in their peripheral vision, focusing their foveal vision just to the side of the image they want to see. They should note that the image becomes clearer and more detailed when they don't look at it dead-on. In dim light, cones in the fovea are not activated, but the rods in the periphery are activated.

Enriching

Our eyes take a significant amount of time to adjust to darkness and back to light because two different types of cells process the different levels of light. Have students follow these steps for a first-hand experience of this phenomenon:

- Have students measure how long it takes to make the light–dark adaptation.
- Divide students into small groups and expose one group member to different levels of light.
- Have groups record the time it took for the student to first see in the dark and first open both eyes without irritation in bright light (after being in the dark).
- Be sure students record results over several trials to get an average time of adaptation. Take the groups' data and combine them into an average class result.

MODULE 9

■ APPLYING THE POINTS

Invite an optometrist or ophthalmologist to your class to discuss diseases and other eye problems people may experience over a lifetime, including astigmatism, cataracts, macular degeneration, and glaucoma. You might want students to write questions they would like to have answered by the professional. These questions may be presented in a question-and-answer format after an initial presentation or in lieu of one.

■ TEACHING TIPS

(1) In Module 7, students learned that neurons usually have only one axon per cell. Bipolar cells in the eye are an exception to this rule. These cells have two axons: one receives information from the rods and cones and the other sends information to the ganglion cells.

(2) Make a connection to neuroscience by reminding students that visual processing occurs in the occipital lobe of the brain rather than in the eye. The occipital lobe is located in the back of the brain, just above the cerebellum.

F•Y•I

The cells that make up the retina seem backward. The rods and cones are located at the very back of the retina. The bipolar and ganglion cells are stacked on top of the rods and cones in layers. The light is interpreted by the rods and cones first, even though the light passes through the bipolar and ganglion cells before it hits those light-sensitive cells.

trb tr A black-line master for Table 9.1, Differences Between the Cone and Rod Receptors in the Human Eye, is available in the **Black-Line Masters Appendix** of the *Teacher's Resource Binder.*

▶ **bipolar cells** Cells that form the middle layer in the retina. Bipolar cells gather information from the rods and cones and pass it on to the ganglion cells.

▶ **ganglion cells** The top layer of cells in the retina. Ganglion cells receive information from bipolar cells and transmit it through their axons, which together form the optic nerve.

▶ **optic nerve** The nerve that carries visual information from the eye to the occipital lobes of the brain.

▶ **blind spot** The point at which the optic nerve travels through the retina to exit the eye. The lack of receptor rods and cones at this point creates a small blind spot.

TABLE 9.1 DIFFERENCES BETWEEN THE CONE AND ROD RECEPTORS IN THE HUMAN EYE

	CONES	RODS
Number	6 million	120 million
Location in retina	Center (fovea)	Edge (periphery)
Color sensitive?	Yes	No
Sensitivity in dim light?	Low	High
Ability to detect sharp detail (acuity)?	High	Low

The rods and cones feed their information into the middle layer of retinal cells, the **bipolar cells.** The bipolar cells in turn pass that information to the **ganglion cells,** which form the final layer in the retina. The axons of the ganglion cells come together to form the **optic nerve,** which carries information from your eyes to your brain's occipital lobes, where extensive visual processing occurs. We tend to think that we see with our eyes, but it is our brains that must process the information that the eyes deliver. Where the optic nerve exits the eye, it creates a **blind spot,** because no rods or cones can occupy that point on the retina. Figure 9.8 will help you identify your own blind spot.

Figure 9.8 **A Blind Spot Detector** A blind spot exists where the optic nerve exits through the retina, because there are no rods or cones at this point. To find your blind spot, close your right eye and look at the cookie monster. Maintain your focus on the cookie monster and slowly adjust the distance of the book from your eyes until the cookie disappears. Under normal circumstances, you are unaware of your blind spot because one eye sees what the other does not. Even with one eye closed, you're not aware of the gap because your brain "fills in" the missing information by making an assumption about what belongs in the void. This assumption is another example of top-down processing.

Demonstrating

BLIND SPOTS Extend the text's blind spot activity by having students notice what exactly fills the space where the blind spot is. The space is actually white, not gray or black, as one would expect.

Students can even draw a line around the cookie in the text. When they do this, they will notice that the line continues as the brain creates what fills the blind spot, based on the surrounding stimuli.

trb At this point, you may wish to use **Enrichment Lesson:** *Blind Spots* (*Teacher's Resource Binder,* p. 9-1).

Color Vision

7. What are the two theories of color vision? Which one offers the better explanation of how we see colors?

Difference thresholds are child's play to the eye. Our visual system is so good at detecting minor variations in color that we can detect 7 *million* separate hues (Geldard, 1972). The richness this ability adds to our visual world is apparent in the array of color chips available at the paint store and the variety of lipstick colors at the cosmetics counter.

Color, as we know, is a function of the cones. According to a theory first proposed in the nineteenth century and based on the work of Hermann von Helmholtz and Thomas Young, cones are "tuned" to be sensitive to three different wavelengths of light, which represent red, green, and blue. According to this **trichromatic (three-color) theory,** all the colors we can discriminate are combinations of these three colors. There is now direct evidence that these three kinds of cones do, in fact, exist. The system is similar to the design used to enable color on television and computer monitors. Embedded in those screens are phosphors that glow red, green, or blue, and all the colors you see on the screen are mixtures of these three basic colors. The cones in the retina operate the same way.

If you've studied art, you may have learned that the primary colors are red, blue, and yellow and wonder why cones aren't "tuned" to these three colors. You'll find the answer in Figure 9.9. Painting produces color by a *subtractive* process: Each paint pigment subtracts—absorbs or "soaks up"—different wavelengths of light. Red paint, for example, absorbs all wavelengths except red, which is reflected back to the eye. If you mix red, blue, and yellow paint together, you end up with black; those three pigments form the minimum combination needed to subtract *all* the wavelengths of light.

▶ **trichromatic (three-color) theory** Theory of color vision that says cones are "tuned" to detect red, green, or blue light. Various levels of stimulation in these three kinds of cones enable us to identify millions of different color combinations.

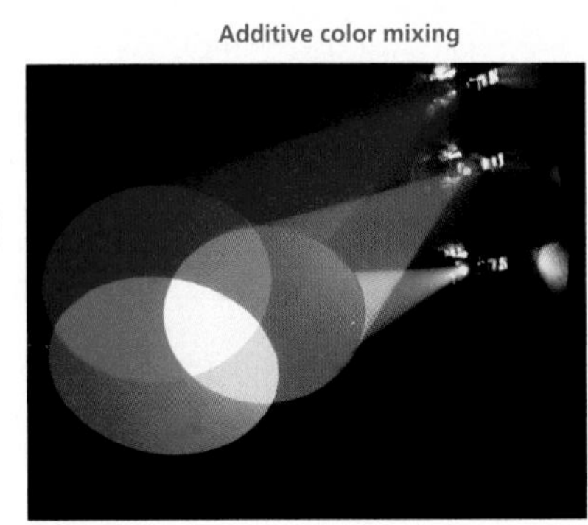

Figure 9.9 **What Are the Primary Colors?** That depends on whether you're mixing paints or lights. Mixing paints is a subtractive process—each new pigment "soaks up" another wavelength of reflected light. All wavelengths are subtracted with a mixture of red, blue, and yellow (the result is black), so they are primary. Mixing colored lights is an additive process—each new color adds another wavelength. In this case, the fewest colors that can be mixed to produce white light (representing all wavelengths) are red, green, and blue, so they are primary for this additive process.

■ APPLYING THE POINTS

If the following professionals are available, they would be interesting guest speakers during a class period:

- An advertising executive, screen printer, or graphic artist could speak about the use of color in print ads.
- Artists who create billboard ads could present examples of images they submit to printers and discuss how billboards, when viewed up close, are made up of different-colored dot combinations, using four basic colors—magenta, cyan, yellow, and black.

■ TEACHING TIPS

tr (1) A four-color transparency of Figure 9.9, What Are the Primary Colors?, is available in the **Overhead Transparencies Set.**

(2) Acquire catalogs from several clothing companies or go to the company Web sites and view their clothes on line. Have students compare similarly hued clothes from different companies. For example: Are "forest" and "hunter" the same shade of green? Students can also make a list of the different names for hues in the same color family (reds, blues, greens, browns, and so forth).

Cross-Curricular Connections

ART AND PAINTING Team-teach a lesson in subtractive and additive color mixing with your school's art teacher. Encourage students to combine colors in different proportions to create some of the 7 million different hues the human eye can see.

tr A four-color transparency of Figure 9.9, What Are the Primary Colors?, is available in the **Overhead Transparencies Set.**

MODULE 9

■ TEACHING TIPS

(1) Using an overhead projector and colored acetate, demonstrate the additive color process. With these you can show how cyan, magenta, and yellow create different colors.

web (2) After images are not limited to color vision. Students can see afterimages of movement as well. For a vivid example of movement aftereffects, invite students to visit **www.sover.net/~manx/spirals.html**. They will view the Counter-Rotating Spirals illusion and learn more of the history of motion aftereffects.

trb At this point, you may wish to use Demonstration Activity: *Movement Aftereffects* (*Teacher's Resource Binder*, p. 9-1; Handout 9–8).

■ LOOKING AT THE ISSUES

Do colorblind people experience discrimination in the workplace? Is this discrimination justified? Explore this issue by working with students to research existing policies for various professions to find those that prohibit colorblind people from working on particular tasks, and why. For example, the military excludes colorblind recruits from working at certain jobs that require color identification, like serving in the infantry, in which seeing different colors at night is important.

trb At this point, you may wish to use Analysis Activity: *The Color Vision Screening Inventory and Colorblindness* (*Teacher's Resource Binder*, p. 9-1; Handout 9–9).

■ MULTICULTURAL CONNECTIONS

Color perception and preference are not necessarily universal. Explore the following questions in a full-class discussion:

- Do people in other cultures see red the same way people in the United States do?
- Do people in other cultures prefer the same colors as people in the United States do? What color do people in different countries call their favorite?
- Does food color matter to people in different cultures? Why or why not?

Stop on Red, Go on Blue? Isn't it interesting that traffic lights use red and green—the two colors most likely to be confused by a person with color deficiencies—as the means of conveying the important information of whether to stop or proceed? If you check, you'll notice that newer traffic signals now have a lot of blue in the "green" light; it's really more of a teal. This slight change helps people with color deficiencies tell the difference between Stop and Go. It also helps, of course, that red and green occupy different positions in the box that houses the lights.

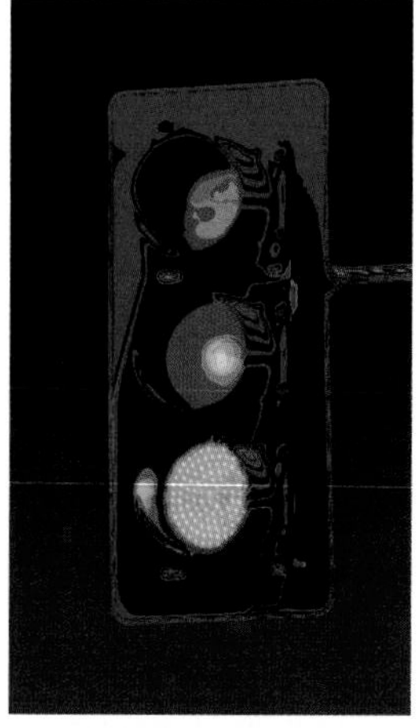

Vision, however, operates on an *additive* process, with each wavelength of light adding a new color to the mix. If you mix red, green, and blue lights, you end up with white, not black! Those three lights are primary because they are the minimum needed to produce white light, which combines all the wavelengths.

"Color-blind" people generally lack one of the three types of cones. A more accurate term is "color deficient," because people with this condition are not really blind to color, they are just limited in the number of colors they can see. Usually they lack either the red or green receptors and have trouble telling the difference between the two (Boynton, 1979). This inherited condition is much more common among males than females. Many times, the person does not even realize a problem exists.

There are some things trichromatic theory does not explain. One of the most fascinating is why we see color afterimages. If you have normal vision, try this for yourself with Figure 9.10, and turn the odd green, black, and yellow American flag into the more familiar red, white, and blue version of the stars and stripes. Ewald Hering proposed an **opponent-process theory** of color to explain such images. Hering's theory argues that color-processing neurons oppose one another. For example, stimulation that turns *on* a green-processing neuron ensures that a red-processing neuron will be *off* (DeValois & DeValois, 1975). Thus, you can see red *or* green at any one spot at a given time, but not both simultaneously. Many color pairs combine easily (red and blue, for example, combine to form violet), but there is no "greenish-red" color.

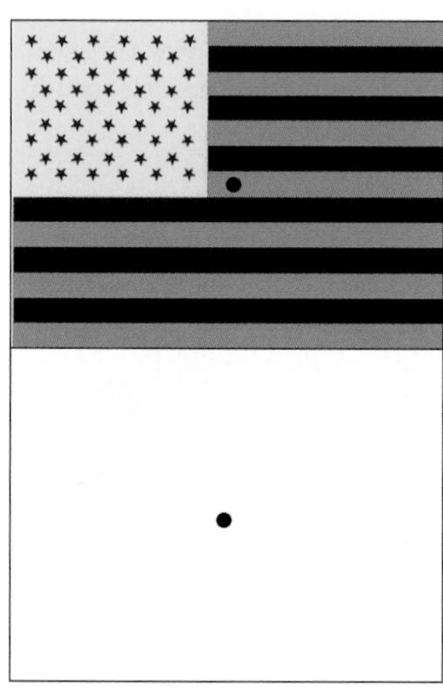

Figure 9.10 Color Afterimages Look at the center dot of the flag for about a minute, then shift your gaze to the dot below it. An afterimage will develop, but it will be in red, white, and blue! The opponent-process theory of color vision can explain this, but the trichromatic theory cannot.

When you stared at the flag in Figure 9.10, you did so long enough to fatigue your green-detection neurons. Then, when you looked at the white space, your

Demonstrating

FOVEAL VERSUS PERIPHERAL COLOR VISION Since cones detect color and rods do not, students might not realize that their peripheral vision is very poor at judging color.

Have a volunteer sit in a chair and fixate on a point straight ahead. Stand to the side of the volunteer, at a 180-degree angle, with a colored marker or piece of colored paper against a neutral background. Move in a semicircle toward the person's center of vision, asking periodically if the volunteer can tell what color the marker is. Repeated guessing will prove incorrect until the marker is close to the center of the field of vision where the cones reside.

trb At this point, you may wish to use Analysis Activity: *The Color Vision Screening Inventory and Color Blindness* (*Teacher's Resource Binder*, p. 9-1; Handout 9–9).

red-detection neurons, which were not tired, produced a red aftereffect that lasted until the green cells recovered. The other two pairs of opponent cells are, as you can tell from the flag demonstration, black–white and yellow–blue.

So, we have two entirely different theories of color vision: the Young-Helmholtz trichromatic theory and Hering's opponent-process theory. Which one is right? They *both* are! Substantial experimental evidence indicates that both systems function to let you see color, and we have no reason to suspect that the existence of one makes the other impossible. Color is clearly important to us.

▶ **opponent-process theory** Theory of color vision that says color is processed in opponent pairs (red-green, yellow-blue, and black-white). Light that stimulates one half of the pair inhibits the other half.

▶ **pitch** A sound's highness or lowness, which depends on the frequency of the sound wave.

▶ **hertz (Hz)** A measure of the number of sound wave peaks per second, or frequency, of a sound wave. Hertz determines the pitch of a sound.

▶ **decibel (dB)** A measure of the height of a sound wave, which determines the loudness of a sound.

Hearing

The Nature of Sound

 8. What is sound?

Light enters the eye as waves of electromagnetic energy. Does sound come in waves, too? Yes, but in this case the waves are produced by vibration. Sound *is* vibration. You can feel your vocal cords vibrate if you touch your neck while singing or talking. Musical instruments all produce vibrations, of strings in the case of guitars and pianos, of reeds in the case of saxophones, of drumskins in the case of tympanis. But you won't hear any of these sounds unless the vibration is carried from its source to your ear. Typically, the vibration travels in pulses of air molecules, but other substances can carry sound waves, too, such as the bones of our skull transmitting the sound of a fast-beating heart to our ears, or water in a pool transmitting the sound of music to the ears of synchronized swimmers. In the case of light, the length of the wave produced hue, and the amplitude (height) of the wave produced brightness. For sound, the length of the wave determines the **pitch** of the sound. Pitch is expressed as **hertz (Hz)**—the number of waves that reach the ear each second. Middle C on the piano, for instance, represents a sound of 256 Hz. Normal human hearing allows us to hear deep, rumbling bass sounds as low as 20 Hz, or high-pitched whistles of 20,000 Hz.

The height, or amplitude, of the sound wave determines *loudness,* which is usually measured in **decibels (dB),** named after Alexander Graham Bell. The absolute threshold for hearing is 0 dB. You can see the decibel level of some common sounds in Figure 9.11 on page 170. Notice that any prolonged sound exceeding 85 dB can produce hearing loss. Sound at the 85 dB level is not painful, and many people play music through headphones at volume levels above 85 dB. This is not a

MODULE 9

■ **CHECKING FOR UNDERSTANDING**

Use any of the following prompts to assess students' understanding of vision:

- Explain how light enters the eye and is sent to the brain for processing.
- Differentiate between the trichromatic and opponent-process theories of color vision. What evidence supports each theory?
- How are rods and cones different?

trb At this point, you may wish to use **Building Vocabulary: Graphic Organizer:** *Parts of the Eye* (*Teacher's Resource Binder,* p. 9-1; **Handout 9–2**) as an assessment tool. Have students fill in the parts of the eye and identify the function of each part.

■ **APPLYING THE POINTS**

(1) One ear specialist suggests a do-it-yourself test for hearing. Hold your hand up to your shoulder as if you're taking a courtroom oath. Then, rub your thumb and forefinger together. If you don't clearly hear a "scritching" sound, you may have some hearing loss in that ear.

trb At this point, you may wish to use **Demonstration Activity:** *Locating Sounds* (*Teacher's Resource Binder,* p. 9-1).

(2) Have band students bring in and play instruments to demonstrate how vibrations work with different instruments. Have students analyze the instruments' sounds by considering the following questions:

- What produces the vibrations in each instrument?
- How does the instrument produce louder and softer sounds?

Meeting Individual Needs

trb **GRAPHIC ORGANIZER: PARTS OF THE EAR** Provide learning opportunities for all levels of learners with **Building Vocabulary: Graphic Organizer:** *Parts of the Ear* (*Teacher's Resource Binder,* p. 9-1; **Handout 9–3**) using one of the following options:

- **Independent Learners.** Students may fill out the organizer on their own or follow along in class during discussion and lecture.
- **Cooperative Learners.** Students may use the textbook as a resource and work in groups to find the answers that fit in the blanks.
- **Exceptional Learners.** The graphic organizer can fill a special education need to provide notes for exceptional students. These students may fill in the blanks independently, with a student or teacher/tutor, or along with class discussion and lecture.

MODULE 9

■ TEACHING TIPS

trb tr (1) A black-line master for Figure 9.11, How Loud Is Loud?, is available in the **Black-Line Masters Appendix** of the *Teacher's Resource Binder.*

(2) Explain to students that deafness occurs in two different ways:

- **Conduction deafness** involves a blockage of the sound as it travels through the ear. Earwax, foreign objects, and damage to the eardrum or ossicles are the main causes of this kind of deafness.
- **Nerve deafness** involves damage to the auditory nerve. Illness, genetic determination, or traumatic head injuries can lead to this type of deafness.

trb At this point, you may wish to use **Enrichment Lesson:** *Hearing Loss* (*Teacher's Resource Binder*, p. 9-1).

F • Y • I

Heather Whitestone of McCallum, Alabama, who was crowned Miss America in 1995, has been profoundly deaf since childhood. In the pageant, she performed ballet, which she learned to do by feeling the vibrations of the music through the floor on which she danced. In 2002, she received a cochlear implant to enhance her sense of hearing. She chose to have this done when she could not hear her young son's cries after he injured himself playing in the yard at their home.

trb At this point, you may wish to use **Technology Application Activity:** *PsychSim:* **"The Auditory System"** (*Teacher's Resource Binder*, p. 9-1).

Figure 9.11 **How Loud Is Loud?** The loudness of sound is measured in decibels. Every 10-decibel increase represents a *tenfold* increase in loudness (a 20-decibel increase is 100 times louder, and a 30-decibel increase is 1000 times louder!). Prolonged exposure to sounds of 85 or more decibels can permanently damage receptor cells in the ear and cause hearing loss.

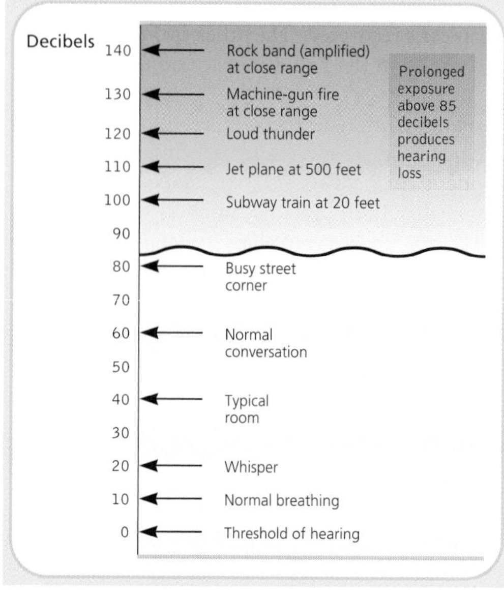

▶ **auditory canal** The opening through which sound waves travel as they move into the ear for processing. The auditory canal ends at the tympanic membrane, or eardrum.

▶ **eardrum (tympanic membrane)** The tissue barrier at the end of the auditory canal. It transfers sound vibration from the air to the three tiny bones of the middle ear.

▶ **ossicles** Three tiny bones (hammer, anvil, and stirrup) that transfer sound waves from the eardrum to the cochlea.

▶ **cochlea** The major organ of hearing, a snail-shaped, bony, fluid-filled structure in the inner ear where sound waves are changed to neural impulses.

▶ **oval window** The point on the surface of the cochlea which receives sound vibrations from the three tiny bones of the middle ear.

good idea. The change will not be noticeable on a day-to-day basis, but exposure to any loud prolonged noise, including good music, will produce gradual, irreversible hearing loss. Many aging rockers from the 1960s—including Pete Townsend of The Who and Steven Stills of Crosby, Stills, Nash, and Young—are now dealing with hearing loss caused by exposure to loud amps at countless concerts. Listen up, music fans, and turn down the volume.

The Structure of the Auditory System

9. What are the major components of the auditory system? What is the function of each?

When your best friend shouts your name across the courtyard at the mall, what happens? First, obviously, the vibrations that constitute the sound must travel through the air from your friend's mouth to your ear. When the sound waves reach your ear, they travel down your **auditory canal** (Figure 9.12) until they reach a piece of tissue that seals the inner workings of the ear from the dirt, Q-tips, and small Lego pieces of the outside world. This tissue is called the **eardrum** (more formally known as the *tympanic membrane*). When sound reaches it, your eardrum begins to vibrate at the same rate as the incoming waves of energy in your

Enriching

Have students research the decibels of different sounds common to school and social activities.

- Do the following sounds in school fall within the safe range of decibels: bells that signal class changes and hall noise?
- Do the following sounds related to music fall within the safe range of decibels: volume used by teens on a typical portable CD player and music heard live at concerts and other festivities?
- Have students develop proposals that might make their school and social activities safer in terms of sound level. These proposals may be submitted to the appropriate group—from student government to the school administration or the parent–teacher association.

friend's greeting. The tissue of the eardrum is quite tough, but it can be damaged, either by direct contact with objects inserted in the ear (this is why you shouldn't insert objects in your ear) or by exceptionally loud noises that can literally cause the eardrum to burst. When the eardrum heals, some hearing loss will remain, because the scar tissue that develops does not conduct vibration as readily as the original tissue.

Attached to the back of the eardrum are the **ossicles,** a tiny mechanism consisting of three small bones that pick up and transmit the sound vibration. These bones are called the *hammer,* the *anvil,* and the *stirrup,* because (if you use your imagination) they vaguely resemble these objects. These three small structures connect the eardrum to the main organ of hearing, a fluid-filled, snail-shaped bony tube called the **cochlea,** which, as you might expect, is the Latin term for "snail."

The stirrup attaches to the cochlea at the **oval window,** a membrane that begins to vibrate at the same frequency as an incoming sound. This, in turn, sets up vibrations in the fluid that fills the cochlea. Finally, the vibrating fluid stimulates thousands of **hair cells,** tiny projections in the

▶ **hair cells** The receptor cells for hearing, located in the cochlea and responsible for changing sound vibrations into neural impulses.

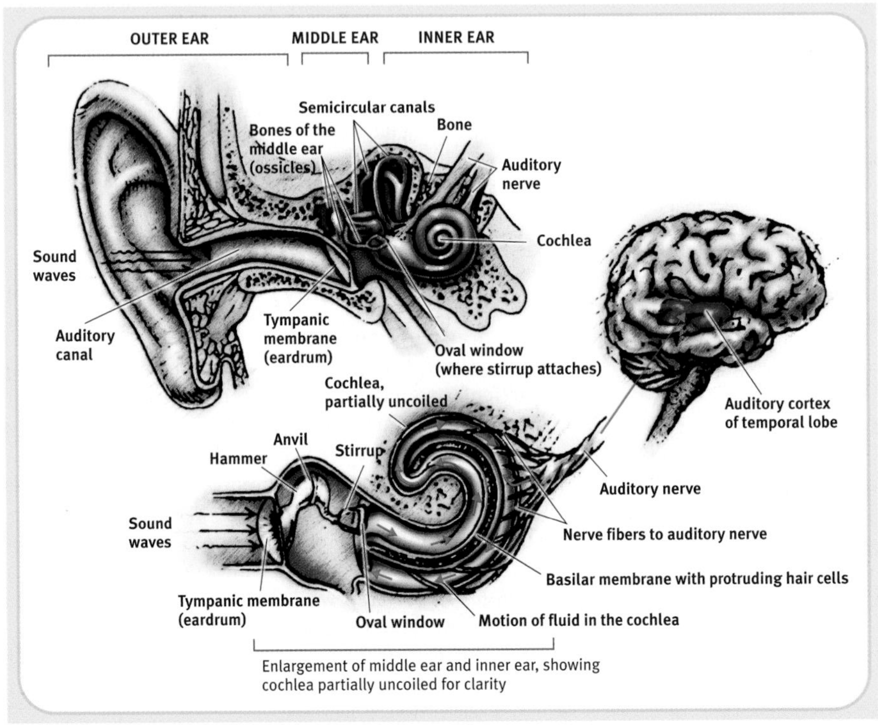

Figure 9.12 The Amazing Journey of a Sound Sound waves must travel through air, tissue, bone, and fluid before the hair cells in the cochlea, the receptor cells for hearing, generate nerve impulses that the brain can interpret. Use this diagram to follow the path of sound as you read about its journey in the text.

Demonstrating

BONE-CONDUCTED SOUND Students can also demonstrate bone-conducted sound with a metal coat hanger tied to the center of a thin string about 4 feet long. They should first press one end of the string into one ear with the tips of their index fingers while plugging the other ear. Then they should ask someone to tap the coat hanger with a knife or fork. John Fisher reports that the effect will sound like the city of London's famous clock, Big Ben.

trb At this point, you may wish to use **Enrichment Lesson:** *Recognizing Our Own Voices* (*Teacher's Resource Binder,* p. 9-1).

tr ■ **TEACHING TIP**

A four-color transparency of Figure 9.12, The Amazing Journey of a Sound, is available in the **Overhead Transparencies Set.**

■ **LOOKING AT THE ISSUES**

People in the deaf community are divided over the role of speech versus sign language in communicating with the hearing world. Some in the deaf community feel that learning to speak and read lips instead of learning sign language denies one's identity as a deaf person. Consider the following questions:

- What are the benefits and limitations of using sign language exclusively in a hearing world?
- What should the hearing world's response be to the use of sign language?

trb At this point, you may wish to use **Enrichment Lesson:** *Hearing Loss* (*Teacher's Resource Binder,* p. 9-1).

■ **MULTICULTURAL CONNECTIONS**

Is sign language a universal language? Do people from cultures with languages other than English use a different sign language than English speakers? Using library or Internet sources, have students research how other cultures view deaf people and how sign language, or other means of communication, are used by the deaf in other cultures.

■ **JOURNAL WRITING**

Invite students to use the following questions as springboards for entries in their psychology journals:

- Imagine that you suddenly lost your hearing. How would you feel? What would you need to do to adapt to your new condition?
- Do you think deaf people should be required to learn how to speak instead of using sign language when in public? Why or why not?

MODULE 9

F • Y • I

Hearing is explained by two different theories, both of which are supported by evidence.

- In the **place theory,** different frequencies of sound waves are said to vibrate different places on the cochlea. These places are wired to different parts of the auditory cortex in the brain so that the sound can be processed correctly.
- In the **frequency theory,** the entire cochlea is believed to vibrate at a particular frequency, thus sending the signal of the quality of sound to the brain.

■ TEACHING TIP

Ask students why dogs cock their heads to one side or another when they listen to sounds. Explain that dogs and other animals do that to identify the direction of the sound and to hear it better.

trb tr A black-line master for Figure 9.13, How Do You Know Where a Sound Is Coming From?, is available in the **Black-Line Masters Appendix** of the *Teacher's Resource Binder.*

tb **■ CHECKING FOR UNDERSTANDING**

After you cover hearing, check students' understanding of this sensory system in any of the following ways:

- Create a quiz from the *Test Bank* that tests students' knowledge of parts and functions of the ear.
- Ask students to write a one-page description of the ear that includes the parts of the ear and the function of each.

trb tr Create and project a transparency of *Graphic Organizer: Parts of the Ear* (*Teacher's Resource Binder,* p. 9-1; **Handout 9–3**) and have students complete it orally.

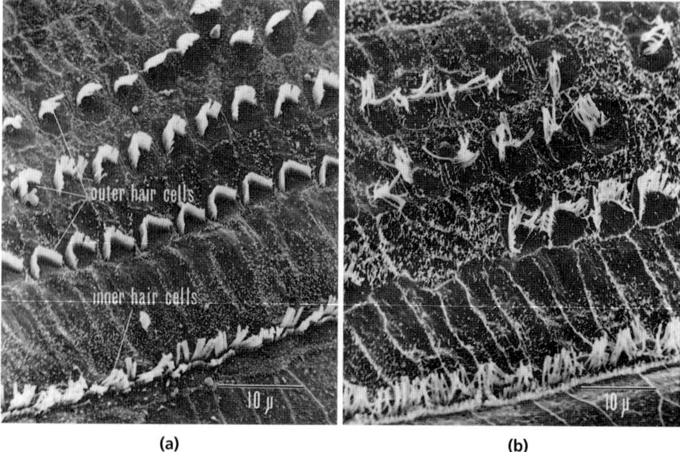

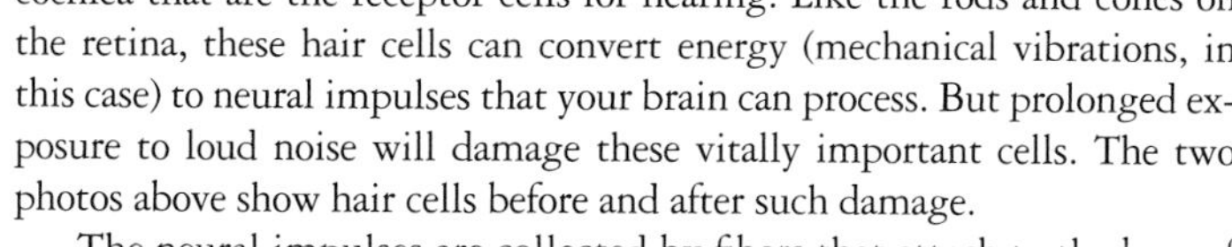

Warning: Rock Concerts Can Be Dangerous to Your Guinea Pig (and You) These scanning electron micrographs of the inner ear hair cells of a guinea pig before (a) and after (b) exposure to 24 hours of loud noise (comparable to that of a loud rock concert) testify to noise's destructive effects.

cochlea that are the receptor cells for hearing. Like the rods and cones on the retina, these hair cells can convert energy (mechanical vibrations, in this case) to neural impulses that your brain can process. But prolonged exposure to loud noise will damage these vitally important cells. The two photos above show hair cells before and after such damage.

The neural impulses are collected by fibers that attach to the base of each hair cell. These fibers join to form the **auditory nerve,** which exits the cochlea and travels to the temporal lobes of the brain, where auditory processing occurs.

Sound Localization

10. How do you identify where a sound is coming from?

If you are a hearing person, close your eyes for a moment and listen to the sounds around you. Do you have any difficulty knowing where a particular sound is coming from—whether it's behind you or in front, to your left or to your right? Localizing sounds is something that we are very good at, and it's important that we are. Sounds often signify important environmental events, including the presence of danger. We'd *better* be able to locate the source quickly. How do we do it?

We rely on two important cues to locate sound sources (Figure 9.13). Step one is to determine which ear hears the sound first. Sound travels through air at about 750 miles per hour. That's fast, but there is still a detectable time lag before sound reaches the farther ear (Brown & Deffenbacher, 1979;

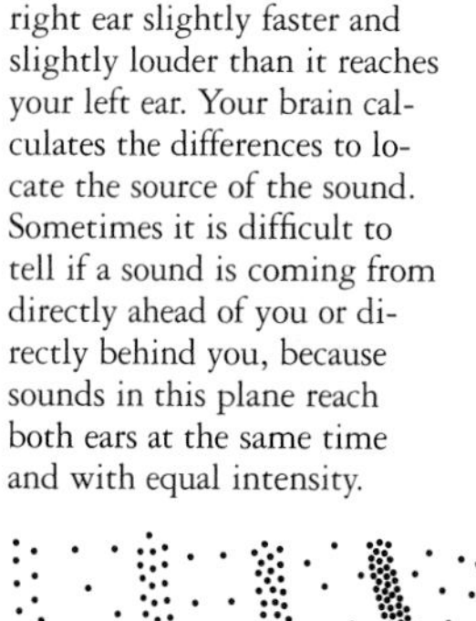

Figure 9.13 **How Do You Know Where a Sound Is Coming From?** When a sound originates from your right, as in this figure, it reaches your right ear slightly faster and slightly louder than it reaches your left ear. Your brain calculates the differences to locate the source of the sound. Sometimes it is difficult to tell if a sound is coming from directly ahead of you or directly behind you, because sounds in this plane reach both ears at the same time and with equal intensity.

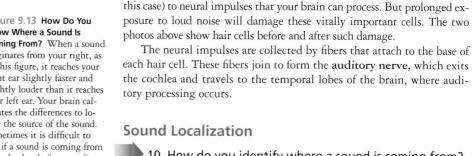

Demonstrating

SOUND LOCALIZATION Invite a volunteer to sit with eyes closed in a chair facing the class. Clap at varying locations around the volunteer's head. The person will confidently and accurately locate sounds coming from either side (which strike the two ears differently) but will have more difficulty locating sounds in the 360-degree plane that is equidistant between the two ears (overhead, in back, or in front).

trb At this point, you may wish to use **Demonstration Activity:** *Locating Sounds* (*Teacher's Resource Binder,* p. 9-1).

Middlebrooks & Green, 1991). Second, we determine which ear hears the louder, more intense sound. By the time a sound gets around to the ear farther from the source, the sound is muted enough for your brain to be aware of the difference. Locating the source of sounds is only one of many determinations your brain makes without any conscious effort on your part.

▶ **auditory nerve** The nerve that carries sound information from the ears to the temporal lobe of the brain.

Other Senses

We have spent considerable time on vision and hearing, which no doubt are vital senses. They also are the best-understood sensory systems, and the ones that first come to mind when the topic of sensation comes up. Think, though, what life would be like with no ability to taste or smell. Without the ability to savor the taste and smell of food, would you still be willing to put effort into preparing meals and eating them? And what would life be like with no sense of touch? You not only would lose "good touch," like the satisfaction of a hug or kiss from someone you care about deeply, you'd also lose the ability to detect pain. This loss may sound like an improvement, but it wouldn't be. Pain is one of the most effective mechanisms we have to protect ourselves from environmental dangers. Without pain, we wouldn't realize that we had placed our hand on a red-hot stove burner until we smelled our flesh burning—far too late to minimize the seriousness of the injury! Finally, what about your sense of balance, and your ability to judge the position of your body parts? Walking would be incredibly difficult if you didn't have a sense of what your legs were doing at each step (excuse the pun) of the process.

Let's take a brief look at some of our remaining senses.

Taste

11. What are the four basic tastes? Which tastes are we naturally attracted to, and why do we naturally avoid others?

Taste is a chemical sense. You have receptor cells located on the surface of the tongue (and, to a lesser degree, elsewhere in the mouth) that respond to the chemical structure of the foods you eat. These cells can detect four different tastes: salty, sweet, sour, and bitter (McBurney & Gent, 1979). Newborn babies have a natural attraction to salty and sweet tastes, a biological predisposition that ensures that they will seek mother's milk (which is sweet) and salt (which is necessary for survival). Babies also have natural dislikes—of sour and bitter tastes—which protect them from substances that are more likely to be poisonous.

F • Y • I

(1) **Synesthesia** is a condition in which people confuse or combine their sensory experiences. Synesthetes often report "smelling colors" or "hearing numbers."

(2) The traditional "tongue map," showing how different regions of the tongue detect different tastes, is not accurate. In the late 1800s, a German PhD student studied the tongue's sensitivity to different tastes, which he plotted on a graph. The graph of his data was done "impressionistically," meaning he didn't rely on his actual data to create the graph. For more than 75 years, scholars took his graph at face value, perpetuating the myth of the tongue map.

trb At this point, you may wish to use **Demonstration Activity:** *Taste—The Four Basic Tastes* (*Teacher's Resource Binder*, p. 9-1).

(3) People seem to have a built-in preference for sweet foods. They find bitter and sour foods unpleasant; they like salty foods at low concentrations but dislike them at high concentrations. In one study of infants, sweet substances elicited sucking and, in some cases, smiling. Sour tastes produced "lip pursing and wrinkling of the nose," and bitter prompted "opening of the mouth with the upper lip elevated and protrusion of the tongue." These reactions make good evolutionary sense since bitter or sour plants are often toxic, while the sweeter ones tend to be nutritious.

trb At this point, you may wish to use **Demonstration Activity:** *Taste: The Four Basic Tastes* (*Teacher's Resource Binder*, p. 9-1).

Meeting Individual Needs

trb GRAPHIC ORGANIZER: PARTS OF THE TONGUE Provide learning opportunities for all levels of learners with **Building Vocabulary: Graphic Organizer:** *Parts of the Tongue* (*Teacher's Resource Binder*, p. 9-1; **Handout 9–4**) using one of the following options:

- **Independent Learners** Students may fill out the organizer on their own or follow along in class during discussion and lecture.
- **Cooperative Learners** Students may use the textbook as a resource and work in groups to find the answers that fit in the blanks.
- **Exceptional Learners** The graphic organizer can fill a special education need to provide notes for exceptional students. These students may fill in the blanks independently, with a student or teacher/tutor, or along with class discussion and lecture.

MODULE 9

■ TEACHING TIP

As a link to neuroscience, inform students that smell is the only sense where the signals do not go directly to the thalamus before being processed. In fact, smell is processed near the prefrontal cortex before it is sent along, which may help explain why smell can trigger powerful memories, since that part of the brain works with the limbic system to process emotional memories.

trb At this point, you may wish to use Demonstration Activity: *Identifying Odors* (*Teacher's Resource Binder*, p. 9-1).

F • Y • I

According to Linda Bartoshuk, taste buds are innervated by two cranial nerves: one carries taste, and the other carries pain and touch. This means that supertasters feel more pain from lesions on the tongue. Supertasters also perceive more pain from oral irritants, including chili peppers, ethyl alcohol, and carbonation. Fat in food is also perceived as a touch sensation. If you're a supertaster, you're a super perceiver of fat in food.

Source: Bartoshuk, L. (1997). *The health report: Supertasters.* Retrieved March 3, 2003, from www.abc.net.au/rn/talks/8.30/helthrpt/stories/s369.htm.

trb At this point, you may wish to use Demonstration Activity: *Temperature and Taste* (*Teacher's Resource Binder*, p. 9-1).

V At this point, you may wish to show Videocassette: *Scientific American Frontiers, Second Edition,* Segment 12: "Tasters and Supertasters" (*Teacher's Resource Binder*, p. 9-1).

Flavor, a Sensory Interaction We often speak of taste when we really mean flavor. Taste can detect only sweet, sour, salty, and bitter. The flavors shown here on these sumptious plates also involve their smell, texture, temperature, and appearance.

Taste receptor cells can be damaged by heat, as you no doubt know if you've ever burned your mouth on hot food you couldn't wait to eat. Tobacco smoke also harms these cells. Fortunately, taste cells do replace themselves within a few days. A short-term benefit of kicking the cigarette habit is that food starts to taste much better as the taste cells regenerate.

One interesting fact about taste is that we don't all have the same sensitivity to taste. About a quarter of the population, dubbed *supertasters* by researcher Linda Bartoshuk and her colleagues (1994), have an abundance of taste receptors that allow them to experience tastes, especially bitter tastes, more intensely than most of us do. Bartoshuk theorizes that these individuals were the poison detectors of ancient civilization. If they avoided a food, it was likely to be dangerous, and others would avoid it as well. Even today, supertasters, with their enhanced sensitivity to alcohol's bitter taste, are less likely to become alcoholics than are those who don't share this trait.

Another quarter of the population are nontasters. They do taste, of course, but with much less intensity than people with more taste cells. These individuals tend to do well in times of food scarcity. Quite literally, they are willing to eat anything, no matter how bad it tastes. In times of plenty this tendency can be dangerous, but it just might allow survival in famine. The majority of us, about half the population, fall in the middle as medium tasters.

Smell

12. How do taste, smell, and flavor differ?

Smell, like taste, is a chemical sense. Molecules given off by many substances circulate in the air (Figure 9.14). When these molecules reach the upper nasal passages, **olfactory cells** that project from the brain can process them. In some ways, smell is more complicated than taste. By triggering various combinations of olfactory cells, thousands of different odors are detectable. Unlike taste cells, olfactory cells do not regenerate when damaged. Thus their number decreases as we grow older; many elderly individuals have a noticeably decreased sense of smell.

► **olfactory cells** The chemical receptor cells for smell, located in the nasal passages.

Taste and smell interact to produce flavor. Perhaps you've noticed that flavor is greatly diminished when you have a head cold with lots of congestion. Odors that normally travel up to the nasal passages from the back

Demonstrating

TASTE BUD COUNT Have students count the number of taste buds they have on their tongues by following these instructions:

- Punch a hole in an index card and place it on the tip of the tongue.
- Using blue food coloring, paint the tongue through the hole.
- Count the number of fungiform pupillae (which will appear as bright pink bumps) in the hole.

Supertasters will have many of these bumps, while nontasters will have few.

trb At this point, you may wish to use Application Activity: *Tasting Salt and Sugar* (*Teacher's Resource Binder*, p. 9-1).

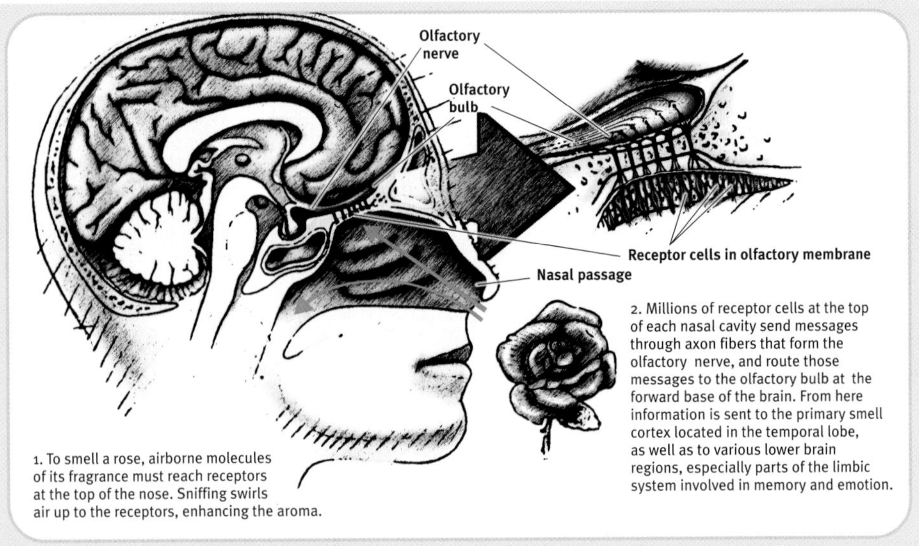

Olfactory nerve
Olfactory bulb
Receptor cells in olfactory membrane
Nasal passage
2. Millions of receptor cells at the top of each nasal cavity send messages through axon fibers that form the olfactory nerve, and route those messages to the olfactory bulb at the forward base of the brain. From here information is sent to the primary smell cortex located in the temporal lobe, as well as to various lower brain regions, especially parts of the limbic system involved in memory and emotion.
1. To smell a rose, airborne molecules of its fragrance must reach receptors at the top of the nose. Sniffing swirls air up to the receptors, enhancing the aroma.

Figure 9.14 **The Sense of Smell**

of the throat are blocked when you have a head cold, and you are left with taste alone. Try plugging your nose the next time you eat a fruit jelly bean or Starburst. You can detect sour (from the citrus) and sweet (from the sugar), but you cannot tell the flavor (cherry, lemon, and so on). As soon as you unplug your nose, though, the flavor becomes instantly apparent! Actually, flavor is an interaction of more than just taste and smell. Appearance is important (how much appeal would blue milk have?), which is why fine restaurants spend so much effort on the visual presentation of their food. Feel or texture is also important (imagine soggy potato chips), as is temperature (how does a steaming hot cup of Coca-Cola sound?).

Touch

13. What are the four basic skin senses? According to gate control theory, how can we effectively reduce pain?

Touch is your physical connection with the outside world. Your skin is embedded with receptors that respond to various kinds of stimulation. The basic skin senses are pain, warmth, cold, and pressure. Your experience of other skin sensations flows from various combinations of these four basic skin senses. Itches, for example, result from gentle stimulation of pain receptors; hot, from simultaneous stimulation of warm and cold (Figure 9.15); and wetness, from simultaneous stimulation of cold and pressure.

Figure 9.15 **When Is Hot Not?** When cold and warm receptors are stimulated at the same time, the result is an eerie sensation of hot.

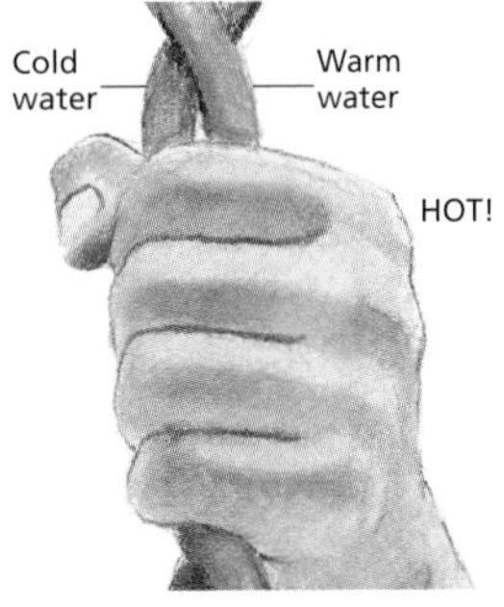

tr ■ **TEACHING TIP**

A four-color transparency of Figure 9.14, The Sense of Smell, is available in the **Overhead Transparencies Set.**

■ **JOURNAL WRITING**

Invite students to use the following questions as springboards for entries in their psychology journals:

- Do you feel that vision and hearing are more important to you than your other senses? Explain.
- Do you like certain foods better because of their taste? Is texture important to you in the type of food you prefer to eat? Do you notice the appearance or color of food? Why or why not?
- Are there certain smells that elicit powerful memories for you? Describe them.
- Relate an experience during which your sense of taste was affected by your sense of smell.

trb At this point, you may wish to use **Demonstration Activity:** *Vision and Taste—Related Senses* (*Teacher's Resource Binder*, p. 9-1) and **Demonstration Activity:** *Taste and Smell—Related Senses* (*Teacher's Resource Binder*, p. 9-1).

F • Y • I

There are two types of skin, the largest organ in the human body.

- **Hairy skin** contains hair cells, which detect movement and pressure.
- **Glabrous skin** contains no hair cells, so the receptors in this type of skin are more sensitive. Glabrous skin is found mainly on the palms of the hand, bottoms of the feet, and on lips.

Demonstrating

IS IT HOT? Skin senses variations of cold and warm, which combined make something feel hot. Donald Mershon suggests a convenient demonstration that utilizes an ice-cube tray (one that makes very small cubes). First, fill every other row with water and freeze. Then, being careful not to slop water to produce melting, fill the empty rows with warm water. Have a student place his or her hand over the surface of the tray to feel the heat.

trb At this point, you may wish to use **Cooperative Learning Activity:** *Warm Plus Cold Equals Hot* (*Teacher's Resource Binder*, p. 9-1).

F • Y • I

The gate-control theory of pain helps explain why people aren't always aware of pain. Pain signals can be controlled by the brain. The brain can choose which pain to consider and which to ignore, blocking off pain signals in the spinal cord that it chooses to ignore. This theory explains why pain is related to the severity of the injury incurred and why athletes can ignore major injuries.

trb At this point, you may wish to use **Enrichment Lesson:** *Pain Control* (*Teacher's Resource Binder*, p. 9-1).

V At this point, you may wish to show **Videocassette:** *The Mind,* **Second Edition, Module 21: "Treating Chronic Pain"** (*Teacher's Resource Binder*, p. 9-1).

■ **MULTICULTURAL CONNECTIONS**

Have students research how other cultures view pain, as well as what type of rituals or traditions these cultures might have that involve pain.

- How are reactions to pain viewed in other cultures?
- Are painful rituals a part of every culture's heritage?

trb At this point, you may wish to use **Enrichment Lesson:** *Cultural Differences in Pain* (*Teacher's Resource Binder*, p. 9-1).

■ **APPLYING THE POINTS**

Phantom limb sensations occur when a person feels the presence of a limb after it has been lost. At times, people can experience intense pain in limbs that are no longer there. Contact a surgeon who specializes in amputations to ask about how doctors treat patients with phantom limb pain and sensations.

trb At this point, you may wish to use **Enrichment Lesson:** *Pain Control* (*Teacher's Resource Binder*, p. 9-1).

V At this point, you may wish to show **Videocassette:** *The Mind,* **Second Edition, Module 20: "Phantom Limb Pain"** (*Teacher's Resource Binder*, p. 9-1).

Psychology or Physics? Firewalking is sometimes presented as an example of mental discipline or "mind over matter." In fact, it has much less to do with psychology (even "pop" psychology) than with basic physics. Burning coals are poor conductors of heat. As long as the firewalker moves at a brisk pace, he is unlikely to burn himself. It's the same principle that allows you to touch a cake in an oven to test for doneness without burning yourself. Cake is a poor conductor of heat. If you touch the metal cake pan, however, you will learn that it conducts heat much more effectively! If you walked across a metal grid placed atop the coals, the result would be severe burns.

Many researchers have studied the complicated and interesting sense of pain. Two of them, Ronald Melzack and Patrick Wall, proposed a gate-control theory of pain (1965). According to this theory, pain messages from the body travel on one set of nerve fibers in the spinal cord, and other kinds of sensory information travel on another set of fibers. The fibers carrying pain messages contain pain gates, which are open when we experience pain. Under some conditions, the nonpain fibers can actually close the pain gates. You may have noticed that other touch sensations (rubbing the area that hurts or icing it, for example) can partially block the sensation of pain.

These incoming pain messages involve bottom-up processing. But pain also involves top-down processing. That is, your brain has a significant impact on whether and how you perceive pain. Athletes in competition may not be fully aware of a painful injury until after their competition is completed. Their level of focus blocks the pain messages from conscious awareness.

Body Senses

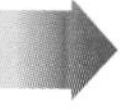

14. What are the two body senses, and how do they differ?

When people speak of the "five senses," they are referring to sight, hearing, taste, smell, and touch, but two additional body senses are critically important to our functioning.

Your **kinesthetic sense** provides information on your body's position and movement. It relies on receptor cells located throughout

Meeting Individual Needs

trb **GRAPHIC ORGANIZER: PARTS OF THE SKIN** Provide learning opportunities for all levels of learners with **Building Vocabulary: Graphic Organizer:** *Parts of the Skin* (*Teacher's Resource Binder*, p. 9-1; **Handout 9–4**) using one of the following options:

- **Independent Learners** Students may fill out the organizer on their own or follow along in class during discussion and lecture.
- **Cooperative Learners** Students may use the textbook as a resource and work in groups to find the answers that fit in the blanks.
- **Exceptional Learners** The graphic organizer can fill a special education need to provide notes for exceptional students. These students may fill in the blanks independently, with a student or teacher/tutor, or along with class discussion and lecture.

your muscles and joints. I experienced a disruption of this sense when I had surgery to repair a tendon in the pinky finger of my right hand. I was fully conscious during the surgery, and the anesthetic was administered via an injection in my armpit—which sounds much worse than it actually was—while I held my hand behind my head. I temporarily lost all sensation in my arm after this injection. The odd thing was that I felt totally dissociated from that arm—even though that arm was stretched straight out to my side during the operation, my brain remembered it as being in the last place it had provided kinesthetic information. In other words, it felt like my hand was still behind my head, even though I could see that my arm was straight. A more common disruption of the kinesthetic sense happens when your leg "falls asleep." This occurs when you've held your leg in the same position for so long that the nerve temporarily stops transmitting kinesthetic information. It is almost impossible to walk smoothly until the link is reestablished.

A second body sense, the **vestibular sense,** located in your inner ear, provides information about your overall orientation. This sense relies on the fluid-filled semicircular canals perched on top of the cochlea, which are visible in Figure 9.12 on page 171. The easiest way to disrupt your vestibular sense is to spin in circles until you become dizzy. After you stop spinning, the fluid in the vestibular system continues to spin, much as water continues to swirl in a beaker after you've stopped moving the container. Quite literally, you won't know which way is up until the fluid settles down.

Your senses are your windows to the world, sources of the raw information you need to guide your thoughts and behaviors. Now that you know a little about how they operate, surely you'll agree they're *sensational*!

▶ **kinesthetic sense** The system for sensing the position and movement of individual body parts.

▶ **vestibular sense** The system for sensing body orientation and balance, located in the semicircular canals of the inner ear.

A Balancing Act Your ability to balance results from the vestibular sense that gets its information from the semicircular canals in the inner ear. You feel dizzy when this sense is disrupted. Professional spinners, such as ballet dancers and ice skaters, are able to avoid dizziness by training their eyes to focus on the same stationary spot after each rotation. This helps them maintain their orientation.

MODULE 9

F • Y • I

People who lose their kinesthetic sense, called **proprioception,** lose the ability to move unless they can see themselves move. When they see their bodies, their brains are able to process what needs to be done to move. Without looking, these people become limp and collapse.

trb At this point, you may wish to use **Enrichment Lesson:** *The Remarkable Case of Ian Waterman* (*Teacher's Resource Binder,* p. 9-1).

V At this point, you may wish to show **Videocassette:** *The Brain,* **Second Edition, Module 11: "Sensing Motion Integration"** (*Teacher's Resource Binder,* p. 9-1).

■ **APPLYING THE POINTS**

Invite a local dance instructor or figure skating instructor to class to discuss how dancers and figure skaters maintain their balance while successfully performing their amazing spins and turns.

trb At this point, you may want to use **Demonstration Activity:** *Nystagmus* (*Teacher's Resource Binder,* p. 9-1) and **Application Activity:** *Vision and Balance* (*Teacher's Resource Binder,* p. 9-1).

Close

To complete this module with a discussion, ask students the following questions about the senses they have just studied:

- If you lost every sense, which one would you miss the most? The least?
- Imagine a world in which humans had to rely on a sense other than vision to process their experience of the world. Which sense would you prefer to be dominant other than vision? How would your life be different?
- Which sense do you appreciate most? Which do you appreciate more now that you have read this module? Why?

Demonstrating

A FINE BALANCE Our ability to maintain balance depends to some extent on visual cues. Students can experience this for themselves by standing on one foot for 30 seconds—first with their eyes open, then with their eyes closed. The latter is more difficult because the vestibular and visual systems work together to enable us to maintain balance. If students spin around a few times (thus disrupting their vestibular sense) and then close their eyes, they will find it impossible to balance on one foot.

trb At this point, you may wish to use **Demonstration Activity:** *Nystagmus* (*Teacher's Resource Binder,* p. 9-1) and **Application Activity:** *Vision and Balance* (*Teacher's Resource Binder,* p. 9-1).

MODULE 9

Checking the Points

■ TEACHING TIPS

web (1) The book companion site for *Thinking About Psychology* at **www.worthpublishers.com/thinkingaboutpsych** contains a module quiz, flashcards of key terms and people, as well as other student activities and resources for this module. You will also find PowerPoint lectures, a quiz grade book, and other teaching resources by logging on as an instructor.

(2) At this point, you may wish to review and confirm concepts about sensation with **Critical Thinking Activity:** *Fact or Falsehood?* (*Teacher's Resource Binder*, p. 9-1; **Handout 9–1**). If students completed this handout earlier, ask them not to refer to that version. Suggest that students complete the handout individually, taking the time needed to look up information in the text to respond correctly to questions. When students have completed the handouts, review the items with the entire class.

REVIEW

Module 9: Sensation

What's the Point?

Sensation is the process by which our sensory systems pick up information from the world around us. Perception is the process by which we organize this raw material into meaningful information. In bottom-up processing, our nervous system reaches conclusions by sifting through the wealth of data that enters through our sensory systems. In top-down processing, we base our conclusions on our experiences and expectations. It might be helpful to think of bottom-up processing as putting together a jigsaw puzzle without knowing what the final image should be, and to think of top-down processing as putting the puzzle together with the aid of the picture on the front of the box.

Thresholds

1. *What are absolute thresholds and difference thresholds, and how do they differ?*

   An absolute threshold is the minimum amount of stimulation a person can detect. A difference threshold (also called a just-noticeable difference, or jnd) is the minimum difference a person can detect between two stimuli. Absolute thresholds describe the smallest amount of light or sound or touch (or some other sensation) that we can detect. The difference threshold describes the smallest changes we can detect in existing sensations.

2. *What is signal detection theory and why is it a significant accomplishment for modern psychology?*

   Signal detection theory is a set of formulas and principles that lets us predict when a person will be able to detect a faint signal if other signals are present in the background. This theory has many practical applications, in medical, air travel, and military fields.

Sensory Adaptation

3. *How does sensory adaptation make your life easier?*

   Sensory adaptation is the ability to filter out unchanging aspects of the environment, such as a persisting smell. Sensory adaptation allows us to focus our attention on changes in the world around us, which frequently are conditions that could put us at risk, such as an approaching automobile.

Selective Attention

4. *How does selective attention relate to effective study skills?*

   We cannot possibly pay attention to all the stimuli in the world around us. Selective attention—the ability to focus on one or a few of these stimuli—lets us block out the world around us when we must study for an exam in a noisy house or busy schoolroom.

The Visual System

5. *What is light?*

   The light we are able to see is the visible spectrum, a tiny portion of a broad spectrum of electromagnetic radiation that exists in our environment. Light travels as waves, and two characteristics of these waves determine the quality of what we see. The length of a wave determines the

Reteaching

trb You may wish to provide students with the following graphic organizers for review of the eye, ear, tongue, and skin:

- Building Vocabulary: Graphic Organizer: *Parts of the Eye* (*Teacher's Resource Binder*, p. 9-1; Handout 9–2)
- Building Vocabulary: Graphic Organizer: *Parts of the Ear* (*Teacher's Resource Binder*, p. 9-1; Handout 9–3)
- Building Vocabulary: Graphic Organizer: *Parts of the Tongue* (*Teacher's Resource Binder*, p. 9-1; Handout 9–4)
- Building Vocabulary: Graphic Organizer: *Parts of the Skin* (*Teacher's Resource Binder*, p. 9-1; Handout 9–5)

color, or hue, we see. The height of the wave determines brightness.

6. *What are the major parts of the visual system, and what roles do these parts play in our ability to see?*

   Both our eyes and our brain are necessary for processing visual images. Light passes first through the cornea, a clear bulge on the front of the eye that begins the process of focusing images so they can be processed. Behind the cornea, the colored iris expands or shrinks the pupil of the eye to adjust the amount of light allowed to enter the inner eye. The lens is a small, flexible disk of tissue that adjusts automatically to focus images on the retina at the back of the eye. The retina contains rods and cones that convert light energy into nerve impulses that our brain can process. Other cells transport these impulses to the optic nerve, which carries the information to the occipital lobes of the brain.

7. *What are the two theories of color vision? Which one offers the better explanation of how we see colors?*

   The trichromatic (three-color) theory states that receptor cells in the eye are "tuned" to detect red, green, or blue light, and that all the colors we see are combinations of these three lights. The opponent-process theory of color vision states that the eye has three pairs of color-processing neurons, and that these pairs oppose one another, just as the on-off positions of a lamp oppose one another—when one member of a pair is "on" or stimulated, the other member must be off. Neither of these theories can explain all aspects of color vision, but each explains some part of how we see colors. Thus, both offer good explanations of color vision.

Hearing

8. *What is sound?*

   What we sense as sound are waves produced by vibrations in air or other substances. The length of the wave determines the pitch of the sound, and the height of the wave determines its loudness.

9. *What are the major components of the auditory system? What is the function of each?*

   The major components of the auditory system start with the auditory canal, which directs sound waves toward the inner ear for processing. Another is the eardrum, at the end of the auditory canal, which vibrates at the same rate as the incoming waves. Others include the three tiny bones behind the eardrum, which transmit this vibration to the cochlea, where hair cells convert the vibrations to neural impulses your brain can process. Fibers from the hair cells form the auditory nerve, a cable that carries the impulses to the temporal lobes of the brain for processing.

10. *How do you identify where a sound is coming from?*

    Your brain relies on two cues to judge the location of a sound. Your brain automatically assesses which ear heard the sound first, for that ear will be on the same side as the origin of the sound. It also assesses which ear hears a louder, more intense sound, because the sound is slightly muted by the time it reaches the ear away from the source of the sound.

Other Senses

11. *What are the four basic tastes? Which tastes are we naturally attracted to, and why do we naturally avoid others?*

    Receptor cells on your tongue and in other parts of your mouth respond to salty, sweet, sour, and bitter tastes. Newborn babies like

Have students test their knowledge by working in small groups to complete each graphic organizer, at first without referring to the text. Then have group members be responsible for checking one of the organizers against the text. Each student responsible for a particular organizer can then answer questions and check organizers about that body part and its relationship to sensation.

MODULE 9

trb ■ TEACHING TIPS

To help students individually review module concepts, suggest they use the flashcards described in **Building Vocabulary: *Flashcards*** (*Teacher's Resource Binder*, p. 9-1).

salty and sweet tastes, but they dislike sour and bitter tastes. These unlearned reactions help protect young humans from substances that could be poisonous, and they attract them to substances that aid their survival, like mother's milk and salt.

12. *How do taste, smell, and flavor differ?*

    Taste and smell are both chemical senses; receptor cells in the mouth and nose process chemical molecules and convert them into neural impulses our brains can process. Taste and smell interact to produce flavor, but our perception of flavor also depends on appearance, feel, and texture of food.

13. *What are the four basic skin senses? According to gate-control theory, how can we effectively reduce pain?*

    The four basic skin senses are pain, warmth, cold, and pressure, and all other skin sensations flow from some combination of these four. The gate-control theory of pain suggests that pain messages travel on one set of nerve fibers in the spinal cord, and that other sensory information travels on a different set of fibers in the spinal cord. The fibers that carry pain messages have gates that are open when we are experiencing pain. Stimulating the fibers on which the other sensory information travels—for example, by rubbing an injured knee—may reduce pain by forcing the pain gates to close so that the other nerve fibers may send their message (the rubbing) to the brain.

14. *What are the two body senses, and how do they differ?*

    Your kinesthetic sense uses receptor cells in your muscles and joints to monitor the position and movement of your body parts. Your vestibular sense relies on the fluid-filled semicircular canals located in your inner ear to provide feedback on your balance and general body orientation.

Key Terms

sensation, p. 157
bottom-up processing, p. 157
perception, p. 157
top-down processing, p. 157
absolute threshold, p. 158
difference threshold (just noticeable difference), p. 159
signal detection theory, p. 159
sensory adaptation, p. 160
selective attention, p. 161
electromagnetic energy, p. 162
hue, p. 162
cornea, p. 164
iris, p. 164
pupil, p. 164
lens, p. 164
retina, p. 165
receptor cells, p. 165
rods, p. 165
cones, p. 165
fovea, p. 165
bipolar cells, p. 166
ganglion cells, p. 166
optic nerve, p. 166
blind spot, p. 166
trichromatic (three-color) theory, p. 167
opponent-process theory, p. 168
pitch, p. 169
hertz (Hz), p. 169
decibel (dB), p. 169
auditory canal, p. 170
eardrum (tympanic membrane), p. 170
ossicles, p. 171
cochlea, p. 171
oval window, p. 171
hair cells, p. 171
auditory nerve, p. 172
olfactory cells, p. 174
kinesthetic sense, p. 176
vestibular sense, p. 177

Self-Test

Multiple-Choice Questions

Choose the *best* answer for each of the following questions.

1. Art sat in one position so long that his leg fell asleep and he had trouble standing on it. Art's leg was no longer sending ________________ messages to his brain.
   a. vestibular
   b. kinesthetic
   c. auditory
   d. electromagnetic

2. Mina has excellent hearing. She can hear musical notes and electronic chimes that her friends all miss. Mina's ________________ for sounds seems to be lower than that of her friends.
   a. difference threshold
   b. jnd
   c. absolute threshold
   d. minimal tolerance

3. The ________________ is a light-sensitive surface that is located at the back of your eye and that contains receptor cells for transforming light waves into neural impulses.
   a. retina
   b. cornea
   c. iris
   d. fovea

4. The point at which the optic nerve exits the eye is known as the
   a. fovea.
   b. bipolor cell cluster.
   c. ganglion cell cluster.
   d. blind spot.

5. Jon had an ear infection and his right eardrum ruptured. Jon's doctor told him that his hearing would be impaired in that ear while the eardrum is healing. Jon may have trouble
   a. localizing sounds.
   b. hearing loud noises.
   c. standing on one leg.
   d. coughing.

6. During the Cold War, researchers who wanted to improve the military's ability to detect incoming nuclear warheads developed ________________ theory.
   a. opponent-process
   b. trichromatic
   c. top-down processing
   d. signal detection

Matching Terms and Definitions

7. For each definition, choose the *best* matching term from the list that follows.

Definitions

a. A just noticeable difference.
b. Theory of color vision that says cones are "tuned" to detect red, green, or blue light.
c. The process by which our sensory systems and nervous system receive stimuli from our environment.
d. Focusing conscious awareness on a particular stimulus to the exclusion of others.
e. Information processing that focuses on how cognitive processes—such as expectations and experiences—influence our interpretation of incoming sensory information.
f. The process of organizing and interpreting sensory information.

(tb) Using the Test Bank

The *Test Bank* that accompanies this textbook offers a wide variety of questions in different formats and levels of complexity. Use the software to construct whole tests or to integrate standardized questions into teacher-made tests.

Self-Test Answers

Multiple-Choice Questions
1. b, 2. c, 3. a, 4. d, 5. a, 6. d

Matching Terms and Definitions
7. a. (13), b. (7), c. (3), d. (12), e. (1), f. (4)

Self-Test Answers

Matching Terms and Definitions (continued)
g. (9), h. (2), i. (5)

Fill-in-the-Blank
8. wavelength; amplitude, 9. Rods; cones, 10. localize, 11. taste; smell

Brief Essay Question
12. Students should describe the parts of the eye in order of how light enters it: cornea, iris, pupil, and retina. Students should also discuss how light hits the back of the retina where the rods and cones are found. The light information then passes from the rods and cones to the bipolar cells and then to the ganglion cells, the axons of which combine to form the auditory nerve, which exits the eye through the blind spot.

g. The system for sensing body orientation and balance, located in the semicircular canals of the inner ear.
h. Information processing that focuses on the raw material that enters through our eyes, ears, and other organs of sensation.
i. Diminished sensitivity as a result of constant stimulation.

Terms
(1) top-down processing
(2) bottom-up processing
(3) sensation
(4) perception
(5) sensory adaptation
(6) signal detection theory
(7) trichromatic theory
(8) opponent-process theory
(9) vestibular sense
(10) kinesthetic sense
(11) olfactory sense
(12) selective attention
(13) difference threshold

Fill-in-the-Blank Questions

8. The ________________ of a light wave determines a light's color; the ________________ of a light wave determines its brightness.
9. The retina contains two types of receptor cells. ________________ detect only black, white, and shades of gray, but they help us see at night. ________________ detect color and fine details, but they require bright light to function properly.
10. To ________________ sounds, your brain assesses two kinds of information: (1) which ear hears the sound first, and (2) which ear hears the sound more loudly than the other.
11. Your sense of ________________ and your sense of ________________ are chemical senses, which convert chemical molecules into neural impulses your brain can process.

Brief Essay Question

12. When a ray of light enters your eye, what path does it take? In about six sentences, describe the parts of the eye that the light passes through, and the path that the information follows to reach your brain.

Performance Standards

Standard Area: Sensation and Perception

Content Standard 1: Basic concepts illustrating the functioning of the different sensory systems

Performance Standard 1.1 Discuss the principles of thresholds, adaptation, and constancy.

- Discuss size, shape, and lightness constancy. Provide real-world examples to illustrate each type of constancy. (Student Text pp. 194–195)
- Figure 10.11, "Size-Distance Relationship," introduces students to the Ponzo illusion which illustrates how depth cues may distort our interpretation of size. (Student Text p. 194)
- Figure 10.12, "Shape Constancy," illustrates how when a door opens the shape changes, but constancy provides that we will continue to perceive the door as a rectangle. (Student Text p. 195)

Content Standard 2: Influence of the individual and the environment on perception

Performance Standard 2.1 Discuss Gestalt principles, such as figure-ground, continuity, similarity, proximity, closure, and so on.

- Define the term "Gestalt." Explain it in relation to perceptual organization. (Student Text p. 183)
- Figure 10.1, "A Gestalt," illustrates the significance of "the whole is greater than the sum of its parts." (Student Text p. 184)
- Present the following principles with examples: figure-ground, similarity, proximity, closure, and continuity. (Student Text pp. 184–186)
- Figure 10.2, "What Do You See?" illustrates reversible figure-ground. (Student Text p. 185)
- Figure 10.3, "Gestalt Grouping Principles," provides illustrations of similarity, proximity, closure, and continuity. (Student Text p. 185)
- Figure 10.4, "Closure and the Blind Spot," allows students to experience how the brain will create a gestalt. (Student Text p. 186)
- Present a number of illusions, for example the Müller-Lyer and the Ames room. Explain the perceptual principles at work. (Student Text pp. 197–201)

Performance Standard 2.2 Explain binocular and monocular depth cues.

- Define depth perception in context of how it affects our lives. Discuss Gibson and Walk's findings on depth perception using the "visual cliff." (Student Text pp. 186–187)
- Discuss the binocular depth cues of retinal disparity. Provide examples of each that illustrate how these cues allow us to see depth. (Student Text pp. 187–189)
- Figure 10.7, "Random Dot Stereogram," illustrate how retinal disparity creates depth. (Student Text p. 189)
- Discuss monocular depth cues, such as relative size, relative motion, interposition, relative height, texture gradient, relative clarity, and linear perspective. Illustrate each cue with pictures or photographs. (Student Text pp. 189–193)
- Explain the perception of motion, when nothing is moving, using the concepts of stroboscopic motion and phi phenomenon. Provide examples of each. (Student Text p. 193)

Performance Standard 2.3 Explain the role of the environment, motivation, past experiences, culture, and expectations on perception.

- Explain the role of expectations in creating perceptual set. Illustrate how perceptual set may influence our everyday perceptions. (Student Text pp. 195–196)
- Figure 10.13, "Perceptual Set," illustrates how perceptual set influences our perceptions of a picture. (Student Text p. 196)
- Explore the effect of context on our perceptions. (Student Text p. 197)
- Focus on claims of extrasensory perception (ESP) and discuss how a large number of people believe in such abilities. Examine how scientists attempt to study such phenomena. Explore alternative explanations for ESP abilities. (Student Text pp. 198–199)

Materials NETWORK

All of the items from the Video, Activity, and Enrichment Centers listed below come from the *Teacher's Resource Binder.* These items will help you teach and expand on concepts presented in Module 10.

trb This logo indicates when an item from the Materials Network may be used in conjunction with a specific note found in this module's *Teacher's Edition.*

Organizational Principles

V Video Center

- **Videocassette:** ***Scientific American Frontiers,*** **Second Edition, Segment 11: "Cockpit Confusion"** Consult the faculty guide from the *Scientific American Frontiers* video series for a description of this segment. (*Teacher's Resource Binder,* p. 10-1)

Activity Center

- **Critical Thinking Activity:** *Fact or Falsehood?* With this activity, students' preconceptions about perception are either exposed as incorrect or reinforced as correct. (*Teacher's Resource Binder,* p. 10-1; **Handout 10–1**)
- **Application Activity:** *Sensation Versus Perception* Sometimes our perceptions don't give us the real picture. These two optical illusions help show how our perceptions can override the sensations that come to us from the world. (*Teacher's Resource Binder,* p. 10-1; **Handout 10–2**)
- **Technology Application Activity:** *The Exploratorium* San Francisco's Exploratorium is a museum dedicated to showcasing human perception. Students can explore the museum's Web site, interact with different illusions, and even create their own versions of the museum's exhibits. (*Teacher's Resource Binder,* p. 10-1)
- **Application Activity:** *Perceptual Organization* Gestalt principles of perception are best understood interactively. The images from this handout will help students understand how these principles work. (*Teacher's Resource Binder,* p. 10-1; **Handout 10–3**)
- **Critical Thinking Activity:** *Object Recognition* Top-down and bottom-up processing are demonstrated with this activity that forces students to identify objects based on their perceptions rather than on their sensory information. (*Teacher's Resource Binder,* p. 10-1; **Handout 10–4**)
- **Application Activity:** *An Auditory Analogue of Visual Reversible Figures* Figure-ground illusions aren't isolated to visual experience. This simple activity demonstrates how auditory stimuli can become a figure-ground illusion. (*Teacher's Resource Binder,* p. 10-1)
- **Application Activity:** *The Ganzfeld* What would the world be like if it were colorless and formless? Interestingly, Gestalt psychologists have studied this phenomenon, called a *Ganzfeld,* and found some fascinating results. This activity replicates a Ganzfeld experience for your students. (*Teacher's Resource Binder,* p. 10-1)
- **Application Activity:** *The Gestalt Law of Pragnanz* The Gestalt law of Pragnanz says that we tend to simplify and perfect figures in our perception. Demonstrate the law using this activity in which students copy a series of figures. (*Teacher's Resource Binder,* p. 10-1; **Handout 10–5**)

Enrichment Center

- **Enrichment Lesson:** *Visual Agnosia* A discussion of visual agnosia, defined as "a syndrome in which all parts of the visual field are seen, but the objects seen are without meaning," provides an excellent introduction to a discussion of perceptual organization and interpretation. (*Teacher's Resource Binder,* p. 10-1)

Depth Perception

Activity Center

- **Cooperative Learning Activity:** *Binocular Vision Versus Monocular Vision* This activity demonstrates our reliance on both eyes to see depth. In it, students try to catch a tennis ball with one eye or both eyes open. (*Teacher's Resource Binder,* p. 10-1; **Handout 10–6**)
- **Technology Application Activity:** *PsychQuest:* **"How Do Athletes Use Perceptual Cues?"** This interactive CD-ROM lesson enables students to explore how much athletes compete by relying on the concepts presented in this module. (*Teacher's Resource Binder,* p. 10-1)
- **Application Activity:** *Autostereograms* Magic Eye illusions, also called autostereograms, work by using retinal disparity. This activity explores this illusion, providing tips for how to see the 3D images found in these pictures. (*Teacher's Resource Binder,* p. 10-1; **Handouts 10–7** and **10–8**)

Motion Perception

Activity Center

- **Application Activity:** *The Oscillating Window Illusion* This easily constructed illusion causes students to see the "window" increase in thickness and then stop and reverse course as it spins around on its axis. (*Teacher's Resource Binder,* p. 10-1)

- Application Activity: *Kinesthetic Capture* Usually, visual perception overrides perception from the other senses. But, with this activity, students can see that vision doesn't dominate our perceptions all the time. (*Teacher's Resource Binder*, p. 10-1)

Enrichment Center

- Enrichment Lesson: *Motion Detection* In this lesson, people's visual sense of motion—as in the childhood game of "statues"—is discussed. (*Teacher's Resource Binder*, p. 10-1)

Perceptual Constancy

Activity Center

- Application Activity: *Perceived Lunar Size* How big must an object be on Earth for it to cover the moon in our visual field? Surprisingly, it is not as big as most students think. (*Teacher's Resource Binder*, p. 10-1; **Handout 10–9**)

Perceptual Set

Activity Center

- Cooperative Learning: Evaluation Activity: *Discovering Personal Bias* Working in groups, students can see that their personal biases influence how they interpret a story presented from one of two contexts. (*Teacher's Resource Binder*, p. 10-1; **Handout 10–10**)
- Application Activities: *Perceptual Set* This collection of activities quickly demonstrates how our perceptual set causes us to make rather silly errors at times. (*Teacher's Resource Binder*, p. 10-1)
- Application Activity: *Social Transmission of a Narrative:* The "gossip" game or "telephone" game from childhood aptly demonstrates how what we hear is not always what we relay to others. (*Teacher's Resource Binder*, p. 10-1)
- Critical Thinking Activity: *Reverse Speech and Speech Complementarity* The textbook introduces the concept of backward masking, where messages are supposedly inserted backward into song lyrics. This activity explores how the power of suggestion (and thus perceptual set) can influence what we hear. (*Teacher's Resource Binder*, p. 10-1)

Enrichment Center

- Enrichment Lesson: *Subliminal Persuasion* Expanding on the text's introduction to subliminal perception, this lesson delves into the real story behind subliminal persuasion techniques used throughout history. (*Teacher's Resource Binder*, p. 10-1)

Context

Activity Center

- Application Activity: *Context Effects* This quick activity demonstrates that the same figure can be perceived as completely different objects, depending on the context. (*Teacher's Resource Binder*, p. 10-1; **Transparency Master 10–1**)
- Application Activity: *Context and Anagrams* Students can experience context effects as they decipher anagrams. They come up with different words for the same combination of letters, depending on the context. (*Teacher's Resource Binder*, p. 10-1; **Handout 10–11**)

Enrichment Center

- Enrichment Lesson: *Context and Perception* Not only are sensory systems vulnerable to the influence of context; our social perceptions can be altered, depending on the context. (*Teacher's Resource Binder*, p. 10-1)

Illusions

V Video Center

- Videocassette: *Scientific American Frontiers*, **Second Edition, Segment 3: "Water, Water Everywhere"** Consult the faculty guide from the *Scientific American Frontiers* video series for a description of this segment. (*Teacher's Resource Binder*, p. 10-1)

Activity Center

- Application Activity: *Belief in ESP Scale* Measure how much your students are likely to believe in extrasensory perception with this handy scale. (*Teacher's Resource Binder*, p. 10-1; **Handout 10–12**)
- Evaluation Activity: *Testing for ESP* This activity uses our inability to predict randomness to expose the logical fallacies of extrasensory perception. (*Teacher's Resource Binder*, p. 10-1)
- Analysis Activities: *ESP Tricks* This collection of extrasensory perception tricks will astound your students and encourage them to use their critical thinking skills. (*Teacher's Resource Binder*, p. 10-1)
- Technology Application Activity: *PsychSim:* **"Visual Illusions"** *PsychSim* is an interactive CD-ROM containing tutorials in different content areas of psychology. A workbook accompanies the disc for extra rehearsal of the information in this tutorial. (*Teacher's Resource Binder*, p. 10-1)
- Application Activity: *The Wundt-Jastrow Illusion* This illusion highlights the distinction between sensation and perception as students view two identical figures that seem to change size as the figures are moved around. (*Teacher's Resource Binder*, p. 10-1; **Handout 10–13**)
- Application Activity: *Horizontal-Vertical Illusion* This illusion demonstrates that vertical lines tend to look longer than horizontal lines. (*Teacher's Resource Binder*, p. 10-1)
- Application Activity: *Poggendorf Illusion* This illusion shows how bisected lines can deceive our visual perception, sometimes with dangerous consequences. (*Teacher's Resource Binder*, p. 10-1; **Handout 10–14**)

Enrichment Center

- Enrichment Lesson: *Belief in ESP* Why do people believe in extrasensory perception when scientific evidence doesn't support it? This lesson presents some reasons why people cling to unsubstantiated beliefs. (*Teacher's Resource Binder*, p. 10-1)
- Enrichment Lesson: *Resources for Obtaining Visual Illusions* This lesson lists a number of resources for obtaining visual illusions that may be used in the classroom. (*Teacher's Resource Binder*, p. 10-1)

MODULE 10 Perception

Have you ever tasted one of your parents' favorite foods and found it disgusting? Or felt that a friend's playful shove was rude or even painful? Or disagreed with the popular opinion about a new music video? We are all exposed to the same audio, motion, and color sensations—indeed, to the same wavelengths of light and sound, the same physical touches and movements, the same chemical tastes and smells. But how very different are our **perceptions**—our interpretations of the stimuli coming in from the world around us.

Our processing of incoming stimulation (*sensation*) is known as *bottom-up processing.* In this module we consider *top-down processing,* the influence that our experiences and expectations have on our perceptions as we organize and interpret incoming sensory information.

Organizational Principles

What's the point? 1. What important contribution did the Gestalt psychologists make to the study of human perception?

In nineteenth-century Germany, the Gestalt psychologists offered an alternative to the approach that Wilhelm Wundt (widely regarded as the "father" of scientific psychology) was taking in his laboratory at the University of Leipzig. Wundt's approach was to break down conscious experience into its most fundamental components. The Gestalt psychologists disagreed, stating that by breaking experiences into their basic parts something important is lost—the **gestalt** or whole—which indeed may be greater than the sum of its parts.

▶ **perception** The process of organizing and interpreting sensory information.

▶ **gestalt** The "whole," or the organizational patterns, that we tend to perceive. The Gestalt psychologists emphasized that the whole is greater than the sum of its parts.

Getting Started

Begin a discussion of perception by asking students if they favor using one sense over another or feel that one sense is keener for them than another. Volunteers may identify the sense they feel most strongly about, and why.

trb You also may wish to use **Critical Thinking Activity:** *Fact or Falsehood?* (*Teacher's Resource Binder*, p. 10-1; **Handout 10–1**) as a prereading strategy to find out what students already know about perception. The activity along with its results will prime students to note terms and concepts in the text that confirm or dispel their preconceptions about perception.

MODULE 10

Perception

Introducing the Module

The Points: Module Objectives

- Identify the important contribution of Gestalt psychologists to the study of human perception.
- Describe how people determine figure and ground, and why it is important.
- Describe the principles of similarity, proximity, closure, and continuity.
- Understand depth perception and how it affects our lives.
- Describe the two major binocular depth cues and how they help us perceive depth.
- Understand cues that let us calculate depth, using only one eye, and how they let us calculate depth.
- Describe what might cause us to perceive motion when nothing is moving.
- Understand the value of perceptual constancy in our lives.
- Analyze how perceptual set affects our everyday interpretations of sensory experiences.
- Determine how context influences our perceptions.
- Appreciate what makes perceptual illusions so interesting.

Building Vocabulary

Because vocabulary for this module is best learned along with sensory experiences of perception, have students create flashcards for module vocabulary and terms related to perception.

MODULE 10

Teaching the Points

■ TEACHING TIPS

web (1) You can log on as an instructor to the book companion site for *Thinking About Psychology* at **www.worthpublishers.com/thinkingaboutpsych**. It contains teacher resources for class presentations as well as review and assessment of module concepts and terms.

(2) Students may more readily identify top-down processing with stereotyping since both use previous expectations to make judgments about the world around us. Help students understand that although stereotyping can be negative, it can also be very efficient for people as they interact with certain stimuli. Without top-down processing, we would have to interpret the world as if it were constantly new.

trb At this point, you may wish to use **Critical Thinking Activity:** *Object Recognition* (*Teacher's Resource Binder*, p. 10-1; **Handout 10–4**) and **Cooperative Learning: Evaluation Activity:** *Discovering Personal Bias* (*Teacher's Resource Binder*, p. 10-1; **Handout 10–10**).

web (3) The following Web sites are good resources for teaching sensation and perception:

- Hugh Foley's page at **www.skidmore.edu/~hfoley/perception.htm**
- Psychology Tutorials at **http://psych.hanover.edu/Krantz/tutor.html**
- Vision Science at **www.visionscience.com/VisionScience.html**
- The Internet Psychology Lab (IPL) at **http://kahuna.psych.uiuc.edu/ipl/index.html**
- *The Joy of Visual Perception: A Web Book* by Peter K. Kaiser at **www.yorku.ca/eye**

trb At this point, you may wish to use **Application Activity:** *Sensation Versus Perception* (*Teacher's Resource Binder*, p. 10-1; **Handout 10–2**).

trb **tr** (4) A black-line master for Figure 10.1, A Gestalt, is available in the **Black-Line Masters Appendix** of the *Teacher's Resource Binder*.

When I was in high school, my biology teacher tried to make this point with an example. He led us through an exercise in which we had to calculate the "value" of a human being. We were to imagine somehow reducing this human to the appropriate quantities of the elements found on the periodic table—hydrogen, oxygen, carbon, calcium, iron, and so on—and to calculate the cost of each quantity. By adding up the various components, we could then determine the cost of the human body. The surprising conclusion was that each of us was "worth" only a few dollars!

This simple biology exercise was a great lesson in how much we miss if we spend too much time breaking things down into smaller and smaller pieces (Figure 10.1). The Gestalt psychologists knew this when they urged their colleagues to look at the whole—the entirety, the gestalt. Furthermore, they believed that this was the way human perception actually occurs. We don't focus on discrete, individual stimuli in our environment; rather, we group them into more meaningful units (Rock & Palmer, 1990). Let's look at some of the ways we group stimuli in our effort to understand the world around us.

Figure 10.1 **A Gestalt** The German Gestalt psychologists of the nineteenth century believed that the whole is different from the sum of its parts. The parts of this figure are rather abstract red shapes on a white background. Yet because of the way those parts are arranged, we perceive much more. The red shapes become circles cut by white lines, and the white lines produce a cube! Even this shape is subject to various interpretations. You can make the tiny X in the center seem to be on either the front edge of the cube *or* the back (but not both at the same time). You can make the cube seem to appear in front of the paper with red circles, *or* behind a paper with holes cut out of it. (From Bradley & others, 1976)

Figure-Ground Relationships

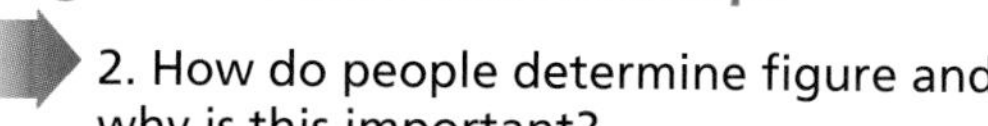

2. How do people determine figure and ground, and why is this important?

Gestalt psychologists pointed out that we naturally organize our environment into **figure-ground** relationships. In most photographs and visual scenes, you can easily pick out the *figure.* It will be some object that stands out or draws your attention, and it probably will be nearer to the center of the visual field than the edge. It may be moving, and it will often be fairly large and colorful. The *ground* consists of the surrounding aspects of the visual field, which we commonly call the background. Thus, in a photo of a jet flying across the sky, the airplane is the figure and the sky is the ground. In a sports photo, the swimmer touching the wall at the end of the race is the

► **figure-ground** The organization of the visual field into objects (the *figures*) that stand out from their surroundings (the *ground*).

► **grouping** The perceptual tendency to organize stimuli into understandable groups.

184 Chapter 4 ■ Sensation and Perception

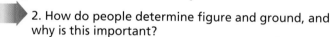

Suggested Readings

Use the following books as teacher-preparation tools or as enrichment for advanced students:

Coren, S., Ward, L. M., & Enns, J. T. (1999). *Sensation and perception* (5th ed.). Fort Worth, TX: Harcourt, Brace. (textbook)

Fisher, J. (1979). *Body magic.* New York: Stein & Day.

Goldstein, E. B. (1999). *Sensation and perception* (5th ed.). Pacific Grove, CA: Brooks/Cole. (textbook)

Gregory, R. L., & Gombrich, E. H. (Eds.). (1973). *Illusion in nature and art.* New York: Scribner.

Grosswirth, M., & Salny, A. (1981). *The Mensa genius quiz book.* Reading, MA: Addison-Wesley.

figure, and the other swimmers, the lane markers, the side of the pool, and the water itself are the ground. Sometimes the relationship between figure and ground is more ambiguous, as in Figure 10.2, and produces a reversible figure.

The tendency to perceive figure and ground is not exclusively visual. We strive to identify the figure in other contexts as well, such as the predominant taste in a casserole or the melody of a song.

Figure 10.2 **What Do You See?** If black is the figure, you see men in a hurry. If black is the ground and white is the figure, you see arrows instead.

Grouping Principles

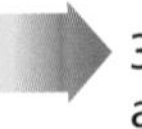

3. Describe the principles of similarity, proximity, closure, and continuity.

The Gestalt psychologists also believed people are predisposed to organize stimuli by **grouping**—placing items into understandable sets. Several principles guide the way we group stimuli (Figure 10.3).

- ***Similarity*** Perhaps the most basic principle is similarity. We place items that look similar in the same group. This is easy to see in team contests: All the players wearing blue shirts are from the University of Michigan; all those wearing red shirts represent the University of Wisconsin.
- ***Proximity*** This term comes from the word *approximate,* which means "close." If objects are close together, we place them in the same group. Not only do the Michigan Wolverines basketball players wear the same uniform, they also share the same bench. It is partially because they are near one another that we put them in the same group.
- ***Closure*** Our brain's tendency to look for the whole, not the parts, drives us to fill in any gaps in a perceptual field. Look at Figure 10.4 on page 186. When you follow the directions to make the object disappear, you will notice that the horizontal line appears to continue right through the area—there is no longer a gap in the line! Your brain doesn't like gaps, assumes this one doesn't belong there, and fills in the space for you. The prin-

Figure 10.3 **Gestalt Grouping Principles** *Similarity* leads us to see two sets of triangles and one set of circles. *Proximity* leads us to see three sets of two lines each. *Closure* leads us to see intact shapes where there are none. *Continuity* leads us to see one long wavy line and one straight one, rather than four half-circles. Our brains are programmed to group objects to help us make sense of the world around us.

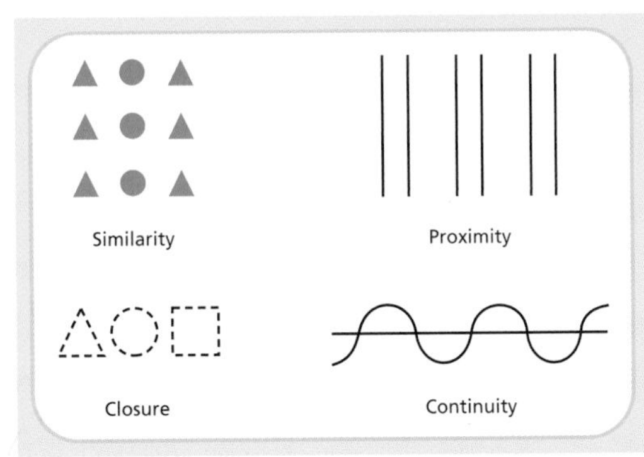

Hoffman, D. D. (1998). *Visual intelligence: How we create what we see.* New York: Norton.
Matlin, M., & Foley, H. (1997). *Sensation and perception* (4th ed.). Boston: Allyn & Bacon. (textbook)
Sacks, O. (1987). *The man who mistook his wife for a hat.* New York: Summit.
Shepard, R. N. (1990). *Mind sights.* New York: Freeman.

■ APPLYING THE POINTS

Have students create their own tessellations, like the one in Figure 10.2 on page 185 of the *Student Edition.* This picture is similar to tessellations created by M. C. Escher. A **tessellation** is a repeating geometric pattern, and the ones in the figure and those that Escher created combine tessellations with figure-ground illusions where two geometric patterns repeat at the same time—one as a figure and one as a ground.

trb **tr** A black-line master for Figure 10.2, What Do You See?, is available in the **Black-Line Masters Appendix** of the *Teacher's Resource Binder.*

web If you are interested in all things Escher, check out the World of Escher Web site at **www.worldofescher.com**.

■ JOURNAL WRITING

Invite students to use the following question and writing prompt as a springboard for an entry in their psychology journals:

- Many Gestalt principles seem more common sense than psychology. Why do you think knowing these principles enhances our understanding of human behavior?

trb **tr** A black-line master for Figure 10.3, Gestalt Grouping Principles, is available in the **Black-Line Masters Appendix** of the *Teacher's Resource Binder.*

■ TEACHING TIP

Students can discover auditory figure-ground illusions by simply repeating aloud a word such as *say.* It will shift abruptly to *ace* and back again to *say.*

trb At this point, you may wish to use **Application Activity:** ***An Auditory Analogue of Visual Reversible Figures*** (*Teacher's Resource Binder,* p. 10-1).

web ■ APPLYING THE POINTS

As an extra-credit assignment, lead students through the step-by-step dissection of a cow's eye that appears on The Exploratorium Web site at **www.exploratorium.edu/learning_studio/cow_eye**.

trb At this point, you may wish to use **Technology Application Activity:** ***The Exploratorium*** (*Teacher's Resource Binder,* p. 10-1).

■ APPLYING THE POINTS

Contact a civil engineer to inquire about the principles that must be kept in mind when designing a highway or road system. If possible, obtain answers to the following questions:

- What optical illusions are most important to avoid in planning a road system?
- What are some techniques that can be used to design a good road system?

Present the information, and then engage your students in a discussion of how these techniques relate to Gestalt grouping principles.

V At this point, you may wish to show **Videocassette:** *Scientific American Frontiers,* **Second Edition, Segment 11: "Cockpit Confusion"** (*Teacher's Resource Binder,* p. 10-1).

F•Y•I

Seeing depth is achieved because we have two eyes in the front of our heads. Animals with eyes on the sides of their heads have excellent peripheral vision, which allows them to scan for danger. Peripheral vision is much better at detecting motion, so having eyes on the sides of the head gives an evolutionary advantage to animals that are typically hunted. Predators do not need to be on the lookout for danger—they *are* the danger! They need to determine distances between them and their prey, which requires the depth perception that binocular vision provides.

trb At this point, you may wish to use **Technology Application Activity:** *PsychQuest:* "How Do Athletes Use Perceptual Cues?" (*Teacher's Resource Binder,* p. 10-1).

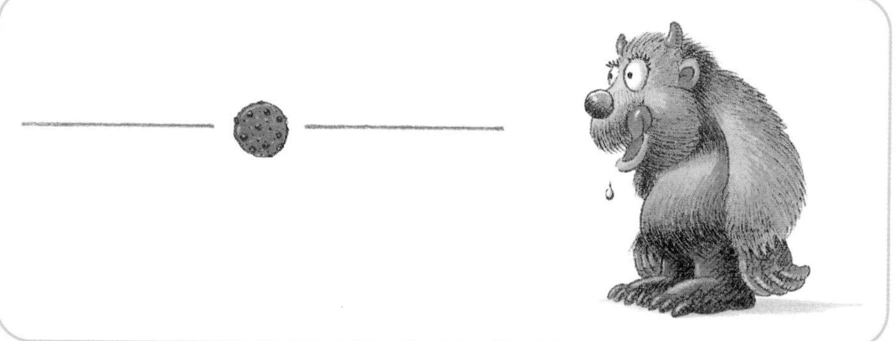

Figure 10.4 Closure and the Blind Spot Close your right eye, look at the monster, and slowly adjust the distance between your eye and the page until the cookie disappears (about a foot). When the cookie disappears, the two line segments will appear to join into one continuous line as your brain strives to create a gestalt.

ciple of closure also allows you to perceive a cube in Figure 10.1 on page 184. The cube is in your head, not on the paper.

- ***Continuity*** Once an object appears to move in a particular direction, your brain assumes that movement continues unchanged. On some of the smaller highways, for example, you can easily miss your turn unless you really pay attention to the signs. We tend to assume the highway continues in the direction we've been moving.

Depth Perception

4. What is depth perception, and how does it affect our lives?

▶ **depth perception** The ability to see in three dimensions and judge distance.

▶ **visual cliff** A laboratory device for testing depth perception in infants and young animals.

▶ **binocular cues** Depth cues that require the use of both eyes.

▶ **monocular cues** Depth cues that require the use of only one eye.

▶ **retinal disparity** A binocular depth cue resulting from slightly different images produced by the separation of the retinas in the left and right eyes.

Consider how difficult life would be if you had no **depth perception** and were therefore unable to see in three dimensions and to judge distance. You would certainly not be able to drive—you rely on your ability to perceive depth in parking, determining when it's safe to pull out onto a busy street, and deciding if you can and should pass another car. Sports would also be impossible. Depth perception guides you when you position your hands to catch a ball, time a volleyball spike, and shoot accurate free throws. And think of the little things: threading a needle, tossing wadded-up paper into a trash basket, and placing clean dishes on a shelf. All these actions depend on depth perception.

Is this vital human skill a product of nature or nurture? Eleanor Gibson and Richard Walk explored this question using a device called the **visual cliff** (Figure 10.5), which ensures the infant's safety while allowing researchers to determine whether an infant perceives depth. Gibson and Walk's (1960) research indicates that even very young in-

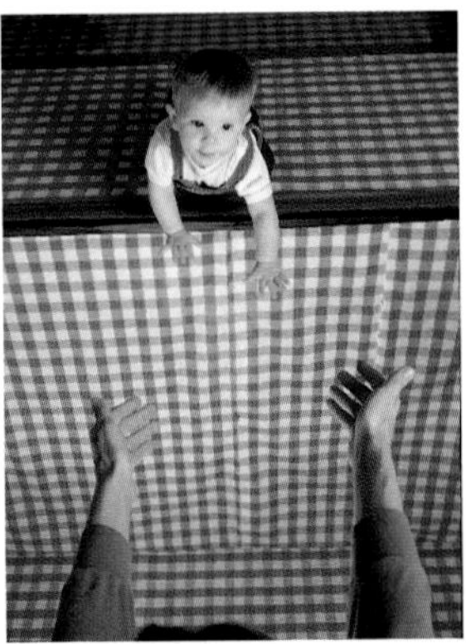

Figure 10.5 The Visual Cliff This device can safely test infants for the ability to perceive depth. Infants are reluctant to crawl onto the glass protecting them from the drop-off, even when their primary caregivers coax them to do so. Depth perception can protect us from falls.

fants just barely able to crawl are reluctant to move past the edge of what appears to be a drop-off, so this ability might be, to some extent, inborn. And research with other species also supports this "nature" view: Depth perception exists even for animals mobile at birth. But research also supports the "nurture" view. By the time children can crawl, they have already had a lot of interaction with the environment, so their reluctance to venture over the edge of a cliff may be learned. Depth perception improves as human children experience increased interaction with the environment (Campos & others, 1992). As is almost always the case, both nature *and* nurture are important.

Given our anatomy, it's amazing that we even have these impressive abilities to perceive depth. The retina is a two-dimensional surface, yet we use it to determine height, width, *and* depth. Working together, your eyes and brain use a number of tricks to create that third dimension. Some of them, known as **binocular cues,** rely on both eyes. Others—the **monocular cues**—require only a single eye.

Binocular Depth Cues

5. What are the two major binocular depth cues, and how do they help us perceive depth?

Do you remember playing with a Viewmaster toy when you were young? To use this toy, you insert a round card containing pictures into a viewer and look through the eyepieces. What you see is an image with astounding depth. How does this seemingly simple toy create these great images? The trick is that the toy's design relies on the binocular depth cue known as **retinal disparity**—the difference between the images you see with the retinas in your left and right eyes. Let's see how this works.

The Viewmaster: A Binocular Depth Toy This classic childhood toy produces an enhanced sense of depth by exaggerating the effect produced by retinal disparity. A separate image is projected to each of the child's two eyes. These images were taken by two cameras placed a couple of feet apart.

web ■ LOOKING AT THE ISSUES

Some people cannot see depth well because of different conditions that hinder the eyes' ability to see in stereo. Have your students check out **www.vision3d.com** to find the answers to the following questions:

- What is amblyopia *(lazy eye)*? What are some treatments for this condition?
- What is strabismus *(eye turns, such as crossed eyes or wall eyes)*? What are some treatments for this condition?
- How are vision problems related to learning disabilities and dyslexia?

■ TEACHING TIPS

(1) Have students bring in their old Viewmasters for an in-class demonstration of retinal disparity. Students can view the images with one eye closed and both eyes open to see how the same image is projected in two slightly different places to capitalize on our perception of depth.

(2) Relate retinal disparity to real life by having students recall a time when they were lying down watching television with their vision in one eye obscured by a pillow or blanket. If so, they probably had to shift their position to correct the obstruction, or they had to close one eye—watching TV and a pillow at the same time is not very enjoyable!

Demonstrating

BINOCULAR VISION Have students close one eye, point their two forefingers toward each other, and then bring them together quickly. They are likely to miss. An even more difficult test is to have them hold a pencil in each hand and bring the pencil points together. It is important, of course, that their hands not be at arm's length. If they repeat either test, they ought to drop their arms out of view before they try again. This will eliminate the perception of any depth cues from the position of the hands and arms.

trb At this point, you may wish to use **Cooperative Learning Activity:** *Binocular Vision Versus Monocular Vision* (*Teacher's Resource Binder*, p. 10-1; **Handout 10–6**).

MODULE 10

■ APPLYING THE POINTS

If possible, have students contact a local film school to discuss how 3-D movies are made. Have them report their findings after asking film school representatives the following questions:

- Are 3-D movies similar to Viewmaster images, where the same shot is taken with two different cameras? *(Yes. The anaglyph process involves filming the same scene with two cameras, printing the film in two different colors, and putting the images on top of each other. The first movie made this way was* The Power of Love, *released in 1922!)*
- Why do people need those red-and-blue glasses to see the 3-D image? *(With movies shot under the anaglyph process, the colored filters in the glasses draw each eye toward the other colored film, causing an overlap. Today's 3-D technology involves more advanced filters that aren't necessarily colored since those colored glasses often gave people headaches.)*

■ LOOKING AT THE ISSUES

Have you ever gotten a headache after reading for a long period of time? If so, you can blame *convergence.* The eye muscles must work harder to read since the material is close to the eyes. Have students respond to the following questions in a class discussion:

- Is reading in the dark a bad idea? *(The evidence is mixed. A British researcher found higher incidence of myopia—nearsightedness—with people who read a lot, while other professionals in the field believe that reading in dim light can strengthen the eye muscles. People who read in dim light can get headaches, but it does not seem to damage the eyes.)*
- Why do older people hold books out at arm's length to read? What aspect of their vision is deteriorating and causes them to do this? *(People gradually lose the ability to focus on near objects as they age. This condition is called presbyopia, and it is usually corrected with reading glasses.)*
- How can people avoid getting headaches after reading for a long time? Are there techniques for reading to minimize this phenomenon? *(People can sit up straight when reading so they do not subject their eyes to awkward focusing positions. Also, taking breaks when reading can keep the muscles from becoming fatigued.)*

► **convergence** A binocular depth cue related to the tension in the eye muscles when the eyes track inward to focus on objects close to the viewer.

If you look closely at the card containing the Viewmaster pictures, you will see that it seems to contain two identical pictures for each scene. Actually, these images differ slightly because they were taken by cameras a couple of feet apart, with slightly different vantage points. The Viewmaster projects the image taken by the left camera only to your left eye, and the image from the right camera only to your right eye. Your brain uses the different views to calculate distance and add depth to the scene.

Your brain does this easily because it uses the same technique all the time in real life. The two "cameras" are your two eyes. Because they are separated by a couple of inches in your head, your eyes receive slightly different views of any given scene. You can demonstrate this for yourself by creating the "finger sausage" described in Figure 10.6. The "sausage" appears to jump back and forth precisely because each of your eyes has its own distinct vantage point. Viewmasters exaggerate the effects of retinal disparity because the two cameras that took the photos were separated by more than the couple of inches separating your eyes. For another example of an image that relies on retinal disparity, try your luck at Figure 10.7. (Don't give up if you don't immediately see it!) Once you're able to produce the 3-D image, close or cover one eye. The effect will end, showing that this image was a creation of your two eyes interacting with your brain.

Retinal disparity is most effective when you are viewing items that are quite close to you. The farther away the object is, the less difference the placement of your eyes makes. The finger sausage jumps more when you hold your hands six inches in front of your face than it does when you extend your arms fully. Try it and you'll see.

The second binocular cue, **convergence,** translates tension in the muscles that control your eyeballs into information about distance. If you were able to draw a line from each eye to a distant object, those lines would be parallel. To maintain your focus on that object as it moved closer to you, your eyes would both have to swing inward. This movement puts tension on the muscles that control your eyeballs, and your brain notices that tension. The more tension that's required to keep both eyes aimed at the object, the closer the object must be. To feel this, focus on your finger with your arm fully extended. At this point, there is not much tension. However, as you continue to

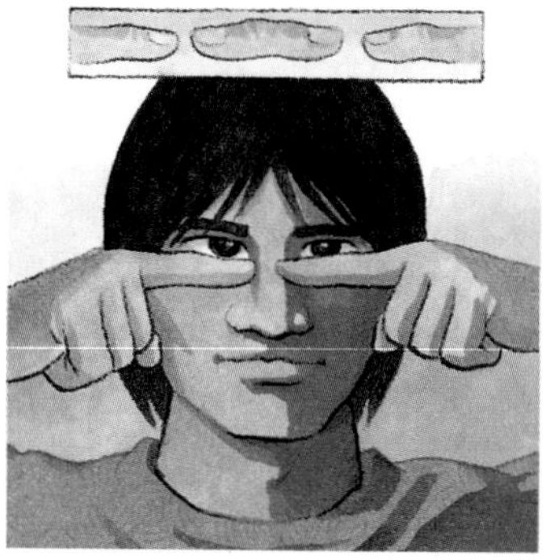

Figure 10.6 **The Binocular Finger Sausage** To see a bizarre illusion created by binocular vision, point your two index fingers together with about a half-inch separation. Look beyond them and you will see a finger sausage. By adjusting the distance separating your fingers or the distance between your fingers and your eyes, you can make the sausage grow and shrink. When you get tired of it, however, simply close one eye. Without binocular vision, there can be no sausage. Note that when you alternately close one eye and then the other, the gap between your fingers jumps from side to side. It's your brain's attempt to combine these two views that creates the sausage in the first place.

Demonstrating

RETINAL DISPARITY Have students roll a sheet of paper into a tube and raise it to their right eye, as if they were holding a telescope. Tell them to look through the tube, focusing on a blank wall in front of them. Next, have them hold their open left hand beside the tube and continue to focus ahead. The images received by the two eyes will fuse, and the hole in the tube will appear to be in the student's hand. They may need to slide the hand alongside the tube until they find the precise spot where the hole appears to go through the very center of the palm.

Source: Fisher, J. (1979). *Body magic.* New York: Stein & Day.

focus and slowly draw your finger closer to your nose, your eyes will "cross." The closer your finger gets, the stronger the tension will be. As you can see, convergence, like relative disparity, predicts depth most effectively at relatively short distances. Depth perception at longer distances relies mostly on the monocular cues, our next topic.

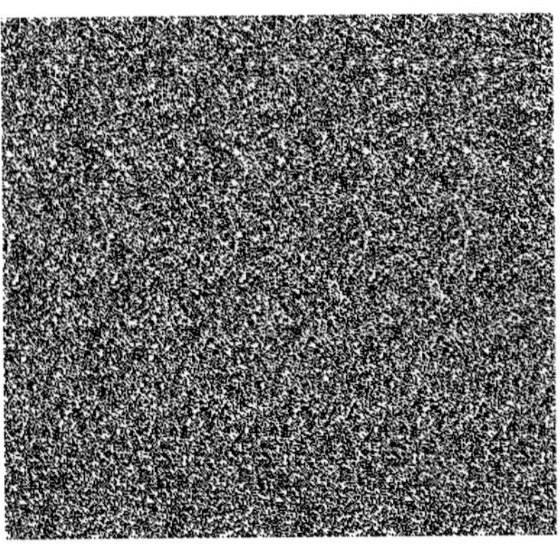

Figure 10.7 Random Dot Stereogram The ability to see an intriguing image in the stereogram to the left depends on retinal disparity. To make the image of the Greek letter psi appear (the image below shows what you are looking for), you must trick your eyes into thinking the paper is either twice as far, or half as far, away from your eyes as it really is. Try relaxing your eyes so they slowly swing outward. When you are at the proper depth, the dots projected to your right eye will align with the dots projected to your left eye to form the 3-D image. The dots that create the psi are among the other dots and become apparent only when your eyes line them up properly. If you have trouble, it simply means your eyes are difficult to trick; they want to focus at the proper depth!

Monocular Depth Cues

6. What cues let us calculate depth using only one eye, and how do they let us calculate depth?

People who have lost vision in one eye cannot use retinal disparity or convergence cues. But they can calculate depth accurately by means of the monocular cues, which continue to operate even if you close one eye. Artists use monocular cues to build a sense of depth into their paintings and drawings. Using them, a painter can "trick" our two-dimensional retinas into seeing three dimensions on a two-dimensional canvas! There are quite a number of these cues. We will discuss seven of them.

- ***Relative size*** One of our best available depth cues is the size of an object. If an object of known size appears large, it is probably close, and if an object appears small, it is probably distant. Passenger jets passing over your home at 35,000 feet appear so tiny it's hard to believe they hold full-size people inside.

Relative Size The fans in the foreground appear much larger than the baseball players or the more distant fans.

web ■ TEACHING TIP

Invite your students to visit the Magic Eye site at www.magiceye.com for additional examples of autostereograms.

Another comprehensive 3-D site is at www. vision3d.com/optical. It includes an extensive gallery of autostereo-grams; a step-by-step tutorial for learning to see them; a visual guide that explains how the brain decodes 3-D images; and information on visual disabilities, including a directory of optometrists and ophthalmologists.

trb At this point, you may wish to use **Application Activity:** ***Autostereograms*** (*Teacher's Resource Binder*, p. 10-1; **Handouts 10–7** and **10–8**).

F • Y • I

Two methods can be used to trick the eyes into seeing hidden images in the random dot autostereogram, featured in Figure 10.7 of the *Student Edition*.

- The **parallel method** involves focusing on a place beyond the autostereogram so the eyes are looking at the picture as if it were two different images.
- The **cross-viewing method** involves crossing the eyes while focusing on the autostereogram. This procedure is the reverse of the parallel method and uses the same principle, except that the area being focused on is in front of the stereogram rather than behind it.

trb At this point, you may wish to use **Application Activity:** ***Autostereograms*** (*Teacher's Resource Binder*, p. 10-1; **Handouts 10–7** and **10–8**).

Demonstrating

web 3-D VISION In a computer lab or as a homework assignment, have students try out some of the 3-D vision games found at www.vision3d.com.

- Eye Hop Game: www.vision3d.com/ehop.html
- Framing Game: www.vision3d.com/frame.html
- Reversible Figures: www.vision3d.com/optical/puzzles.html

MODULE 10

■ TEACHING TIPS

tr (1) A four-color transparency of Figure 10.8, Relative Motion, is available in the **Overhead Transparencies Set.**

(2) Students may feel that the monocular depth cues are more common sense than psychology. Emphasize that without these cues, many forms of entertainment—from art to television to movies—would lack the visual richness and beauty they possess. Monocular depth cues help make the world a more visually interesting place.

trb At this point, you may wish to use **Application Activity:** *Perceptual Organization* (*Teacher's Resource Binder,* p. 10-1; **Handout 10–3**) and **Application Activity:** *The Gestalt Law of Pragnanz* (*Teacher's Resource Binder,* p. 10-1; **Handout 10–5**).

F•Y•I

Many of these depth cues rely on previous knowledge to work. If we don't know already how large an object is, then the relative size cue becomes meaningless. Here is where top-down processing is most useful in helping us accurately understand the world.

Figure 10.8 **Relative Motion** In this example, the passenger is moving past a stable world. If she fixes her gaze on the bridge, objects behind it will appear to move forward. The farther away the object is, the more slowly it will appear to move. Objects in front of the fixation point appear to move backward.

But you know the plane's real size, and the fact that it appears small is one of the main ways you know it is far away. That same plane flying only 20 feet over your home would appear frighteningly large.

- ***Relative motion*** Apparent slowness indicates an object is distant (Figure 10.8). If a passenger jet passed 20 feet over your house, it not only would appear large but also would appear to be moving exceptionally fast. A plane flying high overhead seems to just barely crawl across the sky, yet you know it is moving several hundred miles an hour.
- ***Interposition*** This cue is so obvious that, unless you think about it, you may fail to realize its significance: Closer objects partially obstruct the view of more distant objects. You know a tree is in front of a house because it blocks your view of part of the house. If the tree were more distant than the house, the house would block your view of the tree. If you're thinking, "Well, duh," be impressed that your brain uses even very simple information to assess depth.

Interposition You know number 7 is closer to you than the other horses because number 7 partially blocks the view of the other horses.

- ***Relative height*** Distant objects appear higher in your field of vision than close objects do (Figure 10.9). Thus, trees on the far side of a lake will appear above the lake, which is closer to you.

Cooperative Learning

MONOCULAR DEPTH CUES Divide students into small groups and have them compile a portfolio of examples of monocular depth cues. Have them bring in their own magazines (or collect back issues from your library), look for examples of each type of monocular cue, and collect the examples in a scrapbook or on a poster. Each example should be accompanied by a note that identifies the type of monocular depth cue it exemplifies.

As another option, students can search the Internet for pictures that use monocular depth cues. Have them put together a PowerPoint presentation with these digital pictures.

Figure 10.9 **Relative Height** You know that the trees and houses are farther away than the lake because they are higher up in the drawing than the lake is.

Texture Gradient Individual blades of grass are visible in the foreground, but in the distance the grass looks like a smooth carpet.

- ***Texture gradient*** Distant objects usually have a much smoother texture than nearby objects. A grassy park that from a distance appears to be a smooth carpet of green shows more and more texture as you get closer to it. When you reach the park, you can see individual blades of grass and weeds (and perhaps bugs, twigs, and wads of discarded chewing gum as well!). The Black Hills in South Dakota appear uniformly "black" because of the very dark green color of the fir trees. You can't see the individual trees (or boulders or streams) until you draw close.
- ***Relative clarity*** Distant objects are less clear than nearby objects are. This cue mostly functions outdoors, where distant objects have a bluish, hazy appearance because of the moisture and dust in the air. Smog can exaggerate your perception of depth, causing land-

F•Y•I

Although we can see depth with only one eye, it is much more difficult to perceive depth with one eye closed than with both eyes open. Animals with eyes on the sides of their heads (birds, rabbits, and so forth) tend to compensate for their lack of depth perception by moving their heads a lot as they try to look around objects. This type of movement that creates depth is called **monocular parallax.**

■ **TEACHING TIP**

Cite an interesting example of depth cues working to create an illusion of reality by discussing the proportions of Michelangelo's sculpture *Pieta.* The *Pieta* depicts the Virgin Mary holding her dead son, Jesus. The figure of Christ is lifelike and proportional to reality. If the figure of Mary, however, were to rise to her feet and stand erect, she would be more than 7 feet tall! But to look at the sculpture, one would never notice that Mary was so much larger than her son.

tr A four-color transparency of Figure 10.9, Relative Height, is available in the **Overhead Transparencies Set.**

web For more information on the *Pieta* and a photo of the sculpture, see **www.eleganza.com/detailed/pieta.html**.

Cross-Curricular Connections

ART AND PHOTOGRAPHY Team-teach a lesson on monocular depth cues with your school's art teacher or an art professor from a local college. Students can create a realistic picture in any medium by using monocular depth cues, or they can create a picture that manipulates the monocular cues in an imaginative way.

MODULE 10

web ■ **APPLYING THE POINTS**
Explore how the use of linear perspective was first used in art in the 1400s in Florence, Italy, by browsing the Web site of Boston's Museum of Science at **www.mos.org/sln/Leonardo/ExploringLinearPerspective.html**. On this site, the rules of linear perspective are discussed and demonstrated in two works by Leonardo da Vinci—*The Annunciation* and a study for *The Adoration of the Magi*. In the second painting, you can see the faintly sketched lines da Vinci used to ensure that he employed linear perspective correctly.

■ **CHECKING FOR UNDERSTANDING**
Have students write a response to the following question about depth perception:

- Why can people with only one eye still see depth? *(Make sure students' responses reflect knowledge of monocular depth cues by listing each one discussed in the module and explaining how each one works.)*

Relative Clarity The distant mountains look blue and hazy because of dust and moisture in the atmosphere.

marks to appear farther away than they really are in a city beset by moist, dusty air. In the dry, clear American Southwest, however, distances appear compressed. You may drive over a hill and view mountains that seem close enough to reach for a lunchtime picnic. In reality, you may be lucky to get there by suppertime!

- ***Linear perspective*** Parallel lines seem to draw together in the distance. If you stand on a straight section of highway and look down the road, the shoulders of the road will seem to come ever closer to each other until they eventually merge at a point on the horizon.

Linear Perspective The lights leading the way to the runway seem to come together in the distance.

Enriching

web USING "LEONARDO'S WINDOW" Boston's Museum of Science offers a wonderful on-line lesson in which students can create a realistic and natural picture by using linear perspective. Called "Leonardo's Window," this lesson has students taping some acetate onto a window and tracing the lines found in the natural world outside to create a painting. For more instructions, see **www.mos.org/sln/Leonardo/UsingLeosWindow.html**.

Considered together, these seven monocular cues—relative size, relative motion, interposition, relative height, texture gradient, relative clarity, and linear perspective—and the binocular cues of retinal disparity and convergence provide a small but powerful arsenal of tools to help us judge depth. "Look before you leap" is good advice partially because distance cues allow you to determine how far away your landing spot is.

Motion Perception

7. What might cause us to perceive motion when nothing is moving?

Our ability to perceive motion is just as critical for survival as is our ability to perceive depth. In many ways, motion perception is the more complex task. To perceive motion accurately, you must interpret a large number of variables very rapidly. Not only does the object move, but so does your body. Swing your head from side to side, and you will see a great deal of motion, motion that you correctly conclude is a result of head movement rather than object movement.

Sometimes, however, our conclusions are wrong, and we perceive motion when there is none. These mistakes are not all bad. In fact, we rely on this illusion of movement to make movies "move." When we go to the cinema, we are able to "see" motion from a rapidly projected (24 frames per second) series of slightly varying still images. This illusion is called *stroboscopic motion,* an outcome you've used to your advantage if you've ever created a "flip movie," such as the one that we've begun in Figure 10.10.

A second and equally handy example of an apparent motion effect is the *phi phenomenon,* which creates the illusion of movement when fixed lights are turned on and off in sequence. Highway construction sites often use the phi phenomenon to create signs with arrows that appear to move, directing motorists to merge into a smaller number of lanes. Computerized marquee signs and even strings of holiday lights also use this illusion, as do sports scoreboards. A stadium scoreboard at the University of Northern Iowa, located in my town, is programmed to display a panther, the team mascot, leaping across the display area. The action seems so real that it's easy to forget that all you're really looking at is a whole bunch of light bulbs blinking on and off.

Figure 10.10 Movement That Isn't Movement—Courtesy of Stroboscopic Motion Each of these figures differs only slightly from the ones on either side of it. This is the first step to creating stroboscopic motion: Project each figure rapidly one after the other in order, and the resulting figure would appear to dance. (Source: Brittany Buchholtz)

Demonstrating

MOTION PERCEPTION Instruct your students to focus on a point straight ahead of them. Then, have them hold the forefinger of their right hand directly in front of them. Next, they should move the forefinger slowly to the right until they can no longer see it. (They should continue to stare ahead and keep the forefinger at eye level.) When they can no longer see their finger, they should wiggle it rapidly. They will see the movement.

trb At this point you may wish to use **Enrichment Lesson:** *Motion Detection* (*Teacher's Resource Binder,* p. 10-1).

web ■ **APPLYING THE POINTS**

(1) In 1834, a newfangled device was invented that simulated movement. Called the **zoetrope**, it consisted of a bowl with slits cut vertically all around the edge. A strip of drawings was inserted into the bottom of the bowl, which was then spun around. When a person looked at the drawings through the side of the bowl, they appeared to come to life and move! Have students create their own zoetropes by following the instructions on the Web site at **www.randommotion.com/html/zoe2.html**.

- Why does the eye perceive movement in a zoetrope? *(Because the slits simulate flashes of light, which is essential in perceiving motion. If you look over the top of the bowl of a zoetrope, the perception of movement disappears.)*

(2) Another motion perception device students can construct is a **thaumatrope.** By very quickly spinning a disk with different images on each side, students can see that the two images blend together as one. For instructions on constructing a thaumatrope, see **www.randommotion.com/html/thauma.html**.

- When were thaumatropes first invented? *(In the 1820s, but the device has Greek roots.)*
- Why do thaumatropes create the illusion of one image from two separate ones? *(Each image is projected onto the retina and creates an afterimage, which remains on the retina long enough to blend with the next image. What is popularly known as* persistence of vision *is actually* iconic memory storage.*)*

trb At this point, you may wish to use **Application Activity:** *The Oscillating Window Illusion* (*Teacher's Resource Binder,* p. 10-1) and **Application Activity:** *Kinesthetic Capture* (*Teacher's Resource Binder,* p. 10-1).

MODULE 10

F • Y • I

When Spanish conquistadors explored the southwestern United States, their perception was tricked as they looked down on the Colorado River from the rim of the Grand Canyon. What they perceived to be a small running creek about 6 feet wide was actually a raging river more than a mile wide! The perceptual cues from the top of the canyon fooled them into thinking the river was much smaller than it really was.

tr A four-color transparency of Figure 10.11, Size-Distance Relationships, is available in the **Overhead Transparencies Set**.

trb At this point, you may wish to use **Application Activity:** *Perceived Lunar Size* (*Teacher's Resource Binder*, p. 10-1; **Handout 10–9**).

Figure 10.11 **Size-Distance Relationships** Sometimes size and distance cues make it hard to perceive accurately. (top) The monocular depth cues of relative height and linear perspective force us to see the poodle on the right as more distant. We therefore think that this poodle must be bigger to produce the same size image at our eyes. In fact, all three are the same size. (bottom) This illustration of a trick called the Ponzo illusion works the same way as the poodles. Depth cues force us to see the top bar as more distant, and this assumption leads us to distort our interpretation of size. The bars are actually the same size!

Perceptual Constancy

8. What is the value of perceptual constancy in our lives?

One amazing quality of human perception is **perceptual constancy.** The world would be a much more frightening place if we did not have this ability. It is comforting to have a deep understanding that things will remain constant, despite changes in the distance, angle of view, or level of lighting of an object. There are three major kinds of constancy: *size constancy, shape constancy,* and *lightness constancy.*

Size Constancy

Recall from our discussion of depth perception that an object's size is one of the best cues we have in judging the distance of an object. This relationship between size and distance is one of the most fundamental in perception: Objects that appear big are close and objects that appear small are distant. What happens, however, when an object approaches you? Consider a friend coming into view at the end of the street. Because your friend is some distance away, she appears quite small. But then she appears to grow larger and larger. Is she getting bigger? Of course not! She is getting closer. That's the point of *size constancy:* We expect size to remain constant. Our knowledge of the world leads us to conclude that when the apparent size of an object changes, the actual size is not changing at all. What's changing is the distance.

You can use the flag demonstration on page 168 to explore this size-distance relationship. If you follow the instructions and watch for an afterimage to appear in the white square in your book, you will find that the image is quite small (about the size of the weird color version in the book). If you try the exercise again and watch for an afterimage on a wall across the room, the size of the image will be strikingly different. This time, you will see a very large flag, because your brain knows the wall is farther away than the page in your book. Since the actual image on your retina is exactly the same size in both cases (it was produced by looking at the same stimulus in your book), your brain *concludes the image on the wall must have been produced by a much bigger flag.* Only if the flag itself were larger could the retinal image be the same! Your brain has confused size and distance cues. Other examples of illusions based on a misperception of size and distance cues appear in Figure 10.11.

Demonstrating

RETINAL IMAGE SIZE Have students hold a hand in front of them at arm's length and move it toward their head, then away; they will perceive no change in size. (The size of the retinal image is, of course, changing.) Now, have students hold the forefinger of their left hand about 8 inches in front of their face and focus on it. They should then position their right hand at arm's length, past their left forefinger. While maintaining fixation on their left fingertip, they should move their right hand toward and away from their face. Although their focus should be on the left finger, they should also notice the image of the hand as it moves. It will change dramatically in size.

Source: Coren, S., Ward, L. M., & Enns, J. T. (1999). *Sensation and perception* (5th ed.). Fort Worth, TX: Harcourt Brace.

Consider how frightful the world would be without size constancy. As someone drew closer to you, you would have to stop and wonder whether that person were morphing into a giant before your eyes! Size constancy spares us such thoughts and allows us to be comfortable in our knowledge that the objects around us are not changing.

Shape Constancy

Shape constancy assures us that an object's shape has not changed even though our angle of view indicates it may have done so. As Figure 10.12 illustrates, a closed door viewed straight on appears rectangular, which, of course, it is. But, if someone begins to open the door, that rectangle will look like a trapezoid. Despite the changed appearance, you will have no doubts about the shape of the door. You instantly realize that it's the viewing angle that has changed and not the door itself.

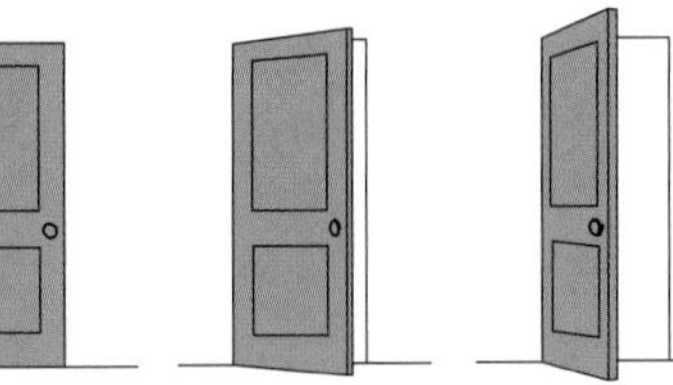

Figure 10.12 Shape Constancy As a door opens, its shape changes from a rectangle to a trapezoid. Shape constancy ensures that we will continue to perceive the door as a rectangle.

We automatically correct for changing angles in a number of different situations. The next time you have to sit off to the side when your teacher uses the overhead projector, note that the screen becomes a trapezoid. Your brain will automatically correct for the distorted angle, and you will perceive the projected images as though you were viewing the objects straight on. Shape constancy lets you make these automatic corrections.

Lightness Constancy

The third type of constancy, *lightness constancy,* gives us the ability to see an object as having a constant level of lightness no matter how the lighting conditions change. If you look at a sheet of typing paper in bright sunlight, it appears blazingly white; view the same sheet in a dimly lit room, and it appears gray. Has the paper changed? Of course not. We know that the "white" paper stays constant no matter what the lighting conditions are. We can make this adjustment even if we are outside, reading a page that is half in sunlight and half in shade. Without lightness constancy, this experience would be quite bizarre.

Perceptual Set

9. How does perceptual set affect our everyday interpretations of sensory experiences?

Have you ever stopped to consider just how important your expectations are in any given situation? What happens in a class if you expect a teacher to be boring? If your favorite band is giving a concert, and you expect it to be wonderful, how much does that influence your percep-

► **perceptual constancy** Perceiving the size, shape, and lightness of an object as unchanging, even as the retinal image of the object changes.

Demonstrating

COLOR AND LIGHTNESS CONSTANCY Bring in two pairs of men's dress socks—one pair dark blue and one pair black. In dim light, have students identify what color the socks are. Do the same in brighter light. Although the task may be easier in the brighter light, the correct match is still not definitive until both colors are compared with each other. Sometimes blue and black are impossible to distinguish in dim light, which is why getting dressed in the dark can often bring about mismatches when choosing dark socks or shoes to wear!

■ **JOURNAL WRITING**

Invite students to use the following questions or ideas as springboards for entries in their psychology journals:

- How have you been affected by sticking falsely to your perceptual set?
- Imagine for a moment what life would be like without perceptual constancy. Describe a "day in the life" of someone who lacked the ability to perceive constancy.

trb At this point, you may wish to use Application Activity: *Perceptual Set* (*Teacher's Resource Binder,* p. 10-1).

■ **TEACHING TIP**

Have students imagine how disturbing the world would be if we suddenly lost our ability to perceive constancy. What if objects seemed to grow larger as they approached? What if objects appeared to change shape when they moved? What if color became different in different levels of light? Their "monster" little brother would be a lot scarier if he grew and changed shapes and colors right before their eyes!

tr A four-color transparency of Figure 10.12, Shape Constancy, is available in the Overhead Transparencies Set.

MODULE 10

trb tr ■ TEACHING TIP
A black-line master for Figure 10.13, Perceptual Set, is available in the **Black-Line Masters Appendix** of the *Teacher's Resource Binder.*

■ CHECKING FOR UNDERSTANDING
Here are several ways to assess students' comprehension of module concepts:

- Assign any or all of the journal questions or prompts as an in-class writing assessment.
- Divide the students into groups and give each one a journal question prompt. Have groups present their answers to the class. Either you or students outside the group should correct any misconceptions in the responses.

■ LOOKING AT THE ISSUES
Although there is little to no scientific evidence to support subliminal persuasion, the belief in it abounds. Have students discuss the appeal of believing that subliminal messages can influence behavior. *(Subliminal messages promise maximum benefit with minimum work; they may offer another avenue of hope for people seeking to quit bad habits, such as smoking, overeating, and gambling.)*

trb At this point, you may wish to use **Critical Thinking Activity:** *Reverse Speech and Speech Complementarity* (*Teacher's Resource Binder,* p. 10-1) and **Enrichment Lesson:** *Subliminal Persuasion* (*Teacher's Resource Binder,* p. 10-1).

Figure 10.13 **Perceptual Set** Cover the side pictures and ask a few friends what they see in the center. You can influence them to see the saxophone player by first having them glance briefly at the picture on the left. Similarly, a glance at the picture on the right will drive them toward interpreting the center picture as a woman's face. (From Shepard, 1990.)

tion of the concert? If you've grown to really like a particular TV show, do your expectations that the show will be good affect how you'll react to tonight's episode?

Expectations such as these produce **perceptual set,** perhaps the clearest example yet of top-down processing. This mindset can profoundly affect our view of the world. Look, for example, at Figure 10.13. You can predispose a person toward seeing either a saxophone player or a woman's face in the middle photo by showing either the left or the right picture first (Boring, 1930). If you show the unambiguous (clear) saxophone player first, the person will be more likely to see the saxophone player in the ambiguous center drawing. If you show the woman's face first, the person will be more likely to see the woman's face in the center drawing.

This "power of suggestion" produced by perceptual set influences us in many ways. It may account for multiple false reports of unidentified flying objects, for example, after people hear a report of one such false incident. The first report creates a perceptual set that influences what other people perceive (see also Thinking Critically: Extrasensory Perception, page 198). Perceptual set also accounts for reports of "subliminal messages" in the media. When I was a college student in the 1960s, my friends and I wiled away many hours playing Beatles music backward on our turntables. We were listening for messages about band member Paul McCartney, who was inaccurately rumored to be dead. We were finding them, too. Once you've determined that the recording *might* say "Paul is dead," it is almost impossible *not* to hear the message in the weird sounds produced when you play recorded music backward. We hear the message we expect to hear. If we'd started with the perceptual set that the ambiguous segments would say "Dolls eat bread," that is what we would have forever heard.

Perceptual set is often guided by **schemas,** concepts or mental frameworks that help us to organize the world. One of our strangest schemas is for faces. We are so driven to create faces that we tend to see them everywhere (Figure 10.14).

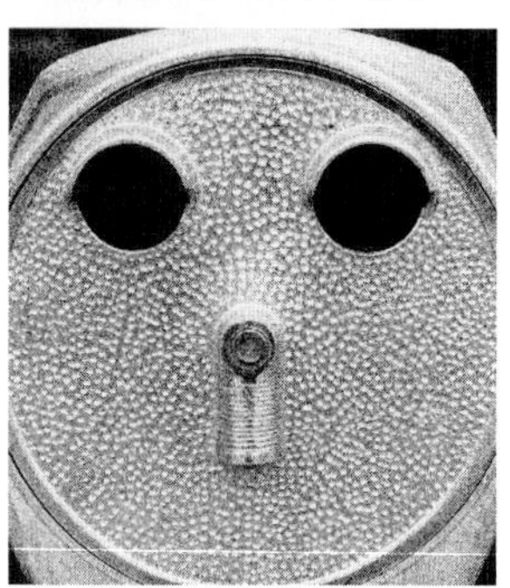

Figure 10.14 **Face Schemas** We have such a strong schema for faces that we tend to see them everywhere.

Demonstrating

PERCEPTUAL SET WITH SOUND Ask your class to shout out the answers to the following questions. "What do these letters spell?" (Write *folk* on the board.) "How about these?" (Write *croak.*) "And what do these letters spell?" (Write *soak.*) "What do we call the white of an egg?" Students will respond "yolk" even though the answer is "egg white."

trb At this point, you may wish to use any of the activities suggested in **Application Activities:** *Perceptual Set* (*Teacher's Resource Binder,* p. 10-1).

Context

 10. How does context influence our perceptions?

Context—the setting or environment in which we interpret sensory stimuli—also affects what we perceive (Figure 10.15). During a visit to Disney World years ago, my wife and I had almost worked our way to the very front of the line for Space Mountain when the ride malfunctioned. To fix the problem, the repair crew turned on all the lights, and we had an opportunity to see the entire roller coaster, normally enshrouded in darkness. We watched as technicians checked the ride and sent an empty car around the entire circuit. Shortly thereafter, they again doused the lights and we were able to board. Somehow, the experience with the lights spoiled our ride. The mystery was gone, and we perceived Space Mountain much differently than we would have in the absence of the malfunction.

Figure 10.15 **Context Effects** How we perceive the size of this fish depends on the context in which we view it. If you cover the man, the fish will fit in the pan. If you cover the hand, this man has caught a real whopper!

Context can have a remarkably subtle effect. One experiment showed that music established a context that could influence a listener's definition of a spoken homophone (two words that are pronounced the same but have different definitions). Listeners who heard sad music were likely to hear *mourning,* not *morning* and *die,* not *dye* (Halberstadt & others, 1995).

Illusions

 11. What makes perceptual illusions so interesting?

Perceptual illusions fascinate almost everyone. We are usually superb at decoding the nuances of the world around us. But sometimes—most often under fairly elaborate conditions—we are "tricked" into misinterpreting sensory stimuli. Psychologists study illusions because they provide clues about how our sensory and perceptual systems work. In this section we will look at several illusions. In each case, some basic perceptual principles help create the illusions. As you consider each illusion, see if you can link it to one or more of the principles you've read about in this module.

▶ **perceptual set** A mental predisposition to perceive something one way and not another.

▶ **schemas** Concepts or mental frameworks that organize and interpret information.

▶ **context** The setting or environment in which we interpret sensory stimuli.

Cross-Curricular Connections

BIOLOGY AND PHYSICS

- Team up with a biology teacher to create a lesson on sensation and perception. The biology teacher can present information on the sensory systems while you focus on perceptual principles related to those systems.
- Team up with a physics teacher to create a lesson on the physics of perception, since many perceptual principles and visual illusions rely on physics for the explanations.

■ **APPLYING THE POINTS**

Have students imagine how context could create different perceptions in the following situations:

- if their favorite rock band held a concert in the school gym instead of an arena
- if they had a date and their grandparents came along for the ride
- if English class were held at someone's house

trb tr At this point, you may wish to use **Application Activity:** *Context Effects* (*Teacher's Resource Binder,* p. 10-1; **Transparency Master 10–1**) and **Application Activity:** *Context and Anagrams* (*Teacher's Resource Binder,* p. 10-1; **Handout 10–11**).

F•Y•I

Research on context shows that situations can have a powerful effect on behavior. Point out these examples:

- Studying should not occur while lying in bed. Students who do this often associate studying with sleeping since they study where they sleep. For effective studying, a designated place should be created where all the necessary supplies are available.
- Sleep researchers also suggest designating the bed for sleeping, instead of watching TV or reading, for people who suffer from insomnia. People can associate the bed with those activities rather than with sleeping, which may hinder their ability to fall asleep easily.

trb At this point, you may want to use **Enrichment Lesson:** *Context and Perception* (*Teacher's Resource Binder,* p. 10-1).

trb ■ **TEACHING TIP**

For information on how to obtain visual illusions for your classroom for display or demonstration purposes, refer to listings provided in **Enrichment Lesson:** *Resources for Obtaining Visual Illusions* (*Teacher's Resource Binder,* p. 10-1).

MODULE 10

trb tr ■ TEACHING TIP

A black-line master for Figure 10.16, The Müller-Lyer Illusion, is available in the **Black-Line Masters Appendix** of the *Teacher's Resource Binder.*

web ■ LOOKING AT THE ISSUES

The following Web sites offer information about scientific testing of psychic phenomena:

- The James Randi Educational Foundation homepage at **www.randi.org**
- The Rhine Research Center Web site at **www. rhine.org**
- Frequently Asked Questions About Parapsychology at **www.psiresearch.org/para1.htm**

After searching these sites, have students discuss the following questions:

- Why are psychics generally unwilling to be scientifically tested?
- Do you think paranormal phenomena is a worthy scientific subject to study? Why or why not?

trb At this point, you may wish to use **Evaluation Activity:** *Testing for ESP* (*Teacher's Resource Binder*, p. 10-1) and **Enrichment Lesson:** *Belief in ESP* (*Teacher's Resource Binder*, p. 10-1).

■ MULTICULTURAL CONNECTIONS

Teaching skepticism about ESP should be tempered so as not to alienate students with various religious beliefs and experiences, such as beliefs in angels, dreams as visions, and so forth. The goal of this skepticism should be to avoid scam artists rather than to dispel particular belief systems.

Thinking Critically

Extrasensory Perception

You've seen the stories about **extrasensory perception (ESP).** Some people claim perceptions beyond the capabilities of our sensory systems. These extrasensory powers break down into three specific areas:

- *precognition*—a knowledge of future events.
- *telepathy*—an ability to exchange thoughts with another person.
- *clairvoyance*—an ability to "see" distant events.

Perhaps you've talked to people who believe they've had an ESP experience. Perhaps you think you have had one yourself! These beliefs are widespread, with several surveys showing that at least half of a variety of populations believe in ESP (Blackmore, 1997; Gallup & Newport, 1991; *George,* 1996; Nishizawa, 1996).

Belief in ESP sustains a billion-dollar industry (Nisbet, 1998). Infomercials by psychics are a staple for late-night and cable TV broadcasters, and advertisements by psychics fill the back pages of countless magazines and *National Enquirer*–type newspapers. Some police departments now call on psychics to help locate missing persons and attempt to solve other difficult crimes. Even former First Lady Nancy Reagan regularly consulted with her astrologer in an effort to protect her husband—structuring his personal schedule according to the astrologer's recommendations. If this sort of thing is good enough for the president of the United States, should we accept such claims, too, or at least give them serious consideration?

Most psychologists would say that yes, we should consider claims of ESP, and some scientists have investigated such claims. Remember, though, that one of the hallmarks of scientific thinking is skepticism. Scientists are much more likely to begin by assuming the claims are false than to assume they are correct. This doesn't mean scientists are somehow "mean" or cynical, only that they require proof before accepting a claim.

It is also true that scientists and the general public may have different standards for evidence. Scientists are unlikely to accept cause-and-effect claims about ESP without *experimental* evidence. The public tends to be impressed with undocu-

Figure 10.16 **The Müller-Lyer Illusion** Which line appears longer—segment AB or segment BC?

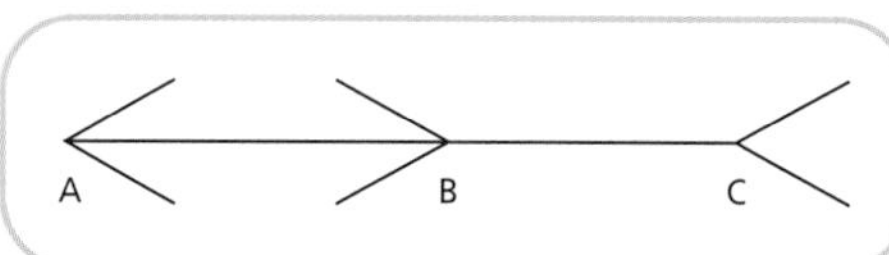

Puzzle 1 This famous puzzle, the Müller-Lyer illusion, has been around since the late 1800s. You will see the illusion if you compare line segment AB with line segment BC in Figure 10.16. Does one appear longer? To most people the lines seem about the same, but if you measure them, you will see that AB is quite a bit longer! There are alternative explanations for this illusion, as there are for most illusion puzzles. One possibility, illustrated in Figure 10.17, is that we have

Enriching

Over a period of time, have students collect horoscopes or other precognitive predictions from publications found in supermarket checkout aisles. Have them record the predictions and compare them with what actually did occur. Students can do this by checking the newspapers for reports related to the predictions or keeping a journal of what happens in their lives to check against their newspaper horoscopes. What students will likely find is that predictions made by astrologers are usually ambiguous enough to apply to multiple situations, which begs the question—can a prediction that applies to many outcomes really be considered accurate if it comes true?

trb At this point, you may wish to use **Analysis Activities:** *ESP Tricks* (*Teacher's Resource Binder*, p. 10-1).

mented *case studies*—single reports of psychic phenomena that they may have read about or personally experienced. When appropriate scientific controls are established in research on ESP, special psychic abilities disappear. No conclusive scientific evidence supports the claims of ESP.

What accounts for this major difference between public opinion and scientific opinion? The answer is that we often misinterpret *correlations,* which are statements of how two events are related. Consider this strange coincidence: I'm thinking about my friend and he suddenly calls. I am likely to notice that these two events—my thoughts and the phone call—occurred together, be impressed with the timing, and perhaps assume I have a psychic ability. But the fact that these two events were correlated does *not* mean that my thoughts caused my friend to call. What I am failing to notice is the number of times I think of my friend and he doesn't call, and the number of times he calls when I haven't been thinking about him. These instances are much less likely to stand in my memory, because they seem much more ordinary. Similarly, you may be impressed when you dream about an event that then occurs the next day. That's impressive, but when you consider how often your dreams do not become reality the next day, this single event seems much more likely to be a simple, quite ordinary coincidence.

If such events were not mere coincidences, shouldn't those who claim to have psychic abilities be able to exercise their powers more reliably? Why can't they demonstrate psychic powers in experiments? Why can't they provide adequate warnings before floods or tornadoes? Why can't they locate missing persons? And, most telling, why are these people with ESP always on TV asking for our credit card numbers instead of picking the winning lottery numbers and living off the proceeds?

▶ **extrasensory perception (ESP)** The controversial claim that perception can occur apart from sensory input.

learned to interpret arrowheads at the ends of a line as an indication of distance, which leads to a misapplication of size-distance relationships.

Puzzle 2 In the next famous illusion, the Ames room, two people seem to change size as they switch positions in the room. A person who appears small on one side of the room

Figure 10.17 **Why Do We See the Müller-Lyer Illusion?** One suggested explanation (Gregory, 1968) for the illusion is that we use the arrows at the ends of the lines to help judge distance and, thus, length.

■ TEACHING TIPS

trb tr (1) A black-line master for Figure 10.17, Why Do We See the Müller-Lyer Illusion?, is available in the **Black-Line Masters Appendix** of the *Teacher's Resource Binder.*

(2) Use the Thinking Critically box (*Student Edition* pages 198–199) to reinforce the idea that correlation does not mean causation, reviewing an important lesson from Module 2. Students should be reminded that two events that occur together should not lead one to conclude that those events have a cause-and-effect relationship.

V At this point, you may wish to show **Videocassette:** ***Scientific American Frontiers,*** **Second Edition, Segment 3: "Water, Water Everywhere"** (*Teacher's Resource Binder,* p. 10-1).

■ APPLYING THE POINTS

Another illusion for students to explore is the Wundt-Jastrow illusion. Why the illusion works remains a mystery. Students can formulate their own hypotheses about its explanation, and they can design appropriate experimental tests to be presented in class.

trb At this point, you may wish to use **Application Activity:** ***Wundt-Jastrow Illusion*** (*Teacher's Resource Binder,* p. 10-1; **Handout 10–13**).

■ APPLYING THE POINTS

Have students use library and Internet resources to research techniques filmmakers employ to create special effects. For example, when students compare how the *Star Wars* trilogy was made compared with the *Lord of the Rings* trilogy, they discover the impact of computer-generated images on filmmaking. Use the following questions to help students discuss their findings:

- How can actors appear taller or shorter than they are in reality, like in the film series *Lord of the Rings*?
- How are the special effects techniques different today than in the past? How has computer technology changed the way people make films?

trb At this point, you may wish to use Technology Application Activity: *PsychSim:* "Visual Illusions" (*Teacher's Resource Binder*, p.10-1).

The Ames Room

is suddenly huge on the other side (see photos above). Figure 10.20 (page 201) reveals the secret. The room is distorted. When we view the room from the perspective of the peephole (as the camera did), however, we assume it is a standard, rectangular room. (Why wouldn't it be?) Therefore we perceive as larger the person who is in fact closer. Our minds don't let us see that person as closer because that would defy what we have learned about the structure of normal rooms.

Puzzle 3 Do you see the light red ring in Figure 10.18? Well, it isn't there. If you look at a section of the "ring" that falls in between the black objects and cover up the black lines, you will see that the area is just as red as the rest of the page. We perceive the red ring because of the Gestalt grouping principles. Our brains try to find closure for all those gaps in the black lines by seeing a ring that connects them all.

Figure 10.18 **An Illusion Based on the Gestalt Principle of Closure**

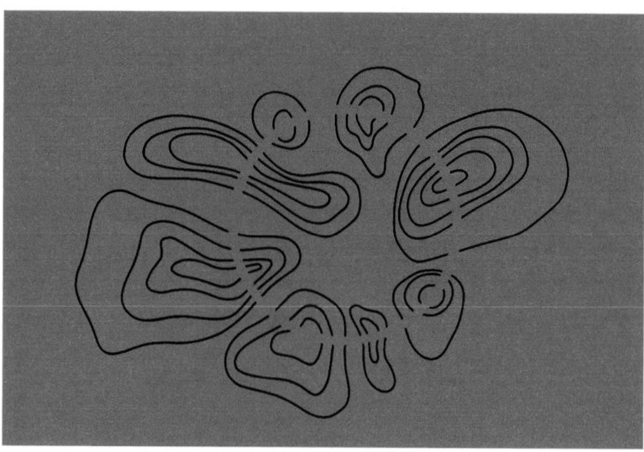

Puzzle 4 The two illusions in Figure 10.19 depend on shadow and light. Notice in Figure 10.19(a) that there appears to be a ripple. Even though this pattern is printed on flat paper, it is very difficult to interpret it as a flat drawing. Note that the ridges change quite impressively if you turn the book upside down. The area of the drawing that had represented a valley now represents a hill! This reversal happens because we assume that light normally comes from above (Hoffman, 1998). You can see a similar light and shadow effect in Figure 10.19(b). The smaller circle in the upper right appears to bulge out from the background. The smaller circle at the lower left appears to dip in. This happens because we perceive the light source to be coming from above. If you turn the diagram upside down, the bulge and the dip reverse themselves, conforming to our assumption that a light is coming from above.

Perception is the road we follow to make sense of the world. The constant stream of sensory input that bombards us is meaningless unless we can interpret it properly. We accomplish this so effortlessly that we are usually aware only of our rare mistakes. Perceptive, aren't we?

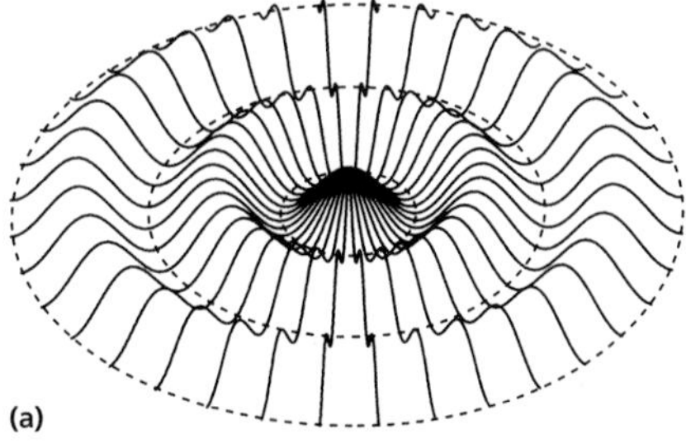
(a)

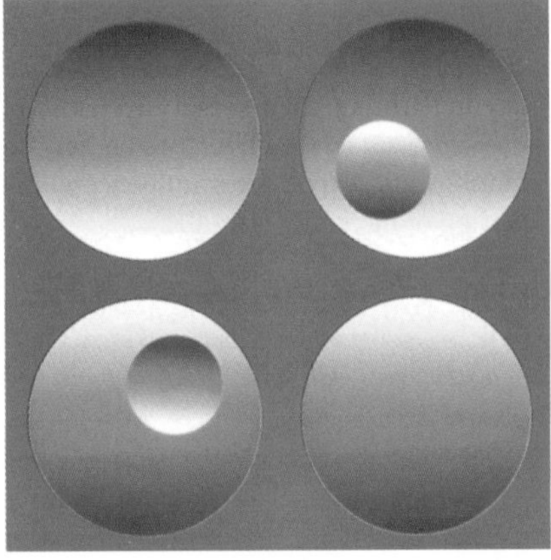
(b)

Figure 10.19 **Two Illusions Based on Our Assumptions About Light**

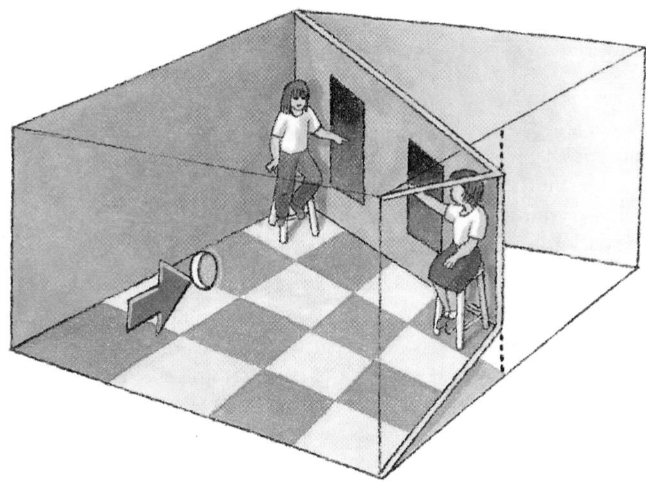

Figure 10.20 **Distorted Size** This view of the specially designed Ames room explains the puzzle on page 200. It violates our expectations for how a room should be constructed, and we're tricked into thinking the size of the girls has changed, rather than the dimensions and angles of the room.

■ TEACHING TIP

A four-color transparency of Figure 10.19, Two Illusions Based on Our Assumptions About Light, is available in the **Overhead Transparencies Set.**

■ JOURNAL WRITING

Invite students to use the following questions as springboards for entries in their psychology journals:

- Many of the activities and demonstrations in this module are designed to trick your perceptions. Have you been tricked? What were some of the more memorable tricks you fell for, and how did you feel about falling for them?
- Have you ever had an encounter with ESP? Describe your experience. What might be a scientific explanation for your experience?

Close

To sum up this module's contents, pose the following question to your students:

- This module has mainly been about how our perceptions aren't necessarily realistic interpretations of the sensory input we receive from the world. What implications will this knowledge have on your lives?

Make sure students understand that perception protects people from many types of harm, provides meaningful information about their place in the world, and helps them navigate through physical and social situations with greater ease. Everyone should be sensitive to the limitations of their perceptions, but they should not ignore the benefits that perceptual cues offer them each and every day.

MODULE 10

Checking the Points

TEACHING TIPS

web (1) The book companion site for *Thinking About Psychology* at **www.worthpublishers.com/thinkingaboutpsych** contains a module quiz, flashcards of key terms and people, as well as other student activities and resources for this module. You will also find PowerPoint lectures, a quiz grade book, and other teaching resources by logging on as an instructor.

trb **tr** (2) At this point, you may wish to use **Critical Thinking Activity:** *Fact or Falsehood?* (*Teacher's Resource Binder*, p. 10-1; **Handout 10–1**) to review with the class concepts about perception. You may either read items from the handout aloud or use the handout as a transparency with an overhead projector. Have a volunteer read the first item and provide a response. Ask students who agree with the response to find a passage in the text that supports it and read it aloud. If students contest the response, have them use the text to find a passage that supports their answer and read it aloud. Once consensus is reached, repeat the process with the next item on the handout.

REVIEW

Module 10: Perception

What's the Point?

Our perceptions are our interpretations of the stimuli coming in from the world around us. We process these stimuli in two ways: by *bottom-up processing,* which focuses on the raw material that enters through our sensory systems; and by *top-down processing,* which focuses on how our expectations and experiences influence our interpretation of incoming stimuli.

Organizational Principles

1. *What important contribution did the Gestalt psychologists make to the study of human perception?*

   The Gestalt psychologists stressed that the whole is more than the sum of its parts. They believed that research that attempts to break human perception into its basic parts—the individual stimuli—misses the point that humans tend to perceive things in meaningful units.

2. *How do people determine figure and ground, and why is this important?*

   We tend to organize our perception of our environment into a figure and the surrounding ground. The figure is the prominent object (or sound, or taste, and so on) and the ground consists of everything else surrounding the figure (the background).

3. *Describe the principles of similarity, proximity, closure, and continuity.*

   Similarity is our tendency to group items that appear to be the same (people wearing the same uniforms must be a team). *Proximity* is the tendency to group items that are near one another (basketball players sitting on a bench must be members of the same team, even if some of them are wearing warm-ups that partially cover the uniform). *Closure* is the tendency to close gaps and perceive a broken image as a whole, not as a collection of parts (bricks set close together on the ground are a path or a road). *Continuity* is the tendency to assume that apparent movement will continue in the way that it started (your dish of spaghetti has lots of long strands with hidden parts; it is not a pile of short pieces).

Depth Perception

4. *What is depth perception, and how does it affect our lives?*

   Depth perception is our ability to judge distance and see the world in three dimensions. To judge depth, your brain uses binocular cues (those that compare information from your two eyes) and monocular cues (those that require information from one eye only). Evidence indicates that some amount of depth perception is present at birth, but experience polishes our ability to perceive depth. Without this ability, we would be unable to function in a three-dimensional world.

5. *What are the two major binocular depth cues, and how do they help us perceive depth?*

   The two major binocular cues are retinal disparity and convergence. *Retinal disparity* is a term describing the slight difference in the images you see with the retinas in your left and right eyes. This difference occurs because your two eyes are separated by

Meeting Individual Needs

Although the terms in this module aren't new, their use in this context may be. Help students who are overwhelmed by the number of terms in this module by having them make flashcards of the concept terms. Each flashcard should focus on one perceptual cue and its description.

- **Independent Learners** To help students link the terms with perceptual cues, have them categorize the flashcard terms by topics presented in the text.
- **Cooperative Learners** Have students work in small groups to categorize flashcard terms by topics. Then, have the groups use their flashcard categories to create a graphic organizer about perception. Groups may present and explain their graphic organizers to the entire class.

about two inches, giving you two slightly different views of the world. Your brain compares these two images and makes assumptions about distance. *Convergence* is a binocular cue that translates the amount of tension in your eye muscles into information about the distance of an object you are viewing. Your brain knows that as you focus on nearby objects, your eyes turn toward your nose and the tension in your eye muscles increases.

6. *What cues let us calculate depth using only one eye, and how do they let us calculate depth?*

   Seven monocular cues—relative size, relative motion, interposition, relative height, texture gradient, relative clarity, and linear perspective—allow us to calculate depth using only one eye. *Relative size* tells us that if we know the size of the object, it will appear small when it is distant and large when it is close. *Relative motion* tells us that an object of known size that appears to be moving slowly is probably at a distance from us. *Interposition* (or overlap) tells us that nearby objects obstruct our view of faraway objects. *Relative height* tells us that objects that appear high in our field of vision are farther away than objects that appear low in that field. *Texture gradient* tells us that the texture of faraway objects is smoother than the texture of similar objects near to us. *Relative clarity* tells us that fuzzy, cloudy things tend to be more distant than objects we can see in clear detail. *Linear perspective* tells us that parallel lines will appear to join together in an upside-down V in the distance.

Motion Perception

7. *What might cause us to perceive motion when nothing is moving?*

   Perceiving motion is a complicated process, because our brain must sort out so many irrelevant movements—those of our own body as well as those in the world around us. Our brain sometimes fails to sort out all this information properly and perceives movement when nothing is really moving. This happens, for example, when we see a series of still images in rapid succession, which appears to be a continuously moving "movie," thanks to the principle of stroboscopic motion. The phi phenomenon is responsible for the illusion of movement produced by lights blinking off and on in a preselected pattern, such as with signs that show animation.

Perceptual Constancy

8. *What is the value of perceptual constancy in our lives?*

   Perceptual constancy—our ability to trust that the size, shape, and lightness of objects will not change—gives us security in assessing the world around us. We also rely on size constancy to perceive distance: We know that objects remain the same size; therefore if they appear to grow larger or smaller, we must be seeing the effects of distance.

Perceptual Set

9. *How does perceptual set affect our everyday interpretations of sensory experiences?*

   Perceptual set is a predisposition, based on past experiences, that leads us to perceive something one way and not another. Part of those expectations consist of schemas, mental concepts of how things should be. For example, if your perceptual set contains a schema that expects dogs to bark and bite, you will be afraid of any dog you meet, no matter how gentle it is. If your schema expects dogs to be your best friends, you will approach dogs that you meet in a welcoming, friendly manner. Perceptual set is somewhat like a pair of glasses that changes the color of things that you view.

MODULE 10

Using the Test Bank

The *Test Bank* that accompanies this textbook offers a wide variety of questions in different formats and levels of complexity. Use the software to construct whole tests or to integrate standardized questions into teacher-made tests.

Self-Test Answers

Multiple-Choice Questions

1. a, 2. d, 3. a, 4. a

Context

10. *How does context influence our perceptions?*

Context—the setting in which we receive sensory stimuli—causes us to interpret stimuli differently, depending on where we are and what we have recently experienced. If you hear a certain tone in an amusement park, you may interpret that as a signal that you won a prize in a game. If you hear that same tone in school, you may interpret the sound as a signal that it is time to go to lunch.

Illusions

11. *What makes perceptual illusions so interesting?*

Our senses play "tricks" on us in the form of illusions. Understanding the conditions that allow these illusions to occur teaches us a lot about our normal sensory and perceptual systems. Some of the more famous illusions studied by psychologists are the Müller-Lyer illusion, the Ames room, and other illusions based on our knowledge of grouping and the normal patterns of light.

Key Terms

perception, p. 183
gestalt, p. 183
figure-ground, p. 184
grouping, p. 185
depth perception, p. 186
visual cliff, p. 186
binocular cues, p. 187
monocular cues, p. 187
retinal disparity, p. 187
convergence, p. 188
perceptual constancy, p. 194
perceptual set, p. 196
schema, p. 196
context, p. 197
extrasensory perception (ESP), p. 198

Self-Test

Multiple-Choice Questions

Choose the *best* answer for each of the following questions.

1. Mrs. Green is organizing the school library so that the history books will be in one section, all the science books in another, all the language books in a third, and so on. She believes students will find books in this arrangement more easily than if she simply alphabetizes everything by author. Mrs. Green is organizing the books according to the principle of
   a. similarity. c. closure.
   b. contiguity. d. relative disparity.

2. Annie recently won a prize for painting the best landscape in all the art classes in school. She probably used all the following depth cues except one to create her realistic painting of the landscape. Which of the following cues would NOT be used in a painting?
   a. Relative size c. Linear perspective
   b. Interposition d. Convergence

3. Paolo injured his left eye when he was a child, and he now is blind in that eye. Paolo cannot use ______________ cues to judge depth.
   a. binocular c. gestalt
   b. monocular d. context

4. Kim's team was thrilled when they won the regional soccer championship. They all cheered when the final scores, the words "Congratulations Blue Team!", and some happy faces rolled across the scoreboard. These images appeared to move because of the ______________ effect.
   a. phi phenomenon c. Ames room
   b. stroboscopic motion d. Müller-Lyer

Alternative Assessment/Portfolio Project

trb VISUAL ILLUSIONS ON THE WORLD WIDE WEB Students can create a portfolio of examples of visual illusions by using sites from the Internet and print media. The portfolio will not only serve as a worthwhile project, but it will also give students a study tool for the module test. By completing this project, students should be able to identify monocular depth cues and visual illusions, as well as explain why these principles work to fool our vision. For details, see *Teacher's Resource Binder*, p.10-1.

Use the general rubric provided in **Handout 10–15** in the *Teacher's Resource Binder* to evaluate the portfolios. Adapt the rubric to suit your needs.

5. David, who lives on a farm, viewed an abstract sculpture and thought it was a chicken. Sean, who lives in the city, viewed the same sculpture and thought it was a motorcycle. David and Sean apparently had different ________________ when they viewed the sculpture.
   a. convergences
   b. binocular cues
   c. monocular cues
   d. perceptual sets

6. Maria is very worried that her grandmother in Argentina will soon be ill, because Maria had a dream that showed her grandmother in a hospital bed. Maria apparently believes in
   a. schemas. c. telepathy.
   b. precognition. d. illusions.

Matching Terms and Definitions

7. For each definition, choose the *best* matching term from the list that follows.

Definition

a. The perceptual tendency to form a group of things that are like each other.
b. The monocular depth cue that tells us that objects that are fuzzy or cloudy are farther away than things we can see in clear detail.
c. The perceptual tendency to organize stimuli into understandable groups.
d. The controversial claim that perception can occur without any sensory input.
e. The binocular cue that judges depth by comparing the two slightly different images that result from the different information received by the retinas in the right and left eyes, which are separated by about two inches.
f. The organization of the visual field into objects that stand out from their surroundings.
g. The perceptual tendency to form a group of things that are close together.
h. A laboratory device for testing depth perception in infants and young animals.
i. The perceptual tendency to close the gaps in images or other perceptions so that we can perceive the whole, not the individual parts.

Term

(1) visual cliff
(2) proximity
(3) figure-ground
(4) similarity
(5) retinal disparity
(6) grouping
(7) continuity
(8) ESP
(9) closure
(10) relative motion
(11) relative clarity
(12) texture gradient

Fill-in-the-Blank Questions

8. ________________ is the process of organizing and interpreting sensory information.

9. ________ ________ processing focuses on the raw material that enters through our sensory systems; ________ ________ processing focuses on how our expectations and experiences influence our interpretation of incoming stimuli.

10. The principle of ________ ________ tells us that objects do not change size, shape, or color.

Brief Essay Question

11. What was the main contribution that the Gestalt psychologists made to the study of perception? How did the Gestalt view differ from the approach Wilhelm Wundt used to study perception? Answer these questions in one paragraph of four to five sentences.

Self-Test Answers

Multiple-Choice Questions (continued)
5. d, 6. b

Matching Terms and Definitions
7. a. (4), b. (11), c. (6), d. (8), e. (5), f. (3), g. (2), h. (1), i. (9)

Fill-in-the-Blank Questions
8. Perception, 9. Bottom-up; top-down, 10. perceptual constancy

Brief Essay Question
11. Students should understand that Gestalt psychology tried to encourage psychologists to look at how people perceive the world rather than at their individual behaviors. They delved into why and how people perceived sensory phenomena to understand people's behavior. Wilhelm Wundt was concerned with analyzing *how* people reacted to stimuli, not why. He also was unconcerned with the stimuli themselves. Gestalt psychologists were fascinated with how different stimuli can produce both similar and different behaviors.

CHAPTER 5 Motivation and Emotion

Biopsychological Domain

Teaching with the Standards

Standard Area: Motivation and Emotion

Breakdown of Module 11: Motivation

Content Standard 1: Application of motivational principles to human and animal behavior Module 11 uses many examples and vignettes to illustrate motivational principles. (Student Text pp. 207–221)

Content Standard 2: Environmental and biological cues that trigger basic motives Module 11 describes homeostasis to help students understand motivated behavior. The authors emphasize the difference between homeostasis and drive reduction theory. (Student Text pp. 210–211)

Content Standard 3: Motivational theories The text discusses many different theories of motivation. Historic explanations, such as instinct and drive-reduction theories, are discussed. In addition, biological theories, such as the Yerkes-Dodson, are presented. Homeostasis is contrasted with drive reduction theory. Intrinsic and extrinsic motivation is also emphasized. Abraham Maslow's "hierarchy of needs" is explained, along with criticisms of this theory. Achievement motivation is defined and its measurement discussed. (Student Text pp. 207–216)

Content Standard 4: Influence of physiological and environmental variables on the development of motives Module 11 explores physiological and environmental factors that influence hunger. The physiology of hunger is examined. The role of the hypothalamus is emphasized. External incentives and cultural influences on hunger are explored. Cultural and biological factors are also considered in a discussion of the causes of anorexia nervosa and bulimia nervosa. (Student Text pp. 217–221)

Content Standard 5: How an individual's values and expectations determine motivational choice and strength Specific strategies that students can use to motivate themselves and others are presented. (Student Text pp. 215–216)

Content Standard 7: Effects of motivation and emotion on cognition, behavior, and perceptions The author explains how learning can be affected by motivation. Module 11 introduces students to the Yerkes-Dodson law and the relationship between the level of arousal and performance. (Student Text pp. 209–211)

Breakdown of Module 12: Emotion

Content Standard 6: Biological, affective, cognitive, and behavioral aspects of emotions and how they interact with one another The author discusses how emotions are a result of physiological activation, expressive behaviors, and conscious experience. The order of these experiences that result in a particular emotion is considered. Various theories of emotion are presented such as the James-Lange and Cannon-Bard theories. The role of cognition on emotion is also discussed. Schachter-Singer's, Robert Zajonc's, and Richard Lazarus' ideas are contrasted. The experience of fear is emphasized. The role of the sympathetic and parasympathetic nervous system in controlling physiological arousal is discussed. (Student Text pp. 227–233)

Content Standard 7: Effects of motivation and emotion on cognition, behavior, and perceptions Module 12 investigates the role of gender and culture on emotion. The concept of display rules is explained. Examples illustrate differing reactions to similar events based on cultural influences. (Student Text pp. 234–238)

Content Standard 2: Structure of the nervous system The division of the autonomic nervous system is presented in the context of how an individual experiences fear. (Student Text pp. 232–233)

Scope and Sequence

	Objectives	Text Reference	Standards Covered
Lesson 1	Introduce the concept of motivation. Look at specific student behaviors and try to explain "why." Introduce early theories of motivation, instinct, and drive reduction. Discuss biological explanations of behavior, such as homeostasis and arousal theory.	Module 11, pp. 207–210.	Standard Area: Motivation and Emotion, Content Standard 1, Performance Standard 1.1, Content Standard 2, Performance Standard 2.1, Content Standard 3, Performance Standard 3.1, Content Standard 7, Performance Standard 7.2
Lesson 2	Investigate cognitive theories of motivation. Discuss intrinsic and extrinsic motivation. Discuss achievement motivation and how achievement is measured.	Module 11, pp. 210–211, 213	Content Standard 1, Performance Standard 1.1, Content Standard 3, Performance Standard 3.1
Lesson 3	Introduce Maslow's hierarchy of needs. Discuss criticisms of Maslow's theory. Explore how we can motivate our own and others behavior.	Module 11, pp. 212, 214–216	Content Standard 1, Performance Standard 1.1, Content Standard 3, Performance Standard 3.1, Content Standard 5, Performance Standard 5.1
Lesson 4	Investigate the physiological and environmental factors that influence hunger. Discuss the development of eating disorders and the characteristics of those suffering from anorexia or bulimia.	Module 11, pp. 216–220	Content Standard 1, Performance Standard 1.1, Content Standard 2, Performance Standard 2.1, Content Standard 4, Performance Standard 4.1
Lesson 5	Introduce the components of emotion. Discuss the different theories of emotion in the context of experiencing fear. Discuss how a polygraph works and the controversy surrounding its use.	Module 12, pp. 226–235.	Standard Area: Motivation and Emotion, Content Standard 6, Performance Standard 6.1 Standard Area: Biological Bases of Behavior, Content Standard 2, Performance Standard 2.2
Lesson 6	Discuss how we express emotion. Investigate nonverbal communication and body language. Discuss Ekman's research on universal facial expressions and display rules. Discuss other cultural and gender differences in emotional expression.	Module 12, pp. 234–238	Standard Area: Motivation and Emotion, Content Standard 6, Performance Standard 6.1, Content Standard 7, Performance Standard 7.1
Lesson 7	Review and test.		

CHAPTER 5

Motivation and Emotion

Introducing the Chapter

The Points: Chapter Objectives

- Discuss the similarities of instinct and drive theories.
- Discuss the difference between drive theory and homeostasis.
- Explain the reasons why intrinsic motivation is more beneficial than extrinsic motivation.
- Analyze the role our physiological and emotional needs have in reaching potential.
- Determine how psychologists measure achievement motivation.
- Identify ways we can motivate others to give their best efforts.
- Analyze how the body regulates weight so effectively.
- Differentiate between historical and modern cognitive theories of emotion.
- Identify the physiological changes that occur when you experience fear.
- Determine criteria for assessing gender differences in emotional expression.

CHAPTER 5

Motivation and Emotion

My tenth-grade English teacher froze after I said, "I think this poem is kinda stupid." She had just read to the class Robert Frost's "Stopping by Woods on a Snowy Evening," and she had asked for my opinion of this poem. My answer was not what she was looking for.

Composing herself, Ms. Stutzman calmly put down her chalk and walked over to my desk. She matter-of-factly told the class, and me, "I don't think you would call the poem stupid if you understood it. Let me help you understand."

She proceeded to explain the *emotion* she felt when she read, *"And I have miles to go before I sleep."* Afterward, our assignment was to write a paragraph, due at the end of the period, explaining why we thought Frost wrote this poem. In essence, we were to explain Frost's *motivation* for writing.

Psychology—like Mrs. Stutzman—is interested in motivation and emotion. In the next two modules, we will look at some of the ways that psychologists study these two concepts, and we will review some of their most important research. Hopefully, the discussion will help you understand both concepts, so that if you're asked to explain either, you won't give the same response I gave to Frost's classic poem.

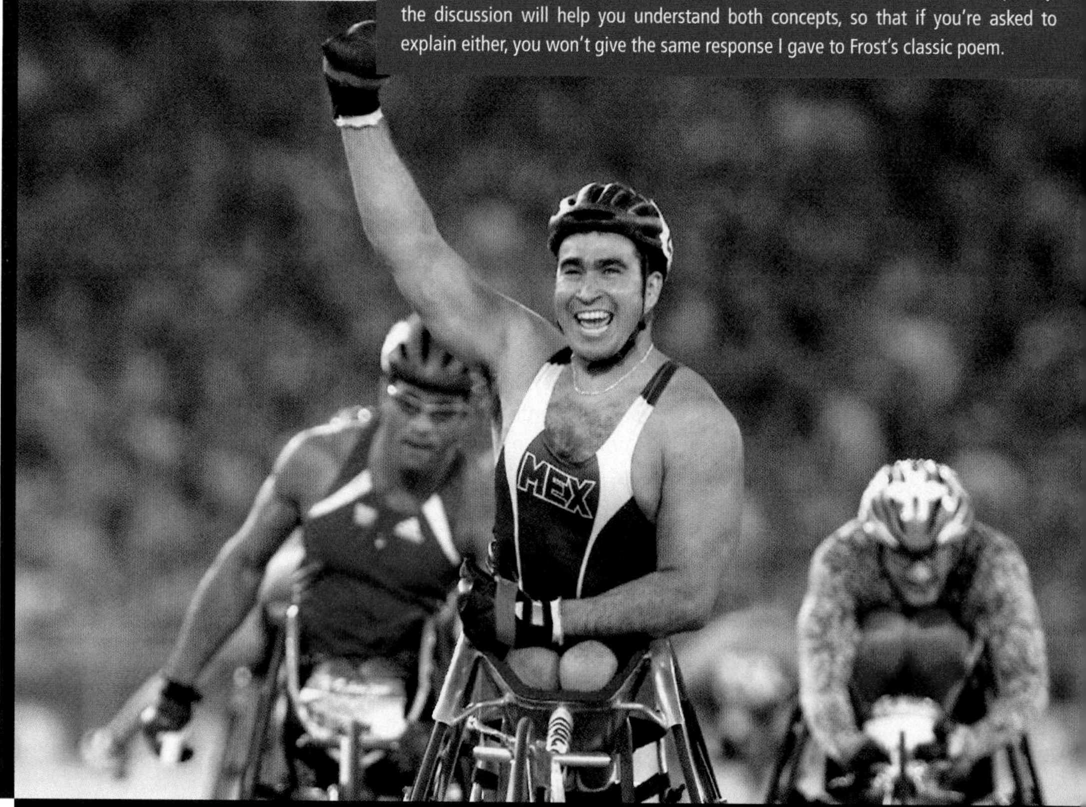

Performance Standards

Standard Area: Motivation and Emotion

Content Standard 1: Application of motivational principles to human and animal behavior

Performance Standard 1.1 Analyze the behavior of humans and other animals by applying motivational concepts.

- Illustrate motivational principles using a number of case studies or vignettes. Introduce the concept of motivation through a discussion of the tragic events of September 11, 2001. In addition, use examples from school settings. Discuss how intrinsic versus extrinsic motivation may influence school success. (Student Text pp. 206, 210–211)

Content Standard 2: Environmental and biological cues that trigger basic motives

Performance Standard 2.1 Investigate the role of internal and external cues that determine motivation stemming from basic drives.

- Explore the concept of homeostasis and arousal theory. (Student Text pp. 208–210)
- Compare the concept of homeostasis with drive-reduction theory. (Student Text pp. 207–210)

Content Standard 3: Motivational theories

Performance Standard 3.1 Discuss one or more motivational theories, such as expectancy value, cognitive dissonance, arousal, Maslow's hierarchy of needs, and drive reduction.

- Examine some historical explanations for human motives. Investigate instinct theory and its drawbacks. Explain drive-reduction theory and its limitations. (Student Text pp. 207–208)
- Explore biological theories for motivation. Discuss arousal theory and the Yerkes-Dodson law. Investigate the role of arousal on performance. (Student Text pp. 209–210)
- Discuss cognitive theories of motivation. Investigate why intrinsic motivation is more beneficial than extrinsic. (Student Text pp. 211–212)
- Investigate Abraham Maslow's hierarchy of needs theory. Discuss criticisms of his research. (Student Text p. 213)
- Figure 11.4, "Maslow's Hierarchy of Needs," summarizes the needs at every level from physiological to self-actualization. (Student Text p. 213)
- Examine Henry Murray's theory of achievement motivation. Discuss the use of TAT's to measure achievement motivation. (Student Text pp. 214–215)

Content Standard 4: Influence of physiological and environmental variables on the development of motives

Performance Standard 4.1 Investigate the development of common motives.

- Explore physiological factors that influence hunger. Examine the role of glucose, insulin, leptin, orexin, and the hypothalamus in triggering hunger. Discuss the concept of set point. Examine how the basal metabolic rate, the number of fat cells, and hormones work together to maintain an animals particular weight. (Student Text pp. 217–219)
- Discuss the role that external incentives play in influencing hunger. Examine research on individuals who are "internals" or "externals" and the effect on eating. Focus on cultural influences on hunger, such as how we learn to shun or enjoy certain foods. (Student Text pp. 219–220)
- Examine both cultural and biological influences in the development of eating disorders. Discuss the characteristics of individuals suffering from anorexia nervosa or bulimia nervosa. (Student Text pp. 220–221)

Content Standard 5: How an individual's values and expectations determine motivational choice and strength

Performance Standard 5.1 Apply expectancy value theory to understand their own or others' actions.

- Focus on strategies that students may use to motivate themselves and others. For example, discuss the benefits of setting specific, challenging goals or cultivating intrinsic motivation. (Student Text pp. 215–216)

Content Standard 7: Effects of motivation and emotion on cognition, behavior, and perceptions

Performance Standard 7.2 Investigate how learning, memory, and problem solving are affected by motivation and emotion.

- Explain how learning can be affected by arousal. Discuss the Yerkes-Dodson law and the relationship between the level of arousal and performance. (Student Text pp. 209–210)

Materials NETWORK

All of the items from the Video, Activity, and Enrichment Centers listed below come from the *Teacher's Resource Binder.* These items will help you teach and expand on concepts presented in Module 11.

trb This logo indicates when an item from the Materials Network may be used in conjunction with a specific note found in this module's *Teacher's Edition.*

Introduction to Motivation

Activity Center

- Critical Thinking Activity: *Fact or Falsehood?* With this activity, students' preconceptions about motivation are either exposed as incorrect or reinforced as correct. (*Teacher's Resource Binder,* p. 11-1; Handout 11–1)
- Building Vocabulary: *Crossword Puzzle* With a crossword puzzle that incorporates a definition-matching exercise, students can learn the concepts from this module while using two different methods of processing. (*Teacher's Resource Binder,* p. 11-1; Handout 11–2)

Historic Explanations

Activity Center

- Critical Thinking Activity: *Evolutionary Motivations* According to evolutionary psychologists, our genes predispose us to act in ways that enhance our chances of survival from generation to generation. Drives and instincts are often discussed within the framework of evolution. Students can use this activity to understand how evolutionary theory can explain our most basic motivations. (*Teacher's Resource Binder,* p. 11-1; Handout 11–3)

Biological Explanations

Activity Center

- Critical Thinking Activity: *Sensation-Seeking Scale* Why do some people risk their lives for entertainment? Popular culture finds such people fascinating, and this activity explores how sensation seeking is one motivation behind daredevil behavior. (*Teacher's Resource Binder,* p. 11-1; Handout 11–4)

Cognitive Explanations: Intrinsic and Extrinsic Motivation

Activity Center

- Critical Thinking Activity: *The Work Preference Inventory* What motivates our work choices can determine the type of career we choose. What do students prefer—work that is challenging or enjoyable? Work for compensation or service to others? Have students respond to this scale, designed by Teresa M. Amabile and her colleagues. (*Teacher's Resource Binder,* p. 11-1; Handout 11–5)
- Analysis Activity: *Intrinsic Motivation and Achievement* Research indicates that people who are oriented toward mastery and hard work may achieve more. This activity analyzes students' motivations toward work and challenging activities. (*Teacher's Resource Binder,* p. 11-1; Handout 11–6)
- Evaluation Activity: *The Purpose-in-Life Test* James Crumbaugh's Purpose-in-Life Test assesses how purposeful one's life is, based on the notion that the greater the sense of purpose, the higher the motivation to achieve. (*Teacher's Resource Binder,* p. 11-1; Handout 11–7)
- Evaluation Activity: *The Hope Scale* Is hope more than just wishful thinking? Hope is determined by goals and plans. People with more hope lead happier, more successful lives. This activity will help students measure the level of hope in their lives. (*Teacher's Resource Binder,* p. 11-1; Handout 11–8)

Enrichment Center

- Enrichment Lesson: *Intrinsic Motivation* This lesson, discussed in full in Module 16's resources, helps define and clarify this important concept. (*Teacher's Resource Binder,* p. 11-1)
- Enrichment Lesson: *Purpose in Life* Viktor Frankl, a Holocaust survivor, found that people who seemed to find purpose in life were able to overcome hardship and live longer, healthier lives. This lesson details Frankl's work, centered on his book *Man's Search for Meaning,* an excellent resource for lectures on this topic. (*Teacher's Resource Binder,* p. 11-1)

Clinical Explanations

V Video Center

- Videocassette: *Scientific American Frontiers,* Second Edition, Segment 30: "The Power of Persuasion" Consult the faculty guide from the *Scientific American Frontiers* video series for a description of this segment. (*Teacher's Resource Binder,* p. 11-1)

Activity Center

- Analysis Activity: *An Assessment of Your Present Needs* Abraham Maslow's hierarchy of needs outlines the needs that must be met on the path to self-actualization. Students can think critically about their own needs in relation to Maslow's hierarchy with this lesson. (*Teacher's Resource Binder,* p. 11-1; Handout 11–9)
- Application Activity: *A Short Measure of Self-Actualization* Have your students achieved Maslow's coveted self-actualization? Use this measure to find out. (*Teacher's Resource Binder,* p. 11-1; Handout 11–10)
- Analysis Activity: *Desire for Control* Achievers often seek control over much of their lives as they try to conquer life's challenges. This measure will help students see how much control they desire over their lives. (*Teacher's Resource Binder,* p. 11-1; Handout 11–11)
- Application Activity: *Measuring Achievement Motivation* Using a photo from the text, students can gain insight into how they explain the achievement motivation of others and gain insight into their own motivations for achievement. (*Teacher's Resource Binder,* p. 11-1)
- Application Activity: *Achievement and Challenge* If given the choice, what level of challenge would you choose in a competition? How much challenge you seek reveals the level of achievement motivation you possess. (*Teacher's Resource Binder,* p. 11-1)
- Analysis Activity: *The Needs Assessment Questionnaire* The Needs Assessment Questionnaire (NAQ), designed by Teresa Heckert and her colleagues, provides an opportunity to introduce the need for achievement and to describe two additional social needs—for autonomy and dominance. (*Teacher's Resource Binder,* p. 11-1; Handout 11–12)
- Application Activity: *Theory X and Y Orientation Scale* Leaders motivate either by building friendly communities or by micromanaging workers. This scale will help students see what type of leader they are and which type of leader they prefer. (*Teacher's Resource Binder,* p. 11-1; Handout 11–13)
- Application Activity: *Assessing Leadership Style* Introduce research on leadership styles with this least preferred worker questionnaire. (*Teacher's Resource Binder,* p. 11-1; Handout 11–14)

Enrichment Center

- Enrichment Lesson: *Maslow's Hierarchy* Maslow recognized that a given motive does not have to be 100 percent satisfied before a person turns to a higher need. He said that our needs are only partially satisfied at any given moment. Maslow's hierarchy of needs is explained and clarified in this lesson about his often-quoted and misunderstood theory. (*Teacher's Resource Binder,* p. 11-1)
- Enrichment Lesson: *Weiner's Attribution Model of Achievement* Our explanations of achievement reveal what type of goals we value. This lesson explains a theory of achievement explanation that explores the stability and focus of our attributions by describing two categories of attributions for success or failure: (1) internal or external (dispositional or situational) and (2) stable or unstable. (*Teacher's Resource Binder,* p. 11-1)
- Enrichment Lesson: *Birth Order, Achievement, and Personality* A disproportionate number of National Merit Scholars, Rhodes Scholars, and astronauts have been first-borns. Do first-born children achieve more than last-born children? Where do only children fit? These questions are explored in this lesson on birth-order theory, a popular explanation for familial relationships. (*Teacher's Resource Binder,* p. 11-1)
- Enrichment Lesson: *Describing Good Leaders* According to Hollander, "leadership is a process, not a person." Although leaders do command greater attention, followers can affect and even constrain leaders' activities in more than passing ways. This lesson explores this theory of good leadership. (*Teacher's Resource Binder,* p. 11-1)

Hunger: A Closer Look

Activity Center

- Technology Application Activity: *PsychSim:* "Hunger and the Fat Rat" *PsychSim* is an interactive CD-ROM containing tutorials in different content areas of psychology. Because this tutorial contains simulated experiments that lesion rat brains, consider whether to use it according to your students' sensitivity to animal rights issues. (*Teacher's Resource Binder,* p. 11-1)

- Technology Application Activity: *PsychQuest:* "How Do We Control How Much We Eat?" *PsychQuest* is a CD-ROM program that encourages critical thinking in students. This program explores the body's ability to control eating habits. (*Teacher's Resource Binder,* p. 11-1)
- Critical Thinking Activity: *A Survey of Eating Habits* Are our attitudes toward food and eating shaped by our childhood experiences? Donn Byrne and his colleagues argued that this may be the case, and they designed this survey. Use this activity to help students explore their childhood experiences with food. (*Teacher's Resource Binder*, p. 11-1; Handout 11–15)

Enrichment Center

- Enrichment Lesson: *Taste Preferences—Learned and Genetic* Taste plays an important role in eating, and our taste preferences are both learned and genetic. M. Harris, an anthropologist at the University of Florida, argues that all taste preferences ultimately result from a careful calculation of rewards and costs. This lesson explains more deeply how taste governs what and how we eat. (*Teacher's Resource Binder*, p. 11-1)
- Enrichment Lesson: *Body Image Survey Results* Why do Westerners find eating bugs disgusting, while other cultures do not? Marvin Harris, an anthropologist at the University of Florida, argues that all taste preferences ultimately result from a careful calculation of rewards and costs. (*Teacher's Resource Binder*, p. 11-1)

MODULE 11

Motivation

Introduction to Motivation

On the morning of September 11, 2001, terrorists hijacked four U.S. passenger planes headed for the West Coast. They deliberately flew three of the aircraft into U.S. buildings, killing all passengers and thousands of people on the ground. The biggest criminal investigation in history followed this horrific crime.

As with most murder cases, investigators in their attempts to bring the guilty to justice began by asking, "Why?" Why would anyone want to do something so devastatingly awful? What drove this suicidal attack? Investigators for what came to be known as "9/11" were seeking to understand the *motives* of the hijackers.

For over a century, psychologists have searched for the roots of behavior, attempting to understand why we do what we do. This quest to understand **motivation** (from the Latin *movere,* meaning "move")—the need or desire energizing and moving behavior toward a goal—has led psychology in several directions. In this module, we will examine biological, cognitive, and clinical explanations for motivation. Then we will see how some of these ideas can help us figure out how to motivate others and ourselves. And finally, we will take a close look at our hunger motivation, and how it goes awry in those with eating disorders.

▶ **motivation** A need or desire that energizes and directs behavior.

Ground Zero Rescue workers raised the American flag at the site of the World Trade Center devastation in New York City.

Getting Started

To start a prereading discussion, have students respond to the following question:

- If you needed to motivate the members of a team or club to which you belong, what would you do, and why? What results would you expect?

trb You may wish to use **Critical Thinking Activity:** *Fact or Falsehood?* (*Teacher's Resource Binder,* p. 11-1; **Handout 11–1**) to get students thinking about what motivates people to behave in certain ways. The activity will prime students to discriminate among the concepts in the module.

MODULE 11

Motivation

Introducing the Module

The Points: Module Objectives

- Discuss in what ways instinct theory and drive-reduction theory are similar and how they differ.
- Discuss the basic idea in arousal theories of motivation as well as whether or not homeostasis is the same as drive reduction.
- Explain why intrinsic motivation is more beneficial than extrinsic motivation.
- Analyze whether some needs are more basic than others.
- Determine how psychologists measure achievement motivation.
- Identify ways in which we can motivate others to give their best efforts.
- Analyze psychological and environmental factors that influence hunger.
- Analyze why peole develop eating disorders.

trb tr Building Vocabulary

Building Vocabulary: *Crossword Puzzle* (*Teacher's Resource Binder,* p. 11-1; **Handout 11–2**) incorporates a definition-matching exercise from which students can learn concepts related to motivation while using two different methods of processing. Invite students at first to work on the puzzle individually and then meet in small groups to receive help in completing and then checking their responses. You may also wish to use the handout as a transparency that can be projected; with the groups, review a correctly completed puzzle.

■ **TEACHING TIP**

Students will have varying degrees of emotions when discussing the September 11 terrorist attacks. Help students be sensitive to each other and students of Arabic or Muslim heritage as you discuss this pivotal event in U.S. history.

MODULE 11

Teaching the Points

■ **TEACHING TIPS**

web (1) You can log on as an instructor to the book companion site for *Thinking About Psychology* at www.worthpublishers.com/thinkingaboutpsych. It contains teacher resources for class presentations as well as review and assessment of module concepts and terms.

(2) An effective way of introducing the nature and diversity of human motivation is to ask students, "Why do you think people go to college?" Answers will cover the full range of human motives, from the belief that they eventually have to earn a living to feed their families to the notion that they may find a spouse in college and the desire to simply increase their knowledge and competence.

The discussion provides an excellent opportunity to illustrate that motivation has both energizing and directional aspects. The diversity of answers will also provide a good lead-in to Maslow's hierarchy of needs.

trb You may wish to use **Evaluation Activity:** *The Purpose in Life Test* (*Teacher's Resource Binder*, p. 11-1; **Handout 11–7**) and **Evaluation Activity:** *The Hope Scale* (*Teacher's Resource Binder*, p. 11-1; **Handout 11–8**).

■ **LOOKING AT THE ISSUES**

Human instincts are hard to pinpoint since humans behave so individualistically. Have students compare and contrast the behavior of animals and humans, trying to isolate what might be considered instincts for humans. Use the following questions to engage students in discussion:

- What types of behavior are inherited, complex behaviors that occur throughout the human and animal species?
- Where can we draw the line between individual behavior and instinctive behavior?
- Does drive-reduction theory help differentiate between what is considered an instinct and what is an individual behavior? Why or why not?

trb You may wish to use **Critical Thinking Activity:** *Evolutionary Motivations* (*Teacher's Resource Binder*, p. 11-1; **Handout 11–3**).

Historic Explanations

What's the Point? 1. In what ways are instinct theory and drive-reduction-theory similar, and how do they differ?

Instincts

An **instinct** is an inherited (unlearned), preprogrammed, complex behavior occurring throughout a species. In the first published psychology textbook, William James (1890) listed 37 human instincts, including the "mental instincts" of jealousy, curiosity, and cleanliness. Thus, instinct theory was the original psychological explanation of motivation. Many theorists back then found James' list inadequate, so they added more and more instincts, such as the desire to dominate and the desire to make things. Eventually, the number of proposed instincts swelled to a mind-boggling 10,000 (Bernard, 1924), making the study of instincts, shall we say, cumbersome. Further, instinct theorists fell into a trap by using instincts both to label *and* to explain a behavior. For instance, they might say that *studying* behavior would be explained by the *studying instinct.* And what's the studying instinct? Well, it's studying behavior. Given this circular reasoning, interest in explaining behavior through instincts understandably dropped off. Filling the void left by 10,000 instincts was drive-reduction theory.

Thirst Quenching Both the young woman and the cat have the same motive, but they inherited different ways to meet this need. The cat's behavior pattern is fixed, and it drinks only by curling its tongue backward as it laps water out of a container. With a more advanced nervous system, humans can learn a variety of ways to quench their thirst.

▶ **instinct** A complex, unlearned behavior that is rigidly patterned throughout a species.

▶ **drives** In drive-reduction theory, aroused tension states created by imbalances that prompt an organism to restore the balance, typically by reducing the drive.

▶ **drive-reduction theory** The idea that a physiological need creates an aroused tension state (a drive) that motivates an organism to satisfy the need.

Drives

Still searching for a way to explain motivation, psychologists looked hopefully at the study of **drives,** states of tension that result from an internal imbalance. Consider hunger, for example. Ever miss breakfast because you got up late? By 10:00 A.M., you're starving. Skipping your Wheaties creates an internal, physiological *need* for food, which leads to hunger, a psychological *drive.* The drive to eat and the need for food disappear after you eat lunch. **Drive-reduction theory** is the idea that a physiological need creates a state of tension (a drive) motivating an organism to satisfy that need (Figure 11.1). Eating and drinking are drive-reducing behaviors: Eating reduces the hunger drive, and drinking reduces the thirst drive. We'll take a closer look at hunger later in this module.

Suggested Readings

Use the following books as teacher-preparation tools or as enrichment for advanced students:

Adler, A. (1959). *The theory and practice of individual psychology.* Totowa, NJ: Littlefield Adams.

Burger, J. (2000). *Personality* (5th ed.). Belmont, CA: Wadsworth.

Burger, J. M. (1992). *Desire for control.* New York: Plenum.

Frankl, V. (1959). *Man's search for meaning.* New York: Washington Square Press.

Harris, M. (1987). *The sacred cow and the abominable pig.* New York: Simon & Schuster.

Snyder, C. R. (1994). *The psychology of hope.* New York: Free Press.

Weiner, B. (Ed.). (1974). *Achievement motivation and attribution theory.* Morristown, NJ: General Learning Press.

Weiner, B. (1992). *Human motivation: Metaphors, theories, and research.* Newbury Park, CA: Sage.

Figure 11.1 **Drive-Reduction Theory**

Like instinct theory, drive-reduction theory did not produce the explanations of motivation many had hoped for. Drive-reduction theory had a great deal of difficulty explaining particular activities. For instance, what drive is reduced when a bungee-jumper pays $30 for the privilege of leaping headfirst off a three-story crane at the state fair? Once again, the search for an explanation of motivation's origins shifted, this time to the biological, cognitive, and clinical arenas.

Biological Explanations

2. What is the basic idea in arousal theories of motivation? Is homeostasis the same as drive reduction?

Some psychologists believed that the key to understanding motivation would be found in biological processes other than instincts and drive-reduction. One group searched for the answer in our level of psychological arousal, and another group looked closely at how we regulate our body chemistry.

Arousal Theories

It's Friday night, and you're sitting at a fast-food restaurant with three friends who have registered to take the same college entrance exam the next morning. You know that all three have about the same level of intelligence and knowledge base, but they seem to have very different approaches to the test-taking process:

- ***Friend A:*** "You know, I don't really care about the test. I'm going to a trade school, and I'm only taking the test because my parents want me to. Can I have some of your fries?"
- ***Friend B:*** "I want to do well, but if I screw up on this test, it's not going to permanently ruin my life. I'll give it my best shot. Where's the ketchup?"
- ***Friend C:*** "It's all on the line tomorrow. If I don't get a good score, it will change my life forever. I'm so nervous, I can't eat."

Each of these three people has a different level of *arousal;* the brain of each has activated different levels of alertness. So, which of them will stand a better chance of acing the exam? One arousal theory, the

Demonstrating

YERKES-DODSON LAW Using jigsaw puzzles, of varying degrees of difficulty, set up three different centers, each having a timer. In each center, have students try to put together a puzzle under varying degrees of stress.

- Students should time themselves putting together each puzzle in 5-, 15-, and 30-second intervals.
- Have them record how many pieces they put in correctly in each timed trial.
- Students should then chart their levels of arousal on a graph similar to that in Figure 11.2 on page 210 in their texts. Did their experience correlate with the Yerkes-Dodson law? Why or why not?

F • Y • I

(1) Positive psychologist Mihayli Csikszentimihalyi (*cheek-sent-me-high*) proposes that activities such as helping others (altruism) and participating in challenging, fulfilling activities (flow) produce good feelings that last well beyond the experience. Satisfying hunger and quenching thirst are activities that feel good, but they do not provide lasting feelings of well-being and happiness.

trb **tr** A black-line master for Figure 11.1, Drive-Reduction Theory, is available in the **Black-Line Masters Appendix** of the *Teacher's Resource Binder.*

(2) Some theorists believe that cognitive tasks require lower levels of arousal since people need more concentration on those types of tasks. Physically demanding tasks would require higher levels of arousal since more motivation is needed to complete those tasks.

■ TEACHING TIP

Arousal and *stimulation* are two words that will probably elicit chuckles from students of varying degrees of maturity. Help students see that these words can mean more than their popular connotations.

trb At this point, you may wish to use **Critical Thinking Activity:** *Sensation-Seeking Scale* (*Teacher's Resource Binder,* p. 11-1; **Handout 11–4**).

■ JOURNAL WRITING

Invite students to use the following questions and writing prompts as springboards for entries in their psychology journals:

- Which level of arousal do you think you will have (or have had) in facing a college entrance exam? What will be (or what were) your "day before" preparations? How will (or how did) these preparations affect your level of arousal?
- Do you experience test anxiety? If so, describe your experience. Why do you feel you experience this anxiety? Does it affect tests in all subjects or just a few? Speculate why and explain your thoughts.

MODULE 11

F • Y • I

The original experiments that led to the Yerkes-Dodson law involved subjecting white mice to different levels of shock as a motivator to get them to learn. It was found that the mice learned fastest with a medium level of shock, which then led to the belief that cognitive processes are carried out more efficiently with medium levels of stress and stimulation.

trb tr A black-line master for Figure 11.2, Arousal and Performance, is available in the **Black-Line Masters Appendix** of the *Teacher's Resource Binder.*

■ TEACHING TIP

Relate biological homeostasis to cognitive dissonance, the mental equivalent to homeostasis, in which people seek a balance between their actions and attitudes. Although **biological homeostasis** focuses on physical conditions such as hunger, thirst, and temperature, **cognitive homeostasis** involves mental conditions, such as consistency, balance, and harmony in one's thinking—that is, such things as seeking racial and social equity, prioritizing one's goals in life, and promoting peace with the self and others.

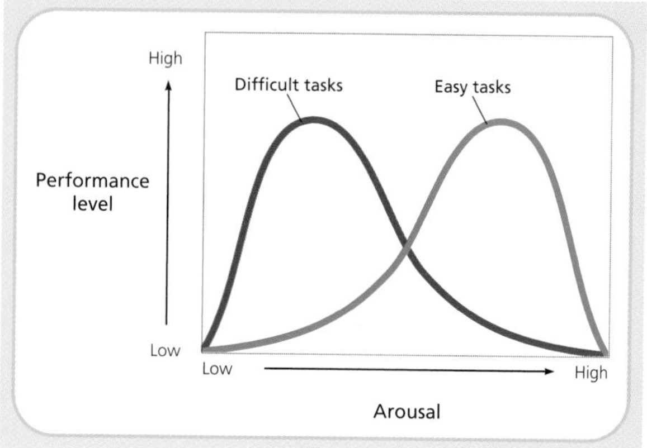

Figure 11.2 **Arousal and Performance** The Yerkes-Dodson law describes the relationship between performance and arousal. In general, arousal will increase performance up to a point, after which further arousal impairs performance. However, optimal arousal changes according to the difficulty of the task. For a simple task, higher arousal leads to optimal performance. Lower arousal is best for difficult tasks.

Yerkes-Dodson law, would predict a better performance by Friend B. The Yerkes-Dodson law is the principle that arousal helps performance, but only up to a point. The optimum level of arousal depends on the difficulty of the task. Too much or too little arousal can decrease performance, as shown in Figure 11.2. Using this reasoning, Friend A would have too low a level of alertness to ace the exam, and Friend C may be too overstimulated to do well.

Arousal theorists state that each of us has an optimal level of stimulation we like to maintain. When you're stressed out (overstimulated), how do you relax? If your optimal level of stimulation is low, perhaps you'll go for a quiet walk or talk casually on the phone. If your optimal stimulation level is high, you might crank your favorite FM station or enjoy a vigorous workout. Arousal theorists explain the motivation behind our behaviors as our attempts to maintain this optimal level of stimulation. And this explanation, they would say, tells us why bungee-jumpers (who presumably have a very high optimal stimulation level) pay good money to leap headfirst through three stories of space! A similar idea is the basis of the next biological motivation theory, which focuses on maintaining a balanced internal state.

▶ **Yerkes-Dodson law** The theory that a degree of psychological arousal helps performance, but only up to a certain point.

▶ **homeostasis** A tendency to maintain a balanced or constant internal state; the regulation of any aspect of body chemistry, such as blood glucose, around a particular level.

Homeostasis

What is your average body temperature? Most of us maintain a fairly constant 98.6 degrees F. as an average. But if you ride a bike, jump rope, or play basketball, your temperature will rise above normal for a while, until perspiration and other body mechanisms kick in and bring your temperature back down to normal. This return to normal is a product of **homeostasis,** the body's tendency to maintain a balanced or constant internal state. Balancing our internal states means regulating such things as hor-

Demonstrating

HOMEOSTASIS Invite your school's nurse (or a local RN) to visit the class and help students find their levels of homeostasis in the following areas: temperature, blood pressure, heart rate, lung capacity and/or breathing rate (number of breaths per minute). Then, have students do some light exercise (10 jumping jacks, jogging in place for 1 minute, and so on) to see how much these measurements change. Students should make note of the answers to the following questions:

- How quickly do their measurements fall back to normal?
- What body reactions occur to help restore homeostasis?
- What do they do to speed up homeostasis?

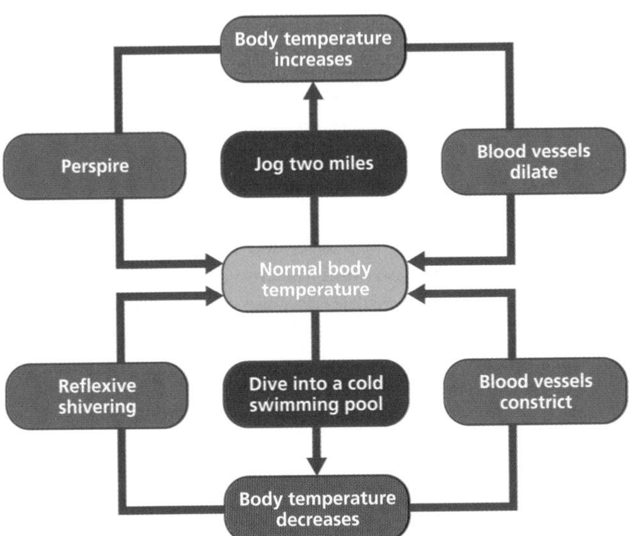

Figure 11.3 **An Example of Homeostatic Regulation** When body temperature increases or decreases, body mechanisms like those illustrated here kick into gear, returning your temperature to normal.

mone levels, water levels in our cells, and blood sugar level. Any change in the normal level, up or down, will be corrected, bringing us back to the comfort zone (Figure 11.3). Is this concept limited to your body? How about the shopping mall? The thermostat there is set at a comfortable temperature, and if the temperature drops below that setting, the heat will come on. A rise in temperature will activate the air conditioner.

The concept of homeostasis sounds like drive-reduction theory, doesn't it? The difference lies in what each emphasizes. Remember that drive-reduction theory focuses on *removing deficits.* Homeostatic regulation focuses on *avoiding both deficits and surpluses.*

The biological pieces to motivation's puzzle help us see parts of motivation's big picture. The cognitive pieces make the picture clearer.

Cognitive Explanations: Intrinsic and Extrinsic Motivation

3. Why is intrinsic motivation more beneficial than extrinsic motivation?

Cognitive theories examine the role our thoughts play in motivating our behavior. Let's take a closer look at one key example of a cognitive theory of motivation—the difference between extrinsic and intrinsic motivation.

At any given time during the school year, you probably have at least one or two tests on the horizon. What motivates you to study for these

■ JOURNAL WRITING

Invite students to use the following questions and writing prompts as springboards for entries in their psychology journals:

- Think of a time when the drive to satisfy basic needs motivated your behavior. What emotions did you feel? How quickly were you motivated to satisfy those needs?
- How would you describe your optimal state of arousal?
- Describe a time during which you felt your body was motivated to achieve homeostasis. What did this feel like?

■ TEACHING TIPS

(1) Be sure to reinforce the difference between *drive reduction* and *homeostasis.* Although the ultimate outcome of both motivations is the same, the way of achieving those goals are very different.

trb tr (2) A black-line master for Figure 11.3, An Example of Homeostatic Regulation, is available in the **Black-Line Masters Appendix** of the *Teacher's Resource Binder.*

Cross-Curricular Connections

BIOLOGY How do biology textbooks discuss *homeostasis* and *drive reduction*? Do the texts differentiate between these concepts? Have students work in small groups to explore these questions, focusing on how biology textbooks treat the cognitive explanations for these theories of motivation. If possible, make a different textbook available to each group, and have groups report their findings to the full class.

trb At this point, you may wish to use **Critical Thinking Activity:** *Evolutionary Motivations* (*Teacher's Resource Binder,* p. 11-1; **Handout 11–3**).

MODULE 11

F • Y • I

Extrinsic motivation can lead to the over**justification effect,** in which people lose the desire to perform an enjoyable behavior because they are rewarded for doing it. As the text notes, sometimes getting a reward can cheapen an experience and make it less likely to be performed without the reward.

trb At this point, you may wish to use Analysis Activity: *Intrinsic Motivation and Achievement* (*Teacher's Resource Binder,* p. 11-1; Handout 11–6).

■ LOOKING AT THE ISSUES

Grades are an integral part of most educational systems. In a full-class discussion, explore the following questions about grades and motivation:

- What effect do grades have on the motivation to learn?
- How could teachers motivate students to learn without giving grades?

trb At this point, you may wish to use Analysis Activity: *Intrinsic Motivation and Achievement* (*Teacher's Resource Binder,* p. 11-1; Handout 11–6)

■ JOURNAL WRITING

Invite students to use the following questions and writing prompts as springboards for entries in their psychology journals:

- What motivates you to do well in school? Are these motivators intrinsic or extrinsic? Explain.
- How did you feel about learning when you were younger? Did you enjoy it more or less than now? Why?

trb At this point, you may wish to use Enrichment Lesson: *Intrinsic Motivation* (*Teacher's Resource Binder,* p. 11-1).

▶ **extrinsic motivation** A desire to perform a behavior because of promised rewards or threats of punishment.

▶ **intrinsic motivation** A desire to perform a behavior for its own sake and to be effective.

tests? Is it because you want an *A,* or is it because you are excited about the material and want to learn as much as you can? If you're studying only to get an *A* (or to avoid an *F*), psychologists would say that your motivation is extrinsic. **Extrinsic motivation** is the desire to perform a behavior because of promised rewards or threats of punishment. The desire to perform a behavior for its own sake, because it is interesting and fun to do (surely the reason you study for your tests!), is **intrinsic motivation.** So, if you work at a fast-food restaurant flipping burgers, are you working because you want the money, or because you're trying to make the best burger possible? Is your motivation in this situation extrinsic or intrinsic? Only you know the answer.

Which is the better form of motivation: extrinsic or intrinsic? Will students learn how to design good Web pages faster if they're promised external rewards, such as money for *A*'s in computer class, or if they're told they can post their site on the Internet as soon as they learn how to make suitable pages? Are the better teachers those who are "in it for the money" or those who love to teach? Research indicates that intrinsic motivation has an edge over extrinsic motivation, at least in some areas. For example, intrinsic motivation often results in high achievement, whereas extrinsic motivation does not (Spence & Helmreich, 1983). The most creative scientists, artists, and teachers are also those working from intrinsic motivation (Amabile, 1996). Does this mean most exemplary actors and writers are oblivious to the extrinsic rewards of success? No, but rather than being the focus of their efforts, the money and fame seem more like a pleasant surprise. Intrinsic and extrinsic motivations surely work together for some of our activities. Sometimes, of course, external rewards can help us achieve a goal. The marching band kids who wash cars every summer weekend to pay for a trip to a New Year's Day parade are extrinsically motivated to earn some extra money.

Paid to Perform This student is receiving an extrinsic reward for his schoolwork. Would he likely learn more or less if his rewards were intrinsic?

A primary concern about external rewards, however, is that behaviors maintained by extrinsic motivation alone may not be effectively sustained once the rewards are removed. That is, will grades go down if a parent stops giving money for anything above a *C*? Evidence suggests removal of an extrinsic motivator may result in behavior levels even lower than before the rewards were given (Lepper & others, 1973). Suddenly introducing external rewards can certainly disrupt the intrinsic pleasure found in certain activities. If your little sister loves to shoot baskets, but you start giving her a piece of candy for every shot she puts in the hoop, she may start playing basketball for the candy instead of the pure joy of the activity itself.

Enriching

Have students work individually or with partners to survey high school students and elementary students about feelings toward school. The surveys should seek answers to the following questions:

- Are elementary school students as concerned about making good grades as high school students?
- What reasons do elementary school children give for why they should come to school? What reasons do high school students give? How are these reasons different? How do the reasons distinguish students of elementary age from students of high school age?
- Ask high school students when, if ever, they stopped liking school. Does there seem to be an age, in general, at which children stop liking school? What seems to precipitate this change?

Have students present their survey findings to the class; then, allow time for the class to compare and contrast the findings.

Clinical Explanations

Clinical psychologists, those who assess and treat people with psychological disorders, have shed additional light on our understanding of motivation. Clinical explanations of motivation do not rely on physiological data. Rather, they base their conclusions on information clinicians have gathered in intensive studies of individuals (often patients) or groups. Here, we'll consider two clinical explanations of motivation: Abraham Maslow's famous needs hierarchy and Henry Murray and David McClelland's views on achievement motivation.

Abraham Maslow

▶ **Abraham Maslow** (1908–1970) Humanistic psychologist who developed the hierarchy of needs.

▶ **hierarchy of needs** Maslow's pyramid of human needs, beginning at the base with physiological needs and proceeding through safety needs and then to psychological needs. Higher-level needs won't become active until lower-level needs have been satisfied.

▶ **self-actualization** According to Maslow, the need to live up to one's fullest and unique potential.

Hierarchy of Needs

4. Are some needs more basic than others?

If you're really sleepy, with your body craving a one- or two-hour nap, you may not feel much like reading *Lord of the Flies*. Similarly, if you're stranded on foot in an unfamiliar city late at night and concerned for your safety, you probably won't be thinking about your next date. Some of your needs are clearly more basic than others. The need for sleep will take precedence over the need to learn, just as the need for safety takes precedence over the need for companionship.

Recognizing that some needs take priority over others, **Abraham Maslow** (1970) designed his famous **hierarchy of needs** (Figure 11.4). The idea behind this pyramid structure is that we must satisfy lower, basic needs (air, water, food, sleep) before the next level of needs can motivate us. The highest need, according to Maslow, is to *actualize* one's abilities and realize one's full and unique potential. He called this topmost level **self-actualization.**

Maslow's hierarchy has been widely applied in business and industry. Nevertheless, critics have found fault with his research methods. His sample size was too small, he selected his own subjects for study, and he defined his terms ambiguously. Moreover, many people behave in ways that don't comform to Maslow's hierarchy. For instance, how does the hierarchy account for the political prisoner who goes on a hunger strike, or the soldier who abandons the need for safety to satisfy the needs for national belongingness and esteem?

Self-actualization needs
Need to live up to one's fullest and unique potential

Esteem needs
Need for self-esteem, achievement, competence, and independence; need for recognition and respect from others

Belongingness and love needs
Need to love and be loved, to belong and be accepted; need to avoid loneliness and alienation

Safety needs
Need to feel that the world is organized and predictable; need to feel safe, secure, and stable

Physiological needs
Need to satisfy hunger, thirst, and other survival needs

Figure 11.4 **Maslow's Hierarchy of Needs** Maslow's theory proposes that we must satisfy our basic physiological needs before we can try to meet higher-level safety and psychological needs.

MODULE 11

(tr) ■ TEACHING TIP

A four-color transparency of Figure 11.4, Maslow's Hierarchy of Needs, is available in the **Overhead Transparencies Set.**

■ APPLYING THE POINTS

Contact a clinical psychologist in your area who uses humanistic therapeutic methods and ask about his or her views on Maslow's hierarchy of needs. Report to the class the psychologist's responses to the following questions:

- How do current psychologists regard Maslow's famous theory?
- How is Maslow's theory used in a clinical setting to help people with their problems?

(trb) At this point, you may wish to use **Enrichment Lesson:** *Maslow's Hierarchy* (*Teacher's Resource Binder*, p. 11-1).

■ JOURNAL WRITING

Invite students to use the following questions and writing prompts as springboards for entries in their psychology journals:

- Describe an experience in which your basic needs weren't met, hindering you from doing well in school. How did you feel about school at that time? What did you do to resolve your needs?
- Do you feel you are self-actualized? Do you know of anyone you would consider self-actualized? Explain.

■ MULTICULTURAL CONNECTIONS

Do people in other cultures believe the fulfillment of basic needs is an important road to self-actualization? Have students research different cultural and religious teachings about how to achieve the ultimate rewards in life. Ask them to compare their findings to the road Maslow described in his hierarchy.

(trb) At this point, you may wish to use **Analysis Activity:** *An Assessment of Your Present Needs* (*Teacher's Resource Binder*, p. 11-1; **Handout 11–9**) and **Application Activity:** *A Short Measure of Self-Actualization* (*Teacher's Resource Binder*, p. 11-1; **Handout 11–10**).

Demonstrating

BIRTH ORDER AND ACHIEVEMENT Ask your students to think of two individuals—a highly motivated, driven overachiever and a somewhat lazy underachiever. Then ask for a show of hands about the latter in response to the question "Is the person a first-born or an only child?" After briefly explaining the birth order–achievement relationship, ask how many of the highly motivated people are first-born or only children. Now ask the questions "Why do you think this relationship between birth order and achievement exists? What differences in the lives and experiences of first- and later-borns might explain this finding?" The exercise stimulates an active discussion, partly because students can readily speculate, based on their own family experiences.

(trb) At this point, you may wish to use **Analysis Activity:** *Desire for Control* (*Teacher's Resource Binder*, p. 11-1; **Handout 11–11**) or **Enrichment Lesson:** *Birth Order, Achievement, and Personality* (*Teacher's Resource Binder*, p. 11-1).

MODULE 11

■ **JOURNAL WRITING**

Invite students to use the following questions and writing prompts as springboards for entries in their psychology journals:

- What would you consider your greatest achievement in life up to this point? How did you achieve it?
- What type of work do you prefer, challenging or easy? Why?

■ **APPLYING THE POINTS**

Contact a local sports psychologist to speak to your students about techniques he or she might use to motivate athletes. Ask your guest to address the following questions in a class presentation:

- How does he or she measure an athlete's level of achievement motivation?
- How might he or she encourage an athlete to increase achievement motivation?
- What coaching strategies might someone use that would lead a team toward higher achievement?

trb At this point, you may wish to use **Application Activity:** *Measuring Achievement Motivation* (*Teacher's Resource Binder,* p. 11-1) and **Application Activity:** *Achievement and Challenge* (*Teacher's Resource Binder,* p. 11-1).

▸ **achievement motivation** A desire for significant accomplishment: for mastery of things, people, or ideas; for attaining a high standard.

▸ **Henry Murray** (1893–1988) Neo-Freudian who first established the concept of achievement motivation and also developed important personality testing tools.

Achievement

5. How do psychologists measure achievement motivation?

Clinical psychologists often find themselves treating people who are struggling to succeed in life. Why do some succeed against all odds, whereas others fail, despite having been given every opportunity? What motivates you to stay in high school, when 20 percent of your peers across the country are dropping out of school? Why do some students persist in their quest for a college degree when so many give up after a year or two? And why do some camp out overnight in line to get tickets to a concert you couldn't pay others to attend? The answer may in part be **achievement motivation,** which, according to **Henry Murray** (1938) includes a desire for

- significant accomplishment.
- mastery of ideas, things, or people.
- attaining a high standard.

Appreciating differences in achievement motivation is one thing; comparing those differences is quite another. Without physiological indicators, how might we measure achievement motivation? David McClelland (1953) and his colleagues devised a way. Look at the photo of the young man in Figure 11.5. If you had to write a story about what was going on in that photo, what would you say? McClelland assumed that people tell stories that reflect their own achievement motivation. Thus, he labeled stories about heroic acts, pride in accomplishment, or pursuit of a goal as having an achievement theme. And he gave people who consistently wrote stories with achievement themes high scores for achievement motivation.

People high in achievement motivation persist in the face of difficulty. Is it any surprise that a study of gifted artists, scholars, and athletes showed that all had impressive, self-disciplined motivation to meet their goals (Bloom, 1985)? What distinguishes these outstanding high achievers is not their raw talent. Rather, their daily practice regimen eclipses that of less-accomplished colleagues. Achievement is much more than ability: Those with a passion to perfect and the discipline to prepare are often the best in their fields. As

Figure 11.5 What's Going on Here? Motivation researchers use people's responses to ambiguous photos like this to assess achievement motivation. They ask research participants to invent stories about the people in the photo, and then the researchers analyze the stories, watching for achievement themes.

Cooperative Learning

Have students form groups with others who are in the same birth position: first-borns, middle-borns, and last-borns. Only children can form a fourth group or join the first-borns. Have one volunteer from each group take notes as each group member state his or her feelings about being in a particular birth-order position. Then have each group discuss the following questions:

- How would you be different had you been born in another position?
- How would you be different if you were of the other sex in your same position?
- How does your position continue to affect you today?

Finally, have the whole class reconvene to discuss their group experiences. Facilitate the discussion by asking students about their feelings toward the other positions, whether they now have improved understanding of their siblings' positions, and how discussion of the effects of birth order might shape their future parenting.

"Maybe they didn't try hard enough."

Storybook Achievers The main character in children's stories often works hard to overcome obstacles. Does this theme help establish an expectation of achievement in children who hear these stories?

my Grandpa Ledbetter used to say, "I think you'll get a lot luckier at baseball, Randy, if you practice a bit more!"

Persisting in spite of difficulties brings rewards to the not-so-rich-and-famous, too: People who were underachievers in high school also tended to have more difficulty later in life holding on to both a job and a spouse, compared with their high-achieving counterparts (McCall, 1994).

Motivating Ourselves and Others

6. How can we motivate others to give their best efforts?

Who are your heroes? Do they hold public office, help keep our communities safe, or help you learn? Perhaps they're exceptionally good at running, acting, or singing. Somewhere along the line, our heroes and role models became motivated to succeed. Judging from their lives, their achievement motivation must be high. Did you ever wonder where such motivation to succeed comes from? Or whether you could increase your own level of motivation? If so, you'll be happy to know that the experts say, "Yes!" Here are three ways you can further develop your self-motivation.

- ***Associate your high achievement with positive emotions.*** If you score high on a test, don't attribute it to luck. Celebrate! You did well because you are bright.
- ***Connect your achievement with your efforts.*** A bad grade may simply mean you need to spend more time studying than you're used to. The best athletes and actors have had to work hard at their craft, even though they make it look effortless when we watch them on TV.

F • Y • I

Hope is a psychological concept related to achievement motivation. According to C. R. Snyder of the University of Kansas, hope is related to a person's goals and how that person plans on achieving them. By setting realistic, achievable goals, people can start on the road to achievement. If people have goals that are 100% attainable ("I hope to watch an hour of TV today," for example), their hope is low because the challenge is not great enough to work toward. People who have completely unrealistic goals ("I hope I can train pigs to fly") also have low levels of hope—not because the challenge isn't great enough, but because they don't have pathways or motivation to achieve their goals

trb At this point, you may wish to use **Evaluation Activity:** ***The Hope Scale*** (*Teacher's Resource Binder*, p. 11-1; **Handout 11–8**).

V ■ TEACHING TIP

At this point, you may wish to show **Videocassette:** ***Scientific American Frontiers*, Second Edition, Segment 30: "The Power of Persuasion"** (*Teacher's Resource Binder*, p. 11-1)

Demonstrating

OPTIMISM AND ACHIEVEMENT MOTIVATION Have students list their last three achievements and their last three failures on a sheet of paper. Next to each item, encourage students to write a one- or two-sentence explanation for that achievement or failure. Then, have them review their explanations. Are the achievement explanations celebrations or not? Do the failure explanations blame a personal fault or chalk it up to circumstances?

Remind students that optimists believe that good events are due to personal accomplishment; the effects will last for a long time and influence other areas of life. If students have pessimistic thinking about their accomplishments and failures, encourage them to come up with alternative explanations for these events that reflect more optimistic thinking.

trb At this point, you may wish to use **Enrichment Lesson:** ***Weiner's Attribution Model of Achievement*** (*Teacher's Resource Binder*, p. 11-1).

MODULE 11

■ **CHECKING FOR UNDERSTANDING** Have students list the suggestions for motivating oneself (along with suggestions of their own) on a sheet of paper. Then have them choose one topic from psychology that reinforces that particular suggestion and write an explanation of their choice. Answers may include the following:

- Associate high achievement with positive emotions—positive reinforcement, conditioning of positive emotions, optimistic thinking
- Connect achievement with effort—optimistic explanatory style, intrinsic motivation
- Raise expectations—achievement motivation, intrinsic motivation
- Cultivate intrinsic motivation—intrinsic motivation, flow, positive reinforcement
- Attend to individual motives—leadership styles, flow, positive reinforcement, intrinsic or extrinsic motivation
- Set specific, challenging goals—hope, flow, achievement motivation, creativity, leadership styles
- Choose an appropriate leadership style—task vs. social leadership, achievement motivation, intrinsic or extrinsic motivation, reinforcement, leadership styles

- ***Raise your expectations.*** Your goals should be high enough so that you are challenged, but not so unreasonably high that you become discouraged.

Motivating yourself is one thing, but what about motivating others? To be an effective leader—with friends, family, or on the job—you will have to know how to motivate others. Motivating others is a four-step process:

1. ***Cultivate intrinsic motivation.*** We know that intrinsic motivation produces greater achievement. You can cultivate intrinsic motivation by providing appropriately challenging tasks that foster curiosity. The other side of this coin is avoiding manipulative extrinsic rewards that *control* behavior (I'll give you $10 for every *A*). Extrinsic rewards can be effective if they *inform* (Look at this great report card! Let's go out to dinner to celebrate!) rather than control. Praising effort more than ability also helps (Mueller & Dweck, 1998).
2. ***Attend to individual motives.*** Not everybody moves to the beat of the same drummer. If you know this, you will try to discover what motivates each individual in your group. You can challenge those who value *accomplishment* to achieve excellence in a variety of settings. You can pay extra attention to those who require *recognition.* And you can provide competitive opportunities for those who value *power.*
3. ***Set specific, challenging goals.*** Several studies show that setting specific, challenging goals motivates higher achievement (Locke & Latham, 1990; Mento & others, 1987; Tubbs, 1986). Clear objectives promote effort, direct attention, and stimulate creative strategies. Help others define their goals while providing consistent feedback on progress.
4. ***Choose an appropriate leadership style.*** Figuring out which leadership style is best for you or for the situation can be a challenge, but the results are worth it. Consider two general styles. **Task leadership** is goal-oriented. Leaders using this style set standards, organize work, and focus attention on goals. **Social leadership** is group-oriented, builds teamwork, mediates conflict, and offers support. Those working with social leaders may buy into the process, feeling more motivated to achieve if they are a part of the decision making.

▶ **task leadership** Goal-oriented leadership that sets standards, organizes work, and focuses attention.

▶ **social leadership** Group-oriented leadership that builds teamwork, mediates conflict, and offers support.

Now that you have a general understanding of how psychologists explain our motivational processes, let's take a closer look at a key motivator: hunger. Hunger obviously has physiological components, but key psychological factors also contribute to our motivation to eat, as evidenced by the devastating effects of eating disorders.

Demonstrating

GOAL SETTING Encourage students to set some short-, medium-, and long-term goals; have them bring their lists to class. To discuss the goals they set, encourage students to respond to the following questions:

- What type of intrinsic motivation do you have for achieving these goals?
- What past experiences help you feel good about your chances of achieving these goals?
- What plans do you have for achieving these goals?

trb At this point, you may wish to use **Evaluation Activity:** *The Hope Scale* (*Teacher's Resource Binder*, p. 11-1; **Handout 11–8**).

Motivate Yourself! Celebrate those good grades or that healthy heart, and know that your hard work is paying off! If your grades or your fitness aren't so great, don't write yourself off. Such feats take dedication and discipline. Setting reasonable daily and long-term goals will help.

Hunger: A Closer Look

7. What physiological and environmental factors influence hunger?

Ever been asked to relate an embarrassing moment from your past? I don't have to think long to come up with several examples, one of which includes my first college date. Friday morning, second week of college. The plan was to "meet at the snack bar after English," where we could have a Coke and work through that early what-do-I-say awkwardness. If things progressed, perhaps a meal and movie would follow.

No sooner did we sit down than my stomach let out a growl so loud that people in both booths across from us turned quickly to look. In hopes of distracting my lovely companion, I started naming movies I'd like to see. But it happened again! Not quite as loud, perhaps, but twice the duration. These empty-stomach pangs, which I was powerless to control, did not make a good impression. I did go out for a meal and a movie that night—with my not-as-lovely roommate, Chad.

Inopportune stomach noise is a fact of life, and it generally indicates hunger. However, other factors—some physiological, some environmental—also tell us when to eat.

PEANUTS

THE EARS HEAR THE CAN OPENER..

RIGHT AWAY THE STOMACH KNOWS THAT SUPPER IS COMING..

HOW DO THE EARS TELL THE STOMACH?

I'VE NEVER BEEN ABLE TO FIGURE THAT OUT..

Physiology of Hunger

For a physiological understanding of hunger, we turn first to some key substances in your body, and then to your brain's control of these substances.

MODULE 11

■ JOURNAL WRITING

Invite students to use the following questions and writing prompts as springboards for entries in their psychology journals:

- Do you eat because of internal or external cues? How have your family's attitudes about food influenced your eating habits?
- What, if any, cultural influences are you aware of that affect how you feel about your weight?
- Have you felt pressure to look a certain way, especially in terms of your weight? If so, what was your experience? How did you feel about this pressure? What was your response to it? What, if anything, would you change about your response?

As students read through the section on hunger, have them review their journal writing. They can confirm or revise their notions about eating habits and self-image in relationship to food and weight based on what they've learned.

trb At this point, you may wish to use Technology Application Activity: *PsychQuest:* "How Do We Control How Much We Eat?" (*Teacher's Resource Binder,* p. 11-1)

■ LOOKING AT THE ISSUES

Have students briefly reflect on the most effective leader they have known. It should be someone they have personally seen in action—it's best if they choose someone they themselves have followed. Ask each student to write down the characteristics and behaviors that make that person an effective leader. After students have completed the assignment (either before or in class), have them meet in small groups and share their written reactions. Have each group record their members' responses with an eye toward common themes. Finally, have each small group report back to the full class.

trb At this point, you may wish to use Application Activity: *Theory X and Y Orientation Scale* (*Teacher's Resource Binder,* p. 11-1; Handout 11–13) and Application Activity: *Assessing Leadership Style* (*Teacher's Resource Binder,* p. 11-1; Handout 11–14).

Cooperative Learning

Divide students into small groups and present them with a situation in which they must come up with a plan to motivate people to work in that situation. Their motivation plan should include concepts discussed in the text, including cultivating intrinsic motivation, attending to individual motives, setting specific yet challenging goals, choosing a specific leadership style for success. Here are some situations you could assign to groups:

- coaching a team in a championship game
- teaching a middle school or high school class about a difficult subject
- leading a choir or orchestra in performing a challenging piece
- motivating a retail store's employees to meet a weekly sales goal
- teaching young children how to share

MODULE 11

F • Y • I

Extremes in blood sugar levels can be harmful to one's health. Here are two conditions related to blood sugar levels:

- **Hypoglycemia** occurs when blood sugar levels run too low due to a lack of food.
- **Hyperglycemia** occurs when blood sugar levels run too high.

LOOKING AT THE ISSUES

Research into the role of the hypothalamus in weight control has raised hope of a weight-control pill that would trigger the appropriate part of this region of the brain to have a person either eat or feel satiated. In a full-class discussion, elicit students' responses to the following questions:

- Would such a pill be popular? Why or why not?
- How would this pill affect eating habits of people over time?
- What might be some long-term effects on health from the use of this pill?

F • Y • I

The **lateral hypothalamus (LH)** is the part of the brain that controls the desire to eat. When its LH is stimulated, a rat will eat without becoming satiated. The **ventromedial hypothalamus (VMH)** is the part of the brain that controls satiety. When its VMH is stimulated, a rat will starve to death, acting as though it has eaten and does not need food.

trb At this point, you may wish to use **Technology Application Activity:** *PsychSim:* **"Hunger and the Fat Rat"** (*Teacher's Resource Binder*, p. 11-1).

► **set point** The point at which an individual's "weight thermostat" is supposedly set. When the body falls below this weight, increased hunger and a lowered metabolic rate may act to restore the lost weight.

► **basal metabolic rate** The body's resting rate of energy expenditure.

- ***Glucose*** This form of sugar circulates throughout your body. Run low on glucose, and you will feel hungry. Glucose is a major source of energy for your body.
- ***Insulin*** This hormone allows our cells to use glucose for energy or convert it to fat. When levels of insulin go up, glucose levels go down.
- ***Leptin*** This protein is produced by bloated fat cells, which send out a "stop eating" message. Artificially increased leptin levels in mice stimulate activity and reduce eating. Obese mice receiving leptin injections lose weight (Halaas & others, 1995). The leptin receptors in obese humans may be insensitive to leptin, however (Considine & others, 1996), and studies are under way to determine whether some drug treatment might help activate those receptors.
- ***Orexin*** This hunger-triggering hormone is produced by the hypothalamus. When glucose levels drop, orexin levels rise, and we feel hungry.

What do all these substances have in common besides hunger? Your brain controls them all in some way. Your hypothalamus, a key structure in your brain, actively regulates your appetite in many ways (Figure 11.6). For example, the hypothalamus monitors leptin level to estimate available fat. We've learned a lot from medical records of people who had tumors near the base of the brain (the location of the hypothalamus) and subsequently became very overweight (Miller, 1995). We've also learned a lot from rats. Damage to parts of the hypothalamus that restrain eating will produce excessive eating in rats. Stimulate those areas and a rat will instead starve to death.

One interesting theory views the hypothalamus as a "weight thermostat." This thermostat is genetically engineered to maintain a **set point,** which is the weight a full-grown active person hovers around when not trying to gain or lose weight (Lissner and others, 1991). (As a teen, your body doesn't yet have a set point because you're still growing and still gaining weight as a part of normal development.) Regardless of how much the person eats in a given day (and calorie intake does vary), the scale will pretty much register the same weight. Set point theory relies on three underlying concepts:

Figure 11.6 **The Hypothalamus** The hypothalamus (colored red in this picture), contains important hunger controls. Depending on the information it receives through substances in your blood, your hypothalamus can send messages that encourage you to eat or stop eating.

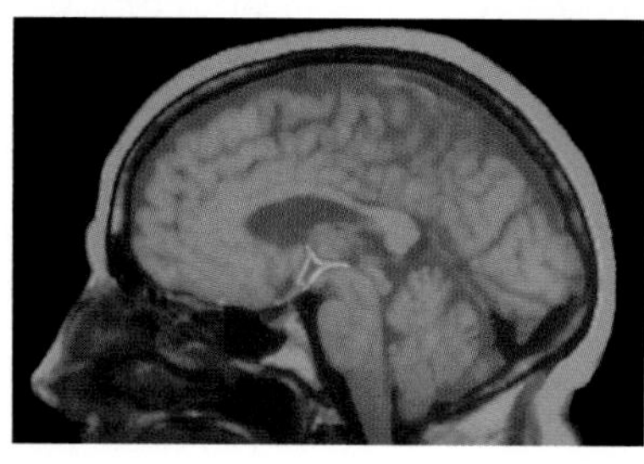

1. We have a **basal metabolic rate** (the resting rate at which we burn calories for energy).
2. We have a specific number of fat cells (which can expand in size and increase in number).
3. We have hormones that work together to keep our weight where it's designed to be.

The metabolism of a normal-weight person who overeats will speed up, preventing weight gain. But an overweight person's metabolism reacts differently. When overweight people diet, their bodies view the reduced intake of calories as starvation. Their metabolism slows down to conserve energy, converting more glucose to fat in preparation for the apparent "famine." Set point theory may help explain why so many people who lose weight dieting gain the weight back: They are returning to their set point.

Hunger in the Brain Damage to the part of the hypothalamus responsible for controlling eating led to a threefold increase in weight for this rat, providing evidence for the brain's control of hunger mechanisms.

Environment and Hunger

Certainly, our body chemistry and the thermostatlike action of the hypothalamus fuel our drive to eat. But physiology is not the only hunger catalyst. We should also consider external incentives and culture.

External Incentives

The sight, sound, and smell of food—all external incentives—seem to affect some people more than others, whose eating habits appear to be triggered more by internal factors. This difference is so striking that researchers have labeled the first group "externals" and the other group "internals." In one study, researchers had "internals" and "externals" fast for 18 hours. They then took the two groups into a laboratory where steak was cooking. Compared with the "internals," "externals" experienced a greater increase in blood insulin levels, in hopeful anticipation of incoming food energy (Rodin, 1984). External stimuli affect the hunger-related physiological states in many individuals.

GARFIELD® **by Jim Davis**

■ **APPLYING THE POINTS**

Using available resources, including the Internet, have students gather information about popular weight-loss programs, such as Weight Watchers, Jenny Craig, the Atkins Diet, and so forth, to see how well these programs address the physiology of hunger. The research should focus on gathering information that allows students to answer the following questions:

- Do the programs focus on what type of food to eat or how much food to eat? What are the reasons behind the recommendations?
- How do the programs address motivational issues, like environment and culture, which are issues that arise in dieting?
- Do the programs address the concept of set point? Why or why not?

trb At this point, you may wish to use **Critical Thinking Activity:** ***A Survey of Eating Habits*** (*Teacher's Resource Binder*, p. 11-1; **Handout 11–15**) and **Enrichment Lesson:** *Body Image Survey Results* (*Teacher's Resource Binder*, p. 11-1).

■ **TEACHING TIP**

Discuss with students whether they believe they are "internals" or "externals" by posing the following questions:

- What foods can they resist? What foods do they find difficult or impossible to resist?
- What environmental or cultural factors influence their eating habits?

This discussion will help students apply this knowledge to their own lives.

MODULE 11

■ **APPLYING THE POINTS**
Invite a local physician or psychologist who specializes in eating disorders to come and speak about anorexia and bulimia. Eating disorders are prevalent among adolescents—both male and female—making such a presentation both timely and relevant.

■ **MULTICULTURAL CONNECTIONS**
The text suggests that culture has a large impact on our eating habits and taste preferences. With permission, interview students from various cultures to find out what foods they eat that are different from foods eaten in general American culture. Also, have students research how other cultures view body images—for example, whether thin is "in" elsewhere in the world.

trb At this point, you may wish to use **Enrichment Lesson:** *Taste Preferences—Learned and Genetic* (*Teacher's Resource Binder*, p. 11-1).

■ **TEACHING TIP**
Be sensitive in your discussion of eating disorders. Disorders like anorexia and bulimia are prevalent among adolescents, and it may or may not be obvious that some students struggle with these problems. Help students see that eating disorders are difficult to diagnose and treat. Prejudices and stereotypes about people with these disorders may lead students to hide their struggles rather than seek the help they need.

trb At this point, you may wish to use **Technology Application Activity:** *PsychQuest:* **"How Do We Control How Much We Eat?"** (*Teacher's Resource Binder*, p. 11-1) and **Critical Thinking Activity:** *A Survey of Eating Habits* (*Teacher's Resource Binder*, p. 11-1; **Handout 11–15**).

▶ **anorexia nervosa** An eating disorder in which normal-weight people (usually adolescent females) suffer delusions of being overweight, put themselves on self-starvation regimens, and become dangerously underweight (15 percent or more).

▶ **bulimia nervosa** An eating disorder characterized by episodes of overeating, usually of high-calorie foods, followed by vomiting, use of laxatives, fasting, or excessive exercise.

Culture

Culture also shapes our attitudes toward eating. White Americans often see obesity as a weakness or a sign of laziness. African-Americans and Latinos tend to be less concerned about weight and generally more accepting of those who are overweight (Crandall, 1988; Hebl & Heatherton, 1998). Culture also affects taste. We tend to shun foods to which we have not been exposed, while not thinking twice about eating the familiar foods we've seen all our lives on the dinner table. I've never eaten horse, dog, or rat meat, but people in other parts of the world readily accept these foods and even prefer them to foods I consider a great treat, such as shrimp. Repeated exposure to new foods increases our willingness to give them a try (Pliner, 1982; Pliner & others, 1993).

Eating Disorders

8. Why do people develop eating disorders?

A member of my daughter's ballet class at the beginning of the year looked like a perfectly normal 15-year-old—5 feet, 5 inches tall, and weighing 120 pounds. As the year went by, this young woman became thinner and thinner, though she continued to make remarks to other members of the class about "how fat" she was. Some wondered if she was ill. Obsessed with losing weight, she eventually hit 90 pounds before finally getting treatment for **anorexia nervosa,** an eating disorder in which a normal-weight person (9 times out of 10, an adolescent female) has a distorted self-perception of being "fat." Anorexia sufferers diet and exercise excessively and become dangerously underweight.

Despite the attention the press has given to eating disorders lately, they aren't confined to the present time. Years ago, I remember hearing stories of how cheerleaders and drill-team members (all girls) at other schools had to "weigh in" every Monday morning as a means of monitoring weight. Rumors also flew that many of these girls were *bulimic,* which meant they had **bulimia nervosa,** an eating disorder characterized by excessive eating (bingeing) followed by vomiting (purging), laxative use, fasting, or excessive exercise. Binge-purge eaters are fearful of gaining weight, preoccupied with food, and often suffer from depression and/or anxiety (Hinz and Williamson, 1987). Individuals with anorexia often display bulimic characteristics as well.

Recipe for Eating Disorders Excessive concern over weight may lead to anorexia or bulimia nervosa. This girl is in an inpatient treatment program for anorexia, and writes in a journal to help her clarify the emotions that contribute to her disorder.

Cross-Curricular Connections

DANCE, CHEERLEADING, AND WRESTLING Have students consult with the dance instructor, cheerleading sponsor, and wrestling coach about how they address weight and food issues with members of their squads. Use the following questions to elicit findings students' discovered during these consultations:

- Are there weight limits for being a member of the squad? Why or why not?
- Do they monitor the weight of squad members? Why or why not?
- Have they ever had to approach a student about weight issues (being either overweight or underweight)? How did they handle that situation?

trb At this point, you may wish to use **Enrichment Lesson:** *Body Image Survey Results* (*Teacher's Resource Binder*, p. 11-1).

The Perfect Form? Because they are surrounded by pictures of what are considered to be perfect body types, many people feel imperfect by comparison.

What causes these eating disorders? For some, there may be a genetic link. Twin studies show that identical twins are much more likely to have the same eating disorder than fraternal twins are (Fichter & Noegel, 1990). Another line of research indicates that some people may be at higher risk because they have abnormal levels of chemicals that facilitate neural communication (Fava & others, 1989).

Without question, however, the genetic factors interact with a cultural pressure to be thin. These pressures are particularly strong in weight-conscious cultures. Mothers who are unusually concerned about their own weight and about the weight and appearance of their daughters are more likely to have a child with an eating disorder (Pike & Rodin, 1991). Anorexia usually starts as a diet, and bulimia often has its origins in a diet broken by gorging.

Our society bombards us with pictures of the "perfect" body in commercials and advertisements, an image unobtainable by nearly everyone. Our weight-obsessed culture worsens the situation, sending the message that fat equals weakness. Susan Wooley and Orland Wooley (1983, p. 884) sum up culture's impact in a nutshell: "An increasingly stringent cultural standard of thinness for women has been accompanied by a steadily increasing incidence of serious eating disorders in women."

The common thread running through these discussions of biological, cognitive, or clinical explanations is the notion of *motives.* The same thread that weaves its way through hunger and eating disorders continues through discussions of terrorism, leadership, and other motivated behaviors. Though hidden like the processor in a computer, motives energize and direct behavior, whether the goal is for good or bad. Understanding motives will help us predict and control all kinds of behaviors.

The noblest motive is the public good.
Virgil (70 B.C.–19 B.C.)

MODULE 11

■ **LOOKING AT THE ISSUES**

Have students explore society's cultural pressure to be thin. Have students, both male and female, take their measurements (chest, waist, hip, and leg and arm circumference) and calculate the averages of these measurements and share that information with the class.

- Into what size clothes would someone with these measurements fit?
- Do magazines portray people who have these measurements?
- Do students feel as though they are the same, smaller, or larger than people featured in magazine ads? Why or why not? How does this make them feel about their body image?

trb At this point, you may wish to use **Enrichment Lesson:** ***Body Image Survey Results*** (*Teacher's Resource Binder*, p. 11-1).

Close

This module closes with a quote from the Roman author Virgil: "The noblest motive is the public good." Motives create the undercurrent for all behavior, good or bad. In a class discussion, have students contemplate the following questions about motives:

- How have the motives of others helped and/or hurt you in your life? How have your own motives helped and/or hurt others?
- Do you agree with Virgil's assessment of the ultimate positive motive? Why or why not?

MODULE 11

Checking the Points

■ TEACHING TIPS

web (1) The book companion site for *Thinking About Psychology* at **www.worthpublishers.com/thinkingaboutpsych** contains a module quiz, flashcards of key terms and people, and other student activities and resources for this module. You will also find PowerPoint lectures, a quiz grade book, and other reaching resources by logging on as an instructor.

trb tr (2) At this point, you can help students review and confirm their understanding of motivation with **Critical Thinking Activity:** *Fact or Falsehood?* (*Teacher's Resource Binder*, p. 11-1; **Handout 11–1**) by using the handout as a transparency to project for the class. Ask students not to refer to a version of the handout they may have completed earlier. Then read each item on the handout and have students respond to the item as *true* or *false*. For items about which students have differing responses, ask those that disagree to cite passages in the text to support the correct answer; wait for a class consensus before moving on to the next item.

REVIEW

Module 11: Motivation

What's the Point?

Historic Explanations

Instinct theory and drive-reduction theory were psychologists' first attempts to explain our motives.

1. *In what ways are instinct theory and drive-reduction theory similar, and how do they differ?*

   Instinct theory and drive-reduction theory both attempted to understand human motives by relating them to underlying urgent physical pushes that point our behavior in certain directions. Instinct theory tried to explain motives in terms of instincts—unlearned, preprogrammed behavior. This theory fell out of favor because the long list of instincts merely described human behavior but did not explain it. Drive-reduction theory tried to connect behavior to human needs, such as hunger, but it could not explain such human motives as curiosity or thrill-seeking behavior.

Biological Explanations

Biological theories of motivation explain behavior as a response to underlying physical states.

2. *What is the basic idea in arousal theories of motivation? Is homeostasis the same as drive reduction?*

   Arousal theories, such as the Yerkes-Dodson law, state that each of us has an ideal level of stimulation, and that we behave in certain ways to maintain that level. Arousal theories explain motives such as curiosity and thrill seeking in this context.

   Homeostasis is the body's tendency to maintain a balanced internal state, by regulating the level of various substances (such as hormones or water) or processes (such as temperature). The concept of drive reduction focuses on removing deficits (lack of water); the concept of homeostasis focuses on avoiding either deficits or excesses (too much water in the system *or* too little water in the system).

Cognitive Explanations: Intrinsic and Extrinsic Motivation

Cognitive theories of motivation attempt to explain behavior in terms of how our thoughts direct our actions.

3. *Why is intrinsic motivation more beneficial than extrinsic motivation?*

   Extrinsic motivation—motivation imposed from outside yourself—is the desire to perform certain behaviors because you believe you will receive a reward or avoid a punishment. Intrinsic motivation—motivation that stems from inside of you—is a desire to perform a behavior for the satisfaction you feel while performing it. Research indicates that internal motivation tends to lead to high achievements, but that extrinsic motivation may not be able to maintain behaviors when the external authority stops offering the reward or threatening the punishment.

Clinical Explanations

Clinical theories of motivation explain behavior in terms of basic human needs for fulfillment. These theories are drawn from intensive studies of relatively small numbers of people.

4. *Are some needs more basic than others?*

   Abraham Maslow's hierarchy of needs states that we must satisfy lower needs, such as the needs for water, food, and safety, before we can attempt to satisfy higher needs that allow us to reach our full potential. Maslow's five levels are physiological needs, safety needs, belongingness and love needs, esteem needs, and self-actualization needs. His theory has been widely applied in the world of business. Maslow's critics note that his research methods did not meet the standards for controlled scientific studies, and that his theory does not explain some behaviors, like fasting in order to make a political point.

5. *How do psychologists measure achievement motivation?*
   Achievement motivation is the desire for significant accomplishments; for the mastery of ideas, things, or people; and for attaining a high standard. David McClelland came up with the idea of measuring a person's achievement motivation by having the individual write a story about what is happening in an ambiguous photo. Researchers then count the number of times that achievement shows up in the story, and this gives them a score that represents the individual's level of achievement motivation.

6. *How can we motivate ourselves to give our best effort? How can we motivate others to do the same?*
   Experts give three tips for motivating yourself: Connect your high achievements with positive emotions; connect all of your achievements with your own efforts, and raise your expectations of what you can achieve. Experts also give four tips for motivating others: Cultivate intrinsic motivation, attend to individual motives, set specific and challenging goals, and choose an appropriate leadership style for yourself and the situation.

Hunger: A Closer Look

7. *What physiological and environmental factors influence hunger?*
   Physiological influences—such as levels of glucose, insulin, leptin, and orexin—contribute to our desire to eat. The hypothalamus, a structure in the brain, may function much like a thermostat, maintaining the set point for weight. But the environment also triggers the desire to eat. External cues (sights, smells, images) and culture (exposure to food defined as appealing) also motivate hunger.

8. *Why do people develop eating disorders?*
   Two common eating disorders are bulimia nervosa, characterized by bingeing and purging, and anorexia nervosa, characterized by a distorted self-perception of being fat and excessive dieting and exercise. We don't yet have a full explanation for these disorders, but researchers who have studied the disorders among twins believe that genetic factors, possibly involving biochemistry, are part of the answer. Cultural pressures to be thin—a particular danger in the United States, which is obsessed with "perfect" bodies and "ideal" weights—may act as a catalyst to trigger the disorders.

Key Terms

motivation, p. 207
instinct, p. 208
drive, p. 208
drive-reduction theory, p. 208
Yerkes-Dodson law, p. 210
homeostasis, p. 210
extrinsic motivation, p. 212
intrinsic motivation, p. 212
hierarchy of needs, p. 213
self-actualization, p. 213
achievement motivation, p. 214
task leadership, p. 216
social leadership, p. 216
set point, p. 218
basal metabolic rate, p. 218
anorexia nervosa, p. 220
bulimia nervosa, p. 220

Key People

Abraham Maslow, p. 213
Henry Murray, p. 214

trb tr ■ **TEACHING TIP**

At this point, you may wish to provide students with a fresh copy of **Building Vocabulary:** *Crossword Puzzle* (*Teacher's Resource Binder*, p. 11-1; **Handout 11–2**). If students have filled in the puzzle earlier in the module, ask them not to refer to that version. In small groups, have students complete the puzzle as a review of vocabulary related to motivation concepts. You may also wish to project the handout as a transparency, providing students with a correctly completed puzzle to use as a check against their group's work.

MODULE 11

tb Using the Test Bank

The *Test Bank* that accompanies this textbook offers a wide variety of questions in different formats and levels of complexity. Use the software to construct whole tests or to integrate standardized questions into teacher-made tests.

Self-Test Answers

Multiple-Choice Questions

1. c, 2. d, 3. a, 4. a

Self-Test

Multiple-Choice Questions

Choose the *best* answer for each of the following questions:

1. Maria loves to swim and is an excellent diver. Mr. Perez, Maria's father, hopes her special skill at swimming will earn her an athletic scholarship to college, and he has decided to pay Maria $3 for every hour she spends in the community pool. Mr. Perez may find that his plan will not work because
   a. $3 an hour is not much to pay as an hourly reward.
   b. Maria's love of swimming may increase so much that he will be unable to pay for all the hours she spends in the pool.
   c. Maria may lose her love of swimming because the reward will take away her intrinsic motivation for this activity.
   d. external rewards are never effective.

2. Former President George Bush celebrated his seventy-second birthday by donning a parachute and a sky-diving suit and jumping from a plane. The type of motivation theory that would best explain this behavior is a(n)
   a. historic theory, like drive-reduction theory; historic theories are old, as is a man who is 72.
   b. clinical theory, like Maslow's hierarchy of needs; the former president apparently wanted to satisfy his basic need for safety.
   c. instinct theory; the former president seemed to have an instinct for flying.
   d. biological theory, like arousal theory; the former president probably wanted to increase his level of stimulation.

3. Thomas has just taken a job as manager of the people who test game software before the programs are released for sale. Thomas wants to be a good manager and keep people happy. He also knows that he is responsible for maintaining quality and holding the schedule. He is thinking of doing the four things listed below. Which of these four is a BAD idea if Thomas wants to motivate the testers to do their best work possible?
   a. Using extrinsic motivation to control the testers so that the testers will know he's aware of how quickly or slowly they are working.
   b. Adopting a social leadership style so that the testers will feel that they are part of the decision-making process.
   c. Finding out what motivates each tester so that he can provide suitable work tasks for each of them.
   d. Setting weekly goals that are just a bit higher than last year's goals so that the testers will feel challenged.

4. Lily works in the psychology department at a local university. She reads stories that research participants have written about some people in a batch of photos. As she reads, Lily counts the number of times that the stories mention heroic acts, pride in accomplishments, or pursuit of a goal. The people who wrote these stories probably participated in a study of
   a. achievement motivation.
   b. homeostatic regulatory mechanisms.
   c. Maslow's hierarchy of needs.
   d. the Yerkes-Dodson law.

Alternative Assessment/Portfolio Project

A WEEK OF FOOD Have students keep a food diary for at least a week. They should record all the food they eat and all the beverages they drink. At the end of the week, have them reflect on the following questions:

- Compare your eating choices with the FDA's food pyramid. Do your eating habits reflect the recommendations for a healthy diet? Why or why not?
- Why did you eat what you ate and drink what you drank? What were the motives that drove your choices?
- Upon reflection on your eating choices, what would you change? Why? What would you keep the same? Why?

5. Andrea visited Ethiopia with her college roommate. Andrea, who loves to eat, lost her appetite at dinner the first night when her roommate's mother served a spicy stew containing cow's stomach, a great delicacy in Ethiopia. Andrea's loss of appetite was an example of the influence of
   a. culture on hunger—Andrea probably had anorexia nervosa, which is common in the United States.
   b. culture on hunger—cow's stomach is a delicacy in Ethiopia, but not in the United States.
   c. physiology on hunger—Andrea's insulin levels were probably too low from not eating properly while on the plane.
   d. physiology on hunger—Andrea had probably reached her set point, and she couldn't eat any more.

Matching Terms and Definitions

6. For each definition, choose the *best* matching term from the list that follows:

Definition

a. An aroused tension state created by an imbalance that prompts an organism to restore the balance.
b. The theory that a degree of psychological arousal helps performance, but only up to a certain point.
c. The point at which an individual's "weight thermostat" is supposedly set.
d. A complex behavior that is rigidly patterned throughout a species and is unlearned.
e. A need or desire that energizes and directs behavior.
f. An eating disorder characterized by episodes of overeating, followed by vomiting or use of laxatives.
g. The body's resting rate of energy expenditure.
h. A need to live up to one's fullest and unique potential.

Term

(1) motivation
(2) instinct
(3) drive
(4) drive-reduction theory
(5) Yerkes-Dodson law
(6) self-actualization
(7) set point
(8) basal metabolic rate
(9) bulimia nervosa
(10) anorexia nervosa

Fill-in-the-Blank Questions

7. A(n) ________________ is a complex, unlearned behavior found throughout a species.

8. ________ ________ theory focuses on removing deficits; ________________ focuses on avoiding both deficits *and* excesses.

9. ________________ leadership focuses on setting standards, organizing work and directing attention toward goals ; ________________ leadership is group-oriented and focuses on building teamwork, mediating conflict, and offering support.

Brief Essay Question

10. What is the principle on which Abraham Maslow constructed his hierarchy of needs? In two paragraphs of three or four sentences each, explain the basic idea, describe the five levels of the hierarchy, and mention one or two points critics raised about Maslow's theory.

Self-Test Answers

Multiple-Choice Questions (continued)

5. b

Matching Terms and Definitions

6. a. (4), b. (5), c. (7), d. (2), e. (3), f. (9), g. (8), h. (6)

Fill-in-the-Blank Questions

7. instinct, 8. Drive-reduction; homeostasis, 9. Task; social

Brief Essay Question

10. Students should understand that the underlying principle behind Maslow's theory is that we must meet more basic needs before we can attend to more complex ones. Ensure that students list the five levels of the hierarchy found on page 213 of their text. They should also point out that several examples exist that refute Maslow's contention that people satisfy basic needs before seeking to fulfill more complex ones.

MODULE 12

Performance Standards

Standard Area: Motivation and Emotion

Content Standard 6: Biological, affective, cognitive, and behavioral aspects of emotions and how they interact with one another

Performance Standard 6.1 Explain the different theories of emotion, such as James-Lange, Cannon-Bard, or cognitive theories.

- Present the James-Lange theory of emotion and criticisms of this theory. (Student Text pp. 228–229)
- Explain the Cannon-Bard theory of emotion. Contrast it with the James-Lange theory. (Student Text pp. 228–229)
- Figure 12.1, "Three Theories of Emotion," contrasts the James-Lange, Cannon-Bard, and Schachter's theories of emotion. (Student Text p. 229)
- Explain Schachter's two-factor theory of emotion. (Student Text p. 230)
- Discuss Robert Zajonc's conclusions that cognition is not always necessary for emotion. (Student Text p. 230)
- Explain Richard Lazarus' beliefs that some emotional responses do not require conscious thought. (Student Text p. 231)
- Figure 12.3, "Two Paths to Emotional Responses," compares the theories of Zajonc and Lazarus on the role of cognition in emotion. (Student Text p. 231)

Content Standard 7: Effects of motivation and emotion on cognition, behavior, and perceptions

Performance Standard 7.1 Explain perceptual differences between those who differ in motivation.

- Consider how gender affects our ability to express and understand emotion. (Student Text pp. 236–237).
- Investigate how culture influences how we express emotions and how we interpret the emotions of others. (Student Text pp. 237–238).
- Discuss how "display rules" affect how we express emotions. (Student Text pp. 237–238)

Standard Area: Biological Bases of Behavior

Content Standard 2: Structure of the nervous system

Performance Standard 2.2 Divide the roles of the different subdivisions of the nervous system.

- Compare the roles of the sympathetic and parasympathetic nervous systems in understanding what physiological changes occur when you experience fear. (Student Text pp. 232–233)
- Figure 12.5, "The Division of Labor in the Autonomic Nervous System," illustrates how these two systems affect change in the body. (Student Text p. 233)

Materials NETWORK

All of the items from the Video, Activity, and Enrichment Centers listed below come from the *Teacher's Resource Binder.* These items will help you teach and expand on concepts presented in Module 12.

trb This logo indicates when an item from the Materials Network may be used in conjunction with a specific note found in this module's *Teacher's Edition.*

Theories of Emotion

Activity Center

- Critical Thinking Activity: *Fact or Falsehood?* With this activity, students' preconceptions about emotions are either exposed as incorrect or reinforced as correct. (*Teacher's Resource Binder,* p. 12-1; **Handout 12–1**)
- Building Vocabulary: *Matching People and Concepts* Students learn about people and concepts in this module through a handout that requires them to match each name or concept with a description or definition. (*Teacher's Resource Binder,* p. 12-1; **Handout 12–2**)
- Graphic Organizer: *Theories of Emotion* The three main theories of emotion are difficult to understand because they use the same terminology but a different sequence of events. Students can clarify each of the three theories of emotion with this graphic organizer. (*Teacher's Resource Binder,* p. 12-1; **Handout 12–3**)
- Analysis Activity: *Brief Measure of Positive and Negative Affect—The Positive and Negative Affect Scales (PANAS)* Studies of affective structure have shown that positive and negative affect are the two primary dimensions of mood. Which do your students experience more—positive or negative emotions? This scale analyzes the quality of their emotional lives. (*Teacher's Resource Binder,* p. 12-1; **Handout 12–4**)
- Application Activity: *Facial Feedback and the James-Lange Theory of Emotion* With a pencil, students can manipulate their facial expression, thereby influencing their emotional responses to newspaper cartoons. (*Teacher's Resource Binder,* p. 12-1; **Handout 12–5**)
- Application Activity: *The Affect Grid* How would students rate their mood right now—pleasant or unpleasant, aroused or sleepy? This quick measure of current affect allows students to discover what their moods really are. (*Teacher's Resource Binder,* p. 12-1; **Handout 12–6**)
- Application Activity: *The Relationship Between Affect and Personality Traits* To assess the content of a person's emotional life, researchers have sometimes asked volunteers to keep a record of their daily experiences over several weeks or even months. Larsen and Diener's Daily Mood Form provides a vehicle for students to measure their daily affect over time and relate it to their personality traits. (*Teacher's Resource Binder,* p. 12-1; **Handout 12–7**)
- Application Activity: *The Mood Awareness Scale* How aware are we of our moods? "High mood monitors" are more likely to show greater self-consciousness, more neuroticism, lower self-esteem, and greater negative affect. Students can use this measure to not only extend the theories of emotion as presented in the text of Module 12 but also to get the inside story on their awareness of mood. (*Teacher's Resource Binder,* p. 12-1; **Handout 12–8**)

Enrichment Center

- Enrichment Lesson: *Opponent-Process Theory and the Psychology of Addiction* Addiction can be explained by the opponent-process theory of emotion—for every positive emotion experienced, a negative emotion will follow. This lesson explains this relationship, shedding light on why addictions are so powerful. (*Teacher's Resource Binder,* p. 12-1)
- Enrichment Lesson: *Cognitive Appraisal and Emotion* The text of Module 12 indicates that emotion researcher Richard Lazarus has emphasized the importance of cognitive appraisal in emotion. Lazarus' work on cognitive appraisal is extended and clarified in this lesson. (*Teacher's Resource Binder,* p. 12-1)
- Enrichment Lesson: *Public and Private Self-Consciousness* The text indicates that cognition is an important element in emotions. You may want to extend this principle by discussing individual differences in self-consciousness, specifically the distinction between private and public aspects of self-consciousness. (*Teacher's Resource Binder,* p. 12-1)

Fear: A Closer Look

Activity Center

- Analysis Activity: *The Affect Intensity Measure* Some people consistently experience their emotions more strongly than do others, and this measure will help your students see how intensely they experience affect. (*Teacher's Resource Binder,* p. 12-1; **Handout 12–9**)

- **Evaluation Activity:** *Envy and Jealousy* Fear can lie at the center of other emotions, namely envy and jealousy. Help students discover their own susceptibility to these emotions with this measure—the Dispositional Envy Scale (DES). (*Teacher's Resource Binder,* p. 12-1; **Handout 12–10**)
- **Analysis Activity:** *What Do You Fear?* Fears are pervasive in most people's lives. This activity will help students discover what they fear—from bugs to lightning to public speaking (which most people fear more than death!). This measure is adapted from the Temple Fear Survey Inventory. (*Teacher's Resource Binder,* p. 12-1; **Handout 12–11**)
- **Application Activity:** *Using the GSR to Detect Deception* Polygraph machines measure, among other things, the galvanic skin response, which is theoretically tied to our emotional responses to lying. This activity allows students to see how the galvanic skin response works in detecting deception. It also introduces students to the polygraph and the controversy surrounding it. (*Teacher's Resource Binder,* p. 12-1)
- **Application Activity:** *The Disgust Scale* The things Americans find disgusting are not universal. This scale helps students see what they find disgusting—which is likely related to what they fear. (*Teacher's Resource Binder,* p. 12-1; **Handout 12–12**)

Enrichment Center

- **Enrichment Lesson:** *The Amygdala and Fear* The amygdala is involved in the learning of both animal and human fears.The amygdala is often referred to as "emotion central." Much research has been done into this brain structure's role in our emotional lives, especially in how we feel and express fear. (*Teacher's Resource Binder,* p. 12-1)
- **Enrichment Lesson:** *Scared to Death* It is possible to be scared to death—literally. Understandably, few drop dead under a researcher's eye. This lesson relates several true stories of this phenomenon as well as explanations as to why it happens. (*Teacher's Resource Binder,* p. 12-1)
- **Enrichment Lesson:** *Government Confidence in the Polygraph* If polygraphs are so unreliable, why do law enforcement agencies and attorneys place such weight on them? This article explores this irony in greater detail, noting that the confidence in the polygraph is both surprising and worrisome. (*Teacher's Resource Binder,* p. 12-1)
- **Enrichment Lesson:** *Detecting Deception* The cues we think indicate deception—such as direct eye contact, excessive smiling, and posture shifts—are not the cues people provide when they are actually trying to deceive us. This lesson highlights the nonverbal cues that do indicate deception and describes the research study that has uncovered these cues. (*Teacher's Resource Binder,* p. 12-1)

The Expression of Emotion

Activity Center

- **Analysis Activity:** *Emotional Expressivity Scale* The Emotional Expressivity Scale (EES), highlighted in this activity, assesses the extent to which people outwardly display their emotions. (*Teacher's Resource Binder,* p. 12-1; **Handout 12–13**)
- **Technology Application Activity:** *PsychSim:* **"Culture and Gestures"** *PsychSim* is an interactive CD-ROM containing tutorials in different content areas of psychology. In this tutorial, students discover how certain gestures are universal while others are unique to a culture. (*Teacher's Resource Binder,* p. 12-1)
- **Cooperative Learning Activity:** *Nonverbal Communication* Students can learn valuable lessons about the importance of nonverbal communication with this team-building activity in which students must accomplish a task without talking to each other. This exercise in nonverbal communication, frequently used in therapeutic settings, also works well in the classroom. (*Teacher's Resource Binder,* p. 12-1)
- **Analysis Activity:** *The Affective Communication Test* Much less research has been done on the complementary process of nonverbal expressiveness as compared to emotional recognition. To measure individual differences in expressiveness, use this Affective Communication Test. (*Teacher's Resource Binder,* p. 12-1; **Handout 12–14**)
- **Technology Application Activity:** *PsychSim:* **"Expressing Emotion"** *PsychSim* is an interactive CD-ROM containing tutorials in different content areas of psychology. In this tutorial, students manipulate facial features to create certain emotions. (*Teacher's Resource Binder,* p. 12-1)

Enrichment Center

- Enrichment Lesson: *Cultural Differences in Emotional Expression* Emotional life is shaped by its cultural context. How are the Japanese different from the Bedouins of Egypt? Why don't Tahitians express sadness? This lesson explores the reasons behind the different ways emotions are expressed in other cultures. (*Teacher's Resource Binder*, p. 12-1)
- Enrichment Lesson: *"Catch the Feeling"* Emotions are contagious! For a long time, researchers have observed that therapists tend to "catch" their clients' feelings. Also, parents communicate their feelings to their children and vice versa. Additionally, friends resonate to each other's needs. This lesson explores the theories behind emotional contagion and the implications for this remarkable phenomenon. (*Teacher's Resource Binder*, p. 12-1)

MODULE 12

Emotion

Introducing the Module

The Points: Module Objectives

- Identify the two main historical theories of emotion, and describe how modern cognitive theories of emotion differ from these older theories.
- Describe the physiological changes that occur when you are frightened.
- Describe how we communicate our emotions to others.
- Analyze how gender and culture affect our ability to express our own emotions and read the emotions of others.

trb Building Vocabulary

Improve and confirm students' knowledge of the module by having them match people and concepts to definitions and descriptions in **Building Vocabulary:** *Matching People and Concepts* (*Teacher's Resource Binder*, p. 12-1; **Handout 12–2**).

■ **TEACHING TIP**

Encourage students to share their emotions regarding the different types of situations presented at the beginning of the module. How did they explain these events? How did they react to others after these types of events? What recommendations would they have for making these experiences more stable, emotionally, for others?

trb At this point, you may wish to use **Application Activity:** *The Mood Awareness Scale* (*Teacher's Resource Binder*, p. 12-1; **Handout 12–8**) and/or **Application Activity:** *The Affect Grid* (*Teacher's Resource Binder*, p. 12-1; **Handout 12–6**).

MODULE 12

Emotion

Every school year, I see lists of names posted by the theater, band room, athletic office, and other locations around the school. Have you ever searched a list looking for your name? The cast list for a play? Honor roll? An election? Chair placements in the band? Did your name appear where you'd hoped—or where you'd feared? Perhaps it was left off altogether.

Having posted a few lists myself for student council elections, I have witnessed students jumping and screaming with happiness, excitement, and surprise. I've seen others, clearly disappointed and with tears in their eyes, force a smile and walk bravely away. Still others did little to disguise their anger.

The **emotions** these students were having were full-body responses, involving physical arousal, expressive behaviors, and conscious experiences. Let's see how this might work. Imagine that you and a good friend check the National Honor Society list to see whether either of you has been chosen. A smile breaks across your face as you see your name. You pump your fist above your head and give a little whoop of joy. Then, checking the list again, you notice your friend's name missing. Reining in your emotions, you start providing explanations, such as, "I was lucky to have made it," or "Maybe your name was left off by mistake." Your shift from personal happiness to shared sadness with your friend contains the three ingredients of emotion:

► **emotions** Whole-organism responses, involving (1) physiological arousal, (2) expressive behaviors, and (3) conscious experience.

Getting Started

Before students read the module, have them come up with a one- or two-sentence response to the question, "What is emotion?" As students work their way through this module, suggest that they compare this written response to what they learn about emotion from the text.

trb You may wish to use **Critical Thinking:** *Fact or Falsehood?* (*Teacher's Resource Binder*, p. 12-1; **Handout 12–1**) as a pre-reading strategy to find out what students already know about emotion. The activity will prime students to note terms and concepts in the text that confirm or dispel their preconceptions about this subject.

- ***Physiological activation***—increased heart rate as you read the good news, decreased heart rate as you console your disappointed friend.
- ***Expressive behaviors***—smiling and pumping your fist after seeing your name, losing the smile and putting an arm around your friend's shoulder when you notice her name is missing.
- ***Conscious experience***—interpreting what it means to be a member, and what it means to your friend to be left out.

Compared with other species, from dolphins to deer to ducks, humans appear to be the most emotional (Hebb, 1980). This rich source of human behavior has intrigued psychologists for more than a century now, and has also sparked some pretty emotional debates. Those debates revolve around two controversies, both addressing the order in which each ingredient is stirred into the recipe for emotions.

1. Which comes first, physiological arousal or the subjective experience of an emotion? Do you feel happy because your heart is pounding, or is your heart pounding because you feel happy?
2. Can we react emotionally before appraising a situation, or does thinking always precede emotion? Did you feel joy at seeing your name on the list before you thought about what that meant, or did you interpret the situation and then feel joy?

To answer these questions, psychologists have been proposing theories and designing experiments to test them for over 100 years.

"I don't sing because I am happy. I am happy because I sing."

Which Comes First? Is it the physiological arousal or the emotional experience? This issue has been widely debated in psychology.

Theories of Emotion

What's the Point? 1. What were the two main historical theories of emotion, and how do modern cognitive theories of emotion differ from these older theories?

As is often the case when several perspectives exist on a given topic, the theories of emotion are complementary: Each provides some insight into why or how we experience emotions.

Historical Approaches

Ask the person with the locker next to yours why she is smiling, and she might say, "Because I'm happy." Why did you slam your locker door? "Because I'm angry." Why are you trembling? "Because I'm afraid." Common sense explains any of these emotions as a result of a *stimulus*

Suggested Readings

Use the following books as teacher-preparation tools or as enrichment for advanced students:

Axtell, R. E. (1991). *Gestures: The do's and taboos of body language around the world.* New York: Wiley.

Carlson, J., & Hatfield, E. (1992). *Psychology of emotion.* Fort Worth, TX: Harcourt Brace Jovanovich.

Deaux, K., Dane, F., & Wrightsman, L. (1993). *Social psychology in the 90s* (6th ed.). Pacific Grove, CA: Brooks/Cole.

LeDoux, J. (1998). *The emotional brain: The mysterious underpinnings of emotional life.* New York: Simon & Schuster.

Parkinson, B., Totterdell, P., Briner, R. B., & Reynolds, S. (1996). *Changing moods: The psychology of mood and mood regulation.* New York: Longman.

MODULE 12

Teaching the Points

web ■ **TEACHING TIP**

You can log on as an instructor to the book companion site for *Thinking About Psychology* at www.worthpublishers.com/thinkingaboutpsych. It contains teacher resources for class presentations as well as review and assessment of module concepts and terms.

■ **JOURNAL WRITING**

Invite students to use the following questions and writing prompts as springboards for entries in their psychology journals:

- Would you like never to be sad again? Why or why not?
- Would you share another person's total life experience? Why or why not?
- Do you want to measure your positive emotions? Why or why not? How would such a measure be used in everyday life?

trb At this point, you may wish to use Analysis Activity: *Brief Measure of Positive and Negative Affect—The Positive and Negative Affect Scales (PANAS)* (*Teacher's Resource Binder*, p. 12-1; Handout 12–4).

■ **APPLYING THE POINTS**

Do animals experience emotion? Invite a zoologist or animal researcher to discuss with students the extent to which animals express emotions.

■ **LOOKING AT THE ISSUES**

Pose the following question to the class: "Are humans the only species to experience complex emotional reactions?" Using available resources, including the Internet, have students research emotions in animal species. Afterward, promote a discussion in which students respond to that question as well as these follow-up questions:

- How do researchers measure emotional responses in animals?
- Why have humans evolved to experience emotions of greater complexity than animals experience . . . or have they?
- Does the idea of animals experiencing emotions make you think differently about them? Why or why not?

MODULE 12

■ TEACHING TIP

The theories of emotion can be difficult to keep straight. Each theory uses the same terminology to discuss emotions—namely, *physiological arousal* and *cognitive labeling.* These concepts, however, are presented in different orders, depending on the theory. Help students organize these theories by presenting them on a flowchart.

trb At this point, you may wish to use **Graphic Organizer:** ***Theories of Emotion*** (*Teacher's Resource Binder*, p. 12-1; **Handout 12–3**) and/or **Application Activity:** ***Facial Feedback and the James-Lange Theory of Emotion*** (*Teacher's Resource Binder*, p. 12-1; **Handout 12–5**).

F • Y • I

William James has long been considered one of the greatest minds in psychology, even though he never took a course in his field. He wrote the first psychology textbook, *Principles of Psychology*; taught the first course in psychology offered in America (at Harvard); and conducted experiments in psychology at about the same time as Wilhelm Wundt (the widely regarded "father of psychology"). Yet James hated doing experiments, feeling they were tedious, and disliked being called a "psychologist." And not only was he related to Walter Cannon—his brother was the famous novelist Henry James.

William James (left) and Carl Lange (right)

► **William James** (1842–1910) American psychologist who believed our awareness of physiological responses leads to our experience of emotion (see *James-Lange theory*).

► **Carl Lange** (1834–1900) Danish physiologist who proposed a theory of emotion similar to, and at about the same time as, William James' theory that our awareness of physiological responses leads to our experiences of emotion (see *James-Lange theory*).

► **James-Lange theory** The theory that our experience of emotion is our awareness of our physiological responses to an emotion-arousing stimulus.

► **Walter Cannon** (1871–1943) American physiologist who, along with Philip Bard, concluded that physiological arousal and emotional experience occur simultaneously (see *Cannon-Bard theory*).

► **Cannon-Bard theory** The theory that an emotion-arousing stimulus simultaneously triggers (1) physiological responses, and (2) the subjective experience of emotion.

(for instance, a fire alarm) leading to a conscious feeling (fear) and a physiological response (shaking, increased heart rate). In other words, using fear as the example, the fire alarm sounds, you experience fear, and your heart starts to race. Early theories on emotion do not agree with this commonsense approach.

Psychologist **William James** and physiologist **Carl Lange** proposed theories at about the same time (the 1890s) challenging the commonsense sequence of emotions. James and Lange wrote that our experience of emotion is our awareness of our bodily responses to the emotion-producing stimulus. So, with the **James-Lange theory,** the fire alarm sounds, you start shaking, you become aware of the shaking, and you label this reaction as fear.

Walter Cannon (James' son-in-law!) disagreed with the James-Lange view of emotion. Cannon (1929) noted that the heart races whether we're frightened, angry, or exhilarated. How, then, can the same physiological reaction trigger such different emotional interpretations? And how do we explain circumstances where we have such reactions without any emotion-provoking stimuli? Peeling onions, for example, produces the bodily response usually associated with sadness, but peeling onions does not cause sadness. Cannon proposed that an emotion-arousing stimulus *simultaneously* triggers (1) physiological responses *and* (2) the subjective experience of emotions. After elaboration by Philip Bard (1934), this view of simultaneous bodily responses and emotional experience became known as the **Cannon-Bard theory** of emotion.

Each of these older *psychophysiological* theories helps us understand emotion. We do in fact feel emotions, to some degree, by observing changes in our bodies, as the James-Lange theory maintains. But the Cannon-Bard theory was also correct in asserting the important role the brain and nervous system play in our conscious feelings (Figure 12.1).

Suggested Readings *(continued from previous page)*

Pinker, S. (1997). *How the mind works.* New York: Norton.

Platt, C. (1989). *When you can live twice as long, what will you do?* New York: Morrow.

Somerville, R. (Ed.). (1994). *Emotions: Journey through the mind and body.* Alexandria, VA: Time-Life Books.

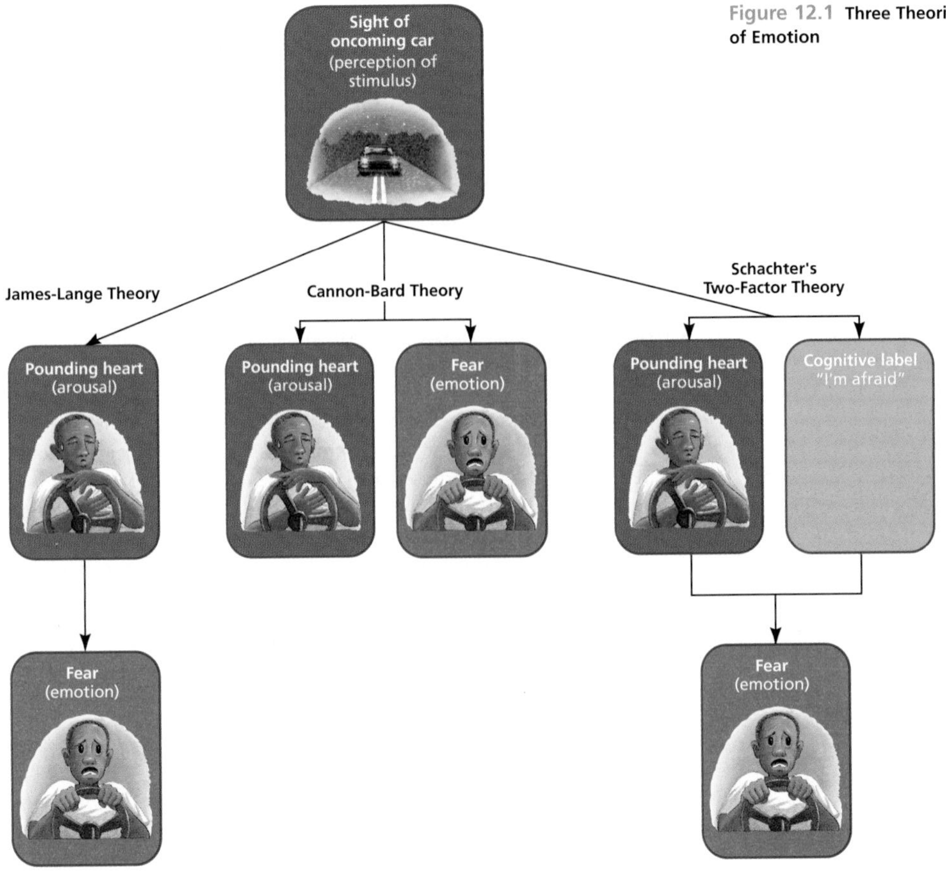

Figure 12.1 **Three Theories of Emotion**

Sight of oncoming car (perception of stimulus)

James-Lange Theory: Pounding heart (arousal) → Fear (emotion)

Cannon-Bard Theory: Pounding heart (arousal) + Fear (emotion)

Schachter's Two-Factor Theory: Pounding heart (arousal) + Cognitive label "I'm afraid" → Fear (emotion)

Modern psychophysiological explanations tie the importance of hormone levels to emotions. Higher levels of testosterone, for example, are linked to aggression. But does aggression cause testosterone levels to increase, do higher levels of testosterone cause aggression, or does some third factor cause both of them? To answer such questions, psychologists have examined the way our thoughts influence our emotions.

Cognition and Emotion

Which comes first—our thoughts about a situation (our *cognitive appraisal*) or our experience of the emotion? This chicken-and-egg dilemma characterizes the second of the two controversies in the study

■ TEACHING TIP

A four-color transparency of Figure 12.1, Three Theories of Emotion, is available in the **Overhead Transparencies Set.**

■ LOOKING AT THE ISSUES

Using available resources, have students research how hormones influence mood and behavior. Guide a discussion of students' findings with the following questions:

- Do higher levels of estrogen lead to mood swings? Why or why not?
- Does more testosterone lead to increased violence? Why or why not?

Demonstrating

EMOTIONAL REACTIONS Have students simulate different emotional reactions to the point where they physically experience the emotion. For example, students can increase their breathing and try to cry to simulate fear or sadness, or they can begin to laugh hysterically to simulate happiness or joy. Conclude the demonstration by asking students the following questions:

- Did this exercise create an emotional feeling in you? Why or why not?
- What theory does this exercise support? Why?

trb At this point, you may wish to use **Application Activity:** *Facial Feedback and the James-Lange Theory of Emotion* (*Teacher's Resource Binder*, p. 12-1; **Handout 12–5**).

MODULE 12

(F • Y • I)

The amygdala is part of the limbic system of the brain, along with the hippocampus and the basal ganglia. A scientist named James Papez (rhymes with "apes") theorized that this part of the brain was responsible for the expression of emotion, and it was originally called *Papez's circuit.* Using advanced technology, researchers have shown that Papez's ideas about the brain regions controlling emotions were correct.

trb At this point, you may wish to use **Enrichment Lesson:** *The Amygdala and Fear* (*Teacher's Resource Binder,* p. 12-1).

■ APPLYING THE POINTS

Have volunteers relate a time when they felt the same type of physical feeling for different emotions. To help students relate their experiences, ask the following questions:

- What emotions have similar physical bases?
- Have you ever tried to convince yourself that you were feeling a different emotion? How did you do it? Were you effective?

■ TEACHING TIP

Make a link between *Robert Zajonc's arguments* and the discussion of *reflexes* in Module 3. Because reflexes work by passing on messages that control movement before processing in the brain occurs, we can avoid dangerous situations without having to take time to think about them.

■ JOURNAL WRITING

Invite students to use the following questions and writing prompts as springboards for entries in their psychology journals:

- Have you ever experienced a reflexive emotional reaction? Describe your experience.
- Does this experience make you agree with a particular theory of emotion? Why?

Stanley Schachter

of emotion. Let's look at some contemporary cognitive approaches to emotion: the two-factor theory, and two different theories that attempt to explain the sequence of events in emotions.

Stanley Schachter (SHACK-ter) and Jerome Singer (1962) developed one of the leading cognitive theories of emotion. In their **two-factor theory,** the first factor is *physiological arousal,* which can be brought about by anything from a loud stimulus to a drug. The second factor is a *cognitive label* of the physiological arousal. The bottom line to this theory is that the only distinguishing characteristic among emotions is how we label the arousal we are feeling. If you're aroused and you believe the appropriate emotion is fear, you'll feel afraid. If you think anger is the appropriate emotion, you'll instead explain your arousal as anger. According to two-factor theorists, our physical experiences of emotions are so similar that we must appraise and label our reactions in order to experience an emotion.

Do all cognitive psychologists agree with this viewpoint? Certainly not. **Robert Zajonc** (ZI-yence) (1980, 1984a) argues that emotion and cognition are separate, and that our interpretations of situations are sometimes slower than our emotional reactions. In other words, before we know what we think about a situation, we know how we feel about it. Complex research supports Zajonc's argument.

▶ **Stanley Schachter** (1922–1997) American psychologist who, with Jerome Singer, concluded that emotion requires a cognitive label of physiological arousal (see *two-factor theory*).

▶ **two-factor theory** The theory that to experience emotion one must (1) be physically aroused, and (2) cognitively label the arousal.

▶ **Robert Zajonc** (1923–) American psychologist who concluded that some emotional reactions involve no deliberate thinking and cognition is not always necessary for emotion.

▶ **Richard Lazarus** (1922–) American psychologist who concluded that some emotional responses do not require conscious thought.

We have pathways in our brain carrying or transmitting messages from one part of our nervous system to another. Certain pathways skip the cortical (thinking) parts of the brain and take a more direct path to the *amygdala,* an emotion control center in the brain (Figure 12.2). Some researchers (LeDoux & Armony, 1999) believe these shortcuts explain why our feelings are more likely to control our thoughts, than our thoughts are to control our feelings, particularly when we're surprised. For example, imagine that you are raking leaves on a fall afternoon. You hear and see some leaves rustling, and you jump back, not knowing whether the rustling was caused by the wind blowing or by a snake in the grass. After your immediate fear response, the thinking part of your brain takes over, and you take steps to determine whether danger is present ("It's a snake! Run!").

Zajonc believes that emotions are basic to human existence, and that they developed before cognition in the history of our species. For these reasons, cognition need not always take place prior to emotion. Not all emotion researchers agree with Zajonc.

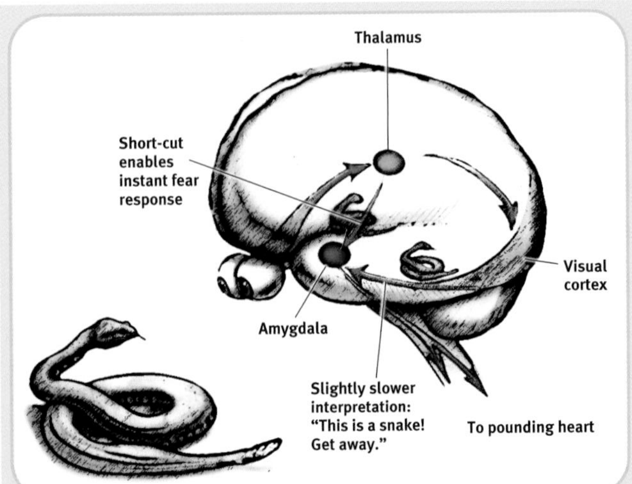

Figure 12.2 **First Run, Then Think!** Your brain has short-cuts that allow you to react almost instantly to a frightening situation instead of thinking about what you should do and why you should do it.

Richard Lazarus (1991, 1998) does agree that our brains can process information outside of our *conscious* awareness, and that some emotional responses do not require conscious thought. However, Lazarus believes there must be at least a minimal amount of *unconscious* thinking, even for emotions we feel instantaneously; how else would we know what we're reacting to? The initial appraisal of the rustling leaves produces an emotion, in this case fear, and an accompanying jump away, based on a snap assessment that the situation may be harmful. A secondary, conscious appraisal involves deciding what to do after the immediate, initial response (Figure 12.3).

Most of the emotions we face daily are much more complex than a primitive fear of snakes, and they require more complex cognitive appraisals. Being the first one in your family *not* to make a select team

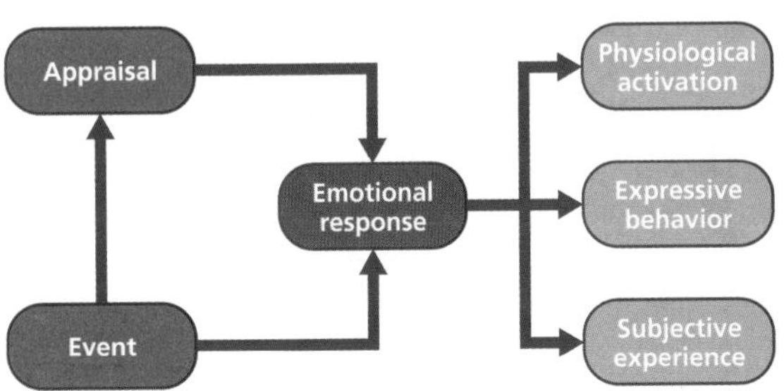

Figure 12.3 **Two Paths to Emotional Responses** According to Robert Zajonc, some emotional responses are immediate and do not require conscious appraisal. However, our appraisal and labeling of events also determine our emotional responses. Lazarus, Schachter, and Zajonc all agree on this last point.

■ TEACHING TIP

Four-color transparencies of Figure 12.2, First Run, Then Think!, and Figure 12.3, Two Paths to Emotional Responses, are available in the **Overhead Transparencies Set.**

F • Y • I

Richard Lazarus conducted experiments using mild electrical shock on his patients. He noticed that they would react to the shock without realizing it. He called this ability to react emotionally without conscious awareness **subception.**

trb At this point, you may wish to use **Enrichment Lesson:** ***Cognitive Appraisal and Emotion*** (*Teacher's Resource Binder*, p. 12-1).

■ LOOKING AT THE ISSUES

Lazarus studied the importance of preparing a person for emotion. He and his associates documented that a person's emotional reactions to witnessing a film on a painful event could be lessened by describing the procedure in a matter-of-fact way or heightened by emphasizing the pain the subject was experiencing. In a full-class discussion, ask the following questions:

- Before surgery, how could this research be used by doctors to help their patients?
- How can parents use this research to help rear their children?
- How could activists use this information to motivate people to join the cause?

Demonstrating

BALLOON REACTIONS Blow up several balloons and have a stickpin ready so you can pop them at a given time. Replicate the procedure Lazarus used to prepare people for emotional reactions. Establish a baseline reaction by popping one balloon at a random point, catching the class off guard. Then, run one trial in which you matter-of-factly explain that you will be popping the balloon, preparing them for the uncomfortable experience of hearing it pop. Next, run another trial in which you emphasize how painful it is to hear a balloon pop. Dramatize the "pain" as much as possible. After the second trial, ask students how your preparation in each instance changed their subception of the event.

trb At this point, you may want to use **Enrichment Lesson:** ***Cognitive Appraisal and Emotion*** (*Teacher's Resource Binder*, p. 12-1).

MODULE 12

trb ■ CHECKING FOR UNDERSTANDING

During class, have students develop oral or written explanations of the differences among the three main theories of emotion. You may also wish to use **Graphic Organizer:** *Theories of Emotion* (*Teacher's Resource Binder*, p. 12-1; **Handout 12–3**) as an assessment tool by having students fill in the spaces with the information that best describes each theory's approach to explaining emotions.

■ JOURNAL WRITING

Invite students to use the following questions and writing prompts as springboards for entries in their psychology journals:

- What do you fear the most? How did this fear develop? Have you tried anything to overcome this fear? Describe your experience.

trb At this point, you may wish to use **Analysis Activity:** *The Affect Intensity Measure* (*Teacher's Resource Binder*, p. 12-1; **Handout 12–9**).

▶ **autonomic nervous system** The part of the nervous system that controls the glands and the muscles of the internal organs (such as the heart). Its sympathetic division arouses; its parasympathetic division calms.

might produce immediate disappointment that, after further analysis, leads to the complex emotion of shame. A note of consolation from a friend who *did* make the team can produce a slow, warming feeling of happiness *if* you choose to see the effort as heartfelt and *if* you have a history of warm exchanges with that friend. Our more complex emotions, such as love, happiness, shame, and guilt, are rooted in our conscious interpretations, appraisals, and memories of earlier experiences. *How* we think about the situations also affects these emotions. Thinking positively about situations makes us feel better; thinking negatively makes us feel worse.

While there are competing theories about our understanding of emotion, there is little debate about how your body reacts to certain emotions, such as fear. It's time now to take an in-depth look at what we know about fear.

Fear: A Closer Look

2. What physiological changes occur when you are frightened?

You know that your body undergoes changes as you experience emotions like fear. Some are obvious: A fire alarm goes off, and your stomach seems to turn inside out, your muscles tense, and your mouth may even go dry. But your body is also busy in other not-so-obvious ways, preparing you for this alarming situation. Your blood is flowing away from organs with momentarily nonessential functions and coursing toward other body parts you may need more in this emergency. For instance, your digestion slows, but blood flow increases to the muscles you'd need to run away. Your pupils dilate, or increase in size, allowing more light into your eyes and improving your vision. Your liver dumps sugar into your bloodstream for energy, and perspiration appears to cool your churned-up body. All of these involuntary activities underscore your body's incredible and wonderful response to a dangerous situation. Perhaps most wondrous of all, you did not have to think about or consciously activate this system of defenses in any way.

Sympathetic Nervous System Arousal?

Your response to dangerous situations is coordinated by a two-pronged arrangement called your **autonomic nervous system.** Your autonomic nervous system has two divisions, one that arouses and one that calms (Figure 12.4). The arousing side, the

Demonstrating

THE DISGUST RESPONSE Many complex emotions have their roots in fear. Disgust is one of these emotional reactions that may have evolutionary explanations. Paul Rozin's taste test demonstrates how the disgust response is very different from simple rejection of unpleasant tastes, smells, and sights. Ask students to consider the following question: "Which of the following glasses of water would you drink?"

- one that contains an odorless, harmless chemical that is terribly bitter
- one that is laced with a lethal dose of arsenic
- one that is sterile and contains only pure water but had previously held a sample of dog feces

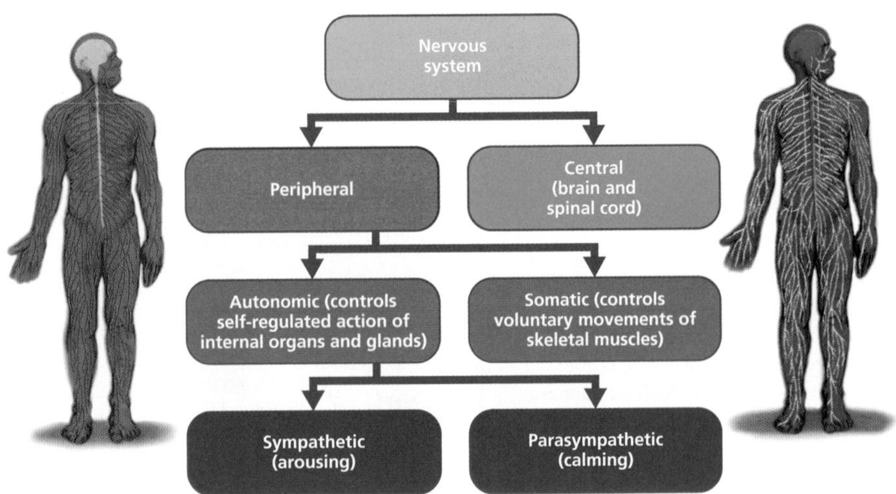

Figure 12.4 The Main Divisions of the Human Nervous System Your autonomic nervous system, which regulates the automatic responses of your organs and glands, is part of your body's overall nervous system.

sympathetic division, accelerates your heart rate, increases respiration (breathing level), and increases the secretion of hormones that help prepare your body for "fight or flight." The calming side, the *parasympathetic division,* slows your breathing, heart rate, and secretion of stress hormones (Figure 12.5).

Measuring autonomic nervous system responses to questions is sometimes used in a misguided effort to detect whether someone is telling the truth (see Thinking Critically: Detecting Lies, pages 234–235).

Autonomic nervous system controls physiological arousal

Sympathetic division (arousing)		Parasympathetic division (calming)
Pupils dilate	EYES	Pupils contract
Decreases	SALIVATION	Increases
Perspires	SKIN	Dries
Increases	RESPIRATION	Decreases
Accelerates	HEART	Slows
Inhibits	DIGESTION	Activates
Secrete stress hormones	ADRENAL GLANDS	Decrease secretion of stress hormones

Figure 12.5 The Division of Labor in the Autonomic Nervous System

"Disgust," explains Rozin, "involves rejection based not on sensory properties but on knowledge of the nature of something." And it is about something other than fear of injury or sickness. The second glass containing poison elicits a different, less violent reaction than knowing what used to be in the third.

trb At this point, you may wish to use **Application Activity:** ***The Disgust Scale*** (*Teacher's Resource Binder,* p. 12-1; **Handout 12–12**).

■ MULTICULTURAL CONNECTIONS

Ask students, "Are fears common the world over?" After a brief discussion, have students choose a culture other than their own to research what people from that culture fear and how they express their fear.

trb At this point, you may wish to use **Technology Application Activity:** ***PsychSim:*** **"Culture and Gestures"** (*Teacher's Resource Binder,* p. 12-1) and/or **Enrichment Lesson:** ***Cultural Differences in Emotional Expression*** (*Teacher's Resource Binder,* p. 12-1).

■ TEACHING TIPS

tr (1) A four-color transparency of Figure 12.4, The Main Divisions of the Human Nervous System, is available in the **Overhead Transparencies Set.**

(2) Have students categorize different reactions to fear as being either *flight* or *fight.* For example, if you jump back when an angry dog lunges at you, you are experiencing a **flight response.** If you stand up to a bully, you are experiencing a **fight response.** This categorization can help students see the link between the autonomic nervous system and behavior.

trb **tr** A black-line master for Figure 12.5, The Division of Labor in the Autonomic Nervous System, is available in the **Black-Line Masters Appendix** of the *Teacher's Resource Binder.*

trb At this point, you may wish to use **Analysis Activity:** ***What Do You Fear?*** (*Teacher's Resource Binder,* p. 12-1; **Handout 12–11**).

F • Y • I

Usually, phobias are learned responses to a stimulus; therefore, they can be extinguished using traditional conditioning techniques, like systematic desensitization. Typically, however, most people do not seek treatment for their phobias, since phobias do not necessarily interfere with one's daily life.

trb At this point, you may wish to use **Analysis Activity:** ***What Do You Fear?*** (*Teacher's Resource Binder,* p. 12-1; **Handout 12–11**) and/or **Enrichment Lesson:** ***Scared to Death*** (*Teacher's Resource Binder,* p. 12-1).

■ **APPLYING THE POINTS**

The following activities will help students better understand the use of polygraph tests in law enforcement:

- Have students interview a lawyer, police officer, and judge to get each person's opinion on the use of polygraphs in criminal investigations.
- Invite a lawyer or law school professor to discuss issues related to polygraph tests with students, such as the admissibility of polygraph results in court.

trb At this point, you may wish to use **Application Activity:** *Using GSR to Detect Deception* (*Teacher's Resource Binder*, p. 12-1) or **Enrichment Lesson:** *Government Confidence in the Polygraph* (*Teacher's Resource Binder*, p. 12-1).

■ **JOURNAL WRITING**

Invite students to use the following questions and writing prompts as springboards for entries in their psychology journals:

- How do you act when you lie? Can others tell when you are lying? How does lying make you feel?
- Do you believe polygraph machines accurately detect lying? Why or why not? Have your thoughts on this subject changed after reading this module? If so, how?

trb At this point, you may wish to use **Enrichment Lesson:** *Detecting Deception* (*Teacher's Resource Binder*, p. 12-1).

Thinking Critically

Detecting Lies

TV newscasts and newspaper front pages carry frequent reports of crime suspects agreeing or refusing to take a **polygraph** or lie-detecting test. Would you agree to take a lie-detector test if you were wrongly accused of committing a crime? Most of us answer this question with a resounding, "Of course!" After all, if we're not guilty, what have we to hide, right? Well, it's not quite that simple. Careful review of the research on polygraphs may cause you to rethink your answer.

A polygraph machine monitors changes in heart rate, respiration, and perspiration to determine whether a person is feeling emotional stress about a particular question. The underlying assumption is that a person will show stronger autonomic nervous system responses when lying than when telling the truth.

Unfortunately, polygraphs measure *all* stress reactions, including those from honest people who are upset by a question, not lying in their answer. Controlled studies of polygraph interpretations have produced some disturbing results. In one study (Kleinmuntz & Szucko, 1984), professional polygraph interpreters judged 37 percent of the innocent people they tested guilty. In the same study, these experts correctly identified the guilty parties only 76 percent of the time, meaning nearly one-fourth of the real liars fooled the machine (Figure 12.6). Hundreds of other studies on the validity of polygraph tests yield similar results (Ben-Shakhar & Furedy, 1990).

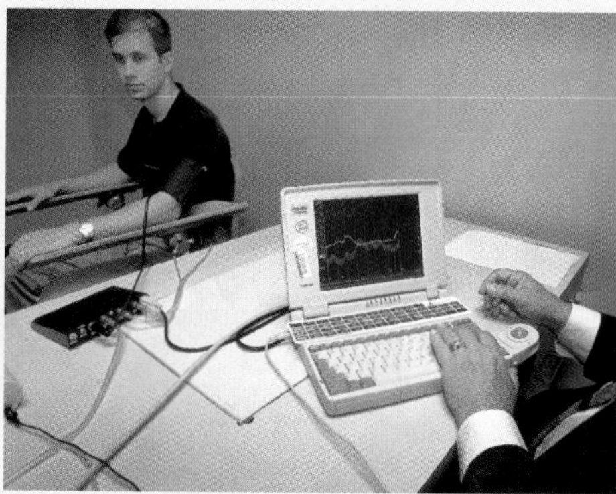

A Typical Polygraph Setup Do tests like this reliably predict who the liars are?

A more effective polygraph test asks questions about details that would be known only by those committing the crime (Bashore & Rapp, 1993). Even this test, however, relies on the same under-

The Expression of Emotion

3. How do we communicate our emotions to others?

Measuring hormone levels or using sophisticated electronic equipment to detect other physiological changes are not the only means of recognizing emotions. We communicate emotions all the time without saying a word.

Cross-Curricular Connections

MASS COMMUNICATIONS Have students watch some "cop shows" over the next week or so to see how these shows handle polygraphs.

- Do they seem to rely on polygraph evidence to investigate and indict suspects or try defendants?
- Do any cite research on polygraphs as an argument against their use?
- Are defendants willing to submit to polygraphs? Why or why not?

trb At this point, you may want to use **Enrichment Lesson:** *Government Confidence in the Polygraph* (*Teacher's Resource Binder*, p. 12-1).

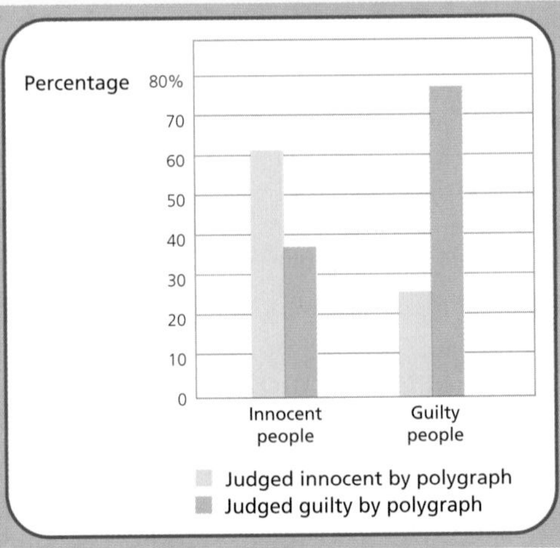

Figure 12.6 How Accurate? One research study (Kleinmuntz & Szucko, 1984) showed that expert interpretations of polygraph tests judged more than one-third of the innocent people taking the tests to be guilty. These experts also declared that almost 25 percent of the guilty were judged innocent by the test.

▶ **polygraph** A machine, commonly used in attempts to detect lies, that measures several physiological responses (such as perspiration, heart rate, blood pressure, and breathing changes) accompanying emotion.

lying assumption: Strong autonomic nervous system responses indicate lying. This means that we must exercise extreme caution in how we use polygraph test results.

"We can't determine if you're telling the truth, but you should have a doctor check your pressure."

Nonverbal Communication

Has this ever happened to you? A teacher calls on you in class to answer a question, and you kind-of-sort-of know the answer. While you stumble your way through your reply, your teacher stops nodding in agreement, turns away with arms crossed and brow furrowed, and looks down at the floor. Meanwhile, the student next to you shoots her arm up in the air, apparently ready to answer after you're through trying. Both

tr ■ **TEACHING TIP**

A four-color transparency of Figure 2.5, Experimental Design, is available in the **Overhead Transparencies Set**.

■ **JOURNAL WRITING**

Invite students to use the following questions and writing prompts as springboards for entries in their psychology journals:

- Has your nonverbal communication ever been misinterpreted? How and why? Did you change your future behavior in light of this misinterpretation? If so, how?
- How well do you think you understand the opposite sex's body language? Do you agree that women are better able to read body language than men? Why or why not?

trb At this point, you may wish to use **Cooperative Learning Activity:** ***Nonverbal Communication*** (*Teacher's Resource Binder*, p. 12-1).

Cross-Curricular Connections

GOVERNMENT Using available library and Internet resources, have students research local, state, and federal laws concerning the use of the polygraph in criminal investigations. Have students address the following questions in their research:

- Have laws regarding the use of polygraphs changed because of research on the tests' ineffectiveness?
- Why are law enforcement officials so confident in their use of the polygraph in investigations?

trb At this point, you may wish to use **Enrichment Lesson:** ***Government Confidence in the Polygraph*** (*Teacher's Resource Binder*, p. 12-1).

■ LOOKING AT THE ISSUES

Does each gender seem to have "rules" for emotional expression? Ask students whether the following would be acceptable in our culture:

- two men kissing when greeting each other
- two women patting each other on the behind during a sports competition
- men crying at a sad movie
- women violently expressing anger
- men hugging each other to celebrate an occasion

Students may giggle at some of these scenarios, but they demonstrate that each gender has "acceptable" rules for expressing emotions with each other.

trb At this point, you may wish to use **Technology Application Activity:** *PsychSim:* **"Expressing Emotion"** (*Teacher's Resource Binder*, p. 12-1).

your classmate and the teacher clearly communicated their feelings, even though they said nothing. You knew *exactly* what they were thinking because they communicated with you *nonverbally.*

Nonverbal communication, or *body language,* is a frequent messenger of our emotions to others. Our facial expressions, tone of voice, and hand gestures often give us away. We tend to look at a person's mouth to detect happiness but at the eyes for anger and fear. When we talk about someone "wearing his heart on his sleeve," we mean that person readily communicates emotions nonverbally. With either a quickly averted glance or an extended gaze, we can communicate everything from submission to dominance, disinterest to intimacy (Kleinke, 1986).

How we communicate and interpret emotions seems to depend on whether we are male or female, and on what our culture has taught us about appropriate public behavior.

Gender and Cultural Effects on Emotion

4. How do gender and culture affect our ability to express our own emotions and read the emotions of others?

Who is better at reading the nonverbal emotions we express, men or women? Studies regularly give the nod to women (Hall, 1987). Women show better skills at detecting emotion in people's facial expressions, body movements, and tone of voice (Blum, 1998). But both males and females find it more difficult to read the body language of the opposite sex than to read the body language of people of their own gender (Buck, 1984).

Men and women also differ in the way they express emotions. North American women smile more, gesture with more expression, and have more expressive faces than their male counterparts (DePaulo & others, 1992; Kring & Gordon, 1998). Women also tend to talk more about their emotions (Grossman & Wood, 1993). North American men, on

Reading Between the Lines Research shows that women are better than men at reading nonverbal emotional cues.

Demonstrating

SOCIAL SELF-CONSCIOUSNESS People who are self-conscious in public are sensitive to social rejection and may be less inclined to express their true emotions. Have students pretend to draw a capital *E* on their forehead using their dominant hand. What direction does the *E* face? If it is oriented so that someone looking at the student would have seen it in the correct position, it is likely that the student is high in public self-consciousness. According to a study by R. Glen Hass, people who are low in public self-consciousness are more likely to draw an *E* from an internal perspective.

trb At this point, you may wish to use **Enrichment Lesson:** *Public and Private Self-Consciousness* (*Teacher's Resource Binder*, p. 12-1).

the other hand, seem to express only one emotion—anger—more openly than women (Coats & Feldman, 1996).

How can we explain these differences? As males and females, are we simply physiologically different, or do we learn to behave differently? Research seems to indicate that at least two factors do affect the way we learn to express and interpret emotions.

1. *Power* is a key issue in interpreting nonverbal communications. In any relationship, from boss-employee to teacher-student, one person always has more power than the other. The person with *less* power will be more motivated to read the nonverbal emotional cues, and will probably read them better, than the person in charge (Fiske, 1993). In one study, Sara Snodgrass (1992) randomly assigned males and females to be either the leader or the follower in two-person teams. She found the followers were more sensitive than the leaders to nonverbal signals, whether the leader was male or female.
2. People raised in expressive families, or in cultures that value being emotionally expressive, are likely to be more expressive, whether they are male or female (Kring & Gordon, 1998).

Culture also influences how we express emotions and how we interpret the emotions of others. Consider the meeting in 1991 between American Secretary of State James Baker and Iraqi Foreign Minister Tariq Aziz. Saddam Hussein, Iraq's president, had sent Aziz, his half-brother, to represent him at this meeting, which followed Iraq's invasion of Kuwait (Triandis, 1994). Baker told Aziz, "If you do not move out of Kuwait, we will attack you." The message was clear and direct, and Baker's body language was calm and subdued. Aziz reported to his brother that Baker was "not at all angry. The Americans are just talking and they will not attack." He misread Baker's nonverbal communication, and thousands of Iraqis died in the war that followed.

What went wrong at this meeting? Baker delivered his message with the restraint customary for an American diplomat. Hussein's brother viewed the communication through the cultural window of his Iraqi heritage, which expects expression to be more emotional. In Iraq, a truly angry person would gesture, shout, and stomp his foot. Neither Baker nor Aziz was aware of the **display rules** for the other's country, the cultural rules governing how and when a person may express emotion (Ekman and others, 1987).

Even the display rules for something as simple as when it's appropriate to smile can vary from one culture to the next. Germans, who smile less often than Americans, often think Americans are hiding their true feelings behind false smiles. Japanese observers of American behavior might disagree, stating that Americans don't smile often enough. In Japan, it is rude to display disappointment or distrust publicly, so the Japanese smile even more than Americans (Hall & Hall, 1990).

▶ **display rules** The cultural rules governing how and when a person may express emotion.

Cross-Curricular Connections

FOREIGN LANGUAGE

- Team-teach a lesson with any or all of the teachers in the foreign-language department. Focus on students' knowledge of the cultures whose languages their classmates might study in school.
- Team-teach a lesson with the ESL/ELL teacher about different cultures that are represented in your school, along with differences and similarities that exist between those cultures and U.S. cultures.

F • Y • I

According to Roger G. Axtell, there is one "ultimate gesture" that carries a certain welcome characteristic, unlike any other single gesture. This ultimate gesture is known everywhere in the world. It is absolutely universal. It is rarely, if ever, misunderstood. Primitive tribes and world leaders alike know and use it. Scientists believe that this particular gesture actually releases chemicals, called endorphins, into the system to create a feeling of mild euphoria.

What is this singular signal, this ultimate giant of all gestures? *(The smile!)*

Source: Axtell, R. E. (1991). *Gestures: The do's and taboos of body language around the world.* New York: Wiley.

trb At this point, you may wish to use Enrichment Lesson: *Cultural Differences in Emotional Expression* (*Teacher's Resource Binder,* p. 12-1).

■ **MULTICULTURAL CONNECTIONS**

Have students explore how people in different cultures express the following emotions: *love* and *affection, fear, discomfort* or *displeasure,* and *anger.*

With permission, students can also interview peers from other cultures about how they express these emotions and how they might be learning to adapt their emotional habits of expression to American cultural standards.

trb At this point, you may wish to use Enrichment Lesson: *Cultural Differences in Emotional Expression* (*Teacher's Resource Binder,* p. 12-1).

■ **APPLYING THE POINTS**

Have students contact the nearest U.S. embassy to ask about rules for diplomatic protocol.

- How does the government prepare diplomats for foreign service?
- What are some common rules of protocol that Americans tend to break when abroad?

MODULE 12

Close

The text challenges students to identify the emotions expressed in the pictures in Figure 12.7. As the text notes, regardless of culture or gender, students should be able to identify correctly what emotion is being expressed. Pose the following questions to students after having them complete this exercise:

- Why is it important to study how and why emotions are expressed?
- Does the knowledge that emotional expression is universal change your attitude about people from other cultures and the opposite gender? Why or why not?

Encourage students to recognize that emotions unify us as a human race. Since we all share these basic responses to the environment, we are really less different than we may appear.

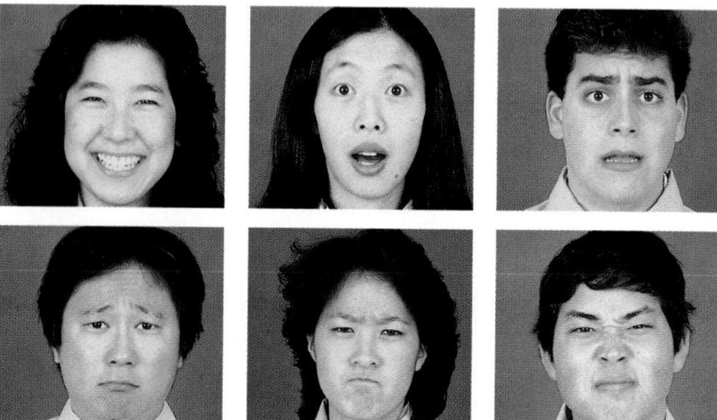

Figure 12.7 **Facial Expressions and Culture** Are facial expressions culturally specific or culturally universal? Can you tell which face shows surprise? Happiness? Sadness? Fear? Disgust? Anger? Find the answers on page 242. (From Matsumoto and Ekman, 1989.)

Cultures also disagree about the meaning behind gestures. Former Presidents Richard Nixon and George H. W. Bush both got themselves in hot water by giving the "OK" sign in countries where this gesture is considered rather vulgar. The hand sign given by University of Texas football fans (index and pinkie fingers up, two middle fingers down) would seriously insult a man in Italy, where that gesture means his wife has been unfaithful.

And what about facial expressions? Are they read differently across cultures? Several studies (Ekman, 1994; Ekman & Friesen, 1975; Izard, 1977, 1994) have attempted to find the answer by showing photographs of different facial expressions to people around the world, asking participants to guess the emotion. How would you do on such a test? Take a minute or two to see if you can label the emotions in the facial expressions in Figure 12.7.

How did you do? Chances are, regardless of your cultural background, you did fairly well. Researchers have found that certain basic expressions rise above culture. Physiological measures of emotion also show consistency across cultures. As in many other areas of study in psychology, we see that while there are significant cultural and gender differences, there is a core of similarity among all people across the globe.

Demonstrating

EXPRESSION IDENTIFICATIONS Have students replicate the study by Matsumoto and Ekman by showing a number of different students the pictures of the emotional expressions in Figure 12.7. Have them choose which emotion goes with each facial expression from a scale that displays the spectrum of emotions. Students can see how well people can identify different emotional reactions.

REVIEW

Module 12: Emotion

What's the Point?

Emotions are full-body responses, involving physical arousal, expressive behaviors, and conscious experience. Theories of emotion have focused on two questions: (1) Which comes first, physiological arousal or the subjective experience of an emotion? and (2) Can we react emotionally before appraising a situation, or does thinking always precede emotion?

Theories of Emotion

1. *What were the two main historical theories of emotion, and how do modern cognitive theories of emotion differ from these older theories?*

   The James-Lange theory proposed that our subjective experience of emotion is our awareness of our body's responses to an emotion-producing stimulus. The Cannon-Bard theory proposed that an emotion-arousing stimulus simultaneously triggers both our body's responses and our subjective experience of the emotion. Each of these theories explains part of how we experience emotion.

   Modern cognitive theories differ from the older theories in their stress on the link between thinking and emotion, and on how our appraisals and interpretations of situations affect our emotions. Some researchers in cognitive psychology also study the structure, function, and biochemistry of the nervous and hormone systems to understand how our bodies change as we experience emotions.

Fear: A Closer Look

2. *What physiological changes occur when you are frightened?*

   We become frightened in situations we define as dangerous. Your body's peripheral nervous system (the part of the nervous system that is *not* the brain and spinal cord) has a built-in, automatic defense system. This defense system is the *autonomic nervous system,* and it has an arousing side (the *sympathetic division*) and a calming side (the *parasympathetic division*). When you are frightened, the sympathetic division puts you on high alert, increasing your heart rate, your levels of breathing and perspiration, and the amount of stress hormones pouring into your bloodstream. It also makes your pupils larger to let in more light, decreases salivation, and closes down processes like digestion, which aren't necessary for your immediate survival. When danger passes, the parasympathetic division turns off the high-alert preparations and returns your body to a calmer state.

The Expression of Emotion

3. *How do we communicate our emotions to others?*

   We express our emotions to others by sending verbal and nonverbal messages. We use facial expressions, tone of voice, hand gestures, and posture to communicate with people around us.

4. *How do gender and culture affect our ability to express our own emotions and to read the emotions of others?*

   Women surpass men at reading nonverbal emotions in facial expressions, body movements, and tone of voice. They also express

Checking the Points

■ **TEACHING TIPS**

web (1) The book companion site for *Thinking About Psychology* at www.worthpublishers.com/thinkingaboutpsych contains a module quiz, flashcards of key terms and people, and other student activities and resources for this module. You will also find PowerPoint lectures, a quiz grade book, and other teaching resources by logging on as an instructor.

trb (2) At this point, you may wish to review and confirm concepts about emotion with **Critical Thinking Activity:** ***Fact or Falsehood?*** (*Teacher's Resource Binder,* p. 12-1; **Handout 12–1**). If students completed a copy of this handout earlier, ask them not to refer to it. Suggest that students complete the handout individually, taking the time to look up information in the text to respond correctly to questions. Then, have them exchange handouts with a classmate to check the answers.

trb (3) With partners, students can also review module concepts in **Graphic Organizer:** *Theories of Emotion* (*Teacher's Resource Binder,* p. 12-1; **Handout 12–3**). They may review organizers they filled out earlier in the module or receive a copy of a blank organizer that they can fill in together as a review. Encourage students to look up information in the text whenever necessary.

MODULE 12

trb **tr** ■ TEACHING TIP

At this point, you may wish to review module vocabulary with the entire class by using **Building Vocabulary:** ***Matching People and Concepts*** (*Teacher's Resource Binder,* p. 12-1; **Handout 12–2**) as a transparency that can be projected. For each item on the handout, have a student read the item aloud and make a match. If other students challenge the answer, have the challengers name the correct match and read aloud a passage from the text that supports their challenge. If the challenge is incorrect, ask students to find a passage from the text that confirms the correct match.

tb **Using the Test Bank**

The *Test Bank* that accompanies this textbook offers a wide variety of questions in different formats and levels of complexity. Use the software to construct whole tests or to integrate standardized questions into teacher-made tests.

Self-Test Answers

Multiple-Choice Questions

1. c, 2. b, 3. d

more emotions (except for anger, which North American men express more readily) and talk more about their emotions. But in reading emotions, men read men's body language better than women's, and women read women's body language better than men's. Two factors influence the way men and women learn a style of nonverbal communication: power in a relationship, and family and cultural traditions about expressing emotions.

Each culture has its own display rules—cultural guidelines that tell how and when people may express emotions. Because these rules vary from one culture to another, it is easy to misinterpret the nonverbal communications—gestures and body language—of a person from another country. Nevertheless, some basic facial expressions—smiling, frowning, showing disgust and fear, for example—seem to be understood by all humans, no matter where they live.

Key Terms

emotions, p. 226
James-Lange theory, p. 228
Cannon-Bard theory, p. 228
two-factor theory, p. 230
autonomic nervous system, p. 232
polygraph, p. 234
display rules, p. 237

Key People

William James, p. 228
Carl Lange, p. 228
Walter Cannon, p. 228
Stanley Schachter, p. 230
Robert Zajonc, p. 230
Richard Lazarus, p. 231

Self-Test

Multiple-Choice Questions

Choose the *best* answer for each of the following questions.

1. Miss Li, the soccer coach at Every High School, just had a terrible experience: She looked in her gym bag and saw a rat snoozing in her shoe. When the team captain asked Miss Li whether she was frightened, she replied, "I don't know. I haven't appraised the situation yet." Miss Li seems to believe in the ________________ theory of emotion.
   a. commonsense
   b. Cannon-Bard
   c. two-factor
   d. subjective physiological

2. Nathan, a new driver, almost ran into another car. When he was safely on the other side of the intersection, he noticed that his heart was racing, he was perspiring heavily, and his mouth was very dry. These reactions are signs that Nathan's ________________ system had kicked in during the near-accident.
   a. parasympathetic c. central
   b. sympathetic d. somatic

3. Shawna was working the register in a convenience store last night when a robber pointed a gun at her and told her to empty all the money in the cash drawer into a paper bag and hand it over. She did as she was told. Every time Shawna thinks of this event, she is afraid all over again. She breaks into a cold sweat, her heart races, and her mouth gets very dry. The owner of the store wants Shawna to take a lie detector test, since there were no other witnesses to the robbery, and the security

camera failed to record it. Should Shawna take the test?

a. Yes. She's innocent and has nothing to hide.
b. Yes. The sweating, rapid heart rate, and dry mouth are signs that a polygraph interpreter would see as evidence of innocence.
c. No. She is clearly lying and the test will prove that.
d. No. A polygraph interpreter could interpret her sweating, rapid heart rate, and dry mouth as evidence of guilt.

4. Molly's family loves games, and one of their favorites is charades. Molly has noticed that when her father and four brothers are on one team, and Molly, her mother, and her three sisters are on the other team, Molly's team usually wins. Pitting men against women in charades may give women a slight edge because
 a. women surpass men at interpreting body language and facial expressions.
 b. women surpass men at expressing emotions.
 c. women read other women's nonverbal communications more easily than they read men's nonverbal communications.
 d. All of the above are true.

5. American psychologist William James and his son-in-law, Walter Cannon, were in the kitchen preparing the trimmings for a family barbeque. Cannon was slicing several onions for the hamburgers; and tears were streaming down his face and down the face of James, who was standing beside him talking about how we experience emotion. Suddenly Cannon shouted, "You see! This is a perfect example of my point!" Cannon was probably referring to his own view that
 a. our experience of emotion is our awareness of our bodily responses. James and Cannon felt sad because they felt the tears rolling down their cheeks.
 b. our experience of emotion is our awareness of our bodily responses. No one felt sad; both James and Cannon realized they were crying because their eyes were irritated by the onion juices.
 c. our experience of emotion is the result of simultaneous bodily responses and a subjective experience of emotion. James and Cannon felt sad because they felt the tears rolling down their cheeks.
 d. our experience of emotion is the result of simultaneous bodily responses and a subjective experience of emotion. No one felt sad; both James and Cannon realized they were crying because their eyes were irritated by the onion juices.

Matching Names and Theories

6. For each theory described below, choose the *best* matching name of the person connected with that theory. (***Hint:*** *Some theories have more than one name connected to them.*)

Definition

 a. The theory that our experience of emotion is our awareness of our physiological responses to an emotion-arousing stimulus.
 b. The theory that an emotion-arousing stimulus simultaneously triggers (1) physiological responses, and (2) the subjective experience of emotion.
 c. The theory that to experience emotion one must (1) be physically aroused, and (2) cognitively label the arousal.
 d. The theory that emotion and cognition are separate, and that our interpretations are sometimes slower than our emotional reactions.
 e. The theory that there must be at least a minimal amount of *unconscious* thought, even for instantaneously felt emotions, so that we know what we're reacting to.

MODULE 12

Self-Test Answers

Multiple-Choice Questions (continued)

4. a, 5. d

Matching Terms and Definitions

6. a. (3) and (8), b. (1), c. (6), d. (4), e. (7)

MODULE 12

Self-Test Answers

Fill-in-the-Blank Questions

7. sympathetic; parasympathetic, 8. nonverbal communication, 9. physical arousal; expressive behaviors; conscious experience

Brief Essay Question

10. Students should discuss the controversy over the order of physical arousal and cognitive labeling and the controversy over whether cognition must occur at all in emotional reactions. They should correctly explain how each theory of emotion addresses these controversies.

Person

(1) Walter Cannon
(2) Tariq Aziz
(3) William James
(4) Robert Zajonc
(5) James Baker
(6) Stanley Schachter
(7) Richard Lazarus
(8) Carl Lange
(9) Sara Snodgrass

Fill-in-the-Blank Questions

7. The autonomic nervous system has two divisions: the ________________, which arouses you when something dangerous happens, and the ________________, which calms you after such events.

8. Facial expressions, tone of voice, and hand gestures are all parts of ________________ ________________.

9. The three components of emotion are physiological activation, ________________ ________________, ________________ and ________________ ________________.

Brief Essay Question

10. What are the two main controversies that appear in most of the debates over the best theory of emotion? In two paragraphs of about three or four sentences each, describe the two controversies and give one or two examples of theories that mention this theme.

Answers to the questions in Figure 12.7 (page 238): From left to right and top to bottom, the emotions displayed in these photos are happiness, surprise, fear, sadness, anger, and disgust.

CHAPTER

Stress and Health

Biopsychological Domain

Teaching with the Standards

Standard Area: Stress, Coping, and Health

Breakdown of Module 13: Effects of Stress

Content Standard 1: Origins of stress Stress is defined in terms of the common stressors and our reactions to stress. Stressors are divided into three major categories: daily stress, significant life changes, and catastrophes. Research on the effects of perceived control on our health is also presented. (Student Text pp. 244–245, 248–251)

Content Standard 2: Physiological changes due to stress Physiological reactions to stress are discussed in Module 13. Walter Cannon's research on the fight-or-flight response is discussed, as well as Hans Seyle's work on the general adaptation syndrome. Focus is on how the body is affected by stress. The author discusses how stress affects an individual's immune system. The possible connection between stress, cancer, and heart disease is also presented. (Student Text pp. 245–247, 251–253)

Content Standard 3: Psychological changes due to stress Emotional reactions to stress are presented in Module 13. Emphasis is placed on how our perceptions of stressors can affect our stress levels. Judith Rodin's research on the importance of perceived control is discussed. In addition, Martin Seligman's work on optimism and health is presented. (Student Text pp. 245–251)

Content Standard 4: Cognitive and behavioral techniques for reducing stress and promoting wellness Cognitive strategies and behavioral strategies for dealing with anger are presented. (Student Text p. 253)

Breakdown of Module 14: Promoting Wellness

Content Standard 4: Cognitive and behavioral techniques for reducing stress and promoting wellness Module 14 focuses on how students can change their lifestyles to improve their health. Emphasis is placed on the importance of exercise, developing good social relationships, the role of faith, and positive experiences in promoting wellness. Positive psychology concepts, such as flow, are discussed along with how optimism contributes to our sense of well-being. Health risks associated with smoking and obesity are discussed. Practical and safe suggestions to stop smoking and lose weight are presented. (Student Text pp. 258–273)

Scope and Sequence

	Objectives	Text Reference	Standards Covered
Lesson 1	Define stress. Discriminate between the stressors and the reaction to stress. Discuss the different types of stressors we encounter, such as daily stress, significant life changes, and catastrophes. Discuss how our perceptions of stress can affect how we deal with it.	Module 13, pp. 244–251	Standard Area: Stress, Coping, and Health, Content Standard 1, Performance Standard 1.1, Content Standard 2, Performance Standard 2.1, Content Standard 3, Performance Standard 3.1
Lesson 2	Investigate our emotional and physiological reactions to stress. Discuss Hans Seyle's general adaptation syndrome. Define the difference between a Type A and a Type B personality and possible health risks.	Module 13, pp. 249–253	Content Standard 2, Performance Standard 2.1, Content Standard 3, Performance Standard 3.1, Content Standard 4, Performance Standard 4.2
Lesson 3	Discuss the importance of a healthy lifestyle. Examine the role of exercise in a happy and healthy life. Investigate how having friends, family, and faith provides social support and contributes to well-being.	Module 14, pp. 258–263	Content Standard 4, Performance Standard 4.2
Lesson 4	Discuss the role of optimism in offering some protections against stress. Discuss the concept of flow. Examine the connection of flow, happiness, and optimism to our well-being. Discuss the characteristics of happy people. Explore how we can overcome pessimism.	Modules 13 and 14, pp. 250–251, 263–268	Content Standard 1, Performance Standard 1.1, Content Standard 4, Performance Standards 4.1, 4.2
Lesson 5	Discuss the dangers associated with smoking and obesity. Investigate behavioral techniques to overcome nicotine addiction and to safely lose weight.	Module 14, pp. 268–273	Content Standard 4, Performance Standard 4.2
Lesson 6	Review and test.		

Stress and Health

One day after school, one of my students came in to ask for an extension on a research project. He explained that play rehearsal had been running late, he had several tests scheduled at the end of the week, and he had let the research paper slide. He also said he was "...feeling really stressed out."

Have you ever used that phrase? We all experience stress, no matter what we call those feelings. And we all know that stress can turn a good day into a bad day. But what will happen if the feelings continue over a long period? Will our health be affected? Are there ways to minimize the "stressed out" feeling when it hits? And how do our emotions affect this stressed-out feeling?

Health psychologists search for answers to these and other health-related questions, and we will review much of their work in the last two modules of the biopsychological domain. In Module 13, we'll see how psychologists link the effects of stress to illness. In Module 14 we'll see whether certain behaviors and thoughts can improve your health and wellness and help prevent illness.

CHAPTER 6

CHAPTER 6

Stress and Health

Introducing the Chapter

The Points: Chapter Objectives

- Define stress.
- Identify emotional and physiological responses to stress.
- Identify three main types of stressors and how they affect our health.
- Evaluate how our outlook and feelings of control influence our health.
- Analyze if there is a connection between cancer and stress.
- Analyze what we know about the link between stress and heart problems.
- Explain how exercise contributes to wellness.
- Evaluate how social support makes a difference in our health and well-being.
- Describe the "faith factor" and how it relates to wellness.
- Analyze how flow, happiness, and optimism contribute to our well-being.
- Explain why smoking is so dangerous, and why it is so hard to give up.

MODULE 13

Performance Standards

Standard Area: Stress, Coping, and Health

Content Standard 1: Origins of stress

Performance Standard 1.1 Explain stress and its origins.

- Define the concept of stress, distinguishing between the stressor and the stress reaction. (Student Text pp. 245–246)
- Discuss how we view a stressor affects how we respond to it. (Student Text pp. 245–246)
- Figure 13.1, "Assessing Stress," illustrates how our appraisal of a stressful event greatly influences how we will respond to it emotionally and physically. (Student Text p. 246)
- Identify the three main types of stressors and how they affect our health. (Student Text pp. 248–249)
- Discuss how the hassles of modern life lead to stress. (Student Text p. 248)
- Examine the role of poverty and racism on stress. (Student Text p. 248)
- Explore how work can produce physical, emotional, and mental exhaustion. Discuss the concept of burnout. (Student Text p. 248)
- Examine how significant life changes that result in stress can lead to illness. (Student Text p. 249)
- Describe the impact that catastrophes have on stress and health. (Student Text p. 249)
- Examine how our outlook and feelings of control influence our health. (Student Text pp. 249–251)

Content Standard 2: Physiological changes due to stress

Performance Standard 2.1 Examine possible physiological responses to stress.

- Discuss Walter Cannon's research on the fight-or-flight response. (Student Text p. 246)
- Investigate Hans Seyle's general adaptation syndrome. (Student Text pp. 246–247)
- Figure 13.2, "Seyle's General Adaptation Syndrome," illustrates how prolonged stress can lead to physical illness. (Student Text p. 247)
- Explore the relationship between stress and cancer. (Student Text p. 251)
- Examine the link between stress and heart problems. Emphasize the difference between Type A and Type B personalities and their risk for heart disease. (Student Text pp. 252–253)

Content Standard 3: Psychological changes due to stress

Performance Standard 3.1 Discuss possible psychological responses to stress.

- Investigate our emotional responses to stress. (Student Text pp. 245–246)
- Discuss how we view a stressor affects how we respond to it. (Student Text pp. 245–246)
- Figure 13.1, "Assessing Stress," illustrates how our appraisal of a stressful event greatly influences how we will respond to it emotionally and physically. (Student Text p. 246)
- Discuss how our perceived control of a situation affects our health. (Student Text pp. 250–251)
- Examine the role of optimism on stress and health. (Student Text pp. 250–251)

Content Standard 4: Cognitive and behavioral techniques for reducing stress and promoting wellness

Performance Standard 4.2 Investigate behavioral techniques to reduce stress and promote wellness.

- Investigate how we can better handle anger and promote better health. For example, the authors suggest that time and exercise can effectively reduce anger. (Student Text p. 253)

Materials NETWORK

All of the items from the Video, Activity, and Enrichment Centers listed below come from the *Teacher's Resource Binder.* These items will help you teach and expand on concepts presented in Module 13.

trb This logo indicates when an item from the Materials Network may be used in conjunction with a specific note found in this module's *Teacher's Edition.*

Stress

V Video Center

Consult the faculty guide from *The Brain* video series for descriptions of these modules.

- Videocassette: *The Brain,* Second Edition, Module 21: "Emotions, Stress, and Health" (*Teacher's Resource Binder*, p. 13-1)
- Videocassette: *The Brain,* Second Edition, Module 22: "Coping with Stress: Control and Predictability" (*Teacher's Resource Binder*, p. 13-1)

Activity Center

- Critical Thinking Activity: *Fact or Falsehood?* With this activity, students' preconceptions about stress are either exposed as incorrect or reinforced as correct. (*Teacher's Resource Binder*, p. 13-1; Handout 13–1)
- Building Vocabulary: *Linking to the Textbook* Students learn the module terminology as they delve deeper into the text, searching for answers to questions presented on the handout. (*Teacher's Resource Binder*, p. 13-1; Handout 13–2)
- Technology Application Activity: *PsychQuest:* "How Does Chronic Stress Affect Us?" This CD-ROM engages students in a lesson about long-term response to stress. (*Teacher's Resource Binder*, p. 13-1)
- Application Activity: *Stress Levels* Students can assess their current levels of stress with this handy measure. (*Teacher's Resource Binder*, p. 13-1; Handout 13–3)
- Application Activity: *Vulnerability to Stress* One's vulnerability to stress, assessed in this activity, can have implications for one's health. (*Teacher's Resource Binder*, p. 13-1; Handout 13–4)
- Application Activity: *Stress Symptoms* Many physical symptoms are related to stress. This measure can help students see if their health is being affected by stress. (*Teacher's Resource Binder*, p. 13-1; Handout 13–5)
- Evaluation Activity: *Hassles and Uplifts Scale* This activity can help students assess their hassles and uplifts, compared with their peers. (*Teacher's Resource Binder*, p. 13-1; Handout 13–6)

Enrichment Center

- Enrichment Lesson: *Hassles and Uplifts* This lesson helps students see how one person's hassle can be another's uplift, and vice versa. (*Teacher's Resource Binder*, p. 13-1)

Effects of Perceived Control

Activity Center

- Evaluation Activity: *The Stress Appraisal Measure* Use this activity to help students see how they appraise the stress in their lives. (*Teacher's Resource Binder*, p. 13-1; Handout 13–7)
- Application Activity: *Perceived Control* This activity will help students assess whether their locus of control is internal or external. (*Teacher's Resource Binder*, p. 13-1; Handout 13–8)

Enrichment Center

- Enrichment Lesson: *Locus of Control and Health* This lesson expands on the concept of locus of control discussed in Application Activity: *Perceived Control.* (*Teacher's Resource Binder*, p. 13-1)

Stress and Disease

V Video Center

- Videocassette: *The Mind,* Second Edition, Module 4: "Cognition and the Immune System: Mind/Body Interactions" Consult the faculty guide from *The Mind* video series for a description of this module. (*Teacher's Resource Binder*, p. 13-1)

Activity Center

- Analysis Activity: *Type A and Type B Personalities* Are your students Type A or Type B personalities? Use this measure to assess this quality as you teach about the relationship between personality and health. (*Teacher's Resource Binder*, p. 13-1; Handout 13–9)
- Evaluation Activity: *Hostility and Its Alleviations* This handout explores how students deal with hostile feelings and can lead to a discussion of the best ways to handle aggressive feelings. (*Teacher's Resource Binder*, p. 13-1; Handout 13–10)

Enrichment Center

- Enrichment Lesson: *A Deeper Look into Type A Personalities* What are the hallmarks of the Type A personality? This lesson explores the phenomenon, listing qualities of the personality type that students may recognize in themselves and others. (*Teacher's Resource Binder*, p. 13-1)
- Enrichment Lesson: *A 12-Step Program for Type A Personalities* This lesson gives practical advice for coping with stress as a Type A. (*Teacher's Resource Binder*, p. 13-1)

MODULE 13

Effects of Stress

Introducing the Module

The Points: Module Objectives

- Define stress.
- Identify emotional and physiological responses to stress.
- Identify the three main types of stressors and explain how they affect our health.
- Explain how our outlook and feelings of control influence our health.
- Discuss whether there is a stress-cancer connection.
- Analyze what we know about the link between stress and heart problems.

trb Building Vocabulary

Students can gain a deeper understanding of the concepts in this module with **Building Vocabulary:** *Linking to the Textbook* (*Teacher's Resource Binder*, p. 13-1; **Handout 13–2**). Have students find information about the module terms in the text to complete the handout. Explain to students that the answers they discover as they read may go against preconceptions they have about stress and health.

MODULE 13

Effects of Stress

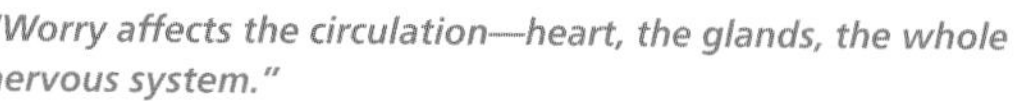

"Worry affects the circulation—heart, the glands, the whole nervous system."

—Dr. Charles Mayo, (1865–1939)

Though the situation was not funny, I must admit I chuckled. For the second consecutive year, Debbie (a former student of mine) had been cast as a female lead in the school musical. And for the second straight year, Debbie lost her voice the Monday before the show opened. Students in the cast and teachers in the hallways wondered, "How could this happen two years in a row?" Was Debbie's condition "all in her head," implying no physiological cause? Was she bluffing in some odd attempt for sympathy? Was she simply "stressed out" and in need of rest? According to the show's director, no other lead in the previous 10 years had experienced this problem.

Well, the show went on, and Debbie sang "Oklahoma" and all her other songs beautifully all three nights, just as she had the year before. Debbie's reaction to her upcoming on-stage performance differed from that of several other actors who were nervously anticipating the show. She never developed any cold symptoms, but she did lose and regain her voice. Why did this happen?

The answer to this question is an example of the effects of stress on health, the topic of this module. This relationship, like so many others that psychologists study, involves both the mind and the body. Let's begin with a closer look at how psychologists define *stress.*

► **stress** The process by which we perceive and respond to certain events, called *stressors,* that we appraise as threatening or challenging.

► **health psychology** A subfield of psychology that focuses on how stress affects our well-being and our health.

Stress

What's the Point? 1. What is stress?

Let's say it's Friday morning, and tonight—after months of wanting to go out with this person—you finally will have that big date, a date that

Getting Started

Before you begin this module, ask students to recall a situation in which a fictional character from literature, film, or television felt stress. What precipitated the stressful situation? What happened because of the stressful situation? How did the character respond to it?

trb You may wish to use **Critical Thinking:** *Fact or Falsehood?* (*Teacher's Resource Binder*, p. 13-1; **Handout 13–1**) as a prereading strategy to find out what students already know about stress and health. The activity will prime students to note terms and concepts in the text that confirm or dispel their preconceptions about the effects of stress.

has made it hard to concentrate at times during the week. You've decided what you're going to wear, and you and your date have decided where you're going to eat and what movie you'll see. Brushing your teeth, you look in the mirror and discover the start of a rather large pimple on the right side of your nose. A perfect situation just got a little less perfect. Welcome to **stress**—the *process* by which we perceive and respond to events that we appraise as threatening or challenging.

A Stress Reaction? Blemishes that appear at inopportune times are often reactions to stress.

Where is the stress in this situation? Is it the date, the pimple, or both? Most psychologists would say that neither the date nor the pimple is stress. Rather, the date is a *stressor*, an event you could appraise as threatening or challenging. The pimple is a *stress reaction,* though it may become a stressor as well. Remember, stress is a process of perceiving and responding. Our appraisal of an event as potentially threatening or challenging can make a huge difference in what we experience and in how effectively we respond.

Health psychology, a subfield of psychology, focuses a lot of attention on how stress affects our well-being and our health, asking such questions as:

- How are stress and illness related?
- How do our perceptions of stress affect our health?
- Can we control our reactions to stress?
- What behaviors and attitudes help prevent health problems?

Let's turn now to our responses to stress and their impact on our health.

Responding to Stress

2. What are our emotional and physiological responses to stress?

Stress is inevitable, but unhealthy responses to it are not. When faced with a stressor, such as a flat tire on your way to school or work, how do you respond? Is the flat tire a *threat?* ("I'll never be able to fix this! I'm sunk.") Or is it a *challenge?* ("I can handle this. Let's see, what are my options?") Your appraisal of the situation is crucial. If you see the stressor as a threat, you're more likely to panic and freeze up, making it far more difficult to solve your problem. If instead you view the stressor as a challenge, your response will be focused, and you're much more likely to overcome the obstacle (Figure 13.1, page 246). Your perception of the stressor directly affects your emotional responses. The top athletes, the best

Everyday Hassles Depending on your response to stressors, your health may suffer from the combined effects of daily hassles.

MODULE 13

Teaching the Points

■ **TEACHING TIPS**

web (1) You can log on as an instructor to the book companion site for *Thinking About Psychology* at **www.worthpublishers.com/thinkingaboutpsych.** It contains teacher resources for class presentations as well as review and assessment of module concepts and terms.

(2) Encourage students to consider how they appraise the stressful events in their lives. Do they consider the daily stressors they endure to be a hassle or an uplift? Help them see that viewing stress as an uplift rather than as a hassle can improve their ability to manage stress successfully.

trb At this point, you may wish to use Evaluation Activity: *Hassles and Uplifts Scale* (*Teacher's Resource Binder*, p. 13-1; Handout 13–6) and Enrichment Lesson: *Hassles and Uplifts* (*Teacher's Resource Binder*, p. 13-1).

Suggested Readings

Use the following books as teacher-preparation tools or as enrichment for advanced students:

Baron, R., & Paulus, P. (1991). *Understanding human relations* (2nd ed.). Boston: Allyn & Bacon.

Friedman, M., & Ulmer, D. (1984). *Treating type A behavior—and your heart.* New York: Knopf.

Maslach, C. (1982). *Burnout: The cost of caring.* Englewood Cliffs, NJ: Prentice-Hall.

Matarazzo, J. (1984). Behavioral immunogens. In B. L. Hammonds & C. J. Scheirer (Eds.), *Psychology and health* (pp. 9–43). Washington, DC: American Psychological Association.

Seligman, M. E. P. (1991). *Learned optimism.* New York: Knopf.

Selye, H. (1976). *The stress of life.* New York: McGraw-Hill.

Williams, R. (1989). *The trusting heart.* New York: Time Books.

Williams, R., & Williams, V. (1994). *Anger kills.* New York: Harper Perennial.

MODULE 13

trb **tr** ■ TEACHING TIP
A black-line master for Figure 13.1, Assessing Stress, is available in the **Black-Line Masters Appendix** of the *Teacher's Resource Binder.*

F • Y • I

(1) Stress comes in two types. **Distress** is stress perceived as being negative—events we think of when we think of stress. **Eustress** is stress perceived as being positive, but it still carries with it heightened arousal.

Both types of stress, endured over a prolonged period of time, can lead to harmful physical effects, even though eustress is more pleasant to endure.

trb At this point, you may wish to use **Technology Application Activity:** *PsychSim:* **"How Does Chronic Stress Affect Us?"** (*Teacher's Resource Binder,* p. 13-1).

(2) Studies of stressors have shown that people's number one fear is speaking in public. Second to this fear is the fear of dying. Citing this finding, comedian Jerry Seinfeld has joked that people are more afraid of giving the eulogy at a funeral than being in the casket!

Figure 13.1 Assessing Stress Your appraisal of a stressful event greatly influences how you will respond to it emotionally and physically.

teachers, and the most effective leaders seem to thrive when faced with what they perceive as a challenge.

Our emotional responses to stressors vary, but our physical responses share some important similarities. Imagine the following scenario. You were supposed to finish reading *Julius Caesar* for English class yesterday, but you forgot your book at school. This morning, your teacher started class by saying, "For today's short-answer quiz, please take out a blank sheet of paper." Surprised by the announcement and unprepared to succeed, you experienced a unified, mind-body stress response. Physiologist **Walter Cannon** (1929) found that a number of situations—from emotion-arousing incidents like a pop quiz to physically stressful conditions like extreme cold—all trigger the release of stress hormones into the nervous system. Your nervous system, as part of its stress response, increases your heart rate, dulls your sensation of pain, and sends more blood to your larger muscles, preparing you either to take action against the challenge (fight!) or to flee from it (flight). Cannon's work on the *fight-or-flight* response paved the way for another scientist, whose highly respected research greatly expanded our understanding of stress.

As a young man in his twenties, **Hans Selye** (SELL-yay) thought he'd discovered a new hormone that, when injected into rats, caused bleeding ulcers and shrinkage of an important, disease-fighting gland. To his dismay, Selye found that the hormone was not the only thing that caused this reaction in rats. A number of substances, completely unrelated to the hormone, caused the very *same* reactions. Initially dejected, Selye reevaluated his results, and wondered whether there might be "a single nonspecific reaction of the body to damage of any kind" (1976). After subjecting animals to other stressors (for example, electric shock or an immobilizing restraint), Selye found a predictable, recurring response that—like a motion detector turning on a light regardless of the motion detected—was so general in nature that he called it the **general adaptation syndrome (GAS).**

▶ **Walter Cannon** (1871–1945) American psychologist who concluded that physiological and emotional experiences occur simultaneously.

▶ **Hans Selye** (1907–1982) Psychologist who researched a recurring response to stress that he called the general adaptation syndrome.

▶ **general adaptation syndrome (GAS)** Selye's concept of the body's adaptive response to stress in three stages—alarm, resistance, exhaustion.

Cooperative Learning

Have students brainstorm about different stressors they encounter in a regular school day. Assign each group a different stressor, and challenge the group members to come up with at least three positive ways to deal with the stress, keeping in mind strategies realistic for people their age. After group members have the opportunity to share their three ideas, have groups discuss why teens don't always handle stress very well.

trb At this point, you may wish to use **Application Activity:** *Stress Levels* (*Teacher's Resource Binder,* p. 13-1; **Handout 13–3**).

The GAS, according to Selye, has three phases (Figure 13.2) Phase 1 is an *alarm reaction,* which happens when your nervous system is activated following an emotional or physical trauma (as explained in Cannon's fight-or-flight research). With your heart pumping faster and all your other resources at the ready, your body mobilizes itself to meet the challenges of Phase 2, *resistance.* The outpourings of stress-related hormones keep your respiration, temperature, and blood pressure high. But your body is not built to sustain this kind of resistance indefinitely. With extended exposure to the traumatic event, your body's reserves become depleted, and Phase 3, *exhaustion,* becomes likely. Exhaustion brings with it greater susceptibility to illness and, under extreme circumstances, death. Selye's bottom line: Although our bodies are built to handle temporary stress, prolonged stress will produce *physical deterioration.* Evidence supporting Selye's bottom line includes brain scans of those who have lived through extended combat conditions or child abuse. The flood of stress hormones accompanying these traumatic events appears to correspond with the shrinking of a brain structure called the *hippocampus.* This brain structure is vital for memory recall. Those experiencing the trauma may experience memory difficulties (Sapolsky, 1999).

Reaction to War With prolonged exposure to warlike conditions, this family's resistance to the stressors of famine and war may lead to exhaustion and increase the likelihood of illness.

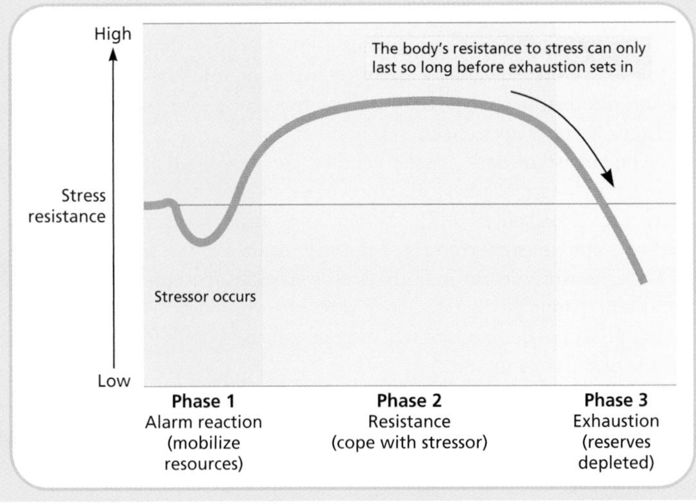

Figure 13.2 **Selye's General Adaptation Syndrome (GAS)** Following a traumatic event, the body enters an initial alarm phase. Over time, the body's resistance to stress decreases.

Reteaching

(tr) A four-color transparency of Figure 13.2, Selye's General Adaptation Syndrome (GAS), is available in the **Overhead Transparencies Set.** Using this transparency, have students identify the different phases of Hans Selye's general adaptation syndrome. Cover up the different phases, having students identify orally or on a sheet of paper what the different phases are called and what they entail. This will help you assess whether students understand the syndrome and which points needs to be readdressed.

(tr) ■ **TEACHING TIP**

A four-color transparency of Figure 13.2, Selye's General Adaptation Syndrome (GAS), is available in the **Overhead Transparencies Set.**

■ **APPLYING THE POINTS**

(1) Contact a local physician or stress researcher to get more information about the biological impact of stress and Selye's general adaptation syndrome. If possible, learn answers to the following questions that you can incorporate into a class lecture:

- What specific health problems are positively correlated with prolonged stress?
- What specific hormones are related to stress?
- What other health factors and habits complicate stress-related health problems?
- How can people reduce stress naturally?

(V) At this point, you may wish to show **Videocassette:** ***The Brain,*** **Second Edition, Module 21: "Emotions, Stress, and Health"** (*Teacher's Resource Binder,* p. 13-1).

(2) Contact a representative of a branch of the military to see how they train their members to handle the stress of combat. If possible, learn answers to the following questions that you can incorporate into a class lecture:

- What specific training techniques does the military use to improve soldiers' ability to handle stress during combat?
- What support in the field is available for soldiers?
- Separation from family and home during combat can compound the stress some soldiers feel. How does the military handle this complication?

MODULE 13

■ **APPLYING THE POINTS**

Here are some suggestions for finding out more about stress in the workplace:

- Contact local companies and interview human resources personnel about how they try to keep their workers from experiencing burnout.
- Interview an industrial/organizational psychologist about methods companies can use to help workers avoid burnout.
- Challenge students to combine the results of the interviews to create a public awareness campaign that teaches people how to avoid burnout in their jobs and in school.

Stressful Events

3. What are the three main types of stressors, and how do they affect our health?

Researchers investigating the relationship between stress and health have been very interested in three types of stressors. These stressful life events include daily stress, significant life changes, and catastrophes.

Daily Stress

Your locker jams. Your lab partner fails to complete his part of the lab. The lunch line is so long you'll probably have all of five minutes to eat by the time you get your food. According to several researchers (Kohn & Macdonald, 1992; Lazarus, 1990; Ruffin, 1993), the most significant sources of stress may be the everyday hassles we regularly face. Ever lose your keys when you were already late? Misplace your ticket to a concert? Wear the exact same shirt to school as someone you don't like? Combine these hassles over time, and depending on your response to these stressors, your health may suffer.

This statement may be no surprise to those living in urban ghettos, where some of the highest rates of blood pressure occur. The overcrowding, unemployment, and poverty found in these areas add up to high levels of daily stress. Add the incidences of racism that members of minority groups often experience while living in these conditions, such as knowing that others doubt your intelligence and your integrity, and the daily pressures are compounded like interest on a bank loan. Researchers have tied abnormally high blood pressure rates in some African Americans to life's daily stressors, especially when the perception of racism and poor living conditions coincide (Clark & others, 1999).

Economic upheaval also brings high levels of daily stress. What happened to life expectancy among Russian men following the collapse of Communism in the 1990s? It fell by five years, while suicide, divorce, and murder rates all went up (Holden, 1996).

The persistent daily hassles that are part of one's daily work life can produce the state of physical, emotional, and mental exhaustion called **burnout** (Maslach, 1982). When you hear someone say they're "burned-out" on something, it typically means they've had enough. Police officers worn down by high-stress situations, parents worn down by persistent parenting hassles, and teachers worn down by the during- and after-school demands of teaching are all candidates for burnout. The results of burnout include

- depression (from the emotional exhaustion).
- decreased performance or productivity (from the physical exhaustion).
- cynicism (from the mental exhaustion).

▶ **burnout** Physical, emotional, and mental exhaustion brought on by persistent job-related stress.

Cross-Curricular Connections

LITERATURE Have students bring in their favorite novel or biography/autobiography. Have them assess how well the main character or subject of the book deals with stress in life. Ask students to address the following questions:

- Does the central figure in the book deal well or poorly with stress? Explain.
- Is this character someone you would want to emulate in terms of coping with stress? Why or why not?
- Does the way this person deals with stress make the book particularly compelling to you? Why or why not?

Significant Changes

Significant personal changes in your life comprise the second kind of life event stressor. The death of a loved one, leaving home to live on your own, and divorce are examples of stressors related to life transitions.

There are at least two different ways to study the health effects of significant life changes. The first is to compare the lives of those who suffer the same illness, such as a stroke, to determine whether they shared similar life changes that would predict the illness. The second and more time-consuming method involves tracking people over time, noting whether a life change precedes an illness. One organization with the time and resources to conduct such a study is the U.S. National Academy of Sciences, which sponsored a review of life changes (Dohrenwend & others, 1982). This review found a greater vulnerability to disease in people who had recently been fired, widowed, or divorced. Another study found that the likelihood of death in widowed people doubles in the week after their partner's death (Kaprio & others, 1987).

Significant Life Change Those who have recently been widowed, fired, or divorced are more vulnerable to disease.

Catastrophes

Earthquakes, floods, and wars are all large-scale, relatively unpredictable, life-threatening events. Do these catastrophic stressors affect health? If the Los Angeles earthquake of 1994 is any indication, the answer is yes. On the day of the earthquake, five times the normal number of sudden-death heart attacks were reported, but only 13 percent of these deaths were deemed a result of running, lifting debris, or some other form of physical exertion. What accounted for the remainder of the increase? The likely answer is stress (Muller & Verrier, 1996).

Catastrophes often mean prolonged exposure to stress. A comprehensive review of studies addressing the psychological effects of disasters showed a 17 percent increase in the likelihood of depression and other disorders (Rubonis and Bickman, 1991). The stress of catastrophes puts us at psychological and physical risk.

Effects of Perceived Control

4. Can our outlook and feelings of control influence our health?

The negative effect of every stressor in our lives—running out of gas, failing an exam, feeling obligated to buy a holiday gift for someone who unexpectedly gave you one at the last minute—is magnified if we think of

HISTORY Have students research some significant historical catastrophes (wars, natural disasters, and so on). Ask them to analyze how well the people and nations affected by the catastrophes dealt with stress before, during, and after the event by addressing the following questions:

- Were general conditions particularly stable before the catastrophe? Why or why not?
- Was someone or something to blame for the catastrophe or was the event completely unpredictable and controllable? Explain. How was the collective psyche of people affected?
- What was the immediate impact of the catastrophe on the people or nation? How long did the effects last? Did the people or nation emerge from the catastrophe stronger? Why or why not?

trb At this point, you may wish to use **Application Activity:** *Perceived Control* (*Teacher's Resource Binder*, p. 13-1; **Handout 13–8**).

■ **JOURNAL WRITING**

Invite students to use the following questions and writing prompts as springboards for entries in their psychology journals:

- Do you feel you have a stressful life? Explain your answer.
- Do you feel stress could sometimes be beneficial to you? Describe a time when stress helped rather than harmed.
- What significant life changes have you dealt with in your life? How would you rate the way you dealt with the stress of those changes? Explain your rating.
- Have you ever experienced a catastrophe? Describe the situation and your feelings in dealing with it.

■ **MULTICULTURAL CONNECTIONS**

Using available resources, including the Internet, have students work independently or with partners to research stress in other countries by considering the following questions:

- What types of daily stressors are common in that country?
- What type of cultural expectation exists about handling stress?
- How has that particular country dealt with a major catastrophic event in its history?
- What are the instances of depression and suicide among people of that country/culture? What do these statistics say about how the country/culture deals with stress?

If permission is granted, international students could be interviewed for personal opinions and information about how other cultures deal with stress.

If students make a formal oral or written presentation of their findings, you may wish to consider giving extra credit for this work.

MODULE 13

TEACHING TIP

A four-color transparency of Figure 13.3, Health or Illness, is available in the **Overhead Transparencies Set.**

F•Y•I

A person's level of optimism is closely linked to their mother's level of optimism. Studies show that if a mother has a high level of optimism, the child will have a high level as well.

APPLYING THE POINTS

If possible, arrange for students to interview the staff of a local nursing home to see if the facility provides residents with ways to control daily routines. Students can also inquire whether the staff knows of the findings of the 1986 Rodin study cited in the text. Students might also ascertain from interviewed staff members whether the Rodin findings have already changed or might someday change the facility's philosophy.

trb At this point, you may wish to use **Application Activity:** *Perceived Control* (*Teacher's Resource Binder*, p. 13-1; **Handout 13–8**) and **Enrichment Lesson:** *Locus of Control and Health* (*Teacher's Resource Binder*, p. 13-1).

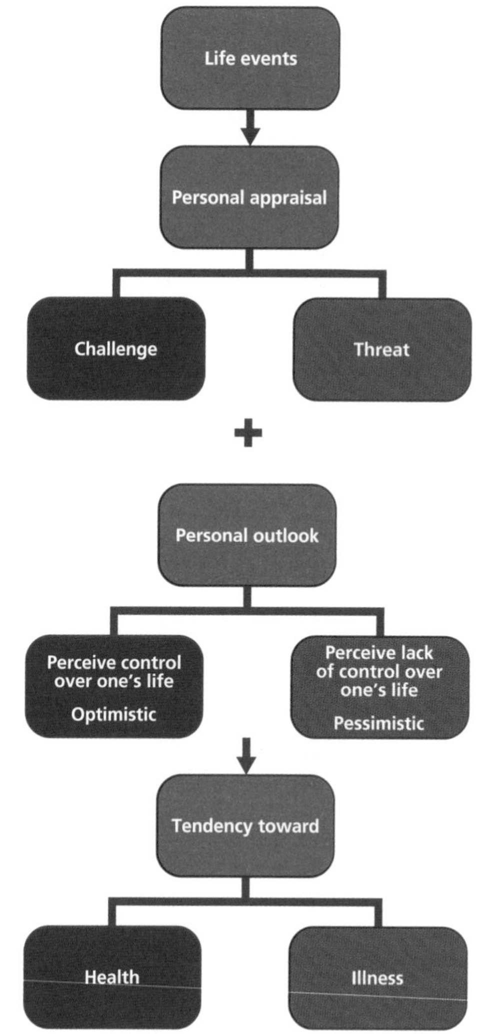

Figure 13.3 Health or Illness The effect of life events depends on several factors, including how you appraise the situation and your own personal outlook.

the stressor negatively and as something that is beyond our control. Let's look at how a sense of control and optimism are linked to stress effects.

Several lines of research demonstrate the importance of *perceived control* on health. One study (Overmier & Murison, 1997) showed that *uncontrollable* stress (along with a bacterial infection) produces the harshest stomach ulcers in humans. Another study by Judith Rodin (1986) compared nursing-home patients who perceived little control over their activities with similar patients who did control some of their daily routines. Rodin found that patients perceiving less control declined in health more rapidly and died sooner than those with more control. Other researchers found lowered immunity to disease among rats exposed to uncontrolled stress. When two rats simultaneously receive the same amount of mild electrical shock, the rat that can turn off the shock stays just as healthy as the rat receiving no shock at all. And these "empowered" rats are much healthier than shocked rats that have no control over the shocking mechanism.

Optimism also seems to offer some protection against the effects of stress. How would you respond to the statement, "In uncertain times, I usually expect the best"? If you agreed, you may have a more optimistic approach to life. Compared with their pessimist counterparts (those with a more negative approach to life), students identified as optimists have stronger immune systems and are less likely to become ill or fatigued during the last month of the semester (Seligman, 1991). Optimists also recover more quickly from heart surgery than pessimists do, and, when stressed, they register lower blood pressure readings (Segerstrom & others, 1998). One study of 2400 Finnish men revealed that those with a hopeless, bleak outlook on life were twice as likely to die during a 10-year span than were those labeled optimists (Everson & others, 1996).

So why are optimism and a perceived sense of control good predictors of better health? And why do pessimism and perceived loss of control predict poor health? The answer, once again, involves the interplay between mind (your perceptions or appraisals) and body (your physiology) (Figure 13.3).

Cooperative Learning

Divide students into groups and have them list the three most stressful things teens deal with every day. Then have them list some explanations of why these things happen and why they are stressful. As students present their reasons to the class, have them analyze whether the attributions are optimistic or pessimistic. Help students see that optimistic thinking empowers people to seek ways to change stressful situations while pessimistic thinking sees no way out of a stressful circumstance.

trb At this point, you may wish to use **Evaluation Activity:** *The Stress Appraisal Measure* (*Teacher's Resource Binder*, p. 13-1; **Handout 13–7**).

Both pessimism and perceived loss of control lead to the production and release of *stress hormones.* Ridding yourself of these hormones uses up your body's reserves of disease-fighting white blood cells. This weakens and thereby hinders your immune system's ability to ward off diseases it would otherwise defeat. Surgical wounds in both humans and animals heal more slowly under stressful conditions. In one ingenious study showing this effect, researchers made a small, precise puncture wound in the skin of dental students (who volunteered for the experiment). Puncture wounds made during summer vacation healed significantly faster than wounds made three days before major exams (Kiecolt-Glaser & others, 1998). Stressed-out students have weaker disease-fighting mechanisms than those who are relatively free of stress. Researchers have also found that cold symptoms are more severe in those under stress (Cohen & others, 1991, 1998). So, if you catch a cold, you'd better chill.

Immune System Ready! A large macrophage (at top) is about to trap and ingest a tiny bacterium (lower right). Macrophages and other cells of our immune system constantly patrol our bodies in search of invaders. People with a pessimistic outlook tend to release excess stress hormones that hamper their immune system's effectiveness and make illness more likely.

Stress and Disease

It's well documented that stress makes minor illnesses, such as colds, worse. Stress also plays a role in more significant diseases.

Cancer and Stress

 5. Is there a stress-cancer connection?

Due to conflicting research, the relationship between stress and cancer is not entirely clear. Some researchers have looked for—but not found—a connection between stress and cancer (Edelman & Kidman, 1997; Fox, 1998). For example, World War II concentration camp survivors underwent prolonged, horrific stress, but they have not shown higher-than-normal cancer rates.

Other researchers have found evidence of a stress-cancer connection. In one study, people with a history of workplace stress were five times more likely to develop colon cancer than were those without workplace stress (Courtney & others, 1993). Cancer patients who verbalize their feelings (presumably releasing stress) have a slightly higher survival rate than cancer patients who keep a cork in emotion's bottle (McKenna & others, 1999; O'Leary, 1990; Temoshok, 1992).

Two things are clear: (1) Stress does not appear to *create* the actual cancer cells. (2) Stress definitely affects the body's malignancy-fighting ability. Stress-weakened immune systems are much more likely to *allow tumor growth* they would otherwise combat.

■ LOOKING AT THE ISSUES

Illness tends to occur around times of stress. For students, exam times are usually stressful times. Have students consider the following questions:

- Do you feel most stressed around exam time at your school? Why or why not?
- How could you reduce your personal stress level at exam time?
- How do your teachers and administrators try to reduce the stress of exam time?
- What other things could be done to make exam time less stressful?

V At this point, you may wish to show **Videocassette: *The Mind,* Second Edition, Module 4: "Cognition and the Immune System: Mind/Body Interaction"** (*Teacher's Resource Binder*, p. 13-1).

■ APPLYING THE POINTS

Ask a local oncologist about his or her thoughts regarding a stress-cancer link. The following questions can guide the informal interview and subsequent presentation of findings to the class:

- Does this professional see a link between cancer and stress in his or her own practice? Why or why not?
- How does this professional suggest that patients deal with stress?
- What support groups are available in the community or region for cancer patients?

trb At this point, you may wish to use **Enrichment Lesson:** *Locus of Control and Health* (*Teacher's Resource Binder*, p. 13-1).

Enriching

Have students research times during the school year when students are absent the most. Students may need to research attendance records for the past few years to see if any patterns of attendance materialize. Help them evaluate their findings by asking the following questions:

- Do dips in attendance occur before or after stressful times, like around exam time?
- Are later days of the week (Thursdays and Fridays) more often missed than earlier days (Mondays and Tuesdays)? Why or why not? If so, could absences be due to stress?

MODULE 13

■ LOOKING AT THE ISSUES

Situational rage has become a national problem, often with devastating consequences. Several different types of rage have emerged in recent years: road rage, workplace rage, even surf rage. Consider the following questions in a full-class discussion:

- Why does expressing instant anger over minor annoyances lead to health problems in the future?
- Why do you think the incidence of rage-related situations has increased in recent years?
- What are some techniques people can use to deal with their feelings of instant rage?
- What are some reasons why "blowing off steam" or expressing rage only intensifies hostile feelings?

trb At this point, you may wish to use **Enrichment Lesson:** *Locus of Control and Health* (*Teacher's Resource Binder*, p. 13-1).

Stress and Heart Problems

6. What do we know about the link between stress and heart problems?

You've heard of one car being hit by another from behind? While I've never been hit from behind while driving, I *have* been rear-ended in a grocery store.

Where I live, grocery shopping on a Saturday morning is neither good nor unique planning. Having waited until the weekend, shoppers flood the aisles, pushing oversized shopping carts from the produce to the pickles. Every Saturday morning, there are always characters trying to set the world record for speed shopping. Walking briskly, they sling food into their carts, and look incredibly annoyed at anyone blocking their path. At the checkout, they dart from one line to the next, looking to minimize wait time. I was in the checkout line when one of these speed shoppers rear-ended me while stealing the spot behind me from a slower shopper.

Speed shoppers—impatient, competitive, and hard-driving—have what Meyer Friedman and Ray Rosenman called **Type A** tendencies. These two researchers contrasted these hard-driving types with another group—the **Type B** personalities, those who are more laid-back, easygoing, and relaxed. The origin of these classifications is intriguing, and their importance in understanding the link between stress and heart attack is significant.

In the mid-1950s, Friedman and his associates initially studied the eating habits of married White couples living in the San Francisco area, and they discovered an interesting fact: The women ate just as much fat and cholesterol as their husbands did, but the men were much more likely to experience heart disease. Friedman ruled out sex differences (for example, female sex hormones) as a reason for this effect after finding that African-American women with similar diets were just as prone to heart disease as the men. Perplexed, Friedman could not figure out what caused the coronary differences.Then, one woman in the study announced,

> If you really want to know what is going to give our husbands heart attacks, I'll tell you. It's stress . . . the stress they have to face in their businesses, day in, day out. Why when my husband comes home, it takes at least one martini just to unclench his jaws.
>
> (Friedman and Ulmer, 1984)

The woman making the statement did not work outside of her home, nor did most of the White women in the study. But most of the African-American women did hold jobs. Could work stress, or stress in general, be the answer?

▶ **Type A** Friedman and Rosenman's term for competitive, hard-driving, impatient, verbally aggressive, and anger-prone people.

▶ **Type B** Friedman and Rosenman's term for easygoing, relaxed people.

To test the stress–heart disease link, Friedman measured blood-clotting speed and cholesterol level (both associated with heart attack risk) in tax accountants in the months leading up to their busiest time of the year, the April 15 tax-filing deadline. In January and February, the readings were normal. However, during the incredibly intense days leading up to the deadline, with the accountants scrambling to meet their clients' deadlines and working long hours, the clotting and cholesterol readings skyrocketed to dangerous levels. In May, the readings were *back to normal.* Stress *did* predict risk of heart attack.

In the nine-year study that followed, Friedman and Rosenman tracked 3000 healthy men between the ages of 35 and 59, labeling each man as either Type A or Type B, based on a 15-minute interview. By the end of the study, 257 men had suffered heart attacks, and 69 percent of them were Type A. None of the "pure" Type Bs, the most easygoing, had heart attacks.

The scientific world clamored for more information regarding Type A and Type B individuals. Which of the ingredients (if any) in the Type A personality concoction—hard-driving, verbally aggressive, anger-prone, competitive—was the toxic chemical? The winner (or loser, depending on how you look at it) turned out to be anger, and one other negative emotion—depression (Miller & others, 1996; Williams, 1993). Consider these findings:

"Typical 'Type A' behavior."

Stressful! There probably aren't too many "Type B" conductors.

- Those experiencing instant anger over minor annoyances, especially for those with aggressive reactive personalities, are the most prone to heart attacks (Williams, 1989).
- A review of 57 studies shows that depression significantly increases the risk of death by heart attack (Wulsin & others, 1999).
- Cynical and hostile college students are five times more likely to die of heart attacks in middle age than are their trusting, gentler classmates (Williams, 1989).

Treatment for depression is readily available from clinical psychologists and physicians, but is there any treatment for anger? Is the anger part of this equation something that those who are Type A should seek to overcome? In both cases, the answer is yes. Psychologists suggest two ways of handling anger that are better than merely "blowing off the steam," which actually tends to amplify hostile feelings (Geen & Quanty, 1977; Hokanson & Edelman, 1966). First, though it sounds simple, if you feel very angry give yourself some time to calm down. I was told as a young boy to "count to 10" before doing anything when I was angry with my brother. The physiological storm that anger stirs up in your body will drop below hurricane level when given time to calm down. Second, try to vent the anger by exercising, confiding in a friend, or writing in a journal. These behaviors will let you sift through your feelings without stifling them and will help you to avoid explosive reactions later (Baumeister & others, 1990). Also, avoid sulking, which simply allows rehearsal of the reasons for being angry.

Actively trying to control anger instead of letting it control you is effort well spent. Keep in mind the words of Charles Spielberger and Perry London (1982) who perhaps put it best when they warned that rage, "seems to lash back and strike us in the heart muscle."

■ JOURNAL WRITING

Invite students to use the following questions and writing prompts as springboards for entries in their psychology journals:

- How in control do you feel about your life? Explain why you feel this way.
- Has stress ever made a sickness you had worse? Explain the circumstances.
- Do you feel you are a Type A or Type B personality? Explain your answer by giving examples of how you deal with stress.

Close

Each generation deals with unique stressors. Students today confront pressures from parents, peers, and teachers as they move from junior high to high school and beyond. The goal of this module is to help students identify and deal with stress in their lives. Have students imagine a stressor they currently deal with. Ask them to write down the different feelings this stressor stirs up in them. Then have them write down at least three different, positive ways of dealing with the stress, based on the suggestions presented in the module. Have students share their newly found ways of dealing with stress in small groups or with the class.

Enriching

Have students conduct research and collect data from a representative sample of peers to see if there is a link between stress, GPA, personality type, and attendance. Survey the students about their personality type (A or B), how they handle typical stressors like studying for exams, what their GPA is, and how many days of school they miss for illness.

- Are students who are high achievers more likely to miss school for illness? Why or why not?
- Do students with higher GPAs experience more stress than those who don't? Why or why not?
- Be sure to obtain permission from an IRB (Institutional Review Board) and informed consent before conducting any research project.

trb At this point, you may wish to use **Analysis Activity:** *Type A and Type B Personalities* (*Teacher's Resource Binder*, p. 13-1; **Handout 13–9**) and **Enrichment Lesson:** *A Deeper Look into Type A Personalities* (*Teacher's Resource Binder*, p. 13-1).

MODULE 13

Checking the Points

■ TEACHING TIPS

web (1) The book companion site for *Thinking About Psychology* at www.worthpublishers.com/thinkingaboutpsych contains a module quiz, flashcards of key terms and people, and other student activities and resources for this module. You will also find PowerPoint lectures, a quiz grade book, and other reaching resources by logging on as an instructor.

trb (2) To review concepts related to stress, ask student pairs to fill in the handout in **Critical Thinking Activity:** *Fact or Falsehood?* (*Teacher's Resource Binder*, p. 13-1; **Handout 13–1**). If students filled out this handout as a prereading activity, have them fill it out again without referring to the previous attempt and then compare and contrast their preconceptions about stress and health to the concepts they learned by reading this module. Have partners work together to agree on the correct response for each item and to then cite passages in the text that confirm their responses.

REVIEW

Module 13: Effects of Stress

What's the Point?

Stress

1. *What is stress?*

   Stress is the process by which we perceive and respond to *stressors,* events we appraise as threatening or challenging. That appraisal will influence not only what we experience, but also how we respond. Health psychology, a subfield within psychology, takes a special interest in how stress affects our well-being and our health.

2. *What are our emotional and physiological responses to stress?*

   Emotional responses to stress vary, depending on how we appraise the stressors in our life. If we judge an event to be threatening, we may panic and freeze up, but if we judge it to be a challenge, we will probably be aroused and focused on the situation. Physiological responses to stressors tend to follow the same pattern, which Walter Cannon called the fight-or-flight response. During this reaction, stress hormones pour into our bloodstream, our heart rate increases, our sensation of pain diminishes, and blood flows toward the large muscles in our body. Hans Selye extended this idea in his general adaptation syndrome (GAS), which describes the three phases of stress reactions: alarm, resistance, and physical deterioration.

3. *What are the three main types of stressors, and how do they affect our health?*

   The three main types of stressors are daily hassles, significant life changes, and catastrophes. Ongoing daily stress, even over small events, can produce physical damage. People who must cope with overcrowding, unemployment, poverty, and racism, for example, show higher-than-normal blood pressure readings. In the workplace, persistent daily hassles can produce burnout—physical, emotional, and mental exhaustion. Significant life changes, such as the death of someone close to you, divorce, or being fired from your job, can increase your vulnerability to disease. Catastrophic events often expose the survivors to prolonged stress, which puts them at risk of psychological and physical harm.

Effects of Perceived Control

4. *Can our outlook and feelings of control influence our health?*

   The simple answer is yes. Research indicates that optimism and a feeling of being able to control our daily routines foster better health. Pessimism and the perception that we have no control can actually harm us. Optimists tend to have stronger immune systems, to recover more quickly from surgery, and to have lower readings on blood pressure tests under stress. The mechanism seems to be the production and release of stress hormones during periods of pessimism and perceived loss of control. The body's attempt to rid itself of these excess amounts of hormones creates conditions that weaken the immune system.

Stress and Disease

5. *Is there a stress-cancer connection?*

   The research on the stress-cancer connection is not conclusive at this time. We know that stress does not create cancer cells, but stress does seem to weaken the body's normal tendency to fight the growth of tumors that have already formed.

6. *What do we know about the link between stress and heart problems?*
   High levels of stress increase the risk of heart disease. Meyer Friedman and Ray Rosenman discovered this link more than fifty years ago, in studies that led to the now-famous terms *Type A* and *Type B* personalities. Type A personalities—who tend to be impatient, competitive, hard-driving, verbally aggressive, and anger-prone—are more likely to have heart attacks than are Type B personalities, who are more laid-back, easygoing, and relaxed. The Type A characteristic that seems most destructive is anger, but studies show that depression also increases the risk of death from heart disease.

Key Terms

stress, p. 245
health psychology, p. 245
general adaptation syndrome (GAS), p. 246
burnout, p. 248
Type A, p. 252
Type B, p. 252

Key People

Walter Cannon, p. 246
Hans Selye, p. 246

Self-Test

Multiple-Choice Questions

Choose the *best* answer for each of the following questions.

1. The principal at Regional High School recently announced that, because of a new state rule, all students must pass a series of tests to be allowed to move into the next higher grade. Since the announcement, the number of absences at the school due to stress-related illnesses has risen dramatically. The school psychologist is now holding special sessions to help students cope better with their stress. Which of the following topics would NOT be appropriate for these sessions?
   a. Threat or challenge? Your perceptions of stress can affect your health.
   b. Stress is a process: You can control the way you react to stress.
   c. Your general outlook can foster good health or lead to poor health.
   d. Be stress-free! You don't have to experience stress.

2. The fight-or-flight response is a
   a. full mind-body reaction that prepares you to take action against the challenge or to flee from it.
   b. purely emotional response to stress that tends to be the same for everyone.
   c. purely physical response to stress that tends to vary from person to person.
   d. the final stage of the GAS sequence, when your body is exhausted and you have to run away.

3. Dr. Cary has been working in United Nations refugee camps in crisis areas for several years. Initially, he was optimistic, full of energy, happy to get up in the morning, and sure he could help people in need. Lately, he has noticed that he feels depressed most of the time, accomplishes only about half of what he used to accomplish in a day, and no longer believes his work is doing much good at all. Dr. Cary is showing the symptoms of

MODULE 13

trb ■ TEACHING TIP

Building Vocabulary: ***Linking to the Textbook*** (*Teacher's Resource Binder*, p. 13-1; **Handout 13–2**) may be used to review module vocabulary and terms. Have students work in small review groups to complete the handout, without referring to a previous version of this same handout they may have completed earlier in the module. Taking turns, group members should use the text to check and confirm responses.

tb Using the Test Bank

The *Test Bank* that accompanies this textbook offers a wide variety of questions in different formats and levels of complexity. Use the software to construct whole tests or to integrate standardized questions into teacher-made tests.

Self-Test Answers

Multiple-Choice Questions

1. d, 2. a, 3. b,

Alternative Assessment/Portfolio Project

trb COPING WITH STRESS Have students create a self-assessment portfolio of their experiences with stress by writing a reflective journal entry to accompany each of the following activities from the *Teacher's Resource Binder*:

- **Application Activity:** *Stress Levels* (*Teacher's Resource Binder*, p. 13-1; **Handout 13–3**)
- **Application Activity:** *Vulnerability to Stress* (*Teacher's Resource Binder*, p. 13-1; **Handout 13–4**)
- **Application Activity:** *Stress Symptoms* (*Teacher's Resource Binder*, p. 13-1; **Handout 13–5**)
- **Evaluation Activity:** *Hassles and Uplifts Scale* (*Teacher's Resource Binder*, p. 13-1; **Handout 13–6**)

MODULE 13

Self-Test Answers

Multiple-Choice Questions (continued)

4. c, 5. c.

Matching Terms and Definitions

6. a. (4), b. (8), c. (9), d. (3), e. (8), f. (10), g. (1), h. (7), i

a. a weakened immune system as a result of a prolonged pessimistic outlook.
b. burnout—a form of physical, emotional, and mental exhaustion brought on by job-related stress.
c. the alarm reaction, the first phase of the general adaptation syndrome, because he is adapting to his new life.
d. the Type A personality syndrome, as evidenced by his depression about his lack of results.

4. Romiro and David, who are participating in a student-exchange program, reached the airport this morning and heard that their scheduled flight was delayed because the plane had engine problems. Romiro thought about the situation and said that their trip would probably be doubly safe now, because their plane would receive a more thorough safety check. David also thought about the situation and said this was surely just a sign of bad things to come, and the trip and the month away from home would probably be a disaster. Who is more likely to feel greater stress and possibly even become sick on the trip, Romiro or David?
   a. Romiro. People with an optimistic outlook release excess stress hormones that can damage their immune system, making illness more likely.
   b. Romiro. His unrealistic remarks suggest that he has not truly appraised the situation, and research shows that the amount of stress we feel about a situation is greatly influenced by our appraisal of the situation.
   c. David. People with a pessimistic outlook release excess stress hormones that can damage their immune system, making illness more likely.
   d. David. His doom-and-gloom statements indicate that he has not taken time to appraise the situation, and research shows that the amount of stress we feel about a situation is greatly influenced by our appraisal of the situation.

5. Friedman and Rosenman found that stress did predict risk of heart attack in men who had Type A personalities. In further investigations, researchers discovered that the aspect of stress most likely to predict heart disease is
   a. stress that disturbs relaxation at home.
   b. stress that makes the workplace less productive.
   c. a general tendency to anger and depression.
   d. a general tendency to indifference and boredom.

Matching Terms and Definitions

7. For each definition, choose the *best* matching term from the list that follows.

Definition

a. A brain structure that is vital for memory recall; seems to shrink when subjected to a flood of stress hormones.
b. The process by which we perceive and respond to certain events that we appraise as threatening or challenging.
c. In Friedman and Rosenman's terminology, a person who is competitive, hard-driving, impatient, verbally aggressive, and anger-prone.
d. A subfield of psychology that deals with how stress affects our well-being
e. The belief that one has some influence over the outcome of one's activities and routines.
f. In Friedman and Rosenman's terminology, a person who is easygoing and relaxed.
g. Events that we appraise as threatening or challenging.
h. Physical, emotional, and mental exhaustion brought on by persistent job-related stress.

Alternative Assessment/Portfolio Project *(continued)*

- Evaluation Activity: *The Stress Appraisal Measure* (*Teacher's Resource Binder,* p. 13-1; Handout 13–7)
- Application Activity: *Perceived Control* (*Teacher's Resource Binder,* p. 13-1; Handout 13–8)
- Analysis Activity: *Type A and Type B Personalities* (*Teacher's Resource Binder,* p. 13-1; Handout 13–9)
- Evaluation Activity: *Hostility and Its Alleviations* (*Teacher's Resource Binder,* p. 13-1; Handout 13–10)

As a culminating focus of this portfolio, have students write a detailed plan for how they can deal with stress better than they have been able to up to this point. Encourage students to apply some of the suggestions from the text to their daily lives and the stress-creating situations in which they might find themselves.

Term

(1) stress
(2) stressor
(3) health psychology
(4) hippocampus
(5) GAS
(6) resistance
(7) burnout
(8) perceived control
(9) Type A
(10) Type B
(11) optimist
(12) pessimist

Fill-in-the-Blank Questions

7. Walter Cannon described the fight-or-flight response, in which an event triggers the release of stress hormones into the nervous system. To prepare you to fight or flee, your nervous system then increases your ______________ ______________, dulls your sense of pain, and pumps more blood to your ______________ ______________.

8. Working with rats, Hans Selye discovered the general adaptation syndrome (GAS), a predictable, recurring response to stress. The GAS has three stages:
(1) an ______________ reaction,
(2) ______________, and
(3) ______________.

Brief Essay Question

9. Your friend Ernie is a very competitive and hard-driving young man, and he often gets angry over things that seem to others to be just minor events. You've read that people with these characteristics have a high risk of having a heart attack. In two short paragraphs of about three or four sentences each, tell Ernie some of the things you've learned about stress, anger, and health. In your answer, offer some advice that might help Ernie get more enjoyment from his life now and could help him avoid heart trouble later.

MODULE 13

Self-Test Answers

Fill-in-the-Blank Questions

7. heart rate; larger muscles, 8. alarm; resistance; exhaustion

Brief Essay Question

9. Student answers should indicate most of the following points: Students should show that they understand that the physiological response to stress (the fight-or-flight response) is much the same from one person to another, but emotional responses vary, depending on how individuals appraise stressors. During the fight-or-flight response, stress hormones pour into the bloodstream, heart rate increases, sensation of pain diminishes, and blood flows to the large muscles. Stress reactions have three phases: alarm, resistance, and physical deterioration. High levels of stress increase the risk of heart disease. Friedman and Rosenman studied thousands of men and found that the personal characteristic that seems most destructive in the Type A personality profile is anger. Helpful advice would include taking enough time to calm down; venting the anger by exercising; confiding in a friend or writing in a journal; and avoiding sulking, which functions as an opportunity for rehearsing reasons for being angry.

Performance Standards

Standard Area: Stress, Coping, and Health

Content Standard 4: Cognitive and behavioral techniques for reducing stress and promoting wellness

Performance Standard 4.1 Investigate cognitive techniques to reduce stress and promote wellness.

- Investigate how an individual's explanatory style can affect the person's health. Discuss the role of optimism and pessimism in health. (Student Text pp. 266–268)
- Discuss how we can overcome pessimism and improve our health. (Student Text p. 267)

Performance Standard 4.2 Explore behavioral strategies to deal with stress and promote wellness.

- Discuss the benefits of exercise to our overall physical and psychological health. (Student Text pp. 258–260)
- Explore the important part that social support plays in our physical and psychological well-being. (Student Text pp. 260–261)
- Investigate the "faith factor." (Student Text pp. 261–263)
- Discuss how flow, happiness, and optimism contribute to our well-being. (Student Text pp. 263–268)
- Examine why smoking is so dangerous. Discuss safe guidelines for quitting smoking. (Student Text pp. 268–270)
- Define obesity. Investigate the physical and emotional health risks of obesity. Discuss why it is so difficult to lose weight and some safe hints that may be helpful. (Student Text pp. 270–273)

Materials NETWORK

All of the items from the Video, Activity, and Enrichment Centers listed below come from the *Teacher's Resource Binder.* These items will help you teach and expand on concepts presented in Module 14.

trb This logo indicates when an item from the Materials Network may be used in conjunction with a specific note found in this module's *Teacher's Edition.*

Healthy Lifestyles

Activity Center

- Critical Thinking Activity: *Fact or Falsehood?* Check students' preconceptions. (*Teacher's Resource Binder,* p. 14-1; **Handout 14–1**)
- Building Vocabulary: *Exploring Root Words* Students explore root words. (*Teacher's Resource Binder,* p. 14-1; **Handout 14–2**)
- Analysis Activity: *Coping with Health Injuries and Problems Scale* This scale measures students' ability to cope with these life events. (*Teacher's Resource Binder,* p. 14-1; **Handout 14–3**)
- Analysis Activity: *Social Support Scale* Measure your students' level of social support. (*Teacher's Resource Binder,* p. 14-1; **Handout 14–4**)
- Evaluation Activity: *Self-Concealment Scale* This scale measures how likely students are to share their lives with others. (*Teacher's Resource Binder,* p. 14-1; **Handout 14–5**)

Enrichment Center

- Enrichment Lesson: *Spirituality and Health* This lesson expands on the text discussion. (*Teacher's Resource Binder,* p. 14-1)

Positive Experiences and Well-Being

V Video Center

- Videocassette: *Scientific American Frontiers,* **Second Edition, Segment 34: "Sport Imports"** Consult the faculty guide from the *Scientific American Frontiers* video series for a description of this segment. (*Teacher's Resource Binder,* p. 14-1)

Activity Center

- Application Activity: *Creating Flow Experiences* Students can practice creating flow with this activity. (*Teacher's Resource Binder,* p. 14-1; **Transparency Masters 14–1** and **14–2**)
- Analysis Activity: *Measuring Optimism* Students can find out how optimistic they are with this measure. (*Teacher's Resource Binder,* p. 14-1; **Handouts 14–6** and **14–7**)
- Critical Thinking Activity: *Unrealistic Optimism About Life Events* This activity helps students see the value of moderation. (*Teacher's Resource Binder,* p. 14-1; **Handout 14–8**)
- Evaluation Activity: *The Hardiness Scale* This scale measures hardiness. (*Teacher's Resource Binder,* p. 14-1; **Handout 14–9**)
- Analysis Activity: *Imagining Your Future: The Hope Scale* Students can infer their own levels of happiness with this hope scale. (*Teacher's Resource Binder,* p. 14-1; **Handout 14–10**)

Enrichment Center

- Enrichment Lesson: *Positive Subjective Experiences* This lesson helps clarify and extend the discussion of these phenomena. (*Teacher's Resource Binder,* p. 14-1)
- Enrichment Lesson: *Flow* The qualities of a flow experience are defined. (*Teacher's Resource Binder,* p. 14-1; **Transparency Master 14–3**)
- Enrichment Lesson: *Hope* This lesson highlights three components of hope. (*Teacher's Resource Binder,* p. 14-1)
- Enrichment Lesson: *The Health Beliefs Model* This lesson describes the science behind the health beliefs model. (*Teacher's Resource Binder,* p. 14-1)

Overcoming Illness-Related Behaviors

Activity Center

- Evaluation Activity: *Why Smoke?* This lesson delves into why people smoke. (*Teacher's Resource Binder,* p. 14-1; **Handout 14–11**)
- Evaluation Activity: *How Healthy Is Your Diet?* This measure will help your students evaluate their diets. (*Teacher's Resource Binder,* p. 14-1; **Handout 14–12**)
- Critical Thinking Activity: *A Nutrition Quiz* This quiz will help your students see how much they know about food and nutrition. (*Teacher's Resource Binder,* p. 14-1; **Handout 14–13**)
- Evaluation Activity: *The Dieting Beliefs Scale* This lesson helps clarify scientifically tested weight-loss strategies. (*Teacher's Resource Binder,* p. 14-1; **Handout 14–14**)

Enrichment Center

- Enrichment Lesson: *Preventing Smoking* This lesson on preventing smoking may help students quit. (*Teacher's Resource Binder,* p. 14-1)
- Enrichment Lesson: *Reading Food Labels* This lesson explains some food labels and consumer rules. (*Teacher's Resource Binder,* p. 14-1)
- Enrichment Lesson: *Obesity* This lesson helps students avoid obesity and understand its health impact. (*Teacher's Resource Binder,* p. 14-1)
- Enrichment Lesson: *Maintaining Weight Loss* This lesson helps students see the value of lifelong, healthy eating habits. (*Teacher's Resource Binder,* p. 14-1)

MODULE 14

Promoting Wellness

Introducing The Module

The Points: Module Objectives

- Explain how exercise contributes to wellness.
- Evaluate how social support makes a difference in our health and well-being.
- Describe the "faith factor" and how it relates to wellness.
- Analyze how flow, happiness, and optimism contribute to our well-being.
- Explain why smoking is so dangerous and why it is so hard to give up.
- Understand obesity and the physical and emotional health risks that accompany this condition.
- Analyze why it is so hard to lose weight.

trb Building Vocabulary

At this point, you may wish to use **Building Vocabulary:** ***Exploring Root Words*** (*Teacher's Resource Binder*, p. 14-1; **Handout 14–2**) to challenge students, working individually or with partners, to relate the meanings of some familiar words with the module terms. By doing so, they will discover that some familiar words are roots for terms related to psychology.

■ APPLYING THE POINTS

Have some students interview local doctors to see if the doctors use psychological "immunizations" in their health care practices. Suggest that students ask how doctors might deal with someone who seems to exacerbate health problems with psychological ones. Have the students who conduct these informal interviews brief the class on their findings.

MODULE 14

Promoting Wellness

Healthy Lifestyles

Positive Experiences and Well-Being

Overcoming Illness-Related Behaviors

Before Jonas Salk created the polio vaccination in 1954, polio terrorized our country. Many thousands were crippled, including President Franklin Delano Roosevelt, and thousands more died. In 1984, research psychologist **Martin Seligman** had a life-changing conversation with the famous Dr. Salk.

Seligman and Salk were together at a conference where immunologists and psychologists were discussing how both fields contribute to making life better. Salk told Seligman, "If I were a young scientist today, I would still do immunization. But instead of immunizing kids physically, I'd do it your way. I'd immunize them psychologically. I'd see if these psychologically immunized kids could then fight off mental illness better. Physical illness too" (Seligman, 1995).

Given the tenfold increase in the rate of clinical depression since the years just before WWII, an "immunization" against this mental illness would, indeed, make life better (Seligman, 1994). Depression makes you feel miserable. It also hurts your productivity at school and work, and it puts your physical health in jeopardy. We could avoid much pain, sickness, and lost work time if we could stay well and never start down depression's dark path.

In this module, we explore the concept of **wellness,** which is the result of a healthy lifestyle and healthy attitudes. We also examine ways to promote psychological and physical well-being and to overcome behaviors that lead to illness. Several roads lead to a healthy lifestyle. Let's take a closer look at three of these roads, starting with exercise.

▶ **Martin Seligman** (1942–) American psychologist and proponent of positive psychology.

▶ **wellness** The common result of a healthy lifestyle and healthy attitudes.

Healthy Lifestyles

Exercise

What's the Point? 1. How does exercise contribute to wellness?

In June of 2002, President George W. Bush asked all Americans to exercise at least 30 minutes each day. His motives included improving the

Getting Started

Start the module by asking students to describe the physical and psychological qualities of a person their age that they consider healthy. As students learn about promoting wellness by reading this module, they might benefit from reviewing and, if need by, revising their initial descriptions.

trb You may wish to use the **Critical Thinking Activity:** ***Fact or Falsehood?*** (*Teacher's Resource Binder*, p. 14-1; **Handout 14–1**) as a pre-reading strategy to find out what students already know about promoting wellness. The activity will prime students to note terms and concepts in the text that confirm or dispel their preconceptions about promoting wellness.

health of U.S. citizens and saving millions of dollars in lost productivity on the job. Time will tell if this presidential request increases our health and lowers our health-care bills.

Do you exercise regularly? If so, you are part of a growing minority in America. The physical benefits of *aerobic exercise,* such as increased lung and heart fitness, are well documented. Are there psychological benefits as well? The answer appears to be a resounding yes.

Mental and Physical Health Studies show aerobic exercise is good for your muscles and your mind.

Several studies suggest exercise is an effective, nonmedical means of reducing anxiety and depression. In one of these studies, Lisa McCann and David Holmes (1984) worked with a group of mildly depressed college women. They assigned the women to one of three groups:

- Group A participated in an aerobic exercise program.
- Group B worked through a series of relaxation exercises.
- Group C received no treatment.

Ten weeks after the treatment programs began, those in the aerobic exercise group showed the greatest decrease in depression (Figure 14.1). This dramatic finding illustrates that exercise can help reduce or prevent depression, the common cold of mental illness.

Physical fitness also leads to greater self-confidence and self-discipline (Stephens, 1988). Unfortunately, many of us bypass daily exercise because we think we need to run 5 miles a day to make a difference. Not true. Even a 10-minute walk increases energy levels and lowers tension (Thayer, 1987, 1993).

So we know exercise boosts mood. But *how* does aerobic exercise make us feel better? Several factors contribute. Exercise

- increases the output of the mood-boosting chemicals your nervous system produces (Jacobs, 1994).
- enhances your cognitive abilities, such as memory, to some degree (Etnier & others, 1997).
- lowers your blood pressure (Perkins & others, 1986).
- has side effects, such as better sleep, that provide an emotional benefit.

Figure 14.1 Exercise for Mental Health Feelings of depression decreased dramatically when exercise was included as a part of the treatment. (Adapted from McCann and Holmes, 1984.)

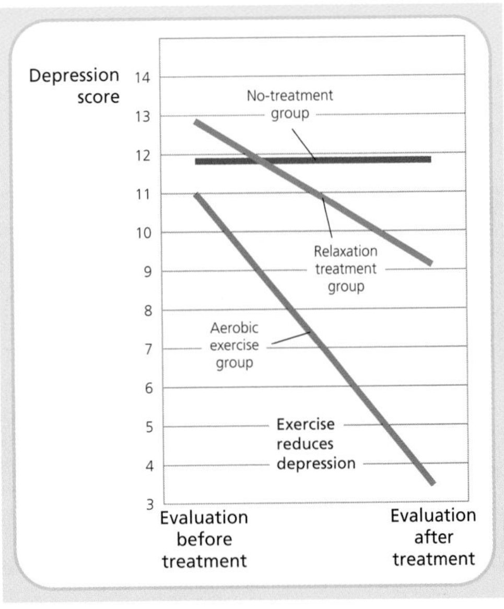

Suggested Readings

Use the following books as teacher preparation-tools or as enrichment for advanced students:

Burger, J. (2000). *Personality* (5th ed.). Pacific Grove, CA: Wadsworth.

Csikszentmihalyi, M. (1990) *Flow: The psychology of optimal experience.* New York: HarperCollins

Edlin, G., & Golanty, E. (1988). *Health and wellness.* Boston: Jones & Bartlett.

Insel, P., & Roth, W. (1985). *Core concepts in health* (4th ed.). Palo Alto, CA: Mayfield.

Myers, D. G. (1992). *The pursuit of happiness: Discovering the pathway to fulfillment, well-being, and enduring personal joy.* New York: Avon.

Seligman, M. E. P. (1998). *Learned optimism: How to change your mind and your life* (2nd ed.). New York: Pocket Books.

Teaching the Points

■ TEACHING TIPS

web (1) You can log on as an instructor to the book companion site for *Thinking About Psychology* at **www.worthpublishers.com/thinkingaboutpsych.** It contains teacher resources for class presentations as well as review and assessment of module concepts and terms.

tr (2) A four-color transparency of Figure 14.1, Exercise for Mental Health, is available in the **Overhead Transparencies Set.**

■ JOURNAL WRITING

Invite students to use the following questions and writing prompts as springboards for entries in their psychology journals:

- Describe your exercise habits. Why are you maintaining your current level of activity? What would you change about your exercise habits?
- What, if anything, has caused you emotional pain in the last 24 hours? What has caused you the most happiness? How much have your family and friends caused your pain and helped you through it?
- How would you describe the quality of your religious or spiritual life? How often do you attend religious or spiritual services per week or month? What would you change about your religious habits?

trb At this point, you may wish to use **Analysis Activity:** ***Social Support Scale*** (*Teacher's Resource Binder,* p. 14-1; **Handout 14–4**) and **Enrichment Lesson:** ***Spirituality and Health*** (*Teacher's Resource Binder,* p. 14-1).

MODULE 14

■ **LOOKING AT THE ISSUES**
Studies show that people living in the United States are overweight and unhealthy because they do not include exercise and a healthy diet in their lifestyles. Have students explore why these two key habits aren't utilized more frequently by addressing the following questions:

- Why would people not see the long-term benefits as "worth it" when faced with short-term "rewards" of poor diet and lack of exercise?
- What are some reasons people give for not exercising and eating right?
- How do the media influence people's decisions about diet and exercise?
- What are some convincing arguments for teens to start eating right and exercising?

■ **APPLYING THE POINTS**
Contact a local cardiologist to see what he or she does to encourage patients to develop and maintain support during illness and recovery. Find out the professional's response to the following questions, which you may incorporate into a class lecture:

- Does the hospital have a policy of letting family members visit a heart attack patient? Why or why not?
- Are there support groups available through the hospital for heart patients? Why or why not?

trb At this point, you may wish to use **Analysis Activity:** ***Coping with Injuries and Health Problems Scale*** **(*Teacher's Resource Binder*, p. 14-1; Handout 14–3).**

■ **TEACHING TIP**
Help students see that social support can come in many forms—extended family (aunts, uncles, grandparents), friends, or religious groups. Also, students should be encouraged to cultivate close relationships with friends and family during times of good health so that the ties are there when they're needed during times of ill health.

trb At this point, you may wish to use **Analysis Activity:** ***Social Support Scale*** **(*Teacher's Resource Binder*, p. 14-1; Handout 14–4).**

Regular exercise cuts heart-attack risk in half (Powell & others, 1987) and increases longevity by as much as two years (Paffenbarger & others, 1986). So why not, after finishing your homework, pump up your bike tires or lace up those running shoes?

Family and Friends

2. Does social support make a difference in our health and well-being?

What, if anything, has caused you emotional strain in the past 24 hours? Think about that for a moment. The most common answer, according to a good-news–bad-news research finding, is "family" (Warr & Payne, 1982). This is understandable. Each day, families juggle time, energy, and resources in an attempt to satisfy each person's needs for food, transportation, and belonging in today's increasingly busy world. The results often include stress, and stress can be toxic to our bodies. It can lead to heart disease, suppress the immune system, and contribute to high blood pressure.

However, the good news is that the family juggling act also brings happy moments. When the same researchers asked *what had prompted pleasure* in the previous 24 hours, the answer once again, by an even *larger* margin, was "family." The close relationships found in families and with some good friends is most often a source of happiness. Family and friends offer *social support,* making us feel liked and wanted. This social support provides the cognitive rewards of happiness and contentment. Several studies have also linked social support to health and wellness.

- People with more social ties (family, friends, support groups) are less likely to die prematurely (Cohen, 1988).
- Heart attack victims living alone are *twice* as likely to have another heart attack within six months as are those living with a family member (Case & others, 1992).
- An amazing study followed children with high IQ scores for 70 years. Regardless of economic status, the children who grew up with parents who did not divorce outlived the children of divorce by an average of 4 years (Schwartz & others, 1995). Do intact families provide more social support for children? Probably so.

Joy and Strife Our family members sometimes bring stress, but they also bring us support and happiness.

Suggested Readings

Use the following works as teacher-preparation tools or as enrichment for advanced students:

Seligman, M. E. P., & Csikszentmihalyi, M. (2000). Positive psychology: An introduction. *American Psychologist, 55,* 5–14.

Snyder, C. R. (2000). *Handbook of hope: Theory, measures, and applications.* New York: Academic Press.

Snyder, C. R. (1994). *The psychology of hope.* New York. Free Press.

Snyder, C. R. (2000). *Handbook of hope: Theory, measures, and applications.* New York: Academic Press.

Taylor, S. (1998). *Health psychology* (4th ed.). New York: McGraw-Hill.

One of the more compelling and ingenious attempts to examine the relationship between social needs and the functioning of our immune systems involved a study of 276 participants. Each participant agreed to allow drops of a cold-germ–laden liquid to be dripped into their healthy noses. What these researchers found is nothing to sneeze at: Those with the most social ties were less likely to catch a cold and produced less mucus. (How they measured the mucus, I'm not quite sure.) The results showed that social support aids in resisting the common cold (Cohen & others, 1997).

So do all these findings mean that your health is destined to fail if you have a messed-up family and no trustworthy friends? Not necessarily. We all have access to support groups, which are widely available and can provide the connectedness and sense of belonging that's proven so beneficial to emotional and psychological health. Many local schools and religious organizations sponsor support groups, and your school counselor should be able to point you in the right direction if you're interested.

Stress is unavoidable, but the support provided by family, friends, and support groups provides a buffer against the ill effects of stress. Another possible buffer is the "faith factor."

The Faith Factor

3. What is the "faith factor," and how does it relate to wellness?

Do religion and spirituality relate to health? A recent poll showed that 80 percent of all Americans believe they do (Matthews & Larson, 1997). But is it possible to assess this relationship scientifically? Several researchers have tried, and they found a *correlation* between being religiously active and longevity. This means the researchers found that certain factors tend to occur together, but they did not do experiments that would show cause and effect. In this case, they found that people who attend religious services regularly, from a variety of religious backgrounds, tend to live longer than those who attend infrequently. One study, for example, followed 21,204 people for eight years (Hummer & others, 1999). Those researchers found that people who did not attend religious services were 1.87 times more likely to have died than were those who attended services weekly (Figure 14.2, page 262). Put another way, the life expectancy of a 20-year-old in this study would be 83 years for the most frequent attenders, and 75 years for nonattenders. This eight-year difference ranks up there with the positive effects of exercise and nonsmoking.

Does this mean that your life expectancy will go up if you start attending religious services frequently? Not exactly. We cannot say that religious involvement guarantees wellness and longevity. What we can

■ MULTICULTURAL CONNECTIONS

Are the benefits of exercise, family, friends, and spirituality recognized the world over? Have students use available resources to research the health attitudes of other cultures. Through their research, have students determine if the Western idea of a healthy lifestyle is the same the world over. With their permission, students may ask students from other cultural backgrounds about the lifestyle habits of their native cultures.

Enriching

Contact several churches, synagogues, and mosques in your area to see if they have an active older adult community that worships with them. If so, ask what the average age is of older people in the congregation and how healthy this group of congregants would rate themselves. Then contact a nursing home or senior adult day-care center to see how many of these people are active in religious activities. Gather data about their average age and health to see if older people who participate in religious services seem to be healthier and to live longer than those who do not.

trb At this point, you may wish to use **Enrichment Lesson:** ***Spirituality and Health*** (*Teacher's Resource Binder*, p. 14-1).

MODULE 14

■ TEACHING TIPS

Some students who do not attend religious services may feel uncomfortable with the idea that being religious is more beneficial to life than not being religious. Help students understand that no one religious viewpoint is being promoted in the text—in fact, studies merely show that any religious faith and service attendance are correlated factors to good health.

Explore ways in which the benefits of being religious can be found in other social institutions, like volunteering and charity work.

trb tr A black-line master for Figure 14.3, Explaining the Faith Factor, is available in the **Black-Line Masters Appendix** in the *Teacher's Resource Binder.*

trb At this point, you may wish to use **Enrichment Lesson:** ***Spirituality and Health*** (*Teacher's Resource Binder*, p. 14-1).

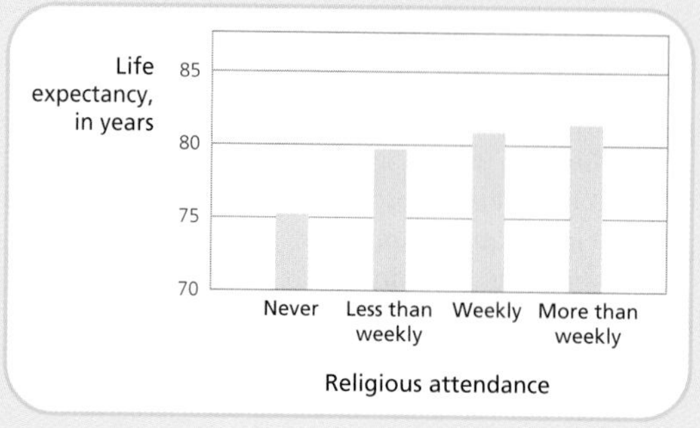

Figure 14.2 **The Faith Factor?** People who frequently attend religious services tend to live longer than those who do not attend. (Data from Hummer & others, 1999.)

say is that at least three factors associated with the religiously active seem to contribute to better health (Figure 14.3):

1. The beliefs of the religiously active often promote healthier lifestyles. That is, religious leaders typically do not encourage smoking, drinking, and staying up all night partying.
2. Attending religious services is a communal, not a solo, experience. Faith communities provide social support, and they tend also to encourage another predictor of wellness and good health: marriage. Married people are more satisfied with life and happier than their unmarried, separated, or divorced counterparts (Coombs, 1991; Gove & others, 1990; Wood & others, 1989).
3. Religiously active people often experience less anxiety and stress due to a worldview promoting optimism, gratitude, and hope for the future. Optimists have stronger immune systems than pes-

Figure 14.3 **Explaining the Faith Factor** The impact of religion on health has many dimensions.

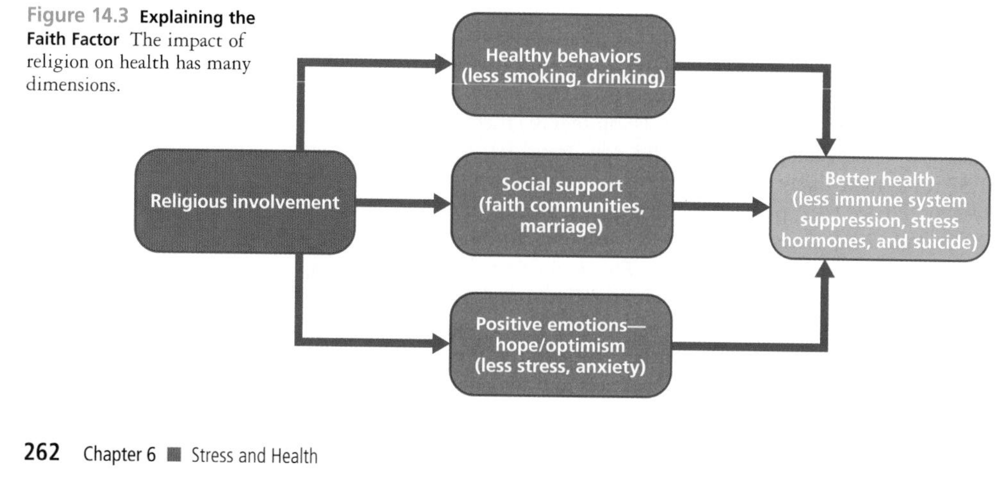

Enriching

If students attend religious services, have them explore what lifestyle choices their particular religious affiliation actively supports or discourages. If students do not attend religious services, have them interview people in their own social support network and reflect on whether their social network supports and discourages the same type of behaviors. Promote a class forum on this topic by posing the following questions:

- What behaviors are actively supported or discouraged in the religious affiliation or social support network you explored?
- How do these behaviors relate to good health?

trb At this point, you may wish to use **Enrichment Lesson:** ***Spirituality and Health*** (*Teacher's Resource Binder*, p. 14-1).

simists do. Religiously active people have stronger immune systems and have fewer hospital stays than religiously inactive people (Koenig & Larson, 1998; Koenig & others, 1997).

The relationship between spirituality and health has not escaped the notice of the nation's medical schools. In 1994, only 3 of America's 126 medical schools offered courses in spirituality and health. Sixty-one of the 126 had a spirituality and health course by 1999 (Levin & others, 1997; McVeigh, 1999). The ongoing research in this area, a direct result of renewed interest in studying the relationship between health and faith, may yield new and helpful information in the coming years.

▶ **positive psychology**
Subfield of psychology that focuses on the study of optimal human functioning and the factors that allow individuals and communities to thrive.

Positive Experiences and Well-Being

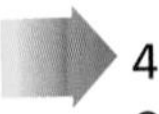

4. How do flow, happiness, and optimism contribute to our well-being?

Experience success in the classroom, on the ball field, or with a GameCube controller in your hands, and you feel some degree of happiness. When we're happy, we're more likely to forgive the friend who borrowed and did not return a pen, to help those who do not understand an assignment, or to tolerate the driver who cuts us off in traffic. Wouldn't it be great if we could "bank" these successes or positive experiences after they occur, building up a reserve that would help get us through rough times? And could this reserve "inoculate" or help prevent us from becoming depressed during difficult times, as Jonas Salk had hoped? The answer, according to Martin Seligman and others doing research in **positive psychology,** is a solid yes.

Years after his conversation with Salk, Seligman, and others, began studying emotions, feelings, and positive experiences that foster well-being and allow us to thrive. Ed Diener (2002) explains *well-being* as a "concept that includes life satisfaction, feelings of fulfillment, pleasant emotions, and a low level of unpleasant emotions." Experiences (including both thoughts and feelings) that produce pleasant emotions lead a person to judge life as satisfying, fulfilling, and "going well." For example, if a goal of yours is to get an A in your psychology class, and you earn a 97 percent on a test, seeing that grade will be a positive experience that promotes your well-being. Why are positive experiences important? Research (Fineburg, 2000) shows that the more positive experiences you have, the more likely you are to

1. have better relationships with others.
2. contribute more to your community.
3. excel in academics and sports.
4. provide leadership.

MODULE 14

■ **TEACHING TIP**

Foster optimistic thinking in your students by encouraging the following attitudes regarding school:

- Failing grades do not mean all hope is lost. Most teachers offer tutoring or additional help in bringing up low grades.
- Poor grades do not mean one is stupid. Grades only indicate that one didn't do well on that particular test, not in life.
- Treat failure as a challenge, not as an obstacle. Evaluate study habits and listening skills that can be changed to help ensure future success.

trb At this point, you may wish to use **Analysis Activity:** *Measuring Optimism* (*Teacher's Resource Binder*, p. 14-1; **Handouts 14–6** and **14–7**).

Cross-Curricular Connections

BIOLOGY AND HEALTH Have students work with partners or in small groups to check in your school's biology and health textbooks for references to the relationship between positive experiences and health. Have them use their findings to respond to the following questions:

- How many references to the relationship between positive experiences and health are there in each text? How many pages are devoted to this relationship?
- Which type of textbook has more references to the positive experience/health link? Why might this be?
- How do these books describe this link? Do they seem biased? If so, how?

trb At this point, you may wish to use **Enrichment Lesson:** *Spirituality and Health* (*Teacher's Resource Binder*, p. 14-1) and **Enrichment Lesson:** *Positive Subjective Experience* (*Teacher's Resource Binder*, p. 14-1).

MODULE 14

■ **JOURNAL WRITING**

Invite students to use the following questions and writing prompts as springboards for entries in their psychology journals:

- When are you in flow? Describe how you feel when you are in flow.
- What makes you happy? How do you try to make others happy? How has a positive experience helped you feel better when you have been sick or down?
- Would you categorize yourself as optimistic or pessimistic? What contributed to you being that way? How has being that way helped or hurt you in life?

F • Y • I

Microflow is a way for people to combat boring situations. **Microflow** activities are those that one can engage in that keep the mind active when having to attend to less than challenging circumstances. Students who engage in a seemingly meaningless activity like doodling, finger tapping, or leg shaking during class may be engaging in microflow.

trb At this point, you may wish to use **Enrichment Lesson:** *Flow* (*Teacher's Resource Binder*, p. 14-1; **Transparency Master 14–3**) and **Application Activity:** *Creating Flow Experiences* (*Teacher's Resource Binder*, p. 14-1; **Transparency Masters 14–1 and 14–2**).

▶ **flow** A state of optimal experience; for flow to occur, the experiences must be a challenge requiring skill, have clear goals, and provide feedback.

5. propose new ideas in such areas as science and business.
6. help others.
7. be less of a drain on psychological and physical health systems.

But note that, as of this writing, most of the research linking well-being and positive experiences is *correlational*. We don't really know which is the cause and which is the effect. Do the positive experiences cause all these wonderful characteristics to exist in the people who have them? Or do people who already have these wonderful characteristics tend to have experiences that are more positive? One thing is clear, however: Our potential for well-being consists of the goals that are important to us and the degree to which we are achieving those goals.

Researchers in positive psychology have found at least three kinds of experiences that have powerful effects on the individual. Flow, happiness, and optimism all contribute to our sense of well-being.

Flow

Flow, defined by Mihaly Csikszentmihalyi (pronounced cheeks-sent-me-hi; 1990), is a state of optimal experience. Activities we perform for the satisfaction of doing them and not for extrinsic rewards put us in a state of flow. Reading a book we can't put down, playing a game of three-on-three basketball in the driveway with friends, or acting in the school play can all be flow experiences. People in flow situations report losing track of time and being hard to distract. They also lose any sort of self-consciousness about their appearance or other people's opinions of them. Let's take a closer look at flow, using the basketball example.

For flow to occur, we need a challenge requiring skill. Playing basketball (a real challenge for me) meets this requirement; watching TV does not. Clear goals (trying to put the ball in the hoop, keeping someone else from scoring, winning the game) and feedback (each basket counts for 1 point, first team to 11 wins) are also flow necessities.

In the Flow A challenge requiring skill, clear goals, and feedback can become a "flow" activity.

Flow can happen in all areas of life, including the workplace. You may have a job where you literally start counting the minutes until it's time to leave. Perhaps you work there only for the money. Such a job borders more on drudgery, a direct contrast to flow. In what kind of job might you experience flow every day? You may want to keep

Enriching

(1) Have students brainstorm about flow activities they regularly engage in. Challenge them to participate in one of these activities within the next few days and reflect afterward about how the flow experience made them feel. In a class discussion, invite volunteers to respond to the following questions:

- How did being in flow make you feel?
- Did being in flow affect your mood for the rest of the day? Why or why not? Did a good mood extend into the next day? Why or why not?
- How can you experience more flow in your life?

trb At this point, you may wish to use **Enrichment Lesson:** *Flow* (*Teacher's Resource Binder*, p. 14-1; **Transparency Master 14–3**) and **Application Activity:** *Creating Flow Experiences* (*Teacher's Resource Binder*, p. 14-1; **Transparency Masters 14–1 and 14–2**).

that question in mind as you think about employment after graduation or select your major in college.

Flow is a subjective experience that contributes to another kind of positive experience: happiness.

Happiness

You walk into school, and the first person you talk to says, "Nice haircut. Looks sharp," bringing a smile to your face. Next, you go to class and find that the project you worked on for two weeks received a better grade than you'd anticipated. Finally, you solve a math problem that is giving most of your classmates a struggle. If you then begin helping your classmates solve that problem, a psychologist would not be surprised. Research shows that when we're happy, we're much more likely to help others (Diener, 2000). Happy people also make decisions more easily (Isen & Means, 1983), cooperate more (Forgas, 1998), and view the world as safer (Johnson & Tversky, 1983).

Of course, not everyone responds to "Nice haircut" in the same way. I'll bet you know someone who would say, "What didn't you like about my hair before?" How can the same event lead to happiness in some and gloom in others? Part of the answer may lie in several qualities and tendencies happy people possess (Table 14.1). Compared with

TABLE 14.1 HAPPINESS IS . . .

RESEARCHERS HAVE FOUND THAT HAPPY PEOPLE TEND TO	HOWEVER, HAPPINESS SEEMS NOT MUCH RELATED TO OTHER FACTORS, SUCH AS
Have high self-esteem (in Western countries)	Age
Be optimistic, outgoing, and agreeable	Gender (women are more often depressed, but also more often joyful)
Have close friendships or a satisfying marriage	Education levels
Have work and leisure that engage their skills	Parenthood (having children or not)
Have a meaningful religious faith	Physical attractiveness
Sleep well and exercise	

Source: Summarized from DeNeve and Cooper (1998), Myers (1993, 2000), and Myers and Diener (1995, 1996).

trb tr ■ **TEACHING TIP**

A black-line master for Table 14.1, Happiness Is . . . , is available in the **Black-Line Masters Appendix** of the *Teacher's Resource Binder.*

■ **LOOKING AT THE ISSUES**

Before World War II, two of psychology's goals focused on studying the positive aspects of life. Since World War II, the field has focused on curing illness rather than identifying positive qualities. Set aside time for small groups of students to discuss the following questions about positive subjective experiences:

- Why are mental illnesses easier to study than positive traits?
- What prejudices might lead some people to disregard the study of positive qualities?
- How might knowing the qualities of positive experiences lead to greater knowledge of our health?

trb At this point, you may wish to use **Enrichment Lesson:** *Positive Subjective Experiences* (*Teacher's Resource Binder*, p. 14-1).

(2) Have students think of the happiest person they know and interview that person about why he or she is so happy. Have students share their interview findings by responding to the following questions in a class discussion:

- Do these people view themselves as happy? Why or why not?
- What is their attitude about taking compliments?
- What is their attitude about handling difficulties in life?
- Do they consciously do anything to maintain happiness in their lives? Why or why not?
- How can you learn to be happier by following their examples?

trb At this point, you may wish to use **Analysis Activity:** *Imagining Your Future: The Hope Scale* (*Teacher's Resource Binder*, p. 14-1; **Handout 14–10**).

MODULE 14

tb ■ CHECKING FOR UNDERSTANDING

Here are several ways to assess students' comprehension:

- Assign any or all of the journal questions or prompts for an in-class writing assessment.
- Divide the students into groups or pairs and give each group a journal question prompt. Have them present their answers to the class, correcting any misconceptions that may arise.
- Use questions from the *Test Bank* to do a quick assessment of their knowledge of the concepts.

their less happy counterparts, happy people tend to be more outgoing, interact more with others, have a larger circle of friends, and participate in more rewarding activities. Having more friends often provides more social support and more opportunities for affection. Happy people also have a higher sense of personal control over their lives and exhibit higher levels of hope when facing challenges. Hope, according to Rick Snyder (1994), is a better predictor of how well a student will do in college than the standardized tests students take to get in. Optimistic attitudes, as we will see next, provide health bonuses as well.

Optimism

You've probably heard phrases like, "Optimists see the glass as half full, pessimists see it as half empty." But what is the difference between an optimist and a pessimist? *Optimism* is the belief that bad events

- are temporary.
- are not your fault.
- will not have broader effects beyond the present circumstances.

Pessimism is the opposite of optimism—the tendency to expect the worst. Let's look more closely at these contrasting attitudes, using the common situation of being let down by a friend. Imagine that the weekend is fast approaching, and you're making plans for Friday night. Your friend Chris says, "I'll call you tonight." You wait for the call, but it never comes. How would you explain this to yourself? Would you assume Chris blew you off and didn't really want to do anything with you? Or would you suppose something came up that kept your friend from calling? More specifically, which of the following phrases would best describe your reaction?

1. "I didn't get a call tonight because Chris really doesn't like me."
2. "Maybe Chris tried to call while someone else was on our phone?"
3. "I wonder what came up that kept Chris from calling?"
4. "Chris doesn't really want to hang out with me Friday or any day."

The way you answered that question may give some clues to whether you are optimistic or pessimistic. Our habits for thinking about causes of good or bad events determine whether we have an optimistic or pessimistic **explanatory style.** People with an optimistic explanatory style are more likely to think of causes like phrases 2 and 3, which provide temporary explanations that do not create a personal reason or fault for Chris's failure to call. Those with a pessimistic explanatory style would choose options 1 and 4, which place the blame on themselves and are permanent in nature. (See "Up Close: Overcoming Pessimism.")

▶ **explanatory style** The habits we have for thinking about the good or bad causes of events.

Demonstrating

(1) HOPE: GOALS, PATHWAYS, AND AGENCY Encourage students to write down five goals they want to accomplish within the next five to ten years. Have them consider the following questions:

- Are these goals concrete or abstract? How can you make abstract goals concrete?
- Are these goals realistic? Why or why not? *(Setting realistic goals starts students down the hopeful road.)*
- Do you have a plan for accomplishing these goals; that is, if your goal is to get a college education, do you know where you will go and how you will pay for it? *(Having concrete, realistic plans to accomplish these goals renders the goals more likely to happen.)* How confident are you that you will achieve these goals? *(Feeling confident that one can act to achieve goals is the key component to having hope.)*

trb At this point, you may wish to use **Enrichment Lesson:** *Hope* (*Teacher's Resource Binder*, p. 14-1).

Up Close

Overcoming Pessimism

Too much optimism can result in an inappropriate lack of responsibility, but pessimism—expecting the worst or explaining bad events in the worst way—can lead to sadness, passivity, and depression. Developing a positive explanatory approach benefits most people.

A series of studies conducted under the supervision of Martin Seligman (1995) have shown that changing from a negative to a positive explanatory style is possible and is especially beneficial for people at risk for depression. Most of these studies dealt with children identified as prone to depression. Those who went through a program to change their thinking style were *far less likely to show depressive symptoms* later in life than those who did not go through the program.

There are at least two techniques for overcoming pessimism (Seligman, 1998). The first technique, *distraction,* attempts to delay the pessimistic thought until a more appropriate time. Distraction is especially useful when a situation requires immediate action and negative thoughts could prove disastrous. Soldiers approaching an enemy outpost, for example, must somehow distract themselves from such thoughts as "I could get killed," thoughts that could cause hesitation and possibly death.

Disputation, a second technique, is arguing with oneself about pessimistic beliefs. A longer-lasting technique than distraction, disputing pessimistic thoughts changes reactions from dejection to optimism. We can dispute pessimism in at least four ways (Fineburg, 2000):

- ***Distancing*** Realizing that negative thoughts are usually unfounded helps distance us from pessimism's destructiveness. We do not tolerate insults about ourselves from others. Why accept them from ourselves? Do not think after a bad test score, "I'm a stupid idiot." Instead, think, "I didn't do well on this test."
- ***Checking for evidence*** Evidence from other times and places can disprove a pessimistic belief. You may have received a bad math score this time, but that doesn't make you a failure at math. What about your score on a previous test, a homework assignment, or the standardized tests?
- ***Considering alternatives*** Bad events often have multiple explanations, but pessimists usually focus on the most harmful and defeating. Instead of thinking, "I'm stupid and will always stink at math"—a very personal and permanent thought if there ever was one—think of explanations that pinpoint nonpersonal, specific, and changeable causes for the event. Your math score was bad, but did you study enough? Did you study effectively? Did other tests scheduled for the same day divide your attention?
- ***Avoiding the End-of-the-World Syndrome*** Finally, what if the negative thought is correct? If math is not your strength, realizing that this is not "the end of the world" can ease the pain brought by this belief. You have other gifts.

(2) ATTRIBUTIONS AND EXPLANATIONS Explore students' own attributions toward circumstances by having them write down three different explanations for getting the grade they made on their most recent test. (You may want to supply the grades to remind them.) Have them list the first explanation that comes to their minds first and then supply two other explanations in addition to the first. Then ask these questions:

- Was the first attribution optimistic or pessimistic? Why? In which explanatory style(s) do the second and third explanations fall?
- Which explanation(s) do you think will help you do better on the next test? Which seem harmful?

trb At this point, you may wish to use **Analysis Activity:** ***Measuring Optimism*** (*Teacher's Resource Binder,* p. 14-1; **Handouts 14–6** and **14–7**).

■ LOOKING AT THE ISSUES

Have students consider how they would respond or how they have responded in a situation like the one the author, Randy, describes with Chris and the Friday night call. Then elicit students' thoughts with the following questions:

- Do teens in your school typically make pessimistic or optimistic attributions? Why?
- How can one learn to be less pessimistic and more optimistic?

trb At this point, you may wish to use **Analysis Activity:** ***Measuring Optimism*** (*Teacher's Resource Binder,* p. 14-1; **Handouts 14–6** and **14–7**).

■ TEACHING TIP

Link *optimistic* and *pessimistic explanatory style* with *dispositional* and *situational attribution.*

- **Dispositional attribution** means that one explains another's behavior by attributing it to a personal quality or flaw. For example, if someone you don't know very well walks by you in the hall and you say "hello" but he or she doesn't respond, you may make a dispositional attribution by saying that he or she is "stuck up" or "rude." We tend to make dispositional attributions toward people we don't know. Options 1 and 4 in the Chris and the Friday night call story are dispositional.
- **Situational attribution** gives more credit and blame to situational factors than to personal ones. In the encounter in the hall, if the person you say hello to doesn't respond, you may make a situational attribution by saying that he or she was distracted by something or didn't see you. We tend to make these attributions about people we know well and ourselves. Options 2 and 3 in the Chris story are more situational.

trb At this point, you may wish to use **Critical Thinking Activity:** ***Unrealistic Optimism About Life Events*** (*Teacher's Resource Binder,* p. 14-1; **Handout 14–8**).

MODULE 14

tr ■ TEACHING TIP

A four-color transparency of Figure 14.4, How Deadly?, is available in the **Overhead Transparencies Set.**

■ LOOKING AT THE ISSUES

Recent laws have limited tobacco companies' ability to market their products to teens. Restrictions on advertising and sponsorship of events are aimed at curbing smoking among teens. Pose the following questions to students regarding this issue:

- How does advertising and sponsorship of events by tobacco companies make tobacco use more attractive to teens?
- Why aren't alcohol companies imposed with the same limits as tobacco companies on advertising and sponsorship?
- Encourage students to use the Internet to find statistics on adolescent tobacco use over the last five to ten years. What kinds of trends exist today in teen smoking and tobacco use?

trb At this point, you may wish to use **Evaluation Activity:** ***Why Smoke?*** (*Teacher's Resource Binder*, p. 14-1; **Handout 14–11**) and **Enrichment Lesson:** ***Preventing Smoking*** (*Teacher's Resource Binder*, p. 14-1).

Why is this optimism-pessimism thing important to wellness? In addition to spending less time in hospitals, healing faster, and living longer, optimists are far less likely to become depressed (Seligman, 1991, 1994). Fortunately, if you lean more to the pessimistic side and want to avoid some of the side effects of the negative explanatory style, there are steps you can take to think more positively about both good and bad events.

Overcoming Illness-Related Behaviors

Some behaviors increase our chances of becoming ill. Two of these behaviors are smoking and being significantly overweight.

Smoking

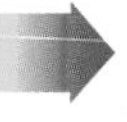

5. Why is smoking so dangerous, and why is it so hard to give up?

If a bus crashed, killing all 100 passengers aboard, this would be tragic. Imagine 100 of those buses crashing every day for 52 weeks and you have the same number of deaths caused by smoking each year in the U.S. alone! With this kind of death rate, you'd think the public outcry to ban the sale of cigarettes would echo around the globe. Sadly, the World Health Organization (1999) predicts 10 million people will be dying annually from smoking within the next few years, doubling our crashing buses example. Smoking is a killer (Figure 14.4).

If you start smoking in your teens and never quit, you have a 50 percent chance of dying a premature and agonizing death from your addic-

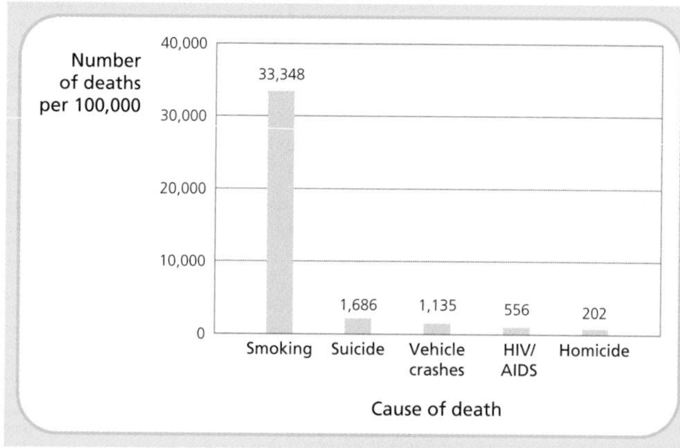

Figure 14.4 **How Deadly?** Smoking accounts for 10 times more deaths than the combined numbers for suicide, auto crashes, HIV/AIDS, and murders. (World Health Organization, 1999).

Enriching

Have volunteers conduct a survey about smoking with a representative sample of students in your school. (Be sure to submit the survey to an Institutional Review Board and obtain informed consent from each subject before conducting any research.)

- Do the students in the sample smoke? Why or why not?
- If they do, how many cigarettes do they smoke in a day? If they do, do they wish they didn't? Why or why not? If they don't, what has kept them from smoking?
- If a younger sibling were to consider smoking, would they encourage it? Why or why not?

trb At this point, you may wish to use **Evaluation Activity:** ***Why Smoke?*** (*Teacher's Resource Binder*, p. 14-1; **Handout 14–11**) and **Enrichment Lesson:** ***Preventing Smoking*** (*Teacher's Resource Binder*, p. 14-1).

tive habit. This is an especially dangerous time for you, because almost all smokers start as adolescents. If your parents, siblings, and friends smoke, the chances are much higher that you'll light up as well. Students who drop out, get poor grades, or feel less control over their futures are also at a high risk (Chassin & others, 1987; Schulenberg & others, 1994). But for those of you who haven't started smoking by the time you graduate from high school, the odds are tremendously low that you'll ever start this habit. And if your best friends and parents are nonsmokers, those odds drop to almost zero (Moss & others, 1992).

We know smoking is bad for our lungs and heart. But smokers also suffer other health risks. Smokers

- have high rates of depression and divorce (Doherty & Doherty, 1998; Vita & others, 1998).
- lose 12 minutes off their life for every cigarette (*Discover*, 1996).
- are three times more likely than nonsmokers to drink alcohol.
- are 17 times more likely than nonsmokers to smoke marijuana (National Center for Health Statistics, 1992).

So why don't teenage smokers throw out their cigarettes when they learn these facts? In part because **nicotine** is even more addictive than cocaine or heroin: One in three who try cigarettes gets hooked (Heishman & others, 1997). The **withdrawal** symptoms that accompany attempts to quit are horrible: Insomnia, anxiety, craving, and irritability are a few of the symptoms, all of which can be relieved by just a few puffs on a grit.

In contrast, the addictive qualities of nicotine are numerous and rewarding. Nicotine suppresses appetite, reduces sensitivity to pain, calms anxiety, and boosts awareness. These effects surely compound the difficulty smokers face when attempting to kick the habit, even when they know death looms as a long-term smoking result.

Almost half of all smokers try to quit each year. For those who try to quit, the success rate is about 14 percent. If you have friends or relatives who would like to quit, you might want to pass along these 10 guidelines, published by the U.S. Agency for Health Care Policy and Research, as a way to improve their odds (Wetter & others, 1998).

1. Set a quit date.
2. Inform family and friends.
3. Get rid of all cigarettes.
4. Review things you learned from previous attempts to quit and anticipate challenges.
5. Use a nicotine patch or gum.

▶ **nicotine** Behavioral stimulant found in tobacco.

▶ **withdrawal** The discomfort and distress that follows discontinuing the use of an addictive drug.

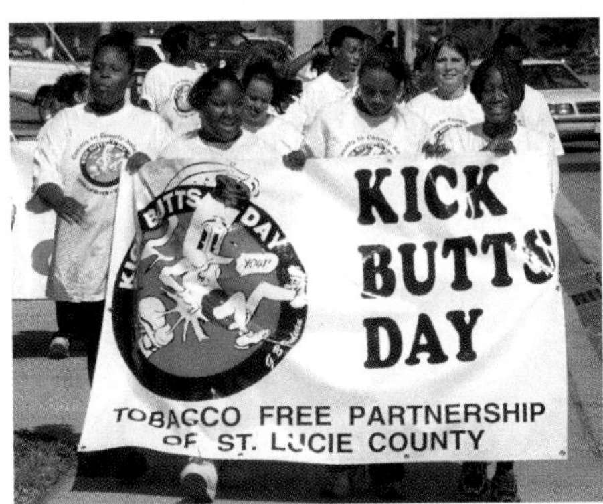

Kick Butts! Some communities plan special days to encourage smokers to kick the habit.

F • Y • I

Nicotine, the addictive substance in tobacco products, is not as physiologically harmful as the other additives and byproducts of smoking and chewing tobacco. **Nicotine** is a stimulant, increasing heart rate and respiration. The additives and byproducts in tobacco are the actual cancer-causing agents. Nicotine's only function is to keep people smoking and chewing tobacco.

■ **JOURNAL WRITING**

Invite students to use the following questions and writing prompts as springboards for entries in their psychology journals:

- Do you or people you know smoke? Why might you or they smoke? Have you or they considered quitting or tried to quit? What methods have you or they used to try to quit? Which methods were successful?
- If you are a nonsmoker, how do you feel around those who smoke? What do you do when you are around smokers?

Cross-Curricular Connections

BIOLOGY With a biology teacher, team-teach a lesson about the physical and psychological impact of smoking and addiction to nicotine. If you both feel comfortable, you can extend the lesson to include other substances that are smoked or inhaled (marijuana, crack cocaine, inhalants, and so on).

trb At this point, you may wish to use **Evaluation Activity:** *Why Smoke?* (*Teacher's Resource Binder,* p. 14-1; **Handout 14–11**) and **Enrichment Lesson:** *Preventing Smoking* (*Teacher's Resource Binder,* p. 14-1).

TEACHING TIP

A four-color transparency of Figure 14.5, Discrimination, is available in the **Overhead Transparencies Set.**

JOURNAL WRITING

Invite students to use the following questions and writing prompts as springboards for entries in their psychology journals:

- How do you feel when you see people who are overweight in public? How do you explain why they are overweight? Do your explanations imply a prejudice against the obese? Explain.
- Have you ever struggled with your weight, trying to either gain or lose pounds? Describe your experiences. How did you feel about your efforts?

▶ **body mass index (BMI)** Your weight in kilograms (pounds multiplied by .45) divided by your squared height in meters (inches divided by 39.4). U.S. government guidelines encourage a body mass index (BMI) under 25. The World Health Organization and many countries define obesity as a BMI of 30 or over.

6. Be totally abstinent—not one puff.
7. Avoid alcohol (which leads to relapse).
8. If other smokers live or work with you, quit together.
9. Avoid places where others are likely to smoke.
10. Exercise; research shows higher success rates in quitters assigned to regular exercise (Bock & others, 1999).

Smoking is an illness-related behavior you can control from the outset: Never try smoking, and you'll never be a smoker. We have less control over our weight, the next topic.

Obesity

6. What is obesity, and what physical and emotional health risks accompany this condition?

Obesity's health risks are not as clear-cut as those connected to smoking. Still, people who are obese, with **body mass indexes** of 30 or more, face an increased risk of diabetes, high blood pressure, heart disease, gallstones, arthritis, sleep disorders, and certain types of cancer, according to the National Institutes of Health (1998). In addition to the physical health risks, there are significant mental health risks as well. Obesity affects how we think about ourselves and how others think about us and treat us. Seriously overweight people are often stereotyped as sloppy, slow, and lazy (Crandall, 1994; Ryckman & others, 1989). Researchers observed this type of discrimination in a study in which professional actors pretended to interview for a job (Pingitore & others, 1994). The researchers videotaped the actors in two different situations, giving exactly the same answers to the same questions and using the same voice intonation and gestures (Figure 14.5).

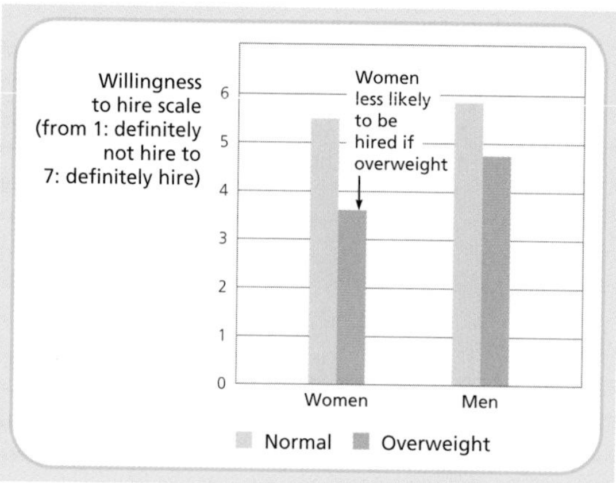

Figure 14.5 **Discrimination** Overweight individuals, especially women, are less likely to be hired than are normal weight individuals. (Data from Pingitore & others, 1994.)

Enriching

(1) Have students record what they eat (if you eat it, write it!) for three days. Elicit students' responses to this experience by asking the following questions about their eating journals:

- How would you characterize your eating habits: healthy or unhealthy? If you answer "healthy," exchange your eating journals with a few other students in class. Do these people agree that your eating habits are healthy? Why or why not?
- What unhealthy foods could you cut out of your life? Would this be easy? Why or why not?
- What healthy foods should you add to your diet? Would this be easy? Why or why not?
- Why do you eat what you eat—convenience or conscious choice?

trb At this point, you may wish to use **Evaluation Activity:** ***The Dieting Beliefs Scale*** (*Teacher's Resource Binder,* p. 14-1; **Handout 14–14**).

The only difference between the two videotapes was the apparent weight of the job applicant. In one tape, the actors were their normal, average-weight selves. In the other, make-up and padding were added to make the actors look 30 pounds heavier. The researchers then assigned participants to view one of the two tapes and rate their willingness to hire the person. Those evaluating the "obese" applicant routinely rated the heavy person as *less worthy* of hiring. Discrimination against obese people rivals race and gender discrimination, and it occurs at every employment step from hiring and compensation to promotion and dismissal (Roehling, 2000). This discrimination is unfair, given the physiology of fat.

Weight Control

7. Why is it so hard to lose weight?

Have you ever wondered, "How does so-and-so eat that much but never gain any weight?" Do you have friends or relatives who always seem to be on some sort of diet but never make much progress in their attempts to lose weight? Are the people who order the "plus-size" clothes merely gluttons who can't control the urge to eat? The mystery that is weight control is worth unraveling.

The thin look has not always been "in," as it is today. Look at the paintings reflecting European high society centuries ago, and you'll see that being round, even rotund, was viewed as desirable. Obesity is still valued in countries where huge supermarkets are not found. In areas where famine strikes regularly, obesity signifies wealth and social status (Furnham & Baguma, 1994).

Our ability to store energy in fat cells reflects the feast-or-famine lifestyle our ancestors faced thousands of years ago. Fat is the perfect fuel reserve. We draw from it when food is scarce. But now that most Americans live in a world where sweets and fatty foods are abundant, our genetic program for storing energy in fat cells is about as outdated as 1980s software. With today's increased food availability, an increasing number of folks are carrying more weight than they should.

Desired Look Compared with similar ads from 50 years ago, today's advertisements promote unrealistic body images.

Physiology of Obesity

So how can we lose our excess pounds? The energy equivalent of a pound of fat is 3500 calories. So can't we assume that cutting 3500 calories from our food intake would drop our weight by one pound? Not so.

■ **MULTICULTURAL CONNECTIONS**

Using available resources, have students explore how people in other cultures feel about food. To discuss students' findings, pose the following questions:

- How do people in other cultures feel about diet and exercise?
- Is food viewed as a valuable resource or a disposable luxury? Why?
- Is obesity a problem for people in other cultures, as it is in the United States? Why or why not?

trb At this point, you may wish to use Enrichment Lesson: *Obesity* (*Teacher's Resource Binder,* p. 14-1).

■ **APPLYING THE POINTS**

Contact your school's cafeteria manager to see what the policies are about what foods are served in the school's lunchroom. Use the following questions to gather information and present your findings in a class lecture:

- How do you decide what to serve each day?
- What types of snack foods are available for students in the lunchroom? Are they "healthy"?
- Are fresh fruits and vegetables available daily?
- What types of food seem to be most popular with students? Are these choices considered healthy?

trb At this point, you may wish to use Enrichment Lesson: *Reading Food Labels* (*Teacher's Resource Binder,* p. 14-1).

(2) Divide the class into groups and have each group take a representative sample of students in your school and calculate their body mass index. After a group calculates the body mass index, have them pose the following questions to the students in their sample. (Make sure groups obtain permission from an Institutional Review Board and informed consent from subjects before conducting any research.)

- What does the average body mass index indicate about the health of the school's students?
- How do you think students feel about the weight in this average? Would they want to lose weight? Do their BMIs support their body images? Why or why not?

trb At this point, you may wish to use Critical Thinking Activity: *A Nutrition Quiz* (*Teacher's Resource Binder,* p. 14-1; Handout 14–13).

MODULE 14

■ **APPLYING THE POINTS**

Through telephone interviews, on-line research, or brochures, have students learn about different local commercial weight-loss programs (Jenny Craig, Weight Watchers, and so forth). Have them present the key components of each, highlighting research-based psychological principles used by these programs.

trb At this point, you may wish to use Enrichment Lesson: *Maintaining Weight Loss* (*Teacher's Resource Binder*, p. 14-1).

■ **TEACHING TIP**

You may have several students who struggle with tobacco use and weight-related issues. Try to alleviate any discomfort they may have about the information in this module by emphasizing the powerful hold addictions like smoking and overeating have on people. Battling nicotine addiction and losing weight take great physical and psychological effort over a long period of time, so help your students be sensitive to the struggles that their peers might experience.

Human Fat Cells Fat cells like these divide after reaching a certain size. Dieting reduces the size of each fat cell, but dieting cannot reduce the overall *number* of fat cells.

To understand why weight loss is not that simple, you have to know a bit more about fat cells, set point, and metabolism.

The average adult has about 30 billion *fat cells*. As we take in more calories than we need, these cells enlarge. Once fat cells reach a certain size, they divide and create more cells. Does dieting reduce the number of fat cells? No. Dieting only reduces the *size* of these cells, all of which remain ready to grow again once we resume a higher-calorie regime (Sjostrom, 1980).

A second reason that reducing your diet by 3500 calories does not automatically cause you to drop a pound relates to your **set point**—a "weight thermostat" set to keep your body weight within a certain range. If your weight drops below your set-point range, your body thinks "Famine!" and attempts to conserve energy by increasing your hunger and slowing down your metabolism—the rate at which you burn calories. To make things worse, when your diet ends and you start eating normally, your body remains in this energy-conservation mode. The amount of food that formerly *maintained* your normal weight may now *increase* your weight.

Metabolic rates vary from person to person. You and a friend who is your height and weight may eat the same amount of food, but one of you may put on pounds while the other does not, even though you both maintain the same activity level. If your resting metabolism is slower than your friend's, you'll be the one who burns fewer calories, making you prone to weight gain.

The roots of your metabolic rate are genetic. Genes may also determine how quickly your brain receives a "full" signal once you start eating, and the efficiency with which you convert extra calories to fat. Will there someday be a pill that blocks the chemical "time-to-eat" messages in your nervous system? For some overweight people, such a pill may be the only way to overcome the physiology of obesity.

Bottom Liners

"It works as well as most other diet plans. . . . I've lost over $200 in less than three weeks."

Losing Weight

Your physiological deck may be stacked against weight loss. Still, if you (or a friend) are looking to shed a few pounds, here are some hints that may prove helpful.

- ***Reduce exposure to tempting food cues.*** Keep the chips and ice cream out of the house, and don't go near sweet shops. Never, never go to the supermarket when you're hungry.
- ***Boost your metabolism.*** Exercise speeds up your metabolism and lowers your set point. Walking, jogging, and swimming empty fats cells, build muscle, and make you feel better.

- *Be patient, realistic, and moderate.* Extreme thinness is more risky than moderate heaviness (Ernsberger & Koletzky, 1999). The National Institutes of Health say that a reasonable amount of time to lose 10 percent of your body weight is six months.
- *Permanently change the food you eat.* You can modify both your hunger and your metabolism by eating foods with more fiber and color (the natural kind!) and less fat, salt, and sugar, and by eating more fruits and vegetables. The sugar in fruits stimulates less hunger-producing insulin than the refined sugar in soft drinks, candy, and Lucky Charms.
- *Control your portions.* Eat slowly to give your body a chance to send "I'm full" signals to your brain. Don't stuff yourself, and don't feel obliged to finish the oversized portions you'll receive in many restaurants.
- *Don't skip breakfast and lunch in order to eat a big dinner.* This eating pattern slows metabolism and is common among overweight people.
- *Set attainable goals.* You guarantee defeat if you set your target weight unrealistically low. Realistic goals, like exercising three times per week, can build a sense of persistence.

YES, THE KIDS WATCH THE TELETUBBIES ON T.V., I WATCH THE ONE IN FRONT OF THE T.V.

Couch Potato? Watching television will not boost your metabolism.

▶ **set point** The point at which an individual's "weight thermostat" is supposedly set. When the body falls below this weight, an increase in hunger and a lowered metabolic rate may act to restore the lost weight.

REVIEW

Module 14: Promoting Wellness

What's the Point?

Healthy Lifestyles

1. *How does exercise contribute to wellness?*

   The physical and psychological benefits of exercise contribute to wellness, which is the result of a healthy lifestyle and healthy attitudes. Exercise reduces anxiety, depression, and the risk of heart attack. It accomplishes these things in part by increasing mood-boosting chemicals, enhancing cognitive abilities, lowering blood pressure, and enabling better sleep. Physical fitness also increases our self-confidence and self-discipline.

2. *Does social support make a difference in our health and well-being?*

   The social support we receive from family and friends seems to have a significant effect on our health and well-being. Some studies indicate that people with social support

Close

Have students imagine what our culture would be like if psychological immunizations were given as much attention as physical ones. Pose the following questions:

- How might our culture be different if this were true?
- What would our cultural leaders have to do to make psychological immunizations more important to the public?

Checking the Points

■ **TEACHING TIPS**

web (1) The book companion site for *Thinking About Psychology* at **www.worthpublishers.com/thinkingaboutpsych** contains a module quiz, flashcards of key terms and people, and other student activities and resources for this module. You will also find PowerPoint lectures, a quiz grade book, and other reaching resources by logging on as an instructor.

trb (2) As a review of concepts about promoting wellness, read aloud the items from **Critical Thinking Activity:** *Fact or Falsehood?* (*Teacher's Resource Binder*, p. 14-1, **Handout 14–1**) and have students determine whether each of the items is true or false. When the answer to an item is unclear, encourage students to find a passage in the module that supports their response. When the class comes to consensus, move on to the next item.

tend to live longer than those who have no social ties. In addition to making us feel liked and happy, social support seems to act as a buffer against the physical effects of stress, possibly by strengthening our immune systems. People who receive little social support from their families often find a similar sense of belonging in support groups, which are available through many local schools and religious organizations.

3. *What is the "faith factor," and how does it relate to wellness?*

   The "faith factor" is an indication that religion and spirituality seem to contribute to a longer life span. Although research producing these results shows a correlation between frequent participation in religious services and longer life expectancy, the research does not show whether this is a cause-and-effect relationship. Three components of religious participation do tend to contribute to better health: (1) the promotion of healthier lifestyles, (2) the social support offered by faith communities, and (3) the optimism associated with a religious worldview.

Positive Experiences and Well-Being

4. *How do flow, happiness, and optimism contribute to our well-being?*

   Well-being includes life satisfaction, feelings of fulfillment, pleasant emotions, and a low level of unpleasant emotions. Flow, happiness, and optimism are all positive experiences that contribute to our sense of well-being. Flow is a subjective, optimal experience. To produce flow, an activity must meet three criteria: it must set a challenge that requires skill, have clear goals, and offer feedback. Happiness contributes to well-being in that happy people tend to be outgoing, to have rich sources of social support, to feel a sense of control over their personal lives, and to exhibit hope when meeting challenges. When we are happy, we tend to help others. Optimism contributes to our well-being by fostering explanations that bad events are temporary, are not our fault, and are confined to a limited set of circumstances. Compared with pessimists, optimists are less likely to become depressed or to be hospitalized for other reasons, and they are more likely to heal faster and live longer. We can overcome pessimism by using two techniques: distraction and disputation.

Overcoming Illness-Related Behaviors

5. *Why is smoking so dangerous, and why is it so hard to give up?*

   People who begin smoking tobacco in their teens have a 50 percent chance of dying a smoking-related death. Nicotine, found in tobacco, is more addictive than cocaine or heroin. One-third of all smokers will try to quit, but only 14 percent of them will actually accomplish their goal. The most effective way to avoid the health-destroying effects of cigarette smoking is not to begin smoking. People who have not started smoking by the time they graduate from high school will probably never acquire this habit.

6. *What is obesity, and what physical and emotional health risks accompany this condition?*

   The World Health Organization and many countries define *obesity* as a body mass index of 30 or more. (Body mass index, or BMI, is your weight in kilograms [pounds multiplied by .45] divided by your squared height in meters [inches divided by 39.4]). Obese people are at high risk for various types of physical diseases, but they also are at risk for mental health problems. Stereotypes of seriously overweight people as sloppy, slow, and lazy produce discrimination in the workplace and in social life.

274

7. *Why is it so hard to lose weight?*

Today's "ideal" body image—an extremely thin person—is not the most desirable goal in other cultures, and has not always been desirable even in our own culture at other times. Many people find it very difficult to lose weight, for several good reasons. First, part of our genetic program regulates energy storage in fat cells as a protection against famine. And as we take in more calories than we use, our fat cells multiply, never again to return to their original number. As food becomes unavailable—whether through famine or through dieting—our body limits access to this potentially life-saving resource by slowing our metabolism. This tendency, helpful as it may have been for our early ancestors, makes it very difficult to shed extra pounds in our modern-day society where food is all too available. A second line of defense against weight loss is our set point—an internal regulatory system that attempts to maintain our weight at a certain level, by increasing or (as in this case) slowing our metabolic rate. The third component that makes weight loss more difficult for some than for others is that our metabolic rates are genetically inherited, and they differ from one person to another. For all these reasons, simply eliminating 3500 calories—the energy equivalent of a pound—will not cause us to lose a pound of our stored fat. The most effective weight-loss plans are those that set realistic and moderate goals; increase exercise to boost metabolism; and make permanent changes in the types, portions, timing, and quantities of food we consume.

Key Terms

wellness, p. 258
positive psychology, p. 263
flow, p. 264
explanatory style, p. 266
nicotine, p. 269
withdrawal, p. 269
body mass index, p. 270
set point, p. 272

Key People

Martin Seligman, p. 258

Self-Test

Multiple-Choice Questions

Choose the *best* answer for each question.

1. Shannon has been feeling depressed lately. Shannon should know that
   a. exercise would increase the output of mood-boosting chemicals produced by her nervous system.
   b. even a 10-minute walk could increase her energy levels and lower any tension she might be feeling.
   c. exercise helps her sleep better, and that could provide an emotional boost.
   d. All of the above statements are true.

2. Sergei recently moved to Pittsburgh, Pennsylvania, from Moscow, Russia. He has no family in the United States, and he has made very few friends, so he has very little social support. Sergei would be well advised to
   a. join a support group, which will give him a sense of belonging and connectedness.
   b. continue to distance himself from family and friends until he gets used to being alone.

MODULE 14

trb ■ TEACHING TIPS

To review vocabulary, distribute to students copies of the handout in **Building Vocabulary:** *Exploring Root Words* (*Teacher's Resource Binder*, p. 14-1; **Handout 14–2**). Have students complete the handouts on their own, without referring to the text or an earlier version of the handout they may have completed. Then, in small groups, students may check and confirm their responses, using the text as a reference whenever necessary.

tb Using the Test Bank

The *Test Bank* that accompanies this textbook offers a wide variety of questions in different formats and levels of complexity. Use the software to construct whole tests or to integrate standardized questions into teacher-made tests.

Self-Test Answers

Multiple-Choice Questions

1. d, 2. a

Alternative Assessment/Portfolio Project

trb PROMOTING HEALTH ON THE WEB Alternative assessment tools are designed to enable students to demonstrate understanding of concepts outside traditional pen-and-paper assessments. Students can research several Web sites to gain information about how to promote wellness. (See *Teacher's Resource Binder*, p. 14-1 for more details about this project.)

Use the general rubric provided by **Handout 14–15** (*Teacher's Resource Binder*, p. 14-1) to evaluate the completed portfolios. Adapt the rubric to suit your needs.

MODULE 14

Self-Test Answers

Multiple-Choice Questions (continued)

3. c, 4. d, 5. a, 6. d

Matching Terms and Definitions

7. a. (5), b. (12), c. (1), d. (3), e. (9)

c. avoid joining clubs and faith communities, where his feelings of loneliness may be magnified.
d. learn that being alone is part of being an American.

3. Kozumi loves baseball, and each day he practices after school to become a better hitter. He often loses track of the time, is unlikely to hear people calling to him, and he doesn't seem to care what others think about his compelling interest in baseball. During batting practice, he has set himself a challenging goal—hitting 9 balls out of 10 into the outfield—and he loves the feedback of hearing the bat smack against the ball. Kozumi is
   a. avoiding the "end-of-the-world" syndrome.
   b. reaching his set point.
   c. having a flow experience.
   d. experiencing a distraction.

4. Meredith wanted very badly to play the lead in the drama club's fall musical, but Sophie got that part. Meredith's first reaction was to think that she never gets what she wants. After a moment, though, Meredith remembered some advice her aunt had given her about fighting off pessimistic thoughts. She thought carefully and retrieved a memory of being elected president of the drama club, something she also badly wanted. Meredith is practicing the technique of ________________ to fight pessimism.
   a. distancing
   b. considering alternative explanations
   c. avoiding the "end-of-the-world" syndrome
   d. checking for evidence

5. Ricardo is in his first year at college, and he's gained the "freshman 15"—15 extra pounds that many young people gain in their first year of dormitory living. Ricardo wants to lose this weight over the next 15 weeks. His best bet is to
   a. increase his level of activity. This additional exercise will increase his metabolism and lower his set point.
   b. cut his intake of calories by 3500 each week. This reduction will burn off one pound of fat for each of the next 15 weeks and return his weight to normal.
   c. eliminate all fat from his diet. This drastic change will cause his fat cells, which have surely increased in number, to return to their original number.
   d. skip breakfast and lunch, and eat only one big meal at dinnertime each day. This change in the timing of his eating will adjust his set point and peel off the pounds.

6. Krissy has a BMI of 35. Krissy is
   a. abnormally thin.
   b. about average.
   c. slightly overweight.
   d. obese.

Matching Terms and Definitions

7. For each definition, choose the *best* matching term from the list that follows.

   Definition

   a. State of optimal experience.
   b. Point at which an individual's "weight thermostat" is supposedly set.
   c. Common result of a healthy lifestyle and healthy attitudes.
   d. Research finding that demonstrates that two or more factors occur together; does NOT demonstrate cause and effect.
   e. Tendency to expect the worst.

f. Weight (in kilograms) divided by squared height (in meters).
g. Technique for fighting pessimism by arguing with oneself.
h. Habits for thinking about the good or bad causes of events.
i. Studies optimal human functioning and factors that allow individuals and communities to thrive.

Term

(1) wellness
(2) aerobic exercise
(3) correlation
(4) positive psychology
(5) well-being
(6) flow
(7) explanatory style
(8) optimism
(9) pessimism
(10) disputation
(11) BMI
(12) set point

Fill-in-the-Blank Questions

8. Martin Seligman and other psychologists who do research in ________________ psychology are interested in the factors that allow individuals and communities to ________________.

9. Aerobic exercise increases lung and heart fitness, and it also reduces ____________ and ________________.

Brief Essay Question

10. Bart is 12, and he wants to look cool. He has decided that smoking will help him achieve this image, and he's pinched a pack of his dad's cigarettes. Each day, on the way home from school, Bart smokes one or two cigarettes, and he's now very happy that he can inhale without choking. In two paragraphs of about three or four sentences each, explain to Bart the risks he's taking.

Self-Test Answers

Matching Terms and Definitions (continued)

f. (11), g. (10), h. (7), i. (4)

Fill-in-the-Blank Questions

8. positive; thrive, 9. anxiety; depression

Brief Essay Question

10. Students should express an understanding of the risks of smoking. People who start smoking in their teens and don't ever stop have a 50 percent chance of dying prematurely from a smoking-related disease. Nicotine is highly addictive, more so than cocaine or heroine, and about one-third of those who try cigarettes become addicted. Short-term rewards—suppressed appetite, reduced sensitivity to pain, a calming effect, and heightened awareness—overcome the nicotine addict's fear of the long-term risk of death. Half of all smokers try to quit each year, but fewer than 15 percent succeed.

Cognitive Domain

Teaching with the Standards

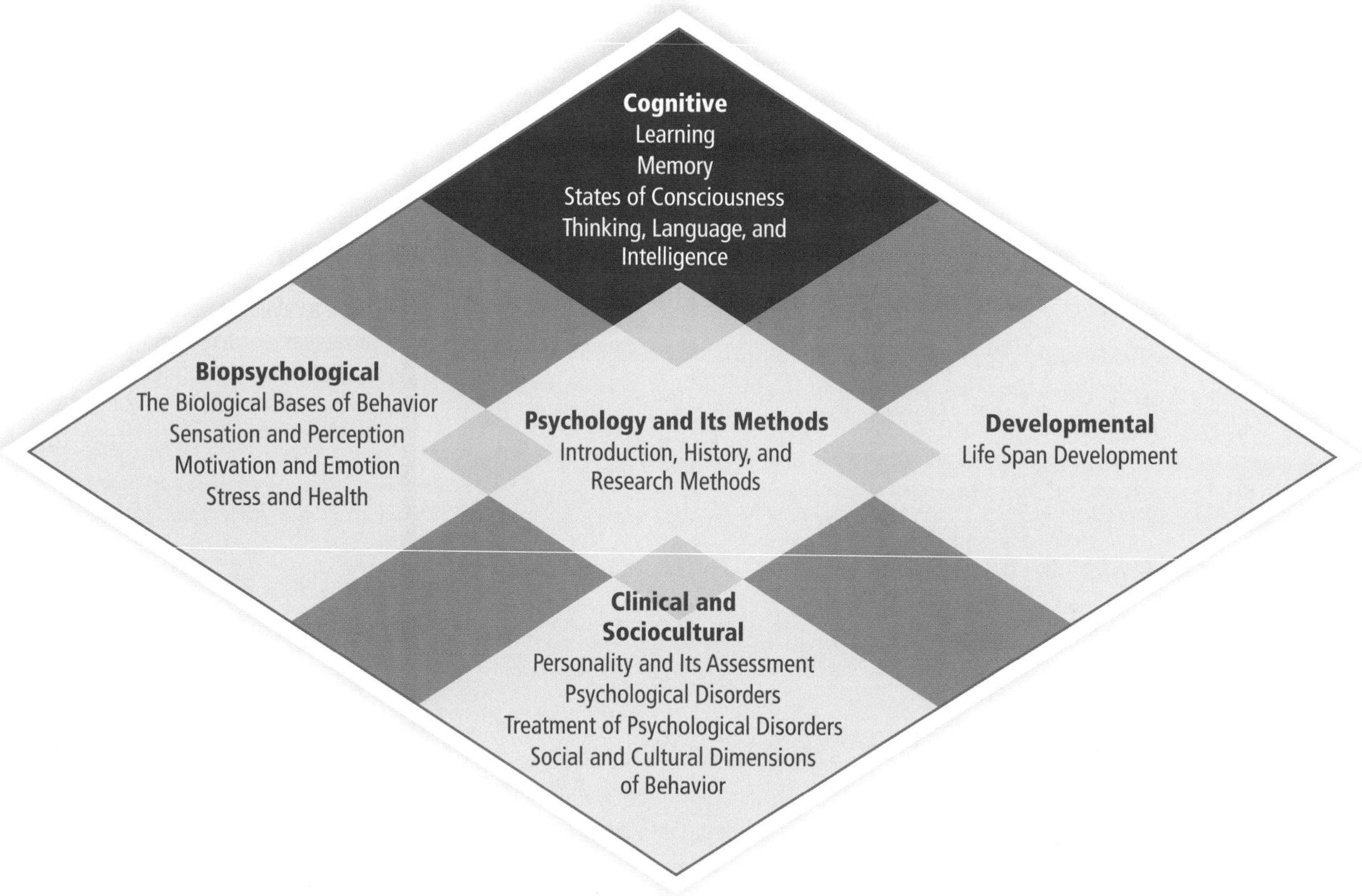

Cognitive
Learning
Memory
States of Consciousness
Thinking, Language, and Intelligence

Biopsychological
The Biological Bases of Behavior
Sensation and Perception
Motivation and Emotion
Stress and Health

Psychology and Its Methods
Introduction, History, and Research Methods

Developmental
Life Span Development

Clinical and Sociocultural
Personality and Its Assessment
Psychological Disorders
Treatment of Psychological Disorders
Social and Cultural Dimensions of Behavior

Scope and Sequence

Background/Significance of the Cognitive Domain

One of the authors, at the beginning of Module 23, asks the question, "What is it that makes us human?" This is a question that has caused both psychologists and philosophers a great deal of thought. The author argues that it is our cognitive abilities to think, know, and remember, that separate us from other species. So much of our daily lives are spent in thinking, learning, and remembering that, to understand ourselves, we must understand our cognitive processes.

The National Standards for the Teaching of High School Psychology also emphasize the importance of understanding cognitive processes. The Memory unit is the one they suggest teachers explore when the time to teach cognition is limited. As the author of our text agrees, "Information processing enables memory, a cognitive skill so important that it's virtually impossible to imagine life without it." Module 18, Information Processing, and Module 19, Forgetting and Memory Construction, help students explore how we remember and how we can improve our memory.

The National Standards also suggest that if instructors can devote more time to teaching cognition they should explore the other units in the domain. Any of the following sections can be taught to help students understand the important role of cognition in their lives. Module 15, Classical Conditioning, Module 16, Operant Conditioning, and Module 17, Observational Learning, address how our behavior changes in response to environmental forces. Module 20, Sleep, Dreams, and Body Rhythms, Module 21, Hypnosis, and Module 22, Drugs, explore our states of awareness, sleep, and other altered states of consciousness. Module 23, Thinking and Language, explores the nature of cognition, the role of language and decision-making in our lives. Module 24, Intelligence and Intelligence Testing, examines our definitions of intelligence and how we assess this psychological construct.

Understanding these cognitive processes is an important part of understanding and defining ourselves.

Cognitive Domain

Introducing the Domain

The Points: Domain Objectives

- Define classical conditioning.
- Describe how John Watson and Rosalie Rayner demonstrated that emotions can be classically conditioned.
- Understand the importance of the roles of cognition and biological predispositions in learning.
- Describe how positive and negative reinforcement work, and how they differ from each other.
- Analyze how punishment influences behavior and why it tends to be ineffective.
- Explain how you can use operant conditioning to teach a new behavior.
- Describe how Bandura's research demonstrated the principles of observational learning.
- Compare how humans and computers utilize the information processing model.
- Identify and describe the two types of sensory storage.
- Describe the techniques to increase the limited capacity and duration of short-term memory.
- Identify the capacity and duration of long-term memory.
- Evaluate the importance of context in memory.
- Define consciousness.
- Identify the different rhythms of the body and how they differ from one another.
- Understand why sleep is so important to daily life.
- Differentiate why subjects carry out hypnotic suggestions according to both the social influence theory and the divided consciousness theory of hypnosis.
- Describe a psychoactive drug.
- Evaluate what avenues help prevent the use of dangerous psychoactive drugs.

Cooperative Learning

Divide students into small groups and have them discuss the following questions, bringing their group answers to the whole class after the discussion:

- What does it mean to think? How do you do it?
- What is an emotion? How many different emotions can you name?
- What does it mean to learn something? How do you know you've learned?
- What are some reasons why people don't remember things? What are some ways you can improve your memory?

Cognitive Domain

- Define a concept, explaining why it is useful.
- Analyze how people learn language.
- Compare and contrast Gardner's and Sternberg's theories of intelligence.
- Evaluate Alfred Binet's, Lewis Terman's, and David Weschler's contributions to intelligence testing.

A tremendous amount of psychology takes place "between your ears." The previous domain focused on the biology that enables these psychological processes. Now we'll move on to the processes themselves. Even within this domain, our topics are amazingly diverse: learning, memory, states of consciousness, thinking, language, and intelligence.

Fundamental issues are at stake in all these areas. How does a child learn appropriate behaviors? How does an airline pilot remember the proper sequence of steps for taking off and landing safely? Why do we sleep, and what accounts for the sometimes bizarre content of our dreams? What makes it possible for us to solve problems ranging from space travel to unplugging the drain on the kitchen sink? How can children so easily learn language, especially considering how challenging it is to master a foreign language later in life? Are there different kinds of "smart," or does one kind of intelligence underlie all of our mental abilities? These are but a few of the issues we will consider in the next chapters. There is plenty to think about!

CHAPTER 7

Learning

Cognitive Domain

Teaching with the Standards

Standard Area: Learning

Breakdown of Module 15: Classical Conditioning

Content Standard 1: Understanding learning Module 15 introduces students to many historical figures in the study of classical conditioning. The work of Ivan Pavlov, John Watson, Rosalie Raynor, Robert Rescorla, and John Garcia are presented along with the impact of their research on our understanding of learning. (Student Text pp. 286–294)

Content Standard 2: Classical conditioning processes Classical conditioning is explained using Pavlov's work with salivating dogs and other examples provided by the author. Acquisition of a new response is explained, as well as discrimination, generalization, extinction, and possible spontaneous recovery of the same behavior. John B. Watson's research on Little Albert is explored along with the ethical questions that resulted. The role of our biological predispositions and cognition on learning is presented. (Student Text pp. 281–294)

Content Standard 4: The role of cognition in learning Robert Rescorla and Allan Wagner's revolutionary research on learning is emphasized. The important role that cognition plays in classical conditioning is explained. (Student Text pp. 293–294)

Content Standard 5: The influence of biology and culture on learning Module 15 presents John Garcia's taste-aversion studies and discusses how learning is constrained by the biological predispositions of a particular species. (Student Text p. 293)

Breakdown of Module 16: Operant Conditioning

Content Standard 1: Understanding learning Module 16 introduces students to many historical figures in the study of operant conditioning. The work of Edward Thorndike and B. F. Skinner are presented along with the impact of their research on our understanding of learning. (Student Text pp. 300–302, 304–305)

Content Standard 3: Understanding operant conditioning Operant conditioning is explained using Edward Thorndike's research on the law of effect. Emphasis is placed on the work of B. F. Skinner. Concepts such as reinforcement, punishment, shaping, discrimination, and extinction are explained. The schedules of reinforcement are also presented along with real-world examples of each. In addition, the role of cognition and biology on operant conditioning is explored. (Student Text pp. 300–318)

Content Standard 4: The role of cognition in learning The role of latent learning and the overjustification effect both illustrate the influence of cognition in operant conditioning. Tolman's research on cognitive maps is discussed. (Student Text pp. 316–317)

Content Standard 5: Investigate how biology and culture influence learning Biology clearly influences how animals learn. Module 16 presents evidence of how species are biologically predisposed to learn some behaviors easily and others only with great difficulty. (Student Text pp. 317–318)

Breakdown of Module 17: Observational Learning

Content Standard 1: Understanding learning Module 17 introduces students to Albert Bandura and his pioneering work on observational learning. (Student Text pp. 325–326)

Content Standard 4: The role of cognition in learning The principles of operant conditioning are emphasized in Module 17. Albert Bandura's research involving an inflatable Bobo doll is presented. The conditions that promote observational learning are discussed. Examples of observational learning in everyday life are presented. The role of the media in violence among teenagers is investigated. (Student Text pp. 325–330)

Scope and Sequence

	Objectives	Text Reference	Standards Covered
Lesson 1	Introduce the concept of learning. Discuss the principles of classical conditioning, illustrating the work of Ivan Pavlov.	Module 15, pp. 281–288	Standard Area: Learning, Content Standard 1, Performance Standard 1.1, Content Standard 2, Performance Standard 2.1
Lesson 2	Introduce generalization, discrimination, and spontaneous recovery. Present John B. Watson's research on Little Albert and its ethical implications. Discuss the role of cognition and biology on classical conditioning.	Module 15, pp. 288–294	Content Standard 1, Performance Standard 1.1, Content Standard 2, Performance Standard 2.1, Content Standard 4, Performance Standard 4.2, Content Standard 5, Performance Standard 5.1
Lesson 3	Compare classical to operant conditioning. Discuss the principles of operant conditioning. Discuss possible problems with the use of punishment to change behavior.	Module 16, pp. 300–310	Content Standard 1, Performance Standard 1.1, Content Standard 3, Performance Standard 3.1
Lesson 4	Introduce the work of B. F. Skinner. Discuss the different partial reinforcement schedules.	Module 16, pp. 310–315	Content Standard 1, Performance Standard 1.1, Content Standard 3, Performance Standard 3.1
Lesson 5	Discuss the role of cognition and biology on operant conditioning. Present application of operant conditioning principles to everyday life.	Module 16, pp. 316–318	Content Standard 3, Performance Standard 3.1, Content Standard 4, Performance Standard 4.2, Content Standard 5, Performance Standard 5.1
Lesson 6	Explore Albert Bandura's research on observation learning. Investigate the relationship between media violence and violence in real life.	Module 17, pp. 325–330	Content Standard 1, Performance Standard 1.1, Content Standard 4, Performance Standard 4.1
Lesson 7	Review and test		

CHAPTER 7

Learning

Introducing the Chapter

The Points: Chapter Objectives

- Define classical conditioning.
- Identify the three basic processes in classical conditioning.
- Describe the role Pavlov played in the study of classical conditioning.
- Describe how John Watson and Rosalie Rayner demonstrated that emotions can be classically conditioned.
- Understand the importance of the role of cognition and biological predispositions in learning.
- Explain the law of effect, and how it can be used to modify behavior.
- Describe how positive and negative reinforcement work, and how they differ from one another.
- Analyze how punishment influences behavior and why it tends to be ineffective.
- Explain how you can use operant conditioning to teach a new behavior.
- Describe the advantages and disadvantages of continuous reinforcement of responses.
- Identify the four partial reinforcement schedules and how they differ.
- Evaluate how latent learning and the overjustification effect demonstrate that mental processes affect operant conditioning.
- Describe how Bandura's research demonstrated the principles of observational learning.
- Analyze how antisocial and prosocial behavior develop as a result of observational learning.
- Determine the connection between violence and the media.

CHAPTER 7

Learning

Many species don't have much to learn. They are born with most necessary behaviors "programmed" in. Thus, earthworms don't have to go to school, and crocodiles don't need tutors.

Humans are different. One of our greatest gifts is to be able to adapt successfully to a wide variety of situations. To do this, we must profit from our experiences. We must draw significant information from the environment. In short, we rely on learning to a greater extent than any other species. This chapter presents what psychology has learned about learning. We will discover how we learn by forming associations and by observing the behavior of others. What does *learning* really mean? Under what circumstances does it occur? How can we control the process to produce more desirable outcomes? Soon you will know, because you're about to learn!

Performance Standards

Standard Area: Learning

Content Standard 1: Understanding learning

Performance Standard 1.1 Understand learning from a psychological paradigm.

- Discuss the influential historical figures in the study of learning. Investigate the findings of such researchers as Ivan Pavlov, John B. Watson, John Garcia, and Robert Rescorla. (Student Text pp. 286–294)

Content Standard 2: Classical conditioning processes

Performance Standard 2.1 Explain the principles of classical conditioning.

- Investigate how a neutral stimulus becomes able to elicit a response through repeated pairings with an unconditioned stimulus. See how yelling "Flush" to a person showering acts as a conditioned stimulus to evoke a jump out of the shower! (Student Text pp. 281–283).
- Figure 15.1, "An Example of Classical Conditioning," illustrates how a previously neutral stimulus (yelling "Flush") can become associated with a new response (jumping out of the shower). (Student Text p. 282)
- Explore the language of classical conditioning. Definitions and examples for unconditioned stimuli, unconditioned response, conditioned stimuli, and conditioned response are presented. (Student Text pp. 283–284)
- Understand the three basic processes of classical conditioning: acquisition, extinction, and spontaneous recovery. (Student Text pp. 284–286)
- Discuss the role that Ivan Pavlov played in the study of classical conditioning. Apply the language of classical conditioning to Pavlov's research on salivating dogs. (Student Text pp. 286–288)
- Figure 15.4, "Pavlov's Experiment," illustrates how Pavlov classically conditioned dogs to salivate to a tone. (Student Text p. 287)
- Explore the processes of generalization and discrimination in learning. (Student Text pp. 288–290)
- Investigate how John B. Watson and Rosalie Raynor classically conditioned Little Albert to fear white furry objects. Explore the role of generalization in this experiment. Discuss the ethical implications of Watson's research on Little Albert. (Student Text pp. 290–293)
- Figure 15.6, "Conditioning Little Albert," reviews the process by which Watson was able to classically condition and generalize fear in Little Albert. (Student Text p. 291)
- Discuss the implications of John Garcia's taste aversion studies on our understanding of classical conditioning. (Student Text p. 293)
- Understand the role cognition plays in the process of classical conditioning. (Student Text pp. 293–294)

Content Standard 4: The role of cognition in learning

Performance Standard 4.2 Explain the role of cognition in learning.

- Explore the research of Robert Rescorla and Allan Wagner. Discuss the role of prediction in the acquisition of a new behavior. (Student Text pp. 293–294)

Content Standard 5: The influence of biology and culture on learning

Performance Standard 5.1 Understand the influence of biology on learning.

- Discuss John Garcia and Robert Koelling's research on taste aversion in rats. Investigate how animals are predisposed to learn certain associations. Explore how certain biological constraints help animals survive in their environments. (Student Text p. 293)

Materials NETWORK

All of the items from the Activity and Enrichment Centers listed below come from the *Teacher's Resource Binder*. These items will help you teach and expand on concepts presented in Module 15.

trb This logo indicates when an item from the Materials Network may be used in conjunction with a specific note found in this module's *Teacher's Edition*.

Components of Classical Conditioning

Activity Center

- Critical Thinking Activity: *Defining Learning* The challenge of this activity is for students to decide which of the presented situations define a learning experience. (*Teacher's Resource Binder*, p. 15-1; Handout 15–1)
- Building Vocabulary: Graphic Organizer: *Concept Web* By completing this concept web, students review vocabulary and make connections among terms related to learning and classical conditioning. (*Teacher's Resource Binder*, p. 15-1; Handout 15–2)
- Application Activity: *Classical Conditioning with Lemonade Powder* Get your students to salivate like Pavlov's dogs with this activity that uses lemonade powder as the unconditioned stimulus and a key word as the conditioned stimulus. (*Teacher's Resource Binder*, p. 15-1)

Classical Conditioning Processes

Activity Center

- Technology Application Activity: *PsychSim:* "Classical Conditioning" *PsychSim* is an interactive CD-ROM containing tutorials in different content areas of psychology. In this tutorial, students review the four basic elements of classical conditioning and perform the eye blink conditioning experiment. (*Teacher's Resource Binder*, p. 15-1)
- Application Activity: *Conditioning the Eye Blink* Students can conduct their own step-by-step classical conditioning experiment as they train their lab partners to blink in response to a conditioned stimulus. (*Teacher's Resource Binder*, p. 15-1; Handout 15–3)

Ivan Pavlov's Discovery

Enrichment Center

- Enrichment Lesson: *Pavlov: The Man Behind the Experiment* Ivan Pavlov was more concerned about making his mark in physiology than psychology. This lesson delves into this fascinating figure in psychology's history. (*Teacher's Resource Binder*, p. 15-1)

Generalization and Discrimination

Activity Center

- Application Activity: *Classical Conditioning with a Water Gun* Demonstrate generalization and discrimination with this fun, interactive activity that uses a water gun and a brave volunteer. (*Teacher's Resource Binder*, p. 15-1)

Classical Conditioning in Everyday Life

Activity Center

- Critical Thinking Activity: *Human Taste Aversions* Would you enjoy your soup less if it were stirred with a flyswatter? Imagine this situation and others with this activity, in which students can experience taste aversions indirectly. (*Teacher's Resource Binder*, p. 15-1)

Enrichment Center

- Enrichment Lesson: *Abnormal Psychology and Classical Conditioning* Many psychological disorders have been successfully treated using classical conditioning procedures, as this lesson points out. (*Teacher's Resource Binder*, p. 15-1)
- Enrichment Lesson: *The Association Principle* Pavlov proved that associations are powerful. This lesson shows how people naturally want to associate themselves with pleasant circumstances and distance themselves from unpleasant ones. (*Teacher's Resource Binder*, p. 15-1)

Cognition and Biological Predispositions

Activity Center

- Critical Thinking Activity: *Classical Conditioning: Preparing for an Important Event* By popping balloons and having students record their responses, you will demonstrate how strong classical conditioning can be—even when associations between stimuli are anticipated. (*Teacher's Resource Binder*, p. 15-1)

Enrichment Center

- Enrichment Lesson: *Cognitive Processing in Learning* Behavioral research into the cognitive angle of classical conditioning by Michael Dawson shows that active participation in the conditioning process helps ensure that associations are formed. (*Teacher's Resource Binder*, p. 15-1)
- Enrichment Lesson: *Biological Predispositions* John Watson believed that it didn't matter what the conditioned stimulus was in order for conditioning to occur. However, studies show that we are predisposed to learn certain associations and not others. (*Teacher's Resource Binder*, p. 15-1)

MODULE 15

Classical Conditioning

What's the Point? 1. What is classical conditioning?

My freshman dormitory in college was a cheaply built affair. One area where the college had really cut costs was the plumbing for the large, communal bathrooms on each floor. The cold water pipes were too small to supply adequate water to both the showers and the toilets, which created a real problem if you were showering when someone flushed a toilet. The toilet would siphon off most of the cold water, and the shower temperature would momentarily turn hot enough to scald.

This reality led to a rule: When someone was about to flush a toilet while a dormmate was in the shower, he was to yell *Flush!* to warn the showerer. This was a simple plan and a good solution, once you had learned to respond appropriately. The morning of my first shower, I had not made the connection. As I languished half asleep in the water, I heard the word *Flush!* but did not associate it with me and my shower. Only after being struck by painfully hot water did I jump out of the way. My jump was a reflexive, automatic response to the hot water. I still had not made the connection.

After I had this experience a few more times, however, **learning** occurred. When a dormmate yelled *Flush!* I instantly jumped to the side, with time to spare before the water temperature spiked. Although I did not realize it at the time, I had been classically conditioned. **Classical conditioning**—is a form of *learning by association.* I had come to associate a new **stimulus** (the word *Flush!*) with another stimulus (hot water). *Flush!* was now a reliable predictor that scalding water was coming, and I began to respond to the word in the same way I had responded to the hot

▶ **learning** A relatively permanent change in behavior due to experience.

▶ **classical conditioning** A type of learning where a stimulus gains the power to cause a response because it predicts another stimulus that already produces the response.

▶ **stimulus** Anything in the environment that one can respond to.

Getting Started

Before students read the module, begin a discussion by asking volunteers to share an early learning experience of which they have a clear memory. Have these students then explain what they think enabled them to learn what they did.

trb You may wish to use **Critical Thinking Activity:** *Defining Learning* (*Teacher's Resource Binder,* p. 15-1; **Handout 15–1**) as a prereading strategy to help students think about the different ways learning occurs. This activity will challenge students to think about learning in plants, animals, humans, and machines.

MODULE 15

Classical Conditioning

Introducing the Module

The Points: Module Objectives

- Define *classical conditioning.*
- Describe how an unconditioned stimulus (UCS) differs from a conditioned stimulus (CS) and how an unconditioned response (UCR) differs from a conditioned response (CR).
- Identify the three basic processes in classical conditioning.
- Describe the role Ivan Pavlov played in the study of classical conditioning.
- Define generalization and discrimination, and explain in what way they can be considered opposites.
- Describe how John Watson and Rosalie Rayner demonstrated that emotions can be classically conditioned.
- Explain the importance of the role of cognition and biological predispositions in learning.

trb tr Building Vocabulary

The handout in **Building Vocabulary: Graphic Organizer:** *Concept Web* (*Teacher's Resource Binder,* p. 15-1; **Handout 15–2**) shows relationships among module concepts and includes module vocabulary associated with classical conditioning. Students can work in small groups to complete the organizer and refer to their texts to both learn the vocabulary and confirm the correct placement of terms from the word bank in the web. To check for correctly completed concept webs, you can use the handout as a transparency with answers inserted and project it for all groups to review.

MODULE 15

Teaching the Points

■ **TEACHING TIPS**

web (1) You can log on as an instructor to the book companion site for *Thinking About Psychology* at **www.worthpublishers.com/thinkingaboutpsych**. It contains teacher resources for class presentations as well as review and assessment of module concepts and terms.

web (2) Mark Plonsky's very useful library at **www.uwsp.edu/acad/psych/dog/lib-sci.htm** has a large number of links organized into the categories of *classical conditioning, operant conditioning, biological constraints on learning,* and *cognitive views,* along with other issues that can be used as preparation for teaching this module.

(3) When students relate classical conditioning learning experiences, they often relate operantly conditioned learning experiences—that is, those that are gained by reinforcement rather than association of two stimuli. Help students understand that **classical conditioning** involves associating a natural response with a new stimulus—that is, one that didn't elicit that response before the association was made.

tr A four-color transparency of Figure 15.1, An Example of Classical Conditioning, is available in the **Overhead Transparencies Set.**

water itself. After repeated pairings, the two stimuli were linked in my mind, and each now produced the same **response**—an immediate jump to the side. This change in behavior was proof that learning had occurred.

Classical conditioning is learning (as evidenced by my changed behavior) where a stimulus (*Flush!*) gains the power to cause a response (Jump!), because it predicts another stimulus (scalding water) that already produces the response (Jump!). Whew, that's a mouthful, but at its center it's really not too complicated (Figure 15.1). One stimulus begins to produce the same response as another stimulus because the learner has developed an association between the two.

For much of the twentieth century, material on classical conditioning helped form the core of introductory psychology textbooks. This type of learning focused on behavior, pure and simple. There was no need to con-

Figure 15.1 **An Example of Classical Conditioning** Classical conditioning led a group of dormmates to respond to the word *Flush!* the same way they responded to painfully hot water.

Two related events:

Stimulus 1: Calling the word "flush" before flushing the toilet warns that water in the shower will soon be scalding.

+

Stimulus 2: When the toilet is flushed, hot water in the shower gets much hotter.

Result after repetition:

Stimulus: We hear "flush"

Response: We jump anticipating hot water

Suggested Readings

Use the following books as teacher-preparation tools or as enrichment for advanced students:

Black, A. H., & Prokasy, W. F. (Eds.). (1972). *Classical conditioning II: Current research and theory.* New York: Appleton-Century-Crofts.

Cialdini, R. B. (1993). *Influence: Science and practice* (3rd ed.). New York: HarperCollins.

Konner, M. (1982). *The tangled wing.* New York: Holt, Rinehart & Winston.

Nisbett, R., & Ross, L. (1980). *Human inference: Strategies and shortcomings of social judgment.* Englewood Cliffs, NJ: Prentice Hall.

sider what happened inside the learner's head. And that was the way a school of psychology known as **behaviorism,** led by American psychologist **John Watson,** felt psychology should operate. By manipulating a stimulus in the environment, the psychologist could control the learner's behavioral response. Indeed, we know that a dog has learned to sit if he does it, that a musician has learned a new piece when she can play it, that a gymnast has learned a new routine when he can perform it, that a child has learned to walk when she can make it across the room on two legs, and that a student has learned psychology when he can perform adequately on a test. In all these cases, learning is reflected in *behavior.*

Watson was very influential in his day, but behaviorism no longer dominates psychology. A growing body of evidence indicates that all kinds of learning, including classical conditioning, can be understood only in light of **cognition**—mental processes. To most of us, this is simply common sense. If you ask a group of friends to define *learning,* they will almost surely tell you that it is something that occurs in your head. "Learning is when you understand something" and "learning occurs when you remember" are typical answers, and they both reflect the importance of cognition. Behaviorists like Watson were suspicious of using such explanations because they thought it was impossible to study cognitive processes scientifically. In contrast, contemporary psychologists believe it is impossible to understand classical conditioning without reference to cognitive processes.

While classical conditioning does not occupy quite the central position it once did, this type of learning through association still helps us understand a variety of behavioral and emotional responses.

▸ **response** Any behavior or action.

▸ **behaviorism** The view that psychology should restrict its efforts to studying observable behaviors, not mental processes.

▸ **John Watson** (1878–1958) Founder of behaviorism, the view that psychology should restrict its efforts to studying observable behaviors, not mental processes.

▸ **cognition** Mental processes; all the mental activities associated with thinking, knowing, and remembering.

▸ **unconditioned stimulus (UCS)** In classical conditioning, a stimulus that triggers a response automatically and reflexively.

Components of Classical Conditioning

2. How does an unconditioned stimulus (UCS) differ from a conditioned stimulus (CS)? How does an unconditioned response (UCR) differ from a conditioned response (CR)?

Classical conditioning is a straightforward, logical process. It is easy to understand *if* you have mastered a few key terms. It is a good idea to read through this section on components and the next section on processes two or three times. Pause at the end of each paragraph and reflect for a moment on the meaning of each term that has been introduced. We will use these terms over and over, and you'll be lost if you haven't taken the time to master their meanings.

- **Unconditioned stimulus** (UCS) The UCS is a stimulus that triggers a response reflexively or automatically, just as scalding hot water in a shower makes someone jump. Very hot shower water is

MODULE 15

■ JOURNAL WRITING

Invite students to use the following questions and writing prompts as springboards for entries in their psychology journals:

- What is learning?
- Describe a time in your life when you "learned from experience." Do you think it was an example of classical conditioning? How?

■ LOOKING AT THE ISSUES

The behaviorists who wanted to isolate the study of psychology to only observable behavior were trying to make psychology "scientific." Psychology has been accused of being a "soft" science in comparison to the "hard" sciences of chemistry, physics, and biology. Have students ponder the differences in these various scientific fields.

- What defines a science?
- What are the differences between "soft" sciences and "hard" sciences? Does psychology fit into either category neatly? Why or why not?
- How has psychology become more scientific than in the beginning of the twentieth century?

Enriching

Have students survey a representative sample of students to get their views on psychology as a science. Elicit students' findings by asking the following questions:

- Do students view psychology as a science? Why or why not?
- How would students compare psychology to chemistry, physics, and biology?
- Do students consider psychologists scientists? Why or why not?

F • Y • I

The UCR and the CR are almost always the same response. The stimulus that elicits the response is the crucial difference—the UCS elicits the UCR, while the CS elicits the CR.

trb At this point, you may wish to use Application Activity: *Classical Conditioning with Lemonade Powder* (*Teacher's Resource Binder*, p. 15-1).

■ **APPLYING THE POINTS**

Contact any of the school's athletic coaches to ask how they get their team members to learn their sports. Typically, coaches will have players practice plays over and over so the teams will perform the learned behavior naturally during a game. Players will associate the names of plays with the behaviors, so they don't have to think twice during a game.

trb At this point, you may wish to use Technology Application Activity: *PsychSim:* "Classical Conditioning" (*Teacher's Resource Binder*, p. 15-1).

► **unconditioned response (UCR)** In classical conditioning, the automatic response to the unconditioned stimulus.

► **conditioned stimulus (CS)** In classical conditioning, a previously neutral stimulus that, through learning, has gained the power to cause a conditioned response.

► **conditioned response (CR)** In classical conditioning, the response to the conditioned stimulus.

► **acquisition** In classical conditioning, the process of developing a learned response.

a UCS for jumping. Classical conditioning cannot happen without a UCS. The only behaviors and emotions that can be classically conditioned are those that are reliably produced by a UCS.

- **Unconditioned response (UCR)** The UCR is, quite simply, the response to the UCS. If hot water is the UCS, jumping out of the way is the UCR. Once again, notice that the stimulus-response relationship between the UCS and the UCR is *reflexive*, not learned.
- **Conditioned stimulus (CS)** The CS is the originally *neutral stimulus* that, through conditioning (learning), gains the power to cause the response. On my first day in the dorm, the word *Flush!* was a neutral stimulus—I did not associate it with showers, and it did not make me jump. Thousands of other sights and sounds around the dormitory were also neutral stimuli. The conditioning process changed the word *Flush!* from a neutral stimulus to a CS. (This constitutes learning!) All those other neutral stimuli remained neutral. In basic classical conditioning, the neutral stimulus and the CS are always the same thing. The term *neutral stimulus* describes the stimulus *before* conditioning and the term *CS* describes the stimulus *after* conditioning.
- **Conditioned response (CR)** The CR is the response to the CS. In basic classical conditioning, it is the same behavior that is identified as the UCR. If I jump because of hot water (a UCS), my jumping is a UCR. However, if I have learned to jump when someone yells *Flush!* (a CS), my jumping is now a CR.

So remember—the five main components of classical conditioning are the *UCS*, the *UCR*, the *neutral stimulus*, the *CS*, and the *CR*.

Classical Conditioning Processes

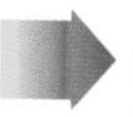

3. What are the three basic processes in classical conditioning?

Now that you understand the five main components of classical conditioning, you need to know a little more about three basic processes in this type of learning: acquisition, extinction, and spontaneous recovery.

Acquisition

Acquisition is the most basic process in classical conditioning, the one that establishes a new, learned response. Acquisition occurs when a neutral stimulus is repeatedly paired with a UCS. Each pairing is called a *trial*.

Reteaching

trb You may wish to use Application Activity: *Classical Conditioning with Lemonade Powder* (*Teacher's Resource Binder*, p. 15-1) to get your students to salivate like Pavlov's dogs. This activity uses lemonade powder as the UCS and a key word as the CS. Get students to identify the appropriate components of classical conditioning to see if they understand what distinguishes each component from the other.

In my dorm, I *acquired* the new CR when a stimulus—the word *Flush!*—was repeatedly paired with the UCS of hot water. Notice that we do not yet refer to the word *Flush!* as a CS because we have yet to demonstrate that the response, jumping, was caused by anything other than the UCS (hot water). We do this by conducting a test.

To see if a CR has actually been acquired, you need to conduct a test. In this case, you would shout the word *Flush!* to a person (me!) in the shower without presenting scalding hot water (meaning you wouldn't flush the toilet). Then you would observe whether anything happened. If there is no response (no jumping), it means the word is not yet a CS. If the person in the shower does jump, however, this means *Flush!* has become a CS. The person's jumping has occurred because of the word, so this jumping is a CR (not a UCR). *Flush!* has become a CS, and the jump has become a CR. You have shown that the acquisition process in classical conditioning has occurred. Once acquired, the CR will be *maintained* only if the CS continues to be paired with the UCS on some trials.

Extinction and Spontaneous Recovery

Extinction is the procedure for reversing the learning that has taken place. Extinction occurs as the CS loses its power to trigger a CR. Recall that when we want someone to *acquire* a CR, we repeatedly pair a neutral stimulus with the UCS. But if we want to reverse this learning, we must weaken the strength of the association between the two stimuli. We do this by repeatedly presenting the CS alone.

In the shower example, if prank-minded friends had repeatedly shouted *Flush!* but never followed the word with a hot water dousing, the CR to the word would eventually have weakened and died. When a CR has completely disapeared, we can say that it has been *extinguished.*

But extinguished responses, like unwanted visitors, tend to linger. The return of an extinguished, classically conditioned response after a rest period is called **spontaneous recovery.** The recovered response is weaker than the original one, however, and it can be extinguished more easily. Assume, for example, that my prankster friends had succeeded in extinguishing my response to the word *Flush!* by the end of the school year. If I returned to the same dorm after summer vacation, chances are good that I would jump, at least slightly, if someone yelled *Flush!* The renewed jump would be evidence of spontaneous recovery. This time though, only a few prank soundings of *Flush!* would produce extinction again.

Figure 15.2 (page 286) illustrates the processes of acquisition, extinction, and spontaneous recovery. The strength of CR, in this case, would be the distance that I jumped.

► **extinction** In classical conditioning, the diminishing of a learned response; when an unconditioned stimulus does not follow a conditioned stimulus.

► **spontaneous recovery** The reappearance, after a rest period, of an extinguished conditioned response.

Cooperative Learning

You may want to use **Application Activity:** ***Conditioning the Eye Blink*** (*Teacher's Resource Binder*, p. 15-1; **Handout 15–3**) so students can conduct their own step-by-step classical conditioning experiment as they train their lab partners to blink in response to a CS. Students can record the following information during the demonstration:

- how many trials it takes for an eye blink to become conditioned
- how many trials without a paired response it takes to extinguish the eye blink
- how many trials it takes to spontaneously recover the eye blink after extinction

■ **LOOKING AT THE ISSUES**

The fable about the boy who cried "wolf" teaches lessons about classical conditioning. The boy who cried "wolf" when no danger was present extinguished the villagers' conditioned response to come to his aid. Remind students of this fable and ask them to relate the lesson of this fable to the following questions:

- Does continuous media coverage decrease public reaction to and sentiment for tragic events?
- Can a lack of empathy for the plight of others be classically conditioned? How?

trb At this point, you may wish to use **Enrichment Lesson:** ***Abnormal Psychology and Classical Conditioning*** (*Teacher's Resource Binder*, p. 15-1).

■ **APPLYING THE POINTS**

Many programs that help people overcome addictions are based on classical conditioning. Suggest a review of literature about these programs to find out how they work and how effective they are. Students may also interview a psychologist who uses these techniques.

trb At this point, you may wish to use **Enrichment Lesson:** ***Abnormal Psychology and Classical Conditioning*** (*Teacher's Resource Binder*, p. 15-1).

■ **CHECKING FOR UNDERSTANDING**

Here are several ways to assess students' comprehension:

- Assign any or all of the journal questions or prompts for an in-class writing assessment.
- Divide the students into groups or pairs and give each group a journal question prompt. When students present their answers to the class, correct any misconceptions that may arise.
- Use questions from the *Test Bank* or the handout for **Building Vocabulary: Graphic Organizer:** ***Concept Web*** (*Teacher's Resource Binder*, p. 15-1; **Handout 15–2**) to do a quick assessment of their knowledge of the concepts.

MODULE 15

TEACHING TIP

A four-color transparency of Figure 15.2, Three Basic Classical Conditioning Processes, is available in the **Overhead Transparencies Set.**

F • Y • I

Ivan Pavlov was a Russian physiologist who earned the 1904 Nobel Prize in Physiology and Medicine. His studies in digestion accidentally led to his famous discovery of classical conditioning.

trb At this point, you may wish to use **Enrichment Lesson:** *Pavlov: The Man Behind the Experiment* (*Teacher's Resource Binder,* p. 15-1).

MULTICULTURAL CONNECTIONS

Have students use library and Internet resources to research how the Russian people view Ivan Pavlov's accomplishments. Then, have students respond to the following questions:

- What are some ways in which Russia has honored Pavlov for his accomplishments?
- Do the Russians regard Pavlov more as a physiologist or psychologist?

trb At this point, you may wish to use **Enrichment Lesson:** *Pavlov: The Man Behind the Experiment* (*Teacher's Resource Binder,* p. 15-1).

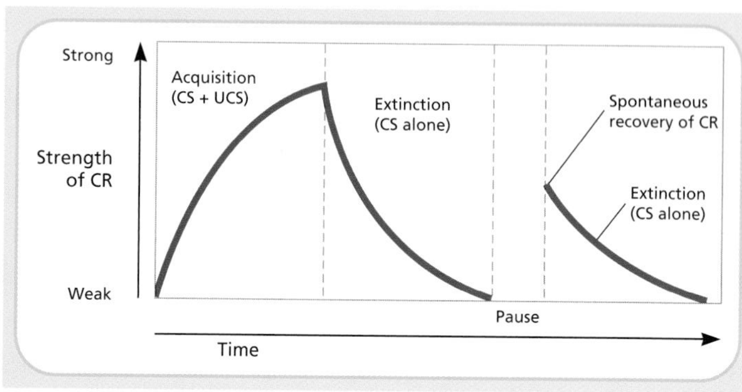

Figure 15.2 **Three Basic Classical Conditioning Processes** *Acquisition* occurs as the CS and the UCS are repeatedly paired. *Extinction* happens if the CS is presented by itself. *Spontaneous recovery* means that the extinguished CR again appears after a rest period.

Ivan Pavlov's Discovery

4. What role did Ivan Pavlov play in the study of classical conditioning?

Ivan Pavlov Pavlov's pioneering studies of the digestive system led to decades of research to identify the principles of classical conditioning.

One of the most famous names in the history of psychology is **Ivan Pavlov.** Pavlov, a Russian physiologist interested in the study of digestion, earned a Nobel prize for his work in this area in 1904. As happens to many good scientists, however, some unexpected findings sparked his curiosity and led him in new directions. He landed squarely in the realm of behavioral psychology.

At the time, Pavlov was investigating the effects of salivation (drool!) on the digestive process. In a surgical procedure of his own design, he installed a shunt (a small tube) to divert and collect salivary secretions from dogs (Figure 15.3). To stimulate the production of saliva, he then introduced meat powder into the dogs' mouths.

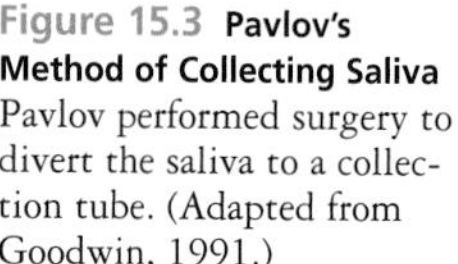

Figure 15.3 **Pavlov's Method of Collecting Saliva** Pavlov performed surgery to divert the saliva to a collection tube. (Adapted from Goodwin, 1991.)

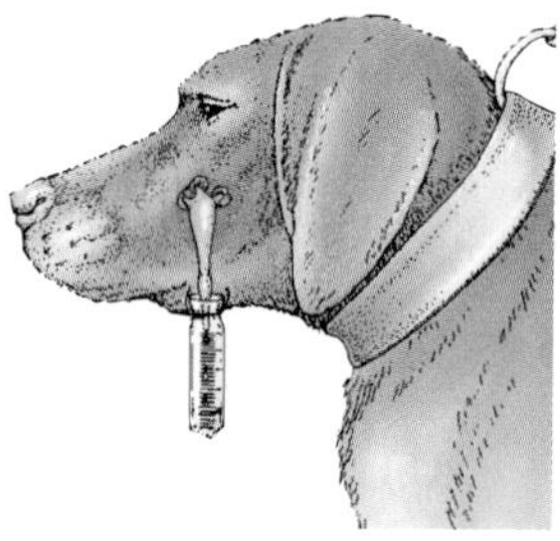

When Pavlov first began working with a dog, the procedure was just fine. Pavlov would restrain the animal in a harness, attach a tube to collect the saliva, and stimulate the production of saliva with the meat powder. But after Pavlov had worked with a dog for a while, problems began to crop up. The more familiar the dog became with the procedure, the less likely he was to wait for the meat powder before salivating. Some dogs began to drool as they were being harnessed. Some even salivated when they heard the experimenter come toward the kennel at about the right time each day. If you have a family dog, you may have noticed this type of learning by association yourself. As dinnertime draws near, does your dog begin to salivate in anticipation as you start to go through the preparations? If so, you may find this behavior funny or interesting. But for Pavlov, the premature drooling was disruptive.

Intrigued with his dogs' "misbehavior," Pavlov began to wonder if he could control the salivation response by manipulating various stimuli in the environment. Would it be possible to choose a stimulus, such as the sound of a tuning fork, and intentionally create a salivation response to that stimulus? As Pavlov began to investigate these new questions about the dogs' behavior, he identified the central features of classical conditioning we know today.

Let's use Pavlov's basic demonstration of classical conditioning to review the concepts we have already discussed. His task was to teach a dog to salivate to the sound of a tuning fork. Think about the *components* of this experiment, and try to identify the neutral stimulus and the UCS, UCR, CS, and CR. Now check your ideas by reading the summaries below and looking closely at Figure 15.4.

- The *unconditioned stimulus* (UCS) is the meat powder, because it produces a salivation response without prior learning.
- The *unconditioned response* (UCR) is salivation, because salivation is the response to the UCS of meat powder. Notice that no learning has yet taken place. The ability of meat to make a hungry dog drool is reflexive, not learned.

▶ **Ivan Pavlov** (1849–1936) Learning theorist famous for the discovery of classical conditioning.

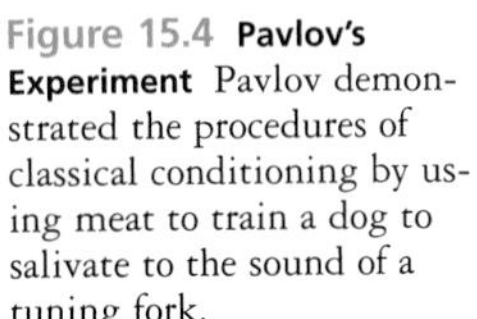

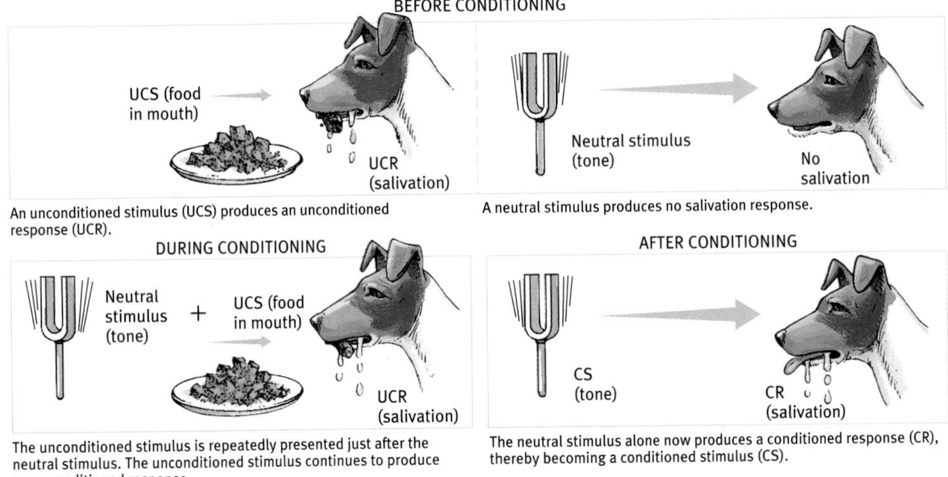

BEFORE CONDITIONING
UCS (food in mouth)
UCR (salivation)
An unconditioned stimulus (UCS) produces an unconditioned response (UCR).
Neutral stimulus (tone)
No salivation
A neutral stimulus produces no salivation response.
DURING CONDITIONING
Neutral stimulus (tone)
+
UCS (food in mouth)
UCR (salivation)
The unconditioned stimulus is repeatedly presented just after the neutral stimulus. The unconditioned stimulus continues to produce an unconditioned response.
AFTER CONDITIONING
CS (tone)
CR (salivation)
The neutral stimulus alone now produces a conditioned response (CR), thereby becoming a conditioned stimulus (CS).

Figure 15.4 **Pavlov's Experiment** Pavlov demonstrated the procedures of classical conditioning by using meat to train a dog to salivate to the sound of a tuning fork.

tr ■ TEACHING TIP

A four-color transparency of Figure 15.4, Pavlov's Experiment, is available in the **Overhead Transparencies Set.**

F • Y • I

Another psychological phenomenon was discovered "by accident" like Pavlov's classical conditioning. *Learned optimism*, described by Martin Seligman, was formulated after Seligman observed that some of the dogs in his experiments on learned helplessness did not give up after many trials of being subjected to uncontrollable shock. Seligman later realized that the dogs that didn't give up give us insight into the psychology of optimism as much as the dogs who gave up give us insight into the psychology of depression.

trb At this point, you may wish to use **Enrichment Lesson:** ***Pavlov: The Man Behind the Experiment*** (*Teacher's Resource Binder*, p. 15-1).

■ APPLYING THE POINTS

Have students share their experiences with their dogs or cats regarding the associations the pets have made with feeding time. Have students share how their pets respond to the opening of a cabinet door or the rattling of a food bag. Do the pets come running? Do the pets behave in certain ways to signal desires for food, water, or going to the bathroom?

Reteaching

tr A four-color transparency of Figure 15.4, Pavlov's Experiment, is available in the **Overhead Transparencies Set.** You may want to use this transparency to see if students need additional instruction in the basic elements of classical conditioning and Pavlov's experimental setup. Cover up key elements of the figure and quiz students orally on each element.

MODULE 15

trb ■ TEACHING TIP

You may wish to use **Application Activity:** ***Classical Conditioning with a Water Gun*** (*Teacher's Resource Binder,* p. 15-1) to demonstrate generalization and discrimination with this fun, interactive activity that uses a water gun and a brave volunteer!

F • Y • I

Timing is very important to successful classical conditioning. Studies have shown that the CS must precede the UCS by about one-half to one second in order to bring about the CR. Other types of timing that can occur with classical conditioning include the following:

- **Delayed conditioning** occurs when the CS precedes the UCS, but they overlap just a little. This is the best situation for conditioning, especially if the time delay between CS and UCS is short.
- **Trace conditioning** occurs when the CS precedes the UCS and they do not overlap. The longer the time delay between the CS and UCS, the more difficult conditioning is.
- With **simultaneous conditioning,** the CS occurs at the same time as the UCS. This is not a good idea because it results in poor conditioning. The CS doesn't predict the UCS at all in this situation.
- With **backward conditioning,** the CS follows the UCS. Little or no conditioning takes place, unless the response is a biological predisposition.

trb At this point, you may wish to use **Application Activity:** ***Classical Conditioning with a Water Gun*** (*Teacher's Resource Binder,* p. 15-1).

- The *neutral stimulus* is the sound of the tuning fork before the dog has been conditioned. This stimulus is neutral because it does not produce a salivation response. Pavlov, of course, could have used many other stimuli—bells, whistles, or even lights—as the neutral stimulus.
- The *conditioned stimulus* (CS) is the sound of the tuning fork after the dog has been conditioned, because that tone now produces the response of salivation. Notice that the tone serves as both the neutral stimulus and the CS at different times in the conditioning process.
- The *conditioned response* (CR) is salivation, because salivation is now the response to the sound of the tuning fork. Notice here that salivation can be either the UCR or the CR, depending on what stimulus led to the salivation.

Now let's look at the *processes* in this classical conditioning experiment. To produce *acquisition,* Pavlov repeatedly sounded the tuning fork just before introducing meat powder into the dog's mouth. He knew acquisition had occurred because he tested for a learned response: He presented the sound of the tuning fork without the meat powder. If the dog salivated (and he did), the salivation was a CR, proving that the sound of the tuning fork had become a CS. To *extinguish* the classically conditioned response, Pavlov repeatedly sounded the tuning fork without the meat powder. The learned association between the sound of the tuning fork and the taste of meat gradually weakened under these circumstances and, as the link weakened, the dog produced less and less saliva. When the salivation response had disappeared, extinction had occurred. If Pavlov sounded the tuning fork the next day and the dog salivated, the renewed CR would signify *spontaneous recovery.* The spontaneously recovered CR would be weaker than the CR before extinction—the dog would produce less saliva.

Now that we've reviewed the components and processes of classical conditioning, let's look at two concepts that broaden our understanding of how we learn.

Generalization and Discrimination

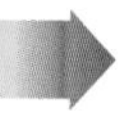

5. What are generalization and discrimination, and in what way can they be considered opposites?

Generalization and discrimination are two of the more useful concepts psychologists apply in thinking about learning. We discuss them here in relation to classical conditioning, but they apply equally well to all kinds of learning.

Reteaching

Some students may find the alphabet soup of acronyms (UCS, CS, UCR, and so forth) found in classical conditioning to be challenging. Display several small posters at the front of the class with the classical conditioning terms on them so that students can see the acronyms as they take notes, participate in activities, and answer questions.

trb At this point, you may wish to use **Building Vocabulary: Graphic Organizer:** ***Concept Web*** (*Teacher's Resource Binder,* p. 15-1; **Handout 15–2**).

Generalization occurs when an organism produces the same response to two similar stimuli. Let's assume for a moment that Pavlov somehow lost the tuning fork he had used with one of his dogs and was forced to substitute a different tuning fork, one with a different tone. Pavlov had progressed far enough so that the tone of the original tuning fork had become a CS that generated a strong CR of salivation. What do you think would happen when Pavlov sounded the substitute tuning fork, producing a tone that had never been paired with meat powder? Pavlov discovered that the dog *did* respond by salivating, and that the more similar the substitute tone was to the original tone, the stronger the salivation response was! Figure 15.5 illustrates some generalization data Pavlov actually collected, using touches to various body parts as stimuli.

Discrimination occurs when an organism produces *different* responses to two similar stimuli. Let's assume Pavlov finally found his missing tuning fork, and he now had two (the original and the substitute) that were capable of producing salivation, thanks to generalization. What might happen if he paired the original tuning fork with the UCS of meat powder on some trials, but never paired the substitute tuning fork with the UCS? Assuming the dog could actually hear the difference between the tones made by the two tuning forks, the conditioned salivation response to the sound of the original tuning fork would be maintained (because this tone tells the dog that food is on the way), but the response to the sound of the substitute tuning fork would be extinguished (because that tone never leads to meat powder). Now the dog is no longer generalizing, he is discriminating.

Generalization and discrimination appear very frequently in the world around us. For example, I know of a little girl named Antonia who developed a classically conditioned fear of buzzing insects after a painful bee sting on the ear. The sting paired pain—a UCS that naturally produces fear—with the buzzing bee. Through this association, the buzzing bee became a CS for the CR of fear. This fear then generalized to all buzzing insects, and for a while Antonia feared everything that buzzed. With additional real-life experience, however, Antonia soon began to make appropriate discriminations. Her CR of fear stayed strong for buzzing things that give painful stings (like bees and hornets), but it was extinguished for buzzing things that don't give these stings (like disgusting flies or merely annoying mosquitoes).

▶ **generalization** A process in which an organism produces the same response to two similar stimuli.

▶ **discrimination** A process in which an organism produces different responses to two similar stimuli.

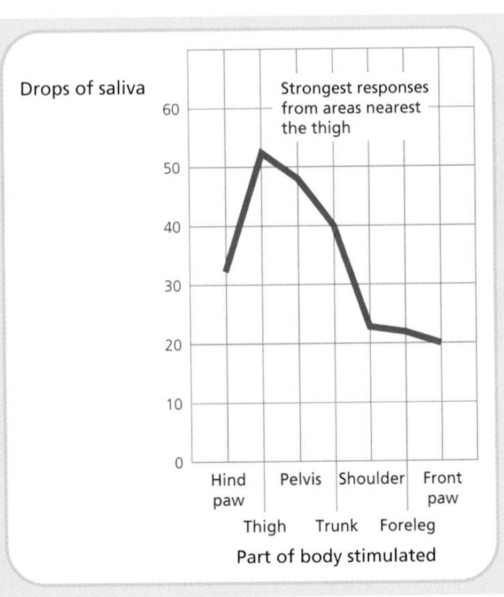

Figure 15.5 Generalization Pavlov conditioned dogs to salivate when their thighs were stimulated by a slight vibration. This graph shows how much saliva was produced when other parts of the dogs' bodies were stimulated. The dogs salivated more when the stimulated spot was nearer to the point of original conditioning.

MODULE 15

trb tr ■ TEACHING TIP

A black-line master for Figure 15.5, Generalization, is available in the **Black-Line Masters Appendix** of the *Teacher's Resource Binder.*

■ LOOKING AT THE ISSUES

Remind students that they respond to stimuli at school every day—for instance, the sound of the bell that signals a class change. Have students hypothesize how students would react if that sound were changed in any way. For example:

- How long would it take for students to realize what the new sound meant?
- Could students be trained to respond to only one type of bell?
- How do they think school administrators use the concepts of generalization and discrimination in daily school situations?

trb At this point, you may wish to use **Application Activity:** *Classical Conditioning with a Water Gun* (*Teacher's Resource Binder,* p. 15-1).

F • Y • I

Many common phobias—like those for bugs, as described in the text—are learned through classical conditioning. They can also be deconditioned, using the same classical conditioning processes. The most common form of therapy for phobias is called systematic desensitization. Clients of psychologists are gradually taught to associate feelings of relaxation rather than anxiety with what they fear.

trb At this point, you may wish to use **Enrichment Lesson:** *Abnormal Psychology and Classical Conditioning* (*Teacher's Resource Binder,* p. 15-1).

Meeting Individual Needs

trb GRAPHIC ORGANIZER Provide learning opportunities for all levels of learners with one of the following options for using the graphic organizer found in **Building Vocabulary: Graphic Organizer:** *Concept Web* (*Teacher's Resource Binder,* p. 15-1; **Handout 15–2**).

- **Independent Learners** Students may fill out the organizer on their own or follow along in class during discussion and lecture.
- **Cooperative Learners** Students may use the textbook as a resource and work in groups to find the answers that fit in the blanks.
- **Exceptional Learners** The graphic organizer can fill a special education need to provide notes for exceptional students. These students may fill in the blanks independently, with a student or teacher/tutor, or during class discussion and lecture.

MODULE 15

■ **CHECKING FOR UNDERSTANDING**
Present students with the following situation, and have them identify the elements of classical conditioning:

- Kim was very nervous about her upcoming chemistry exam. She had studied very hard. On the day of the big exam, she happened to get a stomach flu and subsequently did not do well on her test. Now, when she even begins studying for any exam, she feels sick to her stomach. *(The UCS in this situation is the stomach flu, which made Kim feel sick. The UCR is her upset stomach. The CS is the testing situation and the CR is her upset stomach, which she now associates with the testing condition. She has also generalized her upset stomach to tests in all subjects, not just chemistry.)*

F • Y • I

Because he lost his position at Johns Hopkins University, John Watson ended up applying his knowledge of psychology and behaviorism in the advertising industry, as one can see from how effectively advertisers use classical conditioning to sell their products!

■ **TEACHING TIP**
Have students brainstorm about different stimuli in their own environment that could be used in classical conditioning.

- What are some objects you encounter every day that you do not have a natural aversion to?
- What are some everyday objects that you do have a natural aversion to?
- What would it take to get you to associate an aversive object with a neutral one?

trb At this point, you may wish to use **Enrichment Lesson:** *The Association Principle* (*Teacher's Resource Binder*, p. 15-1).

Did You Flinch? If so, you've been classically conditioned! Try to identify the UCS, UCR, CS, and CR for this example of conditioning. Check your answer on page 292.

Antonia's example involved classical conditioning, but generalization and discrimination can occur for other types of learning as well. I was fascinated when my son, Eric, was learning animals and their names as a one-year-old. He used the word *Bow-wow* to describe all dogs (a generalization), but he could also discriminate among dogs and other animals, like *Meow-meows* and *Moo-moos*.

Classical Conditioning in Everyday Life

The beauty of classical conditioning is not that it explains *all* things, but rather that it explains *some* things *really well.* Psychologists can predict and control classically conditioned responses with great accuracy, and this was one of the first areas where the newly developed field of scientific psychology could do so. One of the most famous demonstrations in the history of American psychology established the importance of classical conditioning in the development of emotions.

Little Albert Meets John Watson and Rosalie Rayner

6. How did John Watson and Rosalie Rayner demonstrate that emotions can be classically conditioned?

John B. Watson Watson established American behaviorism. He believed that all behavior was the result of environmental factors. He and Rosalie Rayner set out to prove it by classically conditioning fear of rats in an 11-month-old boy known as Little Albert.

Earlier in this module, we noted that American psychologist John Watson believed that the proper study of psychology was behavior, not mental processes, which in his view cannot be studied scientifically. He passionately argued that psychology should study only stimulus-response relationships. Watson was therefore not pleased with the growing acceptance of Sigmund Freud's psychoanalytic viewpoint, which relied heavily on the unconscious mind as a means to explain human behavior. Psychoanalysts, for example, viewed phobias (disruptive, irrational fears) as a symbolic result of unconscious fears left over from childhood.

Watson, working with **Rosalie Rayner** at Johns Hopkins University in 1920, set out to demonstrate that such fears could be explained by the principles of classical conditioning. He did this by intentionally establishing a fear of rats in an 11-month-old boy now known as Little Albert. Initially Albert was not afraid of the tame, white laboratory rat. (In the world of classical conditioning, the rat was a neutral stimulus.) Albert did not respond to rats with crying or any facial expressions signifying fear. Watson and Rayner were able to change this quite easily by

Cross-Curricular Connections

LITERATURE Have students bring in a novel or nonfiction work that depicts a character with a fear. Use the following questions to discuss these fictional characters:

- How did the fear develop?
- What explanation for the fear does the character or narrator provide?
- Does the character overcome the fear? If so, how?

trb At this point, you may wish to use **Enrichment Lesson:** *Abnormal Psychology and Classical Conditioning* (*Teacher's Resource Binder*, p. 15-1).

sneaking up behind Albert when he was in the presence of a rat and banging a steel bar to make a startling noise. The noise was a UCS that produced a UCR of fear (crying). Because the UCS was paired with the rat, the rat became a CS to produce the same fear response (Figure 15.6). Watson and Rayner were able to announce that Little Albert's fear was a predictable outcome of an environmental condition. In this case at least, it did not represent some sort of repressed, unconscious conflict.

Watson and Rayner were even able to demonstrate generalization (Albert also showed fear of a furry, white rabbit) and discrimination (he did not show fear of dissimilar toys). Albert's mother apparently began to have some doubts about the research and withdrew the boy before Watson and Rayner were able to extinguish Albert's newly established phobia.

▶ **Rosalie Rayner** (1900–1935) Graduate student of John Watson and co-researcher for the famous Little Albert demonstration of classically conditioned emotion.

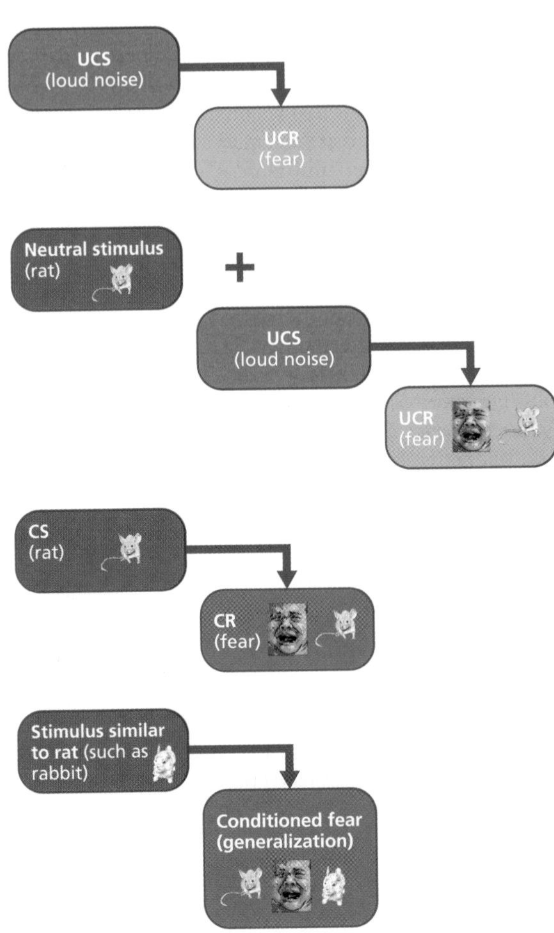

Figure 15.6 **Conditioning Little Albert** By pairing the neutral stimulus of a white rat with the UCS of a loud noise, Watson and Rayner were easily able to classically condition fear. They also demonstrated generalization when little Albert became afraid of other white furry animals.

MODULE 15

■ LOOKING AT THE ISSUES

Watson and Rayner's experiment with Little Albert shed important light on the nature of human emotions. But, as the text notes, this famous experiment also paved the way for limitations on how psychologists can study people and their emotions. To help students think about this experiment, ask the following questions:

- Do you think what Watson and Rayner did to Little Albert was ethical? Could they have changed their procedures to be more ethical? If so, how?
- Do you think the possible beneficial outcomes of a research project are worth the potential risk of harm to the experiment's subjects? Explain.

tr A four-color transparency of Figure 15.6, Conditioning Little Albert, is available in the **Overhead Transparencies Set.**

Reteaching

tr A four-color transparency of Figure 15.6, Conditioning Little Albert, is available in the **Overhead Transparencies Set.** You may want to use this transparency to see if students understand the way Watson and Rayner used classical conditioning to condition fear in Little Albert. Cover up key parts of the diagram to quiz students orally about each element.

MODULE 15

■ **JOURNAL WRITING**

Invite students to use the following questions and writing prompts as springboards for entries in their psychology journals:

- Do you have any phobias that are explained by a classical conditioning experience from your past? Describe the situation. How might you use classical conditioning to decondition your fear?
- Are you loyal to a favorite brand of a product? Might your loyalty be due to classical conditioning? If so, how is this possible?
- Have you experienced a classically conditioned taste aversion? Describe your experience.

trb At this point, you may wish to use **Enrichment Lesson:** *The Association Principle* (*Teacher's Resource Binder*, p. 15-1) and **Critical Thinking Activity:** *Human Taste Aversions* (*Teacher's Resource Binder*, p. 15-1).

Answers to the "Did You Flinch?" questions on page 290: The UCS is the explosion of the popped balloon. The UCR is the flinch produced by the pop. The CS is the sight of the pin approaching the balloon. The CR is the flinch produced by the sight of the pin approaching the balloon.

One of the mysteries of American psychology is what happened to Little Albert. He may still be alive, an old man with a lingering fear of rats because of Watson and Rayner's research. If so, he might be pleased to know that concern for his well-being helped spark the development of modern ethical standards in psychological research to prevent exactly this sort of unfortunate situation.

Aside from these ethical concerns, what can we conclude from Watson's research? The main point is that whenever you associate an emotional response with a particular stimulus, classical conditioning is probably involved. Advertisers learned this point quickly and have used it to their advantage for many years. Nestea commercials, for example, repeatedly pair images of cool, refreshing swimming pools and Nestea instant iced tea. The images of the pools function as a UCS to produce in viewers a feeling of being cool and refreshed. After being repeatedly paired with these images, the product name becomes a CS. Alone, it, too, produces a CR of being cool and refreshed. Thus, when I walk in the grocery store and see a dozen brands of instant iced tea mix, I am more likely to select Nestea because just looking at that label makes me feel cool and refreshed.

Advertisers spend millions of dollars to create classically conditioned emotional responses. Marlboro ads establish a rugged, macho image. Mountain Dew ads establish a youthful image. Victoria's Secret ads establish a sexy image. All are attempts to use the principles of classical conditioning to sell more products!

You don't need a big advertising budget to find other examples of classically conditioned emotions. Let's say you are seeing a new person and things are going delightfully well. The budding relationship is a UCS for positive emotions. During the evening, you hear a new song on the radio. What happens? The song becomes "your song." Whenever you hear it, you feel better, because it produces the same positive emotions that the relationship itself does. The song has become a CS, and classical conditioning is at work. A similar thing happens to me with running shoes. For me, running functions as a UCS for relaxation and stress relief. The more miles I put on a new pair of shoes, the more comforting they become. Eventually all I have to do is put on the shoes (now a CS) to start feeling better. Maybe this is one reason why I generally prefer my old, broken-in clothes to brand new ones. The old jeans are associated with a wealth of pleasant memories that bring me comfort as reliably as the tone of Pavlov's tuning fork made a dog drool.

Classically Conditioned Comfort Because of the many pleasant events that may be associated with their use, old clothes and shoes often become conditioned stimuli that produce a relaxed, comforting response. New clothes may be stylish, but they don't have this ability to help us unwind!

Negative emotions can be conditioned, too. Some women who have been raped destroy the clothes they were wearing at the time of the attack. The act of rape is an extraordinarily powerful UCS for negative feelings—powerful enough to produce conditioning with a single pairing. The clothes, because they were associated with the crime, become a CS that elicits the same feelings. Even buildings can take on emotional bag-

Demonstrating

THE ASSOCIATION PRINCIPLE Classical conditioning principles show that learned associations are strong once established. Robert Cialdini notes that people want to be associated with good news and events and not associated with bad news and events. People associate themselves with their favorite sports team when they win, but not when they lose. When the team wins, people report, "We beat them, 17 to 14." When the team loses, people say, "They lost, 24 to 12." Have students record their friends' reactions to the wins and losses of sports teams in their school over the course of a season. They should see this phenomenon at work in their own environments.

trb At this point, you may wish to use **Enrichment Lesson:** *The Association Principle* (*Teacher's Resource Binder*, p. 15-1).

gage. Watch the facial expressions of students walking into your high school in the morning. Those who find school to be a generally pleasant experience will brighten up as soon as they walk through the door. Because it's a place associated with good things happening, the building itself can produce positive feelings. Unfortunately, the school will have the opposite effect on other students. Their associations are mostly negative, and the building will be a CS for negative emotions. Similarly, places of worship, favorite restaurants, hospitals, and the site of automobile accidents can all trigger emotions—some positive, some negative, but all classically conditioned.

▶ **John Garcia** (1917–) Identified, along with colleague Robert Koelling, the phenomenon of taste aversion, which established that classical conditioning was influenced by biological predispositions.

▶ **Robert Rescorla** (1940–) Developed, along with colleague Allan Wagner, a new theory that emphasized the importance of cognitive processes in classical conditioning.

Taste Aversion

In 1966, **John Garcia** and Robert Koelling showed how classically conditioned taste aversion—avoidance of certain tastes—could develop. While doing radiation research on rats, Garcia and Koelling noticed that the rats began to avoid drinking from the water bottles in the radiation chambers. Like Pavlov, these researchers became intrigued by this unexpected result of their research. In new trials, they discovered that it was possible to use a nausea-producing drug as a UCS to condition an aversion response to a particular taste. Paired with the drug that produced nausea, a particular food or drink became a CS that also produced the feelings of nausea. Have you ever felt sick shortly after eating a certain food? If that food lost its appeal as a result, you experienced a classically conditioned taste aversion.

John Garcia Raised in poverty, Garcia was unable to attend school regularly as a child. He was in his late twenties before starting junior college, and he didn't receive his Ph.D. until he was almost 50. Despite these obstacles, Garcia was elected to the National Academy of Sciences and received the American Psychological Association's Distinguished Scientific Contribution Award for his work in conditioning.

Cognition and Biological Predispositions

7. Why is it so important to understand the role of cognition and biological predispositions in learning?

For several decades before the 1980s, original research in classical conditioning had largely come to a halt. This was one area that researchers figured had been pretty much nailed. From Pavlov on, a growing body of evidence seemed to support the idea that this type of conditioning was purely behavioral and required only that a neutral stimulus be repeatedly paired with an unconditioned stimulus. This way of thinking became so well established that nobody bothered to question it anymore. **Robert Rescorla** and Allan Wagner were the psychologists who began to think out of the box. They realized that certain aspects of classical conditioning

MODULE 15

■ TEACHING TIP

Taste aversions are particularly good for illustrating classical conditioning. Share one of your own and explain it in terms of conditioning principles. If asked, students are sure to volunteer aversions of their own. Martin Bolt of Calvin College tells his students of his aversion to commercially produced frozen chicken dinners. He stored a dinner in the freezer compartment of his department's refrigerator. When he went to retrieve it, he found it in the company of a frozen laboratory rat. A student assistant, not knowing how to dispose of the deceased animal, had carefully packaged it in plastic and temporarily placed it in the freezer. He now finds all such dinners repulsive.

trb At this point, you may wish to use Critical Thinking Activity: *Human Taste Aversions* (*Teacher's Resource Binder*, p. 15-1).

F • Y • I

Secondary disgust is the aversion that reminds a person of something that is considered disgusting in its own right. For example, while okra is a perfectly good food to eat, many people find it disgusting since it becomes slimy when boiled. Paul Rozin notes how subjects in one of his experiments were presented with two pieces of chocolate fudge, one shaped to look like a muffin, the other a replica of dog droppings. Guess which one subjects avoided!

trb At this point, you may wish to use Critical Thinking Activity: *Human Taste Aversions* (*Teacher's Resource Binder*, p. 15-1).

Enriching

Some drug treatment programs use taste aversion techniques to get patients to quit using drugs. Have students investigate these programs.

- How do these treatment programs use taste aversion to get people to quit?
- Are they successful? Why or why not?
- Is it ethical to make someone sick on purpose, even if you are trying to help him or her overcome a devastating illness? Why or why not?

trb At this point, you may wish to use Critical Thinking Activity: *Human Taste Aversions* (*Teacher's Resource Binder*, p. 15-1).

MODULE 15

■ APPLYING THE POINTS

Have some students contact a local oncologist or cancer research center to see how they use knowledge of classical conditioning and taste aversions to help patients deal with nausea associated with chemotherapy and radiation. Encourage them to brief the class on their findings.

Close

Explain to students that the discovery of classical conditioning made behaviorism the dominant perspective in psychology. It seemed to explain the fundamentals of learning and avoided the scientifically messy concepts of consciousness and thinking. Yet Rescorla and Wagner's research showed that cognition also played a key role in determining what associations could and could not be learned. With this in mind, ask students the following questions:

- Why would scientists want to believe that thinking was absent from the process of classical conditioning?
- How can the study of classical conditioning and cognition together help people understand human behavior?

situations simply could not be explained without reference to *cognition*—the dreaded mental processes the behaviorists were trying to avoid.

Rescorla and Wagner (1972) conducted clever experiments showing that a simple pairing of stimuli is not enough to *ensure* conditioning. The key feature appears to be predictability. If a formerly neutral stimulus (*Flush!*) allows the learner to *reliably predict* that a UCS (hot water) is about to occur, the neutral stimulus will morph into a CS. If the UCS is not predictable, the neutral stimulus will stay neutral. If Pavlov's tuning fork tone had sometimes been followed by meat powder and sometimes not, it would not have become a CS, and the CR of drooling would not have developed. The tone would not have *reliably predicted* the UCS (meat powder). Calculating whether an event is predictable is, of course, a cognitive process, a mental assessment that requires thinking.

The biological perspective has influenced our understanding of another aspect of classical conditioning. Originally, psychologists thought the principles of classical conditioning would operate with any stimulus, for any species. This is not the case. Remember Garcia's work on taste aversion? We seem to be biologically predisposed to develop an aversion to the food we ate before getting sick, rather than to the place where we ate the food. I once got very ill the evening after eating cheddar cheese soup, which had been one of my favorite foods. Sure enough, I now have no desire to smell or taste this soup. Note that of all the stimuli that were present the evening I got sick, *only* the smell and taste of the soup produced an aversion. I was with my wife that evening, but I did not develop an aversion to her—thank goodness!

This biological predisposition to develop taste aversions may protect us from revisiting foods that could be poisonous and may be part of our evolutionary heritage. People who easily developed taste aversions were more likely to survive and have offspring. Those who snacked repeatedly on tainted food were less likely to live to reproduce. Other common fears—heights, thunderstorms, and snakes—may offer similar protection against threats that have existed since the beginning of human history (Cook & others, 1986). Perhaps unfortunately, we are less likely to fear modern, technological threats, like automobiles and unseen pollutants in the water supply. These significant threats to our well-being have not been around long enough to become part of the evolutionary "baggage" we will pass on to the next generations.

Classically Conditioned Taste Aversion Have you ever become sick after eating seafood? If so, you probably learned to avoid similar foods in the future. Why are taste aversions likely to develop?

Classical conditioning remains an important aspect of modern psychology. Research has moved us from a purely behavioral explanation of this type of learning to one that is more heavily influenced by cognitive and biological factors. Even so, classically conditioned behaviors and emotions are an important part of the world around us.

Module 15: Classical Conditioning

What's the Point?

1. *What is classical conditioning?*

Learning is any relatively permanent change in behavior due to experience. Classical conditioning is a type of *learning by association.* This means that two stimuli appear together in such a consistent and reliable way that one stimulus gains the power to predict the response that the other stimulus already produces. (A *stimulus* is anything one can respond to; a *response* is any behavior or action.) The behaviorist school of psychology, led by John Watson, was especially interested in classical conditioning because, at least in its early form, this type of learning focused on behavior, not mental processes. Contemporary psychologists are still interested in classical conditioning, but they realize that cognition (mental processes) influences almost all forms of learning.

Components of Classical Conditioning

2. *How does an unconditioned stimulus (UCS) differ from a conditioned stimulus (CS)? How does an unconditioned response (UCR) differ from a conditioned response (CR)?*

The five basic components of classical conditioning are the UCS, the UCR, a neutral response, the CS, and the CR.

A UCS is a stimulus (scalding hot water) that automatically triggers a response (jumping aside). A CS is a formerly neutral stimulus (a shout of *Flush!*) that—after repeated pairings with the UCS—has gained the power to trigger the same response that the UCS triggers.

A UCR is a reflexive, unlearned response (jumping aside) to something in the environment (scalding hot water). A CR does not differ from a UCR in content—the CR is the same as the UCR. But a CR differs in the way it has become linked to the stimulus; a CR is a *learned* response, not a reflexive and unlearned reaction (as the UCR is).

Classical Conditioning Processes

3. *What are the three basic processes in classical conditioning?*

The three basic processes in classical conditioning are

- *acquisition*—the process of developing a learned response through repeated pairings of the neutral stimulus with the UCS. To test whether acquisition has occurred, you would present the neutral stimulus without the UCS. If the response formerly made only to the UCS occurs, you would know that classical conditioning has taken place and the neutral stimulus has become a CS.
- *extinction*—the diminishing of a learned response by repeatedly presenting the CS alone, without presenting the UCS. The object is to weaken the association between the CS and the UCS.
- *spontaneous recovery*—the reappearance, after a rest period, of an extinguished CR (learned response). The "revived" CR will be weaker, and it will diminish more quickly, than the original CR.

Ivan Pavlov's Discovery

4. *What role did Ivan Pavlov play in the study of classical conditioning?*

Ivan Pavlov discovered classical conditioning during his research on the digestive

Checking the Points

■ TEACHING TIPS

web (1) The book companion site for *Thinking About Psychology* at www.worthpublishers.com/thinkingaboutpsych contains a module quiz, flashcards of key terms and people, as well as other student activities and resources for this module. You will also find PowerPoint lectures, a quiz grade book, and other teaching resources by logging on as an instructor.

trb (2) Students can test their understanding of module concepts by working in small groups to review the items in **Critical Thinking Activity:** *Defining Learning* (*Teacher's Resource Binder*, p. 15-1; **Handout 15–1**). Group members can take turns reading items aloud, responding to items, and finding passages in the text to either confirm each response or reveal the correct one. Challenge students to discover what they have learned during this review by not referring to a copy of the handout they may have filled out earlier in the module.

Reteaching

Use the following diagram to clarify the basic concepts of classical conditioning:

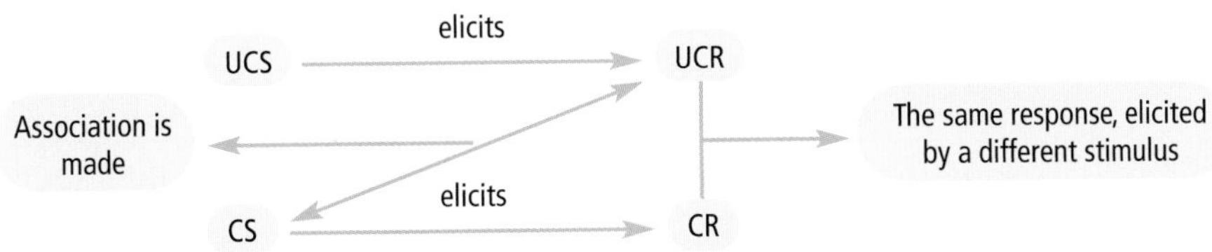

process. As the dogs in his study learned to anticipate eating, they drooled—which complicated Pavlov's research but piqued his scientific curiosity. In the history-making experiments we've discussed, the UCS was meat powder, the UCR was drooling, the (learned) CS was a tone, and the CR was drooling. Pavlov showed the processes of acquisition (the dog learned to drool at the sound of a tuning fork), extinction (the dog stopped drooling when the tone no longer predicted food), and spontaneous recovery (the dog again drooled in response to the sound of the tuning fork after a rest period).

Generalization and Discrimination

5. *What are generalization and discrimination, and in what way can they be considered opposites?*

   Generalization is a process in which we make the same response ("High Five") to two similar stimuli (big win in basketball; big achievement on an exam). Discrimination is a process in which we make different responses to two similar stimuli (High Five to our team's big win in basketball; silence and sad faces to the opponents' big win in basketball). We can consider these two processes to be opposites in the sense that the first (generalization) enlarges the number of occasions on which we make a specific response, but the second (discrimination) diminishes the number of occasions on which we make that response.

Classical Conditioning in Everyday Life

6. *How did John Watson and Rosalie Rayner demonstrate that emotions can be classically conditioned?*

   In their famous "Little Albert" research, Watson and Rayner used classical conditioning to instill a fear of rats in an 11-month-old boy. They first presented a white laboratory rat and showed that the baby had no fear of rats. Then they paired the rat's appearance with loud noises, which by themselves produced a fear reaction in the child. After repeated pairings, the rat alone would produce the fear reaction. In this experiment, the loud noise was the UCS, fear was the UCR, the rat was the CS, and fear was the CR. Watson and Rayner wanted to show that fear could be caused by learning, not by deep Freudian conflicts. Contemporary psychologists would consider this research unethical because it harmed the participant. Nevertheless, the idea of using classical conditioning to associate emotions with specific objects or images is now a major element in product advertising and affects us in many ways in our daily lives.

Cognition and Biological Predispositions

7. *Why is it so important to understand the role of cognition and biological predispositions in learning?*

   Researchers have demonstrated that even learning acquired through classical conditioning is affected by our thought processes. The learner must recognize that the CS reliably predicts the CR, and this recognition is a mental process (cognition). Biological predispositions—our inborn tendencies—make us less likely to do things (playing with snakes and spiders) that might threaten our lives. Ancestors who failed to avoid such dangers did not live to reproduce.

Key Terms

learning, p. 281
classical conditioning, p. 281
stimulus, p. 281
response, p. 282
behaviorism, p. 283
cognition, p. 283
unconditioned stimulus (UCS), p. 283
unconditioned response (UCR), p. 284
conditioned stimulus (CS), p. 284
conditioned response (CR), p. 284
acquisition, p. 284
extinction, p. 285
spontaneous recovery, p. 285
generalization, p. 289
discrimination, p. 289

Key People

John Watson, p. 283
Ivan Pavlov, p. 286
Rosalie Rayner, p. 290
John Garcia, p. 293
Robert Rescorla, p. 293

Self-Test

Multiple-Choice Questions

Choose the *best* answer for each of the following questions:

1. Bert has an old, broken-down vacuum cleaner that frequently shorts out and delivers a painful electric shock to his hand. He has learned that the vacuum's motor always starts to hum loudly just before the shock. Now Bert removes his hand before getting shocked. The hum is a ________________ because it has been repeatedly paired with the shock.
   a. UCS
   b. UCR
   c. CS
   d. CR

2. Charlene's grandparents got a new puppy. Unfortunately, the puppy is not yet trained, and it jumps up on people, including Charlene, who is only three. After being knocked down repeatedly, Charlene became afraid of the puppy. Recently, she has been afraid of all the other dogs she sees, too. Charlene's recent fear of all dogs is a clear example of
   a. discrimination.
   b. generalization.
   c. a biological predisposition.
   d. spontaneous recovery.

3. Ricky was hiking in the woods when he heard a rustling noise in the leaves where he had just stepped. Ricky, who has never been harmed by a snake, instantly jumped forward a full two feet, fearing a snake might be near his foot. Psychologists would explain Ricky's fear of snakes as a(n)
   a. biological predisposition that may help Ricky survive.
   b. example of spontaneous recovery of an old childhood fear.
   c. sensible response based on Ricky's ability to generalize.
   d. example of behaviorism.

4. Mr. X is quite elderly and he lives alone. His nephew, Al (who was named after Mr. X), thinks Mr. X might enjoy having a pet, but he knows Mr. X does not have the energy to take care of a dog or a cat. Al thinks carefully, and he decides a tame white rat in a cage might be just the right choice. When he pulls the cover off the cage and shouts "Surprise!" Mr. X screams and looks terrified. Al seems to have found the man who many years earlier was the child in
   a. Watson and Rayner's experiments on conditioning fear.
   b. Pavlov's experiments on classical conditioning.

MODULE 15

trb tr ■ TEACHING TIP

To help students review module concepts and vocabulary as well as confirm what they have learned about classical conditioning, use **Building Vocabulary: Graphic Organizer:** *Concept Web* (*Teacher's Resource Binder*, p. 15-1; **Handout 15–2**) as a transparency that may be projected for the class to view. Help students fill out the web correctly with the words from the word bank. If students have filled in the handout earlier, ask them not to refer to those earlier versions.

tb Using the Test Bank

The *Test Bank* that accompanies this textbook offers a wide variety of questions in different formats and levels of complexity. Use the software to construct whole tests or to integrate standardized questions into teacher-made tests.

Self-Test Answers

Multiple-Choice Questions

1. c, 2. b, 3. a, 4. a

MODULE 15

Self-Test Answers

Multiple-Choice Questions (continued)

5. d, 6. a

Matching Terms and Definitions

7. a. (11), b. (6), c. (4), d. (2), e. (3), f. (5), g. (1), h. (9), i. (12), j. (7)

Fill-in-the-Blank Questions

8. Unconditioned stimulus; Unconditioned response; Conditioned stimulus; Conditioned response

c. Freud's experiments on the connection between fear and unresolved conflicts.
d. Garcia's experiments on taste aversion and rats.

5. Bob is working as a research assistant in the psychology department for the summer. Dr. Solario, the researcher Bob works for, is studying the effect of thinking on classical conditioning. ________ ________ would approve of Dr. Solario's interests.
   a. Rosalie Rayner
   b. John Watson
   c. Ivan Pavlov
   d. Robert Rescorla

6. Elise's parents read her a bedtime story each night, which is one of Elise's favorite parts of the day. While they read, Elise happily hugs Teddy, her stuffed bear. Today, Elise started preschool, and she insisted on taking Teddy to school with her. Teddy is apparently a ______________ that produces the same response (feeling secure and comfortable) produced by the parents' presence at bedtime, which is a ______________.
   a. CS; UCS
   b. UCS; CS
   c. CS; CR
   d. UCS; UCR

Matching Terms and Definitions

7. For each definition, choose the *best* matching term from the list that follows:

Definition

a. Any behavior or action.
b. In classical conditioning, the response to the conditioned stimulus.
c. A type of learning where a stimulus gains the power to cause a response because it predicts another stimulus that already produces the response.
d. In classical conditioning, the automatic response to the unconditioned stimulus.
e. A relatively permanent change in behavior due to experience.
f. In classical conditioning, a previously neutral stimulus that, through learning, has gained the power to cause a conditioned response.
g. In classical conditioning, a stimulus that triggers a response automatically and reflexively.
h. Anything in the environment that one can respond to.
i. The view that psychology should restrict its efforts to studying observable behaviors and not mental processes.
j. Mental processes associated with thinking, knowing, and remembering.

Term

(1) UCS
(2) UCR
(3) learning
(4) classical conditioning
(5) CS
(6) CR
(7) cognition
(8) taste aversion
(9) stimulus
(10) acquisition
(11) response
(12) behaviorism

Fill-in-the-Blank Questions

8. The five components of classical conditioning are the
   - ______________, a stimulus that triggers a response automatically and reflexively.
   - ______________, the automatic response to the unconditioned stimulus.
   - ______________, a previously neutral stimulus that, through training, has gained the power to cause a conditioned response.
   - ________ ________, the response to the conditioned stimulus.

- _______________, something in the environment that does not trigger the conditioned response.

9. The three main processes that occur during classical conditioning are (a) _______________, the process of developing a CR; (b) _______________, the diminishing of a CR; and (c) ________ ________, the reappearance, after a rest period, of an extinguished CR.

10. The person who is famous for discovering classical conditioning is ________ ________.

Brief Essay Question

11. At the beginning of the school year, a relatively quiet new beeping fire alarm was installed. When it went off one day for a fire drill in September, the students didn't respond to this new sound. Teachers had to usher them out the doors. However, in October the new beeping alarm went off as the halls filled with smoke. Frightened students hurried out of the school to safety. In November, the beeping alarm went off again, and the students again hurried out fearfully. However, this time it was only a fire drill, so there was no fire. Then for 10 days straight in December, the alarm malfunctioned and went off daily. Now no one paid any attention to it again. After Christmas break, the alarm was repaired and went off as scheduled for a drill in January. Several students jumped anxiously, remembering the October fire. In two paragraphs, describe how students in this story were classically conditioned to that new beeping fire alarm. Use the terms *neutral stimulus, UCS, UCR, CR, CS, extinction,* and *spontaneous recovery.*

Self-Test Answers

Fill-in-the-Blank Questions (continued)

8. Neutral stimulus, 9. acquisition; extinction; spontaneous recovery, 10. Ivan Pavlov

Brief Essay Question

11. In their answers, students should show their understanding of classical conditioning, and of the terms *neutral stimulus, UCS, UCR, CR, CS, extinction,* and *spontaneous recovery.* Students should explain that the first time the alarm sounded, it was a neutral stimulus. The second time it went off, it was associated with the UCS of smoke from a real fire, and the alarm became a CS. In November, the alarm functioned as a CS and students fled the building. But then in December, after repeated false alarms, extinction occurred. By January, spontaneous recovery had occurred as students recalled the early association of alarm and smoke.

MODULE 16

Performance Standards

Standard Area: Learning

Content Standard 1: Understanding learning

Performance Standard 1.1 Understand learning from a psychological paradigm.

- Discuss the influential historical figures in the study of learning. Investigate the findings of such researchers as Edward Thorndike and B. F. Skinner. (Student Text pp. 301–302, 304–306)

Content Standard 3: Understanding operant conditioning

Performance Standard 3.1 Understand the principles of operant conditioning.

- Explore a real-world example of operant conditioning, a child crying for candy in a store. (Student Text p. 300)
- Figure 16.1, "An Operant Conditioning System, " illustrates how a child operantly conditions her mother to give her candy. (Student Text p. 301)
- Define Edward Thorndike's law of effect and how it is used to modify behavior. (Student Text pp. 301–302)
- Discuss the role of reinforcement in learning. Distinguish between positive and negative reinforcement through real-world examples. (Student Text pp. 303–306)
- Figure 16.2, "Reinforcement Strengthens Behavior," illustrates the difference between positive and negative reinforcement on behavior. (Student Text p. 303)
- Compare how immediate and delayed reinforcement affect learning. (Student Text pp. 306–307)
- Investigate the differences between primary and secondary reinforcement. (Student Text pp. 307–308)
- Figure 16.3, "Primary and Secondary Reinforcements," illustrates the basic differences between these types of reinforcers. (Student Text p. 307)
- Explore how punishment affects behavior. Discuss how punishment can be ineffective. (Student Text pp. 308–310)
- Compare the two forms of punishment. (Student Text p. 308)
- Figure 16.4, "Punishment Weakens Behavior," illustrates the differences between the two forms of punishment and the results on behavior. (Student Text p. 308)
- Investigate how operant conditioning can be used to teach a new behavior. Explain the concepts of shaping, discrimination, and extinction. (Student Text pp. 310–311)
- Compare continuous and partial reinforcement schedules. Compare fixed-interval, fixed-ratio, variable-interval, and variable-ratio schedules of reinforcement through real-world examples. (Student Text pp. 312–315)
- Figure 16.5, "The Cumulative Record," reveals the patterns of responding for partial schedules of reinforcement. (Student Text p. 313)
- Investigate the role of cognition in operant conditioning. (Student Text pp. 316–317)
- Discuss the role of biology in operant conditioning. (Student Text pp. 317–318)

Content Standard 4: The role of cognition in learning

Performance Standard 4.2 Explain the role of cognition in learning.

- Discuss latent learning as an example of how thinking affects our learning. (Student Text pp. 316–317)
- Investigate Tolman's research on cognitive maps. Discuss how these findings demonstrated that learning occurs cognitively before it is expressed behaviorally. (Student Text pp. 316–317)
- Define the overjustification effect. Discuss how grades can lead to overjustification. (Student Text p. 317)

Content Standard 5: Investigate how biology and culture influence learning

Performance Standard 5.1 Understand the influence of biology on learning.

- Discuss why the principles of operant conditioning don't work equally well for all behaviors in all species, that an animal's biology predisposes it to learn certain behaviors easily and others with difficulty. Explain how a pigeon easily learns to peck at a disc for food but has difficulty learning to flap its wings for food. (Student Text pp. 317–318)

Materials NETWORK

All of the items from the Video, Activity, and Enrichment Centers listed below come from the *Teacher's Resource Binder.* These items will help you teach and expand on concepts presented in Module 16.

trb This logo indicates when an item from the Materials Network may be used in conjunction with a specific note found in this module's *Teacher's Edition.*

What Is Operant Conditioning?

Activity Center

- Critical Thinking Activity: *Consequences and Their Effects* With this activity, students discriminate among the concepts in the module. (*Teacher's Resource Binder*, p. 16-1; Handout 16–1)
- Building Vocabulary: Graphic Organizers: *Concept Flowcharts* (*Teacher's Resource Binder*, p. 16-1; Handouts 16–2 and 16–3)
- Technology Application Activity: *PsychSim:* "Operant Conditioning" Students are exposed to the principles of reinforcement. (*Teacher's Resource Binder*, p. 16-1)

The Law of Effect

Enrichment Center

- Enrichment Lesson: *Beyond Freedom and Dignity* This lesson addresses B. F. Skinner's views. (*Teacher's Resource Binder*, p. 16-1)
- Enrichment Lesson: *Walden Two, Los Horcones, and the Twin Oaks* These communities use operant conditioning principles. (*Teacher's Resource Binder*, p. 16-1)

Reinforcement

Activity Center

- Technology Application Activity: *Positive Reinforcement On-Line Tutorial* This is an on-line tutorial for understanding positive reinforcement. (*Teacher's Resource Binder*, p. 16-1)
- Critical Thinking Activity: *Negative Reinforcement Versus Punishment* Students discriminate among module concepts. (*Teacher's Resource Binder*, p. 16-1; Handout 16–4 and Transparency Master 16–1)
- Critical Thinking Activity: *Examples of Negative Reinforcement* Further explore the concept of negative reinforcement. (*Teacher's Resource Binder*, p. 16-1; Transparency Master 16–2)

Punishment

Enrichment Center

- Enrichment Lesson: *The Self-Injurious Behavior Inhibiting System (SIBIS)* This lesson addresses a system that has been used with austistic children. (*Teacher's Resource Binder*, p. 16-1)

Some Reinforcement Procedures

Activity Center

- Technology Application Activity: *Clicker Training and Operant Conditioning* Karen Pryor developed this technique to train pets. (*Teacher's Resource Binder*, p. 16-1; Handout 16–5)
- Application Activity: *Conditioning the Instructor's Behavior* For the brave instructor only! (*Teacher's Resource Binder*, p. 16-1)
- Cooperative Learning Activity: *Shaping Demonstration* Working together, students train each other. (*Teacher's Resource Binder*, p. 16-1)

Enrichment Center

- Enrichment Lesson: *Transforming Couch Potatoes with Operant Conditioning* This technique encourages children to exercise. (*Teacher's Resource Binder*, p. 16-1)

Schedules of Reinforcement

Activity Center

- Analysis Activity: *Consideration of Future Consequences Scale* Use this scale to measure students' ability to delay gratification. (*Teacher's Resource Binder*, p. 16-1; Handout 16–6)
- Application Activity: *Partial Reinforcement Schedules* This activity allows students to apply their knowledge of partial reinforcement schedules. (*Teacher's Resource Binder*, p. 16-1; Handout 16–7)

New Understandings of Operant Conditioning

Activity Center

- Technology Application Activity: *PsychSim:* "Maze Learning" With this interactive CD-ROM tutorial, students train a rat. (*Teacher's Resource Binder*, p. 16-1)
- Critical Thinking Activity: *The Overjustification Effect* This activity shows how overjustification works in school. (*Teacher's Resource Binder*, p. 16-1)

Enrichment Center

- Enrichment Lesson: *The Overjustification Effect* This lesson details how overjustification works. (*Teacher's Resource Binder*, p. 16-1)
- Enrichment Lesson: *Superstitious Behavior* B. F. Skinner made observations to help explain superstitous behavrior. (*Teacher's Resource Binder*, p. 16-1)

MODULE 16

Operant Conditioning

Introducing the Module

The Points: Module Objectives

- Explain the law of effect, and how it can be used to modify behavior.
- Describe how positive and negative reinforcements work, and how they differ.
- Evaluate which type of reward affects our learning more—immediate rewards or delayed rewards.
- Differentiate between primary and secondary reinforcement.
- Analyze how punishment influences behavior and why it tends to be ineffective.
- Explain how you can use operant conditioning to teach a new behavior.
- Describe how we learn to behave differently in response to similar stimuli, and how we manage to get rid of behaviors we have learned.
- Describe the advantages and disadvantages of continuous reinforcement.
- Identify the four partial reinforcement schedules and how they differ.
- Evaluate how latent learning and the overjustification effect demonstrate that mental processes affect operant conditioning.
- Analyze why the principles of operant conditioning do not work equally well for all behaviors in all species.

trb Building Vocabulary

Building Vocabulary: Graphic Organizers: *Concept Flowcharts* (*Teacher's Resource Binder*, p. 16-1; **Handouts 16–2** and **16–3**) offer students opportunities to improve their understanding of the module's terms.

- *Concept Flowchart—Operant Conditioning: The Basics* (**Handout 16–2**) shows how the core concepts of operant conditioning are related to each other.
- *Concept Flowchart—Reinforcement* (**Handout 16–3**) offers students an opportunity to work with only the concepts related to reinforcement.

MODULE 16

Operant Conditioning

What Is Operant Conditioning?

A few years ago, I was in the grocery store on a busy, preholiday afternoon. In front of me in the checkout line was a mother and her preschool-aged daughter. When the girl spotted the candy bar display, she asked if she could have one. Mom, clearly tired and running out of patience on a hectic day, said, "No." The girl, a wee bit cranky herself, started to fuss, and the battle was on. It quickly escalated to a full-fledged tantrum on the girl's part and yelling on the mom's. A short while later, the mother apparently decided the girl was not about to settle down while they waited to complete their purchase. With an exasperated "Here, just take it and be quiet," she tossed a candy bar toward the girl, who instantly went from tantrum-mode to a bright smile as she tore into the treat.

You may be thinking, "Aha! That little girl certainly had her mother trained." Actually, both the mother's and the daughter's behaviors were affected by a type of learning called **operant conditioning.** In operant conditioning the *frequency* of a behavior (how often it occurs) depends on its *consequence* (the event that follows the behavior). When psychologists do research on operant conditioning, they often manipulate consequences in order to either increase or decrease how often a behavior happens. The mother in the grocery store was inadvertently using operant conditioning to teach her daughter to throw tantrums. At the same time, the daughter was unknowingly using operant conditioning to teach her mother to buy her candy (Figure 16.1). You decide who was the more effective psychologist!

Operant conditioning is not the least bit complicated in its most basic form. Let's say your parents began to hand you a $100 bill each evening if you cleared your own dinner dishes from the table after completing your

▶ **operant conditioning** A type of learning in which the frequency of a behavior depends on the consequence that follows that behavior.

Getting Started

Before students begin reading this module, ask them to imagine themselves as parents of a small child. How would they teach the child to behave well in public places, such as stores, movie theaters, or restaurants? As students learn about operant conditioning, have them review and, if need be, revise their initial teaching strategies.

trb You may wish to use **Critical Thinking Activity:** *Consequences and Their Effects* (*Teacher's Resource Binder*, p. 16-1; **Handout 16–1**) to get students thinking about the relationship between behavior and consequences. The activity will prime students to discriminate among various concepts in the module.

Figure 16.1 **Operant Conditioning for Better or for Worse** This child is using operant conditioning to train her mother to buy candy, while the mother is operantly conditioning the child to have tantrums.

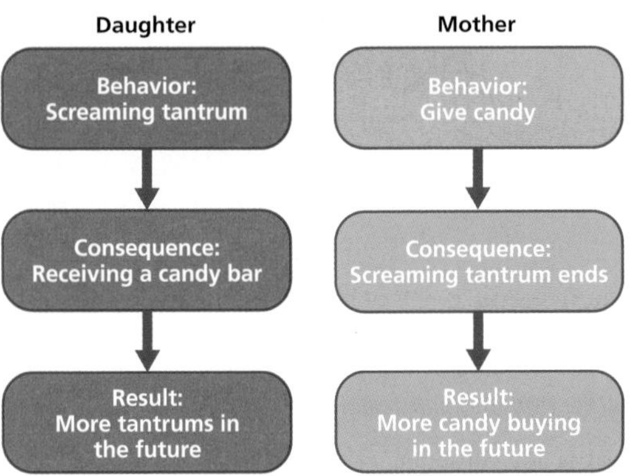

meal. Would this consequence influence your dish-clearing behavior? Most likely you would begin to clear your dishes more regularly and more quickly than before. What if your parents somehow wired the television so you received a painful electric shock every time you touched the power button on the set or the remote? The shock is a consequence, too. Would it influence the frequency with which you touched the power button?

Wouldn't it be great if we could influence others—parents, siblings, friends, teachers, employers—to behave the way we want them to? The pair in the grocery store stumbled upon a powerful behavior-changing tool. Let's take a closer look at how operant conditioning techniques work.

The Law of Effect

What's the Point? 1. What is the law of effect, and how can it be used to modify behavior?

Edward Thorndike, an early American psychologist, first presented the law of effect, from which operant conditioning later developed. The *law of effect* simply states that behaviors with favorable consequences will occur more frequently, and behaviors followed by less favorable consequences will occur less frequently. **B. F. Skinner** built his life's

▶ **Edward Thorndike** (1874–1949) Author of the law of effect, the principle that forms the basis of operant conditioning.

▶ **B. F. Skinner** (1904–1990) Developed the fundamental principles and techniques of operant conditioning and devised ways to apply them in the real world.

MODULE 16

Teaching the Points

■ TEACHING TIPS

web (1) You can log on as an instructor to the book companion site for *Thinking About Psychology* at **www.worthpublishers.com/thinkingaboutpsych.** It contains teacher resources for class presentations as well as review and assessment of module concepts and terms.

(2) Use the following Web sites as teacher-preparation, enrichment, or remediation tools:

- Mark Plonsky's very useful library at **www.uwsp.edu/psych/dog/lib-sci.htm** has a large number of links organized into the categories of classical conditioning, operant conditioning, biological constraints on learning, cognitive views, and other issues.
- John Krantz's Tutorials and Demonstrations (**http://psych.hanover.edu/Krantz/tutor.html**) also contain useful information on operant conditioning, in addition to other topics in psychology.

tr (3) A four-color transparency of Figure 16.1, An Operant Conditioning System, is available in the **Overhead Transparencies Set.**

Suggested Readings

Use the following books as teacher-preparation tools or as enrichment for advanced students:

Allen, B. (2000). *Personality theories: Development, growth, and diversity* (3rd ed.). Boston: Allyn & Bacon.

Bellack, A. S., & Hersen, M. (1977). *Behavior modification: An introductory textbook.* New York: Oxford University Press.

Coon, D. (1977). *Introduction to psychology: Exploration and application.* New York: West.

Deci, E. L. (1980). *The psychology of self-determination.* Lexington, MA: Heath.

Deci, E. L., & Ryan, R. M. (1985). *Intrinsic motivation and self-determination in human behavior.* New York: Plenum.

Grasha, A. F. (1995). *Practical applications of psychology* (4th ed.) New York: HarperCollins.

Hulse, S. H., Deese, J. E., & Smith, H. E. (1980). *The psychology of learning* (5th ed.). New York: McGraw-Hill.

MODULE 16

F • Y • I

web The text mentions that communal societies began using Skinner's operant conditioning principles. Two such societies are still in existence today.

- Los Horcones, in the mountains of Mexico, maintains a Web site at www.loshorcones.org.mx. Of special interest at the site is the section "Misunderstandings About Behavior Analysis and Radical Behaviorism," which tries to refute common objections to the use of Skinnerian concepts in daily life.
- Twin Oaks, a community in rural Virginia, maintains a large Web site at www.twinoaks.org that describes its policies and activities, including Saturday tours and a three-week visitor program.

trb At this point, you may wish to use **Enrichment Lesson:** *Walden Two, Los Horcones, and the Twin Oaks Communities* (*Teacher's Resource Binder*, p. 16-1).

■ **JOURNAL WRITING**

Invite students to use the following questions and writing prompts as springboards for entries in their psychology journals:

- What are some behaviors that you find particularly reinforcing? Punishing? How have these been used effectively in your life?
- In what ways have you conditioned your parents' behavior? In what ways have you been conditioned by them?

Reinforcement and the Law of Effect Fishing crews in the Cayman Islands have cleaned their catch in this bay for years, thus providing an easy meal for the stingrays that live in the surrounding waters. The rays began to hang around, and then divers and swimmers began feeding them by hand, and even petting them. Can you see how the law of effect has been at work in this situation?

work on this idea, developing the fundamental principles and techniques of operant conditioning (see Psychology Is a Science: B. F. Skinner, pages 304–305). Two of the more important concepts used in operant conditioning are *reinforcement* and *punishment.*

- **Reinforcement** is any consequence that *increases* the future likelihood of a behavior.
- **Punishment** is any consequence that *decreases* the future likelihood of a behavior.

Keep in mind that the learner, not the teacher, casts the vote that determines whether a consequence will be a reinforcement or a punishment. When my two children were younger, they had very different feelings about broccoli. Carl really liked broccoli, and if I had given him some after he did a chore, he would have been more likely to do the chore in the future. For him, broccoli was a *reinforcement.* But Eric did *not* like broccoli. If I had given Eric broccoli after he did a chore, he probably would never have done that chore again. Broccoli was a *punishment* for Eric. My feelings about broccoli (which I like, especially with cheese sauce) make no difference.

Hi and Lois

Who Teaches Whom? What behavior has been reinforced!?

Suggested Readings *(continued)*

Lepper, M. R., & Greene, D. (Eds.). (1979). *The hidden costs of rewards.* Hillsdale, NJ: Erlbaum.

Logue, A. W. (1995). *Self-control: Waiting until tomorrow for what you want today.* Englewood Cliffs, NJ: Prentice Hall.

Malott, R. W., Ritterby, K., & Wolf, E. L. C. (1973). *An introduction to behavior modification.* Kalamazoo, MI: Behaviordelia.

Skinner, B. F. (1971). *Beyond freedom and dignity.* New York: Knopf.

Skinner, B. F. (1948). *Walden two.* New York: Macmillan.

Skinner, B. F. (Ed.). (1972). *Cumulative record: A selection of papers* (3rd ed.). New York: Appleton-Century.

Smith, W. I. (1978). *Conditioning and instrumental learning* (2nd ed.). New York: McGraw-Hill.

Parents and other authority figures don't always understand this aspect of consequences. A parent will sometimes yell at a child for misbehavior, thinking that yelling is a form of punishment. However, a child who is usually ignored may view getting yelled at as a form of desired parental attention. If this is the case, the law of effect predicts the behavior that preceded the parent's yelling will be *more* likely to happen again. Likewise, a school administrator might suspend a student from school for skipping class, not realizing that for a student who doesn't care for school, this punishment is not a punishment at all: it may even make future skipping *more* likely!

▶ **reinforcement** Any consequence that *increases* the likelihood of a behavior.

▶ **punishment** Any consequence that *decreases* the likelihood of a behavior.

▶ **positive reinforcement** In operant conditioning, anything that increases the likelihood of a behavior by following it with a desirable event or state.

▶ **negative reinforcement** In operant conditioning, anything that increases the likelihood of a behavior by following it with the *removal* of an undesirable event or state.

Reinforcement

2. How do positive and negative reinforcements work, and how do they differ from each other?

Reinforcement procedures strengthen responses by making them more likely to occur again. There are two ways to reinforce a behavior: *positive reinforcement* and *negative reinforcement* (Figure 16.2).

Positive reinforcement occurs when a behavior is followed by a desirable event or state. For example, if a parent pays her son $10 for the behavior of earning an *A* in psychology, she has positively reinforced his behavior.

Negative reinforcement occurs when a behavior ends an undesirable event or state. This is a tricky concept. Note that the behavior is a means of either *escaping* or *avoiding* an undesirable situation. The words *positive* and *negative* in this context do not mean "good" and "bad." Here, *positive* simply means that something desirable is *presented.* And *negative* means that something undesirable is *removed.* For example, Roshni's headache is undesirable. If taking aspirin provides

POSITIVE REINFORCEMENT

Behavior is followed by a desirable event or state.

$10 for an A makes it more likely a student will earn more As.

NEGATIVE REINFORCEMENT

Behavior ends an undesirable event or state.

Taking aspirin relieves headaches and makes it more likely that aspirin will be taken in the future.

Figure 16.2 **Reinforcement Strengthens Behavior** Positive and negative reinforcement work differently, but both types of reinforcement make a behavior more likely to happen again.

MODULE 16

■ **TEACHING TIP**

To help students understand the goals of negative reinforcement and punishment, summarize the difference between these concepts with the following summary: "Negative reinforcement and punishment are used for entirely different purposes. **Negative reinforcement** strengthens behaviors, whereas **punishment** weakens behaviors."

trb tr A black-line master for Figure 16.2, Reinforcement Strengthens Behavior, is available in the **Black-Line Masters Appendix** of the *Teacher's Resource Binder.*

trb tr At this point, you may wish to use **Critical Thinking Activity:** ***Negative Reinforcement Versus Punishment*** (*Teacher's Resource Binder*, p. 16-1; **Handout 16–4** and **Transparency Master 16–1**).

Cooperative Learning

Have students get into small groups, challenging them to list the different types of behavior modification techniques their parents have used over the years on them and their siblings. Create a master list of the class's answers, analyzing what category of reinforcement or punishment each technique falls under.

trb At this point, you may want to use **Technology Application Activity:** ***PsychSim: Operant Conditioning*** (*Teacher's Resource Binder*, p. 16-1).

MODULE 16

(F • Y • I)

B. F. Skinner's work with animals spurred research and work in training all kinds of animals to serve useful purposes. In World War II, Skinner trained pigeons to guide missiles to their targets. While the military at that time didn't buy into Skinner's pigeons (nobody wanted to admit they used ordinary pigeons to win the war), these animals were more effective than humans at identifying their targets. Jim Simmons, Ph.D., a Navy scientist, trained pigeons for use by the Coast Guard in conducting search and rescue missions. While humans were 38% accurate at identifying targets, pigeons were 93% accurate—and they didn't get bored after being on duty for hours.

Source: Azar, B. (2002, October). Pigeons as baggage screeners, rats as rescuers. *Monitor on Psychology, 33*(9). Washington, DC: American Psychological Association.

trb At this point, you may wish to use **Technology Application Activity:** *PsychSim:* "Operant Conditioning" (*Teacher's Resource Binder*, p. 16-1).

web ■ **TEACHING TIP**

SeaWorld has developed an animal behavior unit targeted for students in grades 4–8. Although not on a high school level, you may find their descriptions of training marine animals relevant to the discussion of animal training that Skinner used with operant conditioning. You can find the unit plan online at **www.seaworld.org/teacherguides/pdf/b&t-4-8.pdf.**

trb At this point, you may wish to use **Technology Application Activity:** *Clicker Training and Operant Conditioning* (*Teacher's Resource Binder*, p. 16-1; **Handout 16–5**).

■ **APPLYING THE POINTS**

Contact a local university to see if their psychology department has any old Skinner boxes in their inventory. Ask if a professor will come to class and demonstrate how the Skinner box works and what studies are done today using Skinner boxes.

Psychology is a Science

B. F. Skinner

Few have done more than B. F. Skinner (1904–1990) to advance the notion of psychology as a scientific discipline. In one recent study, almost 2000 psychologists ranked Skinner as the most eminent psychologist of the twentieth century (Haggbloom & others, 2002). Through his work and his writing, Skinner spent his career developing a behavioral "technology" that did not rely on references to unseen thought processes. His goal was to understand and control the actions of other organisms. His new technology was operant conditioning.

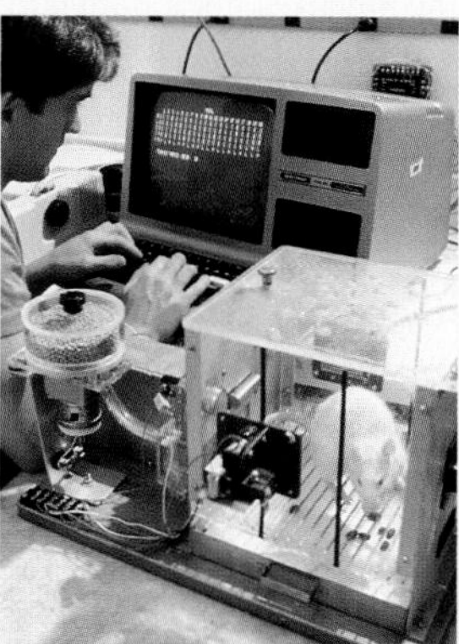

A Rat in an Operant Chamber This rat, in a Skinner box, or operant chamber, has been taught to press a bar for a food reinforcement.

Skinner believed that all behaviors in all species are governed by the same principles. To identify these principles, Skinner studied simple behaviors, mostly of rats and pigeons. He and his assistants taught rats to press a lever with their paws, and pigeons to peck a disk with their beaks. The rats and pigeons performed these acts in an invention that Skinner called an *operant chamber*, but that most others call a *Skinner box*. The box gave the experimenter an opportunity to control the environment and precisely record an animal's responses. Using this arrangement, Skinner identified principles that he felt could be used to understand and control complicated behaviors in the real world.

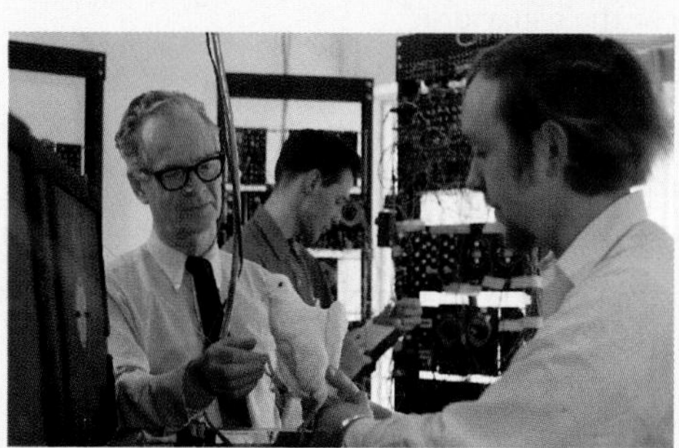

B. F. Skinner in the Laboratory

Skinner, never content to limit himself to the laboratory, became a ceaseless advocate for his point of view. He was frequently the center of controversy because of many books and articles written by and about him. Skinner's public fame started when a 1945 magazine article detailed how he and his wife were using a climate-controlled "air crib" for their

relief from the headache, Roshni's behavior of taking aspirin has been negatively reinforced. Negative reinforcement, like all reinforcement, *strengthens* a behavior. So, Roshni becomes more likely to take aspirin to escape a headache in the future.

The "Baby in the Box" B. F. Skinner's daughter spent time in this specially designed environment. Some thought this was awful, others thought it was less of a problem than a standard baby crib with bars.

daughter (which some felt was too similar to a rat's or pigeon's operant chamber). Skinner stayed in the public eye for the rest of his career. In the late 1940s, he published *Walden Two,* a novel presenting his ideas for a perfect community based on principles of operant conditioning. In the book, Skinner criticized democracy, the nuclear family, the use of money, and religion. But he still managed to inspire a number of groups to actually start communities that avoided punishment and used reinforcement to encourage desirable behaviors. Some are still in existence, including Los Horcones in Sonora, Mexico, where Skinner believed his principles were applied most appropriately. In the 1970s, Skinner published *Beyond Freedom and Dignity,* describing his belief that human freedom was an illusion. This sparked enough public discussion to land him on the covers of national news magazines.

Skinner loved the debate and was passionate about defending his positions and the science on which they were based. His final speech, delivered at the American Psychological Association convention only eight days before he died of leukemia, was a spirited defense of behaviorism and critique of cognitive "science," which he believed wasn't scientific at all (Skinner, 1990).

Skinner's viewpoints were extreme, but his work does have a number of successful, practical applications. As you will see throughout this module, operant conditioning principles affect our behavior at home, in school, and at work. Skinner may not have always won people's hearts and minds, but he did contribute importantly to our understanding of learned behavior and the development of psychology as a science.

The concept of negative reinforcement can be confusing at first. Sometimes students think it is simply a more technical term for punishment, but this is not the case. Punishment, as we will see soon, weakens a behavior. Negative reinforcement always strengthens a behavior that

F • Y • I

(1) Walden Two was also the blueprint for Twin Oaks, a small community founded in 1967 near Richmond, Virginia. Still in existence, it is one of the longest-running and largest communes (Twin Oaks prefers the term "intentional community") in the country. Located on 450 acres of farms, fields, and woods, its present population consists of 87 adults and 13 children (ranging in age from 2 to 75) who share income and property.

(2) Skinner held that our beliefs in human freedom and dignity were illusions. He believed we are slaves to our environment and not actually free to do as we choose. Skinner argued that denial of the fact that our environment controls us leaves us vulnerable to control by subtle and malignant circumstances as well as by malicious people. Governments and political leaders, he contended, may seek to control us for their own benefit rather than to serve our best interests. Recognizing that behavior is shaped by its consequences is the first step in taking control of the environment and ensuring that it delivers consequences promoting desirable behavior. When we demand freedom, argued Skinner, what we really mean is freedom from aversive consequences, not freedom to make choices. In the final analysis, we can have "freedom" but only by arranging our own consequences, not by leaving it to "fate" or the "government."

trb At this point, you may wish to use **Enrichment Lesson:** *Walden Two, Los Horcones, and the Twin Oaks* (*Teacher's Resource Binder,* p. 16-1).

MODULE 16

■ TEACHING TIP

Students may consider "time out" a negative reinforcement technique. Traditional time out is not actually a negative reinforcement technique. Sitting a child in a chair in the corner for a period of time is really **omission training**—depriving someone of something they want in order to teach the person not to do the undesired behavior any longer. Omission training is a form of punishment, not reinforcement. If getting out of time out were tied to a behavior, then it would qualify as negative reinforcement. For example, if a child can get out of time out if he or she agrees to comply with a parental request, then the child would be negatively reinforced to be compliant. If time out were used as a negative reinforcement technique, then it would be a more powerful behavior modification technique.

trb At this point, you may wish to use **Critical Thinking Activity:** *Negative Reinforcement versus Punishment* (*Teacher's Resource Binder*, p. 16-1; **Handout 16–4, Transparency Master 16–1**).

■ LOOKING AT THE ISSUES

Delaying gratification is a skill many parents want their children to have. People who can delay gratification are able to achieve more in life. Have students consider the following questions:

- What types of "real world" rewards occur on a delayed schedule?
- Did you learn to wait for rewards? Why or why not?
- Does the media encourage people to delay gratification? Why or why not?

trb At this point, you may wish to use **Analysis Activity:** *Consideration of Future Consequences Scale* (*Teacher's Resource Binder*, p. 16-1; **Handout 16–6**).

removes an undesirable stimulus. Here are more examples of negative reinforcement:

1. The girl in the grocery store at the beginning of this module used negative reinforcement to teach her mom to buy her candy. The mother found the tantrum undesirable, and she escaped it by buying her daughter candy. The end of the tantrum negatively reinforced the mother's candy-buying behavior, which is likely to recur in the future.
2. Hitting the snooze button on my annoying alarm clock is negatively reinforcing, because the behavior allows me to escape from the alarm. This strengthens the behavior and helps ensure that I will hit the snooze button in the future.
3. For some people, taking alcohol or other drugs is negatively reinforcing. Alcohol provides some escape from stress and anxiety, which are undesirable. The reduction of anxiety that follows negatively reinforces the behavior of drinking and therefore strengthens that behavior. (Note, however, that the problems that led to the anxiety were not reduced.) Alcohol, by the way, is also *positively* reinforcing, to the extent that people find its "buzz" desirable. One reason many drugs are addictive is that they provide both positive and negative reinforcement.

Immediate Versus Delayed Reinforcement

3. Which affects our learning more—immediate rewards or delayed rewards?

If psychologists had designed the warning label on cigarette packs, it might say, "Warning: If you smoke these cigarettes, your breath will smell awful for the rest of the day!" Psychologists know that we are more likely to respond to immediate consequences (bad breath) than to delayed consequences (long-term risk of lung or heart disease). In other words, *immediate reinforcement* is more effective than *delayed reinforcement.* This also helps explain why it is difficult to *quit* smoking cigarettes. The desirable consequence—the "rush" produced by the chemicals in tobacco—is immediate. The undesirable effects on one's lungs and cardiovascular system are much more long term. It's no surprise, then, that drugs that produce the most immediate reinforcement, like nicotine and cocaine, are the most addictive (Marlatt, 1991). You can see the same relationship in those who overeat. The taste of fattening foods provides immediate positive reinforcement, but the effects of obesity are delayed.

Rats and pigeons, like people, prefer immediate reinforcement, and they seem to require it for learning. A rat, for example, will not learn to press a bar if the reinforcement for that behavior is delayed by 30 seconds or more. But humans have a great ability to adapt, and one of the

▶ **primary reinforcement** Something that is naturally reinforcing, such as food (if you are hungry), warmth (if you are cold), and water (if you are thirsty).

▶ **secondary reinforcement** Something that you have learned to value, such as money.

Enriching

Have students survey a representative sample of students to see if they would prefer to delay gratification rather than get immediate gratification. The survey should present different situations that offer a choice of delaying or getting immediate gratification. (Be sure to obtain permission from an Institutional Review Board and informed consent before conducting any research on human subjects.)

things we learn as we develop is that delayed reinforcers are sometimes worth the wait. Paychecks aren't issued until the end of the pay period and grades not until the end of the grading period, yet they still influence us. In fact, the ability to delay gratification is a real advantage. For example, children who prefer a big reward tomorrow over a smaller reward today are likely to become higher achieving adolescents than children who prefer immediate gratification (Mischel & others, 1989).

Primary Versus Secondary Reinforcement

4. How do primary and secondary reinforcement differ?

Primary and secondary reinforcement are similar in that they both affect the frequency of behaviors, but they differ in one important way. A **primary reinforcement** is something that is naturally rewarding, such as food (if you are hungry), warmth (if you are cold), and water (if you are thirsty). A **secondary reinforcement** is something you have *learned* is rewarding because it has been paired with a primary reinforcer (Figure 16.3).

Money, for example, is a secondary reinforcer because you have learned you can use it to purchase various forms of primary reinforcement, such as pizza and clothes. But money itself is not naturally rewarding. If you give a $100 bill to a 6-month-old baby, he will probably put it in his mouth to see if it tastes good. (He's checking for a primary reinforcer!) When the baby discovers it doesn't taste good, he will spit it out and show no further interest. Is this how you respond when given a $100 bill? Not likely! For you, that piece of paper has value—so much so that you would work hard to get more.

Grades are a major influence on student behavior. Are they a primary or a secondary reinforcement? If you said "secondary," you're right. You had to learn the value of grades. Without this learning, grades have no value. (Try training your dog by giving

Figure 16.3 **Primary and Secondary Reinforcements** Primary reinforcers, such as food, are naturally rewarding. Secondary reinforcers are rewarding because we have learned that they are associated with basic rewards.

PRIMARY REINFORCEMENT

Food is a primary reinforcer for a dog.

SECONDARY REINFORCEMENT

An owner's words can become secondary reinforcement when they're associated with petting and approval.

■ **APPLYING THE POINTS**

Invite the local K-9 police unit to visit your class and discuss how it trains dogs to sniff for drugs, explosives, and cadavers. Other options for guest speakers who use operant conditioning may include other types of dog trainers (for obedience schools and dog shows) or psychologists who work with patients in a **token economy**—an operant conditioning procedure that rewards desired behavior in the context of institutional settings, such as schools, hospitals, and homes for the delinquent.

trb At this point, you may wish to use **Technology Application Activity:** *Clicker Training and Operant Conditioning* (*Teacher's Resource Binder*, p. 16-1; **Handout 16–5**).

■ **JOURNAL WRITING**

Invite students to use the following questions and writing prompts as springboards for entries in their psychology journals:

- How much value do you place on earning money? Does the prospect of earning money (or more money) make that task appealing to you? Why or why not?
- Are you planning on choosing a career based on how much money you will make? Why or why not?
- Are high or low grades motivating to you? Do your goals for school involve getting certain grades? Why or why not?

Cooperative Learning

Have students brainstorm about different secondary reinforcers that they find particularly appealing. Make a chart with several columns that represent different general categories of secondary reinforcers (e.g., food, money, attention/affection, and so on). Have students fill in specific reinforcers that fit into each of the categories.

MODULE 16

■ TEACHING TIP

Emphasize to students that the goal of the consequence is what defines whether it is a *reinforcement* or a *punishment.*

- If a behavior is encouraged by the consequence, then it is a **reinforcement**.
- If a behavior is discouraged by the consequence, then it is a **punishment**.

trb A black-line master of Figure 16.4, Punishment Weakens Behavior, is available in the **Black-Line Masters Appendix** in the *Teacher's Resource Binder.*

trb At this point, you may wish to use **Critical Thinking Activity:** ***Negative Reinforcement versus Punishment*** (*Teacher's Resource Binder,* p. 16-1; **Handout 16–4, Transparency Master 16–1**).

trb ■ TEACHING TIP

You may wish to use **Enrichment Lesson:** ***The Self-Injurious Behavior Inhibiting System (SIBIS)*** (*Teacher's Resource Binder,* p. 16-1) to get students thinking about whether punishment can be beneficial. Autistic children often engage in self-injurious behavior. A pair of frustrated parents and scientists at Johns Hopkins developed SIBIS, which uses punishment to almost eliminate such behavior quickly. Is SIBIS a marvel of modern science or cruelty? This lesson seeks answers to this question.

her a B plus for sitting or heeling, instead of a primary reinforcement in the form of attention or a dog biscuit!) Some students have never learned to associate much value with school grades, and grades do not affect their behavior much, either.

Punishment

5. How does punishment influence behavior, and why does it tend to be ineffective?

The Process of Punishment

We noted earlier in this module that punishment *weakens* a behavior, or makes it less likely to occur again in the future. Punishment can take either of two forms (Figure 16.4):

- ***An undesirable event following the behavior.*** For example, if a toddler puts his hand on a painfully hot stove burner, the behavior of touching the burner is punished, because it leads to an undesirable event: getting burned (Ouch!). Because stove touching has been punished, that behavior is less likely to happen in the future.
- ***A desirable state or event ends following the behavior.*** Let's say a young boy pulls his sister's hair while watching TV, and his father takes away TV privileges for the rest of the day. The behavior of hair pulling has ended something desirable—watching TV. The loss of privileges should make the boy's hair-pulling behavior less likely to occur in the future. Traffic fines are another example of punishment that removes something desirable. If I engage in the behavior of illegal parking and am then required to turn over some of my desirable money, I should be less likely to park illegally in the future.

TWO FORMS OF PUNISHMENT

Behavior is followed by an undesirable event.

A toddler burned by a hot stove will be less likely to touch the stove again.

Behavior ends a desirable event or state.

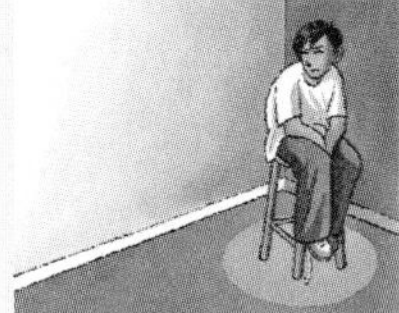

A boy who loses his TV privileges for pulling his sister's hair will be less likely to pull her hair again.

Figure 16.4 **Punishment Weakens Behavior** Here are two forms of punishment. In one, the punished behavior is followed by an undesirable event. In the other form of punishment, the punished behavior is followed by the loss of a desirable event or state. Although the types of punishment differ, each of them decreases the likelihood that the behavior will happen again.

Meeting Individual Needs

trb tr The concepts of negative reinforcement and punishment are difficult for some students to distinguish. You may wish to use the following activities to solidify these concepts for students:

- **Critical Thinking Activity:** *Negative Reinforcement versus Punishment* (*Teacher's Resource Binder,* p. 16-1; **Handout 16–4, Transparency Master 16–1**) With this activity, students clearly distinguish between negative reinforcement and punishment, two quite different concepts that are often considered synonymous.
- **Critical Thinking Activity:** *Examples of Negative Reinforcement* (*Teacher's Resource Binder,* p. 16-1; **Transparency Master 16–2**) Further ingrain the concept of negative reinforcement with these real-life examples of negative reinforcement in action.

Problems with Punishment

Many learning experts in operant conditioning, following the lead of Skinner, oppose the use of punishment to control behavior. They feel that punishment is likely to backfire in the long run, for a variety of reasons. For starters, punishment does not end the desire to engage in a behavior. Children punished for using inappropriate language often continue to use the bad language—just not in the presence of the one who punished them for it. Likewise, adults punished for speeding may just purchase a radar detector rather than driving more moderately.

Punishment can also lead to fear, anxiety, and lower self-esteem. Frequently punished children or animals may learn to engage in *avoidance* behaviors: Harshly punished children may run away from home, and harshly punished students may drop out of school. A final criticism of punishment is that when adult role models use aggression to solve their problems, children learn to model that aggressive behavior as a problem-solving strategy. This may help explain why abusive parents tend to come from abusive families (though, impressively, most abused children do not go on to become abusive parents) (Straus & Gelles, 1980).

So, despite all these problems, why is punishment used so often? One reason seems to be that when a punished individual is obedient or contrite, even for just a few minutes, this consequence positively reinforces the behavior it followed—which in this case is punishment. This desirable consequence in turn makes the behavior more likely to happen in the future. The result is a vicious cycle: Punishment leads to *temporary* suppression of misbehavior, which reinforces the punishment, which is then even more likely to be used when the suppressed misbehavior inevitably returns, which leads to another reinforcing, temporary suppression, and so on.

Is there any role for punishment in learning? Yes—a limited one: Swift, sure punishment can effectively control certain behaviors, especially if the punisher's goal is to protect a child from a dangerous situation. For example, if a toddler has developed the bad habit of running into the street, a harsh reprimand or swat on the behind may be appropriate. A young child needs to develop some fear and avoidance of the street. But punishment is generally most effective when used least. Have you ever had a class where the teacher was constantly punishing by losing his or her temper and yelling at the class? How effective was the teacher's behavior after it occurred several times? Compare that scenario with a class's reaction to angry behavior on the part of a teacher who rarely "loses it." If

Pros and Cons of Punishment Punishment, under the right circumstances, can decrease behavior, but it also has several undesirable side effects. It can lower self-esteem and produce fear and anxiety.

Cross-Curricular Connections

GOVERNMENT Using available library and Internet resources, have students explore the laws in your state governing the use of corporal punishment in schools and by parents. Discuss students' findings by asking the following questions:

- What legal rights do both groups have in using this type of punishment?
- What are your school's policies regarding corporal punishment?
- Does a correlation exist that shows a relationship between whether a state allows the death penalty and allows corporal punishment?

trb At this point, you may wish to use **Enrichment Lesson:** *The Self-Injurious Behavior Inhibiting System (SIBIS)* (*Teacher's Resource Binder*, p. 16-1).

■ LOOKING AT THE ISSUES

The use of punishment on children is very controversial. Have students explore the following questions, related to punishment, in small group discussions:

- If punishment is not as effective in encouraging behavior as reinforcement, why do you think people swear by it? What do you think reinforces the use of punishment?
- What undesirable behaviors do you think punishment might reinforce in children?

■ JOURNAL WRITING

Invite students to use the following questions and writing prompts as springboards for entries in their psychology journals:

- What types of discipline strategies have your parents used to mold your behavior? Have their discipline strategies changed from when you were younger?
- If you could create your own rules and consequences, what would you create? Would it be different if you were crafting a set of rules and consequences for your own children? Why or why not?

■ MULTICULTURAL CONNECTIONS

Using available resources, challenge students to research the use of corporal punishment with children in other countries. To discuss students' findings, pose the following questions in a full-class discussion:

- What countries have made use of corporal punishment by parents and schools legal? What are the specifics of such laws?
- Do you think there is a correlation between the type of government in a country and legalization of corporal punishment?
- If students from other countries attend your school (and only if they care to volunteer the information), ask them to relate some experiences with discipline practices in their native cultures, pointing out practices that are similar to and different from the discipline practices in your school.

MODULE 16

■ LOOKING AT THE ISSUES

Spanking is a controversial punishment technique employed by many parents and school systems across the country. Have students consider the following questions:

- Were you spanked as a child? Why or why not?
- What reasons might parents have for spanking their children?
- What reasons might parents have for not spanking their children?
- Where is the line between spanking and child abuse?
- Is spanking successful? Why or why not?

trb At this point, you may wish to use Enrichment Lesson: *Self-Injurious Behavior Inhibiting System (SIBIS)* (*Teacher's Resource Binder*, p. 16-1).

■ APPLYING THE POINTS

Have students recall their early childhood memories of learning how to do something, like ride a bike. How did they learn? What operant conditioning techniques did their "teacher" use with them?

▶ **shaping** Reinforcement of behaviors that are more and more similar to the one you want to occur. Shaping is the operant technique used to establish new behaviors.

your memories are similar to mine, you'll see that the less often punishment happens, the more effective it is.

For all the reasons we've discussed here, most psychologists recommend *reinforcing an incompatible behavior* as an effective alternative to punishment. Rather than punishing a child for lying, for example, parents might consider reinforcing the child for telling the truth. This will increase the amount of truth telling, and, since a child cannot tell the truth and lie at the same time, the amount of lying must decrease. The basic philosophy here is to "catch the child being good," and reinforce accordingly. This approach will lead to a more gradual change of behavior, but the change will be more permanent than the temporary suppression of behavior that follows punishment. Reinforcement also has two other benefits. First, it tends to lead to *approach* behaviors (one reason why kids are often so eager to see their mostly reinforcing grandparents), rather than feelings of fear, anxiety, and low self-esteem. And second, children who model positive reinforcement are a lot more fun to be with than children who model aggressive behaviors.

Some Reinforcement Procedures

Shaping

6. How can you use operant conditioning to teach a new behavior?

The law of effect says that reinforcing a behavior makes the behavior more likely to occur in the future. But how can you apply operant conditioning to a behavior that hasn't yet occurred? Skinner developed a technique to do this, called **shaping.** When you shape a behavior, you positively reinforce behaviors that move closer and closer to the target behavior.

Shaping When this child falls, as he surely will, Dad will praise her attempt. Parents who give such praise know that it is important to provide reinforcement following the first attempts, even if they are failures, in order to encourage a child to ride farther and farther.

To train a pigeon to turn in clockwise circles, for example, you would start by providing a food reward every time the pigeon turns its head to the right. Pigeons turn their heads frequently, and the law of effect says that reinforcing this behavior will cause the pigeon to turn its head to the right more often. Now the trick is to gradually extend how far the pigeon must turn its head before you give it a food reward. After a series of increasingly longer turns, the pigeon will finally turn all the way around. By breaking

Demonstrating

trb (1) The following activities from the *Teacher's Resource Binder* allow you to demonstrate the power of operant conditioning:

- Application Activity: *Conditioning the Instructor's Behavior* (*Teacher's Resource Binder*, p. 16-1) For the brave instructor only! This activity challenges students to condition their teachers to behave in certain nonembarrassing ways by applying principles of operant conditioning.
- Cooperative Learning Activity: *Shaping Demonstration* (*Teacher's Resource Binder*, p. 16-1) Working together, students can use operant conditioning to train each other to perform a simple task.

the circling behavior into a succession of gradual steps, you can easily shape it.

Many other examples of shaping happen in everyday life. Remember when you learned to ride your bicycle without training wheels? Chances are, someone held the seat and ran along beside you until you were reasonably well balanced, and then let go. You probably managed to roll several feet on your own before falling, at which point you were rewarded with a hearty, "Good job!" It really wasn't that good a job—you only made it a few feet—but for a first attempt it deserved reinforcement. Gradually, as your riding skills improved, your trainer made you ride farther and farther before giving you a compliment. You were being shaped!

▶ **discrimination** The ability to distinguish between two similar signals or stimuli.

▶ **extinction** In operant conditioning, the loss of a behavior when no consequence follows it.

Discrimination and Extinction

7. How do we learn to behave differently in response to similar stimuli, and how do we ever manage to get rid of behaviors we have learned?

Shaping is useful for training behaviors that otherwise probably wouldn't happen. Other important issues in conditioning include **discrimination,** distinguishing between similar stimuli, and **extinction,** the loss of a learned response when there is no longer a consequence.

Life would be fairly chaotic if we made the same response to all stimuli that were similar. For obvious safety reasons, students and teachers need to learn to *discriminate* between class dismissal bells and fire alarm blares. We do this by learning the difference between similar *signals.* What signal tells you it's time to leave the classroom at the end of the period? How does it differ from the fire alarm signal? And "false-alarm" fire drills—where students are immediately called back to class before they've even left the building—need to be kept to a minimum to prevent the extinction of the evacuation response.

Sometimes, however, extinction is a good thing. If the mom in the checkout line in the story at the beginning of this module had ignored her child's tantrums, those behaviors would eventually have died out on their own. Remember, without reinforcement, behaviors learned through operant conditioning will disappear.

Without discrimination, we wouldn't know when to answer the phone and when to answer the door. We wouldn't know whether to say "Hi, Jill" or "Hi, Jane" when a friend comes into view. Without extinction, we wouldn't stop repeating the same unsuccessful chess strategy, or stop flirting with someone who doesn't respond to our interest. These operant conditioning concepts can help us understand why certain behaviors thrive while others die out. Your reading behavior has obviously not extinguished, so let's continue!

Discrimination This trainer is teaching the dolphin to discriminate different hand signals. Reinforcement—a fish treat—is provided only when the animal performs the proper behavior for that signal.

MODULE 16

■ **TEACHING TIP**

Help students understand the meaning of the word *discrimination* in the context of operant conditioning. **Discrimination,** in the simplest sense, means to choose one thing over another. So, in operant conditioning, people are choosing to respond to one stimulus and not to another.

F • Y • I

Another concept related to discrimination is *generalization.* Generalization is the opposite of discrimination.

- With **discrimination,** the person responds to a particular stimulus only.
- With **generalization,** the person responds to stimuli that are similar to each other.

Consider the following example: If your school changed to a different type of signal than a bell to signify a class change, would that throw you off? Maybe at first, but in the long run probably not—as long as the signal came at the appropriate time, you would respond to the signal regardless of how it sounded.

(2) A CONDITIONED RESPONSE While discussing operant conditioning, interrupt your lecture and say, "Oh, by the way, before I forget again . . . " and complete the sentence by asking a question that will get either an almost totally positive or almost totally negative response. All students will usually raise a hand (note that you haven't requested raised hands). Immediately, tell students to freeze in their positions. Explain that students are conditioned to discriminate when to raise their hands in response to a teacher's request but not to others' requests.

Source: Stork, E. (1992). Operant conditioning: Role in human behavior. In R. Brown, D. Franz, B. Ibarra, & M. Sullivan. (Eds.), *Learning: A five-day unit plan prepared by APA teachers of psychology in secondary schools.* Washington, DC.: American Psychological Association.

trb At this point, you may wish to use **Application Activity:** *Conditioning the Instructor's Behavior* (*Teacher's Resource Binder,* p. 16-1) or **Cooperative Learning Activity:** *Shaping Demonstration* (*Teacher's Resource Binder,* p. 16-1).

MODULE 16

■ TEACHING TIP

Help students see the fundamental difference between *continuous* and *partial reinforcement schedules.*

- **Continuous reinforcement** occurs every single time a behavior is performed.
- **Partial reinforcement** only occurs after the behavior has been performed a certain number of times or after a certain amount of time has passed.

trb At this point, you may wish to use **Application Activity:** *Partial Reinforcement Schedules* (*Teacher's Resource Binder,* p. 16-1; **Handout 16–7**).

■ LOOKING AT THE ISSUES

Many teachers give grades on a continuous reinforcement schedule, awarding points for every assignment students turn in. Have students consider the impact of this type of reinforcement on learning.

- Do you get grades for every assignment you turn in? Why or why not?
- How do you feel if a teacher doesn't give grades for every assignment?
- What unintended consequences might occur when teachers use continuous reinforcement?

trb At this point, you may wish to use **Analysis Activity:** *Consideration of Future Consequences Scale* (*Teacher's Resource Binder,* p. 16-1; **Handout 16–6**).

trb ■ CHECKING FOR UNDERSTANDING

You may wish to use **Application Activity:** *Partial Reinforcement Schedules* (*Teacher's Resource Binder,* p. 16-1; **Handout 16–7**) to see whether students can apply their knowledge of partial reinforcement schedules. The handout may be used as an individual or group exercise.

▸ **continuous reinforcement** In operant conditioning, a schedule of reinforcement in which a reward follows every correct response.

▸ **partial reinforcement schedule** In operant conditioning, a schedule of reinforcement in which a reward follows only some correct responses.

▸ **fixed-interval schedule** In operant conditioning, a partial reinforcement schedule that rewards only the first correct response after some defined period of time.

Schedules of Reinforcement

What do buying food from a vending machine and playing the lottery have in common? They are both behaviors maintained by positive reinforcement. However, you're more likely to continue playing the lottery after having purchased a losing ticket than you are to put more money into a vending machine that has just failed to produce the desired potato chips. This is because the two examples illustrate different *schedules of reinforcement—continuous reinforcement* for the vending machine and *partial reinforcement* for the lottery.

Continuous Reinforcement

8. What are the advantages and disadvantages of continuous reinforcement of responses?

In **continuous reinforcement,** you reward every correct response, just as a vending machine is supposed to do. The owner of the machine is training you to behave in a certain way—inserting your money in the machine. If you put the money in properly, you will be reinforced by receiving a bag of potato chips. Since you get your chips every time you put in your money, this is continuous reinforcement.

Continuous reinforcement is most useful for establishing new behaviors. Lots of reinforcement is often necessary when you are trying to teach someone to do something new, such as teaching a child to play tee ball. One problem with behaviors that have been continuously reinforced, however, is that they are quite easy to extinguish. If the learner is accustomed to being reinforced for each correct behavior, and the reinforcement stops, extinction will occur quite rapidly. Think about how you behave when you put money in a vending machine and the machine doesn't dispense your product. Do you quickly put more money in? Probably not! When the goal is to establish behavior that is resistant to extinction, one of the partial reinforcement schedules works better.

Partial Reinforcement

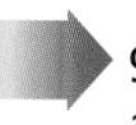

9. What are the four partial reinforcement schedules, and how do they differ?

Partial reinforcement schedules reward only some responses. When our behavior is reinforced intermittently (only some of the time), hope springs eternal and we are reluctant to give up. If a vending machine is a good example of continuous reinforcement, a lottery is a good example of partial reinforcement. People don't expect to win every time they buy a ticket. Therefore, they will continue to buy tickets even if they don't win. As lottery commissions know, partial reinforcement schedules produce responding that is hard to extinguish.

Cooperative Learning

SCHEDULES OF REINFORCEMENT POSTERS Have students work in groups, with each group creating a small poster of a schedule of reinforcement to display in the classroom during this module. The posters should include the definition of the schedule and various real-life applications of it.

Skinner (1961) and others have identified four different partial-reinforcement schedules. Two of the schedules, called *interval schedules*, focus on the time that elapses between reinforcements. The other two schedules, called *ratio schedules*, focus on the number of responses before reinforcement occurs. Let's take a closer look at each of these four partial reinforcement schedules.

Dennis the Menace

"I think Mom's using the can opener."

Signals Can Be Powerful! The dog is occasionally reinforced with a bowl full of food after hearing the can opener. That's enough to send him running every time he hears it!

Fixed-Interval Schedule

A **fixed-interval schedule** reinforces the first correct response after some defined period of time has passed. For example, a researcher might always reinforce a rat's first bar press after 60 seconds. After receiving a food pellet (a reinforcement) for that response, the rat has to wait 60 seconds before it will be reinforced for another correct response. The interval (60 seconds) is fixed, and there is no way the rat can get reinforcement during that 60-second interval—thus the term *fixed-interval schedule.*

A rat with experience on this schedule learns not to respond during the first part of the interval, when there is no way to get a reinforcement. Toward the end of the interval, the rat starts pressing the bar, "checking" to see if the time is up. The rate of checking increases as the end of the interval approaches. The result is the response pattern you can see in Figure 16.5. Skinner used graphs like the one in Figure 16.5

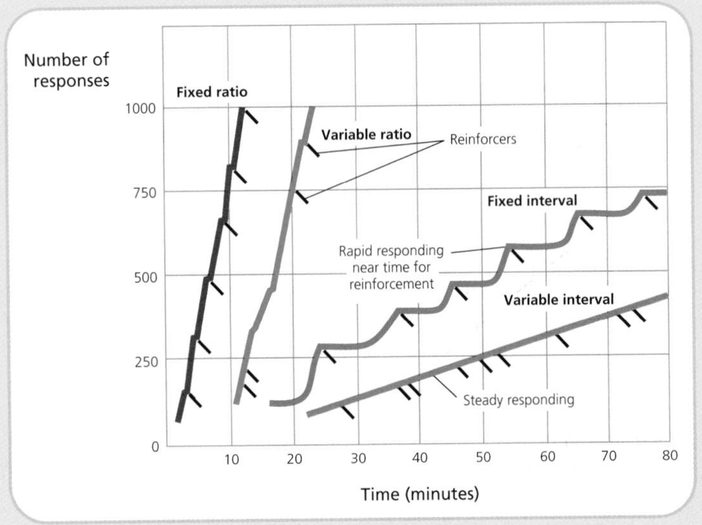

Figure 16.5 The Cumulative Record Skinner's pigeons showed these four patterns of responding for the partial schedules of reinforcement. Notice that the ratio schedules produce a faster response rate (a steeper line) than the interval schedules. (Adapted from "Teaching machines" by B. F. Skinner. Copyright © 1961, Scientific American, Inc. All rights reserved.)

MODULE 16

■ TEACHING TIPS

tr (1) A four-color transparency of Figure 16.5, The Cumulative Record, is available in the **Overhead Transparencies Set.**

(2) Be sure students understand the difference between *interval* and *ratio schedules.*

- **Interval schedules** involve a time element—time must pass before reinforcement will occur. The subject must demonstrate the behavior at the right time to get reinforcement.
- **Ratio schedules** are dependent on the behavior itself—a certain number of behaviors are needed before reinforcement will occur.

trb At this point, you may wish to use **Building Vocabulary: Graphic Organizers:** ***Flowchart—Reinforcement*** (*Teacher's Resource Binder*, p. 16-1; **Handout 16–3**).

■ APPLYING THE POINTS

Ask students to identify the schedule that helps to explain why a teenager who stays at home after school may often wait until the time just prior to his or her parents return before finishing (or even starting!) daily chores and responsibilities. *(a fixed-interval reinforcement schedule)*

Enriching

Have students research how companies pay their employees. Use the following questions to help students focus their research and discuss their findings:

- What different fixed-interval reinforcement schedules are most common: weekly, biweekly, or monthly?
- How do employees feel about their pay schedules? Would they like a different one? Why or why not?

MODULE 16

F • Y • I

The pattern of reinforcement shown during a fixed-interval reinforcement schedule is called **scooping**. Animals and people trained on this schedule tend to wait until the time interval is drawing near before performing the behavior, which results in the scooped look of the graph charting the behavior.

■ LOOKING AT THE ISSUES

Cramming for tests is a result of a fixed-interval schedule of reinforcement. Have students consider the following questions:

- Why do students cram rather than study steadily? What are the benefits and drawbacks of cramming?
- Would pop quizzes be a better system for getting kids to learn? Why or why not?

► **variable-interval schedule** In operant conditioning, a partial reinforcement schedule that rewards the first correct response after an unpredictable amount of time.

► **fixed-ratio schedule** In operant conditioning, a partial reinforcement schedule that rewards a response only after some defined number of correct responses.

► **variable-ratio schedule** In operant conditioning, a partial reinforcement schedule that rewards an unpredictable number of correct responses.

to track the responses of pigeons and rats. The horizontal axis of the graph measures time, and the vertical axis measures total responses. The small slash marks indicate points at which the animal received a reinforcement (such as a food pellet). The slopes of the lines connecting the slashes show the rate of responding—a steeper line indicates more responses per minute.

Do fixed-interval schedules happen in real life? You bet! Have you ever had a class with a quiz every Friday? If so, you were being reinforced (with a good grade) for your behavior (studying) on a fixed-interval (one week) schedule. Did you study much for the quiz on Monday, Tuesday, or Wednesday? Most students don't. Instead, they pack the main part of their responding into the end of the interval, just as the rats did in Skinner's research on fixed-interval schedules.

Variable-Interval Schedule

A **variable-interval schedule** also requires a period of time to pass before a correct response is rewarded, but in this case the amount of time changes after each reinforcement. A bar-pressing rat has no way to know how long the interval will be, so it must keep "checking" by pressing the bar to see if anything happens. When the interval is up, the next correct press on the bar earns the rat its reward.

Recall that on the fixed-interval schedule, the rat (or the student) can sit out the first part of the interval (that is, not respond) without risk. Not so on a variable-interval schedule, where any given interval might be very short. Instead, the rat learns to respond at a moderate, steady rate, as Figure 16.5 shows. Fast responses don't get extra rewards, so speed is not important with a variable-interval schedule.

Pop quizzes use a variable-interval schedule. When a quiz can occur at any time, you have to study a little bit each day. If there is no quiz today, there may be one tomorrow. If there is a quiz today, there may be another one tomorrow. To get the most reinforcement (good grades on your quizzes), you must be a steady studier.

Fixed-Ratio Schedule

A **fixed-ratio schedule** requires a certain number of correct responses before reinforcement occurs. The word *ratio* in the term refers to the ratio of reinforcements to responses, such as one reinforcement for every 20 correct responses. Fixed-ratio schedules do place a premium on speed: The faster the rat makes the required number of responses, the faster it will be fed, which means more to eat for a hungry rat. A rat with some experience on the fixed-ratio schedule will run through the required number of responses very rapidly. As you can see in Figure 16.5, it will take a short break. After "catching its breath," the rat will run through the next set of responses as rapidly as possible.

Reteaching

trb A four-color transparency for Figure 16.5 on page 313, The Cumulative Record, is available in the **Overhead Transparencies Set**. You may wish to use this transparency to assess students' knowledge of the different types of partial reinforcement. Cover up the key terms on the graph to see if students can identify which line goes with which reinforcement schedule.

Video rental stores that run "Rent 10, Get 1 free" specials are using a fixed-ratio schedule of reinforcement. You may have found yourself renting 10 videos pretty quickly to qualify for your reinforcement—the free video. After watching the free video, you may not rent again for a while. (You're probably pretty sick of videos after watching them several nights in a row!) However, after "catching your breath" for a few days, you and your friends may start renting again in order to earn the next free video.

Variable-Ratio Schedule

A **variable-ratio schedule** also requires a number of correct responses before reinforcement, but the number is unpredictable because it changes after each reinforcement. Rats on a variable-ratio schedule tend to respond fast and to continue responding after receiving a reinforcement. After all, the next response *could* always be the response that pays off, and the only way to find out is to make that response! This schedule also produces tremendous resistance to extinction. Skinner (1953) found that pigeons sometimes pecked 150,000 times without a reward after having been on a high variable-ratio schedule.

No wonder, then, that the variable-ratio schedule is sometimes called the "gambler's schedule." Lottery tickets and many other forms of gambling pay off on a variable-ratio schedule. People who buy lottery tickets never know how many tickets will be necessary to win, but they do know that the more tickets they buy, the better their chances of winning will be. The trouble is that the games are designed to give a large number of small payouts, big enough to provide reinforcement for purchasing a ticket but small enough to ensure that the vast majority of people will lose more money than they win. I stood behind a woman in the grocery store one day and watched her spend $5 to purchase and scratch off five tickets. Four were losers, and the fifth paid off with two "free" tickets. One of these paid $2, and as she left she turned to her friend and said, "I won!" She had actually lost $3 ($5 minus her $2 win), yet her small win had reinforced her ticket-buying behavior! Do you think she was motivated to buy additional tickets the next time she was at the store?

Schedules of Reinforcement in Real Life This gambler is being reinforced on a variable-ratio schedule. She does not know how many times she has to play in order to win. The variable-ratio schedule produces a high, steady response rate, much to the delight of the casino owners!

MODULE 16

F • Y • I

Companies that require workers to fulfill a quota before taking a break or getting paid are operating on a fixed-ratio schedule. Typically, workers will rush through the work they must do to meet the quota and get reinforced. While this type of schedule increases productivity, it does not necessarily increase quality.

■ LOOKING AT THE ISSUES

Variable-ratio schedules have been linked to several types of addictions, including gambling and drug and alcohol abuse. As described in the text, pigeons pecked more than 150,000 times an hour to get reinforcement. Have students consider the following questions:

- How might the pigeons' behavior be related to human drug users or addicts?
- Why would a variable-ratio schedule make it so difficult for addicts to quit?
- How could operant conditioning principles be used to help addicts quit?

Reteaching

trb You may wish to use **Application Activity:** *Partial Reinforcement Schedules* (*Teacher's Resource Binder*, p. 16-1; **Handout 16–7**) to allow students to apply their knowledge of partial reinforcement schedules. In this activity, students must identify the reinforcement schedule described in the handout.

MODULE 16

■ TEACHING TIPS

tr (1) A four-color transparency of Figure 16.6, Learning Without Reward, is available in the **Overhead Transparencies Set.**

(2) You may wish to use **Technology Application Activity:** ***PsychSim:* "Maze Learning"** (*Teacher's Resource Binder,* p. 16-1) to reinforce the concept of latent learning. *PsychSim* is an interactive CD-ROM containing tutorials in different content areas of psychology. In this tutorial, students will have fun training a rat by using operant conditioning and cognitive maps.

F•Y•I

Skinner's research on "superstitious" behavior in pigeons can be presented in class to illustrate both the power of reinforcement and its application to everyday life. According to Skinner, a superstitious behavior is a response that is accidentally reinforced—that is, there is no prearranged contingency between the response and reinforcement. Because the behavior and reinforcement occur together, the behavior is repeated and, by chance, is again followed by reinforcement. This process may explain why we carry a half-dollar as a good luck piece, wear the same slacks when taking tests, and step over cracks in the sidewalk.

trb At this point, you may wish to use **Enrichment Lesson:** ***Superstitious Behavior*** (*Teacher's Resource Binder,* p. 16-1).

New Understandings of Operant Conditioning

Despite Skinner's sharpest arguments to the contrary, we now know that *cognition* (our thought processes) affects all types of learning, including operant learning. And our biology also sets boundaries for how and what we can learn.

The Role of Cognition

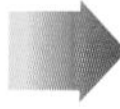

10. How do latent learning and the overjustification effect demonstrate that mental processes affect operant conditioning?

Latent learning, which takes place without apparent reward, is probably the best example of how our thinking—not just whether we are reinforced—affects our learning. In a now-classic experiment (Tolman & Honzik, 1930), researchers demonstrated how a **cognitive map,** or mental representation of one's environment, can influence learning. In this experiment, they trained one group of rats to find its way through a maze by putting a food reward in a box at the end of the maze. As the number of trials increased, the rats in this group gradually decreased the time in which they completed the maze (Figure 16.6). The researchers also placed a second group of rats in the maze, but they did not reward them with food for finding the end of the maze. Rats in this second

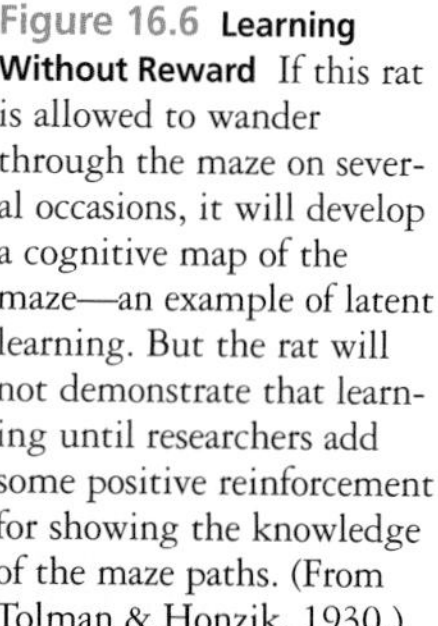

Figure 16.6 **Learning Without Reward** If this rat is allowed to wander through the maze on several occasions, it will develop a cognitive map of the maze—an example of latent learning. But the rat will not demonstrate that learning until researchers add some positive reinforcement for showing the knowledge of the maze paths. (From Tolman & Honzik, 1930.)

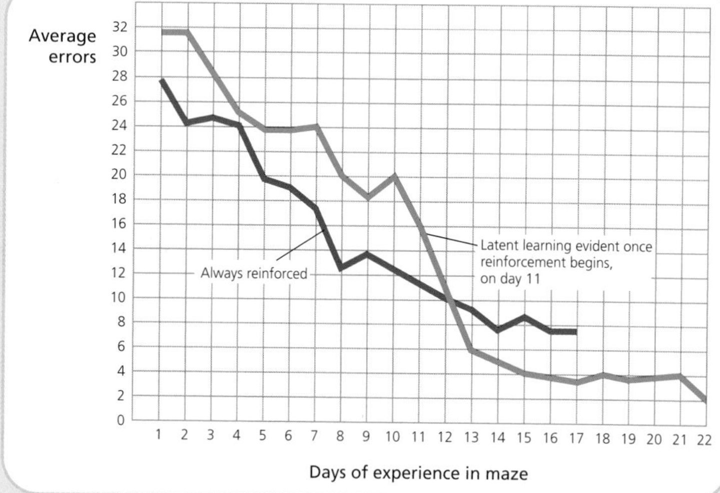

Enriching

Have students replicate the Tolman and Honzik latent learning experiment. Construct two mazes and have one group of laboratory rats run through one maze while the other group doesn't get that opportunity. Then train the rats, using operant conditioning, to run the maze. Time each group to see which one learns the maze the fastest. (Be sure to get approval from an Institutional Review Board and follow the guidelines for caring for animals as defined by the APA Ethics Code.)

group wandered through the maze, exploring it, but their times did not improve during this first phase of the experiment. Then things changed in the second phase of the experiment, when the experimenters put a food reward in the box at the maze's end. Now the second group of rats' performance rapidly improved, until it matched that of the first group. The rats in the second group had developed a cognitive map as they wandered through the maze in the first phase. They had learned, but the learning occurred cognitively before it was expressed behaviorally.

The **overjustification effect** provides more support for cognition's role in operant conditioning. Rewarding an already enjoyable behavior *overjustifies* it and may actually *decrease* the frequency of that behavior. This is the direct opposite of the effect Skinner's principles would predict—an increase in the rewarded behavior. Unfortunately, overjustification sometimes happens in school. Activities like reading, which should be (and are) naturally reinforcing for most young children, can be overjustified if the school provides lots of special rewards, such as gold stars, grades, and special parties for meeting reading goals. The danger is that these rewards may begin to overwhelm the child's natural motivation to read and become the primary means of maintaining the behavior. When the rewards stop, the behavior stops as well. ("What, I don't get a free pizza for reading 10 books?!")

Even grades can lead to overjustification. One experiment divided fifth graders into two groups. The researchers told one group to read a passage and informed students in the group that they would be graded on how much they'd learned. They told the other group that they should read the passage, but they wouldn't be graded, simply questioned to find out what they remembered. There was little difference in how much the two groups remembered, but the second group thought the passage was more interesting (Grolnick & Ryan, 1987). The point is that there seems to be a link between external, environmental rewards and internal, cognitive factors. If we ignore cognition, we won't get the whole picture about how operant conditioning works.

▸ **latent learning** Learning that occurs but is not apparent until the learner has an incentive to demonstrate it.

▸ **cognitive map** A mental representation of a place.

▸ **overjustification effect** The effect of promising a reward for doing what one already likes to do. The reward may lessen and replace the person's original, natural motivation, so that the behavior stops if the reward is eliminated.

The Role of Biology

11. Why don't the principles of operant conditioning work equally well for all behaviors in all species?

Like cognition, biology clearly influences how we learn and what we learn, including what we learn through operant conditioning. Some species are *biologically predisposed* to learn some behaviors easily and other behaviors only with great difficulty.

Pigeons, for example, easily learn to flap their wings to avoid electric shock and to peck at a disc for food. Operant conditioning principles would suggest that you could reverse these two behaviors and teach

■ **TEACHING TIP**

The overjustification effect is related to cognitive dissonance. In **cognitive dissonance,** subjects try to reconcile a conflict between attitudes and actions. In doing so, they often change their attitudes to support the actions others see.

In one experiment, subjects pretended to like a boring task and then were paid either $1 or $20. Afterward, those who were paid $1 said they liked the task more, because they had no other incentive to like it—their payment didn't justify liking the activity for the money.

This effect helps to explain why teachers, police officers, and firefighters devote long, hard hours to their jobs for relatively little pay—and why professional athletes and celebrities often complain about being rich and famous!

trb At this point, you may wish to use **Critical Thinking Activity:** *The Overjustification Effect* (*Teacher's Resource Binder*, p. 16-1) or **Enrichment Lesson:** *The Overjustification Effect* (*Teacher's Resource Binder*, p. 16-1).

■ **JOURNAL WRITING**

Invite students to use the following questions and writing prompts as springboards for entries in their psychology journals.

- Has the overjustification effect ever caused you to dislike school? Explain.
- How could school officials overcome the overjustification effect so that students would like learning for the sake of learning?

■ **APPLYING THE POINTS**

Radical behaviorists felt that psychology would be less of a science if it studied phenomena like consciousness and cognition. With this in mind, have your students imagine they are radical behaviorists from the past. Ask them to participate in a forum in which they respond to the following questions:

- How might you explain the concepts of *latent learning*, *overjustification*, and *biological predispositions* in behaviorist terms?
- Which one of these concepts would fit in your view of psychological science, and which would not? Why?

MODULE 16

Close

Working in small groups, have students consider the following questions about behaviorism and psychology:

- Why didn't behaviorism last as the premier way to study psychology?
- Why did behaviorists seem to ignore evidence of cognition in their own experiments?
- How does an understanding of cognition make operant conditioning principles even more important to our understanding of human behavior?

Visit each group and listen to their discussion. Help clarify confusing issues or details related to module concepts.

Matching the Species to the Behavior Operant conditioning works best when it focuses on behaviors that come naturally to a species, such as jumping-up behaviors in dogs.

the birds to flap for food and peck to avoid shock. This turns out to be very difficult, however, because it defies the biological tendencies of the species (Foree & LoLordo, 1973). Wing flapping is a natural defense mechanism for pigeons and thus lends itself well to avoidance behaviors. Pecking is a response naturally associated with eating, so pigeons easily learn to peck for food.

Operant conditioning offers practical and useful techniques for altering behavior in families, schools, and workplaces. It can indeed change the way people act and, like all science-based theories, it is alive and changing. New research has shed light on cognitive and biological factors that influence operant procedures, which helps us to employ these principles even more effectively.

Individualized Learning Many computerized instructional programs take advantage of operant conditioning principles. This girl will have her answers shaped by a program that breaks instruction down into a series of easy steps. She will receive positive reinforcement for each correct answer.

Enriching

Have students research how circus animals are trained to do the seemingly unnatural behaviors they perform as part of the circus. Help them focus their research and discuss their findings by posing the following questions:

- What operant conditioning techniques do circus trainers use? What training in animal care do they need to have?
- What behaviors are commonly trained in different types of animals? Are these behaviors natural for the animal? Why or why not?

REVIEW

Module 16: Operant Conditioning

What's the Point?

What Is Operant Conditioning?

Operant conditioning is a type of learning in which the frequency of a behavior depends on its consequence—the event that follows the behavior.

The Law of Effect

1. *What is the law of effect, and how can it be used to modify behavior?*

   American psychologist Edward Thorndike gets credit for the discovery of the law of effect—the statement that behaviors followed by favorable consequences will occur more frequently, and behaviors followed by unfavorable consequences will decrease. B. F. Skinner built on Thorndike's work and developed the principles, and many applications, of operant conditioning. Anything that increases the likelihood of a behavior recurring is a reinforcement. Anything that decreases the likelihood of a behavior recurring is a punishment. Whether an event is a reinforcement or a punishment depends on how the learner views the event, not how others view it.

Reinforcement

2. *How do positive and negative reinforcements work, and how do they differ from each other?*

   Any reinforcement increases the future likelihood of a behavior by following the behavior with a consequence that the learner values. When we use positive reinforcement to increase the chances that a behavior will appear again, we *present something desirable* after the behavior appears. For example, when you put coins in a vending machine, the candy bar or soda that pops out is a positive reinforcement for your behavior of giving up your money. When we use negative reinforcement to increase the chances that a behavior will appear again in the future, we *remove something undesirable* after the behavior appears. When you take aspirin to get rid of a headache, the relief from pain is the negative reinforcement for your behavior of taking the aspirin. In each case, you value the consequence of the behavior.

3. *Which affects our learning more—immediate rewards or delayed rewards?*

   Immediate rewards present desirable consequences on the spot, and they are therefore a more effective form of reinforcement than delayed rewards. In laboratory settings, rats and pigeons require immediate reinforcement for learning. Humans learn to wait for delayed rewards, such as paychecks and grades.

4. *How do primary and secondary reinforcement differ?*

   Primary reinforcers are stimuli that do not require any learning to be rewarding. Water is a primary reinforcer for a thirsty person; you don't need to learn to drink water when you are thirsty. Secondary reinforcers are rewarding because we have learned that they have value. The *sight* of a water fountain when you are parched from running in the park is a secondary reinforcer, because you have learned that this machine delivers cool water.

MODULE 16

Checking the Points

■ **TEACHING TIPS**

web (1) The book companion site for *Thinking About Psychology* at **www.worthpublishers.com/thinkingaboutpsych** contains a module quiz, flashcards of key terms and people, and other student activities and resources for this module. You will also find PowerPoint lectures, a quiz grade book, and other teaching resources by logging on as an instructor.

trb (2) Students can test their understanding of operant conditioning by working in small groups to respond to handout items in **Critical Thinking Activity:** *Consequences and Their Effects* (*Teacher's Resource Binder*, p. 16-1; **Handout 16–1**). Provide a handout to each group, and ask students not to refer to earlier versions of this handout they may have worked on. For each response, group members should alternate finding passages in the text that confirm the response as correct or reveal the answer as incorrect, while providing the correct answer with text support.

Punishment

5. *How does punishment influence behavior, and why does it tend to be ineffective?*

Punishment decreases the chances that a behavior will appear in the future. Punishment takes two forms: an undesirable event that follows a behavior (pain from touching a stove), or the end of a *desirable* state or event following a behavior (losing the right to use the phone because you have run up your parents' phone bill). Punishment can suppress behavior temporarily. But in the long term, punishment may just teach the punished person to avoid displaying the behavior when the person who delivered the punishment is present, or simply to avoid that person. Physical punishment also can teach aggressive behavior. Psychologists tend to believe that punishment's role should be limited to occasions that protect the learner from immediately dangerous consequences, like running into traffic. In most other cases, reinforcing desirable behaviors seems a better alternative, because the change that results will be more permanent, even if it does not occur as quickly.

Some Reinforcement Procedures

6. *How can you use operant conditioning to teach a new behavior?*

To teach a new behavior using operant conditioning, you would *shape* the behavior. This means that you would reward behaviors as they become more similar to the one you want to teach. For example, if you want to teach a child to ride a bicycle, you would reward any small step the child makes along the way to independent riding—sitting properly, balancing on the seat, pedaling while you run beside the bike holding the child, and so on.

7. *How do we learn to behave differently in response to similar stimuli, and how do we ever manage to get rid of behaviors we have learned?*

Discrimination is a learned response of behaving differently toward similar signals. Through conditioning, we learn that certain consequences will follow some signaling stimuli (a conversation with friends or family may follow the ringing tone of a phone) but not other similar stimuli (no conversation with friends or family when the microwave signal goes off). Therefore, we learn not to answer the phone when the microwave signals.

Extinction is the loss of a behavior when no consequence follows it. Without reinforcement, behaviors learned through operant conditioning will disappear.

Schedules of Reinforcement

8. *What are the advantages and disadvantages of continuous reinforcement of responses?*

Continuous reinforcement rewards every correct response a learner makes. This type of reinforcement is very successful in teaching something new, when you want the learner to establish a strong association between the behavior and its consequence. The disadvantage of continuous reinforcement is that when you stop rewarding the behavior, it quickly ends. Another way to say this is that continuously reinforced behaviors are easily extinguished.

9. *What are the four partial reinforcement schedules, and how do they differ?*

Partial reinforcement schedules reward only some responses, and the behaviors they reinforce are much harder to extinguish than behaviors that have been continuously reinforced. Two of the four partial reinforcement schedules (fixed-interval and

320

variable-interval schedules) focus on the period of time, or *interval,* between reinforcements. The other two partial reinforcements schedules (fixed-ratio and variable-ratio schedules) emphasize the *ratio*—some fraction of the total—of correct responses that receive a reward.

- In fixed-interval schedules, a response receives a reward only after a defined period of time passes (remember weekly quizzes).
- In variable-interval schedules, a response receives a reward after an unpredictable period of time (remember pop quizzes).
- In fixed-ratio schedules, a response receives a reward only after a defined number of responses (remember rent-10, get-one-free offers).
- In a variable-ratio schedule, a response receives a reward after an unpredictable number of responses (remember lottery tickets).

Fixed-interval and variable-interval schedules do not reward fast responding, because speed doesn't affect when the reward will appear. Fixed-ratio and variable-ratio schedules do reward speed, because the sooner the learner makes the required number responses, the sooner the reward will appear.

New Understandings of Operant Conditioning

10. *How do latent learning and the overjustification effect demonstrate that thought processes affect operant conditioning?*

Skinner believed that the consequences that follow behaviors will determine how often those behaviors occur, and behaviors that are not rewarded will disappear.

Latent learning defies this statement because it takes place with no apparent reward. We know that the learning has occurred because the individual behaves appropriately in situations where this learning is useful. Psychologists demonstrated latent learning in an experiment in which rats learned to navigate a maze but received no apparent reward for their behavior. The rats formed a cognitive map—a mental representation of the maze. This is a mental process influencing behavior.

Overjustifying is rewarding a behavior a person already enjoys. When the new reward no longer follows the behavior, the behavior that used to be enjoyable may disappear. Skinner would have predicted that the additional rewards would make the behavior even stronger. Instead, the additional rewards seem to destroy the person's original, internal motivation, which is further evidence that mental processes influence learning.

11. *Why don't the principles of operant conditioning apply equally to all behaviors in all species?*

Each species is biologically predisposed to learn certain behaviors—this means that our biology places fences around what we can easily learn. No matter how carefully I apply operant principles to reward your responses, I will not be able to teach you to fly by flapping your arms. I could easily teach this to a pigeon, which is biologically prepared to fly at a very young age.

MODULE 16

trb **tr** ■ TEACHING TIP

Have students work individually to complete the graphic organizers in **Building Vocabulary: Graphic Organizer:** *Concept Flowcharts* (*Teacher's Resource Binder*, p. 16-1; **Handouts 16–2** and **16–3**) without referring to the text or to versions of these flowcharts they may have filled in earlier. When students have completed the flowcharts, use the handouts as transparencies and project them (with answers inserted) so the class may review the module vocabulary and the relationship of these terms to operant conditioning.

tb Using the Test Bank

The *Test Bank* that accompanies this textbook offers a wide variety of questions in different formats and levels of complexity. Use the software to construct whole tests or to integrate standardized questions into teacher-made tests.

Self-Test Answers

Multiple-Choice Questions

1. b, 2. d, 3. a, 4. a

Key Terms

operant conditioning, p. 300
reinforcement, p. 302
punishment, p. 302
positive reinforcement, p. 303
negative reinforcement, p. 303
primary reinforcement, p. 307
secondary reinforcement, p. 307
shaping, p. 310
discrimination, p. 311
extinction, p. 311
continuous reinforcement, p. 312
partial reinforcement schedule, p. 312
fixed-interval schedule, p. 313
variable-interval schedule, p. 314
fixed-ratio schedule, p. 314
variable-ratio schedule, p. 315
latent learning, p. 316
cognitive map, p. 316
overjustification effect, p. 317

Key People

Edward Thorndike, p. 301
B. F. Skinner, p. 301

Self-Test

Multiple-Choice Questions

Choose the *best* answer for each of the following questions.

1. B.F. Skinner has asked four students to name their favorite parts of his research. Maria chose negative reinforcement. Charlie chose latent learning. Jamal chose partial schedules of reinforcement. Cynthia chose shaping. Which student will Skinner frown at?
   a. Maria, because Skinner did not believe that a response could be negatively reinforced.
   b. Charlie, because latent learning shows that thought processes affect operant conditioning, an idea Skinner denied.
   c. Jamal, because Skinner did not believe partial reinforcement was effective.
   d. Cynthia, because Skinner did not believe behavior could be shaped.

2. You have had a very rushed, stressful day, and you haven't had time to eat since grabbing a doughnut early this morning. Under these conditions, which of the following will be a secondary reinforcer for you?
   a. a ripe, red apple
   b. lunch with a friend
   c. a coupon for a free sandwich at the local fast-food restaurant
   d. All of the above will be secondary reinforcers.

3. Herb thought he wanted to go out with Molly, but he was feeling a little shy about asking her for a date. To lead up to that request, Herb went out of his way to smile at Molly when he saw her in the hallway, and Molly was beginning to smile back. But now Herb has decided Molly is not his type, and he takes special care to avoid looking at her. Herb is trying to
   a. extinguish Molly's recent interest in him.
   b. reinforce Molly's recent interest in him.
   c. shape Molly's behavior so she will ask him for a date.
   d. give Molly a secondary reinforcement in addition to the earlier primary reinforcement.

4. Brad violated his curfew when he came home two hours late on Saturday, and his parents grounded him for a month. The grounding is a form of
   a. punishment.
   b. negative reinforcement.

Alternative Assessment/Portfolio Project

trb MODIFYING AN EXISTING BEHAVIOR Students can use operant conditioning to change or modify a behavior in their own lives. Using the guidelines found in the *Teacher's Resource Binder*, ask students to apply the concepts of this module in a practical way to make a change in their own behavior. As the guidelines suggest, students may create a journal, a video diary, or a "before-and-after" poster to document their experience (*Teacher's Resource Binder*, p. 16-1; **Handout 16–8**).

c. primary reinforcement.
d. secondary reinforcement.

5. Tina lives in Big City and rides a city bus to Normal High School. The buses arrive at the corner on the hour and on the half hour, and if Tina catches the 7:00 or 7:30 bus, she gets to school on time. Occasionally, Tina misses both buses, and she has to take a cab. The cabs pass her corner on an unpredictable schedule, so she never knows whether she will make it to school on time. The buses run on a _______________ schedule; the cabs run on a _______________ schedule.
   a. fixed-ratio; variable-ratio
   b. variable-ratio; fixed-ratio
   c. variable-interval; fixed-interval
   d. fixed-interval; variable-interval

6. Jose loves to play the violin, and he practices daily so that he'll play his very best. Jose's father really hopes that Jose will become a professional violinist, and he has decided to reward Jose for practicing by giving him $5 each day he practices. Jose's father may be sorry, because
   a. positive reinforcement is rarely effective.
   b. the money for practicing is being given on a partial reinforcement schedule, which will cause Jose to speed up his playing.
   c. he may overjustify his son's behavior, and Jose may lose his own natural motivation to practice.
   d. he may underjustify his son's behavior, and then he will have to increase the reward for daily practicing.

Matching Terms and Definitions

7. For each definition, choose the *best* matching term from the list that follows.

Definition

a. Any consequence that *decreases* the future likelihood of a behavior.
b. Partial-reinforcement schedules that focus on the *number of responses.*
c. In operant conditioning, anything that increases the likelihood of a behavior by following it with the removal of an undesirable event or state.
d. In operant conditioning, a pattern in which reinforcement follows only some correct responses.
e. In operant conditioning, anything that increases the likelihood of a behavior by following it with a desirable event or state.
f. In operant conditioning, a schedule of reinforcement in which a reward follows every correct response.
g. Partial-reinforcement schedules that focus on the *time between correct responses.*
h. A type of learning in which the frequency of a behavior depends on the consequence.
i. Something that you have learned to value, like money.

Term

(1) operant conditioning
(2) positive reinforcement
(3) negative reinforcement
(4) primary reinforcement
(5) secondary reinforcement
(6) discrimination
(7) continuous reinforcement
(8) partial reinforcement
(9) ratio schedules
(10) interval schedules
(11) punishment
(12) shaping

MODULE 16

Self-Test Answers

Multiple-Choice Questions (continued)

5. d, 6. c

Matching Terms and Definitions

7. a. (11), b. (9), c. (3), d. (8), e. (2), f. (7), g. (10), h. (1), i. (5)

MODULE 16

Self-Test Answers

Fill-in-the-Blank Questions

8. E. B. Tolman; B. F. Skinner, 9. latent learning; overjustification effect, 10. biologically

Brief Essay Question

11. Students should demonstrate in their answers that they understand that shaping is based on the principle of positive reinforcement—the idea that you increase the likelihood that a behavior will occur in the future by presenting something desirable after the behavior appears. Immediate rewards are more effective than delayed rewards. Dylan's owner will shape Dylan's behavior by rewarding behaviors that resemble sitting, the desired goal. The owners will do this in small steps, immediately rewarding any small behavior (standing still, dropping the hindquarters even a little, briefly touching the hindquarters to the floor, and so on) that resembles or could lead to full sitting. This plan should work because shaping is widely used to change behavior while also avoiding punishment—Dylan will enjoy learning this new behavior!

Fill-in-the-Blank Questions

8. _________ _________ is the author of the law of effect, which laid the foundation for the work _________ _________ did on operant conditioning.

9. ______________ ______________ and the ______________ ______________ demonstrate that thought processes can affect operant learning.

10. Each species is ______________ predisposed to learn some things easily and to learn others only with great difficulty, if at all.

Brief Essay Question

11. Imagine that your best friend, Joe, is afraid of dogs, including your dog, Dylan, a big friendly golden retriever. You know Dylan would never hurt Joe, but Dylan gets very excited when he sees Joe and he often jumps up on him. You have decided that you will shape Dylan's behavior, so that he sits when he sees Joe, instead of jumping on him. In two or three short paragraphs, describe how you will use operant conditioning to shape Dylan's behavior, and why you think your plan will work.

Performance Standards

Standard Area: Learning

Content Standard 1: Understanding learning

Performance Standard 1.1 Understand learning from a psychological paradigm.

- Discuss the influential historical figures in the study of learning. Investigate the findings of Albert Bandura on observational learning. (Student Text pp. 325–327)

Content Standard 4: The role of cognition in learning

Performance Standard 4.1 Understand how observational learning functions.

- Discuss Albert Bandura's experiment in observational learning involving an inflatable "Bobo" doll. (Student Text pp. 325–327)
- Discuss the four conditions that need to be present for observational learning to occur (attention, retention, ability to reproduce the behavior, motivation). (Student Text p. 327)
- Investigate examples of observational learning in everyday life. (Student Text pp. 328–329)
- Discuss how antisocial and prosocial behaviors can result from observational learning. (Student Text pp. 328–329)
- Investigate the connection between violence in the media and violence in real life. (Student Text pp. 329–330)

Materials NETWORK

All of the items from the Video, Activity, and Enrichment Centers listed below come from the *Teacher's Resource Binder*. These items will help you teach and expand on concepts presented in Module 17.

trb This logo indicates when an item from the Materials Network may be used in conjunction with a specific note found in this module's *Teacher's Edition*.

Albert Bandura and Observational Learning

Activity Center

- Critical Thinking Activity: *Fact or Falsehood?* With this activity, students' preconceptions about observational learning are either exposed as incorrect or reinforced as correct. (*Teacher's Resource Binder*, p. 17-1; Handout 17–1)
- Building Vocabulary: Graphic Organizer: *Concept Web* This concept web includes module vocabulary about observational learning and shows relationships among these terms. (*Teacher's Resource Binder*, p. 17-1; Handout 17–2)

Observational Learning in Everyday Life

Activity Center

- Application Activity: *Acquiring a Skill Through Observation* By choosing a role model who exemplifies a desirable skill, students can use this self-directed activity to apply the concepts of observational learning. (*Teacher's Resource Binder*, p. 17-1)
- Cooperative Learning Activity: *The Power of Role Models in Advertising* In this activity, students explore why celebrities are powerful role models sought after by advertisers. (*Teacher's Resource Binder*, p. 17-1)

Enrichment Center

- Enrichment Lesson: *Germans Who Helped Jews Escape* One reason why some Germans helped Jews during World War II centered on the power of positive parental role models—role models who exemplified prosocial behavior—thereby showing how important positive role models are to forming lifelong altruistic behavior. (*Teacher's Resource Binder*, p. 17-1)

Observational Learning of Violence from the Media

Activity Center

- Analysis Activity: *Violence in Children's Media* Students can gather first-hand data on violence in different forms of children's media with this activity. (*Teacher's Resource Binder*, p. 17-1)

Enrichment Center

- Enrichment Lesson: *Observational Learning* Robert Cialdini's work on the power of influence by others is detailed, exploring how other people can influence our behavior in more ways than we usually want to admit. (Teacher's Resource Binder, p. 17-1)

MODULE 17

Observational Learning

How much have you learned by watching others? Can you imagine what it would be like to drive a car if you had never seen another person do it? Even if you'd been able to read the owner's manual (which explains how the car works) and your state driver's manual (which explains the rules of the road), actually driving the car would be next to impossible. It's one thing to read about transmissions, windshield wipers, and passing lanes, but it's something else entirely to be able to watch other people using them.

This is the stuff of *observational learning,* and thank goodness we are capable of it. Can a child learn from watching her older siblings? You bet. Just as a Little Leaguer can learn from watching his favorite Major League player, a video gamer can learn from watching her expert-level friend, and a new employee can learn on the job from watching a more experienced colleague. Not only can we profit from our own experiences, we can also profit from the experiences of others.

Albert Bandura and Observational Learning

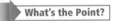

What's the Point? 1. How did Bandura's research demonstrate the principles of observational learning?

Observational learning takes place by watching others. It differs from other kinds of learning in that another person—the **model**—actually practices or repeats behaviors, which the learner observes and mimics in a

▶ **observational learning** Learning by observing others.

▶ **model** The person observed in observational learning.

MODULE 17

Observational Learning

Introducing the Module

The Points: Module Objectives

- Describe how Bandura's research demonstrated the principles of observational learning.
- Analyze how antisocial and prosocial behaviors develop as a result of observational learning.
- Address the connection between violence in the media and violence in real life

trb tr Building Vocabulary

Building Vocabulary: Graphic Organizer: *Concept Web* (*Teacher's Resource Binder,* p. 17-1; **Handout 17–2**) offers students opportunities to improve their understanding of the module's terms by allowing students to see how the terms in the module relate to each other. After students complete the organizer on their own, have them meet in small groups to compare and confirm their answers. You may also use the handout as a transparency to project (with answers inserted) a correctly completed concept web for groups to check their work.

Getting Started

You may want to start this module by asking volunteers to share a childhood experience in which they learned something by watching an older family member.

trb You may wish to use **Critical Thinking Activity:** *Fact or Falsehood?* (*Teacher's Resource Binder,* p. 17-1; **Handout 17–1**) as a prereading strategy to find out what students already know about observational learning. The activity will prime students to note terms and concepts in the text that confirm or dispel their preconceptions about topics in this module.

MODULE 17

Teaching the Points

web ■ **TEACHING TIP**

You can log on as an instructor to the book companion site for *Thinking About Psychology* at **www.worthpublishers.com/thinkingaboutpsych.** It contains teacher resources for class presentations as well as review and assessment of module concepts and terms.

■ **JOURNAL WRITING**

Invite students to use the following questions and writing prompts as springboards for entries in their psychology journals.

- Describe a time when you learned something observationally.
- Describe a time when someone learned something (good or bad) from you observationally.

Modeling Mom

process called **modeling.** It's an amazing thing, isn't it, that I can learn by modeling my behavior after that of another person? My learning is not an observable behavior. It occurs in my brain as a cognitive process.

American psychologist **Albert Bandura** conducted groundbreaking experiments in observational learning in the 1960s (Bandura & others, 1961). In one experiment, the researchers arranged for a young child to be playing in a room when an adult in another part of the room began a series of violent behaviors. The adult directed the behaviors toward an inflatable Bobo doll—the kind that are several feet tall with a weighted base so they right themselves when knocked over. The adult's tirade lasted for about 10 minutes. While tossing poor Bobo around, the adult shouted things like "Sock him in the nose. . . . Hit him down. . . . Kick him."

Albert Bandura Stanford psychologist Albert Bandura conducted groundbreaking research in observational learning.

In the next step of the experiment, the researchers took the child to a play room with many toys. When the child was happily engaged with the toys, the researcher interrupted to say that the playing would have to stop because the cool toys were being saved "for the other children." The child, now frustrated, was then taken to yet another room and left alone with only a few toys—and Bobo.

Bandura, of course, was interested in seeing how the child would now behave. Children who had observed an adult behaving aggressively with Bobo exhibited more aggression than other children in the experiment who hadn't observed the adult model. Those who had observed an attack on Bobo were not only more aggressive but also mimicked the exact behaviors and words they had seen. Observational learning was at work.

In another variation of his research, Bandura (1965) studied the effect of *consequences* delivered to the *model*—in this case, the adult demonstrating aggressive behavior for the youngster. Would such consequences affect the *observer*—in this case, the child observing the aggressive adult? We know that consequences—good and bad—affect how and what we learn. But what happens when we observe *another person* experiencing those consequences? To test this, Bandura produced a film that showed an adult model behaving aggressively ("Sockeroo!") toward the ever-present Bobo doll. For this film, however, the researchers could choose one of three different endings:

1. Another adult rewards the aggressive adult model with praise and candy. One group of children saw this ending.

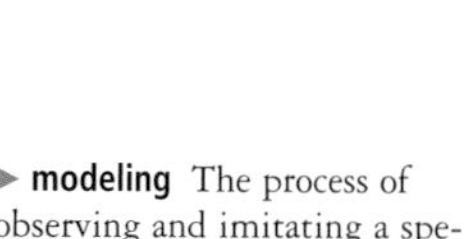

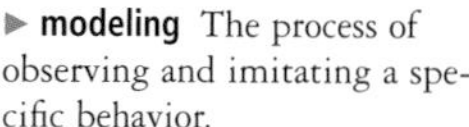

▸ **modeling** The process of observing and imitating a specific behavior.

▸ **Albert Bandura** (1925–) A major figure in the study of observational learning and several other important topics. Former president of the American Psychological Association.

Suggested Readings

Use the following as teacher-preparation tools or enrichment for advanced learners:

Allen, B. (2000). *Personality theories: Development, growth, and diversity* (3rd ed.). Boston: Allyn & Bacon.

Bandura, A. (1997). *Self-efficacy: The exercise of control.* New York: Freeman.

Cialdini, R. (1993). *Influence: Science and practice* (3rd ed.). New York: HarperCollins.

London, P. (1970). The rescuers: Motivational hypotheses about Christians who saved Jews from the Nazis. In J. Macaulay & L. Berkowitz (Eds.), *Altruism and helping behavior.* Orlando, FL: Academic Press.

Oliner, S., & Oliner, P. (1988). *The altruistic personality: Rescuers of Jews in Nazi Europe.* New York: Macmillan.

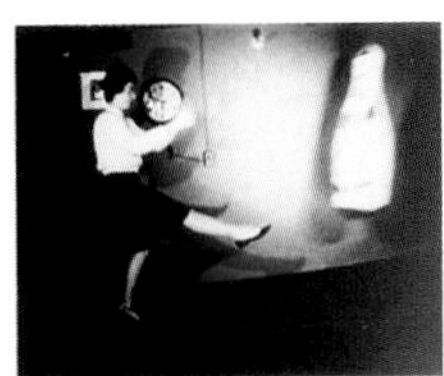

How Would You Treat Bobo? Bandura's research showed that children imitated, with uncanny precision, the behaviors that they saw modeled.

2. Another adult calls the model a "bad person" and spanks the model. A second group of children saw this ending.
3. The model receives neither a reward nor a punishment. A final group saw this neutral ending.

After viewing the video, each child in each group spent time in the play room with the Bobo doll and other toys. Children who saw the model rewarded for aggression behaved most aggressively in the play room, and those who saw the model spanked behaved least aggressively. This is referred to as *vicarious* learning—learning by seeing the consequences of another person's behavior. When the consequence is a reward, the observer is more likely to repeat the behavior.

In variation after variation, Bandura's experiments showed the same results—we learn by watching others *if* the following four conditions are met (Bandura, 1977):

1. ***Attention.*** To learn, you must be aware of the behaviors of those around you. A student who is attentive during PE stands a good chance of actually learning those line dances!
2. ***Retention.*** You must remember the behavior you witnessed. Will the attentive student be able to retain—from one week to the next—all those steps so expertly shown by the PE teacher?
3. ***Ability to reproduce the behavior.*** I have watched my sons skateboard many times, but I do not possess the required skills to do the tricks. Despite all my watching, my minimal sense of balance means I can barely stand on the board, even if it isn't moving!
4. ***Motivation.*** We are more likely to feel motivated to learn if the model we've observed has been rewarded for the behavior and if we like the model. The Nike corporation pays huge endorsement fees to Tiger Woods because its advertising agency believes likable megastars are effective models.

MODULE 17

■ **LOOKING AT THE ISSUES**

Ask students why, from an evolutionary perspective, observational learning is beneficial. Then allow time for a discussion. By the end of the discussion, make sure students understand that without the ability to learn by watching others, people would have to learn things the "hard way," which wouldn't always lead to optimal chances of survival.

■ **TEACHING TIP**

Vicarious learning is a type of observational learning. **Vicarious learning** depends on the learner understanding the consequences he or she has observed. Observational learning can occur without consequences being involved in a learning situation since **observational learning** is learning by observing others.

Meeting Individual Needs

trb GRAPHIC ORGANIZER Provide learning opportunities for all levels of learners with one of the following options for using **Building Vocabulary: Graphic Organizer:** *Concept Web* (*Teacher's Resource Binder*, p. 17-1; **Handout 17–2**):

- **Independent Learners** Students may fill out the organizer on their own or follow along in class during discussion and lecture.
- **Cooperative Learners** Students may use the textbook as a resource and work in groups to find the answers that fit in the blanks.
- **Exceptional Learners** The graphic organizer can fill a special educational need to provide notes for exceptional students. These students may fill in the blanks independently, with a student or teacher/tutor, or along with class discussion and lecture.

MODULE 17

■ JOURNAL WRITING
Invite students to use the following questions and writing prompts as springboards for entries in their psychology journals.

- Are you a role model for someone else? How? Describe both a positive and a negative role-modeling experience that you've been a part of and its effects on you.
- Have you ever been involved in a charity drive? Why did you join or start the campaign? What impact did the drive have on you and those you helped?

trb At this point, you may wish to use Cooperative Learning Activity: *The Power of Role Models in Advertising* (*Teacher's Resource Binder*, p. 17-1).

■ LOOKING AT THE ISSUES
Have students explore the school's administrative policies about handling student pranks. They can interview administration officials and teachers who have been with the school for several years about various pranks that have occurred. Bring the class together after interviews and research have been conducted and ask the following questions:

- Has there been a time in the school's history when a school prank "went wrong"? What happened? What was done about it?
- What rules or policies exist today to deter or handle school pranks?

► **antisocial behavior** Negative, destructive, unhelpful behavior.

► **prosocial behavior** Positive, constructive, helpful behavior.

Observational Learning in Everyday Life

2. How do antisocial behaviors and prosocial behaviors develop as a result of observational learning?

Children are capable of learning by observation almost from the moment of birth. Thus, the cumulative effect this mountain of observations has on behavior is tremendous and can be either positive or negative. Children learn much that's appropriate from models, but—as we saw in the Bobo experiments—they also learn much that's inappropriate.

People are often unaware of the impact they have on others. Retired professional basketball star Charles Barkley repeatedly argued in the early 1990s that he was a basketball player, not a role model. It's easy to understand why he didn't want to be considered responsible for those mimicking his "bad boy" behaviors, but Barkley's position was not realistic. It is impossible to choose *not* to be a role model. If you're in the public eye as a professional athlete or entertainer, you are—by the nature of your position—a powerful role model. Even those of us who are not in the public eye will almost certainly influence others. If you have younger brothers or sisters, rest assured they look up to you and learn from you how to behave in a variety of situations, just as you may have learned from older siblings. If a new person is hired at your place of work, or if you're a senior on a sports team, *you* are a role model. Whether you realize it or not, others are watching and learning from you.

Role Model Music stars such as Eminem create controversy because the public cannot agree about whether the modeled behaviors are appropriate. Can you think of other stars who create such controversy?

But even if you can't control whether or not others will see you as a role model, you do have some control over the *kind* of role model you will be. You can model **antisocial behaviors,** which are negative and destructive, like some students in my school whose "leadership" resulted in a rash of vandalism in the name of "pranks" during homecoming week. Or you can model **prosocial behaviors,** which are positive, constructive, and helpful, like other students in my school whose behavior spearheaded a drive to collect thousands of cans of food

Alternative Assessment/Portfolio Project

OBSERVATIONAL LEARNING EXPERIENCE Students can improve a skill by choosing a role model and observing his or her behavior over a period of time. Application Activity: *Acquiring a Skill Through Observation* (*Teacher's Resource Binder*, p. 17-1) details a project in which students identify someone who possesses a skill that they want to improve in their own lives. Through interviews and observation, students can learn techniques to change their behavior. They can demonstrate these newly found skills in a class "talent show." As a tool for assessment, students can write about their experience in a series of journal entries.

Role Model People will imitate either prosocial or antisocial behavior. The same learning principles apply no matter what behavior is modeled.

when donations to the local food bank dried up after the 9/11 terrorist attacks. In each case, the actions of a few students snowballed into a much bigger trend. Your choices do make a difference!

Observational Learning of Violence From the Media

3. What is the connection between violence in the media and violence in real life?

If you're a typical American teenager, by the time you graduate from high school, you will have spent more time watching television than you spent in school (Elliot, 1996). Not only does almost every home

Real-Life Instant Replay to Follow? Is there a connection between violence in the media and violence in society? Research indicates that we do learn aggression from what we observe.

Enriching

Have students use the questions below to survey a representative sample of students in your school to see how much violent media they have seen in their lives. Afterwards, have students compare the responses of females and males. (Be sure to get permission from an Institutional Review Board—IRB—and to obtain informed consent before pursuing any research project.)

- What type of television shows did you enjoy watching when you were little? What shows do you watch now?
- When did you first see a "violent" movie? Do you like violent movies now? Why or why not?
- What kinds of video games did you play when you were a kid? If you still play video games, what kinds of games do you prefer?

■ JOURNAL WRITING

Invite students to use the following questions and writing prompts as springboards for entries in their psychology journals:

- Do you feel you live in a more violent society than the one your parents lived in? Why or why not?
- Do you feel you are exposed to too much violence? Why or why not? How does watching violence make you feel? Explain.

■ APPLYING THE POINTS

Have students interview their parents and grandparents. These interviews should focus on policies for allowing children to view violence on television, in movies, and in video games. Have students meet in small groups and respond to the following questions:

- Do these policies seem to consider the research findings of Albert Bandura and his colleagues?
- Were their policies different for siblings of different gender and ages? If so, how?
- How different were the policies of your grandparents and parents? Explain the differences.
- What policies will you use in the future for your own children? Why did you choose these policies?

You might want to travel from group to group to clarify issues, answer questions, and listen to responses.

■ MULTICULTURAL CONNECTIONS

European cultures view media violence as taboo and restrict how much violence can be shown on television and in movies. Using library or Internet sources, have students research how other cultures view violence in the media. In particular, have them focus on the following question:

- Are juvenile crime rates higher or lower in cultures that restrict media violence than that in the United States?

trb At this point, you may wish to use **Analysis Activity:** *Violence in Children's Media* (*Teacher's Resource Binder*, p. 17-1) and/or **Enrichment Lesson:** *Observational Learning* (*Teacher's Resource Binder*, p. 17-1).

MODULE 17

■ LOOKING AT THE ISSUES

Is our society more violent today than in the past? Have students use available resources, including the Internet, to research crime statistics from the last 50 to 100 years. On the basis of their research, ask students to hypothesize reasons why violent crime has increased over time or decreased from time to time. The following questions may help focus discussion about students' findings:

- How has the influence of the media changed over the last century?
- In addition to media violence, what are some other variables that might also explain the increase in crime over the last century?

trb At this point, you may wish to use **Enrichment Lesson:** *Germans Who Helped Jews Escape* (*Teacher's Resource Binder*, p. 17-1) to help students see that sometimes violence within one's culture is difficult to identify and combat.

Close

Ask students, "Who becomes a role model?" Even though Charles Barkley didn't want to become one, the research shows that some people can't help but be role models. Have students independently create a list of people for whom they could act as a role model. Then have them reflect whether they would be a positive role model or a negative one for the different people on their lists. Use the following questions to promote class discussion:

- Are there people on your list that you don't normally think you influence? Why?
- On which people that you've listed do you think you exert the most influence? Why?

have a TV set, the vast majority have more than one. And what about the content of all this TV programming? Much of it is undeniably violent. The average U.S. student has witnessed about 8000 murders and well over 100,000 violent acts by the end of elementary school (Huston & others, 1992). Only about half of these cases of violence portray pain or harm to the victim in a realistic way (Mediascope, 1995). Keep in mind that these statistics relate only to television. Movies, video games, print media, and the Internet provide even more exposure to violence.

The key question, of course, is whether all this observation of violence makes any difference in real life. Research indicates it does. Bandura's experiments, and more like them, indicate that we do learn aggression from what we observe. The American Psychological Association's Commission on Violence and Youth (1993) reached these conclusions after an extensive review of the available research:

- Higher levels of viewing violence on television are associated with increased acceptance of aggressive attitudes and increased aggressive behavior.
- Children's exposure to violence in the mass media, particularly at young ages, can have harmful, lifelong consequences.
- Film and TV portrayals of women in victim roles and of ethnic minorities in aggressive and violent roles worsen the violence experienced by women and ethnic minorities.
- The viewing of television programming and commercials affects our concept of reality and how we believe others live.

The commission also concluded that TV *could* be an effective prosocial force. The media are sources of observational learning. Society can, however, choose whether the media will function as a prosocial or antisocial learning model.

We take, we give. We learn, we teach. Others have served as role models for you, and you serve as role models for others. Give some thought to the lessons you are providing for others, and choose carefully the models you will follow.

Cooperative Learning

Have students work in groups to operationally define "violence" as seen in the media. Then have them select several programs to watch and count the number of violent acts committed in each show. Afterward, have group members compare their tallies and discuss their results.

- What type of shows had the most violence? Why?
- What type of shows had the least violence? Why?
- Did students see violent acts that didn't fit the group's operational definition? Why or why not?
- Was the violence presented as entertaining (for comedic purposes) or as a representation of real-world experience?

REVIEW

Review Module 17, Observational Learning

What's the Point?

Albert Bandura and Observational Learning

1. *How did Bandura's research demonstrate the principles of observational learning?*

   Observational learning is learning we acquire by observing models and imitating their behavior. Bandura's research, especially his famous Bobo-doll experiments, demonstrated that children can learn to behave aggressively by observing others behave aggressively. In further experiments, Bandura and his colleagues showed that we learn by watching others, but only if we pay attention, remember the behavior we witnessed, are able to reproduce the behavior, and are motivated because the person we observed either received a reward or was very likable.

Observational Learning in Everyday Life

2. *How do antisocial behaviors and prosocial behaviors develop as a result of observational learning?*

   Whether a model's behavior is "bad" or "good" does not affect another person's ability to mimic that behavior, providing the observer pays attention, remembers the behavior, can reproduce the behavior, and is motivated to reproduce the behavior. Other people serve as role models for us, and each of us is in turn a role model for others. We cannot choose whether we will be role models, but we can choose whether we will model negative and destructive (antisocial) behaviors or positive, constructive, and helpful (prosocial) behaviors.

Observational Learning of Violence From the Media

3. *What is the connection between violence in the media and violence in real life?*

   We all tune into the media—television, newspapers, magazines, the Internet, movies, video games, and so on. Each of these media sources is a window through which we can observe models performing behaviors we may later mimic. These media forms could expose us to prosocial learning models, but they very often flood us with antisocial behaviors, including aggressive and violent acts.

Key Terms

observational learning, p. 325
model, p. 325
modeling, p. 326
antisocial behavior, p. 328
prosocial behavior, p. 328

Key People

Albert Bandura, p. 326

MODULE 17

Checking the Points

■ TEACHING TIPS

web (1) The book companion site for *Thinking About Psychology* at **www.worthpublishers.com/thinkingaboutpsych** contains a module quiz, flashcards of key terms and people, and other student activities and resources for this module. You will also find PowerPoint lectures, a quiz grade book, and other teaching resources by logging on as an instructor.

trb (2) Use **Critical Thinking Activity:** *Fact or Falsehood?* (*Teacher's Resource Binder,* p. 17-1; **Handout 17–1**) as a review activity if you did not use it as a prereading strategy at the beginning of the module. If the handout was used at the beginning of the module, encourage students to look it over to gauge how their preconceptions fared against what they read and learned in Module 17.

trb (3) To review the module vocabulary, you might have students work with partners to complete the concept web presented in **Building Vocabulary: Graphic Organizer:** *Concept Web* (*Teacher's Resource Binder,* p. 17-1; **Handout 17–2**). Otherwise, use the organizer as a transparency, inserting answers and projecting it for the class to use as a review.

MODULE 17

Using the Test Bank

The *Test Bank* that accompanies this textbook offers a wide variety of questions in different formats and levels of complexity. Use the software to construct whole tests or to integrate standardized questions into teacher-made tests.

Self-Test Answers

Multiple-Choice Questions

1. b, 2. a, 3. d

Matching Terms and Definitions

4. a. (6), b. (2), c. (5), d. (3), e. (4)

Brief Essay Question

5. Students' answers should demonstrate that they understand the basic principles of observational learning and that children tend to imitate what they see, not do what they are told to do. People learn most easily if they are aware of the behaviors of those around them, if they remember the behavior they observed, if they are able to reproduce the behavior, and if they are motivated by seeing the behavior rewarded. Younger siblings learn from observing older sisters and brothers. Elsie's little brother and sister will probably learn not only to watch TV programs that contain violent scenes, but also to deceive their parents by watching these programs when the parents are not around.

Self-Test

Multiple-Choice Questions

Choose the *best* answer for each of the following questions:

1. Carla, who works at home, has been very busy lately. Her 5-year-old son, Drew, has been watching TV a lot more, including some old movies starring the Three Stooges. Last week, Drew's teacher phoned to say that Drew was slapping his classmates on the side of the head. Drew is
   a. behaving prosocially in school and antisocially at home.
   b. modeling the behavior he observed in the Three Stooges movies.
   c. showing normal behavior for a 5-year-old boy.
   d. displaying early warning signals of a mental disorder.
2. Every week, Vikram watches a home improvement show on TV, and every week, the main builder puts on ear protectors and safety glasses before running his electric saw. The builder's display of safe behavior in the workshop is an example of
   a. being a role model.
   b. antisocial behavior in the media.
   c. vicarious learning.
   d. nefarious learning.
3. Sam watched carefully as his friend, Joey, yelled a dirty word at their kindergarten teacher. The teacher was angry, and she gave Joey a timeout for using bad words, which made Joey cry. Sam knows what the dirty word means, but he is unlikely to imitate Joey and yell it at their teacher because
   a. Joey is too young to be a role model.
   b. Joey's behavior is too complicated to reproduce.
   c. Sam wasn't paying attention to Joey's behavior.
   d. Joey's behavior was not rewarded, and so Sam won't be motivated to learn it.

Matching Terms and Definitions

4. For each definition, choose the *best* matching term from the list that follows:

Definition

a. Stanford psychologist who conducted groundbreaking research on observational learning.
b. The person who is observed during observational learning.
c. Positive, constructive, helpful behavior.
d. The process of observing and imitating a specific behavior.
e. Negative, destructive, unhelpful behavior.

Term

(1) observational learning
(2) model
(3) modeling
(4) antisocial behavior
(5) prosocial behavior
(6) Albert Bandura
(7) Bobo
(8) vicarious learning

Brief Essay Question

5. Elsie's parents pay her to babysit her little brother and sister two nights a month. Everyone is happy with this arrangement—Elsie enjoys the extra money, her parents feel secure knowing she is with the younger children, and the younger children adore Elsie and look forward to these evenings. Elsie also enjoys the opportunity to watch TV shows that contain a lot of violent scenes—shows that Elsie's parents would not let her watch if they were home. In two paragraphs of about three sentences each, explain to Elsie how this behavior may affect her younger siblings, and why.

CHAPTER

8 Memory

Cognitive Domain

Teaching with the Standards

Standard Area: Memory

Breakdown of Module 18: Information Processing

Content Standard 1: Encoding in memory Module 18 identifies many of the factors involved in encoding. The author discusses the role of automatic and effortful processing in the information processing system. Also, the differences between semantic, visual, and auditory encoding are discussed. Examples also demonstrate the important role of imagery in encoding. (Student Text pp. 335–338, 339–340)

Content Standard 2: Characteristics of short-term and long-term memory Module 18 discusses the duration and capacity of both the short-term and long-term memory systems. Examples are provided of chunking to increase the capacity of short-term memory. Primacy and recency effects are also demonstrated. Hermann Ebbinghaus's research on nonsense syllables is presented. Explicit and implicit memories are also described in the context of the biological process of memory storage. (Student Text pp. 336–337, 342–345, 348–349)

Content Standard 3: Retrieval in memory The text analyzes the importance of retrieval cues in memory. The two forms of memory—recall and recognition—are explained. The effect context has on our ability to retrieve memories is also discussed. The role our physical condition and mood play in the retrieval process is addressed. (Student Text pp. 350–352)

Content Standard 4: Physiological bases of memory The process of getting information into long-term memory is discussed. Emphasis is on the biological bases for memory storage, specifically the concept of long-term potentiation. The role of the hippocampus in processing explicit memories is presented, as well as the role of the cerebellum in storing implicit memories. (Student Text pp. 345–349)

Content Standard 5: Strategies for improving memory Module 18 presents many methods for improving memory ability. The role of rehearsal, overlearning, and the spacing effect are presented. The use of mnemonic devices, such as the method of loci or the peg-word system, are explored as ways to improve memory. (Student Text pp. 336–343)

Breakdown of Module 19: Forgetting and Memory Construction

Content Standard 1: Encoding in memory Examine how lack of encoding causes memory failure. Test your memory skills: Have you encoded what a penny looks like? (Student Text pp. 359–360)

Content Standard 2: Characteristics of short-term and long-term memory Module 19 investigates the effects of time on long-term memory storage. Herman Ebbinghaus' "forgetting curve" is discussed. (Student Text pp. 361–362)

Content Standard 3: Retrieval in memory The role of interference in retrieval failure is explored. Examples are provided of proactive and retroactive interference. In addition, the issues surrounding memory construction are explored. Elizabeth Loftus' research on the misinformation effect is discussed. (Student Text pp. 362–368)

Content Standard 5: Strategies for improving memory Module 19 examines how motivated forgetting can help explain repressed memories. In addition, the factors that may influence the accuracy of a child's recall are explored. The controversy surrounding recovered memories is discussed. Emphasis is on why we should be cautious in trusting the accuracy of memories, including our own. (Student Text pp. 368–371)

Scope and Sequence

	Objectives	Text Reference	Standards Covered
Lesson 1	Introduce the information-processing model. Define and discuss the process of encoding, storage, and retrieval. Introduce sensory, short-term, and long-term memory.	Module18, pp. 334–335, 343–346	Standard Area: Memory, Content Standard 1, Performance standard 1.1, Content Standard 2, Performance Standards 2.1, 2.2
Lesson 2	Discuss memory encoding. Examine the role of automatic and effortful processing in encoding. Discuss the influence of rehearsal, overlearning, the spacing effect and the serial position effect on later memory retrieval. Compare semantic, auditory, and visual cues and later recall.	Module18, pp. 336–343	Content Standard 1, Performance Standards 1.1, 1.2, Content Standard 2, Performance Standards 2.1, 2.2
Lesson 3	Discuss the role of imagery in encoding. Discuss different types of mnemonic devices and how they improve retention. Discuss how organizing memories by chunking or hierarchies when encoding can improve retrieval.	Module18, pp. 340–343	Content Standard 1, Performance Standard 1.2, Content Standard 5, Performance Standard 5.2
Lesson 4	Examine the capacity and duration of sensory, short-term, and long-term memory. Compare explicit and implicit memory. Investigate the role of the hippocampus and cerebellum in memory storage. Explain long-term potentiation.	Module18, pp. 343–349	Content Standard 2, Performance Standards 2.1, 2.2, Content Standard 4, Performance Standard 4.1
Lesson 5	Examine the two processes of retrieval: recall and recognition. Discuss the role of context in memory retrieval. Examine state-dependent and mood-congruent memories. Discuss how organizing memories by chunking or hierarchies can improve retrieval.	Module18, pp. 350–352	Content Standard 3, Performance Standard 3.1
Lesson 6	Examine the factors involved in forgetting. Discuss encoding, storage, and retrieval failure. Discuss proactive and retroactive interference as sources of forgetting.	Module19, pp. 359–364	Content Standard 1, Performance Standard 1.2, Content Standard 2, Performance Standard 2.2, Content Standard 3, Performance Standard 3.2
Lesson 7	Discuss memory construction. Introduce the misinformation effect. Discuss the controversy surrounding recovered memories and the use of testimony given by children.	Module19, pp. 364–371	Content Standard 3, Performance Standard 3.3, Content Standard 5, Performance Standard 5.1
Lesson 8	Review and test		

Memory

Now, where did I leave those car keys? Dang! Why can't I ever remember what I was supposed to pick up at the grocery store? And why do I forget lists and keys but not the time when my favorite TV show is on, or the route I follow to work? (In fact, I can follow that route without even thinking about it!) And what about the accuracy of memories? Sometimes my teenage son and I have entirely different memories of an event we experienced together. We can't both be right, yet we both sincerely believe we are. How can that be explained?

This chapter will give you glimpses of the answers to these questions and more. We'll look at how memories are processed, from encoding (getting the information into memory) to storage (tucking the information away) to retrieval (getting it back when you need it). We'll also examine how memory can fail and be inaccurate. Let's hope you find it memorable!

CHAPTER 8

CHAPTER 8

Memory

Introducing the Chapter

The Points: Chapter Objectives

- Compare how humans and computers utilize the information processing model.
- Differentiate between automatic and effortful processing.
- Evaluate why distributed rehearsal is more effective than massed rehearsal.
- Analyze why semantic encoding improves memory.
- Analyze how mnemonic devices help encode for storage and easy retrieval.
- Apply the use of chunking to memorize information, such as with the 50 states.
- Identify and describe the two types of sensory storage.
- Describe the techniques to increase the limited capacity of short-term memory.
- Identify the capacity and duration of long-term memory.
- Differentiate between explicit and implicit memory.
- Identify the parts of the brain that process different types of memory.
- Analyze how recall and recognition are used to measure memory retrieval.
- Evaluate the importance of context in memory.
- Analyze how the lack of encoding causes memory failure.
- Understand current knowledge about the effects of time on long-term memory storage.
- Describe how memories are disrupted by proactive and retroactive interference.
- Explain why repressed memories are examples of motivated forgetting.
- Analyze how constructed memories combine true and false information.
- Understand why psychologists are cautious about claims of recovered memories.

MODULE 18

Performance Standards

Standard Area: Memory

Content Standard 1: Encoding in memory

Performance Standard 1.2 Describe variables that affect encoding.

- Present the information-processing model. Explain the role of encoding. (Student Text pp. 335–336)
- Figure 18.1, "Memory as Information Processing," illustrates the role of encoding. (Student Text p. 335)
- Discuss the role of automatic and effortful processing in encoding. (Student Text pp. 336–337)
- Discuss the role of rehearsal on memory. (Student Text pp. 336–338)
- Figure 18.3, "Rehearsal and Retention," illustrates Ebbinghaus' research findings. (Student Text p. 337)
- Discuss visual, auditory, and semantic encoding. (Student Text pp. 339–340)
- Figure 18.5, "The Advantage of Semantic Encoding," demonstrates that semantic encoding increases retention. (Student Text p. 340)
- Emphasize the advantage of encoding imagery. (Student Text p. 340)
- Explain memory organization by chunking and hierarchies. (Student Text pp. 342–343)

Content Standard 2: Characteristics of short-term and long-term memory

Performance Standard 2.1 Describe short-term memory.

- Define the primacy and recency effect. (Student Text p. 338)
- Define chunking. (Student Text p. 342)
- Figure 18.7, "Effectiveness of Chunking," allows students to see the usefulness of this tool. (Student Text p. 342)
- Discuss the duration and capacity of short-term memory. (Student Text pp. 344–345)

Performance Standard 2.2 Describe long-term memory.

- Present Hermann Ebbinghaus' research on rehearsal. (Student Text pp. 336–338)
- Figure 18.3, "Rehearsal and Retention," illustrates Ebbinghaus's research findings. (Student Text p. 337)
- Discuss the duration and capacity of long-term memory. (Student Text pp. 345–346)
- Compare explicit and implicit memories. (Student Text pp. 348–349)

Content Standard 3: Retrieval in memory

Performance Standard 3.1 Discuss the role of retrieval cues in memory.

- Compare recall and recognition. (Student Text p. 350)
- Investigate how context affects memory retrieval. (Student Text p. 351)
- Discuss priming. (Student Text pp. 350–351)
- Figure 18.12, "Context and Memory," demonstrates the role context plays in how we remember. (Student Text p. 351)
- Explain state-dependent and mood-congruent memories. (Student Text p. 352)

Content Standard 4: Physiological bases of memory

Performance Standard 4.1 Identify brain regions vital to memory.

- Discuss the process of long-term potentiation. (Student Text pp. 347–348)
- Explore the role of the hippocampus in explicit memory storage. (Student Text pp. 348–349)
- Examine how the cerebellum functions in the memory. (Student Text pp. 348–349)
- Figure 18.10, "Explicitly or Implicitly Remembered?," summarizes the role of the hippocampus and cerebellum in memory. (Student Text p. 349)

Content Standard 5: Strategies for improving memory

Performance Standard 5.2 Methods for improving memory.

- Discuss the value of overlearning. (Student Text pp. 337–338)
- Investigate why distributed rehearsal is effective. (Student Text p. 339)
- Examine the usefulness of mnemonic devices. (Student Text p. 341)
- Discuss how organization improves our memories. (Student Text pp. 342–343)
- Table 18.1, "Tips for Becoming a Better Encoder," provides ideas to improve memory. (Student Text p. 343)

Materials NETWORK

All of the items from the Video, Activity, and Enrichment Centers listed below come from the *Teacher's Resource Binder.* These items will help you teach and expand on concepts presented in Module 18.

trb This logo indicates when an item from the Materials Network may be used in conjunction with a specific note found in this module's *Teacher's Edition.*

The Information-Processing Model

V Video Center

Consult the faculty guide from *The Mind* video series for descriptions of these modules.

- Videocassette: *The Mind,* Second Edition, Module 10: "Life Without Meaning: The Case of Clive Wearing" (Part 1) (*Teacher's Resource Binder,* p. 18-1)
- Videocassette: *The Mind,* Second Edition, Module 11: "Clive Wearing: Living Without Memory" (*Teacher's Resource Binder,* p. 18-1)

Activity Center

- Critical Thinking Activity: *Fact or Falsehood?* With this activity, students' preconceptions about information processing are either exposed as incorrect or reinforced as correct. (*Teacher's Resource Binder,* p. 18-1; Handout 18–1)
- Building Vocabulary: *Mnemonic Devices* Students memorize module terms and their definitions by using mnemonic devices, which are discussed and presented in the text. (*Teacher's Resource Binder,* p. 18-1)
- Graphic Organizers: *Making Sense of Memory—Encoding, Storage, and Retrieval* Each of the three graphic organizers for this module helps students learn concepts about memory in terms of how information is either encoded, stored, or retrieved. (*Teacher's Resource Binder,* p. 18-1; Handouts 18–2a through 18–2c)
- Technology Application Activity: *PsychQuest:* "Can We Rely on Our Memory?" *PsychQuest* is an interactive CD-ROM containing tutorials in different areas of psychology. In this tutorial, students work on the concept of memory. (*Teacher's Resource Binder,* p. 18-1)

Enrichment Center

- Enrichment Lesson: *The World Memory Championships* People actually compete to see who has the world's greatest memory. Students learn more about these championships in this lesson. (*Teacher's Resource Binder,* p. 18-1)
- Enrichment Lesson: *The Case of Clive Wearing* Clive Wearing was a talented musician until encephalitis robbed him of the ability to store memories. (Use *The Mind* video series modules described in the Video Center under The Information-Processing Model to go into further detail.) (*Teacher's Resource Binder,* p. 18-1)

Encoding

Activity Center

- Application Activity: *Serial Position Effect in Recalling U.S .Presidents* This activity has students recall the first 43 U.S. presidents, demonstrating primacy and recency effects in the process. (*Teacher's Resource Binder,* p. 18-1)
- Application Activity: *Visually Versus Auditorally Encoded Information* This activity powerfully demonstrates the benefits of visual imagery as students use different techniques to encode information. (*Teacher's Resource Binder,* p. 18-1; Handout 18–3)
- Application Activity: *The Self-Reference Effect* This activity demonstrates that when we think of a word in terms of ourselves, the word becomes more memorable. (*Teacher's Resource Binder,* p. 18-1; Handout 18–4)
- Application Activity: *Meaning and Memory* Students are more likely to remember complex information if they have a context for that information. This activity, which describes a common experience in abstract terms, is more memorable when put in a meaningful context. (*Teacher's Resource Binder,* p. 18-1)
- Application Activity: *Semantic Encoding of Pictures* Memory for pictures surpasses memory for words; however, both types of memory depend on how well the material is understood. In short, meaning is important for both visual and verbal memory. (*Teacher's Resource Binder,* p. 18-1; Handout 18–5)
- Demonstration Activity: *Mnemonic Devices in Action* To illustrate the power of mnemonic devices, begin your lecture with a classroom demonstration that showcases your own use of mnemonics. (Caution: This activity is for the brave of heart!) (*Teacher's Resource Binder,* p. 18-1)
- Demonstration Activity: *Method of Loci* Take students on a trip through your house or classroom as you demonstrate your memory by using the method of loci. (*Teacher's Resource Binder,* p. 18-1)

- Application Activity: *Chunking* As the text indicates, information organized into chunks is recalled more easily. Chunking often occurs so naturally that we take it for granted. With this activity, you can easily demonstrate how chunking works as students try to memorize an increasingly longer set of numbers. (*Teacher's Resource Binder*, p. 18-1)
- Application Activity: *Meaningful Chunks* With this activity, students discover that meaningful units of information increase the amount of information one can remember. (*Teacher's Resource Binder*, p. 18-1)

Enrichment Center

- Enrichment Lesson: *Mnemonic Devices* Mnemonic devices are of both theoretical and practical importance. They can be used to illustrate the role of meaning, imagery, and organization in successful encoding. If time allows you only one lecture on memory, this topic is a good choice. (*Teacher's Resource Binder*, p. 18-1)
- Enrichment Lesson: *The Keyword Method* With this lesson, highlight the power of a mnemonic device that provides a practical, psychology-related example for students to use. (*Teacher's Resource Binder*, p. 18-1)

Storage

V Video Center

Consult the faculty guide from *The Brain* and the *Scientific American Frontiers* video series for descriptions of these modules and segments.

- Videocassette: *The Brain,* Second Edition, Module 20: "A Super-Memorist Advises on Study Strategies" (*Teacher's Resource Binder*, p. 18-1)
- Videocassette: *The Brain,* Second Edition, Module 16: "The Locus of Learning and Memory" (*Teacher's Resource Binder*, p. 18-1)
- Videocassette: *The Brain,* Second Edition, Module 18: "Living with Amnesia: The Hippocampus and Memory" (*Teacher's Resource Binder*, p. 18-1)
- Videocassette: *The Brain,* Second Edition, Module 17: "Learning as Synaptic Change" (*Teacher's Resource Binder*, p. 18-1)
- Videocassette: *Scientific American Frontiers,* Second Edition, Segment 16: "Remembering What Matters" (*Teacher's Resource Binder*, p. 18-1)

Activity Center

- Technology Application Activity: *PsychSim:* "Iconic Memory" *PsychSim* is an interactive CD-ROM containing tutorials in different content areas of psychology. In this tutorial, students work with the concept of iconic memory. (*Teacher's Resource Binder*, p. 18-1)
- Application Activity: *Memory Capacity* Demonstrate the "Magic Number Seven, Plus or Minus Two" with this activity. (*Teacher's Resource Binder*, p. 18-1)
- Analysis Activity: *Flashbulb Memory* Personally significant events tend to be remembered vividly. Help students recall flashbulb experiences with this activity. (*Teacher's Resource Binder*, p. 18-1)

Enrichment Center

- Enrichment Lesson: *Rajan Mahadevan's Amazing Memory* Learn more about this graduate student from India who memorized an amazing 31,811 digits of pi. (*Teacher's Resource Binder*, p. 18-1)
- Enrichment Lesson: *Episodic, Semantic, and Procedural Memory* This lesson highlights that long-term memory can be broken down even further. (*Teacher's Resource Binder*, p. 18-1)

Retrieval

Activity Center

- Application Activity: *Retrieval Cues* Like information stored in encyclopedias, memories may be inaccessible until we have cues for retrieving them. This activity shows that cue words have power on recall. (*Teacher's Resource Binder*, p. 18-1; **Handout 18–6a** and **18–6b**)
- Demonstration Activity: *Expertise and Retrieval Rates* As people develop expertise in an area, central concepts become increasingly elaborated, organized, and interconnected. By organizing their knowledge in these ways, experts recall information more efficiently. (*Teacher's Resource Binder*, p. 18-1)
- Application Activity: *Déjà vu in the Classroom* Students often ask for an explanation of the déjà vu experience—that eerie sense that "I've been in this exact situation before." Drew Appleby provides a classroom demonstration of the déjà vu experience. (*Teacher's Resource Binder*, p. 18-1)
- Application Activity: *The Pollyanna Principle* The Pollyanna principle states that pleasant items and events are usually processed more efficiently and accurately than less pleasant ones. Although the principle presumably also applies to a variety of phenomena in perception, language, and decision making, it has been best documented in memory. (*Teacher's Resource Binder*, p. 18-1)
- Application Activity: *Remembering the Seven Dwarfs* Students have a harder time recalling the names of the Seven Dwarfs than they do recognizing them. This memory demonstration highlights how difficult processing information can be, even with familiar material. (*Teacher's Resource Binder*, p. 18-1; **Handout 18–7**)

Enrichment Center

- Enrichment Lesson: *Making Doctors' Instructions More Memorable* Studies indicate that patients typically forget up to half the information provided to them by their doctors. Remembering the advice is obviously important to physical well-being; it also correlates highly with a patient's general level of satisfaction with medical care. (*Teacher's Resource Binder*, p. 18-1)

MODULE 18

Information Processing

Introducing the Module

The Points: Module Objectives

- Identify the three basic steps in the information-processing model.
- Differentiate between automatic and effortful processing, and explain how we use them to encode school-related information.
- Explain how an item's position in a list influences the memory of that item.
- Evaluate why distributed rehearsal is more effective than massed rehearsal.
- Analyze how semantic encoding improves memory.
- Explain how encoding imagery aids our memory.
- Analyze how mnemonic devices help us encode memories for storage and easy retrieval.
- Identify two ways of organizing information and how they help us encode large amounts of information.
- Identify and describe the two types of sensory memory.
- Describe techniques we can use to increase the limited capacity and duration of short-term memory.
- Explain the capacity and duration of long-term memory.
- Explain how we get information into long-term memory.
- Explain explicit and implicit memories and which parts of the brain process each of these types of memory.
- Identify two forms of memory retrieval.
- Explain how context affects our ability to retrieve memories.
- Evaluate how our physical condition and mood affect our ability to retrieve memories.

MODULE 18

Information Processing

Information processing enables memory, a cognitive skill so important that it's virtually impossible even to imagine life without it. Before leaving for school this morning, I need to remember to let the dog out. I also need to remember to put the student papers I read last night into my briefcase and bring some ground beef up from the freezer in preparation for tonight's dinner. As I sit here working, I can remember details from my recently completed weekend. The football game I saw on television was close enough to hold my attention all the way to the end. My wife and I went to a pretty good movie on Saturday. On Friday, my recreational league volleyball team won two of three games in a hotly contested match. I actually got both feet off the ground at once to spike the ball a couple times!

We rely on memory all the time, and not just for the details of our daily lives. I need to remember who I am and what I stand for. I need to remember the norms our society has developed—the "proper" rules for behavior: what to do with my trash, how to answer the phone, which side of the hall to walk on, and a thousand other guidelines that let us coexist in a complex society. I also need to remember how to cook, how to balance my checkbook, how to wash my clothes, and how to program the VCR. And, though I am not consciously aware of it, I even need to remember the meanings of words in my language, and the processes necessary for walking or standing upright.

In this module, we will focus on memory, using an information-processing model (Atkinson & Schiffrin, 1968).

Getting Started

Before students read this module, ask them how they think people are able to remember things, from simple tasks like tying their shoes to complex concepts like those they learn in various school subjects. Suggest that as students read the module they compare their initial speculations to the concepts about memory they learn in the text.

trb You may wish to use **Critical Thinking:** *Fact or Falsehood?* (*Teacher's Resource Binder*, p. 18-1; **Handout 18–1**) as a pre-reading strategy to find out what students already know about memory and information processing. The activity will prime students to note terms and concepts in the text that confirm or dispel their preconceptions about these topics.

The Information-Processing Model

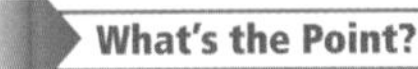

1. What are the three basic steps in the information processing model?

There are certainly differences between how a human brain works and how a computer works, but they both process information in three basic steps (Figure 18.1):

1. **Encoding,** or getting information into the memory system.
2. **Storage,** or retaining information over time.
3. **Retrieval,** or getting information out of storage.

Let's see how these three steps work as computers process information.

To begin with, nothing happens unless you can *encode* information or get it into the computer. There are various options for doing this, but two common devices for encoding information are keyboards and modems. Once encoded, the information must be retained in *storage.* Computers offer two kinds of storage, one temporary and the other more permanent. Temporary storage takes place in the active memory of the computer that keeps the various applications open on your desktop. You know how temporary this memory is if you've ever briefly lost power while working on a project. More permanent storage is available on the computer's hard drive. This storage can even survive the computer's "loss

▶ **encoding** The process of getting information into the memory system. The first stage of the information processing model of memory.

▶ **storage** The retention of encoded information over time. The second stage of the information processing model of memory.

▶ **retrieval** The process of getting information out of memory storage. The third and final stage of the information processing model of memory.

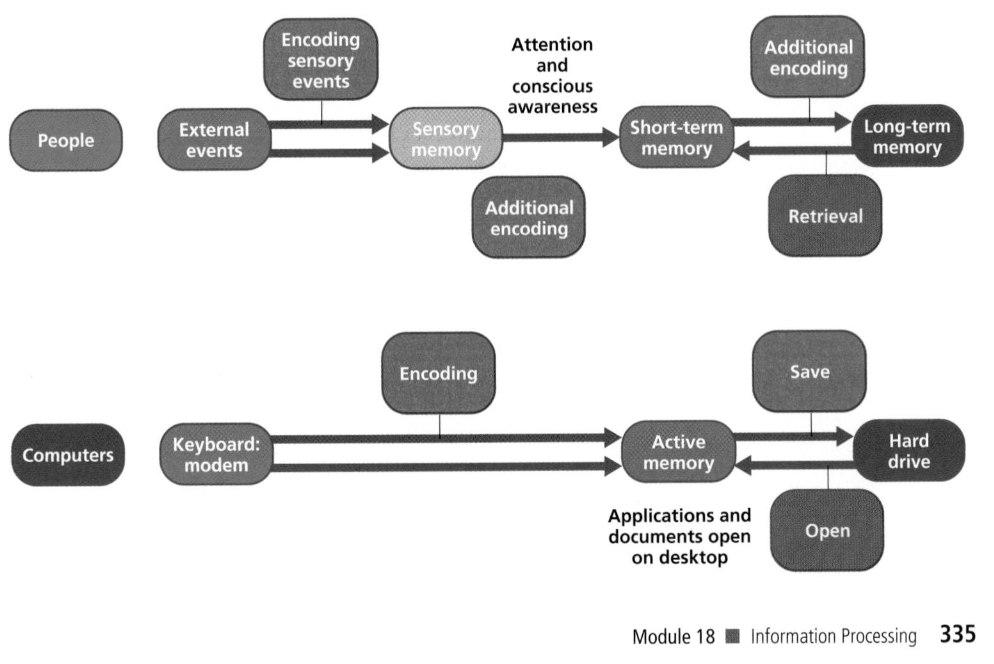

Figure 18.1 Memory as Information Processing Computer memory and human memory differ in many ways, but they share three basic steps: encoding information, storing information for later use, and retrieving information.

Suggested Readings

Use the following books as teacher-preparation tools or as further reading for advanced students:

Baddeley, A. (1998). *Human memory: Theory and practice* (Rev. ed.). Boston: Allyn & Bacon.

Hilts, P. J. (1995). *Memory's ghost: The strange tale of Mr. M. and the nature of memory.* New York: Simon & Schuster.

Matlin, M. (1998). *Cognition* (4th ed.). Fort Worth, TX: Harcourt.

Pinker, S. (1997). *How the mind works.* New York: Norton.

Restak, R. M. (1988). *The mind.* New York: Bantam.

Schacter, D. L. (1996). *Searching for memory: The brain, the mind, and the past.* New York: Basic Books.

Solso, R. (1998). *Cognitive psychology* (5th ed.). Boston: Allyn & Bacon.

Thompson, C., Cowan, T., & Frieman, J. (1993). *Memory search by memorist.* Hillsdale, NJ: Erlbaum.

trb Building Vocabulary

Students can apply the mnemonic techniques suggested in the text as they learn and review the vocabulary terms at the end of the module. You may wish to have students present a brief oral explanation of a device they chose along with the word and definition they committed to memory as described in Building Vocabulary: *Mnemonic Devices* (*Teacher's Resource Binder,* p. 18-1).

Teaching the Points

■ TEACHING TIPS

web (1) You can log on as an instructor to the book companion site for *Thinking About Psychology* at www.worthpublishers.com/thinkingaboutpsych. It contains teacher resources for class presentations as well as review and assessment of module concepts and terms.

(2) Ask your students if they can recite the second sentence of the "Pledge of Allegiance." Everyone will think this is easy, and they will think through the entire pledge before realizing it consists of a single sentence.

trb At this point, you may wish to use Technology Application Activity: *PsychQuest:* "Can We Rely on Our Memories?" (*Teacher's Resource Binder,* p. 18-1).

tr A four-color transparency of Figure 18.1, Memory as Information Processing, is available in the Overhead Transparencies Set.

web ■ APPLYING THE POINTS

The San Francisco Exploratorium site includes a number of fascinating memory demonstrations and activities at www.exploratorium.edu/memory/index.html. Have students work with partners or in small groups to explore this site and choose several of the activities to complete. Afterwards, have students respond to the following questions:

- How well did you do on the memory tasks?
- Are the types of memory games highlighted in the site related to the type of memory you use in school? Why or why not?

MODULE 18

F • Y • I

If studying occurs in 15- to 20-minute intervals with a minimum of 5-minute breaks in between study sessions, information is more likely to be remembered on a test. If students would take 15 to 20 minutes per class a day to review what was learned that day, they would likely see an improvement in their grades and experience a sense that school is easier.

■ **MULTICULTURAL CONNECTIONS**
Have students research these questions at a local university library or on the Internet:

- Are there differences in how people encode information in other cultures?
- Are people from a particular culture more likely to use a particular encoding scheme unique to their culture, or do they use techniques that other cultures also use?

Students who wish to investigate the same culture may work together, pool their research, discuss the questions, and present their findings in a brief oral report to the class, possibly for extra credit.

► **automatic processing** The unconscious encoding of some information, such as space, time, and frequency, without effort.

► **effortful processing** Encoding that requires attention and conscious effort.

► **rehearsal** The conscious repetition of information.

► **Hermann Ebbinghaus** (1850–1909) German philosopher who conducted pioneering memory studies.

► **overlearning** Rehearsal of information beyond the point where it has been learned. Overlearning is an effective strategy for improving memory.

of consciousness" when it's turned off! But all this encoding and storage would be useless if you couldn't *retrieve* information from storage. If you're careful about setting up folders and subfolders, this can be a snap. If you're not careful, you can lose documents. You may know you've stored a project, but if you can't recall its name or the folder where you placed it, you won't be able to retrieve it easily.

Human beings also encode information. Instead of a modem or a keyboard, we use our senses to gather information. Then we must store the information, either temporarily or permanently. Finally, we must gain access to the memories we have permanently stored. Let's take a more detailed look at these three steps in the human system.

Encoding

Encoding is the process in which you move information—the raw material, the "stuff" that you will ultimately remember—into your memory system. Good students are invariably good encoders of information. Fortunately, we can control some of the factors that influence how well we encode information.

Automatic and Effortful Processing

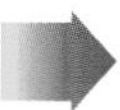

2. How do automatic and effortful processing differ, and how do we use them to encode school-related information?

Automatic processing is an unconscious process of capturing, or encoding, information. Have you ever had the experience of taking a test and being able to remember exactly *where* in your textbook the information is, but not being able to remember *what* the information is? That's because we encode place information automatically (probably because it provides an evolutionary advantage—it's important to remember where threats in the environment came from, for example). We also tend to encode information about time and frequency automatically.

Unfortunately, you can't automatically capture *what* you've written in your notes. To master that information, you must pay attention and work hard, because it requires **effortful processing** (Figure 18.2). Research indicates that some processing strategies are more effective than others, and the most important one seems to be **rehearsal,** or practice.

Hermann Ebbinghaus taught us much of what we know about the importance of rehearsal. Ebbinghaus, a nineteenth-century German philosopher, wanted data to support his ideas about memory. To get those data, he spent a considerable amount of time committing to

Meeting Individual Needs

trb GRAPHIC ORGANIZER Provide learning opportunities for all levels of learners with **Graphic Organizers:** *Making Sense of Memory—Encoding, Storage, and Retrieval* (*Teacher's Resource Binder*, p. 18-1; **Handouts 18–2a** through **18–2c**). Distribute each organizer at the appropriate point in the module, beginning now with the organizer for encoding.

- **Independent Learners** Students may fill out the organizer on their own or follow along in class during discussion and lecture.
- **Cooperative Learners** Students may use the textbook as a resource and work in groups to find the answers that fit in the blanks.
- **Exceptional Learners** The graphic organizer can fill a special education need to provide notes for exceptional students. These students may fill in the blanks independently, with a student or teacher/tutor, or along with class discussion and lecture.

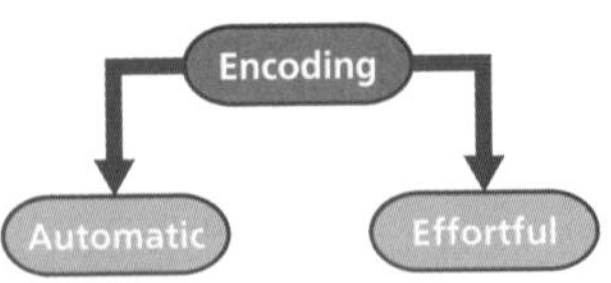

Figure 18.2 Automatic and Effortful Processing Thanks to automatic processing, this student will be able to remember where he studied his textbook with no effort at all. But he will have to pay attention and use effortful processing to encode the information he's trying to learn from the book!

memory lists of three-letter nonsense syllables. If this sounds like nonsense to you, keep in mind that Ebbinghaus wanted to memorize only unfamiliar items. His major conclusion? The more you rehearse, the more you retain (Figure 18.3). Practice, indeed, does make perfect. Here's your first tip for becoming a good encoder: *The more time you invest in rehearsing, the more effective your memory is going to be.*

Another effective processing strategy is **overlearning**—continuing to rehearse even after you have committed something to memory. Students who play musical instruments know they should continue to practice pieces that they can already play without error. And gymnasts

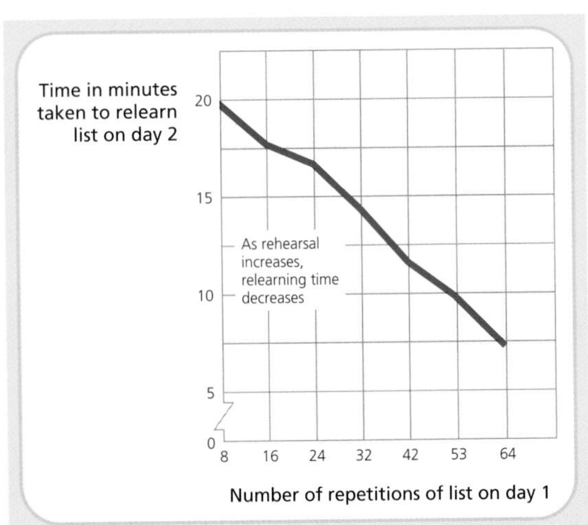

Figure 18.3 Rehearsal and Retention Hermann Ebbinghaus discovered that the more times he rehearsed a list on the first day, the less time it took to be able to repeat the list with no errors on the second day. (From Baddeley, 1982.)

tr ■ TEACHING TIP

A four-color transparency of Figure 18.3, Rehearsal and Retention, is available in the **Overhead Transparencies Set.**

■ JOURNAL WRITING

Invite students to use the following questions and writing prompts as springboards for entries in their psychology journals:

- How much effort do you put into studying? Why?
- Do you spend as much time overlearning schoolwork as you do overlearning skills needed for mastering hobbies or activities? Why?
- What images do you hold in your memory from your elementary school experience? Are the images mostly positive or negative or both? Why?

Demonstrating

Compile a list of words (nonsense or otherwise) and have students spend some time memorizing it each day for a few days. In order to facilitate memorization, challenge students to come up with a mnemonic device for the list and to use it each day. Time students daily to see how long it takes them to recite the list of words. Afterward, have students discuss this experience.

- What mnemonic device did students use? Did they rehearse the list outside of class? Why or why not?
- How long did it take them to remember the list on the first, second, and fifth day? Did their learning curve look like Ebbinghaus'? Why or why not?

trb At this point, you may wish to use **Demonstration Activity:** *Method of Loci* (*Teacher's Resource Binder*, p. 18-1).

MODULE 18

■ **TEACHING TIP**

To remember the difference between *primacy* and *recency effect*, point out that a word drawn from the same root word for **primacy** is *primary*, which means "first." With this kind of memory, we can remember items that come at the beginning of the list. **Recency** is related to the word *recent*. We use this kind of memory for items that come at the end of the list—in other words, items that occurred in the most recent memory.

trb At this point, you may wish to use **Application Activity:** *Serial Position Effect in Recalling U.S. Presidents* (*Teacher's Resource Binder*, p. 18-1).

tr A four-color transparency of Figure 18.4, The Serial Position Curve, is available in the **Overhead Transparencies Set.**

F•Y•I

What would it be like to process every piece of sensory input in the environment? This may be what life is like for people with attention-deficit hyperactivity disorder (ADHD). PET scan studies show that the brains of people with ADHD seem to be unable to filter out what it is important to give their attention to in the environment.

trb At this point, you may wish to use **Technology Application Activity:** *PsychSim:* "Iconic Memory" (*Teacher's Resource Binder*, p. 18-1).

Practice Makes Perfect! Whether in sports, music, or academics, more rehearsal leads to better performance.

know that they must continue to rehearse mistake-free routines in order to give their best performances. Overlearning is just as important for school-related information. So here's your second tip: *Continue to rehearse academic information even after you think you have it mastered.* This is one of the best ways to make sure the information is available under stressful test conditions.

Serial Position Effect

3. How does an item's position in a list influence our memory of that item?

How many times have you taken a test in which you had to remember a list of items? Probably a lot. At such times, the **serial position effect**—the tendency to recall the first and last items on the list more easily—comes into play. Chances are good that you struggled most with recalling the middle items (Figure 18.4). You may also have experienced the serial position effect if you were introduced to a dozen new people at a party. By the end of the evening, which ones were you most likely to remember? The folks you met first and last. Each of these conditions has its own term:

- The *primacy effect* enhances our ability to recall items near the beginning of a list. We have more opportunities to rehearse those first items. Memory researchers who want to minimize the primacy effect may present the list of items quickly, thus eliminating the opportunity to rehearse between items.
- The *recency effect* enhances our ability to recall items near the end of a list. The most recent items are freshest in memory. Memory researchers who want to eliminate the recency effect will delay recall or distract the memorizer by asking several unrelated questions (What is your zip code?) between presenting the final items and asking people to recall the list (from Craik & Watkins, 1973).

Percentage of words recalled: 90%, 80, 70, 60, 50, 40, 30, 20, 10, 0

Recency effect

Primacy effect

1 2 3 4 5 6 7 8 9 10 11 12

Position of word in list

Figure 18.4 The Serial Position Curve People given a list of items and later asked to recall the items had little trouble remembering the first few items (the primacy effect) and the last few items (the recency effect). The hardest items to recall are those in the middle. (From Craik & Watkins, 1973.)

Here is your third tip: *Devote extra rehearsal time to the middle of lists you must memorize.*

Demonstrating

Have students sit in a circle in the classroom. Starting at one point in the circle and going clockwise, have students offer a piece of information about themselves that other students would not likely know. Then, after all students have offered a piece of information, have them write down each student's information. Plot students' information that was remembered best. This graph should reflect the serial position curve, showing the primacy and recency effects.

Spacing Effect

4. Why is distributed rehearsal more effective than massed rehearsal?

Rehearsal can be more or less effective, depending on when you do it. Research on the **spacing effect** (Dempster, 1988) shows **distributed rehearsal**—or spread-out sessions—works better than **massed rehearsal**, rehearsal packed together into longer sessions (cramming). Consider the way performers practice. Do actors or musicians mass all their rehearsals for the week into a single, day-long session? No, because as the performers tire, additional rehearsal becomes less and less valuable. So here's your fourth tip: *If you cram all your studying into one long session the night before an exam, you will not encode the information as effectively as you would if you space your study time fairly evenly throughout the unit.* You may put in as many hours, but you won't learn as much per hour. In fact, the spacing effect is one of the most powerful arguments for the use of comprehensive semester final exams—reviewing the material from a course throughout the semester will actually enhance *lifelong* retention of the material (Bahrick & others, 1993)!

Encoding Meaning

5. How does semantic encoding improve our memories?

If rehearsal is central to encoding, so is meaningfulness. In fact, you might well think of rehearsal and meaningfulness as the twin pillars of encoding. If you're interested in cutting down the amount of time you spend in rehearsal (and what student isn't?), your most effective option is to make the material meaningful, a process known as **semantic encoding.**

Research shows that when we encode according to meaning, we remember more effectively than when we encode either sounds (*acoustic encoding*) or images (*visual encoding*). In one experiment, researchers flashed words to participants and then followed with questions that led to semantic, acoustic, or visual processing of information (Figure 18.5, p. 340). For example, to get participants to process acoustically, the researchers might ask whether the flashed word rhymed with another word. To promote semantic encoding, researchers would ask whether the flashed word would fit in a particular sentence. The participants remembered much better when they had encoded the material semantically (Craik & Tulvig, 1975).

Ebbinghaus himself estimated that it was *10 times* harder to learn nonsense syllables than meaningful material. To search for meaning is therefore a wise investment of your time, but where do you find it? If you're ready for your fifth tip, I'll tell you: *One good way to add meaning to material is to use the* ***self-reference effect*** *by relating it to your own life.*

▶ **serial position effect** Our tendency to recall best the first and last items in a list.

▶ **spacing effect** The tendency for distributed practice to yield better retention than is achieved through massed practice.

▶ **distributed rehearsal** Spreading rehearsal out in several sessions separated by periods of time.

▶ **massed rehearsal** Putting all rehearsal time together in one long session (cramming).

▶ **semantic encoding** The encoding of meaning.

▶ **self-reference effect** The enhanced semantic encoding of information that is personally relevant.

■ **APPLYING THE POINTS**

Ask students what specific techniques they use to study for tests. Most students are likely to use very shallow processing without much meaning involved. Have students bring in material from a class in which they have a test coming up. Spend some time in class helping individual students develop meaningful connections to the material. Reserve some time for students to share with the class how they made the information meaningful. Note what type of encoding techniques (self-reference effect, semantic encoding, and so forth) students used. Encourage them to share how well they did on the test with the class.

 At this point, you may wish to use **Application Activity:** *Meaning and Memory* (*Teacher's Resource Binder,* p. 18-1) and **Application Activity:** *The Self-Reference Effect* (*Teacher's Resource Binder,* p. 18-1; **Handout 18–4**).

tb ■ **CHECKING FOR UNDERSTANDING**

Create a quiz using questions from the *Test Bank* to assess students' knowledge of the concepts in this module. With so many interrelated concepts, giving such short quizzes periodically during this module may prove helpful in keeping students on track.

Demonstrating

MEMORY CAPACITY To give students an idea of how difficult it is to remember a random string of numbers, give them 30 seconds to memorize the following 30 numbers: 2 1 6 9 6 4 6 1 5 1 9 9 7 2 5 2 4 6 8 0 1 2 9 6 1 6 0 8 9 4. (Before class, write the numbers on the chalkboard and cover with a screen, prepare a transparency, or distribute written copies.) After 30 seconds have passed, have students write the numbers down in sequence. Nancy Shulins suggests that 4–9 correct is average, 10–19 is extraordinary, 20–29 is brilliant. Ask those who perform well to indicate how they did it.

trb At this point, you may wish to use **Application Activity:** *Memory Capacity* (*Teacher's Resource Binder,* p. 18-1).

MODULE 18

■ TEACHING TIPS

tr (1) A four-color transparency of Figure 18.5, The Advantage of Semantic Encoding, is available in the **Overhead Transparencies Set.**

(2) Have students recall images of historical events that they have found to be particularly memorable (i.e., pictures of natural disasters, the *Columbia* accident, the war with Iraq, etc.). Pose the following questions to help them speculate about why these images are so compelling:

- Are tragic images more compelling than joyful ones? Why or why not?
- Are photos of historical events you read about in history books less memorable than ones you see "live" on television? Why or why not?
- Does constant news coverage of an event cause you to be more or less interested in the event? Why?

trb At this point, you may wish to use **Application Activity:** ***Visually Versus Auditorially Encoded Information*** (*Teacher's Resource Binder*, p. 18-1; **Handout 18–3**).

■ JOURNAL WRITING

Invite students to use the following questions and writing prompts as springboards for entries in their psychology journals:

- Do you remember elementary school fondly? Middle school? Why or why not?
- Do you feel you've had a good high school experience? In the future, what do you think will be your most memorable experiences from high school?
- Do you look forward to future high school reunions? Why or why not?

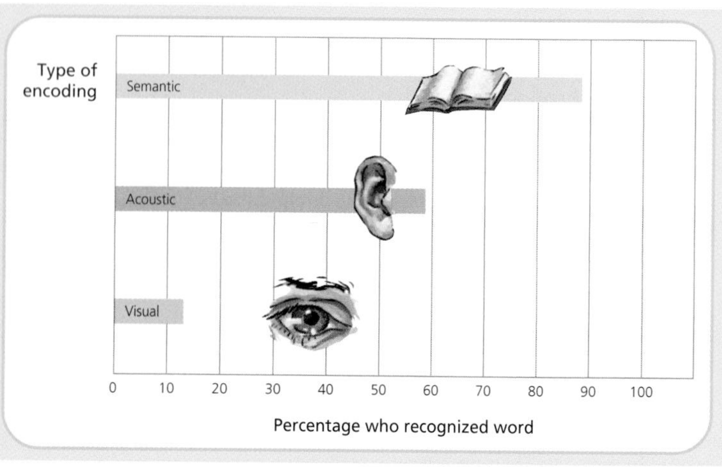

Figure 18.5 The Advantage of Semantic Encoding This graph shows the results of a study in which researchers flashed words and caused people to process the words according to their meaning (*semantic encoding*), sound (*acoustic encoding*), or image (*visual encoding*). They found that people were more likely to remember the words if they had considered their meaning. (From Craik & Tulving, 1975.)

Search for such connections and you will encode, and remember, the material more effectively (Symons & Johnson, 1997). Meaningful connections are particularly easy to find in a psychology course because the subject matter—behavior and mental processes—relates to *you*.

Encoding Imagery

6. How does encoding imagery aid our memory?

Encoding visual images is relatively easy. Our mental pictures tend to stick, as you well know if you've ever struggled to rid your mind of the image of an unpleasant event. The videos of the collapse of the World Trade Center towers will surely remain with us for the rest of our lives. Images of positive events also tend to stick in our minds. Do you have positive images of your elementary school days? For many of us, these happy snapshots overwhelm the less pleasant aspects of grade school. The third-grade roller skating party remains, but the day you suffered through class with a stomach ache does not. This tendency to encode images of the high points while letting the tedious or less joyous moments pass causes us to recall events—like elementary school—more positively than we actually felt about them at the time. Just think, this *rosy retrospection* (Mitchell & others, 1997) will probably apply one day to your high school memories! The tests, relationship hassles, and scheduling difficulties will likely be overwhelmed by more pleasant images.

The Power of Images None of us will forget the horrible images of September 11, 2001.

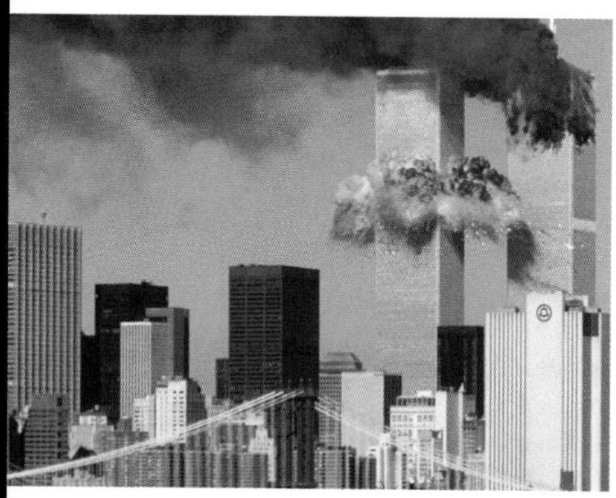

Enriching

Have students interview a parent or grandparent about their high school experience. Suggest students include the following questions in their interviews, and use the same questions to discuss the completed interviews in class:

- Was high school a good experience? Why or why not?
- What was your most memorable experience from that time?
- What significant historical events happened during your high school years? Do you remember any of those events vividly? Which one, and what about it do you remember best? Why?

trb At this point, you may want to use **Application Activity:** ***The Pollyanna Principle*** (*Teacher's Resource Binder*, p. 18-1).

Mnemonic Devices

 7. How do mnemonic devices help us encode memories for storage and easy retrieval?

Which way do you set your clock for daylight savings time? I remember "spring forward." When using a screwdriver, it's "righty-tighty, lefty-loosey." I do well naming the Great Lakes, too, because of the acronym HOMES—Huron, Ontario, Michigan, Erie, and Superior. These are examples of **mnemonic devices** (pronounced nih-MON-ik), a formal term for memory tricks. If you recall that we encode visual images fairly easily, you'll understand why so many of these tricks rely heavily on imagery. The method of loci and the peg-word system are two of the best-known image-based mnemonic devices.

Have you ever heard a speaker preface major points of a talk with phrases like "In the first place I'd like to discuss . . . " or "In the second place let's shift our attention to . . . "? Where are these "places" the speaker is referring to? They are in the imagination, and they relate to an old speaker's technique for remembering major points in the days before Teleprompters. The technique, the **method of loci**, associates items to be remembered with specific locations in the imagination. Let's say I want to remember to remind my classes of an upcoming assignment and a day I'll have to miss class because of a conference. To use the method of loci, I might imagine my living room, with student papers strewn all over my couch, waiting to be corrected. I could "see" myself trying to enter the room and tripping over a suitcase sitting by the door. Later, in school, I would return to this scene in my mind. The couch would remind me of the assignment, and the suitcase would remind me of the trip.

Another mnemonic device that depends on imagery is the **peg-word system.** To use this memory trick, you would learn a set of peg words—words or phrases on which you can "hang" items you want to remember (Figure 18.6). The more striking and unusual the image,

▶ **mnemonic device** A memory trick or technique.

▶ **method of loci** A mnemonic device in which you associate items you want to remember with imaginary places.

▶ **peg-word system** A mnemonic device in which you associate items you want to remember with a list of peg words you have already memorized.

One is a bun.
Two is a shoe.
Three is a tree.
Four is a door.
Five is a hive.
Six is a pile of sticks.
Seven is heaven.
Eight is a gate.
Nine is a line.
Ten is a hen.

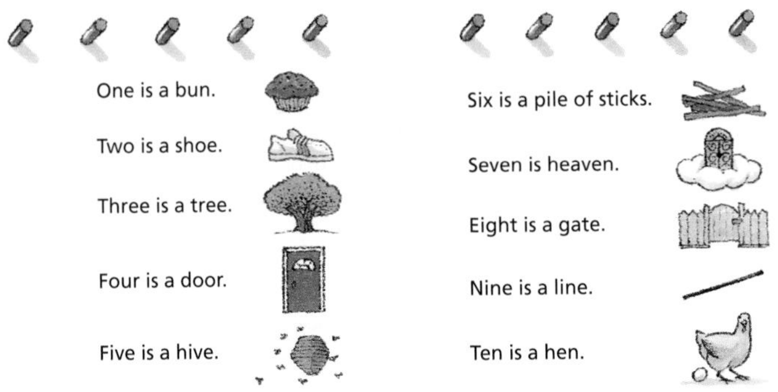

Figure 18.6 **A Simple Peg-Word System** Learn these 10 "pegs" and you can use them to remember any list of 10 items by creating vivid associations between the items and the pegs. Research shows a list learned this way can be remembered in any order with few errors (Bugelski & others, 1968). Notice that the pegs (*bun, shoe,* and so on) rhyme with the numbers (*one, two,* and so on)—a mnemonic device in its own right.

MODULE 18

■ TEACHING TIPS

(1) Have students share mnemonic devices they have developed or learned in the past. For what subjects did mnemonics work for them? Most likely, subjects in which facts and procedures are dominant (math, science, social studies) are more likely to successfully employ mnemonics than subjective or interpretative subjects, like English and drama.

web (2) Michael Tipper provides a Web site for accelerated learning, which includes an extensive treatment of mnemonics—all the way from memory aids for spelling words to ones for remembering rock formations. It can be found at **www.happychild.org.uk/acc/tpr/mne/index.htm**.

trb At this point, you may wish to use **Demonstration Activity:** ***Mnemonic Devices in Action*** (*Teacher's Resource Binder,* p. 18-1) and **Enrichment Lesson:** ***Mnemonic Devices*** (*Teacher's Resource Binder,* p. 18-1).

trb tr A black-line master for Figure 18.6, A Simple Peg-Word System, is available in the **Black-Line Masters Appendix** of the *Teacher's Resource Binder.*

MODULE 18

■ TEACHING TIP

Why are phone numbers divided into groups of three and four numbers? Why are social security numbers divided into three numbers, then two numbers, and then four numbers? The answer is that people can remember more pieces of information in chunks. By dividing the numbers into smaller groups, people are more likely to remember the entire list of numbers.

trb At this point, you may wish to use **Application Activity:** *Chunking* (*Teacher's Resource Binder*, p. 18-1).

trb tr A black-line master for Figure 18.7, Effectiveness of Chunking, is available in the **Black-Line Masters Appendix** of the *Teacher's Resource Binder*.

▶ **chunking** Organizing information into meaningful units.

the less likely you are to forget the item. For example, assume that my first item is carrots, and my peg for item one is *bun*. To come up with a vivid image linking carrots and buns, I could imagine a steaming hot carrot in a hot dog bun and see myself adding ketchup, mustard, onions, and relish before taking a big, delicious bite. Then I'd associate my second item with the peg *shoe*, and so on. You are right if you're thinking this is a lot of effort, but memories encoded with the peg-word system can last a long time. When I use it to teach a 10-item list to my students, they can usually recall the list perfectly more than a month later. So here's your encoding tip on using mnemonics: *Memory tricks like the method of loci and the peg-word system can create vivid images that you won't easily forget.*

Organizing Information

8. What are two ways of organizing information, and how do they help us encode large amounts of information?

I happened to stumble across a NASCAR race on television the other day and was amazed by the efficiency of the pit crews. They were able to accomplish more in a few seconds than my local mechanic can do in an hour. Many factors help explain this, not the least of which is organization. Each member of the pit crew plays a meaningful role in a highly organized structure designed to produce maximum efficiency.

Another tip on becoming a successful encoder: *You can encode more efficiently if you take a few moments to organize your information first.* Organizing information into meaningful units is called **chunking.** You can encode many more letters if they are organized into meaningful words and sentences than you can if they are just randomly grouped (Figure 18.7).

Organizing information into a *hierarchy* is another effective encoding technique. Hierarchies are organizational systems that focus on the relationships between pieces of information. The most familiar example of a hierarchical organization is an outline, which you've probably done for papers or other assignments. By indenting subpoints beneath main points, you get a sense of how each piece of information relates to the rest of the information. Chemistry's periodic table of elements is another example of hierarchical organization. It is so central to the field that it hangs

ROW 1	RNN TYW KTYU ACDF OAHNSOO RTA UO UCR OYO
ROW 2	ASK NOT WHAT YOUR COUNTRY CAN DO FOR YOU

Figure 18.7 **Effectiveness of Chunking** Give yourself 10 seconds to learn the letters in Row 1. How well did you do? Now try Row 2. Did you do any better? The identical letters appear in both rows, but they are easier to encode if they are chunked, or organized into meaningful units—in this case, into words, and then into a meaningful sentence.

Demonstrating

CHUNKING Read aloud the following string of numbers: 1 7 7 6 1 8 1 2 1 8 6 1 1 9 1 7 1 9 4 1 1 9 6 3 1 9 8 6 2 0 0 2. Have students write down as many numbers as they can recall.

Then, read aloud the same numbers, chunking them in the following way: 1776, 1812, 1861, 1917, 1941, 1963, 1986, 2002. Have students write down as many of the numbers as they remember. Their responses will demonstrate the power of chunking to remember large amounts of information.

trb At this point, you may wish to use **Application Activity:** *Chunking* (*Teacher's Resource Binder*, p. 18-1) and **Application Activity:** *Meaningful Chunks* (*Teacher's Resource Binder*, p. 18-1).

TABLE 18.1 TIPS FOR BECOMING A BETTER ENCODER

1. ***Rehearse.*** The more time you invest in rehearsing, the more effective your memory is going to be.
2. ***Overlearn.*** Continue to rehearse academic information even after you think you have it mastered.
3. ***Overcome the serial position effect.*** Devote extra rehearsal time to the middle of lists you must memorize.
4. ***Benefit from the spacing effect.*** If you cram all your studying into one long session the night before an exam, you will not encode the information as effectively as you would if you space your study time fairly evenly throughout the unit.
5. ***Take advantage of the self-reference effect.*** One good way to add meaning to material is to relate it to your own life.
6. ***Use mnemonic devices.*** Memory tricks like the method of loci and the peg-word system can create vivid images that you won't easily forget.
7. ***Chunk material or arrange it in a hierarchy.*** You can encode more efficiently if you take a few moments to organize your information first.

on the wall of every chemistry classroom and is printed inside the cover of every chemistry textbook. Each row and column provides specific meaning to help the user know how the elements relate to one another.

So, did you encode all those tips we gave you on becoming a better encoder? If you need to rehearse them, read through the list in Table 18.1.

Storage

Storage is retention of information, the very core of memory. Humans have three distinct storage systems, each with a different degree of permanence. We will deal with them in order from least to most permanent: *sensory memory, short-term memory* (which includes *working memory*), and *long-term memory.*

Sensory Memory

9. What are the two types of sensory memory?

Our senses are constantly bombarded with sensory input. Consider how many objects are in view right now. If you're in a classroom, there are undoubtedly displays on the wall, scenes visible through windows (if you're lucky enough to have windows in your room!), and people to look at. Each of those people offers much to see—facial features, hairstyle, items of clothing, jewelry, and so forth. And that's just visual

  ■ TEACHING TIP

A black-line master for Table 18.1, Tips for Becoming a Better Encoder, is available in the **Black-Line Masters Appendix** of the *Teacher's Resource Binder.*

F • Y • I

Several documented cases exist of people who have lost the ability to form new memories. One such case involves a musician named Clive Wearing. Having lost his memory because of an illness, Clive lived his life in the momentary present, experiencing fleeting realizations of his condition.

trb At this point, you may wish to use **Enrichment Lesson:** *The Case of Clive Wearing* (*Teacher's Resource Binder,* p. 18-1).

Meeting Individual Needs

trb GRAPHIC ORGANIZER If you did not do so earlier in the module, you can provide learning opportunities for all levels of learners with **Graphic Organizers:** ***Making Sense of Memory—Encoding, Storage, and Retrieval*** (*Teacher's Resource Binder,* p. 18-1; **Handouts 18–2a** through **18–2c**). At this point in the module, have students focus on the organizer for storage.

- **Independent Learners** Students may fill out the organizer on their own or follow along in class during discussion and lecture.
- **Cooperative Learners** Students may use the textbook as a resource and work in groups to find the answers that fit in the blanks.
- **Exceptional Learners** The graphic organizer can fill a special education need to provide notes for exceptional students. These students may fill in the blanks independently, with a student or teacher/tutor, or along with class discussion and lecture.

MODULE 18

■ TEACHING TIP

The next time you call on a student who doesn't seem to be paying attention, pause briefly before asking him or her to recall what you just said or discussed. He or she will be less likely to rely on echoic store to "prove" that he or she was listening.

■ APPLYING THE POINTS

Have students make their own animated movies, using a stack of paper or a Post-It note pad. Have them draw successive figures on several sheets of paper. After they've finished drawing their movies, they can flip the pages rapidly so that their figure "moves," demonstrating how iconic store works.

trb At this point, you may wish to use Technology Application Activity: *PsychSim:* "Iconic Memory" (*Teacher's Resource Binder*, p. 18-1).

input. What can you hear right now? Is anyone talking? Is there machinery operating? Is there music in your environment? Even a quiet environment might include the rustling of papers or the gentle sound of someone breathing. Add to this the smells, tastes, touches, and internal feedback on balance and positions that you receive from your body, and it becomes obvious that we gather much more information at any instant in time than we can possibly cope with or hope to use. **Sensory memory** is a way of encoding this sensory input just long enough to make a decision about its importance.

We can hold visual information in sensory memory for less than half a second, in the *iconic store* (Sperling, 1960). It is the iconic store (think of the little pictures that constitute computer icons to remember that *iconic* is visual) that helps us to hold one image in our visual field until another image replaces it. We hold auditory, or sound, information in sensory memory for perhaps three or four seconds, in the *echoic store* (Cowan, 1988; Lu & others, 1992). Have you ever been spacing off in class and had a teacher ask, with an irritated tone, "What did I just say?" Did you notice that you can generally retrieve that information, even though you truly weren't paying attention? Thank your echoic (from the word "echo") store for this ability.

Short-Term Memory

10. What techniques can we use to increase the limited capacity and duration of our short-term memory?

Your **short-term memory** is more permanent than sensory memory. This part of your memory system contains information you are consciously aware of at any point in time. Sometimes, short-term memory is referred to as *working memory* to emphasize the active processing that occurs there. In this way, it is similar to the active memory on your computer that allows you to manipulate and use several applications at once.

Sensory memory is brief but huge. Short-term memory is far more limited because our consciousness itself is limited—we can attend to only a few things at one time. How many? George Miller (1956) established that short-term memory can maintain roughly seven chunks of information, or—as his classic article put it in the title—*The Magical Number Seven, Plus or Minus Two.* In other words, most people can handle somewhere between five and nine chunks of information at one time. When my co-author spells his name for other people, he can run it all together: E-r-n-s-t. With a five-letter name, people have no problem maintaining the whole thing in their short-term memory at once. When I spell my name for others, however, I can't just run the letters together. *Blair-Broeker* contains 13 characters, including the hyphen, and that is enough to overwhelm short-term memory. I have to pause a couple times

▶ **sensory memory** The brief, initial coding of sensory information in the memory system.

▶ **short-term memory** Conscious, activated memory that holds about seven chunks of information briefly before the information is stored more permanently or forgotten. Also called *working memory.*

▶ **long-term memory** The relatively permanent and limitless storehouse of the memory system.

Reteaching

Have students create the following chart in their notes to help them keep some concepts in this module straight. (You can also supply these charts with blanks for students to fill out during class discussion.)

This chart has a companion chart discussed in a later Reteaching activity on page 346 of this *Teacher's Edition.*

	Iconic Store	Echoic Store
Duration	Less than a second	3 to 4 seconds
Root word	Icon = small picture (visual)	Echo = repeated sound (auditory)

as I spell it if there is to be any hope of the other person getting it down correctly. Notice that the capacity of short-term memory is seven *chunks*. You can hold seven chunks almost as easily as seven individual items. Holding seven words in short-term memory, for example, means that you are actually holding more than seven syllables and a lot more than seven letters. Chunking is an effective technique not only for encoding but also for increasing the capacity of short-term memory.

What about the duration of short-term memory—how *long* can we retain information in this portion of our memory? About as long as you keep rehearsing it. If you meet a new and interesting person at a party, you will retain the person's name as long as you keep repeating it to yourself. But what if you get distracted? How long will the name stay? To answer this question, researchers (Peterson & Peterson, 1959) presented participants with short, three-consonant groups to remember. They then distracted the participants by giving them an arithmetic task that prevented rehearsal. As the results show (Figure 18.8), short-term memory is indeed short term. Even though people had to remember only three consonants, these items disappeared from memory in less than 20 seconds when rehearsal was prevented.

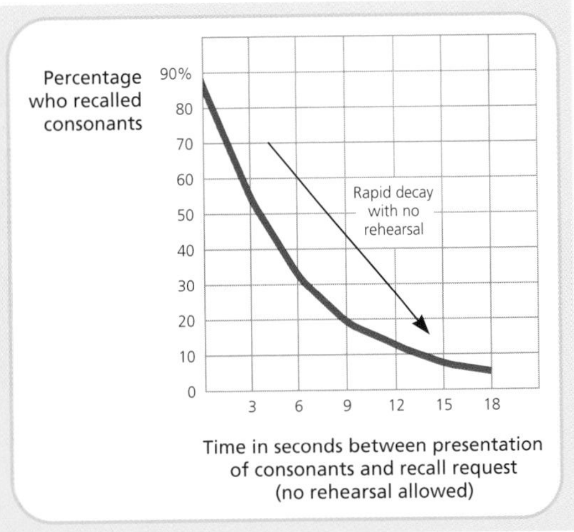

Figure 18.8 How Long Does Short-Term Memory Last? As this graph shows, when people are not allowed to rehearse, short-term memory decays rapidly. Within a few seconds, most people are unable to recall three consonants. (From Peterson & Peterson, 1959.)

Short-term memory, with its limited capacity and short duration, is like a stovetop on which you're preparing your dinner. Having only four burners limits the number of dishes and volume of food you can cook. You also must pay active attention to the food you're preparing if you're going to avoid ruining the meal or burning down the house. All of the rest of the food stored in your cupboards, refrigerator, and freezer—the food you don't need to pay attention to—represents our next topic: long-term memory.

Long-Term Memory

11. What are the capacity and the duration of long-term memory?

Long-term memory represents the vast, amazing memory storehouse that can hold memories without conscious effort. Remember our computer analogy here. Short-term memory is like the active memory on your computer that allows you to deal with the various projects open on your desktop at any moment. Constant power (attention) is necessary to maintain

(tr) ■ TEACHING TIP

A four-color transparency of Figure 18.8, How Long Does Short-Term Memory Last?, is available in the **Overhead Transparencies Set**.

■ LOOKING AT THE ISSUES

If getting distracted during learning is a problem for most people, imagine how difficult it is for people with ADHD to learn in a typical classroom setting. Have students brainstorm about the different distractions that occur during a typical class.

- Which of these distractions bother you? Which can you ignore?
- How many of these distractions are preventable? What does your teacher do to minimize distractions?
- How do you distract the class? Is it purposeful or not? Why?

■ APPLYING THE POINTS

Have students share whether they feel the need for a TV or radio to be on while they study.

- Why do they desire this distraction during learning?
- Do they feel they study better with this distraction? Why or why not?
- If they don't like the distraction, why is that the case?

Demonstrating

Replicate the study by Peterson and Peterson by having students try to memorize a list of words (nonsense or otherwise). Next, have them do some sort of arithmetic problem (counting backwards from 100 by sevens or multiplying two four-digit numbers together), giving them a time limit. Then, have them recall the words. You may want to give them several different durations of time to memorize a group of words to gauge the length of their short-term storage.

(trb) At this point, you may wish to use **Application Activity:** *Meaningful Chunks* (*Teacher's Resource Binder*, p. 18-1) and **Application Activity:** *Memory Capacity* (*Teacher's Resource Binder*, p. 18-1).

MODULE 18

■ JOURNAL WRITING

Invite students to use the following questions and writing prompts as a springboard for entries in their psychology journals:

- Do you have a name that is often misspelled or one that people often ask you to spell out for them? Does this have anything to do with how long your name is? Why or why not?
- Are you good at remembering names? Why or why not?
- What are some flashbulb memories shared by you and all your peers? Describe them. What are some you have personally? Describe them. What are the qualities of these memories—positive or negative?

■ APPLYING THE POINTS

Discuss with students the idea that people of the same generation often share certain flashbulb memories. Have students interview parents, grandparents, and older siblings or friends about flashbulb memories that their generation shares, including those related to the bombing of Pearl Harbor, John F. Kennedy's assassination, the bicentennial celebration of the United States, the attempted assassination of President Ronald Reagan, the *Challenger* explosion, Princess Diana's death, or September 11, 2001.

- How vividly did those being interviewed remember their whereabouts for events that were flashbulb memories for their generation?
- What emotional reactions did those being interviewed have toward an event that served as a flashbulb memory for their generation?

trb At this point, you may wish to use Analysis Activity: *Flashbulb Memory* (*Teacher's Resource Binder*, p. 18-1).

Clark's Nutcracker Do you ever have trouble remembering where you left your psychology book or your wallet? Compare your memory to that of the Clark's Nutcracker. It can remember the location of up to 6000 places where it has stored seeds for the winter (Shettleworth, 1993).

this memory. What happens to your work if the power blinks off? It's gone! As a result, most of us have learned to save our work frequently. This means we make a copy of the project on the computer's hard drive, a device that will retain the information even when the machine is turned off.

Similarly, we can file information away in our long-term memory and have it stay there without paying attention to it. It's available (we hope!) when we want it. Although until I mention it, you probably have not been thinking about these bits of information, but I'll bet you could retrieve with ease your zip code, the name of your English teacher, how you spent last New Year's Eve, and countless other events that you encoded and stored at some point in the past. Note that you effectively encoded these pieces of information either because you rehearsed them frequently or because they held personal meaning for you—two of the factors we identified as crucial when we discussed encoding. And now they are permanent residents in your long-term memory storehouse.

Long-term memory is as expansive as short-term memory is limited. What is its duration? Nobody knows for sure, but it's clear that humans can maintain memories for about a century. (Are you willing to trust your computer's hard drive to last that long?) Short-term memory can hold about seven chunks. What's the capacity of long-term memory? Again, nobody knows. Like a sponge with unlimited capacity, your long-term memory can always absorb more, even on days when you feel you can't possibly take in even one more piece of information.

One especially interesting kind of long-term memory is **flashbulb memory,** a clear, vivid memory of significant, emotional events. I have lived long enough to pick up lots of these: driving home in my first car (a used, powder blue 1965 Mustang GT); the sunshine briefly breaking through in the middle of our outdoor wedding; being left in the hallway as they wheeled my wife in for an emergency C-section on the night our son Carl was born. Sometimes flashbulb memories center around a shared event. People in your grandparents' generation may recall with amazing detail what they were doing when they heard the news of the attack on Pearl Harbor. Your parents may have flashbulb memories of President Kennedy's assassination or the explosion of the space shuttle *Challenger.* Your vivid memories of the September 11 terrorist attacks on the World Trade Center will last a lifetime.

▶ **flashbulb memory** A vivid, clear memory of an emotionally significant moment or event.

▶ **long-term potentiation** An increase in a synapse's firing efficiency. Believed to be the neural basis of learning and memory.

Reteaching

Have students create the following chart in their notes to help them keep some of the concepts in this module straight. (You can also supply these charts with blanks for students to fill out during class discussion.)

This chart has a companion chart discussed earlier in the Reteaching activity on page 344 of this *Teacher's Edition.*

	Sensory Memory	Short-Term Memory	Long-Term Memory
Duration	Less than a minute	20 seconds to 20 minutes (depending on rehearsal)	Unlimited
Capacity	Unlimited	7 ± 2 (5 to 9) chunks of information	Unlimited

Memory and the Brain

12. How do we get information into long-term memory?

How, exactly, does the brain go about storing long-term memories? This mystery has occupied scientists for decades, but in the last several years, researchers have uncovered some important clues. We now know that our brain does not function like a tape recorder, holding permanent, accurate records of every experience, ready to be played back if the right button is pushed. Current memory research indicates that memories are constructed from myriad bits and pieces of information. Our brain *builds* our memories, just as you would assemble a jigsaw puzzle. When pieces are missing, we invent new ones to fill in the spaces. Because of this, some of our memories are accurate, and others are way off.

Another important clue to how memories are stored is that each memory appears to activate a particular, specific pattern of firing in brain cells—neurons. The key to the process lies in the synapses that form the connecting points between the neurons. As the sequence of neurons that represents a particular memory fires over and over, the synapses between these neurons actually become more efficient, a process known as **long-term potentiation** (Figure 18.9). Learning and memory stimulate the neurons to release chemicals (primarily the neurotransmitter serotonin) at the synapses, making it easier for the neurons to fire again in the future (Kandel & Schwartz, 1982). The tracks formed in your brain are almost like a trail blazed through deep snow from a cabin to the woodpile. With repeated trips, the trail becomes easier and easier to follow.

The concept of long-term potentiation helps explain several other memory phenomena. A variety of things, including a blow to the head, can disrupt neural function and the formation of new memories. This is why football players who have suffered concussions may have trouble remembering the play when the injury occurred (Yarnell & Lynch, 1970). Drugs can also disrupt memories, by interfering with

Figure 18.9 **Growing a Memory** These two electron microscope images show one way that long-term potentiation makes a synapse more efficient. The left image, before long-term potentiation, shows only one receptor site (gray shows the receiving neuron). The right image shows two receptor sites. This dual target increases the likelihood that a message from the sending neuron will make it across the synapse to the receiving neuron. The growth of the second site is an indication that something may have been learned and remembered.

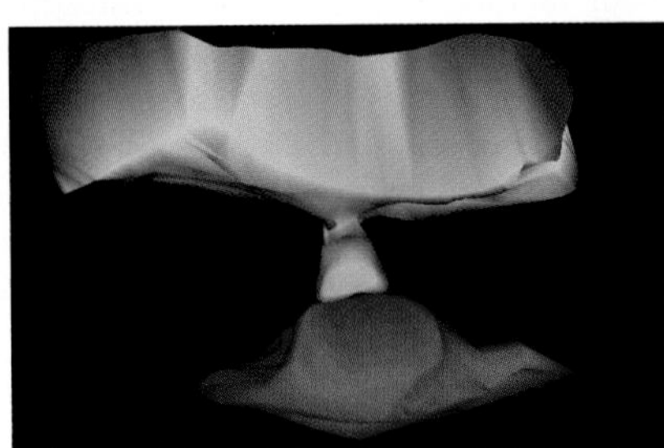

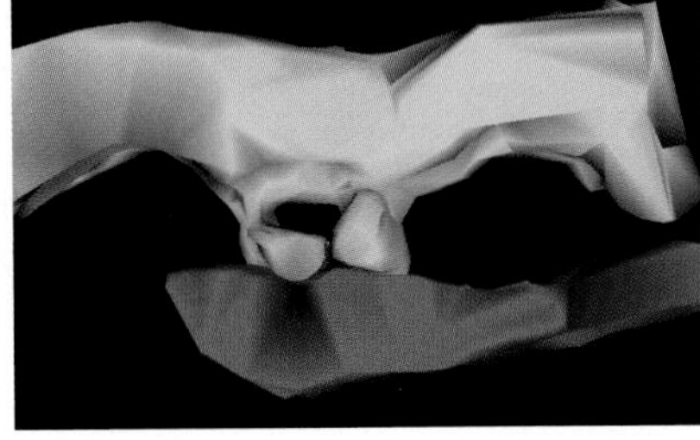

F•Y•I

(1) Many people cling to the myth that new memories create a new wrinkle in the brain. Wrinkles have nothing to do with memories, but it seems that long-term potentiation supports the idea that new trails are blazed in the brain as new memories are formed.

(2) Studies have shown that patients with Korsakoff's syndrome have smaller hippocampi than is normal. Korsakoff's is a dementia-like disease linked to chronic alcoholism. Patients' memories slowly erode, leaving them lost in the past. The long-term memories they would have stored during their years as an alcoholic are lost since alcohol disrupts the forming of new memories.

Enriching

Have students research how the daytime television soap opera programs mythologize amnesia. The following questions will help students focus their research and discuss their findings:

- How do soap operas portray amnesia?
- What are some common causes of these incidents of amnesia?
- How long does the amnesia usually last?
- What leads the person to "recover" their memories?

MODULE 18

■ TEACHING TIP

Link the concept that *stress enhances memory* to Freud's concept of *repression.* Freud believed that traumatic events from childhood caused people to bury the memory of those events in the unconscious, leading to difficulties later in life. Research shows that while people are capable of repressing memories, traumatic memories are typically vividly remembered. People who've experienced abuse or witnessed tragedy usually remember details and feelings years after the event actually occurred.

■ MULTICULTURAL CONNECTIONS

Have students research how people from other countries and cultures perceive events that people in the United States find memorable. Present the following questions for students to use as a guide for research and subsequent discussion of their findings:

- Do people from other countries and cultures find these events as memorable as the majority of those who in live in the United States do? Why or why not?
- What are some events that people from other countries or cultures find memorable? How well do people living in the United States remember these events?

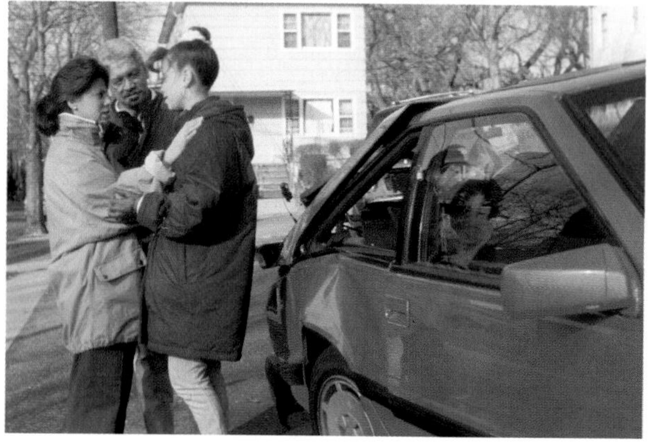

Stress and Memory Stressful events, such as this car accident, stimulate the release of stress hormones that enhance the formation of memories. These drivers are not likely to forget this day. Such memories may help encourage defensive driving in the future.

the neurotransmitters necessary for long-term potentiation. Alcohol is one such a drug, which accounts for the alcohol-induced memory "black-out" that often accompanies a night of heavy drinking (Weingartner & others, 1983).

Stress hormones also affect memory. Do you think they disrupt or enhance the ability to form long-term memories? Here's a hint: Stress is often the body's response to danger. It is important that we retain details of dangerous situations so we can protect ourselves in the future. It's not surprising, then, that stress enhances memories. The hormones tell your body that something significant is happening, and they trigger biological changes that stimulate the formation of memories. People given a drug to block the effect of hormones in a stressful situation tend to remember fewer details of an upsetting story than their counterparts who did not receive the drug (Cahill, 1994).

Explicit and Implicit Memories

13. What are explicit and implicit memories, and what parts of the brain process each of these types of memory?

Let's examine one last aspect of long-term memory. There are many types of memories, but one major division separates explicit from implicit memory (Figure 18.10). **Explicit memory** is what we normally think of when we think of memory: the recall of facts and experiences. At what temperature does water freeze? Where did you eat dinner last night? What is your mother's middle name? Answering all of these questions requires a conscious effort to retrieve and state information. **Implicit memory** requires no such conscious effort. Implicit memory lets us retrieve our knowledge of procedures and skills, such as walking. You don't have to think about how to ride a bicycle before peddling off. Nor do you have to think about how to read or how to button your shirt. Your ability to perform all these tasks depends on memory, but it is implicit, not explicit.

▶ **explicit memory** Memory of facts and experiences that one must consciously retrieve and declare.

▶ **implicit memory** Memory of skills and procedures, like how to walk, that are retrieved without conscious recollection.

Explicit and implicit memory appear to be entirely different systems, controlled by different brain parts. Explicit memories are processed

Cross-Curricular Connections

CREATIVE NONFICTION WRITING Have students write an expository essay that details how to do something that requires implicit memory. Have them share their essays, reflecting on how difficult or easy it was to put implicit memories into words. Facilitate a discussion of students' writing experience with the following questions:

- About which details did you have to think hard in order to remember?
- Were you able to remember every step with ease? Did you have to walk through the process in your mind before you wrote?
- Why are implicit memories more difficult to remember than explicit ones?

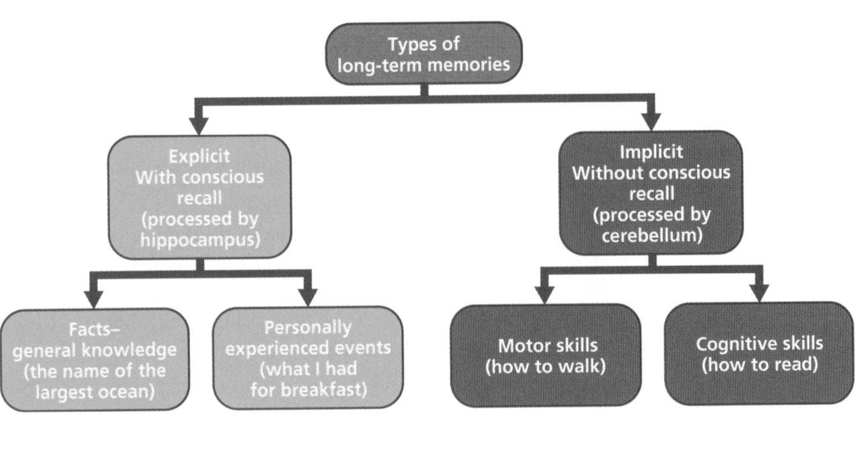

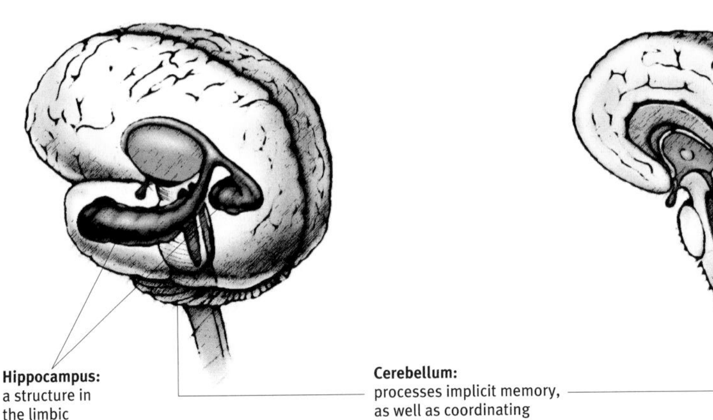

Figure 18.10 **Explicitly or Implicitly Remembered?** Long-term memories can be classified as either explicit or implicit. These two types of memories are processed by different parts of the brain. Explicit memories of facts and experiences are processed through the hippocampus, a part of the limbic system deep in the center of the brain. Implicit memories for procedures and skills, however, are processed by the cerebellum, a structure at the bottom rear of the brain.

through the *hippocampus,* a small structure located in the central region of the brain. Implicit memories are processed through the *cerebellum,* the rounded structure at the bottom rear of the brain (see Figure 18.10). Odd things can happen because of this split. A man who experienced damage to the hippocampus, for example, would be unable to form new explicit memories, but his ability to form implicit memories would remain intact. What would happen if he went to play golf on the same course each day? He would have no explicit memory of the course—it would seem like a brand new place every time. But his scores would gradually improve over time, because his implicit memories would allow him to get better with practice.

■ TEACHING TIPS

tr (1) A four-color transparency of Figure 18.10, Explicitly or Implicitly Remembered?, is available in the **Overhead Transparencies Set.**

V (2) You may wish to show **Videocassette:** ***The Mind,*** **Second Edition, Module 10: "Life Without Meaning: The Case of Clive Wearing" (Part 1)** (*Teacher's Resource Binder,* p. 18-1) and **Videocassette:** ***The Mind,*** **Second Edition, Module 11: "Clive Wearing: Living Without Memory"** (*Teacher's Resource Binder,* p. 18-1) to highlight the life of a man who lost his ability to form new explicit memories.

■ APPLYING THE POINTS

Have students imagine what would happen if they lost the ability to store new explicit memories. Elicit their responses with the following questions:

- How would their relationships with people change?
- What would daily life be like?
- Would they prefer to be blissfully ignorant of their condition? Why or why not?

Reteaching

Help students understand the difference between *explicit* and *implicit memory* by explaining the meanings of the words:

- **Explicit** means "fully and clearly expressed." Facts about information and experiences are clear and real, and some part of our memory tries to store these facts accurately. The hippocampus, where new memories are created and processed, holds explicit memory.
- **Implicit** means "without conscious recall" We often can't explain how we do things that are habitual and routine. Even as these activities are accomplished without much conscious thought, our memories of these activities are stored in a place in the brain that governs autonomic processes. The cerebellum handles information about movement, balance, and coordination.

trb At this point, you may wish to use **Enrichment Lesson:** ***Episodic, Semantic, and Procedural Memory*** (*Teacher's Resource Binder,* p. 18-1).

MODULE 18

(F•Y•I)

Retrieval of certain information can depend on how well we have integrated it into our prior knowledge of a subject or situation. Jean Piaget, the child development pioneer, called this process **assimilation.** Those who assimilate information well tend to retrieve it better, making them more likely to be good students in school.

trb At this point, you may wish to use **Demonstration Activity:** *Expertise and Retrieval Rates* (*Teacher's Resource Binder,* p. 18-1).

▸ **recall** A measure of memory in which you must retrieve information you learned earlier, as on a fill-in-the-blank test.

▸ **recognition** A measure of memory in which you must *identify* items you learned earlier, as on a multiple-choice test.

▸ **context effect** The enhanced ability to retrieve information when you are in an environment similar to the one in which you encoded the information.

Retrieval

14. What are two forms of memory retrieval?

The final step in the information processing model of memory is *retrieval,* the process of getting information out of memory storage. Two forms of retrieval are recall and recognition.

- **Recall** is the kind of retrieval we usually think of as "memory"—searching for information that was previously stored, and calling it back into conscious awareness. This is the literal meaning of the word *re-call.* Test makers use fill-in-the-blank, short-answer, and essay questions to tap recall.
- **Recognition** is also retrieval, but it is an easier process than recall, because you need only identify information. You may struggle to describe an individual you witnessed committing a crime (recall) yet have little trouble picking the person out of a police line-up (recognition). Multiple-choice and matching questions test recognition.

How do we get to the memories we need to retrieve? We follow pathways, often multiple pathways, that lead to the memory. When I need to contact a friend, I can do so by hopping in the car and driving to his house. If I'm feeling relaxed, I can walk over. I can also e-mail him, or call him on the phone, or send a message with a mutual friend I know will see him before I do. The point is, I have lots of ways to reach him. Likewise, there are many pathways I can follow to retrieve a memory. I can "connect" to a memory of, say, Mount Rushmore by remembering a family trip, by thinking of a TV show I might have seen, or by seeing a photo in a magazine. In each case, my memory of Mount Rushmore is *primed,* or triggered, by a memory *retrieval cue* (Figure 18.11).

Memories weave a web of neural pathways inside the brain, and retrieval cues send us down one pathway or another in our search for memories. Have you ever noticed that the more you know about a subject, the easier it is to learn even more about it? Learning and retrieval build on each other. If you know only one or two isolated facts about how the federal government works, you don't have much of a framework upon which to hang new information. But if you already know about the Constitution, the three branches, the role of the civil service, significant Supreme Court decisions, and close presidential elections, it becomes relatively

High School Days Here is how my co-author and I looked when we were your age! Our present students might have difficulty identifying us, but our high school classmates would probably have no trouble at all.

Meeting Individual Needs

trb **GRAPHIC ORGANIZER** If you did not do so earlier in the module, you can provide learning opportunities for all levels of learners with one of the following options for **Graphic Organizers:** *Making Sense of Memory—Encoding, Storage, and Retrieval* (*Teacher's Resource Binder,* p. 18-1; **Handouts 18–2a** through **18–2c**). Each of the three graphic organizers for this module presents concepts about a different step in information processing. At this point in the module, distribute the organizer for retrieval.

- **Independent Learners** Students may fill out the organizer on their own or follow along in class during discussion and lecture.

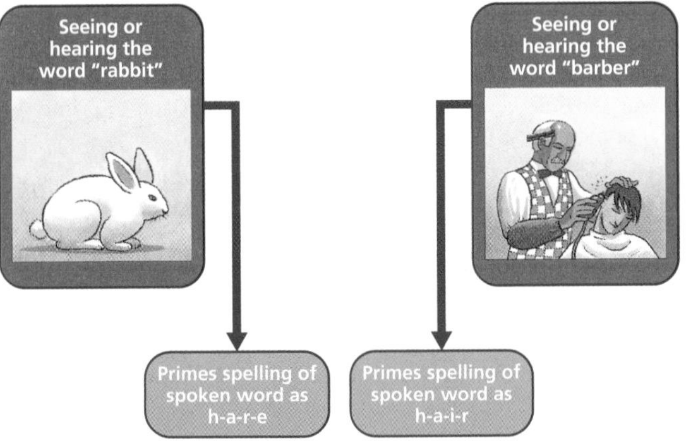

Figure 18.11 **A Hare-Raising Experience** If you show people a picture, you can activate certain associations in their memory pathways—a process known as *priming*. When you later ask them to spell a word that can be spelled in two different ways (*hare* or *hair*), their response may reflect the content of the picture. Thus, a picture of a rabbit is likely to activate the spelling h-a-r-e. A picture of a barber at work is likely to activate the spelling h-a-i-r. (Adapted from Bower, 1986.)

easy to integrate new information. This interrelated web of association allows for easy priming of memory, and thus more effective retrieval.

Context

15. How does context affect our ability to retrieve memories?

Context is the environment in which you encode or retrieve information. When these environments are the same, you may experience the **context effect**—an enhanced ability to retrieve information more effectively. This happened when my wife and I visited a little town in Oregon where her family vacationed many years before. When we arrived, her memories began flooding back, and she was able to direct me to several landmarks around town. Returning to the context where she had encoded the memories primed the retrieval of those memories years later. One experiment carried this idea even further. The researchers divided scuba divers into groups and read each group a list of words. One group heard the list on shore; the other, under water (Figure 18.12).

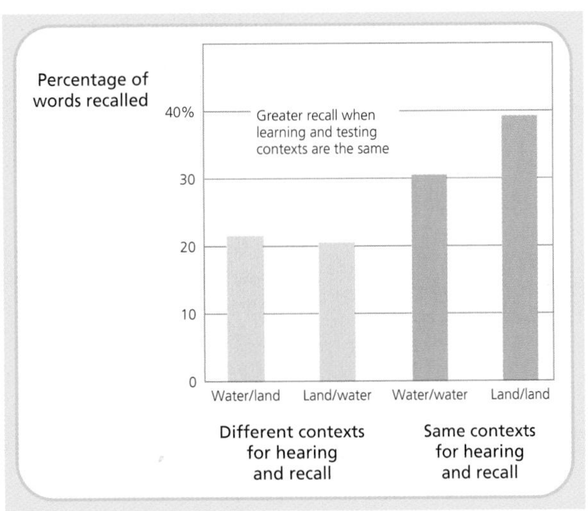

Figure 18.12 **Context and Memory** As this rather odd experiment demonstrated, retrieval is best when it occurs in the same environment where encoding took place. In this case, the two contexts were under 10 feet of water (while scuba diving!) or sitting on the shore. (Adapted from Godden & Baddeley, 1975.)

■ **APPLYING THE POINTS**

How powerful is context to memory? Have students spend some time trying to remember events from their childhood. Challenge students to then visit a place where they spent a lot of time during childhood (an elementary school, a childhood home, a playground, and so forth). Have them spend some time trying to remember the events in the environmental context of those memories. Afterward, explore students' findings with the following questions:

- How much easier was it to remember the events in the environmental context?
- Did other memories come flooding back in the context?

tr A four-color transparency of Figure 18.11, A Hare-Raising Experience, is available in the **Overhead Transparencies Set.**

trb At this point, you may wish to use **Application Activity:** ***Retrieval Cues*** (*Teacher's Resource Binder*, p. 18-1; **Handouts 18–6a** and **18–6b**).

■ **TEACHING TIP**

Encourage students to spend time studying for tests in your classroom, even in the desks they sit in during class. This will capitalize on the context effect when they take the test on the material at a later time.

trb **tr** A black-line master for Figure 18.12, Context and Memory, is available in the **Black-Line Masters Appendix** of the ***Teacher's Resource Binder.***

trb At this point, you may wish to use **Application Activity:** ***Retrieval Cues*** (*Teacher's Resource Binder*, p. 18-1; **Handouts 18–6a** and **18–6b**).

- **Cooperative Learners** Students may use the textbook as a resource and work in groups to find the answers that fit in the blanks.
- **Exceptional Learners** The graphic organizer can fill a special education need to provide notes for exceptional students. These students may fill in the blanks independently, with a student or teacher/tutor, or along with class discussion and lecture.

MODULE 18

■ LOOKING AT THE ISSUES

Does the state-dependent effect work with caffeine and sugar, both of which students might consume while studying? Have students research the literature on state-dependent memories to see if any studies exist on these variables. Students can also do anecdotal research, recording how much caffeine and sugar they consume while studying and whether they consume the same amount before taking the test to see if their recall is less than desirable.

Close

Do you have to have a good memory to be a good student? . . . a good citizen? . . . a good worker? American society seems to value those with good memories for information and skills. In a full-class discussion, have students respond to an often-used quote that summarizes the importance of memory in our society: "Those who do not remember the past are condemned to repeat it."

Later, those who heard the words on shore recalled more of the words when they were on shore, and those who heard the list under water recalled the words best under water (Godden & Baddeley, 1975). Any environment provides countless cues that can later function to prime the retrieval of memories.

State Dependency

16. How do our physical condition and mood affect our ability to retrieve memories?

Our ability to retrieve memories also depends on the physical or mental state we were in at the time we encoded an event. **State-dependent memory** means that retrieval is best when the retrieval state is *congruent* with (that is, the same as) the encoding state. Strangely enough, if you were tired when encoding, retrieval will also be better when you are tired. Note, however, that you will neither encode nor retrieve as well when you are tired as you would if you were not tired. Do you drink caffeinated drinks, like cola, when you study? Chances are you'll retrieve better under the influence of caffeine. This even extends to drugs which normally disrupt learning, like alcohol (Lowe, 1987). Despite its overall negative effects, if you were under the influence of alcohol when encoding, you'll retrieve somewhat better (although not well) with alcohol in your system.

Memories are also *mood-congruent.* If you're happy when you encode, you'll retrieve better when you're happy. On the other hand, if you've been somewhat depressed as you worked your way through a particular unit in a class, you'll probably test better when depressed. Odd, isn't it? Perhaps even more significant is the way our moods bias our memories. If you think back to first grade when you're in a good mood, the mood is likely to prime positive memories. But if you're depressed when you try to remember, your mood is likely to function as a retrieval cue for negative memories (Eich, 1995).

Lose your memories, and you've lost your sense of self. Without the past, both joy and sadness would be fleeting and our world would be shallow indeed. We would have no way to connect events, and we would be unable to learn anything. Our waking hours are a constant progression of encoding important information, storing countless pieces of information on both a short-term and long-term basis, and retrieving needed information from long-term storage. If you remember nothing else about this topic, remember the remarkable, amazing role memory plays in our daily lives.

► **state-dependent memory** The enhanced ability to retrieve information where you are in the same physical and emotional state you were in when you encoded the information.

Meeting Individual Needs

Offer students the choice of taking a quiz on this material in either a recall or recognition format. Some students may find that they prefer one format or the other. After the quizzes are graded, discuss with students the advantages and disadvantages of each type of test. Also analyze what type of studying works better for each type of test.

trb At this point, you may wish to use **Application Activity:** ***Remembering the Seven Dwarfs*** (*Teacher's Resource Binder*, p. 18-1; **Handout 18–7**).

REVIEW

Module 18: Information Processing

What's the Point?

The Information-Processing Model

1. *What are the three basic steps in the information processing model?*

   The three basic steps are *encoding* (getting information into memory), *storage* (retaining encoded information over time), and *retrieval* (getting information out of storage). Computers offer a useful analogy for understanding human memory, because both computers and humans process information using these three steps.

Encoding

2. *How do automatic and effortful processing differ, and how do we use them to encode school-related information?*

   Automatic processing is capturing information with no conscious effort, usually information about place, time, or frequency. Automatic processing won't help us learn facts or figures in school, but it may help keep us safe from threats in the environment. We encode most school-related information by effortful processing—working hard to learn new material by paying attention and using deliberate encoding strategies, such as rehearsal and overlearning. We can become more efficient encoders by spending more time rehearsing material and by continuing to rehearse material even after we think we have mastered it.

3. *How does an item's position in a list influence our memory of that item?*

   Researchers have demonstrated that we most easily remember the first and last items in a list. This tendency is known as the serial position effect, and it has two parts: The primacy effect is the ability to remember the first items, and the recency effect is the ability to remember the last items. Middle items in a list require more rehearsal, because we remember them less easily.

4. *Why is distributed rehearsal more effective than massed rehearsal?*

   The spacing effect shows that rehearsals that are spread out over time encode information better than massed rehearsals do. As people tire during long periods of rehearsal, the additional hours of practice or review become less and less productive. To encode more effectively, spread out your practice or homework sessions evenly over the week instead of cramming just before a test!

5. *How does semantic encoding improve our memories?*

   Semantic encoding is processing information by focusing on its meaning. Semantic encoding is much more effective than acoustic encoding (focusing on sounds) or visual encoding (focusing on images). Another way to become a better encoder is to try to relate new information to your own life to make it memorable.

6. *How does encoding imagery aid our memory?*

   Visual encoding may not be as effective as semantic encoding, but we encode visual images fairly easily. The tendency to recall events more positively than we felt about them while experiencing them is known as rosy retrospection.

Checking the Points

■ TEACHING TIPS

web (1) The book companion site for *Thinking About Psychology* at **www.worthpublishers.com/thinkingaboutpsych** contains a module quiz, flashcards of key terms and people, as well as other student activities and resources for this module. You will also find PowerPoint lectures, a quiz grade book, and other teaching resources by logging on as an instructor.

trb (2) At this point, you may wish to have students review and confirm concepts about information processing with **Critical Thinking Activity:** *Fact or Falsehood?* (*Teacher's Resource Binder*, p. 18-1; **Handout 18–1**). Suggest that students take turns reading items from **Handout 18–1** to a partner, who answers with either "true" or "false." Partners can discuss concepts and refer to the text in order to find passages that confirm the correct responses.

trb **tr** (3) You may also wish to provide students with **Graphic Organizers:** *Making Sense of Memory—Encoding, Storage, and Retrieval* (*Teacher's Resource Binder*, p. 18-1; **Handouts 18–2a** through **18–2c**). Have students fill out these organizers as a tool to review module concepts and their relationship to each step in information processing. Encourage students to fill in the graphic organizers without referring to the text or copies of the organizers they may have filled out earlier in the module. Next, allow time for students to use their texts to help them review concepts they had difficulty with. Finally, in a class discussion, students may ask additional questions about module concepts for which they need clarification. **Handouts 18–2a** through **18–2c** may also be used as transparencies to project correctly filled-in organizers for the class.

7. *How do mnemonic devices help us encode memories for storage and easy retrieval?*

   Many mnemonic devices (memory tricks or techniques) use visual images as memory aids. One such device, the method of loci, has us use our imagination to place items we want to remember in locations that we are familiar with—items on a grocery list spread all around your living room, for example. Another mnemonic device, the peg-word system, has us hang the items we want to remember from mental "pegs" that are actually parts of a previously memorized rhyme or list.

8. *What are two ways of organizing information, and how do they help us encode large amounts of information?*

   We can encode more efficiently if we organize information. One method of organizing information is chunking—grouping it into meaningful units, such as words, sentences, or groups of numbers. Another effective way to encode large amounts of information is to create a hierarchy, organizing your thoughts into major concepts, minor related ideas, and the relationships among all these items.

Storage

9. *What are two types of sensory memory?*

   Sensory memory is the part of the memory system that briefly holds information gathered by our senses (vision, hearing, touch, and so on). Some initial coding happens in sensory memory, but much of this information is quickly discarded. Information remains in the iconic store—the portion of sensory memory that handles visual memories—for less than half a second. Information remains in the echoic store—the portion of sensory memory that handles memories of sounds—for about three or four seconds.

10. *What techniques can we use to increase the limited capacity and duration of our short-term memory?*

    Short-term memory is the conscious, activated memory that you are aware of at any given time. You can hold information in short-term memory longer than in sensory memory, but only as long as you continue to rehearse it. And you can hold only a limited number of items in short-term memory—somewhere between five and seven, though these can be either small items (the individual numbers in a new phone listing, for example), or larger chunks (such as the names of the players on a sports team). To use your short-term memory most efficiently, you can rehearse items (holding them in memory longer) or chunk them (compressing bits and pieces into larger items). But no matter how hard you try, items will slip from short-term memory if you are distracted.

11. *What are the capacity and the duration of long-term memory?*

    The capacity of long-term memory seems to be without limit, for our memory "disks" never fill up. We don't know the duration of long-term memory, but some people reach 100 years old with memories intact. Flashbulb memories are a special kind of long-term memory in which we form vivid, detailed memories of significant emotional events.

12. *How do we get information into long-term memory?*

    Researchers are still studying how the brain stores long-term memories. We now know that memories are stored in parts, not as little video clips in our brain. We also know that the key to learning and memory appears to be long-term potentiation, a term that describes the strengthening of the pathways among neurons in the brain when those neurons are repeatedly used. A simple way to think of this is to compare the pathway to the memory's location in the brain with a pathway that forms near your school when many students walk in a certain direction each day. Whether in the brain or the schoolyard, the path becomes more easily recognized and more easily traveled because of the frequent use. Injuries that jar or damage the brain, or use of drugs that interfere with neurotransmitters, can disrupt long-term potentiation and cause memory loss. Stress can trigger the release of hormones that enhance our ability to form long-term memories.

13. *What are explicit and implicit memories, and what parts of the brain process each of these types of memory?*

    Explicit memories are memories of facts (your age) and experiences (where you were yesterday) that you consciously pull out of memory and "know." The hippocampus processes explicit memories. Implicit memories are memories of skills (walking up stairs) and procedures (turning a key in a lock) that you can accomplish without conscious thought. The cerebellum processes implicit memories.

Retrieval

14. *What are two forms of memory retrieval?*

    Retrieval is the process of getting information out of memory storage, which we need to do in daily life. The two common forms of retrieval are recall and recognition. Recall is scanning our memory and calling information back into conscious awareness (answering the brief essay question in the quiz at the end of this module). Recognition is identifying information that you have stored in long-term memory (identifying the correct answer in the multiple-choice questions in the quiz at the end of this module). Retrieval cues—things that trigger a memory—help us "find" our memories by priming, or activating certain associations in our memory pathways.

15. *How does context affect our ability to retrieve memories?*

    We retrieve memories more easily in the environment in which we formed them. This is called the context effect. Any environment contains retrieval cues that can activate associations in our memory pathways.

16. *How do our physical condition and mood affect our ability to retrieve memories?*

    Our best chance of retrieving a memory is returning to the physical and emotional state we were in when we formed the memory, a concept known as state-dependent memory. The concept of mood-congruent memories is similar, in that we most easily retrieve memories when our mood matches the mood we were in when forming the memory. But mood-congruent memories have another characteristic: When we are in a certain mood, the mood seems to act as a general retrieval cue, priming our search and directing us toward memories that match our mood. Thus, when depressed, we remember our past sorrows; when happy, we retrieve joyful memories.

MODULE 18

■ **TEACHING TIP**

If students have not yet chosen and used a mnemonic device (explained in the text) to learn and memorize one or more module vocabulary words, have them do so now. If they have already reported on the mnemonic device(s) they chose to learn one or more vocabulary words, have them review the mnemonic device now to see if it did encourage correct and efficient information processing.

tb Using the Test Bank

Create a test using the *Test Bank.* Choose from questions about the concepts in the module in varying formats.

Self-Test Answers

Multiple-Choice Questions

1. d, 2. b, 3. a

Key Terms

encoding, p. 335
storage, p. 335
retrieval, p. 335
automatic processing, p. 336
effortful processing, p. 336
rehearsal, p. 336
overlearning, p. 337
serial position effect, p. 338
spacing effect, p. 339
distributed rehearsal, p. 339
massed rehearsal, p. 339
semantic encoding, p. 339
self-reference effect, p. 339
mnemonic device, p. 341
method of loci, p. 341
peg-word system, p. 341
chunking, p. 342
sensory memory, p. 344
short-term memory, p. 344
long-term memory, p. 345
flashbulb memory, p. 346
long-term potentiation, p. 347
explicit memory, p. 348
implicit memory, p. 348
recall, p. 350
recognition, p. 350
context effect, p. 351
state-dependent memory, p. 352

Key People

Hermann Ebbinghaus, p. 336

Self-Test

Multiple-Choice Questions

Choose the *best* answer for each of the following questions:

1. Annalee is the president of the Spanish Club, and she will be introducing the exchange students from Spain at a party tonight. She has been studying the list of names, but she still can't remember the five names in the middle of the list. Annalee's memory is suffering from
   a. overlearning.
   b. the self-reference effect.
   c. the spacing effect.
   d. the serial position effect.
2. Karl has a midterm math test next Monday, and he's been studying for it all semester. He's sure he knows all the material that will be on the test, but he's determined to continue reviewing his math notes and textbook each day between now and the test. Karl is using the encoding technique known as
   a. cramming.
   b. overlearning.
   c. the recency effect.
   d. automatic processing.
3. Nicole has had a me-me-me day. In English, she remembered the meaning of "autobiography" by thinking about what she would say in her own life history. In psychology, she decided she would play the piano better if she rehearsed it daily, instead of only on Saturday mornings before her piano lesson. Nicole is using
   a. the self-reference effect to remember information from her classes.
   b. the recency effect to prime her memory.
   c. massed rehearsal to be the most successful student in school.
   d. automatic processing so that she won't have to spend time doing homework.

Alternative Assessment/Technology Project

web IMPROVING MEMORY WITH THE WEB The Mind Tools site on memory techniques and mnemonics (**www.mindtools.com/memory.html**) will help students apply the concepts taught in Module 18 by helping them to improve their memories. This site reviews the underlying principles of effective mnemonic systems. It introduces several specific mnemonics and applies them to the remembering of names, dates, telephone numbers, and so on. Of special interest to students will be the section called "Using mnemonics for exams." You might ask students to visit the site and write a brief essay that addresses the following aspects of mnemonics:

- Identify the three fundamental principles that underlie the use of mnemonics.
- Describe three specific mnemonic techniques that are not described in the text.
- Show how one of them can be applied to studying for an exam.

4. Antoine's friends are wondering what's wrong with him today. He told them earlier that he had to do some grocery shopping for his grandmother on the way home from school. Then he told them that he could see his granny eating a bun full of raw eggs, drinking milk from her shoe, hanging slices of bread from the limbs of a tree, and slathering butter all over her door. Antoine is not crazy or mean, he's just using the mnemonic device called
   a. flashbulb memory.
   b. mood-congruent memory.
   c. the method of loci.
   d. the peg-word system.

5. Darlene's mother was in an automobile accident and suffered brain damage. The doctors told Darlene that her mother's hippocampus will no longer function properly. Darlene should expect that her mother will now be unable to form new
   a. explicit memories—memories of skills and procedures.
   b. implicit memories—memories of skills and procedures.
   c. explicit memories—memories of facts and experiences.
   d. implicit memories—memories of facts and experiences.

6. Mr. Perry just learned that the principal has lost her voice and he will have to announce the lists of 4 students who were elected officers of the senior class, 6 students who were elected to student council, 9 students who were elected to the cheerleading squad, and 11 students who will play first string on the football team. The principal's secretary will whisper the names to Mr. Perry, and he will announce them over the loudspeaker system. Knowing what you know about short-term memory capacity, what would you tell Mr. Perry about the chances of remembering these names after hearing them only once?
   a. All of the lists will be hard to remember, because the capacity of short-term memory is only 3 items.
   b. The 11 members of the football team will be hard to remember, because short-term memory capacity is 5 to 9 items.
   c. The 9 members of the cheerleading squad will be hard to remember, because short-term memory capacity is only 7 items.
   d. The 6 students elected to student council will be hard to remember, because short-term memory will hold only 3 to 5 items.

7. Martha lost her keys, and she has looked everywhere for them. She's trying one more time to find them, by walking through all the places she walked through earlier and doing all the things she did as she walked. Martha is hoping that she will find her keys with the help of
   a. a flashbulb memory.
   b. a mood-congruent memory.
   c. the context effect.
   d. the serial effect.

Matching Terms and Definitions

8. For each definition, choose the *best* matching term from the list that follows:

   Definition

   a. Putting all rehearsal time together in one long session (cramming).
   b. The tendency for distributed practice to yield better retention than is achieved through massed practice.
   c. A brief sensory memory of sounds, lasting no more than 4 seconds.
   d. A brief sensory memory of visual information, lasting no more than a few tenths of a second.
   e. Organizing information into meaningful units.

Self-Test Answers

Multiple-Choice Questions (continued)

4. d, 5. c, 6. b, 7. c

Matching Terms and Definitions

8. a. (8), b. (6), c. (12), d. (11), e. (10)

MODULE 18

Self-Test Answers

Matching Terms and Definitions (continued)

f. (1), g. (2), h. (4), i. (9)

Fill-in-the-Blank Questions

9. Automatic; effortful, 10. meaning; acoustic, visual, 11. sensory; short-term; long-term

Brief Essay Question

12. Students' answers should note that both computers and humans process information in three steps: encoding (getting information into memory), storage (retaining encoded information over time), and retrieval (getting information out of memory). Keyboards and modems are two devices used to encode information for computers; humans use their senses to encode information. Computers retain information temporarily in active memory and more permanently on a hard drive; humans retain information temporarily in sensory storage and short-term (or working) memory, and more permanently in long-term memory. Computers retrieve information from organized folders and subfolders (or sometimes not at all, if no system of organization was used). Humans retrieve information through recall and recognition, with the aid of retrieval cues that trigger memories.

f. The enhanced ability to retrieve information when you are in the same physical and emotional state you were in when you encoded the information.
g. An increase in a synapse's firing potential. Believed to be the neural basis of learning and memory.
h. Improved recall for the first items in a list.
i. A formal name for a memory trick or technique.

Term

(1) state-dependent memory
(2) long-term potentiation
(4) primacy effect
(5) recency effect
(6) spacing effect
(7) distributed rehearsal
(8) massed rehearsal
(9) mnemonic device
(10) chunking
(11) iconic store
(12) echoic store

Fill-in-the-Blank Questions

9. ________________ processing allows us to encode information about space, time, and frequency unconsciously and without effort; ________________ processing requires us to pay attention and make an effort to encode information.

10. We remember most effectively when we use semantic encoding, the encoding of ________________. Two other forms of encoding are ________________ encoding, in which we encode sounds, and ________________ encoding, in which we encode images.

11. The three big divisions of memory storage are ________________ memory, ________________-________________ memory, and ________________-________________ memory.

Brief Essay Question

12. Your 11-year-old cousin, Mia, loves to work on a computer, and she also is very bright. When she saw you reading this module, Mia noticed that it was about memory. Now she wants you to explain "how memory works." Knowing what you learned from this module, explain to Mia the concepts of encoding, storage, and retrieval. Remember to connect the idea of human memory to Mia's hands-on knowledge of computers, which should help her understand these concepts. Relay this information in two short paragraphs of around four to five sentences each.

Performance Standards

Standard Area: Memory

Content Standard 1: Encoding in memory

Performance Standard 1.2 Describe variables that affect encoding.

- Explain how forgetting can be explained by encoding failure. (Student Text pp. 359–360)
- Figure 19.1, "How Can You Remember What You Haven't Encoded?," illustrates how we fail to encode the details on the face of a penny, and so forget it. (Student Text p. 360)

Content Standard 2: Characteristics of short-term and long-term memory

Performance Standard 2.2 Describe long-term memory.

- Investigate the effects of time on long-term memory storage. (Student Text p. 361)
- Discuss Hermann Ebbinghaus' "forgetting curve." (Student Text p. 361)
- Figure 19.2, "The Forgetting Curve," summarizes the relationship between time and retention, as discovered by Hermann Ebbinghaus. (Student Text p. 361)

Content Standard 3: Retrieval in memory

Performance Standard 3.2 Discuss how interference affects retrieval.

- Define the concept of interference. (Student Text p. 362)
- Contrast proactive and retroactive interference. Real-world examples illustrate these differences. (Student Text pp. 363–364)
- Figure 19.4, "Scenes of Interference," illustrates the differences between these two processes. (Student Text p. 363)

Performance Standard 3.3 Investigate memory construction.

- Investigate how false information is incorporated into constructed memories. (Student Text pp. 365–366)
- Discuss Elizabeth Loftus' research on the misinformation effect. (Student Text pp. 367–368)

Content Standard 5: Strategies for improving memory

Performance Standard 5.1 Examine variables that interfere with memory.

- Explain how motivated forgetting can help explain repressed memories. (Student Text pp. 364–365)
- Investigate the factors that influence the accuracy of children's recall. (Student Text pp. 368–369)
- Discuss the controversy surrounding recovered memories. Explain why researchers are cautious about claims of recovered memories. (Student Text pp. 370–371)
- Figure 19.9, "Don't Always Trust Your Memory!," examines the factors that contribute to the memory process that might influence the accuracy of your memories. (Student Text p. 371)

Materials NETWORK

All of the items from the Video, Activity, and Enrichment Centers listed below come from the *Teacher's Resource Binder.* These items will help you teach and expand on concepts presented in Module 19.

trb This logo indicates when an item from the Materials Network may be used in conjunction with a specific note found in this module's *Teacher's Edition.*

Forgetting as Encoding Failure

Activity Center

- Critical Thinking Activity: *Fact or Falsehood?* With this activity, students' preconceptions about forgetting and memory construction are either exposed as incorrect or reinforced as correct. (*Teacher's Resource Binder*, p. 19-1; Handout 19–1)
- Building Vocabulary: Graphic Organizer: *Concept Web* Enhance students' understanding of the concepts and vocabulary in the module. (*Teacher's Resource Binder*, p. 19-1; Handout 19–2)
- Application Activity: *Memory of a Penny* It's not easy to correctly recall the details of a penny. (*Teacher's Resource Binder*, p. 19-1)
- Critical Thinking Activity: *Encoding Failure* Demonstrate the fact that we don't encode the details of everyday items. (*Teacher's Resource Binder*, p. 19-1)

Enrichment Center

- Enrichment Lesson: *Change Blindness* This lesson explores why we fail to encode on deeper levels. (*Teacher's Resource Binder*, p. 19-1)

Forgetting as Storage Failure

Activity Center

- Application Activity: *Meaning and Memory: An Assignment to Be Forgotten* Students will delight in this activity that instructs them to forget a number for homework! (*Teacher's Resource Binder*, p. 19-1)

Enrichment Center

- Enrichment Lesson: *Losing Stored Memories—Korsakoff's Syndrome and Alzheimer's Disease* Students learn more about these conditions with this lesson. (*Teacher's Resource Binder*, p. 19-1)

Forgetting as Retrieval Failure

Activity Center

- Application Activity: *A Forgetting Journal* Have students record what they've forgotten for a period of time—a twist on the traditional journal. (*Teacher's Resource Binder*, p. 19-1)
- Critical Thinking Activity: *Earliest Recollections* This activity delves into the contents of what we believe to be memories of early childhood. (*Teacher's Resource Binder*, p. 19-1)
- Technology Application Activity: *PsychSim:* "Forgetting" *PsychSim* is an interactive CD-ROM containing tutorials in different content areas of psychology including memory interference. (*Teacher's Resource Binder*, p. 19-1)
- Application Activity: *The Tip-of-the-Tongue Phenomenon and Capital Cities* Using capital cities as the stimuli for recall, demonstrate the phenomenon of tip-of-your-tongue. (*Teacher's Resource Binder*, p. 19-1; Handout 19–3)
- Analysis Activity: *Repression or Inadequate Retrieval Cues?* As this lesson demonstrates, retrieval failure is the largest contributor to forgetting. (*Teacher's Resource Binder*, p. 19-1)

Memory Construction

V Video Center

- Videocassette: *Scientific American Frontiers,* Second Edition, Segment 17: "True or False?" Consult the faculty guide from the *Scientific American Frontiers* video series for a description of this segment. (*Teacher's Resource Binder*, p. 19-1)

Activity Center

- Application Activity: *Creating a False Memory* This activity demonstrates false memories. (*Teacher's Resource Binder*, p. 19-1; Handout 19–4)
- Cooperative Learning Activity: *Constructive Memory: The Rumor Chain* This activity demonstrates our ability to inadvertently change the details of a story. (*Teacher's Resource Binder*, p. 19-1)
- Application Activity: *Eyewitness Recall* Create a video in which students must be eyewitnesses. (*Teacher's Resource Binder*, p. 19-1)
- Application Activity: *Retroactive and Proactive Inhibition* In this activity, students memorize different lists of words at different times. (*Teacher's Resource Binder*, p. 19-1)

Enrichment Center

- Enrichment Lesson: *The Misinformation Effect* Delve deeper into Elizabeth Loftus' findings. (*Teacher's Resource Binder*, p. 19-1)
- Enrichment Lesson: *Constructive Memory* This lesson includes research findings by Loftus and a constructed memory by Piaget. (*Teacher's Resource Binder*, p. 19-1)
- Enrichment Lesson: *Repressing Memories of Abuse* Repressed memories are a dangerous trend in light of recent research. (*Teacher's Resource Binder*, p. 19-1)

MODULE 19

Forgetting and Memory Construction

Forgetting as Encoding Failure
Forgetting as Storage Failure
Forgetting as Retrieval Failure
Memory Construction

"I forgot." When was the last time you used this simple, two-word phrase? Did it relate to a forgotten assignment? A chore you were supposed to have done? A friend's birthday? We all suffer from memory lapses on a fairly regular basis. In this module, we'll see what psychology has learned about forgetting.

We process information into our memory through three stages: **encoding** (getting information into memory), **storage** (retaining that information), and **retrieval** (getting the information back out after it's been stored). When we say "I forgot," we could be describing a failure at any of these three stages: a lack of encoding or ineffective storage or an inability to retrieve what has been adequately stored. Forgetting is complicated!

Forgetting as Encoding Failure

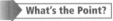

What's the Point? 1. How does lack of encoding cause memory failure?

The cafeteria in my school is in the basement. Its roof is held up by a series of pillars. By the time students reach my class as juniors and seniors, they have been in that room literally hundreds of times, both for lunch and for study halls. When I quiz them on the number of pillars in the cafeteria, however, fewer than half of them can correctly recall that there are 8! Students guess as few as 2 or as many as 15. How can it be

▶ **encoding** The process of getting information into the memory system.

▶ **storage** The retention of encoded information over time.

▶ **retrieval** The process of getting information out of memory storage.

MODULE 19

Forgetting and Memory Construction

Introducing the Module

The Points: Module Objectives

- Analyze how the lack of encoding causes memory failure.
- Discuss current knowledge about the effects of time on long-term memory storage.
- Describe proactive interference and retroactive interference and how they disrupt memories.
- Discuss how motivated forgetting can help explain repressed memories.
- Analyze how false information is incorporated into constructed memories.
- Identify some of the factors that influence the accuracy of children's recall.
- Discuss the memory principles that lead psychologists to be cautious about claims of recovered memories.

trb tr Building Vocabulary

With **Building Vocabulary: Graphic Organizer:** *Concept Web* (*Teacher's Resource Binder*, p. 19-1; **Handout 19–2**), students can learn the definitions of concepts in the module as they see how the concepts relate to one another. You may use the handout as a transparency to project and discuss with the entire class before having students fill in the concept web independently.

Getting Started

Before students begin reading the module, ask them whether they think they have a good memory. For those who answer yes, have them list possible factors that create good memories. For those who answer no, have them list possible factors that create poor memories. Encourage students to compare the factors on their lists to the concepts about forgetting and memory construction they discover as they read this module.

trb You may wish to use **Critical Thinking:** *Fact or Falsehood?* (*Teacher's Resource Binder*, p. 19-1; **Handout 19–1**) as a pre-reading strategy to find out what students already know about forgetting. The activity will prime students to note terms and concepts in the text that confirm or dispel their preconceptions about forgetting.

MODULE 19

Teaching the Points

■ TEACHING TIPS

web (1) You can log on as an instructor to the book companion site for *Thinking About Psychology* at **www.worthpublishers.com/thinkingaboutpsych**. It contains teacher resources for class presentations as well as review and assessment of module concepts and terms.

(2) Test students' knowledge of everyday places and items from around your school to demonstrate encoding failure. For a model of how to proceed with this exercise, review the author's example of students' recall of the number of pillars in a school cafeteria.

trb At this point, you may wish to use **Application Activity:** *Memory of a Penny* (*Teacher's Resource Binder*, p. 19-1) and/or **Enrichment Lesson:** *Change Blindness* (*Teacher's Resource Binder*, p. 19-1).

tr A four-color transparency of Figure 19.1, How Can You Remember What You Haven't Encoded?, is available in the **Overhead Transparencies Set**.

■ LOOKING AT THE ISSUES

Anticipate the findings discussed later in the module by asking students how people can rely on memories of isolated events if they can't remember details about everyday events and places. Research by Elizabeth Loftus on eyewitness testimony shows that people's recollections of events are often inaccurate, like our memories about the details of currency or coins.

that these bright young people do so poorly remembering something they have seen so often? Despite numerous exposures to the 8 pillars, few students encode this information into memory because it is relatively unimportant to them. As long as there are enough pillars to hold up the roof (an issue of trust for almost everyone), they don't need to care how many there are.

We all fail to encode information in our environment, as you'll see if you try this simple quiz. On the back of a United States penny, you will find the value listed as "one cent."

- What is the similar value statement on the back of a dime? How about on a quarter?
- Which way does Lincoln face on the penny—to the left or right? (After you answer this question, try your luck at identifying the real penny in Figure 19.1.)
- Which way does Jefferson face on the nickel?
- Finally, which way does Washington face on the quarter?

Think of how many hundreds and hundreds of times you have seen and used these coins. Yet, unless you have a particular interest in coin collecting, you may not be able to answer any of these questions (you can find the answers on page 362). You probably haven't *forgotten* the answers. Rather, you never bothered to encode this information, because you don't need to know these details to be able to spend the coins.

Encoding failure may contribute to the increasing "forgetfulness" some older people experience. As we age, the parts of the brain active during encoding respond more slowly (Grady & others, 1995). Older people may be more forgetful because they are encoding less information.

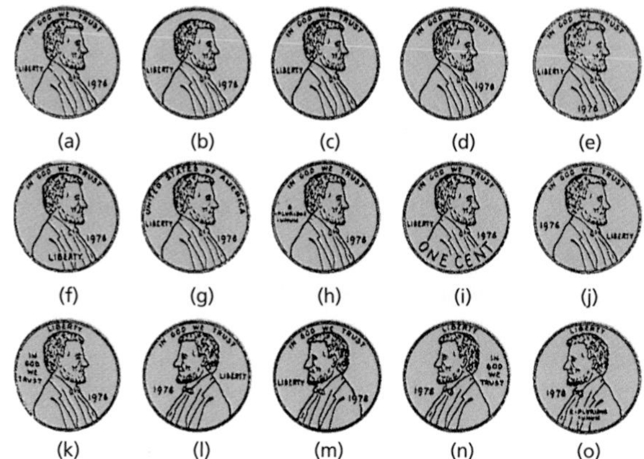

Figure 19.1 **How Can You Remember What You Haven't Encoded?** Can you pick out the real deal? (See page 362 for the answer.) Most of us can't, because we've never bothered to encode this information. The penny spends just as well whether we can identify the correct version or not. (From Nickerson & Adams, 1979.)

Suggested Readings

Use the following as a teacher-preparation tool or as enrichment for advanced students:

Albrecht, K. (1980). *Brain power.* Englewood Cliffs, NJ: Prentice Hall.

Baddeley, A. (1982). *Your memory: A user's guide.* New York: Macmillan.

Bower, G. (1990). Awareness, the unconscious, and repression: An experimental psychologist's perspective. In J. Singer (Ed.), *Repression and dissociation: Implications for personality theory, psychopathology, and health.* Chicago: University of Chicago Press.

Halonen, J. S. (1986). *Teaching critical thinking in psychology.* Milwaukee: Alverno Productions.

Hilts, P. J. (1995). *Memory's ghost: The strange tale of Mr. M. and the nature of memory.* New York: Simon & Schuster.

MODULE 19

Forgetting as Storage Failure

2. What do we know about the effects of time on long-term memory storage?

I've long been fascinated by the compost pile that we keep behind our house. A never-ending stream of grass clippings, leaves, weeds, egg shells, grapefruit rinds, celery stalks, and other organic rubbish makes its way into the pile, only to rapidly decompose to a small fraction of its original bulk. Are memories like that, decaying like the material in the compost pile?

This idea of decay is consistent with the results obtained by **Hermann Ebbinghaus** (1885), famous for his early studies of memory. His "forgetting curve" (Figure 19.2) indicates that most forgetting happens quite rapidly and then levels off. Most of the loss occurs early on, just as it does in the compost pile, and then slows down considerably. More recent research has looked at the process of forgetting far beyond the 30 days Ebbinghaus examined (Bahrick, 1984) (Figure 19.3 on page 362). The researcher was interested in how well people remembered the vocabulary they had learned in Spanish class decades earlier. He found that most of the vocabulary was lost in three years, but after that initial loss, the forgetting curve leveled off. Words people remembered after three years were likely to remain in their memories a quarter-century later! The term **permastore memory** is used to describe these especially long-lasting memories.

We still don't know enough about how long-term memories are stored in the brain to understand if they actually do decay with time.

▶ **Hermann Ebbinghaus** (1850–1909) German philosopher who conducted pioneering memory studies.

▶ **permastore memory** Long-term memories that are especially resistant to forgetting and are likely to last a lifetime.

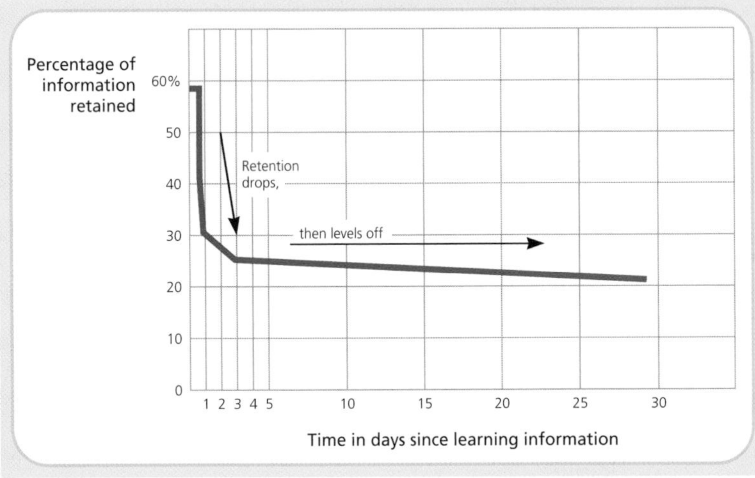

Figure 19.2
The Forgetting Curve
Hermann Ebbinghaus demonstrated over a century ago that most forgetting occurs soon after learning. After a steep initial drop, we retain most of the remaining information. (Adapted from Ebbinghaus, 1885.)

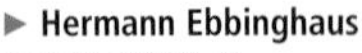

■ **APPLYING THE POINTS**
How can students decrease the forgetting curve studied by Ebbinghaus? If students would take several minutes to review information they learned right after a particular class, they would retain more information for a longer period of time, thereby increasing the likelihood that long-term storage would occur.

tr ■ **TEACHING TIP**
A four-color transparency of Figure 19.2, The Forgetting Curve, is available in the **Overhead Transparencies Set.**

Loftus, E. (1979). *Eyewitness testimony.* Cambridge, MA: Harvard University Press.

Loftus, E., & Ketcham, K. (1991). *Witness for the defense: The accused, the eyewitness, and the expert who puts memory on trial.* New York: St. Martin's Press.

Loftus, E., & Ketcham, K. (1994). *The myth of repressed memory: False memories and allegations of sexual abuse.* New York: St. Martin's Press.

Piaget, J. (1962). *Play, dreams, and imitation in childhood.* New York: Norton.

MODULE 19

■ TEACHING TIPS

tr (1) A four-color transparency of Figure 19.3, Permastore Memory, is available in the **Overhead Transparencies Set.**

(2) Link the discussion of *permastore* to *long-term potentiation* discussed in Module 18. **Long-term potentiation** is the biological component of memory. As a person learns a new task, the brain develops a pathway that controls and stores the information for accomplishing that task. With each repetition of the task, the pathway becomes more efficient. New pathways are formed and strengthened as learning and memory continue, making it more difficult to lose a well-rehearsed task or memory.

trb ■ APPLYING THE POINTS

At this point, you may wish to use **Critical Thinking Activity:** *Encoding Failure* (*Teacher's Resource Binder,* p. 19-1) to further demonstrate our lack of encoding the details of everyday items. This quick activity tests students' knowledge of watches, money, and telephones.

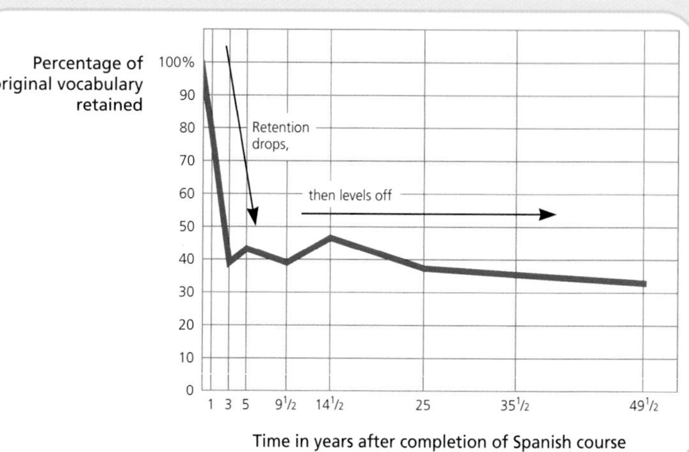

Figure 19.3 **Permastore Memory** This graph shows how well people retained Spanish vocabulary they had learned in school a half-century earlier. Note that although the timeline differs, this forgetting curve has the same shape as the one, in Figure 19.2, which Ebbinghaus identified. (Adapted from Bahrick, 1984.)

Answers to the questions in the list about coins on page 360: A dime reads "one dime," a quarter reads "quarter dollar," Lincoln faces to his left, and both Jefferson and Washington face right.

Answer to the penny exercise (Figure 19.1) on page 360: Penny (a) is the real penny.

The work on permastore seems to indicate that even if some memories do decay, others do not. It will be interesting to see if future research demonstrates a change in the physical storage of the memories that do decay. What we do know for sure is that we sometimes also forget because we are unable to retrieve memories that are still stored.

Forgetting as Retrieval Failure

Retrieval failure probably accounts for most of our forgetting. You've encoded and stored the information. It's in there, but you can't get it out.

Interference

3. What are proactive interference and retroactive interference, and how do they disrupt memories?

Interference is a retrieval problem that occurs when one memory gets in the way of another. Have you ever traveled in a car from one city to another, happily listening to music on your favorite radio station? As you approach the new city, you may find that the music begins to turn into some other kind of music you'd never listen to. The two types of music will compete for your attention because two stations with similar radio frequencies are sharing the air waves. If neither is strong enough to dominate, interference occurs and you won't be able to receive either station clearly.

Meeting Individual Needs

trb **GRAPHIC ORGANIZER** Provide learning opportunities for all levels of learners with one of the following options for using **Graphic Organizer:** *Concept Web* (*Teacher's Resource Binder,* p. 19-1; **Handout 19–2**):

- **Independent Learners** Students may fill out the organizer on their own or follow along in class during discussion and lecture.
- **Cooperative Learners** Students may use the textbook as a resource and work in groups to find the answers that fit in the blanks.
- **Exceptional Learners** The graphic organizer can fill a special education need to provide notes for exceptional students. These students may fill in the blanks independently, with a student or teacher/tutor, or along with class discussion and lecture.

A similar thing happens with memories. When an older memory disrupts a newer memory, you experience **proactive interference** (Figure 19.4). Have you ever moved and had to learn a new phone number? When you get the new number, you sit down and rehearse it until you commit it to memory. Later on, though, when somebody asks you for your new number, you may be unable to retrieve it. When you follow the retrieval pathway in your brain to "my phone number," the only number you can find is the old one. Your earlier learning is interfering with your retrieval of the more recent information—your new number. Here are some other examples of proactive interference.

- Remembering last year's locker combination proactively interferes with remembering this year's combination.
- Calling your current girlfriend's house on the phone and asking to speak to your *former* girlfriend. (This actually happened to me when I was in high school—not a pleasant experience!)
- Remembering the word for something in the first foreign language you studied, but not being able to recall the word for that item in the most recent foreign language you studied.

You can also suffer from **retroactive interference**, which occurs when a more recent memory reduces your ability to retrieve an older memory. I have had the same phone number now for over 20 years.

▶ **proactive interference** The disruptive effect of earlier learning on the recall of recently stored information.

▶ **retroactive interference** The disruptive effect of new learning on the recall of previously stored information.

Figure 19.4 **Scenes of Interference** Because his memory of last year's locker combination (a) produces proactive interference, this boy can't remember this year's combination. He gets so caught up in the details of this year's game (d) that retroactive interference prevents him from remembering the details of last year's game (c).

MODULE 19

■ TEACHING TIP

Help students remember the difference between *proactive* and *retroactive interference* by using the following mnemonics:

- The prefix *pro-* means "before," and **proactive interference** is defined by previous memories—those coming *before* now—blocking newer memories.
- The prefix *retro-* means "backward," and **retroactive interference** is defined by previous memories being blocked by newer memories—newer memories *go back* and seemingly erase older ones.

trb At this point, you may wish to use **Application Activity:** ***Retroactive and Proactive Inhibition*** (*Teacher's Resource Binder,* p. 19-1).

tr A four-color transparency of Figure 19.4, Scenes of Interference, is available in the **Overhead Transparencies Set.**

Demonstrating

TRANSCRIPTS To demonstrate retrieval, obtain a copy of each student's transcript from the guidance counselor. Have students list the classes they took and the grades they received each year, beginning in ninth grade. Once they feel they've exhausted their memories, give them a copy of their transcript. Have them compare their remembered list with the actual one and count the number of errors. Have them determine which type of information was more memorable—classes or grades?

trb At this point, you may wish to use **Application Activity:** ***The Tip-of-the-Tongue Phenomenon and Capital Cities*** (*Teacher's Resource Binder,* p. 19-1; **Handout 19–3**).

MODULE 19

■ JOURNAL WRITING

Invite students to use the following questions and writing prompts as springboards for entries in their psychology journals:

- Have you experienced proactive interference? Retroactive interference? Describe these experiences.
- Have you ever realized that you had been motivated to forget something? Why did you seemingly forget it?
- Do you believe that repression is a real phenomenon? Why or why not?

■ MULTICULTURAL CONNECTIONS

How do other cultures deal with painful memories? Have students research by interviewing students from other cultures (from whom they receive permission) or using available resources in the library or on the Internet. In a class forum, have students share their findings by posing the following questions:

- Do they emphasize putting bad experiences behind them and moving on? Or is there time allotted for them to confront a problem?
- Are there some forms of psychoanalysis-type therapy evident in non-Western cultures?

■ CHECKING FOR UNDERSTANDING

To check students' understanding of forgetting, have them describe, either orally or in writing, the three different ways information can be forgotten.

I have rehearsed it so well that I find it impossible to retrieve my earlier phone numbers. When I was in college, I easily retrieved my dorm phone number, but I no longer have any idea what it was. My current phone number retroactively interferes with it. There are lots of examples of this phenomenon, too.

- Your memory of your class schedule for this year has overwhelmed the schedule you followed last year.
- Your memory of current sports champions (World Series, Super Bowl, NCAA basketball, and so forth) will probably displace memories of champions from previous years.
- You can remember the sequence of buttons necessary to activate your current electronic devices (microwave, VCR, and so on), but you probably can't remember how to operate the ones you had five years ago.

Motivated Forgetting

4. How can motivated forgetting help explain repressed memories?

Sometimes, you might have a reason to forget. The act of forgetting can provide protection from anxiety or from potentially distressing information. If you're trying to exercise more, those two days you were a couch potato last week might just slip your mind. If you're trying to cut calories, that candy bar your friend shared with you between classes may not make it into your daily calorie count. To remember these things would be to admit that you hadn't quite lived up to your goals. That's motivation to forget them.

Does scientific evidence support the idea of motivated forgetting? Yes. In one experiment, students took a study skills course in which they were asked to recall their previous study habits. They remembered studying less than they actually had, which allowed them to think the study skills course was more effective (Conway & Ross, 1984).

There is less scientific support for **Sigmund Freud**'s theory of psychoanalysis, a famous attempt to understand motivated forgetting. Freud viewed the unconscious mind as a storehouse for ideas that threaten us with anxiety. Freud thought such ideas were moved to the unconscious in a process called **repression** (Figure 19.5). This, he thought, may be how we protect ourselves from painful memories, though the memories continue to lurk beneath the level of consciousness and can haunt us in a variety of ways. One goal of therapy, Freud thought, is to bring these buried memories to the surface so they can be fully understood.

▸ **Sigmund Freud** (1856–1939) Founder of psychoanalysis, a controversial theory about the workings of the unconscious mind.

▸ **repression** In Sigmund Freud's psychoanalytic theory, the process of moving anxiety-producing memories to the unconscious.

Enriching

trb At this point, you may wish to use Application Activity: *A Forgetting Journal* (*Teacher's Resource Binder*, p. 19-1). With this activity, students record what they've forgotten for a period of time—a twist on the traditional journal, in which memories are usually recorded.

Figure 19.5 **Repression** Sigmund Freud argued that we block from consciousness—or repress—memories that could cause us anxiety. Research evidence is mixed on this issue, making the concept of repression controversial.

Many of Freud's ideas about the unconscious mind have worked their way into the popular culture. Movies and novels often illustrate how repression is supposed to work. Despite the reality that there is little experimental evidence to support this theory, 90 percent of college students still believe that the process of repression does protect people by pushing painful memories to the unconscious (Kihlstrom, 1990). Actually, stressful incidents tend to stimulate the release of stress hormones that *enhance* the encoding and storage of memories (Cahill, 1994). So, while we do seem readily able to forget minor details when motivated, we are, unfortunately, more, not less, likely to remember painful events.

Memory Construction

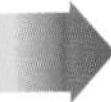

5. How is false information incorporated into constructed memories?

Many people believe that memories are like video tapes. As long as you can find the right tape to replay, you can access the recorded memory. Not so. Retrieving a memory is more like building a jigsaw puzzle (Figure 19.6, page 366), and that's because of the way we store memories in the first place. When you commit an event to memory, your brain breaks the memory into tiny pieces. Some of the pieces are invariably lost, so that when you try to reassemble the puzzle, there are holes. Like a creative carpenter, your brain builds new pieces to fill in those gaps. The new pieces may or may not represent what was there originally, but once they take their place in the assembled puzzle, you have no way of determining whether they are real or fictional.

■ APPLYING THE POINTS

(1) Have students research repressed memories, basing their exploration on elements of movies and television shows they've seen that depict people who have experienced repressed memories. Present the following questions to guide research and subsequent class discussion:

- How research-based were these depictions of repressed memories?
- What did the therapists in these movies or television shows do to get their patients to "remember"?

trb (2) You may wish to use **Analysis Activity:** ***Repression or Inadequate Retrieval Cues?*** (*Teacher's Resource Binder,* p. 19-1) to demonstrate that empirical evidence for the Freudian concept of repression as the unconscious blocking of painful memories and unacceptable impulses is meager. As this lesson demonstrates, retrieval failure is the largest contributor to forgetting.

trb ■ **TEACHING TIP**

You may wish to use **Critical Thinking Activity:** ***Earliest Recollections*** (*Teacher's Resource Binder,* p. 19-1) to get students thinking about Freudian theory and memory. Students can explore their earliest memories with this lesson that delves into the contents of what we believe to be memories of early childhood. Have students share their memories with their parents to see if their memories are accurate.

Demonstrating

trb You may wish to use **Cooperative Learning Activity:** ***Constructive Memory: The Rumor Chain*** (*Teacher's Resource Binder,* p. 19-1) to demonstrate how memories are constructed. The childhood game of "gossip" is the basis for this robust activity that demonstrates our ability to inadvertently change the details of a story according to our expectations and prejudices.

MODULE 19

■ APPLYING THE POINTS

(1) Have students try out the memory construction word list with friends who are not currently enrolled in this class to see how many of the friends fall victim to remembering words that don't appear on the list. Help students share this experience by asking the following questions:

- How sure were the friends of remembering the words?
- What words did the friends "remember"?
- Were the friends surprised at their ability to construct memories of words? Why or why not?

trb (2) You may also wish to use **Application Activity:** *Creating a False Memory (Teacher's Resource Binder,* p. 18-1; **Handout 19–4**) to demonstrate memory construction. False memories are easy to create, as this simple activity demonstrates.

Figure 19.6 **How Does Memory Work?** Memory is less like a videotape than like a jigsaw puzzle with missing pieces. Your brain "manufactures" new pieces to fill in the holes and construct a complete memory.

Shall we try it? You need a piece of paper and a pencil. When you're all set, give yourself 30 seconds to commit to memory as many of the following words and phrases as possible. Don't continue reading until you've spent your 30 seconds memorizing.

textbook, all-nighter, quiz, flashcards, review, lecture, vocabulary, GPA, outline, essay, notes, semester exam, due date, grading scale, assignment, unit test, memorize, class project, handouts, tutor, chapter guide

Now, in whatever order you can, and without referring to the original list, see how many of the words you can write on your paper. Take as long as you like. Then go back and check your list against the original. Chances are you will have remembered quite a few of the items. You are also likely to have left off some of the items—that was a lot to learn in 30 seconds! Now, without looking at the list, answer these four questions:

1. Was the word *lecture* on the list?
2. Was the word *grading scale* on the list?
3. Was the word *study* on the list?
4. Was the word *school* on the list?

Study and *school* were not on the original list, but people often "remember" them anyway.

If you said *study* and *school* were on the original list, you might be thinking that I fooled you. After all, these two words seem to belong on this list! That's just the point. As you struggled with the difficult memory task and my follow-up questions, you began to speculate on items that reasonably belonged on the list. Now you've got a problem—which items were really there at first, and which were imagined? Your

► **Elizabeth Loftus** (1944–) University of California, Irvine, psychologist whose research established the constructed nature of memory.

► **misinformation effect** Incorporating misleading information into one's memory of an event.

Demonstrating

TRY TO REMEMBER To demonstrate how memory works, videotape an event in your classroom. (It can either be a typical activity, like a daily lesson, or an event you construct to create some excitement.)

- After the event has been captured on video, have students take a few moments to write down their recollections of the event.
- Then, show the video to the students to see how many of their recollections are accurate.
- Repeat this activity several days later to see if their memories have become more or less accurate.

memory was constructed out of some things that were real and some that were not, and distinguishing between the two categories will now be very difficult.

University of California, Irvine, psychologist **Elizabeth Loftus** was the first to demonstrate in the laboratory this tendency to construct memories. She and her colleague John Palmer (1974) showed participants a film of a car accident (Figure 19.7). They varied the wording in their questions, asking one group, "How fast were the cars going when they *smashed* into each other?" and the other, "How fast were the cars going when they *hit* each other?" This seemingly minor difference was enough to produce significantly greater speed estimates by the "smashed" group. The researchers were able to alter memory, simply by the way they phrased the question, and the participants were never aware of the manipulation.

Loftus and Palmer demonstrated another important aspect of memory a week later, when they asked participants whether they recalled seeing broken glass at the scene of the accident. The "smashed" group was more than twice as likely as the "hit" group to recall broken glass. There was no broken glass. The question led participants to construct memories of broken glass, because this is a reasonable outcome of an accident, especially one in which the cars had "smashed." Incorporating misleading information into a memory, as occurred here, is known as the **misinformation effect.**

Hundreds of experiments have verified the tendency to construct memories. Misinformation can cause a hammer to be recalled as a screwdriver and breakfast cereal to be recalled as eggs, among a myriad of similar transformations (Loftus & others, 1992). And the more time that passes before the misleading information is provided, the greater the misinformation effect will be (Loftus, 1992).

Think for a minute how important this finding is. If memory can be altered by the

Elizabeth Loftus Elizabeth Loftus is a memory researcher from the University of California, Irvine.

Depiction of actual accident

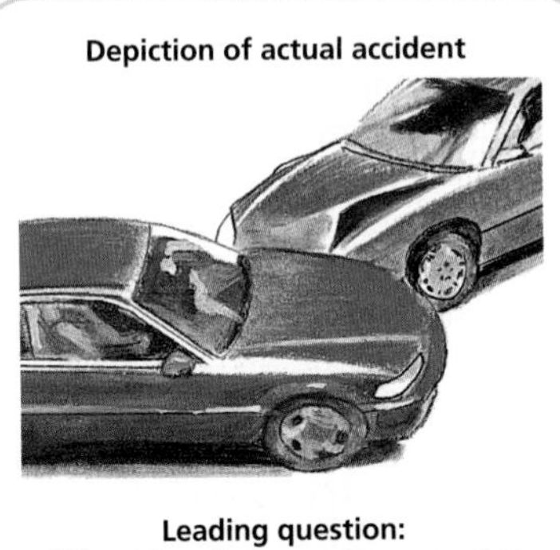

Leading question:
"About how fast were the cars going when they smashed into each other?"

Memory construction

Figure 19.7 **The Nature of Memory** What we remember depends partly on the wording of the questions we are asked. People who were asked questions about cars "smashing" remembered a worse collision than those who were asked questions about cars "hitting" each other. (From Loftus, 1979.)

■ TEACHING TIPS

tr (1) A four-color transparency of Figure 19.7, The Nature of Memory, is available in the **Overhead Transparencies Set.**

(2) Link *memory construction* to *construction of survey questions.* Surveys can be manipulative if they contain *loaded questions.* **Loaded questions** are those questions intended to lead a subject to respond in a certain way. For example, say that you don't find littering that serious of a problem, in light of other far more serious problems in your community. If a group wants you to say you are against littering, they might phrase a question to you as follows: "Do you think people who throw their nasty trash into your front yard should pay a hefty fine?" Chances are you will answer "Yes," even if littering, compared to other problems, wasn't that big of a concern of yours before the question was asked.

Demonstrating

QUESTIONING MEMORIES Have volunteers create a brief video of an incident—for example, two students accidentally bump into one another in the hall and one or both drop their belongings. Show this video to two groups of students outside of your class. (Be sure to get Institutional Review Board approval and informed consent from subjects before embarking on any research project.)

- Have your students work in one of two groups, with each group preparing differently worded questions to ask about the incident on video. (Encourage them to use the Loftus and Palmer questions about a car accident as a model.)
- Have each group present their questions to a group of viewers, who will provide answers.
- Have the full class meet to discuss the differences between the memories of the subjects in each viewing group.

way questions are asked, this has major implications for courtroom testimony. A skillful attorney can actually change a witness's memory by carefully wording the questions, and the witness will probably be completely unaware of the manipulation. When you realize that eyewitness testimony is one of the most damning kinds of evidence in a criminal trial, you can see that everyone involved—particularly the jury—should be aware of the basic processes that control memory and forgetting. This is but one of many reasons why psychology is such a relevant course.

The media spotlight has been shining on two related areas of interest in recent years: children's testimony in alleged cases of child abuse, and recovered memories of abuse. Let's look at what researchers have learned about these two important topics.

Children's Recall

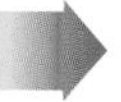

6. What are some of the factors that influence the accuracy of children's recall?

Child abuse occurs with alarming regularity, and people who abuse children must be identified and prosecuted as the criminals they are. Yet, as important as it is to punish abusers, we must also protect innocent adults from being falsely accused of crimes they did not commit—a situation that also happens regularly. When people are charged with abuse, their innocence or guilt may be determined by the testimony of young children. Is such testimony reliable? Are children's memories accurate? Let's look at some evidence.

Researchers who have set out to intentionally alter children's memories have been remarkably successful, especially in demonstrating the misinformation effect. Two of the leading researchers in this area (Ceci & Bruck, 1993) were able to plant false memories in preschoolers by interviewing them once a week for 10 weeks and repeatedly asking questions like, "Can you remember going to the hospital with a mousetrap on your finger?" Eventually, a large number of the children constructed stories that ended up with mousetraps and hospital visits. The stories were false but convincing, and they were almost impossible to distinguish from true memories.

Researchers have established two general principles about children's memory (Figure 19.8). First, children's memories grow more accurate with age. Compared with older children and adults, preschool-age children are more susceptible to suggestion—and therefore less accurate—90 percent of the time (Bruck & Ceci, 1999). For example, studies report that younger children are more likely than older children to falsely report that someone had licked their knee or that something "yucky" had been put in their mouth.

web ■ **TEACHING TIP**

Gary Wells's Web site at www.psychology.iastate.edu/faculty/gwells/homepage.htm provides numerous resources for extending the text discussion of eyewitness recall. Included are video clips for students to test their own eyewitness accuracy, current research reports, and the recently published U.S. Department of Justice national guidelines on eyewitness evidence.

trb At this point, you may wish to use Enrichment Lesson: *Constructive Memory* (*Teacher's Resource Binder*, p. 19-1).

■ **APPLYING THE POINTS**

Invite a local criminal attorney, prosecutor, and/or criminal court judge to discuss how research in eyewitness testimony has affected the legal world and the judicial system in the United States.

trb At this point, you may wish to use Application Activity: *Eyewitness Recall* (*Teacher's Resource Binder*, p. 19-1).

■ **MULTICULTURAL CONNECTIONS**

Do legal systems in other parts of the world value eyewitness testimony as much as the U.S. legal system? Using available resources, including the Internet, ask volunteers to research laws from other cultures that concern the weight eyewitness testimony is given in criminal proceedings. Encourage those who conducted research to report their findings in an informal oral presentation.

Enriching

web Have students investigate the work of Northwestern University law professor Lawrence C. Marshall, whose Web site for the Center for Wrongful Convictions and the Innocence Network is at www.law.northwestern.edu/wrongfulconvictions. Professor Marshall has his students review cases to see if a person was wrongly convicted. His classes have found that several innocent people have been sent to prison and even put to death as a result of a variety of problems, many of which relate to eyewitness memory problems.

- How does the work of this professor affect the integrity of our legal system?
- If you were convicted of a crime, how would you defend yourself if eyewitness testimony was the only evidence against you?
- What would you do to enhance your memory of a crime if you were a witness?

Figure 19.8 **The Accuracy of Children's Recall** Older children recall events more accurately than younger children do. Children's memories are also more accurate if the adult uses words the child can understand and refrains from using leading or suggestive questions.

The second and more important principle is that there are ways to minimize these false memories in children. The key is to eliminate the suggestibility and misinformation that can lead children, in their effort to please the adults asking questions, to construct false memories. One surprising example of suggestibility involved the anatomically correct dolls (dolls with realistic sexual details) that investigators often use when asking children about possible abuse. The problem is that these unusual dolls, *in and of themselves,* may suggest to children that they should talk about genital contact. In one study, researchers asked 3-year-olds to use anatomically correct dolls to illustrate how they had been touched during a doctor's examination. Although none of these children had been touched in their genital area, more than half of them reported such contact, apparently because the dolls suggested to the children that such a response was desired (Ceci & Bruck, 1993).

Eager to Please Children crave the approval of adults. This attempt to please makes it more likely that children will remember things the way they think an adult wants them to.

Knowing that young children are prone to constructing false memories, investigators should develop techniques to minimize the misinformation effect. Studies (Howe, 1997; Pipe, 1996) show that children's testimony is most likely to be accurate when the interviewing adult:

1. phrases questions using words the child can understand.
2. has had no contact with the child prior to the investigation.
3. uses neutral language and does not ask leading or suggestive questions.

If interviewers violate these rules, children may construct false memories. And when that happens, it will be almost impossible to undo the damage and determine what parts of the memories are real. In most cases, children who construct these memories are sincerely trying to do what is right—there is no intentional lying involved.

LOOKING AT THE ISSUES

How much influence does the media have on our beliefs about eyewitness testimony in children and adults?

Have students work in small groups to choose any of the crime dramas on network television today and then watch an episode or two. Groups can evaluate whether their chosen television series accurately portrayed what the research suggests about eyewitness testimony and memory construction.

After groups have viewed their chosen show, have each focus on the following questions in a report of their conclusions to the class:

- Did the police in the show ask leading questions of witnesses?
- Did the attorneys rely too heavily on the word of witnesses?
- Was a line-up used? If so, did it follow what research suggests is proper procedure? (See Gary Wells's Web site, cited on page 368 of the *Teacher's Edition* for details of this research.)

JOURNAL WRITING

Invite students to use the following question as a springboard for entries in their psychology journals:

- Have you ever experienced a constructed memory? Describe your experience.

MODULE 19

trb ■ TEACHING TIP

You may wish to use **Analysis Activity:** *Repression or Inadequate Retrieval Cues?* (*Teacher's Resource Binder,* p. 19-1) to show that empirical evidence for the Freudian concept of repression as the unconscious blocking of painful memories and unacceptable impulses is meager. As this lesson demonstrates, retrieval failure is the largest contributor to forgetting.

■ LOOKING AT THE ISSUES

As the author, Charlie, points out, the ways therapists uncover repressed memories include hypnosis, imagery, and dream analysis. Have students examine each of these therapeutic practices to see whether or not they are scientifically valid. To help guide research and subsequent class discussion of findings, present these questions to your students:

- How are these techniques controversial?
- What certification does one need to be able to use these techniques?
- What studies have been done to prove their effectiveness?

Recovered Memories

7. What memory principles lead psychologists to be cautious about claims of recovered memories?

Perhaps you know something about recovered memories from watching the talk shows on daytime TV, for this issue has received a great deal of attention in such forums. Celebrities such as Roseanne have claimed that, as adults, they recovered long-repressed memories of childhood abuse. They argue that the trauma of abuse caused the memories to be repressed—buried in the unconscious mind—only to be recovered when triggered by some event years later.

The one indisputable fact in this issue is that childhood physical and sexual abuse unfortunately does occur, with devastating impact on the victims. Beyond this, things become murkier. Many sincere, legitimate therapists are convinced that some of their patients have experienced such repression and that they have helped them recover these memories through therapy. Other psychologists are skeptical and worry that well-meaning therapists are leading suggestible people into constructing false memories. Can research on memory help shed light on the truth? Let's break it down into two specific questions.

1. **Can repression of memories occur?** In other words, can a memory of a traumatic event be lost from consciousness? To find out, one researcher (Williams, 1995) located over 100 adult women who were documented victims of sexual abuse as children. When interviewed, most women did recall the abusive event, but over a third of them were not able to. Sometimes they recalled other abusive events or were confused about the event in question. Although the victims may have been too young to remember, this research at least leaves the door open—repression of traumatic events may be possible. And, if it is possible to repress the memories into unconsciousness, it may also be possible to recover them.
2. **Can recovered memories be false?** Some therapists, unfortunately, use techniques that seem to increase the likelihood of false memories. As reports of childhood abuse became more common in the 1980s and 1990s, some therapists believed it was important to frame questions in a way that tapped into the possibility of repression. Patients were told that "denial" and "repression" could happen easily. One popular book suggested, "If you are unable to remember any specific instances . . . but still have a feeling that something abusive happened to you, it probably did" (Bass & Davis, 1988, pp. 21–22). The techniques used to "uncover" memories include hypnosis (creating a state of suggestibility and asking the patient about possible past experiences), imagery (having the patient imagine and try to re-create possible past experiences), and dream analysis (ex-

Recovered Memory? The controversy over recovered memories has received widespread media attention because of the claims of entertainers like Roseanne, who said that as an adult, she recovered memories of childhood abuse. It has been impossible to determine under what circumstances such recovered memories are accurate or false.

Enriching

trb You may want to use any of the following lessons to expand the instruction on memory construction:

- **Enrichment Lesson:** *The Misinformation Effect* (*Teacher's Resource Binder,* p. 19-1)
  Delve deeper into Elizabeth Loftus' findings about the misinformation effect with this lesson.
- **Enrichment Lesson:** *Constructive Memory* (*Teacher's Resource Binder,* p. 19-1)
  Loftus' original research in constructive eyewitness memory is detailed in this lesson as well as Piaget's famous constructed memory of his own kidnapping from when he was a small child.
- **Enrichment Lesson:** *Repressing Memories of Abuse* (*Teacher's Resource Binder,* p. 19-1)
  Numerous people throughout recent history have spent time in jail as a result of constructed "repressed" memories—a dangerous trend in light of research on how susceptible our memories are to influence, as this lesson discusses.

ploring the patient's dreams for hidden hints of possible past experiences). In each of these techniques, therapists make suggestions to their patients, which we now know can lead people to unwittingly construct false memories. The authority and prestige of the therapist makes these suggestions even more powerful.

These two conflicting lines of evidence leave the recovered memory debate mired in an unsatisfying and potentially dangerous lack of clarity. Memories may be created, lost, and recovered, which seems to suggest that therapy could be used as a tool to identify previously undiscovered cases of child abuse. However, recovered memories are often inaccurate, and memories relating to events that occurred before the age of 3 (before most people's brains have matured enough to be physically capable of long-term storage) are especially likely to be inaccurate. If a therapist suggests childhood abuse as a possible source of adult difficulties, this suggestion may function as misinformation that produces false memories.

Victims of child abuse have suffered tremendously. Yet adults falsely accused of abuse based on the "evidence" of recovered memories have suffered, too. Families have been torn apart based on unprovable allegations of childhood abuse that may or may not be true.

Perhaps psychological science will one day identify a more reliable way to sort out the false memories. For now, we clearly need to be cautious and avoid jumping to conclusions about recovered memories.

Maybe it is the mysteries about memory that make it so fascinating. Our memories have tremendous power to keep the past alive. They can also deceive us (Figure 19.9). Even experts suffer from falsely constructed memories. Famous child psychologist Jean Piaget remembered in detail an attempt to kidnap him in a park when he was a child. He had for years been grateful for his nursemaid's efforts to successfully foil the kidnapping. But as an adult, he learned that this vivid memory was false! He had constructed it from a story told by his nursemaid, who later admitted she had lied about the kidnapping attempt. We are accustomed to dealing with fact or fiction, yet memory seems to be fact *and* fiction, with no clear way to distinguish the former from the latter. Should we trust our memories? Yes, but we should also be aware that they are not perfectly reliable.

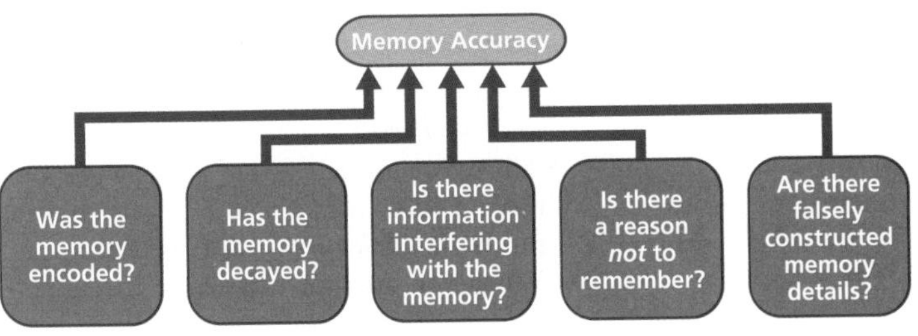

Figure 19.9 **Don't Always Trust Your Memory!** Why aren't memories more accurate? Many factors contribute to the complicated process of memory. When you consider all that can go wrong, maybe the remarkable thing is that our memories are as accurate as they are!

trb tr ■ TEACHING TIP

A black-line master for Figure 19.9, Don't Always Trust Your Memory!, is available in the **Black-Line Masters Appendix** of the *Teacher's Resource Binder.*

Close

After studying this module, how can we ever trust our memories? This question may arise as students process the implications of forgetting and memory construction on our legal system and daily lives. Help students realize that although memory is malleable, students can use techniques to increase the likelihood of remembering events accurately. Also, students can use this awareness of the fallibility of memory to become better consumers and critical thinkers.

Reteaching

trb tr A black-line master of Figure 19.9, Don't Always Trust Your Memory!, is available in the **Black-Line Masters Appendix** of the *Teacher's Resource Binder.* You can use this transparency to see how well students understand the different reasons why memory is not so much a videotape of life as it is a jigsaw puzzle. Discuss with them ways they can improve their recall of facts and events by reviewing the tips from Module 18.

MODULE 19

Checking the Points

■ TEACHING TIPS

web (1) The book companion site for *Thinking About Psychology* at www.worthpublishers.com/thinkingaboutpsych contains a module quiz, flashcards of key terms and people, as well as other student activities and resources for this module. You will also find PowerPoint lectures, a quiz grade book, and other teaching resources by logging on as an instructor.

trb (2) To help students review module concepts, have them work in groups to respond with either "true" or "false" to statements about forgetting and memory construction in **Critical Thinking Activity:** *Fact or Falsehood?* (*Teacher's Resource Binder*, p. 19-1; **Handout 19–1**). If students filled in this handout before reading the module, ask them not to refer to it and to answer based on what they have learned. To confirm responses, group members can take turns finding passages in the text that support each correct response.

REVIEW

Module 19: Forgetting and Memory Construction

What's the Point?

We process information into memory through three stages: encoding (getting information into memory), storage (retaining the information), and retrieval (getting the information back out of storage when we need it). At any of these stages, our memory can fail, causing us to forget.

Forgetting as Encoding Failure

1. *How does lack of encoding cause memory failure?*

   We may not remember information because we never paid attention to it long enough to encode it. We don't attend to information we consider unimportant. Older people may be especially susceptible to encoding failure because the parts of the brain active during encoding respond more slowly as we age.

Forgetting as Storage Failure

2. *What do we know about the effects of time on long-term memory storage?*

   More than a century ago, Hermann Ebbinghaus showed that storage failure tends to occur in a predictable pattern. We lose most of the information we are going to lose shortly after we learn it. After this initial period, the loss tends to level off. Some memories lodge in permastore memory, where they remain for decades. Researchers have not yet demonstrated whether the storage areas involved in memory actually change physically over time.

Forgetting as Retrieval Failure

Most instances of forgetting result from our inability to retrieve information we have previously stored.

3. *What are proactive interference and retroactive interference, and how do they disrupt memories?*

   Proactive interference occurs when an old memory of information interferes with a memory of something you learned recently. *Pro* comes from a Greek word meaning "before," or "in front"; the memory "before" your current memory is blocking your new memory. Retroactive interference is just the opposite—a new memory blocks your ability to retrieve an older memory. *Retro* comes from a Latin word meaning "backward" or "back." Thus your new memory prevents you from looking backward on your memory pathways and finding an old memory.

4. *How can motivated forgetting help explain repressed memories?*

   Research indicates that we do sometimes forget some information that might cause us anxiety if we brought it into conscious awareness. Sigmund Freud based his theory of psychoanalysis on the concept of motivated forgetting. Although current research provides limited support for our ability to forget anxiety-producing events, it does not support Freud's view that repression protects people by pushing painful memories to the unconscious.

Memory Construction

5. *How is false information incorporated into constructed memories?*

   When you initially store a memory, your brain tucks it away in bits and pieces, much like the pieces of a jigsaw puzzle. When you attempt to retrieve that memory, your brain must reconstruct it, and sometimes some of the pieces are not retrieved properly. When this happens, your brain will fill in the gaps, often with false information. Once this false information is in place, it becomes a part of the memory, and you probably won't be able to distinguish it from the true portion of the memory. By asking leading questions, other people can introduce misleading information into your memories and cause you to misremember. This process is called the misinformation effect.

6. *What are some of the factors that influence the accuracy of children's recall?*

   Children, especially young children, are very susceptible to the misinformation effect, or the construction of false memories. Children may answer questions by providing information they think an adult questioner expects to hear. This can have disastrous consequences when a child testifies against a falsely-accused person and tries to please the investigators who are guiding the child's testimony. Research indicates that we can minimize false memories in children by ensuring that the adult who interviews children (1) uses wording they can understand, (2) has had no contact with the children prior to the investigation, and (3) refrains from asking leading or suggestive questions.

7. *What memory principles lead psychologists to be cautious about claims of recovered memories?*

   Recovered memories of abuse are memories that people claim to have repressed but later retrieved, often in the context of therapy. The evidence on the reliability and accuracy of recovered memories is mixed. Researchers have shown that a small percentage of people who were abused as children cannot recall the abuse. But the research on false memories shows that another person—in this case, a therapist—can, even with the best intentions, plant thoughts that lead people to construct memories of events that never happened. Further research is needed to answer this question. What we do know for certain is that many factors contribute to the complicated process of memory, and memory can fail us at many points along the way.

Key Terms

encoding, p. 359
storage, p. 359
retrieval, p. 359
permastore memory, p. 361
proactive interference, p. 363
retroactive interference, p. 363
repression, p. 364
misinformation effect, p. 367

Key People

Hermann Ebbinghaus, p. 361
Sigmund Freud, p. 364
Elizabeth Loftus, p. 367

trb tr ■TEACHING TIP

To review module vocabulary and concepts, use **Building Vocabulary: Graphic Organizer:** ***Concept Web*** (*Teacher's Resource Binder*, p. 19-1; **Handout 19–2**). The handout can be used as a transparency and projected for the class to view together. Help students fill in the web correctly and find passages in the text that define the terms and explain the relationship of one term with another.

MODULE 19

tb Using the Test Bank

The *Test Bank* that accompanies this textbook offers a wide variety of questions in different formats and levels of complexity. Use the software to construct whole tests or to integrate standardized questions into teacher-made tests.

Self-Test Answers

Multiple-Choice Questions

1. a, 2. a, 3. c, 4. b, 5. d

Matching Terms and Definitions

6. a. (7), b. (9)

Self-Test

Multiple-Choice Questions

Choose the *best* answer for each of the following questions:

1. Selina and her family have moved to a new apartment, and now Selina must take a different bus home from school. Today, Selina was talking and laughing with a friend and accidentally boarded her old bus. Selina's mistake is an example of
   a. proactive interference.
   b. retroactive interference.
   c. permastore memory.
   d. the misinformation effect.

2. Alex learned French in high school almost 30 years ago. He recently traveled to France on business, and he was very pleased to discover that he could remember many basic words and phrases. Alex's remaining French vocabulary is an example of
   a. permastore memory.
   b. repression.
   c. a constructed memory.
   d. proactive interference.

3. Mina is taking an intelligence test, and one of the questions asks students to choose which of the following is kept in a silo: corn, cars, cats, or cucumbers. Mina grew up in the city, and although she once read a book about farms, her memory of silos seems to have faded away. Mina is likely to give the wrong answer to this question because of
   a. a memory retrieval failure.
   b. a memory storage failure.
   c. a memory encoding failure.
   d. the misinformation effect.

4. Manny is 43, and he's very irritated because one of his favorite songs from the 1970s is now being used with different words in a popular commercial. Manny is especially frustrated because when he tries to sing this song now, he often sings the words from the commercial instead of the original words. Manny is experiencing
   a. proactive interference.
   b. retroactive interference.
   c. a recovered memory.
   d. permastore memory.

5. It's Monday, and your assignment for your psychology class is due today. You haven't finished, but you've heard that your instructor is sometimes sympathetic to students who explain that they didn't do their work because they had a memory encoding failure. Which of the following would be your best excuse?
   a. "I thought the assignment was due today, but then Larry planted false information in my memory by asking me if I'd finished next Monday's assignment. I would have given you the work next Monday—really!"
   b. "Larry and I were talking about how worried we were about this assignment, and I guess I just repressed the memory that it was due today because I was so anxious."
   c. "My dog ate my homework."
   d. "I never heard you say that the assignment was due today."

Matching Terms and Definitions

6. For each definition, choose the *best* matching term from the list that follows:

   Definition

   a. Memories of abuse that people claim to have repressed but later retrieved, often in the context of therapy.
   b. The retention of encoded information over time.

Alternative Assessment/Technology Project

web FALSE MEMORY SYNDROME Search engines will provide, literally, thousands of sites that students can explore for false memory syndrome. Students can do a project of their own choice that relates to this controversial memory phenomenon. Or they can do a more specific project focusing, say, on the False Memory Syndrome Foundation (FMSF).

FMSF has a large Web site at **www.fmsfonline.org**. It defines false memory syndrome; describes the purpose, programs, and activities of the foundation; and provides information regarding its scientific and professional advisory board. Additional sections answer FAQs (*F*requently *A*sked *Q*uestions), provide a newsletter archive, a list of upcoming events, and links to other Internet resources. Students can use any of these articles as a springboard for projects, which may take one of the following forms:

c. Long-term memories that are especially resistant to forgetting and likely to last a lifetime.
d. The process of incorporating misleading information into one's memory of an event.
e. The disruptive effect of new learning on the recall of previously stored information.
f. The process of getting information into the memory system.
g. The disruptive effect of earlier learning on the recall of more recently stored information.

Term
(1) retrieval
(2) proactive interference
(3) retroactive interference
(4) encoding
(5) permastore memory
(6) repression
(7) recovered memories
(8) misinformation effect
(9) storage

Fill-in-the-Blank Questions

7. _______________ _______________ was the first to demonstrate that forgetting happens rapidly and then levels off.

8. _______________ _______________ and colleagues first performed laboratory experiments that demonstrated the tendency to construct memories.

Brief Essay Question

9. You are serving as the lead investigator in a case where a preschool teacher has been accused of child abuse, and part of your job is to question the children who attend this preschool. In three paragraphs of two or three sentences each, explain how you plan to question these children, and why you will use this approach. Be sure to use your knowledge about memory storage and memory construction in explaining your plan.

Self-Test Answers

Matching Terms and Definitions (continued)
c. (5), d. (8), e. (3), f. (4), g. (2)

Fill-in-the-Blank Questions
7. Hermann Ebbinghaus, 8. Elizabeth Loftus

Brief Essay Question
9. Students should demonstrate an understanding of the dangers of leading questions and the constructed memories that can result from such questions. An investigator who questioned children in a case like this would have to be very careful because leading questions can actually plant false information and change a child's memory of an event. Once stored, this information will not be recognizable as false information. Children want to please adults, and this makes them especially susceptible to unknowingly constructing false memories. A careful investigation would adhere to three guidelines: (1) The investigator would phrase questions in language children can understand. (2) The interviewing adult would be someone who has not had any contact with the child prior to the investigation. (3) The interviewer would use neutral language and not ask leading or suggestive questions.

- a literature review of research relevant to this topic
- a poster presentation about memory construction or false memory syndrome
- a research paper on how well law enforcement heeds research findings in this area
- a PowerPoint presentation about how the media seem to ignore research in memory construction

CHAPTER

States of Consciousness

Cognitive Domain

Teaching with the Standards

Standard Area: States of Consciousness

Breakdown of Module 20: Sleep and Dreams

Content Standard 1: Characteristics of sleep stages and theories of why we sleep Module 20 investigates the characteristics of the N-REM and REM stages of sleep. The EEG patterns for the different stages are presented. The theories—preservation and restoration—that explain why we sleep are also detailed. Emphasis is on the biological mechanisms involved in sleep. Common sleep disorders, such as insomnia, sleep apnea, and narcolepsy, are discussed. Other less common sleep disorders, such as somnambulism (sleep walking) and night terrors, are also presented. (Student Text pp. 379–386, 389–391)

Content Standard 2: Explaining and interpreting dreams The three modern explanations of dreaming—information-processing, physiological function, and activation-synthesis—are presented. Freud's theory of dream interpretation is also addressed. (Student Text pp. 387–388)

Breakdown of Module 21: Hypnosis

Content Standard 3: Hypnosis and its uses Module 21 defines hypnosis and compares the social influence and divided consciousness theories in explaining the phenomenon. Specific hypnotic techniques, including induction, are presented. Deep sleep and hypnosis are compared. Hypnotizability, as measured by the Stanford Hypnotic Susceptibility Scale, is discussed. The author examines whether hypnosis can make us do things we would not normally do and if posthypnotic suggestions can lead to lasting behavioral changes, such as losing weight. The psychological applications of hypnosis (specifically, pain control) are also addressed. The author also investigates the controversy surrounding the use of hypnosis to enhance memory recall. (Student Text pp. 396–403)

Breakdown of Module 22: Drugs

Content Standard 4: Psychoactive drugs and their psychological and physiological effects Module 22 examines what psychoactive drugs are and how they work in the body. Specifically, the author explains how drugs affect the brain at the neural level. In addition, the five main drug categories—depressants, opiates, stimulants, hallucinogens, and marijuana—are presented. Specific drugs, such as alcohol, are discussed within their category, in alcohol's case with depressants. The psychological and physiological effects of each drug are described. (Student Text pp. 408–423)

Scope and Sequence

	Objectives	Text Reference	Standards Covered
Lesson 1	Define consciousness. Discuss our body's natural rhythms. Focus on the circadian rhythm and its role in the sleep-wake cycle. Discuss the importance of sleep and the effects of sleep deprivation.	Module 20, pp. 378–381	Standard Area: States of Consciousness, Content Standard 1, Performance Standards 1.1, 1.2
Lesson 2	Discuss the theories of why we sleep. Examine the N-REM and REM sleep stages. Discuss the different sleep disorders, such as insomnia, apnea, and narcolepsy.	Module 20, pp. 382–386, 389–391	Content Standard 1, Performance Standards 1.1, 1.3
Lesson 3	Contrast the purposes of N-REM and REM sleep. Focus on dreaming and possible explanations for why we dream.	Module 20, pp. 384–388	Content Standard 1, Performance Standard 1.1, Content Standard 2, Performance Standard 2.2
Lesson 4	Define hypnosis. Discuss the social influence and divided consciousness theories of hypnosis. Examine the various hypnotic techniques and susceptibility to hypnosis. Present the different psychological applications of hypnosis and the controversy surrounding the use of hypnosis.	Module 21, pp. 396–403	Content Standard 3, Performance Standards 3.1, 3.2
Lesson 5	Define psychoactive drugs and dependence. Examine how drugs act in the brain. Present the five major categories of drugs.	Module 22, pp. 408–411	Content Standard 4, Performance Standards 4.1, 4.2
Lesson 6	Discuss the psychological and physiological effects of depressants (alcohol, sedatives), opiates (morphine, heroin), and stimulants (caffeine, nicotine, cocaine, amphetamines).	Module 22, pp. 412–419	Content Standard 4, Performance Standards 4.1, 4.2
Lesson 7	Discuss the psychological and physiological effects of hallucinogens (LSD, ecstasy) and marijuana. Discuss how to prevent the use of psychoactive drugs.	Module 22, pp. 419–423	Content Standard 4, Performance Standards 4.1, 4.2
Lesson 8	Review and test		

CHAPTER 9

States of Consciousness

Introducing the Chapter

The Points: Chapter Objectives

- Define consciousness.
- Identify the different body rhythms of the body and how they differ from each other.
- Understand why sleep is so important to daily life.
- Identify the different stages of sleep, including REM and N-REM sleep, and analyze their differences.
- Identify the different types of sleep disorders and determine the causes and consequences of those disorders on people's lives.
- Differentiate why subjects carry out hypnotic suggestions, according to both the social influence theory and the divided consciousness theory of hypnosis.
- Explain what posthypnotic suggestions are and how they might be used to help people.
- Describe how hypnosis can help control pain.
- Analyze why researchers are skeptical of other claims of hypnotic effects.
- Describe a psychoactive drug.
- Explain how psychoactive drugs work.
- Identify the five main drug categories.
- Evaluate what avenues help prevent the use of dangerous psychoactive drugs.

CHAPTER 9

States of Consciousness

I had been unfairly accused of taking something though I couldn't really remember what it was. Nobody wanted to hear my side of the story. My friends and family wouldn't listen, and they actually started chasing me in hopes of turning me into the authorities. Presumed guilty instead of innocent, I feared I was going to be arrested, tried, and convicted without any hope of legal assistance. Cornered and frightened, with no place to hide, I thankfully woke up.

The emotions and events of this dream seemed so real that I had a lot of trouble getting back to sleep. There was even a slight moment of pause, after waking, where I had to reassure myself, "That was a dream, right? Yes. Phew!"

Dreaming is merely one of the altered states of consciousness we will examine in this three-module chapter. We also will be taking a close look at the research and beliefs about hypnosis, and drug use and addiction.

Performance Standards

Standard Area: States of Consciousness

Content Standard 1: Characteristics of sleep stages and theories of why we sleep

Performance Standard 1.1 Investigate the N-REM and REM stages of sleep.

- Describe the four stages of N-REM, nondreaming sleep. (Student Text pp. 384–385)
- Discuss how an EEG measures brain waves during sleep. Analyze how EEGs reveal different sleep patterns during a 90-minute cycle. (Student Text pp. 384–385)
- Figure 20.5, "Brain Waves and Sleep Stages," illustrates the different EEG patterns for the stages of N-REM and REM sleep. (Student Text p. 385)
- Describe REM sleep and discuss why REM is often called paradoxical sleep. (Student Text pp. 385–386)
- Figure 20.7, "A Good Night's Sleep," illustrates how we cycle through sleep stages all night and how stages 3 and 4 decrease while REM increases during a night's sleep. (Student Text p. 386)

Performance Standard 1.2 Discuss theories of why we sleep.

- Discuss the role of circadian rhythms in our sleep-wake cycle. (Student Text p. 378)
- Investigate the importance of sleep to our daily functioning. Discuss the consequences of sleep deprivation. (Student Text pp. 379–381)
- Present the biological mechanisms that contribute to sleeping. Focus on the role of the hypothalamus and the hormone melatonin in initiating sleep. (Student Text pp. 382–383)
- Discuss the two different theories of why we sleep: preservation and restoration. (Student Text p. 383)

Performance Standard 1.3 Investigate different sleep disorders.

- Discuss the three most common sleep disorders: insomnia, sleep apnea, and narcolepsy. Emphasize treatment of these different disorders. (Student Text pp. 389–391)
- Discuss less common sleep problems, such as somnambulism (sleepwalking), night terrors, bruxism (teeth grinding), enuresis (bed wetting), and myoclonus (sudden jerking). (Student Text p. 391)

Content Standard 2: Explaining and interpreting dreams

Performance Standard 2.2 Compare theories of dream use and interpretation.

- Discuss Freud's theory that dreams are the key to understanding our unconscious conflicts. (Student Text p. 387)
- Present more modern theories of dreaming. Compare the information-processing, physiological function, and activation-synthesis theories of dreaming. (Student Text pp. 387–388)

Materials NETWORK

All of the items from the Video, Activity, and Enrichment Centers listed below come from the *Teacher's Resource Binder.* These items will help you teach and expand on concepts presented in Module 20.

trb This logo indicates when an item from the Materials Network may be used in conjunction with a specific note found in this module's *Teacher's Edition.*

Body Rhythms

V Video Center

- Videocassette: *The Brain,* Second Edition, Module 13: "Sleep and Circadian Rhythms" Consult the faculty guide from *The Brain* video series for a description of this module. (*Teacher's Resource Binder,* p. 20-1)

Activity Center

- Critical Thinking Activity: *The Sleep IQ Test* With this activity, students' preconceptions about sleep will either be exposed as incorrect or reinforced as correct. This test comes from the National Sleep Foundation, a nonprofit organization "that promotes public understanding of sleep and sleep disorders and supports sleep-related education, research, and advocacy to improve public health and safety." (*Teacher's Resource Binder,* p. 20-1; Handout 20–1)
- Building Vocabulary: *Flashcards* Question-and-answer flashcards help students review both familiar and unfamiliar vocabulary related to sleep that appears in this module. (*Teacher's Resource Binder,* p. 20-1)
- Graphic Organizer: *Sleep Stages, Waves, and REM* With this organizer, students identify the individual stages of sleep and the relationship of one stage to another in the context of sleep. The graphic organizer serves a dual purpose as a learning device for module concepts and a note-taking tool. (*Teacher's Resource Binder,* p. 20-1; Handout 20–2)
- Technology Application Activity: *Visiting SleepNet* Students can explore the SleepNet Web site. It provides direct and indirect access to a variety of topics, including sleep disorders and support groups, sleep deprivation, dream links, sleep labs, and research links, professional organizations, and last but not least, the *Snooze Paper,* which discusses news events involving sleep. They can also take a quick assessment of their sleep habits to determine whether they may have a problem with sleep. (*Teacher's Resource Binder,* p. 20-1; Handout 20–3)
- Application Activity: *Keeping a Sleep Diary* Students can gain insight into their actual sleep habits by keeping a record of how much sleep they get each night. (*Teacher's Resource Binder,* p. 20-1; Handout 20–4)
- Application Activity: *Larks or Owls?* Our daily schedule of waking and sleeping is timed by a body clock known as circadian rhythm. The short assessment on the handout in this activity will help students determine their preference for morning or evening activity and encourage them to plan tasks for optimal performance according to their preferences. (*Teacher's Resource Binder,* p. 20-1; Handout 20–5)
- Analysis Activity: *School Start Times: An Informal Debate* This activity, which includes a reprint of a newspaper article, enables students to research and debate the controversial issue of pushing back school start times to optimize teenagers' sleeping habits. (*Teacher's Resource Binder,* p. 20-1; Handouts 20–6 and 20–7)

Enrichment Center

- Enrichment Lesson: *Melatonin* Melatonin is a hormone secreted by the pea-sized pineal gland, located at the center of the brain. It seems to play an important role in the synchronization of the sleep-wake cycle. Melatonin, the hormone responsible for helping people fall asleep, is also a popular dietary supplement used to overcome sleeping problems. This lesson focuses on the benefits of using melatonin and cautions students about its potential adverse effects. (*Teacher's Resource Binder,* p. 20-1)

Sleep and Sleep Deficit

Activity Center

- Evaluation Activity: *Sleep Deficit Scale* On a large scale, students today suffer from sleep deprivation. This activity will help students assess their sleep debt. It also leads to a discussion of the reasons why people their age do not get enough sleep. (*Teacher's Resource Binder,* p. 20-1; Handout 20–8)

Enrichment Center

- Enrichment Lesson: *A Case of Extreme Sleep Deprivation: Randy Gardner* In 1964, a young high school student began a science project. For the project, he stayed awake for 11 days to learn the effects of sleep deprivation on the body. Physically he suffered only minor problems. Psychologically, Randy Gardner experienced bizarre and disturbing problems, ranging from lack of concentration to hallucinations. (All of his symptoms disappeared after he got some sleep.) In this lesson, students learn about this famous story in the psychology of sleep. (*Teacher's Resource Binder,* p. 20-1)

Why We Sleep

Ⓥ Video Center

Consult the faculty guide from the *Scientific American Frontiers* video series for descriptions of these segments.

- Videocassette: *Scientific American Frontiers,* Second Edition, Segment 15: "Can You Beat Jet Lag?" (*Teacher's Resource Binder,* p. 20-1)
- Videocassette: *Scientific American Frontiers,* Second Edition, Segment 13: "Catching Catnaps" (*Teacher's Resource Binder,* p. 20-1)

Enrichment Center

- Enrichment Lesson: *Afternoon Naps* Most small children take afternoon naps, but those naps are phased out by the time children hit elementary school. The afternoon siesta has been common in many cultures around the world, particularly those in tropical climates. This lesson shows how we actually need the afternoon nap to feel energized throughout the day. (*Teacher's Resource Binder,* p. 20-1)

Sleep Stages, REM, and Dreaming

Video Center

Consult the faculty guides from *The Brain* and the *Scientific American Frontiers* video series for descriptions of these modules or segments.

- Videocassette: *The Brain,* Second Edition, Module 14: "Sleep: Brain Functions" (*Teacher's Resource Binder,* p. 20-1)
- Videocassette: *Scientific American Frontiers,* Second Edition, Segment 14: "What's in a Dream?" (*Teacher's Resource Binder,* p. 20-1)
- Videocassette: *The Brain,* Module 15: "REM Sleep and Dreams" (*Teacher's Resource Binder,* p. 20-1)

Activity Center

- Technology Application Activity: *PsychSim:* "EEG and Sleep Stages" *PsychSim* is an interactive CD-ROM containing tutorials in different content areas of psychology. This tutorial contains descriptions of the characteristic wave patterns of sleep stages 1 through 4 and REM sleep, as well as a simulation of sleep research in which the student awakens a subject at different stages of sleep to check for dreams. (*Teacher's Resource Binder,* p. 20-1)
- Critical Thinking Activity: *Remembering Night Dreams* Popular culture has latched onto Freud's idea that "dreams are the royal road to the unconscious." Because dreams are fascinating to students, the content and impact of dreams on people's daily lives often provokes lively class discussion. This activity will provide a profile of your students' dreams and offer a comparison to the dreams of others. (*Teacher's Resource Binder,* p. 20-1; Handout 20–9)
- Application Activity: *Dream Journal* Some students say they never dream, while others claim frequent dreams and offer vivid descriptions. Students can more closely evaluate their dream life with this activity that challenges them to keep a journal of their dreams over a period of time. (*Teacher's Resource Binder,* p. 20-1; Handouts 20–10 and 20–11)
- Application Activity: *Dreams and Problem Solving* Nobel prize winner Albert Szent-Gyorgyi said, "My work is not finished when I leave my workbench in the afternoon. I go on thinking about my problems all the time, and my brain must continue to think about them when I sleep because I wake up sometimes in the middle of the night, with answers to questions that have been puzzling me." Can we solve problems in our dreams? This activity will help students see that the old adage "sleep on it" might just be true after all. (*Teacher's Resource Binder,* p. 20-1; Handout 20–12)
- Application Activity: *Remembering Daydreams* Jerome Singer notes that daydreams are more conscious and controllable than night dreams. They are also a much-neglected source of information about a person's inner life and potential. This activity challenges students to keep a diary of daydreams that will help them better understand themselves and may even lead them to change some aspects of their lives. (*Teacher's Resource Binder,* p. 20-1)

Enrichment Center

- Enrichment Lesson: *Gender and Cultural Differences in Dreams* Not all people dream about the same things. Woman and people from different cultures report dream content that is different from men in Western countries. This lesson highlights some of those differences. (*Teacher's Resource Binder,* p. 20-1)

Sleep Disorders and Sleep Problems

Activity Center

- Critical Thinking Activity: *Sleep Strategies* The exercise in this activity provides a good introduction to a classroom discussion of the causes and treatment of insomnia. (*Teacher's Resource Binder,* p. 20-1; Handout 20–13)

Enrichment Center

- **Enrichment Lesson:** *Sleep Disorders* This lesson offers deeper coverage of insomnia, narcolepsy, and sleep apnea—three of the most common sleep disorders. (*Teacher's Resource Binder*, p. 20-1)
- **Enrichment Lesson:** *Treating Insomnia* Effective treatment for insomnia involves a multifaceted approach, including sleep restriction, stimulus control, and relaxation response training—all of which are detailed in this lesson. (*Teacher's Resource Binder*, p. 20-1)

MODULE 20

Sleep, Dreams, and Body Rhythms

What's the Point? 1. What is consciousness?

Has this ever happened to you? You're watching a movie with friends or family late at night, and no matter how hard you fight it, you simply cannot keep your eyes open. Or perhaps you've waged a similar struggle while reading a textbook (but certainly not your psychology text) late at night. You fight it, but soon you nod off—sleep wins again.

You don't stand much of a chance in the tiredness battle; virtually every night, sleep wins. And when you do stay up later than you should, the effects are often obvious. The day a 10-page term paper is due, I can easily spot those who, having waited until the last minute, spent most of the previous night at a keyboard. Fighting the "nods," heads bobbing downward, they suddenly jerk upright after a brief trip to never-never land.

Bored Senseless or Sleep-Deprived? This student has clearly lost any struggle to stay awake.

Getting Started

trb You may wish to use **Critical Thinking Activity:** *The Sleep IQ Test* (*Teacher's Resource Binder*, p. 20-1; **Handout 20–1**) as a prereading strategy to find out what students already know about sleep. This activity, along with results from the *Sleep IQ Test* handout, will prime students to note terms and concepts in the text that confirm or dispel their preconceptions about sleep.

web An on-line version of the *Sleep IQ Test* handout is also available from **www.sleepfoundation.org/nsaw/sleepiq99i.html**, courtesy of the National Sleep Foundation.

MODULE 20

Sleep, Dreams, and Body Rhythms

Introducing the Module

The Points: Module Objectives

- Define consciousness.
- Distinguish how the body's natural rhythms differ from one another.
- Determine the costs to your body when you don't get enough sleep.
- Understand why we benefit from sleep.
- Identify the four stages of nondreaming sleep.
- Explain why REM sleep is sometimes called paradoxical sleep.
- Identify three modern explanations of dreaming.
- Determine some common sleep disorders and their consequences.

Building Vocabulary

Have students find meanings of the terms and create flashcards. Students may use the flashcards independently or with partners to learn or review vocabulary.

trb At this point, you may also wish to use **Building Vocabulary:** *Flashcards* (*Teacher's Resource Binder*, p. 20-1).

Teaching the Points

web ■ **TEACHING TIP**

You can log on as an instructor to the book companion site for *Thinking About Psychology* at **www.worthpublishers.com/thinkingaboutpsych**. It contains teacher resources for class presentations as well as review and assessment of module concepts and terms.

■ **JOURNAL WRITING**

Invite students to use the following questions and writing prompts as springboards for entries in their psychology journals:

- Describe your sleeping habits.
- On average, why don't teens today get enough sleep?
- If you could plan how much and when you sleep, what would you plan and why?

MODULE 20

■ TEACHING TIP

The three types of body rhythms discussed here can be easily distinguished by thinking of them in terms of a clock face.

- **Circadian rhythms,** those that occur once a day, correspond with the hour hand on a clock. The short hour hand rotates around the clock face twice each day to indicate the passing of 24 hours, the approximate length of a circadian rhythm.
- **Ultradian rhythms,** those that occur more than once a day, correspond to the minute hand of a clock. The long minute hand revolves around the clock face once an hour, more often than the once-a-day circadian rhythm.
- **Infradian rhythms,** those that occur once a month or season, correspond to the date found on most wristwatches. The date indicating the time of the month or year indicates when an infradian rhythm might occur.

■ JOURNAL WRITING

Invite students to use the following questions and writing prompts as springboards for entries in their psychology journals:

- At what times during the day do you feel most sleepy and most awake? Does your daily schedule capitalize on these periods of sleepiness and energy? Why or why not?
- The box on pages 380–381 discusses premenstrual syndrome and some common myths associated with this phenomenon. Why do you think our society continues to believe that a woman's menstrual cycle adversely affects her life (and the lives of people around her), despite evidence to the contrary?

To nod off is to temporarily lose waking **consciousness,** or awareness of yourself and your environment. Depriving yourself of sleep alters your body's natural rhythms, making it difficult to maintain normal, waking consciousness. Indeed, your body has several naturally occurring rhythms affecting wakefulness and sleep.

Body Rhythms

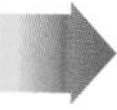

2. How do your body's natural rhythms differ from one another?

An e-mail titled "Reliably Predict Your Mood for Free" once caught my eye. Closer investigation showed the predictions were anything but reliable, and certainly not free. This advertisement pitched something called a "biorhythm chart," which was a good example of a **pseudoscientific claim**—an assertion that attempts to appear scientific but is not really based on science.The e-mail guaranteed that after I typed in the time and date of my birth, their chart could accurately predict my good and bad days, my illnesses and accidents, and even the days when I should gamble. (Gullibility level was not predicted.)

Researchers have found that pseudoscientific biorhythm charts are useless (Hines, 1998). Researchers who have drawn random samples from regular users of these charts could not produce replicable results—meaning that if you recreate the same test, under the same conditions, the results will vary. Your body does, however, have real **biological rhythms,** which affect physiological processes such as body temperature, blood pressure, and the effectiveness of medicines. These rhythms fall into three main categories:

- **Circadian rhythms** occur approximately once during a 24-hour period (*circa* and *dies* in Latin mean "about" and "day," respectively). The sleep-wake cycle is an example of a circadian rhythm.
- **Ultradian rhythms** occur more than once a day. The most studied ultradian rhythm is the way we cycle through various stages of sleep each night. (You'll read more about these stages very shortly.)
- **Infradian rhythms** take place less than once a day. They may occur once a month, as with a woman's menstrual cycle (see Thinking Critically: Infradian Rhythms and PMS, pages 380–381), or once a season, as with a bear's winter hibernation.

We are aware of some of these rhythms as we cycle through them, but most run on autopilot, rarely generating a second thought. An understanding of your body's natural rhythms may help you get more out of your day—and night.

► **consciousness** Awareness of yourself and your environment.

► **pseudoscientific claim** Any assertion that is not based on science, even though in some circumstances, attempts are made to appear scientific.

► **biological rhythms** Periodic physiological fluctuations

► **circadian (ser-KAY-dee-un) rhythms** Biological rhythms (for example, of temperature and wakefulness) that occur approximately every 24 hours.

► **ultradian (ul-TRAY-dee-un) rhythms** Biological rhythms that occur more than once each day.

► **infradian (in-FRAY-dee-un) rhythms** Biological rhythms that occur once a month or once a season.

Suggested Readings

Use the following books as teacher-preparation tools or as enrichment for advanced students:

Coren, S. (1996). *Sleep thieves.* New York: Free Press.

Dement, W. C. (1978). *Some must watch while some must sleep.* New York: Norton.

Dement, W. C., & Vaughan, C. (1999). *The promise of sleep.* New York: Delacorte.

Maas, J. B. (1998). *Power sleep.* New York: Villard.

Singer, J., & Switzer, E. (1980). *Mind-play.* Englewood Cliffs, NJ: Prentice-Hall.

Sleep and Sleep Deficit

3. What are the costs to your body when you don't get enough sleep?

Live to be 90, and you will have spent roughly 30 years of your life with your eyes closed, mostly oblivious to your surroundings. Ironically, few of us know much at all about the gentle tyrant that drives us to bed each night. We may know even less about what happens to our mind and body if we don't get the sleep we need. The research on sleep deprivation, however, could not be clearer:

- Lack of sleep decreases the levels of hormones necessary for proper immune system functioning. Sleep deprivation also increases levels of the stress hormone cortisol, which has been linked to the damage of brain cells responsible for learning and memory (Leproult & others, 1997).
- Citing the number of road deaths related to truck drivers and others who fall asleep while driving, the National Transportation Safety Board (1995) considers driver fatigue a bigger safety problem than alcohol use. Figure 20.1, which dramatically illustrates the effect of one hour of lost sleep, supports this position.
- Sleep debt contributes to hypertension, impaired concentration, irritability, suppression of cancer-fighting immune cells, and premature aging (Dement, 1999; Horne, 1989; Spiegel & others, 1999).

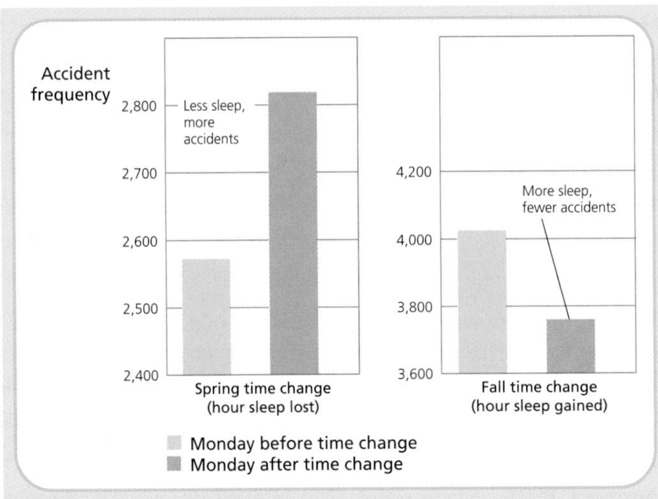

Figure 20.1 **Spring Forward, Fall Back?** Compare the frequency of accidents on the Mondays before and after we lose an hour to daylight saving time in the spring. In the fall, the opposite trend appeared (National Transportation Safety Board, 1995).

MODULE 20

■ TEACHING TIPS

tr (1) A four-color transparency of Figure 20.1, Spring Forward, Fall Back?, is available in the **Overhead Transparencies Set.**

(2) Have students calculate roughly how much of their lives they have spent sleeping up to this point. Suggest that students interview their parents to find out how many hours of sleep they averaged when they were infants and toddlers. Parents or guardians may also help them recall their daily bedtimes and waking times during elementary and middle school. Students can also track the hours they sleep each night for about a week to average the amount of time they sleep at this point in their lives.

trb At this point, you may want to use **Application Activity:** *Keeping a Sleep Diary* (*Teacher's Resource Binder*, p. 20-1; **Handout 20–4**).

F • Y • I

trb Relate for students the story of Randy Gardner, who, as a teenager in 1964, spent over 11 days awake for a school project. You can find more about Randy and his experience in **Enrichment Lesson:** *A Case of Extreme Sleep Deprivation: Randy Gardner* (*Teacher's Resource Binder*, p. 20-1). Physically, Randy suffered only minor problems. Psychologically, though, he experienced bizarre and disturbing problems, ranging from lack of concentration to hallucinations. (All his symptoms disappeared after he got some sleep.)

Cross-Curricular Connections

GOVERNMENT Have students research laws and policies regarding how long people in certain jobs can work without breaks and sleep. Suggest that they then make contact with local companies to find out about company policies related to work hours. In particular, students should focus on companies that employ truck drivers, air traffic controllers, pilots, doctors and nurses, and factory workers. The following questions may guide research and interviews as well as subsequent discussion of students' findings:

- What government regulations relate to work without breaks or sleep?
- What are the policies of some companies related to work without breaks or sleep? For what kinds of workers do these policies apply? Compare and contrast the companies' policies with the government regulations.
- How do these policies affect the efficiency and well-being of workers in these companies? How do they reflect what you've learned about a person's need for sleep?

MODULE 20

■ LOOKING AT THE ISSUES

The importance of sleep cannot be ignored, especially in today's fast-paced society. Use the following activity to help students evaluate how sleep may positively affect their lives.

On the left half of a piece of paper, have students list three ways in which they would like to improve in school subjects or extracurricular and social activities. After you discuss the importance of getting enough sleep, have students speculate how the three items they listed might improve if they changed or modified some of their sleep habits. Encourage them to write the possible improvements on the right side of the piece of paper. These comparisons may help students determine ways in which they can correct unhealthy sleep habits.

■ TEACHING TIP

A four-color transparency of Figure 20.2, PMS or Normal Variation?, is available in the **Overhead Transparencies Set**.

Thinking Critically

Infradian Rhythms and PMS

Controversy surrounds the concept of PMS, or "premenstrual syndrome." Over the objection of psychologists, PMDD (premenstrual dysphoric disorder) was added to the list of potential disorders (requiring further study) listed in the book that thousands of health-care officials use to diagnose mental illness. To understand why psychologists objected, you need to know a bit more about PMS and infradian rhythms.

A woman's menstrual cycle is, on average, a 28-day infradian cycle. During this cycle, the woman's uterine wall is preparing for possible pregnancy. If conception does not occur, the uterine wall sloughs off its thickened lining and the cycle starts again. Do emotional or intellectual changes accompany these physical changes? Tradition says "yes," but psychologists doing research in this area give us reasons to reconsider this assumption.

Several studies (for example, Gallant & others, 1991; Hardie, 1997; McFarlane & others, 1988; Slade, 1984) have gathered data by polling women about their psychological and physical health. To avoid biasing the results, the researchers did not tell the women why they were gathering the data. They asked each woman for a single day's data, and

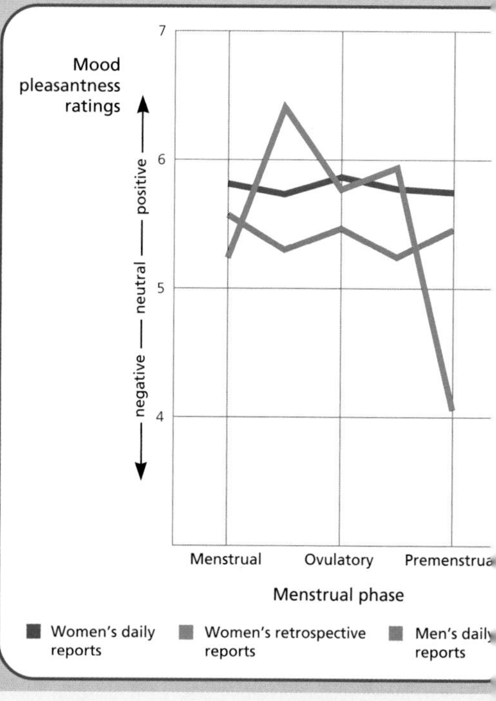

Figure 20.2 PMS or Normal Variation? Men's and women's moods fluctuate at about the same rate during any given month. However, the moods recalled by women do not match the actual moods reported day-by-day during the month (McFarland & others, 1989).

With the evidence mounting against late nights, you'd think that a movement toward turning lights out earlier would gain momentum. Wrong. Teenagers are getting almost two hours less sleep now than they did 70 years ago, before the days of all-night drive-throughs, the Internet, and late-night TV channels (Maas, 1998). Four out of five students are "dangerously sleep deprived," according to sleep researcher **William Dement** (1999). Dement states, "The brain keeps an accurate count of

Cross-Curricular Connections

ECONOMICS, HEALTH, GOVERNMENT, AND DEBATE School start times have become a popular discussion topic as studies show how little sleep students receive. Some schools across the country have adjusted their start times to help improve attendance and academic performance. The following cross-curricular projects can help students explore the effects of start times in your school:

- Working with an economics teacher, students can calculate the financial and economic impacts of different school start and finish times on the school and the community by interviewing parents, community/business leaders, and school administrators.
- Working with an anatomy or health teacher, students can assess the impact of later start times on students' health by conducting a research project comparing students' energy levels during the school week and on the weekends or a holiday.

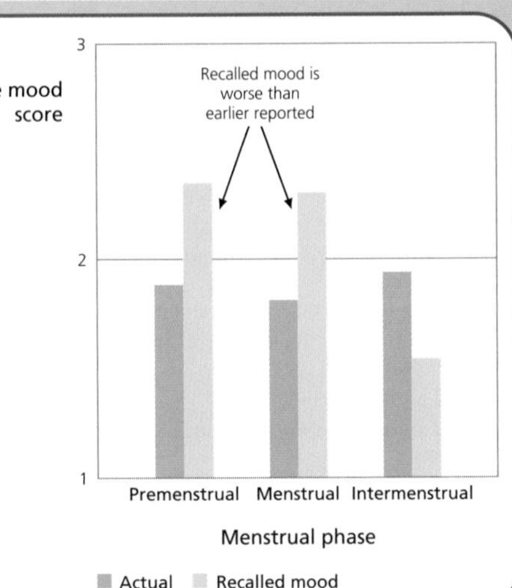

Figure 20.3 Actual Mood Versus Perceived Mood This graph shows that women's *recalled* moods do not reflect the *actual* moods they reported during the menstrual cycle.

later they ascertained the corresponding day of the woman's menstrual cycle. Some of the researchers compared their results with data from men and data from women in other cultures. The findings were remarkably consistent:

- Gender differences in mood are nonexistent (Figure 20.2). In one study (McFarlane & others, 1988), women and men report the same number of actual mood swings each month, although women later recalled having more mood swings (McFarland & others, 1989).
- The menstrual cycle has little effect on actual mood (Figure 20.3) (McFarland & others, 1989).
- There is no reliable relationship between the menstrual cycle and memory, creativity, exam scores, problem solving, or work efficiency (Golub, 1992).
- From a cultural standpoint, the idea of a premenstrual set of symptoms is a uniquely Western phenomenon (Parlee, 1994).
- Women complaining of PMS and given a placebo (inactive pill) report just as much relief as those given an actual drug (Richardson, 1993).

These findings are out of sync with our traditional assumptions. Perhaps the definition of PMS can offer some insight. Checklists for PMS include sadness, irritability, headaches, insomnia, and lethargy. Doesn't everybody at some time or another experience these symptoms? Does that mean we all have PMS? Or could it mean that we need to reconsider PMS altogether?

sleep debt," which helps explain why many high school students sleep effortlessly until noon on weekends if allowed. He matter-of-factly adds that, given the damage improper rest inflicts on your brain, a large sleep debt "makes you stupid." Are you getting the sleep you need? To find out, answer the questions in Table 20.1, page 382. Most teens need nine hours sleep each night. If you need an alarm to interrupt the sleep your body still wants, you're not getting enough.

▶ **William Dement** (1928–) Sleep researcher who coined the term *REM*.

- Working with a government teacher, students can find out the legal procedures the school system would have to go though to allow school to start at a different time.
- Working with a debate teacher, students can conduct a debate about starting school at a later time to optimize teenagers' sleeping habits and needs.

Students' findings may lead them to interesting proposals about their school start times. Encourage these students to prepare a letter, using their research as support, that presents a proposal for school start times. These letters may be distributed to the student government, school administration officials, and parent-teacher association for review.

■ **JOURNAL WRITING**

Invite students to use the following questions as springboards for entries in their psychology journals:

- If you could take a nap every afternoon, would you? Why or why not?
- How can the school's schedule be changed to maximize the research associated with sleep and sleep debt?

(tr) ■ **TEACHING TIP**

A four-color transparency of Figure 20.3, Actual Mood Versus Perceived Mood, is available in the **Overhead Transparencies Set.**

MODULE 20

■ **APPLYING THE POINTS**

Have students take the sleep deprivation quiz in Table 20.1 on page 382. Have them evaluate whether their answers indicate sleep deprivation. Then have them reflect on why they may be sleep deprived. Challenge them to consider ways in which lack of sleep has adversely affected their lives and what they can realistically do to add more sleep to their daily schedules.

trb At this point, you may want to use **Evaluation Activity:** *Sleep Deficit Scale* (*Teacher's Resource Binder*, p. 20-1; **Handout 20–8**).

■ **TEACHING TIPS**

trb tr (1) A black-line master for Table 20.1, Are You Sleep Deprived?, is available in the **Black-Line Masters Appendix** of the *Teacher's Resource Binder*.

trb (2) You may wish to use **Application Activity:** *Larks or Owls?* (*Teacher's Resource Binder*, p. 20-1; **Handout 20–5**) as a short assessment that will help students determine their preference for morning or evening activity and encourage them to plan tasks for optimal performance based on their preferences.

TABLE 20.1 ARE YOU SLEEP DEPRIVED?

Cornell University psychologist James Maas reports that most college students suffer the consequences of sleeping less than they should. To see if you are headed toward being in that group, answer the following true-false questions:

TRUE	FALSE	
___	___	1. I need an alarm clock in order to wake up at the appropriate time.
___	___	2. It's a struggle for me to get out of bed in the morning.
___	___	3. Weekday mornings I hit the snooze bar several times to get more sleep.
___	___	4. I feel tired, irritable, and stressed out during the week.
___	___	5. I have trouble concentrating and remembering.
___	___	6. I feel slow with critical thinking, problem solving, and being creative.
___	___	7. I often fall asleep watching TV.
___	___	8. I often fall asleep in boring meetings or lectures or in warm rooms.
___	___	9. I often fall asleep after heavy meals.
___	___	10. I often fall asleep while relaxing after dinner.
___	___	11. I often fall asleep within five minutes of getting into bed.
___	___	12. I often feel drowsy while driving.
___	___	13. I often sleep extra hours on weekend mornings.
___	___	14. I often need a nap to get through the day.
___	___	15. I have dark circles around my eyes.

If you answered "true" to three or more items, you probably are not getting enough sleep. To determine your sleep needs, Maas recommends that you "go to bed 15 minutes earlier than usual every night for the next week—and continue this practice by adding 15 more minutes each week—until you wake without an alarm clock and feel alert all day." (Quiz reprinted with permission from James B. Maas, *Power sleep: The revolutionary program that prepares your mind and body for peak performance* [New York: HarperCollins, 1999].)

Why We Sleep

4. How do we benefit from sleeping?

What causes us to sleep? One hundred years ago, Russian physiologist Ivan Pavlov believed sleep resulted from what he called "massive inhibition." Others suggested that neurons disconnected from one another, causing us to "drift off." Though we have come a long way technologi-

Enriching

Have students conduct a sleep survey with a representative sample of students at your school. They should ask about how much sleep students get each night, whether they nap in class or feel extremely tired during the day, and why they may or may not get enough sleep each night. (Be sure to get approval from an Institutional Review Board and obtain informed consent from subjects before embarking on any research project.)

cally since the days of Pavlov, we still have no complete answer to this question. But scientists have gathered some partial answers by looking at the brain and nervous system.

The control center for the 24-hour rhythm of sleep appears to be the brain's *hypothalamus.* You have a sort of sensor in your hypothalamus, which monitors changes in light and dark. Perceiving certain key changes in light level, your hypothalamus sends neurological messages to parts of your brain and body, initiating the changes that will put you to sleep. These physiological changes often involve the increase or decrease of *hormones* (chemical messengers) in your bloodstream.

One such hormone, **melatonin,** has been linked to regulation of the sleep-wake cycle (Haimov & Lavie, 1996). Wake up in the morning, turn on the light or open the curtains, and the melatonin levels that built up while you slept will start to drop again. Your melatonin levels will continue to drop until the next time you turn out the lights, close your eyes, and go to sleep. Some people with insomnia respond favorably to medically controlled amounts of melatonin supplements.

So, we know something about *how* we go to sleep, but *why* do we need to sleep? Why can't we simply stay up, day after day, doing the things we want to do? Two possible answers to these questions revolve around the concepts of *preservation* and *restoration.*

If you've ever walked through your home in the dark without turning on lights and crashed into something, you can understand how sleep might help keep us safe. Such night-time crashes must have been even more common for our ancestors, who lived in caves and on cliffs. Traveling or hunting at night (well before the invention of the flashlight) was treacherous, and perhaps those who attempted it did not survive long enough to reproduce and pass along their genes. Sleep provides *protection* from nighttime's dangers, at least for daytime mammals like us. The sleep cycles of other animals have adapted in different ways, depending on such factors as ability to hide, species-specific habits, and need for nourishment (Webb, 1982). Bats, for example, sleep 20 hours a day. Cats sleep 15, but elephants drift off for only 3 to 4 hours. The adaptation theory holds that we sleep at times of the night or day that maximize our safety and survival.

Another prominent theory suggests that sleep is restorative, allowing us to recuperate from the everyday wear and tear we put ourselves through. Our brain and body remain active while we sleep. We may undergo a rebuilding process, as tissues are restored, memories are consolidated, and things learned on the previous day are reorganized.

► **melatonin** A hormone that helps regulate daily biological rhythms.

Sleep Command Center The hypothalamus, colored red in this MRI brain scan photograph, sends messages to other parts of the brain, saying "Time to sleep."

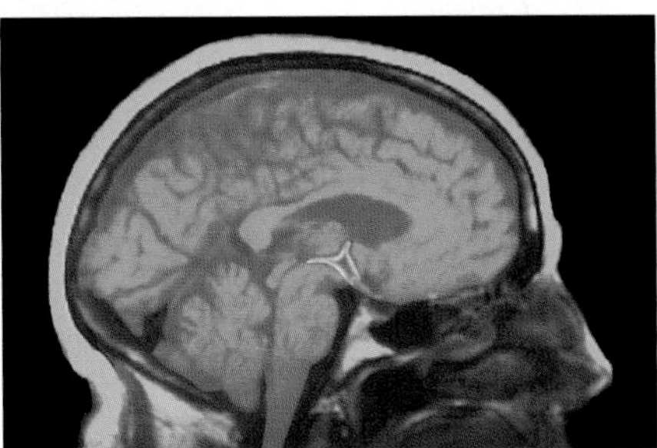

MODULE 20

tb ■ **CHECKING FOR UNDERSTANDING**

Here are several ways to assess students' comprehension:

- Assign any or all of the journal questions or prompts for an in-class writing assessment.
- Divide the students into groups or pairs and give each group a journal question prompt. Have them present their answers to the class, correcting any misconceptions that may arise.
- Use questions from the *Test Bank* to do a quick assessment of their knowledge of the concepts.

Enriching

trb Have students research the hormone melatonin, which is reponsible for helping people fall asleep, and government regulations that pertain to melatonin. You may also wish to use **Enrichment Lesson:** *Melatonin* (*Teacher's Resource Binder*, p. 20-1), which describes this hormone. This lesson focuses on the benefits of using melatonin and cautions students about its potential adverse effects.

MODULE 20

■ TEACHING TIPS

trb (1) This section of the module is highly technical, so students may benefit from using the graphic organizer about the sleep cycle discussed in Meeting Individual Needs at the foot of this page.

tr (2) A four-color transparency of Figure 20.4, Measuring Sleep, is available in the **Overhead Transparencies Set.**

F • Y • I

Another instrument used to measure sleep is the electromyograph. The **electromyograph** measures muscle movements. The device is attached to the body in much the same way as an EEG. Electrodes are attached to different muscles and record how much the muscles tense during sleep. Since muscles are completely relaxed during REM sleep, the EMG shows this muscle relaxation to indicate the patient has entered REM.

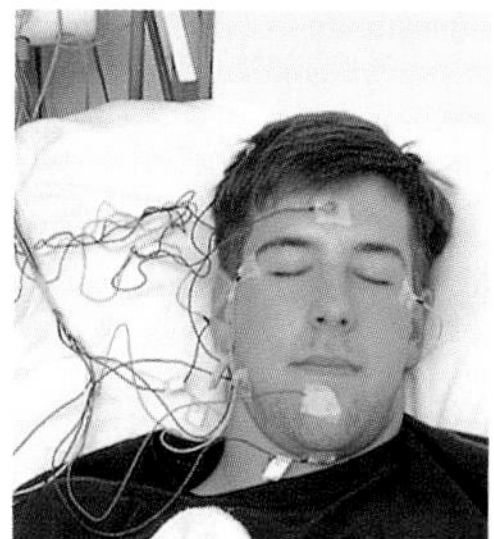

Nap Time? Could you sleep with electrodes attached to your face and head? Sleep research participants must and do adapt to this inconvenience.

Sleep Stages, REM, and Dreaming

The Stages of Sleep

5. What are the four stages of nondreaming sleep?

The sleep-wake cycle itself is circadian, but we all have a 90-minute *ultradian* rhythm cycling throughout our night's sleep. During the 90-minute cycle, two types of sleep occur, in a series of regular, repeating stages. How do we know this? Because sleep researchers have measured the brain waves, eye movements, and muscle tension of sleeping people. The challenges in gathering sleep data are twofold:

1. The person whom you're studying must be asleep.
2. The person must also agree to have a minimum of five electrodes glued to his or her head (Figure 20.4)! The electrodes, which are connected to an **electroencephalograph (EEG),** are collecting brain wave measurements (not delivering shocks!), so the procedure is painless.

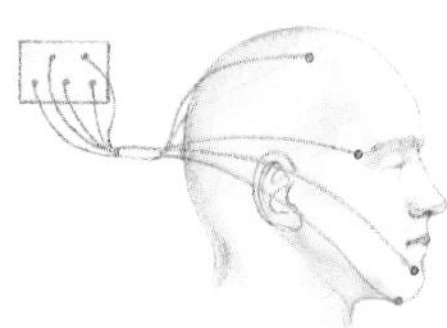

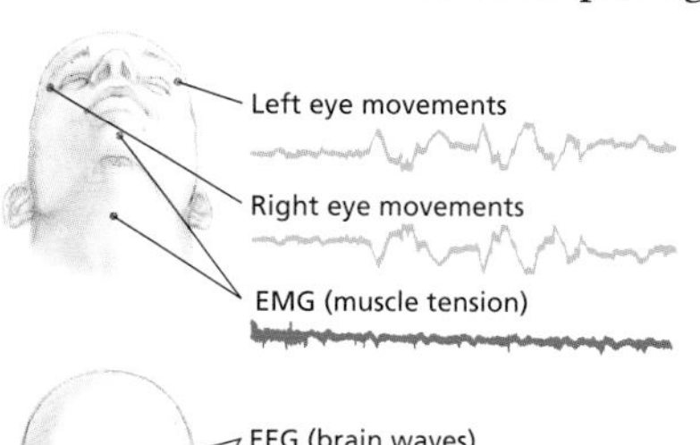

Figure 20.4 **Measuring Sleep** Sleep researchers use electrodes to measure brain waves, eye movements, and muscle tension while we sleep. They can use the changes in these measurements to label the different stages of sleep and dreaming.

Fortunately, thousands of volunteers have submitted to sleeping under observation with electrodes on. Would you volunteer to be a participant in a sleep study? For a few minutes, let's suppose you would. Here's what would happen.

As you try to relax, drifting from wakefulness to sleep, your brain waves cycle more and more slowly. As you nod off for the benefit of science, you will cycle through four stages of relatively quiet sleep before you go into a more active dreaming state (Figure

Garfield

I LOOK BACK ON MY LIFE WITH REGRETS

ALL THOSE WASTED YEARS

ALL THAT TIME SPENT AWAKE

JIM DAVIS 11-19

Meeting Individual Needs

trb **GRAPHIC ORGANIZER** Provide learning opportunities for all levels of learners with one of the following options for using **Graphic Organizer:** *Sleep Stages, Waves, and REM* (*Teacher's Resource Binder*, p. 20-1; **Handout 20–2**):

- **Independent Learners** Students may fill out the organizer on their own or follow along in class during discussion and lecture.
- **Cooperative Learners** Students may use the textbook as a resource and work in groups to find the answers that fit in the blanks.
- **Exceptional Learners** The graphic organizer can fill a special education need to provide notes for exceptional students. These students may fill in the blanks independently, with a student or teacher/tutor, or along with class discussion and lecture.

20.5). You will not be able to tell the exact moment you enter *Stage 1,* but a sleep researcher, noticing your slowed breathing and irregular brain waves, could accurately point to these first moments of sleep, which rarely last longer than five minutes (Figure 20.6). It would be easy to awaken you from this stage, and if we did, you'd probably insist you had not been sleeping. You may also report that you had fantastic, dreamlike sensations, such as falling.

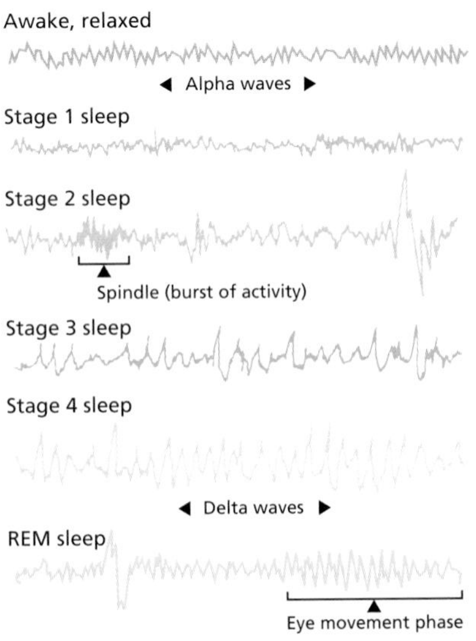

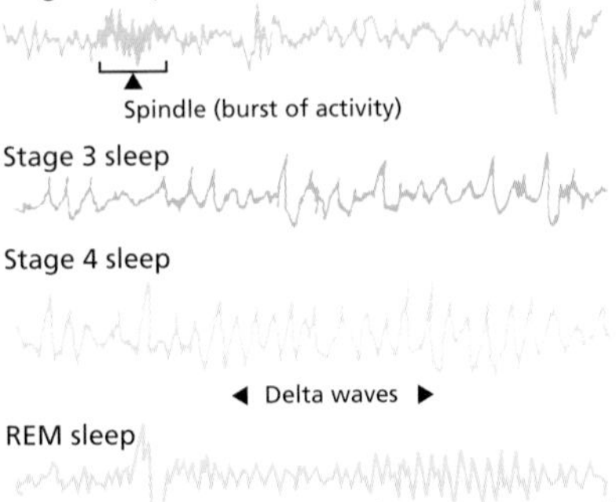

Figure 20.5 **Brain Waves and Sleep Stages** Brain waves slow down as we cycle into the deeper stages of sleep.

But let's imagine that we did not awaken you. As you exit Stage 1, your brain waves cycle more slowly, and you slide into the deeper sleep of *Stage 2.* Little brain wave bursts called **spindles** characterize this stage. The first time you enter Stage 2, your stay lasts 20 minutes. Over the course of the night, you will spend up to half of your entire time asleep in this stage.

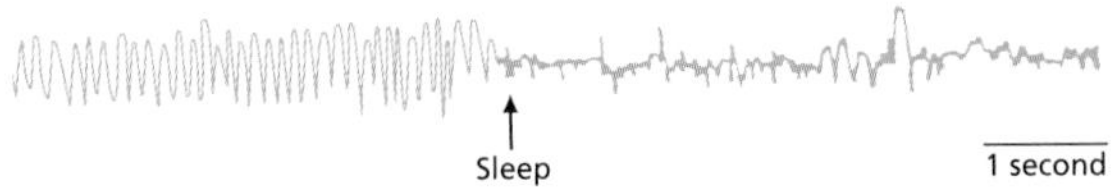

Sleep

1 second

Figure 20.6 **Entering the Land of Nod** You wouldn't be able to say precisely when you fell asleep last night, but a sleep researcher charting your brain waves could pinpoint the time very accurately.

About 30 minutes after you fall asleep, your brain waves begin to slow way down as you drop into *Stages 3* and *4.* These two stages, identified by the increasing percentage of large, slow *delta wave* cycles per second, together are called *slow-wave sleep,* or **delta sleep.** Your brain waves slow down to less than one cycle per second in delta sleep, compared with the 15 or so cycles per second you experienced just after you closed your eyes. The first time you travel through this ultradian cycle, your rejuvenating delta sleep will last about 30 minutes.

► **electroencephalograph (EEG)** A machine that amplifies and records waves of electrical activity that sweep across the brain's surface. Electrodes placed on the scalp measure these waves.

► **spindles** Bursts of brain-wave activity that characterize Stage 2 of N-REM sleep.

► **delta sleep** Stages 3 and 4 of N-REM sleep, characterized by large, slow delta waves; delta sleep is minimal during the last four hours of sleep.

► **N-REM sleep (non–rapid eye movement sleep)** The period of sleep in which sleep Stages 1 through 4 occur; not characterized by eye movement or vivid dreams.

REM Sleep

6. Why is REM sleep sometimes called "paradoxical" sleep?

Up to this point, you've been cycling down through the four stages of **N-REM sleep,** or *non–rapid eye movement sleep.* After you reach Stage 4, your brain waves will begin to pick up a little speed and strength. You will move back up through Stages 3, 2, and 1, and then you will enter

■ JOURNAL WRITING

Invite students to use the following writing prompt as a springboard for entries in their psychology journals:

- Describe any experiences you've had falling asleep in class. Were they embarrassing? Funny?

F • Y • I

(1) The brain waves people exhibit when they are awake and active are called beta waves. **Beta waves** are high-frequency, low-amplitude waves. **Theta waves** characterize the transition from stage 1 to stage 2. Theta waves are slower, so they have higher amplitude and lower frequency than **alpha waves**—the type of waves that are present as people move from relaxation to deeper sleep.

(2) Another type of wave characteristic of sleep stage 2 is the **K-complex.** As you can see in Figure 20.5, in stage 2 there is a sharp upturn followed by a rapid downturn of the wave, which looks similar to a heartbeat pattern on an EKG. This wave is the precursor to the large delta waves that characterized stages 3 and 4.

■ TEACHING TIP

tr A four-color transparency of Figure 20.5, Brain Waves and Sleep Stages, is available in the **Overhead Transparencies Set.**

Reteaching

tr A four-color transparency of Figure 20.5, Brain Waves and Sleep Stages, is available in the **Overhead Transparencies Set.** Using the transparency, have students identify the brain wave patterns characteristic of the different stages of sleep. Help them identify the following important concepts:

- alpha waves that characterize wakefulness
- sleep spindles found in stage 2
- delta waves that characterize stages 3 and 4
- how REM is different from the other stages of sleep

MODULE 20

tr ■ TEACHING TIP

A four-color transparency of Figure 20.7, A Good Night's Sleep, is available in the **Overhead Transparencies Set.**

F•Y•I

(1) Dreams do not usually occur in N-REM sleep, but they can and do happen. Have you ever just fallen asleep in class and started "dreaming" about something mundane—like walking down the sidewalk or talking with a friend—only to jerk awake when you dream you are tripping or falling? This experience can be explained as an N-REM dream. Normally, in REM sleep, the body is completely relaxed, so people do not react physically to their dreams. But if we dream during N-REM, then our bodies may interpret our dreams as reality and react to them, causing us to jump or startle at an apparent fall.

(2) REM is also known as *emergent stage 1* sleep. As we go through the sleep cycle each night, the body starts with the twilight sleep of stage 1 and moves into deeper, slow-wave sleep patterns. When the body cycles back up to stage 1, it experiences brain waves like stage 1 again, only this time it is in REM, the most restful sleep. So while it appears that the body is coming out of sleep every 90 minutes, it is actually cycling into emergent stage 1 or REM sleep.

► **REM sleep** Rapid eye movement sleep; a recurring sleep stage during which vivid dreams commonly occur. Also known as *paradoxical sleep,* because muscles are relaxed but other body systems are active.

your first period of rapid eye movement sleep, or **REM sleep,** a type of sleep in which your eyes move rapidly under your closed lids, and you dream vividly. Your initial REM period will not last long, and after it ends, the cycle will start again from Stage 1. This 90-minute ultradian rhythm continues all night, though delta sleep drops out of the cycle after the second or third time through. The last four hours of sleep, assuming you get the eight to nine hours you're supposed to, are pretty much spent alternating between Stage 2 and REM (Figure 20.7).

REM sleep is very different from any N-REM sleep stage. During REM sleep, your brain patterns more closely resemble those of relaxed wakefulness than any of the other sleep stages. Not only do the eyes dart about under closed eyelids, but also the pulse quickens and breathing becomes faster and irregular. Blood flows into the genitals at a rate faster than it can be removed. But despite all this internal activity, the electrode measuring muscle tension in your chin would show a flat line on the EEG, because you are, in essence, temporarily paralyzed during REM sleep. Your brainstem blocks messages from your motor cortex, the brain structure that controls your movements. This is why REM sleep is sometimes called *paradoxical* sleep: Internally, your body is aroused; externally, you're the picture of calm, and hard to awaken.

What's going on in our brains to produce all that internal activity? We're dreaming. Over 80 percent of people awakened during REM sleep report that the wak-up call interrupted a dream. REM sleep consumes about 25 percent of your nightly sleep, which means that you spend 100 minutes each night dreaming, whether you remember a second of it or not. This holds true for everyone. We *all* dream every night of our lives.

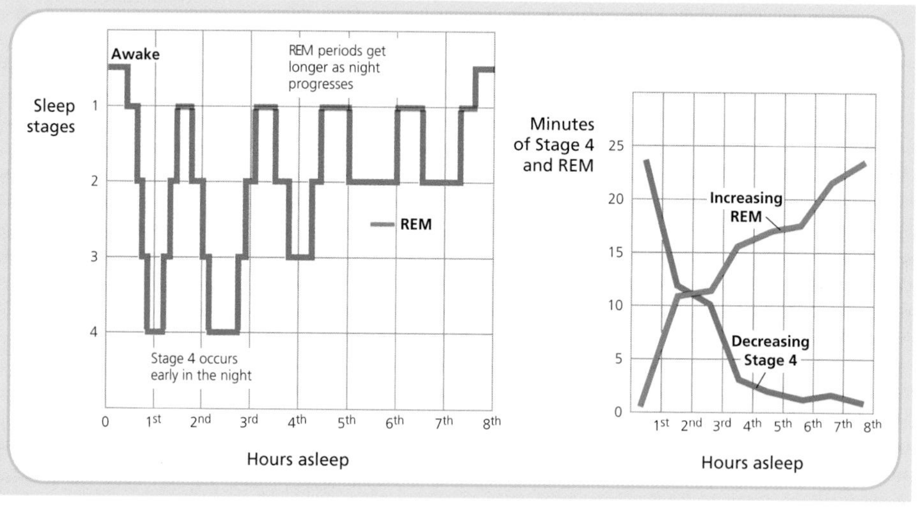

Figure 20.7 **A Good Night's Sleep** We cycle through sleep stages all night. The graph on the left shows that as we sleep, we cycle down into deeper stages of sleep and back up, where we enter REM sleep. The graph on the right shows how REM sleep increases as the night wears on.

Meeting Individual Needs

Students who have difficulty with vocabulary may need help in understanding why REM is called paradoxical sleep. Explain to students that a *paradox* is something that seems to contradict itself. It seems illogical for the brain to be so active while it is asleep, but this is true during REM. When we are at our most relaxed physically, we are experiencing one of our most active times mentally, a contradictory or *paradoxical* state.

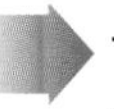

Why Do We Dream?

7. What are three modern explanations of dreaming?

There are several theories of why we dream. Sigmund Freud contributed psychology's earliest dream theory. In his book *The Interpretation of Dreams,* published over a century ago, Freud wrote that dreams were the key to understanding our inner conflicts. He believed that dreams were expressions of wish fulfillment, and that most dreams could be "traced back through analysis to erotic wishes." Modern theories of dreaming offer at least three more plausible explanations:

- ***Information-processing*** Dreams serve an important memory-related function by sorting and sifting through the day's experiences and tying up loose ends. Research shows REM sleep facilitates memory storage, and the amount of REM sleep increases following stressful times (McGrath & Cohen, 1978; Palumbo, 1978).
- ***Physiological function*** Neural activity during REM sleep provides periodic stimulation for our brains. Infants, whose brains are developing at a fantastic rate, spend significantly more time than their adult counterparts do in REM sleep (Figure 20.8). The discovery that the pituitary gland secretes a growth hormone *during* delta sleep supports this theory. Weren't we always told as young children, "If you don't get your sleep, it will stunt your growth"? The growth hormone secreted while we sleep suggests we should have listened to this advice.

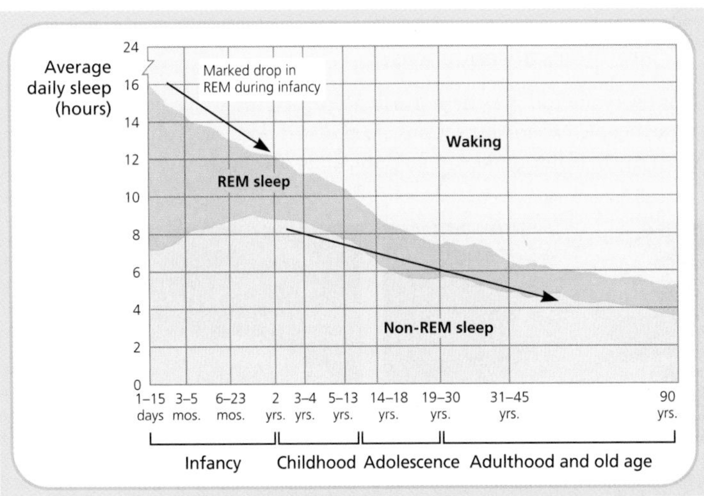

Figure 20.8 **Sleep and Age** Sleep patterns change as we grow older (Snyder & Scott, 1972).

F•Y•I

Students are fascinated by dream analysis. Popularized by Sigmund Freud as being the key to understanding our unconscious thoughts, dream analysis is still used by some psychoanalysts to help clients determine the causes of their current life problems. Typically, however, these professionals leave most of the interpretation up to the client, forgoing the practice of imposing symbolic interpretation on the patient. Most dream interpretation books on the market today are not based on scientific testing and shouldn't be used as evaluation tools.

tr ■ TEACHING TIP

A four-color transparency of Figure 20.8, Sleep and Age, is available in the **Overhead Transparencies Set.**

Enriching

Have students conduct a telephone interview of local psychologists and doctors to see what theory of dreaming they believe in. Students can come up with a script to control for confounding variables or they can simply collect the data for class discussion. (Be sure to obtain approval from an Institutional Review Board and informed consent from all subjects before embarking on any research project.)

■ **JOURNAL WRITING**

Invite students to use the following questions as springboards for entries in their psychology journals:

- Why are people fascinated by dreams?
- What might be some evolutionary reasons for dreaming?
- Why is REM sleep called "paradoxical" sleep? Why is REM sleep so important to our lives?

What happens when we don't get REM sleep? Students may have seen movies or TV shows that depict people going insane if they are deprived of dreaming. Some studies have shown that REM deprivation can lead to confusion, irritability, and lack of concentration. Others have shown that very few ill effects occur when one is deprived of REM. Studies in animals seem to indicate that they behave as though they are acting out dreams when they are REM deprived. Regardless, when people or animals are deprived of REM, they experience REM rebound, where they fall more easily into REM and stay in REM longer than normal.

The Meaning of Dreams? Marc Chagall's painting *I and the Village* captures what a dream can look like to the dreamer: colorful, confusing, and possibly filled with meaning.

- ***Activation-synthesis*** Rather than ascribing any physiological or memory-related status to dreams, this theory suggests that dreams are simply the mind's attempt to make sense out of random neural firing in the various regions of the "sleeping" brain. That is, the brain's attempt to interpret random neural activity during sleep creates a dream.

We are not the only animals who experience REM sleep. We don't know if other animals are actually having dreams, but nearly all animals, from sheep to walruses, show measurable REM periods while hooked up to an EEG during sleep. (Just how do they keep the electrodes on the walruses?) Such evidence suggests a biological *need* for REM sleep. We do know that people don't feel rested unless their sleep has contained REM periods. Also, when finally allowed to sleep after a period of sleep deprivation, we tend to dive straight into REM sleep rather than following the normal cycle. Further, REM does not occur in fish, whose behavior (unlike mammals) is governed more by instinct and less by learning, supporting the information-processing model. The truth behind dreams, once discovered, will surely encompass both psychological and biological explanations.

Sleep Disorders and Sleep Problems

8. What are some common sleep disorders, and what are their consequences?

Not everyone follows the normal sleep patterns we've been discussing. Some people experience serious sleep disruptions or problems related to sleep, such as insomnia, sleep apnea, and narcolepsy.

Cat Nap The cat in N-REM sleep (left) is sleeping comfortably. On entering REM sleep, the cat's brain stops sending the signals to the muscles that let the cat hold its head off the floor.

Cross-Curricular Connections

ART Have students explore the relationship between modern art and dreaming in one of the two following ways:

- Research how modern artists used dream imagery or their own dreams to create their works. In particular, the Spanish painter Salvador Dali (1904–1989), the Italian painter Giorgio de Chirico (1888–1974), and Russian-born Marc Chagall (1887–1985) became famous for their paintings based on dreams.
- Create their own piece of art (drawing, painting, sculpture, or photo) reflecting their most memorable dreams.

Insomnia

Who among us has never spent a restless night, tossing and turning, unable to get the sleep we so desperately desire? Thoughts of taking an important exam, anticipation of a special trip, or distress brought on by concern for a loved one all carry the potential to block the sleep we'd like to have. Fortunately for most, difficulty in getting to sleep is a rare event. For those less fortunate, who suffer **insomnia,** getting to sleep or staying asleep can be a real nightmare.

Oral medications for insomnia may actually worsen the problem. Sleeping pills can be addictive, and they inhibit or suppress REM sleep, leaving the sleep-hungry person feeling even worse than before. Alcohol also suppresses REM sleep: those who have a drink at bedtime to "help me sleep" will find the cure to be worse than the disease.

Stanley Coren's (1996) research sheds some interesting light on insomnia. After collecting EEG data on those who complained about insomnia and those who did not, he asked both groups to estimate how long it took to get to sleep. Insomnia complainers estimated that it took them twice as long to get to sleep than it actually did. Further, they dramatically miscalculated the amount of time they slept, estimating they'd slept half the time they actually had. Perhaps we should keep this research in mind the next time we think we haven't slept much the night before. It's a lot easier to remember, and exaggerate, the times during the night when we were awake than the times we were asleep!

Still, there are several things you can do to increase the quality of your sleep:

- Do not consume caffeinated beverages or foods after 3:00 P.M. Skip that soda with dinner, and turn away from late-night chocolate snacks.
- Get up at the same time every morning. Sleeping late on weekends can make it difficult to get to sleep on Sunday night, leaving you extra tired on Monday morning. Naps can have the same effect: You may not be able to fall asleep at your normal bedtime.
- Avoid nighttime activities that rile you up. Video games, arguments, or a 10-mile run right before attempting to sleep? Not a good idea.
- Try not to sweat it when you can't get to sleep. Remember that it's normal to take 15 minutes or more to fall asleep at night. Besides, sleeping poorly for one night won't cause any great harm, and often you'll be able to sleep better the following night.

▶ **insomnia** Recurring problems in falling asleep or staying asleep.

■ **APPLYING THE POINTS**

Here are two suggestions for having outside professionals enhance the material on sleep disorders for students:

- Invite a guest speaker from a sleep clinic to talk to the class about the treatment of various sleep disorders.
- Schedule a field trip to a sleep clinic so that students can see firsthand how sleep disorders are studied and treated.

You may wish to use **Enrichment Lesson:** ***Treating Insomnia*** **(*****Teacher's Resource Binder,*** p. 20-1), which outlines the multifaceted approach necessary for effective treatment of insomnia, including sleep restriction, stimulus control, and relaxation response training.

Cross-Curricular Connections

HISTORY Have students research the sleep patterns of famous people throughout history. Some examples:

- Leonardo da Vinci
- Salvador Dali
- Thomas Edison
- Winston Churchill
- Presidents Lyndon Johnson and Bill Clinton

MODULE 20

■ LOOKING AT THE ISSUES

Some people have theorized that sleep apnea is related to SIDS (sudden infant death syndrome). This disturbing and controversial problem occurs when infants die in their sleep seemingly without cause. Throughout the years, parents have been given conflicting advice about how to prevent SIDS. Have students explore what researchers know about SIDS and its link to sleep disorders. Use the following questions to help students focus their research and discuss their findings in class:

- What are some possible causes of SIDS? How might one explanation be related to sleep apnea?
- What is the current advice to parents about avoiding SIDS? How has this advice differed over the years?
- What are some recent research projects into the causes and preventions of SIDS?

F • Y • I

Some studies have shown a link between Type 2 diabetes and sleep apnea. Dr. Arthur Friedlander (2001) published a study showing that diabetic patients were three times more likely to have sleep apnea. The link is correlational, which may mean that weight is the factor linking these two disorders.

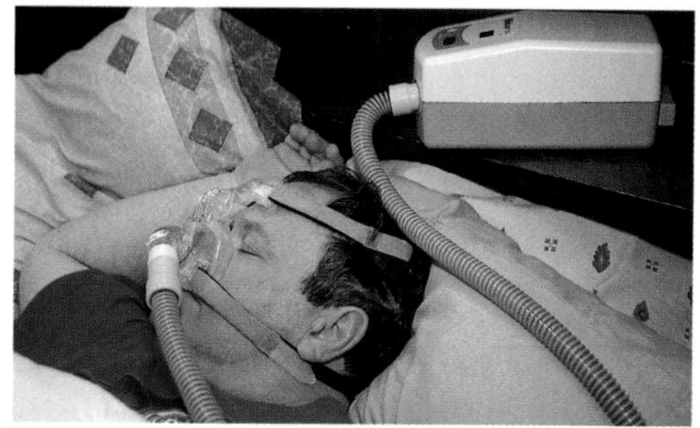

Sleeping Aid Those with sleep apnea can turn to this Continuous Positive Airway Pressure (CPAP) machine (and others like it) to help them get the sleep they need.

Sleep Apnea

Losing one night's sleep may not cause significant damage, but **sleep apnea**—a disorder characterized by repeated awakenings throughout the night as a result of not being able to breathe—can leave you exhausted. A person with sleep apnea is a loud snorer who stops breathing at the peak of a heavy, inhaled snore. Breathing may cease for as long as a minute. The only way the person can breathe again is to briefly awaken, which may happen more than 400 times a night. Apnea sufferers (usually male, overweight, and over 40) experience dreadful sleepiness even after a full night's sleep, but they may be unaware they are having such poor-quality sleep.

Some of you are probably thinking, "My dad is heavy and snores like a freight train. Does he have sleep apnea?" I'm not going to advise you to play sleep diagnostician, but if you have a relative or friend who fits this profile, you might want to find out a little more about sleep apnea, and perhaps even suggest that the person be checked for this disorder. Roughly 4 percent of the population suffers from sleep apnea. The most common treatment involves use of a CPAP (Continuous Positive Airway Pressure) machine, which helps the person breathe during the night.

► **sleep apnea** A sleep disorder characterized by temporary cessations of breathing during sleep and consequent momentary reawakenings.

► **narcolepsy** A sleep disorder characterized by uncontrollable sleep attacks. The sufferer lapses directly into REM sleep, often at inopportune times.

Narcolepsy

Can you imagine what it would be like to suddenly fall asleep because something made you laugh, cry, or feel infuriated? Such is the life of a person with **narcolepsy** (*narco* meaning "numbness," *lepsy* meaning "seizure"), a rare disease (striking 1 in 2000 people) that runs in families. Those with narcolepsy experience sleep attacks when their nervous systems get aroused, often from a strong emotion (Dement, 1978). When an attack occurs, they fall immediately into REM sleep, often at the most inopportune or dangerous times. Imagine being cut off in traffic, getting angry at the other driver, and lapsing into sleep! Fortunately, such incidents are avoidable because narcolepsy is treatable with prescription drugs. If you don't have narcolepsy now, chances are you never will; the onset of this disorder accompanies puberty.

Other Sleep Problems

Other sleep-related problems don't qualify as sleep disorders, but they can be very disruptive, nonetheless. The first four on this list typically occur during N-REM delta sleep (Stages 3 and 4).

- **Somnambulism** is sleepwalking. Is it dangerous to wake a sleepwalker? No, but it is difficult to awaken someone who is walking around with brain waves revving up at 1 cycle per second. Is the sleepwalker acting out a dream? Again, no. Remember, most dreams occur during REM sleep, and during that type of sleep, we lose our ability to move around.
- **Night terrors** most often afflict children, who look to all the world like they are awake and terrified, even though they are sound asleep. The child rarely has any memory of the event when told about it in the morning. Nightmares are dreams, so they occur during REM sleep. Night terrors are different. They occur within a few hours of falling asleep, during Stage 4 sleep.
- *Bruxism* is teeth grinding that sounds as though two bricks are being rubbed together. Adults with this problem often wear some kind of tooth guard to keep from wearing away enamel.
- *Enuresis* is bed wetting.
- *Myoclonus* is a sudden jerking of a body part occurring in Stage 1 or 2. Everyone experiences myoclonus now and then, but acute cases can result in daytime symptoms similar to those accompanying sleep apnea.

Some people appear to get by on as few as four hours of sleep per night. However, the vast majority of these brief sleepers experience negative effects on their bodies, such as memory loss and premature aging, that we cannot immediately see. So, when you're tired and it's time to sleep, pay attention to your body. Cut that last phone call to a friend short, turn off the TV, and give in to the gentle tyrant that is your need for sleep.

► **somnambulism** Sleepwalking, which usually starts in the deeper stages of N-REM sleep. The sleepwalker can walk and talk and is able to see but rarely has any memory of the event.

► **night terrors** A sleep-related problem characterized by high arousal and an appearance of being terrified; unlike nightmares, night terrors occur during Stage 4 sleep, within 2 or 3 hours of falling asleep, and are seldom remembered.

Is It Dangerous to Awaken a Sleepwalker? No. It's simply difficult to awaken someone whose brain waves are revving along at 1 cycle per second.

"Wait! Don't! It can be dangerous to wake them!"

MODULE 20

Close

Encourage a class discussion by posing the following question:

- What would need to change about our society for people in this country to place a greater value on getting enough sleep?

As you discuss this question, encourage students to use the information they learned from the text, as well as the videos, activities, and lessons in the *Teacher's Resource Binder* to support their arguments.

Cooperative Learning

Have students work in groups with each group researching a different sleep disorder. Students should collect information on the causes, treatments, and symptoms of each disorder. Challenge them to go beyond the information in the text. Also, suggest that each group find at last one person undergoing treatment and learn (if the patient gives permission) what day-to-day life is like for a person with his or her particular sleep disorder. There are several ways group members can combine their work and make a class presentation of their findings:

- create a poster for display that educates other students about the sleep disorder
- write a newspaper item for the school or local newspaper about the sleep disorder
- create a PowerPoint presentation for a sleep disorder seminar sponsored by the psychology club

MODULE 20

Checking the Points

trb ■ TEACHING TIPS

web (1) The book companion site for *Thinking About Psychology* at www.worthpublishers.com/thinkingaboutpsych contains a module quiz, flashcards of key terms and people, as well as other student activities and resources for this module. You will also find PowerPoint lectures, as well as other student activities and resources by logging on as an instructor.

(2) Critical Thinking Activity: *Fact or Falsehood?* (*Teacher's Resource Binder*, p. 20-1; Handout 20–1) can help students review concepts about sleep. Ask them not to refer to a version of the *Sleep IQ Test* they may have completed earlier. In groups, have students discuss the correct response to each item and support their answers with passages from the text.

tr (3) Graphic Organizer: *Sleep Stages, Waves, and REM* (*Teacher's Resource Binder*, p. 20-1; Handout 20–2) can help students review module concepts and their relationship to one another and the experience of sleep. Students may either review a previously completed organizer or apply what they have learned in the module by filling in a blank copy of the organizer. You can review a correctly completed organizer by using the handout as a transparency and projecting it for the entire class to view.

REVIEW

Module 20: Sleep, Dreams, and Body Rhythms

What's the Point?

1. *What is consciousness?*
   Consciousness is awareness of yourself and your environment. In sleep, we lose waking consciousness.

Body Rhythms

2. *How do your body's natural rhythms differ from one another?*
   Our bodies have naturally recurring biological rhythms that affect physical processes. Circadian rhythms, such as the sleep-wake cycle, occur approximately once during a 24-hour period. Ultradian rhythms, such as the sleep stages, occur more than once a day. Infradian rhythms, such as bears' hibernation, occur once a month or once a season.

Sleep and Sleep Deficit

3. *What are the costs to your body when you don't get enough sleep?*
   About 80 percent of all students get too little sleep, according to William Dement, a leading sleep researcher. Sleep deprivation decreases the levels of hormones that the body requires for proper functioning, and increases the level of the stress hormone, cortisol, which has been linked to damaged brain cells. Sleep deprivation also is associated with higher risk of accidents, hypertension, concentration problems, and other health problems.

Why We Sleep

4. *How do we benefit from sleeping?*
   Although we know some of the consequences of sleep deprivation, we don't completely understand why sleep is necessary or what sleep does for our bodies. We do know that part of the brain, the hypothalamus, monitors light patterns and triggers bodily changes that make us sleep. The adaptation theory suggests that we sleep at times that help us stay safe, and that sleep aids survival. Others believe that sleep lets our bodies rebuild tissues, consolidate memories, and organize thoughts.

Sleep Stages, REM, and Dreaming

5. *What are the four stages of nondreaming sleep?*
   We have two types of sleep, N-REM sleep, in which we dream very little, and REM sleep, in which we have vivid dreams. The N-REM portion of our sleep has four stages that repeat throughout the night:
   - Stage 1, which lasts about 5 minutes and may contain sensations like the feeling of falling.
   - Stage 2, characterized by spindles (little bursts of brain-wave activity) and higher-amplitude waves.
   - Stages 3 and 4, which combined are known as slow wave, or delta, sleep. Delta sleep diminishes in the second half of a normal night of sleep.

6. *Why is REM sleep sometimes called "paradoxical" sleep?*
   REM (rapid eye movement) sleep usually appears after the first full cycle of N-REM sleep, though it may appear earlier if the sleeper is seriously sleep-deprived. REM sleep is the period of sleep in which we have vivid dreams. The term "paradoxical sleep" reflects two seemingly contradictory and coexistent physical states: internal arousal (rapid eye movements, high pulse and breathing rates, and so on), and external calm and absence of movement. The brainstem blocks messages from the motor cortex during REM sleep, producing temporary paralysis.
7. *What are three modern explanations of dreaming?*
   Sigmund Freud proposed that all dreams are the expression of conflicts over erotic wishes. Modern theories of dreaming propose instead that dreams perform one or more of the following functions: processing information we have collected during waking periods; stimulating the brain and enabling growth; and attempting to make sense of random firing of brain cells in a sort of "connect-the-dots" exercise.

Sleep Disorders and Sleep Problems

8. *What are some common sleep disorders, and what are their consequences?*
   Insomnia is difficulty getting to sleep or staying asleep, often because we are preoccupied with some problem or upcoming event. Medications, alcohol, and other drugs can suppress REM sleep and worsen insomnia. Sleep apnea is characterized by loud snoring and repeated short periods in which breathing stops. Sleep quality is poor, because these sleepers must briefly wake up and catch their breath each time breathing stops. Most people with sleep apnea are middle-aged, overweight men. Narcolepsy is the most dramatic sleep disorder. A person with narcolepsy falls into REM sleep with no warning, usually in the middle of some strongly emotional situation. Other more common sleep problems include sleepwalking (somnambulism), night terrors, teeth grinding (bruxism), bed wetting (enuresis), and sudden jerking movements (myoclonus).

Key Terms

consciousness, p. 378
pseudoscientific claim, p. 378
biological rhythms, p. 378
circadian rhythms, p. 378
ultradian rhythms, p. 378
infradian rhythms, p. 378
melatonin, p. 383
electroencephalograph (EEG), p. 384
spindles, p. 385
delta sleep, p. 385
N-REM sleep, p. 385
REM sleep, p. 386
insomnia, p. 389
sleep apnea, p. 390
narcolepsy, p. 390
somnambulism, p. 391
night terrors, p. 391

Key People

William Dement, p. 380

MODULE 20

trb ■ TEACHING TIP

If students have already prepared question-and-answer flashcards as described in **Building Vocabulary:** *Flashcards* (*Teacher's Resource Binder*, p. 20-1), they may benefit from exchanging their flashcards with a partner for a vocabulary review. If students have not yet prepared question flashcards, have them do so now, and then use the flashcards individually or with partners to review vocabulary.

MODULE 20

tb Using the Test Bank

The *Test Bank* that accompanies this textbook offers a wide variety of questions in different formats and levels of complexity. Use the software to construct whole tests or to integrate standardized questions into teacher-made tests.

Self-Test Answers

Multiple-Choice Questions

1. d, 2. b, 3. a, 4. c, 5. c

Matching Terms and Definitions

6. a. (6), b. (7), c. (10), d. (5), e. (3), f. (8), g. (1), h. (2)

Self-Test

Multiple-Choice Questions

Choose the *best* answer for each of the following questions:

1. Every year, monarch butterflies migrate from all over the United States to a part of Mexico, which has become very famous as a tourist attraction. This migration is an example of
   a. a pseudoscientific rhythm.
   b. a circadian rhythm.
   c. an ultradian rhythm.
   d. an infradian rhythm.

2. Leslie has been hooked up to a machine that monitors melatonin, which is linked to regulation of the sleep-wake cycle. This morning, Leslie woke up and felt the warm sun streaming in through the bedroom curtains. If the machine is working properly, it will register ________________ ________________ levels of melatonin.
   a. very high
   b. gently rising
   c. gently dropping
   d. very low

3. Alberto has volunteered for a sleep experiment, and the researchers are looking at a printout showing Alberto's brain waves a few minutes ago. The printout shows a pattern of long, slow waves—so long that he appears to have only one wave each second. Alberto is in
   a. delta sleep.
   b. Stage 2 sleep.
   c. REM sleep.
   d. Stage 1 sleep.

4. Katie has a new baby boy, and she warns everyone who comes to see the baby that they must not make any noise if the baby is sleeping. Katie says that a lot of noise at this stage might stunt the baby's growth. Katie seems to believe that sleep has
   a. an information-processing function.
   b. an activation-synthesis function.
   c. a physiological function.
   d. All of the above.

5. Alisha just read an article on sleep disorders, and now she is very worried about her father. Last year he turned 50, and he's gained a lot of weight recently. He also looks very tired, and Alisha can hear him snoring loudly at night. Alisha is probably worried that her father has
   a. narcolepsy.
   b. enuresis.
   c. sleep apnea.
   d. bruxism.

Matching Terms and Definitions

6. For each definition, choose the *best* matching term from the list that follows:

   Definition

   a. Sleep in which you have vivid dreams and darting eye movements, but your body is temporarily paralyzed.
   b. Sleepwalking.
   c. Stages 3 and 4 of N-REM sleep, characterized by long, slow waves.
   d. Sleep in which you cycle through the four sleep stages.
   e. Regular body rhythm that occurs more than once each day.
   f. A sleep disorder in which a person suddenly goes directly from a fully awake state to REM sleep.
   g. An assertion that sounds scientific but is not based on science.
   h. Regular body rhythm that occurs approximately every 24 hours.

Alternative Assessment/Portfolio Project

trb SLEEP PROFILE Students often don't realize how much their sleeping habits affect their lives. Having them document their sleep patterns, analyze their sleep deficits, and develop strategies to improve their sleeping routine will help them realize sleep's impact and importance.

Use revised and finished projects from any or all of the following activities found in the *Teacher's Resource Binder* to compile a sleep profile portfolio:

- Application Activity: *Keeping a Sleep Diary* (*Teacher's Resource Binder*, p. 20-1; Handout 20–4)
- Application Activity: *Larks or Owls?* (*Teacher's Resource Binder*, p. 20-1; Handout 20–5)

Term

(1) pseudoscientific claim
(2) circadian rhythm
(3) ultradian rhythm
(4) infradian rhythm
(5) N-REM sleep
(6) REM sleep
(7) somnambulism
(8) narcolepsy
(9) insomnia
(10) delta sleep

Fill-in-the-Blank Questions

7. The adaptation theory of why we sleep holds that we sleep at times of day or night that offer us the most _______________.

8. Another theory of sleep holds that sleep is _______________ because it allows our bodies to rebuild tissues, consolidate memories, and organize our recent learning.

9. Sleep researchers use a(n) _______________ to study brain waves of people while they are asleep.

Brief Essay Question

10. Rita will be starting college next year, and she'd like to have her own apartment instead of living with her parents. She plans to work full time on the night shift at a local manufacturing plant to pay her rent and have lots of spending money. Rita knows that a full-time class schedule, lots of homework, and a full-time job will be very challenging, but she thinks she can handle it by cutting back her sleep hours from eight hours to six hours each day. In two paragraphs of about three or four sentences each, share your knowledge of sleep deprivation with Rita and tell her what might happen if she carries out this plan.

Self-Test Answers

Fill-in-the-Blank Questions

7. safety, 8. restorative,
9. electroencephalograph

Brief Essay Question

10. Students should remember that sleep deprivation can have physical and mental consequences. People can experience lack of concentration, irritability, and heart murmurs. Rita should keep in mind that while she may be able to function normally for a time without sleep, she will need to take naps to compensate for her lack of sleep.

- Application Activity: *Dream Journal* (*Teacher's Resource Binder*, p. 20-1; **Handouts 20–10** and 20–11)
- Application Activity: *Remembering Daydreams* (*Teacher's Resource Binder*, p. 20-1)

A discussion of how to compile and assess these portfolios appears in **Alternative Assessment/Portfolio Project:** *Sleep Profile* (*Teacher's Resource Binder*, p. 20-1; **Handout 20–14**). Use the general rubric provided by **Handout 20–14** to evaluate the portfolios. Adapt the rubric to suit your needs.

MODULE 21

Performance Standards

Standard Area: States of Consciousness

Content Standard 3: Hypnosis and its uses

Performance Standard 3.1 Explain different hypnotic phenomena.

- Define *hypnosis*. (Student Text p. 396)
- Examine the social influence and divided consciousness theories of hypnosis. (Student Text pp. 397–398)
- Discuss the idea of a "hidden observer," as presented by Ernest Hilgard. (Student Text p. 398)
- Explain the induction process. (Student Text pp. 398–399)
- Investigate the differences between deep sleep and being hypnotized. (Student Text p. 399)
- Present the Stanford Hypnotic Susceptibility Scale and the characteristics of individuals with high and low hypnotizability scores. (Student Text p. 399)
- Figure 21.1, "Stanford Hypnotic Susceptibility Scale," reveals how the population breaks down into low, medium, and high hypnotizability. (Student Text p. 399)
- Discuss whether hypnosis can make us do things we otherwise would not do. (Student Text p. 400)
- Investigate whether posthypnotic suggestions can help us lose weight or stop smoking. (Student Text pp. 400–401)

Performance Standard 3.2 Discuss applications of hypnosis.

- Discuss whether hypnosis can make us do things we otherwise would not do. (Student Text p. 400)
- Investigate whether posthypnotic suggestions can help us lose weight or stop smoking. (Student Text pp. 400–401)
- Examine whether hypnosis can enhance memory recall. Discuss why psychologists are suspicious of hypnotically enhanced memories. (Student Text pp. 401–402)
- Discuss how hypnosis can be used to help control pain. (Student Text pp. 402–403)
- Investigate why researchers are skeptical about claims of hypnotic effects such as feats of strength and age regression. (Student Text p. 403)
- Discuss the role of the placebo effect when analyzing claims of hypnosis to solve problems ranging from headaches to warts. (Student Text p. 403)

Materials NETWORK

All of the items from the Video, Activity, and Enrichment Centers listed below come from the *Teacher's Resource Binder.* These items will help you teach and expand on concepts presented in Module 21.

trb This logo indicates when an item from the Materials Network may be used in conjunction with a specific note found in this module's *Teacher's Edition.*

What Is Hypnosis?

Activity Center

- **Critical Thinking Activity:** *Fact or Falsehood?* With this activity, students' preconceptions about hypnosis are either exposed as incorrect or reinforced as correct. (*Teacher's Resource Binder,* p. 21-1; **Handout 21–1**)
- **Building Vocabulary: Graphic Organizer:** *Concept Web* Students can fill in this graphic organizer to interact with and visually process the concepts in this module. (*Teacher's Resource Binder,* p. 21-1; **Handout 21–2**)
- **Application Activity:** *Hypnosis as Heightened Suggestibility* Demonstrate for students that they can be easily led to believe that a simple task is difficult to accomplish—by listening to powerful suggestion. (*Teacher's Resource Binder,* p. 21-1)

Hypnotic Techniques

Activity Center

- **Application Activity:** *The Relaxation Response* Relaxation is the basis for hypnosis. With this activity, students discover how quickly and easily a person may become completely relaxed. (*Teacher's Resource Binder,* p. 21-1)
- **Analysis Activity:** *The Creative Imagination Scale* Researchers have developed an alternative to the Stanford Hypnotic Suggestibility Scale that relies less on coercion and more on voluntary behavior. (*Teacher's Resource Binder,* p. 21-1)

Applications of Hypnosis

V Video Center

- **Videocassette:** *The Mind,* **Second Edition, Module 2: "Hypnotic Dissociation and Pain Relief"** Consult the faculty guide from *The Mind* video series for a description of this module. (*Teacher's Resource Binder,* p. 21-1)

Activity Center

- **Demonstration Activity:** *Hypnosis—A Stage Demonstration* Use this activity to show how seemingly impossible feats of strength can be performed with a little practice and showmanship. (*Teacher's Resource Binder,* p. 21-1)

Enrichment Center

- **Enrichment Lesson:** *Is Hypnosis an Altered State of Consciousness?* This lesson addresses the question by citing research that shows what hypnosis is and is not capable of. (*Teacher's Resource Binder,* p. 21-1)

MODULE 21

Hypnosis

Introducing the Module

The Points: Module Objectives

- Evaluate how social influence theory explains why subjects carry out a hypnotist's suggestions.
- Evaluate how divided consciousness theory explains why subjects carry out a hypnotist's suggestions.
- Discuss whether hypnosis makes us do things we otherwise would not do.
- Explain what posthypnotic suggestions are and how they could help us lose weight or stop smoking.
- Analyze why psychologists are suspicious of hypnotically enhanced memories.
- Describe how hypnosis can help control pain.
- Analyze why researchers are skeptical about other claims of hypnotic effects.

trb Building Vocabulary

Working individually or with partners, students can complete **Building Vocabulary: Graphic Organizer:** *Concept Web* to visually process the terms in the module (*Teacher's Resource Binder*, p. 21-1; **Handout 21–2**).

Teaching the Points

web ■ TEACHING TIP

You can log on as an instructor to the book companion site for *Thinking About Psychology* at **www.worthpublishers.com/thinkingaboutpsych**. It contains teacher resources for class presentations as well as review and assessment of module concepts and terms.

web ■ LOOKING AT THE ISSUES

What do contemporary researchers believe about hypnosis? Have students check out the Web site **www.hypnosis-research.org/hypnosis/index.html** to find out more about clinical applications of hypnosis. Students can also browse the Society for Psychological Hypnosis's Web site at **www.apa.org/divisions/div30**.

MODULE 21

Hypnosis

Ever been hypnotized? For several years, my school's postprom party has featured an entertainer who uses hypnosis as part of his act. Students always return to class on the following Monday tired but full of questions about what they've seen and, in some cases, what they've experienced. Can psychology shed any light on what happens during hypnosis?

What Is Hypnosis?

Hypnosis is a social interaction between a hypnotist and a subject. Suggestibility plays a key role. The hypnotist's suggestions may alter the subject's perceptions, feelings, thoughts, or behaviors. Researchers, therapists, and entertainers—and most of the rest of us—are interested in why these suggestions seem to have such power over people. Psychologists have proposed two key theories: social influence and divided consciousness.

Equally Reliable? Stage hypnotists such as the one who suggested these students were on the beach in need of sunscreen fascinate their audiences with many of the same techniques researchers examine in the laboratory. This module will explain some of what the researchers have learned.

Getting Started

Begin a discussion by asking students whether they've ever had an experience with hypnosis. Students may have seen a stage hypnotist, been hypnotized as a result of therapy, or just seen people being hypnotized on television. Ask students whether they believe hypnosis is real and something that can help people.

trb You also may wish to use **Critical Thinking Activity:** *Fact or Falsehood?* (*Teacher's Resource Binder*, p. 21-1; **Handout 21–1**) as a prereading strategy to find out what students already know about hypnosis. The activity along with its results will prime students to note terms and concepts in the text that confirm or dispel their preconceptions about hypnosis.

Social Influence Theory

What's the Point? 1. How does social influence theory explain why subjects carry out a hypnotist's suggestions?

Social influence theory argues that powerful social influences produce the state we call hypnosis. As evidence, proponents of this theory note that no special physiological condition marks hypnosis as anything other than normal consciousness—the natural state of awareness we experience when we're fully awake and alert (Lynn & others, 1990; Spanos & Coe, 1992). Our social environment can indeed have a huge effect on our behavior and experiences. One day this year I was feeling fine until my wife said my voice sounded scratchy and asked if my throat hurt. All of a sudden, I started to feel as though I was getting ill. I never did get sick, so it was apparently only my wife's suggestive question that made me feel less than 100 percent.

Peer pressure, one of the many forms of social influence, can lead people to behave in ways they wouldn't normally. A "mob mentality," for example, may lead otherwise law-abiding sports fans to engage in destructive behavior while "celebrating" a big win. Social influence is also apparent in religious cults. A charismatic leader may seem to "cast a spell" on followers, who then behave in ways they would have had difficulty imagining before the cult experience.

Is hypnosis governed by similar social pressures? Certainly the hypnotist's status and authority increase the likelihood that subjects will be influenced by suggestions. And subjects often want to appear cooperative, which increases their suggestibility. Keep in mind that neither the hypnotist nor the subject is necessarily "faking" it—both may believe strongly in the powers of hypnosis. In fact, the stronger their beliefs, the more likely they are to experience results—real results! The strongest support for the social influence theory is that behaviors produced with hypnosis can often be produced in other ways. You may hypnotize me into believing I have a "suggested illness," but I might also acquire this belief by reading a list of symptoms or seeing a program on TV. I might even succumb to an offhand comment like my wife's.

Divided Consciousness Theory

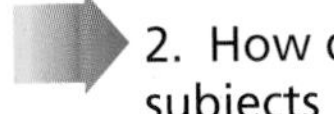

2. How does divided consciousness theory explain why subjects carry out a hypnotist's suggestions?

Opposing social influence theory are psychologists who believe hypnosis is a state of **divided consciousness.** We are all capable of dividing our consciousness to some extent. When I go out for a long run, for example,

▶ **hypnosis** A social interaction in which one person (the hypnotist) makes suggestions about perceptions, feelings, thoughts, or behaviors, and another person (the subject) follows those suggestions.

▶ **social influence theory** The theory that powerful social influences can produce a state of hypnosis.

▶ **divided consciousness theory** The theory that during hypnosis, our consciousness—our awareness of ourselves and others—splits, so that one aspect of consciousness is not aware of the role other parts are playing.

F • Y • I

Stage hypnotists make ready use of the fact that they can successfully suggest to their audience that it will begin to experience, say, itching sensations on various parts of their bodies—possibly on the head, arms, back, or legs. To underscore a suggestion, the performer may casually (but not obtrusively) scratch the body part that was suggested. Before long, many in the audience start to follow suit.

trb At this point, you may wish to use Application Activity: *Hypnosis as Heightened Suggestibility* (*Teacher's Resource Binder*, p. 21-1).

■ TEACHING TIP

Link the concept of *mob mentality* to *social psychology* and *diffusion of responsibility.* When people are in a big group, they tend to lose individual identity and responsibility for their actions. If the crowd starts to behave in a particular way, people get carried away because they feel anonymous—that no one will hold them responsible if everyone is participating.

■ LOOKING AT THE ISSUES

(1) Have students research incidents of brainwashing by cult leaders. Students can meet in small groups to discuss their findings, centering the discussion on the following questions:

- How have famous examples of cult mentality (Branch Davidians, the Jonestown Massacre, and so forth) demonstrated the use of social influence techniques to persuade people to behave in particular ways?
- What types of people tend to fall prey to cult leaders?

(2) What other explanations can students come up with to explain hypnotic behavior? Before students respond to the question, have them research the following social psychology concepts related to the social influence theory:

- conformity
- peer pressure
- groupthink
- social desirability

Suggested Readings

Use the following books as teacher-preparation tools or as enrichment for advanced students:

Benson, H. (1975). *The relaxation response.* New York: Morrow.

Fisher, J. (1979). *Body magic.* New York: Stein & Day.

Fromm, E., & Nash, M. R. (Eds.). (1992). *Contemporary hypnosis research.* New York: Guilford.

Gauld, A. (1992). *A history of hypnotism.* New York: Cambridge University Press.

Lynn, S. J., & Rhue, J. W. (Eds.). (1991). *Theories of hypnosis: Current models and perspectives.* New York: Guilford.

Lynn, S. J., Rhue, J. W., & Kirsch, I. (Eds.). (1993). *Handbook of clinical hypnosis.* Washington, DC: American Psychological Association.

Tinterow, M. M. (Ed.). (1970). *Foundations of hypnosis.* Springfield, IL: Charles Thomas.

MODULE 21

■ **TEACHING TIP**

Link the author's experience with running marathons to *flow.* **Flow** occurs when people are engaged in challenging activities for which they have some skill. Like the author's running experience, people in flow will lose track of time, feel caught up in the moment, and lack feelings of self-consciousness that might distract them from their task.

F • Y • I

Ernest Hilgard is considered one of the most influential psychologists of the twentieth century. After joining the faculty at Stanford in 1933, he pursued many interests, one of which was hypnosis. Hypnosis was viewed largely as the tool of magicians and quacks, but Hilgard's scientific studies of the phenomenon shed light on why it worked for some people and what applications of it were beneficial. He developed the Stanford Hypnotic Suggestibility Scale, which helped to standardize the study of hypnosis.

■ **APPLYING THE POINTS**

If possible, contact a psychologist who uses hypnosis in his or her practice to see what applications and techniques are used today. Report findings from your discussion with the professional to the class.

trb At this point, you may wish to use **Application Activity:** ***The Relaxation Response*** (*Teacher's Resource Binder*, p. 21-1).

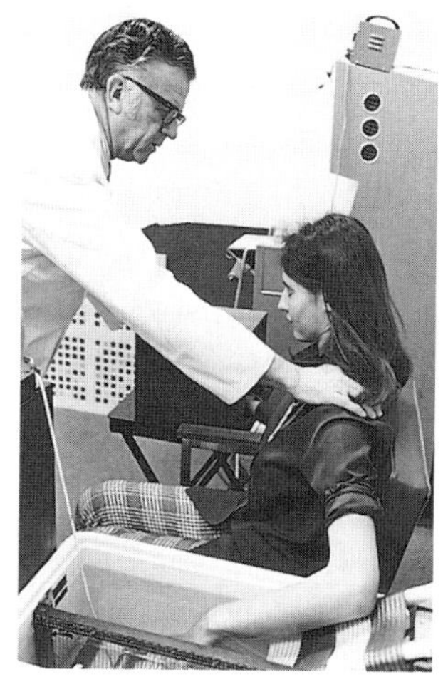

Hypnosis as Divided Consciousness Ernest Hilgard has demonstrated that some part of the consciousness of hypnotized subjects like this one remain aware of pain (induced here by ice water), even though she behaves as though pain does not exist. Hilgard called the part that remained aware the "hidden observer."

I sometimes get so caught up in thinking about things that a mile goes by unnoticed. Some tiny part of my consciousness continues to monitor traffic, curbs I might trip over, and the route, so that the rest of my mind can spin free on other topics.

Ernest Hilgard argued that hypnosis is a more dramatic form of this division (1986, 1992). He stumbled on this idea while demonstrating hypnosis to his class at Stanford University one day. He used a suggestion to produce deafness in a hypnotic subject, then challenged the class to prove that the young man was not deaf. Class members tried the sorts of things you probably would, such as sneaking up behind the young man and making loud noises, and insulting him in hopes of getting a response. Nothing worked, until one student asked if there was a part of the subject that was still listening. Hilgard himself was skeptical, but he asked the subject to raise his finger if some part of him could still hear. Up went the finger. The odd thing is that even the subject did not know why he had raised his finger until it was explained to him after the demonstration. The part that could hear, which Hilgard called the *hidden observer,* was so effectively split from the rest of his consciousness that even the subject was unaware of it.

The key difference between the two explanations of hypnosis is this: social influence theory says that hypnosis is a result of *external* social variables; divided consciousness theory says that hypnosis is the result of a special exaggerated division of one's *internal* consciousness. It's possible, of course, that both positions may be partially correct. Hypnosis is complex enough that several variables may be interacting to produce the effects (Kihlstrom & McConkey, 1990).

By now you may be wondering just how someone enters into this complex state of being hypnotized. Let's consider some of the techniques used.

Hypnotic Techniques

▶ **Ernest Hilgard** (1904–2001) Pioneering hypnosis researcher and an advocate of the divided consciousness theory of hypnosis.

▶ **hypnotic induction** The process in which a hypnotist creates a state of hypnosis in a subject, generally by voicing a series of suggestions.

Have you seen hypnosis depicted in cartoons? Perhaps the hypnotist was swinging a pocket watch on a chain back and forth or using a spiraling disc. The zombielike hypnotized person muttered "Yes, master" and lurched forward with outstretched arms to do the hypnotist's bidding. As you may have guessed, the reality of **hypnotic induction** is far different. It requires nothing more than the hypnotist's voice and is so easily accomplished that the Federal Communication Commission set up rules preventing the procedure from being broadcast on TV. If someone performed a hypnotic induction on TV,

Demonstrating

trb RELAXING Lead students through a relaxation exercise similar to the one described in **Application Activity:** ***The Relaxation Response*** (*Teacher's Resource Binder*, p. 21-1). Afterward, discuss with them how easy it was to become relaxed and what factors contributed to their ability to become relaxed. Some factors that will be evident include dim lighting, your soothing voice, and the students' own levels of fatigue.

people at home in their living rooms could become hypnotized! In fact, stage hypnotists do experience this problem. They frequently find that some members of the audience become as deeply hypnotized as the volunteers on stage.

There is nothing magical or mystical in the process—the "secret" is a calm, rhythmic tone in the hypnotist's voice, which becomes a focal point for the subject's attention. The hypnotist begins by giving easy, logical suggestions ("Your eyes are getting tired. You feel very relaxed."). Most people find the state of hypnosis to be very relaxing, so these suggestions are particularly easy to follow. Continuing to focus the subject's attention, the hypnotist then gradually moves on to more difficult tasks.

Hypnosis is sometimes falsely characterized as a "deep sleep." During hypnosis, subjects sometimes do physically slump in their chairs. However, it is possible to talk, move, and open your eyes while hypnotized.

Certain tests help determine in advance who may be a good hypnotic subject. The Stanford Hypnotic Susceptibility Scale, in which subjects respond to a series of suggestions (for example, that your hands are glued together and you cannot separate them), is one such test. This test indicates that most people are moderately hypnotizable. About 10 percent are very poor subjects and an equal number are highly hypnotizable; the rest fall in the middle (Figure 21.1). The higher you score on this scale, the more easily you can be hypnotized and the more easily you will respond to suggestions.

Hypnotizability also depends on the circumstances of the hypnotic session. It is more difficult to achieve hypnosis in front of an audience than in a one-on-one private office session. Less susceptible subjects who do not become hypnotized on stage may respond differently in an office setting.

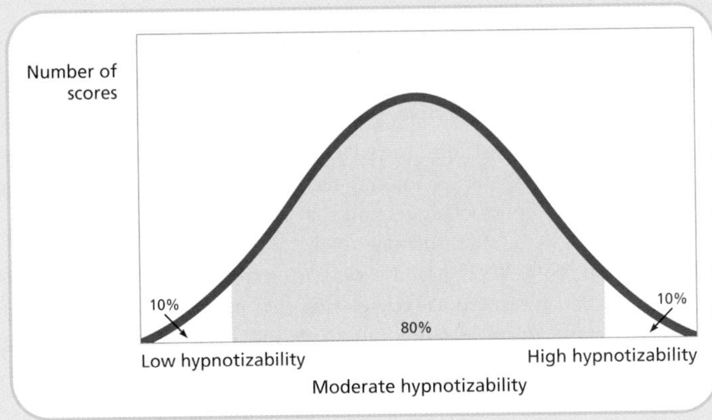

Figure 21.1 Stanford Hypnotic Susceptibility Scale Can everyone be hypnotized? People differ in their ability to be hypnotized. About one-tenth of all people make excellent subjects, and an equal number are very difficult to hypnotize. Most people are moderately susceptible to hypnosis.

Enriching

In his book, *The Relaxation Response*, Dr. Herbert Benson suggests four basic components necessary to elicit the relaxation response.

- A quiet, calm environment with as few distractions as possible.
- A mental device to prevent "mind wandering".
- A passive, "let-it-happen" attitude.
- A comfortable position to prevent muscular tension.

trb To find out more about the relaxation response and to apply these four components use **Application Activity:** *The Relaxation Response* (*Teacher's Resource Binder*, p. 21-1).

MODULE 21

F • Y • I

The text notes that there are individual differences in hypnotic responsiveness and that the Stanford Hypnotic Susceptibility Scale (SHSS) provides a measure of a person's hypnotizability. Sheryl Wilson and Theodore Barber designed the Creative Imagination Scale (CIS) as an alternative to earlier scales (including the SHSS). They claimed the earlier scales were too authoritarian, usually requiring a trance induction, and could not be administered in a group setting. Given the emergence of a more democratic culture and a more educated public, few people, they reasoned, like to be told, "You are under my control, and you will behave as I tell you."

trb At this point, you may wish to use **Analysis Activity:** *The Creative Imagination Scale* (*Teacher's Resource Binder*, p. 21-1).

■ TEACHING TIP

Be sure to emphasize to students that high suggestibility does not mean one is weak-minded or gullible. People who value respect for authority may submit to hypnotic suggestion because they want to please the hypnotist. Environment and attitude play important roles in how suggestible someone may be.

trb tr A black-line master for Figure 21.1, Stanford Hypnotic Susceptibility Scale, is available in the **Black-Line Masters Appendix** of the *Teacher's Resource Binder.*

■ CHECKING FOR UNDERSTANDING

Have students write a persuasive paper arguing for one of the two theories of hypnosis—the *social influence theory* or the *divided consciousness theory.* Have them compare and contrast each theory as they try to persuade their audience about which theory is a better explanation of hypnosis.

MODULE 21

■ LOOKING AT THE ISSUES

Have students use available resources, including the Internet, to research the propaganda techniques of different regimes throughout history, including those found in pre–World War II Germany, fascist Spain and Italy, the Soviet Union, Iran, and Iraq. In a full class discussion, have students present their findings in response to the following questions:

- How did the charismatic leaders of these regimes use the power of suggestion and authority to control people?
- What emotions, both good and bad, came into play for people living under such regimes?
- How were the regime's propaganda and political techniques similar to techniques used with hypnotic suggestion?

■ TEACHING TIP

Link the *power of suggestion* to Stanley Milgram's studies of obedience. Milgram was able to show that a mere suggestion by an authority figure could lead someone to subject someone else to a supposedly harmful dose of electric shock. Were those people evil? Not likely—just subject to the power of the request of someone in authority.

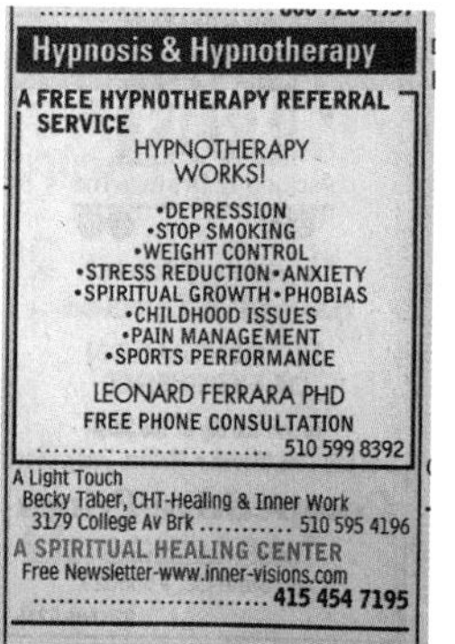

A Magical Cure? Many people turn to hypnosis for help in stopping smoking or losing weight. How effective are these programs? It turns out that people enrolled in other programs that try to help without hypnosis fare just as well.

Hypnotic Suggestions

3. Can hypnosis make us do things we otherwise would not do?

The key technique in hypnosis is making suggestions that the subject follows. These suggestions can influence a wide variety of behaviors, sensations, thoughts, and emotions (Bowers, 1976). Thus, hypnotized people can be made to flap their arms like birds, hallucinate the smell of roses, believe that it's midnight in the middle of the day, or be angry about something that supposedly happened at school. The hypnotist creates a new and interesting reality for the subject. Sometimes the results are entertaining, which explains the popularity of stage hypnotists like the one who performs at our postprom party.

How powerful are these suggestions? Could they lead you to do something against your will? Could an evildoer hypnotize you to commit crimes on his or her behalf? The answer to these questions is complicated. In one study (Orne & Evans, 1965), hypnotized people did dip their hands into what they were told was acid and then threw the "acid" into the face of another person. Proof that hypnosis could be used to do evil deeds, right? Not necessarily. There are other explanations for this behavior. Perhaps the hypnotized participants knew that—because they were involved in an experiment—they wouldn't be asked to do something truly harmful. Or perhaps our natural tendency to obey an authority figure could by itself produce these results. In fact, when nonhypnotized subjects were asked to engage in the same acid-throwing behavior, they were just as likely as the hypnotized subjects to do so. This seems to indicate that hypnosis alone does not cause the behavior. Hypnosis *can* lead people to do things they otherwise wouldn't, but so can powerful suggestions of any kind.

Posthypnotic Suggestions

4. What are posthypnotic suggestions, and could they help us to lose weight or stop smoking?

▶ **posthypnotic suggestion** A suggestion, made during a hypnosis session, that the subject will carry out when no longer hypnotized.

Some hypnotic suggestions, called **posthypnotic suggestions,** don't take effect until *after* the session has ended. Entertainers may, for example, make a posthypnotic suggestion that a subject bark like a dog on a prearranged signal after returning to the audience. Therapists also use this technique to help clients lose weight or stop smoking. The hypnotist may plant a posthypnotic suggestion that certain foods or the cigarettes will taste terrible, like rancid meat. Research indicates that people with low hypnotic susceptibility benefit just as much from posthypnotic suggestions as do those with high hypnotic susceptibility

Demonstrating

LEMON SUGGESTION Tell your students to close their eyes and imagine they are cutting a lemon. Speak slowly and methodically while you tell them that this lemon is ". . . a large . . . sour . . . bitter lemon . . . so full of juice that it drips over your fingers onto the floor. Now imagine sucking the juice from the same fruit." After students experience your suggestion, ask the following questions:

- What's happening? Are you salivating? Why or why not?
- How does this demonstration mimic hypnotic suggestion?
- What about this demonstration was particularly vivid?

trb At this point, you may wish to use Demonstration Activity: *Hypnosis—A Stage Demonstration* (*Teacher's Resource Binder*, p. 21-1).

(Bowers & LeBaron, 1986). This finding suggests that the therapist's attention may be as important as the posthypnotic suggestion itself. People in therapy programs that don't rely on hypnosis may show as much improvement as those who opt for hypnosis.

Hypnotists also use posthypnotic suggestions to save time, money, and stress for subjects they meet with regularly. The hypnotist may suggest that at the next session the subject will be hypnotized as soon as the hypnotist provides a particular signal, such as a touch to the left shoulder.

It's also interesting that hypnotized subjects usually report remembering what occurred while they were hypnotized unless the hypnotist produces **posthypnotic amnesia** by suggesting they will not.

Are these techniques reliable and useful? Let's see what the research suggests.

▸ **posthypnotic amnesia** The supposed inability to remember what happened during hypnosis because the hypnotist suggests that the subject will have no memory of that period of time.

Applications of Hypnosis

Memory and pain control are the two bookends of hypnosis. On the one side, researchers are skeptical of claims that hypnosis can enhance memory. On the other, they accept claims that hypnosis can help control pain. As you might imagine, other claims tend to fall somewhere in the middle of this bookshelf.

Hypnosis and Memory

5. Why are psychologists suspicious of hypnotically enhanced memories?

Many people believe that hypnosis is a good way to retrieve lost memories. The idea is that if memories can somehow become "lost," hypnosis may provide a way to retrieve them from the subconscious (a proposed storehouse for ideas and memories you cannot easily access) or wherever else they may be hiding. This idea has appeared in the media so often that a majority of college students agree that "under hypnosis a person [can] recall childhood events with very high accuracy" (Furnham, 1993). Some police departments have even used hypnosis to try to uncover details witnesses may have lost.

There *have* been instances when individuals recovered seemingly lost memories during hypnotic sessions. For example, Ed Ray, a bus driver who had been kidnapped and held captive with 26 children in 1977, was able, when hypnotized, to remember enough of the kidnappers' license plate to lead to an arrest.

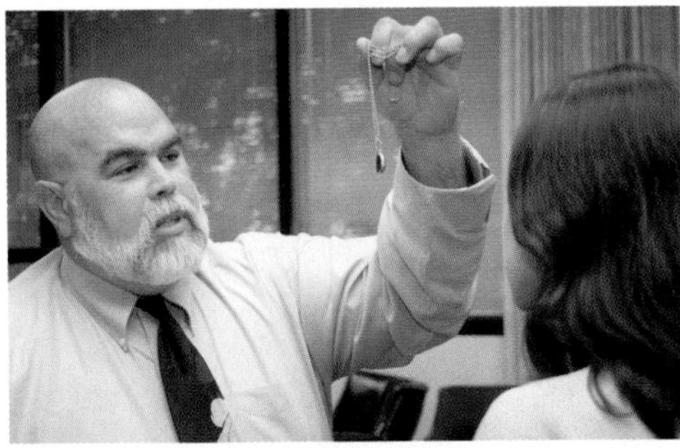

Hypnosis and Memory The use of hypnosis to retrieve memories is controversial. It is difficult to tell if this police hypnotist will help the witness accurately recall the details of a crime, or suggest details that the witness will later be unable to distinguish from reality.

Cooperative Learning

HYPNOSIS IN TELEVISION AND FILM Divide students into groups and have them use available resources, including the Internet, to research how hypnosis is portrayed in different types of movies and television shows. If possible, have them bring in clips to demonstrate their conclusions. The presentations should address the following questions:

- How do legal shows and movies portray hypnosis?
- How do comedic and cartoon shows and movies portray hypnosis?
- Does either type of media cite the drawbacks or limitations of hypnosis? What claims are made about what hypnosis is capable of providing?

■ **LOOKING AT THE ISSUES**

If the use of hypnosis during therapy yields much the same results as therapy without hypnosis, why is it still used? Discuss with students how the power of belief in something can be very effective. Cite the placebo effect as an example of this phenomenon.

■ **APPLYING THE POINTS**

Have students work individually or with partners to research any studies that have been done to show the effectiveness of hypnosis for different physical and psychological problems. For extra credit, students can write a report to showcase their findings. The report should address the following questions (which may also prompt a class discussion):

- How many studies exist?
- What does the research suggest are problems that can be helped by hypnosis?
- Do programs offered in classified ads (as shown in the photo on page 400 of the *Student Edition*) claim benefits beyond what the research suggests? How?

trb At this point, you may wish to use **Enrichment Lesson:** ***Is Hypnosis an Altered State of Consciousness?*** (***Teacher's Resource Binder***, p. 21-1).

■ **TEACHING TIP**

Link the concept of *lost or hidden memories* with *Freudian theory*. Sigmund Freud developed the idea that people repress difficult experiences from childhood in the subconscious (or unconscious), which must be brought to consciousness so the early experiences do not interfere with adult life. Hypnosis and dream interpretation were two ways in which Freud believed these experiences and memories could be revealed.

MODULE 21

■ **LOOKING AT THE ISSUES**

Some obstetricians have begun teaching their pregnant patients to self-hypnotize to alleviate the pain of labor. Some patients who have used self-hypnosis in this way report feeling no pain at all, without using drugs. Suggest students research the extent of the use of self-hypnosis for women going through labor. Have them address the following questions as they present their findings in oral reports:

- What techniques are important for success with self-hypnosis?
- Are the results just as likely to occur with relaxation techniques? Why or why not?
- How popular is the technique? Have there been any studies of its effectiveness?
- Are there concerns about the use of drugs during labor that would prompt women to choose hypnosis over drugs?
- Are there dangers with self-hypnosis? How does one come out of it? Are there liability issues or ethical obligations with doctors who advocate this practice?

V At this point, you may wish to show **Videocassette:** ***The Mind,*** **Second Edition, Module 2: "Hypnotic Dissociation and Pain Relief"** (*Teacher's Resource Binder,* p. 21-1).

■ **APPLYING THE POINTS**

Working in small groups, ask students to survey local dentists about whether they use hypnosis in their practices. To help groups compare findings, ask the following questions:

- How many use hypnosis? How do they use it?
- What results have they seen in using it?
- Do they use other methods of pain relief and relaxation? What methods do they use?
- What kind of training did they receive to be certified to use it? Is it part of or separate from dental school preparation?

V At this point, you may wish to show **Videocassette:** ***The Mind,*** **Second Edition, Module 2: "Hypnotic Dissociation and Pain Relief"** (*Teacher's Resource Binder,* p. 21-1).

However, we need to be cautious about generalizing from these specific cases. First, they are quite rare. Second, we cannot be sure that hypnosis was the reason for the retrieval—maybe the memory would have come back anyway. The most substantial problem is that hypnosis is a state of suggestibility. In an effort to please the hypnotist, the subject may inadvertently manufacture *untrue* details and then later be unable to distinguish the real from the unreal. This happens even without hypnosis, because your brain stores memories in pieces, much like a jigsaw puzzle. When you try to retrieve a memory, your brain may not be able to locate all the pieces, and then it fills in the "holes" with plausible events that could have occurred. When this happens, psychologists say that you have constructed a false memory. Hypnosis increases the likelihood of constructing false memories and may also give subjects a false sense of confidence in the accuracy of these "retrieved" memories (McConkey, 1992). Many courts now recognize the significant problems associated with using "hypnotically refreshed" memories and have banned testimony from witnesses who have been hypnotized (Druckman & Bjork, 1994; Gibson, 1995; McConkey, 1995).

Hypnosis and Pain Control

6. How can hypnosis help control pain?

For a clear success story about the use of hypnosis, look no further than pain control. Here there is solid evidence that hypnosis works. Holding your arm in ice water for a half-minute or so generally produces intense discomfort. If you don't believe it, fill your sink with ice water and try it! Hypnotized subjects, however, report little pain under the same circumstances (Druckman & Bjork, 1994; Kihlstrom, 1985). They are apparently able to separate themselves from the pain they are experiencing, much as an injured athlete may be able to set aside feelings of pain until after the competition ends.

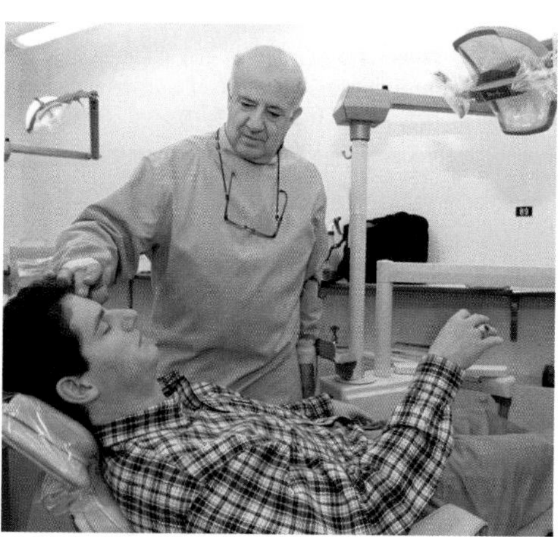

A Hypnotic Experience Some dentists use hypnosis to help patients deal with anxiety and discomfort during dental procedures.

These pain-management strategies have been applied to several real-life settings. For example, some dentists use light hypnosis to help their nervous patients relax and deal more effectively with discomfort. Hypnosis has also helped relieve chronic pain associated with arthritis, migraine headaches, and cancer (Hilgard, 1980; Long, 1986). These techniques may allow people to avoid painkilling drugs, which often have unwanted side effects, such as dependence and the loss of mental sharpness.

Demonstrating

ICY RELIEF Follow the author's suggestion on this page, and have a bucket of ice water handy for students to stick their hands in to see how much pain can be alleviated by hypnosis. Have students try to relax to see if that takes the pain away at all.

V At this point, you may wish to show **Videocassette:** ***The Mind,*** **Second Edition, Module 2: "Hypnotic Dissociation and Pain Relief"** (*Teacher's Resource Binder,* p. 21-1).

Other Hypnotic Claims

7. Why are researchers skeptical about other claims of hypnotic effects?

Hypnosis has been used in a wide variety of therapeutic settings in which subjects have experienced relief with problems ranging from headaches to warts (Bowers, 1984). The problem is that we have no way of knowing for sure that hypnosis caused these improvements. Many studies have shown that people who receive treatment of *any* kind (even sugar pills) tend to show more improvement than those who receive no treatment, thanks to the power of our positive expectations. This is called the *placebo effect.* Hypnosis may function as a type of placebo—producing an effect simply because people expect it to. For example, in the study in which hypnosis proved beneficial in getting rid of warts, a control group given positive suggestions *without* hypnosis showed similar improvement (Spanos, 1991).

Researchers are particularly skeptical of two types of claims for the power of hypnosis: feats of strength and age regression. A favorite claim of those who believe feats of strength can be achieved through hypnosis is to have someone stand on a subject who stretches rigid and planklike between two chairs. The problem is that this feat is also possible without hypnosis. *Age regression* under hypnosis is an attempt to turn back the clock to an earlier time in one's life. Psychologists consider this feat equally unreliable, and for the same reasons. Hypnotically enhanced memories are unreliable. The hypnotist's suggestions could lead the subject to unknowingly but falsely manufacture the regression to some earlier time. This happened in one study that tried to demonstrate how subjects could be regressed to the day of their fourth birthday party, at which point they could remember the day of the week with great accuracy (True, 1949). A follow-up analysis revealed that typical 4-year-olds don't know what day of the week it is. The hypnotist in this case was actually communicating the correct answer to his subjects by asking the days of the week in order ("Is it Monday? Is it Tuesday?") (Orne, 1982). Since the hypnotist knew the correct answer, he may have inadvertently signaled that answer to subjects with slight changes in the inflection of his voice. In any case, hypnotic age regression could not have led the subjects to the correct answer because, as 4-year-olds, they wouldn't have known it!

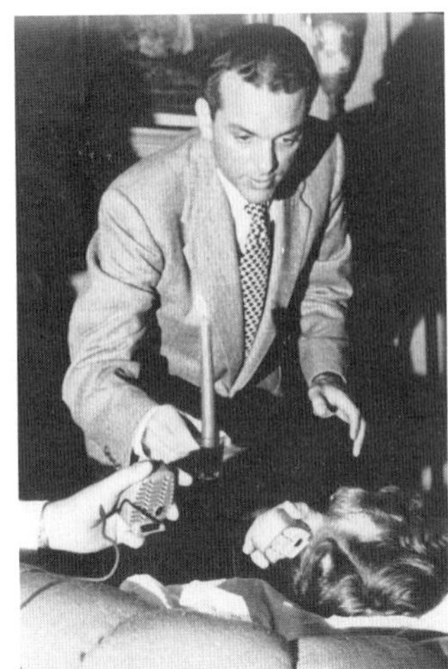

Age Regression? The case of Bridey Murphy took hypnotic age regression to a new level in the 1950s. Bridey is a young Irish woman who "appeared" when a hypnotist regressed his subject, Virginia Tighe, to before her birth, and Tighe began giving details of nineteenth-century life in Ireland. Is this evidence for reincarnation? Hardly. Investigators discovered that one of Virginia's childhood neighbors in Wisconsin was Bridey Murphy Corkell, who proved to be the source of much of the information Virginia reported when later hypnotized.

Hypnosis remains one of the more fascinating topics studied by psychologists. Researchers may disagree on the "best" theory for explaining hypnosis, but they agree on one thing: We can be influenced by suggestions. With that in mind, let me just leave you with the thought that things are going quite well today, you're enjoying your psychology class, and the time you spend studying will be effective and productive!

F•Y•I

As the author notes, hypnosis has also been used to regress people back to an earlier age to bring out certain painful childhood memories. Although people who are hypnotically "age regressed" appear to be a childlike version of themselves, they often exhibit qualities that suggest an adult version of a child's behavior. They will write with a childlike handwriting but will not make errors in spelling like children. Also, they will use adult vocabulary in describing and explaining the childhood memory. This type of behavior leads many researchers to believe that age regression is more playacting than reality.

■ MULTICULTURAL CONNECTIONS Is hypnosis as controversial in other cultures as it is in the United States? Using available print and Internet resources, have students explore the use of hypnosis as a means of therapy in different cultures. Ask students to focus their research on responses to the following questions, which you can use to prompt a full-class discussion:

- Do psychological and psychiatric associations in other countries advocate the use of hypnosis more strongly or less strongly than here in the United States? If so, why or why not?
- Do graduate schools in psychology offer courses in hypnosis? How many? How do these numbers compare with the number of graduate schools?

Close

Have students discuss the following questions about hypnosis:

- Do you now question the validity and helpfulness of hypnosis? Why or why not?
- How does knowing about the power of suggestion make you feel about your ability to be influenced by suggestions?
- If you were asked to be hypnotized for either entertainment or therapeutic purposes, would you accept? Why or why not?

Cooperative Learning

DISSOCIATIVE IDENTITY DISORDER LEGITIMACY The problems of hypnotic suggestion have called into question the diagnosis of dissociative identity disorder (DID), formerly known as multiple personality disorder. Working in groups, have students research criticism against DID as a legitimate psychological disorder and come up with group responses to the following questions:

- Why has DID come into question? What are some arguments for and against its legitimacy?
- What role does hypnosis play in this debate?
- What position has the American Psychiatric Association taken on this disorder? Is it still included in the current version of the *Diagnostic and Statistical Manual of Mental Disorders?* Why or why not?

trb At this point, you may wish to use **Enrichment Lesson:** *Is Hypnosis an Altered State of Consciousness?* (*Teacher's Resource Binder*, p. 21-1).

MODULE 21

Checking the Points

■ TEACHING TIPS

web (1) The book companion site for *Thinking About Psychology* at **www.worthpublishers.com/thinkingaboutpsych** contains a module quiz, flashcards of key terms and people, and other student activities and resources for this module. You will also find PowerPoint lectures, a quiz grade book, and other teaching resources by logging on as an instructor.

trb (2) At this point, you may wish to review concepts about hypnosis with **Critical Thinking Activity:** *Fact or Falsehood?* (*Teacher's Resource Binder*, p. 21-1; **Handout 21–1**) If students completed this handout earlier, ask them not to refer to earlier versions. Have a volunteer read the first item and provide a response. Ask students who agree with the response to find a passage in the text that supports it and read it aloud. If students contest the response, have them use the text to find a passage that supports their answer and read it aloud. Once consensus is found, repeat the process with the next item on the handout.

REVIEW

Module 21: Hypnosis

What's the Point?

What Is Hypnosis?

Hypnosis is a social interaction in which one person (the hypnotist) makes suggestions—about perceptions, feelings, thoughts, and behaviors—that another person (the subject) carries out.

1. *How does social influence theory explain why subjects carry out a hypnotist's suggestions?*

   Social influence theory maintains that hypnosis is not a special physiological condition, but rather an extreme case of social influence. Social influence operates in many parts of our life, including the influence of peer pressure. Those who explain hypnosis using this theory do not imply that the hypnotist or the subject is faking the behavior. Instead, they propose that the hypnotist's status and authority influence the subject—who wants to please the hypnotist—to unknowingly follow the suggestions. In this view, hypnosis is a result of external variables.

2. *How does divided consciousness theory explain why subjects carry out a hypnotist's suggestions?*

   Divided consciousness theory maintains that hypnosis is a state of divided consciousness, in which one part of the mind is unaware of the roles played by the other parts. In this view, hypnosis is a result of a special exaggerated division of one's internal consciousness.

Hypnotic Techniques

Hypnotic induction is the process in which a hypnotist creates a state of hypnosis in a subject, generally by voicing a series of suggestions. The secret is a calm rhythmic tone that invites relaxation, a suggestion most people find easy to follow. People are more or less susceptible to hypnosis, and the Stanford Hypnotic Susceptibility Scale tests these tendencies.

3. *Can hypnosis make us do things we otherwise would not do?*

   In some experiments, people have done things (such as throwing a liquid they thought was acid at others) that they would probably not have done outside of hypnosis. The difficulty comes in explaining why these events happened, because nonhypnotized subjects asked to perform the same behaviors also obeyed. Hypnosis alone does not seem to cause these behaviors; rather, powerful suggestions may be able to influence us in this way.

4. *What are posthypnotic suggestions, and could they help us to lose weight or stop smoking?*

   A posthypnotic suggestion is a suggestion planted during hypnosis, to be carried out after the hypnotic session has ended—usually triggered by some cue the hypnotist plants during hypnosis. Some research indicates that people—those with low hypnotic susceptibility as well as those with high susceptibility—do carry out such suggestions. But again, people enrolled in programs that encourage cessation of smoking but do not use hypnosis tend to fare just as well as those who receive posthypnotic suggestions that cigarettes will taste foul or make them sick.

Applications of Hypnosis

5. *Why are psychologists suspicious of hypnotically enhanced memories?*

   Instances of memories accurately retrieved under hypnosis are rare. Because hypnosis is a state of suggestibility, the subject may unknowingly construct false memories to please the hypnotist. Although these memories are false, the subject will believe they are real once they have been constructed. Most courts now ban testimony obtained under hypnosis.

6. *How can hypnosis help control pain?*

   Hypnosis does help control pain, apparently because the person experiencing the pain is able to disconnect from it. Many health-care professionals use hypnosis to help relieve chronic pain and to avoid the use of pain-killing drugs and their side effects.

7. *Why are researchers skeptical about other claims of hypnotic effects?*

   Hypnotists have made some extreme claims, such as their ability to "regress" a person to a previous life in an earlier historical period, or the ability to cause others to perform amazing feats of strength. Psychologists are skeptical of such claims because there is no evidence supporting age regression, and the evidence for feats of strength can be duplicated by simply suggesting to unhypnotized people that they are capable of these acts.

Key Terms

hypnosis, p. 396
social influence theory, p. 397
divided consciousness theory, p. 397
hypnotic induction, p. 398
posthypnotic suggestion, p. 400
posthypnotic amnesia, p. 401

Key People

Ernest Hilgard, p. 398

Self-Test

Multiple-Choice Questions

Choose the best answer for each of the following questions.

1. Nita has just finished watching a TV program about a young woman with a rare form of brain cancer. After hearing the young woman, her family, and her doctors discuss the symptoms of the disease, Nita decided she, too, has this rare form of cancer. She says she can feel the tumor growing in her brain, although she had no such symptoms before watching the program. Nita's belief that she is seriously ill is an example of the kind of suggestibility that supporters of the ____________ ____________ theory of hypnosis often cite.

   a. hypnotic induction
   b. placebo effect
   c. social influence
   d. divided consciousness

2. Joey pedaled to school on his bike today, weaving in and out of traffic in the school driveway and passing groups of students on their way to the entrance. He did this without thinking much about any of the people or events in his surroundings; instead, he was thinking about some formulas he expected to find on his chemistry quiz this morning. Joey's ability to ride his bike and prepare for his quiz is an example of the kind of split attention that proponents of the ____________ ____________ theory of hypnosis often cite.

MODULE 21

trb tr ■ TEACHING TIP

Building Vocabulary: Graphic Organizer: *Concept Web* (*Teacher's Resource Binder*, p. 21-1; **Handout 21–2**) provides a good review of module vocabulary. Students can study a completed concept web they filled out earlier in the module. Otherwise, you may wish to project the concept web (using the handout as a transparency) and review the module vocabulary with the entire class.

tb Using the Test Bank

The *Test Bank* that accompanies this textbook offers a wide variety of questions in different formats and levels of complexity. Use the software to construct whole tests or to integrate standardized questions into teacher-made tests.

Self-Test Answers

Multiple-Choice Questions

1. c, 2. d

Meeting Individual Needs

Help students overwhelmed by the terms in this module by having them make flashcards of the vocabulary. One side of each flashcard should identify an aspect of hypnosis, while the other side should provide its definition.

- **Independent Learners** To help students link the terms with hypnosis, have them categorize the flashcard terms by topics presented in the text.
- **Cooperative Learners** Have students work in small groups to categorize flashcard terms by topics. Then, have the groups use their flashcard categories to create their own graphic organizer about hypnosis. Groups may present and explain their graphic organizers to the entire class.

MODULE 21

Self-Test Answers

Multiple-Choice Questions (continued)

3. b, 4. c, 5. a

Matching Terms and Definitions

6. a. (4), b. (2), c. (7), d. (5), e. (3), f. (6)

a. hypnotic induction
b. placebo effect
c. social influence
d. divided consciousness

3. Todd attended a postprom party last night, where a hypnotist performed. Today, Todd is behaving strangely. Every time someone says "Todd," he begins to quack like a duck. Apparently the hypnotist gave Todd a
   a. hypnotically refreshed memory.
   b. posthypnotic suggestion.
   c. manufactured memory.
   d. test using the Stanford Hypnotic Susceptibility Scale.

4. Tania and Kasey are attempting to stop smoking cigarettes. Tania has enrolled in a program that uses posthypnotic suggestions (that cigarettes will taste like rotten meat) to discourage smoking. Kasey has also enrolled in a program to help her stop smoking, but it does not include any form of hypnosis. Which girl has the better chance of stopping her smoking?
   a. Tania; research shows that posthypnotic suggestions are the most effective way to break the smoking habit.
   b. Kasey; research shows that programs that do not use hypnosis are more effective in breaking the smoking habit.
   c. Their chances are about equal; research indicates that people show about as much improvement in programs that use hypnosis as in those that do not use hypnosis.
   d. Neither Tania nor Kasey. Smoking is an individual problem, and programs cannot help one to break the habit.

5. Studies of the use of hypnosis to control pain have shown that hypnosis
   a. is an effective pain-management strategy.
   b. reduces pain a little, but not enough to justify its use.
   c. does nothing to control pain.
   d. may actually worsen pain.

Matching Terms and Definitions

6. For each definition, choose the best matching term from the list that follows:

Definition

a. A suggestion, made during a hypnosis session, that the subject will carry out when no longer hypnotized.
b. The theory that, during hypnosis, our awareness of ourselves and others splits, so that one aspect of our mind is not aware of the role other parts are playing.
c. A person who makes suggestions about perceptions, feelings, thoughts, or behaviors that another person will carry out.
d. The supposed inability to remember what happened during hypnosis because the hypnotist has suggested that the subject will have no memory of that period of time.
e. The process in which a hypnotist creates a state of hypnosis in a subject, generally by voicing a series of suggestions.
f. An effect that occurs because we expect it to occur; for example, feeling relief from a headache after being given a pill that we believe will be effective but that in reality contains only sugar.

Term

(1) social influence theory
(2) divided consciousness theory
(3) hypnotic induction
(4) posthypnotic suggestion
(5) posthypnotic amnesia
(6) placebo effect
(7) hypnotist
(8) subject

Fill-in-the-Blank Questions

7. Ernest Hilgard researched hypnosis and was an advocate of the ________ __________ theory of hypnosis.

8. Critics of Hilgard's theory of hypnosis proposed the __________ __________ theory, the idea that powerful social effects can produce a state of hypnosis.

Brief Essay Question

9. It's four years from today, and you were lucky enough to be admitted to the class of a famous defense lawyer. Each term, this lawyer has his students review the trials of two people waiting to be executed for murder. Your job is to participate in a decision about whether the person received a fair trial. In reading the records of one trial, you notice that the prosecution's main witness had been placed under hypnosis to "refresh" her memory of the crime. In two paragraphs of about three sentences each, explain how many courts now view testimony based on "hypnotically refreshed" memories, and state some of the evidence from psychology that led to those views.

MODULE 21

Self-Test Answers

Fill-in-the-Blank Questions

7. divided consciousness, 8. social influence

Brief Essay Question

9. Students should discuss the limitations that psychologists feel exist with hypnosis. Although psychologists find hypnosis can benefit pain sufferers and some addicts, it is not reliable or valid to support age regression or refreshed memories.

MODULE 22

Performance Standards

Standard Area: States of Consciousness

Content Standard 4: Psychoactive drugs and their psychological and physiological effects

Performance Standard 4.1 Classify the major psychoactive drugs and their effects.

- Define psychoactive drugs and the concept of dependence. (Student Text pp. 408–409)
- Discuss the five main drug categories and why some drugs defy their categories. (Student Text p. 410)
- Table 22.2, "A Guide to Selected Psychoactive Drugs," summarizes the various drugs (example: alcohol), their type (depressant), pleasurable effects ("initial high"), and adverse effects ("depression"). (Student Text p. 423)

Depressants

- Examine the physiological and psychological effects of alcohol. (Student Text pp. 412–414)
- Define "sedatives" and discuss when they are prescribed. Discuss some of the dangers of barbiturate use. (Student Text pp. 414–415)

Opiates

- Define "opiates." Discuss why opiates are so addictive. (Student Text p. 415)
- Compare opiates to endorphins. (Student Text p. 415)
- Discuss the physiological effects of morphine and heroin. Examine the dangers of opiate use. (Student Text pp. 415–416)

Stimulants

- Discuss the effects of stimulants. Examine which stimulants are considered most dangerous. (Student Text pp. 416-419)
- Discuss the physiological and psychological effects of caffeine, nicotine, cocaine, and amphetamines. Examine the dangers of stimulant use. (Student Text pp. 416–419)

Hallucinogens

- Define "hallucinogens." Discuss what dangers they pose to users. (Student Text pp. 419–420)
- Discuss the physiological and psychological effects of LSD and ecstasy. (Student Text p. 420)

Marijuana

- Compare and contrast marijuana with the other drugs discussed in Module 22. (Student Text p. 421)
- Discuss the physiological and psychological effects of marijuana use. (Student Text pp. 421–422)

Performance Standard 4.2 Evaluate the effects of psychoactive drug use.

- Define psychoactive drugs and the concept of dependence. (Student Text p. 408)
- Table 22.2, "A Guide to Selected Psychoactive Drugs," summarizes the various drugs (example: alcohol), their type (depressant), pleasurable effects ("initial high"), and adverse effects ("depression"). (Student Text p. 423)
- Examine the physiological and psychological effects of alcohol. (Student Text pp. 412–414)
- Discuss some of the dangers of barbiturate use. (Student Text pp. 414-415)
- Examine the dangers of opiate use. (Student Text pp. 415–416)
- Discuss the physiological and psychological effects of caffeine, nicotine, cocaine, and amphetamines. Examine the dangers of stimulant use. (Student Text pp. 416–419)
- Discuss the physiological and psychological effects of LSD and ecstasy. (Student Text p. 420)
- Discuss the physiological and psychological effects of marijuana use. (Student Text p. 421–422)

Materials NETWORK

All of the items from the Video, Activity, and Enrichment Centers listed below come from the *Teacher's Resource Binder.* These items will help you teach and expand on concepts presented in Module 22.

trb This logo indicates when an item from the Materials Network may be used in conjunction with a specific note found in this module's *Teacher's Edition.*

Psychoactivity and Dependence

Activity Center

- Critical Thinking Activity: *Fact or Falsehood?* With this activity, students' preconceptions about drugs are either exposed as incorrect or reinforced as correct. (*Teacher's Resource Binder*, p. 22-1; Handout 22–1)
- Building Vocabulary: *Crossword Puzzle* Students can learn the concepts in the module by completing this crossword puzzle. (*Teacher's Resource Binder*, p. 22-1; Handout 22–2)
- Analysis Activity: *Signs of Drug Abuse* This activity presents two brief surveys. (*Teacher's Resource Binder*, p. 22-1; Handout 22–3)
- Analysis Activity: *The Internet Addiction Test* This survey will help students analyze whether Internet addiction falls into the same category as drug addiction. (*Teacher's Resource Binder*, p. 22-1; Handout 22–4)

Enrichment Center

- Enrichment Lesson: *Factors in Drug Abuse* This lesson enumerates some factors that enhance a person's likelihood of becoming addicted. (*Teacher's Resource Binder*, p. 22-1)

Drugs and Neurotransmission

Activity Center

- Technology Application Activity: *PsychQuest:* "How Do Psychoactive Drugs Affect Us?" *PsychQuest* is an interactive CD-ROM that students can use to learn more about various topics in psychology. (*Teacher's Resource Binder*, p. 22-1)

Drug Classifications

V Video Center

Consult the faculty guide from *The Mind* video series for descriptions of these modules.

- Videocassette: *The Mind,* Second Edition, Module 22: "Depressants and Their Addictive Effects on the Brain" (*Teacher's Resource Binder*, p. 22-1)
- Videocassette: *The Mind,* Second Edition, Module 29: "Alcohol Addiction: Hereditary Factors" (*Teacher's Resource Binder*, p. 22-1)

Activity Center

- Cooperative Learning Activity: *Blood Alcohol Concentrations* Students can explore the blood alcohol concentrations in both men and women. (*Teacher's Resource Binder*, p. 22-1; Handouts 22–5 and 22–6)

Enrichment Center

- Enrichment Lesson: *Alcohol Consumption Among College Students* This eye-opening lesson presents survey results of college students about their alcohol consumption. (*Teacher's Resource Binder*, p. 22-1)
- Enrichment Lesson: *Rohypnol—A Date Rape Drug* This lesson explores the drug. (*Teacher's Resource Binder*, p. 22-1)
- Enrichment Lesson: *Wonder Drugs—Aspirin and Heroin* Bayer pharmaceutical company developed these two drugs in the 1800s. (*Teacher's Resource Binder*, p. 22-1)
- Enrichment Lesson: *Caffeine—Is It Harmful?* This lesson enlightens students about the effects of caffeine on their health. (*Teacher's Resource Binder*, p. 22-1)
- Enrichment Lesson: *The LSD Experience* This drug's dangerous properties and effects on people are outlined in this lesson. (*Teacher's Resource Binder*, p. 22-1)
- Enrichment Lesson: *Is Marijuana Good Medicine?* This lesson will help clarify what marijuana can and cannot do for people who are sick. (*Teacher's Resource Binder*, p. 22-1)

Prevention

V Video Center

- Videocassette: *The Mind,* Second Edition, Module 30: "Treating Drug Addiction: A Behavioral Approach" Consult the faculty guide from *The Mind* video series for a description of this module. (*Teacher's Resource Binder*, p. 22-1)

Activity Center

- Application Activity: *Eyescube Drug Simulation* This activity helps students experience firsthand the complicated lifestyle of drug users. (*Teacher's Resource Binder*, p. 22-1; Handout 22–7)

MODULE 22

Drugs

Introducing the Module

The Points: Module Objectives

- Describe a psychoactive drug.
- Explain how psychoactive drugs work.
- Identify the five main drug categories, and analyze why some drugs defy their categories.
- Describe the physiological and psychological effects of drinking alcohol, as well as what sedatives are and when they are prescribed.
- Identify opiates, and explain why they are so addictive.
- Explain the effects of stimulants, and identify which are considered most dangerous.
- Identify hallucinogens, and describe the dangers they pose to users.
- Distinguish the similarities and differences between marijuana and other drugs discussed in this module.
- Evaluate ways to prevent the use of dangerous psychoactive drugs.

trb tr Building Vocabulary

Have students complete **Building Vocabulary:** *Crossword Puzzle* (*Teacher's Resource Binder*, p. 22-1; **Handout** 22–2) to interact with the definitions and terms for the concepts in the module. Students can work on the puzzles with partners, or you can use the handout as a transparency if you prefer to work on the puzzle with the entire class.

Teaching the Points

web ■ TEACHING TIP

You can log on as an instructor to the book companion site for *Thinking About Psychology* at **www.worthpublishers.com/thinkingaboutpsych**. It contains teacher resources for class presentations as well as review and assessment of module concepts and terms.

MODULE 22

Drugs

Psychoactivity and Dependence

What's the Point? 1. What is a psychoactive drug?

Most adults and young adults in this country regularly take **psychoactive drugs,** substances that affect mood, behavior, or perceptions. Surprised? If so, perhaps you don't associate the phrase "psychoactive drug" with the three most commonly used psychoactive substances: caffeine, alcohol, and nicotine. These everyday chemical substances are drugs, and, as such, they can induce an *altered state of consciousness.* They also can lead to **dependence**—a state of *physiological or psychological need* for a drug. Notice that I said *dependence,* not *addiction.* The concept of addiction, which has been applied freely to so many social behaviors, has lost much of its meaning. Addicted to love? Addicted to television? Addicted to popcorn? Actually, true addictions seriously disrupt a person's ability to function in everyday life. Gambling and Internet use can sometimes fit this description, but very few other behaviors do. For our purposes in this module, I'll use the term *dependence* instead of *addiction* to discuss psychoactive drugs.

► **psychoactive drug** A chemical substance that alters perceptions, mood, or behavior.

► **dependence** A state of physiological and/or psychological need to take more of a substance after continued use. Withdrawal follows if the drug is discontinued.

"Just tell me where you kids get the idea to take so many drugs."

Getting Started

Have students list the drugs that they believe are problems among people their age. Allow time for them to brainstorm reasons why people choose to use drugs in the first place, as well as factors in life that lead some to become drug addicts.

trb You also may wish to use **Critical Thinking Activity:** *Fact or Falsehood?* (*Teacher's Resource Binder*, p. 22-1; **Handout 22–1**) as a prereading strategy to find out what students already know about drugs. The activity, along with its results, will prime students to note terms and concepts in the text that confirm or dispel their preconceptions about drugs.

Dependence is accompanied by symptoms of **withdrawal** when a user is deprived of that drug. You may experience this yourself if you normally drink a few cans of caffeinated cola daily and then go on a weekend camping trip where no soda is available. If you experience grogginess, get a headache, and "miss" your cola, you are demonstrating caffeine dependence.

Withdrawal symptoms often resemble the opposite of a psychoactive drug's intended effect. For a heroin user, this means that the brief, drug-induced episodes of euphoria, relaxation, and slowed breathing will give way to prolonged depression, restlessness, and abnormally rapid breathing after the drug wears off (Feldman & others, 1997). Withdrawal is even worse in those with a long history of drug use. Regular drug use leads to **tolerance,** a reduced response to the drug, which prompts the user to take larger doses to achieve the same pleasurable effects (Figure 22.1). So, for example, a new drinker may get a "buzz" from one beer, but after drinking regularly over a period of weeks, the person will develop a tolerance for alcohol and may require two or three beers to achieve that same feeling. With this increased intake, the person's body must struggle to clean out the increased toxins and cope with the rising blood alcohol level. You'll read more about the effects of alcohol in a few pages.

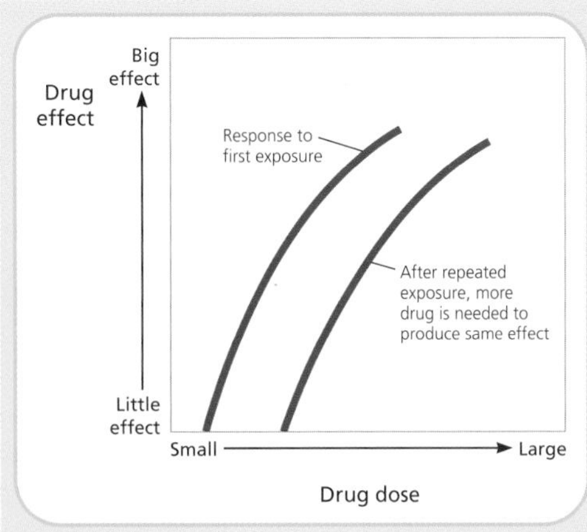

Figure 22.1 **Tolerance** The initial effect of a psychoactive drug is not the same as the effect that occurs with repeated use. As the user's body develops tolerance to the drug, larger and larger amounts will be needed to achieve the same effect.

Drugs and Neurotransmission

 2. How do psychoactive drugs work?

You probably didn't expect to read about biochemistry when you registered to take psychology. In fact, every memory, thought, and behavior you've ever had has resulted from biochemical interactions between **neurons** (or nerve cells) in your brain and spinal cord, which together make up your **central nervous system (CNS).** Neurons communicate through a process called *neurotransmission.*

So what does all this have to do with psychoactive drug use? A lot. Without neurotransmission, none of your behaviors or thought processes would be possible. And psychoactive drugs interfere with *normal* neurotransmission. To understand how they do this, we need to know more about how neurons and psychoactive drugs each work.

The 90 billion or so neurons in your CNS control everything from breathing and sensing pain to understanding sensory input from your eyes and nose. Neurons communicate with one another through

▶ **withdrawal** The discomfort and distress that follow when a person who is dependent on a drug discontinues the use of that drug.

▶ **tolerance** Reduced responsiveness to a drug, prompting the user to increase dosage to achieve effects previously obtained by lower doses.

▶ **neuron** A nerve cell; the basic building block of the nervous system.

▶ **central nervous system (CNS)** The brain and spinal cord.

Suggested Readings

Use the following books as teacher-preparation tools or as enrichment for advanced students:

Bachman, J. (1997). *Smoking, drinking, and drug use in young adulthood: The impact of new freedoms and new responsibilities.* Mahwah, NJ: Erlbaum.

Carroll, C. (1996). *Drugs in modern society* (4th ed.). Madison, WI: Brown & Benchmark.

Insel, P., & Roth, W. (1998). *Core concepts in health* (8th ed.). Mountain View, CA: Mayfield.

Wallace, B., & Fisher, L. (1991). *Consciousness and behavior* (3rd ed.). Boston: Allyn & Bacon.

Young, K. S. (1998). *Caught in the net: How to recognize the signs of Internet addiction and a winning strategy for recovery.* New York: Wiley.

■ TEACHING TIPS

tr (1) A four-color transparency of Figure 22.1, Tolerance, is available in the Overhead Transparencies Set.

(2) Drug use can be a difficult topic to discuss since the social stigma of drug use is so profound. If students are using drugs illegally, then they or their parents may be in denial about their problem, or their parents may be unaware of the problem. In discussing drug use and addiction, be sensitive about accusing anyone of being a drug user, but be open to privately discussing any personal concerns students may have about their own problems or those of family and friends.

(3) If a student approaches you about problems with drugs, help him or her understand your obligations as a teacher. Although you can assure the student a certain level of confidentiality, you may be obligated to report behaviors that you feel may cause the student or someone the student cares about personal harm to a guidance counselor, school psychologist, and/or parent. Inform the student, up front, that you will do everything in your power to help but that, for his or her safety, that may involve other, more qualified people.

trb At this point, you may wish to use Analysis Activity: *Signs of Drug Abuse* (*Teacher's Resource Binder,* p. 22-1; Handout 22–3).

■ CHECKING FOR UNDERSTANDING

To evaluate students' understanding, have them discuss the possible physical and psychological effects of withdrawal and tolerance. *(Withdrawal involves physical symptoms that are typically opposite to the drug's effects. Tolerance leads to greater dependence on a particular drug since it must be taken with increasing amounts and frequency. Overdose is common with drugs that produce tolerance since the user must take more and more of the drug to get an effect.)*

trb At this point, you may wish to use Analysis Activity: *The Internet Addiction Test* (*Teacher's Resource Binder,* p. 22-1; Handout 22–4).

MODULE 22

■ **TEACHING TIP**

Link the discussion of *drugs and neurotransmission* to the discussion of *agonists and antagonists* in Module 7.

- Drugs that mimic a neurotransmitter's function are known as **agonists**.
- Drugs that nullify a neurotransmitter's function are called **antagonists**.

trb At this point, you may wish to use **Technology Application Activity:** *PsychQuest:* **"How Do Drugs Affect Us?"** (*Teacher's Resource Binder,* p. 22-1).

F•Y•I

Drugs can have such an effect on the body because they are chemically similar to the brain's natural neurotransmitters. Some commonly known drugs and the neurotransmitters they are similar to are as follows:

- Cocaine is chemically similar to dopamine.
- LSD is chemically similar to serotonin.
- Opiates, like morphine, are chemically similar to endorphins. The name *endorphins* is a combination of the neurotransmitter's technical name *endogenous morphines. Endogenous* means "naturally occurring."

■ **APPLYING THE POINTS**

If possible, have volunteers contact a medical professional who specializes in brain chemistry to ask how common drugs work in the brain. Suggest that students ask the following questions of the specialist:

- What specific kinds of drugs act to bind with receptor sites?
- What specific kinds of drugs act to block a neurotransmitter's release?
- What specific kinds of drugs act to block neurotransmitter reabsorption?

Students who have gathered this information may convey their findings in a brief oral report.

▶ **neurotransmitter** Chemical messengers that cross synaptic gaps between neurons. When released by the sending neuron, neurotransmitters travel across the synapse and bind to receptor sites on the receiving neuron, setting up the next link in the chain of communication.

▶ **synapse** The junction between the tip of the sending neuron and the receptor sites on the receiving neuron. The tiny gap at this junction is called the synaptic *gap* or *cleft.*

chemical messengers called **neurotransmitters,** which are released from one neuron to the next. All bodily messages—the sleepiness that pulls your eyelids closed at midnight or the pain you feel when you step on a piece of broken glass—pass from one neuron to the next in this way. In each case, a neuron releases neurotransmitters into the **synapse** (SIH-naps), or gap, separating the sending neuron from a neighboring neuron. The neurotransmitter moves across the synapse and binds to a *receptor site* on the neighboring neuron. Once the chemical messenger binds with the receptor site, the message is "received" and your body responds accordingly. The neurotransmitter does not stay bound to the receptor indefinitely. The chemical is either broken down and washed away, or more likely, *reabsorbed* by the neuron that sent it into the synapse. This reabsorption allows the same neuron to release its neurotransmitter.

Psychoactive drugs get into your synapses and affect neurotransmission in three different ways (Figure 22.2):

1. *Binding with receptors (mimicking a neurotransmitter's effects),* which causes neurons to fire in the absence of normal stimulation.
2. *Blocking receptor sites (preventing neurotransmitters from binding),* and thereby not allowing neurotransmission to occur.
3. *Blocking neurotransmitter reabsorption* thereby intensifying the neurotransmitter's effects in the synapse.

Psychoactive drugs often bind *better* and stay attached to receptors *longer* than normal neurotransmitters do, intensifying the drug's impact on bodily processes.

Now that you understand the three main ways that psychoactive drugs can interfere with normal patterns of neurotransmission, let's look at some specific classes of drugs and how they work.

Drug Classifications

3. What are the five main drug categories, and why do some drugs defy their categories?

We'll study five different categories of psychoactive drugs: *depressants, opiates, stimulants, hallucinogens,* and *marijuana.*

Most discussions of drugs and their effects use these five categories, but the drug-taker's *expectations* and *mood* can cause some drugs to jump outside the boundaries of any one classification. For example, alcohol is a depressant, but it can have a wildly stimulating effect on a drinker who expects to feel stimulated, such as a highly excited fan celebrating a winning basketball team after the state tournament.

Cross-Curricular Connections

GOVERNMENT Have students participate in either an informal or formal debate about the legalization of illegal drugs. To prepare for the debate, allow time for students to research the following questions, using Internet or print resources:

- What laws currently exist regarding illegal drugs?
- What possible societal and psychological effects would result if currently illegal drugs were legalized?
- What can the government do now to encourage more people not to use drugs?

trb At this point, you may wish to use **Enrichment Lesson:** *Is Marijuana Good Medicine?* (*Teacher's Resource Binder,* p. 22-1).

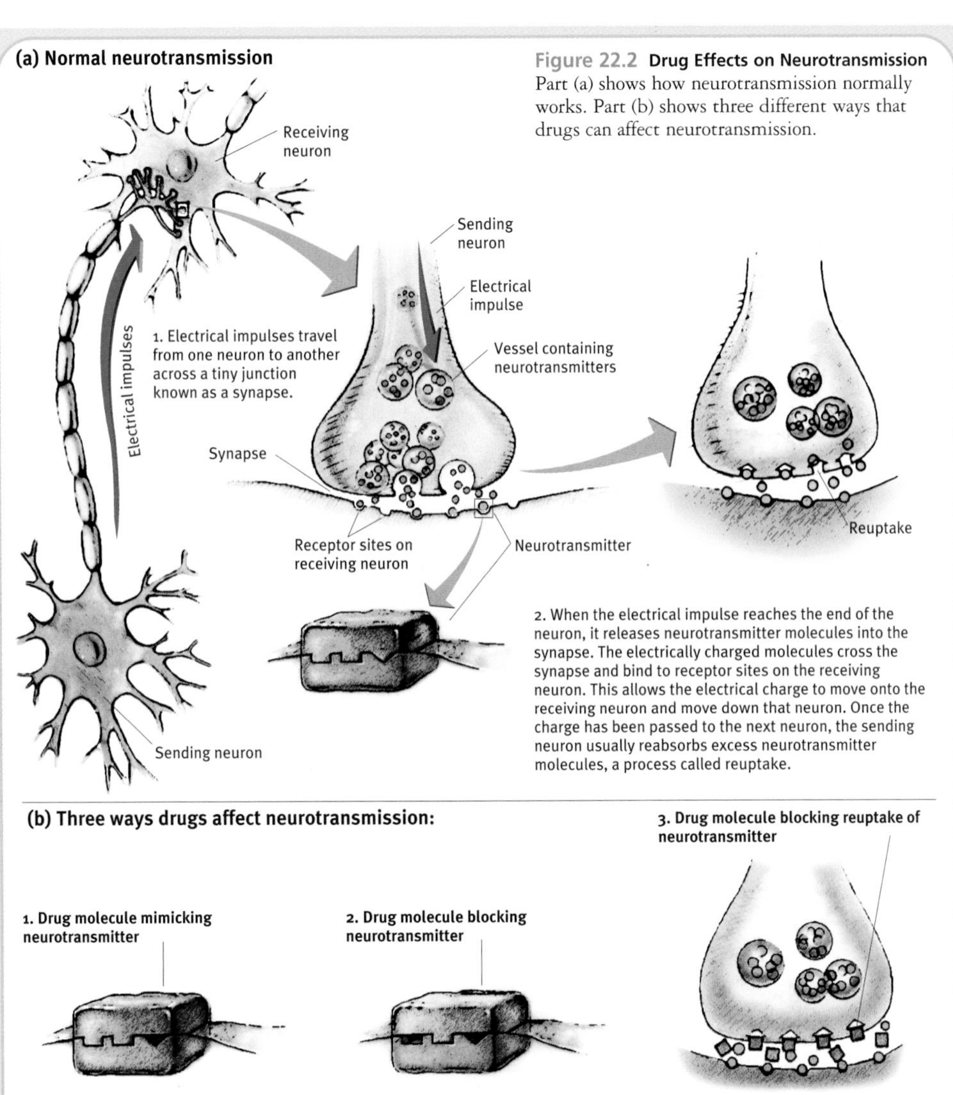

(a) Normal neurotransmission
Receiving neuron
Sending neuron
Electrical impulse
Electrical impulses
1. Electrical impulses travel from one neuron to another across a tiny junction known as a synapse.
Vessel containing neurotransmitters
Synapse
Receptor sites on receiving neuron
Neurotransmitter
Reuptake
Sending neuron
2. When the electrical impulse reaches the end of the neuron, it releases neurotransmitter molecules into the synapse. The electrically charged molecules cross the synapse and bind to receptor sites on the receiving neuron. This allows the electrical charge to move onto the receiving neuron and move down that neuron. Once the charge has been passed to the next neuron, the sending neuron usually reabsorbs excess neurotransmitter molecules, a process called reuptake.
(b) Three ways drugs affect neurotransmission:
1. Drug molecule mimicking neurotransmitter
2. Drug molecule blocking neurotransmitter
3. Drug molecule blocking reuptake of neurotransmitter
This drug molecule is similar enough in structure to a neurotransmitter that it mimics the electrically charging effects a neurotransmitter usually has on a receiving neuron. Morphine, for instance, mimics the action of our body's natural endorphins by stimulating neurons in brain areas involved in mood and pain sensations.
This drug molecule has a structure similar enough to a neurotransmitter to occupy the receptor site and block its action, but not similar enough to continue the electrical charge down the receiving neuron. Botulin poisoning paralyzes its victims by blocking receptors involved in muscle movement.
This drug molecule binds to the sites that normally reabsorb neurotransmitter molecules, thus blocking reuptake. Cocaine blocks reuptake of three neurotransmitters that affect mood. The extra neurotransmitter molecules remain in the synapse, intensifying their normal mood-altering effects. When the cocaine level drops, the absence of these neurotransmitters produces a crash.

Figure 22.2 Drug Effects on Neurotransmission Part (a) shows how neurotransmission normally works. Part (b) shows three different ways that drugs can affect neurotransmission.

MODULE 22

■ TEACHING TIPS

(1) Link the description of *neural transmission* with the information presented in Module 7. Review for students the parts of the neuron, the role of neurotransmitters in behavior, and how action potentials work.

 (2) Four-color transparencies of Figures 22.2a and 22.2b, Drug Effects on Neurotransmission, are available in the **Overhead Transparencies Set.**

tr ■ **CHECKING FOR UNDERSTANDING**

Show the transparency of Figure 22.2 with some of the key terms and processes blocked out. Orally quiz students about the parts and processes to determine how well they understand drug effects on neurotransmission.

F • Y • I

web Many antidepressants are classified as selective serotonin reuptake inhibitors (SSRIs). These drugs block the reabsorption of serotonin so that serotonin remains in the synapse longer. These drugs are used to treat depression, bulimia nervosa, obsessive-compulsive disorder, anorexia nervosa, and panic disorder. Learn more about any of the following SSRIs by visiting their respective Web sites:

- Prozac: **www.prozac.com**
- Zoloft: **www.zoloft.com**
- Celexa: **www.celexa.com**
- Luvox: **www.solvaypharmaceuticals-us.com/Products/Mental_Health/LUVOX/default.asp**
- Paxil: **www.paxil.com**

V At this point, you may wish to show **Videocassette: *The Mind,* Second Edition, Module 22: "Depressants and Their Addictive Effects on the Brain"** (*Teacher's Resource Binder*, p. 22-1).

MODULE 22

■ **LOOKING AT THE ISSUES**

In small groups, have students explore the following questions related to alcohol consumption:

- Are current laws that regulate alcohol sale and consumption effective? Why or why not? What laws or enforcement techniques should be enacted to have an effect?
- Should there be different blood alcohol limits for men and women, considering how the drug affects each sex differently? Why or why not?
- What are some of the health benefits of alcohol consumption for adults? What recommendations do doctors give for healthful alcohol consumption by adults?

V At this point, you may wish to show **Videocassette:** ***The Mind,*** **Second Edition, Module 20: "Alcohol Addiction: Hereditary Factors"** (*Teacher's Resource Binder,* p. 22-1).

■ **JOURNAL WRITING**

Invite students to use the following questions and writing prompts as a springboard for an entry in their psychology journals:

- Has your life been affected by the misuse of alcohol? How has it been affected?
- Do you feel the law goes far enough to combat teen alcohol use and abuse? Why or why not?

■ **APPLYING THE POINTS**

Invite a member of the local police department to class. Ask the guest to discuss the following questions:

- What legal procedures must be followed if intoxication is suspected?
- What tests are used to determine if someone is intoxicated?
- What punishments exist for people who are found to be intoxicated?

trb At this point, you may wish to use **Cooperative Learning Activity:** ***Blood Alcohol Concentrations*** (*Teacher's Resource Binder,* p. 22-1; **Handouts 22–5** and **22–6**).

Depressants

4. What are the physiological and psychological effects of drinking alcohol? What are sedatives, and when are they prescribed?

Depressants are drugs that reduce neural activity and slow body function. We'll focus mainly on alcohol but also discuss sedatives.

Alcohol

The alcohol found in beer, wine, and liquor, is really *ethyl alcohol,* or ethanol. Ethanol is very different from the antiseptic variety (isopropyl alcohol) you put on your finger after removing a sliver. In this module we'll use the word *alcohol* when we mean *ethanol.*

In the competition for most-used psychoactive drug in the world, alcohol places second. (Caffeine is first.) Like any depressant, alcohol slows thinking and impairs physical activity. Alcohol is unique among the depressants in that its use is largely recreational: People drink to "unwind," for the taste, or to increase sociability at a party.

Alcoholic beverages vary widely in the amount of alcohol they contain. Beer is 3.5 to 5 percent alcohol, wine between 9 and 12 percent, and the hard stuff like whiskey a whopping 40 percent. One 12-ounce can of beer would have about the same effect as 4 ounces of wine or 1 ounce of hard liquor (Figure 22.3). The average 150-pound man takes about an hour to metabolize the alcohol from one beer. If he drinks more than one beer per hour, his *blood alcohol content* (BAC) quickly increases.

Alcohol also affects women and men differently. A man and a woman who both weigh the same and drink the same amount of alcohol will have very different amounts of alcohol in their bloodstreams an hour later for at least three reasons (Julien, 2001):

- Men typically have 50 percent more of an enzyme responsible for breaking down (*metabolizing*) alcohol. Men rid themselves of alcohol faster.
- Pound for pound, men have more blood in their vascular systems. Alcohol is diluted more in men.
- A higher percentage of body fat in women tends to concentrate more alcohol in blood plasma than in men, which raises BAC in women.

In most states, a BAC of .08 percent is legal intoxication. However, the selection of .08 as the cut-off point is arbitrary, which means a person may not necessarily be able to drive safely with a lower BAC. According to the Federal Department of Transportation, truck drivers are not allowed to drive at .04, and pilots, after going 24 hours without a

▶ **depressants** Drugs (such as alcohol and sedatives) that reduce neural activity and slow body function.

Enriching

Have students work individually or with partners to explore the advertising techniques alcohol distributors use.

- Is there a common theme about the type of scenes depicted in the ads? Describe it.
- For what type of audience is the ad aiming?
- Are there laws that limit what alcohol advertising can depict? Are there limits to where they can advertise?

Challenge interested students to write letters to newspaper editors and argue the positions they developed from this activity about the advertising of alcohol.

drink, should test no higher than .02. Behavioral impairment can begin at .01. Even at this low BAC level, the time it takes to react increases, as does the likelihood of accidents.

But if alcohol depresses the nervous system, why do so many people report feeling "enlivened" or stimulated after drinking small amounts? Indeed, how do we explain the following:

- René is normally quiet but talks a mile a minute after drinking a wine cooler.
- Nicholas is usually mild mannered but becomes aggressive after downing a couple beers.
- Juanita is a penny pincher but leaves the server a huge tip after an evening of scotch on the rocks at a restaurant.

Figure 22.3 **What Do We Mean by "One Drink"?** One 12-ounce can of beer has about the same amount of alcohol as 4 ounces of wine or 1 ounce of whiskey.

The answer lies in the brain area most affected by alcohol. Alcohol tends to shut down the parts of your brain responsible for controlling inhibitions and making judgments. So, poor decisions and unrestrained behaviors are typical in those under the influence. This helps explain another example of alcohol-induced bad judgment: Most drinkers, even after scoring at or above .08 on a Breathalyzer test, judge themselves capable of driving home from the bar (Denton & Krebs, 1990; MacDonald & others, 1995). It also may help explain the many fights, accidents, and unwanted sexual advances that involve drinking. Alcohol intoxication dramatically increases the probability that we will act out the inappropriate or dangerous urges we keep in check while sober.

Alcohol also impairs memory. I remember a former college classmate who, when questioned on Saturday morning after a night of drinking, couldn't remember what he'd done, where he'd been, and who he'd been with the night before. He would vigorously deny statements I had heard him make just 12 hours earlier. My classmate lost these Friday night memories in part because alcohol suppresses the processing of recent events into long-term memory. Alcohol also plays another peculiar trick with our memory: Experiences from the intoxicated state may not transfer to the sober state (Eich, 1980). Finally, alcohol suppresses REM (dream) sleep, which further disrupts memory storage.

Preventing Problems Students, faculty, and chaperones at this Nebraska high school are all required to take a Breathalyzer test to gain entry to the prom.

Enriching

Have students research drug education programs that are available through your school and/or school district. Students may also compare your district's drug education programs with those in nearby school districts. Have students use the following questions to focus research and present the findings in a class discussion:

- What age group do these programs target? Why? Does research support the choice?
- What is the philosophy of the programs? What does research say about this approach?
- Who teaches these programs? Do the teachers need special certification? Why or why not?
- Has drug use declined in your area since these programs have been instituted? Why or why not?

web ■ **TEACHING TIP**

Surf the Web site at **www.ncadd.com/index.html**, which houses information from the National Commission Against Drunk Driving. This site provides useful information about alcohol consumption laws, by state, and resources for educators and students to learn more about the effects of drunk driving.

F • Y • I

Alcohol has been shown to affect the hippocampus, the area of the brain that is responsible for forming new memories. This effect helps explain why people who drink heavily lose their memories of the time they were intoxicated.

■ **LOOKING AT THE ISSUES**

Have students research the rates of violent crime that occur among those under the influence of alcohol. Pose the following questions:

- What percentage of murders occur while either the victim or assailant is under the influence?
- What percentage of sexual assaults occur while either the victim or assailant is under the influence? Does this percentage change depending on the age of either person?
- What about other violent crimes, such as theft, battery, or domestic abuse?

trb At this point, you may wish to use **Enrichment Lesson:** *Alcohol Consumption Among College Students* (*Teacher's Resource Binder*, p. 22-1).

■ **MULTICULTURAL CONNECTIONS**

Explain to students that many religious groups forbid alcohol use while alcohol consumption is a part of some cultural traditions and lifestyles. Pose the following questions that may be verified with research:

- Which cultures view alcohol consumption in a negative light? Do these cultures experience the same problems with alcohol abuse as does U.S. culture?
- Which cultures view alcohol as being positive—or part of everyday life? Do these cultures deal with the same issues as U.S. culture? Why or why not?

MODULE 22

■ **TEACHING TIP**

Encourage students to take the test in Table 22.1. Be sensitive to students' questions about either their own use of alcohol or the use of alcohol by friends or loved ones. Avoid being judgmental, but emphasize that alcohol abuse leads to problems in many areas of life. It can be especially harmful if a person drinks heavily during key developmental phases of life, such as the teen years.

trb tr A black-line master for Table 22.1, Do You Have an Alcohol Problem?, is available in the **Black-Line Masters Appendix** of the *Teacher's Resource Binder.*

■ **APPLYING THE POINTS**

Contact a variety of alcohol treatment programs in your area to ask them about techniques used to treat alcohol addiction.

- How do the programs differ? How are they similar?
- How many of them rely on the 12-step concept popularized by Alcoholics Anonymous?
- What tools do they provide their patients for dealing with the life-long temptations that alcohol provides?

V At this point, you may wish to show **Videocassette:** *The Mind,* **Second Edition, Module 30: "Treating Drug Addiction: A Behavioral Approach"** (*Teacher's Resource Binder,* p. 22-1).

■ **LOOKING AT THE ISSUES**

Barbiturates are not as commonly prescribed today as they have been in the past. Have students explore the reasons why barbiturates are used today and what drugs have replaced them.

- What are some additional side effects of barbiturate use?
- How are barbiturates and benzodiazepines different chemically?
- How do doctors help patients avoid addiction to these types of sedatives?

trb At this point, you may wish to use **Enrichment Lesson:** *Rohypnol—A Date Rape Drug* (*Teacher's Resource Binder,* p. 22-1).

TABLE 22.1 DO YOU HAVE AN ALCOHOL PROBLEM?

If you can answer yes to even one of these questions, consider seeking advice about your use of alcohol.

1. Has someone close to you sometimes expressed concern about your drinking?
2. When faced with a problem, do you often turn to alcohol for relief?
3. Are you sometimes unable to meet home or work responsibilities because of drinking?
4. Have you ever required medical attention as a result of drinking?
5. Have you ever experienced a blackout—a total loss of memory while still awake—when drinking?
6. Have you ever come in conflict with the law in connection with your drinking?
7. Have you often failed to keep the promises you have made to yourself about controlling or cutting out your drinking?

The recreational use of alcohol often gets out of hand, leading to dependence, health problems, accidental injuries, or death. In fact, no other drug has generated more problems, concern, or controversy than alcohol has in this country. For evidence, look no further than our Constitution, where two of the 27 amendments deal solely and directly with alcohol. The combined yearly deaths from all illegal drugs is still less than the number of alcohol-related deaths each year (Siegel, 1990).

Half of all beer, wine, and liquor consumed in this country is swallowed by only 10 percent of the population. Many of those included in that 10 percent are alcohol dependent. If you suspect that a family member or friend is dependent on alcohol (an "alcoholic"), you might ask that person to read the questions distributed by the National Institute on Alcohol Abuse and Alcoholism (Table 22.1). Answering "yes" to any of the questions indicates an alcohol problem of some sort. Answering "yes" to several of the questions may indicate alcoholism.

Sedatives

Alcohol reduces mental and physical activity, but the terms *tranquilizer* and *sedative* are reserved for drugs prescribed by a physician to reduce anxiety or induce sleep. In 1912, physicians first began prescribing **barbiturates** as sedatives. But since that time, we've learned several important dangers of barbiturate use (Julien, 2001).

▶ **barbiturates** Drugs that depress the activity of the central nervous system, reducing anxiety but impairing memory and judgment.

- They are lethal in overdose.
- They interact dangerously with other drugs, especially alcohol.

Cross-Curricular Connections

(1) GOVERNMENT Research the two amendments to the Constitution that have dealt with alcohol consumption.

- What is the history behind these amendments? What do these amendments say?
- When and why was Prohibition repealed?

Encourage interested students to create a multimedia presentation about alcohol consumption. The presentation should include the history of alcohol use in the United States, including how alcohol consumption went beyond being a subject of law and became a constitutional issue.

- They impair memory and judgment.
- They are much more likely to create tolerance and dependence than newer sedatives.

As a result, barbiturates have mostly been replaced by newer forms of sedatives known as **benzodiazepines.** You've heard of Valium or Xanax? Both are anti-anxiety drugs, and both are benzodiazepines. Safer than barbiturates, benzodiazepines can still create dependency, so they are prescribed only for *short-term* treatment of anxiety and insomnia.

Opiates

5. What are the opiates, and why are they so addictive?

Opiates are drugs that depress neural activity. When used correctly, opiates can relieve pain without addictive after-effects. When used as recreational drugs, they can be deadly. The opiates are all derivatives of opium, a product of the poppy plant. Read the millenniums-old writings of Homer, Hippocrates, and Virgil, and you'll find opium mentioned as a sleep aid. Opium has been used as a medicine (stops pain, coughs, and diarrhea) and abused as a recreational drug for thousands of years.

The active ingredient in opium is **morphine,** which has been used around the world to treat severe pain since the early 1800s. Its use was so widespread during the Civil War that opium or morphine dependence was called "soldier's disease." The United States banned nonmedical uses of opium derivatives, including morphine, heroin (which is three times stronger than morphine and highly addictive), and codeine, during Woodrow Wilson's presidency in the early 1900s.

So how does morphine work? You have millions of pain-signaling neurons that are activated when you sprain your ankle or undergo dental surgery. Morphine prevents these neurons from firing, or releasing pain-signaling neurotransmitters into the synapse. (See Figure 22.2b, part 2, page 411.) Without release of the neurotransmitters, the pain message cannot travel to your brain. Your ankle is still sprained, but thanks to the morphine in your system, your brain doesn't feel the pain.

Is it necessary to take something like morphine to prevent pain neurons from firing? No. Under certain circumstances, your body naturally produces **endorphins,** chemicals with morphinelike qualities that act on the same neural receptors as opium or morphine. Endorphins are your body's natural pain-killing substance, and neurons in your system may release them if you experience serious trauma or long-term strain, which produces the "runner's high" sometimes felt by long-distance runners. Endorphins are thought to produce a state of peaceful oblivion in critically wounded people.

▶ **benzodiazepines** Drugs (such as Valium) that depress the activity of the central nervous system without most of the side effects associated with barbiturates.

▶ **opiates** Opium and its derivatives, such as morphine and heroin; they depress neural activity, temporarily lessening pain and anxiety.

▶ **morphine** Strong sedative and pain-relieving drug derived from opium.

▶ **endorphins** "Morphine within"—natural, opiatelike neurotransmitters linked to pain control and to pleasure.

(2) **HISTORY** Two different wars were fought in China over opium. Have students research these wars between China and Great Britain to see how the opium trade affected both European and Asian culture. For extra credit, students may write a report in which the following questions are answered:

- Why were the wars fought in the first place?
- What did China lose in these wars?
- What did Great Britain lose in these wars?
- What impact does opium have in China today?

F • Y • I

Laudanum was a medicine used commonly in the Victorian era to treat a variety of ailments. It was used most successfully as a painkiller and a cough suppressant. It was also found to help with loose stool. Mothers often used it to soothe their fussy babies. What made laudanum so effective? It was a special mixture of alcohol and opium. Doctors in the Victorian period were so impressed with the medicinal properties of straight opium and laudanum that they neglected to tell their patients about the addictive properties. Officials in the United States banned the practice of prescribing heroin in 1914; therefore, laudanum also became illegal.

■ **APPLYING THE POINTS**

Contact a local surgeon, ask the following questions about the medical use of morphine, and report your findings to the class:

- What are some situations in which morphine is widely used?
- How is the drug administered? Can patients self-medicate with morphine? How is addiction controlled in these situations?
- How long is a patient allowed to be on morphine? Can it only be used in the hospital setting or can patients take some home to dispense?
- What alternatives for pain regulation are used instead of morphine? What are the side effects of these drugs?

■ **TEACHING TIP**

Link the discussion of *endorphins* to concepts discussed in Module 7. **Endorphins** are the body's naturally occurring opiates. When the body experiences pain, endorphins are produced; they cause the person to feel less and less pain as time passes. When a user takes an opiate, the body stops making endorphins on its own, which makes withdrawal a very painful experience as the body's ability to relieve its own pain is lost for a time.

MODULE 22

F • Y • I

Heroin launched the term "junkie" into English vocabulary. In the late 1800s, people addicted to heroin, which had been marketed as a wonder drug by the Bayer Corporation, would collect and sell off scrap metal to get money to buy the drug. Hence, users of heroin became known as "junkies."

trb At this point, you may wish to use **Enrichment Lesson:** *Wonder Drugs—Aspirin and Heroin* (*Teacher's Resource Binder*, p. 22-1).

■ **MULTICULTURAL CONNECTIONS**

The British have a different view of heroin addiction than people in the United States. Instead of viewing drug addicts as criminals, they are viewed in Great Britain as sick people who need to be treated medically. The British government has established a series of drug clinics that dispense drugs to people in an effort to wean users off of drugs. This system has led to a decrease in heroin addiction and black market trade in heroin over the last 30 years.

V At this point, you may wish to show **Videocassette:** *The Mind,* **Second Edition, Module 30: "Treating Drug Addiction: A Behavioral Approach"** (*Teacher's Resource Binder*, p. 22-1).

■ **JOURNAL WRITING**

Invite students to use the following questions and writing prompts as a springboard for entries in their psychology journals:

- Are you addicted to caffeine? Give the reasons why or why not.
- Why do some students take stimulants? Do the drugs really seem to help people remain alert?
- Have you ever gone through caffeine withdrawal? What was your experience?

Feeling No Pain "Runner's high" may be a result of endorphin production, your body's natural painkiller.

The use of morphine and other opiates is, unfortunately, not limited to temporary pain killing under medical supervision. Opiates have powerful side effects, such as euphoria and relaxation, which pave the way for the insatiable cravings of dependence with repeated use and abuse of drugs such as heroin. Tolerance soon develops, making it more and more difficult to get enough of the opiate to stave off withdrawal symptoms. Heroin's withdrawal symptoms include a week's worth of intense pain, hyperventilation, depression, high blood pressure, and explosive diarrhea. Thousands die each year from overdoses in their desperate attempt to avoid the agony of withdrawal. Heroin is right at the top of the list of psychoactive drugs to avoid.

Stimulants

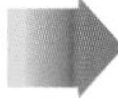

6. What effects do stimulants have, and which stimulants are considered most dangerous?

We've reviewed several psychoactive drugs that depress and relax. On the other side of the bridge are **stimulants,** drugs that excite neural activity and speed up body functions. This category includes caffeine, nicotine, cocaine, and the amphetamines. And one of those—caffeine—is the number one most-used psychoactive drug in the world.

Caffeine

From coffee to tea, cocoa to cola, as many as 80 percent of the adults in this country consume some form of **caffeine** daily (Julien, 2001). Many choose coffee as their delivery system. Coffee causes bad breath, stains your teeth, looks like motor oil, keeps you from sleeping, and tastes awful the first several times you drink it. Even after getting hooked, many coffee drinkers require cream and sugar to get it down. So why do millions drink it every day? Because a 5-ounce cup of coffee contains about 100 milligrams of caffeine. Caffeine rewards the user with a sense of increased energy, mental alertness, and forced wakefulness, which

► **stimulants** Drugs (such as caffeine, nicotine, and the more powerful amphetamines and cocaine) that excite neural activity and speed up body functions.

► **caffeine** Stimulant found in coffee, chocolate, tea, and some soft drinks.

Demonstrating

CAFFEINE SURVEYS Have students work with partners to create surveys whose results would allow them to respond to the following questions:

- How many students at your school would consider themselves addicted to caffeine?
- How do students generally get their caffeine "fix"?
- Is there a stigma associated with caffeine consumption? Why or why not?
- Why do students consume caffeinated products? Are students concerned about their caffeine consumption? Why or why not?

Have the full class meet to respond to the questions and discuss the surveys.

trb At this point, you may wish to use **Enrichment Lesson:** *Caffeine—Is It Harmful?* (*Teacher's Resource Binder*, p. 22-1).

prompts continued use regardless of taste. Caffeine accomplishes this by blocking neurological receptors that, if activated, would sedate your central nervous system. (See Figure 22.2b, part 2, page 411.) With sluggishness sent packing, a caffeine dependency settles in.

Unfortunately, as with so many psychoactive drugs, regular caffeine use produces tolerance as well as dependence. One cup no longer provides the artificial lift, so the caffeine drinker pours another cup or buys another soda. And then another. If you take in 200 or more milligrams of caffeine per day, you will probably experience withdrawal symptoms on a day when you go without. Caffeine withdrawal includes headache, agitation, and tiredness, and the intensity of the withdrawal is tied directly to the normal amount of caffeine ingested daily. When the coffee pot runs dry, even mild-mannered tempers wind up on a short fuse.

Drug Dependence? Caffeine dependence may occur with as little as two cups of coffee (200 milligrams) per day.

I greatly underestimated the power of caffeine dependence early in my teaching career. It was my turn to have the 100-cup coffee maker in the teacher's lounge ready by 7:00 A.M., and I simply forgot to do it. You've never seen so many adults get cranky so quickly as withdrawal set in, with no caffeine fix in sight. At lunch that day, a caffeine-deprived teacher jokingly suggested I be arrested for failure to percolate.

While researchers have not found long-term damaging effects from small daily doses of caffeine (the equivalent of two cups of coffee), you are wise to avoid becoming a prisoner in caffeine's jail. Getting the sleep you need is infinitely better for your body (and attitude) than artificially stimulating a sleep-deprived brain.

Nicotine

Nicotine, the primary active ingredient in tobacco, ranks up there with alcohol and caffeine in the most-used drug category. The stimulating effects of nicotine are similar to those of caffeine, but nicotine usually enters the body in a cloud of thick, deadly smoke from a cigarette. Nicotine is extremely addictive and does not stay long in the body. For a nicotine-dependent smoker, this means lighting up frequently to sustain the effect. The statistics on smoking are bone-chilling (Julien, 2001):

- 6000 American teenagers will light up for the first time today.
- 3000 of them will develop a smoking habit.
- 1000 of them will die from smoking-related diseases.

▶ **nicotine** Stimulant found in tobacco.

MODULE 22

F • Y • I

Studies have shown that pregnant women can consume the equivalent of up to one cup of coffee per day without affecting their growing fetus. Some studies, though, have linked caffeine consumption during pregnancy to miscarriage and low birth weight. Some women elect to eliminate caffeine entirely from their diets entirely just to be safe.

trb At this point, you may wish to use **Enrichment Lesson:** *Caffeine—Is It Harmful?* (*Teacher's Resource Binder*, p. 22-1).

■ MULTICULTURAL CONNECTIONS

Using available print and Internet resources, have students research whether caffeine is as widely consumed abroad as it is in the United States. Afterward, in a class forum, have students respond to the following questions and support their responses with findings from their research:

- How do people in other countries get their caffeine "fix"?
- Is there a relationship between the level of caffeine consumption and level of income? Are developing countries less likely to have high rates of caffeine addiction?

■ LOOKING AT THE ISSUES

Tobacco companies have come under intense scrutiny over the last decade as states have sued them to get reimbursement for the medical expenses of tobacco users. The companies agreed to a record-setting settlement of claims brought by the states as the legal costs began to mount. Using available print and Internet resources, have students research the following questions:

- What were the details of this settlement?
- What did the companies have to do differently as a result?
- What benefits did the states get from settling? What rights did they relinquish regarding future litigation?

Cooperative Learning

Tobacco companies were banned from advertising on television in the 1960s. Their advertising efforts today appear in print media and through sponsorship of sporting events. The recent tobacco settlement put limits on such advertising since those ads could be seen by teens.

Divide students into two groups. Have each group make an oral presentation of its responses, supported by research, to one of the following sets of questions:

- One group can study magazine ads. In what magazines do tobacco ads regularly appear? To what demographic do they seem to try to appeal? Do antismoking ads also appear in the same magazines?
- Another group can study tobacco company sponsorship of events. What events do tobacco companies directly sponsor? Who do these events appeal to? What events do subsidiaries of tobacco companies sponsor? Is a relationship with a tobacco company mentioned?

MODULE 22

■ JOURNAL WRITING

Invite students to use the following questions and writing prompts as a springboard for entries in their psychology journals.

- Is smoking prevalent among teens at your school? Why or why not?
- Do your parents smoke? How has their habit affected your view of smoking?
- Is cocaine and/or crack use prevalent among teens in your school? Why or why not?

web ■ LOOKING AT THE ISSUES

Several groups have instituted public awareness campaigns against smoking, with many campaigns targeting teens. Have students research the type of campaigns that are being waged, analyzing how effective they, as teens, believe each campaign to be.

- The Truth: **www.thetruth.com**
- American Lung Association's School Programs: **www.lungusa.org/school**
- Philip Morris USA (a tobacco company): **www.philipmorrisusa.com/responsible_marketing**

F•Y•I

(1) Some of the carcinogenic chemicals inhaled by tobacco smokers include formaldehyde, ammonia, and tar—all of which are potentially lethal if ingested into the body separately. Over time, the buildup of these chemicals in the lungs is what leads to lung cancer.

(2) Sigmund Freud was indeed a strong advocate of the use of cocaine in his early years. He took the drug himself on a daily basis and advised its use as a treatment for mental and physical disorders (such as asthma), as an aphrodisiac, and as a local anesthetic. Freud was even hired by two pharmaceutical firms, Merck and Parke-Davis, to promote the use of their cocaine-based products.

Smoker's Lung The lung on the left was a healthy, normal lung. The lung on the right belonged to a smoker. We can't always see the damage smoking causes.

- 37,000 nonsmokers will die this year from heart disease contracted by inhaling passive smoke.
- Another 4000 nonsmokers will contract lung disease from second-hand smoke this year.

Nearly 450,000 smokers will die in the United States this year alone because of their tobacco use. The good news about smoking, if that's possible, is that we've seen a 90 percent decline in the number of adults who smoke or chew tobacco (also a deadly habit) over the past 35 years (Rose & others, 1999). Nicotine replacement therapies, where nicotine comes into the body through chewing gum, nasal sprays, or patches worn on the skin, have helped thousands kick the tobacco habit.

Cocaine

For centuries, some South American people have chewed the leaves of the coca plant for medicinal and religious purposes and to increase endurance. It wasn't until the 1850s that scientists identified, purified, and named the active ingredient—**cocaine** (Julien, 2001). In the 1880s, Americans used cocaine as a surgical anesthetic, among other medical uses.

Austrian physician Sigmund Freud prescribed cocaine in the early 1900s as a treatment for depression and chronic fatigue. He quickly reversed his stance after discovering cocaine's horrible side effects, which include dependence, tolerance, and depression after you quit taking it. Freud then declared cocaine the "third scourge," after alcohol and heroin.

Like Freud, Coca Cola endorsed cocaine during the late 1800s, including about 60 milligrams of the active ingredient from the coca plant in every serving. Coke ran an advertising campaign several years ago calling itself, "the real thing." Well, from 1896 to 1904, Coke was indeed the real thing. The company changed the formula, replacing cocaine with caffeine.

In 1910, President Taft labeled cocaine "Public Enemy Number One" and soon after, the drug was banned. The advent of less expensive but still illegal *amphetamines* in the 1930s replaced recreational cocaine use for many Americans. Cocaine made a regrettable comeback in the late 1970s, with the introduction of inexpensive cocaine crystals called *crack.*

Cocaine and crack cocaine produce a strong euphoric effect, but an even stronger crash. Here's how it works: The cocaine user snorts, smokes, or injects the cocaine. Cocaine blocks the reabsorption of certain neurotransmitters, including dopamine, into the sending neurons at the synapse (see Figure 22.2b, part 3, on page 411). The cocaine high from the excess dopamine quickly wears off. The dopamine is eventually absorbed by the body, but it is not quickly replaced because the neurons re-

► **cocaine** Stimulant derived from leaves of the coca plant.

Enriching

Have interested students contact directors of local homeless shelters for an interview about how shelters deal with clients who have a history of drug addiction. Have those students make a presentation of their findings to the class, which should include responses to the following questions:

- How do shelters handle people who seem to be under the influence? Do shelters offer treatment programs for people seeking help for substance abuse? What programs do shelters offer?
- What types of drugs do shelters see abused most often by homeless people? Do there seem to be more drug addicts who are homeless than not? Why or why not?
- What is the biggest obstacle to a homeless person successfully beating a drug addiction?

trb At this point, you may wish to use Application Activity: *Eyescube Drug Simulation* (*Teacher's Resource Binder*, p. 22-1; Handout 22–7).

laying the pleasure messages no longer work properly. The user is instantly dependent, craving more cocaine to temporarily overcome the crash. All this places a considerable strain on the cardiovascular system, leading to instant death in some cases. Crack and cocaine users also can experience frightening feelings of paranoia and suspiciousness.

Amphetamines

I grew up hearing **amphetamines** called *speed* or *uppers,* words that still characterize amphetamines' stimulating effects. What I didn't grow up hearing about was the cheaper and more dangerous amphetamine derivative, *methamphetamine* (also called *crystal* and *crank*).

Amphetamines basically mimic *adrenaline,* a neurotransmitter that stimulates body functions, by *forcing* the release of stored adrenaline that would otherwise remain in storage. (See Figure 22.2b, part 1, page 411.) Amphetamines' effects include restlessness, high blood pressure, insomnia, agitation, loss of appetite, and a state of hyperalertness. As with most stimulants, use leads to a depletion of normal neurotransmitter levels. Withdrawal symptoms occur as the affected neurons attempt to send messages but cannot. Tolerance builds quickly, and to get high, long time amphetamine abusers have been known to take doses 10 times the amount that would be lethal for a first-time user (Julien, 2001).

Methamphetamine is more potent than regular amphetamines. And "ice" is to methamphetamine as "crack" is to cocaine. A major difference is that ice stays in your system much longer than crack cocaine. Drug researcher Robert Julien (2001) warns of methamphetamine's dangers:

> Repeated high doses of methamphetamine are associated with violent behavior and paranoid psychosis. Such doses cause long-lasting decreases in dopamine and serotonin in the brain. These changes appear to be irreversible.

When referring to fast runners who help improve a team's chances of victory, football, soccer, and track coaches often use the colorful figure of speech, "Speed kills." For high doses of methamphetamine, "Speed kills" is not a figure of speech.

Hallucinogens

7. What are the hallucinogens, and what dangers do they pose to users?

Hallucinogens—sometimes called *psychedelics*—are drugs that produce bizarre perceptions in the absence of corresponding sensory input. The most commonly used hallucinogens were first made in a laboratory. Most of the labs producing these drugs today are illegal. We'll take a closer look at LSD and ecstasy.

▶ **amphetamines** Drugs that stimulate neural activity, speeding up body functions, and associated energy and mood changes.

▶ **hallucinogens** Psychedelic ("mind-manifesting") drugs, such as LSD, that distort perceptions and evoke sensory images in the absence of sensory input.

Enriching

Brainstorm with students about the reasons why people might be tempted to use drugs.

- What rationalization techniques might be used to justify first-time or repeat drug use?
- What type of lifestyle choices might people employ to avoid being tempted to use drugs?
- What can your school do to limit the temptation to do drugs?

trb Based on this discussion, challenge students to work individually or with partners to create public service posters about drug use. These posters could become part of a public awareness campaign about drug abuse students might create at the end of this module for **Alternative Assessment/ Portfolio Project:** ***Public Awareness Campaigns*** **(*Teacher's Resource Binder,*** p. 22-1; **Handout 22–8).**

■ MULTICULTURAL CONNECTIONS

The U.S. relationship with some countries is strained because of cocaine trafficking. In Peru, for example, cultivation of the coca bush is legal, as long as farmers sell their crop to the state. But studies show that farmers can make much more money selling to illegal markets, making cocaine a problem in the developing world. Some leaders in foreign countries and groups within the United States argue that if the U.S. government would crack down on the demand of people who use drugs, then drug traffickers would not find dealing as profitable, thus ending the drug problem altogether. Have students meet in small groups to discuss the following questions:

- What should the U.S. government do to curb the drug trade? Have efforts been successful in the past? Why or why not?
- Should the U.S. government cut off diplomatic and economic ties with drug-trafficking countries? Why or why not?

■ APPLYING THE POINTS

Contact a local narcotics detective about the prevalence of methamphetamine use in your area. You can either invite the detective to address the class or you can report the detective's responses to the following questions:

- Is meth use a problem in your area?
- What are some signs of meth abuse? What are clues signaling that a house is being used as a meth lab?
- What laws exist that prohibit the creation, distribution, and use of meth?

■ TEACHING TIP

Link information about *amphetamines* to *neuroscience* by pointing out that recent research has shown that detoxified former methamphetamine users have lost some key dopamine transporters, which are crucial to movement, verbal performance, and memory. Patients with Parkinson's disease have similar decreases in these dopamine transporters.

MODULE 22

F•Y•I

Flashbacks are associated with LSD use. These experiences can occur days, months, or years after an initial trip. Flashbacks can be as intense as the original trip, but because of their unpredictable nature, they are often terrifying for the user.

trb At this point, you may wish to use Enrichment Lesson: *The LSD Experience* (*Teacher's Resource Binder*, p. 22-1).

■ **MULTICULTURAL CONNECTIONS**

Members of the Native American Church enjoy First Amendment protection to use peyote in their religious worship practices. The church insists that the use of peyote in its services is akin to the use of wine in Catholic Church services.

Explain why the Supreme Court voted 6–3 in 1990 to strike down an Oregon law that banned the use of peyote, thereby supporting its religious use by the Native American Church. Also explain why a Hispanic church in New Mexico has fought to use hallucinogenic tea in its worship services but has been unsuccessful.

■ **JOURNAL WRITING**

Invite students to use the following questions and writing prompts as a springboard for entries in their psychology journals:

- Is LSD, ecstasy, or marijuana prevalent at your school? Why or why not?
- Does illicit drug use by your peers make you feel less safe at school? Why or why not?

web ■ **TEACHING TIP**

Ecstasy has been shown to cause permanent brain damage in even first-time users. It seems to deplete the neurotransmitter serotonin in the brain. PET scans comparing normal brains with the brains of those who use ecstasy show a significant difference in the amount of serotonin in the brain. For more information and an image of a PET scan comparing two brains, see the *Scientific American* article online at **www.sciam.com/article.cfm?chanID=sa004&articleID=000863F7-5165-1C75-9B81809EC588EF21.**

► **LSD (lysergic acid diethylamide)** Powerful hallucinogenic drug; also known as *acid.*

► **ecstasy** Also called *MDMA,* this hallucinogenic drug produces lowered inhibitions, pleasant feelings, and greater acceptance of others. Even moderate use may result in permanent brain damage.

LSD

The first **LSD (lysergic acid diethylamide)** experience by a human was an accident. Albert Hoffman, a Swiss chemist who first synthesized LSD in 1938, accidentally ingested the drug in April 1943 and found himself "seized by a peculiar sensation of vertigo and restlessness. Objects, as well as the shape of my associates in the laboratory, appeared to undergo optical changes" (Hoffman, 1994). Hoffman's experience is similar to those who have taken an "acid trip," where visual distortions, detachment from reality, and panic are common. Acid trips vary from person to person. Some people experience a mildly pleasant or mildly unpleasant reaction; others have nightmarish or deadly experiences. A panic-stricken LSD user, unable to detect the difference between reality and fabrication, can be dangerous not only to himself or herself but also to others.

Consciousness-altering LSD is made in the laboratory, but other hallucinogens are found in nature. *Mescaline* (from the peyote cactus) and *psilocybin* (from certain mushrooms) both produce perceptual disruption of time and space. Some states allow the use of these drugs for centuries-old religious ceremonies, but all states outlaw them for recreational use.

Ecstasy

The hallucinogenic drug **ecstasy** (*MDMA*—or 3, 4-methylendioxy-N-methylamphetamine) was first manufactured more than 80 years ago. This amphetamine derivative is experiencing a rebirth of sorts today. It is closely associated with "rave" dances, where hundreds of partygoers pack in shoulder to shoulder and dance to techno music for most if not all of the night. The stimulating effects of the drug enable dancers to maintain the frenzied pace longer than they normally could.

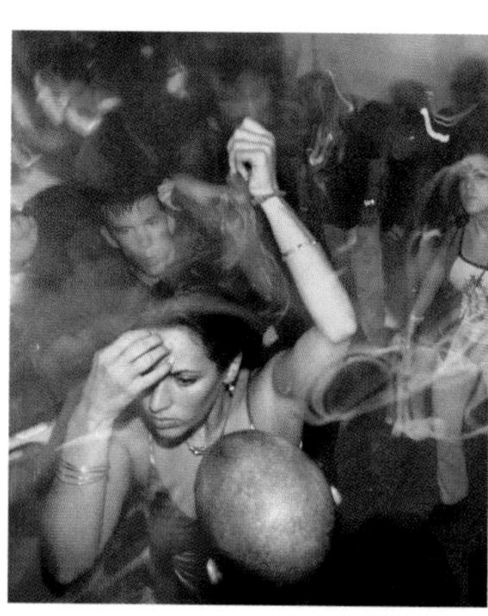

Dance 'Til You Drop? Those attending a rave dance often take MDMA or "ecstasy." The long-term consequences of this drug include permanent brain damage and memory loss.

Ecstasy users report lowered inhibitions, pleasant feelings, and greater acceptance of others. The drug is seductive because it is relatively inexpensive, but its physiological and mental costs can be extremely high. Even moderate users may experience *permanent* brain damage, losing memory, concentration, and verbal reasoning skills (McCann, 1999; Morgan, 1999).

Enriching

Have students research how flashbacks have affected people who used hallucinogenic drugs in the 1960s and early 1970s. The following questions can help students focus their research and discuss their findings with the rest of the class:

- What types of flashbacks do people report having?
- How long after the drug's use have people reported having a flashback?
- In particular, how did LSD use affect Vietnam War veterans?

Marijuana

8. What are some of the similarities and differences between marijuana and the other drugs discussed in this module?

▶ **marijuana** Leaves, stems, resin, and flowers from the hemp plant that, when smoked, lower inhibitions and produce feelings of relaxation and mild euphoria.

It was used to make rope as far back as 8000 BC. It was used for medical purposes in China in 5000 BC, and for religious purposes in India in 2000 BC. It comes from the *cannabis sativa* or hemp plant, and is called *ganja, sinsemilla, pot, hash, Mary Jane, dope, weed, bhang,* and many more names. Most often, it's called **marijuana,** and its use among high school seniors is on the rise.

Marijuana doesn't fit neatly into any of the categories we've discussed thus far, for several reasons:

- Its behavioral effects are similar to that of low doses of alcohol, but different in that high doses do not suppress breathing and are not lethal.
- Compared with LSD, it produces only mild hallucinogenic experiences.
- Its chemical structure does not resemble that of sedatives or hallucinogens.

For these reasons, I've chosen to give marijuana its own category in this module.

Marijuana's active ingredient, *THC (delta-9-tetrahydrocannabinol),* was isolated in 1964. When smoked, THC causes a lowering of inhibitions, relaxation, mild euphoria, and heightened sensitivity to tastes, smells, and sounds. THC can stay in a regular user's body for months, producing a kind of reverse-tolerance effect. That is, the user can take smaller subsequent doses to induce the "high" feeling again because of the amounts of THC already stored in the body. Withdrawal is unpleasant and occurs within 48 hours of nonuse. Symptoms include depression, insomnia, nausea, cramping, and irritability.

As with most psychoactive drugs, marijuana's temporary pleasures come at a long-term cost:

- Pot smoke is far harder on your lungs than cigarette smoke (Wu & others, 1988).
- Brain cell loss accelerates with large doses (Landfield & others, 1988).
- Memory is still impaired long after marijuana's effect has worn off (Pope & Yurgelun-Todd, 1996; Smith, 1995).
- Marijuana seems to suppress the immune system, making it harder for your body to fight off disease and infection (Childers & Breivogel, 1998).

MODULE 22

F • Y • I

(1) Students may have heard before that marijuana is considered to be a "gateway drug," which means that it leads users to desire harder drugs, like heroin. A study of 311 sets of identical and fraternal twins in Australia found that those teens who used marijuana early (before age 17) were two to five times more likely to use harder drugs later in life. In each of these sets of twins, one twin was a user while the other was not, which helped to control for confounding factors like genetics and environment.

(2) Pot smoke is harder on the lungs than cigarette smoke for a few possible reasons. Marijuana smokers typically take longer drags than do cigarette smokers. Also, marijuana cigarettes are not usually filtered as most tobacco cigarettes are.

(3) A study released by the Substance Abuse and Mental Health Services Administration (SAMHSA) showed that teen marijuana use increased by approximately 20 percent during the last half of the 1990s. In 1994, 43 percent of teens treated for substance abuse used marijuana, but in 1999, the number of teens treated for marijuana was 60 percent.

■ LOOKING AT THE ISSUES

Studies have shown that students who are subject to random drug testing are almost four times less likely to use drugs as their nontested counterparts. Have students respond to the following questions, using research when necessary:

- What has the Supreme Court ruled concerning random drug tests in schools?
- Who is subject to random drug testing at your school? How does the school conduct these tests?
- Should students who participate in extracurricular activities be required to submit to drug testing? Why or why not?
- Should all students be subjected to random drug testing? Why or why not?

To verify students' responses, make available a copy of your school handbook.

Cross-Curricular Connections

GOVERNMENT Cancer and AIDS advocacy groups have been pushing for the legalization of marijuana for medicinal purposes. Marijuana has been shown to help curb the nausea associated with AIDS and chemotherapy for cancer, helping patients to keep their strength up as they endure uncomfortable treatments. Using print or Internet resources, have students explore laws across the country that address the medical use of marijuana.

- How many states authorize the medical use of marijuana?
- How does the federal government handle cases of people authorized to use marijuana medicinally?
- Does the federal government supply the drug to people authorized to use marijuana medically? Why or why not?

trb At this point, you may wish to use **Enrichment Lesson:** *Is Marijuana Good Medicine?* (*Teacher's Resource Binder*, p. 22-1).

MODULE 22

■ CHECKING FOR UNDERSTANDING

A four-color transparency of Table 22.2, A Guide to Selected Psychoactive Drugs, is available in the **Overhead Transparencies Set.** Show the transparency with blanks placed over several items in the chart for students to fill in. Use this graphic outline as a quiz in which students fill in the missing items.

■ LOOKING AT THE ISSUES

More and more teens are being treated for substance abuse. A study published by the Substance Abuse and Mental Health Services Administration (SAMHSA) showed that the number of teens admitted to substance abuse treatment programs increased by 20 percent in the late half of the 1990s. With the class, discuss the following questions:

- How might this news be good news?
- Half of the teens in treatment were ordered there by the court. What does this information say about law enforcement efforts regarding teen drug use?
- How does your school handle students who are under the influence? Students who are in possession of drugs? Students who are dealing drugs at school?
- Does your school offer or recommend any particular treatment programs? Why or why not?

■ APPLYING THE POINTS

Have a class volunteer contact your local police station to see if it offers any drug education programs. Ask the volunteer to answer the following questions based on his or her findings:

- What are the components of the program(s)?
- How successful has (have) the program(s) been?

- The structure of every hair on your body is detectably damaged with even a single marijuana experience, and no amount of conditioner will hide the damage.

Several states have passed laws allowing marijuana to be administered under a physician's supervision for certain medical conditions. There is some evidence suggesting THC counteracts both the nausea accompanying cancer's chemotherapy treatments and several of the terrible side effects of AIDS (Benson & Watson, 1999).

Prevention

9. Are there ways to help prevent the use of dangerous psychoactive drugs?

Consider these questions:

1. Is education related to psychoactive drug use?
2. Is hopelessness related to dependence?
3. Is genetics a factor in the development of dependence?
4. Are your peers' attitudes toward drugs important?

The answer to all of these questions is "yes."

1. ***Education is related to drug use.*** Roughly 15 percent of U.S. college dropouts smoke, as do a whopping 42 percent of high school dropouts (Ladd, 1998).
2. ***Hope matters.*** Those who believe their lives are meaningless are more likely to do drugs (Newcomb & Harlow, 1986).
3. ***Genetics plays a role.*** Geneticists have, for example, found a gene occurring more frequently among alcohol-dependent people than among others (Noble, 1993).
4. ***Peers count.*** If the friends you hang out with *never* light up or drink alcohol, there is a good chance you won't either.

If a person is already dependent on some psychoactive substance, effective treatment is essential. However, prevention, or inoculation against ever getting started on drugs, is even more important. There are three vital sides to prevention's triangle:

- A clear understanding of the painful long-term costs of psychoactive drug use, despite pleasurable, short-term rewards (Table 22.2).
- Positive environments that increase self-esteem and foster determination in teens.
- Associating with peers who are adept at saying "no" or willing to learn how to refuse.

Cooperative Learning

DRUG ABUSE PREVENTION Divide students into three groups to explore your community's resources dedicated to preventing drug abuse.

- Have one group outline the long-term costs of the use of psychoactive drugs, adding to the information in Table 22.2.
- Have another group create a chart outlining the positive environments your school and community offer to children and teens. Some examples may include Boys and Girls Clubs, extracurricular activities at school, and scouting.
- Have a third group should come up with several techniques students can successfully employ to refuse offers to use drugs. Their ideas may be presented in role-playing demonstrations for the class.

TABLE 22.2 A GUIDE TO SELECTED PSYCHOACTIVE DRUGS

DRUG	TYPE	PLEASURABLE EFFECTS	ADVERSE EFFECTS
Alcohol	Depressant	Initial high followed by relaxation and disinhibition	Depression, memory loss, organ damage, impaired reactions
Heroin	Depressant	Rush of euphoria, relief from pain	Depressed physiology, agonizing withdrawal
Caffeine	Stimulant	Increased alertness and wakefulness	Anxiety, restlessness, and insomnia in high doses; uncomfortable withdrawal
Methamphetamine ("speed," "crank," "ice")	Stimulant	Euphoria, alertness, energy	Irritability, insomnia, hypertension, seizures
Cocaine	Stimulant	Rush of euphoria, confidence, energy	Cardiovascular stress, suspiciousness, depressive crash
Nicotine	Stimulant	Arousal and relaxation, sense of well-being	Heart disease, cancer (from tars)
Marijuana	Mild hallucinogen	Enhanced sensation, relief of pain, distortion of time, relaxation	Disrupted memory, lung damage from smoke
Ecstasy (MDMA)	Hallucinogen	Euphoria, disinhibition	Brain damage, depression, fatigue

Drug use among high school seniors dropped steadily from 1979 to 1992 but, as Figure 22.4 indicates, marijuana use has unfortunately been on the rise since (Johnston & others, 2002). However, peer groups who disapprove, an understanding of the physiological and psychological costs of drug use, and positive self-regard could help renew a downward trend. Will you be a part of the solution?

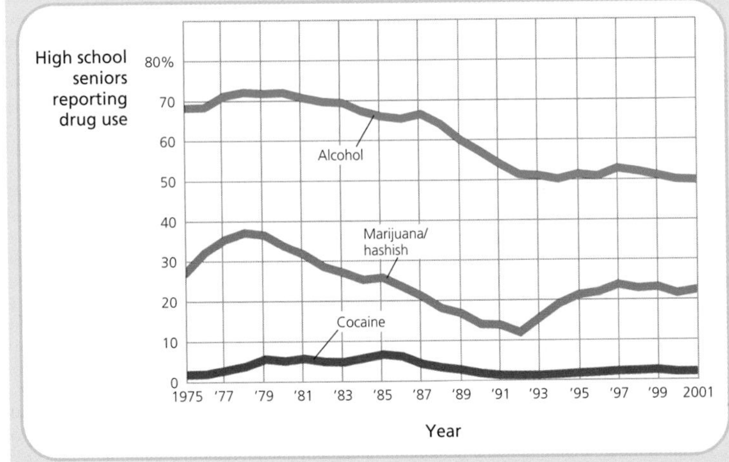

Figure 22.4 **Self-Reports of Drug Use Among High School Seniors** Reported use of alcohol, marijuana, and cocaine declined among high school seniors from 1979 to 1992. Since then, alcohol and cocaine use have declined slightly or held steady, but marijuana use has increased, with drug paraphernalia becoming easier to purchase in local stores.

■ TEACHING TIPS

tr (1) A four-color transparency of Figure 22.4, Self-Reports of Drug Use Among High School Seniors, is available in the **Overhead Transparencies Set.**

trb **tr** (2) A black-line master for Table 22.2, A Guide to Selected Psychoactive Drugs, is available in the **Black-Line Masters Appendix** of the *Teacher's Resource Binder.*

Close

The author of this module asks whether students will become part of the problem or part of the solution. Pose this question seriously to your students. Since some students may be uncomfortable addressing these questions, you may ask them rhetorically or have students brainstorm about ways they can help curb drug use among their peers.

- What behaviors do you need to change or adapt to avoid abusing drugs?
- How can you be a positive influence on your peers regarding drug use?
- How can you be a positive influence on younger children regarding drug use?

■ APPLYING THE POINTS

(1) Using available resources, including the Internet, have students work together in small groups to research what addiction support groups are available in your area. Encourage each group to contact one or more of these support groups to learn their philosophy of what addiction is and how addiction can be effectively treated.

(2) Contact a local psychologist who specializes in substance dependence and get his or her thoughts on various addictions found in the U.S. population, as well as treatments he or she prefers for some of those addictions

trb At this point, you may wish to use Application Activity: *Eyescube Drug Simulation* (*Teacher's Resource Binder*, p. 22-1; Handout 22–7).

MODULE 22

Checking the Points

TEACHING TIPS

web (1) The book companion site for *Thinking About Psychology* at www.worthpublishers.com/thinkingaboutpsych contains a module quiz, flashcards of key terms and people, as well as other student activities and resources for this module. You will also find PowerPoint lectures, a quiz grade book, and other teaching resources by logging on as an instructor.

trb (2) At this point, you may wish to use **Critical Thinking Activity:** *Fact or Falsehood?* (*Teacher's Resource Binder*, p. 22-1; **Handout 22–1**) to review concepts about drugs. If students completed this handout earlier in the module, ask them not to refer to earlier versions. Have a volunteer read the first item and provide a response. Ask students who agree with the response to find a supporting passage in the text and read it aloud. If students contest the response, have them use the text to find a supporting passage for their response and read that passage aloud. Once consensus is reached, repeat the process with the next item on the handout.

REVIEW

Module 22: Drugs

What's the Point?

Psychoactivity and Dependence

1. *What is a psychoactive drug?*

Psychoactive drugs are substances that affect mood, behavior, and perceptions. These substances can lead to dependence, a state of physiological or psychological need for the drug. Continued use can lead to tolerance, which means that larger and larger amounts of the drug are needed to achieve the same effect. A person dependent on a psychoactive drug may undergo withdrawal when deprived of that drug. Withdrawal symptoms are often the direct opposite of the drug's intended effects. Some psychoactive drugs are illegal street drugs, but others, like the caffeine in colas, tea, and coffee, are ingredients in products sold legally.

Drugs and Neurotransmission

2. *How do psychoactive drugs work?*

Neurotransmission is a communication process within the nervous system. In this process, a sending neuron releases chemical messengers (neurotransmitters) into a small gap (a synapse) between the tip of the sending neuron and receptor sites on a receiving neuron. Psychoactive drugs alter this process in one of three ways: by mimicking a neurotransmitter's effects; by blocking a neurotransmitter's effects; or by preventing the reabsorption of a neurotransmitter.

Drug Classifications

3. *What are the five main drug categories, and why do some drugs defy their categories?*

The five categories of psychoactive drugs are depressants, opiates, stimulants, hallucinogens, and marijuana. A user's expectations and mood can cause some drugs to straddle more than one category.

4. *What are the physiological and psychological effects of drinking alcohol? What are sedatives, and when are they prescribed?*

Alcohol and sedatives are both depressants, drugs that reduce neural activity and slow body functions. Alcohol is also a disinhibitor, loosening a person's control over urges that might be kept in control while sober. Alcohol impairs memory and interferes with sleep. Women have stronger reactions to alcohol than men do and retain the substance in their bloodstream longer. The second-most-used psychoactive drug, alcohol is related to more deaths each year than all other drugs combined.

Sedatives are designed for short-term use, to reduce anxiety or induce sleep. The benzodiazepines (such as Valium and Xanax) are the modern alternatives to the barbiturates, which were formerly the leading prescribed sedatives. Physicians now prescribe barbiturates rarely, because they are lethal in overdose, interact with other drugs, and quickly lead to tolerance and dependence.

5. *What are the opiates, and why are they so addictive?*

Opiates are derived from a part of the opium poppy plant. They depress neural activity by

Alternative Assessment/Portfolio Project

PUBLIC AWARENESS CAMPAIGNS Invite a media or marketing consultant from a local drug prevention group to discuss components of a good public awareness campaign. Divide students into small groups and assign each group a different drug. Each group should create a public awareness campaign aimed at preventing use of that drug among high school students. Students should include information about the painful, long-term costs of the use of that drug, environments students should avoid and participate in to limit their exposure to that drug, and ways students can refuse the drug when offered. Since this is a campaign, have students vary the media through which their message is sent.

preventing neurons from firing and sending pain-signaling messages to the brain. Morphine, the active ingredient in opium, is widely used as a painkiller. Heroin, an opium derivative three times stronger than morphine, is illegally used to induce feelings of euphoria and relaxation. Opiates are highly addictive, and dependence develops quickly. Withdrawal is intensely painful, and many heroin users die from overdoses each year. Our bodies produce morphinelike substances, endorphins, that have many of the opiates' good effects without their dangers.

6. *What effects do stimulants have, and which stimulants are considered most dangerous?*

Stimulants excite neural activity and speed up body functions. Caffeine, found in coffee, tea, colas, and chocolate, is both a stimulant and the most popular psychoactive drug in the world. Caffeine works by blocking receptors for neurotransmitters that would otherwise cause you to feel tired and sleepy. Caffeine in moderate amounts has no known long-term damaging effects, but it does lead to dependence and, if use is discontinued, the resulting withdrawal symptoms.

Nicotine is a stimulant found in tobacco, and it, too, leads to withdrawal symptoms. Because nicotine is usually consumed by smoking, use of this drug can lead to cancer and heart and lung problems.

Cocaine and crack (smokable cocaine crystals) produce strong feelings of euphoria by preventing the reabsorption of dopamine and other neurotransmitters. The excess dopamine is eventually absorbed, but new dopamine does not immediately replace it because the neurons no longer work properly. At this point, the user experiences a very strong crash and craves more cocaine.

Amphetamines stimulate neural activity, speeding up body functions, increasing energy, and triggering mood changes. These drugs accomplish their effects by forcing the body to release adrenaline that would normally remain in storage after the body's normal needs have been met. Dependence and tolerance accompany continued use. Methamphetamine is a superamphetamine that is extremely dangerous because it permanently decreases the brain's ability to produce dopamine and serotonin.

7. *What are the hallucinogens, and what dangers do they pose to users?*

Hallucinogens distort perceptions and create sensory images in the absence of sensory input. The hallucinogen LSD is created in laboratories, but other hallucinogens are found in plants, such as the peyote cactus and certain mushrooms. Ecstasy is also a laboratory product. Its stimulating effects are offset by its ability to produce permanent brain damage, even with moderate use.

8. *What are some of the similarities and differences between marijuana and the other drugs discussed in this module?*

Marijuana, like low doses of alcohol, lowers inhibitions, but marijuana is not lethal in high doses, as alcohol is. Like some of the other psychoactive drugs, marijuana produces feelings of relaxation and mild euphoria; because it can suppress nausea, marijuana is used for medical purposes in some states. Like the hallucinogens, marijuana produces heightened sensitivity to tastes, smells, and sounds, but the effects are milder than those of LSD or the other hallucinogens. Marijuana's chemical structure differs from those of the sedatives and hallucinogens. The active ingredient in marijuana is THC, which can remain in the body for months. Like other psychoactive drugs, THC can lead to dependence, and withdrawal can be unpleasant. And like nicotine, THC is delivered in a cloud of smoke that can damage lungs. Marijuana also seems to impair memory and suppress the immune system.

Some media to consider for the drug awareness campaign include the following:

- Pamphlets
- Posters
- Infomercials or short commercials
- Documentaries

trb A full discussion of this project can be found in **Alternative Assessment/Portfolio Project:** *Public Awareness Campaigns* (*Teacher's Resource Binder*, p. 22-1; **Handout 22–8**). Use the general rubric provided in **Handout 22–8**, and adapt it to suit your needs.

MODULE 22

trb ■ TEACHING TIP

Provide a fresh copy of **Building Vocabulary:** *Crossword Puzzle* (*Teacher's Resource Binder*, p. 22-1; **Handout 22–2**) for students use in reviewing module concepts and vocabulary. After students complete the puzzle independently, have them confirm their answers by working with a small group of classmates.

tb Using the Test Bank

The *Test Bank* that accompanies this textbook offers a wide variety of questions in different formats and levels of complexity. Use the software to construct whole tests or to integrate standardized questions into teacher-made tests.

Self-Test Answers

Multiple-Choice Questions

1. a, 2. d

Prevention

9. *Are there ways to help prevent the use of dangerous psychoactive drugs?*

The three factors that seem to help prevent drug use are (1) a clear understanding of the long-term costs of drug use; (2) positive environments that increase self-esteem and foster determination; and (3) associating with peers who disapprove of drug use.

Key Terms

psychoactive drugs, p. 408
dependence, p. 408
withdrawal, p. 409
tolerance, p. 409
neuron, p. 409
central nervous system (CNS), p. 409
neurotransmitter, p. 410
synapse, p. 410
depressants, p. 412
barbiturates, p. 414
benzodiazepines, p. 415
opiates, p. 415
morphine, p. 415
endorphins, p. 415
stimulants, p. 416
caffeine, p. 416
nicotine, p. 417
cocaine, p. 418
amphetamines, p. 419
hallucinogens, p. 419
LSD (lysergic acid diethylamide), p. 420
ecstasy, p. 420
marijuana, p. 421

Self-Test

Multiple-Choice Questions

Choose the *best* answer for each of the following questions:

1. Pat woke up very tired this morning, so she hurried to brew a pot of coffee. With her morning cup of coffee, she had three cigarettes. Realizing that she wouldn't have time for lunch, Pat shoved a fudge brownie and a teabag into her purse, knowing she could brew the tea at the office. By midafternoon, stress from her busy job had built up, so Pat took one of the Valium tablets her doctor had prescribed. That evening, she had two glasses of wine with her dinner. How many categories of psychoactive drugs did Pat cover in her day's consumption?
   a. Two—depressants (Valium and alcohol) and stimulants (caffeine in the coffee, tea, and chocolate, and nicotine in the cigarettes).
   b. Three—depressants (nicotine in the cigarettes), stimulants (Valium), and hallucinogens (alcohol in the wine and caffeine in the chocolate, coffee, and tea).
   c. Four—depressants (alcohol), stimulants (caffeine in the chocolate, coffee, and tea), opiates (Valium), and hallucinogens (nicotine in the cigarettes).
   d. None—all of these substances are legal products or prescription drugs.

2. Since his girlfriend dumped him, Maurice has been feeling very sad. He finds it difficult to get through the day, and he has no energy. His friend, Bill, suggested that

Meeting Individual Needs

trb Help students overwhelmed by the number of terms in this module by having them complete **Building Vocabulary:** *Crossword Puzzle* (*Teacher's Resource Binder*, p. 22-1; **Handout 22–2**). If they completed the puzzle earlier, ask them not to refer to those earlier versions.

- **Independent Learners** Students can complete the handout on their own as a homework or in-class assignment, checking the answers in class. You may want to use **Handout 22–2** as a transparency, inserting the correct answers in the puzzle and projecting the puzzle for students to check their answers.
- **Cooperative Learners** Have students work in small groups to fill out the crossword puzzle. Students can tutor each other about the concepts in the module, or you can create a competition in which students see how quickly their team can complete the puzzle correctly.

Maurice might have more energy and feel happier if he went running with him every morning. But another friend, Kim, thinks Maurice should go to a "rave" dance and take a little ecstasy, which produces happy feelings in a social context. Whose idea is more likely to help Maurice?

a. Kim's, because Maurice needs to move on with his life, and one dose of ecstasy won't hurt him.
b. Kim's, because the ecstasy has no serious side effects, and it will let Maurice stay up and dance all night, which will make him forget his sad feelings.
c. Bill's, because running exercises more muscles than dancing does.
d. Bill's, because running will increase Bill's energy level and also trigger the production of endorphins, the body's natural pain killers, which create good feelings without dangerous side effects.

3. In the movie *The Wizard of Oz,* Dorothy falls asleep in a field of poppies. She may have been feeling the effect of ________________, which is (are) derived from parts of the poppy plant.
   a. LSD
   b. barbiturates
   c. opiates
   d. THC

4. Luis has been drinking a giant-size cola at his mid-morning break, with lunch, immediately after school, and with dinner this past year. He recently began dating Julia, who thinks he drinks too much soda and wants him to drink juice or water instead. To please Julia, Luis has stopped cold turkey—no soda at all. What effects is Luis likely to experience?
   a. feeling tired and groggy
   b. agitation
   c. having some serious headaches
   d. All of the above.

5. Montel's friends suspected that he was taking a psychoactive substance. He was always begging money from his family and friends, and sometimes he seemed so relaxed and happy that it was clear he was high. The friends talked to Montel and he promised they would see a change. They did—for almost a week now, Montel has been experiencing intense pain, terrible diarrhea, and depression, and he says he is breathing so fast he can't catch his breath properly. Montel's friends should seek help because these symptoms suggest that Montel was
   a. drinking alcohol and is continuing to do so.
   b. taking heroin and is in withdrawal.
   c. smoking marijuana, and now he's dependent on it.
   d. taking LSD and is on an acid trip.

6. Mrs. Sapolsky's doctor just prescribed something to counteract the nausea she feels when she takes the very strong drugs used to treat her cancer. Mrs. Sapolsky has noticed that after she takes this substance, she feels very relaxed. Her nausea disappears, and she seems to be able to appreciate the color, smell, and taste of food more than she did before she took the substance. Mrs. Sapolsky's doctor seems to have prescribed
   a. beer, for the relief alcohol brings as a medical treatment for some diseases.
   b. coffee, for the stimulating effects of the caffeine it contains.
   c. marijuana, for the nausea-fighting effects of the THC it contains.
   d. cigarettes, for the stimulating effects of the nicotine contained in cigarette smoke.

Self-Test Answers

Multiple-Choice Questions (continued)

3. c, 4. d, 5. b, 6. c

MODULE 22

Self-Test Answers

Matching Terms and Definitions

7. a. (6), b. (12), c. (4), d. (8), e. (11), f. (7), g. (1), h. (5), i. (3)

Fill-in-the-Blank Questions

8. stimulants, 9. endorphins, 10. depressants

Brief Essay Question

11. Students should note the three primary ways drugs affect the neurons in the central nervous system. Drugs can bind with receptors (mimicking a neurotransmitter's effect), block a neurotransmitter's release, or block neurotransmitter reabsorption.

Matching Terms and Definitions

7. For each definition, choose the *best* matching term from the list that follows:

Definition

a. The active ingredient in marijuana.
b. Psychoactive substances that distort perceptions and evoke sensory images in the absence of sensory input.
c. Reduced responsiveness to a drug, prompting the user to increase dosage to achieve the same result.
d. Junction between the tip of a sending neuron and the receptor sites on a receiving neuron.
e. Concentrated, smokable form of cocaine.
f. Chemical messenger that crosses the synaptic gap between neurons.
g. The brain and spinal cord.
h. Strong sedative and pain-relieving drug derived from opium.
i. The discomfort and distress that follow discontinuing the use of an addictive drug.

Term

(1) central nervous system
(2) nicotine
(3) withdrawal
(4) tolerance
(5) morphine
(6) THC
(7) neurotransmitter
(8) synapse
(9) LSD
(10) ecstasy
(11) crack
(12) hallucinogens

Fill-in-the-Blank Questions

8. Amphetamines, cocaine, and crack are classified as ________________, psychoactive substances that excite neural activity and speed up body functions.

9. Your body produces natural opiatelike substances known as ________________, which are linked to pain control and pleasurable feelings.

10. Barbiturates and benzodiazepines, prescribed to relieve anxiety, are two varieties of ________________, a broad category of drugs that dampen activity in the central nervous system.

Brief Essay Question

11. Imagine that you are a tiny alien from outer space, and you have been sent on a mission to disrupt communication in my nervous system. (Never mind why I'm so important that you have to do this—it's your mission.) You have been told that if you take the shape of a psychoactive drug, you can accomplish your mission easily. In three paragraphs of about two sentences each, describe three ways that you can alter neurotransmission in my brain and succeed at your mission.

CHAPTER 10

Thinking, Language, and Intelligence

Cognitive Domain

Teaching with the Standards

Standard Area: Thinking and Language

Breakdown of Module 23: Thinking and Language

Content Standard 1: Fundamental elements of cognition Module 23 defines the principle elements that comprise thinking. Focus is on how cognition separates us from other species. The various components of thinking, such as concepts, prototypes, concept formation, and concept hierarchies are described and their usefulness discussed. (Student Text pp. 430–433)

Content Standard 2: Strategies and obstacles in problem solving Various strategies that help us solve problems, such as algorithms, heuristics, and insight, are presented in Module 23. In addition to investigating strategies, emphasis is also on obstacles, such as fixation, confirmation bias, heuristics, overconfidence, framing, and belief perseverance that hinder our problem solving abilities. (Student Text pp. 433–441)

Content Standard 3: Language structure Module 23 examines the basic properties of language. Phonemes and morphemes are defined. Examples are provided of how morphemes are combined to form words, phrases, and sentences. The role of grammar in language is also considered. (Student Text pp. 441–444)

Content Standard 4: Stages and theories of language development Noam Chomsky's and B. F. Skinner's differing theories of language acquisition are discussed. In addition, the stages that children go through, from babbling to the two-word stage, are presented. Emphasis is also on how a child's overgeneralization of language supports Chomsky's view of language acquisition. Module 23 also focuses on the controversy surrounding whether animals can acquire and use language. (Student Text pp. 445–449)

Content Standard 5: Connections between thought and language Module 23 considers the influence of language on cognition and behavior. Benjamin Whorf's language relativity theory is discussed. Examples are presented that demonstrate how our language has changed over time. Thought without language, or the importance of mental images to cognition, is also presented. (Student Text pp. 449–450)

Standard Area: Individual Differences

Breakdown of Module 24: Intelligence and Intelligence Testing

Content Standard 1: Concepts related to assessment of differences among individuals Module 24 introduces students to various historical attempts to measure intelligence. The work of Alfred Binet, Lewis Terman, William Stern, and David Wechsler are presented. In addition, basic statistical concepts related to test construction, such as validity and reliability, are discussed. (Student Text pp. 459–463)

Content Standard 2: Discuss the influence of nature and nurture on individual differences The influence of heredity and environment on intelligence is examined. Studies of twins raised together and those raised apart—identical or fraternal—and of adopted children are considered in answering this nature and nurture question. (Student Text pp. 470–471)

Content Standard 3: Understanding intelligence Module 24 compares the traditional theories of intelligence to more modern approaches. Charles Spearman's theory of *g* is compared with Howard Gardner's theory of multiple intelligences, Robert Sternberg's triarchic theory of intelligence, and Daniel Goleman's theory of emotional intelligence. (Student Text pp. 456–459)

Content Standard 4: Concepts related to intelligence testing Module 24 explores how group tests differ from individual tests. In addition, the differences between achievement and aptitude tests are explained. Also, Module 24 investigates the limitations of conventional intelligence tests by exploring labels derived from testing, such as "genius," "normal," and "mental retardation." (Student Text pp. 464–465)

Scope and Sequence

	Objectives	Text Reference	Standards Covered
Lesson 1	Define cognition. Discuss the basis of thought. Define concepts and examine concept formation. Explain the role of prototypes in classifying information. Discuss how concept hierarchies form and their usefulness.	Module 23, pp. 430–433	Standard Area: Thinking and Language, Content Standard 1, Performance Standards 1.1, 1.2
Lesson 2	Define and give examples of algorithms, heuristics, and insight. Examine possible obstacles to problem solving.	Module 23, pp. 433–441	Content Standard 2, Performance Standards 2.1, 2.3
Lesson 3	Discuss how phonemes combine to form morphemes and how morphemes combine to form words and sentences. Discuss language development. Compare Chomsky's and Skinner's theories of language acquisition.	Module 23, pp. 441–449	Content Standard 3, Performance Standards 3.1, 3.2, Content Standard 4, Performance Standards 4.1, 4.2
Lesson 4	Discuss the relationship between thought and language. Present Whorf's linguistic relativity hypothesis. Discuss how language shapes our expectations. Examine the role of mental imagery in cognition. Investigate the controversy surrounding animal language.	Module 23, pp. 448–450	Content Standard 4, Performance Standard 4.3, Content Standard 5, Performance Standard 5.1
Lesson 5	Define intelligence. Compare traditional and modern views of intelligence. Discuss the work of Spearman, Gardner, Sternberg, and Goleman.	Module 24, pp. 455–459	Standard Area: Individual Differences, Content Standard 3, Performance Standard 3.3
Lesson 6	Trace the history of intelligence testing. Discuss the work of Binet, Terman, Stern, and Wechsler. Discuss the extremes of intelligence and the consequences of labeling.	Module 24, pp. 459–465	Content Standard 1, Performance Standard 1.1, Content Standard 4, Performance Standard 4.3
Lesson 7	Compare achievement and aptitude tests. Discuss test construction. Explore the concepts of reliability, validity, and standardization.	Module 24, pp. 468–469	Content Standard 1, Performance Standard 1.2, Content Standard 4, Performance Standard 4.2
Lesson 8	Explore the influences of the environment and heredity on intelligence. Investigate research into the roles of nature and nurture. Discuss bias in testing.	Module 24, pp. 469–472	Content Standard 4, Performance Standards 4.1, 4.3
Lesson 9	Review and Test		

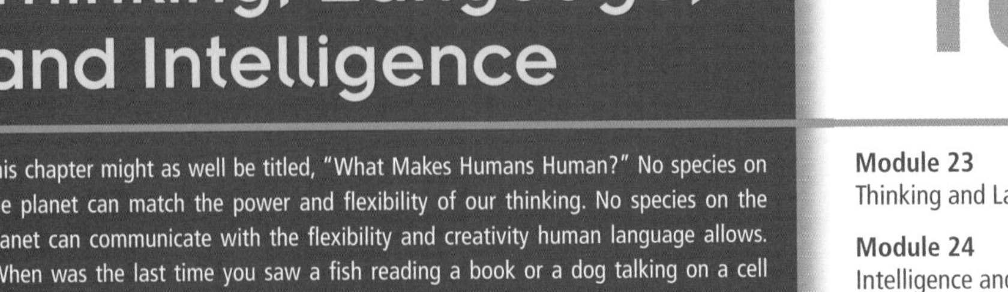

CHAPTER 10

Module 23
Thinking and Language

Module 24
Intelligence and Intelligence Testing

This chapter might as well be titled, "What Makes Humans Human?" No species on the planet can match the power and flexibility of our thinking. No species on the planet can communicate with the flexibility and creativity human language allows. (When was the last time you saw a fish reading a book or a dog talking on a cell phone?) Human intelligence has even allowed us to escape the planet and walk on the surface of the moon. Most of us like to think, communicate, and solve problems; we're good at it. We can't swim as efficiently as sharks or fly with the soaring grace of eagles, but our cognitive skills allow us to construct submarines and airplanes. The topics of this chapter represent the ultimate human abilities.

Thinking, Language, and Intelligence

Introducing the Chapter

The Points: Chapter Objectives

- Define a concept, explaining why it is useful.
- Differentiate between algorithms and heuristics, determining how they help solve problems.
- Analyze how fixation, confirmation bias, heuristics, overconfidence, framing, and belief perseverance influence the ability to solve problems.
- Describe the roles that phonemes, morphemes, and grammar play in the structure of language.
- Analyze how people learn language.
- Describe the linguistic relativity hypothesis, determining whether it is possible to think without language.
- Compare and contrast Gardner's and Sternberg's theories of intelligence.
- Evaluate Alfred Binet's contribution to intelligence testing.
- Evaluate Lewis Terman's role in the development of intelligence tests.
- Describe David Wechsler's contribution to intelligence testing.
- Explain the terms reliable and valid in the context of intelligence testing.
- Analyze the reasons for the differences in test scores among gender, racial, or ethnic groups.

MODULE 23

Performance Standards

Standard Area: Thinking and Language

Content Standard 1: Fundamental elements of thought

Performance Standard 1.1 Define cognition as a mental process.

- Define cognitive abilities. Demonstrate how such abilities separate us from other species. (Student Text p. 430)

Performance Standard 1.2 Explore the process of concept formation.

- Define concept. (Student Text p. 431)
- Define why a concept is useful. (Student Text p. 431)
- Discuss how we classify objects by comparing them with our prototypes. (Student Text pp. 431–432)
- Investigate how and why we develop concept hierarchies. (Student Text pp. 432–433)
- Figure 23.1, "A Concept Hierarchy," provides an example of how children use hierarchies. (Student Text p. 433)

Content Standard 2: Strategies and obstacles in problem solving

Performance Standard 2.1 Investigate problem-solving processes.

- Discuss how algorithms, heuristics, and insight allow us to solve problems. (Student Text pp. 433–435)

Performance Standard 2.3 Investigate obstacles to problem solving.

- Discuss how fixation, mental set, functional fixedness, confirmation bias, heuristics, overconfidence, framing, and belief perseverance affect problem solving. (Student Text pp. 435–440)
- Figure 23.3, "The Luchins Water Jar Problem," is an interactive demonstration of fixation. (Student Text p. 436)

Content Standard 3: Language structure

Performance Standard 3.1 Define language.

- Define language as an extension of cognition. (Student Text p. 441)

Performance Standard 3.2 Investigate the hierarchical structure of language.

- Discuss how phonemes are combined to form morphemes. (Student Text pp. 442–443)
- Examine how morphemes are combined to form words and sentences. (Student Text pp. 442–443)
- Investigate the role of grammar. (Student Text pp. 443–444)

Content Standard 4: Stages and theories of language development

Performance Standard 4.1 Investigate the stages of language development.

- Trace language development through childhood. (Student Text pp. 445–447)
- Table 23.1, "Stages of Language Development," summarizes developmental milestones. (Student Text p. 447)
- Discuss the existence of a critical period for language development. (Student Text p. 449)

Performance Standard 4.2 Evaluate the theories of language acquisition.

- Compare the language acquisition theories of Noam Chomsky and B. F. Skinner. (Student Text pp. 445–446)
- Discuss current theories of language development. (Student Text p. 445)
- Discuss how language overgeneralization supports Chomsky's theory. (Student Text pp. 446–447)

Performance Standard 4.3 Examine the phenomenon of animal language.

- Discuss the controversy surrounding animal language. (Student Text p. 448)
- Discuss early research teaching primates sign language. (Student Text p. 448)

Content Standard 5: Connections between thought and language

Performance Standard 5.1 Investigate the influence of language on thought.

- Discuss Benjamin Whorf's language relativity theory. (Student Text p. 449)
- Examine how sexist language can influence cognition. (Student Text pp. 449–450)
- Understand how we can think without language. (Student Text p. 450)

Materials NETWORK

All of the items from the Video, Activity, and Enrichment Centers listed below come from the *Teacher's Resource Binder.* These items will help you teach and expand on concepts presented in Module 23.

trb This logo indicates when an item from the Materials Network may be used in conjunction with a specific note found in this module's *Teacher's Edition.*

Thinking

V Video Center

- **Videocassette:** ***Scientific American Frontiers,*** **Second Edition, Segment 28: "Teaching Computers to Think"** Consult the faculty guide from the *Scientific American Frontiers* video series for a description of this segment. (*Teacher's Resource Binder,* p. 23-1)

Activity Center

- **Critical Thinking Activity:** *Fact or Falsehood?* With this activity, students' preconceptions about thinking and language are either exposed as incorrect or reinforced as correct. (*Teacher's Resource Binder,* p. 23-1; **Handout 23–1**)
- **Building Vocabulary:** *Crossword Puzzle* Students learn about people and concepts from this module through a crossword puzzle completed when a correct name or concept is matched to the appropriate definition. (*Teacher's Resource Binder,* p. 23-1; **Handout 23–2**)
- **Analysis Activity:** *Cognitive Complexity* Cognitive complexity refers to how simple or elaborate a person's system of personal constructs may be. With this activity, students can analyze their personal constructs. (*Teacher's Resource Binder,* p. 23-1)
- **Technology Application Activity:** *The Tower of Hanoi Problem* Students can test their powers of reason and math as they try to solve a problem that legend says, if solved, could signal the end of the world! (*Teacher's Resource Binder,* p. 23-1)
- **Demonstration Activity:** *Dice Games to Demonstrate Problem Solving* Challenge your class to a construct mind game as they try to figure out the rule that solves the problem of "Petals Around a Rose." (*Teacher's Resource Binder,* p. 23-1)
- **Critical Thinking Activity:** *Problem-Solving Strategies* Students can apply strategies for problem solving, and have a little fun in the process, with this activity that involves trying to solve three complex logic problems. (*Teacher's Resource Binder,* p. 23-1; **Handout 23–3**)
- **Critical Thinking Activity:** *Solving Puzzles* Sometimes people need to reorganize their patterns of thinking to solve problems. If they think "outside the box," they may then see the answer clearly. This simple activity challenges students to do just that. (*Teacher's Resource Binder,* p. 23-1)
- **Demonstration Activity:** *Confirmation Bias* People tend to look for evidence that confirms their hypotheses, which can lead to reinforcing false beliefs. If people would look for evidence that disproves their thinking, they would be more likely to make correct decisions. This simple activity helps students see the power of confirmation bias. (*Teacher's Resource Binder,* p. 23-1)
- **Critical Thinking Activity:** *Confirmation and Custody Decisions* If making a crucial decision about the custody of a child, how would a person make that decision? Research suggests that the decision would depend on how the question was framed. (*Teacher's Resource Binder,* p. 23-1; **Handout 23–4**)
- **Demonstration Activity:** *Demonstrating Mental Set* Mental set is like perceptual set except it affects problem solving. Michael Wertheimer provides a classroom exercise that shows how, in solving a problem, we pay attention only to some aspects of information input and ignore the rest. (*Teacher's Resource Binder,* p. 23-1)
- **Technology Application Activity:** *PsychSim:* **"Rational Thinking"** *PsychSim* is an interactive CD-ROM containing tutorials in different content areas of psychology. In this tutorial, students engage in skill-building exercises to focus on likelihood estimation. (*Teacher's Resource Binder,* p. 23-1)
- **Demonstration Activity:** *The Representativeness Heuristic* Although representativeness works well much of the time, it leads to error when its conclusions run counter to the laws of chance. You can demonstrate the power of the representativeness heuristic in class with one of Amos Tversky and Daniel Kahneman's problems. (*Teacher's Resource Binder,* p. 23-1)
- **Demonstration Activity:** *The Base-Rate Fallacy* You may want to extend the text discussion of the representativeness heuristic to include the **base-rate fallacy**—the tendency to ignore or underuse base-rate information and, instead, be influenced by the distinctive features of the case being judged. (*Teacher's Resource Binder,* p. 23-1)
- **Analysis Activity:** *The Availability Heuristic* The role of vividness in shaping availability is demonstrated in this quick activity. (*Teacher's Resource Binder,* p. 23-1; **Handout 23–5**)

- Critical Thinking Activity: *Framing Decisions* This activity clearly demonstrates that the way a problem is presented can have a profound effect on the decisions people will make in response to it. (*Teacher's Resource Binder*, p. 23-1; Handout 23–6)
- Analysis Activity: *Risk Averse Versus Loss Averse* Amos Tversky and Daniel Kahneman developed the Nobel Prize–winning idea that people are more averse to losing than to taking risks. This activity expands on that idea as students make decisions based on risk versus loss. (*Teacher's Resource Binder*, p. 23-1; Handout 23–7)
- Analysis Activity: *Belief Bias* Syllogisms, or logic puzzles, can help students see how illogical people are when solving problems. (*Teacher's Resource Binder*, p. 23-1; Transparency Master 23–1)

Enrichment Center

- Enrichment Lesson: *The Confirmation Bias and Social Judgment* Our tendency to search for confirming information may have important implications for our social judgments, as this lesson explains. (*Teacher's Resource Binder*, p. 23-1)
- Enrichment Lesson: *The Disjunction Fallacy or Irrational Prudence* A good way to extend the text discussion of thinking errors is to describe the **disjunction fallacy,** or what might be called **irrational prudence.** People tend to make decisions that seem prudent but are actually irrational. (*Teacher's Resource Binder*, p. 23-1)
- Enrichment Lesson: *The Computer and Common Sense* Some psychologists argue that computers are inherently limited by their lack of common sense—that vast store of knowledge that we habitually use to interpret everyday experience. (*Teacher's Resource Binder*, p. 23-1)

Language

V Video Center

Consult the faculty guides from *The Mind* or the *Scientific American Frontiers* video series for descriptions of these modules or segments.

- Videocassette: *The Mind,* Second Edition, Module 28: "Language and Culture" (*Teacher's Resource Binder*, p. 23-1)
- Videocassette: *The Mind,* Second Edition, Module 25: "Human Language: Signed and Spoken" (*Teacher's Resource Binder*, p. 23-1)
- Videocassette: *The Mind,* Second Edition, Module 23: "Infant Speech Sound Discrimination" (*Teacher's Resource Binder*, p. 23-1)
- Videocassette: *The Mind,* Second Edition, Module 24: "Language Predisposition" (*Teacher's Resource Binder*, p. 23-1)
- Videocassette: *Scientific American Frontiers,* Second Edition, Segment 18: "Talking Babies" (*Teacher's Resource Binder*, p. 23-1)
- Videocassette: *Scientific American Frontiers,* Second Edition, Segment 21: "Born to Talk" (*Teacher's Resource Binder*, p. 23-1)

Activity Center

- Critical Thinking Activity: *Simple Language Device* Students can see just how diverse our language can be by creating grammatically correct sentences using the Simple Language Device. (*Teacher's Resource Binder*, p. 23-1; Handout 23–8)

Enrichment Center

- Enrichment Lesson: *Universals of Language* How are all languages the same? Two noted psychologists outline aspects of language that are universal. (*Teacher's Resource Binder*, p. 23-1)
- Enrichment Lesson: *Language Development* Ronald Macaulay discusses the interesting complexity of language development in his fascinating book *The Social Art.* Macaulay notes that children do not learn language totally anew nor do they learn it like a parrot by memorizing complete utterances. Rather, in the early stages, they do a little of both. (*Teacher's Resource Binder*, p. 23-1)
- Enrichment Lesson: *The Smart-Talk Syndrome* Williams syndrome can be discussed either as part of language development or in connection with the relationship between thought and language. This intriguing disorder could be labeled language without thought. (*Teacher's Resource Binder*, p. 23-1)

Thinking and Language Together

V Video Center

Consult the faculty guides from the *Scientific American Frontiers* or *The Mind* video series for descriptions of these segments or modules.

- Videocassette: *Scientific American Frontiers,* Second Edition, Segment 19: "If Only They Could Talk!" (*Teacher's Resource Binder*, p. 23-1)
- Videocassette: *Scientific American Frontiers,* Second Edition, Segment 20: "Who Needs Words, Anyway?" (*Teacher's Resource Binder*, p. 23-1)
- Videocassette: *The Mind,* Second Edition, Module 27: "Animal Language" (*Teacher's Resource Binder*, p. 23-1)

Activity Center

- Critical Thinking Activity: *Doublespeak* How we label things can determine how we perceive them—for example, garbagemen as sanitation engineers. Lead students through this activity that challenges them to decipher doublespeak. (*Teacher's Resource Binder*, p. 23-1; Handout 23–9)
- Application Activity: *Flaws in Mental Imagery* Our ability to create mental pictures of verbal descriptions might not be as good as we think it is. (*Teacher's Resource Binder*, p. 23-1; Handout 23–10)
- Application Activity: *Creating Mental Pictures from Verbal Descriptions* This activity, used in conjunction with the previous one (Application Activity: *Flaws in Mental Imagery*) can help students see just how good they are at creating a mental picture when given a verbal description. (*Teacher's Resource Binder*, p. 23-1)

- Demonstration Activity: *Two Aspects of Visual Imagery* In his book *Experiences in Visual Thinking*, Robert McKim suggests that two aspects of visual imagery are important. The first is clarity—the sharpness of our mental pictures. The second is control—the degree to which we can manipulate our images. (*Teacher's Resource Binder*, p. 23-1)
- Technology Application Activity: *PsychSim:* "Maze Learning" *PsychSim* is an interactive CD-ROM containing tutorials in different content areas of psychology. In this tutorial, students have a wonderful time using cognitive maps to direct a rat to cheese. (*Teacher's Resource Binder*, p. 23-1)
- Application Activity: *Creating a Mental Model* Margaret Matlin notes that when we hear a description of a place, we actively create a mental model that represents the important features of the scene. Research suggests that those who have been asked to draw maps of environments they have merely read about are just as accurate as those who have studied maps. (*Teacher's Resource Binder*, p. 23-1)

Enrichment Center

- Enrichment Lesson: *The Impact of Language on Thought* Beth Azar reviews recent research that shows how language influences the way people think about and approach the world. (*Teacher's Resource Binder*, p. 23-1)
- Enrichment Lesson: *Kanzi and Mulika, Remarkable Pygmy Chimps* This lesson relates the story of Kanzi and Mulika, two pygmy chimps who learned how to communicate in very complex ways. (*Teacher's Resource Binder*, p. 23-1)

MODULE 23

Thinking and Language

Introducing the Module

The Points: Module Objectives

- Define *concept,* and explain why it is useful.
- Define algorithms and heuristics, and explain how they help us solve problems.
- Analyze how fixation, confirmation bias, heuristics, overconfidence, framing, and belief perseverance influence our ability to solve problems.
- Describe the role that phonemes, morphemes, and grammar play in the structure of language.
- Analyze how we learn language.
- Delineate the stages children go through in the development of language.
- Describe the linguistic relativity hypothesis, and discuss whether it is possible to think without language.

trb tr Building Vocabulary

Working with partners or in small groups, have students improve their knowledge of the concepts in the module by having them complete the crossword puzzle presented in the handout for **Building Vocabulary:** *Crossword Puzzle* (*Teacher's Resource Binder*, p. 23-1; **Handout 23–2**). You may wish to use the handout as a transparency and project a correctly completed puzzle for students to use as an answer guide.

Teaching the Points

web ■ TEACHING TIP

You can log on as an instructor to the book companion site for *Thinking About Psychology* at **www.worthpublishers.com/thinkingaboutpsych**. It contains teacher resources for class presentations as well as review and assessment of module concepts and terms.

MODULE 23

Thinking and Language

Thinking

Language

Thinking and Language Together

What is it that makes us human? Are there characteristics that separate us from other species, characteristics uniquely human that only we can claim? How about our thinking abilities and powers of communication? Indeed, in **cognitive abilities**—the mental activities associated with thinking, knowing, and remembering—humans have no equals. Consider how much of your day you spend in thought, and how much of that thought relies on language. Where would you be without cognition? School wouldn't exist. There would be no computers, television, or radio—they all depend on language processing. Thinking is involved in almost every aspect of our day-to-day life, from deciding what clothes to put on in the morning (Does this shirt match my pants? It's cold—maybe I need a sweater) to making the judgments necessary for safe driving to ironing out differences of opinion with friends.

In this module we will first think about thinking, a topic so central to psychology and being human that it has found a place in the title of this book. Then we will turn our attention to language—one of the most remarkable aspects of our ability to think.

Thinking

▶ **cognitive abilities** All the mental activities associated with thinking, knowing, and remembering.

We organize and process vast amounts of information with ease. Sensory information—the processing of depth and color, for example, and the monitoring of balance, body temperature, and other internal systems—often takes place subconsciously, without our being actively aware it's occurring. On the conscious level, we turn our attention to solving

Getting Started

Thinking about thinking, which this module asks students to do, is a very abstract concept that is difficult for many to ponder. In addition, this module also challenges students to determine whether language is necessary for thought. Pose the following questions to students as an introductory activity:

- What separates humans from other forms of life—cognition or language or both?
- Can humans think without language? Does that make one more important than the other? Why or why not?

trb You may wish to use **Critical Thinking:** *Fact or Falsehood?* (*Teacher's Resource Binder*, p. 23-1; **Handout 23–1**) as a prereading strategy to find out what students already know about thinking and language. The activity will prime students to note terms and concepts in the text that confirm or dispel their preconceptions about thinking and language.

countless problems in the course of a day. We exercise judgment regularly. We do make mistakes, sometimes, but most of the time our thinking is remarkably accurate. Let's look at some of the components of thinking.

▶ **concept** A mental grouping based on shared similarity.

▶ **prototype** A typical best example incorporating the major features of a concept.

Concepts

What's the Point? 1. How do we define *concept,* and why is a concept useful?

Psychologists define a **concept** as a mental group based on shared similarities. This definition differs from the more general definition of concept as "an idea" that we hear in everyday speech. Psychologists use the more precise term when they study the conceptual categories we form when we use our built-in capacity to group objects, events, and people that share some similar characteristics. Your kitchen is more efficient with its various items sorted—silverware in one place, canned goods in another. Your brain also sorts information into conceptual categories. Thus, you have a concept for trees, another for bicycles, and yet another for balls. These mental categories let you make instant judgments about new objects you've never seen before. When you come across a new tree, you know in a split second that it belongs in the concept "tree." You know this because it is in some ways similar (a bark-covered, wooden cylinder with branches and, in the right season, leaves) to other trees you have seen. Effortlessly grouping objects into concepts certainly beats wondering, "Gee, what is that tall thing with the green top?"

Encountering new information for which you have no matching concepts is awkward. Perhaps you remember the character Pat from *Saturday Night Live*? Pat was funny because you couldn't determine whether he (or she) was male (or female). Clothing, mannerisms, language, and even the name left you wondering. The uncertainty created the humor. Other examples abound. I can remember being invited to a friend's room during my first year in college. Steve had been given a beanbag chair. They had just been invented, and I had never seen one before. He said, "How do you like my new chair?" I actually argued that it wasn't a chair. My concept of chair included many kinds of chairs, but not beanbags. This glaring inability to classify the new object was memorable because we typically categorize almost effortlessly.

One of the ways we decide whether something belongs in a concept is by matching it with our **prototype**, a typical best example of the concept that incorporates all its key features (Rosch, 1978). The closer the new object is to our prototype, the faster and more easily we can categorize it. We are quicker to recognize an oak tree as a tree than we are to assign a tiny Japanese bonsai tree to this category. Both qualify as trees, but

Male or Female? We have well-defined concepts of male and female that normally help us to quickly and efficiently categorize new people into proper groups. Pat, a character who appeared on the TV show *Saturday Night Live*, was funny because s/he did not clearly fit into either group.

Cooperative Learning

Have students work in small groups, and give each group a couple of simple concepts—for example, *tree, flower, girl, boy, athlete, president.* Have each group come up with a prototype for the concepts by creating drawings, collages, or computer-generated images. Allow time for groups to make presentations of their prototypes, accompanied by brief explanations of how they came to a consensus for each concept prototype.

MODULE 23

■ TEACHING TIPS

(1) Ask students what it means to think. This concept may be too abstract for some of your students. But challenging them to think about the basics of thought and language is central to developing mental maturity and to understanding psychology.

trb At this point, you may wish to use Analysis Activity: *Cognitive Complexity* (*Teacher's Resource Binder*, p. 23-1).

(2) Link the discussion of concepts with Jean Piaget's idea of schemas—basic units of cognition. As people process information, they either assimilate it or accommodate it.

- Assimilation involves putting the new information into an existing category.
- Accommodation requires one to change or adapt a category to suit the new information that conflicted with or added to the old category.

(3) Create a list of the different concepts that are represented in your classroom. Try to narrow down all the objects into the simplest concept possible—such as *furniture, floor covering, shelving, books,* and so forth. Do not share your list with students. Rather, have students look around the classroom and create lists of their own. Combine all the students' lists into one complete list of classroom concepts. Then compare the class list with yours. Debate will surely ensue over what the simplest concepts are and how to categorize certain items.

■ JOURNAL WRITING

Invite students to use the following questions and writing prompts as springboards for entries in their psychology journals:

- How would you explain thoughts to someone visiting from another planet?
- Have you ever come across something that didn't match your existing concept? Describe your experience.

MODULE 23

■ APPLYING THE POINTS

(1) Contact a professor at a local medical school to see if the school has any courses or experience in helping medical students diagnose illnesses that don't necessarily fall into a particular prototype. Ask the professor what advice he or she gives medical students about how to diagnose illnesses accurately. Incorporate what you learn from this informal interview into class discussion.

trb At this point, you may wish to use Demonstration Activity: *Confirmation Bias* (*Teacher's Resource Binder*, p. 23-1).

(2) On their next visit to a store of any kind, have students notice the number of different categories into which the store's personnel have divided the items they sell. Challenge students to write down the different categories they notice and bring the lists to class. Then, have them compare how different stores categorize merchandise.

■ TEACHING TIP

Students can study more effectively if they are adept at making concept hierarchies. Point out that textbooks are commonly divided into these hierarchies. Main concepts often appear as headings that are boldfaced. Subconcepts look different from the main concepts. In addition, important terms, even though the same print size as running text, often appear italicized or boldfaced. If students recognize these concept hierarchies as they study, they will see the big picture the textbook authors are trying to communicate—and that can lead to a better understanding of the textbook material.

trb At this point, you may wish to use Analysis Activity: *Cognitive Complexity* (*Teacher's Resource Binder*, p. 23-1).

When Is a Chair Not a Chair? We are quicker to recognize the item on the left as a chair because it more closely resembles our prototype than does the beanbag chair on the right.

the oak is much closer to our prototype—it is somehow more treelike than a bonsai (to us, at least; the Japanese bonsai grower might pause at the sight of a giant California sequoia). I struggled to identify my friend's beanbag as a chair because it was much further from my prototype than the desk chair and old armchair that furnished my dorm room. Some prototype biases are more serious. For example, we may not recognize an illness as quickly if the symptoms don't match our prototype for that disease (Bishop, 1991). This can be a fatal error for people who don't realize they are having a heart attack because their symptoms don't match their prototype for this condition.

We develop *concept hierarchies* to keep mental information organized. Consider our hierarchy for organizing food in our culture. We begin by learning basic concepts like bread and cake. From there, we identify more specific concepts that fit under each of the basic ones—bread includes white bread, French bread, and banana bread, and cake includes angel food cake, sheet cake, and cupcakes. Bread and cake, in turn, fit into the larger category of baked goods. Similarly, we can break the basic concepts of cheese and milk into more specific concepts (cheddar and skim) or lump them into a broader concept (dairy products). This organizational hierarchy, which we begin to build as we learn the basic concepts (bread, cake, cheese, and milk) as young children, helps us process information about food quickly and efficiently. Grocery stores organize their products to take advantage of our understanding of broad categories, such as frozen food and canned goods. We develop similar hierarchies to deal with concepts as diverse as tools, vehicles, and recreation (Figure 23.1). Our brains have a strong tendency to keep information neat and tidy. Most of us organize our computer files in a similar fashion, with folders representing a few broad categories (school, music, correspondence, and so on) each containing more

Suggested Readings

Use the following as teacher-preparation tools or as enrichment for advanced students:

Adams, J. (1976). *Conceptual blockbusting.* San Francisco: San Francisco Book Company.

Budiansky, S. (1998). *If a lion could talk: Animal intelligence and the evolution of consciousness.* New York: Free Press.

Gilovich, T. (1991). *How we know what isn't so: The fallibility of human reason in everyday life.* New York: Free Press.

Hunt, M. (1982). *The universe within: A new science explores the human mind.* New York: Simon & Schuster.

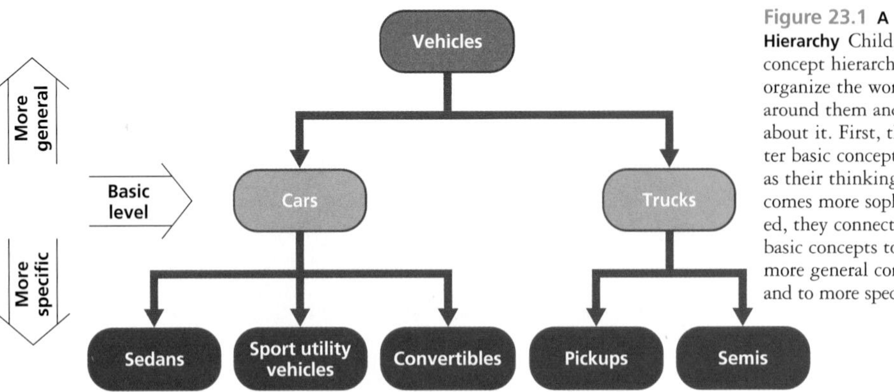

Figure 23.1 **A Concept Hierarchy** Children use concept hierarchies to organize the world around them and learn about it. First, they master basic concepts. Then, as their thinking becomes more sophisticated, they connect those basic concepts to both more general concepts and to more specific ones.

folders with ever more specific topics. When you organize your computer's folders and files, you are creating a hierarchy. (I wonder why the one on my computer is less well organized than the one in my head?)

Problem Solving

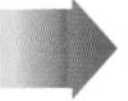

2. What are algorithms and heuristics, and how do they help us solve problems?

Are there enough problems in your life? Probably so. Problems exist when something blocks you from achieving a desired outcome. If you need to get to school but are caught in traffic, that's a problem. If you want a B in your psychology class but are 30 points short, that's a problem. Problems can range from trivial (deciding which of two well-liked albums to put on the CD player) to serious (figuring out what path will allow you to achieve your goals after graduating). We all have several strategies we apply when problems arise in our lives. Many of these strategies fall into the broad categories of *algorithms* and *heuristics*.

Algorithms

An **algorithm** is a strategy that guarantees a solution to a problem. Here are some examples of algorithms:

- Applying the formula "length times height" to determine the area of a rectangle. Many mathematical formulas are algorithms.
- Systematically trying every possible combination on someone's locker until you come across the correct one.
- Checking every shelf of every aisle in a grocery store until you find the Gatorade.

▶ **algorithm** A problem-solving strategy that guarantees the solution to the problem.

Levy, D. (1997). *Tools of critical thinking: Metathoughts for psychology.* Boston: Allyn & Bacon.

Lutz, W. (1989). *Doublespeak.* New York: HarperCollins.

Pinker, S. (1997). *How the mind works* (pp. 284, 293). New York: Norton.

Restak, R. M. (1988). *The mind.* New York: Bantam.

Stanovich, K. (1998). *How to think straight about psychology* (5th ed.). New York: HarperCollins.

Tversky, A., & Kahneman, D. (1980). Causal schemas in judgments under uncertainty. In M. Fishbeinn (Ed.), *Progress in social psychology* (Vol. 2). Hillsdale, NJ: Erlbaum.

Wade, C., & Tavris, C. (1993). *Critical and creative thinking: The case of love and war.* New York: HarperCollins.

■ **CHECKING FOR UNDERSTANDING**

Give students a concept and have them form a hierarchy for it, getting as detailed as they can and progressing from the general to the specific. For variety, give each student a different concept or divide the class into small groups, with each group assigned a different concept. By evaluating this endeavor, you can determine whether students understand concepts, prototypes, and concept hierarchies.

trb tr ■ **TEACHING TIP**

A black-line master for Figure 23.1, A Concept Hierarchy, is available in the **Black-Line Masters Appendix** of the *Teacher's Resource Binder.*

■ **JOURNAL WRITING**

Invite students to use the following questions and writing prompts as springboards for entries in their psychology journals:

- Think of your favorite store. Would you change anything about the way personnel organize the merchandise? Are the categories too specific or too general? Why do you think so?
- How have your organized the files on your computer? Are these categories specific or general? Why or why not?
- What are some problems you have in your life that need solving? Do you have a plan to solve any of them? If so, what is the plan? Do you think it will succeed? Why or why not?

F•Y•I

How students view problems can determine whether they will succeed in solving them. If students are generally pessimistic, then they will view problems as obstacles that pervade and ruin their lives. If students are optimistic, they will tend to view problems as challenges they have the power to overcome.

trb At this point, you may wish to use Critical Thinking Activity: *Problem-Solving Strategies* (*Teacher's Resource Binder*, p. 23-1; Handout 23–3).

MODULE 23

■ **LOOKING AT THE ISSUES**

Heuristics are very useful and efficient, but they can be a problem when they lead people to jump to conclusions. For instance, racial profiling has come under scrutiny as certain ethnic groups claim they are being singled out for suspicion solely on the basis of their race. Explore racial profiling in a class forum by asking the following questions:

- How is racial profiling a heuristic?
- What benefits and problems does racial profiling create?
- If you were in charge, would you allow the police to use racial profiling? Why or why not?

trb At this point, you may wish to use Demonstration Activity: *The Representativeness Heuristic* (*Teacher's Resource Binder*, p. 23-1) or Analysis Activity: *The Availability Heuristic* (*Teacher's Resource Binder*, p. 23-1; Handout 23–5).

F • Y • I

Notice that three heuristic rules exist in the following poem about a spelling rule:

i before *e* except after *c*
Or when it sounds like *a* as in *neighbor* and *weigh*
Isn't that weird?

The first is the most commonly known and the most commonly applied in spelling words like *receive* or *believe*. The second involves an aspect of spelling that can be applied to a wide variety of words, but is lesser known. The third line shows just how complex English spelling can be since the word *weird* doesn't follow either heuristic, but it is spelled correctly.

Sometimes, using algorithms and memorizing spelling words is more effective in learning correct spelling than using heuristics!

trb At this point, you may wish to use Demonstration Activity: *The Representativeness Heuristic* (*Teacher's Resource Binder*, p. 23-1) or Analysis Activity: *The Availability Heuristic* (*Teacher's Resource Binder*, p. 23-1; Handout 23–5).

Algorithms and Heuristics If your problem is to find a particular sports book as a gift for your younger brother, would you be better off systematically checking every book on every shelf—an algorithm—or starting in the sports section—a heuristic? If you're like me, you may even try another heuristic—asking for help!

As you can tell from these examples, algorithms are not always efficient. They may eventually yield a solution to the problem, but only after a long and tedious process. Knowing this, computer programmers may build algorithms into their software. The computers do the tedious work, and we benefit from the solutions.

Heuristics

A **heuristic** is a rule-of-thumb guide that increases our efficiency but does not always lead us to the correct solutions. Here are some examples of heuristics:

- Using spelling rules such as "*i* before *e* except after *c*."
- Checking in the canned goods section of a grocery store to find a particular brand of baked beans.

Heuristics are shortcuts. When they work, we are likely to reuse them the next time we need to save time and increase our mental efficiency in a similar situation.

Insight

Sometimes the solution to a problem pops into your head so quickly that you don't have time to employ a strategy. These wonderfully rewarding moments are examples of **insight**, the sudden realization (Aha!) of a solution. Cartoons often express a moment of insight as a light bulb over the character's head. Insight is fun, satisfying, and one of the reasons most of us enjoy working on word jumbles and other types of mental puzzles—we experience a very pleasing excitement when that answer pops into our head (Figure 23.2). Chimpanzees appear to share

► **heuristic** A rule-of-thumb problem-solving strategy that makes a solution more likely and efficient but does not guarantee a solution.

► **insight** The sudden realization (Aha!) of the solution to a problem.

Cross-Curricular Connections

MATHEMATICS AND SCIENCES Mathematics and the sciences are disciplines that contain numerous heuristics and algorithms. Have students brainstorm all the different heuristics and algorithms they have learned over the years in these classes. Since students may be taking different levels of math and science, have them brainstorm about particular types of concepts at each level of math or science and then make comparisons to see which concepts are retained as the level of courses in a subject progress.

JUMBLE
THAT SCRAMBLED WORD GAME
by Henri Arnold and Mike Argirion
Unscramble these four Jumbles, one letter to each square, to form four ordinary words.
UFYSS
©2002 Tribune Media Services, Inc. All Rights Reserved.
WHAAS
PANDEM
www.jumble.com
SPOXEE
Good dog
7-19
WHEN HE STOPPED TO "SHAKE" WITH THE DOGS HE SAID IT WAS---
Now arrange the circled letters to form the surprise answer, as suggested by the above cartoon.
Answer: A

Figure 23.2 **Insight** Enjoy the "Aha!" as the solutions to these jumbled words pop into your head (see page 437 for answers).

with humans the ability to form insights. In one classic study (Köhler, 1927), a chimp suddenly realized he could stack several boxes to form a platform from which he could reach bananas that had been suspended from the ceiling.

Problems Solving Problems

3. How can fixation, the confirmation bias, heuristics, overconfidence, framing, and belief perseverance influence our ability to solve problems?

A variety of very normal tendencies can hinder our ability to solve problems effectively. Many of them give us tunnel vision, preventing us from searching for alternatives that might offer terrific solutions. Let's look at six of these tendencies.

Fixation

We often approach similar problems with a consistent strategy known as a **mental set**. Mental sets are helpful a lot of the time because they are efficient and may lead to a rapid solution. Many chess players, for example, have a particular move they like to open with because they have learned it usually leads to a win. Engine mechanics often employ a particular approach to diagnosing and repairing problems. Technical

▶ **mental set** A tendency to approach a problem in a particular way. A mental set may or may not be helpful in solving a new problem.

Cross-Curricular Connections

WORLD LANGUAGES STUDY If students take a foreign language course or speak more than one language, have them share the heuristics used for those languages that help both native and non-native speakers learn them. Then, compare and contrast the heuristics used in other languages with those used in English. What similarities exist? In what approximate proportion are the similarities to the differences?

■ APPLYING THE POINTS

(1) Ask students to bring in puzzles from newspapers, magazines, or puzzle books. Have them work in small groups to share and then compare the puzzles and problem-solving strategies they come up with for solving the puzzles. Ask groups to explore the following questions:

- How are the strategies similar from one puzzle to the next? How are the strategies similar or different among different group members?
- With which type of puzzle problems would you use algorithms? With which type would you use heuristics?
- How effective and efficient are these strategies? Are you faster using heuristics or algorithms?

trb At this point, you may wish to use Critical Thinking Activity: *Solving Puzzles* (*Teacher's Resource Binder*, p. 23-1).

(2) You may want students to bring in a particular type of puzzle (a word search, crossword puzzle, or cryptogram) and solve it in class. As students work on puzzles, ask them to think about the specific strategies they are employing. Review their work by asking the following questions:

- Did you start out using heuristics and then employ algorithms when the heuristics didn't work?
- Was the strategy you used when solving your puzzle similar to the strategy you used to solve the Jumble puzzle in Figure 23.2 on page 435 of the *Student Edition*?

trb At this point, you may wish to use Technology Application Activity: *The Tower of Hanoi Problem* (*Teacher's Resource Binder*, p. 23-1) or Demonstration Activity: *Dice Games to Demonstrate Problem Solving* (*Teacher's Resource Binder*, p. 23-1).

MODULE 23

■ TEACHING TIP

Have students try to figure out the water jar problem showcased in Figure 23.3 and the nine-dot problem in Figure 23.4. To solve the problems successfully, students will have to break free of conventional ways of thinking—in one, they will literally have to "go outside the box"!

tr A four-color transparency of Figure 23.3, The Luchins Water Jar Problem, is available in the **Overhead Transparencies Set.**

trb **tr** A black-line master for Figure 23.4, The Nine-Dot Problem, is available in the **Black-Line Masters Appendix** of the *Teacher's Resource Binder.*

trb At this point, you may wish to use **Critical Thinking Activity:** *Solving Puzzles* (*Teacher's Resource Binder*, p. 23-1).

■ APPLYING THE POINTS

Riddles and jokes are a great way to engage students and challenge their mental sets. In addition to the riddles and jokes posed in the book, you may also wish to pose to students any of the following jokes and riddles:

(1) The maker doesn't want it, the buyer doesn't use it, and the user doesn't see it. What is it? *(A coffin.)*

(2) Something extraordinarily unusual happened on the 6th of May in 1978 at 12:34 P.M. What was it? *(At that moment, the time and day could be written as 12:34, 5/6/78.)*

(3) What occurs once in every minute, twice in every moment, yet never in a thousand years? *(The letter* m.*)*

(4) A man left home one morning. He turned right and ran straight ahead. Then, he turned left. After a while, he turned left again, running faster than ever. Then he turned left once more and decided to go home. In the distance, he could see two masked men waiting for him. Who were they? *(The umpire and the other team's catcher.)*

▶ **fixation** A mental set that hinders the solution of a problem.

▶ **functional fixedness** The tendency to think of things only in terms of their usual functions; an impediment to problem solving.

▶ **confirmation bias** The tendency to focus on information that supports one's preconceptions.

support personnel learn mental sets to help them help customers with computer problems. They ask questions designed to focus on specific problems, usually beginning with very basic, but sometimes overlooked, issues ("Is the computer plugged in?").

Sometimes, however, mental set can get in the way. Instead of becoming an efficient problem-solving strategy, it becomes a **fixation**—a rigidly applied recipe that constitutes an obstacle. Have you heard the expression "thinking outside the box"? It implies breaking away from routine, conventional ways of thinking—away from your mental set. Even though these old ways of thinking may have worked in the past, something new and different may now be required. Henry Ford was able to see that cars could be mass-produced by having workers specialize in a single task as an assembly line brought each vehicle past them. By thinking outside the box, he was able to manufacture cars far more cheaply than he could have if a small team of individuals had built one car at a time from the ground up. Ford revolutionized manufacturing by breaking free from old traditions. Can you break free from your own fixations? Find out by trying your hand at the puzzles in Figures 23.3 and 23.4.

Figure 23.3 **The Luchins Water Jar Problem** Can you measure out the amount of water in the right-hand column, using any of the three jars (A, B, and C) with volumes as shown in the middle column? The solution appears as Figure 23.6 on page 438. (From Luchins, 1946.)

Problem	Given jugs of these sizes A	B	C	Measure out this much water
1	21	127	3	100
2	14	46	5	22
3	18	43	10	5
4	7	42	6	23
5	20	57	4	29
6	23	49	3	20
7	15	39	3	18

Figure 23.4 **The Nine-Dot Problem** Make a copy of this figure on a piece of scratch paper (don't even *think* about writing in this book!) and try to connect all nine dots with four straight lines without lifting your pen or pencil from the paper. The solution appears as Figure 23.7 on page 438.

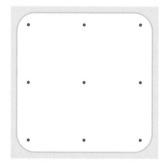

A special kind of fixation is known as **functional fixedness**, the inability to think of different uses for objects. What if you need to remove a screw, but you don't have access to a screwdriver? If you have trouble thinking of other things that can be used to perform this function, you are suffering from functional fixedness. However, if you are mentally flexible enough to realize that a coin, a butter knife, the edge of a

Demonstrating

FIXATION AND GLASSES To further demonstrate fixation on problem solving, draw six drinking glasses in a row on the chalkboard. Shade the contents of the first three to indicate water, but do not shade the last three (indicating that they are empty). Then, pose the following situation:

- Six glasses are in a row. The first three are filled with water, and the last three are empty. By moving only one glass, can you arrange them so that the full and the empty glasses alternate? *(Pour the water from the second glass into the fifth glass.)*

trb At this point, you may wish to use **Demonstration Activity:** *Demonstrating Mental Set* (*Teacher's Resource Binder*, p. 23-1).

credit card, or a paper clip (among many other items) can all be used as a substitute screwdriver, you are good at overcoming functional fixedness. If there's no molasses for the cookies, a clever baker substitutes honey. If there's no bracket for a loose tailpipe, a clever mechanic substitutes a coat hanger. If there's no toilet paper in the supplies box, a clever camper substitutes a leaf (a solution employed long ago by a friend of mine, who, unfortunately, had never learned to identify poison ivy!). Finding new uses for duct tape has produced a cult following. Ready for a functional fixedness challenge? See Figure 23.5.

Figure 23.5 **The Candle-Mounting Problem** Can you think of a way to use these materials to mount the candle on a bulletin board? The solution appears as Figure 23.8 on page 440. (From Duncker, 1945.)

Confirmation Bias

Confirmation bias is our tendency to notice information that supports our hunches more readily than we notice information that conflicts with our hunches. I had a student drop by the other day because she was concerned about her grade in my class. She felt she must be doing better than the grade indicated. I sometimes do make mistakes in calculating a student's grade, but in this case, the problem was hers. She was recalling accurately the quizzes on which she had done well, but she had forgotten several on which she had performed poorly at the beginning of the quarter. She knew she was a bright, capable student. This preconception made her more likely to notice (and remember) the quiz scores that confirmed this idea than the ones that refuted it. As a result, her own estimate of what her grade should be was inflated.

Confirmation bias can have a serious impact on juries in criminal trials. As testimony unfolds, each member of the jury begins to develop a hypothetical story to explain what happened. One juror may speculate, for example, that the defendant acted out of fear. From this point on, the

Answers to Jumble puzzle in Figure 23.2, page 435: Fussy, awash, dampen, expose; A paws pause.

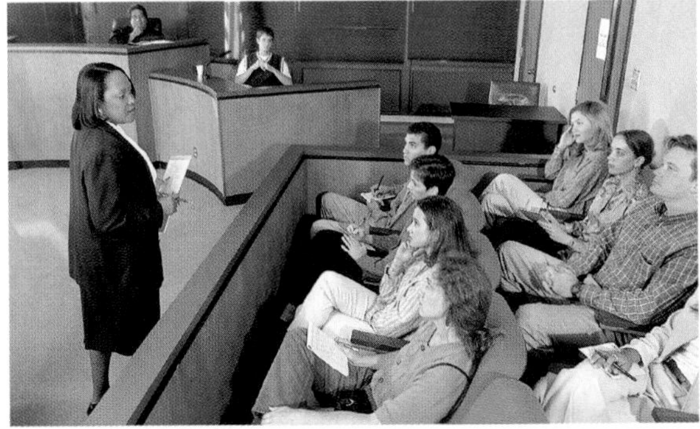

Confirmation Bias As testimony unfolds, each member of this jury will develop a personal story to explain the crime and will then focus more on the evidence that supports that personal story. When the jury meets later to deliberate, the jurors may be surprised to discover how individual their stories are and how different pieces of evidence and testimony stood out as a result.

MODULE 23

■ JOURNAL WRITING

Invite students to use the following questions and writing prompts as springboards for entries in their psychology journals:

- Describe a time when fixation caused you to fail in solving a problem.
- Do you like puzzles, or do you shy away from them in general? Why?
- Have you ever been fooled by someone who turned out to be different than he or she appeared to be? How did confirmation bias play into your gullibility?

■ TEACHING TIPS

tr (1) A four-color transparency of Figure 23.5, The Candle-Mounting Problem, is available in the **Overhead Transparencies Set.**

(2) Present several common objects—for instance, scissors, a paper clip, a wad of chewing gum, and a spoon. Have students form groups and brainstorm about different, nontraditional uses for each item. Compile a master list for each item and its possible uses. Everyone will notice the variety of clever uses for each item as group members break set to come up with different uses.

trb At this point, you may wish to use **Demonstration Activity:** ***Demonstrating Mental Set*** (***Teacher's Resource Binder***, p. 23-1).

■ APPLYING THE POINTS

Contact a local attorney or judge to ask about legal issues involved in jury deliberations. Present in class the responses you learn to the following questions:

- What are the basic procedures that must be followed by juries during deliberations?
- What legal obligations do juries have when deliberating? What types of evidence must they consider over others?
- What type of evidence is excluded from trials to keep juries from becoming biased?
- What rules must jury members follow during the course of a trial to keep from becoming biased?

Demonstrating

MENTAL SET AND A BEAR Use the following riddle to encourage breaking mental set in your students even more:

> A hunter sees a bear 1 mile due south. He shoots, misses, and the bear runs off. The hunter walks the 1 mile south to where the bear had been, then 1 mile due east, then 1 mile due north—at which point, the hunter is standing, again, at exactly the same spot from which the gun had been fired. Question: "What color was the bear?"

If necessary, provide the additional question, "Where on the globe is the hunter? Where can one go, successively, 1 mile due south, then 1 mile due east, then 1 mile due north, and end up at the same place one started from?" *(Only the North Pole satisfies this requirement. The bear is a polar bear and, thus, white.)*

MODULE 23

(F • Y • I)

Daniel Kahneman, a professor of psychology and public affairs at Princeton University, won the 2002 Nobel Prize in Economics for his work with the late Amos Tversky on counterproductive heuristics as they apply to money. Kahneman and Tversky's work showed how people tend to make decisions that aren't predictable, using standard probability formulas. (Amos Tversky was ineligible for the award because the Nobel Prizes are not awarded posthumously.)

■ **LOOKING AT THE ISSUES**

People perceive certain situations as dangerous once a memorable tragedy occurs, even though the actual activity may not be as dangerous as more common activities. For example, people will be afraid of flying because they've seen coverage of a plane crash, but they will have no fear of driving in a car, in which there is a greater likelihood of accident. In light of recent publicized tragedies, invite students to share their feelings about situations like flying in airplanes, working in tall buildings, traveling in space vehicles, and being kidnapped.

trb At this point, you may wish to use Analysis Activity: *Risk Averse Versus Loss Averse* (*Teacher's Resource Binder*, p. 23-1; Handout 23–7).

■ **TEACHING TIP**

The FBI classifies crime in the United States into two categories: violent crimes, such as murder, rape, armed robbery, and assault; and property crimes, such as burglary, larceny, and car theft. Here are some interesting related statistics:

- In 1996, 12 percent of all reported crimes were violent.
- Of accused felons, 1 percent plead insanity—and of those only 25 percent are ultimately acquitted.
- Less than 10 percent of convictions for felony crimes result from jury trials—over 90 percent result from plea-bargaining.

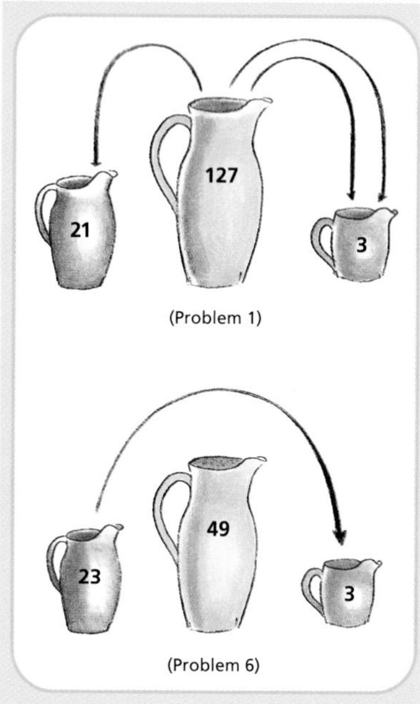

Figure 23.6 **Solution to the Luchins Water Jar Problem on Page 436.** Problems 1 through 7 can all be solved by filling Jar B, then pouring off enough water to fill Jar A once and Jar C twice (desired volume = B − A − 2C). However, Problem 6 can be solved with a simpler formula (A − C), and so can Problem 7 (A + C). Many people miss these easy solutions because the mental set from the first several problems becomes fixated. Did your thinking stay flexible? (From Luchins, 1946.)

juror will be more likely to notice testimony that supports this particular story and will be less likely to consider nonconfirming testimony. Once the testimony is complete and deliberations begin, the assembled jury is often surprised to learn that various members have generated (and confirmed) several different stories during the trial (Kuhn & others, 1994; Pennington & Hastie, 1993).

Counterproductive Heuristics

"Look before you leap." "A stitch in time saves nine." "Don't judge a book by its cover." No doubt you've been hearing expressions such as these since you were a little kid. Such statements are designed to lead you to better decisions and judgment. Your elders wanted to give you rule-of-thumb guidelines that would help you survive and thrive in the world. These guidelines qualify as *heuristics*, which you may recall are quick rule-of-thumb problem-solving strategies.

We all regularly use heuristics to get through the countless decisions we must make each day. Sometimes, however, our brain can fall in the trap of using seemingly helpful heuristics that actually lead us to inaccurate or harmful decisions. **Amos Tversky** and **Daniel Kahneman** (1974) identified several counterproductive heuristics. One of them, the **availability heuristic**, uses information from our memory to judge the likelihood of events. Information that is readily available in our memory can indeed be a good indicator that an event is likely. When I hear thunder, I am quick to assume that rain will follow because I have many instances available in my memory when thunder signaled rain. Sometimes, though, the information available in memory is not such a good indicator.

The lottery commission in my state of Iowa intentionally uses the availability heuristic to influence people's judgment of their likelihood of winning. The commission does this by run-

Figure 23.7 **Solution to the Nine-Dot Problem on Page 436.** This problem literally requires you to "think outside the box." Only by leaving the square created by the outer dots can you solve the problem.

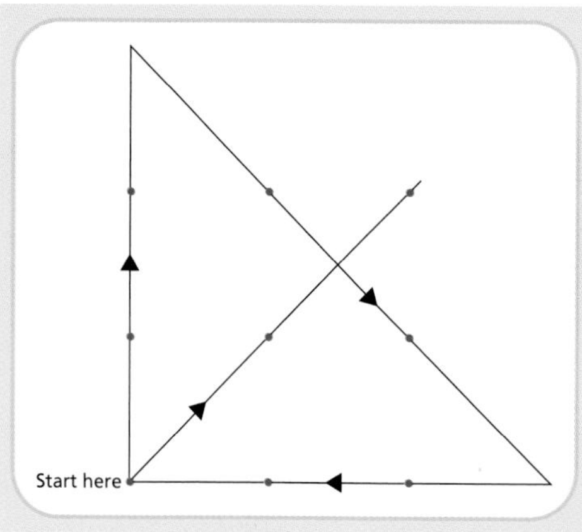

Demonstrating

HEURISTICS AND A BET You can also demonstrate how heuristics leads to error by asking students to imagine they are offered a bet. A die with four green sides and two red ones will be rolled several times. They can be paid $25 if RGRRR or GRGRRR occurs. (Write each sequence on the chalkboard.) Which sequence do they think is more likely to pay off? Most will choose GRGRRR.

In fact, when Tversky and Kahneman posed this choice, either hypothetically or by offering hard cash, at least two-thirds chose that sequence (GRGRRR). Although the sequence is more representative of a die with four green faces (because green sides outnumber red sides), in actuality it is only two-thirds as likely because it is the same as the first alternative with the addition of a "G" (which has the probability of two-thirds on any given roll).

You're a Winner Available images can distort our thinking. Many people buy lottery tickets regularly because images such as this one lead them to believe winning big is much more likely than it actually is.

ning ads and commercials featuring the gleeful winners. Often these winners are holding huge million-dollar cardboard checks and talking about the wonderful ways in which the money will improve their lives. These images are readily available in viewers' memories when they next think about playing the lottery. (Big winners must be common because we see them on TV all the time!) Unfortunately, the commission does not show an equal number of dramatic images of a much more common category—lottery losers. As a result, many people greatly overestimate their chances of winning, which encourages them to play more than they otherwise would have. In these cases, the availability heuristic has clouded people's judgment. Kahneman's work on how such cognitive factors influence judgment led to a Nobel prize in economics in 2002.

Overconfidence

More often than not, people overestimate the likelihood that they are correct. **Overconfidence** occurs when our confidence is greater than our accuracy. One study (Kahneman & Tversky, 1979) asked participants to estimate answers to factual questions by completing such statements as, "I feel 98 percent certain that the population of New Zealand is more than ______ but less than ______." Did the instruction to be 98 percent certain produce answers that were correct 98 percent of the time? Not even close. People were able to "trap" the correct answer—3.7 million people—only two-thirds of the time. The gap between certainty (98 percent) and accuracy (66 percent) was nicely concealed by overconfidence. Even when participants are 100 percent certain of their answers, they are right only 85 percent of the time (Fischhoff & others, 1977).

▶ **Amos Tversky** (1937–1996) Psychologist who, along with Daniel Kahneman, conducted research to discover factors that influence human judgment and decision making.

▶ **Daniel Kahneman** (1934–) Psychologist who, along with Amos Tversky, conducted research to discover factors that influence human judgment and decision making. He won the Nobel prize for this work in 2002.

▶ **availability heuristic** Estimating the likelihood of events based on their availability in memory. We are sometimes right and sometimes wrong in assuming events available in memory are likely.

▶ **overconfidence** The tendency to be more confident than correct when estimating the accuracy of one's beliefs and judgments.

Cross-Curricular Connections

MATH Team teach a lesson about probability with a math teacher. In the lesson, make sure the answers to the following questions related to module concepts are covered:

- What are some basic premises of probability?
- Why does buying more lottery tickets not lead one to a greater chance of winning?

■ LOOKING AT THE ISSUES

Using print or Internet resources, have students research the probability of winning the lottery or winning at any number of casino games like blackjack, slot machines, or craps. Have them also research how many lottery tickets are sold in a year and how much revenue different casino games bring in. In a class discussion, explore students' findings by asking the following questions:

- Do the odds of winning seem good or bad?
- How do the revenues that gambling brings in compare with the odds of winning?
- Would you participate in any of these games, considering the odds of winning? Why or why not?
- Does buying more lottery tickets increase one's chances of winning? Why or why not?

trb At this point, you may wish to use Analysis Activity: *The Availability Heuristic* (*Teacher's Resource Binder*, p. 23-1; Handout 23–5).

F • Y • I

Most of us are more fearful of flying than driving because airplane crashes are vivid and memorable; but flying is, in fact, safer. At the time of its release, the movie *Jaws* produced a fear of sharks in swimmers that no factual data would support. When Abraham Lincoln met Harriet Beecher Stowe, whose book *Uncle Tom's Cabin* dramatically described the effects of slavery, he commented, "I'm happy to meet the little lady who started the Civil War." Consider this: When someone is thinking of buying a new car, whose testimony is usually most persuasive—a neighbor who has had problems with a particular model or *Consumer Reports*, whose conclusions about each model are based on dozens, perhaps hundreds, of reports?

MODULE 23

■ **TEACHING TIP**

Perhaps the simplest demonstration of overconfidence is to have students predict their score on a multiple-choice or another type of short-answer test immediately after they have completed it. (Have them note their estimate at the top of the test.) The majority will overestimate the number of questions they got right. Although the strength of this tendency will depend to some degree on the amount of feedback they have received on previous tests, some students continue to overestimate throughout the semester.

Consumers can be seduced by the way products are framed. For example, people may buy more during a "25 percent off" sale even though they may end up spending more money than they would if there hadn't been a sale. Also, people tend to overeat foods that are labeled "low-fat." They believe more of the food is the same as smaller servings of higher-fat foods, instead of realizing that the amount of fat they consume in either case is about the same.

trb At this point, you may wish to use **Critical Thinking Activity:** ***Framing Decisions*** (*Teacher's Resource Binder*, p. 23-1; **Handout 23–6**).

■ **JOURNAL WRITING**

Invite students to use the following questions as a springboard for entries in their psychology journals:

- How would you feel about beef that is 20 percent fat instead of 80 percent lean? Surgeons who had a 2 percent death rate versus a 98 percent success rate? Explain why you feel the way you do.

tb ■ **CHECKING FOR UNDERSTANDING**

Construct a quiz on the various terms in this module by using the *Test Bank*. Questions can range from multiple-choice to matching. By quizzing students at this point in the module, you can determine whether they understand the concepts thus far.

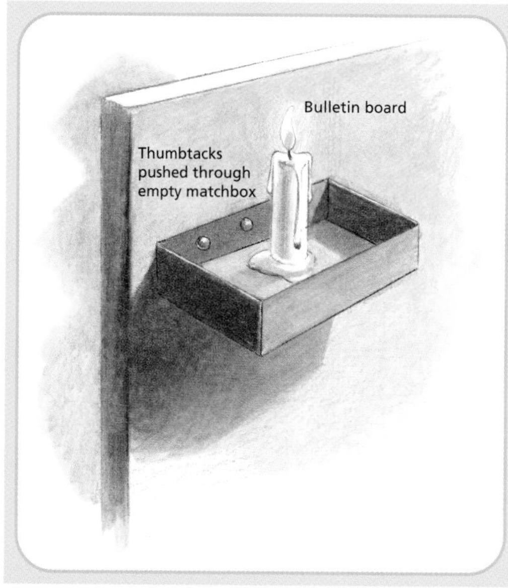

Figure 23.8 **Solution to the Candle-Mounting Problem on Page 437.** If you could not imagine using the box as anything other than a container to hold matches, functional fixedness impaired your problem-solving ability. (From Duncker, 1945.)

It's not just experiments that produce overconfidence. Decisions tainted by overconfidence work their way into everyday life on a regular basis. A friend of mine, psychologist Charles Brewer, frequently reminds people that "everything takes longer than it takes" to help dampen the frustration borne of overconfident planning. One study (Buehler & others, 1994) showed that students typically took twice as many days to complete a project as they originally predicted. I can relate. The work I'm doing on this module tonight is taking much longer than I anticipated.

Why do so many of us appear "programmed" to make false, overconfident judgments so regularly? It may be a way to protect our well-being. Overconfidence is associated with happiness and making tough decisions more easily (Baumeister, 1989; Taylor, 1989). Thinking everything will work out and believing in our own judgment can keep us from fretting and stewing about things.

Framing

Framing is the way we present an issue, and it can have a profound effect on judgment. Framing exactly the same issue in two different ways can produce two very different results. Consider these two statements:

1. Condoms have a 95 percent success rate in stopping HIV, the virus that causes AIDS.
2. Condoms have a 5 percent failure rate in stopping HIV, the virus that causes AIDS.

The two statements are equally true, yet 90 percent of college students who read only the first statement rated condoms as effective. Only 40 percent did so after reading the second statement (Linville & others, 1992).

Can you imagine what would happen if ground beef were marketed as 20 percent fat instead of 80 percent lean? What if a surgeon bragged about a 2 percent death rate, rather than a 98 percent success rate? Framing does make a difference!

Belief Perseverance

A final factor that influences our judgment and decision making is **belief perseverance**, the tendency to stick with our initial idea even if we receive information that discredits it. One study (Lord & others,

Enriching

Have students create and distribute two different surveys on the same topic. Each survey should differ in how the questions are framed. For example, your students may conduct a survey about food preferences. In these surveys, they would frame one set of questions with a more healthful slant, such as the "80 percent lean beef" and "95 percent less fat" examples from the text. The other survey would have questions referring to food that is "20 percent fat beef" and "5 percent fat remaining."

- Students should distribute the surveys randomly to matched sets of subjects—meaning subjects of similar qualities are divided into two groups to ensure that similar types of people answer each type of survey.
- Conduct some statistical analysis on each set of data. Find out how different each group was in their answers. Did students see a framing effect? Why or why not?

1979) focused on two groups of people, one that believed in capital punishment and another that didn't. Participants in each group were shown two supposedly new studies—one indicating that capital punishment does help prevent crime and the other indicating that it does not affect crime rates. Members of each group focused on the study that supported their point of view, and they discounted the value of the opposing study. Both groups started with a belief and read the same evidence for and against that belief. Thanks to confirmation bias, these people used the same evidence to reach two different conclusions. Beliefs last. First impressions can be important, because once established they are likely to persevere.

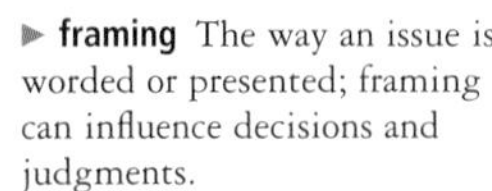

▸ **framing** The way an issue is worded or presented; framing can influence decisions and judgments.

▸ **belief perseverance** Clinging to one's initial beliefs even after new information discredits the basis on which they were formed.

▸ **language** Our spoken, written, or gestured words and the ways we combine them to communicate meaning.

Language

We've spent some time discussing aspects of thinking, one of the more distinctive human qualities. But would our thoughts seem quite as rich, quite as important, if we were unable to share them with others? Our awesome ability to communicate is perhaps the only aspect of cognitive ability that is more impressive than thinking. **Language** is an extension of cognition, a way of combining speaking, writing, and gesturing to communicate meaningfully. Without language, a tremendous amount of our technology would be useless—telephones, computers, radios, DVD and MP3 players, and televisions are all, in essence, machines to help us communicate. The technological revolution enhanced our ability to use language, but communication was healthy and well long before the advent of high-tech tools. Books, newspapers, and letters all depend on language, and the relationships we cherish with family and friends do too. Remove language and we sever our link to our past, forcing each generation to rethink, reinvent, and reexperience all the things our ancestors could have taught us.

Lessons in Culture Language is one important way children learn about their culture. Human culture as we know it would not exist without language, which lets us transmit our ideas across barriers of time and space.

Demonstrating

LANGUAGE SENSE Show students that even language that doesn't make meaningful sense can still be grammatically correct—and be understood.

What is so unusual about the sentence below (aside from the fact it does not make a lot of sense)?

- Jackdaws love my big sphinx of quartz. *(It's the shortest sentence in the English language that includes every letter of the alphabet!)*

trb At this point, you may wish to use **Critical Thinking Activity:** ***Simple Language Device*** (*Teacher's Resource Binder*, p. 23-1; **Handout 23–8**).

MODULE 23

■ TEACHING TIP

Link the concept of *belief perseverance* to that of *group polarization*. With group polarization, the beliefs of a group become enhanced when the group members get together to discuss their beliefs. Instead of opening up dialogue about different views, confirmation bias and belief perseverance set in, causing group members to feel validated about their own beliefs as others in the group support and affirm them. This often happens when two opposing groups sit down to discuss their views. They often end up disagreeing more since they have support of other group members to keep them polarized.

trb tr At this point, you may wish to use **Analysis Activity:** ***Belief Bias*** (*Teacher's Resource Binder*, p. 23-1; **Transparency Master 23–1**).

F•Y•I

Some scholars have called language the most complex body of knowledge known to humanity. Consider this: Languages are comprised of a limited number of symbols that can be combined according to particular rules. These symbols and rules can then be put together to create an unlimited number of messages. As long as someone is using the basic symbols and following the basic rules of the language, he or she can be understood. What an amazing ability we have!

V At this point, you may wish to show **Videocassette:** ***The Mind,*** **Second Edition, Module 25: "Human Language: Signed and Spoken"** (*Teacher's Resource Binder*, p. 23-1).

■ LOOKING AT THE ISSUES

Some historians believe that the fifteenth-century invention of the printing press by Johannes Gutenberg was the greatest invention of the last millennium. Using the questions below, discuss with students why such an invention would make that big of an impression.

- Why is the printing press considered such an important invention? What needs did the printing press meet?
- How much of your life is affected by the printed word? What would school be without the printing press?

MODULE 23

■ MULTICULTURAL CONNECTIONS
The total number of phonemes in languages varies from as few as 11 in Rotokas (spoken in Papua New Guinea) and 12 in Hawaiian to as many as 141 in !Xu~ (spoken in southern Africa, in the vicinity of the Kalahari desert).

- In some languages, there are only 2 or 3 vowel sounds, as in some dialects of the Abkhaz language (spoken in the republic of Georgia), in Arabic, in some Australian Aboriginal languages, and in many Native American language groups. By contrast, in the Punjabi language (spoken in India), there are over 25 vowel sounds. The most common vowel system contains the five main vowels found in English: *a, e, i, o,* and, *u.*
- Consonant sounds vary. Rotokas contains only 6 consonants; !Xu~ contains more than 100, along with several click consonants. The most common consonants are *p, t,* and *k,* but not all languages have these. For example, the Hawaiian language lacks the *t* sound, and the Mohawk language lacks the *p* sound, but all known languages have at least two of the three.
- One of the rarest sounds is represented in the Czech language by the sound *r hacek* (found in the name Dvořák).

Source: *Wikipedia: The Free Encyclopedia,* www.wikipedia.org/wiki/Phoneme

trb At this point, you may wish to use Enrichment Lesson: *Universals of Language* (*Teacher's Resource Binder,* p. 23-1).

■ TEACHING TIP
Take a sample sentence and lead the class through the identification of the different morphemes. For example: "Sometimes a single phoneme can be a morpheme, as in *I.*" This sentence has 15 morphemes. *Sometimes* has three—*some, time,* and *-s. Phoneme* and *morpheme* each have two since *-eme* is a suffix meaning "a unit of something," and the roots *phon* ("sound") and *morph* ("meaning") are both meaningful parts of the words. The rest of the words contain only one morpheme each.

Building Blocks of Language

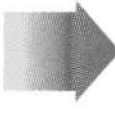

4. What role do phonemes, morphemes, and grammar play in the structure of language?

To build a house, you need materials and knowledge of the rules required to assemble the materials properly. A particular house might require concrete, wood, wires, shingles, windows, and so forth. If you try to assemble these parts without following construction and engineering principles, the house probably won't survive the first windstorm. Language is similar—we build our language from elements and follow rules to determine how we can combine the pieces.

The most basic building block is the **phoneme**, the smallest unit of sound in a particular language. Some languages have hundreds of phonemes, including clicks or tones. The English language has about 40. Notice that phonemes are *spoken* sounds, not written symbols. (We'll have more to say about written symbols later.)

As a young baby, you could produce all the phonemes of all the languages in the world—but only for a short time. The basic rule here is "use 'em or lose 'em." By the time you reached your first birthday, you had lost your remarkable ability to babble in multiple languages and had settled into using the phonemes of your native tongue. If you are a Japanese-speaker, you may find distinguishing the English *r* and *l* sounds challenging, because these sounds are not part of the Japanese language. English-speakers, have trouble with German's breathy *ch* sound (found in *Ich,* the German word for *I*). German speakers may struggle with the English *th* and thus pronounce *this* as *dis*.

***Fun with Language:* How do you pronounce "ghoti"? (see page 445).**

Phonemes don't have meaning in and of themselves—the *p* sound doesn't mean anything, nor does the *f* sound. But we can combine phonemes to form a **morpheme**—the smallest unit of meaning in a language. Sometimes a single phoneme can be a morpheme, as in *I*. More often several phonemes combine to form a morpheme like *water,* which has four phonemes: *w, a, t,* and *r* (the written *e* has no sound of its own). Words often have more than one morpheme. *Waterfall,* for example, has two: *water,* the liquid that fills lakes and rivers, and *fall,* the idea that the water is going over an edge and cascading downward. How many may morphemes do your think there are in *watered?* If you said two, you're right. In this case, the second morpheme is the *-ed* suffix, indicating an event that happened in the past. Every time you add a prefix or suffix to a word (like *un-* in *unwind* or *-less* in *motionless*) you've added a new morpheme. The important thing to note is that these two building blocks—phonemes and morphemes—allow for almost infinite flexibility in language. In spoken English, we use our 40 phonemes to construct an estimated

Cross-Curricular Connections

WORLD LANGUAGES AND PHONEMES Have students research the number of phonemes in languages taught in your school and make a comparison to the number of phonemes in English. In addition, have students from other cultures that are represented in your student body discuss the sound structure of their native languages. Explore students' findings with the following questions:

- What languages have more phonemes than English? What languages have less?
- What are some of the phonemes in the languages taught at your school not found in English?
- What languages, other than English, do students in your school speak? What are some unique phonemes found in those languages?

V At this point, you may wish to show Videocassette: *The Mind,* Second Edition, Module 28: "Language and Culture" (*Teacher's Resource Binder,* p. 23-1).

100,000 morphemes. With those building blocks of meaning, we can generate hundreds of thousands of words. From here the estimates almost seem silly, with literally trillions of possible unique sentences (Figure 23.9).

Of course, as you know, just stringing several words together does not create a sentence. To have a sentence, you must follow the rules of **grammar**—a set of rules for combining phonemes, morphemes, and words to produce meaningful communication. Despite these elaborate rules, language can still be hopelessly, and sometimes humorously, unclear (Figure 23.10, page 444). Consider the phrase, "Don't threaten someone with a chainsaw." This sentence has perfect grammar, but it is still impossible to know which of the two possible meanings the speaker intended. (I think either interpretation constitutes good advice!)

It's important to notice that the grammar we've been talking about is not a set of rules you learn in your English or writing classes. Those classes did teach some rules of English grammar, but you were able to put sentences together long before you ever entered a classroom. Written language is a separate question altogether, because it's a system by which we use symbols (in a visual representation or code) to represent spoken sounds. Even people who live in remote areas of the world with no ability to read or write use complicated grammars in their everyday speech. These grammars, for example, have very specific rules for placing adjectives (red rose or rose red?) or for indicating the gender and status of someone you are addressing (respected female relative or little

▶ **phoneme** In spoken language, the smallest distinctive sound unit.

▶ **morpheme** In language, the smallest unit that carries meaning; may be a word or a part of a word.

▶ **grammar** A system of rules governing how we can combine morphemes and words and arrange them in sentences to communicate with others.

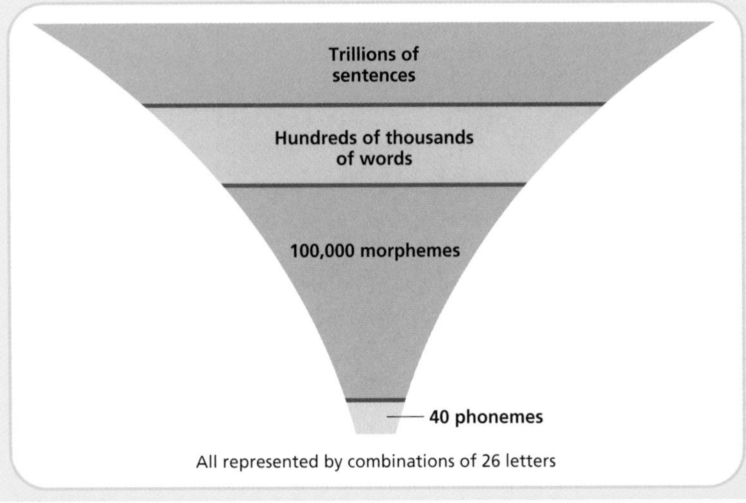

Figure 23.9
Flexibility in Language
The phonemes and morphemes of the English language can be combined in countless ways to produce an almost infinite number of meaningful sentences, which we write using an alphabet of only 26 characters.

Cross-Curricular Connections

WORLD LANGUAGES AND GRAMMAR Using their foreign language texts, have students research the different grammar rules in languages taught in your school and compare those rules to English grammar rules. In addition, have students from other cultures that are represented in your student body discuss the grammatical rules of their native languages. Explore students' findings with the following questions:

- What are some unique grammar rules found in languages other than English? What grammar rules in those languages are the same as English grammar rules?
- When and how is grammar taught in other cultures?

trb At this point, you may wish to show **Videocassette:** ***The Mind,*** **Second Edition, Module 28: "Language and Culture"** (*Teacher's Resource Binder*, p. 23-1).

■ TEACHING TIPS

(1) It may take students a few moments to comprehend the two meanings of "Don't threaten someone with a chainsaw!" To help them along, have them consider who might have the chainsaw. This hint should bring along students who are *fixated* on a particular interpretation.

tr (2) A four-color transparency of Figure 23.9, Flexibility in Language, is available in the **Overhead Transparencies Set.**

■ LOOKING AT THE ISSUES

Students don't often speak in a grammatically correct way, even though they know the correct way to speak, almost intuitively. Have students discuss ways they do not use grammar correctly in everyday speech by having them respond to the following questions:

- What are some common grammatical mistakes people make in everyday speaking? *(You may want to jumpstart the conversation by pointing out the sentence "Me and him are going to the store," which employs incorrect grammar—wrong pronoun case usage to be exact. Another rule often ignored in everyday speech involves pronoun-antecedent agreement; for example, "Everybody has their notebook in class".)*
- Have certain cultural and ethnic groups changed or adapted the standard rules of English grammar? Why? How? *(Point out to students that Ebonics, a dialect of English used by urban African-Americans, uses* be *as a common present tense verb. Other ethnic groups may have adapted English to make the transition smoother from their native language to English.)*
- How have teen slang and jargon infiltrated English language and grammar? *(Point out that many nouns and adjectives have become verbs or taken on new meanings. For example, the word* bad *has several connotations, meaning both "good" and "bad." For teens adept at using the Google search engine on the Internet, the brand name* Google *has become a verb; for example, "I've been googled!")*

(F•Y•I)

Grammar is more than just rules students learn in English class.

- **Syntax** involves how words are grouped together into meaningful sentences. In English, the subject is typically placed before the verb, and adjectives are found before nouns they modify. Other languages use different syntax, such as Spanish, where verbs come before subjects (and can even be both subject and verb, depending on the conjugation of the verb) and adjectives come after the nouns they modify.
- **Mechanics** are rules that govern how language is written. These are the concepts around which most English grammar lessons are structured. Comma, capitalization, and end mark rules are considered part of English mechanics.
- **Pragmatics** are the unwritten rules about what type of language is appropriate to use at particular times. For example, people use language differently in a job interview than they do in informal conversations with friends.

trb At this point, you may wish to use **Enrichment Lesson:** *Universals of Language* (*Teacher's Resource Binder*, p. 23-1).

■ **TEACHING TIP**

Have students create their own ambiguous sentences by playing with *dangling modifiers.* **Dangling modifiers** are a grammatical error where a word or phrase is not located in front of or near the word it modifies.

On the chalkboard, write the sentence "Happy to be home, the bed looked like a comfortable place to take a nap." Now, ask students just who is happy to be home? Explain that according to the organization of words in this sentence (which uses a dangling modifier), the bed is happy to be home!

tr A four-color transparency of Figure 23.10, Grammar Isn't Everything, is available in the **Overhead Transparencies Set.**

Figure 23.10 **Grammar Isn't Everything** Despite being grammatically correct, this sentence is open to several different interpretations: *The artist painted me on the front porch.*

boy baby—perhaps even a barking dog!). Grammar is part of our spoken language, and the question of how we learn it and everything else we call language has generated a lot of debate in psychology. You probably won't be surprised to find out that the debate focuses on nature and nurture.

Cross-Curricular Connections

LANGUAGE ARTS Team-teach a lesson with an English teacher about how grammar is taught in high schools today. Invite the English teacher to respond to the following questions:

- Do all English teachers in the school teach the rules of grammar directly, or do teachers integrate grammar instruction within a writing or reading program? Why do teachers choose to teach one way versus another?
- In general, how skilled are students in using correct grammar?
- What are the most important grammar skills students should possess? Why?

Language Acquisition

5. How do we learn language?

Linguist **Noam Chomsky** (1959, 1987) believes that our brains are "wired" to process vocabulary and rules of grammar virtually without effort. According to this view, we have a predisposition to language—it's part of our heritage as a human species, just as flying is part of a bird's heritage.

But is it part of our heritage to speak a *particular* language? If you are a native English-speaker, imagine bending over the crib of your first-born child, putting the baby to sleep for the night, and the child looks up at you, smiles sleepily, and says, "Guten nacht!" or "Bonne nuit!" Wouldn't you be amazed—perhaps even a little nervous? Babies from English-speaking homes are supposed to speak English, not some other language. Why? This is where nurture steps in. **B. F. Skinner**, famous for his studies of the effects of rewards on behavior, maintained that language learning is nothing special—we learn it just as we learn everything else. Thus, he said (1957), we learn our language through *association* (linking certain sounds with certain people or objects), *imitation* (doing what we see others doing, including their manner of speaking), and receiving (or not receiving) *rewards* (hugs, smiles, and so on).

Most psychologists today believe that Chomsky and Skinner were each right and also each wrong. Chomsky's view that humans have a predisposition to learn language helps explain why all languages in the world have complicated sets of rules that children seem to master at amazingly young ages. Skinner's view that we learn language through association, imitation, and rewards helps explain why we speak the language we hear at home. As is the case in so many parts of psychology, language is neither simply nature nor simply nurture. It's both, interacting to give us a rich tool with which we communicate events, feelings, beliefs, and emotions to other human beings.

Let's look now at how and when children master this wonderful tool we call language.

▶ **Noam Chomsky** (1928–) Linguist who argues that children have a predisposition to learn language, as though their brains were hard-wired to pick up vocabulary and rules of grammar.

▶ **B. F. Skinner** (1904–1990) American psychologist who argued that children learn language through associations, imitation, and reinforcement.

Answer to question on page 442. Consider how "gh" is pronounced in the word **enough**, *how "o" is pronounced in the word* **women**, *and how "ti" is pronounced in the word* **emotion**. *That's right—"ghoti" is pronounced "fish"!*

Language Stages

6. What stages do children go through in the development of language?

Have you ever tried to learn a second language? If so, you're surely aware that language is immensely complicated. There's a lot of work involved, and even if you're diligent about it, progress is usually pretty slow if you are a teenager or older. If you travel to an area where the language is spoken, you'll quickly realize that, despite your efforts, you're nowhere near fluent. The few students who do become fluent still do not

F • Y • I

Noam Chomsky has been one of the most cited persons in academia over the last century. His study of language as a brain function rather than as a social phenomenon led to the emergence of cognitive science as a dominant perspective in psychology.

■ LOOKING AT THE ISSUES

(1) Linguists and educators debate how to teach young children the essentials of grammar and language in elementary school. Some believe a *whole language* approach is better since it more closely models how children originally learn how to talk as infants. Others value a *phonics-based* approach, one that emphasizes learning the phonemes of the language and the grammar rules that dictate how language is spoken and written. Encourage students to share their memories about learning language and grammar.

trb At this point, you may wish to use **Enrichment Lesson:** ***Language Development*** (*Teacher's Resource Binder*, p. 23-1).

(2) Since children can learn languages more easily than adults, many educators and linguists believe that second (and even third) languages should be taught in elementary school rather than in high school. Explore this issue with your students:

- Are world languages taught in elementary schools in your district? Why or why not?
- Is world language instruction the same in elementary schools as it is in high schools—that is, with an emphasis on grammar, vocabulary, and conversational speaking? Why or why not?

Cross-Curricular Connections

WORLD LANGUAGES Invite a teacher of a language other than English to facilitate and clarify a discussion with students about learning a second language. After students answer each of the following questions, ask the language teacher to respond with factual and anecdotal comments:

- Have you tried learning a second language? How successful were you? How well do you think you would communicate with and understand others if you found yourself in the country where that language is spoken? What makes you think this?
- How easy or difficult is it to learn a second language fluently?
- If you could pick up any other language and speak it fluently today, which would you choose? Why?

MODULE 23

■ **APPLYING THE POINTS**
Ask interested students to contact a local day-care center to record the different types of language children at the center use. Have students present their findings in an oral report that addresses the following language usages: consonants most used by infants in the babbling stage, common words young children use in the one-word stage, verbs and modifiers added most by children in the two-word stage, and examples of overgeneralized words children in the center use. Students should also learn whether or not the caregivers correct the children and why or why not.

V At this point, you may wish to show **Videocassette: *The Mind,* Second Edition, Module 24: "Language Predisposition"** (*Teacher's Resource Binder,* p. 23-1) and **Videocassette: *Scientific American Frontiers,* Second Edition, Segment 18: "Talking Babies"** (*Teacher's Resource Binder,* p. 23-1).

F•Y•I

Babies even younger than 4 months old use language. *Cooing* occurs at around 3 to 5 weeks of age. Infants at this age will repeat basic vowel sounds without using consonants.

V At this point, you may wish to show **Videocassette: *Scientific American Frontiers,* Second Edition, Segment 21: "Born to Talk"** (*Teacher's Resource Binder,* p. 23-1).

■ **TEACHING TIP**
Link discussion of *overgeneralization* to Piaget's concepts of *assimilation* and *accommodation.* As children learn the rules of language, they assimilate them into their language schemas. But, with the exceptions to language rules inherent in every vibrant language, some rules don't apply to all words. As children try to use their assimilated knowledge in speaking, adults and older children correct them, and they gradually accommodate their schemas to include these exceptions, eventually learning how to speak in a more grammatically correct fashion as they age.

speak like native speakers. Why does this happen? Because—although we have a predisposition to learn language, we can learn it easily only during the early years of our childhood. Just as we go through a maturational sequence of learning how to walk, we also go through one for learning how to talk. Here are the steps involved.

1. ***Babbling*** By 4 months of age, amazing human language skills are already becoming apparent. Babies are spontaneously producing phonemes and are sophisticated enough to be able to discriminate speech sounds made by others (Kuhl & Meltzoff, 1982). When babbling, children will produce phonemes they have never heard before, but within a few months they will begin to specialize in the sounds used in the languages they hear spoken. By 10 months of age, an expert can identify the language spoken in a home by merely listening to the babbling baby (de Boysson-Bardies & others, 1989).
2. ***One-Word Stage*** At about the time of their first birthday, most babies begin to use their new ability to produce sounds to communicate meaning. They start with very short, one-syllable words like *ma* or *da*, and they may produce them so unreliably that other members of the family argue over whether the child is really communicating intentionally. Baby's skills rapidly improve, however, and soon there is a vocabulary of single words used to describe both things (*kitty*) and actions (*swing*). The pace at which children learn words accelerates rapidly, and by 18 months the average child is learning a new word every day.
3. ***Two-Word Stage*** By the time most babies reach their second birthday, they have entered the two-word stage. Now they are building two-word sentences. Amazingly, the way they arrange these words shows an appreciation for the grammatical rules of their native language. English-speaking children put adjectives before nouns (*big house*), but Spanish speakers put the noun first (*casa grande*).

The two-word stage marks the end of the language stages. As Table 23.1 indicates, after age 2, children then build on the phonemes, morphemes, words, and grammatical rules they have already mastered to develop longer and more complex sentences (Fromkin & Rodman, 1983). And their vocabulary continues to grow, too. Throughout childhood, an average person learns 5000 words a year, the vast majority outside of school (Miller & Gildea, 1987). That's more than 13 words a day! By the time they hit grade school, children understand complex sentence structures.

As children develop their language skills, they drop interesting clues that support Chomsky's theory of language acquisition. One of the most interesting is *overgeneralization*, which occurs when children apply a grammatical rule they have learned too broadly. For example, English

TABLE 23.1 STAGES OF LANGUAGE DEVELOPMENT

AGE IN MONTHS (APPROXIMATE)	ACHIEVEMENT
4	Babbling of many speech sounds
12	One-word sentences
24	Two-word sentences
24+	Rapid development of complete sentences

allows us to turn nouns into verbs. The object I use to play baseball is called a *bat*, and when I am standing at the plate I am *batting*. Once children master this principle they sometimes apply it where they shouldn't (Figure 23.11). A child who knows what a *broom* is may say he is *brooming*, rather than *sweeping*, the floor. The child has never been encouraged to use the word *brooming*, and in fact has never heard it before. Likewise, children will say that they *goed* to the store rather than *went* to the store. Beyond being kind of cute and amusing, this overgeneralization points to the brain's ability to soak up language.

Notice again that the natural, easy learning of language applies to *spoken* language. Spoken language appeared long before written language in human history. Our brains are equipped to handle it easily but we have not

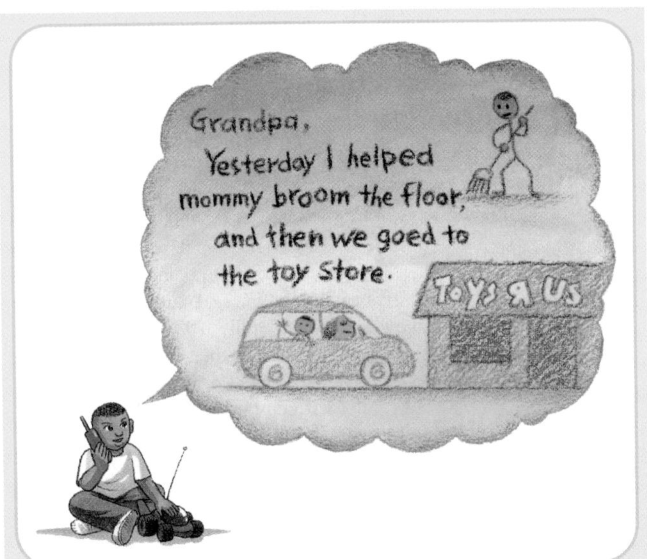

Figure 23.11
Overgeneralization This 4-year-old is making mistakes by applying rules to instances that are considered exceptions in English. These mistakes show he has internalized the grammatical rules of the language.

F • Y • I

Overgeneralization occurs in a couple of different ways. Sometimes children overextend rules in the ways the author points out in the text. In addition, children may call all four-legged animals "doggies" or all flying machines "airplanes." At other times, children **underextend** language rules. They will identify a certain object with a word and insist that only that object fits that description. For example, they may believe a "cookie" is a particular type of cookie, like chocolate chip.

■ **TEACHING TIPS**

trb tr (1) A black-line master for Table 23.1, Stages of Language Development, is available in the **Black-Line Masters Appendix** of the *Teacher's Resource Binder.*

(2) A good example of overgeneralization occurs in the Disney movie Bambi. Young Bambi is learning the vocabulary of the words around him, and he encounters a skunk in a field of flowers. Instead of waiting to learn what the name of the creature is, Bambi calls it "flower." The name sticks and the skunk is forever known as "Flower."

Enriching

Have students research neurological disorders that affect the ability to speak correctly. Students should focus on causes and treatments, as well as descriptions of the typical language errors the victims make. Listed here are some possible disorders students may consider for research:

- strokes that damage left hemisphere areas of language ability, including Broca's and Wernicke's areas
- Williams syndrome
- autism
- aphasia
- deafness

trb At this point, you may wish to use **Enrichment Lesson:** ***The Smart-Talk Syndrome*** (*Teacher's Resource Binder*, p. 23-1).

F • Y • I

Many child development experts recommend teaching sign language to all infants to improve the ability to communicate their wants and needs. Many parents study sign language and teach their young children to sign for objects like "juice," "water," or "toy," as well as for needs like "more," "eat," or "want." Studies show that this practice helps young children and their parents feel less frustrated in the months before spoken language is mastered.

trb At this point, you may wish to use Enrichment Lesson: *Kanzi and Mulika, Remarkable Pygmy Chimps* (*Teacher's Resource Binder*, p. 23-1).

TEACHING TIP

Have students share their experiences of communicating with pets. In a class discussion, invite students to respond to the following questions:

- Have they developed a sign language or verbal command system for communicating with their pet?
- How do they know what their pets want? How do their pets communicate needs to them?

V At this point, you may wish to show **Videocassette:** *Scientific American Frontiers*, **Second Edition, Segment 19: "If Only They Could Talk!"** (*Teacher's Resource Binder*, p. 23-1).

APPLYING THE POINTS

Invite an animal trainer to class to demonstrate methods used to teach animals how to obey commands. The guest can also address what his or her experience has been with animal communication. If possible, have the guest respond to the following questions:

- How do different animal species communicate their wants, needs, and emotions?
- What human behaviors are effective in communicating messages to animals?

V At this point, you may wish to show **Videocassette:** *Scientific American Frontiers*, **Second Edition, Segment 20: "Who Needs Words, Anyway?"** (*Teacher's Resource Binder*, p. 23-1).

Up Close

Animal Language

Do animals have language? I frequently sense that my golden retriever is trying to tell me something, and she often appears to understand what I tell her. Sometimes she even obeys! With enough time and effort, could we expand our communication into a full-fledged language?

Psychologists have been trying to answer this question for over a century, most frequently with chimpanzees. In the 1930s Winthrop Kellogg and Luella Kellogg (1933) raised an infant chimpanzee, Gua, in their home, along with their son Donald. They wondered whether the chimpanzee might develop language abilities if they raised it as a human. The Kelloggs did learn some interesting things from their work with Gua, but—despite eating in a high chair and wearing clothes like little Donald's—the chimpanzee never did learn to talk.

Maybe Gua didn't learn to talk because chimpanzees' vocal structure differs from those in humans. To get around this problem, later researchers, most notably Beatrix Gardner and Allen Gardner (1969), launched a project to teach chimpanzees American Sign Language (ASL), used by deaf humans. The Gardners' first student was the now-famous Washoe, who soon acquired a vocabulary of 132 signs. Roger Fouts, who, with Deborah Fouts, would later become the leading spokesperson for chimpanzees, was one of the Gardners' assistants in the late 1960s, charged with making baby Washoe's life "as stimulating and linguistic" as possible. In 1970, Washoe—and the research program that grew up around her—became Roger Fouts's primary responsibility. He and Deborah Fouts set up a program in which many of the people caring for Washoe and other chimpanzees were themselves deaf and whose first language was ASL. Washoe continued to thrive, and by the late 1990s she had increased her vocabulary to almost 200 signs (Sanz & others, 1998). She has sometimes used amazing creativity to combine these signs to describe items. And, perhaps most amazing of all, Washoe taught signs to her adopted son, Loulis, who picked up 55 signs while under her care. Here is a sample conversation between Loulis and his chimpanzee playmate, Dar (R. Fouts, 2003):

1. Loulis asks for a water balloon from Dar by holding his hand toward the balloon and signing, "Hurry, hurry."
2. When Dar moved away, Loulis signed, "Want."
3. When Dar moved away again, Loulis signed, "Hurry, hurry. Gimme."
4. Dar gave the balloon to Loulis and the two chimpanzees separated.

Nobody doubts that these accomplishments are remarkable. The key question is, do they constitute language? The answer depends on how you define *language.* Even with a loose definition of language, psychologists are skeptical that any chimpanzee's communication skills can come close to matching those of a young human. One trained chimpanzee used 16 signs to ask for an orange: "Give orange me give eat orange me eat orange give me eat orange give me you" (Jolly, 1985). The idea comes across, but hardly with the type of efficiency one would hope for. A great deal of effort produces limited results with chimpanzees, whereas humans master language almost effortlessly. As amazing as these communicating chimpanzees are, their very limitations help illustrate how astounding human language ability is.

Enriching

Learning about animals that have learned to communicate with humans through sign language might lead students to wonder how animals communicate with each other. For extra credit, interested students can explore what researchers know about animal communication. Have these students present their findings to the class in an oral report. Ask the presenters to include responses to the following questions:

- What do scientists know about the structure and meaning of whale songs?
- How do different species of animals communicate with each other about their social order?
- Do any species use any type of symbols (such as signs or body movements) to communicate?

V At this point, you may wish to show **Videocassette:** *The Mind*, **Second Edition, Module 27: "Animal Language"** (*Teacher's Resource Binder*, p. 23-1).

yet developed mechanisms to handle the written word as easily. We learn to speak without conscious effort as young children, yet we must go to school and work to master reading and writing. Even spoken language becomes much more difficult after about age 10—when a critical developmental window seems to slam shut. In rare, tragic cases where a child has been raised in isolation through the first decade of life, language development does not proceed normally. After this window of opportunity closes, those of us who easily developed a first language must struggle to learn a second one. Knowing this, linguists often argue that it makes much more sense to introduce foreign languages in preschool than in middle or high school.

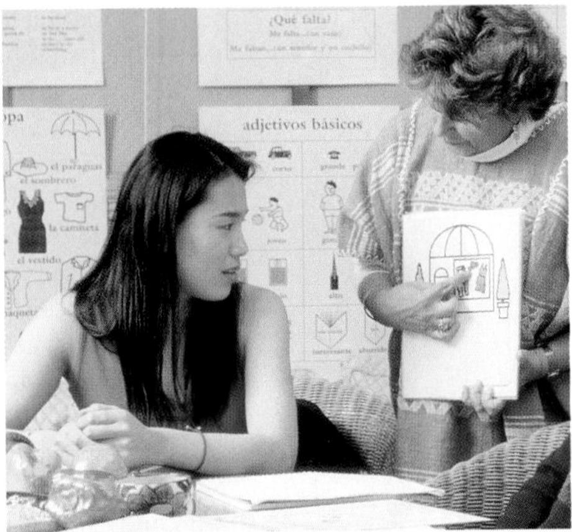

Beyond the Critical Period We can learn language as a natural, automatic process when we are children because we are born with a predisposition to learn language. But there seems to be a catch—if we haven't learned language by the time we reach high school, the window of easy learning seems to slam shut, and we have to work hard to master grammar and vocabulary. We should be offering foreign language in preschool!

Thinking and Language Together

7. What is the linguistic relativity hypothesis? Can we think without language?

Psychologists like to consider thought and language together because it's difficult to consider them apart. Human cognitive skills enable language. Language researcher **Benjamin Whorf** (1956) was so convinced of that connection that he proposed the **linguistic relativity hypothesis**—the idea that our language determines what we can be aware of or think about. He argued, for example, that people who live in areas that are covered in snow most of the year would have many more words for "white," based on different kinds or stages of snow. Those of us who do not have those words in our vocabulary, he maintained, would be unable to perceive these subtle differences in color. Whorf probably went too far in claiming that language *governs* our thinking. Research does not support his observations on snow and colors, but studies have shown that language can influence our thoughts. People who speak two or more languages often report having a different sense of self depending on which language they are using (Matsumoto, 1994). They may even score differently when they take a personality test twice using different languages for each (Dinges & Hull, 1992).

Language can also shape our expectations. In the past, writers used *he, mankind,* and other masculine words to refer to both men and women. When reformers in the 1960s and 1970s urged the public to replace words like *chairman* and *fireman* with *chairperson* and *firefighter,* many thought they were going overboard in being politically correct. Since that time, however, at least 20 studies have consistently shown that gender

▶ **Benjamin Whorf** (1897–1941) Linguist who developed the linguistic relativity hypothesis—the idea that our language structures the way we can think about the world.

▶ **linguistic relativity hypothesis** Benjamin Whorf's hypothesis that language determines the way we think.

Enriching

For homework, have students draw a map of the school from memory. In class, have students compare and contrast the maps that they all drew. They are likely to find wide individual differences. Previous research has shown that people tend to expand the size and detail of the buildings most important to them. Also, compare the maps of new students with those of students who have been on campus for some time.

trb At this point, you may wish to use **Application Activity:** *Creating a Mental Model* (*Teacher's Resource Binder,* p. 23-1).

F•Y•I

In one famous case from the 1970s, a young girl named Genie lived an isolated life with an abusive father until she was 13 years old. Now an adult living in a group home in California, Genie's language skills are not much better than those of a preschooler. She was able to learn rudimentary communication skills, but her vocabulary is not extensive or complex. Her case seems to show that the critical period for language indeed exists before children hit puberty.

■ JOURNAL WRITING

Invite students to use the following questions and writing prompts as springboards for entries in their psychology journals.

- If you didn't have language, how would you think? What would you think about?
- Can you think without language? What are some types or kinds of thoughts that you have that don't require language?
- Have you ever experienced a time when you couldn't describe how you felt or what you were thinking? Why was it so hard? Were you ever able to find a way to express that thought or feeling? Why or why not?

■ TEACHING TIP

Cognitive maps provide a good basis for introducing thought without language. **Cognitive maps** are mental representations of the spatial environment. They represent the world as we believe it to exist. If students are asked to think of the layout of the house in which they grew up or the shortest route from class to the library, they think in terms of images, not words. Sometimes our cognitive maps are very detailed and accurate; at other times, they may be sketchy and bear little resemblance to reality.

trb At this point, you may wish to use **Technology Application Activity:** *PsychSim:* **"Maze Learning"** (*Teacher's Resource Binder,* p. 23-1).

MODULE 23

■ TEACHING TIP

When you ask students the following questions, most will tell you that they answer the questions by using a mental picture: How many windows are in your living room? Which is darker, a Christmas tree or a frozen pea? Which is larger, a guinea pig or a gerbil?

trb At this point, you may wish to use Application Activity: *Creating Mental Pictures from Verbal Descriptions* (*Teacher's Resource Binder*, p. 23-1).

F•Y•I

In *The Image of the City*, Kevin Lynch introduced the use of sketch maps to assess people's representation of the environment. He was especially interested in identifying the architectural and geographical characteristics that make some places more "imageable" and thus easier to remember. He found that this depends on **legibility**, or the ease with which specific parts can be recognized and organized into a coherent pattern. Legibility, in turn, depends on the form and arrangement of five physical elements. These include the following:

- **paths** along which the observer moves
- **edges** or boundaries, such as walls, shores, and railroad tracks
- **districts** into which the observer mentally enters
- **nodes** or strategic points to and from which the observer travels
- **landmarks**, or clearly defined physical objects, such as buildings, signs, or statues

Source: Lynch, K. (1960). *The image of the city.* Cambridge, MA: MIT Press.

Close

Bring students back to the philosophical issues brought up in the beginning of the module.

- Can we think without language?
- Is language meaningful without thought?
- How do you answer these questions now that you have read the module?

▶ **image** A mental picture.

terms do make a difference (Henley, 1989). Masculine words produce images of males. Young girls imagining themselves in a variety of roles later in life may find it difficult to think of themselves as a chairman or fireman because they can't match their own image to the one produced by the word. Doors of opportunity slam shut when this happens.

Although language has a profound influence on thought, we can think without language. We often do so in the form of mental pictures or **images.** Let's say you were buying some new electronic equipment and were concerned about where you would plug it in. You could imagine the room where the equipment would go to "see" the location of the plug sockets. You could pull up this image much more quickly and easily than you could analyze the situation in words: "I remember there is a socket about three feet from the southwest corner of the south wall. . . . "). Sometimes a picture is worth a thousand words. Sports psychologists who understand the power of imagery often have their clients use mental pictures to rehearse their skills and enhance their preparation. Studies from sports as different as figure skating and basketball show that mental practice—seeing yourself performing at your top level—can improve performance (Garza & Feltz, 1998; Savoy & Beitel, 1996).

Your introductory psychology course barely scratches the surface when it comes to the wonders of human thought and language, but one thing is certain: The course could not exist without them. The very fact that you can contemplate and discuss language and thought proves their importance—which, of course, extends to every aspect of human interaction.

REVIEW

Module 23: Thinking and Language

What's the Point?

Thinking and language are aspects of our cognitive abilities—all the mental activities associated with thinking, knowing, and remembering.

Thinking

1. *How do we define* concept, *and why is a concept useful?*

   Psychologists define *concept* as a mental group based on shared similarities. Concepts help us sort information into categories that enable us to make instant judgments about objects we have never seen before. We put things into conceptual categories by matching them with our prototypes, or "best examples" of items. We develop hierarchies for concepts to organize information in our memory.

Demonstrating

VISUAL IMAGES The ability to control visual images can be developed with practice. Have students evaluate their ability to control or manipulate their mental pictures by visualizing the following:

- a pot of water coming to a boil and boiling over
- a running cow changing slowly into a galloping racehorse
- an elderly person you know, perhaps a grandparent, changing back into a teenager
- a speeding motorcycle colliding with a giant feather pillow
- the picture of a "4" in reverse.

Source: McKim, R. (1972). *Experiences in visual thinking.* Monterey, CA: Brooks/Cole.

trb At this point, you may wish to use Demonstration Activity: *Two Aspects of Visual Imagery* (*Teacher's Resource Binder*, p. 23-1).

2. *What are algorithms and heuristics, and how do they help us solve problems?*

An algorithm is a strategy, such as a mathematical formula, that guarantees a solution to a problem. Algorithms are thorough but not always efficient. A heuristic is a rule-of-thumb guide, such as "*i* before *e* except after *c*," which increases our efficiency but does not always lead to the correct solution. Insights are sudden realizations of solutions that pop into our heads (Aha!) without the aid of algorithms, heuristics, or any other strategy.

3. *How can fixation, the confirmation bias, heuristics, overconfidence, framing, and belief perseverance influence our ability to solve problems?*

We can have problems solving problems when we use strategies so consistently that they become mental sets. Efficient strategies that become so routine that they interfere with our ability to consider any other option are known as *fixations*. Functional fixedness is a special kind of fixation in which we are unable to "think outside the box"—to see usefulness in things beyond their usual functions. Thus, we are unable to see a penny as an emergency screwdriver, or a rock as an emergency key to a burning house. *Confirmation bias* is our unconscious tendency to look for evidence for what we believe to be true. This bias prevents us from considering all available options. The quick rule-of-thumb strategies that we know as *heuristics* cause us to form habits, so that we jump to faulty conclusions. The availability heuristic, for example, leads us to make decisions based on information that comes readily to mind, such as thinking we will win the lottery because we have recently seen photos of the few people who do win large lottery prizes. *Overconfidence* is our tendency to be more sure of ourselves than we should be. This unwarranted self-confidence can lead to bad decisions. *Framing* is the way an issue is worded or presented, and it can tilt our mental scale toward one decision versus another. Belief perseverance is our tendency to stick with our initial beliefs even after new information discredits those beliefs. *Belief perseverance* and an open mind cannot coexist.

Language

4. *What role do phonemes, morphemes, and grammar play in the structure of language?*

Phonemes are the smallest units of sound in a particular language. Morphemes are the smallest units of meaning in a particular language. Grammar is a system of rules governing how we can combine morphemes and words and arrange them in sentences to communicate to others. As psychologists use the term, grammar is a set of rules for spoken language, not a written set of rules you learn in school. Very young children learn grammar before they can read, and people with no access to reading and writing speak languages with complex grammars.

5. *How do we learn language?*

Linguist Noam Chomsky believes our brains are "prewired" to learn vocabulary and rules of grammar—that this is part of our human heritage. Learning theorist B. F. Skinner maintained that we learn language as we learn anything else: through association, imitation, and receiving (or not receiving) rewards. Most psychologists now believe that each of these researchers had part of the answer right—Chomsky on our predisposition to learn language, and Skinner on why we learn a particular language.

Checking the Points

■ TEACHING TIPS

web (1) The book companion site for *Thinking About Psychology* at www.worthpublishers.com/thinkingaboutpsych contains a module quiz, flashcards of key terms and people, as well as other student activities and resources for this module. You will also find PowerPoint lectures, a quiz grade book, and other teaching resources by logging on as an instructor.

trb (2) At this point, you may wish to review and confirm concepts about emotion with **Critical Thinking Activity:** ***Fact or Falsehood?*** (*Teacher's Resource Binder*, p. 23-1; **Handout 23–1**). Suggest that students complete the handout individually, taking the time to look up information in the text to respond correctly to questions. (Ask them not to refer to a version of the handout that may have been completed earlier in the module.) Students may exchange completed handouts with classmates to check and confirm responses.

MODULE 23

trb **tr** ■ **TEACHING TIP**

At this point, you may wish to review module vocabulary with the entire class by using **Building Vocabulary:** *Crossword Puzzles* (*Teacher's Resource Binder*, p.23-1; **Handout 23–2**) as a transparency. For each puzzle clue, have a student read the clue aloud and come up with the correct word. If other students challenge the answer, have the challengers give the correct answer and read aloud a passage from the text that supports their challenge. If the challenge is incorrect, ask students to find a passage from the text that identifies the correct answer.

6. *What stages do children go through in the development of language?*

   Children go through three distinct stages as they develop language. In the babbling stage, they babble phonemes and can make all the sounds heard round the world. By 10 months of age, they babble using only the phonemes in their native language. In the one-word stage, which begins around age one, children speak in single words, which describe both things and actions. In the two-word stage, beginning at about age 2, children are forming two-word sentences, and the words follow the order dictated by the rules of grammar for their native language. After the two-word stage, children rapidly acquire new vocabulary words and use more complex grammatical structures in their communications. They show their knowledge of grammar by overgeneralizing ("I goed to the store"), in which they apply the rules too rigidly. If humans do not learn language during the appropriate childhood years, a window of opportunity seems to close. This critical period—like the critical period ducks go through just after birth, when they will follow any moving object—seems to support Chomsky's view of language as part of the built-in characteristics that make us human.

Thinking and Language Together

7. *What is the linguistic relativity hypothesis? Can we think without language?*

   Language researcher Benjamin Whorf proposed the linguistic relativity hypothesis, the idea that language *determines* the way we think. Research has not supported this idea, though language does influence our thoughts and shape our expectations. We are however, able to think without language. We often think in images, and sports psychologists encourage athletes to use mental pictures to rehearse before games.

Key Terms

Key People

Self-Test

Multiple-Choice Questions

Choose the *best* answer for each of the following questions:

1. Myra heard that a new clothing store has opened in her town, but she doesn't know its location. She has decided to drive up and down each street in her town looking for the store. Myra is using a (an) ____________ to find the new store.
   a. prototype
   b. heuristic
   c. algorithm
   d. insight

2. Annie is going to the prom, and her parents have given her money to buy a prom dress. Annie found a two-piece outfit she loves—a long black leather skirt trimmed with small chains, and a matching sleeveless jacket. But Annie's mother vetoed the outfit, saying it was not appropriate. The outfit apparently did not fit Annie's mother's
   a. feelings of overconfidence about children's clothing.
   b. concept hierarchy for prom outfits.
   c. prototype of a prom dress.
   d. availability heuristic.

3. A recent news report told the tale of a man who had been trapped in his car in deep snow and freezing temperatures for two days. The man kept himself warm by cutting the upholstery from the car roof and using it as a blanket. In using his imagination to save his life, this man showed he was not hindered by
   a. functional fixedness.
   b. framing.
   c. insight.
   d. algorithms.

4. Edith, 6 months old, can make all the sounds used in all the languages in the world. Edith's parents want to have her listed in the Guinness Book of Records. They may be disappointed to know that before their first birthday, all babies can make these sounds, which are called ____________, but they lose this ability by their first birthday.
   a. grammar
   b. phonemes
   c. morphemes
   d. suffixes

5. Ernie and Felix will be living with their parents in Paris for two years while their mother is attached to the U.S. Embassy there. Ernie is 6 years old, and Felix is 17. The boys will have classes in both French and English, and they will be exposed to both languages at home and with friends. Who is more likely to become fluent in French, Ernie or Felix?
   a. Felix, because he will be able to understand the complicated rules of French grammar and read higher-level texts on the language.
   b. Ernie, because there is a critical period for learning languages, and it ends in the early teens.
   c. Both Felix and Ernie will learn at the same rate and be equally fluent.
   d. Neither Felix nor Ernie will be able to master French in such a short period of time.

6. Juan is four years old, and he often makes his parents smile when he talks with them. He seems to know the rules of English grammar, but he sometimes applies them in funny ways. For example, when his

MODULE 23

(tb) Using the Test Bank

The *Test Bank* that accompanies this textbook offers a wide variety of questions in different formats and levels of complexity. Use the software to construct whole tests or to integrate standardized questions into teacher-made tests.

Self-Test Answers

Multiple-Choice Questions

1. c, 2. c, 3. a, 4. b, 5. b, 6. a

MODULE 23

Self-Test Answers

Matching Terms and Definitions

7. a. (6), b. (3), c. (11), d. (9), e. (4), f. (1), g. (8), h. (10), i. (7)

Fill-in-the-Blank Questions

8. Noam Chomsky; B. F. Skinner, 9. Daniel Kahneman

Brief Essay Question

10. Jacinthe could start with an algorithm that addresses her problem. With an algorithm, she will need to try every possible solution in order to find the right answer. If that proves too challenging, she may want to try a heuristic, or rule of thumb, that helps her sift through the unrealistic or unlikely solutions to her problem. As she is searching for the solution to her problem, she may suddenly "see" the solution in her mind's eye—that is, experience insight—and move toward implementing a solution based on that insight without having to try out additional alternatives.

father came in the door this evening, Juan ran to him and shouted, "Daddy, Daddy, we goed to the zoo today!" Juan's use of "goed" is an example of

a. overgeneralization.
b. the linguistic relativity hypothesis.
c. babbling.
d. fixation.

Matching Terms and Definitions

7. For each definition, choose the best matching term from the list that follows:

Definition

a. Estimating the likelihood of events based on their availability in memory.
b. A tendency to approach a problem in a particular way; may or may not be helpful in solving a new problem.
c. The proposal that language determines the way we think.
d. Clinging to one's initial beliefs even after new information discredits the basis on which they were formed.
e. A problem-solving strategy that guarantees the solution to the problem.
f. The sudden realization (Aha!) of the solution to a problem.
g. The way an issue is worded or presented; can influence decisions and judgments.
h. The smallest unit of meaning in a given language.
i. The tendency to be more confident than correct when estimating the accuracy of one's beliefs and judgments.

Term

(1) insight
(2) prototype
(3) mental set
(4) algorithm
(5) confirmation bias
(6) availability heuristic
(7) overconfidence
(8) framing
(9) belief perseverance
(10) morpheme
(11) linguistic relativity hypothesis
(12) phoneme

Fill-in-the-Blank Questions

8. __________ __________ proposed that humans are predisposed to learn language, which explains why children master the grammar of their native language at such a young age. __________ __________ proposed that we learn language as we learn everything else—through associations, imitation, and rewards—which best explains why we speak a particular language.

9. __________ __________, working with Amos Tversky, researched factors that influence human judgment and decision making, and received a Nobel prize for this work in 2002.

Brief Essay Question

10. Your friend Jacinthe saw you reading about "problem-solving" and said, "Boy, have I got a problem that needs solving!" In three paragraphs of two to three sentences each, outline for Jacinthe the three different methods of problem-solving that you learned about in this module.

Performance Standards

Standard Area: Individual Differences

Content Standard 1: Concepts related to assessment of differences among individuals

Performance Standard 1.1 Define intelligence.

- Define intelligence. (Student Text p. 456)

Performance Standard 1.2 Understand statistic concepts related to testing.

- Discuss how intelligence test scores form a normal distribution. (Student Text pp. 464–465)
- Figure 24.4, "Intelligence and the Normal Distribution," illustrates how frequently various intelligence test scores occur in the general population. (Student Text p. 464)
- Discuss the concept of test reliability. (Student Text pp. 468–469)
- Investigate the importance of test validity. (Student Text p. 469)

Content Standard 2: Discuss the influence of nature and nurture on individual differences

Performance Standard 2.1 Examine how intelligence is influenced by nature and nurture.

- Discuss how studies of identical and fraternal twins provide evidence for the role of heredity on intelligence. (Student Text p. 471)
- Figure 24.5, "Twins and Intelligence," illustrates the role of heredity on intelligence. (Student Text p. 471)
- Describe the role of the environment in studies of fraternal twins raised together. (Student Text p. 471)

Content Standard 3: Understanding intelligence

Performance Standard 3.3 Explore various theories of intelligence.

- Discuss Charles Spearman's theory of general intelligence, or *g*. (Student Text p. 459)
- Compare traditional theories to modern approaches to understanding intelligence. (Student Text pp. 456–463)
- Investigate Howard Gardner's theory of multiple intelligences. (Student Text pp. 456–457)
- Figure 24.1, "Howard Gardner's Multiple Intelligences," summarizes his theory. (Student Text p. 456)
- Examine Robert Sternberg's triarchic theory of intelligence. (Student Text pp. 457–458)
- Figure 24.2, "Robert Sternberg's Three-Type Theory of Intelligence," summarizes his theory. (Student Text p. 457)
- Explore Daniel Goleman's theory of emotional intelligence. (Student Text pp. 458–459)

Content Standard 4: Concepts related to intelligence testing

Performance Standard 4.1 Explain how intelligence tests reflect individual differences.

- Explore how psychologists explain differences in average test scores among gender, racial, or ethnic groups. (Student Text pp. 469–472)

Performance Standard 4.2 Understand the relationship between test scores and achievement.

- Examine the differences between an achievement and an aptitude test. (Student Text p. 468)

Performance Standard 4.3 Discuss the limitations of traditional intelligence tests.

- Examine cultural bias in conventional testing. (Student Text pp. 469–470)
- Examine the concepts and consequences of using labels created from testing, such as *genius,* and *mental retardation.* (Student Text pp. 464–465)

Materials NETWORK

All of the items from the Video, Activity, and Enrichment Centers listed below come from the *Teacher's Resource Binder*. These items will help you teach and expand on concepts presented in Module 24.

trb This logo indicates when an item from the Materials Network may be used in conjunction with a specific note found in this module's *Teacher's Edition*.

The Nature of Intelligence

Activity Center

- Critical Thinking Activity: *Fact or Falsehood?* With this activity, students' preconceptions about intelligence and intelligence testing are either exposed as incorrect or reinforced as correct. (*Teacher's Resource Binder*, p. 24-1; Handout 24–1)
- Building Vocabulary: *Matching Terms and Definitions* This vocabulary handout requires students to match a definition or statement with a person, concept, or term from the module. (*Teacher's Resource Binder*, p. 24-1; Handout 24–2)
- Critical Thinking Activity: *The Factor Analysis Approach* Factor analysis is a statistical procedure that identifies clusters of related items on a test (any test, not just an intelligence test). It is used to identify the different dimensions of performance that underlie a person's total score. (*Teacher's Resource Binder*, p. 24-1; Handout 24–3)
- Application Activity: *Questionnaire for Business Management* Sternberg and Wagner's test of practical managerial intelligence assesses our tacit knowledge—that is, the knowledge we pick up, by osmosis, from our experience—which determines our ability to manage ourselves, to manage others, and to manage tasks. (*Teacher's Resource Binder*, p. 24-1; Handout 24–4)
- Critical Thinking Activity: *Assessing Creativity* The Remote Associates Test is another popular test of creativity. Students can use this test to gauge the creativity of their own thinking. (*Teacher's Resource Binder*, p. 24-1; Handout 24–5)

Enrichment Center

- Enrichment Lesson: *Gardner's Theory of Multiple Intelligences* Go into greater detail about the components of Gardner's theory and how Gardner arrived at his ideas. This lesson provides a chart that outlines the theory's eight areas of intellectual competence, along with examples of careers each area may lead to and well-known people in those careers. (*Teacher's Resource Binder*, p. 24-1)
- Enrichment Lesson: *Ego-Resiliency and Intelligence* Research indicates that the most central qualities of social intelligence may be the following: understanding people, being good at dealing with people, being warm and caring, being open to new experiences and ideas, having perspective-taking ability, knowing social rules and norms, and having social adaptability. Jack Block and Adam M. Kremen believe that these various aspects of social intelligence may be subsumed under their concept of ego-resiliency. (*Teacher's Resource Binder*, p. 24-1)
- Enrichment Lesson: *Successful Intelligence* Robert Sternberg identifies three aspects of intelligence: analytical, creative, and practical. Together, they make up what he calls "successful intelligence," which is "the ability to adapt to, shape, and select environments to accomplish one's goals and those of one's society and culture." (*Teacher's Resource Binder*, p. 24-1)
- Enrichment Lesson: *Why Do Intelligent People Fail?* Robert Sternberg has studied why people with high IQs often fail miserably at work, home, and life. Enhance discussion of this phenomenon with this lesson that provides Sternberg's conclusions regarding this question. (*Teacher's Resource Binder*, p. 24-1)
- Enrichment Lesson: *Fostering Children's Emotional Intelligence* Psychologist John Gottman suggests that helping a child master his or her emotional world is crucial to helping that child succeed in adult life. This lesson describes Gottman's research into how crucial that mastery is. (*Teacher's Resource Binder*, p. 24-1)
- Enrichment Lesson: *The Psychology of Wisdom* The study of wisdom has moved from the philosophical to the empirical. By presenting a person with certain dilemmas, researchers can assess that person's level of wisdom. (*Teacher's Resource Binder*, p. 24-1)
- Enrichment Lesson: *Creative People—Ten Antithetical Traits* Mihaly Csikszentmihalyi describes creative people as having the unusual capacity to adapt to almost any situation and to make do with whatever is at hand to reach their goals. (*Teacher's Resource Binder*, p. 24-1)

Intelligence Testing

Activity Center

- Analysis Activity: *"How Smart Are You?"* Mensa is an organization of people with a certain IQ, and this quick test can help students see if they might be candidates for membership. In addition, this activity can spark discussion of what a good intelligence test might measure. (*Teacher's Resource Binder*, p. 24-1; Handout 24–6)

- Analysis Activity: *Analogies and Intelligence* Several standardized aptitude tests use analogies to measure a person's ability to do well in college and graduate school. Students can test their ability to solve analogies with this activity. (*Teacher's Resource Binder*, p. 24-1; Handout 24–7)

Enrichment Center

- Enrichment Lesson: *Savant Syndrome* Savant syndrome is a condition in which people with serious mental handicaps, stemming from either retardation or major mental illness, have spectacular islands of ability or brilliance. Often, someone with this condition can perform extraordinarily in fields such as mathematics, music (almost exclusively limited to the piano), art, or mechanics. This lesson contains some theories as to the causes of savant syndrome and some examples of people with this condition. (*Teacher's Resource Binder*, p. 24-1)
- Enrichment Lesson: *Reaction Time and Intelligence* Some researchers believe that reaction time is positively related to a person's level of intelligence. In this lesson, students see for themselves the case for such a connection. (*Teacher's Resource Binder*, p. 24-1)
- Enrichment Lesson: *Intelligence and Glucose Metabolism in the Brain* Researchers using PET scans showed that people who use less brain energy are more likely to be of higher intelligence. (*Teacher's Resource Binder*, p. 24-1)

Test Construction

Activity Center

- Critical Thinking Activity: *Designing and Administering an Intelligence Test* Explore the nature of intelligence and good test construction with this activity that challenges both you and your students to come up with a good measure of intelligence. (*Teacher's Resource Binder*, p. 24-1)
- Critical Thinking Activity: *Remote Associates Test* The test in this activity provides students with a vehicle to determine whether the test construction was sound by using the principles of reliability, validity, and randomization. (*Teacher's Resource Binder*, p. 24-1; Handout 24–8)

Group Differences in Intelligence Test Scores

V Video Center

- Videocassette: *The Brain*, Second Edition, Module 4: "Intelligence and Culture" Consult the faculty guide from *The Brain* video series for a description of this module. (*Teacher's Resource Binder*, p. 24-1)

Activity Center

- Critical Thinking Activity: *Culture-Biased and Culture-Fair Tests* In response to the criticism that tests are culturally biased, several psychologists have attempted to devise instruments that are culture-fair. In the handout for this activity, students see examples of some of these test questions. (*Teacher's Resource Binder*, p. 24-1; Handout 24–9)

Enrichment Center

- Enrichment Lesson: *Blacks as a "Caste-like" Minority* John Ogbu's "caste" point of view extends the text discussion of most expert psychologists' agreement that the racial gap in intelligence scores is environmentally determined. Socioeconomic differences in intelligence test scores can be seen in several cultures throughout the world. (*Teacher's Resource Binder*, p. 24-1)
- Enrichment Lesson: *The National Commission of Testing and Public Policy* In May 1990, the National Commission on Testing and Public Policy released a study highly critical of standardized, multiple-choice tests. It called for a restructuring of educational and employment testing to promote the talents of all Americans. (*Teacher's Resource Binder*, p. 24-1)
- Enrichment Lesson: *The Case Against the SAT* *The Chronicle of Higher Learning* has reported that seven colleges and graduate schools that dropped or modified their use of standardized admissions tests were extremely happy with the results of their decision. The SAT, the nation's premier college entrance exam, is a questionable measure of the academic potential of all types of people, as this lesson points out. (*Teacher's Resource Binder*, p. 24-1)
- Enrichment Lesson: *Genes, Group Differences, and Bias* The controversial book *The Bell Curve* is discussed in this lesson, highlighting the authors' claims of genetic differences that lead to IQ differences and focusing on the theory and research that argue against such a view. (*Teacher's Resource Binder*, p. 24-1)
- Enrichment Lesson: *Genes and Intelligence* Although virtually everyone agrees that both genes and environment influence intelligence scores, Sandra Scarr proposes that differences among people can be best explained as genotype-environment effects. That is, genotype is the driving force behind development, determining how responsive people are to environments, and thus how they develop different levels and profiles of intelligence. (*Teacher's Resource Binder*, p. 24-1)

- **Enrichment Lesson:** *Teaching Intelligence* Several programs exist that seek to teach students skills that can raise IQ scores—and likely increase other aspects of intelligence. (*Teacher's Resource Binder*, p. 24-1)

- **Enrichment Lesson:** *Unanswered Questions About Intelligence* Intelligence, even with the boom in research seen over the past few years, is still a misunderstood and controversial topic. In this lesson, students learn more about psychology's pursuit of answers. (*Teacher's Resource Binder*, p. 24-1)

MODULE 24

Intelligence and Intelligence Testing

Think of some intelligent people. Do they share the same ways of thinking and mental qualities? Would your friends all agree that these people are intelligent, or do you think some might disagree? Questions such as this have challenged psychologists for over a century. Here are the basic issues:

- What, exactly, is intelligence?
- Where does intelligence come from?
- Can we use relatively simple tests to reliably and validly measure intelligence?
- Are there ethnic or gender differences in intelligence test scores, and, if so, what do the differences mean?

These are important questions that have significance for society. Even though we can't fully answer some of these questions, the use of intelligence tests has grown dramatically since they were first introduced. You and most other high school students have probably taken intelligence tests many times as you worked your way through the school system. The results of those tests, in combination with other standardized test scores, have regularly been used to make decisions about students' future education. Let's see what we can learn about intelligence and the tests designed to measure it. Then perhaps we will be in a better position to reap their benefits and avoid their pitfalls.

Do Your Scores Add Up? Most schools use a program of standardized testing, including intelligence tests, to track the performance of students and identify problems that can be solved. Have you ever seen the scores in your guidance folder? You have a right to know what's in there, and this module will help you understand what you'll find if you choose to check it out.

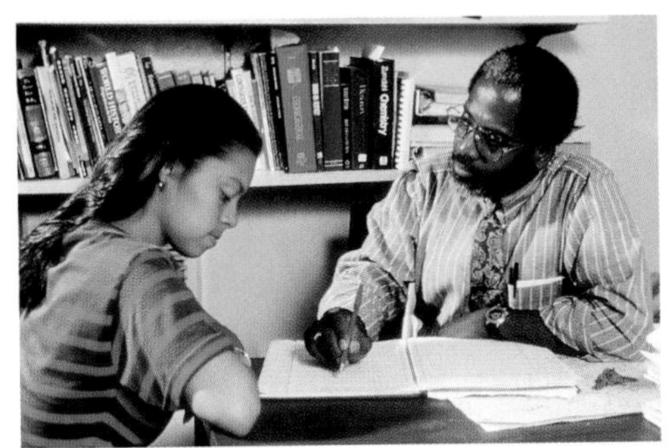

Getting Started

Introduce this module by asking your students to list behaviors they believe to be distinctively characteristic of either particularly intelligent or particularly unintelligent people. In research studies, the behaviors normally listed generally fall into three general classes: practical problem-solving skills, verbal skills, and social competence.

trb You may wish to use **Critical Thinking:** *Fact or Falsehood?* (*Teacher's Resource Binder*, p. 24-1; **Handout 24–1**) as a prereading strategy to find out what students already know about intelligence and intelligence testing. The activity will prime students to note terms and concepts in the text that confirm or dispel their preconceptions about intelligence and intelligence testing.

MODULE 24

Intelligence and Intelligence Testing

Introducing the Module

The Points: Module Objectives

- Compare and contrast Gardner's and Sternberg's theories of intelligence.
- Evaluate Alfred Binet's contribution to intelligence testing.
- Evaluate Lewis Terman's role in the development of intelligence tests.
- Describe David Weschler's contribution to intelligence testing.
- Explain how group tests of intelligence differ from individual tests.
- Differentiate between an achievement test and an aptitude test.
- Explain what we mean when we say a test is reliable and/or valid.
- Analyze the reasons for the differences in average test scores among gender, racial, or ethnic groups.

trb tr Building Vocabulary

Improve and confirm students' knowledge of the concepts in the module by having them work individually to complete the matching exercise presented in **Building Vocabulary:** *Matching Terms and Definitions* (*Teacher's Resource Binder*, p. 24-1; **Handout 24–2**). To help students check their work, you can use the handout as a transparency to project the correctly matched items.

Teaching the Points

web ■ TEACHING TIP

You can log on as an instructor to the book companion site for *Thinking About Psychology* at **www.worthpublishers.com/thinkingaboutpsych**. It contains teacher resources for class presentations as well as review and assessment of module concepts and terms.

MODULE 24

F • Y • I

Although Gardner presents evidence from a variety of research sources to support his theory, perhaps his most intriguing argument is that separate neural centers underlie these various intelligences. For example, he provides numerous case studies of patients who retain the capacity to be musicians, visual artists, and engineers; but these same patients have lost all language abilities because of damage to the speech centers in the left hemisphere of the brain. Similarly, he describes patients who retain their linguistic abilities; but these same patients have difficulty with spatial representation and other visual tasks because of right hemisphere damage. Gardner even provides supporting neurologic data for personal intelligences. For example, a lobotomy may cause little impairment to linguistic or logical-mathematical intelligence, but it can be disastrous for self-understanding and interpersonal relationships.

trb At this point, you may wish to use **Enrichment Lesson:** *Gardner's Theory of Multiple Intelligences* (*Teacher's Resource Binder*, p. 24-1).

■ **TEACHING TIP**

Thomas Armstrong's *7 Kinds of Smart: Identifying and Developing Your Many Intelligences, Revised and Updated with Information on 2 New Kinds of Smart* is a very useful resource for classroom lectures, discussions, and exercises that relate to Gardner's theory. Written as a self-help book, it describes the intelligences, provides checklists for assessing one's strengths and weaknesses, includes suggestions for developing each of the intelligences, and concludes with an extensive list of additional resources.

trb tr A black-line master for Figure 24.1, Howard Gardner's Multiple Intelligences, is available in the **Black-Line Masters Appendix** of the *Teacher's Resource Binder*.

Source: Armstrong, T. (1999). *7 kinds of smart: Identifying and developing your many intelligences, revised and updated with information on 2 new kinds of smart.* New York: Penguin.

▸ **intelligence** The ability to learn from experience, solve problems, and use knowledge to adapt to new situations.

▸ **Howard Gardner** (1943–) Author of a contemporary theory of multiple intelligences consisting of eight separate kinds of intelligence.

The Nature of Intelligence

What's the Point? 1. How do Gardner's and Sternberg's theories of intelligence differ, and what do they have in common?

This is an easy question, right? Everyone knows what intelligence is. To be intelligent is to be smart, bright, "with it," quick, on top of things. Psychologists consider **intelligence** to be the ability to learn from experience, solve problems, and use knowledge to adapt to new situations. They disagree, however, about what this general definition actually entails. For example, we speak of intelligence as though it were one thing, but it may be more accurate to speak of *multiple intelligences*.

Howard Gardner

One leading intelligence theorist, **Howard Gardner,** argues that there are at least eight independent kinds of intelligence, as illustrated in Figure 24.1 (1983, 1993, 1995). Traditionally, schools have tended to emphasize

Intelligence	Examples
Verbal-Linguistic	Reading comprehension Writing
Logical-Mathematical	Solving math and logic problems
Bodily-Kinesthetic	Balance Strength Endurance
Visual-Spatial	Judging distance Map reading Geometry
Musical-Rhythmic	Appreciating and creating music Music theory
Interpersonal	Listening Cooperation Sensitivity to others
Intrapersonal	Knowledge of self
Naturalistic	Appreciate nature Ability to work with plants and animals

Figure 24.1 **Howard Gardner's Multiple Intelligences** (From Gardner, 1999.)

Suggested Readings

Use the following as teacher-preparation tools or as enrichment for advanced students:

Budiansky, S. (1998). *If a lion could talk: Animal intelligence and the evolution of consciousness.* New York: Free Press.

Csikszentmihalyi, M. (1996). *Creativity: The work and lives of 91 eminent people.* New York: HarperCollins.

Csikszentmihalyi, M., Rathunde, K., & Whalen, S. (1993). *Talented teenagers: The roots of success and failure.* Cambridge: Cambridge University Press.

Deary, I. J. (2001). *Intelligence: A very short introduction.* Oxford: Oxford University Press.

Gardner, H. (1993). *Creating minds.* New York: Basic Books.

Gardner, H. (1999). *Multiple intelligences for the 21st century.* New York: Basic Books.

Gottman, J. (1997). *The heart of parenting: Raising an emotionally intelligent child.* New York: St. Martin's Press.

"reading, writing, and arithmetic," which, in Gardner's model, are represented by *verbal linguistic* and *logical-mathematical* intelligence. Gardner sees them as two different intelligences, which may explain why some students are good in math classes but not English classes, or vice versa. Schools may not place an equal value on other kinds of intelligence, such as an actor's *intrapersonal* abilities, a woodworker's *bodily-kinesthetic* skills, or the *naturalistic* intelligence represented by a wildlife biologist.

Some critics argue that Gardner has moved well beyond what is normally considered to be intelligence, which is usually classified as *mental* ability. By adding things like musical ability and bodily-kinesthetic ability, these critics say, he is broadening the concept of intelligence to include areas that used to be considered skills or talents.

▶ **Robert Sternberg** (1949–) Author of a contemporary theory of multiple intelligences consisting of analytical, creative, and practical intelligence.

Robert Sternberg

Psychologist **Robert Sternberg** has a different way of organizing multiple intelligences. His theory (1985, 1997) defines three separate types (Figure 24.2):

- ***Analytic intelligence*** This is the kind of intelligence most often stressed in schools. It helps the individual do things like analyze, compare, and evaluate, and it matches closely with most people's traditional view of intelligence. If you study published reports of various makes and models of cars to determine which would be the best purchase, you have used analytic intelligence.

Intelligence	Examples
Analytic	Analyzing Comparing Evaluating
Practical	Applying Using
Creative	Inventing Designing

Figure 24.2 **Robert Sternberg's Three-Type Theory of Intelligence** (From Sternberg, 1999.)

Gould, J. (1981). *The mismeasure of man.* New York: Norton.

Halonen, J. (1986). *Teaching critical thinking in psychology.* Milwaukee, WI: Alverno Productions.

Roach, M. (1989). *Extraordinary people: Understanding "idiot savants."* New York: Harper & Row.

Sternberg, R. (1986). *Intelligence applied.* New York: Harcourt Brace Jovanovich.

Sternberg, R. (1988). *The triarchic mind.* New York: Viking Penguin.

Sternberg, R. J., Forsythe, G. B., Hedlund, J., Horvath, J., Snook, S., Williams, W. M., et al. (2000). *Practical intelligence.* New York: Cambridge University Press.

Wade, C., & Tavris, C. (1993). *Critical and creative thinking: The case of love and war.* New York: HarperCollins.

Wallace, D. B., & Gruber, H. E. (Eds.). (1989). *Creative people at work: Twelve cognitive case studies.* New York: Oxford University Press.

trb tr ■ **TEACHING TIP**

A black-line master for Figure 24.2, Robert Sternberg's Three-Type Theory of Intelligence, is available in the **Black-Line Masters Appendix** of the *Teacher's Resource Binder.*

F • Y • I

Howard Gardner recently added to his theory *naturalistic intelligence*, which is the ability to understand, categorize, and explain patterns encountered in the natural world.

trb At this point, you may wish to use **Enrichment Lesson:** *Gardner's Theory of Multiple Intelligences* (*Teacher's Resource Binder*, p. 24-1).

■ **LOOKING AT THE ISSUES**

On the chalkboard, write the following criteria used by Howard Gardner to define each "intelligence." Ask students if they agree with Gardner.

- potential isolation by brain damage
- existence of savants, prodigies, and other exceptional individuals
- an identifiable core set of operations—basic kind of information-processing operations or mechanisms that deal with one specific kind of input
- a distinctive developmental history, along with a definite set of "end-state" performances
- an evolutionary history and evolutionary plausibility
- support from experimental and psychological tasks
- support from psychometric findings
- susceptibility to encoding from a symbol system

Source: Project Zero Web site http://pzdev.harvard.edu/AMI/mi.htm.

trb At this point, you may wish to use **Critical Thinking Activity:** *The Factor Analysis Approach* (*Teacher's Resource Binder*, p. 24-1; **Handout 24–3**).

MODULE 24

■ TEACHING TIP

Robert J. Gregory provides an excellent illustration of intelligent behavior as reflecting the ability to learn from experience, to solve problems, and to use knowledge to adapt to new situations. With the example below, you can share a good example of Sternberg's idea of practical intelligence:

- There was a moderately retarded 61-year-old newspaper vendor who, although well-known to community mental health professionals, managed his own affairs with minimal supervision. Both eccentric and fiercely independent, he stored canned goods in his freezer and swore at caseworkers who stopped by to inquire about his well-being. He maintained his fragile independence and tenuous adaptation to his environment by selling papers from a street-side newsstand. The papers cost a quarter, which he recognized as proper payment. He also had learned that three quarters were proper change for a dollar. He refused payment other than a quarter or a dollar—an arrangement his customers had learned to live with. However, one day the price of a newspaper increased to 35 cents. He now had to learn to deal with nickels and dimes, as well as quarters and dollars. The amount of learning required to adapt to this new environmental demand exceeded his intellectual abilities and, sadly, he was soon out of business.

Source: Gregory, R. (1992). *Psychological testing: History, principles, and applications.* Boston: Allyn & Bacon.

trb At this point, you may wish to use **Enrichment Lesson:** *Why Do Intelligent People Fail?* (*Teacher's Resource Binder*, p. 24-1).

■ JOURNAL WRITING

Invite students to use the following questions and writing prompts as springboards for entries in their psychology journals:

- Do you feel you receive a "multiple intelligences" education? If so, how?
- Which of the intelligences do you feel you have more of—analytical, creative, or practical? Which one of them do you think is most important to have? Why?

How Many Intelligences? Howard Gardner of Harvard (left) and Robert Sternberg of Yale are two of the leading cognitive psychologists in the United States today. Each of them believes it is accurate to speak of multiple intelligences, but they disagree on how many kinds of intelligence there are.

I once heard Robert Sternberg tell a joke to illustrate practical intelligence: Two men were walking through the North Woods when a large, mean-looking bear appeared on the other side of a clearing. One of the men sat down, opened his backpack, and took out his tennis shoes. When he started to change his heavy hiking boots for the lighter shoes, his friend said, "What are you doing? You can't possibly outrun that bear." The friend replied, "I don't have to outrun the bear; I only have to outrun you!" Now that's practical intelligence.

- ***Creative intelligence*** Individuals high in creative intelligence can do things like create, invent, and design—they come up with new ideas and adapt to new situations. If you develop clever budgeting or borrowing strategies to be able to buy a new car, you have used creative intelligence.
- ***Practical intelligence*** Practical intelligence is the sort of "common sense" that helps you complete the various tasks you face. It allows you to apply, use, and do. If you successfully negotiate a great deal at the local car dealership, you have used practical intelligence.

Traditional intelligence tests focus on analytic intelligence. They do a reasonably good job of predicting school grades, but they don't do a good job of predicting occupational success. There is a practical intelligence test that predicts managerial success more successfully than traditional intelligence tests do—it focuses on tasks like keeping workers motivated and writing effective memos (Sternberg & Wagner, 1993; Sternberg & others, 1995).

Emotional Intelligence

Yet another theory, popularized in a book by Daniel Goleman (1995), distinguishes between academic intelligence and **emotional intelligence**—the ability to perceive, express, understand, and regulate emotions (Mayer & Salovey, 1993). People with high emotional intelligence are more in touch with their feelings. They can face setbacks without losing their motivation or optimism, and they can manage their emotions in a way that allows them to get along well with others. Academic skills seem very different from the social skills that

Reteaching

You can use this activity to help students evaluate their definitions of intelligence.

Divide students into small groups and have them share their ideas about the following situation:

- Think of a time that you learned something significant and the way that you learned it.
- What did you do to learn this significant thing?
- Were you changed afterward? If so, how?

After groups have had sufficient time to share ideas, ask a representative from each to summarize their group's discussion for the rest of the class. Interesting debate may ensue as members in the groups compare and contrast responses to the same set of questions.

trb At this point, you may wish to use **Enrichment Lesson:** *Successful Intelligence* (*Teacher's Resource Binder*, p. 24-1).

flow from emotional intelligence. Perhaps this is why academically bright people are not much better than average folks when it comes to success in occupations, marriages, child-rearing, and maintaining their own mental health (Epstein & Meier, 1989).

As you can see, psychologists have not yet reached a consensus about the nature of intelligence. It's a complicated concept, and it won't be settled until more research is done. One question that has not been fully answered is whether some underlying factor fuels all of the various multiple intelligences (whatever they may be), much as AAA batteries can power up everything from flashlights to MP3 players. Over a half-century ago, **Charles Spearman** proposed just such a factor, which he called **general intelligence**, or *g*. Spearman was impressed by the tendency of people who excelled in one area to also excel in others. Gardner, Sternberg, and others who emphasize multiple intelligences are more impressed by the very different and separate nature of their various proposed factors. All of these theories give us wonderful glimpses of what intelligence may really entail.

▶ **emotional intelligence** The ability to perceive, express, understand, and regulate emotions.

▶ **Charles Spearman** (1863–1945) Theorized that a general intelligence factor, *g*, underlies other, more specific aspects of intelligence.

▶ **general intelligence (*g*)** A general intelligence factor that Spearman believed underlies specific mental abilities and is therefore measured by every task on an intelligence test.

Intelligence Testing

Have you ever taken an intelligence test? Chances are that you have, but—if you're like many of my students—you don't realize it. The vast majority of schools in the United States have a standardized testing program for their students, and some of these tests are indeed intelligence tests. Even though intelligence tests are widely used, there is much misunderstanding about what the tests can, and cannot, tell us. Let's continue our own quest for understanding by looking at the history of intelligence tests.

Intelligence Research and Testing Left to right, Alfred Binet, Lewis Terman, and David Wechsler, who all contributed to the development of intelligence tests as we know them today.

Cross-Curricular Connections

GUIDANCE COUNSELING AND PSYCHOMETRICS Invite your school's guidance counselor or psychometrist to discuss how intelligence testing is used in your particular school district and state. In the presentation, ask your guest to respond to and cover topics addressed in the questions below:

- What types of intelligence tests are used in this school?
- What qualifies a student as needing special education services?
- What qualifies a student as needing gifted education services?
- What programs are available for both types of special needs identification?

trb At this point, you may wish to use **Enrichment Lesson:** ***The National Commission on Testing and Public Policy*** (*Teacher's Resource Binder*, p. 24-1).

web ■ **TEACHING TIP**

Emotional intelligence is introduced at the *Utne Reader* Web site at www.utne.com/azEQ.tmpl. This site provides a brief 10-question test that students can complete, including explanations for each answer. It also provides links to recent magazine articles that discuss Daniel Goleman's concept.

trb At this point, you may wish to use **Enrichment Lesson:** ***Ego-Resiliency and Intelligence*** (*Teacher's Resource Binder*, p. 24-1).

F•Y•I

Daniel Goleman suggests that no psychological skill is more fundamental than impulse control. He cites the marshmallow challenge, used by psychologist Walter Mischel during the 1960s at a preschool on the Stanford University campus. Mischel invited 4-year-olds into a small room and offered them each a marshmallow. They were told, however, that if they were willing to wait while he ran an errand, they could each have two marshmallows on his return. Some children grabbed the single treat the minute he was out the door. Some lasted a few minutes before they gave in. Others were determined to wait. In the seemingly endless 15- to 20-minute interval, they resisted temptation in a variety of ways. They covered their eyes, they sang to themselves, they played games with their hands and feet, and some even tried to go to sleep.

The importance of how children reacted to the marshmallow challenge became clear some 12 to 14 years later. As adolescents, those who resisted temptation at 4 were more socially competent, personally effective, and self-assertive. They were less likely to freeze under stress and more likely to pursue challenges even in the face of difficulties. They were more self-reliant, confident, trustworthy, and dependable. When they were evaluated again as high school graduates, those who resisted were far superior students to those who acted on whim. They also had dramatically higher scores on their SAT tests (more than 200 points higher than the other group).

trb At this point, you may wish to use **Enrichment Lesson:** ***Fostering Children's Emotional Intelligence*** (*Teacher's Resource Binder*, p. 24-1).

MODULE 24

■ LOOKING AT THE ISSUES

Intelligence tests were created to help students—which they still do by identifying students who need more help and enrichment. But they have also hurt some students since identification for special services can lead to prejudice. Pose the following questions and discuss with students the benefits and drawbacks of intelligence testing in today's schools:

- Is it better to separate students into ability groups or to have mainstreamed classes? Why?
- Are intelligence tests the only or main way students are identified for special services in school? What other assessments are used to identify students who need extra help?
- How can intelligence tests hold students back? How can they help students succeed?

trb At this point, you may wish to use Enrichment Lesson: *Fostering Children's Emotional Intelligence* (*Teacher's Resource Binder*, p. 24-1).

F•Y•I

(1) Alfred Binet believed that intelligence equaled good judgment. He was quoted in a publication written with Theodore Simon: "A person may be a moron or an imbecile if he is lacking in judgment; but with good judgment he can never be either."

Source: University of Indiana. (1997). *History of influences in the development of intelligence theory and testing.* Retrieved March 1, 2003, from www.indiana.edu/~intell/index.html.

(2) Binet and Simon's work with intelligence tests influenced another famous developmental psychologist—Jean Piaget. Theodore Simon put a young Jean Piaget in charge of standardizing another colleague's reasoning test for Parisian schoolchildren, a move which many believe led Piaget to become fascinated with how children develop intellectually.

▶ **Alfred Binet** (1857–1911) Developer of the first test to classify children's abilities using the concept of mental age.

▶ **mental age** The chronological age that corresponds to the difficulty level of the questions a child can answer. In Terman and Stern's intelligence quotient (IQ) formula, mental age is abbreviated as MA.

▶ **chronological age** Actual age. In Terman and Stern's intelligence quotient (IQ) formula, chronological age is abbreviated as CA.

Alfred Binet

2. What was Alfred Binet's contribution to intelligence testing?

Testing has been around for a long time, but we can trace the roots of modern, standardized intelligence tests back to nineteenth-century France. That's when **Alfred Binet** (1857–1911) developed the test that would lead to today's intelligence tests. At that time, France had new laws requiring education for all children. In the face of such overwhelming numbers, teachers needed an efficient way to place children in the proper classes. The French government was also concerned that some teachers would be biased in their placement of students. Wouldn't it be better to give each child a fast and fair test? Government officials asked Binet and a colleague, Théodore Simon, to develop a test that could spot any student likely to struggle in an age-grouped classroom.

Binet and Simon started by assuming that children's intellectual abilities grow year by year. Thus, a typical 7-year-old should be able to answer harder questions than a typical 6-year-old, a typical 8-year-old should answer harder questions than a typical 7-year-old, and so on. However, not every member of each age group is typical—some 7-year-olds can successfully answer questions that are usually appropriate for 8- or even 9-year olds. Other 7-year-olds may struggle with questions most 6- or even 5-year-olds can easily answer.

Binet and Simon used these assumptions to measure **mental age**, a short-hand description of the difficulty level of the questions a child can answer. Thus, a child who can answer 8-year old questions has a mental age of 8, no matter what the child's **chronological age** (actual age) is. Binet and Simon predicted that children who fell significantly behind their age-mates in mental age were the ones who would struggle in an age-grouped classroom. Even at this early time, Binet was concerned that his test, developed for such noble purposes, would be used to label some children as "backward" and to limit their opportunities (Gould, 1981).

Mental Age Everyone in this group is 5 years old and will start school soon. They are not all the same, though. Some of them have more advanced mental abilities than others. Alfred Binet designed his tests to tap this quality—children's mental age—as contrasted with their chronological age (5 years, for these children).

Cross-Curricular Connections

GOVERNMENT Have students research laws regarding special education in the classroom. You may wish to assign each of the following questions to a group of students.

- What criteria has the federal government established to identify children who need special education services?
- What are teachers required by law to provide to those who are identified as "special education" students?
- What is the "least restrictive environment"? How does that affect classrooms at your school?
- Has mainstreaming been successful? Why or why not?

trb At this point, you may wish to use Enrichment Lesson: *The National Commission on Testing and Public Policy* (*Teacher's Resource Binder*, p. 24-1).

Lewis Terman

3. What role did Lewis Terman play in the development of intelligence tests?

Binet was right to be concerned about future applications of his tests. Those who followed him were convinced that intelligence was largely determined by genetics, which meant they were less interested in providing remedial programs for less capable students. Binet, believing that intelligence is determined mostly by environment, felt that slow children could be provided exercises to help them increase their mental abilities.

Stanford University's **Lewis Terman** (1877–1956) was one psychologist who disagreed with Binet and believed that intelligence was reasonably fixed. Terman revised the original Binet and Simon test for use with American children. The revision was called the **Stanford-Binet intelligence test,** and a modern version is still in wide use today. Terman, in collaboration with William Stern, devised a way to express an individual's performance on the test with a single, easy-to-interpret number, the **intelligence quotient (IQ)**. This formula was as famous in psychology as Einstein's $E = MC^2$ was in physics—and it became widely known by the public at large. IQ was calculated as follows:

$$IQ = \frac{MA}{CA} \times 100$$

In this formula, MA represents mental age, determined by the difficulty level of questions a child could answer. CA is chronological age, or the child's actual age. Thus, a child whose mental age and chronological age matched (in other words, a child with average mental development) would have an IQ score of 100. Children whose MA had advanced beyond their CA would have an IQ score above 100. For example, a 10-year-old child who could answer questions suited to the average 11-year-old would have an IQ of $\frac{11}{10} \times 100$, or 110. Similarly, a child who lagged behind agemates in mental development would slip below 100. An 8-year-old who could answer only 6-year-old questions would have an IQ of $\frac{6}{8} \times 100$, or 75. This simple measuring stick proved handy and easy to apply.

Modern intelligence tests all use this same basic technique—comparing a person's actual age with that person's level of mental development. Scores are adjusted so that 100 represents average intelligence for one's age group. The original formula, however, is no longer used. And the term "IQ" is now a shorthand way of saying "intelligence test score." One problem with the formula is the assumption that mental abilities increase a little bit every year; this statement holds true only for children. If a 12-year-old boy attempts to learn calculus and finds it too difficult, it makes sense for him to wait a few years and try again—his mental abilities will continue to grow during his teen years. But if a

▶ **Lewis Terman** (1877–1956) Adapted Binet's tests for use in the United States as the Stanford-Binet intelligence test, which reported intelligence as a calculated IQ score.

▶ **Stanford-Binet intelligence test** The widely used American revision (by Terman at Stanford University) of Binet's original test.

▶ **intelligence quotient (IQ)** The number that results from Terman and Stern's formula for computing the level of a person's intelligence: mental age (MA) divided by chronological age (CA) multiplied by 100.

Enriching

web Have students view the government site at **www.ed.gov/inits/commissionsboards/whspecialeducation**. Then have them create a survey about the role of intelligence tests in schools. The survey should elicit responses to the following questions:

- How would students feel if intelligence tests were used only to place them in particular classes?
- Should students be allowed to choose whatever classes they want to take without regard for intellectual ability?
- How would the social environment change if intellectual ability grouping were the norm at your school?

trb At this point, you may wish to use Enrichment Lesson: *The National Commission on Testing and Public Policy* (*Teacher's Resource Binder*, p. 24-1).

F • Y • I

People in Terman's time believed that bright children became maladjusted adults. Terman's Termites were a group of gifted children chosen to test if precocious children could become talented, adjusted adults. Terman found, among other things, that the gifted were taller, healthier, better developed physically, and superior in leadership and social adaptability—dispelling the popular, contrary opinion. Listed below are ways in which Terman believed that gifted children should be treated differently:

- They should be identified as early as possible in childhood.
- They should be accelerated through school.
- They should have a differentiated curriculum and instruction.
- They should have specially trained teachers.
- They should be viewed as a national resource for the betterment of society.
- They should be allowed to develop in whatever directions their talents and interests dictated.

Source: University of Indiana. (1997). *History of influences in the development of intelligence theory and testing.* Retrieved March 1, 2003, from www.indiana.edu/~intell/index.html.

trb At this point, you may wish to use Enrichment Lesson: *Creative People—Ten Antithetical Traits* (*Teacher's Resource Binder*, p. 24-1).

■ **TEACHING TIP**

Emphasize to students that 100 is considered a "normal" score on an intelligence test. Intelligence tests are routinely restandardized so that the 100 score is the accurate normal score. That way, generational effects in nutrition, education, and knowledge can be accounted for.

MODULE 24

F • Y • I

Lewis Terman was part of the eugenics movement, which started in the nineteenth century. The **eugenics movement** believed that only the "fit" should be allowed to reproduce. They believed that societal problems like poverty, hunger, and unemployment were the results of feebleminded people reproducing at a faster rate than the mentally strong. Terman believed that people from certain ethnic groups and cultures were more feebleminded than others, as evidenced by immigrants from those groups who were more likely to be poor and destitute. He pushed to have his intelligence tests used as a requirement for entry into the United States. The tests would limit entry of those of lower intelligence. He was also part of a committee that used intelligence testing on military recruits for World War I to identify which recruits would be trained for specialized jobs and which ones would be sent to the front lines as regular infantry.

■ LOOKING AT THE ISSUES

Eugenics was taken to a horrible extreme during Hitler's Nazi regime. By selectively eliminating certain ethnic groups and people with "undesirable" traits (such as handicaps, diseases, and low intelligence levels), the Nazis hoped to create a "master race." Today's growing research in genetic therapy to eliminate disease has come under scrutiny as a possible rebirth of the eugenics movement. Some critics believe that gene therapy could just as easily be used for genetic enhancements as it could be used to treat genetic disorders. Explore the following questions about genetic therapy with your students:

- Would you support gene therapy to combat diseases like Alzheimer's and Parkinson's? Why or why not?
- Would you support gene therapy to enhance traits like intelligence and height? Why or why not?
- Should ethical limits be placed on genetic research? Why or why not?

V At this point, you may wish to show Videocassette: *The Brain,* Second Edition, Module 4: "Intelligence and Culture" (*Teacher's Resource Binder,* p. 24-1).

▶ **David Wechsler** (1896–1981) Developer of the Wechsler intelligence scales, which have become the most widely used individual intelligence tests in the United States. These were the first tests to report scores for both verbal and performance intelligence.

▶ **Wechsler intelligence scales** A series of intelligence tests tailored to three different age groups (adults, children, and preschoolers); currently the most widely used individual intelligence tests in the United States.

20-year-old man finds calculus too difficult, waiting probably won't increase his chances of becoming a math whiz—material that is too hard at 20 will probably remain so. This leveling-off process caused problems when people became interested in giving IQ tests to adults as well as children. An average 20-year-old woman would have an IQ of 100, calculated by dividing 20 (MA) by 20 (CA) and multiplying by 100. By age 40, though, her IQ would drop to 50 because her CA has doubled but the MA has stayed the same!

Beyond the problem of adjusting for adult scores, the notion of an IQ formula is perhaps too simplistic. It reduces the complex concept of intelligence to a single number without considering other characteristics that can influence its interpretation. As public interest focused on the new IQ scores, people began to draw inappropriate conclusions: "Your IQ is 103? Hah—mine is 104. I'm smarter than you are!" These conclusions were particularly destructive when leveled by one ethnic group against another. Terman's personal beliefs, however, fostered such comments.

Unlike Binet, Terman assumed intelligence was largely fixed by heredity—he lined up on the nature side of the nature-nurture debate. He also worked hard to promote the wide use of IQ testing, and his ultimate goal was to discourage the spread of what he called "feeble-mindedness" (intellectual weakness) through indiscriminate "breeding" (Terman, 1916). Terman and others shared the belief that measured differences in IQ among various ethnic and national groups were largely inborn, and these beliefs partially accounted for the restrictive U.S. immigration policies of the 1920s. Policymakers never considered cultural and personal factors that might have accounted for the differences. Terman later acknowledged that such factors were significant, but his early belief that people could and should be categorized by the IQ averages of their native country shows how easily values and beliefs can influence science.

David Wechsler

4. What was David Wechsler's contribution to intelligence testing?

In the 1930s, **David Wechsler** (1896–1981) began work on a battery of intelligence tests that have become the most widely used individual intelligence tests in America. The **Wechsler intelligence scales** introduced several innovations, including the following:

- ***Different tests for different age groups*** Rather than trying to test all people with the same instrument, Wechsler developed three tests for different age groups: the Wechsler Adult Intelligence Scale (WAIS), the Wechsler Intelligence Scale for Children (WISC), and the Wechsler Preschool and Primary Scale of Intelligence (WPPSI).

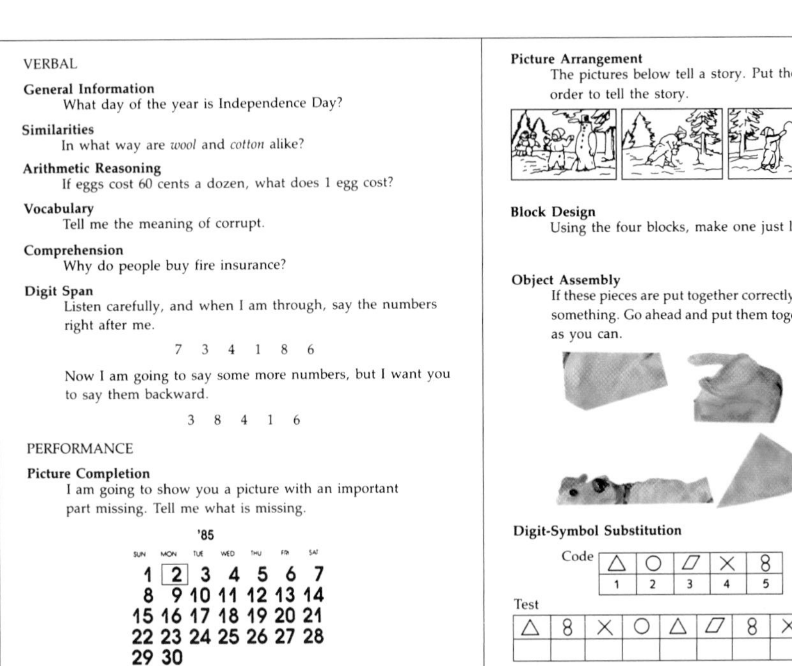

VERBAL
General Information
What day of the year is Independence Day?
Similarities
In what way are *wool* and *cotton* alike?
Arithmetic Reasoning
If eggs cost 60 cents a dozen, what does 1 egg cost?
Vocabulary
Tell me the meaning of corrupt.
Comprehension
Why do people buy fire insurance?
Digit Span
Listen carefully, and when I am through, say the numbers right after me.
7 3 4 1 8 6
Now I am going to say some more numbers, but I want you to say them backward.
3 8 4 1 6
PERFORMANCE
Picture Completion
I am going to show you a picture with an important part missing. Tell me what is missing.
'85
1 2 3 4 5 6 7
8 9 10 11 12 13 14
15 16 17 18 19 20 21
22 23 24 25 26 27 28
29 30
Picture Arrangement
The pictures below tell a story. Put them in the right order to tell the story.
Block Design
Using the four blocks, make one just like this.
Object Assembly
If these pieces are put together correctly, they will make something. Go ahead and put them together as quickly as you can.
Digit-Symbol Substitution
Code
1 2 3 4 5
Test
8 8 8

Figure 24.3 The Wechsler Adult Intelligence Test Here are some sample items from the verbal and the performance sections of a Wechsler test. (From Thorndike & Hagen, 1977.)

- ***Separate scores for verbal and nonverbal abilities*** In addition to providing an overall intelligence score, the Wechsler tests divide intelligence into verbal and performance categories (Figure 24.3). The verbal intelligence section tests vocabulary, math, and similar skills. The performance section tests abilities on tasks such as the assembly of objects.
- ***Subtests*** The Wechsler tests are really a battery of about a dozen individual tests, some of which tap verbal abilities and others performance abilities. Each subtest is separately scored, so people using the results can more easily determine the test-taker's strengths and weaknesses.

Taking an Intelligence Test In individual intelligence tests, such as the Wechsler tests, the tester works one on one with the person taking the test. This child is working on the block design subtest of the Wechsler Intelligence Scale for children. The tester has set up the equipment and will time the child as one measure of performance.

F•Y•I

(1) David Wechsler developed a new formula for intelligence called the **deviation quotient**. This number represents a person's mental ability at a particular age, as well as how that person's score compares with the average score for his or her age.

(2) The Stanford-Binet and the Wechsler tests are not the only ones on the market. Other intelligence tests available today use newer theories of brain function. Some of these tests are listed below:

- Kaufman Assessment Battery for Children (K-ABC)
- Woodcock-Johnson Tests of Cognitive Ability
- Differential Ability Scales
- Cognitive Assessment System (CAS)
- Sternberg Triarchic Abilities Test (STAT)

■ LOOKING AT THE ISSUES

David Wechsler's approach to intelligence testing deviated from Binet's and Terman's in that instead of measuring one type of intelligence for all ages, Wechsler produced a battery of tests that measured both verbal and nonverbal ability for different age groups. Have students discuss whether this is a better approach by responding to the following questions:

- What type of people would do better at verbal items?
- What type of people would do better at performance items?
- How would this approach to testing identify those people who needed special services?

Enriching

Have students construct their own version of the Wechsler tests by coming up with different items for each of the subtests highlighted in Figure 24.3 on page 463 of the *Student Edition*. Invite them to try to administer their tests and compare people's scores with their GPAs.

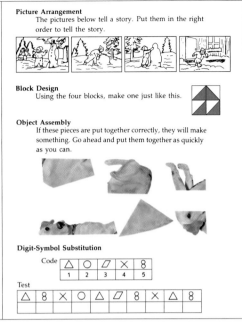

- *Verbal:* General Information, Similarities, Arithmetic Reasoning, Vocabulary, Comprehension, Digit Span
- *Performance:* Picture Completion, Picture Arrangement, Block Design, Object Assembly, and Digit-Symbol Substitution

trb At this point, you may wish to use **Critical Thinking Activity:** ***Designing and Administering an Intelligence Test*** (*Teacher's Resource Binder*, p. 24-1).

MODULE 24

■ LOOKING AT THE ISSUES

More whites are identified as gifted than any other racial or ethnic group. More African-American boys are identified as needing special education services than any other racial, ethnic, or gender group. Have students research legal and political topics brought up by the following questions:

- Are intelligence tests the only thing to blame for this disparity? Explain.
- What legal problems have schools faced because of these disparities? What have been the courts' solutions?
- How can schools shrink the achievement gap?

F • Y • I

(1) Mensa was founded in 1946 by two British barristers who thought it might be an interesting experiment to gather together people of exceptionally high intelligence. *Mensa* is the Latin word for "table"; it symbolizes the coming together of equals. Its original agenda was to discuss and arrive at ways of preserving world peace.

trb At this point, you may wish to use **Analysis Activity:** *How Smart Are You?* (*Teacher's Resource Binder*, p. 24-1; **Handout 24–6**) and *Analysis Activity: Analogies and Intelligence* (*Teacher's Resource Binder*, p. 24-1; **Handout 24–7**).

(2) Just as mental retardation is stratified into different categories, gifted intellectual ability is also divided into stratified categories.

- An IQ score of 110–119 is considered "bright normal."
- A score of 120–129 is considered "superior."
- A score higher than 130 is considered "very superior."

Some groups consider a score higher than 150 to be truly "gifted."

trb tr A black-line master for Figure 24.4, Intelligence and the Normal Distribution, is available in the **Black-Line Masters Appendix** of the *Teacher's Resource Binder.*

Up Close

Extremes of Intelligence: The Ends of the Normal Curve

Most people score near the middle of the range of human intelligence, but what about those who are far below, or far above, the middle? If you look at Figure 24.4 you will see that intelligence test scores show a *normal distribution,* or bell-shaped curve. In any normal distribution, whether of intelligence test scores or some measure of friendliness, most scores pile up near the middle—the farther away you move from the middle, the fewer people are represented.

About 2 percent of the population has an intelligence test score below 70. According to the American Psychiatric Association (1994), half of this 2 percent has mental retardation, defined as having a score of less than 70 and difficulty adapting to the demands of independent living. Within this category, individuals are further classified as having mild, moderate, severe, or profound retardation (Table 24.1). Notice that the vast majority of individuals with retardation are in the mild category, and that most people with mild retardation can, with proper training, lead largely independent lives. People with moderate retardation often thrive living in group homes and doing productive work in sheltered workshops. Independence is very limited or impossible for people with severe and profound retardation.

Nothing Gets Him Down Jimmy Nelson's Down's Syndrome may be his least interesting attribute. Classmates call this prominent member of the cheerleading squad "the most popular kid in school."

What causes mental retardation? Hundreds of factors can contribute, including genetics (*Down*

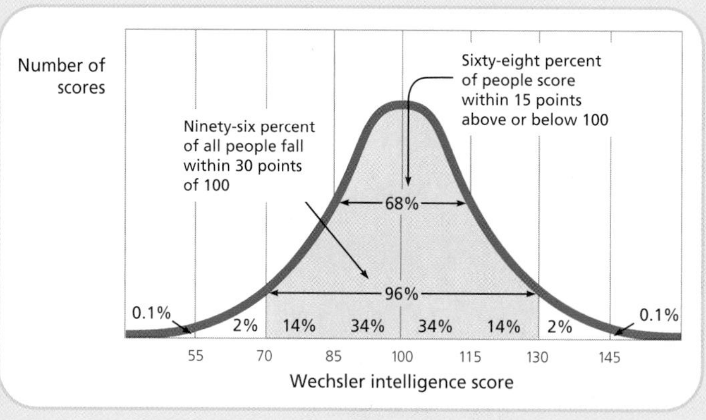

Figure 24.4 Intelligence and the Normal Distribution This graph shows how frequently various intelligence test scores occur in the general population. The average score is 100, and about two-thirds of the population score within 15 points of this average. The further away from average you get, the fewer people achieve that score. It is rare to have scores below 55 or above 145.

Enriching

web (1) Mensa, an organization of intellectually superior individuals, has a huge presence on the World Wide Web. The Mensa International Homepage provides background information on the organization, a description of membership benefits, and a listing of national groups.

Have students complete the Mensa Workout (which takes about 30 minutes) at **www.mensa.org/workout.html**.

TABLE 24.1 DEGREES OF MENTAL RETARDATION

LEVEL	TYPICAL INTELLIGENCE SCORES	PERCENTAGE OF PERSONS WITH RETARDATION	ADAPTATION TO DEMANDS OF LIFE
Mild	50–69	85%	May learn academic skills up to sixth-grade level. Adults may, with assistance, achieve self-supporting social and vocational skills.
Moderate	35–49	10%	May progress to second-grade level academically. Adults may contribute to their own support with employment in sheltered workshops.
Severe	20–34	3–4%	May learn to talk and to perform simple work tasks under close supervision but are generally unable to profit from vocational training.
Profound	Below 20	1–2%	Require constant aid and supervision.

Source: Reprinted with permission from the *Diagnostic and Statistical Manual of Mental Disorders,* Fourth Edition. Copyright 1994 American Psychiatric Association.

syndrome is caused by an extra chromosome) and problems during pregnancy (excessive use of drugs or alcohol, for example) or childbirth. Environmental problems, such as malnutrition during childhood, can also produce retardation.

On the opposite end of the normal curve are those who score above average on intelligence tests. There is no universally agreed upon definition for *genius*, but psychologists have extensively studied high-scoring individuals. Lewis Terman in 1921 began the most famous of these studies, tracking 1500 California schoolchildren with scores over 135. Stereotypes about exceptionally bright children being "nerdy," deficient in social skills, or unhealthy proved untrue as their lives played out over seven decades. These high-scoring children were healthy and well-adjusted in school, and as adults they generally succeeded in such challenging professions as law and medicine (Holahan & Sears, 1995).

Intelligence tests are important tools that help psychologists measure a quality we all share. Fascinating human beings populate the entire range of intelligence.

Chess Champ Ten-year-old Fabiano Caruana is already a candidate for U.S. grand master of chess. Here he won 14 matches out of the 15 he had been playing simultaneously!

(2) Have students do a literature review of studies that survey the demographics of and programs for "giftedness." In their reviews have them consider the following questions.

- Do gender differences exist in those identified as gifted? What are those differences? *(Although overall intelligence scores are equal, average differences do exist between the genders in terms of spatial, social, and analytical intelligences.)*
- Do cultural or socioeconomic differences exist in those identified as gifted? *(Overall, black and rural white children do worse on intelligence tests than suburban white children, but the reasons behind this difference seem to be more socioeconomic than racial.)*
- Should gifted students skip grades in school or just attend enrichment, pull-out classes? Why? *(Research shows that grade acceleration is a positive intervention for highly gifted students, but many educators resist such programs because of social progress concerns.)*

F•Y•I

The American Association for Mental Retardation (AAMR) is an international organization of professionals dedicated to the study of mental retardation. The group's mission statement reads, "AAMR promotes progressive policies, sound research, effective practices, and universal human rights for people with intellectual disabilities." The group was founded in 1876, but it has been responsible for defining mental retardation since 1921.

trb At this point, you may wish to use **Enrichment Lesson:** ***Savant Syndrome*** (*Teacher's Resource Binder*, p. 24-1).

■ TEACHING TIP

As you teach about differences in intelligence, keep in mind that **mainstreaming** brings students of different intellectual abilities into each classroom, a practice that fosters intellectual achievement and causes prejudice at the same time. As you discuss differences in intellectual ability, challenge students to avoid using pejorative words when referring to those people with lower ability. Help students see that this module emphasizes *intelligence* as a controversial term that encompasses a wide range of skills and abilities—including the likelihood that the same person may possess intelligence in some areas and not in others.

trb **tr** A black-line master for Table 24.1, Degrees of Mental Retardation, is available in the **Black-Line Masters Appendix** of the *Teacher's Resource Binder.*

web ■ APPLYING THE POINTS

Have students go to the AAMR's Web site at **www.aamr.org/Policies/faq_mental_retardation.shtml**. There they will learn the current definition for *mental retardation.* After allowing time for exploring this site, engage students in a full-class discussion by posing the following questions:

- Does this definition fit into their schema for mental retardation? Why or why not?
- How does this definition change their perspective of people considered mentally retarded?
- How are the intellectual and adaptive components of the definition different from one another?

MODULE 24

F • Y • I

The Army Alpha tests were first developed in World War I to help the army identify which recruits were capable of specialized training and which were not. Some of the members of the committee who developed the tests read like a who's who of intelligence testing—David Wechsler, Lewis Terman, E. G. Boring, and Robert Yerkes.

trb At this point, you may wish to use **Enrichment Lesson:** *Reaction Time and Intelligence* (*Teacher's Resource Binder*, p. 24-1).

■ APPLYING THE POINTS

Consult your school's psychometrist or guidance counselor to find out how long it takes to administer intelligence tests to students. You can use the following questions to elicit the information, which you can then incorporate into class discussion:

- How often are individual and group tests administered?
- Who is qualified to administer these tests?
- How much does it cost to administer each individualized test? How much does it cost to administer each group test?
- How are the results used?

trb At this point, you may wish to use **Enrichment Lesson:** *The National Commission on Testing and Public Policy* (*Teacher's Resource Binder*, p. 24-1).

▶ **group intelligence tests** Originally developed by the U.S. army to efficiently assess recruits during World War I and now widely used by schools. Usually administered by teachers in their classrooms, these tests are not as reliable as individually administered tests such as the Stanford-Binet or Wechsler tests.

Both the Stanford-Binet and the Wechsler tests are individual intelligence tests, which means that a trained examiner gives the test to one person at a time. The tests are periodically revised to remain current and competitive with one another. It is a little like the Coke and Pepsi competition—just as those two major brands of cola account for most of the market, these two tests account for most of the individual intelligence tests given in the United States.

Group Tests

5. How do group tests of intelligence differ from individual tests?

Although the Stanford-Binet and Wechsler tests are the most widely given *individual* intelligence tests, most people have never taken either of them. The tests given so regularly in many school districts are **group intelligence tests**. These tests were originally developed by the U.S. Army in the early 1900s to help evaluate the massive number of recruits during World War I. The army used these tests because they are very efficient. Many people can take them at one time, using nothing more than a test booklet and an answer sheet. The person supervising the test needs no extensive training, which is required for people who give the individual tests. Scoring is equally easy, with the help of an answer key or a computer program.

It is this tremendous efficiency that makes group tests appealing to schools, too. Schools cannot afford to hire trained testers to give individual tests to each student, but most school budgets can cover group tests administered in a classroom under the supervision of teachers. The answer sheets can be sent to the test supplier for economical computer scoring. And there are lots of choices available, including the Cognitive Abilities

Tests and More Tests It's hard to get through a day without being tested for something!

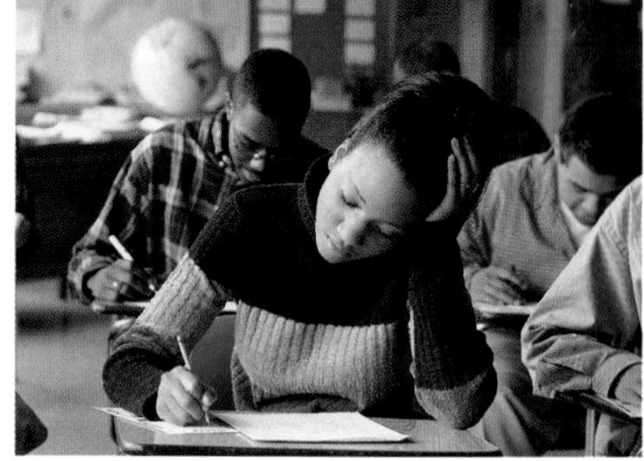

Enriching

Students take standardized tests each year, but do they really know what they are for? Have volunteers contact those in charge of tests in your school to learn more about the testing practices of your school district and state. The following questions may elicit the desired information. In a class presentation have volunteers present the questions along with the responses they learned.

- What standardized tests do students take each year? How do the tests differ with each grade level?
- Are students notified of their scores each year? How?
- How do the schools use the disaggregated data from these scores? Do they have to report them to the state? For what purpose?

trb At this point, you may wish to use **Enrichment Lesson:** *The National Commission on Testing and Public Policy* (*Teacher's Resource Binder*, p. 24-1).

Test, the Differential Aptitude Test, and the Otis-Lennon School Ability Test. If the Stanford-Binet and Wechsler individual tests are comparable to Coke and Pepsi, the various group tests more closely resemble the wide array of makes of automobiles. The U.S. Army, of course, sticks with its original vehicle—the Army Alpha test—to evaluate recruits.

But there is a trade-off with group tests. Have you heard the expression, "There is no such thing as a free lunch"? It applies quite well to group intelligence tests. Their economic efficiency comes at the cost of test reliability. We cannot count on the results of these tests to the same extent that we can count on the results of individual tests. Most school districts compromise by using both kinds of tests. Every child takes a group test every year or two through the elementary school years. If the results fall within the normal range, the results are filed away and nothing further is done. However, if the test indicates some problem, most districts follow up by having the school psychologist administer the more expensive but more reliable individual test, usually the Wechsler or the Stanford-Binet. If that test also indicates special needs, school officials may recommend special programming for that child.

But a question remains: What makes one test more reliable than another? To answer that question, we need to take a closer look at test construction.

Test Construction

Probably no generation in the history of the world has been tested as much as yours. Can you remember when you took your first test? Probably not. If you were born in a hospital, as my sons were, chances are very good that you were tested within the first minute of your life. Newborns are given the Apgar test to determine their overall physical condition and whether medical intervention is necessary. My older son, Carl (who has grown up fine and healthy, I'm happy to say), "failed" this early test—because he was not breathing! After Apgar, the tests came fast and furiously, as people checked your hearing and vision, watched you swim to determine whether you could go in the deep end of the pool, assessed your readiness for kindergarten, judged your intelligence, measured what you had achieved in the classroom, and put you behind the wheel to watch you drive. And your tests aren't over yet—you can still look forward to high school exit exams, college entrance exams, graduate school admission exams, and various professional tests, like the bar exam required of lawyers or the certificate exams to become a master electrician. Is it any wonder we all get tired of being tested? But since we can't avoid them, let's try to understand the general principles behind test design and applications.

F • Y • I

The Apgar test is standard procedure for assessing newborn development. Apgar is an acronym referring to the following abilities all newborns should possess in the first moments of life:
A = **activity** (muscle tone). Babies should move actively from the very beginning
P = **pulse.** A pulse rate higher than 100 beats per minute is considered ideal.
G = **grimace.** When a puff of air is blown in the babies' faces, they should sneeze, cough, and pull away.
A = **appearance.** Skin color should be normal over the entire body.
R = **respiration.** Babies should be breathing well and crying.

■ TEACHING TIP

Ask your students whether they think SAT scores should be used in determining college admissions or in the awarding of scholarships. The question is likely to stimulate a lively debate.

trb At this point, you may wish to use **Enrichment Lesson:** *The Case Against the SAT* (*Teacher's Resource Binder*, p. 24-1).

Cooperative Learning

Divide students into small groups and assign each group a different age group from the life span. Have students brainstorm about the different types of tests they have taken or think they might take at their group's assigned period of life. Encourage group members to discuss what the tests they've identified measure and how those tests have affected or might affect their lives. Bring the groups together, and ask each one to present a brief overview of its discussions. Continue with a class discussion by asking students to hypothesize the impact tests from the past as well as those in the future might have had or might have on their emotional and financial futures, and why.

MODULE 24

F • Y • I

(1) Studies have shown that standardized aptitude tests like the SAT and ACT are not as good at predicting future college success as GPA and class rank. Robert Sternberg and his colleagues have recently been testing a new version of the SAT that takes into account Sternberg's theory of successful intelligence. Initial findings show that the new version seems to do better at predicting college success.

(2) Students can take standardized college admissions tests as many times as they'd like to get higher scores, but they do not take the same test each time. Companies, like the Educational Testing Service, administer several versions of tests that have undergone tests of reliability against each other so that students don't compromise their results by remembering items from previous test-taking opportunities.

trb At this point, you may wish to use Enrichment Lesson: *The Case Against the SAT* (*Teacher's Resource Binder*, p. 24-1).

(3) Remind students that reliability should play into how well they do on standardized college admission tests. Although students can take tests like the ACT and SAT as many times as they wish, their scores shouldn't vary by too many points. In fact, if on one version a student scores too many points higher than on previous attempts at the tests, that student's scores may be flagged and investigated for possible cheating.

trb At this point, you may wish to use Enrichment Lesson: *The Case Against the SAT* (*Teacher's Resource Binder*, p. 24-1).

■ TEACHING TIP

It might be helpful to have students use their own test-taking experiences to brainstorm qualities of bad tests. Ask them to identify what, in particular, they hated about bad tests. Also have them identify specific problems with multiple-choice, matching, fill-in-the-blank, and essay questions on tests. End the discussion by asking students how they think bad tests could be made better.

trb At this point, you may wish to use Critical Thinking Activity: *Designing and Administering an Intelligence Test* (*Teacher's Resource Binder*, p. 24-1).

▶ **achievement tests** Tests that attempt to measure what the test-taker has accomplished.

▶ **aptitude tests** Tests that attempt to predict the test-taker's future performance.

▶ **reliability** The extent to which a test yields consistent results.

▶ **validity** The extent to which a test measures or predicts what it is supposed to.

Achievement and Aptitude Tests

6. What's the difference between an achievement test and an aptitude test?

One major way of characterizing tests is to distinguish between those that assess achievement and those that gauge aptitude. **Achievement tests** attempt to *measure* something. The classroom tests you take on a regular basis measure how much you've achieved in your various units of study. Standardized achievement tests you and other students around the country take are attempts to determine what each of you has accomplished in relation to your classmates. These standardized tests also help schools or districts know how their students are doing in comparison with state and national reference groups. One widely used achievement test battery is the Iowa Tests of Educational Development (ITED).

Aptitude tests are designed to make a *prediction* about future performance. College entrance exams like the American College Test (ACT) and Scholastic Assessment Test (SAT) are both aptitude tests. Intelligence tests are also considered aptitude tests because they attempt to assess the test-taker's ability to learn.

Reliability and Validity

7. What do we mean when we say a test is reliable and/or valid?

Have you ever taken a bad test? Almost every student can relate stories about poorly constructed or unfair tests. Have you heard the expression "garbage in, garbage out"? It applies equally well to computers and poorly designed tests. Bad tests provide bad results. Knowing this, psychological testing experts have worked hard to eliminate problems, especially from widely used standardized tests that are used to make decisions about individuals' futures. Good tests—those that are well designed—are both *reliable* and *valid.*

Test Reliability

In tests, **reliability** equals consistency—no matter who gives the test, the results will be the same. Just as a reliable friend is one you can count on, so is a reliable test. Here are some ways that test designers assess whether a test is reliable:

- *Does it have test-retest reliability?* If so, a person who retakes a test will get almost the same score the second time as the first. For example, if you take an intelligence test twice in 3 months, your score should be roughly the same each time.
- *Does it have split-half reliability?* If so, your score on the even-numbered items should be about the same as your score on the

Reteaching

web There are many Web sites that provide visitors the opportunity to test intelligence. Perhaps most important, these sites provide students with the opportunity to apply what they have learned about the principles of sound test construction. Try the tests at either or both of these sites:

- www.brain.com provides tests of fluid intelligence, crystallized intelligence, short-term memory, and mental quickness.

odd-numbered items. For example, if I give you a 100-point multiple-choice test, you should get about the same number of correct answers on the odd-numbered questions as you do on the even-numbered questions.

- *Does it have scorer reliability?* If so, two people should be able to score the same test and get the same result. My co-author and I, given two identical copies of your exam, should give you the same grade.

Test Validity

Validity is a test's ability to measure or predict what it is supposed to. What if I designed a test to measure your intelligence by checking your hat size. I could do this fairly reliably—I would get consistent answers every time I checked the size label on the inside of your hat. Would you be satisfied with my statement about your intelligence? Maybe—if you have a really big head! But most people would object, saying that this is a bad test. And they'd be right. This is not a *valid* test of intelligence because people with big heads are not necessarily more intelligent than people with small heads. This test does not measure what it is supposed to measure. Reliability alone does not guarantee a good test.

One of the best indicators of test validity is a test's ability to make accurate predictions. College admissions tests are considered somewhat valid because they do a tolerably good job of predicting how well a student will do in the first year of college. It is generally true that students who do well on the tests are those who also do well in college. There are enough exceptions, however, that the use of the tests remains controversial.

Notice that you cannot determine whether a test is valid *unless you know its purpose.* A test can be valid for some purposes but not for others. Intelligence tests, for example, have more validity for predicting how well children will do in elementary school than they do for predicting occupational success for adults. It's interesting that the purpose for which Alfred Binet developed the first test—predicting school success—is still the one that is most valid!

Group Differences in Intelligence Test Scores

8. How can we explain differences in average test scores among gender, racial, or ethnic groups?

Can tests be biased? Can they put certain individuals at a disadvantage because of their gender, race, or cultural background? Psychologists who design tests are very concerned about these questions because some groups do tend to outscore others on some tests. Males do better than females on tests of math problem solving (Hedges & Nowell, 1995). Israeli Jews do better than Israeli Arabs on intelligence tests (Zeidner,

■ LOOKING AT THE ISSUES

Students can now use a computer to take many standardized tests offered by the Educational Testing Service. These tests are adaptive in nature, meaning that each question is chosen to adapt to the abilities of the test taker. Test takers can also schedule the tests at their convenience, instead of waiting until a particular Saturday at different points in the year. Use the following questions to engage students in a discussion of the benefits and drawbacks of adaptive computerized tests:

- How can adaptive tests be both good and bad?
- How could the use of technology be a factor in taking computerized tests?
- What benefits and drawbacks could be possible in scheduling your own test-taking time?

■ TEACHING TIP

Another very valid test students take is the driver's test. To get a driver's license, one must demonstrate knowledge of the rules of the road, as well as the ability to drive. A test can't be more valid than that! Have students brainstorm about other performance-based tests that validly measure what they are designed to measure.

■ CHECKING FOR UNDERSTANDING

Have students write a quick paragraph explaining the difference between aptitude and achievement tests and reliability and validity. Use these paragraphs to assess whether students can distinguish among these important terms.

- IQ Tests Online at www.2h.com/Tests/iq.phtml sorts its Web links into "traditional" and "alternative" IQ tests. The latter category includes humorous tests on everything—from jewelry IQ to garbage IQ.

In addition to having students assess their own intelligence, ask them to determine whether any of the sites provide evidence of standardization, reliability, or validity.

MODULE 24

F • Y • I

For more than 25 years, James R. Flynn, a professor and social activist in New Zealand, has questioned the notion that non-White ethnic groups are intellectually inferior because of their poor scores on intelligence tests. Flynn proceeded to document the intelligence tests scores from more than 20 countries and found that overall intelligence test scores have risen anywhere from 5 to 25 points from the beginning of the twentieth century, regardless of race, ethnicity, or cultural background. This rise in test scores has perplexed researchers and caused many to question whether intelligence tests actually measure intelligence. Flynn believes that intelligence tests actually measure problem-solving skills, which weakly correlate to intelligence.

■ MULTICULTURAL CONNECTIONS Sternberg and Kaufman show how, in contrast to Western cultures, African and Asian cultures are much more likely to emphasize social skills in their conception of intelligence. For example, in Africa, intelligence includes skills that help to establish and maintain harmonious and stable intergroup relations. Chewa adults in Zambia emphasize social responsibility, cooperation, and obedience as important to intelligence. Intelligent children are expected to be respectful to adults. Similarly, Kenyan parents emphasize responsible participation in family and social life as important aspects of intelligence. In Zimbabwe, the word for intelligence, *ngware*, has to do with being prudent and cautious, particularly in social relationships.

Source: Sternberg, R. J., & Kaufman, J. C. (1998). Human abilities. In J. T. Spence, J. M. Darley, & D. J. Foss (Eds.), *Annual Review of Psychology, 49,* 479–502.

trb At this point, you may wish to use Critical Thinking Activity: *Culture-Biased and Culture-Fair Tests* (*Teacher's Resource Binder*, p. 24-1; Handout 24–9).

Group Differences in Intelligence Test Scores On some intelligence tests, different groups have different average scores. The question is, why? Most psychologists believe that environmental factors, not heredity, account for these group differences.

1990). Israeli Arabs, like black Americans, are a minority group within a larger, dominant culture. In the United States, as in Israel, the minority group's scores are lower. In 1994, a group of over 50 researchers (Avery & others, 1994) looked at a series of studies and concluded that the average score for black Americans was roughly 15 points lower than for white Americans. Some evidence indicates that this IQ gap has closed to about 10 points among children tested more recently (Neisser & others, 1996). But the bigger question is why this gap is appearing. Group differences like the three cited here deserve very close study so that we don't leap to inappropriate conclusions about the people involved.

Are the tests biased? Are they testing intelligence, or something else? We know that different groups in the United States have different experiences as participants in American society. Do members of disadvantaged minority groups have the same kinds of experiences that the white, middle-class, Americans who designed these tests have? Probably not. So to the extent that these tests require a knowledge of mainstream American culture, the tests are not valid intelligence tests. In that sense, the tests are biased. Lower scores on the part of some groups reflect the fact that those groups have not had the same kind of "preparation." Notice that we are talking about group differences here, and that scores among the individuals within each group vary tremendously. Some black American children score higher than almost all white American children, and some white American children score lower than almost all black American children. We cannot predict how any individual child will do, based on the group the child comes from—just as we cannot predict how long any individual person will live, even though we know that women, in general, live longer than men.

So does heredity also play a role in racial differences on intelligence test scores? Let's look at what psychologists have discovered about the extent to which intelligence is inherited. This area, as much as any, illustrates the importance of the nature-nurture debate. Is intelligence determined by *nature*—the inborn influence of heredity—or is it determined by *nurture*—the influence of the environment we are raised in? The answer has profound significance for our society. If certain racial groups are likely to be less intelligent because of the genes they were born with, an argument could be made that they are less qualified to hold positions of responsibility. But if environmental factors cause the lower intelligence scores, no such argument can be made, because the differences will disappear if opportunities become more equal. So, which is it—nature or nurture?

Cross-Curricular Connections

SOCIAL STUDIES To help students link concepts about intelligence and intelligence testing to cultures in other regions of the world, provide the anecdote that follows from a study by Joseph Glick.

Liberia's Kpelle tribesmen provides a classic example of adaptive intelligence. Glick asked the tribesmen to sort a group of objects sensibly. To his puzzlement, they insisted on grouping the objects by function (for example, placing a potato with a hoe) rather than by taxonomy (placing the potato with other foods). On the basis of Western standards, this indicated an inferior style of sorting and lower intelligence. After Glick demonstrated the "correct" answer, one of the tribesmen remarked that only a stupid person would sort things that way. When Glick thereafter asked tribesmen to sort items the way a stupid person would, they sorted them taxonomically without hesitation or difficulty.

The answer is that both nature *and* nurture shape an individual's intelligence. How do we know this? From studies that used a number of techniques to untangle the threads linking environment and heredity to intelligence. Studies of identical twins, for example, are useful because identical twins share exactly the same heredity (Figure 24.5). Any differences between them cannot be genetic and must be environmental. Fraternal twins are no more genetically similar than any brothers and sisters are. They are less similar in intelligence test scores than identical twins, but more similar than nontwin siblings. Why? It's because twins—whether fraternal or identical—share a more similar environment, being exposed to a variety of experiences together, than other siblings. Adoption studies are also useful. If an adopted child is more similar to the biological parents than the adoptive parents, there is support for the impact of heredity.

When we roll together the results of the studies of twins—those raised together and those raised apart, identical or fraternal—and of adopted children, it becomes clear that heredity plays a big role in our intelligence. But it also becomes clear that environment plays a role significant enough to explain why group differences exist. In fact, genetics researchers (Cavalli-Sforza & others, 1994; Lewontin, 1982) have established that individual differences within a race are much greater than differences among racial groups. Racists have tried but have been unable to find conclusive support in the research to establish that some groups are superior to others because of their genes. Just as you can't judge a book by its cover, you can't judge a human by color. After all, 99.9 percent of your genes are an exact match to every other human's (Plomin & Crabb, 2000)! Similar problems arise when you try to analyze gender differences. Males

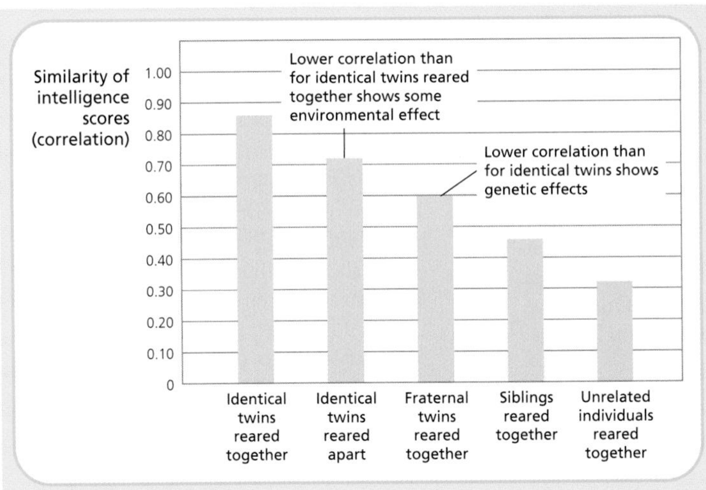

Figure 24.5 **Twins and Intelligence** Twin studies show that intelligence test scores for twins are more similar than scores for either siblings who grow up together or unrelated individuals who grow up together. Environmental effects are apparent in the studies of identical twins reared apart. Heredity's role is apparent in studies of fraternal twins raised together. (Data from McGue & others, 1993.)

V At this point, you may wish to show **Videocassette:** ***The Brain,*** **Second Edition, Module 4: "Intelligence and Culture"** (*Teacher's Resource Binder,* p. 24-1).

Interested students may research to find other anecdotes that are examples of adaptive intelligence. Suggest they write a report of their findings for extra credit.

MODULE 24

F • Y • I

The existence of hereditary variation within a group does not necessitate a hereditary explanation for the differences between groups. You can extend the text illustration of this important point with a similar example, provided by Stephen Jay Gould. He argued that even if intelligence were 70 percent heritable, this would not prove that racial or cultural differences were genetic. For example, height is about 95 percent heritable. Imagine now, he says, a group of malnourished Africans whose average height is several inches less than that of North Americans. The Africans would not remain shorter if they were properly fed. Similarly, the average height in Japan has gone up several inches since World War II, but no one argues that the Japanese gene pool has changed.

Source: Gould, S. J. (1981). *The mismeasure of man.* New York: Norton.

trb At this point, you may wish to use **Enrichment Lesson:** ***Genes and Intelligence*** (*Teacher's Resource Binder,* p. 24-1) and **Enrichment Lesson:** ***Genes, Group Differences, and Bias*** (*Teacher's Resource Binder,* p. 24-1).

tr A four-color transparency of Figure 24.5, Twins and Intelligence, is available in the **Overhead Transparencies Set.**

■ **JOURNAL WRITING**

Invite students to use the following questions and writing prompts as springboards for entries in their psychology journals:

- Do you believe in a "nature" or "nurture" view of intelligence? Why?
- Have you experienced or witnessed prejudice and discrimination because of a perceived racial or cultural difference in intelligence? Describe your experience.

MODULE 24

Close

Create a chart with two columns—one labeled *benefits* and the other labeled *drawbacks*. Have students list, in the appropriate columns, reasons supporting and rejecting the use of intelligence tests in schools, for college admissions, and for job placement.

- Has their view of intelligence tests changed after reading this module? Why or why not?
- Would they recommend people submit to intelligence tests for any purpose? Why or why not?
- How can schools make good, responsible use of intelligence test information?

Checking the Points

■ TEACHING TIPS

web (1) The book companion site for *Thinking About Psychology* at **www.worthpublishers.com/thinkingaboutpsych** contains a module quiz, flashcards of key terms and people, and other student activities and resources for this module. You will also find PowerPoint lectures, a quiz grade book, and other teaching resources by logging on as an instructor.

trb (2) At this point, you may wish to review and confirm concepts about intelligence and intelligence testing with **Critical Thinking Activity:** *Fact or Falsehood?* (*Teacher's Resource Binder*, p. 24-1; **Handout 24–1**). Suggest that students complete the handout individually, disregarding handouts they may have completed at the beginning of the module. Have students take the time to look up information in the text to respond correctly to questions. Invite them to exchange handouts with classmates to check answers.

and females *do* show some differences in mental abilities. Girls, for example, show more verbal fluency (Halpern, 1997), and boys score higher on solving math problems (Hedges & Nowell, 1995). Some part of these gender differences may be biological, but differing social expectations for boys and girls certainly have an effect as well.

The easy answers intelligence tests were supposed to provide have never been quite as easy as some had hoped they would be. The unanswered questions about intelligence and the tests that attempt to measure it remain more interesting than the questions on the tests themselves.

REVIEW

Module 24: Intelligence and Intelligence Testing

What's the Point?

The Nature of Intelligence

1. *How do Howard Gardner's and Robert Sternberg's theories of intelligence differ, and what do they have in common?*

   Psychologists define *intelligence* as the ability to learn from experience, solve problems, and use knowledge to adapt to new situations. Both Howard Gardner and Robert Sternberg have proposed theories of multiple intelligences, rather than one underlying general intelligence factor, as Charles Spearman theorized. Gardner has proposed eight different intelligences: verbal-linguistic, logical-mathematical, bodily-kinesthetic, visual-spatial, musical-rhythmic, interpersonal, intrapersonal, and naturalistic. Sternberg has proposed three intelligences: analytic, creative, and practical. Others have suggested a separate emotional intelligence.

Intelligence Testing

2. *What was Alfred Binet's contribution to intelligence testing?*

   At the request of the French government, Alfred Binet designed the first test to assess children's ability to succeed in school. Binet firmly believed that intelligence is determined mainly by environment, and he worried that his test would be used to label children and limit their opportunities. Binet was the first to use the concept of mental age to describe the level of difficulty of questions a child can answer.

3. *What role did Lewis Terman play in the development of intelligence tests?*

   Terman, an American, adapted Binet's test for use with American children. Terman believed that intelligence is inherited and is firmly fixed. He intended his test, known as the Stanford-Binet test of intelligence, to be used not only to place children in school but also to discourage "breeding" among the "feeble-minded." Terman's test, which was not adjusted to education or cultural background, was used to deny certain groups of people the right to move to the United States and become citizens here. Terman, working with William Stern, devised the formula that gave the score that has become known as the "IQ." This formula divides mental age (MA) by actual age (CA) and multiplies by 100. Current intelligence tests do not use this formula, which works with children but not with adults. A single-number score as an indication of one's mental abilities is also now seen as too simple a way of describing intelligence.

4. *What was David Wechsler's contribution to intelligence testing?*

   Wechsler designed a series of tests, the Wechsler intelligence scales, which offered different tests for different age groups, separate scores for verbal and nonverbal abilities, and a battery of subtests to profile particular strengths and weaknesses. These tests are now the most widely used individual intelligence tests, with the Stanford-Binet test in second place in that competition.

5. *How do group tests of intelligence differ from individual tests?*

   An individual test of intelligence is a one-on-one interaction between a trained tester and a single test-taker. As a result of this individual attention, these tests are expensive and time consuming. Group intelligence tests are paper-and-pencil tests given to groups of people (often students and members of the armed forces) by someone who has not had extensive training in giving the test. Group tests are easy to score because an answer key or a computer program supplies the correct answers. Such tests are quick, efficient, and relatively inexpensive, but they are not as reliable as individual tests.

Test Construction

6. *What's the difference between an achievement test and an aptitude test?*

   An achievement test (like the quiz at the end of this module) attempts to measure what you have accomplished. An aptitude test (like the intelligence tests we've discussed in this module) attempts to predict what you could do in the future.

7. *What do we mean when we say a test is reliable and/or valid?*

   A test is reliable if it consistently assesses the same thing, giving the same scores, no matter who gives the test. A test is valid if it assesses what it is intended to assess. Tests can be reliable without being valid. Good tests are both reliable and valid.

Group Differences in Intelligence Test Scores

8. *How can we explain differences in average test scores among gender, racial, or ethnic groups?*

   Psychologists study the effect of heredity and environment in research on genetically identical twins raised separately or together; genetically different fraternal twins raised separately or together; and adopted children and their biological and adoptive parents. The results show that heredity and environment tend to interact to produce intelligence in individuals. The differences in average test scores could, most psychologists believe, be the result of environment. No research supports the superiority of one racial group over another.

MODULE 24

trb tr ■ TEACHING TIP

At this point, you may wish to review module vocabulary with the entire class by using **Building Vocabulary:** ***Matching Terms and Definitions*** (*Teacher's Resource Binder*, p.24-1; **Handout 24–2**) as a transparency. Have a student read an item aloud on the handout and provide the correct match. If other students challenge the answer, have them identify what they believe is the correct match and support their answer with a passage from the text. If the challenge is incorrect, ask the class to find a passage from the text that identifies and confirms the correct answer.

tb Using the Test Bank

The *Test Bank* that accompanies this textbook offers a wide variety of questions in different formats and levels of complexity. Use the software to construct whole tests or to integrate standardized questions into teacher-made tests.

Self-Test Answers

Multiple-Choice Questions

1. a, 2. a, 3. d, 4. a, 5. d

Key Terms

intelligence, p. 456
emotional intelligence, p. 458
general intelligence (*g*), p. 459
mental age (MA), p. 460
chronological age (CA), p. 460
Stanford-Binet intelligence test, p. 461
intelligence quotient (IQ), p. 461
Wechsler intelligence scales, p. 462
group intelligence tests, p. 466
achievement tests, p. 468
aptitude tests, p. 468
reliability, p. 468
validity, p. 469

Key People

Howard Gardner, p. 456
Robert Sternberg, p. 457
Charles Spearman, p. 459
Alfred Binet, p. 460
Lewis Terman, p. 461
David Wechsler, p. 462

Self-Test

Multiple-Choice Questions

Choose the *best* answer for each of the following questions:

1. Ramir is very proud of his daughter Shukla's beauty and intelligence. Anyone can see her beauty, he says, and her general intelligence is evident in her above-average verbal, mathematical, artistic, and dance talents. Ramir seems to believe in ______________ view of intelligence.
   a. Gardner's c. Spearman's
   b. Sternberg's d. Binet's

2. Mark is such a good electrician that he is booked for two months in advance. People building new houses offer to give him bonuses if he will just squeeze them into his tight schedule. Robert Sternberg would say that Mark has a high degree of ______________ intelligence.
   a. practical c. emotional
   b. intrapersonal d. general

3. Babs has been the main person on the desk at the very busy Emergency Animal Hospital for five years. Everyone—vets, staff members, visitors, and pet owners—loves Babs because she has a very special ability to listen carefully and sensitively and to cooperate with everyone to make things happen quickly and efficiently. Howard Gardner would say that Babs has a high degree of ______________ intelligence.
   a. practical c. intrapersonal
   b. general d. interpersonal

4. Esteban has designed a new test of intelligence based on people's bank balances. He's pretty sure this will be a good test, because he remembers that his father used to shout at people, "If you're so smart, why aren't you rich?" Esteban is especially pleased that this test will yield consistent results, no matter who gives it: To score a person's test, all anyone has to do is look at the balance on that person's bank statement. Esteban may be disappointed to discover that his new test is
   a. reliable but not valid.
   b. valid but not reliable.
   c. neither valid nor reliable.
   d. both valid and reliable.

5. Miss O'Malley, Greatest High School's new guidance counselor, wants to institute some changes in how the school district tests students' intelligence. In the past, Greatest School District used group tests, administered by classroom teachers and scored by computers. Miss O'Malley thinks testing each student individually will give teachers a better view of that per-

son's abilities. She may not be able to make this change because

a. trained testers must administer individual tests.
b. trained testers must score individual tests.
c. most school districts cannot afford the costs of individual testing for all students.
d. All of the above.

Matching Terms and Definitions:

6. For each definition, choose the *best* matching term from the list that follows:

Definition

a. The score that results from dividing a person's mental age by the person's chronological age and multiplying by 100.
b. The chronological age that corresponds to the difficulty level of the questions a test-taker can answer.
c. The extent to which a test measures or predicts what it is supposed to.
d. A test that attempts to predict a test-taker's future performance.
e. The ability to perceive, express, understand, and regulate emotions.
f. The ability to learn from experience, solve problems, and use knowledge to adapt to new situations.
g. The extent to which a test yields consistent results.

Term

(1) achievement test
(2) aptitude test
(3) IQ
(4) emotional intelligence
(5) MA
(6) CA
(7) reliability
(8) validity
(9) intelligence

Fill-in-the-Blank Questions

7. Unlike Charles Spearman, both ________ ________ and ________ ________ believe that there are multiple kinds of intelligence.

8. French psychologist ________ ________ developed the first test to classify children's abilities using the concept of mental age.

9. American psychologist ________ ________ modified an earlier test for use with American children, and his test reported intelligence as a calculated IQ score. He also encouraged the use of his test to discourage "breeding" among the "feeble-minded."

10. American psychologist ________ ________ developed tests that were the first to report scores for both verbal and performance intelligence; these tests have become the most widely used individual intelligence tests in the United States.

Brief Essay Question

11. Jennifer and Sara are identical twins raised apart but reunited in their early twenties. Harry and Halle are fraternal twins raised together. Jan, a psychologist, wants these four people to volunteer for a study of the effects of heredity and environment on intelligence. Jan is also recruiting Jordan, who is adopted, for this study, as well as Jordan's biological parents and his adoptive parents. In three paragraphs of about three sentences each, explain why Jan would be interested in having all these people in his study, and what other categories of people might especially interest him.

Self-Test Answers

Matching Terms and Definitions

6. a. (3), b. (6), c. (8), d. (2), e. (4), f. (9), g. (7)

Fill-in-the-Blank Questions

7. Howard Gardner; Robert Sternberg, 8. Alfred Binet, 9. Lewis Terman, 10. David Wechsler

Brief Essay Question

11. Students should understand that each group could lend some value to a study delving into the nature versus nurture debate over intelligence. Identical twins reared apart can help shed light on which factors are due to nature and which are due to nurture since identical twins share 100% of the same gene code. Fraternal twins reared together can show how a similar environment can affect behavior since fraternal twins share the same environment but only a portion of their genes. Adopted children compared with both their biological and adoptive parents can also shed light on the impact of environment versus genes. If an adopted child is more similar in intelligence to his or her adopted parents, then environment is a likely culprit. If that child is more similar to biological parents, then genes are likely the determining factor.

Clinical and Sociocultural Domain

Teaching with the Standards

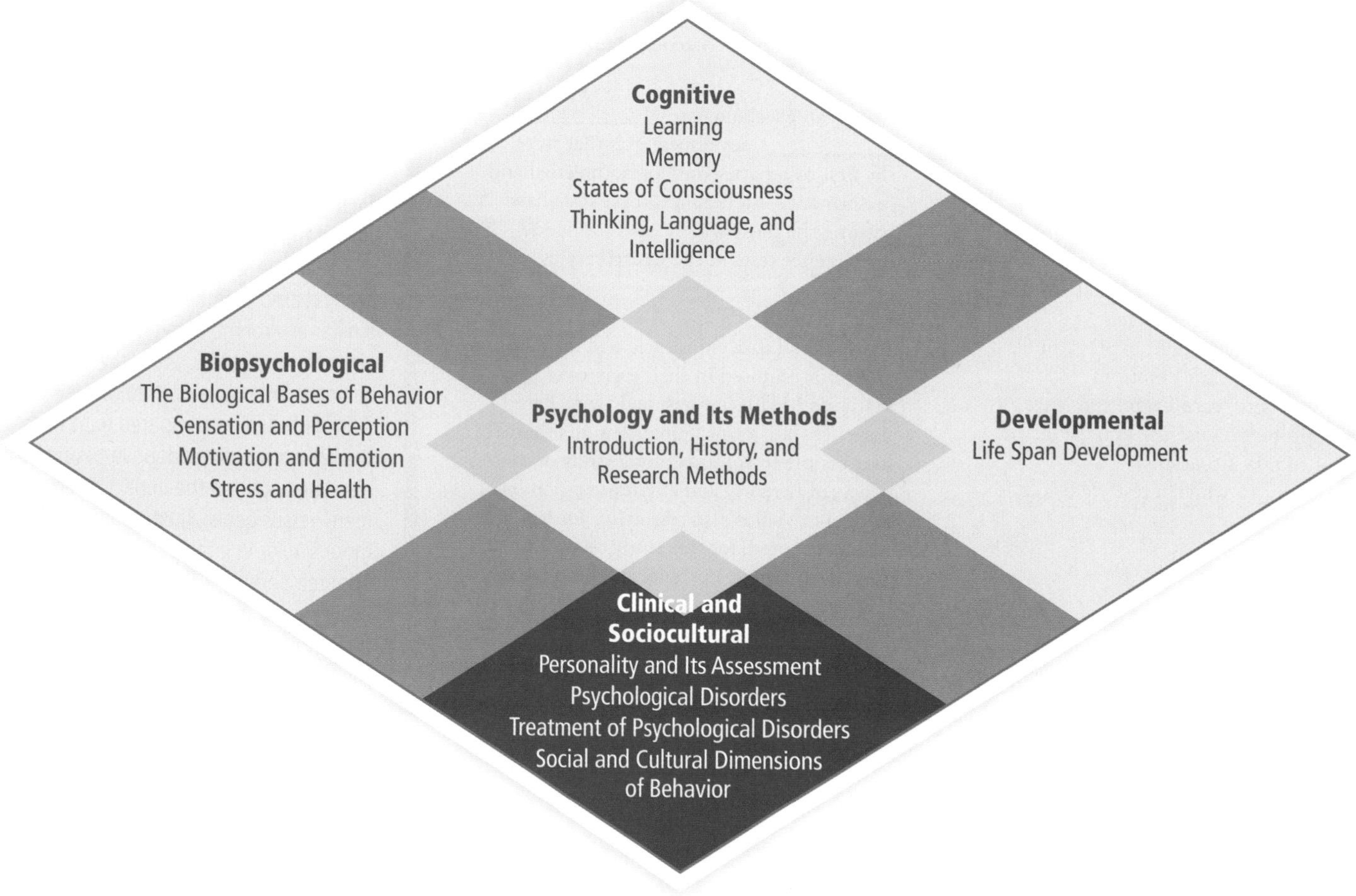

Cognitive
Learning
Memory
States of Consciousness
Thinking, Language, and Intelligence

Biopsychological
The Biological Bases of Behavior
Sensation and Perception
Motivation and Emotion
Stress and Health

Psychology and Its Methods
Introduction, History, and Research Methods

Developmental
Life Span Development

Clinical and Sociocultural
Personality and Its Assessment
Psychological Disorders
Treatment of Psychological Disorders
Social and Cultural Dimensions of Behavior

Scope and Sequence

Background/Significance of the Clinical and Sociocultural Domain

Students who enroll in psychology courses are often interested in learning more about themselves and their relationships with others. The writers of the American Psychological Association's National Standards for the Teaching of High School Psychology recognized this desire. They suggest that the sociocultural domain has "intrinsic appeal" to high school students. They also believe that any of the content areas—personality and assessment, psychological disorders and treatment, and social and cultural dimensions of behavior—cover the dominant themes and concepts of this domain. They recommend that teachers provide students with a solid understanding of specific psychological concepts, as well as opportunities for students to examine their own attitudes. Such an approach will help students better understand forces that influence their behavior, as well as individual differences.

Any of the following sections could be taught to help students understand the sociocultural dimension of their psychological lives. Module 25, Psychodynamic and Humanistic Perspectives, and Module 26, Trait and Social-Cognitive Perspectives on Personality, examine theories of personality development and personality assessment. Module 27, Introduction to Psychological Disorders, Module 28, Anxiety and Mood Disorders, and Module 29, Dissociative, Schizophrenia, and Personality Disorders, explores symptoms and possible causes of abnormal behavior patterns. Module 30, Psychological Therapies, and Module 31, Biomedical Therapies, cover various methods of treatment for psychological disorders. Module 32, Social Thinking and Social Influence, Module 33, Social Relations, and Module 34, Cross-Cultural Psychology, examine how we understand the social world and our interaction with others.

Clinical and Sociocultural Domain

Introducing the Domain

The Points: Domain Objectives

- Explain the psychodynamic perspective's view of psychology.
- Determine how psychodynamic psychologists attempt to assess personality.
- Delineate some major goals of the humanistic perspective, explaining how this perspective views personality development.
- Determine how humanistic psychologists attempt to assess personality.
- Analyze how the study of traits helps us understand personality.
- Describe how psychologists assess a person's enduring personality traits, and evaluate whether those assessment techniques are reliable and valid.
- Describe the factors that social-cognitive psychologists believe interact to form personality.
- Determine how psychologists assess the effect of particular situations on behavior.
- Identify the criteria psychologists use to diagnose psychological disorders.
- Differentiate among the different perspectives psychologists take to understand psychological disorders, and analyze why some object to the medical model.
- Describe how mental disorders develop according to Sigmund Freud.
- Identify the techniques used by psychoanalysis to reveal and resolve conflicts.
- Compare and contrast psychodynamic and interpersonal therapies with psychoanalysis.
- Differentiate between psychoanalytic and humanistic therapy.
- Analyze how cognitive therapies help patients with depression.

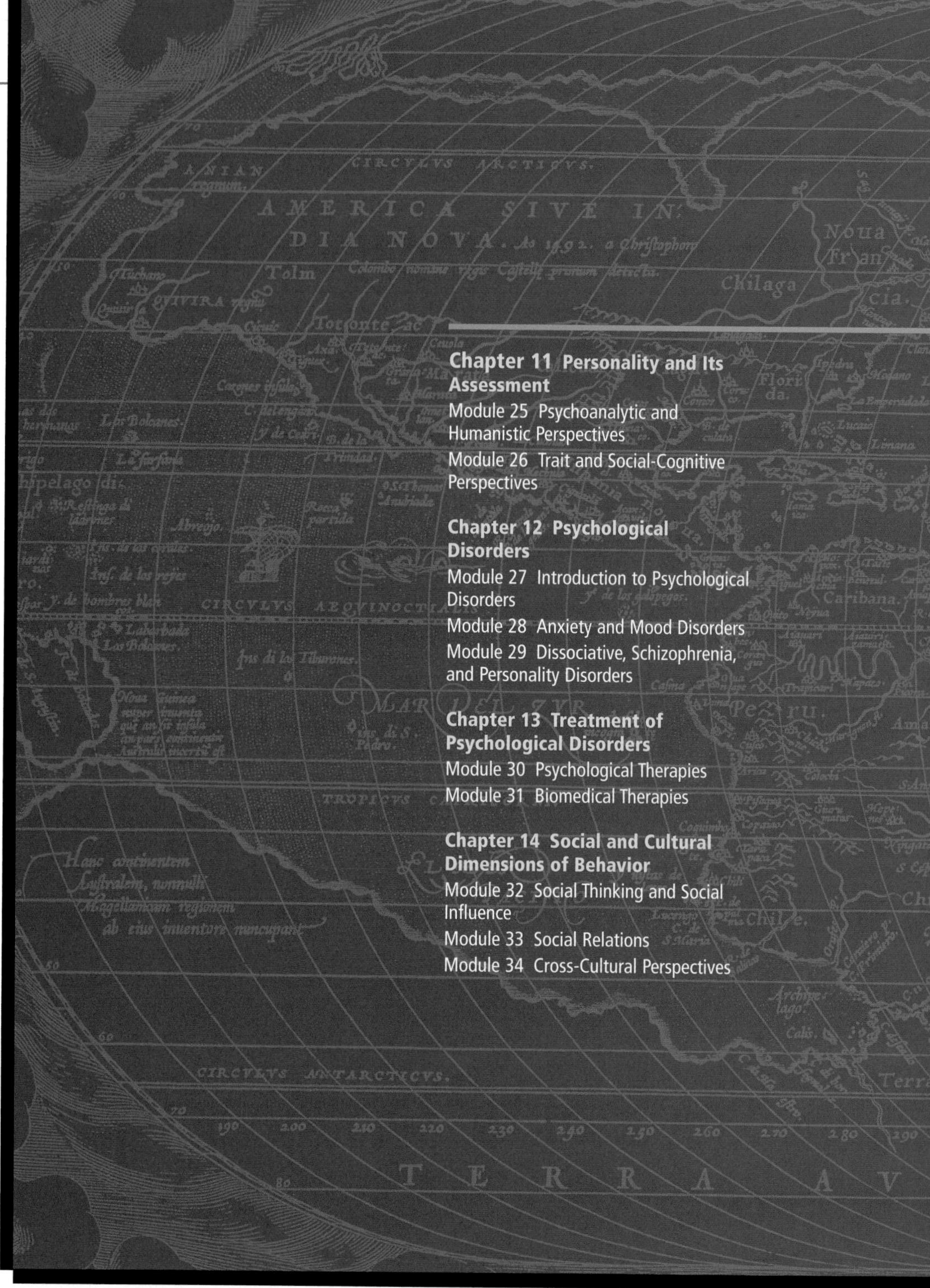

Enriching

Have students consider the question "What is culture?" Many will define it within national, ethnic, or racial parameters. Guide them to consider culture as more specific and defined than those broad categories.

- How does the culture of your region of the country differ from those of other regions?
- Does your family background give you a different cultural perspective from those around you? If so, how?

Clinical and Sociocultural Domain

This domain, consisting of 10 modules, covers the topics that many people think of when they hear the word *psychology*. We'll look first at personality. How do psychologists define and study this basic part of us—the very foundation of what makes each of us a unique person? We'll think about some of the perspectives from which psychologists have theorized about and studied personality, and we'll follow those perspectives into the study of psychological disorders and therapy. In the disorders and therapy modules, you may be tempted to play therapist and analyze yourself or others. Be warned in advance, though, that most psychological disorders are just extreme versions of feelings and behaviors we all display in our "normal" lives. Reading these modules will help you gain some perspective on how psychologists decide that a behavior indicates a disorder. Now let's begin this last—but very interesting—section of your tour of the world of psychology.

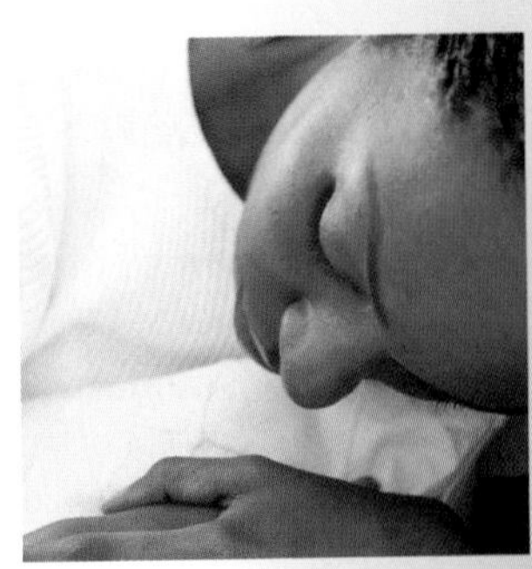

- Identify the advantages of therapy conducted in groups.
- Evaluate the research into psychotherapy's effectiveness.
- Identify alternative therapies, evaluating their effectiveness.
- Explain how antipsychotic drugs work, pointing out some of their negative effects.
- Analyze how attitudes and actions interact.
- Determine how the presence of others influences actions.
- Examine why people are attracted to some people and not to others.
- Describe the conditions under which people are more likely to help others.
- Differentiate among the terms prejudice, stereotype, and discrimination.
- Determine how genetics, the nervous system, and biochemistry contribute to aggression.
- Explain how aggression is learned.
- Describe what helps foster cooperation among groups.
- Define culture, describing how it develops.

CHAPTER 11

Personality and Its Assessment

Clinical and Sociocultural Domain

Teaching with the Standards

Standard Area: Personality and Assessment

Breakdown of Module 25: Psychodynamic and Humanistic Perspectives

Content Standard 1: Define personality Module 25 introduces the concept of personality through examples and is defined as the "characteristic pattern of thinking, feeling, and acting." (Student Text p. 479)

Content Standard 2: Theories of personality Module 25 introduces students to the psychodynamic and humanistic theories of personality. Emphasis is on Sigmund Freud's view of the mind, the interactions of the id, ego, and superego, defense mechanisms, and the psychosexual stages of personality development. The views of the "neo-Freudians," Alfred Adler, Carl Jung, and Karen Horney, are also discussed. Module 25 also emphasizes the humanistic theories of Abraham Maslow and Carl Rogers. Both theories are evaluated for their contributions to personality psychology. (Student Text pp. 479–493)

Content Standard 3: Personality assessment Assessment techniques used by psychodynamic and humanistic psychologists are compared and discussed. Focus is on defining projective assessments, like the TAT and Rorschach inkblot tests. (Student Text pp. 487–488, 492)

Breakdown of Module 26: Trait and Social-Cognitive Perspectives

Content Standard 1: Define personality Module 26 introduces the concept of personality through examples and is defined as "characteristic pattern of thinking, feeling, and acting." (Student Text p. 499)

Content Standard 2: Theories of personality Module 26 introduces students to the trait and social-cognitive theories of personality. Emphasis is on how trait theorists identify traits. The theories of Gordon Allport, Raymond Cattell, Hans Eysenck, and the "Big Five" are discussed. Module 26 also emphasizes the social-cognitive perspective. Focus is on the research of Albert Bandura. Students learn the impact our own feelings of personal control and learned helplessness have on our personalities. The positive psychology movement is also introduced. Both theories are evaluated for their contributions to personality psychology. (Student Text pp. 499–512)

Content Standard 3: Personality assessment Assessment techniques used by trait and social-cognitive psychologists are compared and discussed. Focus is on defining objective assessments, like the Minnesota Multiphasic Personality Inventory (MMPI-2). (Student Text pp. 503–505, 511)

Scope and Sequence

	Objectives	Text Reference	Standards Covered
Lesson 1	Define personality. Present psychodynamic theory. Investigate the role of the id, ego, and superego in personality development. Introduce Freud's psychosexual stages of development.	Module 25, pp. 479–486	Standard Area: Personality and Assessment, Content Standard 1, Performance Standard 1.1, Content Standard 2, Performance Standards 2.1, 2.2
Lesson 2	Finish Freud's psychosexual stages of development. Discuss the role of the defense mechanisms. Compare the neo-Freudians to Freud. Discuss the theories of Jung, Adler, and Horney. Evaluate theory.	Module 25, pp. 483–489	Content Standard 2, Performance Standards 2.1, 2.2
Lesson 3	Compare psychodynamic and humanistic theories. Discuss the theories of Carl Rogers and Abraham Maslow. Evaluate humanistic theory.	Module 25, pp. 489–493	Content Standard 2, Performance Standards 2.1, 2.2
Lesson 4	Introduce the trait perspective. Discuss the theories of Allport, Cattell, Eysenck, and the "Big Five." Evaluate trait theory.	Module 26, pp. 499–505	Content Standard 2, Performance Standards 2.1, 2.2
Lesson 5	Present the views of the social-cognitive psychologists on personality. Explore the research of Bandura, Rotter, and Seligman. Evaluate social-cognitive theory.	Module 26, pp. 505–512	Content Standard 2, Performance Standards 2.1, 2.2
Lesson 6	Explore new directions in psychology. Discuss the positive psychology movement. Introduce research on optimism by Seligman and other positive psychology concepts.	Module 26, pp. 510–511	Content Standard 2, Performance Standards 2.1, 2.2
Lesson 7	Discuss the assessments used by each of the perspectives. Explore the strengths and weaknesses of each technique.	Modules 25 and 26, pp. 487–488, 492, 503–506, 511	Content Standard 2, Performance Standards 2.1, 2.2, Content Standard 3, Performance Standards 3.1, 3.2
Lesson 8	Review and test		

CHAPTER 11

Personality and Its Assessment

Introducing the Chapter

The Points: Chapter Objectives

- Explain the psychodynamic perspective's view of psychology.
- Differentiate among Freud's views of the conscious, preconscious, and the unconscious regions of the mind.
- Describe how the id, ego, and superego interact according to the psychoanalytic theory.
- Identify Freud's stages of personality development.
- Identify the neo-Freudians, differentiating their views from Freud's view.
- Determine how psychodynamic psychologists attempt to assess personality.
- Explain how the humanistic perspective views personality development.
- Uncover the basic ideas behind Maslow's hierarchy of needs.
- Analyze how Carl Rogers believed human growth could best be fostered.
- Determine how humanistic psychologists attempt to assess personality.
- Evaluate the drawbacks of the humanistic perspective.
- Analyze how the study of traits helps us understand personality.
- Identify the "Big Five" traits.
- Describe how psychologists assess a person's enduring personality traits, evaluating whether those assessment techniques are reliable and valid.
- Evaluate the drawbacks of the trait perspective.
- Describe the factors that social-cognitive psychologists believe interact to form personality.
- Determine how psychologists assess the effect of certain situations on behavior.
- Evaluate the drawbacks of the social-cognitive perspective.

CHAPTER 11

Personality and Its Assessment

In the classic teen movie *Ferris Bueller's Day Off,* Matthew Broderick plays a high school senior (Ferris) who appears to take on several different "personalities." He is quiet, modest, and reserved to his parents as he fakes an illness. He is assertive with his friends as he talks them into skipping school and cunning as he lies to a head waiter to get seated for lunch. He is outgoing as he jeers the other team's batters at a Cubs game. He is outlandish as he lip-syncs "Twist and Shout" during a downtown Chicago parade. Will the real Ferris please stand up?

Your personality includes your patterns of acting, thinking, and feeling. Characterizing Ferris' personality is a challenge, because it appears to change from situation to situation.

Psychologists study personality from many directions. Developmental psychologists study personality across the life span. Biological psychologists look for nature's influence on personality. Health psychologists research the impact of personality on well-being.

The next two modules explore personality from four different directions. In Module 25, we'll look at Freud's psychoanalytic theory and its emphasis on unconscious motives, and we'll see how that approach contrasts with the humanist perspective and its focus on self-fulfillment. In Module 26, we'll see how trait theorists search for the factors that make up personality. The final perspective we consider in that module is the social-cognitive approach, in which researchers investigate the influence of environmental factors and thought processes on personality.

Performance Standards

Standard Area: Personality and Assessment

Content Standard 1: Define personality

Performance Standard 1.1 Define personality.

- Personality is defined as "an individual's characteristic pattern of thinking, feeling, and acting." (Student Text p. 479)

Content Standard 2: Theories of personality

Performance Standard 2.1 Identify the psychodynamic, cognitive-behavioral, humanistic, and trait perspectives.

- Discuss Sigmund Freud's view of the mind. Review the concepts of a conscious, preconscious, and unconscious mind. (Student Text pp. 480–482)
- Figure 25.1, "The Mind According to Freud," is an illustration of Freud's theory. (Student Text p. 481)
- Present the Freudian concepts of free association and a slip of the tongue. (Student Text pp. 481–482)
- Explore how the id, ego, and superego interact according to psychoanalytic theory. (Student Text pp. 482–483)
- Explain how defense mechanisms are helpful. (Student Text pp. 483–484)
- Discuss Freud's psychosexual stages of development. (Student Text pp. 484–486)
- Table 25.1, "Freud's Psychosexual Stages," summarizes Freud's theory of personality development. (Student Text p. 485)
- Discuss how the views of the "neo-Freudians" differed from those of Freud. (Student Text pp. 486–487)
- Present the theories of Alfred Adler. (Student Text p. 486)
- Discuss the theories of Carl Jung. (Student Text p. 486)
- Explore the ideas of Karen Horney. (Student Text p. 487)
- Evaluate the psychodynamic perspective from a modern viewpoint. (Student Text pp. 488–489)
- Describe the goals of the humanistic perspective. (Student Text pp. 489–490)
- Investigate Abraham Maslow's theory of a hierarchy of needs. (Student Text pp. 490–491)
- Figure 25.2, "Maslow's Hierarchy of Needs," summarizes this theory. (Student Text p. 490)
- Describe Carl Rogers' belief that human growth could best be fostered by unconditional positive regard. (Student Text p. 491)
- Discuss the greatest contributions and weaknesses of the humanistic perspective on personality. (Student Text pp. 492–493)

Content Standard 3: Personality assessment

Performance Standard 3.1 Compare objective and projective assessment techniques.

- Explain how projective tests are designed to provide insight into the test-taker's unconscious motives. (Student Text pp. 487–488)

Performance Standard 3.2 Describe specific assessment tools.

- Explain the features of the Thematic Apperception Test (TAT). (Student Text pp. 487–488)
- Describe the features of the Rorschach inkblot test. (Student Text p. 488)
- Investigate how humanists attempted to assess personality through self-reports and interviews. (Student Text p. 492)

Materials NETWORK

All of the items from the Activity and Enrichment Centers listed below come from the *Teacher's Resource Binder*. These items will help you teach and expand on concepts presented in Module 25.

trb This logo indicates when an item from the Materials Network may be used in conjunction with a specific note found in this module's *Teacher's Edition*.

The Psychodynamic Perspective

Activity Center

- Critical Thinking Activity: *Fact or Falsehood?* With this activity, students' preconceptions about the psychodynamic and humanistic perspectives are either exposed as incorrect or reinforced as correct. (*Teacher's Resource Binder*, p. 25-1; **Handout 25–1**)
- Building Vocabulary: Graphic Organizer: *Concept Charts* Students learn about people and concepts related to the two prominent theories discussed in this module. (*Teacher's Resource Binder*, p. 25-1; **Handouts 25–2a** and **25–2b**)
- Cooperative Learning Activity: *Introducing Personality* Students can explore the question "Who am I?" and others related to personality theory. (*Teacher's Resource Binder*, p. 25-1)
- Analysis Activity: *Your Theory of Personality* This activity will help students see what their personal theory is. (*Teacher's Resource Binder*, p. 25-1; **Handout 25–3**)
- Critical Thinking Activity: *Fifteen Freudian Principle Statements* This activity demonstrates Sigmund Freud's tremendous impact on popular culture. (*Teacher's Resource Binder*, p. 25-1; **Handout 25–4**)
- Application Activity: *Defense Mechanisms* This activity will help students apply Freud's theory to everyday circumstances, making the theory more concrete. (*Teacher's Resource Binder*, p. 25-1; **Handout 25–5**)
- Cooperative Learning Activity: *Defense Mechanisms Miniskits* With this role-playing activity, students act out different defense mechanisms. (*Teacher's Resource Binder*, p. 25-1; **Handouts 25–6a** and **25–6b**)

Enrichment Center

- Enrichment Lesson: *Issues in Personality Theory* In the course of their work, personality theorists address fundamental issues of human nature and individual differences. (*Teacher's Resource Binder*, p. 25-1)
- Enrichment Lesson: *Freudian Slips* Freud believed that slips of the tongue were the result of a person's unconscious drives and motives coming to the surface. (*Teacher's Resource Binder*, p. 25-1)
- Enrichment Lesson: *The Case of Little Hans* How did Freud come up with such controversial concepts as the *Oedipus complex* and *castration anxiety*? Follow Freud's analysis of Little Hans, his famous case study that lead to these ideas. (*Teacher's Resource Binder*, p. 25-1)

The Humanistic Perspective

Activity Center

- Analysis Activity: *Rosenberg Self-Esteem Scale* Students can see how high their self-esteem is with this activity. (*Teacher's Resource Binder*, p. 25-1; **Handout 25–7**)
- Analysis Activity: *Self-Concept Clarity* Self-esteem is related to one's self-concept clarity, which the scale in this activity measures. (*Teacher's Resource Binder*, p. 25-1; **Handout 25–8**)
- Demonstration Activity: *Three Quick Examinations of Biased Self-Ratings* Students can quickly complete any or all of these assessments to discover the extent of bias in their self-concepts. (*Teacher's Resource Binder*, p. 25-1; **Handouts 25–9** through **25–11**)
- Analysis Activity: *Self-Handicapping* Self-handicapping—protecting one's self-image by creating a ready excuse for failure—can hinder one from becoming self-actualized. (*Teacher's Resource Binder*, p. 25-1; **Handout 25–12**)
- Analysis Activity: *Taking Credit for Success, Denying Responsibility for Failure* Studies indicate that people readily accept credit for success but attribute failure to such external factors as bad luck or a problem's inherent "impossibility." Handing back a psychology test provides a good opportunity to demonstrate this self-serving bias. (*Teacher's Resource Binder*, p. 25-1; **Handout 25–13**)

Enrichment Center

- Enrichment Lesson: *Obstacles to Self-Actualization* Maslow estimated that only 1 percent of adults are self-actualized, the reasons for which are outlined in this lesson. (*Teacher's Resource Binder*, p. 25-1)
- Enrichment Lesson: *The Dark Side of Self-Esteem* The drive toward achieving self-esteem may be more harmful than good, as much research on this topic suggests. (*Teacher's Resource Binder*, p. 25-1)
- Enrichment Lesson: *The Sociometer Theory of Self-Esteem* The construct of self-esteem has long occupied a central place in psychology. Learn how some psychologists believe self-esteem is a measure of how people's lives are going. (*Teacher's Resource Binder*, p. 25-1)

MODULE 25

Psychodynamic and Humanistic Perspectives

The Psychodynamic Perspective

The Humanistic Perspective

"Life moves pretty fast. If you don't stop and look around for a while, you just might miss it."

— Ferris Bueller

What is "personality"? I hear students use this word all the time. Meredith likes how J. J. looks but laments, "If only he had a personality." And for those who don't suffer J. J.'s problem, personalities have been labeled everything from "rotten" to "winning." These everyday notions of personality are fine for discussing friends between classes or at lunch, but psychologists use the term more carefully.

Psychologists define **personality** as an individual's characteristic pattern of thinking, feeling, and acting. In this module, we'll consider the psychodynamic and humanistic perspectives, two very different viewpoints on how personality develops and how it can be assessed.

▶ **personality** An individual's characteristic pattern of thinking, feeling, and acting.

▶ **Sigmund Freud** (1856–1939) Founder of psychoanalysis.

The Psychodynamic Perspective

What's the Point? 1. What is the psychodynamic perspective, and how does it view personality?

After going out for three months and then breaking up, Tyler says, "I know I'm in *denial*, but I think we'll get back together." Mei refuses to talk about a past relationship, saying she doesn't remember much about it. "I've *repressed* that whole thing." In a class full of ill-mannered students, the teacher might say, "You've all *regressed* to eighth grade." These three commonly used terms—*denial*, *repression*, and *regression*—can all be traced back to **Sigmund Freud** (1856–1939), an Austrian physician who proposed psychology's first and most famous theory of personality. Freud believed

Sigmund Freud Freud's theory of psychoanalysis was the first comprehensive theory of personality.

MODULE 25

Psychodynamic and Humanistic Perspectives

Introducing the Module

The Points: Module Objectives

- Explain the psychodynamic perspective and how it views personality.
- Differentiate among Freud's views of the conscious, preconscious, and unconscious regions of the mind.
- Describe how the id, ego, and superego interact, according to psychoanalytic theory.
- Analyze how defense mechanisms are helpful, according to Freud.
- Identify Freud's stages of personality development.
- Identify the neo-Freudians and explain how their views differ from Freud's.
- Explain how psychologists working from a psychodynamic perspective attempt to assess personality.
- Evaluate how Freud's ideas hold up in light of modern research.
- Identify some major goals of the humanistic perspective, and explain how this perspective views personality development.
- Discuss the basic ideas underlying Maslow's hierarchy of needs.
- Identify the three qualities that foster human growth according to Rogers.
- Determine how humanistic psychologists attempt to assess personality.
- Evaluate the greatest contributions and greatest weaknesses of the humanistic perspective on personality.

trb Building Vocabulary

Improve students' knowledge of the concepts in the module by having them complete **Building Vocabulary: Graphic Organizer:** *Concept Charts* (*Teacher's Resource Binder*, p. 25-1; **Handouts 25–2a** and **25–2b**).

Getting Started

Just as Ferris Bueller exhibited several different "personalities" in the movie *Ferris Bueller's Day Off*, so do we exhibit various personalities in different situations and with different people. Have students list the different types of personality they exhibit in a particular day. Ask them the following questions about their lists:

- Why do you exhibit these different types of personality?
- Do all the different personality types fit together to form "the real you"? Why or why not?

trb You may wish to use the **Critical Thinking:** *Fact or Falsehood?* (*Teacher's Resource Binder*, p. 25-1; **Handout 25–1**) as a prereading strategy to find out what students already know about psychodynamic and humanistic psychology. The activity will prime students to note terms and concepts in the text that confirm or dispel their preconceptions about psychodynamic and humanistic psychology.

MODULE 25

Teaching the Points

web ■ TEACHING TIPS

(1) You can log on as an instructor to the book companion site for *Thinking About Psychology* at **www.worthpublishers.com/thinkingaboutpsych**. It contains teacher resources for class presentations as well as review and assessment of module concepts and terms.

(2) William Revelle of Northwestern University directs the Personality Project at **http://fas.psych.nwu.edu/personality.html**. It is a huge site that is designed to "guide those interested in personality theory and research to the current personality research literature."

(3) Students interested in learning more about the personality theorists discussed in Modules 25 and 26 might visit **www.wynja.com/personality/theorists.html**.

■ APPLYING THE POINTS

Write the following terms on the board or create a transparency that you can project. Ask students to describe the meanings of the terms—all of which are part of our common vocabulary, thanks to Freud!

- Fixated *(to be stuck on a particular object or way of behaving)*
- Repressed *(to have suppressed thoughts, feelings, or memories that are too painful to bear)*
- Regressed *(to act in a more immature way)*
- Anal-retentive *(to be obsessively neat and organized)*
- Oedipus complex *(a condition where a boy loves his mother and hates his father)*
- Rationalize *(to explain away a problem or to justify one's own behavior)*

trb At this point, you may wish to use Critical Thinking Activity: *Fifteen Freudian Principle Statements* (*Teacher's Resource Binder*, p. 25-1; Handout 25–4).

▶ **psychoanalysis** Freud's theory of personality; also, a therapeutic technique that attempts to provide insight into one's thoughts and actions by exposing and interpreting the underlying unconscious motives and conflicts.

▶ **psychodynamic perspective** A view of personality that retains some aspects of Freudian theory (such as the importance of unconscious thought processes) but is less likely to see unresolved childhood conflicts as a source of personality development.

▶ **free association** In psychoanalysis, a method of exploring the unconscious in which the person relaxes and says whatever comes to mind, no matter how trivial or embarrassing.

▶ **preconscious** According to Freud, a region of the mind holding information that is not conscious but is retrievable into conscious awareness.

▶ **unconscious** According to Freud, a region of the mind that is a reservoir of mostly unacceptable thoughts, wishes, feelings, and memories.

that an individual's personality—the person's characteristic thoughts and behaviors—emerges from tensions generated by unconscious motives and unresolved childhood conflicts (many of them sexual). To uncover these conflicts and help patients resolve them, Freud used an approach he called **psychoanalysis.** Between 1888 and 1939, Freud published 24 volumes of material on his psychoanalytic theory.

Over the past three-quarters of a century, a more moderate **psychodynamic perspective** on personality has emerged, incorporating some aspects of Freud's views on personality—such as the beliefs that many of our thought processes occur unconsciously and that childhood experiences affect our adult personality—but rejecting others. Theorists viewing personality from a psychodynamic viewpoint are, for example, less likely than Freud to dwell on unresolved childhood conflicts and more likely to consider the person's immediate problems.

Yet, thanks to Freud's continuing popularity in "pop" psychology, you are more likely to be familiar with Freud's outdated terminology than with almost any other set of terms we introduce in this book! In this module, I'll outline Freud's original ideas so you know how the buzz got started.

Freud's View of the Mind

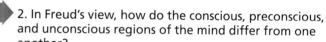

2. In Freud's view, how do the conscious, preconscious, and unconscious regions of the mind differ from one another?

Freud's theory of psychoanalysis grew from his early observations that some patients who consulted him had problems that seemed to have no clear physical cause. A neurologist in France who was treating patients

Freud's Office Freud wanted his patients to relax in a reclining position, facing away from him, while he conducted his version of psychotherapy.

Suggested Readings

Use the following books as teacher-preparation tools or as enrichment for advanced students:

Burger, J. (2000). *Personality* (5th ed.). Belmont, CA: Wadsworth.

Dolnick, E. (1998). *Madness on the couch: Blaming the victim in the heyday of psychoanalysis.* New York: Simon & Schuster.

Gay, P. (Ed.). (1989). *The Freud reader.* New York: Norton.

Gay, P. (1997). *Freud: A life for our time.* New York: Norton.

Hall, C. S. (1982). *A primer of Freudian psychology.* New York: Mentor. (Original work published 1954)

Hall, C. S., & Nordby, V. J. (1973). *A primer of Jungian psychology.* New York: Mentor.

Hergenhahn, B. R., & Olson, M. H. (1999). *An introduction to theories of personality* (5th ed.). Upper Saddle River, NJ: Prentice Hall.

using hypnosis intrigued Freud. (Hypnosis is a social interaction in which one person—the hypnotist—makes forceful suggestions to another person that certain events or responses will occur.) Freud was amazed to find that some patients' physical symptoms disappeared after the hypnotic experience.

Freud experimented with hypnosis but he found that some patients could not be hypnotized. As an alternative to hypnosis, Freud asked his patients to relax and say whatever came to mind, regardless of how trivial or embarrassing the statement seemed. Freud viewed this technique, which he called **free association,** as a window into the *unconscious* mind.

Not Much Help! Cartoonists have joked about Freud's methods for decades.

Freud compared the human mind to a big iceberg consisting of three regions: the conscious, preconscious, and unconscious (Figure 25.1). Just as most of an iceberg is below sea level and unseen, Freud felt that most of the mind is hidden from view. The *conscious* mind, the thoughts and feelings we're aware of, is comparable to the visible part of the iceberg above sea level. Just below the water line is the **preconscious,** consisting of the thoughts and memories not in our current awareness but easily retrieved. And finally, at the deepest level is the **unconscious,** a vast region of

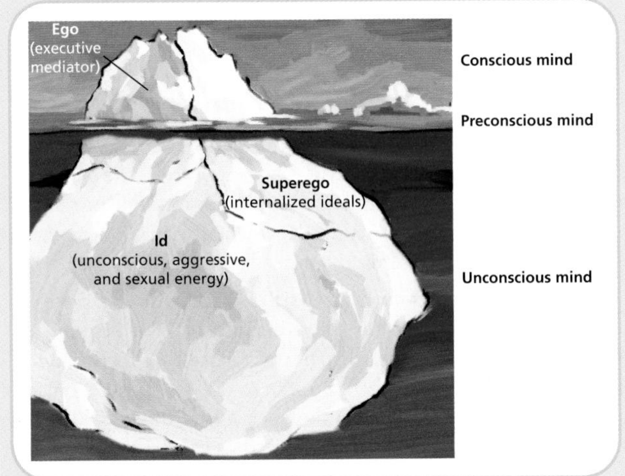

Figure 25.1 **The Mind According to Freud** Freud thought only a small part of the mind or personality, the thoughts and feelings we attend to, was "visible." Freud represented the part of the mind we're aware of using a "tip of the iceberg" comparison.

Loftus, E., & Ketcham, K. (1994). *The myth of repressed memory: False memories and allegations of sexual abuse.* New York: St. Martin's Press.

Nye, R. D. (1992). *Three psychologies: Perspectives from Freud, Skinner, and Rogers* (4th ed.). Pacific Grove, CA: Brooks/Cole.

■ APPLYING THE POINTS

Read a series of random words to your students. These words can be a series of everyday items or just random words taken from a dictionary. Have students free associate with each word, writing down the first word that comes to mind. Discuss this experience by asking the following questions:

- Do any of these words seem to reveal any hidden feelings you might have about something or someone in your life? Why or why not?
- Would you want people to read into this list of freely associated words? Why or why not?

■ TEACHING TIPS

tr (1) A four-color transparency of Figure 25.1, The Mind According to Freud, is available in the **Overhead Transparencies Set.**

(2) Link this discussion of *hypnosis* with Module 21's treatment of the workings of this controversial psychotherapeutic technique. Module 21 discusses why some people are more likely to be hypnotized than others, which involves one's susceptibility to suggestion by authority figures.

trb At this point, you may wish to use **Enrichment Lesson:** *Issues in Personality Theory* (*Teacher's Resource Binder*, p. 25-1).

■ JOURNAL WRITING

Invite students to use the following questions and writing prompts as springboards for entries in their psychology journals:

- Do you feel most of your personality is hidden beneath the surface? Why or why not?
- Do you believe your behavior is guided by experiences buried in your unconscious? Why or why not?

trb At this point, you may wish to use **Analysis Activity:** *Your Theory of Personality* (*Teacher's Resource Binder*, p. 25-1; **Handout 25–3**).

MODULE 25

F•Y•I

Freud thought that people were born with an active id, but they developed the ego and superego through experiences in childhood. Because infants are such needy creatures, Freud saw their behavior as evidence of the innate id, calling infants a "seething cauldron" of desires.

trb At this point, you may wish to use **Enrichment Lesson:** *Issues in Personality Theory* (*Teacher's Resource Binder*, p. 25-1).

■ LOOKING AT THE ISSUES

Have students take note of Figure 25.1 in which almost 90 percent of the iceberg rests beneath the surface of the water. Freud believed that people were like icebergs—only allowing a small bit of their personalities to be seen and keeping the rest hidden from others. Encourage students to meet in small groups to discuss this metaphor of the iceberg and personality. To begin a discussion, you might pose the following questions to the class:

- Do you feel others around you know "the real you"? Why or why not?
- What types of things do people keep hidden from casual friends and acquaintances? Why?
- What types of things do people most often share? Why?

trb At this point, you may wish to use **Analysis Activity:** *Your Theory of Personality* (*Teacher's Resource Binder*, p. 25-1; **Handout 25–3**) and **Cooperative Learning Activity:** *Introducing Personality* (*Teacher's Resource Binder*, p. 25-1).

Hidden? How much of your personality is visible for all to see?

mostly unacceptable thoughts, wishes, feelings, and memories. If he could help patients open the door to this unconscious region, Freud believed, they could recover painful childhood memories and healing could occur.

Thus, treating someone with a psychological disorder meant delving into the unconscious, revealing the nature of that person's inner conflicts and releasing tensions. Through free association and dream analysis, Freud tried to catch glimpses of the unconscious. He also searched for evidence in people's habits and slips of the tongue. These "Freudian slips," as they are often called today, are supposed to reflect something you'd *like* to say. Freud illustrated this concept with an example of a money-strapped patient who did not want any large pills: "Please do not give me any bills, because I cannot swallow them."

Freud's view of personality also had three parts. All three fit into the iceberg.

The Id, Ego, and Superego

3. How do the id, ego, and superego interact, according to psychoanalytic theory?

► **id** According to Freud, the part of personality that consists of unconscious, psychic energy and strives to satisfy basic sexual and aggressive drives. The id operates on the *pleasure principle*, demanding immediate gratification.

► **superego** The part of personality that, according to Freud, represents internalized ideals and provides standards for judgment (the conscience) and for future aspirations.

► **ego** The largely conscious, "executive" part of personality that, according to Freud, mediates among the demands of the id, superego, and reality. The ego operates on the *reality principle*, satisfying the id's desires in ways that will realistically bring pleasure rather than pain.

Freud believed that personality grows out of a basic human conflict. Each of us is born with aggressive, pleasure-seeking biological impulses. But we live in a society, and—as we grow up—we internalize social roadblocks that restrain these impulses. The way each of us resolves the conflict between social restraints and pleasure-seeking impulses shapes our individual personality. Three forces interact during this conflict.

- The **id**, present at birth, consists of unconscious energy from basic aggressive and sexual drives. Operating from the *pleasure principle*, the id demands immediate gratification. For instance, a newborn cries for whatever it needs, whenever it needs it, regardless of what anybody else wants or needs.
- The **superego** consists of the internalized ideals and standards for judgment that develop as the child interacts with parents, peers, and society. It is the voice of conscience that focuses on what we *should* do, not what we'd like to do. The superego wants perfection, and those with a weak superego are likely to give into their urges and impulses without regard to rules. On the other hand, an overly strong superego often produces someone who is virtuous yet guilt-ridden.

Enriching

Have students contemplate reasons why Freudian theory is so popular. Interested students might write reports for extra credit in which they address the following questions:

- Why would people believe that Freud's different levels of consciousness and different types of personality are true?
- Why would people in the Victorian era accept such open talk about sex? Why are people today still fascinated by it?

Invite those who write reports to make their work available for interested classmates to read. If a report sparks issues of interest among students in relation to Freud's theories, further encourage the writer and readers to extend the report by taking part in a class forum or a debate on Freud's theory.

trb At this point, you may wish to use **Enrichment Lesson:** *Issues in Personality Theory* (*Teacher's Resource Binder*, p. 25-1).

- The **ego** is the mediator that makes decisions after listening to both the demands of the id and the restraining rules of the superego. Operating from the *reality principle*, the ego satisfies the id in a realistic way that does not lead to personal strife. The ego, Freud thought, represented good sense and reason.

Freud believed that these three abstract psychological concepts could help us understand the mind. Roughly speaking, the id is the "child" in you, the superego "your parent," and the ego "the adult" that results from the mix. Freud thought that a healthy personality is one that could successfully express pleasure-seeking impulses while avoiding punishment or guilt. This task is not an easy one, though, and to achieve it, the ego must sometimes resort to defensive tactics.

Defense Mechanisms

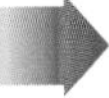

4. According to Freud, how are defense mechanisms helpful?

Anxiety, wrote Freud, is the price we pay for living in a civilized society. The conflict between the id's wishes and the superego's social rules produces this anxiety. However, the ego has an arsenal of unconscious **defense mechanisms** that help get rid of this anxious tension by distorting reality. You have probably heard of several of these. We'll consider seven:

1. *Repression* banishes anxiety-arousing thoughts, feelings, and memories from consciousness. Freud believed repression was the basis for all the other anxiety-reducing defense mechanisms. The aim of psychoanalysis was to draw repressed, unresolved childhood conflicts back into consciousness to allow resolution and healing.

▸ **defense mechanisms** In psychoanalytic theory, the ego's protective methods of reducing anxiety by unconsciously distorting reality.

MODULE 25

F • Y • I

In the 1960s and 1970s, Freudian analysis took on a new face as transactional analysis became popular. Eric Berne developed transactional analysis three years earlier, but in 1967 Thomas Harris, the author of *I'm OK, You're OK*, put a new twist on it. **Transactional analysis** focuses on internal scripts we use when we interact with people. We have certain ways of speaking to others, either from our "Child" script, our "Parent" script, or our "Adult" script. Harris believed that if our conversations with other people were analyzed, a therapist could learn which scripts were used with whom. With that discovery people would be able to use their Adult script more often. Harris took the traditional id, ego, and superego personality traits and renamed them to make them more reader-friendly. *I'm OK, You're OK* has sold more than 10 million copies since its publication, making it one of the most popular self-help books ever published.

■ LOOKING AT THE ISSUES

Repressed memories have come under fire in recent years as research in eyewitness testimony and dissociative identity disorder put the reliability of human memory into question. Have students research these two issues to see whether repressed memories uncovered in therapy can be relied on as accurate recollections of the truth. To direct research and focus subsequent discussion, ask students the following questions:

- What have studies by Elizabeth Loftus and others revealed about the reliability of eyewitness testimony?
- How much do therapists rely on repressed memories in diagnosing dissociative identity disorder?
- Why can't repressed memories be relied on as accurate recollections of the truth?

trb At this point, you may wish to use **Enrichment Lesson:** *Issues in Personality Theory* (*Teacher's Resource Binder*, p. 25-1).

Reteaching

Another way to help students remember the relationship of id, ego, and superego is to think of those old Warner Brothers cartoons where a character would have a devil on one shoulder and an angel on the other. Each would give the character advice, and the character would have to choose to listen to either the devil or the angel. The devil represents the id, which encourages more licentious, uncensored behavior. The angel represents the superego, the part that advises obedience to moral and ethical principles. The character represents the ego, which must take in both types of advice and make the most realistic decision.

You might ask volunteers to develop their own simple drawing of this cartoon situation on the chalkboard, including appropriate labeling of *id, ego,* and *superego.*

MODULE 25

■ JOURNAL WRITING

Invite students to use the following questions and writing prompts as springboards for entries in their psychology journals:

- Have you ever used any of the defense mechanisms described in this section (repression, regression, denial, reaction formation, projection, rationalization, displacement)? Describe your experience(s).
- Have you ever noticed anyone using defense mechanisms? Describe how you handled that experience.

■ TEACHING TIP

Have students come up with an original seven-word sentence in which each word starts with the first letter of a defense mechanism. Challenge them to create a sentence that in some way describes the function of defense mechanisms. This sentence can serve as a mnemonic device. In fact, you may want to have a contest to see who can come up with the best sentence—by doing this, all students may firmly commit these defense mechanisms to memory!

trb At this point, you may wish to use **Cooperative Learning Activity:** *Defense Mechanism Miniskits* (*Teacher's Resource Binder*, p. 25-1; **Handouts 25–6a** and **25–6b**).

2. *Regression* allows an anxious person to retreat to a more comfortable, infantile stage of life. The 6-year-old who wants to sit in Mom's lap while she reads to him after a new baby is born into the family may be regressing to a more comfortable time.
3. *Denial* lets an anxious person refuse to admit that something unpleasant is happening. Thoughts of invincibility, such as "I won't get hooked on cigarettes. It can't happen to me," represent denial. The drinker who consumes a six-pack a day but claims not to have a drinking problem is also using the defense mechanism of denial.
4. *Reaction formation* reverses an unacceptable impulse, causing an anxious person to express the opposite of the anxiety-provoking unconscious feeling. To keep the "I hate him" thoughts from entering consciousness, the ego generates an "I love him" feeling. If you're interested in someone who is already going out with another, and you find yourself feeling a curious dislike instead of fondness for the unobtainable, Freud would say you're experiencing reaction formation.
5. *Projection* disguises threatening feelings of guilty anxiety by attributing the problem to others. "I don't trust him" really means, "I don't trust myself." Hamlet, in the Shakespearean play of the same name, thinks his mother is guilty of murder after she denies wrongdoing. "The lady doth protest too much," he says. The thief thinks everyone else is a thief.
6. *Rationalization* displaces real, anxiety-provoking explanations and replaces them with more comforting justifications for one's actions. Rationalization makes mistakes seem reasonable and often sounds like an excuse. The smoker insists she smokes "just to look older" or "only when I go out with friends." After becoming addicted to cigarettes, she might say, "It's no big deal; I can quit whenever I want."
7. *Displacement* shifts an unacceptable impulse toward a more acceptable or less threatening object or person. The classic example is the company owner who gets upset and yells at the manager, who yells at the clerk, who goes home and yells at the kids, who end up kicking the dog. All except the dog have been displacing.

Freud's Psychosexual Stages

5. What were Freud's stages of personality development?

Freud's analyses of his patients led him to conclude that personality forms during the first five or six years of life. He believed that his patients' problems originated in conflicts that had not been resolved during childhood years. In Freud's view, the patient had become "stuck" or *fixated* in one of

Meeting Individual Needs

Students may be familiar with the defense mechanisms as they are described in the text, but the terminology may be confusing or difficult to remember. Suggest that students create narratives that use the defense mechanisms as characters. Each character/mechanism should behave according to the description given in the text. The narratives may be developed as an oral story, a written story, a poem, a dance, a dramatic skit, or a role-playing exercise. As students create their narratives, you can assess which of the defenses students need more help in grasping.

trb At this point, you may wish to use **Cooperative Learning Activity:** *Defense Mechanism Miniskits* (*Teacher's Resource Binder*, p. 25-1; **Handouts 25–6a** and **25–6b**).

TABLE 25.1 FREUD'S PSYCHOSEXUAL STAGES

STAGE	FOCUS
Oral (1–18 months)	Pleasure centers on the mouth—sucking, biting, chewing
Anal (18–36 months)	Pleasure focuses on bowel and bladder function; coping with demands for control
Phallic (3–6 years)	Pleasure zone is the genitals; coping with incestuous feelings
Latency (6 to puberty)	Dormant sexual feelings
Genital (puberty on)	Maturation of sexual interests

the **psychosexual stages** of development (Table 25.1). Each stage is marked by the id's pleasure-seeking focus on a different part of the body.

The *oral stage* lasts through the first 18 months of life. Pleasure comes from chewing, biting, and sucking. Weaning can be a conflict in this stage.

The *anal stage* lasts from age 18 months to 3 years. Gratification comes from bowel and bladder function. Potty training can be a conflict in this stage.

The *phallic stage* lasts from age 3 to 6 years. The pleasure zone shifts to the genitals. Freud believed boys felt love for their mothers and hatred, fear, or jealousy for their fathers. Viewing Dad as a rival for Mom's love, the phallic-stage boy fears punishment from his father. Freud called this collection of feelings the *Oedipus* (ED-uh-pus) *complex*, named after the Greek tragedy where Oedipus unwittingly kills his father and marries his mother (and pokes his eyes out after realizing what he has done). Freud did not believe in a parallel process for girls, though other psychoanalysts have written about an Electra complex, in which girls love Dad and fear Mom.

During the *latency* period, which lasts from 6 years to puberty, children repress their feelings for the rival parent. Instead of fearing the same-sex parent, girls and boys start to "buddy up" to Mom or Dad. The result is girls learn to do girllike things and boys learn boylike behaviors. Freud called this the *identification process*. This process offers one explanation of *gender identity*, which is our sense of what it means to be either male or female.

The *genital stage* starts at puberty, as the person begins experiencing sexual feelings toward others.

Freud thought that unresolved conflicts in any of the stages could cause problems later in life. The adult who had not worked through

▶ **psychosexual stages** The childhood stages of development (oral, anal, phallic, latency, genital) during which, according to Freud, the id's pleasure-seeking energies focus on different parts of the body.

MODULE 25

trb tr ■ **TEACHING TIP**

A black-line master for Table 25.1, Freud's Psychosexual Stages, is available in the **Black-Line Masters Appendix** of the *Teacher's Resource Binder.*

F • Y • I

(1) Freud based his theory about the Oedipus complex on the case study of a little boy named Hans. Five-year-old Hans had developed a fear of horses, which Freud believed was actually a displaced fear of his father. In addition, Hans had developed castration anxiety, a fear of having his penis cut off. His parents had told him that if he continued to play with his penis, it would be cut off. He had noticed that his sister lacked a penis, so he concluded that his parents had cut her penis off.

trb At this point, you may wish to use **Enrichment Lesson:** ***The Case of Little Hans*** (*Teacher's Resource Binder*, p. 25-1).

(2) While Freud did not develop the concept of the Electra complex, he did believe that girls developed penis envy—never forgiving their mothers for castrating them at birth. This concept, like most Freudian concepts, has woven its way into the public consciousness. In the Disney/Pixar movie *Toy Story*, when Buzz Lightyear arrives in Andy's room, all the toys but Woody are impressed with Buzz's laser light. As Woody protests that his laser is "just a light bulb," Hamm, the piggy bank, asks Mr. Potato Head, "What's with Woody?" Mr. Potato Head leans over and whispers, "Laser envy."

Enriching

web Sigmund Freud's ideas were perhaps some of the most influential and controversial of the twentieth century. Have students prepare reports on Freud and his influence on popular culture. Students can use Freud Net: The Abraham A. Brill Library at **www.psychoanalysis.org** as a rich Internet resource for information about Freud. Maintained by the New York Psychoanalytic Institute, it contains a huge collection of books and articles on the life and work of Freud, as well as links to "Sigmund Freud on the Internet."

MODULE 25

F • Y • I

(1) Freud believed that if a person experienced a problem during one of the psychosexual stages of development, then he or she would become fixated in that stage. Some of the most famous fixations occur during the oral and anal stages.

- If someone was weaned too early, then he or she would show signs of oral fixation later in life—that is, always putting objects in his or her mouth, chain smoking, or overeating.
- In the anal stage, fixation occurs in one of two ways. If potty training occurs too early, a person can become anal-retentive (overly neat and fussy about organization and details). If potty training is not encouraged or allowed to happen haphazardly, the person can become anal-expulsive (overly slovenly and messy).

trb At this point, you may wish to use Enrichment Lesson: *Freudian Slips* (*Teacher's Resource Binder*, p. 25-1).

(2) Jung developed his theories of the **collective unconscious** by studying people who experienced hallucinations as a result of a mental disorder. These hallucinations could not be explained by a past experience, which would fit in with traditional Freudian analysis. Therefore, Jung hypothesized that we must share a collective unconscious buried deep in our brains. The collective unconscious contains experiences from the past that are part of shared human evolutionary history.

trb At this point, you may wish to use Enrichment Lesson: *Issues in Personality Theory* (*Teacher's Resource Binder*, p. 25-1).

■ TEACHING TIP

Link Alfred Adler's view of the importance of social tensions to Erik Erikson's theory of psychosocial development. Erikson was a student of Freud. He supported many of Freud's primary ideas but rejected the emphasis on sexuality in childhood. His eight-stage theory outlines different social crises people must overcome to proceed to the next stage of development.

▶ **Alfred Adler** (1870–1937) Neo-Freudian who thought social tensions were more important than sexual tensions in the development of personality.

▶ **inferiority complex** According to Alfred Adler, a condition that comes from being unable to compensate for normal inferiority feelings.

▶ **Carl Jung** (1875–1961) Neo-Freudian who believed that humans share a *collective unconscious*.

▶ **collective unconscious** Carl Jung's concept of a shared, inherited reservoir of memory traces from our ancestors.

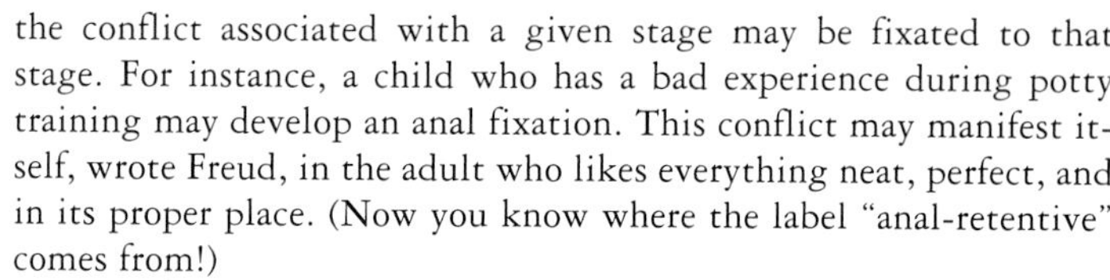

the conflict associated with a given stage may be fixated to that stage. For instance, a child who has a bad experience during potty training may develop an anal fixation. This conflict may manifest itself, wrote Freud, in the adult who likes everything neat, perfect, and in its proper place. (Now you know where the label "anal-retentive" comes from!)

The Neo-Freudians

6. Who were the "neo-Freudians," and how do their views differ from Freud's?

Sigmund Freud attracted many followers. Those who agreed with the basic ideas of psychoanalysis but disagreed with specific parts of Freud's theory were known as *neo-Freudians*. Three of these pioneering psychoanalysts were Alfred Adler, Carl Jung, and Karen Horney.

Alfred Adler

Alfred Adler

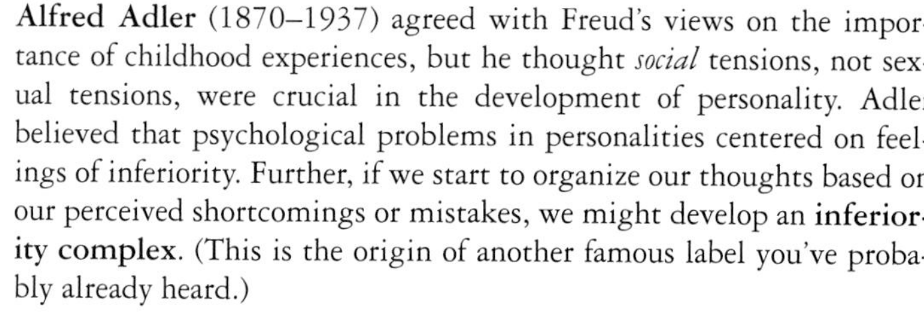

Alfred Adler (1870–1937) agreed with Freud's views on the importance of childhood experiences, but he thought *social* tensions, not sexual tensions, were crucial in the development of personality. Adler believed that psychological problems in personalities centered on feelings of inferiority. Further, if we start to organize our thoughts based on our perceived shortcomings or mistakes, we might develop an **inferiority complex**. (This is the origin of another famous label you've probably already heard.)

Carl Jung

Unlike Adler, **Carl Jung** (1875–1961) (pronounced Yoong) discounted social factors, but he broke with Freud over the importance of the role of the unconscious in personality development. Jung kicked the idea up a notch, saying we not only have an individual unconscious but—as a species—we also have a **collective unconscious**. This is a shared, inherited reservoir of memory traces from our ancestors. Jung thought the collective unconscious included information hard-wired from birth on things we all know. He saw evidence of the collective unconsciousness in the *archetypes* (AR-kuh-types), or universal symbols, found in stories, myths, and art. For instance, the *shadow* archetype is the darker, evil side of human nature. Supposedly, we hide this archetype from the world and ourselves.

Carl Jung

Contemporary psychologists reject the notion of inherited memory. However, many believe that our shared evolutionary history has contributed to some universal behavior tendencies (like hiding our worst secrets from others) or dispositions (evil).

Cross-Curricular Connections

LITERATURE Archetypes can be found in many classic and modern works of literature. Have students bring in their favorite piece of literature and identify archetypes found in those works. Some common archetypes include the following:

- the hero (savior or deliverer)
- the quest (undertaking of a long journey in which battles, trials, and challenges take place to accomplish some lofty purpose)
- the scapegoat (when the hero must die or sacrifice something to save others)
- the great or good mother (representing warmth, fertility, abundance)
- the terrible mother or witch (representing danger, fear, or death)
- the soul mate or princess (representing inspiration or fulfillment)

Karen Horney

Karen Horney

Trained as a psychoanalyst, **Karen Horney** (1885–1952) (HORN-eye) broke from Freud in several ways. She deftly pointed out that Freud's theory was male dominated, and that his explanation of female development was inadequate. She also stated that social variables, not biological variables, are the foundation of personality development. She felt that social expectations, not anatomy, created the psychological differences between males and females. *Basic anxiety*, wrote Horney, is the helplessness and isolation people feel in a potentially hostile world, brought on by the competitiveness of today's society (Horney, 1950). Horney and the other neo-Freudians started the movement toward revising Freud's psychoanalysis into the psychodynamic perspective that is primarily used today.

▶ **Karen Horney** (1885–1952) Neo-Freudian who found psychoanalysis negatively biased toward women and believed cultural variables are the foundation of personality development.

▶ **projective tests** A personality test, such as the Rorschach or TAT, that provides ambiguous stimuli to trigger projection of one's inner thoughts and feelings.

▶ **Thematic Apperception Test (TAT)** A projective test in which people express their inner feelings and interests through the stories they make up about ambiguous scenes.

Assessing Personality from a Psychodynamic Perspective

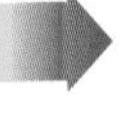

7. How do psychologists working from the psychodynamic perspective attempt to assess personality?

Before providing therapy for a personality disorder, psychologists need to assess personality characteristics. Techniques for assessing personality differ from one perspective to another because the tests are tailored to a particular theory of personality. Psychoanalytic and psychodynamic therapists want assessments that reach into and reveal elements of the unconscious. True-false tests are of no interest, as they would only tap into surface elements of the conscious. Instead, Freud turned to assessment techniques such as dream analysis, which he called the "royal road to the unconscious." Later psychodynamic theorists became interested in **projective tests** designed to provide insight into the test-taker's unconscious motives. Therapists use several different kinds of projective tests. Two are particularly well known:

- **Thematic Apperception Test (TAT)** In this test, the test-taker views images that are deliberately ambiguous—you can't really tell what's happening. If you were taking a TAT, you might be shown a picture of two men in a room, one seated and looking out a window and the other standing with his back turned to the camera.

The TAT Some psychologists believe that patients who tell stories about ambiguous pictures are actually projecting feelings they have about themselves.

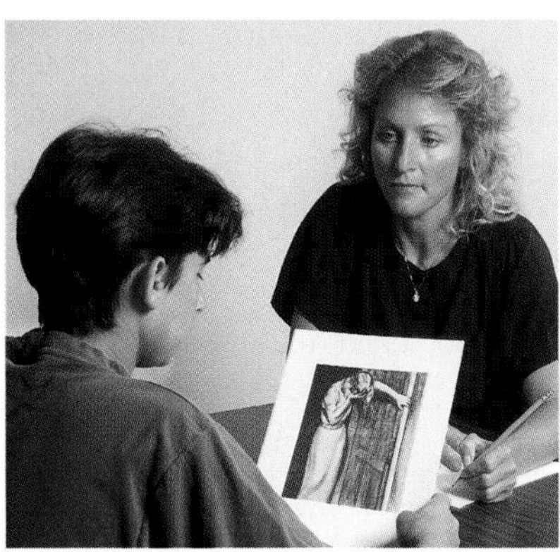

Enriching

web Suggest that students interested in the contributions of Carl Jung and Alfred Adler explore the following two Web sites that offer copious amounts of information on these men:

- The C. G. Jung Page at **www.cgjungpage.org** is edited by Donald William. It provides a helpful introduction to Carl Jung and analytical psychology. In addition to numerous articles on Jung's work, it includes archives, a bulletin board, and links to related Web sites.
- The Alfred Adler Institute of San Francisco maintains a Web site at **http://ourworld.compuserve.com/homepages/hstein** that is devoted to the contributions of Alfred Adler. It provides a brief overview of classical Adlerian psychology and contrasts it with other approaches. Readings on theory and practice, demonstrations of the "Socratic Method in Classical Adlerian Psychotherapy," and Web links are among the other important features at the site.

F • Y • I

Karen Horney fully developed the idea of **neurosis,** or a driving need for something or someone. She believed neuroses helped to make life bearable, giving us a sense of something to strive for. Only when people didn't fulfill a need or became obsessed with a particular neurotic need did these needs become problematic and interfere with life. The ten neurotic needs she identified can be divided into three main categories:

- **Compliance** includes needs for affection, a partner, and simplification of one's life.
- **Aggression** includes needs for power, exploitation of others, prestige, personal admiration, and personal achievement.
- **Withdrawal** includes needs for independence and perfection.

■ APPLYING THE POINTS

Have students contact a psychologist who uses any of the Freudian or neo-Freudian therapeutic approaches. In an informal telephone, letter, or E-mail interview, they may ask the following questions:

- How similar to classic psychoanalytic approaches are modern therapy sessions?
- What training must one have to be certified as a psychoanalyst?

Have students share their findings in brief oral presentations, followed by a class discussion in which the Freudian therapeutic practices of individual psychologists are compared and contrasted.

■ TEACHING TIP

Help students remember the term *projective tests* by linking that term to Freud's defense mechanism of projection. With projection, an analyst's client would attribute negative feelings to someone or something else, making it safer to acknowledge those types of feelings. **Projective tests** enable people to apply their feelings to a picture, which the analyst interprets to explain hidden feelings and experiences.

MODULE 25

■ **LOOKING AT THE ISSUES**

Psychoanalysis has fallen in scientific credibility in recent years since Freud and his students based most of their theories on case studies rather than experimentation. Pose the following questions for a class discussion about the importance of scientific investigation:

- Why are case studies not as reliable as experimentation?
- What type of people did Freud and his students analyze? How might this population skew the development of the theory?
- How might modern scientists test Freud's theory more scientifically?

F•Y•I

Hermann Rorschach was a Swiss psychoanalyst who developed the famous inkblot test. Even though the test enjoyed popularity in the 1940s, 1950s, and 1960s, Rorschach did not experience success with the test in his lifetime; also, he had difficulty finding a publisher. When his book *Psychodiagnostik* did come out in 1921, it was poorly received. He died of complications from appendicitis in 1922, at the age of 37.

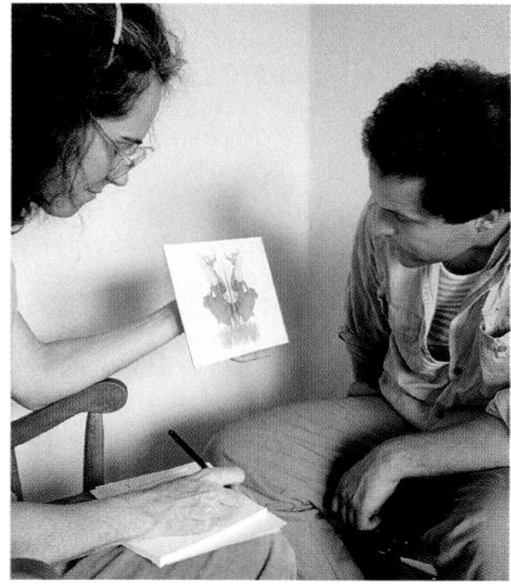

The Rorschach Look at an inkblot and what do you see? Some psychologists believe your responses to this question will provide information about your personality.

The person administering the test would ask you to tell stories about the image, describing what is going on in the picture, as well as what happened before and after the scene. The idea is that you would express your inner feelings and interests in the story you told.

- **Rorschach** (ROAR-shock) **inkblot test** This is the most widely used projective test. Those administering this test assume that a person's responses to a set of 10 inkblots will reveal that individual's inner feelings. If you were taking this test, you would be asked to look at an inkblot and tell what you see. If you see a bat on a part of the inkblot where most people see a bat, your response would be considered "normal." But if you see a gun where most people see a bat, you might be showing aggressiveness.

Are there problems with tests like the Rorschach? Yes. Different therapists interpret the same inkblot responses in different ways, which means the test is not very reliable. No one has developed any single, universally accepted scoring system for this test. Further, the Rorschach is not the emotional X-ray some hoped it would be. The scientific community now agrees that the Rorschach does not accurately predict personality characteristics (Sechrest & others, 1998).

Some clinicians use the Rorschach to break the ice of a therapy session; others use it as part of a series of personality tests and look for trends among all the results. But critics maintain there is "no scientific basis for justifying the use of the Rorschach scales in psychological assessments" (Hunsley & Bailey, 1999).

Evaluating the Psychodynamic Perspective

8. How do Freud's ideas hold up in light of modern research?

No discussion of Freud's work would be complete without at least a simple update and critique. Indeed, most contemporary psychodynamic theorists do not believe Freud's assertion that sex is the basis of personality (Westen, 1996). Nor do they classify patients as "oral" or "anal." They do agree with Freud that much of our mental life is unconscious; that we struggle with inner conflicts among values, wishes, and fears; and that childhood experiences shape our personalities.

Freud's personality theory was comprehensive, unlike any personality theory before. It influenced psychology, literature, religion, and even medicine. Still, we need to be aware of some of the weaknesses of this perspective:

► **Rorschach inkblot test** The most widely used projective test, a set of 10 inkblots, designed by Hermann Rorschach; seeks to identify people's inner feelings by analyzing their interpretations of the blots.

Enriching

web Have students visit one of the many Web sites that provide interactive tests and quizzes. Ask them to take a test to see if it provides an accurate assessment of some aspect of their personality. They can make determinations about these tests, such as: Is there any evidence of the inventory's validity or reliability? Are norms provided and, if so, on whom are they based? Is the test empirically derived?

- Personality Online at **www.personalityonline.com** distinguishes between serious tests, such as the Kiersey Temperament Sorter, and entertaining tests, such as the Love-Type Test and the Color Test.
- Personality Tests at **www.2h.com/Tests/personality.phtml** provides dozens of links to interactive tests that measure such constructs as self-esteem, lifestyle, and assertiveness.
- QueenDom.com at **http://queendom.com** provides links to advice columns and articles on personality and mental health.

- Freud's work was based on individual case studies of troubled upper-class, Austrian white women who lived 100 years ago. Are their experiences applicable to a population, of say, today's middle-class Japanese men? Were the results even applicable to the vast majority of Austrian women outside Freud's study a century ago? Probably not.
- Development is a lifelong process; it is not simply fixed in childhood.
- Boys' gender identity does not result from an Oedipus complex around the time of kindergarten. Gender identity is achieved even without a same-sex parent around the house (Frieze & others, 1978).
- Freud underestimated peer influence on personality development, and he overestimated parental influence.
- The neural network of children under age 3 is insufficiently developed to sustain the kind of emotional trauma Freud described.
- Freud asked his patients leading questions that may have led to false recall of events that never really happened (Powell & Boer, 1994). These same concerns exist today over reports of "repressed memories" of childhood sexual abuse. Evidence suggests therapists may inadvertently implant false memories of abuse in the way they ask clients questions (Ofshe & Watters, 1994).
- Freud's personal biases are evident in his focus on male development.
- Freud's theory is not scientific. It's difficult to submit concepts such as the Oedipal complex or the id to the rigors of scientific testing.

Freud, nevertheless, left a lasting legacy. Our language is filled with psychoanalytic terms, from *repression* to *inferiority complex*. Freud's ideas have steadily declined in importance in the academic world for years, but some therapists, talk shows, and the public still love the concepts (Seligman, 1994).

The Humanistic Perspective

9. What are some major goals of humanistic psychology, and how does this perspective view personality development?

In contrast to Freud's focus on troubled people, **humanistic psychology** focuses on fulfilled individuals, with the goal of helping us all reach our full potential. This movement began gaining credibility and momentum in the United States in the 1960s. Humanistic psychologists wanted a psychology that (Schultz & Schultz, 1996)

▸ **humanistic psychology** A perspective that focuses on the study of conscious experience and the individual's freedom to choose and capacity for personal growth.

Demonstrating

LIMITATIONS OF CASE STUDY RESEARCH Demonstrate the limitations of case study research. (Have all research approved by an Institutional Review Board and receive consent from all participants.)

- Have teams of two or three students select a few easily measured qualities of people, such as height, shoe size, favorite food or color.
- Teams should then choose three or four people for an in-depth interview about these issues.
- Next, have teams take a formal, randomized survey of these issues from a representative population of students in the school.
- Finally, students should compare the results from the case study and the survey. *(Students should see that information from a few people does not accurately reflect information from the population at large.)*

■ **MULTICULTURAL CONNECTIONS**
Have students research how Freudian theories are viewed in other cultures. To guide students' research and subsequent discussion, pose the following questions:

- Do people in other cultures believe Freudian theory has any value in explaining personality development?
- How do people in other cultures view the role of sex in development? Is it similar to or different from what Freud proposed?

■ **LOOKING AT THE ISSUES**
Freud's theory has not stood up well under scrutiny from many sources. Scientific testing of many of his ideas has yielded little or no support for his claims.

Have students work in groups to find references to Freud's theory in several introductory psychology textbooks (including this one), as well as research contradicting his claims. Have groups report back to the class on their findings, which should include responses to the following questions:

- How many references to Freud and his theoretical ideas are found in most psychology textbooks? Do older textbooks have more references than newer ones? Why or why not?
- What information from Modules 4–6 of this text contradicts or supports Freud's ideas about development?
- What information from Modules 32–34 of this text contradicts or supports Freud's ideas about social influence, culture, and gender?
- What information from Modules 7 and 8 of this text contradicts or supports Freud's ideas about brain chemistry and structure?
- What information from Modules 18–19 of this text contradicts or supports Freud's ideas about repressed memories?
- What information from Module 2 of this text contradicts or supports Freud's research practices?

trb At this point, you may want to use **Enrichment Lesson:** *Issues in Personality Theory* (*Teacher's Resource Binder*, p. 25-1).

MODULE 25

F • Y • I

Humanistic psychology is often called the "third force" in psychology. Prior to the 1960s, psychologists were divided into two main camps—behaviorists and psychoanalysts. When the humanistic psychologists came to the forefront, their perspective on human behavior felt like a breath of fresh air.

LOOKING AT THE ISSUES

Before World War II, psychology had three main areas of focus: to cure mental illness, to cultivate genius and talent, and to discover what makes life fulfilling. After the horrors of World War II, psychology focused, full throttle, on diagnosing and treating mental illness—with much success. Promote a discussion that compares and contrasts these differing focuses of psychology by posing the following questions to the class:

- Is the study of positive qualities in life just as important as understanding illness? Why or why not?
- Is the study of positive qualities more difficult than the study of negative ones? Why or why not?

trb At this point, you may wish to use **Analysis Activity:** ***Taking Credit for Success, Denying Responsibility for Failure*** (*Teacher's Resource Binder*, p. 25-1; **Handout 25–13**).

MULTICULTURAL CONNECTIONS

Have students find examples of self-actualized people who have lived in other cultures, both within and outside the United States. Encourage them to discuss their examples with responses to the following questions:

- What roles in society did these people hold?
- What types of things were they able to accomplish?
- Did they inspire others to follow their examples?
- Did people outside their culture recognize them for their efforts? Why or why not?

trb At this point, you may wish to use **Enrichment Lesson:** ***Obstacles to Self-Actualization*** (*Teacher's Resource Binder*, p. 25-1).

Abraham Maslow

1. emphasized conscious experience.
2. focused on free will and creative abilities.
3. studied all factors (not just observable behaviors) relevant to the human condition.

Humanistic psychologists thought psychology in the 1960s was ignoring human strengths and virtues. Freud studied the motives of "sick" people, those who came to him with psychological problems. Humanists, such as Abraham Maslow and Carl Rogers, thought we should also study "healthy" people. They believed human personality was shaped more by our unique capacity to determine our future than by our unconscious conflicts or past learning.

Abraham Maslow and Self-Actualization

10. What is the basic idea underlying Maslow's hierarchy of needs?

Studying psychologically healthy people, **Abraham Maslow** constructed a *hierarchy of needs* (1970) to help explain personality and personal growth (Figure 25.2). Maslow believed we must satisfy our basic physiological needs for food, water, and air before attempting to meet the security and safety needs of the second level of the hierarchy, and the love and belongingness of the third level. Then, after meeting our needs for self-esteem, we could finally strive to fulfill our potential as humans and obtain **self-actualization,** the highest level of his hierarchy. The self-actualized person works toward a life that is challenging, productive, and meaningful.

Figure 25.2 **Maslow's Hierarchy of Needs** (From Maslow, 1970)

Self-actualization needs
Need to live up to one's fullest and unique potential

Esteem needs
Need for self-esteem, achievement, competence, and independence; need for recognition and respect from others

Belongingness and love needs
Need to love and be loved, to belong and be accepted; need to avoid loneliness and alienation

Safety needs
Need to feel that the world is organized and predictable; need to feel safe, secure, and stable

Physiological needs
Need to satisfy hunger and thirst

Searching for examples of self-actualized people, Maslow studied paragons of society, like Eleanor Roosevelt and Abraham Lincoln. He found that those who live productive and rich lives are

- self-aware and self-accepting.
- open and spontaneous.
- loving and caring.
- not paralyzed by others' opinions.
- focused on a particular task they often see as a mission.
- involved in a few deep relationships, not many superficial ones.
- likely to have been moved by personal peak experiences that surpass ordinary consciousness.

Cooperative Learning

tr A four-color transparency of Figure 25.2, Maslow's Hierarchy of Needs, is available in the **Overhead Transparencies Set.**

Working in groups ask students to come up with experiences that contradict Maslow's hierarchy of needs. For instance:

- Can students learn when they are hungry?
- Why do people go on hunger strikes to protest for causes they believe in?
- Why are some considered "starving artists"?

Have a spokesperson from each group share the items. Combine the group lists and then see whether students can add even more experiences to it.

These mature adult qualities, wrote Maslow, are found in those who have "acquired enough courage to be unpopular," discovered their calling, and learned enough in life to be compassionate. These individuals have also outgrown any mixed feelings toward their parents and are "secretly uneasy about the cruelty, meanness, and mob spirit so often found in young people" (Shultz & Shultz, 2000).

Carl Rogers and the Person-Centered Approach

11. In Rogers' view, what three qualities foster human growth?

Humanistic psychologist **Carl Rogers** agreed with Maslow that people are good and strive for self-actualization. Rogers (1980) viewed people much like seeds that thrive when they have the right mixture of ingredients. Just as seeds flourish when given water, soil, and sun, Rogers said, people will flourish when given acceptance, genuineness, and empathy.

And how do we nurture proper human growth in others? By being *accepting*—ideally, through **unconditional positive regard,** or an attitude of total acceptance toward the other person. This attitude values others even though we are aware of their faults and failings. Rogers thought that family members and close friends who express unconditional positive regard for us provide us with great relief. We can let go, confess our most troubling thoughts, and not have to explain ourselves.

We also nurture growth by being *genuine,* according to Rogers. Genuine people freely express their feelings and aren't afraid to disclose details about themselves.

And, finally, we nurture growth by being *empathic*. Empathy involves sharing thoughts and understanding and reflecting the other person's feelings. The key to empathy is listening with understanding. When the listener shows understanding, the person sharing feelings has a much easier time being open and honest. Rogers wrote, "Listening, of this very special kind, is one of the most potent forces for change that I know" (Shultz & Shultz, 2000).

Acceptance, genuineness, and empathy help build a strong relationship between parent and child, teacher and student, manager and employee, or any two people. Rogers believed these three qualities are particularly important in the relationship between a client and a therapist.

Carl Rogers

▶ **Abraham Maslow** (1908–1970) Humanistic psychologist who proposed the hierarchy of needs, with self-actualization as the ultimate psychological need.

▶ **self-actualization** According to Abraham Maslow, the ultimate psychological need that arises after basic physical and psychological needs are met and self-esteem is achieved; the motivation to fulfill one's potential.

▶ **Carl Rogers** (1902–1987) Humanistic psychologist who stressed the importance of acceptance, genuineness, and empathy in fostering human growth.

▶ **unconditional positive regard** According to Carl Rogers, an attitude of total acceptance toward another person.

F • Y • I

In Rogers's person-centered therapy, not much analysis occurs. To facilitate unconditional positive regard, genuineness, and empathy, Rogers would answer questions with questions. "How does that make you feel?" was a common question Rogers would ask when clients would discuss their feelings. Rogers felt that if people received the attention and acceptance that they needed, they could cure themselves. The therapist was merely there to provide support.

trb At this point, you may wish to use Cooperative Learning Activity: *Introducing Personality* (*Teacher's Resource Binder,* p. 25-1).

■ JOURNAL WRITING

Invite students to use the following questions and writing prompts as springboards for entries in their psychology journals:

- Are you on the road to becoming self-actualized? Why or why not?
- Do you think that Maslow put our needs in the right order? Why or why not?
- Do you feel you get unconditional positive regard from your family? Your friends? Why or why not?
- Do you feel you give unconditional positive regard to your family? Your friends? Why or why not?

trb At this point, you may wish to use Enrichment Lesson: *Obstacles to Self-Actualization* (*Teacher's Resource Binder,* p. 25-1).

MODULE 25

■ LOOKING AT THE ISSUES
Humanistic therapy is individual, personal, lengthy, and extensive; because of these factors, it can also be expensive. With managed-care costs skyrocketing, this type of therapy might not be viewed as practical or efficient for most people. Have students explore the questions below to learn what insurance companies typically cover regarding psychotherapy:

- What type of therapy is generally covered by insurance plans?
- How long can a patient participate in therapy?
- Does the therapist have discretion to increase the length of time a person can stay in therapy? Why or why not?

■ LOOKING AT THE ISSUES
Humanistic psychology laid a foundation for the study of positive traits. What legacy have Maslow and Rogers left for psychology today? Have students work in groups to track references in introductory psychology textbooks (including this one). Have each group respond to the following questions:

- How many references to humanistic psychology and its leading proponents are found in most psychology textbooks? Do older textbooks have more references than newer ones? Why or why not?
- What evidence can students find in other textbooks that contradicts or supports Maslow's hierarchy of needs?
- How is Rogers's person-centered therapy viewed in comparison with modern therapeutic techniques?

▶ **self-concept** All our thoughts and feelings about ourselves, in answer to the question, "Who am I?"

Assessing Personality and the Self

12. How do humanistic psychologists attempt to assess personality?

If Rogers, Maslow, or any humanistic psychologist wanted to assess your personality, they probably would ask you to answer questions that would help them evaluate your **self-concept.** Your self-concept includes all your thoughts and feelings about yourself, in answer to the question "Who am I?" Rogers, for example, often asked clients to describe themselves first as they actually were and then as they would ideally like to be. He believed that the closer the actual self was to the ideal self, the more positive the person's self-concept. Assessing personal growth during therapy was a matter of measuring the difference between ratings of ideal self and actual self.

For some humanistic psychologists, any kind of structured personality test is simply too impersonal and detached from the real human being. For them, only a series of lengthy interviews and personal conversations can allow us to understand a person's unique experiences and personality.

Evaluating the Humanistic Perspective

13. What are the greatest contributions—and the greatest weaknesses—of the humanistic perspective on personality?

Carl Rogers once said, "Humanistic psychology has not had a significant impact on mainstream psychology. We are perceived as having relatively little importance" (Cunningham, 1985). Was Rogers correct?

Society has benefited from humanistic psychology. Therapy practices, child-rearing techniques, and workplace management can all attest to a positive humanistic influence.

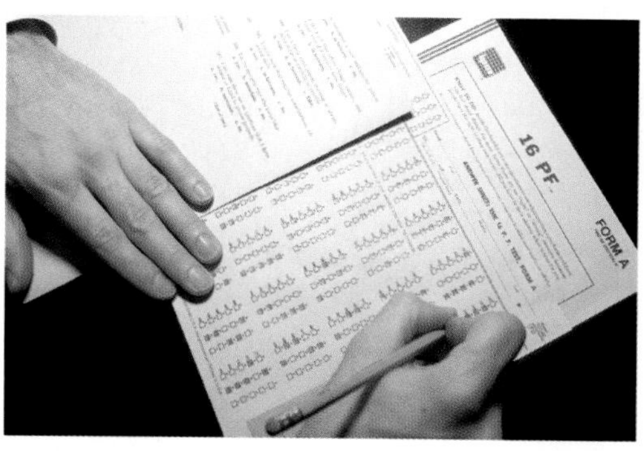

Too Impersonal? Most humanistic psychologists believe that written personality tests are not an adequate way to assess personality. They prefer conversations and interviews that reveal the individual's uniqueness.

But there have been unintentional negative effects as well. Some people have mistakenly interpreted unconditional positive regard for children as meaning that we should never offer constructive criticism to a child, or worse, never tell a child no. Critics also point out that many humanistic terms are vague and hard to define precisely so that other researchers can test them. Maslow, for example, stated that the self-actualized person is *spontaneous, loving,* and *productive.* How do we define these terms to allow Maslow's assumptions to be tested

Enriching

Have students create two columns on a piece of paper—one labeled "Ideal Self" and one labeled "Actual Self." Students should then describe what they want their ideal self to be like and then describe what they believe their actual self is like. Next, encourage students to compare their ideal to their actual selves through the details in the descriptions.

trb At this point, you may wish to use **Demonstration Activity:** *Three Quick Examinations of Biased Self-Ratings* (*Teacher's Resource Binder,* p. 25-1; **Handouts 25–9** through **25–11**) and **Analysis Activity:** *Self-Concept Clarity* (*Teacher's Resource Binder,* p. 25-1; **Handout 25–8**).

scientifically? Without such tests, how do we know whether these terms simply reflect Maslow's personal values?

Whatever its impact on mainstream psychology, humanistic psychology laid the foundation for the *positive psychology* movement of the past few years. As a result, many researchers are now studying the human strengths and virtues, like courage and hope, of healthy people, rather than just the disorders of those who are not psychologically healthy.

REVIEW

Module 25: The Psychodynamic and Humanistic Perspectives

What's the Point?

Your personality is your characteristic pattern of thinking, feeling, and acting. Psychologists study personality from many perspectives, including the psychodynamic and humanistic perspectives.

The Psychodynamic Perspective

1. *What is the psychodynamic perspective, and how does it view personality?*

   The psychodynamic perspective grew out of Sigmund Freud's theory of personality, known as *psychoanalysis.* Those who study personality from the psychodynamic perspective share with Freud the beliefs that many of our thought processes occur unconsciously and that our childhood experiences influence our adult personality. But psychodynamic theorists tend to consider unresolved childhood conflicts (especially sexual conflicts) as less important than Freud did.

2. *In Freud's view, how do the conscious, preconscious, and unconscious regions of the mind differ from one another?*

   Freud compared the human mind to an iceberg; in each case, most of the entity is hidden from view. The conscious mind holds the thoughts and feelings we are aware of. Just below the surface is the preconscious mind, holding the thoughts and memories not in our current awareness but easily retrievable. At the deepest, unseen level is the unconscious, a vast region of mainly unacceptable thoughts, wishes, feelings, and memories. Freud studied the unconscious by having people free associate (relax and say whatever came into their mind), by observing their habits and accidental misstatements, and by analyzing their dreams.

MODULE 25

■ **TEACHING TIP**

Martin Seligman, who as APA president in 1998 brought the study of positive psychology to the forefront, believes that positive psychology does owe a great debt to the pioneering work of the humanistic psychologists such as Maslow and Rogers. However, their research techniques lacked the scientific rigor that characterized psychology during the behaviorist era and that dominates psychological study today. Positive psychologists strive to study strengths within experimental boundaries instead of through case studies.

Close

Two different views about human behavior come together in this module. These two theoretical perspectives are almost diametrically opposed in their views of human nature, the causes of mental illness, and the goals of therapy. Yet they also share many similarities. Have students create a chart comparing and contrasting these two forces in psychological thought. *(Students may point out that the psychodynamic perspective holds that people are born with a strong, selfish id and develop a sense of morality and reality. Humanistic psychologists believe people are naturally good and full of potential, which must be drawn out with love and empathy. Additionally, Freudian thinkers seek to uncover the past, while humanistic psychologists are concerned with helping clients discover how they can maximize present circumstances.)*

MODULE 25

Checking the Points

■ TEACHING TIPS

web (1) The book companion site for *Thinking About Psychology* at **www.worthpublishers.com/thinkingaboutpsych** contains a module quiz, flashcards of key terms and people, and other student activities and resources for this module. You will also find PowerPoint lectures, as well as other student activities and resources by logging on as an instructor.

trb (2) At this point, you may wish to review concepts about the psychodynamic and humanistic perspectives with **Critical Thinking Activity:** *Fact or Falsehood?* (*Teacher's Resource Binder*, p. 25-1; **Handout 25–1**). If students filled in a handout earlier, ask them not to refer to previous versions. Suggest that students complete the handout individually, taking the time to look up information in the text to respond correctly to questions. Have them exchange handouts with a classmate to check answers.

3. *How do the id, ego, and superego interact, according to psychoanalytic theory?*

   Freud believed that personality grows out of a conflict between our pleasure-seeking biological impulses and our internalized social restraints. He proposed a three-part model of personality, consisting of the id, the ego, and the superego. The id, operating from the pleasure principle, demands immediate gratification. The superego is the voice of conscience, prodding us to conform to social ideals and standards. The ego, operating from the reality principle, acts as mediator, attempting to satisfy the demands of the id within the limits that society will tolerate. A person who successfully expresses the pleasure-seeking impulses while avoiding punishment or guilt has a healthy personality.

4. *According to Freud, how are defense mechanisms helpful?*

   Freud believed that defense mechanisms help us reduce the anxious tension that arises from the conflict between the id's wishes and the superego's social rules. The seven defense mechanisms covered in this module are repression, regression, denial, reaction formation, projection, rationalization, and displacement.

5. *What were Freud's stages of personality development?*

   In Freud's view, personality develops during the early years of childhood, as the individual moves through a series of psychosexual stages. These are the oral stage (birth through 18 months), the anal stage (18 months to 3 years), the phallic stage (3 to 6 years), the latency period (6 years to puberty), and the genital stage (from puberty on). Failure to resolve a conflict in any of these stages could, according to Freud, leave the individual fixated at that stage and cause problems in later life.

6. *Who were the "neo-Freudians," and how do their views differ from Freud's?*

   We use the term "neo-Freudians" to refer to personality researchers who agreed with many of Freud's basic ideas but modified some parts of his theory. Three neo-Freudians discussed in this module are Alfred Adler, Carl Jung, and Karen Horney. Adler believed social tensions, not sexual tensions, shaped the development of personality, and he was particularly interested in feelings of inferiority. Jung did not stress social factors, but he extended Freud's ideas about the unconscious, proposing that the human species has a collective shared unconscious. Horney found Freud's view of the development of women's personality lacking, and she also believed that social variables, not sexual anatomy, shaped personality development.

7. *How do psychologists working from the psychodynamic perspective attempt to assess personality?*

   Techniques for assessing personality are tailored to the theory of personality that dominates a particular perspective. Freud used dream analysis and free association to assess his patients' unconscious. Later psychodynamic theorists were interested in projective tests. These tests present images with no clear meaning; the test-taker supposedly projects his or her own meaning, drawn from unconscious motives, onto the image. Two well-known projective tests are the Thematic Apperception Test (TAT), which asks test-takers to tell stories about an ambiguous picture, and the Rorschach test, which asks the meaning of a shape formed by an inkblot. These tests have been criticized for failing to test what they are meant to test and for failing to give the same results when administered by different people at different times.

8. *How do Freud's ideas hold up in light of modern research?*

   Contemporary psychodynamic theorists would tend to agree with Freud that mental life is in large part unconscious, that we struggle with inner conflicts, and that our childhood experiences shape our personalities. But they would not agree that sex is the basis of personality development or that personality development ends in early childhood. Critics also note that Freud's theory has not held up to recent research on peer influence (which he underestimated) and parental influence (which he overestimated). Contemporary research on memory and gender identity formation also fails to support Freud's theory. Freud also studied a very small, specialized group of people, and his own biases are apparent in his theory. Finally, Freud's theory cannot be tested scientifically.

The Humanistic Perspective

9. *What are some major goals of humanistic psychology, and how does this perspective view personality development?*

   Humanistic psychology, which reached a peak in the United States in the 1960s, wanted a psychology that emphasized conscious experience, free will and creativity, and all factors relevant to the human condition. They also believed that psychologists should be basing theories of personality on the study of healthy people, not on studies of people with mental disorders, as Freud had done.

10. *What is the basic idea underlying Maslow's hierarchy of needs?*

    Maslow's hierarchy of needs rests on an assumption that we must meet basic needs before we can attend to higher needs. First we must satisfy physiological needs (food, water, air), then safety needs, then needs for love and belongingness, then needs for self-esteem. Only after satisfying all these needs can we strive for self-actualization—achieving our full potential.

11. *In Rogers' view, what three qualities foster human growth?*

    Rogers believed that people are basically good and strive for self-actualization. We can help others to flourish by giving them acceptance, genuineness, and empathy. Rogers believed his approach could build strong relationships between parent and child, teacher and student, manager and employee, or any two people.

12. *How do humanistic psychologists attempt to assess personality?*

    Humanistic psychologists tend to believe that personality assessment is possible only by understanding a person's uniqueness. Most would reject tests in favor of lengthy interviews and personal conversations, focused on the "Who am I?" question.

13. *What are the greatest contributions—and the greatest weaknesses—of the humanistic perspective on personality?*

    The humanistic perspective restored balance to the study of personality, following Freud's focus on psychosexual stages. This perspective's focus on studying healthy personalities as well as disorders has contributed to the positive psychology movement. And the basic concepts of humanistic psychology have influenced therapy practices, child-rearing techniques, and workplace management. But critics of this viewpoint note that humanistic psychology has presented its ideas in terms that are vague and difficult to define precisely, so that other psychologists cannot test these ideas.

MODULE 25

trb **tr** ■ TEACHING TIP

At this point, you may wish to review module vocabulary with the entire class by using the concept webs in **Building Vocabulary: Graphic Organizer:** ***Concept Charts*** (*Teacher's Resource Binder*, p.25-1; **Handouts 25–2a** and **25–2b**) as transparencies for projection. For each item on the handouts, have a student read the item aloud and provide an answer. If other students challenge the answer, have the challengers identify the correct answer and read aloud a passage from the text that supports the challenge. If the challenge is incorrect, ask students to find a passage from the text that confirms the correct answer.

tb Using the Test Bank

The *Test Bank* that accompanies this textbook offers a wide variety of questions in different formats and levels of complexity. Use the software to construct whole tests or to integrate standardized questions into teacher-made tests.

Self-Test Answers

Multiple-Choice Questions

1. d, 2. d, 3. a

Key Terms

personality, p. 479
psychoanalysis, p. 480
psychodynamic perspective, p. 480
free association, p. 481
preconscious, p. 481
unconscious, p. 481
id, p. 482
superego, p. 482
ego, p. 483
defense mechanisms, p. 483
psychosexual stages, p. 485
inferiority complex, p. 486
collective unconscious, p. 486
projective tests, p. 487
Thematic Apperception Test (TAT), p. 487
Rorschach inkblot test, p. 488
humanistic psychology, p. 489
self-actualization, p. 490
unconditional positive regard, p. 491
self-concept, p. 492

Key People

Sigmund Freud, p. 479
Alfred Adler, p. 486
Carl Jung, p. 486
Karen Horney, p. 487
Abraham Maslow, p. 490
Carl Rogers, p. 491

Self-Test

Multiple-Choice Questions

Choose the *best* answer for each of the following questions.

1. Sigmund Freud has magically appeared at a dinner where a group of psychologists are discussing current psychodynamic views on personality development. Freud is most likely to *disagree* with the contemporary belief that
   a. childhood experiences influence adult behavior.
   b. much of our mental life is unconscious.
   c. we struggle with inner conflicts among values, wishes, and fears.
   d. sex is not the basis of personality.

2. Sima has been having some problems, and she is visiting Dr. Do-Good today. He has asked her to relax and say whatever comes into her mind, no matter how silly, unimportant, or embarrassing it seems to her. Dr. Do-Good is asking Sima to
   a. organize her thoughts in a hierarchy of needs.
   b. take the TAT test to reveal her personality.
   c. express unconditional positive regard toward herself.
   d. free associate so that he can understand her problems.

3. You just passed an open window where your neighbor was cooling a hot apple pie. You immediately had two thoughts. The first was "Grab the pie and run!" The second was "Never, never take your neighbor's pie—bad, bad, bad!" Freud would say that your ________ was responsible for the "Grab the pie" thought, and your ________ was responsible for the "Never, never" thought.
   a. id; superego
   b. superego; id
   c. ego; superego
   d. superego; ego

4. Carla is very worried that she might fail the psychology test. As she looks around the room, she is quite sure that most of the other students are cheating. She thinks she can hear whispering, and some students look as though they might be peeking at other people's answers. What defense mechanism is Carla using to protect herself from realizing that she herself is tempted to cheat?
   a. Reaction formation
   b. Regression
   c. Projection
   d. Rationalization

5. In the musical *The Threepenny Opera*, a character sings these words: "First feed the face, and then talk right or wrong." Which of the following people had a theory that would agree with this thought?
   a. Alfred Adler, in his work on the inferiority complex
   b. Abraham Maslow, in his work on the hierarchy of needs
   c. Karen Horney, in her work on personality development in women
   d. Carl Jung, in his work on the collective unconscious

6. Jamal loves going to his grandfather's house, and he feels he can tell him anything. Grandpa Jefferson really listens to Jamal, and he seems to accept and care about him, even though he knows Jamal's faults and failings. Carl Rogers would say that Grandpa Jefferson is
   a. regressing and is therefore able to be a friend to Jamal.
   b. rationalizing Jamal's behavior in an attempt to make it seem reasonable.
   c. showing unconditional positive regard toward Jamal.
   d. teaching Jamal to strive for self-actualization.

Matching Terms and Definitions

7. For each definition, choose the *best* matching term from the list that follows:

Definition

a. An individual's characteristic pattern of thinking, feeling, and acting.
b. All our thoughts and feelings about ourselves, in answer to the question, "Who am I?"
c. In psychoanalytic theory, the ego's protective methods of reducing anxiety by unconsciously distorting reality.
d. The part of personality that, according to Freud, represents internalized ideals and provides standards for judgment; the conscience.
e. A projective test in which people express their inner feelings and interests through the stories they make up about ambiguous scenes.
f. The part of personality that, according to Freud, is largely conscious and that operates on the reality principle; the mediator between the two other parts of personality.
g. The region of the mind that, according to Freud, is a reservoir of mostly unacceptable thoughts, wishes, feelings, and memories.
h. Carl Jung's concept of a shared, inherited reservoir of memory traces from our species' history.
i. A contemporary view of personality that retains some aspects of Freudian theory (such as the importance of unconscious thought processes) but is less likely to see unresolved childhood conflicts as a source of personality development.

Self-Test Answers

Multiple-Choice Questions (continued)

4. c, 5. b, 6. c

Matching Terms and Definitions

7. a. (3), b. (5), c. (8), d. (12), e. (4), f. (11), g. (1), h. (9), i. (7)

MODULE 25

Self-Test Answers

Fill-in-the-Blank Questions

8. Karen Horney, 9. Carl Rogers, 10. Abraham Maslow

Brief Essay Question

11. Fixation is the idea that a person experienced some type of trauma in a childhood stage of development and therefore their personality development stopped at that point. This idea is outdated since scientific experimentation has not been able to demonstrate that the stages of development proposed by Freud actually exist, casting doubt on the idea of fixation as well.

Term

(1) unconscious
(2) preconscious
(3) personality
(4) TAT
(5) self-concept
(6) psychoanalysis
(7 psychodynamic perspective
(8) defense mechanisms
(9) collective unconscious
(10) id
(11) ego
(12) superego

Fill-in-the-Blank Questions

8. ____________ ____________ rejected parts of Freud's original theory of psychoanalysis because it was negatively biased toward women and underestimated the influence of culture on personality development.

9. ____________ ____________ stressed the importance of acceptance, genuineness, and empathy in fostering human growth.

10. ____________ ____________ proposed the hierarchy of needs, with self-actualization as the ultimate psychological need.

Brief Essay Question

11. Your friend, Ed, has gained a lot of weight, and his elderly uncle, who took some psychology classes when he went to college 50 years ago, has suggested to Ed that he may need therapy because he seems to be fixated at the oral stage. Ed (knowing that you are taking psychology) has asked you what his uncle is talking about. In three paragraphs of three or four sentences each, explain to Ed what Freud meant by "fixation" in one of the psychosexual stages, and tell him why his uncle's views would be considered outdated today.

Performance Standards

Standard Area: Personality and Assessment

Content Standard 1: Define personality

Performance Standard 1.1 Define personality.

- Personality is defined as "an individual's characteristic pattern of thinking, feeling, and acting." (Student Text p. 499)

Content Standard 2: Theories of personality

Performance Standard 2.1 Identify the psychodynamic, social-cognitive, humanistic, and trait perspectives.

- Explain how the study of traits helps us understand personality. (Student Text pp. 499–505)
- Explore how researchers use factor analysis to identify traits. (Student Text pp. 501–505)
- Discuss Gordon Allport's trait theory. (Student Text pp. 500–501)
- Explore Raymond Cattell's 16 personality traits theory. (Student Text p. 501)
- Investigate Hans Eysenck's personality factors theory. (Student Text pp. 501–502)
- Figure 26.1, "Eysenck's Personality Factors," illustrates this trait theory of personality. (Student Text p. 502)
- Identify and discuss the "Big Five" personality traits. (Student Text pp. 502–503)
- Figure 26.2, "The 'Big Five' Personality Factors," illustrates this trait theory of personality. (Student Text p. 502)
- Discuss some of the drawbacks of the trait perspective. (Student Text p. 505)
- Investigate the factors that social-cognitive psychologists believe are important to personality development. (Student Text pp. 505–512)
- Explore the theory of reciprocal determinism, suggested by researcher Albert Bandura. (Student Text pp. 505–508)
- Figure 26.4, "Reciprocal Determinism," illustrates Albert Bandura's theory. (Student Text p. 507)
- Discuss Julian Rotter's research contrasting individuals with an internal versus an external locus of control. (Student Text pp. 508–509)
- Present Martin Seligman's research on learned helplessness. Examine the tie between learned helplessness and depression. (Student Text pp. 509–510)
- Introduce the positive psychology movement. Present the concept of "optimism" and its effect on personality. (Student Text pp. 510–511)
- Evaluate the impact of the social-cognitive perspective on personality theory. (Student Text pp. 511–512)

Content Standard 3: Personality assessment

Performance Standard 3.1 Compare objective and projective assessment techniques.

- Explain how personality inventories are objective tests. (Student Text p. 503)

Performance Standard 3.2 Describe specific assessment tools.

- Discuss the main features of the Minnesota Multiphasic Personality Inventory (MMPI-2). (Student Text pp. 504–505)
- Figure 26.3, "A Minnesota Multiphasic Personality Inventory (MMPI-2) Profile," demonstrates its use in diagnosis. (Student Text p. 504)
- Discuss how social-cognitive psychologists assess the effect of particular situations on our behavior. (Student Text pp. 511–512)

Materials NETWORK

All of the items from the Activity and Enrichment Centers listed below come from the *Teacher's Resource Binder*. These items will help you teach and expand on concepts presented in Module 26.

trb This logo indicates when an item from the Materials Network may be used in conjunction with a specific note found in this module's *Teacher's Edition*.

The Trait Perspective

Activity Center

- Critical Thinking Activity: *Fact or Falsehood?* With this activity, students' preconceptions about trait and social-cognitive perspectives on personality are either exposed as incorrect or reinforced as correct. (*Teacher's Resource Binder*, p. 26-1; **Handout 26–1**)
- Building Vocabulary: *Matching Terms and Definitions* Students can test their knowledge of terms in this module by matching terms with their definitions. (*Teacher's Resource Binder*, p. 26-1; **Handout 26–2**)
- Cooperative Learning Activity: *Introducing Personality* Students can explore the question "Who am I?" to delve into fundamental questions related to personality theory. (*Teacher's Resource Binder*, p. 26-1)
- Analysis Activity: *Your Theory of Personality* In a once popular text on personality, Charles Potkay and Bem Allen provided a brief questionnaire that enabled students to explore their own personality theory. This activity helps students discover their own theory of human behavior. (*Teacher's Resource Binder*, p. 26-1; **Handout 26–3**)
- Analysis Activity: *Extraversion and Emotional Stability* Surveys of people around the world show that extraversion and emotional stability are enduring personality traits. With this activity, students assess their own levels of these traits. (*Teacher's Resource Binder*, p. 26-1; **Handout 26–4**)
- Critical Thinking Activity: *Shyness* Shyness is a trait that 80 percent of Americans at some time claim to have possessed and that 40 percent say currently causes them problems. Indeed, some entertainers—such as the singer Michael Jackson—consider themselves shy. With this activity, students assess their own level of shyness. (*Teacher's Resource Binder*, p. 26-1; **Handout 26–5**)
- Analysis Activity: *The "Big Five" Inventory* Oliver P. John and his colleagues designed the "Big Five" Inventory as a quick assessment of the Big Five personality dimensions. The Big Five traits are extraversion, agreeableness, conscientiousness, emotional stability, and openness. Students can take this assessment to find out how much of each of the Big Five traits they possess. (*Teacher's Resource Binder*, p. 26-1; **Handout 26–6**)
- Application Activity: *Personality Traits in the Workplace* Psychologists have long debated the usefulness of personality tests to predict occupational success. Recent studies show that conscientiousness is the one personality trait that predicts success in the business world. With this activity, students discover how much conscientiousness they possess. (*Teacher's Resource Binder*, p. 26-1; **Handout 26–7**)
- Critical Thinking Activity: *Correlations and Personality Traits* Certain behaviors are correlated with the Big Five personality traits. With this activity, students can correlate common teenage behaviors with their own personality traits. This exercise also provides a good review of the correlational approach in psychological research that was first introduced in Module 2. (*Teacher's Resource Binder*, p. 26-1; **Handouts 26–6** through **26–9**)
- Critical Thinking Activity: *Empirically Derived Tests and the Importance of Cross-Validation* Testing a large pool of items and then selecting those that are found to differentiate particular groups' results in an empirically derived inventory. When the original pool contains a large number of items, there is the real possibility that some of the items will distinguish between the criterion groups by chance alone. To deal with this problem, researchers cross-validate items and use only those that pass the test. This activity helps students see the importance of this technique. (*Teacher's Resource Binder*, p. 26-1; **Handout 26–10**)
- Critical Thinking Activity: *Assessing Social Desirability* One problem with self-report personality inventories is that some respondents tend to give socially desirable rather than honest responses. Another problem is an acquiescence response set in which people tend to agree with test questions regardless of the questions' content. The Marlowe-Crowne Social Desirability Scale attempts to assess this response tendency. (*Teacher's Resource Binder*, p. 26-1; **Handout 26–11**)
- Demonstration Activity: *The Barnum Effect* The Barnum effect is our tendency to accept as valid those descriptions of our personality that are generally true of everyone. This tendency is strongest, of course, when the descriptions are generally favorable. This activity, which includes the North Dakota Null-Hypothesis Brain Inventory, shows the power of this effect. (*Teacher's Resource Binder*, p. 26-1; **Handout 26–10**)

- Critical Thinking Activity: *Astrology and the Barnum Effect* Our tendency to accept astrologers' descriptions of our personality can be explained in terms of the Barnum effect. William Balch provides a classroom exercise that permits testing the validity of astrology. (*Teacher's Resource Binder*, p. 26-1; **Handout 26–12**)

Enrichment Center

- Enrichment Lesson: *Issues in Personality Theory* While many psychologists are concerned with human perception, intelligence, motivation, and development, personality theorists are in the unique position of studying the entire person. They have the monumental task of synthesizing the best information from the diverse fields of the discipline into a coherent, holistic configuration. In the course of their work, personality theorists address fundamental issues of human nature and individual differences. (*Teacher's Resource Binder*, p. 26-1)
- Enrichment Lesson: *The NEO Personality Inventory* The NEO Personality Inventory and its successors, the NEO-PI-R and the NEO Five Factor Inventory (NEO-FFI), were developed in an effort to assess the major domains in the five-factor model of personality described in the text. In contrast to the Minnesota Multiphasic Personality Inventory (MMPI), which measures psychological disorders, the NEOs are designed to measure "normal" personality. These inventories have been among the most popular for research on personality and for clinical use. (*Teacher's Resource Binder*, p. 26-1)
- Enrichment Lesson: *William Sheldon and the Controversy of the Posture Photos* One of the most dubious yet enduring theories of personality is William Sheldon's body type theory. How he gathered evidence of body types is an amazing and disturbing story of eugenics, obedience, and privacy. More than 20,000 photographs by Sheldon, related to this story, are stored in the archives of the Smithsonian Institute. (*Teacher's Resource Binder*, p. 26-1)

The Social-Cognitive Perspective

Activity Center

- Analysis Activity: *The Self-Monitoring Scale* People who perceive themselves as strongly inner-directed tend to act more consistently across different situations than do people who perceive themselves as shaping their behavior to fit specific situations. Mark Snyder has developed the Self-Monitoring (SM) Scale to assess the extent to which people observe and control their expressive behavior and self-presentation out of a concern for social appropriateness. In this activity, students complete the scale and score their own responses. (*Teacher's Resource Binder*, p. 26-1; **Handout 26–13**)
- Application Activity: *Locus of Control* Researchers find that respondents' sense of personal control may vary across different situations. Have students measure their own levels of personal control with the Personal Efficacy Subscale provided in the handout. (*Teacher's Resource Binder*, p. 26-1; **Handout 26–14**)
- Application Activity: *The Life-Orientation Test and Optimism* The Life-Orientation Test assesses a person's optimism, or, more specifically, a person's expectations regarding the favorability of future outcomes. Have students complete this activity to see how much they expect from future outcomes. (*Teacher's Resource Binder*, p. 26-1; **Handout 26–15**)
- Analysis Activity: *Measuring Optimism* The level of optimism people possess is a predictor of depression, both currently and in the future. This test of optimism, developed by Martin Seligman of the University of Pennsylvania, will help your students see their overall levels of optimism and the area—permanence, pervasiveness, or personal—in which they have more pessimistic thoughts. (*Teacher's Resource Binder*, p. 26-1; **Handouts 26–16** and **26–17**)
- Analysis Activity: *Unrealistic Optimism About Life Events* One obstacle to implementing strategies that foster health may be that we are unrealistically optimistic about our health. You can readily demonstrate this with this activity, which is based on Neil Weinstein's research. (*Teacher's Resource Binder*, p. 26-1; **Handout 26–18**)
- Analysis Activity: *ESP Trick—Clairvoyance* This trick serves to underline the necessity for rigid experimental control in evaluating ESP (extrasensory perception) claims. (*Teacher's Resource Binder*, p. 26-1)
- Analysis Activity: *ESP Trick—Mental Telepathy (Gray Elephant in Denmark Trick)* This activity provides a quick and dramatic demonstration of mental telepathy using mathematical formulas that yield the same result regardless of initial number chosen. (*Teacher's Resource Binder*, p. 26-1)
- Analysis Activity: *ESP Trick—Mental Telepathy (Telephone Book Trick)* This activity uses a simple telephone book to demonstrate mental telepathy. Like it's two predecessors, it shows how mental telepathy and clairvoyance can be explained by probability or by just plain trickery. (*Teacher's Resource Binder*, p. 26-1)

Enrichment Center

- Enrichment Lesson: *George Kelly's Personal Construct Theory* George Kelly's basic assumption is that we are strongly motivated to make sense of our worlds. Like scientists, we are always attempting to make better predictions about what will happen to us. Thus we generate and test bipolar personal constructs to interpret and predict events. (*Teacher's Resource Binder*, p. 26-1)
- Enrichment Lesson: *Belief in ESP* Why do people believe in ESP when it has not passed the test of scientific experimentation? Belief in ESP shows how easily people believe in vivid examples and how ignorant people are of how chance works. (*Teacher's Resource Binder*, p. 26-1)

MODULE 26

Trait and Social-Cognitive Perspectives on Personality

The Trait Perspective

The Social-Cognitive Perspective

Remember the last time a friend asked for your opinion of another person? Perhaps you said that person was generous, friendly, and sweet, or maybe self-centered, cranky, and mean. Terms like these describe **traits,** or characteristic patterns of behavior. Some psychologists who study **personality**—an individual's characteristic pattern of thinking, feeling, and acting—find traits a useful tool for describing different personality types. Psychologists taking this *trait perspective* tend to consider our enduring patterns of behavior, those that we're born with and that stay fairly constant across situations.

Other psychologists believe we can better understand personality by studying how people are affected by a particular situation, and by what they've learned, how they think, and how they interact socially. Psychologists who take this **social cognitive perspective** would consider how the same person could be generous in one situation and self-centered in another, or friendly and sweet on one day and cranky and mean the next.

In this module, we'll take a closer look at these two perspectives on personality.

▶ **trait** A characteristic pattern of behavior or a disposition to feel and act, as assessed by self-report inventories and peer reports.

▶ **personality** An individual's characteristic pattern of thinking, feeling, and acting.

▶ **social-cognitive perspective** Perspective stating that understanding personality involves considering situation and thoughts before, during, and after an event.

The Trait Perspective

What's the Point? 1. How does the study of traits help us understand personality?

Think of the last car you rode in, perhaps on your way to or from school. What kind of car was it? What about the color? Was it a compact, small, medium, or large car? Note how we are using descriptive techniques to classify the cars as distinct *types.* Can we use similar techniques to classify personalities? People have been attempting to do so for centuries.

MODULE 26

Trait and Social-Cognitive Perspectives on Personality

Introducing the Module

The Points: Module Objectives

- Analyze how the study of traits helps us understand personality.
- Determine how psychologists identify traits.
- Identify the "Big Five" traits.
- Describe how psychologists assess a person's enduring traits, and explain what we mean when we say an assessment technique is "reliable" or "valid."
- Evaluate the drawbacks of the trait perspective.
- Describe the factors that social-cognitive psychologists believe interact to form personalities.
- Analyze how feelings of personal control affect our behavior, and discuss whether we can learn to feel helpless or optimistic.
- Determine how psychologists assess the effect of particular situations on our behavior.
- Evaluate the drawbacks of the social-cognitive perspective.

trb Building Vocabulary

Students can reinforce their knowledge of trait and social-cognitive perspectives of personality by completing **Building Vocabulary:** *Matching Terms and Definitions* (*Teacher's Resource Binder*, p. 26-1; **Handout 26–2**).

Getting Started

Ask students to list individual traits they believe to be positive and negative. In groups have students compare their lists to see how many traits they listed in common. Then, compile a class list of desirable and undesirable traits. Discuss the list by posing the following questions:

- Were more positive than negative qualities present? Why or why not?
- Do students strive to cultivate any of these qualities? Why or why not?
- Are these traits inborn or learned? Why do you think so?

trb You may wish to use the **Critical Thinking Activity:** *Fact or Falsehood?* (*Teacher's Resource Binder*, p. 26-1; **Handout 26–1**) as a pre-reading strategy to evaluate what students already know about the trait and social-cognitive perspectives of personality. This activity will prime students to look out for information that could prove or disprove their preconceptions about these perspectives.

MODULE 26

Teaching the Points

■ **TEACHING TIPS**

web (1) You can log on as an instructor to the book companion site for *Thinking About Psychology* at **www.worthpublishers.com/thinkingaboutpsych**. It contains teacher resources for class presentations, as well as review and assessment of module concepts and terms.

(2) The debate between trait psychologists and social-cognitive psychologists focuses on how we attribute (or explain) people's behavior. **Trait psychologists** focus on dispositions—inborn qualities that are relatively consistent over a lifetime. **Social-cognitive psychologists** emphasize the power of situations, which change from moment to moment, on human behavior.

trb At this point, you may wish to use **Analysis Activity:** *Your Theory of Personality* (*Teacher's Resource Binder*, p. 26-1; **Handout 26–3**).

F • Y • I

William Sheldon, who developed the body type personality theory, arrived at his conclusions in a controversial way. From the late 1800s to the mid-1900s, Ivy League universities, their Sister schools for women, and other prestigious universities across the country would take "posture photos" of every freshman entering each year. These were nude photos taken at all angles (front, back, and side views), supposedly to determine who had correct posture. (If you were found lacking, you had to take remedial posture classes.) In reality, eugenics theorists from this time period wanted to develop a database of the elite to reinforce notions of the racial superiority of white people. Sheldon, who took many of these photographs, used them to develop his theory of the relationship of body type to personality. More than 20,000 of these photographs are stored in Smithsonian archives.

trb At this point, you may wish to use **Enrichment Lesson:** *William Sheldon and the Controversy of the Posture Photos* (*Teacher's Resource Binder*, p. 26-1).

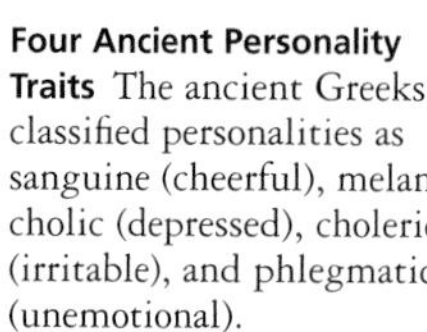

Four Ancient Personality Traits The ancient Greeks classified personalities as sanguine (cheerful), melancholic (depressed), choleric (irritable), and phlegmatic (unemotional).

Thousands of years ago, the ancient Greeks classified personalities using four types: sanguine (cheerful), melancholic (depressed), choleric (irritable), and phlegmatic (unemotional). And how did the ancient Greeks explain whether you were cheerful or irritable? They spoke of your body fluids or "humors." If melancholic humor filled your body, for example, you had a depressive personality.

Today, psychologists still use descriptive techniques to classify personality, but they now attempt to identify characteristic and enduring patterns of behavior, using valid and reliable assessment techniques. (Don't confuse these techniques with the tests you find in teen magazines. Unfortunately, most of those "personality assessments" are no more valid or reliable than the ancient Greeks' descriptions of "humors.")

Identifying Traits

2. How do psychologists identify traits?

One early attempt to classify personality made assumptions based on a person's body type. Thus, plump *endomorphs* were viewed as jolly, and skinny *ectomorphs* as high-strung (Sheldon, 1954). Further study revealed that oversimplified classification systems that lump large numbers of people into a few neat categories tend to eliminate each person's individuality. Three researchers—**Gordon Allport, Raymond Cattell** (kuh-TELL), and **Hans Eysenck** (EYE-zink)—offered broader alternatives to account for these individual variations.

Gordon Allport

Gordon Allport's Trait Theory

After graduating from college, Gordon Allport traveled to Vienna to visit Sigmund Freud, the Austrian physician famous for his theory of psychoanalysis. Their meeting had a profound impact on the trait theory Allport developed years later.

At the time, Freud was developing his theory of the *unconscious*, a hidden reservoir of unacceptable thoughts and feelings. He viewed personality as the result of a long history of interactions between a person's unconscious and conscious minds. Freud often studied people with psychological conflicts, and he searched for answers in childhood experiences.

Suggested Readings

Use the following books as teacher-preparation tools or as enrichment for advanced students:

Burger, J. (2000). *Personality* (5th ed.). Belmont, CA: Wadsworth.

Cohen, D. B. (1999). *Stranger in the nest: Do parents really shape their child's personality, intelligence or character?* New York: Wiley.

Hergenhahn, B. R., & Olson, M. H. (1999). *An introduction to theories of personality* (5th ed.). Upper Saddle River, NJ: Prentice Hall.

Seligman, M. E. P. (1998). *Learned optimism: How to change your mind and your life* (2nd. ed.). New York: Pocket Books.

Snyder, M. (1987). *Public appearances/private realities: The psychology of self-monitoring.* New York: Freeman.

Zimbardo, P. G. (1977). *Shyness.* Reading, MA: Addison-Wesley.

Allport disagreed with Freud in many ways. First, Allport played down the role of the unconscious in healthy people. In fact, unlike Freud, Allport believed personality should only be studied in normal adults, not in those suffering from a psychological problem. Further, wrote Allport, current experiences have far more impact on an adult than early childhood experiences, which Freud dwelled upon.

Allport also resisted the idea of a "personality law" that would apply to everyone. Instead, he strongly believed that individual personalities are unique. This belief, which manifested itself in his trait theory, led psychology in two directions. First, Allport identified several different kinds of traits, which paved the way for other personality researchers and brought respectability to the study of personality (Schultz & Schultz, 1996). But the second direction was more problematic: Allport's emphasis on individual uniqueness made it difficult to produce general ideas that could be tested by others. With over 18,000 ways to describe people even in the unabridged dictionary of Allport's day (Allport & Odbert, 1936), would it be possible to condense all the possible traits into a manageable few? The answer is "yes," according to Raymond Cattell.

▶ **Gordon Allport** (1897–1967) American psychologist and trait theorist who researched the idea that individual personalities are unique.

▶ **Hans Eysenck** (1916–1997) German psychologist who researched the genetically influenced dimensions of personality, including extraversion and introversion.

▶ **Raymond Cattell** (1905–1998) English psychologist who researched whether some traits predicted others. He proposed 16 key personality dimensions or *factors* to describe personality.

Raymond Cattell's Factor Analysis

English psychologist Raymond Cattell's contribution to the trait perspective flowed from his interest in knowing whether some traits predicted others. For instance, if you identify yourself as pessimistic, are you more likely to report feeling sad? Cattell used statistical techniques to compute the relationships among traits until he came up with 16 core personality dimensions, which he called *factors* (Wiggins, 1984). Each factor can be measured, using a questionnaire, and plotted on a continuum—for instance, Factor H, the shy/bold dimension. How would you rate yourself on a scale of 1 to 10 on the shy/bold contiuum, where 1 equals shy and 10 equals bold? Such ratings produce a profile for the individual being assessed.

How many dimensions are there to personality? Cattell insisted personality should be assessed using 16 traits (Cattell & Krug, 1986). Hans Eysenck thought 16 were too many.

Hans Eysenck's Biological Dimensions

German psychologist Hans Eysenck searched for personality dimensions in biology, and his model of genetically influenced dimensions has broad research support. Like Cattell, Eysenck used statistical analysis to come up with his dimensions. Two of his findings are the

Enriching

web Have students learn more about Gordon Allport's contributions to psychology by having them visit **www.ship.edu/~cgboeree/allport.html**. Allport was the first person to use the word *trait* to describe personality, and his theory is considered to be fundamental to the modern study of personality. At this site, students can also take a quiz modeled after Allport's original personality tests.

F • Y • I

Gordon Allport's meeting with Sigmund Freud was a memorable one. Biographies of Allport relate that when Allport went to visit Freud, the esteemed psychoanalyst sat quietly waiting for the younger man to start the conversation. After a long period of time, an antsy Allport impulsively told the story of seeing a young boy become upset on the bus because he had to sit in the same seat a dirty old man had occupied earlier. Allport proposed that maybe the boy had learned to be preoccupied with neatness from his apparently domineering mother. Freud went even further with the story, commenting, "And that little boy was you?" Allport, from then on, felt that psychoanalysis tried to delve too deeply into behavior, just as behaviorism didn't delve deeply enough.

■ TEACHING TIPS

(1) Cattell took three different measurements from people to arrive at a factor analysis of their personality. These different data sets would be correlated to determine a person's personality:

- **L-data** were comprised of events from a person's daily life. He would collect statistical information on daily behavior (number of accidents, visits to the doctor, and so forth)
- **Q-data** were quantitative, resulting from answers to self-report questionnaires. Subjects would take several different personality tests as part of his research.
- **T-data** came from more "objective" measures of personality that didn't rely on self-report (which could be unreliable or incorrect). He would use the Thematic Apperception Test, Rorschach inkblot test, and word association tests for this component.

trb At this point, you may wish to use **Analysis Activity:** *Extraversion and Emotional Stability* (*Teacher's Resource Binder*, p. 26-1; **Handout 26–4**).

(2) Link Raymond Cattell with the concepts he named: **fluid intelligence** (one's ability to reason speedily and abstractly) and **crystallized intelligence** (one's accumulated knowledge and verbal skills).

MODULE 26

■ **LOOKING AT THE ISSUES**

Personality theories do not seek to place value judgments on people's behavior. They merely describe how people behave and try to categorize those behaviors so we can all understand each other better. Have students study Figure 26.1 and respond to the following questions:

- Which personality dimensions seem more desirable than others? Why?
- Do you see some personality traits as being linked to the behavior of women or men? How could this be limiting to either gender?

trb **tr** A black-line master for Figure 26.1, Eysenck's Personality Factors, is available in the **Black-Line Masters Appendix** of the *Teacher's Resource Binder.*

trb At this point, you may want to use **Enrichment Lesson:** *Issues in Personality Theory* (*Teacher's Resource Binder,* p. 26-1).

■ **MULTICULTURAL CONNECTIONS**

If people all over the world tend to describe personality according to the "Big Five," what words from those cultures are used? Do they translate the same into English? Ask non-native speakers to share the words from their home language for *extraversion, stability, openness, agreeableness,* and *conscientiousness* with the class. Also ask students taking world languages to look up these words in their foreign language/English dictionaries.

trb At this point, you may want to use **Analysis Activity:** *The "Big Five" Inventory* (*Teacher's Resource Binder,* p. 26-1; **Handout 26–6**) and **Critical Thinking Activity:** *Correlations and Personality Traits* (*Teacher's Resource Binder,* p. 26-1; **Handouts 26–6** through **26–9**).

tr ■ **CHECKING FOR UNDERSTANDING**

A four-color transparency of Figure 26.2, The "Big Five" Personality Factors, is available in the **Overhead Transparencies Set.** Cover up some of the concepts in the chart and have students fill in the blanks to assess students' knowledge of the Big Five personality traits.

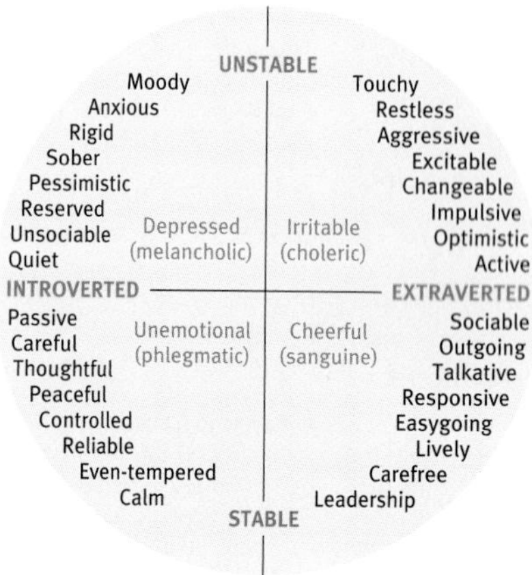

Figure 26.1 **Eysenck's Personality Factors** Hans Eysenck predicted that personality traits were inherited. (From Eysenck & Eysenck, 1963.) Notice how Eysenck's four quadrants align with the four personality types of the ancient Greeks.

extraversion-introversion dimension and the emotional stability-instability dimension.

Extraverts, according to Eysenck, are outgoing and sociable; *introverts* keep to themselves and are quiet. Emotionally stable people are generally relaxed and calm, whereas emotionally unstable people are anxious and tend to worry. Analyzing data from his own questionnaire, Eysenck found he could predict personality traits along these biologically inherited dimensions (Eysenck & Eysenck, 1963) (Figure 26.1).

Eysenck, Cattell, and Allport were all leaders in personality assessment. Building on their work, researchers in this field have now identified a new core set of personality factors.

The "Big Five" Traits

3. What are the "Big Five" traits?

Clearly, there is some debate over the number of fundamental personality traits. How many traits would it take to adequately describe your best friend? Would three be enough to paint this picture? Would 16 cause you to start repeating yourself? In the mid-1980s, researchers decided that an adequate description of personality relied on five essential factors now usually referred to as the "Big Five" (Jang & others, 1998; Wiggins, 1996). Try it for yourself. Can you give an adequate description of your best friend using the five dimensions in Figure 26.2? Findings from around the world show that most people tend to mention these five traits when describing one another (McCrae & others, 1998).

Figure 26.2 **The "Big Five" Personality Factors** Adapted from McCrae & Costa (1986, p. 1002).

EXTRAVERSION
Sociable ↔ Retiring
Fun-loving ↔ Sober
Affectionate ↔ Reserved

OPENNESS
Imaginative ↔ Practical
Preference for variety ↔ Preference for routine
Independent ↔ Conforming

AGREEABLENESS
Soft-hearted ↔ Ruthless
Trusting ↔ Suspicious
Helpful ↔ Uncooperative

EMOTIONAL STABILITY
Calm ↔ Anxious
Secure ↔ Insecure
Self-satisfied ↔ Self-pitying

CONSCIENTIOUSNESS
Organized ↔ Disorganized
Careful ↔ Careless
Disciplined ↔ Impulsive

Meeting Individual Needs

tr A four-color transparency of Figure 26.2, The "Big Five" Personality Factors, is available in the **Overhead Transparencies Set.** Create copies of this transparency for students who have difficulties in reading comprehension or concept mastery. Create blanks for certain terms on the chart, having students fill in the blanks on their own or with assistance from a student tutor.

The Big Five traits—agreeableness, conscientiousness, emotional stability, extraversion, and openness—appear to be stable in adults. Thus, it's unlikely an agreeable 30-year-old will suddenly become suspicious and uncooperative at age 60. In fact, agreeableness and conscientiousness tend to increase as you get older, although the other three may decline a bit (McCrae & others, 1999). Genetic predispositions influence personality traits (Loehlin & others, 1998). *Predisposition* merely means that a tendency to develop a trait exists. Whether the trait actually will develop may depend on environmental factors (such as stress or upbringing). The Big Five traits also predict other personal attributes. For example, marital satisfaction is often high for those who score high on agreeableness, stability, and openness (Botwin & others, 1997).

Do the Big Five represent all we need to know about personality traits? Some psychologists argue the Big Five should be expanded to include dimensions such as positive-negative emotion or femininity-masculinity. Further assessment of traits may some day expand the Big Five to the Big Six or Big Seven. But for now, the Big Five do a good job of describing personality's essential factors.

Testing for Traits

4. How do psychologists assess a person's enduring traits? What do we mean when we say an assessment technique is "reliable" or "valid"?

Some personality researchers try to assess personality by asking people to tell stories about ambiguous pictures—images where the meaning is not clear. Trait researchers prefer **personality inventories,** questionnaires that assess a number of enduring characteristics. These approaches differ in important ways. *Projective tests*, like the personal interpretation of a photo with no clear meaning, ask the person being tested to "project" unconscious motives onto an ambiguous image, in a free-flowing, narrative style. In contrast, personality inventories are *objective tests.* Test-takers provide written answers to standardized, usually true-false or multiple-choice, questions. These objective tests have shown greater **validity** than the projective assessments: They are more likely to measure what you're looking for. If you are a clinical psychologist trying to assess anxiety or depression in a patient, the objective test is more likely than the projective test to measure these conditions accurately. Objective tests also offer greater **reliability:** They yield consistent results, regardless of who is giving the test or when it is being given (Dawes, 1994). And finally, the two types of tests differ in the training required to score them. Scoring or interpreting projective tests requires months, even years, of extensive training, but scoring objective tests is very simple and uncomplicated.

▸ **personality inventories** Questionnaires (often with true-false or agree-disagree items) on which people respond to items designed to gauge a wide range of feelings and behaviors; used to assess selected personality traits.

▸ **validity** The extent to which a test measures or predicts what it is supposed to test.

▸ **reliability** The extent to which a test yields consistent results, regardless of who gives the test or when or where it is given.

■ APPLYING THE POINTS

Conscientiousness has been shown to be the best predictor of successful job performance. Have students contact human resources departments, personnel managers, and job placement specialists to explore how many of these professionals use personality testing to hire and promote people in their organizations. The following questions can help students interview professionals and later discuss findings:

- What types of organizations use personality testing? If they don't use personality tests, why don't they?
- What types of personality tests do employers use?
- What personality traits are they looking for specifically? What traits have they found to be most indicative of successful employees?

trb At this point, you may wish to use **Application Activity:** ***Personality Traits in the Workplace*** **(*Teacher's Resource Binder*, p. 26-1; Handout 26–7).**

■ TEACHING TIP

Remind students of the two types of projective tests discussed in this module. These tests are based on Freud's ideas that free association can unlock the memories and feelings buried in the unconscious part of the mind:

- **The Thematic Apperception Test (TAT)** presents a person with an ambiguous picture. The person relates a story about that picture, which is interpreted according to Freudian principles.
- **The Rorschach inkblot test,** developed in the 1920s, presents a person with blots of ink. The person identifies what they believe the blot looks like. Again, interpretation is based on Freudian concepts.

MODULE 26

F • Y • I

The publisher of the MMPI-2, Pearson Assessments, recommends the following applications for their test:

- Assess major symptoms of social and personal maladjustment.
- Identify suitable candidates for high-risk public safety positions.
- Support classification, treatment, and management decisions in criminal justice and correctional settings.
- Give a strong empirical foundation for a clinician's expert testimony.
- Assess medical patients and design effective treatment strategies, including chronic pain management.
- Evaluate participants in substance abuse programs and select appropriate treatment approaches.
- Support college- and career-counseling recommendations.
- Provide valuable insight for marriage and family counseling.

Source: The Pearson Assessments Web site at www.pearsonassessments.com/assessments/tests/mmpi_2.htm.

trb tr A black-line master for Figure 26.3, A Minnesota Multiphasic Personality Inventory (MMPI-2) Profile, is available in the **Black-Line Masters Appendix** of the *Teacher's Resource Binder.*

trb At this point, you may wish to use **Critical Thinking Activity:** *Empirically Derived Tests and the Importance of Cross-Validation* (*Teacher's Resource Binder*, p. 26-1; **Handout 26–10**).

▸ **Minnesota Multiphasic Personality Inventory (MMPI)** The most widely researched and clinically used of all personality tests. Originally developed to identify emotional disorders (still considered its most appropriate use), this test is now used for many other screening purposes.

The best-known personality inventory has more than 500 questions. It's called the **Minnesota Multiphasic Personality Inventory** (mercifully abbreviated as the **MMPI**), and it is the most widely researched and clinically used of all personality tests. The MMPI was originally developed to assess abnormal behavior. The second version of the test, the MMPI-2, was standardized on a much more diverse sample of people than the original MMPI.

The MMPI-2 assesses test-takers on 10 clinical scales used to diagnose psychological disorders (Figure 26.3). An additional 15 content scales measure all kinds of attributes, including anger, attitude toward work, and whether a person is trying to fake illness.

Therapists are not the only people administering the MMPI-2. Many school admissions officers and personnel departments use the MMPI-2 to assess potential students or employees. Unfortunately, these agencies may be using the test in ways that were not intended (Matarazzo, 1983).

Is it possible to beat the MMPI-2, presenting yourself as something you are not? You bet. Although objective tests have greater validity (they are more likely to measure what you're looking for) than projective tests, they aren't always valid. It may be difficult to fake illness on the MMPI-2, but it is possible to fake near-perfection on some of the other scales by answering in socially desirable ways. If you were applying for a job, and your potential employer gave you a test asking how often you get angry, what would you say? A person with an anger prob-

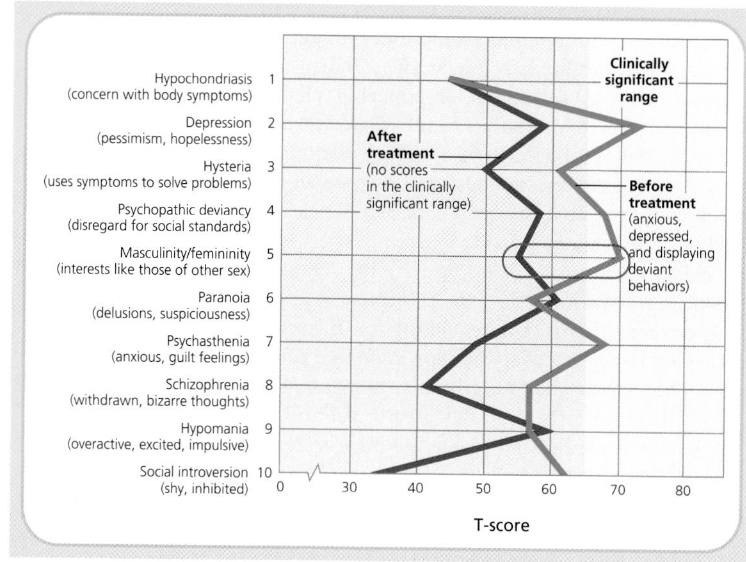

Figure 26.3 A Minnesota Multiphasic Personality Inventory (MMPI-2) Profile These are the scores of a young man suffering depression and anxiety—before and after treatment for his disorders. An average "T-score" is 50, and scores over 65 suggest a psychological disorder.

Enriching

Psychological tests providing false results are a problem in many areas of study. Lie detectors have been shown to be unreliable, and people regularly give false answers to many psychological surveys, both intentionally and unintentionally. What do psychologists do about this problem?

Encourage students to research and discuss the questions below. If possible, present these questions to a local psychologist who can visit your class and facilitate a discussion.

- How do psychologists evaluate the reliability and validity of tests they give? How does standardization and norming help provide better results?
- How do psychologists avoid problems with test responses, such as social desirability and lying?

trb At this point, you may wish to use **Critical Thinking Activity:** *Empirically Derived Tests and the Importance of Cross-Validation* (*Teacher's Resource Binder*, p. 26-1; **Handout 26–10**) and **Demonstration Activity:** *The Barnum Effect* (*Teacher's Resource Binder*, p. 26-1; **Handout 26–10**).

lem who wants a job might say "sometimes" or "almost never" in order to look more favorable to the boss.

This anger example hints at a potential problem with self-report data: How honest are we when assessing ourselves? Can you accurately say how helpful you are? Some researchers suggest peer reports are more likely than self-reports to provide valid and reliable information (Funder, 1991, 1995). What if you say you're not helpful, but all your friends and relatives rate you high in helpfulness? Chances are, you *are* helpful.

▶ **Albert Bandura** (1925–) Canadian-American psychologist who developed the social-cognitive perspective. He believed that to understand personality, one must consider the situation and the person's thoughts before, during, and after an event.

Evaluating the Trait Perspective

5. What are some drawbacks of the trait perspective?

The technique of understanding personality through traits has at least a couple of faults. One criticism of the trait perspective is that it does not consider how important the *situation* is to a particular trait. Do you act the same way in the classroom as you do when you're at lunch with friends? Students seem to vary from classroom to classroom as well. On several occasions, I've had colleagues tell me how quiet or outgoing a student is, only to see the opposite behavior in my class. Trait behavior seems to be related to where we are and whom we're with.

Trait theories also have a glaring weakness in their inability to explain *why* we behave the way we do. Traits may describe us well, but they limit themselves to statements of *how* we behave. Felicia is calm and secure, so we label her as high in emotional stability. Trait theories do not explain why Felicia is calm and secure.

Trait theories also do not consider the effects of our thoughts on our behavior. The social-cognitive perspective, however, has a lot to say about how thoughts and situations affect personality.

The Social-Cognitive Perspective

6. What factors do social-cognitive psychologists believe interact to form our personalities?

The social-cognitive perspective is an interactive theory that combines research on social behavior, cognition, and learning. Some call this theory the *cognitive social learning theory* or the *cognitive-behavioral approach,* but we'll stick with the *social-cognitive perspective,* a name **Albert Bandura** (1986) used. Bandura and other social-cognitive theorists believe we learn by observing and modeling the behaviors of others, or by having certain behaviors reinforced, or rewarded. Proponents of this perspective believe that to understand personality, we need to consider the situation we're in and our thoughts before, during, and after an event.

Albert Bandura

■ **JOURNAL WRITING**

Invite students to use the following questions and writing prompts as springboards for entries in their psychology journals:

- How would you describe your personality according to the "Big Five" traits? Do you think people who know you would describe you this way? Why or why not?
- Do you feel your personality is determined more by your traits or by the situations you find yourself in? Why?
- Have you ever learned by modeling the behaviors of others? Describe your experience.

web ■ **APPLYING THE POINTS**

Students can see trait theory and the controversies surrounding it in action by visiting the Keirsey Temperament Web site at http://keirsey.com. Students can take the Keirsey Temperament Sorter II, a personality test similar to the Myers-Briggs Type Inventory. It includes four scales assessing the dimensions of extraversion versus introversion, intuiting versus sensing, feeling versus thinking, and judging versus perceiving.

After students visit the site, discuss their experience by asking the following questions:

- Is there reason to believe that the Keirsey Temperament Sorter has validity?
- Does the site offer empirical support for its claims?

trb At this point, you may wish to use Enrichment Lesson: *The NEO Personality Inventory* (*Teacher's Resource Binder,* p. 26-1).

■ **TEACHING TIP**

Albert Bandura is most famous for studying how the observation of violence relates to aggression. His famous experiment exposed children to a video of an adult who played either aggressively or nonaggressively with a Bobo clown doll—that is, a tall, inflated doll with sand in the bottom to keep it upright. Children who watched the aggressive play were more likely to play aggressively with the Bobo doll than children who watched the more gentle play.

Cross-Curricular Connections

DEBATE Invite the debate coach to help you structure a formal debate about personality theory. Students can construct a resolution to debate the affirmative and the negative. The debate may either be structured like a policy debate (which would involve teams of students) or a Lincoln-Douglas debate (which pits individual students against each other). One resolution you might consider could be, "Resolved: Personality is made up of inborn, biological traits rather than learned social behaviors."

MODULE 26

F • Y • I

Former President Reagan and his wife consulted astrologers to gain insight into certain political situations with which they were dealing. Is he the only influential world leader who has relied on astrology for insight into the future?

One famous case you might have students research in depth regards the last czar of Russia, Nicholas II, and his wife, Alexandra. Alexandra fell under the influence of the infamous Rasputin, a mystic who led her to make controversial decisions that some blame for the downfall of the monarchy in Russia and the rise of Communism with Lenin and the Bolsheviks.

trb At this point, you may wish to use **Critical Thinking Activity:** *Astrology and the Barnum Effect* (*Teacher's Resource Binder*, p. 26-1; **Handout 26–12**).

■ LOOKING AT THE ISSUES

Psychics advertise on late-night television with frequency, and students may have seen some of these ads and been amazed at the accuracy of the predictions and insights the television psychics made. Have students investigate what limitations the FCC places on psychics for advertising.

- What can psychics offer? What can't they offer?
- Many ads appear with the disclaimer, "for entertainment purposes only." Do the ads suggest that the services of the psychic are strictly for entertainment? Why or why not?
- Psychics have recently come under fire for making certain claims. What laws did they violate? What punishment(s) did they receive?

trb At this point, you may wish to use **Analysis Activities:** *ESP Tricks* (*Teacher's Resource Binder*, p. 26-1).

trb ■ TEACHING TIP

Demonstrate how easily regular people can be fooled by suggestion, manipulation, and plain trickery by showing students your skills with ESP. Instructions for several easy ESP tricks can be found in **Analysis Activities:** *ESP Tricks* (*Teacher's Resource Binder*, p. 26-1).

Thinking Critically

Planets, Palms, and Personalities

Perhaps you've seen people on TV who for a mere $4.99 per minute will take your phone call, telling you all you need to know about yourself and what you should do with your life. They often do this by consulting the position of the stars and planets, and the phase of the moon after you tell them your birth date. Others deliver the message in person, telling you the type of person you are after looking at your handwriting, reading the wrinkles in your palm, or feeling the bumps on your head. Is there anything to these methods? Do these techniques really reveal who you are? Psychologists have seriously considered these questions and have thus far found no scientific support for astrologers' claims.

I'll admit, the other day I read my Capricorn horoscope and agreed with what it said. But that same day, I also read Sagittarius, Libra, and Leo and thought those descriptions applied equally well to me! Not surprising, since few people can pick out their own horoscope when all 12 are presented without labels (Carson, 1985; Kelly, 1997). Similar studies have shown handwriting analysis "experts" do no better than chance in predicting people's occupations from their handwriting samples (Beyerstein & Beyerstein, 1992; Dean & others, 1992).

With such a bad track record, how do astrologers and palm readers stay in business? One former palm reader, Ray Hyman, provides some insight into their apparently successful techniques (1981). The "seer" often starts by offering generally true statements few of us would disagree with. For instance:

- "You worry about things more than you let on."
- "I sense you are nursing a grudge against someone; you really ought to let that go."
- "You are adaptable to social situations and your interests are wide-ranging."

Any of those sound like you? I was in a class once where we were all given a "personality test" that would provide us with a personal character analysis. The next day, we were all handed our individual analyses, then asked how much we agreed with what had been said. Almost all of us said the character analysis closely described our personalities, and some were amazed at the accuracy. Imagine our surprise when the instructor revealed that we had all received the same analysis, taken at random from an astrology magazine!

"Seers" also pay close attention to your body language, clothing, and physical features. Therapeutic shoes may indicate physical discomfort. Haircut or clothing could indicate music preference. Facial expressions can indicate mood. Expensive jewelry? Wealth. After sizing you up, the seer may then say something like, "I can tell you're dealing with a problem, and that you are not sure what to do about it." This sympathy technique builds trust. If the person seeking insight gives a positive nod in response, the seer will reassert the statement even more strongly. Seers are also good at deflecting negative responses. If the statement seems inaccurate, you will just have to work harder to make sense of the "vision" or message.

The bottom line is that we should all beware of those who use these techniques. Reading your horoscope and chuckling at the generalized statements is one thing. Planning your life around them is not a good idea.

Demonstrating

HOROSCOPE IDENTIFICATION Bring in horoscopes for several different zodiac signs. Code each horoscope so only you know which prediction belongs to which sign. Place them all on one piece of paper, and have students rate which one they think is their horoscope. Then, calculate whether students were right.

trb At this point, you may wish to use **Critical Thinking Activity:** *Astrology and the Barnum Effect* (*Teacher's Resource Binder*, p. 26-1; **Handout 26–12**).

Interacting With Our Environment: Three Influences

▶ **reciprocal determinism** The mutual influences between personality and environmental factors.

I had a colleague who taught down the hall from me who, by most accounts, was a very tranquil person. Students described him as "calm" and "gentle." One Saturday afternoon, my daughter's recreational league basketball team played against the team coached by my serene colleague, and I witnessed a completely different person. He looked sternly at his players as they warmed up. He yelled constantly at the teen referee during the game. After the game, he huddled with his players and, in a very loud voice, he told each what she had done wrong during the game—even though they had won by eight points. What would explain the difference in behavior between teacher and coach?

Social-cognitive theorists would likely explain that my colleague's behavior differences were due to the differing *situations.* **Reciprocal determinism** is the name given to the process of interacting with our environment (Bandura, 1986). This process includes the mutual, back-and-forth (that is, reciprocal) interaction of three factors that shape personality:

1. Your thoughts or cognitions
2. Your environment
3. Your behaviors

Each factor interacts with the others (Figure 26.4), according to social-cognitive theorists, in determining your personality. To understand the teacher/coach's changing personality, we would then need to consider the following questions:

- ***How does his behavior change in different situations?*** Does he act the same way at home as he does on the basketball court, or is his home behavior more like his classroom behavior? Would he have been calmer if the referee had been an adult?
- ***How does he perceive each situation?*** Is he more confident in the classroom, and thus more in control? Is coaching so

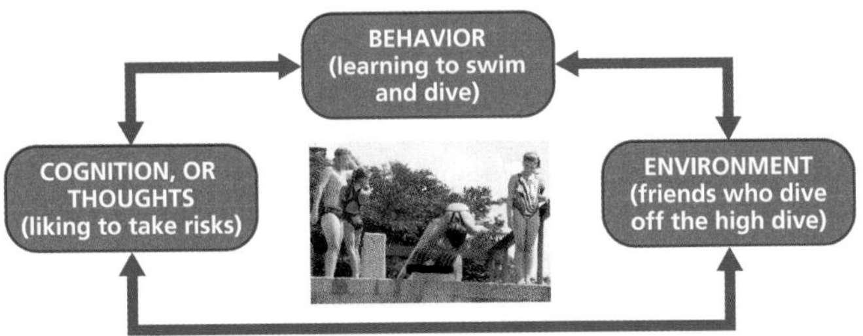

Figure 26.4 **Reciprocal Determinism** Bandura's social-cognitive perspective suggests that personalities are shaped by the interaction of environment, behaviors, and thoughts (cognitions).

MODULE 26

■ JOURNAL WRITING

Invite students to use the following questions and writing prompts as springboards for entries in their psychology journals:

- Have you or a friend ever behaved vastly differently in one situation than in another? Describe the behavior. Why did you or your friend behave so differently?

■ TEACHING TIP

After students have studied Figure 26.4, suggest that they can remember the *reciprocal determinism* theory with the following acronym:

A = *A*ffect or thoughts and emotions
B = *B*ehaviors
C = *C*onsequences

trb tr A black-line master for Figure 26.4, Reciprocal Determinism, is available in the **Black-Line Masters Appendix** of the *Teacher's Resource Binder.*

trb At this point, you may wish to use **Analysis Activity:** *The Self-Monitoring Scale* (*Teacher's Resource Binder*, p. 26-1; **Handout 26–13**).

■ LOOKING AT THE ISSUES

People act differently in different situations. Using the following questions as an interview guide, have students contact a practicing psychologist and a legal expert to ask how they deal with people's changing behavior:

- Do psychologists try to see the patient in different situations to get a full picture of his or her behavior before making treatment decisions? Do they interview family members and friends before making treatment decisions? Why or why not?
- Are defendants forced to dress in prison garb when they appear in court? How does this dress make jurors and judges perceive the defendant?
- How much weight is given to character witnesses in trials? Are they integral to a person's defense? Why or why not?

trb At this point, you may wish to use **Analysis Activity:** *The Self-Monitoring Scale* (*Teacher's Resource Binder*, p. 26-1; **Handout 26–13**).

Meeting Individual Needs

The term *reciprocal determinism* may be difficult for some students to understand. Help them understand this term by breaking down each word within it, then bringing the words together again for a full understanding of the term's definition. Be sure they understand what the words *reciprocal* and *determinism* means.

- *Reciprocal* refers to two or more parties exchanging information. So in this theory, thoughts, environment, and behaviors are interacting, exchanging information about how and why we behave.
- *Determinism* refers to the inevitable consequences of actions. Consequences are determined by actions that precede them

The theory of **reciprocal determinism** refers to actions determined by the interaction of the environment and our thoughts.

MODULE 26

■ TEACHING TIP
Link discussion of *locus of control* with *motivation.*

- **Intrinsic motivation** is similar to internal locus of control. When we are motivated by internal factors, such as the desire to learn or personal feelings of goodness, then we are likely to feel in control of our feelings toward a situation.
- When we experience factors related to **extrinsic motivation**, such as getting good grades or receiving other rewards, then we are at the mercy of others to determine our feelings of self worth. This becomes an integral factor in creating an external locus of control.

trb At this point, you may wish to use **Application Activity:** *Locus of Control* (*Teacher's Resource Binder*, p. 26-1; **Handout 26–14**).

■ APPLYING THE POINTS
Have students imagine that they have just failed a psychology test. Have them write down two or three reasons why they would have failed. Then have them look over the reasons to determine what type of locus of control they feel those reasons indicate.

trb At this point, you may want to use **Application Activity:** *Locus of Control* (*Teacher's Resource Binder*, p. 26-1; **Handout 26–14**).

■ JOURNAL WRITING
Invite students to use the following questions and writing prompts as springboards for entries in their psychology journals:

- In general, do you feel in control of your life? Why or why not?
- Do you feel you have more control in some areas of life than others? Describe and explain one difference.

overwhelming that he loses track of his emotions? Did he sense weakness in the 14-year-old referee and alter his approach to the game?

- ***How do the elements of the situation affect his behavior?*** Do parents breathe down his neck, demanding a victory? Had this same referee called a poor game the week before?

We can't expect to know a person's personality by observing that individual in one situation or at one point in time. All behavior is the result of the interplay between external (environment) and internal factors (thoughts, perceptions).

Personal Control

7. How do our feelings of personal control affect our behavior, and can we learn to feel helpless or optimistic?

Do you feel as though your environment controls you, or do you believe you are in control of your environment? Social-cognitive psychologists who study personal control believe that the way you answer this question can provide clues to your personality. Psychologists who study personality from this perspective are especially interested in two questions:

1. How do feelings of control predict achievement and behavior?
2. How does explanatory style affect our well-being?

Locus of Control
Consider the following statements:

- There's no reason to vote in an election—your vote doesn't really count.
- When you try to get a job, it's not *what* you know that matters, but *whom* you know.
- One person can make a difference in the way elected representatives think.
- If you want to be a success, depend on hard work, not luck.

Which two are closest to what you believe? For a social-cognitive psychologist, these four statements are clues to your *locus of control.* (*Locus* is from a Latin word meaning "place.") The first two reflect what Julian Rotter called an **external locus of control,** the perception that chance, or forces outside yourself and beyond your control, determines your fate. If you feel more comfortable with the second two statements, you probably have an **internal locus of control,** a perception that you

▶ **external locus of control** The perception that chance, or forces beyond your control, controls your fate.

▶ **internal locus of control** The perception that you control your own fate.

Cooperative Learning

V Show students the clip from *Schindler's List* described in **Videocassette:** *Schindler's List and Personal Control* (*Teacher's Resource Binder*, p. 26-1) in which Oskar Schindler talks to the commandant's maid about loss of personal control. In small groups, have students discuss the following questions:

- Briefly describe a time in your life when your efforts seemed to make little difference. What effects did those feelings have on you?
- Concentration camp and prison inmates experience little control over their lives. What other groups are likely to feel the same? What do you think are the long-term effects on them?
- How do you think gender, age, race, or faith might influence one's feelings of control?
- What are the most important factors that influence one's sense of control?

control your own fate. Dozens of studies have compared how an external or internal locus of control correlates with behavior and achievement. Look at these results. Compared with externals, internals

- are less depressed (Presson & Benassi, 1996)
- are more likely to be healthy (Lachman & Weaver, 1998)
- achieve more in school, and act more independently (Lefcourt, 1982)
- cope better with stress, including serious stressors like marital problems (Miller & others, 1986).

Internal vs. External Control People with an internal locus of control—the perception that you control your own fate—are healthier, cope better with stress, and are less likely to be depressed, compared with people with an external locus of control, who attribute their fate to chance or other outside forces.

Good news for internals, but not for externals. If you are an external, is it possible to change your locus of control? Researchers today are working on that very question, which we'll explore in our next section.

Learned Helplessness and Learned Optimism

Researcher Ellen Langer (1983) once said, "Perceived control is basic to human functioning." Indeed, depressed people often feel a lack of control (Seligman, 1975, 1991). People or animals who experience no control over repeated bad events tend to develop **learned helplessness.** In a landmark study, **Martin Seligman** (1975) demonstrated the development of learned helplessness in dogs that had no control over such events. The researchers placed one group of dogs in individual cages divided by a low barrier. These dogs received an electric shock, but they could jump over the barrier to the other side of the cage to escape the shock. A second group of dogs, in similar cages, received the same shocks, but they were restrained in harnesses that prevented escape. After several trials in which shocks were administered but escape was impossible, the researchers removed the harnesses. Sadly, the dogs in this second group did not even attempt to escape from the shocks, even though they could now easily jump over the barrier to the other side of the cage. Instead, most cowered on the cage floor. The dogs had developed a sense that they had no control over their environment. They had learned helplessness (Figure 26.5, page 510).

People learn helplessness, too. Depression and hopelessness emerge in people who face traumatic events over which they have no control. However, several studies show that morale and health can be boosted by giving people control where they had none before, such as control of the TV in a prison, or control over the arrangement of personal belongings in a nursing home (Rodin, 1986; Ruback & others, 1986). And according to one study (Inglehart, 1990), those living in a stable democracy,

▶ **learned helplessness** The hopelessness and passive resignation an animal or human learns when unable to avoid repeated bad events.

▶ **Martin Seligman** (1942–) American psychologist who researched helplessness early in his career before turning his interests to optimism. He has been the primary proponent of positive psychology.

F • Y • I

Martin Seligman's research with the depressed dogs led to his revolutionary identification of *learned helplessness.* But his move to research in optimism also had its beginnings in the study of these depressed dogs. Most dogs developed learned helplessness when they were placed in a situation over which they had no control. But some of the dogs in the uncontrollable situation would not lie down and give up. They would continually try to escape the situation even though their efforts were unsuccessful. This observation led Seligman to want to understand why the dogs behaved this way and whether such inextinguishable optimism could be learned.

Have students apply what they learned about Seligman's experience with depressed dogs to Figure 26.5.

trb **tr** A black-line master for Figure 26.5, Learned Helplessness, is available in the **Black-Line Masters Appendix** of the *Teacher's Resource Binder.*

trb At this point, you may wish to use **Analysis Activity:** *Measuring Optimism* (*Teacher's Resource Binder,* p. 26-1; **Handouts 26–16** and **26–17**).

■ APPLYING THE POINTS

Contact local human resource officers and inquire about how they boost morale in their organizations. Students may use the following questions to guide their inquiries and to discuss their findings in class:

- Do these professionals offer employees opportunities to give suggestions that might increase productivity or better the work environment? What type of program is offered to get feedback from employees?
- Are lower-level employees asked for feedback on management's performance? Why or why not?
- Does the organization offer flex time or telecommuting opportunities? Why or why not? Has the organization developed a mission statement and/or strategic plan? Were all types of employees involved in the process of development?

MODULE 26

■ TEACHING TIP

Link discussion of *explanatory style* with Module 14's discussion of *promoting well-ness.* The positive health effects of optimistic thinking are discussed in detail in that module.

trb At this point, you may wish to use **Analysis Activity:** *Measuring Optimism* (*Teacher's Resource Binder*, p. 26-1; **Hand-outs 26–16** and **26–17**).

F•Y•I

Explanatory style, or the way we explain events in our lives, falls into three categories:

- **Permanence** is the belief that life events will have a permanent effect on us. Optimists believe that the effects of bad events are temporary and the effects of good events are permanent. Pessimists believe the opposite—the effects of bad events are permanent and the effects of good events are transient.
- **Pervasiveness** is the belief that life events have ripple effects on other areas of life. Optimists believe that good experiences will spill over into other areas, while bad events are isolated to a particular circumstance. Pessimists believe that bad events will affect other areas, expecting failure in one area to cause problems in others.
- **Personal** is the belief that life events are due to some personality trait that is unchangeable. Optimists believe that good events are personal, while bad events are due to circumstances. Pessimists believe that good events are circumstantial and bad events are due to personal faults.

trb At this point, you may wish to use **Analysis Activity:** *Measuring Optimism* (*Teacher's Resource Binder*, p. 26-1; **Hand-outs 26–16** and **26–17**).

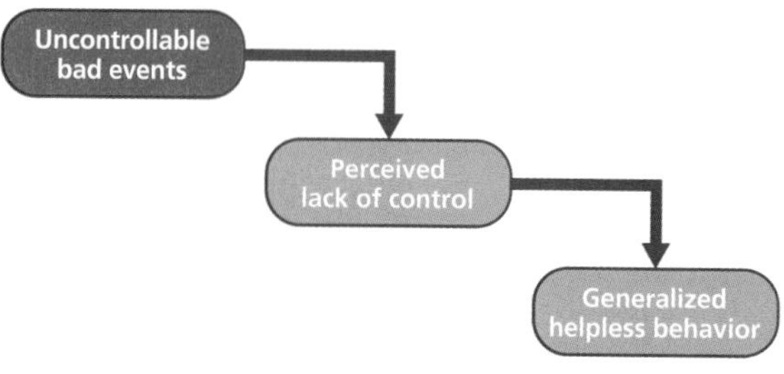

Figure 26.5 Learned Helplessness People and animals are likely to learn helplessness when they repeatedly experience bad events over which they have no control.

where empowerment and personal freedom are more likely, report higher levels of happiness.

After demonstrating learned helplessness, Seligman wondered if optimism could also be learned. His interests led him to found the **positive psychology** movement. Positive psychology studies how we can function most effectively and what factors enable individuals or communities to thrive. Could an optimistic attitude be one of those factors? Let's see what Seligman and others have discovered.

Each of us has, to some degree, an optimistic or pessimistic *explanatory style.* If you have an optimistic style and something goes wrong, you are more likely to explain the problem as (1) temporary, (2) not your fault, and (3) something that will not spread beyond present circumstances. In contrast, those with a pessimistic explanatory style tend to blame themselves, catastrophize the event, and see the problem as something beyond their control. Researchers have found a link between pessimistic style and an external locus of control. Pessimists also are more likely than optimists to get bad grades, experience depression, and have a shorter life span due to poorer health (Seligman, 1991, 1994).

Fortunately for some of us, Seligman has found that pessimists can work to overcome this deficit in their outlook. One successful method is *disputing* pessimistic thoughts (Fineburg, 2000). Arguing with yourself about pessimistic beliefs can turn dejection into optimism. Negative thoughts are often unfounded. Coming to terms with this can help us distance ourselves from pessimism's destructiveness. We also need to check for evidence that disproves pessimistic beliefs and consider alternative explanations for bad events. Finally, it's important not to generalize too much from a bad situation. After a bad test score, don't think, "I'm a stupid idiot and I'll never do well." Instead, think, "I didn't do well on this particular test because I didn't study hard enough." Note the alternative explanation provided in the second answer, which gives the test-taker a more hopeful approach. (Study harder and do better next time.)

Martin Seligman Martin Seligman leads the positive psychology movement, which focuses on how we can function at optimal levels and on the factors that help us to reach those levels.

There are advantages to adjusting your thinking from pessimistic to optimistic, but can you have too much optimism? Yes. One researcher notes, "an unrealistic optimism about future life events" is a common bias among optimistic thinkers (Weinstein, 1980, 1982, 1996). Optimism in its worst form may lead to a false sense of invincibility. For instance, optimistic, sexually active college women who do not use contraception actually believe they are less likely to get pregnant than their pessimistic counterparts (Burger & Burns, 1988). And perhaps too

Enriching

Have students work in small groups to come up with some pessimistic explanations for failing a test. Then have them apply the following methods to counter these thoughts:

- With **alternative seeking**, students should come up with alternative explanations that are more optimistic.
- With **evidence seeking**, students should cite evidence that disputes negative thoughts, such as "I am stupid."
- With **decatastrophizing**, students should come up with reasons why this particular test grade is not the end of the world.

much optimism is a factor for those who enter into and maintain ill-fated relationships, even though they are well aware of the United States' 50 percent divorce rate. Aristotle's observation—"Nothing in excess"—applies to optimism as well as to pessimism.

▶ **positive psychology** A movement in psychology that focuses on the study of optimal human functioning and the factors that allow individuals and communities to thrive.

Assessing Behavior in Situations

8. How do psychologists assess the effect of particular situations on our behavior?

Social-cognitive theorists believe there are better ways to assess a person's personality than the trait theorist's multiple-choice personality inventory (Mischel, 1981). They prefer experiments that study how differing situations affect people's attitudes and behavior. Do you want to know whether children will be more aggressive with their peers after observing videotaped boxing? Or whether children would help one another more after watching a *Mr. Rogers' Neighborhood* program on helpfulness? Social-cognitive psychologists say that the way to know such things is to run an experiment: Vary the situation and look for personality consistencies.

In another kind of assessment, social-cognitive psychologists look at a person's past behavior patterns to predict the person's future behavior (Ouellette & Wood, 1998; Schmidt & Hunter, 1998). If the person and the situation remain the same, the best predictor of future behaviors is previous actions. The classmate most likely to drink beer at a party is the classmate who drank beer at the last party. The teacher most likely to turn back papers the day after picking them up is the teacher who handed them back within one day on the last set of papers. Schools that train teachers know that student teaching is a way of putting prospective teachers in real teaching situations to gather data for predicting how they will perform in the future. Similarly, if you live in a city of 50,000 or more people, your city probably has an assessment center for evaluating fire fighters and police officers (Lowry, 1997). An assessment *simulating* actual conditions—whether of teaching, policing, or some other set of behaviors—is second only to assessing behavior under the demands of the real task.

Evaluating the Social-Cognitive Perspective

9. What are the drawbacks of the social-cognitive perspective?

The social-cognitive approach draws upon cognition and learning research for its conclusions (Mischel, 1993). Its objective, scientific approach to understanding personality makes it an attractive perspective.

■ APPLYING THE POINTS

In order for students to assess their optimism in regards to their expectations of favorable future outcomes, have them identify a career that they would be interested in pursuing. Have them contact local colleges or universities, career-technical colleges or training centers, or academies to find out what type of internship programs are required for completion of a degree or certification in that field.

- Are internships or apprenticeships required? Why or why not?
- How many credit hours are needed to complete the program?
- What skills or knowledge must the trainee demonstrate to complete the internship?
- What is the success rate of people completing the internship? What is the failure rate?

Have students write a paper that responds to the above questions and assesses their optimism toward this possible career.

trb At this point, you may wish to use Application Activity: *The Life-Orientation Test and Optimism* (*Teacher's Resource Binder*, p. 26-1; Handout 26–15).

MODULE 26

Close

The two theories of personality presented in this module try to be more scientific than intuitive. Using the following questions, challenge students to evaluate the scientific practices of the trait and social-cognitive perspectives:

- Is the use of objective tests or real-life simulations better scientific practice? Why?
- What are the limitations of each type of scientific practice in explaining human behavior?
- How can a union of the two perspectives lead to a greater understanding of human behavior?

Checking the Points

■ **TEACHING TIPS**

web (1) The book companion site for *Thinking About Psychology* at www.worthpublishers.com/thinkingaboutpsych contains a module quiz, flashcards of key terms and people, as well as other student activities and resources for this module. You will also find PowerPoint lectures, a quiz grade book, and other teaching resources by logging on as an instructor.

trb (2) At this point, you may wish to review and confirm module concepts with **Critical Thinking Activity:** *Fact or Falsehood?* (*Teacher's Resource Binder*, p. 26-1; **Handout 26–1**). If students filled in the handout earlier, ask them to set it aside. Suggest that students complete the handout in small groups, taking the time to look up information in the text to respond correctly to questions. Have all the groups meet to review the handout together, again asking students to use the text to support their responses.

It has also sensitized researchers to the importance of considering the situation in the assessment of personality.

But wait a minute. Are we merely a product of what we learn? Are we stimulus-response creatures who act a certain way, based on the rewards and punishments we receive? Even if situations do guide our behavior, what role does *emotion* play? What impact do our unseen motives, such as revenge or greed, have on our behavior? Further, are there enduring traits, such as shyness or openness, which get lost in social-cognitive explanations of behavior?

While the experts continue to seek answers to personality's questions, one fact appears indisputable: We can view personality from several perspectives, and each perspective fills in a piece of the puzzle that is personality. The trait and social-cognitive perspectives on personality have strengths and weaknesses, but each helps us understand human behavior. Like so many other parts of psychology—and human life—personality is best understood if we view it from several directions.

REVIEW

Module 26: Trait and Social-Cognitive Perspectives on Personality

What's the Point?

Psychologists who study personality—an individual's characteristic pattern of thinking, feeling, and acting—do so from a number of viewpoints. Two of these are the trait perspective, which considers our enduring patterns of behavior, and the social-cognitive perspective, which considers the effects of the particular situation, our past learning, and our ways of thinking.

The Trait Perspective

1. *How does the study of traits help us understand personality?*

   Identifying a person's characteristic and enduring patterns of behavior can help us to describe people. Such descriptions can lead to classifications based on types of behavior.

2. *How do psychologists identify traits?*

   Typing people by their behavior can lead to oversimplified classification systems. Three researchers—Gordon Allport, Raymond Cattell, and Hans Eysenck—are known for their attempts to develop more useful classification systems. Allport, one of the first psychologists to identify several different kinds of traits, emphasized individual uniqueness, which made it difficult to apply personality types to large numbers of people. Cattell, interested in knowing whether some traits predicted others, used statistical analysis to arrive at 16 traits, or core personality factors, which he believed would yield reliable assessments of personality. Eysenck, who searched for biological bases for personality dimensions, attempted to demonstrate universal trait dimensions. Two of his most famous findings relate to the extravert-introvert dimension and the emotional stability-instability dimension.

3. *What are the "Big Five" traits?*

   Current research in personality psychology generally supports the idea that we can adequately describe personality by locating people on five dimensions: openness, extraversion, agreeableness, emotional stability, and conscientiousness. They also believe that people are genetically predisposed—born with a tendency—to have certain personality traits, but the actual presence or absence of these traits will depend on influences in our environment that encourage or discourage their development.

4. *How do psychologists assess a person's enduring traits? What do we mean when we say an assessment technique is "reliable" or "valid"?*

   Social-cognitive psychologists use objective tests—such as the Minnesota Multiphasic Personality Inventory (MMPI)—to assess traits. Objective tests do not depend on personal interpretations; the questions have been standardized—tested on particular groups of people who provide a standard for scoring answers—so the results should be the same no matter who scores the test or where the scoring takes place. The term *reliable* means that a test yields consistent results, no matter who gives it or where or when it is given. The term *valid* means that a test is indeed measuring what it is meant to test. A reliable test may give consistent results but not measure what it is meant to measure.

5. *What are some drawbacks of the trait perspective?*

   Critics have pointed out that the trait perspective does not consider the influence of different situations on behavior. Critics also note that trait theories do not explain *why* we behave as we do; they merely label our behaviors. And, finally, trait theories do not consider the way our thoughts influence our behaviors.

The Social-Cognitive Perspective

6. *What factors do social-cognitive psychologists believe interact to form our personalities?*

   Psychologists who view personality from the social-cognitive perspective believe that we cannot understand personality unless we consider the influence of situations and our own thoughts on our behavior. Albert Bandura, a leading theorist in this tradition, called the interaction among thoughts, environment, and behavior *reciprocal determinism.* He believed this interaction shapes personality.

7. *How do our feelings of personal control affect our behavior, and can we learn to be helpless or optimistic?*

   People with an external locus of control feel that forces outside themselves control their destiny. People with an internal locus of control believe they control their own fate. Studies indicate that perceptions of control (or lack of control) are very important. People or animals who repeatedly experience bad events and have no control over them will stop trying to control their environments—a state known as learned helplessness. Other studies indicate that conditions that foster control can boost morale and mood. The positive psychology movement conducts research on the ingredients that help people to function effectively and that foster well-being. One outcome of this research has been increases in our understanding of optimistic and pessimistic explanatory styles, which tend to bias our views of the world around us. One interesting discovery is that we apparently can learn optimism, through learning techniques such as disputing (arguing with) our pessimistic thoughts.

MODULE 26

trb ■ TEACHING TIP

At this point, you may wish to provide students with the handout from **Building Vocabulary:** *Matching Terms and Definitions* (*Teacher's Resource Binder*, p. 26-1; **Handout 26–2**). As a tool for reviewing the concepts in the module, students may work individually to fill out the answers in the handout. If they filled out this handout earlier in the module, have them set that copy aside and fill out the fresh copy to challenge their understanding of module vocabulary. Afterward, students may meet in small groups to receive help with any concepts or terms that confused them and to check for correct matches.

tb Using the Test Bank

The *Test Bank* that accompanies this textbook offers a wide variety of questions in different formats and levels of complexity. Use the software to construct whole tests or to integrate standardized questions into teacher-made tests.

Self-Test Answers

Multiple-Choice Questions

1. c, 2. b

8. *How do psychologists assess the effect of particular situations on our behavior?*

   Psychologists studying personality from a social-psychological perspective believe that the best way to assess personality is to conduct experiments to study how differing situations affect people's attitudes and behavior. When experiments are not appropriate, these psychologists may examine people's past behavior to predict their future behavior. Assessments simulating actual conditions can also yield insights into how a person would behave in real situations.

9. *What are the drawbacks of the social-cognitive perspective?*

   Critics of the social-cognitive perspective point out that it fails to consider the influence of emotion and motivation on behavior. They also note that this perspective can overlook enduring traits, such as shyness and openness, that may affect personality.

Key Terms

trait, p. 499
personality, p. 499
social cognitive perspective, p. 499
personality inventories, p. 503
validity, p. 503
reliability, p. 503
Minnesota Multiphasic Personality Inventory (MMPI), p. 504
reciprocal determinism, p. 507
external locus of control, p. 508
internal locus of control, p. 508
learned helplessness, p. 509
positive psychology, p. 510

Key People

Gordon Allport, p. 500
Raymond Cattell, p. 500
Hans Eysenck, p. 500
Albert Bandura, p. 505
Martin Seligman, p. 509

Self-Test

Multiple-Choice Questions

Choose the *best* answer for each of the following questions.

1. Nancy has opened an astrology business, and she's dedicated to the idea that her astrology techniques will be trustworthy and will predict people's future. To that end, she has designed a questionnaire with multiple-choice questions that she has her clients answer. Nancy provides a handout with the answers and the meaning of the scores, so that any of her helpers can score the test, at any time, in any place. Nancy's test is
   a. both reliable and valid.
   b. neither reliable nor valid.
   c. reliable, but not valid.
   d. valid, but not reliable.

2. Jerry was thrilled to be called back for a second interview at a job he really wants. After three levels of bosses interviewed him, the personnel director asked Jerry to take a test. The test was very long, and it asked many true-false and agree-disagree questions about Jerry's personal feelings and thoughts. Some of the questions seemed to ask the same thing, but with different wordings. The test was probably
   a. a projective test.
   b. the Minnesota Multiphasic Personality Inventory.
   c. the California Standardized Employment Inventory.
   d. a simulation meant to predict and assess Jerry's behavior on the job he's applying for.

3. Mrs. Hsu is training to be an emergency medical technician. She will be graded on her participation in a mock rescue, in which her team will respond to an imaginary explosion in a downtown building. The mock rescue is a form of assessment that social-cognitive psychologists recommend, and is
   a. a simulation meant to predict Mrs. Hsu's behavior as an EMT in a real emergency.
   b. one variation of the Minnesota Multiphasic Personality Inventory.
   c. a projective test.
   d. the California Standardized Employment Inventory.

4. Abby is not very attractive, and she is extremely overweight. She hates going to school because the other children make fun of her and play practical jokes on her. Abby has learned that nothing she does gives her any control over how the other children treat her. Today, when a new girl in school approached Abby and invited her to have lunch, Abby just stared at her shoes and looked as though she was going to cry. Abby is showing signs of
   a. learned helplessness.
   b. reciprocal determinism.
   c. an internal locus of control.
   d. a sanguine personality.

5. Ahman and Darlene just got their grades on their psychology midterm. Each of them received a C plus on the test. Ahman said that the teacher had graded him down on the essay question for no good reason, the lighting was poor in the room where he took the test, and his chances of getting into college were now ruined. Darlene said that she was disappointed with her grade, but she really had not studied enough for the midterm and she would do better on the final exam. Ahman seems to have a (n) _______ explanatory style and an _______ locus of control. Darlene seems to have a (n) _______ explanatory style and an _______ locus of control.
   a. pessimistic; internal; optimistic; external
   b. pessimistic; external; optimistic; internal
   c. optimistic; internal; pessimistic; external
   d. optimistic; external; pessimistic; internal

Matching Terms and Definitions

6. For each definition, choose the *best* matching term from the list that follows:

Definition

a. A technique for eliminating pessimistic thoughts.
b. A test's ability to give the same results no matter who scores the test, where the test is given, or when it is given.
c. A test's ability to measure what it is meant to measure.
d. Openness, extraversion, agreeableness, emotional stability, and conscientiousness.
e. A movement within psychology that focuses on the study of optimal human functioning and the factors that allow individuals and communities to thrive.
f. A personality assessment that a trait perspective psychologist might use.
g. Outgoing and sociable people.
h. A characteristic pattern of behavior.
i. Quiet people who keep to themselves.

Term

(1) the Big Five
(2) trait
(3) personality inventories
(4) validity
(5) reliability
(6) decatastrophizing
(7) projective test
(8) learned helplessness
(9) positive psychology
(10) reciprocal determinism
(11) extraverts
(12) introverts

MODULE 26

Self-Test Answers

Multiple-Choice Questions (continued)

3. a, 4. a, 5. b

Matching Terms and Definitions

6. a. (6), b. (5), c. (4), d. (1), e. (9), f. (3), g. (11), h. (2), i. (12)

Fill-in-the-Blank Questions

7. ________________ ________________ developed the social-cognitive perspective, stressing that we must consider the ways that our behaviors, our environment, and our thoughts interact to shape personality.

8. ________________ ________________ was interested in the genetically influenced dimensions of personality, including extraversion and introversion.

9. ________________ ________________ proposed 16 key dimensions, or factors, to describe personality, and his goal was to discover whether some traits predicted others.

10. ________________ ________________ was an early trait theorist who firmly believed that individual personalities are unique.

Brief Essay Question

11. Imagine that your friend has been asked to take a personality test as a part of the application procedure for an important job, but she knows nothing about personality or its assessment and is somewhat apprehensive. In three paragraphs, use what you have just learned to explain what personality is, and how your friend's personality might be studied from the perspectives of two different types of personality psychologists—trait researchers and social-cognitive psychologists.

MODULE 26

Self-Test Answers

Fill-in-the-Blank Questions

7. Albert Bandura, 8. Hans Eysenck, 9. Raymond Cattell, 10. Gordon Allport

Brief Essay Question

11. Your friend will need to know the definition of personality, the two perspectives outlined in this module, and the study of personality scientifically through objective tests and simulations. Trait theories would ask your friend a series of questions, likely taken from several reliable and valid measures of personality, like the MMPI-2; social-cognitive theorists would place your friend in different circumstances to see how he or she would behave.

CHAPTER 12

Psychological Disorders

Clinical and Sociocultural Domain

Teaching with the Standards

Standard Area: Psychological Disorders

Breakdown of Module 27: Introduction to Psychological Disorders

Content Standard 1: Origins and characteristics of psychological disorders Module 27 investigates the criteria that psychologists use to diagnose psychological disorders. The discussion begins by considering four case studies. Each case is discussed in the context of generally accepted criteria for abnormal behavior. The author introduces students to the DSM-IV-TR and its use in classifying disorders. Also, the author discusses the medical and bio-psycho-social perspectives to help students understand the different views psychologists use to understand psychological disorders. The effect of culture on judging abnormality and the effects of labels are also considered. (Student Text pp. 518–525)

Content Standard 3: Major categories of psychological disorders The challenges associated with making an accurate diagnosis are considered. The author examines how the definitions of abnormal behavior differ across cultures and over time. In addition, the author discusses how a medical or bio-psycho-social perspective can influence diagnosis and the treatment of a specific disorder. (Student Text pp. 519–523)

Content Standard 4: Understanding the impact of psychological disorders Module 27 examines how sociocultural and hereditary factors influence the risk of developing a psychological disorder. In addition, the author discusses the stigma associated with a diagnosis of mental illness and considers whether our society has become more accepting of those with specific mental illnesses. (Student Text pp. 525–527)

Breakdown of Module 28: Anxiety and Mood Disorders

Content Standard 3: Major categories of psychological disorders Module 28 covers two of the most common categories of psychological disorders: anxiety and mood disorders. The author identifies symptoms and possible causes of each of the following disorders: generalized anxiety disorder, panic disorder, phobias, obsessive-compulsive disorder, posttraumatic stress disorder, major depressive disorder, and bipolar disorder. In addition, the author discusses the tragedy of suicide. (Student Text pp. 533–549)

Breakdown of Module 29: Dissociative, Schizophrenia, and Personality Disorders

Content Standard 3: Major categories of psychological disorders Module 29 identifies the symptoms and possible causes of dissociative, schizophrenia, and personality disorders. The author also examines the connection between the mind and body in discussing somatoform disorders. (Student Text pp. 554–567)

Scope and Sequence

	Objectives	Text Reference	Standards Covered
Lesson 1	Define disorder. Compare the medical and bio-psycho-social models. Present the DSM-IV-TR. Discuss the pros and cons of labeling.	Module 27, pp. 518–528	Standard Area: Psychological Disorders, Content Standard 1, Performance Standards 1.1, 1.2, 1.3, 1.4, Content Standard 3, Performance Standard 3.2, Content Standard 4, Performance Standard 4.2
Lesson 2	Discuss the symptoms, causes, and treatment of the anxiety disorders.	Module 28, pp. 533–542	Content Standard 3, Performance Standard 3.1
Lesson 3	Discuss the symptoms, causes, and treatment of the mood disorders. Discuss suicide.	Module 28, pp. 542–549	Content Standard 3, Performance Standard 3.1
Lesson 4	Discuss the symptoms, causes, and treatment of dissociative and personality disorders.	Module 29, pp. 555–557, 565–567	Content Standard 3, Performance Standard 3.1
Lesson 5	Discuss the symptoms, types, causes, and treatment of schizophrenia.	Module 29, pp. 560–567	Content Standard 3, Performance Standard 3.1
Lesson 6	Review and test.		

Psychological Disorders

Perhaps you've been surprised at some of the topics you've studied so far in your psychology course—many people don't realize how broad the science of mind and behavior is. This chapter, though, covers a topic you almost certainly expected to find in this class. There are many types of psychological disorders, just as there are many types of physical disorders. Some, such as depression, are relatively common; others, such as multiple personality disorder, are rare and controversial. Many involve common symptoms, such as anxiety, that you can probably relate to personally. But others have symptoms you are not likely to have experienced, such as the bizarre hallucinations that sometimes accompany schizophrenia.

Psychologists and other therapists group disorders into broad, related categories. In the next modules we will explore general issues related to psychological disorders and then turn our attention to some of their major categories. If you or someone you know has struggled with one of these disorders, you know that they can be devastating and frightening. Psychological science is gradually shedding welcome light on the nature of these problems, and this light is showing us the path to more effective treatments. As we learn more, we are better able to address these disturbances of the human condition and to understand the suffering of the victims, their families, and their friends.

CHAPTER 12

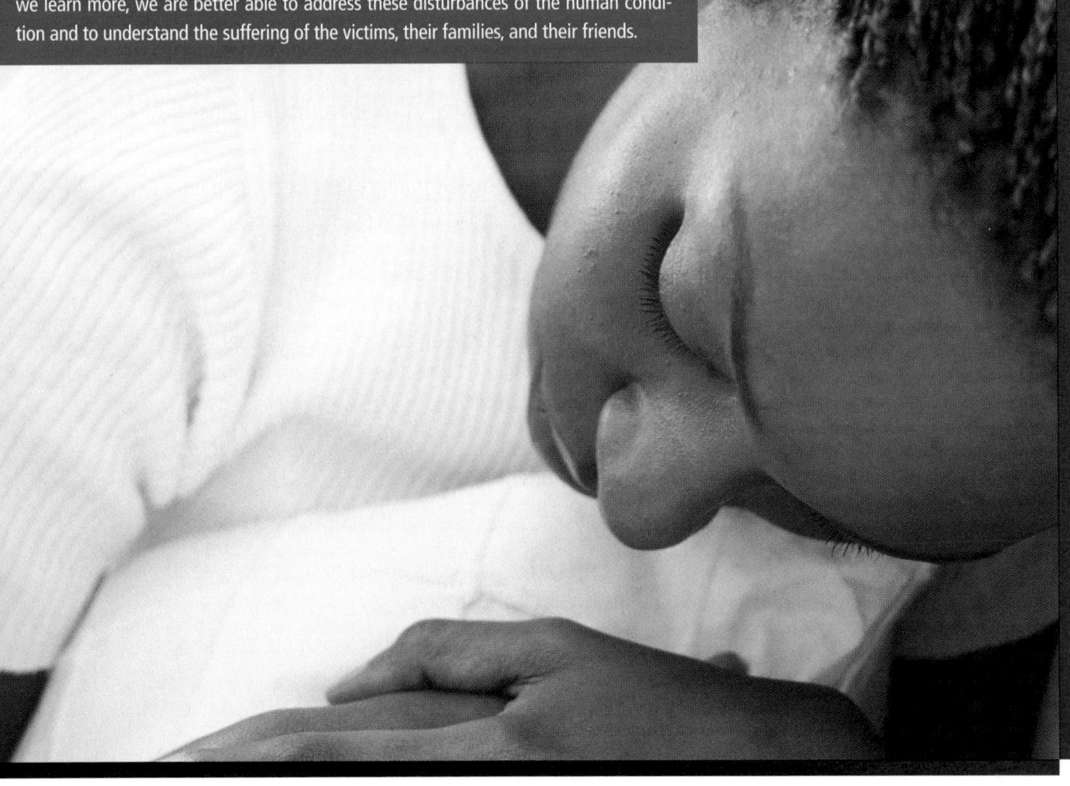

CHAPTER 12

Psychological Disorders

Introducing the Chapter

The Points: Chapter Objectives

- Identify the criteria psychologists use to diagnose psychological disorders.
- Differentiate among the different perspectives psychologists take to understand psychological disorders, and analyze why some object to the medical model.
- Evaluate the drawbacks and advantages of labeling psychological disorders.
- Describe the characteristics of generalized anxiety disorder and panic disorder.
- Identify the characteristics of phobic disorder.
- Delineate the characteristics of obsessive-compulsive disorder.
- Describe the characteristics of post-traumatic stress disorder.
- Analyze what factors contribute to the development of anxiety disorders.
- Describe the characteristics of major depressive disorder.
- Identify the characteristics of bipolar disorder.
- Analyze the factors that may contribute to development of mood disorders.
- Differentiate dissociative amnesia from other forms of amnesia.
- Differentiate dissociative fugue from dissociative amnesia.
- Evaluate why dissociative identity disorder is a controversial diagnosis.
- Explain schizophrenia and identify its major symptoms.
- Describe the four types of schizophrenia, pointing out the main characteristics of each.
- Synthesize the different biological and psychological factors that could interact to produce schizophrenia.
- Differentiate among the three major clusters of personality disorders.

MODULE 27

Performance Standards

Standard Area: Psychological Disorders

Content Standard 1: Origins and characteristics of psychological disorders

Performance Standard 1.1 Investigate the characteristics of abnormal behavior.

- Discuss the criteria psychologists use to diagnose psychological disorders. Define abnormal behavior as behaviors that are maladaptive, unjustifiable, disturbing, and atypical. (Student Text pp. 518–519)
- Discuss how a definition of abnormal behavior is affected by culture and time period. (Student Text pp. 518–521)

Performance Standard 1.2 Examine examples of abnormal behavior.

- Consider four case studies and decide if they show evidence of a psychological disorder. (Student Text pp. 518–520)

Performance Standard 1.3 Discuss how judgments of abnormality are affected by context.

- Discuss the effect of context on judging abnormal behavior. (Student Text pp. 518–520)
- Explore how social and cultural beliefs can affect the behaviors and beliefs characterizing disorders. (Student Text pp. 521–523)

Performance Standard 1.4 Compare the major perspectives for understanding psychological disorders.

- Describe the medical model for understanding psychological disorders. (Student Text pp. 521–522)
- Examine the bio-psycho-social perspective for understanding psychological disorders. (Student Text pp. 522–523)
- Discuss how the DSM-IV-TR is used by mental health professionals to classify mental disorders. (Student Text pp. 524–525)
- Consider the positive and negative impact of diagnostic labels. (Student Text pp. 525–527)

Content Standard 3: Major categories of psychological disorders

Performance Standard 3.2 Discuss the problems with making an accurate diagnosis.

- Examine how definitions of abnormality change across cultures and over time. (Student Text pp. 518–528)

Content Standard 4: Understanding the impact of psychological disorders

Performance Standard 4.1 Discuss variables that influence vulnerability to mental illness.

- Discuss how heredity and sociocultural factors influence vulnerability to abnormal behavior. (Student Text pp. 521–523)

Performance Standard 4.2 Investigate the stigma associated with mental illness.

- Explore the case of Thomas Eagleton as the vice-presidential candidate in 1972 when it was discovered he had been treated for "nervous exhaustion." (Student Text p. 525)
- Discuss research that shows bias toward those labeled with a psychological disorder. (Student Text pp. 526–528)
- Examine Rosenhaun's study on labeling. (Student Text pp. 526–527)

Performance Standard 4.3 Discuss efforts to promote greater understanding of psychological disorders.

- Consider whether American culture has become more accepting of psychological disorders. (Student Text p. 527)

Materials NETWORK

All of the items from the Video, Activity, and Enrichment Centers listed below come from the *Teacher's Resource Binder*. These items will help you teach and expand on concepts presented in Module 27.

trb This logo indicates when an item from the Materials Network may be used in conjunction with a specific note found in this module's *Teacher's Edition*.

Defining *Disorder*

Activity Center

- Critical Thinking Activity: *Fact or Falsehood?* With this activity, students' preconceptions about abnormal psychology are either exposed as incorrect or reinforced as correct. (*Teacher's Resource Binder*, p. 27-1; Handout 27–1)
- Building Vocabulary: Graphic Organizer: *Concept Web* Students can test their knowledge of terms in this module by completing the graphic organizer that gives students more exposure to concepts related to psychological disorders. (*Teacher's Resource Binder*, p. 27-1; Handout 27–2)
- Critical Thinking Activity: *Normality and the Sexes* Through the years, the qualities in men and women that define normality have differed. Have students see if their perceptions of male and female normality differ as well. (*Teacher's Resource Binder*, p. 27-1; Handout 27–3)

Enrichment Center

- Enrichment Lesson: *Defining Psychological Well-Being* This module delves into what it means to be abnormal. But, what qualities define someone as normal? Is happiness just the absence of illness? Explore these questions with this lesson on defining psychological well-being. (*Teacher's Resource Binder*, p. 27-1)

Understanding Disorders

V Video Center

- Videocassette: *Scientific American Frontiers,* Second Edition, Segment 33: "Cop Psychiatrists" Consult the faculty guide from the *Scientific American Frontiers* video series for a description of this segment. (*Teacher's Resource Binder*, p. 27-1)

Activity Center

- Critical Thinking Activity: *Multiple Causations* What causes our behavior? Multiple events cause us to behave both abnormally and normally each day. This activity asks students to ponder how their own behavior could be interpreted if their sanity were questioned. (*Teacher's Resource Binder*, p. 27-1; Handout 27–4)

Enrichment Center

- Enrichment Lesson: *Tourette Syndrome* The bio-psycho-social perspective of psychological illness is captured in a discussion of Tourette Syndrome, a disorder with biological causes as well as psychological and social effects. (*Teacher's Resource Binder*, p. 27-1)
- Enrichment Lesson: *Culture-Bound Disorders* Disorders common in the Western world aren't necessarily common elsewhere—and some disorders that exist elsewhere don't exist in the Western world. Explore some unique disorders with this lesson. (*Teacher's Resource Binder*, p. 27-1)

Classifying Disorders

Activity Center

- Technology Application Activity: *PsychSim:* "Mystery Client" *PsychSim* is an interactive CD-ROM containing tutorials in different content areas of psychology. In this tutorial, students determine what psychological disorder a mystery client has. (*Teacher's Resource Binder*, p. 27-1)

Labeling Disorders

Activity Center

- Analysis Activity: *The Effects of Labeling* Nobel prize-winning scientist Daniel Kahneman and his colleague Amos Tversky propose this activity that exposes students to the detrimental effects of labeling. (*Teacher's Resource Binder*, p. 27-1; Handout 27–5)

Enrichment Center

- Enrichment Lesson: *The Commonality of Psychological Disorders* Psychological disorders are very common, more common than people believe. This lesson highlights the most common psychological disorders—depression, alcohol dependence, and phobias. (*Teacher's Resource Binder*, p. 27-1)

MODULE 27

Introduction to Psychological Disorders

Introducing the Module

The Points: Module Objectives

- Identify the criteria psychologists use to diagnose psychological disorders.
- Differentiate among the perspectives psychologists take in their attempt to understand psychological disorders, and analyze why some psychologists object to the medical model of psychological disorders.
- Identify the DSM-IV-TR.
- Evaluate the drawbacks and advantages in labeling psychological disorders.

trb Building Vocabulary

Students can reinforce their knowledge of the psychological disorders by completing the **Building Vocabulary: Graphic Organizer:** *Concept Web* (*Teacher's Resource Binder*, p. 27-1; **Handout 27–2**). Compared with other modules, the number of terms related to psychological disorders is small. Working individually, students can learn the terms and better understand the relationship among them as they fill in the concept web.

■ TEACHING TIP

Have students brainstorm about behaviors that, when taken out of context, would be considered abnormal. Some ideas to get them started might include the following:

- having a heated argument with someone
- praying aloud or chanting outside of a religious service
- dancing in excitement over getting a good grade or hearing good news

V At this point, you may wish to show **Videocassette:** *Scientific American Frontiers*, **Second Edition, Segment 33: "Cop Psychiatrists"** (*Teacher's Resource Binder*, p. 27-1).

MODULE 27

Introduction to Psychological Disorders

Defining *Disorder*

Understanding Disorders

Classifying Disorders

Labeling Disorders

Observing people's strange-seeming behaviors, we may wonder what is going on inside their heads. Consider the following behaviors, and then decide whether you think they are evidence of a psychological disorder:

1. A man walks up to a window carrying a chair. He puts down the chair, opens the window, takes off his clothes, and seats himself on the chair. Why? He says he feels the need for an "air bath."
2. Every morning, a woman who lives in a Boston suburb asks her husband to bring in the morning newspaper, which the carrier throws just inside their fence. She does this because she is terribly afraid of encountering a poisonous snake. Her husband, concerned about her behavior, repeatedly tells her that there are no poisonous snakes living in their town. Nevertheless, she is afraid to leave the house.
3. A teenaged boy packs a blanket and a bottle of water. Ignoring near-freezing temperatures, he climbs a nearby mountain, spreads the blanket on the ground, sits cross-legged on it, closes his eyes, and remains there throughout the night. In the morning, he runs home and tells his father he has seen a vision.
4. A teenaged girl misses school for three days. She periodically breaks into tears. She finds it nearly impossible to get out of bed in the morning, though she cannot sleep for more than an hour or two at a time. She has no appetite and becomes nauseated if her family urges her to eat.

Most people would say these behaviors are out of the ordinary—perhaps even puzzling or disturbing. But are they so abnormal that we can attribute them to a psychological disorder? Before attempting to answer that question, we must first decide what *psychological disorder* means. Let's see how psychologists define this term.

Getting Started

Before students read this module, have them form small groups of four or five and come up with a definition for *psychological disorder*. Instruct them to be specific, identifying the criteria they would apply in drawing the line between normality and abnormality. After they have finished, ask each group to report its definition to the class.

The rest of this introductory session can be spent in considering the difficulty of satisfactorily defining the term. Present the four criteria identified on page 519–520 of the text. Behavior is considered disordered when it is atypical, disturbing, maladaptive, and unjustifiable.

trb You may wish to use **Critical Thinking Activity:** *Fact or Falsehood?* (*Teacher's Resource Binder*, p. 27-1; **Handout 27–1**) as a prereading strategy to evaluate what students already know about psychological disorders. This activity will prime students to look out for information that could prove or disprove their preconceptions about disorders.

Defining *Disorder*

1. What criteria do psychologists use to diagnose psychological disorders?

Psychologists define a **psychological disorder** as a *harmful dysfunction* in which behaviors are maladaptive, unjustifiable, disturbing, and atypical (Spitzer, 1997, Wakefield, 1997). Let's consider each of these terms.

- *Maladaptive, or destructive to oneself or others.* The behavior of the woman whose fear of snakes prevented her from leaving her home meets this criterion. In some cases, fear of poisonous snakes is a wise and practical response: If bitten, you could die from their deadly venom. But the woman's extreme fear is destructive to her because it restricts her ability to lead a normal life. As you can see, maladaptive behaviors are sometimes—though not always—an exaggeration of normal, acceptable behavior. The behavior of the teenaged girl may also be maladaptive. She is showing some classic symptoms of depression—an inability to sleep, eat, or function normally. And what about the teenaged boy who sat on a blanket all night in near-freezing temperatures? This behavior seems self-destructive, too. Finally, what can we say about the man who sat naked to get an air bath? His behavior may seem strange, but he wasn't really doing anything that could be considered destructive to himself or others (no one else could see him naked), so we can't classify his behavior as maladaptive.
- *Unjustifiable—without a rational basis.* Here again, the woman with the extreme fear of snakes qualifies. It is not rational to refuse to leave your home to avoid a snakebite in an area that has no poisonous snakes. And the teenage girl with symptoms of depression? What if I tell you that her entire family died three days ago, when her home was destroyed by fire? Suddenly, her inability to sleep, eat, or function seems perfectly understandable: These behaviors have a rational basis. And the young man who sat on the blanket all night? What if I tell you that he was a young member of the Navajo nation, living in Arizona in 1920, and a vision quest was part of his religion? In this case, too, the behavior seems quite rational, at least to other members of his culture and to any of those who did understand what he was doing. But surely, you say, the man taking the air bath was performing an act with no rational base. Not so. That man was Benjamin Franklin, signer of the Constitution and one of our country's greatest philosophers and thinkers. His "air bath" was an accepted practice in his day, and, in that context, not an unjustifiable behavior.

▶ **psychological disorder** A "harmful dysfunction" in which behaviors are maladaptive, unjustifiable, disturbing, and atypical.

MODULE **27**

Teaching the Points

web ■ **TEACHING TIP**

You can log on as an instructor to the book companion site for *Thinking About Psychology* at **www.worthpublishers.com/thinkingaboutpsych**. It contains teacher resources for class presentations, as well as review and assessment of module concepts and terms.

■ **JOURNAL WRITING**

Invite students to use the following questions and writing prompts as springboards for entries in their psychology journals:

- Was there a time when your behavior or feelings caused a significant disruption to your normal life? Describe your experience. How did you handle these feelings?
- Do you have an irrational fear of something? What do you fear? Why do you fear it? How have you handled your fear in the past?

■ **MULTICULTURAL CONNECTIONS**

Some cultures have social practices that may be considered abnormal compared with most social practices in contemporary U. S. culture. Help students appreciate this diversity in terms of culture and historical eras.

- Hissing is a polite way to show respect for superiors in Japan.
- Public displays of affection between men and women in Thailand are unacceptable. Interestingly, however, men holding hands is considered a sign of friendship. Additionally, the use of straws is considered vulgar.
- Ancient cultures used *trephining*—a practice of cutting a hole in the skull to release evil spirits that caused migranes or epilepsy.

Suggested Readings

Use the following books as teacher-preparation tools or as enrichment for advanced students:

Balter, M., & Katz, R. (1987). *Nobody's child.* Reading, MA: Addison-Wesley.

Baur, S. (1991). *The dinosaur man: Tales of madness and enchantment from the back ward.* New York: HarperCollins.

Chesler, P. (1989). *Women and madness.* San Diego: Harcourt Brace Jovanovich. (Original work published 1972)

Johnson, A. B. (1990). *Out of Bedlam: The truth about deinstitutionalization.* New York: BasicBooks.

Comer, R. J. (2003). *Abnormal psychology* (5th ed.). New York: Freeman

Rothenberg, A. (1990). *Creativity and madness: New findings and old stereotypes.* Baltimore: Johns Hopkins University Press.

Szasz, T. S. (1994). *Cruel compassion: Psychiatric control of society's unwanted.* New York: Wiley.

MODULE 27

■ LOOKING AT THE ISSUES

(1) Respect for diversity, including norms practiced by cultures radically different from our own, sounds like a wonderful ideal; but how should we react when concepts clash with some of our own deeply held values, such as gender equality? Consider and discuss the following issues:

- Should the U.S. government be accepting of the genital mutilation of women that is common in African countries?
- Female U.S. military personnel in Saudi Arabia have fought against regulations that require them to wear a veil outside their bases. Should these personnel be forced to follow Saudi law or U.S. customs? Should we object to the law in Saudi Arabia that forbids women to drive?
- What are the limits to tolerance? Which types of cultural practices should we accept from other cultures? To which ones should we object? Why?

trb At this point, you may wish to use **Critical Thinking Activity:** *Normality and the Sexes* (*Teacher's Resource Binder*, p. 27-1; **Handout 27–3**).

(2) Have students consider that, statistically speaking, any behavior is atypical if it is not exhibited by 68 percent of the people in a particular group or culture. What common behaviors would be considered abnormal if we followed this definition of *abnormality*? Who would suffer discrimination if this standard were enforced? Guide a class discussion further with the following questions:

- What religious practices or ethnic groups would be considered abnormal for your community?
- What ways of life would be abnormal—homosexuality, single-parent households, or two-parent households?
- What styles of dress would be considered abnormal? What music preferences? What post–high school choices?

trb At this point, you may wish to use **Enrichment Lesson:** *Defining Psychological Well-Being* (*Teacher's Resource Binder*, p. 27-1).

- *Disturbing—troublesome to other people.* This criterion is fairly easy to score for all four individuals. The woman's fear of snakes disturbs at least her husband, who worries about her. The young girl's reaction to her loss probably disturbs her concerned family. The young Navajo's vision quest probably pleases his father and other relatives. Benjamin Franklin's air bath, which was unobserved by others, did not disturb anyone.
- *Atypical—so different that they violate a norm.* Notice that this definition has two parts, and they are equally important: The behavior is not like other people's behavior, and it violates a *norm*—a rule for accepted and expected behavior *in a particular culture.* In terms of defining psychological disorders, it doesn't matter if my behavior is unlike yours if we live in *different* cultures; it only matters whether people in *my* culture think my behavior is abnormal. So let's look again at our four examples. The woman who can't leave her suburban home because of her fear of nonexistent snakes is definitely behaving differently from almost all people in her culture. The grief-stricken girl is behaving in a way that most people in her culture would consider within the typical range for someone who had recently suffered such a loss. The young man who had a vision is behaving in a way that Navajo culture would consider acceptable and typical for males his age. And Benjamin Franklin was bathing in a way that we may consider strange three centuries later, but his eighteenth-century friends would have found it unexceptional.

So how many of these people meet the four criteria for having a psychological disorder? Only one: the woman with the extreme fear of snakes. As these examples illustrate, a behavior may be maladaptive or unjustifiable or disturbing or atypical. But to be judged part of a psychological disorder, it has to meet all four of these criteria. [If you have trouble remembering these four points, try my memory trick: I form a "word"—*MUDA*—from the first letter of each point (maladaptive, unjustifiable, disturbing, and atypical).]

Disordered? This rabid sports fan may behave in an atypical way, but psychologists would not label him disordered because his behavior is not maladaptive, unjustifiable, or disturbing (except to the other team's players!).

Now that we have some agreement on what we mean by *psychological disorder,* we can take a closer look at how psychologists attempt to understand and classify these disorders.

Meeting Individual Needs

Words like *maladaptive* and *atypical* may be difficult for some students who have trouble with reading comprehension or processing language. Help these students break down these words into their meaningful morphemes:

- **Maladaptive:** *mal-* is Greek for "bad." So *maladaptive* means "to adapt badly." People's behavior is maladaptive if the behavior causes them to adjust poorly to new situations, people, or places.
- **Atypical:** The prefix *a-* means "not." So if behavior is *atypical,* it is not typical. Atypical behavior, then, does not match behavior a person previously exhibited or behavior that is common for others in their culture or general environment.

Understanding Disorders

2. What perspectives do psychologists take in their attempt to understand psychological disorders? Why do some psychologists object to the medical model of psychological disorders?

► **Philippe Pinel (1745–1826)** French physician who worked to reform the treatment of people with mental disorders.

Perspectives on psychological disorders have changed through the centuries. Written records of attempts to understand abnormal behavior go back at least 4000 years (Brems & others,1991). Ancient Babylonians viewed disorders as the result of demonic possession and treated them with prayer and magic. Ancient Hebrews saw psychological disorders as punishment for sin, and they, too, looked to religion for a cure. Socrates and other ancient Greek philosophers blamed faulty thought processes for such disorders and believed in the healing power of words. All three cultures used humane treatment methods (Schultz & Schultz, 1996).

Unfortunately, not all approaches to treatment have been humane. Fifteenth-century Europeans suspected that people showing symptoms of psychological disorders were possessed by demons, and they often tortured or executed the sufferers to oust these bad spirits. By the eighteenth century, conditions had improved (at least the executions had stopped), but mentally ill people were often chained and locked up in filthy institutions or displayed like zoo animals. Humane treatment was rare—at least until French physician **Philippe Pinel** (1745–1826) and other reformers worked to eliminate this institutionalized brutality. Pinel and others helped change Europe's view of psychological disorders. Dorothea Dix (1802–1887) worked for similar goals in the United States.

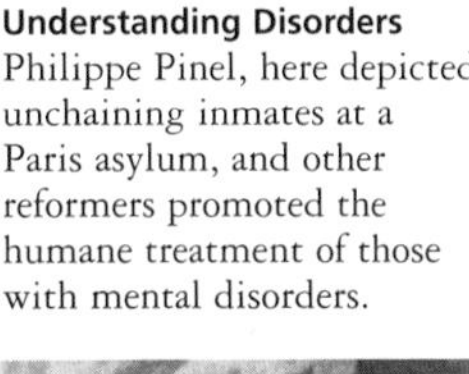

Understanding Disorders Philippe Pinel, here depicted unchaining inmates at a Paris asylum, and other reformers promoted the humane treatment of those with mental disorders.

The Medical Model

Pinel saw psychological disorders as sickness, not demonic possession. Pinel favored talking to patients, treating them gently, and providing clean living conditions. Still, the question lingered: If psychological disorders resulted from sickness, what caused the sickness?

This question was particularly pointed in the 1800s, because medical researchers had recently discovered the brain-damaging and

trb tr Help students understand how the terms in this module are related by having them complete **Building Vocabulary: Graphic Organizer:** *Concept Web* (*Teacher's Resource Binder*, p. 27-1; Handout 27–2).

- **Independent Learners** Students can complete the handout on their own as homework or a class work assignment. You may want to use **Handout 27–2** as a transparency, projecting a correctly completed handout for students to check their answers.
- **Cooperative Learners** Have students work in small groups to fill out the concept web. Students can tutor each other about the concepts in the module, or you can create a competition in which students see how quickly their team can fill out the web correctly.

F • Y • I

(1) Phillipe Pinel, once the personal physician to Napoleon, changed the way the mentally ill were treated across Europe. He devoted his life to helping the mentally ill when he became director of the men's asylum in Paris. He found patients who had been chained to the walls for 30 or 40 years. He ruled that those who weren't violent should be released from chains and treated with modern medicine. During his tenure, death rates for patients went from 60 percent to 10 percent.

(2) Dorothea Dix began her crusade against ill treatment of mental patients when she began tutoring inmates at a women's prison. Hardened female criminals were housed with the mentally ill and mentally retarded, without regard for gender. She campaigned the Massachusetts legislature to change the laws that governed how the mentally ill were housed. She took her reforms to all states east of Mississippi and across the Atlantic Ocean to Europe.

■ **LOOKING AT THE ISSUES**

Have students research the treatment of the mentally ill throughout history. The author mentions different humane practices exhibited in some eras and the inhumane ones practiced by people in more recent centuries. Pose these questions as a research starting point:

- When and where was the first hospital for the mentally ill opened? *(The Society of Friends— the Quakers—opened the first private institution in 1813. The oldest government-run mental institution is St. Elizabeth's in Washington, DC.)*
- What qualified a person to be committed in earlier times? *(People could be committed for any reason. Men would have their wives committed if they wanted a divorce, and girls who became pregnant out of wedlock were also institutionalized.)*
- What laws exist in your state governing commitment conditions and living conditions for the mentally ill?

MODULE 27

■ **APPLYING THE POINTS**

Contact a physician who specializes in treating sexually transmitted diseases and ask him or her about how syphilis causes dementia. The following questions may be used to guide your informal interview as well as to present your findings during class:

- What is syphilis?
- How is it treated? Is it curable?
- How do people develop dementia from having syphilis?

■ **LOOKING AT THE ISSUES**

The medical model of mental illness has led to the development of several drugs for treating a wide variety of mental disorders—from schizophrenia and depression to obsessive-compulsive disorder. Ask students to work in pairs or small groups to research what drugs treat which illness, focusing on the brain chemistry linked to each disorder. Present the following questions to guide the research and the subsequent discussion of students' findings:

- What drugs treat schizophrenia most successfully? What neurotransmitters are linked to this disease?
- What drugs treat depression and bipolar disorder most successfully? What neurotransmitters are linked to these diseases?
- What drugs treat anxiety disorders successfully? What neurotransmitters are linked to these diseases?

trb At this point, you may wish to use **Critical Thinking Activity:** ***Multiple Causations*** (*Teacher's Resource Binder*, p. 27-1; Handout 27–4).

mind-altering syphilis germ. If the dementia that accompanies syphilis had a physical cause, might it be that *all* mental disorders could be traced to diseases of the body? This question led to the **medical model** of "mental illness"—the concept that mental diseases have physical causes that can be diagnosed on the basis of their treatable symptoms. The reforms started by Pinel and others like him, combined with the new medical model, replaced the ugliness of asylums and torture with the humaneness of hospitals and therapy.

The medical model is alive and well today. Contemporary research has uncovered physical causes, both genetic and biochemical, for symptoms of some of the more troubling psychological disorders, including schizophrenia, a group of severe disorders characterized by disturbed thinking, perceiving, feeling, and acting. This new level of understanding has led to new treatments, often involving drug therapy. But the medical model has not always led to the miracle cures some health workers hoped for. In its quest to find physiological explanations for "mental diseases," the medical model focuses almost exclusively on nature, and almost not at all on nurture. By failing to consider environment or culture, the medical model overlooks the influence of such factors as stress, upbringing, and personal history. Another approach, the bio-psycho-social model, offers a more inclusive view of the causes of disorders.

The Bio-Psycho-Social Model

Psychologists who use the **bio-psycho-social perspective** (Figure 27.1) study how biological, psychological, and social factors combine to produce specific psychological disorders. This approach studies both nature *and* nurture, and it focuses on their interaction.

The bio-psycho-social model agrees that there is a biological or physiological component to psychological disorder, but it views it as one leg of a three-legged stool. This component includes your genetic *predisposition,* or hereditary susceptibility to a disorder. Genetic predisposition may help explain why some young people endure break-ups with a boyfriend or girlfriend without getting too depressed, but others become so sad that they can't go to school. The second group of students may have a greater genetic predisposition to depression than the first group.

The psychological part of the bio-psycho-social model includes our thoughts or thinking patterns. Staying with the break-up example, perhaps these two groups of students differ in the way they explain the break-up to themselves. The first group, for example, may explain things in terms of the situation ("I'll really miss being with her [or him], but we're going to be 200 miles apart this summer, and it wouldn't have worked"). Perhaps the second group explains bad events by defining them as examples of permanent faults ("I'm stupid and ugly and I always

► **medical model** The concept that diseases have physical causes that can be diagnosed, treated, and, in most cases, cured. When applied to psychological disorders, the medical model assumes that these "mental" illnesses can be diagnosed on the basis of their symptoms and cured through therapy, which may include treatment in a psychiatric hospital.

► **bio-psycho-social perspective** A contemporary perspective which assumes that biological, psychological, and sociocultural factors combine and interact to produce psychological disorders.

Cross-Curricular Connections

HISTORY Scientific research into mental illness has not always been handled ethically. In the 1930s, the U.S. government withheld treatment from several dozen African-American men who had contracted syphilis in Tuskegee, Alabama, so that they could study the long-term effects of the disease. The discovery of this unethical research many years later unearthed decades of prejudice in mental health research on the basis of both race and gender.

Suggest that interested students research the history of the Tuskegee experiment and changes in mental health research that have occurred as a result of this tragic event. These students may develop oral or written reports for extra credit that can be made available for the rest of the class to hear or read.

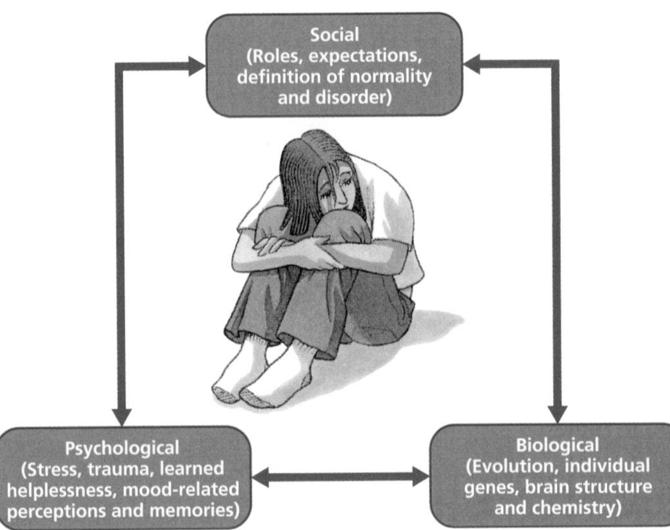

Figure 27.1 **The Bio-Psycho-Social Perspective** Most psychologists today believe that biological, psychological, and sociocultural factors interact to produce mental disorders.

say the wrong thing. It's all my fault"). If so, they are more likely to feel bad about the break-up. How you think about an event can shape your feelings and your actions.

Finally, there is the social part of the bio-psycho-social model. Perhaps the students in the two groups had different expectations about the relationships. If the first group of students saw the break-up as the end of a casual dating arrangement, it might not seem so serious. But if the second group of students saw the break-up as the end of a long-term and permanent bond, they might react more intensely.

Social and cultural beliefs can affect even the behaviors and beliefs characterizing disorders. Most people your age have heard of anorexia nervosa, an eating disorder in which a person becomes significantly underweight but continues to diet. This disease appears to be a Western phenomenon: In countries where food is scarce, no term for this disease exists. Now, have you ever heard of *susto*? Probably not. Few people in the United States have ever been diagnosed with, or even heard of, *susto*. But residents of certain Latin American countries are very much aware of this psychological disorder. They know that *susto* is characterized by a fear of black magic, resulting in extreme restlessness and severe anxiety. As these examples illustrate, cultures have their own unique sources of stress, leading to their own unique disorders (Beardsley, 1994; Castillo, 1997).

The bio-psycho-social model reminds us that, to understand and classify psychological disorders, we need to account for the interaction of physiological, psychological, and sociocultural forces, all of which help shape our behaviors.

Meeting Individual Needs

trb tr Provide students with handouts created from the black-line master of Figure 27.1, The Bio-Psycho-Social Perspective, available in the **Black-Line Masters Appendix** of the *Teacher's Resource Binder*. Have students blank out some of the terms and concepts so that they can fill in the blanks as they learn the material. Students may work independently or with the help of a tutor. You can also use the black-line master to create a quiz with blanked out areas to see how well students have learned the components of this theory of mental illness.

- **Exceptional Learners** The handouts of Figure 27.1 can fill the need to provide notes for exceptional learners. These students may review terms with a student or teacher/tutor. They may refer to the handout during class discussion or lecture.

trb tr ■ **TEACHING TIP**

A black-line master for Figure 27.1, The Bio-Psycho-Social Perspective, is available in the **Black-Line Masters Appendix** of the *Teacher's Resource Binder*.

■ **MULTICULTURAL CONNECTIONS**

Some other culturally specific disorders that students may not be aware of include:

- **Latah** occurs among uneducated middle-aged or elderly women in Malaya. Unusual circumstances (such as hearing someone say "snake" or even being tickled) produce a fear response that is characterized by repeating the words and actions of other people, uttering obscenities, and doing the opposite of what other people ask.
- **Winigo,** the intense fear of being turned into a cannibal by a supernatural monster, was once common among Algonquin Indian hunters. Depression, lack of appetite, nausea, and sleeplessness were common symptoms. This disorder could be brought on when hunters came back from an expedition empty-handed. Ashamed of failure, the hunter might fall victim to deep and lingering depression. Some afflicted hunters would kill and eat members of their own households.

trb At this point, you may wish to use **Enrichment Lesson:** *Culture-Bound Disorders* (*Teacher's Resource Binder*, p. 27-1).

■ **APPLYING THE POINTS**

Treatment options open up when practitioners who follow the bio-psycho-social model care for patients. Have students contact local psychologists and psychiatrists to see what types of treatment options they offer their patients. They may also contact local mental hospitals to see what roles psychologists and psychiatrists play in the treatment of patients. Have students compare and contrast their findings in a class discussion.

trb At this point, you may wish to use **Enrichment Lesson:** *Tourette Syndrome* (*Teacher's Resource Binder*, p. 27-1).

MODULE 27

■ TEACHING TIP

Students may benefit from knowing the different steps clinicians must consider as they diagnose a mental illness:

- Axis I is *Clinical Disorders and Other Conditions That May Be Focus of Clinical Attention.* This area of diagnosis identifies the disorder a patient primarily has, such as schizophrenia, depression, or anxiety disorder. This diagnosis is the basis for insurance coverage. Multiple diagnoses can be made, but the clinician should note a "principal diagnosis."
- Axis II is *Mental Retardation and Personality Disorders.* If patients exhibit low mental ability or a personality disorder, that is noted in this axis.
- Axis III is *Medical Conditions Related to Presenting Problem.* If patients exhibit medical conditions—such as pancreatic cancer—when they have depression, they have a notation in this axis. Unless there is a specific link between a medical condition and a psychological disorder, an Axis III diagnosis will not be made.
- Axis IV is *Psychosocial and Environmental Problems.* If people have problems in life as a result of their disorder, they receive an Axis IV diagnosis. Problems may include having trouble holding down a job or being homeless.
- Axis V is *Global Assessment of Functioning.* A person's overall level of functioning is reported here. If a person has been admitted to the hospital recently or has trouble with daily activities, he or she will be diagnosed as having low global functioning.

trb At this point, you may wish to use Critical Thinking Activity: *Multiple Causations* (*Teacher's Resource Binder*, p. 27-1; Handout 27–4).

Classifying Disorders

▶ **DSM-IV-TR** The American Psychiatric Association's *Diagnostic and Statistical Manual of Mental Disorders* (Fourth Edition, Text Revision), a widely used system for classifying psychological disorders.

3. What is the DSM-IV-TR?

All sciences classify information to create a sense of order within the discipline. Chemistry classifies elements to keep track of atomic weight and the number of electrons orbiting the nucleus. Biology classifies living things in various ways, telling us, for example, whether animals are hatched or born live, cold-blooded or warm-blooded. Clinical psychologists and psychiatrists (physicians who treat psychological disorders) classify psychological disorders according to their symptoms, in order to:

1. describe the disorder.
2. predict the future course of the disorder.
3. treat the disorder appropriately.
4. provide a springboard for research into the disorder's causes.

DSM-IV-TR The American Psychiatric Association publishes and periodically revises the *Diagnostic and Statistical Manual of Mental Disorders* (now in its fourth edition). This volume lists all of the currently accepted categories of mental disorders and their descriptions. U.S. health-care providers require a DSM-IV-TR classification for all treatments they prepay or reimburse.

The American Psychiatric Association developed the most accepted and widely used classification system for psychological disorders. The publication, the *Diagnostic and Statistical Manual of Mental Disorders*, is in its fourth edition, and recently had a text revision, hence its nickname, **DSM-IV-TR**. As of this writing, the fifth edition is still in the works. The DSM-IV-TR also has a practical application: U.S. insurance companies require a DSM-IV-TR classification before they will cover therapy for a disorder.

The DSM-IV-TR divides mental disorders into 17 major categories, with descriptions and estimates of the number of people who have the disorder. It does not list causes. The manual is subject to change and revision. Look in the first edition, and you won't see anorexia nervosa, though the fourth edition now lists this disorder. The DSM-III dropped "homosexuality" as a disorder. The terminology also changes occasionally. When I was in college, we used the term "manic-depressive" to describe those who today are diagnosed with bipolar disorder. And when Sigmund Freud's influence was greater than it is now, we might have wondered if people were "passive-aggressive" or had a "neurosis." The authors of the DSM's third and fourth editions dropped both these terms from the list of disorders.

Do the DSM categories work? Are they reliable? That is, could two psychologists independently interview someone and come up with the same diagnosis? Researchers attempting to answer this question had one group of psychologists interview 75 psychiatric patients face to face and assign DSM categories. They videotaped these interviews (but not the final diagnoses) and

Enriching

Revision allows the DSM to remain up-to-date. Below are Fourth Edition revisions. Have students research to learn of any further DSM revision plans.

- Patients who experience a personality change because of a general medical condition, such as Alzheimer's disease, are now treated psychologically as well as physically.
- Patients with Tourette's syndrome no longer need to demonstrate that their condition impairs daily functioning to be given the diagnosis.
- Several paraphilias (sexual disorders such as exhibitionism and voyeurism) can be diagnosed when they are acted on, not only when patients exhibit these actions to the point of distress or impaired functioning.

asked a second group of psychologists to diagnose the patients, again using DSM categories and guidelines. Both groups assigned the identical diagnosis 83 percent of the time (Riskind & others, 1987). Research of this sort indicates that the DSM categories and guidelines work most, but not all, of the time.

The DSM approach has its critics. Some point out that this classification system is biased in favor of the medical model of psychological disorders. Because it classifies disorders by their "symptoms," the diagnosis of an "illness" is predetermined. Others note that the number of disorder categories has ballooned. In the 1950s, the first edition of the DSM listed 60 categories. In the 1990s, the DSM-IV listed over 400. One survey, conducted the year the DSM-IV came out, found that 48 percent of the people living in the United States would qualify for a DSM diagnosis at some point during their lives (Kessler & Zhao, 1999; Kessler & others, 1994). Finally, critics add that the DSM-IV has an additional problem: Diagnoses can create labels, which are often hard to shake.

Labeling Disorders

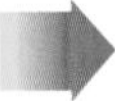

4. What are the drawbacks and advantages in labeling psychological disorders?

In the election of 1972, Republican President Richard Nixon was running for reelection. Senator George McGovern of South Dakota won the top spot on the opposing Democratic party's ticket, and he chose Thomas Eagleton as his running mate. The McGovern-Eagleton ticket was doing relatively well in national polls until rumors surfaced about Eagleton's mental health.

In a flurry of activity, the media reported that Eagleton had suffered "nervous exhaustion" in the previous decade and had twice received electroconvulsive shock therapy (ECT). The stigma attached to the disorder and ECT was so grave that McGovern asked Eagleton to drop out of the race. McGovern's candidacy never rallied, and he lost every state except Massachusetts in that election.

Research suggests we view people differently after they have been labeled (Farina & Fisher, 1982).

Running Mates Nominated by the Democratic party to run for President in 1972, George McGovern chose Thomas Eagleton (left) as his vice-presidential nominee. Eagleton left the ticket amid rumors about his mental health.

Cooperative Learning

Divide students into groups and give each group a different label commonly used in schools, such as "learning disabled," "emotionally conflicted," "gifted," or "at risk." Have each group research what qualifies a person for such a label. In addition, encourage group members to express how they would feel about themselves and school if they were given such a label.

trb At this point, you may wish to use **Analysis Activity:** ***The Effects of Labeling*** (*Teacher's Resource Binder*, p. 27-1; **Handout 27–5**).

■ APPLYING THE POINTS

Contact a psychiatrist and a psychologist to ask them about how they feel about the diagnostic classification system that the DSM-IV-TR offers. Use the following questions as a guide to your conversation and a presentation of your findings to the class:

- Do they feel the criteria are reliable? Why or why not?
- Do they feel the diagnoses rely too much on the medical model? Why or why not?
- Are diagnoses dependent on insurance needs rather than necessary diagnoses? Why or why not?
- Do they feel too many diagnoses are included in the DSM-IV-TR? Why or why not?

■ LOOKING AT THE ISSUES

Several U.S. presidents have experienced physical and mental illness during their tenure that may or may not have been known to the general public. Have students research illnesses of different presidents or presidential candidates to find out whether the illnesses affected administrations or reelection efforts. Following are some examples:

- Abraham Lincoln suffered from depression, and his wife was institutionalized during her life.
- Franklin Delano Roosevelt had polio and tried to hide his disability from the general public.
- John F. Kennedy experienced severe back pain as a result of a birth defect. He also suffered from Addison's disease (a withering of the adrenal glands), which required daily injections of cortisone.
- Ronald Reagan was diagnosed with Alzheimer's disease after his presidency was over, but questions about whether it affected him during the Iran-Contra controversy linger.

trb At this point, you may wish to use **Enrichment Lesson:** ***The Commonality of Psychological Disorders*** (*Teacher's Resource Binder*, p. 27-1).

MODULE 27

LOOKING AT THE ISSUES

(1) How might the issue of labeling affect teachers? Studies show that labeling of students can bias a teacher's treatment of a particular student. Knowing a student's diagnosis, however, can help a teacher get that student the help he or she needs to succeed. How can a balance be reached? Present the questions listed below to the class. Have students brainstorm ways teachers can be aware of labels but be sensitive to the limitations labels can place on students.

- What type of training should teachers go through to help them be more sensitive to the power of labels?
- Should teachers and students be informed of their labels? Why or why not?
- How can teachers and students be proactive about learning disabilities?

trb At this point, you may wish to use **Analysis Activity:** ***The Effects of Labeling*** (*Teacher's Resource Binder*, p. 27-1; **Handout 27–5**).

(2) Therapists must be careful that they don't lead patients they are treating toward a diagnosis or memory that isn't warranted. Contact some psychologists and ask what steps they take to avoid influencing a patient's memory. The following questions may be used as a guide for this conversation as well as a subsequent class presentation on your findings:

- Is there a specific way diagnostic questions need to be asked to avoid leading a patient's answers?
- What steps do therapists take to avoid creating false memories in patients?
- Have they ever had a patient try to fake a mental illness? How was that person caught?

Studies have shown a clear bias against those labeled with a psychological disorder. Think about this: If you owned an apartment complex, would you rent a room to someone who had been in a mental institution? One study (Page, 1977) put this very question to 180 people in Toronto, Ontario, using phone numbers from ads listing furnished rooms for rent. Check out these results:

- If the caller merely asked if the room was available, the answer was usually "Yes."
- If the caller said she was about to be released from a mental hospital, three out of four people told her the room was not available.
- If the caller had someone else call back after she had been turned down, asking if the room was available, the answer was usually "Yes."
- If the caller said she was calling to rent the room for her brother, who was about to get out of jail, three out of four people told her the room was not available.

The stigma against released prisoners and mental health patients appears to produce the same results.

The power of labeling is clear in other research as well. In one controversial study (Rosenhan, 1973), eight *healthy* people from Stanford University went to a local mental hospital to check themselves in. All eight gave false names and occupations, and they acted as they normally would—with one exception: Each complained to the interviewer of hearing voices that said "Thud," "Hollow," or "Empty." Hospital personnel diagnosed all eight as mentally ill and admitted them to the hospital. Once admitted to the hospital, the eight people exhibited no further symptoms.

We should not be surprised that these eight were admitted. After all, if you complained of a headache and sore throat, you'd probably be allowed to stay home from school, even if you really felt fine. What is surprising is that *after* these eight were admitted, clinicians "discovered" the causes of the disorders after analyzing their quite normal life histories. For example, one of the eight was said to be reacting to mixed emotions about his parents. And the clinicians perceived abnormal behavior in very ordinary acts, such as taking notes, which were often mistakenly labeled as symptoms. Though the eight "patients" did not report hearing voices again or having similar symptoms, they had average stays of 19 days.

So how much do labels influence our perceptions? Apparently quite a bit. In another study (Langer & others, 1974, 1980), researchers asked participants to judge a videotaped interview and rate the person in the video. All participants saw the same videotape, but they did not receive the same information *before* viewing and rating the person in the tape. Some participants were therapists who believed they were viewing pa-

Enriching

Have students develop a survey that measures how peers respond to labels that are often used in school. (An Institutional Review Board should approve research, and consent should be obtained from all participants.) The survey should include the following questions:

- How would students feel if they knew the new kid in class was labeled "learning disabled"? Would your feelings be different if he or she were labeled "gifted"? Why or why not?
- Would students invite a learning disabled or gifted student to study with them? Why or why not?
- What feelings would students have if they were labeled as "learning disabled," "emotionally conflicted," or "gifted"?

trb At this point, you may wish to use **Analysis Activity:** ***The Effects of Labeling*** (*Teacher's Resource Binder*, p. 27-1; **Handout 27–5**).

MODULE 27

■ APPLYING THE POINTS

As compared with 30 years ago, when most chronic mental patients were institutionalized, it is now much more likely students will have encountered a person with a chronic mental disorder in the supermarket, at the shopping mall, on the bus, or on the street corner. Ask your students to recall one incident in which they have personally encountered a chronically "mentally ill" person. Present the questions below to help students reflect on and write a description that details such an encounter:

- What made you decide the person was mentally ill?
- Did you feel comfortable or uncomfortable?
- Did the person's behavior seem predictable or unpredictable?
- Did the person seem dangerous or nondangerous?

Collect these descriptions and save them for use in the Close discussion on page 528 of this *Teacher's Edition.*

trb tr ■ TEACHING TIP

A black-line master for Table 27.1, Percentage of Americans Who Have Experienced Psychological Disorders, is available in the **Black-Line Masters Appendix** of the *Teacher's Resource Binder.*

Psychology is a **Science**

Psychological Disorder Rates

No known culture is free of depression or schizophrenia (Castillo, 1997; Draguns, 1990 a, b, 1997). In the United States, 2.1 million people are admitted to mental hospitals each year, and another 2.4 million who are troubled (but not disabled) receive outpatient care from clinics and other mental health organizations. Most of us will eventually have some experience with the mental health care system, either personally or indirectly by way of close friends or relatives.

Poverty seems to be connected with disorder rates. People below the poverty line are twice as likely as their wealthier counterparts to have a serious psychological disorder (Centers for Disease Control, 1992). But this is a correlation, so we cannot assume anything about cause and effect. Does poverty cause the disorder? Does the disorder cause poverty? Or are both caused by something else? The answer varies from disorder to disorder. Schizophrenia, a series of disorders in which a person loses touch with reality, is likely to lead to job loss and poverty. But the stressful and demoralizing conditions of poverty may also contribute to disorders such as substance abuse in men and depression in women (Table 27.1), which are common among Americans today (Dohrenwend & others, 1992).

TABLE 27.1 PERCENTAGE OF AMERICANS WHO HAVE EXPERIENCED PSYCHOLOGICAL DISORDERS

	MEN	WOMEN
Alcohol abuse or dependence	23.8	4.6
Mood disorders (like depression)	5.2	10.2
Schizophrenia	1.2	1.7

Source: Data from Robins & Regier, 1991.

tients. Others were observers who thought they were seeing job applicants. Those who thought they were evaluating a psychiatric patient saw the interviewee as a "passive-dependent type," or "frightened of his own impulses" or something similar. Those who thought the person was interviewing for a job saw none of these qualities. Yes, labels can be helpful, but they also hold the potential to shape our thoughts and lead us astray.

Cooperative Learning

Divide the class into small groups of students, giving each group a different day's copy of a local or national newspaper. Have groups scan the papers for stories that report about the mental condition or history of criminals or victims of crime. Then, have students address the following questions:

- Of all the crimes reported, how many depicted the criminal as having a history of mental illness? How many depicted the victim as suffering from a mental illness?
- Were there any human-interest stories about people who suffer from mental illness? If so, how many? Were these people depicted in a positive light? Why or why not?

Allow time for groups to share their responses, using specific articles they discovered as examples.

MODULE 27

■ JOURNAL WRITING

Invite students to use the following writing prompt as a springboard for entries in their psychology journals:

- Have you ever been unfairly labeled by parents, teachers, or employers? Describe your experience.

trb At this point, you may wish to use Analysis Activity: *The Effects of Labeling* (*Teacher's Resource Binder*, p. 27-1; Handout 27–5).

■ MULTICULTURAL CONNECTIONS

Some mental illnesses are common worldwide. Others are culture-specific. Present the following questions to the class and ask students to use available resources to explore the answers:

- How do other cultures view and label mental illness?
- What disorders are recognized in the United States as well as abroad?
- What type of health care is offered to people with mental illness? Is coverage better or worse than in the United States?

Close

Use the accounts students wrote about an encounter with a chronically "mentally ill" person for the Applying the Points note on page 527 of this *Teacher's Edition*. Tabulate the number of students who found the encounters uncomfortable, unpredictable, and dangerous. Tell students that research on public attitudes has shown that most people feel uncomfortable with the mentally ill and find their behavior to be both unpredictable and dangerous. Then present your tabulations.

Use the students' descriptions to remind them of the definition of *psychological disorder*. The students' examples will illustrate how behavior is considered psychologically disordered when it is atypical, disturbing, maladaptive, and unjustifiable.

Source: Sarason, I., & Sarason, B. (1999). *Abnormal psychology* (9th ed.). Upper Saddle River, NJ: Prentice Hall.

Perhaps the media should shoulder some blame for the way we view those with psychological disorders. One 1980s report found that TV programs portrayed 70 percent of the people with psychological disorders as criminals or violent (Gerbner, 1985). This percentage is way out of line with real life, in which 90 percent of the people with disorders are *not* dangerous. Anxious, withdrawn, or depressed? Yes, that's common. Dangerous? Very unlikely. If those released from mental hospitals stay away from alcohol and other drugs, they are no more likely to become violent than the people they live around (Steadman & others, 1998). Former U.S. Surgeon General David Satcher reinforced this point clearly when he wrote, "There is very little risk of violence or harm to a stranger from casual contact with an individual who has a mental disorder" (1999, page 7).

So are labels good or bad? Helpful or harmful? It depends. Labels describe abnormal behavior; they don't explain it. If I tell you my friend has bipolar disorder, you can read the list of symptoms in the DSM-IV-TR and know how he behaves. But you won't have a clue about how or why he developed this disorder. And as we've seen, those who diagnose disorders must be aware of the dangers and drawbacks of labeling, including their effect on our perceptions. The misdiagnosis of eight healthy people (Rosenhan, 1973) shows us just how easily misdiagnosis can occur.

But we must also remember the benefits of labeling. As we noted earlier in this module, classifications are helpful in giving us thumbnail sketches that let us understand and communicate quickly. A lead author of the current classification system (Spitzer, 1975) points out that psychiatric diagnosis helps mental health professionals communicate with one another about disorders, understand some of the processes at work, and help guide people toward better outcomes in their treatment.

Have we made any progress since 1972, when the stigma of receiving treatment for a psychological disorder drove Thomas Eagleton out of a presidential campaign? The answer, it is to be hoped, is yes. Seeking treatment for disorders such as depression is now more likely to be seen as a strength than a weakness. In 1999, Tipper Gore, wife of then–Vice President Al Gore, told the world, "I had a clinical depression, recognized it, and went to a social worker. I got diagnosed and then successfully treated. I hope that will encourage people to seek treatment if they think they are suffering from depression." As of this writing, Tipper Gore has not ruled out running for office herself.

Many have endured the bewilderment of psychological disorder and flourished in some ways, including Leonardo da Vinci, Isaac Newton, and the Nobel prize–winning economist, John Nash, who was the subject of the Oscar-winning movie, *A Beautiful Mind.* Nash was fortunate in that he was able to overcome his symptoms and behave in ways that were not maladaptive, unjustifiable, disturbing, and atypical. For others, hope rests with increased understanding of disorders and improved treatments.

Cross-Curricular Connections

HISTORY Have students do research about different historical figures, in addition to those mentioned in the text, who battled or who are suspected of battling mental illness. Some people who may have suffered from mental disorders include the following:

- Vincent van Gogh
- King George III of England
- Rosemary Kennedy (sister of John F. Kennedy)
- Sylvia Plath

REVIEW

Module 27: Introduction to Psychological Disorders

What's the Point?

Defining Disorder

1. *What criteria do psychologists use to diagnose psychological disorders?*

   Psychologists define *psychological disorders* as harmful dysfunctions in which behaviors are maladaptive (destructive to oneself or others), unjustifiable (without a rational basis), disturbing (troublesome to other people), and atypical (so different that they violate a norm). A behavior that qualifies for only one or some of these criteria is not necessarily evidence of a disorder; it must satisfy all four points to justify suspicion of a disorder.

Understanding Disorders

2. *What perspectives do psychologists take in their attempt to understand psychological disorders? Why do some psychologists object to the medical model of psychological disorders?*

   Perspectives on psychological disorders have changed since the first records of treatment attempts were recorded in ancient Babylon thousands of years ago. Some of the early views were that mental problems were evidence of demonic possession (Babylon), or punishment for sin (early Hebrews), or faulty thought processes (ancient Greece). Treatments looked to prayer, magic, or healing words, depending on the probable cause. Fifteenth-century Europeans also believed psychological disorders were evidence of demonic possession, but their treatment, designed to drive out demons, was brutal torture or even death. Conditions had improved by the 1800s, and French physician Philippe Pinel and other reformers worked to bring about more humane treatment of people with psychological disorders. This new outlook, combined with other advances in understanding the cause of physical diseases, led to the creation of a medical model of disorders—the idea that "mental illnesses" had physical causes that can be diagnosed on the basis of their treatable symptoms. The medical model, though a humane breakthrough in its time, does not consider the influence of environment or culture on behavior. Because modern versions of this perspective regard disorders as illnesses, treatment may consist of drugs or, in some cases, surgery. Psychologists who disagree with the medical model tend to prefer the more inclusive bio-psycho-social model, a perspective that views psychological disorders as the result of an interaction among biological, psychological, and social forces.

Classifying Disorders

3. *What is the DSM-IV-TR?*

   DSM-IV-TR is an abbreviation used for the *Diagnostic and Statistical Manual of Mental Disorders* (Fourth Edition, Text Revision). The DSM-IV-TR, published by the American Psychiatric Association, contains descriptions of psychological disorders, along with estimates of the number of people who have those disorders. The number and details of the list of disorders change, depending on the current understanding of what is and is not a disorder. The categories and guidelines are, according to one study,

MODULE 27

Checking the Points

■ **TEACHING TIPS**

web (1) The book companion site for *Thinking About Psychology* at www.worthpublishers.com/thinkingaboutpsych contains a module quiz, flashcards of key terms and people, as well as other student activities and resources for this module. You will also find PowerPoint lectures, a quiz grade book, and other teaching resources by logging on as an instructor.

trb (2) At this point, you may wish to review and confirm concepts about the psychological disorders with **Critical Thinking Activity:** *Fact or Falsehood?* (*Teacher's Resource Binder*, p. 27-1; **Handout 27–1**). If students filled in this handout earlier in the module, ask them to set it aside. Suggest that students complete the handout in small groups, taking the time to look up information in the text to respond correctly to questions. Have all the groups meet to review the handout, again using the text to support the responses.

MODULE 27

trb ■ TEACHING TIP

At this point, you may wish to provide students with **Building Vocabulary: Graphic Organizer:** *Concept Web* (*Teacher's Resource Binder*, p. 27-1; **Handout 27–2**). If students completed this organizer earlier, have them set it aside. As students fill in the answers, they will be using the handout as a tool for reviewing module concepts. Suggest that students exchange handouts with classmates to check and confirm the accuracy of their completed concept webs.

tb Using the Test Bank

The *Test Bank* that accompanies this textbook offers a wide variety of questions in different formats and levels of complexity. Use the software to construct whole tests or to integrate standardized questions into teacher-made tests.

Self-Test Answers

Multiple-Choice Questions

1. c, 2.b

more than 80 percent reliable, meaning that independent therapists using this manual tend to assign the same diagnoses. Critics of the DSM-IV say that it supports the medical model of psychological disorders, that its contents are now so extensive that most Americans could fit into one category or another, and that the list of diagnoses can lead to labeling people with psychological problems.

Labeling Disorders

4. *What are the drawbacks and advantages in labeling psychological disorders?*

One of the drawbacks in labeling people is that labels influence our expectations of how people will behave. As a result, we see what we expect to see. In the media, "psychological disorder" has become a label associated with violence. Despite this stereotype, 90 percent of people with psychological disorders are nonviolent. Nevertheless, the stereotype leads many Americans to expect violence from people with mental disorders.

Labels do have some advantages, however. Scientists can do their work more easily if they have common access to a classification of things they study. Chemists use the periodic table of elements to understand and communicate their views on the chemical elements. Biologists use classifications of plants and animals for these purposes. Similarly, psychologists and psychiatrists use the classification, or set of labels, found in the DSM-IV-TR to communicate with one another, to understand the processes at work in the various disorders, and to guide people toward better outcomes in their treatment.

Key Terms

psychological disorder, p. 519
medical model, p. 522
bio-psycho-social perspective, p. 522
DSM-IV-TR, p. 524

Key People

Philippe Pinel, p. 521

Self-Test

Multiple-Choice Questions

Choose the *best* answer for each of the following questions.

1. Angie has a quiz today in her psychology class. Her friends heard her mumbling to herself "MUDA, MUDA, MUDA" on the way through the school halls this morning. Angie is
   a. demonstrating symptoms of a psychological disorder.
   b. repeating her mother's name because it makes her feel less anxious.
   c. trying to remember the four criteria that a behavior must meet before it qualifies as evidence of a psychological disorder.
   d. trying to remember the four main perspectives psychologists take in trying to understand psychological disorders.
2. Joe wants to buy a copy of the *Diagnostic and Statistical Manual of Mental Disorders* (DSM) because he will be working as a therapist after he gets his Ph.D. in psychology three years from now. Joe's uncle, who was a therapist for 40 years, has offered Joe a 1950s copy of the DSM. Joe should turn down his uncle's offer because
   a. insurance companies prefer a medical model of disorders and refuse to pay for therapy for the disorders listed in the DSM.

Alternative Assessment/Portfolio Project

web EXPLORING PSYCHOLOGICAL DISORDERS ON THE WORLD WIDE WEB Students can search the Web for information on the different disorders presented in Modules 27 through 29. Assign each student or group of students a different disorder and have them gather information on it, creating a presentation to share with the class, school, or community. Some presentation options include the following:

- a formal research paper
- a poster presentation
- a public awareness campaign to educate people about the illness
- a documentary about someone with the disorder that educates people about the day-to-day life of people with the illness

b. the DSM classification is constantly updated; it listed only 60 disorders in the 1950s, but it now lists more than 400.
c. the DSM classification is not reliable; Joe should reach his own independent decisions about the people who ask for his help.
d. None of the above. Joe should accept his uncle's offer because the 1950s classification will be almost identical to the current classification.

3. Noah has been washing his hands more than 30 times each day. His family took him to see Dr. Johnson, who is now searching for possible genetic and biochemical causes for Noah's compulsive hand washing. Dr. Johnson has also prescribed medications that Noah must take daily. Dr. Johnson seems to believe in the ___________ model of psychological disorders.
   a. medical
   b. bio-psycho-social
   c. fifteenth-century European
   d. ancient Babylonian

4. For the past two months, Carly has been feeling very sad, for no apparent reason. She is unable to sleep for more than three or four hours at a time, has lost her appetite, and cannot concentrate on her assignments in school. Carly's parents have taken her to see Dr. Diaz, who asked Carly whether other members of her family had ever suffered from depression. Dr. Diaz also wanted to know whether Carly's social life had changed recently. Dr. Diaz now meets with Carly each week to discuss her thoughts about her life and her moods. Dr. Diaz appears to believe in the ___________ model of psychological disorders.
   a. medical
   b. bio-psycho-social
   c. fifteenth-century European
   d. ancient Hebrew

5. Ruthie's mother was recently diagnosed with a psychological disorder. Ruthie's best friend, Brianna, refuses to visit Ruthie at her home because she's afraid Ruthie's mother will attack her. Brianna is
   a. right to avoid Ruthie's mom; about 80 percent of people with psychological disorders become violent.
   b. right to avoid Ruthie's mom; about 50 percent of people with psychological disorders become violent.
   c. probably worrying needlessly; 60 percent of people with psychological disorders are nonviolent.
   d. probably worrying needlessly; 90 percent of people with psychological disorders are nonviolent.

Matching Terms and Definitions

6. For each definition, choose the best matching term from the list that follows:

Definition

a. Contemporary perspective which assumes that biological, psychological, and sociocultural factors combine and interact to produce psychological disorders.
b. A hereditary susceptibility to a disorder.
c. View that psychological disorders are illnesses with physical causes, and that the disorders can be diagnosed on the basis of their symptoms and cured through treatment that may include hospitalization.
d. Disorder labels allow psychologists to communicate with one another more easily.
e. Widely used system for classifying psychological disorders.
f. Disorder labels influence our expectations of how people will behave.

MODULE 27

Self-Test Answers

Multiple-Choice Questions (continued)
3. a, 4. b, 5. d

Matching Terms and Definitions
6. a. (3), b. (7), c. (2), d. (5), e. (4), f. (6)

trb Refer to **Alternative Assessment/Portfolio Project:** *Exploring Psychological Disorders on the World Wide Web* (*Teacher's Resource Binder*, p. 27-1; **Handout 27–6**) for helpful Web sites and a rubric to aid in evaluating students' projects. Revise the rubric to suit your needs.

MODULE 27

Self-Test Answers

Fill-in-the-Blank Questions

7. Phillipe Pinel, 8. Dorothea Dix

Brief Essay Question

9. Students should demonstrate how Kenny's behavior is maladaptive (he refuses to leave his house), unjustified (birds should be more afraid of him than he of them), disturbing (others around him are upset by his behavior), and atypical (most children his age are not afraid of birds like he is).

Term

(1) psychological disorder
(2) medical model
(3) bio-psycho-social perspective
(4) DSM-IV-TR
(5) advantage of labeling
(6) disadvantage of labeling
(7) predisposition

Fill-in-the-Blank Questions

7. ____________ ____________ was a French physician who opposed the institutional brutality of eighteenth-century mental institutions.

8. ____________ ____________ was a reformer who worked to eliminate brutal treatment of people with psychological disorders in the United States.

Brief Essay Question

9. Kenny is worried that he might have a psychological disorder and wonders if he should see a therapist. When Kenny was four years old, he was running barefoot in his back yard and he stepped on a baby bird, killing it. Now he is a junior in high school, but he still feels very frightened and anxious when he is near birds. He sometimes refuses to leave the house if he sees birds in his yard, although his mother and father (who are very upset by Kenny's fear) offer to walk with him to the sidewalk.

What is your view of Kenny's situation? In two paragraphs of about three or four sentences each, explain the four criteria for behaviors that signal psychological disorders, and give your opinion of whether (and why) Kenny's fear of birds and his efforts to avoid them may be evidence of a disorder.

Performance Standards

Standard Area: Psychological Disorders

Content Standard 3: Major categories of psychological disorders

Performance Standard 3.1 Discuss the major categories of psychological disorders.

- Define *anxiety*. Compare normal with abnormal feelings of anxiety. (Student Text p. 534)
- Table 28.1, "Symptoms of Anxiety," reviews the major characteristics of anxiety. (Student Text p. 535)
- Discuss the characteristics of generalized anxiety disorder. (Student Text pp. 535–536)
- Discuss the characteristics of phobic disorder. (Student Text pp. 536–537)
- Table 28.2 reviews "Some Common—and Not-So-Common—Phobias." (Student Text p. 537)
- Discuss the characteristics of obsessive-compulsive disorder. (Student Text pp. 538–539)
- Table 28.3 reviews "Common Obsessions and Compulsions Among Children and Adolescents with Obsessive-Compulsive Disorder." (Student Text p. 539)
- Discuss the characteristics of posttraumatic stress disorder. (Student Text pp. 539–540)
- Examine some of the biological and learning factors that contribute to the development of anxiety disorders. (Student Text pp. 540–542)
- Compare normal sadness to depression. (Student Text p. 542)
- Discuss the characteristics of major depressive disorder. (Student Text pp. 542–543)
- Investigate the tragedy of suicide. (Student Text pp. 544–545)
- Discuss the characteristics of bipolar disorder. (Student Text p. 546)
- Examine some of the biological and social-cognitive factors that contribute to the development of mood disorders. (Student Text pp. 546–549)

Materials NETWORK

All of the items from the Video, Activity, and Enrichment Centers listed below come from the *Teacher's Resource Binder.* These items will help you teach and expand on concepts presented in Module 28.

trb This logo indicates when an item from the Materials Network may be used in conjunction with a specific note found in this module's *Teacher's Edition.*

Anxiety Disorders

V Video Center

- **Videocassette:** *Scientific American Frontiers,* **Second Edition, Segment 32: "Arachnophobia"** Consult the faculty guide from the *Scientific American Frontiers* video series for a description of this segment. (*Teacher's Resource Binder,* p. 28-1)

Activity Center

- **Critical Thinking Activity:** *Fact or Falsehood?* With this activity, to which students respond "true" or "false" to statements, their preconceptions about anxiety and mood disorders are either exposed as incorrect or reinforced as correct. (*Teacher's Resource Binder,* p. 28-1; **Handout 28–1**)
- **Building Vocabulary: Graphic Organizer:** *Concept Chart* Students can test their knowledge of terms in this module by completing this graphic organizer, which in this case is a concept chart. The chart gives students more exposure to the concepts and related vocabulary in the module. (*Teacher's Resource Binder,* p. 28-1; **Handout 28–2**)
- **Analysis Activity:** *Taylor Manifest Anxiety Scale* Learning theorists have explained the development of anxiety in terms of classical conditioning. Psychoanalysts have a very different view of anxiety. Existential theorists have yet another view of anxiety. This measure combines the common theories that attempt to explain the roots of anxiety, including learning theory and trait theory. (*Teacher's Resource Binder,* p. 28-1; **Handout 28–3**)
- **Application Activity:** *Fear Survey* What do we fear? Psychiatrists and psychologists have labeled over 700 specific fears and estimate that there are thousands more. When fears are persistent and debilitating, they are considered phobias. James Geer has developed a scale to measure fear, which is featured in this activity. (*Teacher's Resource Binder,* p. 28-1; **Handout 28–4**)
- **Analysis Activity:** *Social Phobias* Socially anxious people tend to avoid potentially embarrassing social situations. If they cannot avoid contact, they often experience physical symptoms, such as trembling, profuse perspiration, and nausea. For some, the greatest fear is that others will detect their signs of anxiety, such as blushing, hand tremors, and shaking voice. Lorne Hartman's Social Anxiety Thoughts Questionnaire can be given to students to see how much social phobia they may exhibit in daily life. (*Teacher's Resource Binder,* p. 28-1; **Handout 28–5**)
- **Analysis Activity:** *Obsessive-Compulsive Disorder* Obsessive-compulsive disorder traps people in seemingly endless cycles of repetitive thoughts (obsessions) and in feelings that they must repeat certain actions over and over (compulsions). Approximately 20 percent of those with OCD have only obsessions or only compulsions; all others experience both. Use this scale to measure the amount of obsessive-compulsive behavior students exhibit. (*Teacher's Resource Binder,* p. 28-1; **Handout 28–6**)

Enrichment Center

- **Enrichment Lesson:** *Concentration Camp Survival* Examining the coping skills American Jews who survived the Holocaust used in the concentration camps provides an intriguing case study that reinforces much of the literature of this module. Researchers have identified seven major strategies that seem to have contributed to their survival. Those major strategies are differential focus on the good, survival for some purpose, psychological distancing, mastery, will to live, hope, and social support. These strategies are highlighted in this lesson. (*Teacher's Resource Binder,* p. 28-1)
- **Enrichment Lesson:** *Obsessive Thoughts* Typically, we deal with unwanted thoughts by trying to suppress them. Research by Daniel Wegner and his colleagues indicates that this strategy may backfire. The more we attempt to suppress obsessive ideas, the more likely we are to become preoccupied with them. This lesson discusses obsessive thoughts and provides students with information on how to obtain advice, information, newsletters, and referrals to treatment centers from the OCD (Obsessive-Compulsive Disorder) Foundation. (*Teacher's Resource Binder,* p. 28-1)

Mood Disorders

V Video Center

Consult the faculty guide from *The Mind* video series for a description of these modules.

- **Videocassette:** *The Mind,* **Second Edition, Module 31: "Mood Disorders: Mania and Depression"** (*Teacher's Resource Binder,* p. 28-1)
- **Videocassette:** *The Mind,* **Second Edition, Module 32: "Mood Disorders: Hereditary Factors"** (*Teacher's Resource Binder,* p. 28-1)

Activity Center

- Application Activity: *The Zung Self-Rating Depression Scale* The Zung Self-Rating Depression Scale is the most widely used scale for self-rating depression. Students can take this test, and learn more about National Depression Screening Day, a national effort to increase depression awareness. (*Teacher's Resource Binder*, p. 28-1; Handout 28–7)
- Analysis Activity: *The Automatic Thoughts Questionnaire* Philip Kendall and Steven Hollon designed the Automatic Thoughts Questionnaire to measure the frequency of automatic negative thoughts associated with depression and to "identify the covert self-statements reported by depressives as being representative of the kinds of cognitions that depressed persons experience." The Automatic Thoughts Questionnaire was developed with a sample of undergraduate college students. It provides a measure of depression and highlights some of the most important symptoms of this condition. (*Teacher's Resource Binder*, p. 28-1; Handout 28–8)
- Critical Thinking Activity: *Depression and Memory* When we are in a bad or sad mood, we are more likely to remember unpleasant events. Jerry Burger suggests a simple classroom replication of D. M. Clark and J. D. Teasdale's study demonstrating this effect. In this exercise, students will associate past experiences with lists of individual words. After they respond, they will determine the number of pleasant and unpleasant experiences recalled before analyzing the relationship of the memories to the tenor of the day. (*Teacher's Resource Binder*, p. 28-1; Handout 28–7)
- Critical Thinking Activity: *The Revised Facts on Suicide Quiz* The Revised Facts on Suicide Quiz, designed by John McIntosh and his colleagues, is a useful tool for introducing classroom discussion of research on suicide. The information communicated in the answers to the questions goes well beyond research on suicide. You may choose to use the entire quiz or create your own version by selecting items from it. (*Teacher's Resource Binder*, p. 28-1; Handout 28–9)
- Analysis Activity: *The Body Investment Scale and Self-Mutilation* Working primarily with adolescents and young adults between the ages of 13 and 19, the authors found the scale featured in this activity to be predictive of self-destructive behaviors, including suicidal tendencies. (*Teacher's Resource Binder*, p. 28-1; Handout 28–10)
- Analysis Activity: *Loneliness* Loneliness is a common and distressing problem for many people. In one national survey, 26 percent of Americans reported having felt "very lonely or remote from other people" during the previous few weeks. While we have a stereotype in our culture of the elderly as being lonely, research indicates adolescents and young adults are actually the loneliest. Use the Revised UCLA Loneliness Scale to measure your students' levels of loneliness. (*Teacher's Resource Binder*, p. 28-1; Handout 28–11)
- Technology Application Activity: *PsychQuest:* "Why Do We Feel Depressed?" *PsychQuest* is an interactive CD-ROM that students can use to learn more about various topics in psychology. This tutorial presents the topic of depression. (*Teacher's Resource Binder*, p. 28-1)

Enrichment Center

- Enrichment Lesson: *Self-Mutilation* You may want to extend the discussion of suicide to a consideration of recent research on self-mutilation. Experts estimate that there are approximately 2 million self-mutilators in the United States, with the vast majority being women. (*Teacher's Resource Binder*, p. 28-1)
- Enrichment Lesson: *The Sadder-But-Wiser Effect* A number of studies have shown that depressed persons may see certain events more accurately than do those who are happy and optimistic. Lauren Alloy and Lyn Abrahamson initially labeled it the *sadder-but-wiser effect*. Today it is also known as *depressive realism*. Fred Hapgood suggests that depressed people may feel as they do not because of low ego defenses or learned helplessness, but because they see themselves as "lost in a society of cockeyed optimists who barge through life with little grasp of the consequences of their actions or words." (*Teacher's Resource Binder*, p. 28-1)
- Enrichment Lesson: *Cognitive Errors in Depression* Aaron Beck's work with depressed patients convinced him that depression is primarily a disorder of thinking rather than of mood. He argued that depression is best described as a cognitive triad of negative thoughts about oneself, the situation, and the future. The depressed person misinterprets facts in a negative way, focuses on the negative aspects of any situation, and has pessimistic expectations about the future. (*Teacher's Resource Binder*, p. 28-1)
- Enrichment Lesson: *Postpartum Depression* A woman in Texas drowns her five children, believing she is saving them from harm. Was it postpartum depression that caused her to commit this awful act—or an illness more troubling? Learn more about this special type of depression with this lesson. (*Teacher's Resource Binder*, p. 28-1)

- **Enrichment Lesson:** *Commitment to the Common Good* Martin Seligman argues that the present epidemic of depression stems in part from a rise in individualism and a decline in commitment to the common good. Learned optimism has to be coupled with a renewed commitment to the common good. To stem the tide of depression in our society, Seligman observes, "Optimism is a tool to help the individual achieve the goals he has set for himself. It is in the choice of the goals themselves that meaning—or emptiness—resides. When learned optimism is coupled with a renewed commitment to the common good, our epidemic of depression and meaninglessness may end." (***Teacher's Resource Binder***, p. 28-1)

MODULE 28

Anxiety and Mood Disorders

Anxiety Disorders

Mood Disorders

This module covers two of the most common categories of psychological disorders. There is little doubt that you know individuals who struggle mightily with problems related to anxiety and mood. In fact, if you are "normal," you have probably struggled occasionally with such problems yourself.

An odd and sometimes troubling aspect of psychological disorders is that it's easy to see the symptoms—almost all of the symptoms—in yourself. The symptoms of psychological disorders usually fall along a continuum. They can be mild, serious, or anything in between. Typically, there is a "gray area" where it's difficult to decide if there is a significant problem. This is different from many medical conditions that are more likely to be either present or absent, with nothing in between. It doesn't make sense to talk about a woman being "kind of" pregnant, but it is surely possible to be "sort of" anxious.

So I'm going to give you the warning I was given years ago: Don't overreact if you begin to discover in yourself the symptoms we discuss in this module. That's typical, and there's even a name for it—"psychology student's disease." The point to remember is that we all have some of these symptoms some of the time. But they don't suggest a disorder unless they meet four important criteria: symptoms must be *maladaptive,* (disrupting normal functioning) *unjustifiable, disturbing,* and *atypical*. For most people most of the time, they are not. However, if you become concerned that you might be one of the large numbers of people affected by the disorders we discuss in this module, you owe it to yourself to have it checked out. Talk to your parents or your guidance counselor for a referral to a mental health professional who can either set your concerns to rest or help you resolve a problem if it does exist.

Getting Started

Have students consider the following questions:

- What does it mean to be anxious? What behaviors do anxious people exhibit?
- How many different moods do people normally experience in a day?

trb You may wish to use **Critical Thinking Activity:** *Fact or Falsehood?* (*Teacher's Resource Binder*, p. 28-1; **Handout 28–1**) as a prereading strategy to evaluate what students already know about anxiety and mood disorders. This activity will prime students to look out for information that could prove or disprove their preconceptions about these disorders.

MODULE 28

Anxiety and Mood Disorders

Introducing the Module

The Points: Module Objectives

- Describe the characteristics of generalized anxiety disorder and panic disorder.
- Identify characteristics of phobic disorder.
- Delineate the characteristics of obsessive-compulsive disorder.
- Describe the characteristics of post-traumatic stress disorder.
- Analyze some of the factors that may contribute to the development of anxiety disorders.
- Describe the characteristics of major depressive disorder.
- Identify the characteristics of bipolar disorder.
- Analyze the factors that may contribute to the development of mood disorders.

trb Building Vocabulary

Students can reinforce their knowledge of the anxiety and mood disorders by completing **Building Vocabulary: Graphic Organizer:** *Concept Chart* (*Teacher's Resource Binder*, p. 28-1; **Handout 28–2**). Students can learn the terms in this module and understand the relationship among them as they fill in the concept chart.

■ TEACHING TIP

Remind students that you and the counselors at your school are available to talk about anything that might concern students as they study this and the successive modules. Students may begin to self-diagnose disorders in their own lives, and they may also feel that friends and loved ones have these disorders. Develop a list of resource personnel you can refer students to for various issues they may want to discuss with a qualified professional.

MODULE 28

Teaching the Points

■ TEACHING TIPS

web (1) You can log on as an instructor to the book companion site for *Thinking About Psychology* at **www.worthpublishers.com/thinkingaboutpsych**. It contains teacher resources for class presentations, as well as review and assessment of module concepts and terms.

trb **tr** (2) A black-line master for Figure 28.1, Anxiety Disorders, is available in the **Black-Line Masters Appendix** of the *Teacher's Resource Binder*.

■ JOURNAL WRITING

Invite students to use the following questions and writing prompts as springboards for entries in their psychology journals:

- Describe a time when you have been anxious. What situation made you anxious? What were you afraid of? How did you react to this anxiety?
- In general what causes you the most anxiety —school, family, friends, the future, or your work? Explain why.

trb At this point, you may wish to use **Analysis Activity:** *Taylor Manifest Anxiety Scale* (*Teacher's Resource Binder*, p. 28-1; **Handout 28–3**).

Anxiety We all experience anxiety in our lives, often as a response to stressful events. Anxiety is not a disorder unless it begins to create significant difficulties in a person's life.

Now let's take a look at the anxiety disorders and the mood disorders. These disorders, like all others, are diagnosed according to the criteria established in the American Psychiatric Association's *DSM—The Diagnostic and Statistical Manual of Mental Disorders* (Fourth Edition Text Revision, 2000). This guide identifies the symptoms that must be present for a diagnosis to be made.

Anxiety Disorders

When psychologists speak of **anxiety,** they are referring to a vague feeling of apprehension and nervousness. You've probably experienced anxiety in relation to specific events—big tests, school projects, or important medical tests, for example. You may also have experienced a more general anxiety, such as feeling ill at ease about the changes that college or a new job might bring, or concern about how troubling world events will play out. These are both normal types of feelings. Anxiety disorders differ from them in that anxiety—or one's effort to control it—begins to take control and dominate life. We'll discuss five of these disorders (Figure 28.1):

- **Generalized anxiety disorder,** marked by persistent, unexplained feelings of apprehension and tenseness.

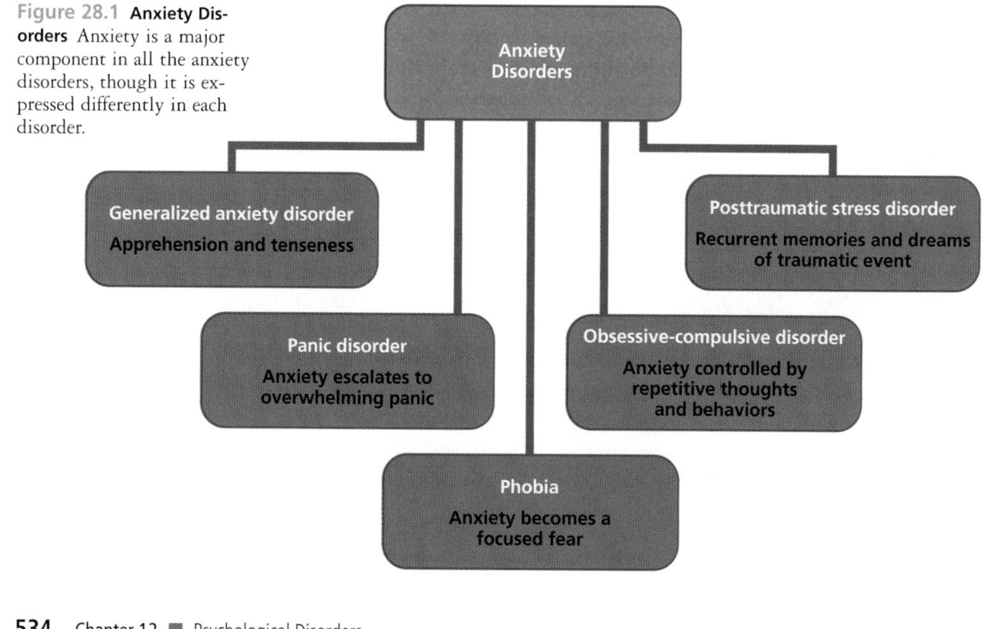

Figure 28.1 **Anxiety Disorders** Anxiety is a major component in all the anxiety disorders, though it is expressed differently in each disorder.

Suggested Readings

Use the following books as teacher-preparation tools or as enrichment for advanced students:

Barondes, S. H. (1998). *Mood genes: Hunting for origins of mania and depression.* New York: Freeman.

Duke, P., & Hochman, G. (1992). *A brilliant madness: Living with manic-depressive illnesses.* New York: Bantam.

Jamison, K. R. (1995). *An unquiet mind.* New York: Knopf.

Raine, N. V. (1998). *After silence: Rape and my journey back.* New York: Crown.

Seligman, M. (1990). *Learned optimism.* New York: Knopf

Summers, M., & Hollander, E. (2000). *Everything in its place: My trials and triumphs over obsessive compulsive disorder.* New York: J.P. Tarcher.

Wedding, D., & Boyd, M. A. (1999). *Movies and mental illness.* New York: McGraw-Hill.

- **Panic disorder,** marked by sudden bouts of intense, unexplained panic.
- **Phobia,** marked by disruptive, irrational fears of objects or situations.
- **Obsessive-compulsive disorder,** marked by unwanted, repetitive thoughts and actions.
- **Posttraumatic stress disorder,** characterized by reliving a severely upsetting event in unwanted recurring memories and dreams.

Generalized Anxiety Disorder and Panic Disorder

What's the point? 1. What are the characteristics of generalized anxiety disorder and panic disorder?

Until pharmaceutical companies began a hard-sell TV ad campaign for drugs to combat *generalized anxiety disorder* many people had never heard of this condition. It doesn't have the dramatic symptoms of many other disorders and until recently escaped public attention. The drug company commercials probably leave many people uneasy because most of us have physical and psychological symptoms that characterize this disorder. However, the symptoms are more lasting for those who suffer generalized anxiety disorder, and are often not attached to any specific event. Table 28.1 lists the symptoms of anxiety. Individuals with generalized anxiety disorder must experience at least three of these symptoms.

Sometimes the anxiety is accompanied by *panic attacks*—episodes of unexplained terror and fear that something bad is going to happen. The attacks, which may last several minutes, usually involve such physical symptoms as choking sensations or shortness of breath. Have you ever

TABLE 28.1 SYMPTOMS OF ANXIETY

Symptoms
Restlessness
Feeling on edge
Difficulty concentrating or mind going blank
Irritability
Muscle tension
Sleep disturbance

Source: Adapted from APA (1994).

▶ **anxiety** A vague feeling of apprehension or nervousness. The basis of the anxiety disorders.

▶ **generalized anxiety disorder** Characterized by disruptive levels of persistent, unexplained feelings of apprehension and tenseness.

▶ **panic disorder** Characterized by sudden bouts of intense, unexplained panic.

▶ **phobia** Characterized by disruptive, irrational fears of objects or situations.

▶ **obsessive-compulsive disorder** Characterized by unwanted, repetitive thoughts and actions.

▶ **posttraumatic stress disorder** Characterized by reliving a severely upsetting event in unwanted recurring memories and dreams.

trb tr ■ TEACHING TIP

A black-line master of Table 28.1, Symptoms of Anxiety, is available in the **Black-Line Masters Appendix** of the *Teacher's Resource Binder.*

tr ■ CHECKING FOR UNDERSTANDING

You can use the black-line master to create a transparency of Table 28.1, covering up terms in the chart for students to identify during class discussion. Use this figure to create a handout for students.

F • Y • I

Patients who have *generalized anxiety disorder (GAD)* often also have major depression, an illness discussed later in this module. Effexor, a drug manufactured by Wyeth-Ayerst, has been shown to be effective in treating both GAD and major depression. Paxil, an antidepressant drug in the same class as Prozac and Zoloft (they are all selective serotonin reuptake inhibitors), is also approved for use to treat GAD as well as social phobia and panic disorder.

Meeting Individual Needs

trb tr Help students understand how the terms in this module are related by having them complete **Building Vocabulary: Graphic Organizer:** ***Concept Chart*** (*Teacher's Resource Binder*, p. 28-1; **Handout 28–2**).

- **Independent Learners** Students can complete the handout on their own as a homework or in-class work assignment. You may want to use **Handout 28–2** as a transparency, projecting a correctly completed chart for students to check their answers.
- **Cooperative Learners** Have students work in small groups to fill out the concept web. Students can tutor each other about the concepts in the module, or you can create a competition in which students see how quickly their team can fill out the web correctly.

MODULE 28

■ JOURNAL WRITING

Invite students to use the following questions and writing prompts as springboards for entries in their psychology journals:

- Have you ever had a panic attack? Describe the experience.
- What are some things that you have a legitimate reason to be afraid of? How did the fear develop?
- What are some things that you have an irrational fear of? How did that fear develop?

F • Y • I

Agoraphobia, or the fear of being in open spaces or in public, often accompanies panic disorder. Since people experience panic attacks at uncontrollable times and in uncontrollable situations, they will often develop a fear of being out in public and having a panic attack. This fear leaves them suffering in their homes, afraid to leave at all.

trb At this point, you may wish to use **Application Activity:** *Fear Survey* (*Teacher's Resource Binder*, p. 28-1; **Handout 28–4**).

■ LOOKING AT THE ISSUES

Phobias are one of the most successfully treated disorders around, yet few people with phobias seek treatment for them. In a class discussion, have students contemplate the following questions that touch on why this might be:

- Why would people be reluctant to get treatment for their everyday fears? *(Everyday fears might not be crippling or disruptive. Also, people may successfully avoid their fear object, not seeing the need to rid themselves of the fear.)*
- What types of fears are more crippling than others? Why?

V At this point, you may wish to show **Videocassette:** *Scientific American Frontiers,* **Second Edition, Module 32: "Arachnophobia"** (*Teacher's Resource Binder*, p. 28-1).

experienced panic? I can recall an episode when I was about 12 years old. My parents were out and I had watched a frightening show on TV. Although I had no reason to do so, I became temporarily convinced that something horrible had happened to my parents. They were fine, of course, but the panic I experienced was so intense that I still remember it clearly more than 40 years later.

We may all feel panic at some point in our lives, but imagine having these attacks several times each day. You're sitting in class, trying to take notes, and the waves of fear start to wash over you for no apparent reason. Your ability to concentrate is totally destroyed; all of your energy is directed toward trying to regain control. Such is the life of a person with *panic disorder,* another of the anxiety disorders.

Phobia

2. What are the characteristics of phobic disorder?

Almost everyone has heard the word *phobia,* which many people use to mean "fear" ("I have a phobia about taking tests.") To psychologists, however, a *phobia* is more than just a fear—it is a fear that is both irrational and disruptive. If you were being stalked on a dark street late at night, your fear of the stalker would not be irrational. But note that irrational fear alone is not enough to define *phobia*—the fear must also be disruptive. Most of us have irrational, nondisruptive fears, of harmless snakes or closed-in spaces, for example. My own particular irrational fear is the step from a ladder to a roof. Despite knowing that I can make the step safely, I hate it. I hate it to the extent that I have never been on the roof of the house in which I have lived for over 20 years! If I were a roofer or a fireman, this fear would be disruptive. But I'm a teacher, and I seldom need to climb onto my roof. On those rare occasions when this becomes necessary, I simply have one of my sons do it or call someone else to do the job. My fear is intense and irrational, but it's not disruptive.

Most phobias involve fear of a particular object, and their names are formed by combining the Greek word for the object with *phobia,* which is the Greek word for fear. Broader phobias also occur.

Social phobias produce fear in social situations. For example, some people have extreme difficulty speaking in public, even to the extent of being unable to respond to questions from a clerk in a store. Others cannot eat in the presence of others, or use public restrooms. As you might imagine, social phobias can seriously impair a person's ability to lead a normal life.

Agoraphobia is fear of situations the person views as difficult to escape from if panic begins to build. Many people with this disorder become trapped in their own homes or in similar safe zones. I once had

Enriching

trb Conduct a study by using **Analysis Activity:** *Taylor Manifest Anxiety Scale* (*Teacher's Resource Binder*, p. 28-1; **Handout 28–3**) and/or **Application Activity:** *Fear Survey* (*Teacher's Resource Binder*, p. 28-1; **Handout 28–4**). Students can even create their own survey to see what students in your school typically fear.

- An Institutional Review Board (IRB) should approve research, and consent should be obtained from all participants.
- Have students write up their findings to publish in a high school journal or as a news item for the school's newspaper. Be sure their report discusses research-based facts about anxiety.

dinner with a woman from my town who was recovering from agoraphobia. She was a middle-aged widow who lived by herself and could not leave her home without experiencing intense fear. She described to me the difficulty of ordinary tasks like grocery shopping, which was to her similar to a military commando raid. Only with intense planning and determination could she leave her car, quickly collect the two or three items she needed most, and make it through checkout before dashing back to the parking lot. Often she began to feel panicky during her few minutes in the store, and sometimes she had to abandon her quest, only to face another trial the next day. Over the course of the last 15 years she has largely conquered her agoraphobia through therapy. She was very happy to say she had actually been able to take a European vacation a few years ago.

Other common (and some not so common!) phobias appear in Table 28.2. Why are phobias considered anxiety disorders? Because they focus general feelings of anxiety onto a feared object or situation. It's as though diffuse light has been passed through a lens to produce a sharp, well-defined image.

TABLE 28.2 SOME COMMON—AND NOT-SO-COMMON—PHOBIAS

These are common:	
Blood	hematophobia
Darkness	nyctophobia
Enclosed space	claustrophobia
Germs	spermophobia
Heights	acrophobia
Mice	musophobia
Snakes	ophidiophobia
Spiders	arachanophobia
Wasps	spheksophobia
Phobias can *develop to almost anything, including:*	
Air	aerophobia
Churches	ecclesiaphobia
Eyes	ommatophobia
Frost	cryophobia
Shadows	sciophobia
Swallowing	phagophobia
Trees	dendrophobia

Source: Adapted from Melville, 1978.

Have students explore the Internet to see how many different types of phobias they can find. In an oral report of their findings, have them respond to the following questions:

- What is the most obscure phobia you found?
- What was the most common phobia listed?

Volunteers may want to combine report results from the class and develop a bar graph or pie chart of phobia findings that can be used as a class display.

trb tr ■ **TEACHING TIP**

A black-line master for Table 28.2, Some Common—and Not-So-Common—Phobias, is available in the **Black-Line Masters Appendix** of the *Teacher's Resource Binder.*

■ **APPLYING THE POINTS**

Contact a psychologist who specializes in treating anxiety disorders and ask about treatment options. The following questions can be used as a guide for this conversation as well as a presentation of findings to your class:

- What types of medication are available?
- What types of behavioral or cognitive therapy are used?
- Do patients typically get completely rid of their fear through therapy? Or is the goal of therapy to get patients to a comfortable level of functioning?

■ **MULTICULTURAL CONNECTIONS**

Using available resources, have students explore whether the objects people in the United States fear most are similar to those things that are feared most in other countries. Pose the following questions to guide students in a discussion of their findings:

- Do people in other cultures fear speaking in public as much as people seem to in the United States?
- Do fears differ among people of different socioeconomic groups? Why or why not?
- Do people in countries that have experienced war have higher incidences of certain anxiety disorders? What kinds?

trb At this point, you may wish to use **Analysis Activity:** *Social Phobias* (*Teacher's Resource Binder*, p. 28-1; **Handout 28–5**).

MODULE 28

F•Y•I

Former Nickelodeon game show host Marc Summers suffers from obsessive-compulsive disorder. Students may remember him as the host of *Double Dare* and *Family Double Dare*, game shows that subjected him to getting splattered with slime and goo. He often felt consumed by anxiety as he struggled to put on a cheerful face as the shows' host. Currently, he hosts a nationally syndicated talk show and is the national spokesman for the Obsessive-Compulsive Foundation.

trb At this point, you may wish to use Analysis Activity: *Obsessive-Compulsive Disorder* (*Teacher's Resource Binder*, p. 28-1; Handout 28–6).

■ JOURNAL WRITING

Invite students to use the following questions and writing prompts as springboards for entries in their psychology journals:

- What behavior do you exhibit that might be considered "compulsive"? Why do you behave that way?
- What compulsive behaviors do you exhibit that are helpful to you? What behaviors are hurtful?

■ TEACHING TIP

Have students recall old childhood "rules" similar to "step on a crack and break your mother's back." Some rules they remember could include "cootie shots" and superstitions like being careful not to break mirrors (or you'll get seven years of bad luck!) or not walking under ladders. Guide a discussion with the following questions:

- Why do children develop these rules? What purpose do they serve?
- How do children learn these rules?
- Do you remember being compulsive about these rules? How did you feel when you broke the rules? What would you do to "make it right"?

Obsessive-Compulsive Disorder

3. What are the characteristics of obsessive-compulsive disorder?

The two major symptoms of obsessive-compulsive disorder are, as you might imagine, obsessions and compulsions. *Obsessions* are repetitive thoughts and *compulsions* are repetitive actions. Almost everyone experiences both symptoms to some degree on a harmless level. In my classroom, I notice a lot of faraway stares as homecoming and prom and other big dating weekends approach. I know many of these students are unable to stop thinking about the upcoming event (at least that was the case for me when I was a student!). Other times a song may begin to play in our head, and we find ourselves unable to rid ourselves of it.

We all have compulsions, too. One day I watched a student walk down the hall tapping the eraser of his pencil on every locker. Somehow he missed the last locker in the row and managed to get about 10 yards down the hall before having to return to tap that last locker. You could almost feel his discomfort until the task was complete. You may have done something similar as a child. Remember that old rhyme about "Step on a crack and break your mother's back"? Were you able to step on sidewalk cracks easily after learning that rhyme?

Obsessive-compulsive tendencies can be helplful sometime. Most good athletes are obsessed with winning and compulsive about training. And, most good students are a bit obsessed with grades and a bit compulsive about studying. These tendencies help us develop important routines, such as fastening our safety belt when we get in a car or brushing our teeth on a regular basis.

Obsessions and compulsions, however, begin to take control with some people, and this is when helpful tendencies become obsessive-compulsive disorder. One common obsession focuses on germs and develops with a compulsion in the form of repetitive hand washing. Individuals may wash their hands literally hundreds of times each day. Often, they engage in a hand-washing ritual that may take many minutes to complete, much like a surgeon scrubbing up before an operation. As long as such people have the opportunity to engage in their rituals, their anxiety re-

Upset by Dog Germs In the 1997 film *As Good as It Gets,* Jack Nicholson plays the part of a person with obsessive-compulsive disorder.

Cross-Curricular Connections

HISTORY Have students research how the diagnosis and treatment of posttraumatic stress disorder (PTSD) has changed over the last century. Have students discover through historical research how people experiencing traumas like war, assassinations, and accidents were expected to behave after such traumas and whether services were available for treating the symptoms of PTSD. Consider the following events that may have caused PTSD to occur for people in the United States:

- World Wars I and II
- Korean and Vietnam conflicts
- Gulf War

TABLE 28.3 COMMON OBSESSIONS AND COMPULSIONS AMONG CHILDREN AND ADOLESCENTS WITH OBSESSIVE-COMPULSIVE DISORDER

THOUGHT OR BEHAVIOR	PERCENTAGE* REPORTING SYMPTOM
Obsessions (repetitive thoughts)	
Concern with dirt, germs, or toxins	40
Something terrible happening (fire, death, illness)	24
Symmetry, order, or exactness	17
Compulsions (repetitive behaviors)	
Excessive hand washing, bathing, tooth brushing, or grooming	85
Repeating rituals (in/out of a door, up/down from a chair)	51
Checking doors, locks, appliances, car brake, homework	46

*Seventy children and adolescents reported their symptoms.
Source: Adapted from Rapoport, 1989.

mains under control. If they are somehow prevented from engaging in their ritual behavior, anxiety and panic rapidly build.

Other common patterns of obsessive-compulsive disorder involve dressing rituals, where a person may take hours to shower and dress each morning because of hundreds of required steps that must be followed. Another common pattern is checking and rechecking a lock or an electrical switch. The person might return to the car 10 times in a row to make sure the lights are off and the door is locked. Table 28.3 lists some common obsessions and compulsions of children and adolescents suffering with this disorder.

Posttraumatic Stress Disorder

4. What are the characteristics of posttraumatic stress disorder?

What do military combat veterans, rape victims, abused children, and rescue workers who have to clean up gruesome accident sites have in common? They are all at increased risk for *posttraumatic stress disorder*. Intense stress is the trigger, and symptoms include nightmares, persistent fear, difficulty relating normally to others, and troubling memories or flashbacks of the traumatic event (American Psychiatric Association,

- the assassinations of John F. Kennedy and Martin Luther King, Jr.
- September 11, 2001
- the *Challenger* and *Columbia* accidents

For extra credit, suggest interested students choose a historical event and turn their research into an oral or written presentation.

trb At this point, you may wish to use **Enrichment Lesson:** *Concentration Camp Survival* (*Teacher's Resource Binder*, p. 28-1).

■ TEACHING TIPS

trb tr (1) A black-line master of Table 28.3, Common Obsessions and Compulsions Among Children and Adolescents with Obsessive-Compulsive Disorder, is available in the **Black-Line Masters Appendix** of the *Teacher's Resource Binder.*

(2) Help students differentiate between *obsessive-compulsive disorder* and *obsessive-compulsive personality disorder*, which is discussed in Module 29.

- **OCD** is an anxiety disorder characterized by obsessive thoughts with corresponding compulsions. People with OCD are likely to lead very routine lives, repeating tasks over and over again to find relief from their anxieties.
- **OCPD** is a personality disorder characterized by an obsessive need for neatness, order, and symmetry. People with OCPD are more likely to be called "neat freaks" or "anal-retentive."

F • Y • I

Compulsions manifest in several different ways:

- **Hoarders** collect things and have a hard time throwing anything away. They are usually plagued by fears of losing things. So they keep everything, including leftovers and broken items.
- **Checkers** will check (and recheck) actions they have performed, like turning off the oven or locking the door. Unfortunately, the number of times needed to relieve anxiety increases with each experience.
- **Counters** will count everything, from steps they take to words people say to them. This preoccupation with counting may stop their daily progress in life.
- **Cleaners** will clean either their hands or surfaces excessively. Often, this cleaning will need to be done a certain number of times to relieve the anxiety.

trb At this point, you may wish to use **Analysis Activity:** *Obsessive-Compulsive Disorder* (*Teacher's Resource Binder*, p. 28-1; **Handout 28–6**).

MODULE 28

■ LOOKING AT THE ISSUES

Media coverage of important historical events has become pervasive in U.S. culture since the 1950s and 1960s. Today, 24-hour news channels are popular media outlets that show up-to-the-minute coverage of war, disaster, and tragedy. Although this capability represents advances in journalism, it also exposes everyday people to the kinds of experiences that could lead to PTSD. Pose the following questions to the class:

- How does viewing trauma on TV affect people who haven't experienced the tragedy or conflict first-hand?
- Can people develop PTSD vicariously? How different are experiences of PTSD for those who developed it vicariously versus those who developed it through first-hand experience with trauma?

trb At this point, you may wish to use **Enrichment Lesson:** *Concentration Camp Survival* (*Teacher's Resource Binder*, p. 28-1).

■ TEACHING TIPS

(1) Link *posttraumatic stress disorder* to *flashbulb memories.* For many people who experience trauma, the events occurring before, during, and directly after the event become etched into their minds, forming a flashbulb memory of the event. Have students recall a powerful memory of a traumatic event that they've experienced and ask if they remember vividly where they were during the event.

(2) Remind students that studies of identical twins provide insight into which behaviors are genetically predisposed and which behaviors are environmentally influenced. Identical twins share 100 percent of their DNA, so comparisons of their behaviors can shed light on what might be passed on in our genetic code.

(3) Remind students that the frontal lobes are responsible for judgment and decision making. If people with OCD have overactive frontal lobes, then they are controlled by overzealous decision making. They cannot control what decisions they should be making, so they allow their behavior to be ruled by repetitive thoughts.

1994). The 9/11 attacks on the Twin Towers and Pentagon were events with the potential to produce many cases of posttraumatic stress disorder, not only among those who escaped the buildings or witnessed the tragedy firsthand, but also in those who followed the events on TV. Children may be particularly vulnerable, because witnessing or experiencing trauma may instill a sense of hopelessness about the future and harm their ability to trust. The negative consequences of bad experiences can produce increased anxiety and other symptoms for many years.

Causes of Anxiety Disorders

5. What are some of the factors that may contribute to the development of anxiety disorders?

Anxiety disorders could be caused by nature—the impact of our inherited biology—or nurture—the influence of the environment. As is almost always the case, both factors are important.

Biological Factors

Anxiety disorders, like so many other areas that psychologists study, illustrate the interaction between our biology and our environment. Some of the biological factors that contribute to anxiety disorders are these:

- ***Heredity*** Some of us inherit a *predisposition,* or likelihood, for developing anxiety disorders. Evidence for this comes from studies of identical twins, who are genetically the same. Even when raised in different families, identical twins sometimes have similar phobias (Carey, 1990; Eckert & others, 1981). The influence of heredity is also apparent in monkey studies demonstrating that fearful parents are likely to have fearful children (Suomi, 1986). The specific fear is not inherited, but the predisposition to be fearful is.

Heredity and Fear We don't appear to inherit specific fears, but we do inherit a predisposition to develop fears. This is why identical twins are more likely than other siblings to share the same fears, even if they are not raised together.

- ***Brain function*** Brain-scanning techniques show that people with anxiety disorders have brains that literally function differently from those of people who do not have anxiety disorders. As Figure 28.2 illustrates, brain scans show a higher degree of activity in the frontal lobes of people with obsessive-compulsive disorder (Rauch & Jenike, 1993; Resnick, 1992). An emotion center called the amygdala also shows differences for people with phobias (Armony & others, 1998).

Enriching

Have students interview people who experienced trauma in the last century to find out how they coped with the stress involved with a particularly tragic event. Students might consider interviewing people who had the following experiences:

- surviving the Holocaust or battles in World War II
- experiencing wars in Korea, Vietnam, or the Persian Gulf
- experiencing the Kennedy assassination in the media
- surviving or witnessing September 11, 2001
- experiencing the *Challenger* or *Columbia* accidents in the media

trb At this point, you may wish to use **Enrichment Lesson:** *Concentration Camp Survival* (*Teacher's Resource Binder*, p. 28-1).

Because brain function is involved, anxiety disorders often respond to treatment with medication.

- ***Evolution*** We are likely to fear situations that posed danger to the earliest humans. Dangerous animals, heights, and storms were threats, and people who didn't have a healthy dose of fear were less likely to survive. Those who did survive passed on to us—their descendants—their tendency to fear these dangers. Many of us share these fears to this day, even though our modern world has made these threats less dangerous than they once were. Unfortunately, we don't have a similar inherited tendency to fear threats that have developed more recently. Cars, for example, kill far more people in the modern world than snake bites do, yet more people fear snakes than fear cars.

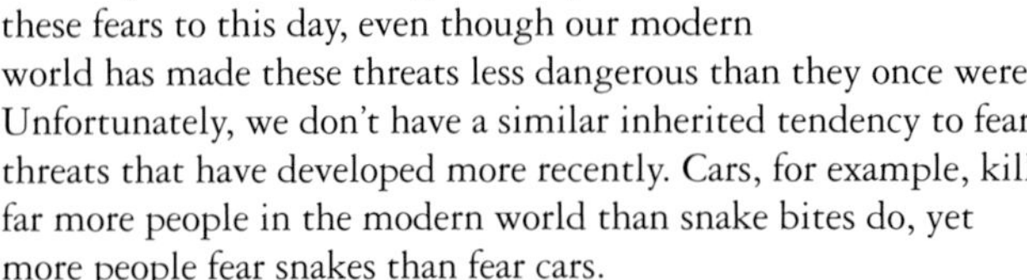

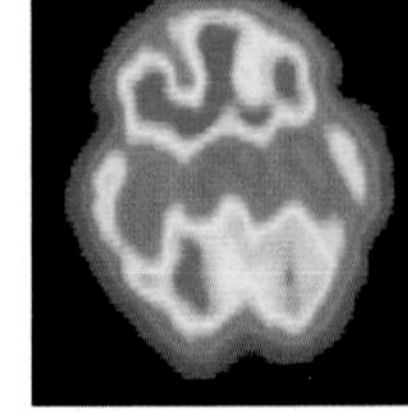

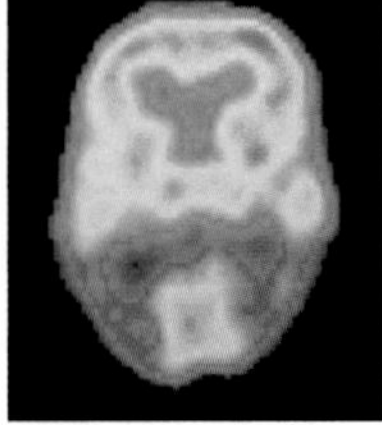

With OCD No OCD

Figure 28.2 **The Brain and Obsessive-Compulsive Disorder** These PET scans show the difference in brain function between a person who has obsessive-compulsive disorder (OCD) and a person who does not. The red areas on the scan on the left indicate higher than normal amounts of activity in the frontal lobes of the brain, a characteristic of obsessive-compulsive disorder.

Learning Factors

Learning gone awry can also produce anxiety disorders. Sometimes we learn to respond well in stressful situations, but if we learn maladaptive responses they can blossom into anxiety disorders. These factors can contribute:

- ***Conditioning*** Ivan Pavlov became famous for his studies in which dogs learned to associate the sound of a tuning fork with the taste of meat, salivating equally to both. Humans can also learn to associate fear with certain places or things. John Watson and Rosalie Rayner (1920) demonstrated this in their famous research with "Little Albert," an infant who learned to fear white rats. Watson and Rayner established the fear by pairing the sight of a rat with loud, frightening noises. Few of us would deliberately teach a child fear, but the child might learn to associate fear and dogs if exposed to a menacing growl or bite when young.
- ***Observational learning*** Children can also learn fears at their parents' knees. If a child sees a parent or older sibling responding with fear to thunderstorms, bees, or high places, the child may well begin to experience the same fear. Even young monkeys learned to fear snakes when given the opportunity to watch other monkeys avoid situations where a snake was present (Mineka, 1985).
- ***Reinforcement*** We also learn to associate emotions with actions, depending on the results that follow those actions. A person with a fear of heights can reduce the fear by avoiding heights. That release from anxiety makes it more likely that the person will avoid heights in the future. A person with an obsessive-

Nature or Nurture? The baby may be biologically predisposed to fear heights, but she may also learn this fear by watching her mother.

Enriching

What would life be like without fear? Have students offer scenarios in which fear is detrimental and useful in daily life. If fear weren't an issue, how would these situations be different?

trb At this point, you may wish to use **Application Activity:** ***Fear Survey*** (*Teacher's Resource Binder*, p. 28-1; **Handout 28–4**).

MODULE **28**

■ LOOKING AT THE ISSUES

Have students research fears that have evolved to help further our species, including public speaking, flying, germs, and failure.

Interested students can present their findings in an oral or written report, which you may consider for extra credit.

V At this point, you may wish to show **Videocassette:** ***The Mind,*** **Second Edition, Module 32: "Mood Disorders: Hereditary Factors"** (*Teacher's Resource Binder*, p. 28-1).

■ TEACHING TIPS

(1) Review with students the components of classical conditioning that led to Little Albert developing a fear of white, furry objects.

- **Unconditioned stimulus (UCS)** = loud "bang" that occurred when the lead pipes were struck
- **Unconditioned response (UCR)** = fear of the loud "bang"
- **Conditioned stimulus (CS)** = white, furry objects
- **Conditioned response (CR)** = fear, but this time in response to the white, furry objects

(2) Have students recall that the fear response John Watson cultivated so easily was reversed in other patients by his student Mary Cover Jones. She used classical conditioning to remove a fear response from individuals who had developed a fear of a certain object. She used a pleasant UCS, like candy or food, so patients could associate the pleasant feeling with the object they had come to fear.

■ JOURNAL WRITING

Invite students to use the following questions and writing prompts as springboards for entries in their psychology journals:

- When would it be good to teach children to fear something?
- What fears have you learned in your life? From whom have you learned them? Do you have any desire to get rid of these fears? Why or why not?

MODULE 28

F • Y • I

Barbara Fredericksen of the University of Michigan has proposed a theory of negative and positive emotions and how those emotions affect other emotions and circumstances in our lives. Although negative emotions narrow our lives and make us selfish and closed to the world around us, positive emotions broaden and build our lives. After experiencing positive emotions, people tend to savor the moment. They are more likely to be helpful and spread their good feelings around.

■ LOOKING AT THE ISSUES

There are several different types of mood disorders that are not classified in the DSM. Have students research the following disorders, concentrating on why they are not included in the DSM:

- seasonal affective disorder
- postpartum depression

■ JOURNAL WRITING

Invite students to use the following questions and writing prompts as springboards for entries in their psychology journals:

- Have you ever felt depressed? What caused your depression? How did you handle it?
- Are certain points in your day, week, month, or year more likely to leave you depressed? Why?

compulsive hand-washing ritual can reduce anxiety by washing and will therefore repeat that action. We tend to repeat responses that have good results and avoid those that have bad results.

No one has an anxiety-free life. But when the anxiety begins to take control (as in the case of a generalized anxiety disorder), refocus as fear (as in the case of a phobia), drive us to rigidly repeated thoughts and behaviors (as in the case of obsessive-compulsive disorder), or make it impossible to escape an earlier horror (as in the case of posttraumatic stress disorder), anxiety has crossed the line and has become a psychological disorder.

Mood Disorders

Mood disorders are disturbances of emotions. Like other disorders you've read about in this module, these conditions are magnifications of our normal reactions. The magnified states in mood disorders are *mania* and *depression*. Mania is a period of abnormally high emotion and activity. Has anyone ever said to you, "Don't be so manic!" People often use that statement when they simply mean "Calm down—don't be so excited!" Life would be very dull if we could never feel elated or excited or wildly enthusiastic. But what if you felt intense mania for days or even weeks and just couldn't "come down"? As you'll see later in this section, some people do, and it's not pleasant.

Depression Anguished depression can be a normal response to tragic events. Specific criteria must be met before a diagnosis of major depression is made.

It is a rare individual who never feels depressed. Can any of us say that we never feel "down," or sad, or listless and drained of energy? Depression is a normal response to many of the things life hands us, including the death of loved ones, the end of important relationships, transitions such as the loss of a job or even graduation, or stress. We can even become depressed over distant events, such as famines or outbreaks of violence in far corners of the world. How do we know where to draw the line between normal reactions and a mood disorder? Keep this question in mind as we consider the two main mood disorders, *major depressive disorder* and *bipolar disorder* (Figure 28.3).

Major Depressive Disorder

6. What are the characteristics of major depressive disorder?

► **major depressive disorder** A mood disorder in which a person, for no apparent reason, experiences at least two weeks of depressed moods, diminished interest in activities, and other symptoms, such as feelings of worthlessness.

Major depressive disorder is the most common mood disorder and one of the more common psychological disorders. Therapists say that depression has crossed the line from a normal reaction to major depres-

Cooperative Learning

Divide the class into small groups of students and have each group create a continuum of the different types of mood, with *depression* on one extreme and *mania* on the other. Have students come up with at least five different levels of mood between the two extremes. When the continuums are completed, have each group present its continuum to the class. Then, pose the following questions to the class:

- Could your group come to a consensus about what the different types of mood were called? Why or why not? How did you decide which moods to place on the continuum?

V At this point, you may wish to show Videocassette: *The Mind*, Second Edition, Module 31: "Mood Disorders: Mania and Depression" (*Teacher's Resource Binder*, p. 28-1).

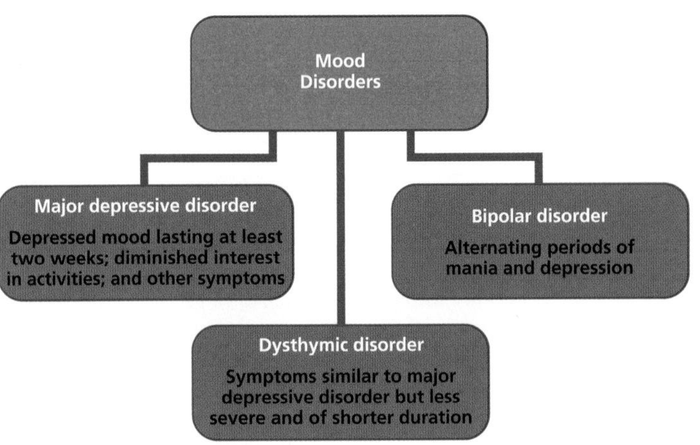

Figure 28.3 **Mood Disorders**

sive disorder when five of the following nine symptoms have been present for two or more weeks (one of the first two symptoms must be included in those five) (DSM-IV-TR, 2000):

- Depressed mood most of the day, nearly every day. (In children and adolescents, an irritated mood satisfies this requirement.)
- Little interest or pleasure in almost all activities.
- Significant changes in weight or appetite.
- Sleeping more or less than usual.
- Agitated or decreased level of activity.
- Fatigue or loss of energy.
- Feelings of worthlessness or inappropriate guilt.
- Diminished ability to think or concentrate.
- Recurrent thoughts of death or suicide.

These symptoms must also produce distress or impaired functioning to qualify as indicators or major depressive disorder. One of the main differences between major depressive disorder and normal grief is the apparent reason for the emotions. Grief over the loss of a loved one is an understandable reaction. In contrast, there may be no apparent trigger for major depressive disorder.

Dysthymic disorder, which shares many of the symptoms of major depressive disorder, doesn't quite have the same overwhelming feel. Major depressive disorder feels like an inescapable weight affecting every aspect of life.

Meeting Individual Needs

trb tr You can provide students with a copy of the black-line master of Figure 28.3, Mood Disorders, available in the **Black-Line Masters Appendix** of the *Teacher's Resource Binder.* Students can fill in terms you have obscured as a quick assessment of their knowledge. Students with special needs may work with a student tutor to complete the handout after class lecture and/or discussion.

- **Exceptional Learners** A handout created from the black-line master for Figure 28.3 can fill the need to provide notes for exceptional learners. These students can review the terms with a student or teacher/tutor. They may also refer to the handout during class discussion or lecture.

trb tr ■ **TEACHING TIP**

For use with the notes that follow, a black-line master of Figure 28.3, Mood Disorders, is available in the **Black-Line Masters Appendix** of the *Teacher's Resource Binder.*

F • Y • I

National Depression Screening Day, created by Harvard psychiatrist Dr. Douglas G. Jacobs in 1991, has since been repeated every year in early October. Each year, the number of sites staffed by mental health professionals has grown. The free screening includes completion of a self-rating depression scale; a 20-minute talk on the causes, symptoms, and treatment of the disorder (during which participants may ask questions) and 5 minutes alone with a mental health professional. Based on the scale scores and the clinician's probing, participants learn whether they need more evaluation. No diagnosis or treatment is provided.

trb At this point, you may wish to use **Application Activity:** *The Zung Self-Rating Depression Scale* (*Teacher's Resource Binder,* p. 28-1; **Handout 28–7**).

■ **TEACHING TIP**

Go into more detail about **dysthymic disorder**, a depressive state lasting more than two years. To make the diagnosis in children and adolescents, the depressive state need only last one year. Patients must also present two or more of the following symptoms: poor appetite or overeating, insomnia (lack of sleep) or hypersomnia (too much sleep), low energy or fatigue, low self-esteem, poor concentration or difficulty making decisions, feelings of hopelessness.

tr ■ **CHECKING FOR UNDERSTANDING**

Create a transparency of Figure 28.3, Mood Disorders, and cover up terms in the chart for students to identify during class discussion. This can help you determine what students grasp well and what they may need to review for better understanding.

MODULE 28

■ TEACHING TIPS

tr (1) A four-color transparency of Figure 28.4, Teen Suicide Rates, on page 545, is available in the **Overhead Transparency Set.**

(2) Suicide may be a sensitive subject, especially if students have known someone who has committed suicide. Students may also have attempted suicide and not shared that experience with others. Be aware that students generally struggle with questions about the meaning of life; although these feelings are normal, ending one's life is not a solution. Remind students that any indication that someone may be contemplating suicide should be taken seriously, not as a joke.

trb At this point, you may wish to use **Critical Thinking Activity:** *The Revised Facts on Suicide Quiz* (*Teacher's Resource Binder,* p. 28-1; **Handout 28–9**).

■ APPLYING THE POINTS

Invite your school's guidance counselor to discuss what your school's plan would be in the event that a student committed suicide. Ask the counselor to address the following questions:

- What plan is now in place? How was it developed?
- What outside resources would be called in?
- Is this plan similar to ones that would be in place if a student died in some other way? How would it be different?

trb At this point, you may wish to use **Critical Thinking Activity:** *The Revised Facts on Suicide Quiz* (*Teacher's Resource Binder,* p. 28-1; **Handout 28–9**).

Up Close

Suicide

When I was a junior in high school, back in the late 1960s, a fellow student didn't appear for class one day shortly after breaking up with a long-time girlfriend. As the day wore on, rumors that he had committed suicide began to travel through the student body. The rumors proved to be true, but nobody ever dealt with the issue openly. Teachers, counselors, administrators, and parents seemed united in their desire not to talk about something they found disturbing and unexplainable. Students were left to sort out their questions and feelings on their own, and the school never even issued an official acknowledgement of what had happened.

Teen suicide rates increased during the last half of the twentieth century, though they have begun to drop off in the past decade or so (Figure 28.4). There have also been student suicides, and suicide attempts, in the school where I now teach. Seeing this important issue brought into the open has been gratifying. In recent years, the administration put into place a crisis response plan to help both students and faculty members cope with the emotional impact of the loss or injury of a student. Instead of pretending that nothing has happened, the school issues announcements, runs articles in the school newspaper, and ensures that counselors are available to help friends with their grief and questions. Bringing the topic of suicide into the light of day may prevent others from making this tragic choice.

One interesting fact about suicide is that people who are deeply depressed rarely kill themselves until after the depression starts to lift. This is confusing to friends, because the suicide occurs just as the person seems to be getting better. Ironically, this lifting of depression gives the person the energy to execute a plan developed when depression was so overwhelming that it effectively stopped action.

For adolescents to have occasional, passing thoughts of suicide is neither unusual nor a cause for concern. But becoming obsessed with thoughts of suicide, or starting to develop plans for committing suicide, is. It's quite likely that a suicide or suicide attempt of someone you know will touch your life, if it has not already done so. If you have a friend who appears deeply depressed, is preoccu-

Symptoms of Depression One symptom of depression is the diminished ability to think or concentrate.

Enriching

trb Conduct a study using **Application Activity:** *The Zung Self-Rating Depression Scale* (*Teacher's Resource Binder,* p. 28-1; **Handout 28–7**). Survey a sample of students to determine the rate of depression among students in your building.

- An Institutional Review Board (IRB) should approve research, and consent should be obtained from all participants.
- Have students write up their findings in a high school journal or as a news item for the school's newspaper. Be sure their report discusses research-based facts about depression.

pied with death, begins to give away prized possessions, or talks openly about suicide, take the signs seriously. Encourage the person to seek help immediately, and consult with a parent, teacher, counselor, physician, or religious leader to make sure you have done all that you can. If *you* begin to feel suicidal, seek help. I rarely encourage students to procrastinate, but when it comes to attempting to end your own life, there is no better thing you can do than delay acting and seek professional help. The dark mood *will* lift, and better days *do* lie ahead.

Consider these differences in suicide rates for different groups:

- In general, Western countries have a higher rate of suicide than non-Western countries, but there is a great deal of variation even among Western countries. The rate in England is about half the U.S. rate, and the rate in Finland is about double (Bureau of the Census, 1998).
- In most parts of the world (other than China), men are more likely than women to commit suicide. Women, however, are at least twice as likely to *attempt* suicide. Men succeed more often because their method of choice is firearms, which are more lethal than the drug overdoses preferred by women.
- White Americans have a higher suicide rate than other racial groups (Bureau of the Census, 1998).
- Suicide rates increase with age. In the United States, the highest rate of suicide is among the elderly. Elderly men commit suicide at a rate of about 60 per 100,000 people.
- There is a strong link between drug and alcohol use and suicide. The risk of suicide is 100 times greater among alcoholics (Murphy & Wetzel, 1990).

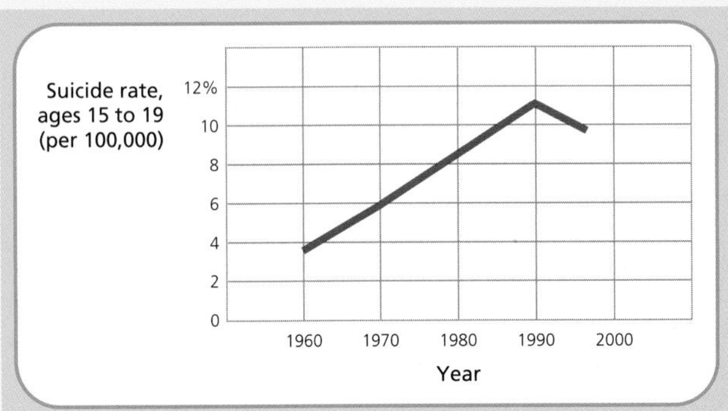

Figure 28.4 Teen Suicide Rates Teen suicide rates increased throughout most of the second half of the twentieth century, but they have been dropping since 1990. (From National Center for Health Statistics.)

Cooperative Learning

After students have read Up Close: Suicide on pages 544 and 545 and studied Figure 28.4, have them meet in groups and come up with several serious, helpful responses they might give to a friend, family member, or acquaintance who might communicate the contemplation of suicide. Present the following questions as a guide for group discussion:

- What would their response be to someone who seems preoccupied with death?
- What would their response be to someone who tried to give them a prized possession?
- What would they say to someone who told them they were contemplating suicide?

tr A four-color transparency of Figure 28.4, Teen Suicide Rates, is available in the **Overhead Transparency Set.**

■ TEACHING TIP

What reasons do people give for being lonely? One survey sorted them into five major categories.

1. **Being unattached:** having no spouse or partner, particularly just after breaking up with a spouse or significant other
2. **Alienation:** being misunderstood and feeling different; not being needed and having no close friends
3. **Being alone:** coming home to an empty house
4. **Forced isolation:** being hospitalized or housebound; having no transportation
5. **Dislocation:** being away from home; starting a new job or school; traveling often

trb At this point, you may wish to use **Analysis Activity:** *Loneliness* (*Teacher's Resource Binder*, p. 28-1; **Handout 28–11**).

F • Y • I

How do people cope with loneliness? Rubenstein and Shaver have found four major strategies.

1. "Sad passivity" includes sleeping, drinking, overeating, and watching TV.
2. "Social contact" may involve calling a friend or visiting someone.
3. "Active solitude" takes the form of studying, reading, exercising, or going to a movie.
4. "Distractions" include spending money and going shopping.

Source: **Rubenstein, C. M., & Shaver, P.** (1982). *In search of intimacy*. New York: Delacorte.

trb At this point, you may wish to use **Analysis Activity:** *Loneliness* (*Teacher's Resource Binder*, p. 28-1; **Handout 28–11**).

■ MULTICULTURAL CONNECTIONS

Have students use available resources to investigate reasons why suicide rates differ in different cultures. Pose the following questions as a guide for research and a subsequent discussion of students' findings:

- Do some cultures view suicide as an honorable way of ending life?
- What is it about Finnish culture that seems to encourage suicide? What about British culture discourages it?

MODULE 28

F • Y • I

(1) David Rosenhan and Martin Seligman identify the following symptoms of *mania*:

- **Mood** or **emotional symptoms**—The mood is typically euphoric, expansive, and elevated. In some cases, the dominant mood is irritability, particularly if the manic person is thwarted.
- **Grandiose cognition**—Manics believe they have no limits to their abilities and, what's worse, do not recognize the painful consequences of trying to carry out their plans. Sometimes manics have delusional thoughts about themselves.
- **Motivational symptoms**—The manic's hyperactivity has an intrusive, dominating, and domineering quality. In the manic state, some engage in compulsive gambling, reckless driving, or poor financial investment.
- **Physical symptoms**—With the hyperactivity comes a greatly lessened need for sleep. After a few days, however, exhaustion settles in, and the mania slows down.

Source: Rosenhan, D., & Seligman, M. (1995). *Abnormal psychology* (3rd ed.). New York: Norton.

(2) *Bipolar disorder* comes in two types:

- **Bipolar Disorder I** is the classic diagnosis of this disorder. Patients experience cyclic periods of inflated mood followed by depressive episodes.
- **Bipolar Disorder II** is a milder form of bipolar disorder in which patients experience at least one episode of hypomania (a period of elevated mood, but without psychosis) and at least one major depressive episode.

▸ **bipolar disorder** A mood disorder (formerly called *manic depressive disorder*) in which the person alternates between the hopelessness of depression and the overexcited and unreasonably optimistic state of mania.

Bipolar Disorder

7. What are the characteristics of bipolar disorder?

People with **bipolar disorder** (previously known as *manic depressive disorder*) also experience the oppressive down periods of major depression. But these depressed times alternate with manic episodes in which the person is unrealistically optimistic and displays wildly hyper behavior.

It's good to be optimistic, but these manic phases are well beyond normal. During mania, a person may go long periods without sleeping, experience changeable, racing thoughts, be easily distracted, and set impossible goals.

These manic phases, like the bouts of depression that occur in major depressive disorder, tend to have hills and valleys. Moods generally follow cyclical patterns—most people find that they swing through some periods when they feel a little down and others where they feel great. In fact, mania is sometimes associated with bursts of creative energy (Jamison, 1993, 1995). Many well-known creative people, from Mark Twain to Vincent van Gogh, are believed to have suffered from bipolar disorder.

Causes of Mood Disorders

8. What factors may contribute to the development of mood disorders?

As with anxiety disorders, no single explanation sheds light on all mood disorders. And again, biology and environment interact. Stress also seems to play a role, providing a trigger that sparks mood disorders when other factors are present.

Vincent van Gogh It is difficult to diagnose mental illness in historical figures, but van Gogh quite possibly suffered from bipolar disorder. His life alternated between periods of blazing creativity—sometimes he finished more than a painting a day—and periods of deep depression. He committed suicide in 1890.

Biological Factors

Our physical and psychological future is not written in our genes, but genetics does set limits on some of our choices. For mood disorders, both heredity and brain function appear to be important biological factors.

- ***Heredity*** Many disorders run in families, and mood disorders are no exception. We can see the influence of heredity in twin studies. Genetically, fraternal twins differ from each other as much as any two other siblings. If one fraternal twin has major depressive disorder, the other twin has a 20 percent chance of developing depression. The odds are significantly higher for identical twins, who have identical genes. If one identical twin has major depressive disorder, the second twin's chances rise to about 50 percent. The trend is even more pronounced for bipolar disorder, with the second identical twin having a 70 percent chance of developing bipo-

Cross-Curricular Connections

ART Invite your school's art teacher in to discuss how the creative genius of several famous artists might have been the outlet for a mental illness. Ask the speaker to include a response to the following questions in his or her talk:

- Does the fact that the artist has a mental illness seem to diminish the quality of the art, according to viewers or critics?
- How have artists of the past defined or described their creativity? In what way are those definitions similar to mania?

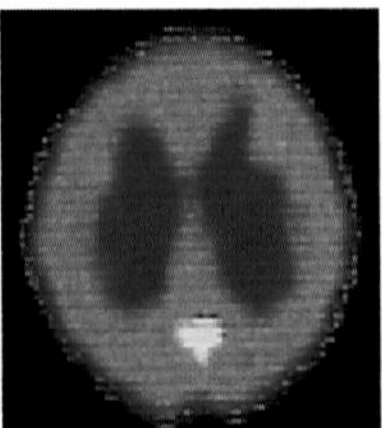
Depressed state (May 17)

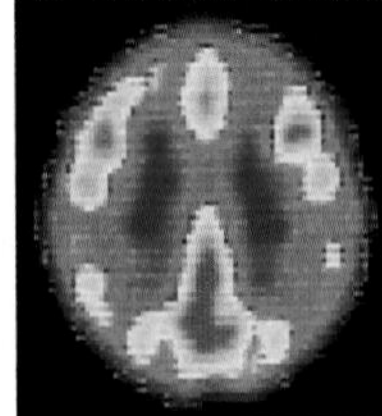
Manic state (May 18)

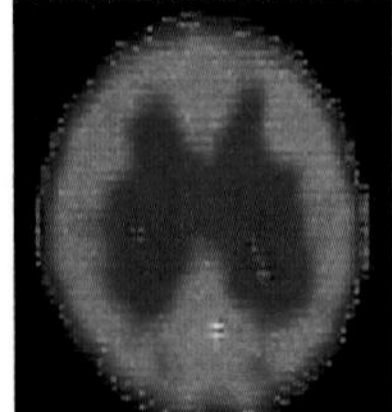
Depressed state (May 27)

Figure 28.5 **Bipolar Disorder and Brain Scans** These PET scans show that mood and brain activity are correlated. The yellow and red areas of the middle scan indicate that the brain is more active during the manic phase of bipolar disorder. (Courtesy of Lewis Baxter and Michael E. Phelps, UCLA School of Medicine.)

lar disorder if the first twin has it (Tsuang & Faraone, 1990). Note, however, that genes are not determining the disorder. For major depressive disorder, 50 percent of identical twins do *not* develop the condition. For bipolar disorder, 30 percent do not develop it.

- ***Brain function*** Depressed people have depressed brains (Figure 28.5). PET scan studies indicate that the brain is less active during major depression, especially in frontal lobe regions that are normally active during positive emotions (Davidson, 1999). It is also true that certain neurotransmitters—the chemical messengers that allow individual neurons in the brain to communicate with one another—appear to be out of balance in the case of mood disorders. The two neurotransmitters that are most important for depression are *serotonin* and *norepinephrine*, which are lacking during times of depression. Prozac and other antidepressant medications help restore the proper levels of these neurotransmitters.

Social-Cognitive Factors

Psychologists operating from the biological and cognitive perspectives have made tremendous progress explaining behavior and mental processes in recent years. In addition to the biological influences described in the previous paragraphs, researchers have identified a number of other important influences. Cognitive psychologists are looking closely at the interplay between the way we think, the situations we find ourselves in, and the way we feel. These social and cognitive factors actually affect brain chemistry and are affected by it. Complicated? Yes, but mood disorders are complex, and we would be unrealistic to expect simple explanations for these conditions. Let's consider a few social-cognitive influences:

1. ***Learned helplessness*** People develop a sense of helplessness when subjected to unpleasant events over which they have little or no control. As they acquire this feeling of helplessness, they give up and no longer try to improve their situation, because they learned in the past that efforts to improve the situation will not work. This, in and of itself, can produce depression. Learned helplessness may be one reason women suffer higher rates of depression than

Enriching

To give students some idea of the manic state of a bipolar disorder, read the following account:

"When I start going into a high, I no longer feel like an ordinary housewife. Instead, I feel organized and accomplished, and I begin to feel I am my most creative self. I can write poetry easily. I can compose melodies without effort. I can paint . . . I see myself as being able to accomplish a great deal for the good of people . . . I feel able to accomplish a great deal for the good of my family and others. I feel pleasure, a sense of euphoria or elation. I want it to last forever. I don't seem to need much sleep. I've lost weight and feel healthy, and I like myself. I've just bought six new dresses, in fact, and they look quite good on me...I feel capable of speaking and doing good in politics. I would like to help people with problems similar to mine so they won't feel hopeless."

Source: Fieve, R. R. (1975). *Mood swing*. New York: Morrow. (p. 17)

F•Y•I

Bipolar disorder is difficult to treat since the same medications aren't very effective at treating depression and mania at the same time. Lithium has been successful in treating bipolar disorder and seems to have anti-suicidal effects. Antidepressants seem to have mixed effects, sometimes enhancing manic episodes.

■ **LOOKING AT THE ISSUES**

Martin Seligman argues that people would be more successful at alleviating depression if they invested in others or the "common good." You might ask your class to reflect on the psychological benefits of the recent bipartisan effort to promote the common good through volunteer service. Pose the following questions to students for a class discussion:

- What might be the psychological payoff for those who participate in community-sponsored "random acts of kindness" days or weeks?
- Does requiring volunteer service negate its benefit? Why or why not?

trb At this point, you may wish to use Enrichment Lesson: *Commitment to the Common Good* (*Teacher's Resource Binder*, p. 28-1).

■ **APPLYING THE POINTS**

Invite a psychologist to class who specializes in treating mood disorders. In the talk, ask him or her to address the following questions:

- What method or methods of treatment does he or she prefer?
- What current research is being done on mood disorders?
- What are the rates of mood disorders among high school students?

MODULE 28

■ TEACHING TIPS

(1) Link the terms *stable*, *internal*, and *global* to *learned optimism*:

- Stable = permanent. Pessimists believe that bad events will become a permanent fixture in their lives.
- Internal = personal. Pessimists believe that bad events are a result of some personal flaw that cannot be changed.
- Global = pervasive. Pessimists believe that a bad experience in one area of life will influence other areas, causing havoc throughout one's life.

trb At this point, you may wish to use **Enrichment Lesson:** *Cognitive Errors in Depression* (*Teacher's Resource Binder*, p. 28-1).

trb tr (2) A black-line master for Figure 28.6, Attributions and Depression, is available in the **Black-Line Masters Appendix** of the *Teacher's Resource Binder*.

■ LOOKING AT THE ISSUES

Attribution and learned helplessness help explain depression, but what about explanations for mania? Using the following questions as a guide, have students brainstorm about different psychological explanations for mania:

- How might learning theorists explain mania?
- What attributions might a manic make about his or her behavior? Would they be optimistic or pessimistic?

Learned Helplessness When people find themselves in unpleasant situations over which they have little control, learned helplessness can set in. This, in turn, is associated with depression.

men do. Compared with men, women are more likely to be abused (Hamida & others, 1998) and twice as likely to feel overwhelmed (Sax & others, 1999). These statistics may help explain women's higher levels of learned helplessness and depression.

2. ***Attributions*** When things go wrong, we try to explain them. These explanations, or attributions, can vary from person to person. It turns out that depressed people are likely to make attributions with the following characteristics (Figure 28.6):

- *Stable*—The bad situation will last for a long time.
- *Internal*—This happened because of my actions, not someone else's, and not because of the circumstances.
- *Global*—My explanation applies to many areas of my life.

If I fail a history test and explain this by saying, "I'm stupid," I've met all these conditions. This attribution is stable (stupidity doesn't come and go, it stays with me), internal (stupidity is a personal characteristic), and global (being stupid affects most of the things I do). One theory (Abramson & others, 1989) says that these attributions lead to a sense of hopelessness that produces depression.

Notice that this sense of hopelessness is much less likely if attributions change. If I say I failed a history test because I was sick that day, even though being sick is internal and global, my explanation is not stable (I haven't said I'll *always* be sick). Thus, I'm less likely to feel hopeless and depressed. If I say I failed the history test because I have a bad teacher, my attribution is not internal—I haven't taken personal responsibility. Again, I avoid depression. Teaching people to change their attributions can be an effective way of treating depression.

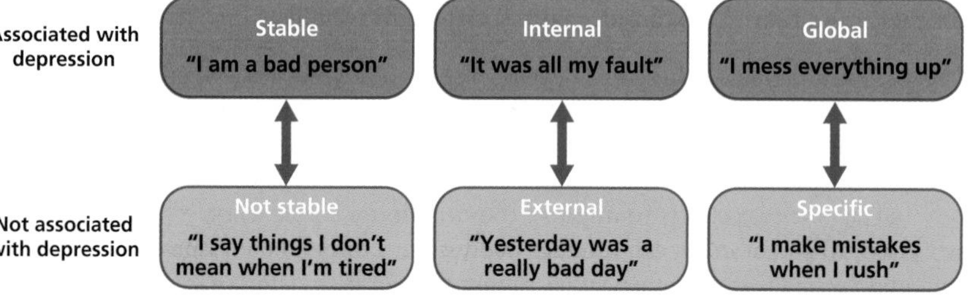
HOW COME YOU GOT FIRED?
Associated with depression
Stable
"I am a bad person"
Internal
"It was all my fault"
Global
"I mess everything up"
Not associated with depression
Not stable
"I say things I don't mean when I'm tired"
External
"Yesterday was a really bad day"
Specific
"I make mistakes when I rush"

Figure 28.6 Attributions and Depression How we explain events—such as losing a job—is associated with depression. People with depression are likely to explain with stable, internal, and global statements.

Demonstrating

ATTRIBUTIONS Ask students to imagine that they have just been notified by their bank that their checking account is overdrawn. Have them write down in a sentence or two what they believe to be the single most important cause. Then, in thinking about what they have written, have them answer the following questions to better understand their attributions:

- Does the cause you describe reflect more about you or more about other people or circumstances (internal or external)?
- Is the cause something that is permanent or temporary; that is, is the cause likely to be present in the future (stable or unstable)?

All these factors, biological and social-cognitive, can interact to form a vicious cycle of depression (Figure 28.7). A person's heredity might predispose depression by allowing the balance of neurotransmitters to operate in a range associated with mood disorders, or by "programming" the brain to function differently. The environment might be stressful and full of situations over which a person has little control. This might produce learned helplessness and discouragement which—coupled with attributions that are stable, global, and internal—pave the way to mood disorders. It is possible that the mood disorders, environmental conditions, or the way one thinks can produce further alterations of brain chemistry and function, making negative thinking and emotions even more likely in the future. These factors, working together, become a trap.

In this module, we've examined two of the more common categories of psychological disorders: anxiety disorders and mood disorders. According to some estimates, roughly one-quarter of us will experience a disorder from one of these two broad categories at some point in our life (Robins & Reigier, 1991). Researchers have begun to unravel the complicated story of what causes anxiety and mood disorders. As they continue to make progress, even more effective treatment options will become available to help those who suffer from these widespread conditions.

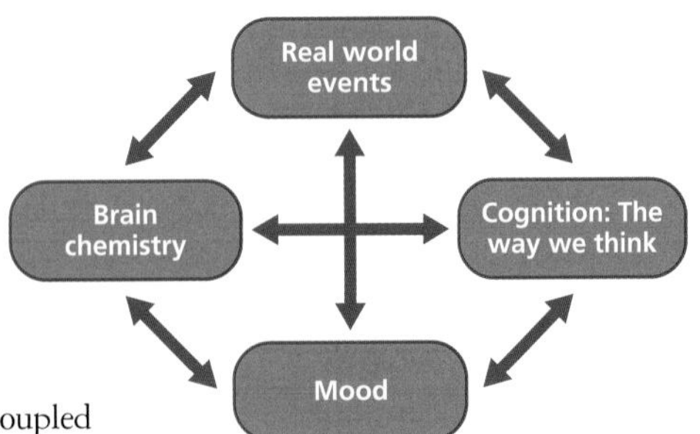

Figure 28.7 **What Determines Mood?** Mood flows from a complex interaction of biological and cognitive factors. These factors influence each other and are influenced by external events and internal moods. Attempts to improve mood can focus on controlling the environment, prescribing medications to change brain chemistry, or changing the way the person thinks.

REVIEW

Module 28: Anxiety and Mood Disorders

What's the Point?

The anxiety and mood disorders considered in this module are only a small portion of the disorders covered by the American Psychiatric Association's *Diagnostic and Statistical Manual of Mental Disorders* (fourth edition, Text Revision). Everyone studying psychological disorders must be careful not to overreact if they discover they have some of the symptoms of the disorders. For a symptom to rise to the level where it may be a sign that a disorder is present, it must be: maladaptive, unjustifiable, disturbing, and atypical.

Anxiety Disorders

Anxiety is a vague feeling of apprehension and nervousness. This module discussed four anxiety disorders: generalized anxiety disorder, panic disorder, phobia, obsessive-compulsive disorder, and posttraumatic stress disorder.

1. *What are the characteristics of generalized anxiety disorder and panic disorder?*

   Generalized anxiety disorder is marked by persistent, unexplained feelings of apprehension and tenseness. People with generalized anxiety disorder must experience at

- Is the cause something that influences other areas of your life or only your checking account balance (global or specific)?

Ask for volunteers to share some of their answers and reiterate that attributions for events that are internal, stable, and global are most likely to be associated with depression.

trb tr ■ TEACHING TIP

A black-line master for Figure 28.7, What Determines Mood?, is available in the **Black-Line Masters Appendix** of the *Teacher's Resource Binder.*

Close

This module focused on two of the most common psychological disorders—*anxiety* and *mood disorders*. In the right balance, these disorders can be adaptive and beneficial. Out of balance, they can be devastating to one's daily life and progress. Have students create a chart with two columns—one column labeled *Benefits/Needs Met* and the other column labeled *Drawbacks/Hindrances*. Students should brainstorm about how the right levels of anxiety and different moods can be beneficial or necessary to daily life and how they can be harmful if not in balance.

Checking the Points

■ TEACHING TIPS

web (1) The book companion site for *Thinking About Psychology* at www.worthpublishers.com/thinkingaboutpsych contains a module quiz, flashcards of key terms and people, as well as other student activities and resources for this module. You will also find PowerPoint lectures, a quiz grade book, and other teaching resources by logging on as an instructor.

trb (2) At this point, you may wish to review and confirm concepts about the psychological disorders with **Critical Thinking Activity:** ***Fact or Falsehood?*** (*Teacher's Resource Binder*, p. 28-1; **Handout 28–1**). If students filled in this handout earlier in the module, ask them to put it away. Suggest that students complete the handout in small groups, taking the time to look up information in the text to respond correctly to questions. Have all the groups meet to review the handout, again using the text to support the responses.

MODULE 28

Checking the Points

tb Using the Test Bank

The *Test Bank* that accompanies this textbook offers a wide variety of questions in different formats and levels of complexity. Use the software to construct whole tests or to integrate standardized questions into teacher-made tests.

least three of the following symptoms: restlessness; feeling on edge; difficulty concentrating or mind going blank; irritability; muscle tension; and sleep disturbance.

Panic disorder is also characterized by anxiety, but in addition is marked by sudden bouts of intense, unexplained panic.

2. *What are the characteristics of phobic disorder?*

   Phobic disorder, or phobia, is marked by disruptive, irrational fears of objects or situations. Phobias focus general feelings of anxiety onto feared objects or situations. Social phobias, which produce fear in social situations, such as public speaking, are common. So is agoraphobia, a fear of situations the person defines as anxiety-producing because the individual would be unable to escape if he or she experienced a panic attack.

3. *What are the characteristics of obsessive-compulsive disorder?*

   Obsessive-compulsive disorder is marked by unwanted, repetitive thoughts and actions. Obsessions are repetitive thoughts; compulsions are repetitive actions. Engaging in these rituals allows individuals to control their anxiety. When the person is deprived of these rituals, anxiety and panic build very rapidly.

4. *What are the characteristics of posttraumatic stress disorder?*

   Posttraumatic stress disorder is characterized by reliving a severely upsetting event in unwanted recurring memories and dreams. It may be triggered by any traumatic event, including combat, rape, abuse, and disasters.

5. *What are some of the factors that may contribute to the development of anxiety disorders?*

   In many disorders, including the anxiety disorders, biology and environment interact. The biological factors influencing the anxiety disorders include heredity (one may inherit a predisposition, or tendency to develop the disorder) and brain function (high levels of activity in the frontal lobes, and differences in function in the amygdala, an area of the brain involved in emotion). Some psychologists believe obsessive-compulsive disorders may have a link to our history as a species, when fearing certain dangerous situations offered advantages for survival.

   Other psychologists believe obsessive-compulsive disorders may be learned behaviors. Having acted in certain ways in the presence of stress, and having the stress reduced following those reactions, may produce learning through association. If it worked last time, do it again. Alternatively, we may learn to associate fear with certain places or objects. And finally, we may learn fear by watching others' fear. If learning creates obsessive-compulsive thoughts and behaviors, say these psychologists, new learning can change those thoughts and behaviors.

Mood Disorders

Mood disorders are disturbances of emotions. They differ from normal emotions primarily in degree, not in kind. The two primary emotional states that are magnified in mood disorders are mania (a period of abnormally high emotion and activity) and depression.

6. *What are the characteristics of major depressive disorder?*

   Major depressive disorder is the more common mood disorder and one of the most common psychological disorders. It differs from ordinary depression by interfering with normal functioning, by having no obvious cause, and by having five of the following symptoms present for two or more weeks:

   - depressed mood most of the day almost every day
   - little interest or pleasure in most activities
   - significant weight or appetite changes
   - increase or decrease in sleeping

Alternative Assessment/Portfolio Project

web EXPLORING PSYCHOLOGICAL DISORDERS ON THE WORLD WIDE WEB Students can search the Web for information on the different disorders presented in Modules 27 through 29. Assign each student or group of students a different disorder and have them gather information on it, creating a presentation to share with the class, school, or community. Some presentation options include the following:

- a formal research paper
- a poster presentation
- a public awareness campaign to educate people about the illness
- a documentary about someone with the disorder that educates people about the day-to-day life of people with the illness

- agitated or decreased level of activity
- fatigue or loss of energy
- feelings of worthlessness or inappropriate guilt
- diminished ability to think or concentrate
- recurrent thoughts of death or suicide

7. *What are the characteristics of bipolar disorder?*
   People with bipolar disorder alternate between periods of major depression and manic periods, in which they display unrealistic optimism and wildly hyper behavior.
8. *What factors may contribute to the development of mood disorders?*
   There is no single complete explanation for mood disorders. We know that heredity plays a role, because studies show that mood disorders can run in families. PET scans show that the frontal lobe regions of the brain are less active during major depression. Low levels of serotonin and norepinephrine, two neurotransmitters, are associated with periods of depression.

   The ways we think, the situations in which we find ourselves, and the ways we feel all interact to produce or relieve depression. For example, people who repeatedly experience unpleasant events that they cannot control may develop learned helplessness, a condition in which they stop trying to avoid the bad events. Another way our thoughts influence our emotions is through attributions—the way we try to explain things that go wrong. If we always attribute bad events to our own permanent characteristics, we will probably experience depression. Biological, social, and cognitive factors interact to produce a cycle of depression.

   Estimates indicate that one in four people will at some time have either an anxiety disorder or a mood disorder.

Key Terms

anxiety, p. 534
generalized anxiety disorder, p. 534
panic disorder, p. 535
phobia, p. 535
obsessive-compulsive disorder, p. 535
posttraumatic stress disorder, p. 535
major depressive disorder, p. 542
bipolar disorder, p. 546

Self-Test

Multiple-Choice Questions

Choose the *best* answer for each of the following questions:

1. Annette was riding the bus to her friend's vacation cottage, when suddenly she was overwhelmed by a sudden feeling of terror. She was sure that something terrible was about to happen. She could feel her heart pounding, she couldn't catch her breath, and she felt as though she was choking. Annette was showing symptoms of
   a. a bipolar attack.
   b. an obsession.
   c. a compulsion.
   d. a panic attack.
2. Leon quit his job last month to stay home and clean his house. Every day when he gets up, he puts on his old clothes and begins washing the walls and floors, vacuuming rugs, dusting furniture, and doing laundry over and over again. Leon would like to stop his cleaning, but when he tries

MODULE 28

trb tr ■ TEACHING TIP

At this point, you may wish to provide students with **Building Vocabulary: Graphic Organizer:** *Concept Chart* (*Teacher's Resource Binder*, p. 28-1; **Handout 28–2**). Have students fill out the answers as a tool for reviewing the concepts in the module. If students filled in the concept web earlier in the module, ask them to put it aside. Encourage students to fill in the handout individually. When they are finished, you may wish to use the handout as a transparency. Project the concept chart completed correctly for students to check and confirm their handouts.

Self-Test Answers

Multiple-Choice Questions

1. d, 2. a

trb Refer to **Alternative Assessment/Portfolio Project:** *Exploring Psychological Disorders on the World Wide Web* (*Teacher's Resource Binder*, p. 27-1; **Handout 27–6**) for helpful Web sites and a rubric to aid in evaluating students' projects. Revise the rubric to suit your needs.

MODULE 28

Self-Test Answers

Multiple-Choice Questions (continued)
3. b, 4. a, 5. d, 6. c

Matching Terms and Definitions
7. a. (3), b. (9), c. (10), d. (8), e. (7), f. (2), g. (6), h. (1)

to, he becomes terribly anxious. Leon is showing symptoms of
a. obsessive-compulsive disorder.
b. agoraphobia.
c. major depressive disorder.
d. bipolar disorder.

3. Helen never leaves the house. Her daughter does her grocery shopping and runs her other errands. Helen has learned to use the Internet so that she can shop for clothes and buy her prescriptions on-line. On the few occasions Helen has tried to leave the house, she's been overwhelmed by feelings of fear and anxiety. Helen is showing symptoms of
a. bipolar disorder.
b. agoraphobia.
c. obsessive-compulsive disorder.
d. major depressive disorder.

4. Fred is sometimes great fun to party with. During those times, he's very optimistic, enthusiastic, and full of energy, and no one else in the group can keep up with him. At other times, though, Fred crashes and is in black moods, unable to get out of bed for days at a time. Fred is showing symptoms of
a. bipolar disorder.
b. obsessive-compulsive disorder.
c. agoraphobia.
d. panic attacks.

5. Rolando has been very sad for the past two days. His sister was diagnosed with leukemia two days ago, and Rolando knows she may not make it through the year. Rolando appears to be
a. on the verge of major depressive disorder.
b. entering the depressed stage of bipolar disorder.
c. suffering from a mood disorder.
d. displaying emotions that are normal in his situation.

6. The police and fire fighter rescue teams who helped people escape from the 9/11 attack on the World Trade Center may relive that event in recurring thoughts and dreams. Recurring thoughts and dreams about stressful events are symptoms of
a. panic attacks.
b. phobias.
c. posttraumatic stress disorder.
d. bipolar disorder.

Matching Terms and Definitions

7. For each definition, choose the *best* matching term from the list that follows:

Definition

a. Our explanations for situations or events.
b. Repetitive thoughts.
c. Repetitive actions.
d. Anxiety disorder marked by persistent, unexplained feelings of apprehension and tenseness, including at least three of the following symptoms: restlessness, feeling on edge, difficulty concentrating or mind going blank, irritability, muscle tension, and sleep disturbance.
e. Most common mood disorder, and one of the more common psychological disorders.
f. Period of abnormally high emotion, overexcitement, and unreasonable optimism.
g. The tendency to find the symptoms of psychological disorders in your own behavior.
h. State that may develop if people are repeatedly subjected to unpleasant events over which they have little control.

Term

(1) learned helplessness
(2) mania
(3) attributions
(4) anxiety

(5) social phobia
(6) psychology student's disease
(7) major depressive disorder
(8) generalized anxiety disorder
(9) obsessions
(10) compulsions

Fill-in-the-Blank Questions

8. ________________ disorders, such as generalized anxiety disorder, panic disorder, phobias, and obsessive-compulsive disorder, are characterized by maladaptive, unjustifiable, disturbing, and atypical behaviors connected to feelings of apprehension and nervousness.

9. ________________ disorders, such as major depressive disorder and bipolar disorder, are characterized by maladaptive, unjustifiable, disturbing, and atypical behaviors connected to emotional disturbances.

Brief Essay Question

10. Some psychologists believe that disruptive, irrational fears of snakes, storms, and heights can be explained by our history as a species. In two paragraphs of about two sentences each, explain how such fears could have helped our ancestors survive.

Self-Test Answers

Fill-in-the-Blank Questions

7. Anxiety, 8. Mood

Brief Essay Question

9. Fears can be explained as being developed through evolution. Fearing objects that would harm or kill is explained as adaptive. By avoiding such dangers, people would have been more likely to survive.

MODULE 29

Performance Standards

Standard Area: Psychological Disorders

Content Standard 3: Major categories of psychological disorders

Performance Standard 3.1 Discuss the major categories of psychological disorders.

- Define *dissociate*. (Student Text p. 555)
- Discuss how dissociative amnesia compares with other forms of amnesia. (Student Text pp. 555–556)
- Compare dissociative amnesia and dissociative fugue. (Student Text pp. 556–557)
- Discuss the controversial diagnosis of dissociative identity disorder. (Student Text pp. 557, 560)
- Examine the relationship between the mind and body. Discuss the somatoform disorders where physical problems occur for psychological reasons. (Student Text pp. 558–559)
- Define *schizophrenia*. (Student Text p. 560)
- Discuss the major symptoms and types of schizophrenia. (Student Text pp. 560–563)
- Discuss some of the biological and psychological factors that interact to produce schizophrenia. (Student Text pp. 563–565)
- Compare the three major clusters of personality disorders. (Student Text pp. 565–567)

Materials NETWORK

All of the items from the Video, Activity, and Enrichment Centers listed below come from the *Teacher's Resource Binder.* These items will help you teach and expand on concepts presented in Module 29.

trb This logo indicates when an item from the Materials Network may be used in conjunction with a specific note found in this module's *Teacher's Edition.*

Dissociative Disorders

V Video Center

- **Videocassette:** *The Brain,* **Second Edition, Module 23: "Multiple Personality"** Consult the faculty guide from *The Brain* video series for a description of this module. (*Teacher's Resource Binder*, p. 29-1)

Activity Center

- **Critical Thinking Activity:** *Fact or Falsehood?* With this activity, students' preconceptions about dissociative, schizophrenia, and personality disorders are either exposed as incorrect or reinforced as correct. (*Teacher's Resource Binder*, p. 29-1; **Handout 29–1**)
- **Building Vocabulary: Graphic Organizer:** *Crossword Puzzle* Students can test their knowledge of terms in this module by completing this crossword puzzle based on module concepts. (*Teacher's Resource Binder*, p. 29-1; **Handout 29–2**)
- **Analysis Activity:** *Questionnaire of Experiences of Dissociation* Students are likely to find it more difficult to identify with those experiencing dissociative disorders than those suffering from anxiety disorders. The former are not only less common but more controversial. Students can complete this activity for greater insight into this class of disorders. (*Teacher's Resource Binder*, p. 29-1; **Handout 29–3**)

Enrichment Center

- **Enrichment Lesson:** *Psychogenic Versus Organic Amnesia* Students are likely to be aware that amnesia may be physically or psychologically based. *Dissociative amnesia* is often referred to as *psychogenic amnesia*, with four characteristics that distinguish it from *organic amnesia*. (*Teacher's Resource Binder*, p. 29-1)
- **Enrichment Lesson:** *The Dissociative Disorders Interview Schedule and Multiple Pesonality* Colin Ross and his colleagues developed the Dissociative Disorders Interview Schedule to refine and standardize the diagnosis of *multiple personality*, now called *dissociative identity disorder*. The controversy surrounding this disorder led the authors of the DSM-IV-TR to attempt to increase the precision of diagnosis. (*Teacher's Resource Binder*, p. 29-1)

Schizophrenia Disorders

V Video Center

Consult the faculty guide from *The Brain* video series for a description of these modules.

- **Videocassette:** *The Brain,* **Second Edition, Module 26: "Schizophrenia: Symptoms"** (*Teacher's Resource Binder*, p. 29-1)
- **Videocassette:** *The Brain,* **Second Edition, Module 29: "Autism"** (*Teacher's Resource Binder*, p. 29-1)
- **Videocassette:** *The Brain,* **Second Edition, Module 27: "Schizophrenia: Etiology"** (*Teacher's Resource Binder*, p. 29-1)

Activity Center

- **Demonstration Activity:** *The Referential Thinking Scale* Students may have some difficulty identifying with the delusional belief system often characterizing schizophrenia. Referential thinking demonstrates a process of reality distortion in which environmental events that would be regarded as casual or indifferent by most people take on special and significant meaning for the subject. (*Teacher's Resource Binder*, p. 29-1; **Handout 29–4**)
- **Demonstration Activity:** *Magical Ideation Scale* The scale is based on the idea that schizophrenia-prone people often show a belief in magical influences. (*Teacher's Resource Binder*, p. 29-1; **Handout 29–5**)

Enrichment Center

- **Enrichment Lesson:** *Infantile Autism* The autistic condition appears similar to schizophrenia, in that social withdrawal is a prominent characteristic of both. There are, however, important differences, as this lesson delineates. (*Teacher's Resource Binder*, p. 29-1)

Personality Disorders

V Video Center

- **Videocassette:** *The Mind,* **Second Edition, Module 35: "The Mind of the Psychopath"** Consult the faculty guide from *The Mind* video series for a description of this module. (*Teacher's Resource Binder*, p. 29-1)

Activity Center

- **Demonstration Activity:** *Antisocial Personality Disorder* Many regard Hervey Cleckley's *The Mask of Sanity* to be the classic work on antisocial personality disorder. Recasting Cleckley's clinical criteria for the disorder in the form of self-referential or opinion statements, Michael Levenson designed an inventory to assess this antisocial posture. (*Teacher's Resource Binder*, p. 29-1; **Handout 29–6**)

MODULE 29

Dissociative, Schizophrenia, and Personality Disorders

Introducing the Module

The Points: Module Objectives

- Differentiate dissociative amnesia from other forms of amnesia.
- Differentiate dissociative fugue from dissociative amnesia.
- Evaluate why the diagnosis of dissociative identity disorder is controversial.
- Explain what schizophrenia is.
- Identify the major symptoms of schizophrenia.
- Describe the four major types of schizophrenia and the main characteristics of each.
- Identify the biological and psychological factors that can interact to produce schizophrenia.
- Differentiate among the three major clusters of personality disorders.

trb Building Vocabulary

Students can reinforce their knowledge of dissociative, schizophrenia, and personality disorders by completing **Building Vocabulary:** *Crossword Puzzle* (*Teacher's Resource Binder*, p. 29-1; **Handout 29–2**). As students fill in the puzzle, they learn the module terms and the relationship among these concepts.

MODULE 29

Dissociative, Schizophrenia, and Personality Disorders

Consider Gene Saunders. Gene was a manager at a manufacturing company. Work had become a struggle, with missed production goals, criticism from his supervisor, and disappointment when an expected promotion didn't come through. The stress at work led to additional problems at home, including a violent argument with his teenage son. Two days after the argument, Gene disappeared. A year and a half later, police in a town hundreds of miles away picked up a drifter who had been working as a short-order cook. The drifter's name was Burt Tate, and while Burt knew what town he was in, he had no knowledge of his life prior to arriving in town. There were no physical or drug problems that would account for the memory loss. You guessed it—Gene and Burt were the same person (Spitzer & others, 1989).

Consider Emilio. His twelfth hospitalization occurred when he was 40 because his mother, with whom he lived, feared him. He dressed in a ragged old coat and bedroom slippers, with several medals around his neck. Much of what he says is simply nonsense. When interviewed, he claimed he had been "eating wires and lightning fires." He alternates from being angry toward his mother to childlike giggling, and he hears nonexistent voices. Emilio has been unable to hold a job since his first hospitalization at age 16 (Spitzer & others, 1989).

Consider Mary. She was 26 years old when referred for hospitalization by her therapist because she had urges to cut herself with a razor. For over 10 years Mary struggled with issues related to religion and philosophy. Her academic performance in college dropped off when she began experimenting with a variety of drugs. When Mary entered therapy, she became both hostile and demanding, sometimes insisting on two therapy sessions a day. She did not exhibit stability in her moods or relationships (Spitzer & others, 1989).

Getting Started

The disorders featured in this module are the ones most commonly associated with having a mental illness. Ask students to consider what it means to lose touch with reality. Have them consider behaviors someone would exhibit if they had lost touch.

trb You may wish to use **Critical Thinking Activity:** *Fact or Falsehood?* (*Teacher's Resource Binder*, p. 29-1; **Handout 29–1**) as a prereading strategy to evaluate what students already know about dissociative, schizophrenia, and personality disorders. This activity will prime students to look out for information that could prove or disprove their preconceptions about these disorders.

Gene, Emilio, and Mary suffer from disorders we will discuss in this module. These disorders are not nearly as common as *anxiety disorders* (such as phobias) and *mood disorders* (such as depression), but they represent an interesting sample of the types of disturbances that can plague people. Keep in mind that when we are done, we will have not come near examining all disorders—the American Psychiatric Association's *Diagnostic and Statistical Manual of Mental Disorders,* Fourth Edition, Text Revision (DSM-IV-TR), lists well over 200 specific disorders! Several of the people you will read about in this module have lost some aspect of their sense of self (dissociative disorders). Others have lost contact with reality (schizophrenia disorders). And still others have developed lasting and counterproductive patterns of behavior (personality disorders).

► **dissociative disorders** Disorders in which the sense of self has become separated (dissociated) from previous memories, thoughts, or feelings.

Dissociative Disorders

Dissociate is the opposite of *associate* (to make connections). Individuals with **dissociative disorders** have in some way broken away from their sense of self—from their memories, thoughts, or feelings. These disorders are quite rare and usually represent a response to overwhelming stress. Three specific forms are *amnesia, fugue state,* and *dissociative identity disorder* (Figure 29.1).

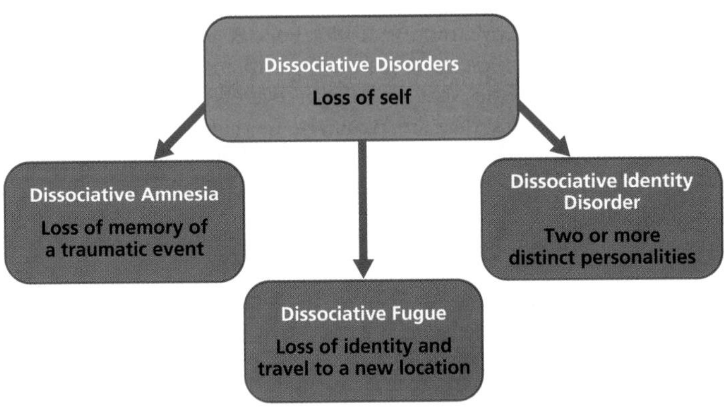

Figure 29.1 **Three Types of Dissociative Disorders**

Dissociative Amnesia

What's the Point? 1. How does dissociative amnesia differ from other forms of amnesia?

Can you remember the meaning of the word *amnesia?* Amnesia is memory loss, and any number of factors, including drug use, can cause it. Drinking too much alcohol, for example, can lead to a "blackout" of all memories of the drinking episode. Head injury, fatigue, and physical disorders such as

MODULE 29

Teaching the Points

■ **TEACHING TIPS**

web (1) You can log on as an instructor to the book companion site for *Thinking About Psychology* at www.worthpublishers.com/thinkingaboutpsych. It contains teacher resources for class presentations as well as review and assessment of module concepts and terms.

(2) Students should understand that *dissociation* is not the same as *psychosis.*

- **Dissociation** involves breaking away from the sense of self by either losing memory and identity or adding personalities.
- **Psychosis** involves a break with reality by believing things that are untrue or having hallucinations about things that aren't there.

trb At this point, you may wish to use **Analysis Activity:** *Questionnaire of Experiences of Dissociation* (*Teacher's Resource Binder,* p. 29-1; **Handout 29–3**).

trb **tr** A black-line master of Figure 29.1, Three Types of Dissociative Disorders, is available in the **Black-Line Masters Appendix** of the *Teacher's Resource Binder.*

■ **CHECKING FOR UNDERSTANDING**

Use the case study vignettes featured in the text on page 554 as a tool to see how well students read and whether they can "diagnose" the disorders found in this book. *(Gene Saunders suffers from dissociative fugue. Emilio suffers from disorganized schizophrenia. Mary suffers from borderline personality disorder.)*

F • Y • I

The DSM-IV-TR lists 14 different categories of disorders, a number of which aren't discussed in detail in this textbook. Interested students can conduct research to learn these different categories. For extra credit, invite students to create a poster that identifies and briefly describes each of the 14 DSM-IV-TR categories.

Meeting Individual Needs

trb **tr** Provide students with a black-line master for Figure 29.1, Three Types of Dissociative Disorders, available in the **Black-Line Masters Appendix** of the *Teacher's Resource Binder.* On the black-line masters, create blanks for students to fill in during class discussion or, later, on their own to help them process the terms related to dissociative disorders. You may also wish to create a transparency from the black-line master of Figure 29.1, covering up the terms so students can call out the answers during an informal assessment of their knowledge of this class of disorders.

- **Exceptional Learners** A handout created from the black-line master for Figure 29.1 can fill the need to provide notes for exceptional learners. These students may review the terms with a student or teacher/tutor. They may refer to the handout during class discussion or lecture.

MODULE 29

■ **TEACHING TIP**

Link the vivid memories trauma victims experience to flashbulb memories. Because of the intense amount of stress and emotional turmoil victims experience during trauma, their memories of those events become like pictures in their minds, which record sensory details very well.

■ **APPLYING THE POINTS**

Have students recall an early childhood memory. Then, have them try to confirm whether that memory is true. Have them interview parents, grandparents, or teachers about the details of their memory to see if their recall is accurate about such early experiences.

(1) A famous case of dissociative amnesia centers on the assassination of Tsar Nicholas II of Russia and his family by the Bolsheviks in 1918. A woman named Anna Anderson surfaced in 1920, and speculation immediately began to point to her as the youngest daughter of the tsar, Anastasia.

trb At this point, you may wish to use Enrichment Lesson: *Psychogenic Versus Organic Amnesia* (*Teacher's Resource Binder*, p. 29-1).

(2) *Amnesia* comes in two different forms:

- **Retrograde amnesia** occurs when old memories are lost. This is the most common type of amnesia. Memories of experiences that occurred in the time surrounding an event fall under this type of amnesia.
- **Anterograde amnesia** occurs when the ability to form new memories is lost. This form is less common, but some types of head trauma or brain disease can affect a person's ability to form new memories.

trb At this point, you may wish to use Enrichment Lesson: *Psychogenic Versus Organic Amnesia* (*Teacher's Resource Binder*, p. 29-1).

(3) The Latin root word for *fugue* and *fugitive* means "flight," which makes *dissociative fugue* an appropriate name for this disorder.

Trauma and Amnesia People under extreme stress, such as soldiers in combat, may experience dissociative amnesia.

Alzheimer's disease can also cause amnesia. To qualify as **dissociative amnesia,** however, the memory loss must be a reaction to a specific, stressful event. Serious personal threats are the most frequent causes of dissociative amnesia. Combat soldiers may report losing their memory for hours or days (van der Hart & others, 1999). Survivors of natural disasters, such as floods or wildfires, sometimes experience similar losses (Kihlström & others, 1993).

In one case of dissociative amnesia, an 18-year-old man lost his memory of a sailing cruise with friends off the coast of Florida. A storm had come up, and only he had the foresight to put on a life jacket and tie himself to the boat. His friends were swept overboard in the high waves. Due to the emotional trauma, the young man lost all memory of the tragic storm and the several days he spent hoping to be rescued.

Sigmund Freud labeled this type of psychologically based amnesia *repression*. As indicated by many media reports in recent years, repressed memories of childhood abuse have become a major controversy in psychology. There is evidence that a percentage of victims of sexual abuse do have trouble remembering the details of the abuse (Chu & others, 1999). More often, however, sexual abuse etches itself permanently into memory, just as witnessing the murder of a parent or being highjacked in a school bus does (Malmquist, 1986; Pope & Hudson, 1995). Most children remember these traumatic events all too well. Furthermore, the accuracy of memories that are later "recovered" is questionable. Previously lost memories that are recovered in therapy tend to be false memories. Therapists may unintentionally plant suggestions in the minds of their clients, resulting in the formation of memories that seem real but actually are not (Loftus, 2000). Although psychologists question the concept of repression, they do not question the horrific reality of child abuse in the lives of too many Americans.

► **dissociative amnesia** A dissociative disorder characterized by loss of memory in reaction to a traumatic event.

► **dissociative fugue** A dissociative disorder characterized by loss of identity and travel to a new location.

► **dissociative identity disorder** A rare and controversial dissociative disorder in which an individual experiences two or more distinct and alternating personalities.

Dissociative Fugue

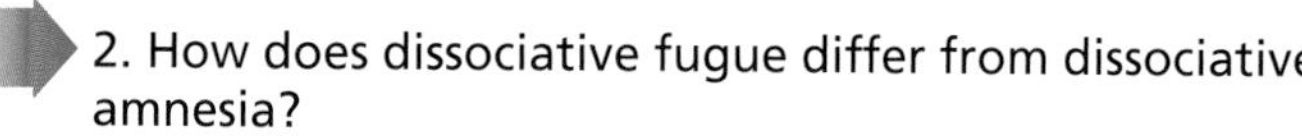

2. How does dissociative fugue differ from dissociative amnesia?

Dissociative fugue is an extended form of dissociative amnesia, in which the loss of one's identity is accompanied by travel to a new location. (The word *fugue* comes from the same root as *fugitive*.) A fugue state can be short, lasting only a few hours, or long, lasting months or even years. The person may develop a new identity, form new friendships, or even enter a new line of work. As with other dissociative disorders, the development of a fugue state is an unconscious response to

Suggested Readings

Use the following books as teacher-preparation tools or as enrichment for advanced students:

Barron, J., & Barron, S. (1992). *There's a boy in here.* New York: Avon.

Baur, S. (1988). *Hypochondria: Woeful imaginings.* Berkeley, CA: University of California Press.

Capote, T. (1994). *In cold blood.* New York: Vintage.

Cleckley, H. (1982). *The mask of sanity.* New York: Plume.

North, C. S. (1987). *Welcome silence: My triumph over schizophrenia.* New York: Simon & Schuster.

Sacks, O. (1983). *Awakenings.* New York: Dutton.

Spanos, N. P. (2001). *Multiple identities and false memories: A socio-cognitive perspective.* Washington, DC: American Psychological Association.

Torrey, E. F. (1995). *Surviving schizophrenia: A manual for families* (3rd ed.). New York: HarperCollins.

extreme stress. The case of Gene Saunders at the beginning of this module represents dissociative fugue. His stressful work and home situations led to his disappearance, and even he was not aware of the history behind his transformation into Burt Tate.

Dissociative Identity Disorder

3. Why is the diagnosis of dissociative identity disorder controversial?

Have you ever felt like a different person? Have you ever said, "I have no idea why I did that"? Magnified to an extreme, these feelings are central features of **dissociative identity disorder** (formerly known as *multiple personality disorder*). In this controversial disorder, a person is said to exhibit two or more distinct and alternating personalities. These subpersonalities reportedly can differ in age, sex, and self-perception of physical characteristics. Some researchers have even reported changes in brain function (Putnam, 1991) or handedness (Henninger, 1992) as a patient switches from one personality to another. Sometimes subpersonalities seem to be aware of one another, and sometimes they do not.

Diagnosed cases of dissociative identity disorder have increased dramatically in recent years. Prior to the 1970s, fewer than 100 cases had ever been reported in professional journals. Then, in the 1980s alone, reports of more than 20,000 diagnosed cases appeared, almost all of them in North America (McHugh, 1995). The average number of subpersonalities has also increased—from 3 to 12 (Goff & Sims, 1993). In some cases, dozens or even 100 different personalities have been reported.

Psychologists debate whether dissociative identity disorder really exists. Are today's clinicians simply more knowledgeable about and willing to make the diagnosis? Are better diagnostic rules reducing the number of cases that in the past were misdiagnosed as other disorders, such as schizophrenia? Skeptics believe the power of suggestion has worked here, just as it has in attempts to recall "repressed" memories. Clinicians, who now have read a great deal about these fascinating cases, may be unintentionally suggesting multiple personalities to their clients. Questions such as "Have you ever felt another part of you is in control?" may lead the patient (who has also read about the disorder or seen depictions on television) to construct subpersonalities in an effort to please the therapist by responding to perceived expectations. This, of course, is also unintentional.

The Media and Mental Disorders The controversy about dissociative identity disorder has been partially fueled by the public's interest in the disorder. Two films—*The Three Faces of Eve* (top) and *Sybil* (bottom)—have showcased "multiple personality." Some are concerned that the films and other forms of media attention lead to false diagnoses of this disorder.

MODULE 29

■ **JOURNAL WRITING**

Invite students to use the following questions and writing prompts as springboards for entries in their psychology journals:

- Have you ever wanted to pick up, move, and start all over somewhere else? Why? What would be the advantages and disadvantages of such a move?
- Do you behave differently in different situations? Have people ever accused you of having different personalities? How did that make you feel?

trb At this point, you may wish to use **Enrichment Lesson:** ***The Dissociative Disorders Interview Schedule and Multiple Personality*** (*Teacher's Resource Binder*, p. 29-1).

■ **LOOKING AT THE ISSUES**

Dissociative identity disorder (DID) is so controversial partly because the claims of patients are so difficult to confirm. Typically, DID is not diagnosed until later in life, when evidence of past abuse or trauma may have disappeared. Using available resources, students can research and then discuss their findings related to the following questions:

- Does such difficultly in confirming this disorder necessarily deny the claims of patients?
- How do investigators prove claims of abuse that happened long ago?

V At this point, you may wish to show **Videocassette:** ***The Brain,*** **Second Edition, Module 23:"Multiple Personality"** (*Teacher's Resource Binder*, p. 29-1).

Meeting Individual Needs

trb tr Help students understand how the terms in this module are related by having them complete **Building Vocabulary:** *Crossword Puzzle* (*Teacher's Resource Binder*, p. 29-1; **Handout 29–2**).

- **Independent Learners** Students can complete the handout on their own as a homework or in-class assignment, checking the answers in class. You may wish to use **Handout 29–2** as a transparency, inserting the correct answers in the web and projecting the completed puzzle for students to check their answers.
- **Cooperative Learners** Have students work in small groups to complete the crossword puzzle. Students can tutor each other about the concepts in the module, or you can create a competition in which students see how quickly their team can complete the puzzle correctly.

MODULE 29

■ TEACHING TIPS

trb tr (1) For use with the notes on this page, a black-line master of Figure 29.2, Somatoform Disorders, is available in the **Black-Line Masters Appendix** of the *Teacher's Resource Binder.*

(2) Hypochondriacs aren't just people who fake sickness to get attention. They truly believe they are sick from a horrible illness that doctors just haven't discovered. They move from doctor to doctor, seeking a diagnosis that will confirm their horrible condition. People who fake illness are said to be **malingering**. With this disorder, patients will fake illness to avoid trouble, to achieve financial gain, or to avoid imprisonment.

■ APPLYING THE POINTS

Invite a doctor to discuss with students what procedures are supposed to be followed when confronted with a suspected hypochondriac.

■ MULTICULTURAL CONNECTIONS

Are somatoform disorders common in non-Western cultures? Have students research and report back to the class on the incidence of hypochondriasis and conversion disorder in different cultures and in each gender within a culture.

F • Y • I

Other forms of *somatoform* disorders include the following:

- Patients with **body dysmorphic disorder** are preoccupied with defects of their bodies. When they are faced with an imperfection of some sort, their concern about it seems overly excessive.
- Patients with **pain disorder** present complaints of severe pain that don't seem to be caused by any particular physical condition.
- Patients with **somatization disorder** are those younger than 30 years old who exhibit a variety of physical symptoms that are unexplained.

Mind and Body in Psychological Disorders

The relationship between mind and body has fascinated psychologists since this science was born. Psychological disorders are a good place to look for this interaction, because such disorders almost always have both psychological and physical components. This is most dramatic in the **somatoform disorders,** in which physical problems occur for psychological reasons. (*Somatic* comes from a Greek word for "body.")

You're probably already familiar with one of these disorders, **hypochondriasis,** which you may know as—*hypochondria* (Figure 29.2). People with this disorder experience symptoms of physical illness, such as headaches and fleeting joint pains, but medical exams reveal nothing physically wrong with their bodies. The disorder is, quite literally, all in the mind. People with hypochondriasis *do* suffer, because they really *believe* they are sick. All of us occasionally have hypochondriacal feelings, worrying that we may be sick but then turning out to be fine. Athletes, who must be tuned in to their bodies, may experience these worries quite frequently, but not usually to the extent seen in this mine-body disorder. And let's be clear about one more thing: *Pretending* to be sick to avoid responsibility or to gain attention also does not qualify as hypochondriasis!

Another somatoform disorder, *conversion disorder,* gets its name from its main symptom—the change, or conversion, of a psychological factor (typically anxiety) into an actual loss of physical function. A

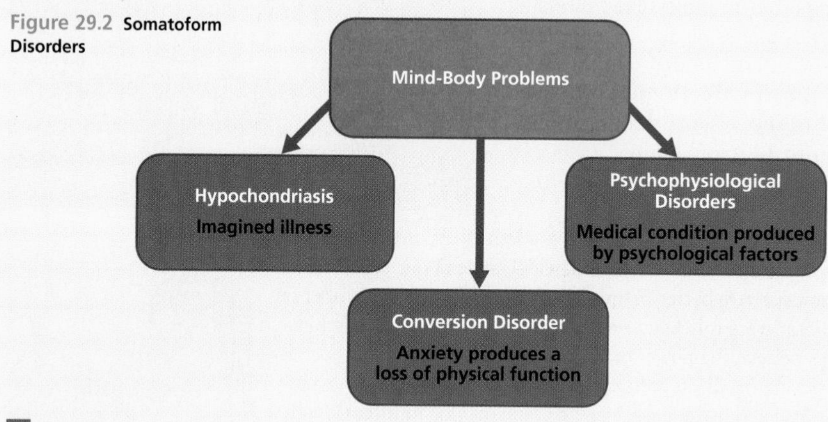

Figure 29.2 **Somatoform Disorders**

Psychophysiological Disorders Stress, combined with a bacterial infection, can cause ulcers—a true medical condition.

person with conversion disorder might suddenly experience blindness, laryngitis, or paralysis, but with no physical cause. Have you ever been so frightened you momentarily lost the ability to move, or so stunned you momentarily lost the ability to speak? Then you've experienced, on a minor, short-term level, the core requirement of conversion disorder—loss of function for psychological reasons.

This disorder and others with no physical basis intrigued Sigmund Freud and helped inspire his theory of psychoanalysis. Until the 1970s, these conditions were known as *hysteria,* a name derived from the Greek word for "uterus." Why? Because some Greeks noticed that these difficult-to-explain symptoms usually happened to women, and they theorized that the symptoms were caused when the uterus broke free and drifted around the body causing problems! By the late 1800s, Freud and other physicians were well aware that the uterus stayed put. Freud recognized that somatoform disorders can occur in women *and* men and reasoned that psychological forces must be producing the symptoms. Although some disorders, such as major depression, appear to be increasing in modern times, conversion disorder has become quite rare.

The symptoms of hypochondriasis and conversion disorder have no real physical basis. But sometimes psychological factors can lead to or aggravate real medical conditions. Stress, for example, contributes to asthma, ulcers, headaches, and high blood pressure. Such conditions, called *psychophysiological* or *psychosomatic disorders,* involve a more complete interaction of mind and body. With these disorders, as with other somatoform disorders, it's not mind *or* body—it's mind *and* body interacting to produce trouble.

▶ **somatoform disorders** Psychological disorders in which the symptoms take a somatic (bodily) form without apparent physical cause.

▶ **hypochondriasis** A somatoform disorder characterized by imagined symptoms of illness.

Cross-Curricular Connections

BIOLOGY AND HEALTH Team-teach a lesson with your school's biology or health teacher to explore the mind-body connection. In the lesson, the teaching team should address the following questions:

- How does stress cause problems in the body?
- What long-term conditions can stress exacerbate?

F • Y • I

(1) People with conversion disorder will typically suffer problems with parts of their bodies that directly relate to the stress they are under. For example, a quarterback for a football team might lose sensation in his throwing hand before the big game. Otherwise, he may report feeling fine and not admit to having stress about the event. *La belle indifference,* a French phrase meaning "beautiful indifference," is used to describe the apathy these patients feel about their condition.

(2) Women's health issues have only recently begun to be distinguished from men's health issues. Contemporaries of Freud believed that women who attended college suffered from shrunken ovaries since they did not bear as many children as less educated women. Using available resources, have students explore old stereotypes about and new advances in women's health.

■ JOURNAL WRITING

Invite students to use the following question as a springboard for an entry in their psychology journals:

- Have you ever gotten sick because of stress? Describe your experience.

■ TEACHING TIP

Link *psychophysiological illness* to Hans Selye's *general adaptation syndrome.* Selye has shown that as people cope with stress, they go through three distinct stages:

- With **alarm,** the body notices the stress and gears up for the reaction to it.
- With **resistance,** the body fights the stress and maintains a high level of arousal. It is during the resistance phase that the body is most susceptible to illness.
- With **exhaustion,** the body loses its ability to maintain the high-energy state and begins to shut down.

MODULE 29

■ TEACHING TIP
If you show any of the popular films that depict dissociative identity disorder, help students watch with a critical eye. Point out that the goal of movies is not to depict reality but to entertain and tell a compelling story.

■ APPLYING THE POINTS
Arrange a field trip to a local mental health care facility to learn more about the most common illnesses of patients in mental institutions. Students can tour the facility and meet with staff psychologists or psychiatrists to learn more about how schizophrenia is treated. You may also want to bring donations of clothing, personal hygiene products, and games for hospital patients.

F • Y • I
Children as young as 12 have developed symptoms of schizophrenia. The onset of the disorder typically occurs during the late teen and early adult years. Full-blown psychotic episodes (where patients lose touch with reality) may not occur until the patient is out on his or her own, away from family and friends who have supported that person in the past.

V At this point, you may wish to show Videocassette: *The Brain,* Second Edition, Module 27: "Schizophrenia: Etiology" (*Teacher's Resource Binder,* p. 29-1).

Sybil Dorsett's famous case of dissociative identity disorder was the subject of a book (*Sybil*) and a made-for-TV movie in the 1970s. However, after the death of Sybil's psychiatrist, a different picture emerged. After reading her recently released records, some experts have come to believe that Sybil's multiple personalities were the result of her therapist's suggestions. By giving names to Sybil's emotional states and asking her to take on these roles as part of the therapeutic process, the psychiatrist could have led Sybil to believe that she possessed multiple personalities.

Schizophrenia Disorders

4. What is schizophrenia?

Schizophrenia is perhaps the most frightening and most misunderstood psychological disorder. Here are some facts to help dispel the myths:

- **Schizophrenia** is not one disorder. It is a family of related disorders involving disorganized and delusional thinking, disturbed perceptions, and inappropriate emotions and behaviors.
- Schizophrenia is not "split personality." "Schiz" does come from a word that means "split," but the split represents a breaking away from reality, not a division of personality. (There is no psychological disorder called *split personality.* Dissociative identity disorder, discussed earlier in this module, comes closest.)
- Schizophrenia occurs in about 1 percent of the population. It affects both men and women at the same rate, and it occurs around the world at about the same rate. Schizophrenia typically develops in late adolescence or early adulthood.

Symptoms of Schizophrenia

5. What are the major symptoms of schizophrenia?

A variety of symptoms characterize schizophrenia (Figure 29.3). No one will experience them all, but everyone with the disorder will experience some of them. Common symptoms include *delusions, hallucinations,* and *inappropriate emotions or behaviors.*

▶ **schizophrenia** A group of severe disorders characterized by disorganized and delusional thinking, disturbed perceptions, and inappropriate emotions and actions.

▶ **delusions** False beliefs that are symptoms of schizophrenia and other serious psychological disorders.

Delusions

A **delusion** is a false belief. Of course, we all believe false things sometimes, but the delusions of schizophrenia are more extensive, more complex, and often more long term. They fall into several broad categories:

Enriching

Students can learn about the lives of Chris Sizemore and Sybil Dorsett by using the following questions as a guide to research and subsequent discussion of the findings:

- What abuse did they say they experienced?
- What type of relationships did they have with their therapists?
- What were the results of their therapy sessions? Did they experience personality integration? Why or why not?
- What impact did the movie versions of their lives have on them?
- What are the current scholarly views about their experiences?

trb At this point, you may wish to use Enrichment Lesson: *The Dissociative Disorders Interview Schedule and Multiple Personality* (*Teacher's Resource Binder,* p. 29-1).

- *Delusions of grandeur* are false beliefs that you are more important than you really are. People with schizophrenia may actually believe they are someone else, such as a famous political leader (Abraham Lincoln, for example) or religious figure (Jesus).
- *Delusions of persecution* are false beliefs that people are out to get you. People may believe they are being followed, or that the CIA is engaging in an elaborate plot to capture them.
- *Delusions of sin or guilt* are false beliefs of being responsible for some misfortune. For instance, a person might believe he is responsible for a plane crash because he failed to brush his teeth one morning.
- *Delusions of influence* are false beliefs of being controlled by outside forces: "The devil made me do it."

▶ **hallucinations** False perceptions that are symptoms of schizophrenia and other serious psychological disorders.

Hallucinations

A **hallucination** is a false perception. The hallucinations people with schizophrenia most often experience are *auditory*. Many report hearing voices, and sometimes the voices tell them what to do. If the hallucination is *visual* the person sees nonexistent objects, or distorted images of items or people. *Tactile* hallucinations occur when people feel skin stimulation, such as a tingling or burning or touch that is not real. Hallucinations can also distort *taste* and *smell*. Note the difference: Delusions are beliefs with no logical basis; hallucinations are perceptions with no outside stimulation. But hallucinations often provide "evidence" for delusions—it's quite logical to believe someone is plotting to kill you if you can taste poison in your food. Life becomes difficult if we can't trust the input from our own senses.

Hallucinations John Nash, the brilliant mathematician featured in the 2001 movie *A Beautiful Mind*, suffered many classic symptoms of schizophrenia, including visual, auditory and tactile hallucinations, which he is shown visibly experiencing here.

Inappropriate Emotions or Behaviors

A wide number of specific symptoms fit into this broad category. Schizophrenia can produce wildly inappropriate emotions. A patient might laugh uncontrollably when sadness is called for. Another suf-

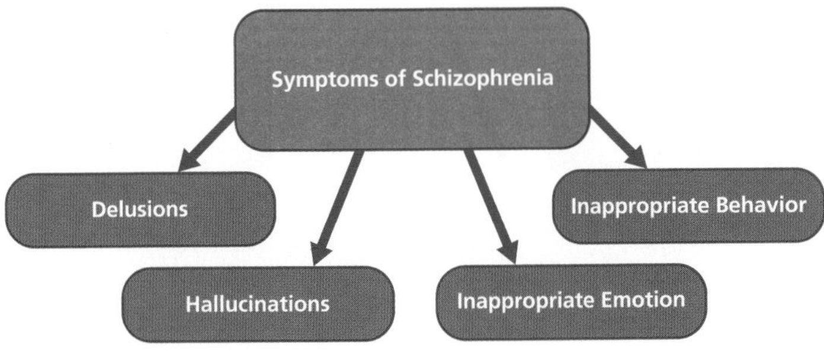

Figure 29.3 **Symptoms of Schizophrenia** It would be unusual for a person with schizophrenia to experience all of these symptoms, but some of them will be present.

trb tr ■ **TEACHING TIP**

A black-line master of Figure 29.3, Symptoms of Schizophrenia, is available in the **Black-Line Masters Appendix** of the *Teacher's Resource Binder.*

■ **LOOKING AT THE ISSUES**

Some famous criminals have claimed that voices told them to commit their crimes. They also held ideas that seemed delusional. Have students research the following cases:

- David Berkowitz (the Son of Sam)—This New York City case involved a young man who claimed that his dog was possessed by Satan. Berkowitz claimed the dog told him to kill.
- John Hinkley—Hinkley attempted to assassinate President Ronald Reagan to attract the attention of Jodie Foster, the Hollywood actress and director.
- John David Chapman—Chapman killed John Lennon because he believed the "devil" side of him told him to do it.

V At this point, you may wish to show **Videocassette:** ***The Brain,*** **Second Edition, Module 26: "Schizophrenia: Symptoms"** (*Teacher's Resource Binder*, p. 29-1).

Demonstrating

HEARING "VIRTUAL HALLUCINATIONS" With help from neuropsychologist Michael Green and his colleagues at the University of California, Los Angeles, Janssen Pharmaceutica produced the audiotape "Virtual Hallucinations," which simulates the auditory hallucinations heard by up to 70 percent of people with schizophrenia. The scene is a job interview. Green states, "Most of us have some insight into the problems suffered by people with extreme anxiety or depression, but few of us have heard voices that no one else can hear. This tape gives us the opportunity to develop empathy for an experience that is not otherwise available to us." Originally produced to give policymakers, family members of people with schizophrenia, and professionals who work with them a first-hand understanding of the disorder, the tape is now available to the public. The tape can be ordered for $9.23 (which includes shipping and handling) from Virtual Hallucinations, P.O. Box 580, New York, New York 10013.

MODULE 29

■ TEACHING TIPS

trb tr (1) A black-line master of Figure 29.4, Types of Schizophrenia, is available in the **Black-Line Masters Appendix** of the *Teacher's Resource Binder.*

(2) Paranoid schizophrenia is the most widely recognizable form of the disorder. Movies depicting paranoids as either bumbling oddballs or psychopathic killers reinforce stereotypes of these patients.

F•Y•I

Schizophrenic patients will exhibit other striking symptoms of their disorder.

- Loose associations occur in patients with disorganized schizophrenia as they tie together events and memories that don't seem to logically fit together.
- *Neologisms* are words that patients create, usually as part of the "word salad" symptom. They will make up words that make no logical sense.

trb At this point, you may wish to use **Demonstration Activity:** *The Referential Thinking Scale* (*Teacher's Resource Binder,* p. 29-1; **Handout 29–4**) and **Demonstration Activity:** *Magical Ideation Scale* (*Teacher's Resource Binder,* p. 29-1; **Handout 29–5**).

trb tr ■ CHECKING FOR UNDERSTANDING

Create a handout from the black-line master for Figure 29.4 in the **Black-Line Masters Appendix** of the *Teacher's Resource Binder* to assess whether students know the different types of schizophrenia. Have students cover some terms and then fill in blanks to reinforce their knowledge of concepts related to this disorder.

ferer might have very flat emotions, showing little or no emotional response. Inappropriate behaviors may be verbal or physical. Some people may not speak at all. Others may produce *word salad,* nonsense talk characteristic of some types of schizophrenia. (Remember Emilio at the beginning of this module? His claim of "eating wires and lightning fires" was one of several symptoms of schizophrenia he exhibited. Can you identify the others?) People with schizophrenia may act in inappropriate ways, or be almost completely inactive. In rare cases, *waxy flexibility* occurs, a state in which you could place the person's arm, as you would place a doll's arm, in some position of your choice. The person would hold that position for hours on end. Quite frequently, people with schizophrenia withdraw from the affairs of the real world. This withdrawal further limits their knowledge of current events and their social skills.

Types of Schizophrenia

6. What are the four major types of schizophrenia, and what are their main characteristics?

The family of disorders known as schizophrenia is broken into four major types (Figure 29.4):

- *Paranoid schizophrenia*, characterized by delusions, particularly delusions of grandeur and persecution. Auditory and other hallucinations often support the delusions.
- *Catatonic schizophrenia,* characterized largely by variations in voluntary movements. A person with this type of schizophrenia alternates between two phases—*catatonic excitement*, consisting of rapid movement, delusions and hallucinations—and *catatonic stu-*

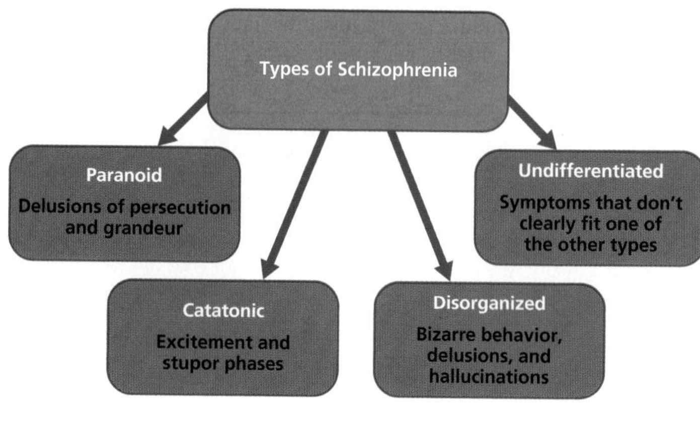

Figure 29.4 Types of Schizophrenia Schizophrenia is a family of related disorders.

Cross-Curricular Connections

LITERATURE Michael Gorman reports a highly successful student project in which students were asked to read Mark Vonnegut's *The Eden Express* and relate it to the psychological literature on schizophrenia. The book is an autobiographical account of the author's schizophrenic breakdown and eventual recovery. Challenge students to complete any of the following projects, which you may assign extra credit:

- a critical analysis of the book's depiction of schizophrenia in light of modern knowledge about the condition
- a reflective paper focusing on the student's reaction to Vonnegut's story
- a creative story based on Vonnegut's account

Source: Gorman, M. (1984). Using *The Eden Express* to teach introductory psychology. *Teaching of Psychology, 11*(1), 39–40.

por, with very little activity or speech. Flat emotion and waxy flexibility often are part of the stupor phase.

- *Disorganized schizophrenia*, characterized by bizarre behavior, delusions, and hallucinations. Individuals with this type of schizophrenia are visibly disturbed. In historical times they were thought to have "gone mad." The case of Emilio from the beginning of this module illustrates disorganized schizophrenia.
- *Undifferentiated schizophrenia,* characterized by symptoms that are disturbed but are not clearly consistent with the paranoid, catatonic, or disorganized types of schizophrenia. Individuals in this category nevertheless show clear evidence of the symptoms of schizophrenia.

Causes of Schizophrenia

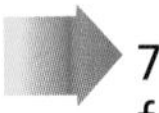

7. What are some of the biological and psychological factors that can interact to produce schizophrenia?

Complex disorders have complicated causes, and there is probably no psychological disorder more complex than schizophrenia. As is so often the case, biological factors and psychological factors seem to interact to produce this disorder.

Biological Factors

The biological approach to schizophrenia has received so much research support in recent years that some experts say we are wrong to call it a psychological disorder. Rather, it is a brain disorder that produces changes in a person's mind. Let's examine the biological factors in more detail.

Genetics The risk of schizophrenia increases substantially if relatives have the disorder (Figure 29.5, page 564). While roughly 1 percent of the general population has schizophrenia, the risk rises to about 10 percent if one's parent or sibling has schizophrenia. These odds are even higher—almost 50 percent—if the relative with schizophrenia is an identical twin (Plomin & others, 1997). Notice that this evidence shows that, while genetics is an important factor, there is no single gene or set of genes that guarantees schizophrenia will develop. If there were, the risk for an identical twin whose co-twin had the disorder would be 100 percent, because identical twins have identical genes. Instead, genetics seems to produce a *predisposition*—an increased likelihood that the disorder will develop. Other factors, as we will see, determine whether the increased likelihood will actually become a full-fledged disorder. A similar situation exists for various kinds of heart disease. Genetics may put a person at risk, but factors such as exercise, diet, and smoking play a critical role in determining whether the disease will develop.

Enriching

Have students examine how heritable other mental illnesses are by asking them to find statistics related to how likely a child is to develop a disorder his or her parent has. Have students conduct research and, afterward, discuss their findings on the following conditions:

- depression and bipolar disorder
- anxiety disorders
- somatoform disorders
- substance-related disorders
- personality disorders

F•Y•I

Recent research using brain imaging techniques have shed some light on the biological basis of schizophrenia.

- People who develop schizophrenia later in life have abnormal brain activity before the onset of symptoms, showing that schizophrenia may be a developmental disorder.
- MRI studies show that gray matter in the brains of schizophrenic patients is markedly less dense than in normal patients.
- Studies have also shown that patients who have auditory hallucinations experience temporal lobe activation, indicating that they really are hearing voices that aren't there.

■ TEACHING TIPS

(1) Remind students that a genetic predisposition does not guarantee that one will get a disorder like schizophrenia. A combination of environmental and behavioral influences helps to determine whether someone with a predisposition will develop the disorder.

trb At this point, you may wish to use **Enrichment Lesson:** ***Infantile Autism*** (***Teacher's Resource Binder***, p. 29-1).

(2) Link discussion of *dopamine* to Module 7's discussion of *neurotransmitters* and their functions. Dopamine is similar in its chemical makeup to cocaine, which explains why abusers of the drug experience schizophrenic-like symptoms. Also linked to dopamine is Parkinson's disease, which is thought to result from a lack of dopamine channels in the brain. Some patients who take medicine to treat schizophrenia will develop Parkinsonian-like symptoms, such as hand tremors.

MODULE 29

F•Y•I

When they became recurrent schizophrenia research subjects, the first and last names of the quadruplets (featured in Figure 29.5) were changed to Genain to protect their privacy. They claim the unique distinction of being the only set of multiples who share this mental illness. All of them became schizophrenic by age 25. In addition to sharing the same gene code, they also shared a nightmarish family life, having suffered abuse from their father and ambivalence from their mother. The least ill of the four, Myra, seems to have been her mother's favorite. Myra managed to avoid some of her father's abuse, reinforcing the idea of the interplay between heredity and environment.

tr A four-color transparency of Figure 29.5, Genetics and Schizophrenics: The Genain Quadruplets, is available in the **Overhead Transparencies Set.**

■ **TEACHING TIP**

Students may be curious about the other personality disorders identified in the DSM-IV-TR.

- Cluster A includes *paranoid, schizoid,* and *schizotypal* disorders. This group contains those disorders that involve odd or eccentric behavior.
- Cluster B includes *antisocial, borderline, histrionic,* and *narcissistic* disorders. This group contains those disorders that include dramatic or impulsive behavior.
- Cluster C includes *avoidant, dependent,* and *obsessive-compulsive* disorders. These are the anxiety-related disorders.

trb At this point, you may wish to use **Demonstration Activity:** ***Antisocial Personality Disorder*** (*Teacher's Resource Binder*, p. 29-1; Handout 29–6).

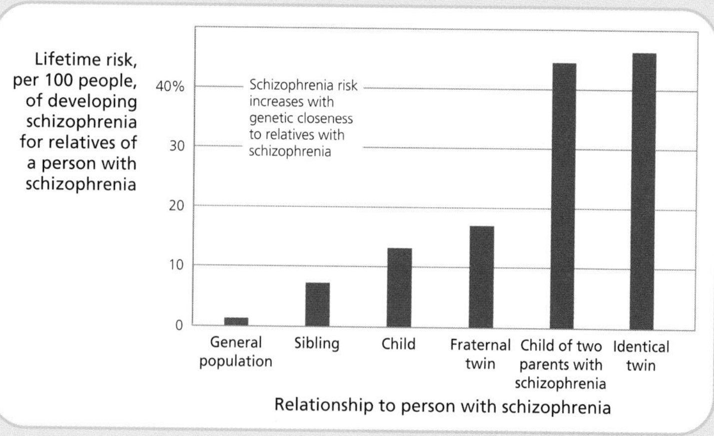

Figure 29.5 **Genetics and Schizophrenia: The Genain Quadruplets** Nora, Iris, Myra, and Hester Genain, identical quadruplets, have all developed schizophrenia. If they had been randomly selected, the risk of this would be 1 in 100 million! We can assume that no single gene or set of genes is directly responsible for schizophrenia, though. If such a direct cause existed, the figure for identical twins, who are genetically identical, would be 100 percent. Since two of the sisters have more serious forms of schizophrenia, it is likely that both heredity and environment—nature and nurture—are involved.

Brain Structure The brain structure of people with schizophrenia differs markedly from normal brain structure. Brain scans show that schizophrenia is often associated with smaller amounts of brain tissue and larger fluid-filled spaces around that tissue (Cannon & Marco, 1994). Particular brain structures may be affected by this disorder. The thalamus, responsible for the routing of incoming sensory information, is smaller when schizophrenia is present and may hinder the person's ability to focus attention (Andreasen & others, 1994).

Brain Function PET scans, which show the parts of the brain that are active during particular tasks, reveal that the brain of a person with schizophrenia actually operates differently than does the brain of someone without the disorder. One difference appears in the frontal lobes—the center of our most advanced thinking abilities—which show less activity when schizophrenia is present (Resnik, 1992). Brain chemistry also differs. Researchers have discovered as many as six times the normal number of receptor sites for the neurotransmitter *dopamine* when they

Schizophrenia and Brain Structure These two brain scans are from identical twins, one who has schizophrenia and one who does not. Note that the open space (this is actually a cavity in the brain filled with fluid) is larger for the twin with schizophrenia (Suddath & others, 1990). Since identical twins have indentical genes, this difference must have been caused by some environmental factor, such as a virus.

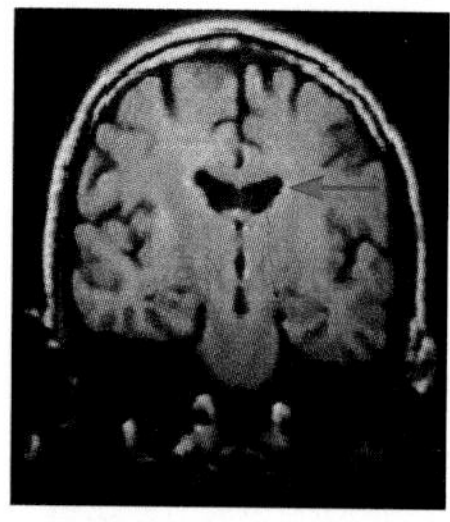

Schizophrenia

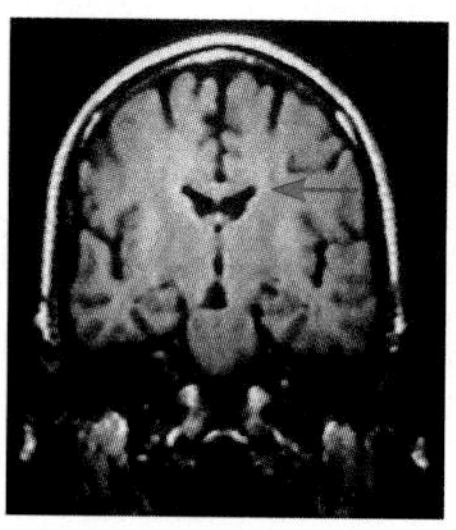

No schizophrenia

examined the brains of people with schizophrenia after death (Seeman & others, 1993). These abnormally high numbers of receptors may explain the delusions and hallucinations associated with schizophrenia. Medication that blocks these receptor sites reduces such symptoms.

Prenatal Viruses A viral infection during the middle of pregnancy may also cause schizophrenia (Waddington, 1993). The evidence for this is circumstantial but persuasive. Rates of schizophrenia rise for individuals who were born a few months after a flu epidemic (Mednick & others, 1994), and the riskiest birth months in general follow the flu season (Torrey & others, 1997). In fact, in the Southern Hemisphere, where the seasons are reversed, the high risk months are reversed as well (McGrath & Welham, 1999).

Psychological Factors

For many years, explanations of schizophrenia focused mainly on psychological factors. Freud targeted the relationship between mother and child as the primary cause of the disorder. He mistakenly thought that mothers who were cold, domineering, and selfish caused schizophrenia in their children (Fromm-Reichmann, 1948).

Are there any psychological factors that *do* appear important? The two areas that seem most significant are stress and disturbed family communication patterns. Recall that the major genetic contribution to schizophrenia seems to be a predisposition—a tendency to develop the disorder. Stress may well be the trigger that sets off the series of events that convert schizophrenia from a possibility into a reality. Disturbed family communications are also correlated with the development of schizophrenia, but at this point it's impossible to tell whether they are a *cause* of schizophrenia or a *result* of the disorder.

The bizarre world of schizophrenia has puzzled and fascinated students of human behavior for centuries. We are making progress both in understanding and effectively treating this devastating disorder. It seems to result from a complex interaction of biological and psychological factors. To be effective, treatment will have to address both of these components.

Personality Disorders

8. How do the three major clusters of personality disorders differ from one another?

Personality disorders are lasting, rigid patterns of behavior that seriously impair one's social functioning. The DSM-IV-TR lists 10 personality disorders, divided into three clusters (Figure 29.6, page 566). The specific disorders are often difficult to diagnose because there is a lot of overlap among them. The behavior patterns are usually evident

▶ **personality disorders** Psychological disorders characterized by inflexible and lasting behavior patterns that disrupt social functioning.

MODULE 29

■ LOOKING AT THE ISSUES

Personality disorders are difficult to diagnose and treat since the behaviors related to them are enduring and rigid. Have students discuss why people may be unable to recognize that someone has a personality disorder by posing the following questions:

- Where is the line between being eccentric, anxious, or odd, and having a personality disorder?
- How might treatment be difficult?

■ APPLYING THE POINTS

Invite a psychologist to class to discuss treatment options for people with personality disorders. In the talk, ask him or her to address the following questions:

- How can people be treated for personality disorders?
- How successful is treatment for these conditions?
- Are personality disorders normally identified in conjunction with other disorders? Why or why not?

■ JOURNAL WRITING

Invite students to use the following questions and writing prompts as springboards for entries in their psychology journals.

- Do you feel you would qualify as someone who might have a personality disorder? Why or why not?
- Have you ever known someone that you suspect might have a personality disorder? What behaviors of theirs lead you to this conclusion?

Cooperative Learning

Divide the class into small groups of students and provide the groups with case studies of people with different personality disorders. After students read each case study, have them work with their group to decide which disorder is being described. Then, have the class come together to see if all the groups agree on the diagnoses for all the case studies. Suggest that groups also come up with their own case studies to see if the class can correctly diagnose the disorders.

MODULE 29

■ **TEACHING TIPS**

trb tr (1) A black-line master of Figure 29.6, Three Main Clusters of Personality Disorders, is available in the **Black-Line Masters Appendix** of the *Teacher's Resource Binder.*

(2) *Paranoid personality* and *schizoid personality* are different from schizophrenia only by a matter of degree. Although people with schizophrenia experience psychotic episodes during which they lose touch with reality, people with these personality disorders do not have these experiences. Their behavior is odd, eccentric, and disturbing, but it does not impair daily life in the way that schizophrenia does.

■ **MULTICULTURAL CONNECTIONS**

Using available print and Internet resources, have students research the occurrence of personality disorders in other cultures. Use the following questions as a guide for students' research and subsequent discussion of their findings:

- What is the incidence of personality disorders in other cultures?
- Are these disorders more common in Western culture? U.S. culture? Why or why not?

Figure 29.6 **Three Main Clusters of Personality Disorders**

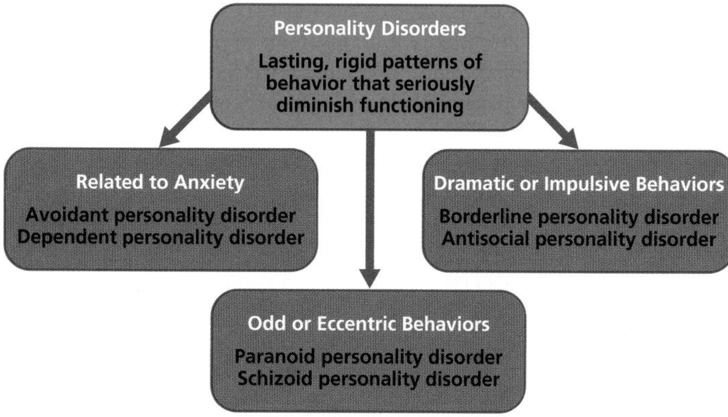

by adolescence and obvious to others, but the person with the disorder often does not recognize the problem exists, which can make treatment difficult. Let's take a look at the three clusters of personality disorders and a sample of the specific disorders included in each cluster.

Personality Disorders Related to Anxiety

Individuals with *avoidant personality disorder* are so sensitive about being rejected that personal relationships become difficult. Those with *dependent personality disorder* behave in clingy, submissive ways and display a strong need to have others take care of them.

Personality Disorders With Odd or Eccentric Behaviors

Individuals with *paranoid personality disorder* (which is different from paranoid schizophrenia) show deep distrust of other people. This suspiciousness gets in the way of personal relationships. Those with *schizoid personality disorder* are detached from social relationships. They are the true hermits, preferring the life of the loner and avoiding intimate interactions with others at all costs.

► **antisocial personality disorder** A personality disorder in which the person (usually a man) shows a lack of conscience for wrongdoing and a lack of respect for the rights of others.

Personality Disorders with Dramatic or Impulsive Behaviors

Those with *borderline personality disorder* exhibit, above all else, instability—of emotions, self-image, behavior, and relationships. Mary, who is featured in one of the cases that opens this module, is an example of a person with borderline personality disorder. Her academic struggles in

Meeting Individual Needs

trb tr As you begin a discussion about personality disorders, distribute to students a handout you've create from the black-line master of Figure 29.6, Three Main Clusters of Personality Disorders, which is available in the **Black-Line Masters Appendix** of the *Teacher's Resource Binder.* This handout will help those students who may have trouble learning the information from this portion of the module. Suggest that students fill in blanks you create on the graphic either individually or with the help of a peer tutor.

- **Exceptional Learners** A handout created from the black-line master for Figure 29.6 can fill the need to provide notes for exceptional learners. These students may review the terms with a student or teacher/tutor. They may refer to the handout during class discussion or lecture.

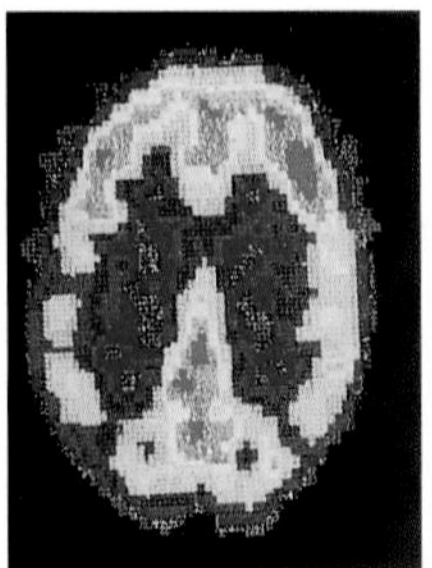

Normal

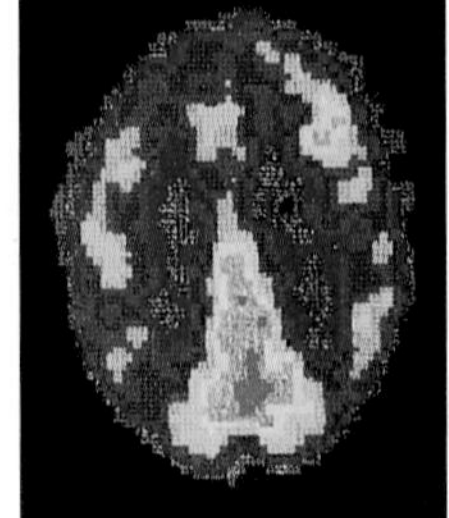

Murderer

The Criminal Brain Biological factors may help explain the criminal behavior of individuals with antisocial personality disorder. These PET scans show reduced activity (less red) in the frontal lobes of a murderer. This may result in a lack of judgment and less ability to control impulsive or aggressive impulses. (From Raine, 1999.)

college, inability to resolve religious and philosophical issues, unrealistic demands, and suicide attempt all add up to a life filled with instability.

Antisocial personality disorder (also known as psychopathic or sociopathic personality disorder) is the most dramatic and troubling of all the personality disorders. People with antisocial personality disorder show absolutely no concern for the rights or feelings of other people. Because of this lack of conscience, they are willing to engage in wide-ranging criminal behaviors about which they show no remorse. This disorder is much more likely to occur in males than in females, and it usually develops by adolescence. People with the disorder are often charming and clever, which helps them get away with their misdeeds. In extreme forms, this disorder may manifest itself in serial killing, where the murderer has no regard for the victims. Vicious crimes are committed for trivial reasons and dismissed with such excuses as, "Once I've done a crime, I just forget it," or "I think of killing like smoking a cigarette, like another habit" (Darrach & Norris, 1984). The horribly counterproductive behavior patterns of antisocial personality are caused by a combination of biological, psychological, and social factors. Once in place, the disorder is extremely difficult to treat effectively. As you can imagine, people with antisocial personality disorder often end up in jail instead of in treatment.

Dissociative disorders, schizophrenia disorders, and personality disorders help us understand that abnormal functioning is as varied as normal functioning, and that the reasons for it are just as complex. Just as psychology can help us understand and promote productive behavior and mental processes, it can help us comprehend the fascinating and sometimes frightening world of mental disorders. This is the first step on the road to effective treatment.

■ TEACHING TIPS

(1) The terms *psychopath* and *sociopath* are synonymous. These words are actually legal terms, not psychological diagnostic terms.

(2) Although all serial killers are antisocial, not all who are antisocial are also serial killers.

V At this point, you may wish to show Videocassette: *The Mind,* Second Edition, Module 35: "The Mind of the Psychopath" (*Teacher's Resource Binder,* p. 29-1).

F • Y • I

Harvey Cleckley identifies the following characteristics of antisocial personality:

1. Superficial charm and good intelligence
2. Poise, rationality, absence of neurotic anxiety
3. Lack of a sense of personal responsibility
4. Untruthfulness, insincerity, callousness, manipulativeness
5. Antisocial behavior without regret or shame
6. Poor judgment and failure to learn from experience
7. Inability to establish lasting, close relationships with others
8. Lack of insight into personal motivations

Source: Cleckley, H. (1976). *The mask of sanity* (5th ed.). St. Louis: Mosby.

trb At this point, you may wish to use Demonstration Activity: *Antisocial Personality Disorder* (*Teacher's Resource Binder,* p. 29-1; Handout 29–6).

Close

Have students ponder the following questions about the disorders discussed in this module:

- How much of a role would you say biology plays in contributing to these disorders? Why?
- How much of a role would you say environment plays in contributing to these disorders? Why?
- How does knowledge of what contributes to these disorders lead to greater compassion for those who suffer from them?

MODULE 29

Checking the Points

■ TEACHING TIPS

web (1) The book companion site for *Thinking About Psychology* at www.worthpublishers.com/thinkingaboutpsych contains a module quiz, flashcards of key terms and people, as well as other student activities and resources for this module. You will also find PowerPoint lectures, a quiz grade book, and other teaching resources by logging on as an instructor.

trb (2) At this point, you may wish to review and confirm concepts about these disorders with **Critical Thinking Activity:** *Fact or Falsehood?* (*Teacher's Resource Binder*, p. 29-1; **Handout 29–1**). If students completed the handout earlier in the module, ask them to set those copies aside. Suggest that students complete the handout in small groups, taking the time to look up information in the text to respond correctly to questions. Have all the groups meet to review the handout, again using the text to support their responses.

REVIEW

Module 29: Dissociative, Schizophrenia, and Personality Disorders

What's the Point?

This module considered dissociative, schizophrenia, and personality disorders, which are only a small part of the disorders covered by the American Psychiatric Association's *Diagnostic and Statistical Manual of Mental Disorders,* Fourth Edition, Text Revision (DSM-IV-TR).

Dissociative Disorders

Dissociative disorders are those in which a person's sense of self separates from the individual's memories, thoughts, or feelings.

1. *How does dissociative amnesia differ from other forms of amnesia?*

   In dissociative amnesia, memory loss is a reaction to a specific, stressful event, rather than to head injury, fatigue, or physical diseases. Sigmund Freud believed dissociative amnesia is due to repressed memories. Many psychologists now believe that "recovered" memories are in fact false memories, sometimes unknowingly planted by therapists.

2. *How does dissociative fugue differ from dissociative amnesia?*

   Dissociative fugue is similar to dissociative amnesia in that both involve loss of memory in response to extreme stress. In dissociative fugue, however, the loss of memory takes the form of a loss of identity (not being able to remember who you are), accompanied by travel to a new location.

3. *Why is the diagnosis of dissociative identity disorder controversial?*

   Dissociative identity disorder was formerly called *multiple personality disorder,* because the person with this condition is said to exhibit two or more distinct and alternating personalities. Many psychologists believe that this disorder results from the interaction between the therapist and the client, and that the therapist's leading questions may cause the clients to search for other personalities within themselves. Diagnoses of this disorder have increased dramatically as reports of the condition have appeared in the popular media and in scientific journals. But dissociative identity disorder is not a pretended illness; clients really believe they have multiple personalities, and therapists believe they are treating an authentic condition.

   Other disorders, the somatoform disorders, are conditions in which physical problems occur for psychological reasons. These disorders include hypochondriasis and conversion disorder. Like dissociative identity disorder, conversion disorder was diagnosed very frequently during one historical period. For conversion disorder, that period coincided with the time of Freud's greatest popularity.

Schizophrenia Disorders

4. *What is schizophrenia?*

   Schizophrenia is a family of related disorders that occur equally often in men and women and that are found in all cultures. About one person in 100 will be diagnosed with schizophrenia, typically in late adolescence or early adulthood.

5. *What are the major symptoms of schizophrenia?*

   The disorders known as schizophrenia share the symptoms of disorganized and delusional thinking, disturbed perceptions, and inappropriate emotions and behaviors. Delusions are false beliefs. Hallucinations are false perceptions. Behaviors and emotions are judged to be inappropriate because they have no apparent relationship to things that are happening to the person. People may talk too much, though not making sense, or not talk at all. They may behave inappropriately or be completely inactive.

6. *What are the four major types of schizophrenia, and what are their main characteristics?*

   A person with *paranoid schizophrenia* has delusions and may have auditory or other hallucinations. Someone with *catatonic schizophrenia* will alternate between periods of excitement (with rapid movements, delusions, and hallucinations) and periods of stupor (with little activity—possibly even waxy flexibility—or speech and flat emotions). A person with *disorganized schizophrenia* will be visibly disturbed, behaving in bizarre ways and having delusions and hallucinations. Someone with *undifferentiated schizophrenia* will have some combination of disorganized and delusional thinking, disturbed perceptions, and inappropriate emotions and behaviors, but the person will not fall neatly into any of the three previous categories.

7. *What are some of the biological and psychological factors that can interact to produce schizophrenia?*

   The biological components of schizophrenia include genetics, brain structure, brain function, and viral infections. Genetics does not *determine* that a person will develop schizophrenia, but twin studies and adoption studies indicate that heredity makes some people more prone to this disorder than others are. Brain scans show that the brain structure of people with schizophrenia differs from normal brain structure. PET scans show that the frontal lobes are less active during periods of schizophrenia. Brain chemistry in these individuals also differs from normal brain chemistry: They have abnormally high numbers of dopamine receptors. Dopamine blockers reduce delusions and hallucinations in people with schizophrenia. There is some indication that a child may be at higher risk for schizophrenia if the child's mother contracts a viral infection during the middle of her pregnancy.

   Stress and disturbed patterns of family communication are the leading psychological factors that may contribute to schizophrenia.

Personality Disorders

8. *How do the three major clusters of personality disorders differ from one another?*

   Personality disorders are lasting, rigid patterns of behavior that seriously impair social functioning. The three clusters are personality disorders related to anxiety, personality disorders with odd or eccentric behaviors, and personality disorders with dramatic or impulsive behaviors. People with antisocial personality disorder show no concern for the rights or feelings of others. This disorder occurs more in males than in females and may lead to criminal behavior.

Key Terms

dissociative disorders, p. 555
dissociative amnesia, p. 556
dissociative fugue, p. 556
dissociative identity disorder, p. 557
somatoform disorders, p. 558
hypochondriasis, p. 558
schizophrenia, p. 560
delusions, p. 560
hallucinations, p. 561
personality disorders, p. 565
antisocial personality disorder, p. 567

trb ■ TEACHING TIP

At this point, you may wish to provide students with **Building Vocabulary: Graphic Organizer:** ***Crossword Puzzle*** **(*Teacher's Resource Binder*, p. 29-1; Handout 29–2).** If students completed the crossword puzzle earlier in the module, ask them to set that version of the puzzle aside. Have students complete the puzzle as a tool for reviewing module concepts. After students have completed a review of module terms by completing the crossword puzzle, have them meet in small groups to ask questions, clarify confusing concepts, and check their answers.

MODULE 29

(tb) Using the Test Bank

The *Test Bank* that accompanies this textbook offers a wide variety of questions in different formats and levels of complexity. Use the software to construct whole tests or to integrate standardized questions into teacher-made tests.

Self-Test Answers

Multiple-Choice Questions

1. d, 2. d, 3. a, 4. c, 5. b

Matching Terms and Definitions

6. a. (4), b. (10), c. (5)

Self-Test

Multiple-Choice Questions

Choose the *best* answer for each of the following questions.

1. When Ike N. Runfast, a famous football star, was picked up for shoplifting, he claimed that he hadn't stolen anything—that he has dissociative identity disorder, and his multiple personalities Mia and Hugo worked together to steal the goods. The prosecutor has hired a psychologist to give an expert opinion on dissociative identity disorder. The psychologist is likely to testify that
   a. fewer than 100 cases of this disorder were reported before 1970, but novels and media coverage have popularized the disorder since that time.
   b. most cases were reported in North America, where the disorder became well known in the media.
   c. clinicians may unintentionally lead patients into believing they have multiple personalities.
   d. The psychologist will probably state all of the above.

2. Whitney has just been diagnosed with schizophrenia. Of the following family members, who is *most* likely to also be diagnosed with schizophrenia at some point?
   a. Whitney's mother.
   b. Whitney's child.
   c. Whitney's brother.
   d. Whitney's identical twin.

3. Carl has been in trouble since he was a little boy, and he seems to have no conscience or feeling of responsibility toward other people's well-being or their possessions. At 17, Carl set fire to an elderly neighbor's house, and the neighbor almost died from smoke inhalation. Carl showed no remorse when he was caught. Carl is showing symptoms of
   a. antisocial personality disorder.
   b. paranoid schizophrenia.
   c. dissociative amnesia.
   d. conversion disorder.

4. Alanna hears voices when no one is speaking, and she believes she is Cleopatra. Hearing voices is a (an) ______________; believing you are a famous person is a (an) ______________.
   a. obsession; compulsion
   b. compulsion; obsession
   c. hallucination; delusion
   d. delusion; hallucination

5. Khalil stayed home from school today because he hadn't finished his term paper and didn't want to receive a failing grade. He told his mother that he had a terribly sick stomach and a severe headache. Khalil is suffering from
   a. a conversion disorder.
   b. a somatoform disorder.
   c. nothing; he's just pretending to be sick.
   d. hysteria.

Matching Terms and Definitions

6. For each definition, choose the *best* matching term from the list that follows:

   Definition
   a. Disorder in which a person experiences symptoms of physical illness, but there is nothing physically wrong with the person.
   b. Disorganized and meaningless nonsense talk that occurs with some forms of schizophrenia.
   c. False beliefs; a symptom of schizophrenia.

Alternative Assessment/Portfolio Project

(web) Students can search the Web for information on different disorders presented in Modules 27 through 29. Assign each student or group of students a different disorder. Students should gather information on their assigned disorder and create a presentation to share with the class, school, or community. Some presentation options include the following:

- a formal research paper
- a poster presentation
- a public awareness campaign to educate people about the illness
- a documentary about someone with the disorder that educates people about day-to-day life of people with the illness

d. Memory loss due to some specific, stressful event.
e. False perceptions; a symptom of schizophrenia.
f. Disorder in which the person seems to have no conscience or feelings of respect for the rights of others.
g. Condition in which a person exhibits two or more distinct and alternating personalities.
h. Type of schizophrenia in which rapid movement, delusions, and hallucinations alternate with very little activity or speech.

Term

(1) dissociative amnesia
(2) dissociative identity disorder
(3) repression
(4) hypochondriasis
(5) delusions
(6) hallucinations
(7) antisocial personality disorder
(8) disorganized schizophrenia
(9) catatonic schizophrenia
(10) word salad

Fill-in-the-Blank Questions

7. In __________________ disorders, the sense of self has become separated from the individual's previous memories, thoughts, or feelings.
8. People with __________________ disorders experience physical problems that have no apparent physical cause.
9. __________________ is a group of disorders marked by disorganized and delusional thinking, disturbed perceptions, and inappropriate emotions and actions.
10. __________________ disorders are characterized by inflexible and lasting behavior patterns that disrupt social functioning.

Brief Essay Question

11. Your cousin Emilee has just learned that her oldest son has schizophrenia. She is feeling very guilty that she might have been a bad mother, perhaps not showing enough warmth or being too domineering or selfish. In two or three paragraphs of about three sentences each, explain to Emilee why she should not feel so guilty, and what current research teaches us about the causes of schizophrenia.

Self-Test Answers

Matching Terms and Definitions (continued)

d. (1), e. (6), f. (7), g. (2), h. (9)

Fill-in-the-Blank Questions

7. dissociative, 8. somatoform, 9. Schizophrenia, 10. Personality

Brief Essay Question

11. Students should discuss the genetic, biological, and viral links to schizophrenia. These explanations for the disorder have more scientific evidence supporting them than the "bad mothering" view espoused by Freud and others.

trb Please refer to **Alternative Assessment/Portfolio Project:** *Exploring Psychological Disorders on the World Wide Web* (*Teacher's Resource Binder*, p. 29-1; **Handout 29–7**) for helpful Web sites as well as a rubric to aid in evaluating students' projects. Revise the rubric to suit your needs.

CHAPTER 13 Treatment of Psychological Disorders

Clinical and Sociocultural Domain

Teaching with the Standards

Standard Area: Treatment of Psychological Disorders

Breakdown of Module 30: Psychological Therapies

Content Standard 1: Treatment methods for psychological disorders Module 30 discusses the psychological options available for individuals with psychological disorders. Treatment options include Freudian psychoanalysis, Rogerian client-centered therapy, and behavior and cognitive therapies. The author also discusses the advantages of group therapy. Emphasis is also on evaluating the effectiveness of psychotherapy, and the module considers alternative therapies like therapeutic touch and light exposure. (Student Text pp. 573–592)

Content Standard 2: Mental health professionals who treat psychological disorders Module 30 discusses common signs, cited by the American Psychological Association, of individuals who may need professional help. The author also considers how one may go about finding the right therapist to help in times of need. In addition, the author differentiates various types of therapists and their training. (Student Text p. 589)

Breakdown of Module 31: Biomedical Therapies

Content Standard 1: Treatment methods for psychological disorders Module 31 focuses on the biomedical approach to treating psychological disorders. Historical attempts to treat mental illness are compared with the development of drug therapies. Deinstitutionalization, as a result of the use of drug therapies, is discussed along with the implications for the homeless population in the United States. Antipsychotic, antianxiety, and antidepressant drugs are described. Focus is on how these drugs affect the brain at the neural level. The negative side effects of these drugs are also considered. Other biomedical techniques, such as electroconvulsive therapy and psychosurgery are discussed. (Student Text pp. 598–607)

Scope and Sequence

	Objectives	Text Reference	Standards Covered
Lesson 1	Discuss the psychoanalytic and humanistic approaches to treating psychological disorders.	Module 30, pp. 573–579	Standard Area: Treatment of Psychological Disorders, Content Standard 1, Performance Standard 1.1
Lesson 2	Discuss the behavior and cognitive therapies for treating psychological disorders. Investigate the effectiveness of psychotherapy.	Module 30, pp. 579–592	Content Standard 1, Performance Standards 1.1, 1.2
Lesson 3	Present historical treatments of psychological disorders. Discuss the use and effectiveness of the drugs and psychosurgery. Discuss how drugs affect the brain.	Module 31, pp.598–607	Content Standard 1, Performance Standards 1.1, 1.2
Lesson 4	Review and test		

CHAPTER 13

Treatment of Psychological Disorders

Introducing the Chapter

The Points: Chapter Objectives

- Describe how mental disorders develop, according to Sigmund Freud.
- Identify the techniques used by psychoanalysis to reveal and resolve conflicts.
- Compare and contrast psychodynamic and interpersonal therapies with psychoanalysis.
- Differentiate between psychoanalytic and humanistic therapy.
- Define unconditional positive regard, determining why it is important to humanistic therapy.
- Differentiate behavior therapies from humanistic therapies.
- Determine the basic assumption underlying behavior therapy based on classical conditioning.
- Determine the basic assumption underlying behavior therapy based on operant conditioning.
- Analyze how cognitive therapies help patients with depression.
- Delineate the advantages of therapy conducted in groups.
- Evaluate the research into the effectiveness of psychotherapy.
- Identify alternative therapies, evaluating their effectiveness.
- Explain how antipsychotic drugs work, pointing out some of their negative effects.
- Evaluate the dangers of extended use of antianxiety medications.
- Analyze why it is difficult to determine the effectiveness of antidepressant drugs.
- Determine why electroconvulsive therapy is used, explaining how it works.
- Examine why lobotomies were performed so frequently in the first half of the twentieth century.

CHAPTER 13

Treatment of Psychological Disorders

Ever had back problems? It's one thing to know that your back hurts, but something entirely different to know what to do about it. Maybe special exercises are the answer, or losing a few pounds to reduce stress on the spine. Maybe a trip to the chiropractor is in order, or the use of a back brace. Maybe you should even consider surgery.

The point is that even when you have identified a disorder—whether it's a physical problem such as a backache or a psychological problem such as depression—there are likely to be several options for treatment. This chapter presents some of the treatments available for psychological disorders. Module 30 focuses on treatments with a psychological basis and Module 31 highlights therapy through drugs or medical procedures available from physicians. As you'll soon see, psychologists have found that some treatments are particularly effective for certain disorders.

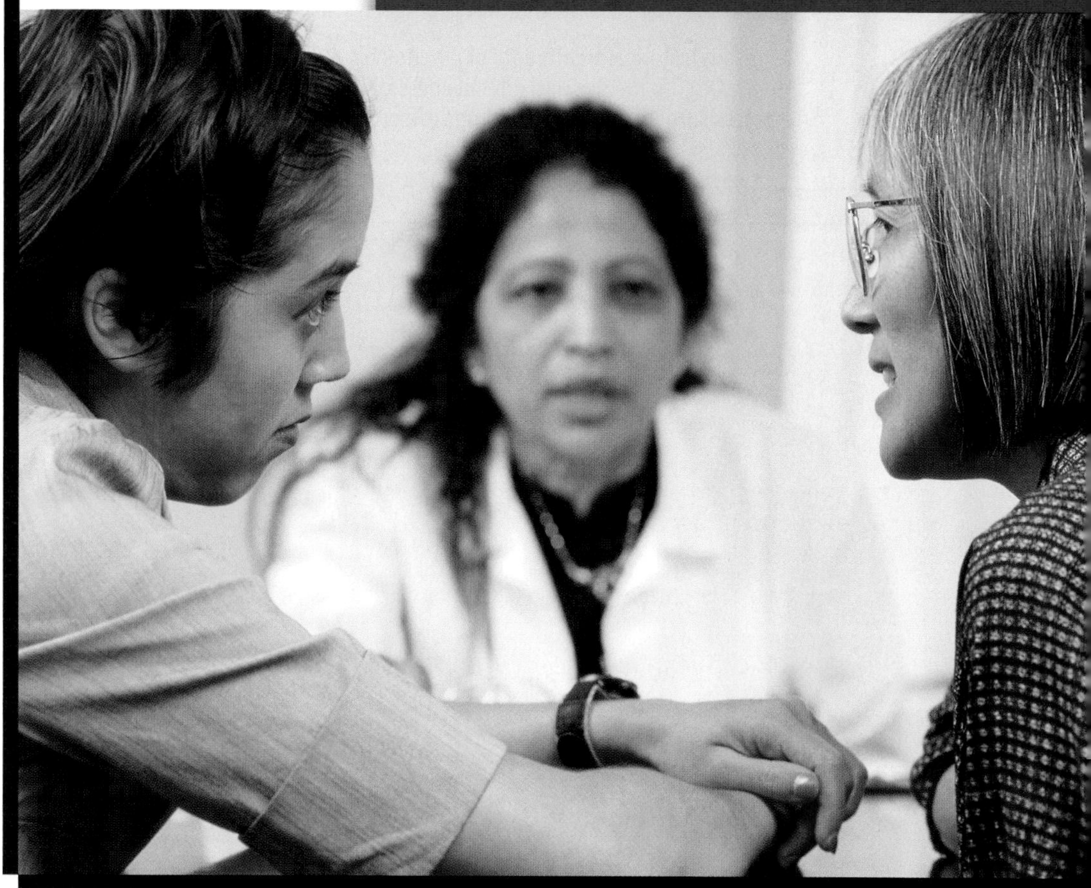

Performance Standards

Standard Area: Treatment of Psychological Disorders

Content Standard 1: Treatment methods for psychological disorders

Performance Standard 1.1 Describe the various treatment techniques for those with psychological disorders.

- Define "psychotherapy." Discuss how many therapists use techniques from a variety of approaches. Define "eclectic" approach. (Student Text pp. 573–574)
- Review psychoanalytic assumptions about the structure of the mind. (Student Text p. 574)
- Discuss the techniques used by psychoanalysts to reveal and resolve conflicts. Emphasize free association, resistance, interpretation, dream analysis, and transference. (Student Text pp. 575–576)
- Discuss criticisms of psychoanalysis. (Student Text p. 576)
- Discuss what psychodynamic and interpersonal therapies share with psychoanalysis and how they differ. (Student Text pp. 576–577)
- Compare psychoanalytic and humanistic approaches to psychotherapy. (Student Text pp. 577–578)
- Present Carl Rogers's client-centered therapy. Focus on active listening techniques and unconditional positive regard. (Student Text pp. 578–579)
- Discuss criticisms of humanistic therapy techniques. (Student Text p. 579)
- Compare behavior therapies with humanistic and psychoanalytic approaches. (Student Text p. 579)
- Focus on the classical conditioning techniques in behavior therapy. Emphasize systematic desensitization and aversive conditioning techniques. (Student Text pp. 580–583)
- Explore operant conditioning techniques in behavior therapy. Focus on the use of token economies to change behavior. (Student Text pp. 583–584)
- Investigate how cognitive therapists help those that are depressed. Focus on explanatory styles. (Student Text pp. 584–586)
- Discuss the use of cognitive-behavior therapy. (Student Text p. 586)
- Explore the advantages of therapy conducted in groups. Focus on family and group therapies. (Student Text pp. 586–587)

Performance Standard 1.2 Assess the effectiveness of various types of therapies and prevention.

- Explore what research tells us about psychotherapy's effectiveness. (Student Text pp. 588–591)
- Explore the effectiveness of alternative therapies. Discuss therapeutic touch and light exposure therapies. (Student Text pp. 591–592)

Content Standard 2: Mental health professionals who treat psychological disorders

Performance Standard 2.1 Therapists and their training.

- Table 30.1, "Therapists and their training," differentiates various types of mental health professionals. (Student Text p. 589)

Performance Standard 2.2 Identify strategies for finding appropriate mental health professionals.

- Discuss the common signs of trouble that may require professional help as cited by the American Psychological Association. (Student Text p. 589)
- Discuss how individuals can locate and evaluate mental health care professionals. (Student Text p. 589)

Materials NETWORK

All of the items from the Video, Activity, and Enrichment Centers listed below come from the *Teacher's Resource Binder.* These items will help you teach and expand on concepts presented in Module 30.

trb This logo indicates when an item from the Materials Network may be used in conjunction with a specific note found in this module's *Teacher's Edition.*

Psychoanalysis

Activity Center

- Critical Thinking Activity: *Fact or Falsehood?* With this activity, students' preconceptions about psychological therapies are either exposed as incorrect or reinforced as correct. (*Teacher's Resource Binder*, p. 30-1; Handout 30–1)
- Building Vocabulary: Graphic Organizer: *Concept Web* By completing this concept web, students are exposed to module concepts and can test their knowledge of module terms. (*Teacher's Resource Binder*, p. 30-1; Handout 30–2)
- Critical Thinking Activity: *Fifteen Freudian Principle Statements* Marianne Miserandino has designed an exercise to introduce the psychoanalytic perspective and, more specifically, to help students appreciate the impact of Sigmund Freud on modern American culture. (*Teacher's Resource Binder*, p. 30-1; Handout 30–3)
- Application Activity: *Defense Mechanisms* This activity will help students' thinking move from the abstract to the concrete as they learn to recognize the operation of defense mechanisms in everyday behavior. (*Teacher's Resource Binder*, p. 30-1; Handout 30–4)
- Cooperative Learning Activity: *Defense Mechanism Miniskits* Mary Inman uses role-playing in miniskits to provide students with the opportunity to apply their understanding of the major defense mechanisms. (*Teacher's Resource Binder*, p. 30-1; Handouts 30–5a and 30–5b)

Enrichment Center

- Enrichment Lesson: *Good Candidates for Psychoanalysis* Psychoanalysis is long and costly. Thus, before psychoanalysis begins, the therapist often uses a series of sessions to determine how appropriate the treatment may be for the client. (*Teacher's Resource Binder*, p. 30-1)
- Enrichment Lesson: *Freudian Slips* Freud believed that Freudian slips were motivated by unconscious conflicts. A hidden motive could presumably be found for even the most innocuous mistake if it were investigated with psychoanalytic methods. (*Teacher's Resource Binder*, p. 30-1)
- Enrichment Lesson: *Interpersonal Therapy* Interpersonal therapy evolved in the 1970s as a structured, brief form of psychoanalysis. Focusing on current relational issues, this form of therapy has been shown to be as effective in the short term as antidepressant drugs in treating depression. (*Teacher's Resource Binder*, p. 30-1)

Humanistic Therapies

Activity Center

- Technology Application Activity: *PsychSim:* "Computer Therapist" *PsychSim* is an interactive CD-ROM containing tutorials in different areas of psychology. In this tutorial, students interact with a computer as they would a nondirective therapist. (*Teacher's Resource Binder*, p. 30-1)
- Application Activity: *Role-Playing to Demonstrate Client-Centered Therapy* William Balch uses student volunteers to demonstrate Rogers's client-centered therapy (also called person-centered therapy), which seems particularly well suited for role-playing. (*Teacher's Resource Binder*, p. 30-1; Handout 30–6)
- Analysis Activity: *The Self-Concealment Scale* An important factor in effective humanistic therapy is providing clients with a safe environment in which they feel free to express themselves. This scale is designed to measure the existence of a safe environment. (*Teacher's Resource Binder*, p. 30-1; Handout 30–7)
- Analysis Activity: *The Imposter Phenomenon* This exercise is appropriate for discussions of either humanistic or cognitive therapies. Fritz Perls has used the term *catastrophic fantasy* to refer to our tendency to deprive ourselves of present joy because of a largely unconscious fear of being unmasked. (*Teacher's Resource Binder*, p. 30-1; Handout 30–8)

Enrichment Center

- Enrichment Lesson: *Computer-Assisted Therapy* There have been many attempts to use computers in therapy. Roger Gould, a psychiatrist at UCLA, has designed the Therapeutic Learning Program (TLP) to help patients clarify their problems and, gradually, to resolve conflicts by developing plans of action. (*Teacher's Resource Binder*, p. 30-1)

Behavior Therapies

 Video Center

Consult the faculty guide from *The Mind* and the *Scientific American Frontiers* video series for descriptions of this module and segment.

- Videocassette: *The Mind,* Second Edition, Module 30: "Treating Drug Addiction: A Behavioral Approach" (*Teacher's Resource Binder*, p. 30-1).
- Videocassette: *Scientific American Frontiers,* Second Edition, Segment 31: "Virtual Fear" (*Teacher's Resource Binder*, p. 30-1).

Activity Center

- Demonstration Activity: *Using Systematic Desensitization to Treat Eraser Phobia* Timothy Lawson and Michael Reardon describe a delightful classroom demonstration of systematic desensitization in treating a chalkboard eraser phobia. (*Teacher's Resource Binder*, p. 30-1)
- Application Activity: *Practicing Systematic Desensitization* Students may practice systematic desensitization on themselves. First, they must identify a specific fear they would like to overcome—for example, the fear of taking tests. Next, they must construct an anxiety hierarchy, which can be readily adapted to fit their own situation. (*Teacher's Resource Binder*, p. 30-1; **Handouts 30–9** and **30–10**)
- Demonstration Activity: *Modeling* Nigel Barber describes a classroom demonstration in which modeling is used to reduce many students' fear of a laboratory rat. (*Teacher's Resource Binder*, p. 30-1; **Handout 30–11**)
- Demonstration Activity: *Assessing Assertiveness* An important behavior therapy is assertiveness training. Jim Eison designed this activity to help students distinguish among assertive, nonassertive, and aggressive responses to common situations. (*Teacher's Resource Binder*, p. 30-1; **Handout 30–12**)

Enrichment Center

- Enrichment Lesson: *The Self-Injurious Behavior Inhibiting System* Ask your students whether aversives should ever be used in altering the behavior of children. Approach the subject by citing the controversy over the Self-Injurious Behavior Inhibiting System (SIBIS), a device that is used to control self-destructive behavior in autistic children. (*Teacher's Resource Binder*, p. 30-1)
- Enrichment Lesson: *Therapy and Totalitarian Control* The behavior therapies—specifically aversive conditioning—may have some students conjuring up images of George Orwell's *1984* and Stanley Kubrick's *A Clockwork Orange*. (*Teacher's Resource Binder*, p. 30-1)

Cognitive Therapies

Activity Center

- Application Activity: *Frequency of Self-Reinforcement Questionnaire* To extend the text treatment of cognitive therapy, you may want to introduce students to the concept of self-reinforcement and its importance in preventing and overcoming depression. (*Teacher's Resource Binder*, p. 30-1; **Handout 30–13**)

Enrichment Center

- Enrichment Lesson: *Strategies to Correct One's Thinking* In *The Feeling Good Handbook*, David Burns, MD, a psychiatrist, suggests ten ways to untwist the common cognitive distortions that typically underlie anxiety and depression. (*Teacher's Resource Binder*, p. 30-1)
- Enrichment Lesson: *Overcoming the Fear of Public Speaking* Survey research indicates that the greatest fear of most Americans is speaking before a group. Michael Motley's practical advice may not only help your students in dealing with their own public speaking phobia, but it can also be used to introduce them to cognitive therapies. (*Teacher's Resource Binder*, p. 30-1)

Family and Group Therapies

Enrichment Center

- Enrichment Lesson: *Psychodrama* A form of group therapy that is certain to interest students is psychodrama. In this technique, developed in the 1920s by Jacob Moreno, group members role-play or reenact emotionally laden scenes from each other's lives in the form of stage plays. (*Teacher's Resource Binder*, p. 30-1)

Evaluating Psychotherapy's Effectiveness

V Video Center

- Videocassette: *The Mind,* Second Edition, Module 3: "Placebo Effect: Mind-Body Relationship" Consult the faculty guide from *The Mind* video series for a description of this module. (*Teacher's Resource Binder*, p. 30-1).

Activity Center

- Analysis Activity: *Attitudes Toward Seeking Professional Psychological Help* Psychologists Edward Fischer and Amerigo Farina have developed a scale to assess people's attitudes toward seeking psychological help. (*Teacher's Resource Binder*, p. 30-1; **Handout 30–14**)

Enrichment Center

- Enrichment Lesson: *The Virtual Couch* Martha Ainsworth believes that online therapy "does not replace face-to-face therapy—it never will. That does not mean it's not a good thing. It's an additional thing." See if students agree after you have taught this lesson. (*Teacher's Resource Binder*, p. 30-1)
- Enrichment Lesson: *The Consumer Reports Study* The November 1995 issue of *Consumer Reports* reported survey results on the effectiveness of psychotherapy. Students learn more about the survey in this lesson. (*Teacher's Resource Binder*, p. 30-1)
- Enrichment Lesson: *Fringe Medicine* The text discusses the difficulty of answering the question "Is psychotherapy effective?" Clients and clinicians alike may have biased perceptions and, hence, selective and biased recall. Karl Sabbagh's analysis of "fringe medicine" supports the text's argument that we need controlled research studies to assess the effectiveness of therapy. (*Teacher's Resource Binder*, p. 30-1)

- **Enrichment Lesson:** *Thinking Errors and Clinical Judgments* The text describes how the judgments of psychiatrists and clinical psychologists about the success of therapy may reflect common errors in thinking. Consideration of these errors not only stimulates students to think critically about the clinical process but also serves to reinforce material from earlier modules. (*Teacher's Resource Binder*, p. 30-1)
- **Enrichment Lesson:** *Can Self-Help Materials Provide Effective Therapy?* More than 2000 self-help books are published annually, and many psychologists include these publications, as well as audiotapes, in the therapeutic process. Do they help? In their recent review of the effectiveness of nonprofessional therapies, Andrew Christensen and Neil Jacobson attempt to answer that question. (*Teacher's Resource Binder*, p. 30-1)
- **Enrichment Lesson:** *Therapy and the Nature of the Problem* The text concludes that therapy is most effective when the problem is specific. Those who suffer phobias can hope for improvement; those who want to change their whole personality are unlikely to benefit from psychotherapy alone. (*Teacher's Resource Binder*, p. 30-1)
- **Enrichment Lesson:** *Writing About Emotional Experiences as Therapy* In reviewing the success of many forms of psychotherapy, James Pennebacker suggests that the mere act of disclosure may be a powerful therapeutic agent. Research indicates that writing about personally upsetting experiences produces consistent and significant health benefits. (*Teacher's Resource Binder*, p. 30-1)
- **Enrichment Lesson:** *From a Disease Focus to a Wellness Model* Emory Cowen believes we must replace the pervasive "disease" model in psychology with a "wellness" model. We must shift from emphasizing people's weaknesses to shoring up their strengths. (*Teacher's Resource Binder*, p. 30-1)
- **Enrichment Lesson:** *Prevention Science* A task force set up by the American Psychological Association to study programs that focus on prevention rather than treatment reported that such programs are effective. (*Teacher's Resource Binder*, p. 30-1)

Module 30 Psychological Therapies

When you think of *therapy,* what do you envision? Perhaps someone lying on a couch, reflecting on childhood memories, with a therapist listening intently nearby, notebook in hand? **Sigmund Freud** devised this once-innovative mode of healing nearly 100 years ago, and for many Americans, this image represents a prototype for therapy. While traditional Freudian-style therapy is still popular in movies and cartoons, only a few key remnants of his methods can still be found in a therapist's office today.

Have you ever wondered whether therapy of any kind really works? Psychologists concerned with this question have developed many different approaches in their attempt to help people cope with psychological problems. As a result, therapists can select from a variety of techniques to find the one best suited to resolving a particular problem.

Therapy sometimes involves prescription medications and even medical procedures in severe cases, but more often, it involves nonmedical options, which are the focus of this module. Psychological therapy, or **psychotherapy,** is "a planned, emotionally charged, confiding interaction between a trained, socially sanctioned healer and a sufferer" (Frank, 1982). All told, there are around 250 types of psychotherapy (Parloff, 1987)! But each centers on one or more of four major approaches: *psychoanalytic, humanistic, behavioral,* and *cognitive.* Depending

Sigmund Freud "I set myself the task of bringing to light what human beings keep hidden within them, not by the power of hypnosis, but by observing what they say and show."—1901

▶ **Sigmund Freud** (1856–1939) Founder of psychoanalysis.

▶ **psychotherapy** An emotionally charged, confiding interaction between a trained therapist and someone who suffers from psychological difficulties.

Getting Started

Have each student imagine that a friend describes behaviors that might lead to a diagnosis of clinical depression. Assuming the role of therapist, have students write down some possible interventions for the friend. As a therapist, what would be some common recommendations? Do any of these recommendations reflect students' theories about the causes of depression? What perspective do they seem to favor?

Source: Osberg, T. (1996, August). *Students as therapists: An activity for abnormal and clinical psychology courses.* Paper presented at the Annual Convention of the American Psychological Association, Toronto.

trb You may wish to use **Critical Thinking Activity:** *Fact or Falsehood?* (*Teacher's Resource Binder,* p. 30-1; **Handout 30–1**) as a prereading strategy to evaluate what students already know about psychological therapies. This activity will prime students to look out for information that could prove or disprove their preconceptions.

MODULE 30

Psychological Therapies

Introducing the Module

The Points: Module Objectives

- Describe how mental disorders develop, according to Sigmund Freud.
- Identify techniques used by psychoanalysis to reveal and resolve conflicts.
- Compare and contrast psychodynamic and interpersonal therapies with psychoanalysis.
- Differentiate between psychoanalytic and humanistic therapy; describe unconditional positive regard, and explain why it is important.
- Differentiate behavior therapies from humanistic therapy and psychoanalysis.
- Identify the basic assumption in behavior therapy that uses classical conditioning techniques.
- Identify the basic assumption in behavior therapy that uses operant conditioning techniques.
- Analyze how cognitive therapy works.
- Delineate the advantages of therapy conducted in groups.
- Evaluate what research tells us about psychotherapy's effectiveness.
- Identify alternative therapies, and evaluate whether they are effective.

trb Building Vocabulary

Students can reinforce their knowledge of psychological therapies by completing **Building Vocabulary: Graphic Organizer:** *Concept Web* (*Teacher's Resource Binder,* p. 30-1; **Handout 30–2**). As they fill in the organizer, students can learn the terms in this module and better understand the relationships among them.

MODULE 30

Teaching the Points

■ TEACHING TIPS

web (1) You can log on as an instructor to the book companion site for *Thinking About Psychology* at www.worthpublishers.com/thinkingaboutpsych. It contains teacher resources for class presentations as well as review and assessment of module concepts and terms.

web (2) "ABC's of Internet Therapy" at www.metanoia.org/imhs is a comprehensive site dealing with every type of "on-line therapy." For each, it presents advantages, limitations, ethics, and advice for protecting a person from quacks.

trb At this point, you may wish to use Enrichment Lesson: *The Virtual Couch* (*Teacher's Resource Binder*, p. 30-1).

tr (3) A four-color transparency of Figure 30.1, Freud's View of the Mind, is available in the Overhead Transparencies Set.

■ LOOKING AT THE ISSUES

With the pervasiveness of the Internet, many therapists have begun offering their services on line. Russ Newman, executive director of the APA, argues that nonverbal cues that a therapist can interpret are lost in an on-line therapy session. Have students' discuss whether people should rely solely on on-line therapy for help with mental disorders.

trb At this point, you may wish to use Enrichment Lesson: *The Virtual Couch* (*Teacher's Resource Binder*, p. 30-1).

F•Y•I

Before Freud, psychology was a new science concerned more with describing the human experience than with developing effective therapeutic techniques. **Structuralism,** the school founded by Wilhelm Wundt in 1879, sought to describe what consciousness was. **Functionalism,** a school favored by G. Stanley Hall in the United States, believed in knowing how the mind worked.

▶ **eclectic approach** An approach to psychotherapy that, depending on the person's problems, uses techniques from various forms of therapy.

▶ **psychoanalysis** Freud's theory of personality and therapeutic technique that attributes our thoughts and actions to unconscious motives and conflicts.

on the person's problems, a therapist may use techniques from two or more of these forms of therapy, in an **eclectic approach.**

We'll begin our explanation of psychotherapy by considering the four individual perspectives. Then we'll see how families and groups may benefit from going through therapy together. Finally, we'll evaluate the effectiveness of psychotherapy and some alternative therapies. Let's start with the first comprehensive approach to therapy, Freud's psychoanalysis.

Psychoanalysis

Very few practice psychotherapy the way Freud did at the turn of the century, but his influence is easy to spot in the treatment methods of several current therapies. Let's take a closer look at Freud's **psychoanalysis** so that we can better understand its broad influence.

Psychoanalytic Assumptions

What's the point? 1. In Freud's view, how do mental disorders develop?

Freud liked to compare personality to an iceberg, composed of three primary elements; the pleasure-seeking *id,* the reality-oriented *ego,* and the *superego,* a set of internalized ideals (the conscience). Just as the vast body of an iceberg floats beneath the water and is invisible, so the greater portion of personality is impossible to see (Figure 30.1). The

Figure 30.1 **Freud's View of the Mind** Freud compared the mind to an iceberg. Just as the greater part of an iceberg floats out of sight, so the greater portion of the mind is concealed from view. The "water line" represents the boundary between conscious and unconscious regions of the mind. The id operates at a totally unconscious level, while the ego and superego are partially revealed and partially submerged. (Adapted from Freud, 1933, page 111.)

Suggested Readings

Use the following books as teacher-preparation tools or as enrichment for advanced students:

Axline, V. (1964). *Dibs: In search of self.* Boston: Houghton Mifflin.

Balter, M., & Katz, R. (1987). *Nobody's child.* Reading, MA: Addison-Wesley.

Baur, S. (1991). *The dinosaur man: Tales of madness and enchantment from the back ward.* New York: HarperCollins.

Burgess, A. (1986). *A clockwork orange.* New York: Norton. (Original work published 1962.)

Burns, D. (1999). *The feeling good handbook* (rev. ed.). New York: Plume.

Dolnick, E. (1998). *Madness on the couch: Blaming the victim in the heyday of psychoanalysis.* New York: Simon & Schuster.

Gay, P. (1997). *Freud: A life for our time.* New York: Norton.

Hall, C. S. (1982). *A primer of Freudian psychology.* New York: Mentor. (Original work published 1954.)

"water line" separating the visible parts of personality from the invisible parts, Freud said, is the boundary between the conscious and unconscious regions of our mind. We are conscious of the portion of personality above the water line, but not of the portion below.

The iceberg represents the structure of personality. But how does personality develop? According to Freud, personality forms during our early childhood, when we pass through a series of stages, such as the oral stage (0 to 18 months) and the anal stage (18 to 36 months). Each stage is a time of potential conflicts, and failure to adequately resolve these conflicts, Freud believed, could result in problems in later adult years. Relief from these psychological problems is possible, Freud believed, if the analyst helps patients bring the repressed, unconscious conflicts and impulses of childhood "to the surface" or into the conscious mind. Freud thought that *insight* into the origin of the disorder would allow the person to work through previously buried feelings. Wellness and health, according to this theory, result from the release of the energy previously (and unconsciously) devoted to resolving these conflicts.

▶ **resistance** In psychoanalysis, the blocking from consciousness of anxiety-laden material.

▶ **interpretation** In psychoanalysis, the analyst's noting supposed dream meanings, resistances, and other significant behaviors in order to promote insight.

Psychoanalytic Methods

2. What techniques does psychoanalysis use to reveal and resolve conflicts?

Psychoanalysis aims to dig up the past to clarify the present. Analysts dig with several different therapeutic tools, and one of the most useful is *free association*. How does free association work? First, the analyst asks the patient to relax, perhaps on a couch, with head slightly elevated. The analyst, seated close by, may ask the patient to think of a childhood memory as a starting point, and to say whatever comes to mind—perhaps a favorite game, childhood friends, or dreams. Sound easy? What if you were the patient and you thought of something embarrassing? Would you hesitate before talking about it? Would you leave something out of your story, change the subject, or joke your way out of the situation? What if your mind went blank? A psychoanalyst would probably classify all of these free association interruptions as **resistance,** or the blocking of anxiety-laden material from consciousness. It is the analyst's job to make patients aware of these sensitive areas, offering insights by exploring their meanings and interpreting them. This **interpretation** includes the analyst's ideas on the meaning behind dreams, resistances, and other significant behaviors. Why did you stop in the middle of a story about your father? Is there an unresolved childhood conflict buried in your memory? Analysts dig for these conflicts and the meaning underneath them.

"Of course I'm feeling uncomfortable. I'm not allowed on the couch."

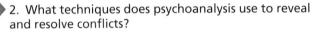

Harvey, J. (1985). *If I'm so successful, why do I feel like a fake?* New York: St. Martin's Press.

Johnson, A. B. (1990). *Out of Bedlam: The truth about deinstitutionalization.* New York: BasicBooks.

Loftus, E., & Ketcham, K. (1994). *The myth of repressed memory: False memories and allegations of sexual abuse.* New York: St. Martin's Press.

Orwell, G. (1990) *1984.* New York: Signet Classics. (Original work published 1948.)

Seligman, M. E. P. (1994). *What you can change and what you can't.* New York: Knopf.

Smith, M. J. (1975). *When I say no I feel guilty.* New York: Bantam Books.

Yates, B. (1985). *Self-management.* Belmont, CA: Wadsworth.

■ **TEACHING TIP**

Refresh students' memories of Freudian principles by reviewing the stages of development in which people could become fixated, thus causing problems later in life:

- **Oral stage** spans from birth to approximately 1 year. Infants are gratified by oral activities, like sucking and drooling. Weaning too early may cause a person to develop bad oral habits, like overeating or smoking, to satisfy that missing need.
- **Anal stage** spans the potty-training years. Children have to balance societal demands with their own desires. Trained too early, anal-retentive personality develops. Trained too late, a person could become anal-expulsive.
- **Phallic stage** lasts until school starts. Young children deal with such famous Freudian issues as the *Oedipus complex, penis envy,* and *castration anxiety.*
- **Latency stage**, occurring during the elementary school years, is a quiet time for development. Children learn their gender roles by associating with same-sex friends.
- **Genital stage** starts at puberty. If they don't engage in sexual experiences, people could have problems later in life.

trb At this point, you may wish to use **Critical Thinking Activity:** *Fifteen Freudian Principle Statements* (*Teacher's Resource Binder,* p. 30-1).

■ **LOOKING AT THE ISSUES**

The "digging" is what makes Freudian analysis so controversial. Critics argue that therapists can easily create memories in their clients, leading those clients to believe that they have experienced some deeply repressed childhood trauma. The following questions can guide students in research and subsequent discussion on this issue:

- How has the research of Elizabeth Loftus brought doubt to the existence of repressed memories?
- How do modern psychoanalysts counteract the possibility of suggesting memories in their clients?

MODULE 30

(F • Y • I)

Traditional Freudian analysis calls for the therapist to be out of the patient's view. Freud believed that seeing the therapist would lead to resistance. If a patient hesitated during free association or didn't share his or her innermost thoughts, then that patient was perceived by the analyst to be resisting treatment, which was also viewed as reflecting a deep-seeded psychological problem.

trb At this point, you may wish to use **Application Activity:** *Defense Mechanisms* (*Teacher's Resource Binder*, p. 30-1; **Handout 30–4**).

■ LOOKING AT THE ISSUES

Insurance coverage for mental health limits the amount of time a person can spend in therapy. Have students find out what mental health coverage they have through their parents or legal guardians. In addition, have them use available print or online resources to find out what coverage is provided for jobs they'd like to have after graduation or college. In a class discussion, pose the following questions:

- How much time in outpatient therapy can a person use in a calendar year?
- How much time in inpatient therapy can a person use in a calendar year?
- Do insurance companies specify what type of mental health therapy they will provide for?
- What type of coverage does the state pay for through Medicaid?

■ TEACHING TIP

Students may wonder why never losing an argument is not good for establishing the credibility of psychoanalysis. Remind students that confirmation bias is a danger to critical thinking. People tend to look for evidence that confirms their preconceptions rather than searching for evidence that disputes their ideas, meaning that they will often miss even glaring evidence that refutes strongly held theories. With Freudian analysis, no alternative explanations for behavior are accepted since all resistance to treatment is simply confirmation of a repressed problem.

Costs of Therapy Traditional psychoanalytic therapy typically costs more than $100 per session and continues for months, even years. Insurance companies will not cover so many sessions, and few people can afford it on their own.

Freud thought dreams were a rich source of information about unconscious conflicts. He called them the "royal road" to the unconscious. Dream analysis is a key element of the psychoanalytic process, and Freud was particularly interested in the *latent content,* or censored meaning, of dreams. This was why Freud spent so much time trying to figure out what his patient's dreams *really* meant. Did that dream about being trapped in a room really mean the patient felt stuck in a bad relationship?

Freud anticipated that patients would develop strong positive or negative emotions toward the analyst. He viewed these feelings as **transference** of the dependency or the love/hate mix patients felt toward important people in their lives. Freud felt that patients could gain insight into current and past relationships by exploring these feelings for their analyst and dealing with the long-repressed issues they represent.

Critics of psychoanalysis note several problems with Freud's methods.

- The foundation of psychoanalysis rested on Freud's belief in *repressed memories.* However, many psychologists doubt that we repress important memories. This topic has sparked intense debate.
- Traditional psychoanalysis is expensive, requires several sessions a week, and can last for years. With sessions typically costing more than $100 per visit, this kind of therapy is available only to the wealthy.
- Refuting psychoanalytic interpretation gets you nowhere. If you disagree with the interpretation, your analyst might say, "Ah, more resistance. You confirm my interpretation." And if you agree, well, you might hear something like. "Ah, no more resistance. You confirm my interpretation." The analyst does not lose many arguments.

The Psychodynamic Perspective

3. What do psychodynamic and interpersonal therapies share with psychoanalysis, and how do they differ from it?

► **transference** In psychoanalysis, the patient's transfer to the analyst of emotions (such as love or hatred) linked with other relationships.

Although few therapists practice strict psychoanalysis today, Freud's innovative techniques for healing have broadly influenced many therapists' work. These therapists make *psychodynamic assumptions* (related to psychoanalysis). They try to understand a person's problems by looking

Meeting Individual Needs

trb tr Help students understand how the terms in this module are related by having them complete **Building Vocabulary: Graphic Organizer:** *Concept Web* (*Teacher's Resource Binder*, p. 30-1; **Handout 30–2**).

- **Independent Learners** Students can complete the handout on their own as a homework or in-class assignment, checking the answers in class. You may want to use **Handout 30–2** as a transparency, projecting a completed concept web for students to use in checking their answers.
- **Cooperative Learners** Have students work in small groups to fill out the concept web. Students can tutor each other about the concepts in the module, or you can create a competition where students see how quickly their team can fill out the web correctly.

at childhood experiences, unconscious drives, and unresolved conflicts. But those working from a psychodynamic perspective today are more likely to request weekly meetings for only a few months, in contrast to Freud's recommendation of several meetings weekly for many years.

Freud's techniques have also influenced *interpersonal psychotherapy.* Therapists using this 12- to 16-session method try to foster insight into the origins of a problem, but they focus on what's going on in the patient's life *now,* rather than trying to untie the knots of a childhood conflict. Interpersonal therapy asks how current relationships can be mended and social skills improved. This attempt to find relief for symptoms caused by today's conflicts has proven effective against depression (Weissman, 1999).

To see how psychoanalytic, psychodynamic, and interpersonal therapies differ, let's consider the case of Serena, a college senior two months from graduation. She has been going out with the same person for two squabble-free years, but recently they've had regular disagreements. Serena has developed trouble sleeping, and she reports feeling easily irritated and depressed. How would therapists from the three approaches treat Serena?

- A psychoanalyst would want to delve completely into Serena's childhood over the course of many visits. The analyst might ask her about her dreams or watch to see if she transfers her feelings toward the boyfriend to the analyst.
- A psychodynamic therapist would also be interested in Serena's childhood and how that may be affecting her relationships, but this therapist would meet with Serena in far fewer sessions and would focus more on her current issues.
- An interpersonal therapist would also seek insight but would encourage Serena to think almost exclusively about her current symptoms and problems. Thus, attention might focus on how she can assess the relationship, resolve disputes with her boyfriend, and better express her emotions.

Humanistic Therapies

4. How do the psychoanalytic and humanistic approaches to therapy differ? What is unconditional positive regard, and why is it important?

To a humanistic therapist, the potential for self-fulfillment already exists in each one of us. Humanistic therapy aims to promote self-fulfillment by increasing self-acceptance and self-awareness. Humanists differ from psychoanalysts in their approach to therapy by

F • Y • I

Interpersonal psychotherapy (IPT) is a short-term therapy that is effective for treating depression. Depression isn't caused by interpersonal events alone, but it usually has an interpersonal component, affecting relationships. Types of interpersonal events that are concentrated on in IPT include the following:

- interpersonal disputes and conflicts
- role transitions (such as becoming a parent or losing a parent)
- grief that goes beyond the normal bereavement period
- deficits patients have in starting and maintaining relationships

trb At this point, you may wish to use **Enrichment Lesson:** *Interpersonal Therapy* (*Teacher's Resource Binder,* p. 30-1).

■ **CHECKING FOR UNDERSTANDING**

Present case studies from various abnormal psychology textbooks and have students explain each person's behavior from a particular perspective. Alternately, you may assign students a particular perspective and have them come up with a case study that reflects common disorders that therapists with that perspective would be likely to treat. Have students then describe what type of treatment that type of therapist would recommend to the patient.

Cooperative Learning

Have students collect and bring to class cartoons, advertisements, and movie or TV references to Freudian ideas. Students can work in groups to identify the particular concept in each, analyzing whether the depiction is positive or negative. Students can also determine whether the depiction is presented in a factual or comedic way.

trb At this point, you may wish to use **Critical Thinking Activity:** *Fifteen Freudian Principle Statements* (*Teacher's Resource Binder,* p. 30-1; **Handout 30–3**).

MODULE 30

■ **LOOKING AT THE ISSUES**
Have students consider the effect of calling people *patients* instead of *clients.*

- How does each of these terms affect the whole therapeutic relationship?
- In what other situations have semantics (the meaning of different words) affected how different jobs, issues, and roles in society are viewed? *(To get the conversation started, point out the following: garbage collectors may be called* sanitation engineers; *overthrowing a political leader may be called* regime change; *and a comedienne once called herself a* domestic goddess *rather than a housewife.)*

F•Y•I

Not much analysis occurs in person-centered therapy. To facilitate unconditional positive regard, genuineness, and empathy, Rogers would answer questions with questions. For example, "How does that make you feel?" was a common question Rogers would ask when clients would discuss their feelings. Rogers felt that if people received the attention and acceptance that they needed, they could cure themselves. He believed that the therapist was merely there to provide the necessary support.

trb At this point, you may wish to use Technology Application Activity: *PsychSim:* "Computer Therapist" (*Teacher's Resource Binder,* p. 30-1).

■ **TEACHING TIP**
Link *humanistic therapy* to Abraham Maslow's *hierarchy of needs.* Instead of explaining behavior in terms of buried unconscious feelings and desires, Maslow believed that full human potential could be achieved if certain basic needs were met. Maslow theorized that people could not appreciate beauty if they were worried about where their next meal was coming from or if they did not have a loving relationship with others.

▶ **Carl Rogers** (1902–1987) Humanistic psychologist who developed client-centered therapy.

▶ **client-centered therapy** A humanistic therapy, developed by Carl Rogers, in which the therapist uses techniques such as active listening within a genuine, accepting, empathic environment to facilitate the client's growth. (Also called *person-centered therapy.*)

▶ **active listening** Empathic listening in which the listener echoes, restates, and clarifies. A feature of Rogers' client-centered therapy.

- fostering growth instead of relieving illness; thus, these therapists refer to people in therapy as "clients," not "patients."
- focusing on the present and future instead of the past.
- emphasizing conscious thoughts instead of unconscious thoughts.

Humanistic therapists typically use *nondirective* methods: Therapists listen without interpreting and do not direct clients to any particular insight. **Carl Rogers** developed the most famous form of humanistic therapy. His **client-centered therapy** stresses *empathy, acceptance,* and *genuineness* during therapy. Rogers believed that for client-centered therapy to be successful, therapists must provide a supportive environment. **Active listening** is crucial and consists of the following:

- ***Paraphrasing*** The therapist uses the words of the client to summarize the conversation.
- ***Clarifying*** Therapists encourage clients to say more by asking questions like, "Could you give me an example of what you're saying?"
- ***Reflecting feelings*** The therapist mirrors the feelings of the client with statements like, "That must really be frustrating."

The following excerpt is an example of an interaction between a Rogerian therapist and a client. See if you can spot where the therapist paraphrases, clarifies, or reflects feelings.

> ***Client:*** *I really feel bad today . . . just terrible.*
> ***Therapist:*** *You're feeling pretty bad.*
> ***Client:*** *Yeah, I'm angry and that's made me feel bad, especially when I can't do anything about it. I just have to live with it and shut up.*
> ***Therapist:*** *You're very angry and feel like there's nothing you can safely do with your feelings.*

Carl Rogers Psychologist Carl Rogers (far right) practicing client-centered therapy.

Cooperative Learning

Have students work with partners or in small groups to create scripts that utilize the principles of active listening. They can present their "conversations" to class, discussing whether their interpretations of Rogerian technique would be helpful.

trb At this point, you may wish to use Application Activity: *Role-Playing to Demonstrate Client-Centered Therapy* (*Teacher's Resource Binder,* p. 30-1; Handout 30–6).

> ***Client:*** *Uh-huh. I mean . . . if I yell at my wife, she gets hurt. If I don't say anything to her, I feel tense.*
> ***Therapist:*** *You're between a rock and a hard place—no matter what you do, you'll wind up feeling bad.*
> ***Client:*** *I mean she chews ice all day and all night. I feel stupid saying this. It's petty, I know. But when I sit there and try to concentrate I hear all these slurping and crunching noises. I can't stand it . . . and I yell. She feels hurt—I feel bad—like I shouldn't have said anything.*
> ***Therapist:*** *So when you finally say something you feel bad afterward.*
> ***Client:*** *Yeah, I can't say anything to her without getting mad and saying more than I should. And then I cause more trouble than it's worth. (Duke & Nowicki, 1979, p. 565)*

The therapist is accepting and understanding while becoming this client's psychological mirror. The goal is for the client to be able to see himself more clearly at the conclusion of therapy.

Can therapy be *completely* nondirective? Rogers said no, but added that nondirectivity was not the most important element of therapy. Rather, the client should feel *unconditional positive regard,* a feeling of being accepted that does not depend on any specific behaviors. This feeling will follow, Rogers believed, from the therapist's nonjudgmental, accepting environment. Unconditional positive regard allows clients to feel valued and accept themselves.

If you want to become a more active listener in your own relationships, look back at the three suggestions Rogers made to achieve this result. Active listening is not reserved only for therapists. Think of your best friends. Chances are, you like them because they are good listeners.

▶ **behavior therapy** Therapy that applies learning principles to the elimination of unwanted behaviors.

Orientations The psychoanalytic therapist may ask questions about childhood, whereas the behavior therapist asks about current actions and activities.

Behavior Therapies

5. How do behavior therapies differ from humanistic therapy and psychoanalysis?

Let's say you have a fear of dogs. A psychoanalyst might try to trace this fear to some unresolved childhood conflict. A Rogerian might offer you unconditional positive regard while helping you to get in touch with your feelings. Behavior therapists would reject both of these approaches and instead attempt to replace your fearful thoughts and related behaviors with constructive, relaxing thoughts and actions. **Behavior therapy** applies learning principles to the elimination of unwanted behaviors. Both *classical conditioning* and *operant conditioning* principles have contributed to the behavior therapy methods.

MODULE 30

■ JOURNAL WRITING

Invite students to use the following questions and writing prompts as springboards for entries in their psychology journals:

- Are you a good listener? What do you do to listen actively?
- Should therapy focus on present circumstances rather than past issues? Why or why not?

■ APPLYING THE POINTS

Contact a humanistic therapist to see how the technique has evolved since Carl Rogers's time. The following questions may be used as a guide for the informal interview as well as a presentation of your findings in class discussion:

- What different techniques does this therapist use?
- How prevalent is the therapeutic technique?
- Is it successful in treating any particular disorders? If so, which ones, and why?

■ LOOKING AT THE ISSUES

Would too much unconditional positive regard be a bad thing? Have students consider the following questions:

- How could unconditional positive regard lead to unwarranted self-esteem?
- Why would people in therapy benefit most from unconditional positive regard?

Cross-Curricular Connections

NONFICTION LITERATURE Virginia Axline, a student of Carl Rogers, has extended the client-centered approach to the treatment of children in play therapy. She has written *Dibs: In Search of Self,* a book that is extremely popular with students. This book can be assigned in preparation for class discussion of the humanistic therapies, and particularly of Rogers's nondirective approach. The more general humanistic themes of becoming aware of one's feelings as they occur, of emphasizing conscious rather than unconscious material, of encouraging responsibility for one's actions, and of promoting growth and fulfillment are also clearly evident in the book.

For extra credit, you can have students write a paper identifying the important elements of client-centered therapy used with Dibs (for example, *active listening, genuineness, acceptance,* and *empathy*).

MODULE 30

■ TEACHING TIP

(1) Remind students that Mary Cover Jones, a student of John Watson, did original work with counterconditioning in the 1930s. In 1929, Watson demonstrated that fear could be learned, through classical conditioning, with his infamous Little Albert study. Mary Cover Jones later showed that people could unlearn fear by associating that object with positive stimuli—work that undergirds the premise of systematic desensitization.

tr (2) For use with the notes to follow about systematic desensitization, a four-color transparency of Figure 30.2 (on page 581), Systematic Desensitization, is available in the **Overhead Transparencies Set.**

■ JOURNAL WRITING

Invite students to use the following questions and writing prompts as springboards for entries in their psychology journals:

- What makes you feel the most anxious?
- What makes you feel the most relaxed?

■ APPLYING THE POINTS

Challenge students to go through the exercise the author describes on this page.

- Have them imagine a situation in which they feel anxious. They should concentrate on their feelings about it. Ask them if they feel those emotions intensely or not.
- Then have the students think of a situation in which they are relaxed and feeling good. They should also concentrate on their emotions in this situation. Are these emotions as intense as the anxious ones? Why or why not?

F•Y•I

An extreme and controversial form of systematic desensitization is called *flooding*. In flooding, patients are immersed in the object or situation that they fear. Imagine being thrown into a swimming pool if you fear the water. The idea of this type of therapy is to show the person that he or she has no reason to fear the item. Experiencing it in this way will lead to less fear later.

trb At this point, you may wish to use **Demonstration Activity:** ***Using Systematic Desensitization to Treat Eraser Phobia*** (*Teacher's Resource Binder*, p. 30-1).

Classical Conditioning Techniques

6. What is the basic assumption in behavior therapy that uses classical conditioning techniques?

Classical conditioning is a type of learning in which we associate two things that occur together. Classical conditioning pioneer John B. Watson showed that we can learn to associate most emotions and some behaviors, such as fear with public speaking or with small, enclosed places. If we can learn such fears, can we "unlearn" them? In some cases, yes, through the process of *counterconditioning,* a behavior therapy technique that teaches us to associate new responses to places or things that have in the past triggered unwanted behaviors. Two popular counterconditioning techniques are *systematic desensitization* and *aversive conditioning.*

Systematic Desensitization

Think of something that makes you feel anxious. Perhaps it's a difficult test you have to take, the opening night of a show you're in, or the first minute of an athletic contest you've suited up for? Now, imagine the most relaxing place for you on Earth. Is it a secluded beach on a beautiful, sunny day? A quiet valley between mountains? A hillside close to a pond? Now then, can you think of the anxious situation and the relaxing situation at the same time? If you're like most people, you won't be able to. You might be able to alternate between the two settings very quickly, but you won't be able to imagine both simultaneously. The most widely used behavior therapy is based on just this idea: You can't feel relaxed and anxious at the same time. **Systematic desensitization** is a type of counterconditioning that associates a pleasant, relaxed state with gradually increasing, anxiety-triggering stimuli (Jones, 1924; Wolpe, 1958; Wolpe & Plaud, 1997). If you can repeatedly relax when faced with higher and higher levels of the anxiety-producing stimulus, you can gradually overcome your problem. Let's apply this technique to a common fear: flying in an airplane.

A behavior therapist using systematic desensitization may start by having you write down a hierarchy of anxiety-triggering flying situations. What flying-related event would cause you the worst anxiety? How about being seated in an airplane while it takes off? If so, this would be the top item on your list. And what flying-related event would cause very little anxiety? Perhaps looking at an airplane from a mile away? This would be the bottom item on your list. Your fear-of-flying hierarchy would include a range of situations from least to most anxiety-provoking.

After establishing your hierarchy, you would be trained to relax using *progressive relaxation.* With this technique, you learn to relax different sets of muscle groups until you approach a near-complete state of relaxation. While you are in that state, your therapist tells you to close

► **systematic desensitization** A type of counterconditioning that associates a pleasant relaxed state with gradually increasing anxiety-triggering stimuli. Commonly used to treat phobias.

Enriching

Classical and operant conditioning techniques can be used for many different disorders and issues, from addictions to laziness. Have students research how classical conditioning is used in popular treatment programs for a variety of life problems, including the following:

- self-injurious behavior in autistic children
- addictions
- children who are couch potatoes

V At this point, you may wish to show **Videocassette:** ***The Mind,*** **Second Edition, Module 30: "Treating Drug Addiction: A Behavioral Approach"** (*Teacher's Resource Binder*, p. 30-1).

Figure 30.2 Systematic Desensitization Systematic desensitization helps people overcome fears, such as a fear of flying. Patients work through a hierarchy of anxiety-producing events associated with flying, and learn to relax at each level of the hierarchy. For instance, once the photo of an airplane no longer produces anxiety, the person with the fear may go to an airport and look at a real airplane from far away. Eventually, the patient works up to touching the plane, boarding the plane, and hopefully, becoming a confident flyer.

your eyes and to imagine the first (least troublesome) item on your hierarchy. If imagining this scene causes you to feel anxious, you signal by raising an index finger. The therapist then instructs you to quit thinking about the situation and to practice deep relaxation again. You would repeat these steps until imagining the scene does not cause anxiety. At that point, you move to the second situation on your hierarchy—perhaps looking at a photo of a plane (Figure 30.2). After several therapy sessions, thoughts and photos are replaced by experience, beginning with somewhat easy tasks like watching planes land a mile away and leading gradually to boarding an airplane. Eventually, you become a confident flyer. Conquering the fear of the actual event increases self-confidence (Foa & Kozak, 1986; Williams, 1987).

A breakthrough in systematic desensitization occurred with the introduction of *virtual reality technology.* Virtual reality is more vivid than your imagination, as you wear a headset projecting a three-dimensional virtual world into your visual field. Virtual reality exposure therapy has effectively helped people cope with fear of flying, public speaking, heights, and animals (North & others, 1998; Rothbaum & others, 1995, 1997; Vincelli & Molinari, 1998).

Modeling has been combined with systematic desensitization to help some patients overcome disruptive fears. For instance, someone with a fear of dogs could watch another person playing with and petting a dog. Gradually, the person learns to model the coach's behavior and touches and handles the dog (Bandura & others, 1969).

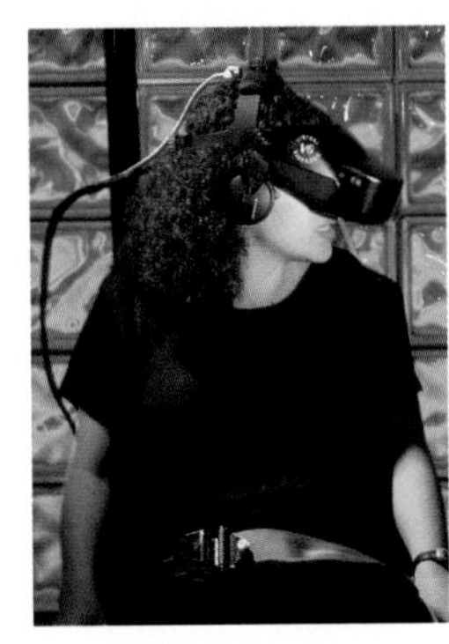

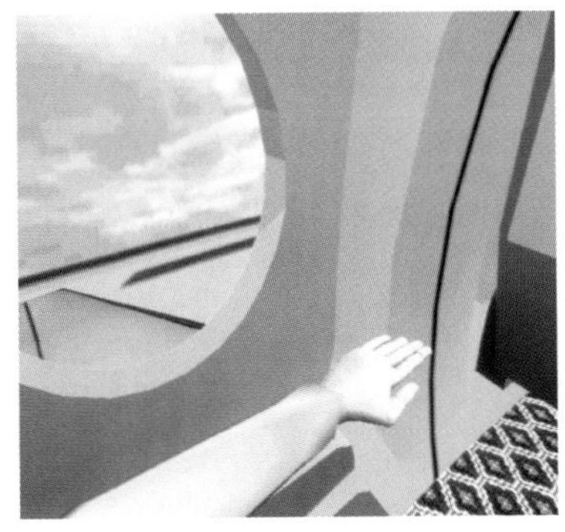

A 3-D Virtual World? Virtual reality techniques help people overcome fears.

Alternative Assessment

trb MODIFYING A PHOBIA Students can apply behavioral techniques by trying to eradicate a fear of their own. Students can use mental imagery or deep breathing as they attempt to use systematic desensitization to alleviate their learned fears. More details are available in **Alterative Assessment:** ***Modifying a Phobia*** (*Teacher's Resource Binder*, p. 30-1; **Handout 30–15**).

■ TEACHING TIPS

(1) Emphasize that self-esteem is most healthy when it is coupled with accomplishment. Unwarranted self-esteem can lead to an inflated sense of self, which might lead people to make bad decisions about relationships, jobs, and finances.

(2) Remind students that Albert Bandura's research on the influence of observed aggression on children's behavior provides the foundation for applications of modeling in therapeutic situations. By watching others behave, people can learn what the appropriate responses are and that the perceived danger they fear is really nothing to fear.

F • Y • I

Virtual reality therapy has experienced a boon as advances in technology make virtual reality seem more real. Virtual reality provides people with an opportunity to face their fears without putting themselves or others in danger when they hesitate. Patients who formerly were using drugs to relax as they faced their fears can now rely on learned techniques instead.

V At this point, you may wish to show **Videocassette:** ***Scientific American Frontiers,*** **Second Edition, Segment 31: "Virtual Fear"** (*Teacher's Resource Binder*, p. 30-1).

■ LOOKING AT THE ISSUES

Traditional behaviorists were not concerned with the thoughts and feelings people had that established fears. They believed that all behavior resulted from a stimulus-response relationship and that concepts like the unconscious mind were irrelevant to people's current situations. Have students respond to the following questions in a class discussion:

- Why would the behaviorist viewpoint be more appealing to scientists than Freudian views?
- Does the underlying cause of a behavior really matter if the therapy is successful in eliminating it? Why or why not?
- Should people focus on experiences from the past or current circumstances? Why?

MODULE 30

F • Y • I

Students may find it amusing that even *The Simpsons* has delved into aversive conditioning. In the first season in 1990, in an episode entitled "There's No Disgrace Like Home," Homer Simpson, the family patriarch, decides that this family needs therapy after a disastrous experience at his company's picnic. At the end of the show, each family member is hooked up to an electroshock therapy machine and gets to administer a shock to another whenever an unwelcome comment or action occurs.

TEACHING TIPS

tr (1) A four-color transparency of Figure 30.3, Unwanted Reactions, is available in the **Overhead Transparencies Set.**

(2) Share your own experiences with taste aversions. If asked, students are sure to volunteer aversions of their own. Martin Bolt, of Calvin College, tells his students of his aversion to commercially produced frozen chicken dinners. He once stored a dinner in the freezer compartment of his department's refrigerator. When he went to retrieve it, he found it in the company of a frozen laboratory rat. A student assistant, not knowing how to dispose of the deceased animal, had carefully packaged it in plastic and temporarily placed it in the freezer. Bolt now finds all frozen chicken dinners repulsive.

APPLYING THE POINTS

(1) Have students contact a local oncologist or cancer research center to see how they use knowledge of classical conditioning and taste aversions to help patients deal with the nausea associated with chemotherapy and radiation.

(2) Contact local alcohol treatment centers and programs to see if they use taste aversions to help clients become sober. The following questions can be used as a guide for an interview as well as a presentation of your findings in class discussion:

- How effective have these methods been?
- What type of aversives do they use?

▶ **aversive conditioning** A type of counterconditioning that associates an unpleasant state (such as nausea) with an unwanted behavior (such as drinking alcohol).

Whether using desensitization or modeling, behavior therapists do not spend a lot of time looking for the cause of the problem, trying to find out when you first experienced it, or considering your level of self-awareness. They believe that overcoming the maladaptive behavior helps you feel better about yourself.

Aversive Conditioning

My second year in college, I suffered a days-long stomach illness. The last food I ate before getting sick was a grilled cheese sandwich. Weeks later, the smell of a grilled cheese sandwich cooking could still nauseate me. The smell of the sandwich had become an unpleasant thing to avoid because I had learned to associate it with vomiting and stomach pain. Do you have trouble eating some food because you associate it with illness?

Aversive conditioning is a type of counterconditioning that purposefully associates an unpleasant state (such as nausea) with an unwanted behavior (such as drinking alcohol). The process is the opposite of systematic desensitization, which replaces a negative (fearful) response with a positive (relaxed) response. Aversive conditioning replaces a *positive* response to a harmful experience (like drinking alcohol) with a *negative* (aversive) response. Aversive conditioning has been used to treat nail biting and the sexual deviancy of child molesters, but let's use the treatment of alcoholism to see in more detail how this form of therapy works.

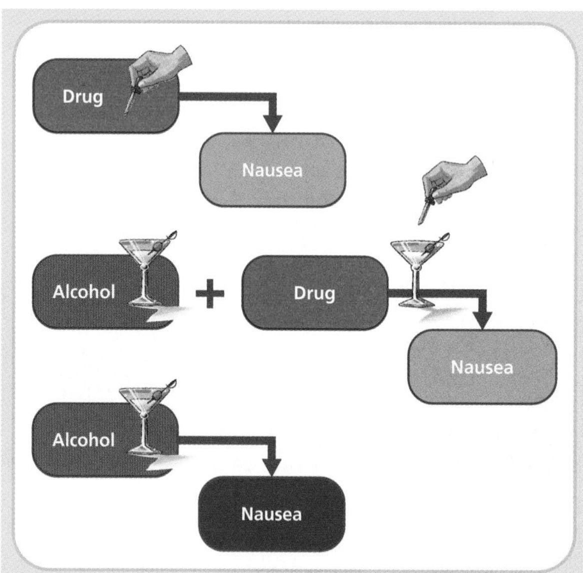

Figure 30.3 Unwanted Reactions In an example of aversive conditioning, alcoholics agree to have a substance put in their drink that makes them vomit. In theory, the person associates the vomiting with drinking and becomes less inclined to drink substances containing alcohol.

In treating alcoholism with aversive conditioning, therapists give people their drink of choice, but with a little twist. Added to the drink is a tasteless, odorless drug that produces severe nausea. The goal is to link drinking with violent nausea, so that the person develops an aversion to the smell and taste of the drink. The formerly positive reaction to drinking becomes negative (Figure 30.3).

Does this treatment for alcoholism last? In one study, 63 percent of the people treated with aversive conditioning were still abstaining from alcohol one year later (Wiens & Menustik, 1983).

Enriching

Challenge students to use available print and on-line resources to research how aversive conditioning has been used to treat other conditions, like nail biting and sexual deviancy, which are mentioned in the text.

trb At this point, you may wish to use **Enrichment Lesson:** ***The Self-Injurious Behavior Inhibiting System*** (*Teacher's Resource Binder*, p. 30-1).

These people had received several booster treatments during that year. Unfortunately, only 33 percent of them were successfully abstaining from alcohol after three years.

Therapists recognize the limitations of aversive treatment. They often combine it with another form of treatment to produce the best results.

Operant Conditioning Techniques

7. What is the basic assumption in behavior therapy that uses operant conditioning techniques?

Our voluntary behaviors are greatly influenced by their consequences. Therapists have applied this basic principle of operant conditioning to help people solve problems at home, at school, and in other settings. This simple principle—reward desired behaviors, and withhold rewards for unwanted behaviors or punish them—has even helped those with disorders learn to function in normal settings. People with schizophrenia, for example, have been taught to act more rationally and behave more appropriately with others. Individuals with mental retardation have learned basic self-care. In both cases, therapists shaped behavior by reinforcing small steps in the right direction.

Operant conditioning techniques give hope to parents of children with *autism.* Children with autism are typically unresponsive to others, lack communication skills, and often engage in unusually repetitive behaviors. In one study (Lovaas, 1987), 19 uncommunicative, withdrawn 3-year-olds with autism took part in an intensive, two-year study. Parents worked 40 hours per week reinforcing appropriate or desired behavior while ignoring or punishing self-abusive and aggressive behaviors. By first grade, 39 of 40 children with autism *who did not* undergo treatment showed no improvement. However, 9 of the 19 receiving treatment became successfully functioning first graders with normal intelligence. Once again, therapy provides hope.

One operant conditioning technique has been used in institutions to encourage getting out of bed on time, getting dressed, cleaning a room, and cooperating with others. This form of *behavior modification* is called a **token economy,** because it rewards desired behaviors with some kind of token. Patients (or in some cases, inmates) earn the tokens by behaving appropriately, and then exchange them for simple things like candy, or privileges like watching TV. Token economies have been successfully used with various populations (people with schizophrenia, delinquent teens, and other groups) and in various settings, including day-care centers, schools, hospitals, and my own home!

► **token economy** An operant conditioning procedure that attempts to modify behavior by giving rewards for desired behaviors. These tokens can be exchanged for various privileges or treats.

Demonstrating

A TOKEN ECONOMY Ask students whether they have ever participated in a token economy. If they say yes, have them list different situations in which a token economy is used. If they say no, ask them if they have ever received a report card or a "conduct grade." Students are not paid to go to school and behave themselves while there, but teachers do give grades that are designed to evaluate the performance of students both academically and behaviorally.

F • Y • I

Diana Woodruf-Pak and Michelle Papka have found that Alzheimer's patients have difficulty being conditioned to blink in response to a tone that previously signaled an impending air puff. In class you might note that Joseph E. Steinmetz and his colleagues at Indiana University have found just the opposite in people with obsessive-compulsive disorder (OCD). Under certain conditions, people with OCD symptoms condition three times faster than people without OCD. "Normally, people show consistent conditioned responses after 10 to 15 trials," reports Steinmetz. "Our OCD subjects showed consistent conditioned responses after as few as three to five trials." He notes that the finding is consistent with theories stating that victims of anxiety disorders suffer a general susceptibility to aversive conditioning.

Several years ago, Steinmetz reported that people with autism also condition much faster than those without autism. Those with autism seemed to over-attend to neutral stimuli, which facilitated the conditioning process and caused mistimed learned responses. Together, these findings demonstrate how research on the very basic mechanisms of learning can lead to practical information about the human condition.

Source: Azar, B. (1999, March). Classical conditioning could link disorders and brain dysfunction, researchers suggest. *APA Monitor,* p. 17.

■ APPLYING THE POINTS

Present to students information you learn about token economies through contact with a local mental health care facility. Find out the tokens used in these economies and how well patients respond to this type of therapy. Furthermore, inquire about the goal of this therapy and the speed at which patients move out of the hospital. Finally, ask if the lessons learned through the token economy are maintained outside the hospital.

MODULE 30

■ LOOKING AT THE ISSUES

Why did psychology experience a cognitive revolution in the 1960s and 1970s? Have students look back into the history of psychology to see why psychologists began focusing on cognition, as well as observable behavior. The following questions can guide students' research and subsequent discussion of their findings:

- How is the cognitive perspective different from the traditional behaviorist view?
- What technological advances have made it easier to study cognition scientifically?

■ APPLYING THE POINTS

If possible, survey college professors in psychology departments at universities near your school to learn with what area(s) of psychology they ally themselves. The following questions can help you gather information and present your findings in class discussion:

- Do the professors in your area reflect the percentages shown in Figure 30.4? Why or why not?
- What specialties do the psychology departments in your area focus on?

tr A four-color transparency of Figure 30.4, Psychologists' Orientations, is available in the **Overhead Transparencies Set**.

▶ **cognitive therapy** Therapy that teaches people new, more adaptive ways of thinking and acting; based on the assumption that thoughts intervene between events and our emotional reactions.

Critics point to two problems with behavior modification, one practical and the other ethical. First, what happens after a person is no longer reinforced for proper behavior? People who leave an institution will not receive tokens for getting out of bed on time. Behavior modification therapists are aware of this problem, and they attempt to shift patients away from tokens and other external rewards and move them toward more internal rewards, such as satisfaction from receiving others' approval.

The second criticism asks whether behavior modification is ethical. Is it right to deprive someone of a privilege, television program, or dessert in order to obtain a desired behavior? Or is this process too controlling? Proponents insist they are working to eliminate or modify destructive behaviors, and that an improved life ultimately outweighs the temporary loss of privileges. The debate continues.

Cognitive Therapies

8. How does cognitive therapy work?

A revolution has taken place in psychology in the last half-century, as psychologists have refocused their interest on thought processes—*cognition*—as well as behavior. This revolution is apparent in therapy, where almost half of all clinical psychologists working in university settings refer to themselves as having some sort of cognitive orientation (Figure 30.4) (Mayne & others, 1994). These therapists believe our thinking affects how we feel. Cognitive explanations of illnesses like depression include the idea that self-blame ("I lost my job because I'm worthless") and overgeneralization ("I'm worthless at everything") set the stage for feeling depressed. Cognitive therapists assume that our thoughts filter the events in our lives and influence our emotional reactions to them. **Cognitive therapies** teach people new, more adaptive ways of thinking and acting.

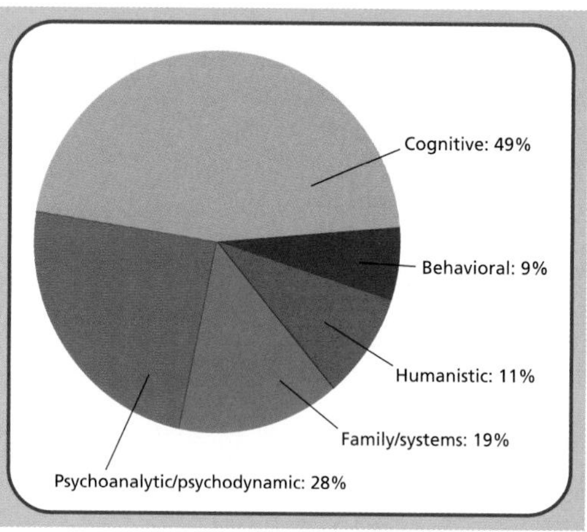

Figure 30.4 **Psychologists' Orientations** Almost half of all psychologists who conduct therapy say they have some sort of cognitive orientation. (Mayne & others, 1994).

The best psychological therapies for depression, especially major depression, appear to be cognitively based. A depressed friend might interpret your friendship as pity, your suggestions as

Reteaching

trb **tr** Provide students with copies of the black-line master of Figure 30.5 (on page 585), Constructive Interpretations, available in the **Black-Line Masters Appendix** in the *Teacher's Resource Binder.* Create blanks on the copies so that students can fill in the ways to create constructive interpretations of events in their lives. Students can also practice different ways of thinking by filling in other situations instead of failing a test. For instance, they may want to substitute situations that they are dealing with. They can work with a partner or counselor on different ways of thinking about the situation. On the next page is a graphic example of another situation students may consider.

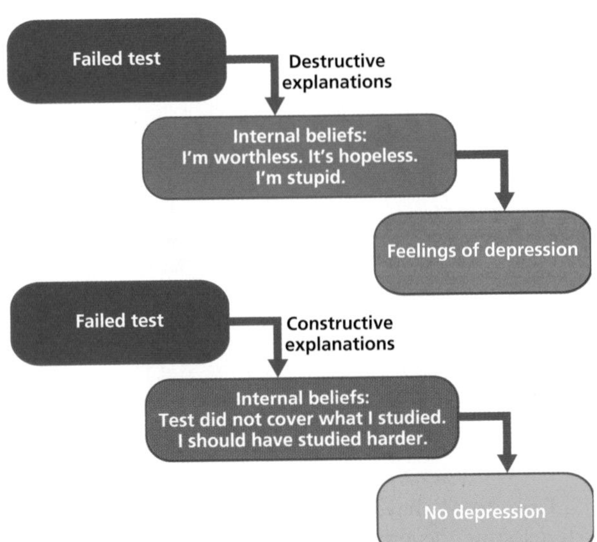

Figure 30.5 Constructive Interpretations Cognitive therapists help people explain bad events constructively instead of destructively.

criticism, and your questions as blame. These negative thoughts fuel depression, sustaining and worsening negative moods. In addition, whereas most of us tend to judge ourselves favorably, this *self-serving bias* is absent during depression. When something good happens, people with depression do not give themselves credit. The person might, for example, explain away an award for being helpful in class as the result of an external circumstance: "They probably drew my name out of a hat." But people with depression are very good at blaming themselves squarely for any failure. What was the reason for the failing grade on the U.S. history test? "Because I'm stupid." (Not "Because I didn't study hard enough," or "Because the test covered material the teacher hadn't gone over in class.")

Cognitive therapists teach clients to think constructively instead of destructively (Figure 30.5). They try to help depressed people take more responsibility for things that go well and to encourage them to give less permanent and devastating explanations for failure. One researcher and her colleagues showed depressed adults the advantages of optimistic *explanatory styles* (Rabin, 1986). The researchers trained these adults to reform their negative thinking patterns and asked them to record each day's good events and the role they played in each event. Depression in these newly trained positive thinkers dropped significantly, compared with levels of depression in people waiting for treatment to become available (Figure 30.6, page 586).

■ TEACHING TIP

Optimistic thinking has three important qualities:

- Permanent—Pessimists believe that bad events will become a permanent fixture in their lives, whereas optimists believe that bad events are temporary.
- Personal—Pessimists believe that bad events are a result of some personal flaw that cannot be changed, while optimists believe that bad events are the result of circumstances that can be controlled.
- Pervasive—Pessimists believe that a bad experience in one area of life will influence other areas, causing havoc throughout one's life. Optimists, however, believe that bad events will remain isolated in time, not affecting later decisions or opportunities as much.

trb At this point, you may wish to use Enrichment Lesson: *Strategies to Correct One's Thinking* (*Teacher's Resource Binder*, p. 30-1).

■ JOURNAL WRITING

Invite students to use the following questions and writing prompts as springboards for entries in their psychology journals.

- How do you feel when you fail tests? Do you feel like a failure or do you look for ways to improve your performance, based on what you missed? Why?
- How easy is it for you to think differently about a situation? Are you easily swayed by other's opinions or are you resolute in your outlook? Why?

Friend is angry about a mistake you made. → **Internal Belief:** I am a bad friend. Nobody wants to be my friend. I am unreliable. → Feelings of depression

Friend is angry about a mistake you made. → **Internal Belief:** I should try to make it up to her somehow. I'll apologize for my mistake and do better next time. → No depression

MODULE 30

LOOKING AT THE ISSUES

Combination therapies tend to be more effective than single therapeutic approaches. Have students ponder the following questions that touch on why this might be so:

- How do combination therapies address the different explanations for human behavior?
- For what disorders are combination therapies effective?

trb At this point, you may wish to use **Application Activity:** *Frequency of Self-Reinforcement Questionnaire* (*Teacher's Resource Binder*, p. 30-1; **Handout 30–13**).

F•Y•I

Compulsions manifest in a several different ways:

- **Hoarders** collect things and have a hard time throwing anything away. People who hoard are usually plagued by fears of losing something, missing something, or needing something that they've thrown away. So they keep everything, including leftover food, papers, and broken items.
- **Checkers** will recheck actions they have performed over and over again. They may fear they did not turn off the oven or lock the door, and they will recheck a certain number of times before they feel better. Unfortunately, the number of times needed to relieve anxiety increases with each experience.
- **Counters** will count everything, from steps they take to words people say to them. They will become preoccupied with counting something seemingly unimportant to the point of stopping their daily progress in life.
- **Cleaners** will clean either their hands or surfaces excessively. Often, this cleaning will need to be done a certain number of times to relieve the anxiety.

tr **TEACHING TIP**

A four-color transparency of Figure 30.6, Optimistic Outlook, is available in the **Overhead Transparencies Set.**

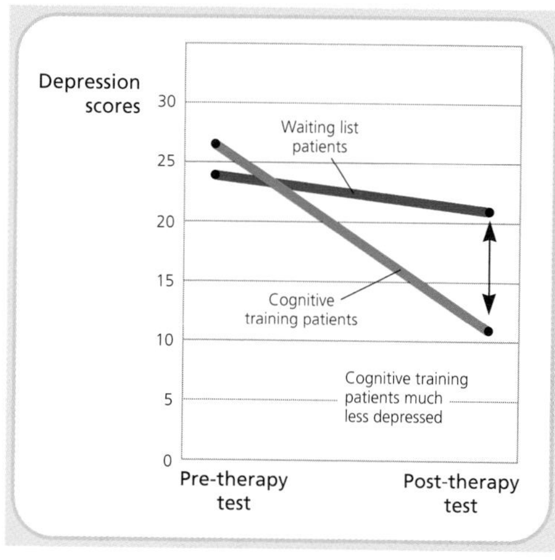

Figure 30.6 Optimistic Outlook Participants who learn optimistic ways of explaining negative events stand a good chance of seeing depression levels decline (Rabin, 1986).

Cognitive-behavior therapy combines cognitive therapy (changing self-defeating thoughts) with behavior therapy (changing inappropriate behaviors). With this therapy, people become aware of their irrationally negative thoughts and are taught to practice a better everyday approach. Let's work through an example of cognitive-behavior therapy.

Obsessive-compulsive disorder (OCD) is characterized by unwanted repetitive thoughts (obsessions) and/or actions (compulsions). In one study, therapists had people with this disorder view a PET (positive emission tomography) scan that showed abnormal activity in their brain when a compulsive urge, like the desire to repeatedly wash hands, was present (Schwartz & others, 1996). Next, the therapists taught these people to relabel their compulsions, saying to themselves, "I'm having a compulsive urge" and attributing the urge to their brain's abnormal activity. Finally, these people learned to engage in a pleasant alternative behavior, like gardening or taking a walk, instead of acting on the urge to wash their hands. The goal was to "unstick" the brain by focusing attention on something else and using a different part of the brain. After two or three months of weekly therapy sessions and practice at home, most participants showed normal brain activity on their PET scans and a decrease in OCD symptoms.

► **cognitive-behavior therapy** An integrated therapy that combines cognitive therapy (changing self-defeating thinking) with behavior therapy (changing inappropriate behaviors).

► **family therapy** Therapy that treats the family as a system. Views an individual's unwanted behaviors as influenced by or directed at other members of the family; attempts to guide the family toward positive relationships and improved communication.

Family and Group Therapies

9. What are the advantages of therapy conducted in groups?

Most of the therapies we've examined so far can occur either individually, one on one with a therapist, *or* in small groups of 6 to 10 people. Cognitive, behavior, and humanistic therapists lead sessions that typi-

Helpful Group Therapy

THE SEVEN DWARFS AFTER THERAPY

cally run for up to 90 minutes per week. Participants discuss and react to one another's issues. Families in conflict are often recommended for group therapy.

Compared with one-on-one therapy, group therapy has some advantages:

- Therapists can help more people in less time.
- Therapy sessions typically cost less.
- The social context of the therapy allows people to discover that others have problems similar to their own. Simply finding that others share the same troublesome feelings can bring great relief.
- Group meetings foster a sense of community. Bereaved, addicted, or divorced people often have a longing for the connectedness found in a group (Yalom, 1985).

Family therapy, which treats the family as a system, is a special kind of group therapy. Families sometimes need outside help when the group's need to connect emotionally conflicts with one individual's need to be more independent. A child who rebels inappropriately adds to and is affected by family tension. Family therapy views an individual's unwanted behaviors as influenced by or directed at other members of the family. Family therapists help the members of the family discover the roles they play inside their family's social unit. They try to guide the family toward positive relationships and improved communication. Opening up the communication pathways within a family helps its members learn new ways of resolving and preventing conflicts (Hazelrigg & others, 1987; Shadish & others, 1993).

Family Therapy When a family receives therapy, relationships and communication typically improve.

■ APPLYING THE POINTS

Many support groups, whose members depend on one another, utilize therapeutic techniques. Contact local support group organizations to ask what type of therapeutic techniques they use in their sessions. The following questions may be used as a guide for an informal interview and subsequent presentation of findings to the class:

- Are sessions led by a qualified or certified therapist? Why or why not?
- What rules for discussion does the group follow?
- How much contact do members have outside of the support group meetings?
- What types of planned activities does the group participate in?

trb At this point, you may wish to use Enrichment Lesson: *Psychodrama* (*Teacher's Resource Binder*, p. 30-1).

■ TEACHING TIP

Have students discuss the advantages and disadvantages of family therapy. Some questions they may consider in their discussion include the following:

- If a patient has a dysfunctional family life, how might individual therapy be only partially effective?
- Would patients be less willing to open up about personal issues if their families knew about their feelings? Why or why not?

■ CHECKING FOR UNDERSTANDING

As an informal assessment, have students identify fictional characters from print and media who seem to have some type of mental disorder. For each identified character, ask the student the following questions:

- What disorder does this character have? How did you draw your conclusion? If possible, give an example.
- What type of treatment would you recommend for this disorder? Why?

With this activity, you can learn whether students know the symptoms of major mental illnesses and some appropriate treatments for those disorders.

Cooperative Learning

Have students form groups based on particular issues about which support groups form. Each student group can contact a local support group and ask permission to sit in on a therapy session. If students can attend a meeting, have them keep the following questions in mind:

- How many people attended the meeting? Was the attendance average? If not, why?
- Who seemed to be in charge of the session? Was it a therapist or a group member?
- What were the qualifications of the group's leader?
- Did there seem to be a lesson or objective to the meeting or was the session open to free discussion? Why was this particular method used?

Suggest that interested students who visited a support group therapy session answer the questions in a written report for extra credit.

MODULE 30

■ **APPLYING THE POINTS**

Have students research how many nonpsychiatric services are available in your city or area. They can use the phone book to find listings of clinical psychologists in private practice, community mental health centers, halfway houses, crisis hotlines, and similar services that do not rely on psychiatrists to perform psychotherapy.

■ **LOOKING AT THE ISSUES**

Psychologists are moving into the realm of psychiatry as the APA pushes states to allow psychologists to become licensed to prescribe medication for mental disorders. New Mexico became the first state to allow such licensure in 2002, and the Department of Defense trained 10 military psychologists to receive endorsement to prescribe drugs. Have students research this turn of events by using the following questions as a guide for research and subsequent discussion:

- How do psychiatrists view these new colleagues?
- Are the training programs for psychologists similar to the training psychiatrists get in medical school? Why or why not?
- Have other states introduced legislation or passed laws allowing psychologists to obtain prescribing privileges? If so, which ones?
- How might this change the practice of psychiatry in the future?

web For more information about prescription privileges in the military, see the article entitled "Psychology's First Prescribers," in the February 2003 *Monitor on Psychology* found on line at **www.apa.org/monitor/feP3/prescribers.html**.

Evaluating Psychotherapy's Effectiveness

10. What does research tell us about psychotherapy's effectiveness?

Before the 1950s, psychiatrists (medical doctors who treat psychological disorders) conducted most of the psychotherapy in this country. But demand for psychological services outgrew the psychiatric profession long ago. Now, clinical and counseling psychologists; clinical social workers; psychiatric nurses; and marital, abuse, and pastoral (religions) counselors conduct most psychotherapy. *Community mental health programs,* which provide outpatient therapy, crisis hotlines, and halfway houses for those moving out of institutionalized settings, are essential in the delivery of psychological services. As psychology's reach has extended further into our communities, researchers have continued to assess the effectiveness of various types of psychological therapies. Here is a sampling of what we've learned thus far:

> ***Clients believe in the effectiveness of psychotherapy.*** In one study, 75 percent of the clients said they were "satisfied" with their therapy (Lebow, 1982). *Consumer Reports* (1995) printed that 89 percent of 2900 readers were at least "fairly well satisfied" with their treatment.
>
> ***Clinicians believe in the effectiveness of psychotherapy.*** Most patients enter therapy very unhappy. After therapy is over, patients usually leave feeling less unhappy. Case study after case study, written by therapists, reports therapeutic success stories.
>
> ***Researchers have debated the effectiveness of therapy.*** Hans Eysenck (1952) noted in a controversial study that two-thirds of those suffering nonpsychotic (less serious) disorders improved with therapy. However, he also reported that those on waiting lists who *did not* receive therapy improved at about the same rate. Wait a minute! Does this mean psychotherapy is just as good as doing nothing? Is time just as good as Carl Rogers at healing? What are we to believe?
>
> Research on the effectiveness of therapy continues. After analyzing the results of over 400 studies, one researcher found evidence that "overwhelmingly supports" the use of psychotherapy as beneficial to overcoming mental illness (Smith & others, 1980). This study found that those who received therapy were better off

FREUD AT A CROSSROADS
Psychoanalysis should relieve stress and anxiety...but so does looking at fish.

Enriching

In a collaborative class brainstorming session, have students come up with an experiment that tests the efficacy of a therapeutic intervention. The intervention does not have to be specific, but the experimental methodology should include a control and experimental group, blind or double-blind procedures, and randomization techniques. Have students also discuss the ethical considerations involved in conducting an efficacy experiment.

Close

Who's Who in Psychotherapy?

Chances are that you or someone you know will need psychological services at some point. The ups and downs of a hectic world are inevitable, but the downs are sometimes a little more than we can handle alone. The American Psychological Association cites the following as common signs of trouble that may require professional help:

- Thoughts of suicide
- Self-destructive behavior, such as abuse of alcohol or another drug
- Disruptive fears
- Deep and lasting depression or feelings of hopelessness
- Sudden mood shifts
- Compulsive rituals, such as hand-washing

Knowing you need some help getting over a rough time in your life is a sign of strength, not weakness. If you do consider contacting a therapist, you need to know where to go. The different kinds of therapists and their training are described in Table 30.1. Counselors at school or school psychologists would be able to recommend names of therapists they trust. After contacting a therapist, you should describe your situation or concerns and ask the therapist to describe his or her treatment approach. It is also wise to ask about the therapist's credentials (is he or she licensed?) and fees. If you think the therapist is a good fit for you, consider setting up an appointment.

TABLE 30.1 THERAPISTS AND THEIR TRAINING

TYPE	DESCRIPTION
Clinical psychologist	Most are psychologists with a Ph.D. and expertise in research, assessment, and therapy, supplemented by a supervised internship. About half work in agencies and institutions, half in private practice.
Clinical or psychiatric social worker	A two-year Master of Social Work graduate program plus postgraduate supervision prepares some social workers to offer psychotherapy, mostly to people with everyday personal and family problems. About half have earned the National Association of Social Workers' designation of clinical social worker.
Counselor	Marriage and family counselors specialize in problems arising from family relations. Pastoral (religious) counselors provide counseling to countless people. Abuse counselors work with substance abusers and with spouse and child abusers and their victims.
Psychiatrist	Physicians who specialize in the treatment of psychological disorders. Not all psychiatrists have had extensive training in psychotherapy, but as M.D.s they can prescribe medications. Thus, they tend to see those with the most serious problems. Many have a private practice.

■ **APPLYING THE POINTS**

Have students contact your state's licensure board to find out what types of training one must receive to practice psychotherapy legally. Students may use the following questions as a guide for an interview with their board contact, and you may use the same questions to guide a class discussion of students' findings:

- What is the smallest amount of training one must receive to gain licensure?
- How many licensed practitioners are in the state? In the community where your school is located?
- Do people have to pass an exam to get licensed? Which one(s)? Do they get an opportunity to take it again if they fail the first time? How many times can they take it?
- What should potential clients look for to ensure their therapist is state-licensed?

trb tr A black-line master of Table 30.1, Therapists and Their Training, is available in the **Black-Line Masters Appendix** in the *Teacher's Resource Binder*.

■ **JOURNAL WRITING**

Invite students to use the following questions and writing prompts as springboards for entries in their psychology journals:

- Have you ever felt any of the "signs of trouble" outlined in the Up Close box? What did you do about them?
- Would you recommend a therapist to a friend if the friend exhibited any of these signs? Why or why not?

■ **TEACHING TIP**

Remind students that feeling or acting in any one of these ways does not indicate a problem that must be dealt with in therapy. All of these behaviors should be taken seriously, whether in isolation or not. In order to be considered a mental illness, though, these experiences must be maladaptive, unjustified, disturbing, and atypical.

MODULE 30

■ TEACHING TIPS

tr (1) A four-color transparency of Figure 30.7, Therapeutic Outcomes, is available in the **Overhead Transparency Set.**

(2) Remind students of the *placebo effect.* This effect, in which people's belief in a therapy can lead to actually feeling better, helps explain why 29 percent of people did get better while on a placebo. A success rate of almost 30 percent is not bad, but it does not compare with the 50 percent success rate of real treatment programs.

V At this point, you may wish to show **Videocassette:** ***The Mind,*** **Second Edition, Module 3: "Placebo Effect: Mind-Body Relationship"** (*Teacher's Resource Binder,* p. 30-1).

■ LOOKING AT THE ISSUES

Unfortunately, many people who have psychological disorders do not have a clear-cut diagnosis. Elicit students' ideas about why clear-cut diagnoses are difficult to make by asking the following questions:

- How does a patient's level of candor or openness contribute to the ability of the therapist to diagnose the problem?
- How might substance abuse interfere with an accurate diagnosis?

trb At this point, you may wish to use **Enrichment Lesson:** *The Consumer Reports Study* (*Teacher's Resource Binder,* p. 30-1).

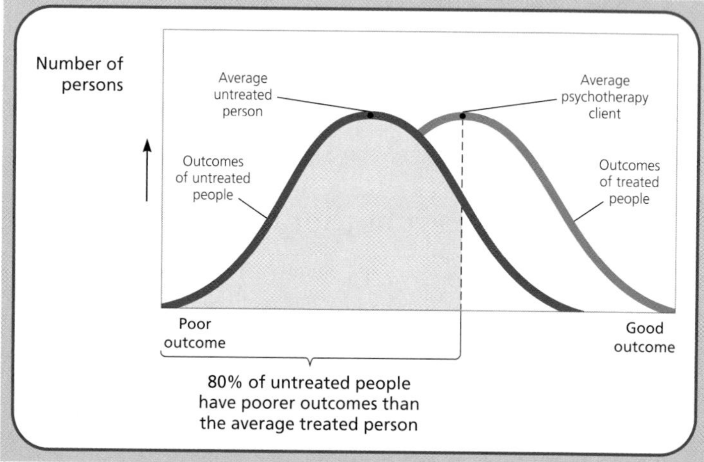

Figure 30.7 Therapeutic Outcomes These overlapping normal curves represent data from 475 studies comparing the outcomes in untreated people and psychotherapy clients. The average psychotherapy client had a better outcome than 80 percent of the untreated individuals (Smith & others, 1980).

than 80 percent of those who did not (Figure 30.7). Another study (Elkin & others, 1989) randomly assigned 239 people with depression to either a control group that received placebo medication (a "sugar pill" or inert substance) and supportive attention *or* to one of three treatment programs: drug therapy, cognitive therapy, or interpersonal therapy. At the end of the 16-week treatment program, depression had lessened in over half of those in the treatment programs, but in only 29 percent of those in the control group. This finding sums up what so many studies have found: Therapy makes a difference. Time is a great healer, but therapy is likely to help time along.

The more clear-cut the psychological problem, the more effective the therapy is likely to be (Singer, 1981). A task force of the Society of Clinical Psychology (Chambless & others, 1997; DeRubeis & Crits-Christoph, 1998) offered several specific suggestions, including the following:

- Cognitive, interpersonal, and behavior therapy work best for depression.
- Cognitive-behavior therapy works well for the eating disorder bulimia.
- Behavior modification works best for enuresis (bed-wetting).

No one kind of therapy or therapist is absolutely more effective than all others. Whether treated by a social worker or a psychiatrist, patients tend to be equally satisfied. And regard-

Enriching

(1) What can we change and what can't we change? Martin Seligman wrote a book with a similar title in which he explored therapeutic evidence to determine which disorders had high rates of successful treatment and which did not. Have students read his book, reflecting on the impact of the power of belief. Have students also contemplate the level of expectation people should have when going into therapy to treat certain conditions and disorders.

Source: Seligman, M. E. P. (1994). *What you can change and what you can't.* New York: Knopf.

trb At this point, you may wish to use **Enrichment Lesson:** *Therapy and the Nature of the Problem* (*Teacher's Resource Binder,* p. 30-1).

less of the type of therapy patients receive, they also report about the same amount of satisfaction (Consumer Reports, 1995). Finally, one recent study found that a clinician's training, experience, or licensing did not predict client outcome (Bickman, 1999). The reality appears to be that just seeking therapy is a step toward feeling better, which may help explain why a clinician's training does not predict results.

Are Alternative Therapies Effective?

11. What are alternative therapies, and are they effective?

You may have noticed that we haven't yet discussed many of the therapy techniques you see advertised in magazines, newspapers, on the psychic news network, and on the Internet. Have you heard of aromatherapists, reflexologists, or anger-release therapists? Princess Diana sought psychological relief from representatives of all three (Smith, 1999). The world is filled with would-be healers making claims that do not stand up to scientific research. Here, at least as much as anywhere else, you will need to apply your critical thinking skills to assess these claims. Testimonials and popular interest aside, what does the evidence say about alternative therapies? Let's take a closer look at two of them: therapeutic touch therapy and light exposure therapy.

Therapeutic Touch Therapy

In *therapeutic touch therapy* therapists move their hands above the person's body to "push energy fields into balance." Touch therapists (who don't actually touch the body) believe balanced energy fields help cure burns, headaches, cancer, and other ailments (Kreiger, 1993). Skeptics find no evidence to support these claims (Scheiber & Selby, 1997). One of these skeptics, James Randi, offered over $700,000 to any therapeutic touch therapist who could "detect a human energy field" under experimental conditions. Only one person agreed to be tested, and walked away empty-handed after failing to detect the presence of a human at a rate better than chance would predict. The *Journal of the American Medical Association* published a study showing similarly dismal results from touch therapists (Rosa & others, 1998). The editor of this prestigious journal urged potential therapeutic-touch patients to save their money. He concluded that this supposed human energy field "does not exist." So, at least for now, the scientific verdict is that this alternative therapy does not work.

(2) Ask students to comb through magazines and newspapers to see what types of alternative therapy are advertised. Allow time for students to describe the advertisements or show actual copies they have cut out. Then ask the following questions:

- What claims of effectiveness do these ads make?
- What type of credentials do the practitioners possess?
- What type of disorders do these therapies claim to treat?

■ **TEACHING TIP**

Students may wonder why therapists even need to get licensed at all if training does not predict the outcome of therapy. Emphasize to students that licensing is designed to reinforce effective treatment practices and to keep untested therapies from harming people. Although seeking treatment is a major step on the road to getting better, a patient usually can only go so far on his or her own without guidance from a trained professional.

trb At this point, you may wish to use Enrichment Lesson: *Fringe Medicine* (*Teacher's Resource Binder*, p. 30-1).

F • Y • I

web *Therapeutic touch therapy* should not be confused with *touch therapy* itself. Although therapeutic touch practitioners seek to bring the human energy fields into balance, using either no contact or light skin contact, **touch therapy** involves actual massage therapy to treat several different types of illness. Touch therapy has been shown to increase birth weight in premature babies, alleviate depression, reduce stress hormone levels, and improve immunosuppression. For more information about touch therapy, refer to Dr. Tiffany Field's Touch Research Institute Web site at **www.miami.edu/touch-research**.

trb At this point, you may wish to use Enrichment Lesson: *Fringe Medicine* (*Teacher's Resource Binder*, p. 30-1).

web ■ **APPLYING THE POINTS**

Have students explore James Randi's efforts at debunking pseudoscience on the Web at **www.randi.org**. Students can read articles about his latest debunking efforts and get updates on his ongoing challenge with psychic Sylvia Browne.

MODULE 30

■ **JOURNAL WRITING**

Invite students to use the following questions and writing prompts as springboards for entries in their psychology journals.

- Do you believe in the existence of human energy fields? Why or why not?
- Do you get the wintertime blues? Have you ever felt down after several days of overcast weather? Describe your feelings.

F • Y • I

Melatonin, a hormone secreted by the pea-sized pineal gland, which is located at the center of the brain, seems to play an important role in the synchronization of the sleep-wake cycle. As our eyes register the fall of darkness, the pineal gland increases its production of melatonin, which circulates to all parts of the body and causes the slowing of biological activity. When light again hits the retina, neural impulses signal the pineal gland to slow melatonin production.

■ **LOOKING AT THE ISSUES**

Seasonal affective disorder (SAD) is not included in the DSM-IV-TR. Have students consider why it isn't and, indeed, what qualifies a disorder to be included in this diagnostic tool. Use the following questions to guide research and a subsequent discussion of students' findings:

- How many people suffer from SAD?
- How do psychiatrists decide which disorders are included in the DSM-IV-TR?

Close

Pose the following questions to your students:

- Has your view of therapy changed? Why or why not?
- If you were experiencing a mental, relational, or social problem, would you seek help from a licensed professional therapist? Why or why not?
- If you were to see a therapist, which perspective would you prefer he or she followed? Why?

Light Exposure Therapy

Some call it the wintertime blahs. Others call it the cold weather blues. Therapists recognize this legitimate form of depression as *seasonal affective disorder* (SAD). Whatever you call it, the feelings accompanying this condition seem to result from the decreased amount of sunlight during the winter months.

About 20 years ago, therapists working for the National Institute of Mental Health came up with a treatment idea. What if SAD patients received a daily dose of bright light? Would the extra light nudge their natural body rhythms back into a normal pattern? Clinical studies indeed reported that light brought relief of winter blues. Now you can buy or rent "light boxes" to increase your exposure to light and brighten your winter days. But wait a minute. Doesn't this sound like yet another example of an *expectation effect* (I feel better because I thought I would feel better)? In this case, additional research has shown that there is more to light-exposure therapy than meets the eye.

One of these studies exposed SAD patients to either bright light treatments or a phony placebo treatment ("negative ion generator"). Investigators displayed equal enthusiasm about each treatment. After four weeks, 61 percent of the participants receiving bright light in the morning had improved tremendously, while only 32 percent of those receiving "negative ion" treatment had improved (Eastman, 1998). Alfred Lewy and his colleagues (1998) reported a biological link between morning light exposure and levels of melatonin, a hormone that plays a role in body rhythm regulation. It turns out that increased exposure to light was indeed a bright idea for treating people with SAD.

Note that applying scientific reasoning and critical thinking while considering new claims does not necessarily mean you will debunk the claim. It does mean you will know with more confidence whether the claim had merit.

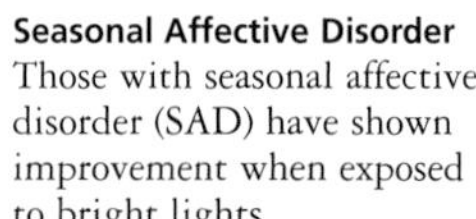

Seasonal Affective Disorder Those with seasonal affective disorder (SAD) have shown improvement when exposed to bright lights.

Those who seek therapy usually feel better after getting help. And of course, there are people who could use professional therapy, do not seek it, but recover anyway. This spontaneous recovery ability shows that humans are resourceful, and that we have a capacity to care for one another. Still, we know that those who receive therapeutic help are more likely to get well than those who do not. Effective therapists possess empathy for their clients, show care and concern, listen respectfully, and reassure. They help make hope available for those who have lost hope, while providing a new perspective on life that is fresh and believable.

REVIEW

Module 30: Psychological Therapies

What's the Point?

Psychotherapy is an emotionally charged, confiding interaction between a trained therapist and someone who suffers from psychological difficulties. Researchers have developed a variety of approaches to therapy, and this module focuses on four of them: psychoanalysis, humanistic therapy, behavior therapy, and cognitive therapy. Therapists who combine two or more perspectives in their work are taking an eclectic approach.

Psychoanalysis

1. *In Freud's view, how do mental disorders develop?*

   Sigmund Freud, the founder of psychoanalysis, believed that personality develops during the early childhood years, as we make our way through a series of stages. Each of these stages can be a source of conflict, and failure to resolve a conflict in a particular stage can produce problems that carry over to later adult life. The three parts of personality—the id, ego, and superego—interact during these conflicts, which may exist at an unconscious level of the mind.

2. *What techniques does psychoanalysis use to reveal and resolve conflicts?*

   Psychoanalysis searches for clues to unconscious conflicts. Two important tools in this search are free association and dream analysis. In free association, the patient relaxes on a couch and says anything that enters his or her mind. The analyst interprets the content of the statements, pointing out interruptions that may indicate resistance, or blocking of topics that cause anxiety. Similarly, the analyst interprets the hidden content of the patient's dreams. In therapy sessions, the patient may transfer to the therapist feelings from other relationships.

   Critics of psychoanalysis point out that Freud's theory rests on a belief in repressed memories, a belief not well supported by current research. Other criticisms are that this form of therapy is very expensive (and therefore beyond the reach of most people) and can be dogmatic (the analyst is always right).

3. *What do psychodynamic and interpersonal therapies share with psychoanalysis, and how do they differ from it?*

   Psychodynamic therapists retain some parts of Freud's theory, such as an emphasis on childhood experiences, unconscious drives, and unresolved conflicts. But they meet less often with patients, and they place less emphasis on some aspects of childhood stages. Interpersonal psychotherapists also try to understand the origins of disorders, but they focus on a shorter resolution (within 12 to 16 weeks) of troublesome symptoms stemming from current problems.

Humanistic Therapies

4. *How do the psychoanalytic and humanistic approaches to therapy differ? What is unconditional positive regard, and why is it important?*

   Humanistic therapists differ from psychoanalytic therapists in stressing personal growth, not recovery from illness; in focusing on the future instead of the past; in emphasizing conscious thoughts rather than unconscious processes; and in being nondirective rather than directive (interpreting for the patient).

MODULE 30

Checking the Points

■ **TEACHING TIPS**

web (1) The book companion site for *Thinking About Psychology* at **www.worthpublishers.com/thinkingaboutpsych** contains a module quiz, flashcards of key terms and people, as well as other student activities and resources for this module. You will also find PowerPoint lectures, a quiz grade book, and other teaching resources by logging on as an instructor.

trb (2) At this point, you may wish to review and confirm concepts about psychological therapies with **Critical Thinking Activity:** *Fact or Falsehood?* (*Teacher's Resource Binder*, p. 30-1; **Handout 30–1**). If students filled out this handout earlier in the module, ask them not to refer to that version. Suggest that students complete the handout in small groups, taking the time to look up information in the text to respond correctly to questions. Have all the groups meet to review the handout, again using the text to support their responses.

MODULE 30

Unconditional positive regard is Carl Rogers's term for communicating to clients the feeling of being accepted without a need to behave in any specific way. Rogers's client-centered therapy stressed empathy, acceptance, and genuineness, which would be communicated through active listening.

Behavior Therapies

5. *How do behavior therapies differ from humanistic therapy and psychoanalysis?*

   Behavior therapists are not interested in childhood conflicts or self-awareness. Instead, they believe that the goal of therapy is to eliminate unwanted behaviors by teaching people to apply learning principles to solving problems.

6. *What is the basic assumption in behavior therapy that uses classical conditioning techniques?*

   Therapy based on classical conditioning assumes that we learn to associate certain stimuli—such as an emotion with a certain place or behavior. If we can learn these associations, we should also be able to unlearn them—through counterconditioning, or forming new associations to old stimuli. Two techniques that attempt to achieve this end are systematic desensitization and aversive conditioning. Systematic desensitization attempts to replace a negative response (such as fear) to a stimulus (such as a dog) with a positive response (such as relaxation) to that stimulus. Aversive conditioning attempts to replace an inappropriate positive response (pleasure) to a stimulus (such as an alcoholic drink) with a negative response (such as nausea) to that same stimulus.

7. *What is the basic assumption in behavior therapy that uses operant conditioning techniques?*

   Therapy using operant conditioning techniques assumes that our voluntary behaviors are influenced by their consequences. Therefore we should be able to change behaviors by rewarding those we desire and withholding rewards for unwanted behaviors, or punishing them. Operant conditioning techniques have been used in a variety of settings, sometimes in the form of token economies—systems in which people who behave appropriately receive tokens that can be traded for something they value.

Cognitive Therapies

8. *How does cognitive therapy work?*

   Cognitive psychologists focus on thoughts, and cognitive therapies assume that people's thoughts act as filters between events and our reactions to those events. Cognitive therapists attempt to teach people to think in more adaptive ways. This approach has been particularly successful in working with people with depression. In those cases, the therapist will attempt to get the person to assume more responsibility for things that go well and to explain failures in less permanent and devastating ways.

   Cognitive-behavior therapy attempts not only to change self-defeating thoughts, but also to eliminate inappropriate behaviors, such as the compulsive hand-washing that occurs in obsessive-compulsive disorder.

Family and Group Therapies

9. *What are the advantages of therapy conducted in groups?*

   Cognitive, behavior, and humanistic therapies are often conducted in groups. A therapist can help more people in the same time, at a lower cost to each individual. People also benefit from seeing that others have problems like their own, and they may find a sense of community in the group setting. Family therapy has the additional advantage of offering insight into the roles family members play and they way those roles contribute to problems individuals are having with the family. The therapist tries to help the family improve their relationships and their ways of communicating.

Evaluating Psychotherapy's Effectiveness

10. *What does research tell us about psychotherapy's effectiveness?*

    Various research studies show that clients and therapists believe that psychotherapy is effective. But studies also show that people with less serious problems tend to improve on their own, sometimes while waiting for therapy. In studies that show that those who receive therapy definitely improve, one important factor seems to be that clients have clear-cut problems. Some therapies work better for some conditions, but no one form of therapy or type of therapist is better than another for all people, at all times.

Are Alternative Therapies Effective?

11. *What are alternative therapies, and are they effective?*

    Alternative therapies are nontraditional approaches to healing. This module covered two of them: therapeutic touch therapy and light exposure therapy—and reported on clinical studies of their effectiveness. There is no evidence that therapeutic touch therapy has any power to help people resolve psychological problems. Light exposure therapy—exposure to artificial sunlight during periods of low natural sunlight—does, however, relieve seasonal depression.

Key Terms

psychotherapy, p. 573
eclectic approach, p. 574
psychoanalysis, p. 574
resistance, p. 575
interpretation, p. 575
transference, p. 576
client-centered therapy, p. 578
active listening, p. 578
behavior therapy, p. 579
systematic desensitization, p. 580
aversive conditioning, p. 582
token economy, p. 583
cognitive therapy, p. 584
cognitive-behavior therapy, p. 586
family therapy, p. 587

Key People

Sigmund Freud, p. 573
Carl Rogers, p. 578

trb tr ■ **TEACHING TIP**

At this point, you may wish to provide students with the **Building Vocabulary: Graphic Organizer:** *Concept Web* (*Teacher's Resource Binder*, p. 30-1; **Handout 30–2**). If students filled in the handout earlier in the module, ask them not to refer to that version. Have them complete the concept web as a tool for vocabulary review. Encourage students to fill in the handout individually. You can then project a transparency of a correctly completed concept web for students to use in checking their work.

MODULE 30

tb Using the Test Bank

The *Test Bank* that accompanies this textbook offers a wide variety of questions in different formats and levels of complexity. Use the software to construct whole tests or to integrate standardized questions into teacher-made tests.

Self-Test Answers

Multiple-Choice Questions

1. b, 2. d, 3. a, 4. c, 5. a

Self-Test

Multiple-Choice Questions

Choose the *best* answer for each of the following questions.

1. Mary has been meeting with a therapist for several months. When she enters the therapist's office, she sits in a chair opposite the analyst and says anything that comes into her mind, regardless of how embarrassing it may feel. Mary's therapist is using
   a. active listening.
   b. free association.
   c. systematic desensitization.
   d. aversive conditioning.

2. Angelo has an intense fear of spiders. His therapist encouraged Angelo to talk about this fear, and she reworded what Angelo said, repeating it back to him. She then asked Angelo to try to remember his earliest childhood experiences with spiders. Finally, she began a program in which she gradually introduced Angelo to photos of spiders, toy spiders, dead spiders, and real spiders to reduce his fear. Angelo's therapist is using
   a. free association.
   b. aversive conditioning.
   c. a token economy approach.
   d. an eclectic approach.

3. Beth told her therapist that she had just had a major fight with her father about her 10 P.M. curfew on Fridays and Saturdays, and that her father had grounded her for a month. Beth is very angry because no one else her age has a 10 P.M. curfew. Beth's therapist responded, "Your curfew makes you feel as though your father is treating you like a little child, doesn't it? And you feel it's unfair because your friends can stay out later. And this makes you feel very angry toward your father, doesn't it?" Beth's therapist is using
   a. active listening.
   b. counterconditioning.
   c. aversive therapy.
   d. free association.

4. Trent has been skipping classes, hanging out with some really tough kids, and getting into a lot of trouble during school hours when he does attend. Mrs. Ramsden, the guidance counselor, thinks Trent is having a problem at home. She has arranged for the school psychologist to meet with Trent, his sisters and brothers, and his parents. She has set up a ________________ therapy session.
   a. psychodynamic
   b. humanistic
   c. family
   d. cognitive-behavioral

5. The principal of Everybody's Favorite High School is tired of seeing food spilled on furniture and on the floor in the cafeteria. He has decided to put a locked gate in the doorway to a room in which all desserts, snacks, and soft drinks will be located. Students who leave their eating area spotless in the cafeteria will receive a slip of paper each day. Five of these slips of paper will admit the student to the locked snack and soft drink area. The principal is
   a. instituting a token economy.
   b. counterconditioning the students.
   c. conducting a systematic desensitization program.
   d. using cognitive therapy to change students' eating behavior.

Matching Terms and Definitions

6. For each definition, choose the *best* matching term from the list that follows.

Definition

a. In psychoanalysis, the patient's transfer to the analyst of emotions linked to other relationships.
b. Type of counterconditioning that associates an unpleasant state with an unwanted behavior.
c. In psychoanalysis, the portion of personality that represents the set of internalized ideals, or conscience.
d. Therapies that try to teach more adaptive ways of thinking and acting, based on the assumption that thoughts intervene between events and our emotions.
e. In psychoanalysis, the pleasure-seeking part of personality.
f. Acceptance that does not depend on any special behavior; a recommended attitude in client-centered therapy.
g. Habitual way of looking at the world and explaining yourself and your actions; may be optimistic or pessimistic.
h. In psychoanalysis, the reality-oriented portion of personality.
i. Alternative therapy that has been shown to be effective in treating seasonal depression.
j. Perspective that tries to understand a person's problems by looking at childhood experiences, unconscious drives, and unresolved conflicts, but that schedules weekly therapy for only a few months, rather than several years.

Term

(1) superego
(2) ego
(3) id
(4) transference
(5) psychodynamic perspective
(6) humanistic therapy
(7) unconditional positive regard
(8) aversive conditioning
(9) systematic desensitization
(10) explanatory style
(11) cognitive therapies
(12) light exposure therapy
(13) therapeutic touch therapy

Fill-in-the-Blank Questions

7. ______________ ______________ was the founder of psychoanalysis, a theory that attributes our thoughts and actions to unconscious motives and conflicts. Therapy based on this theory attempts to resolve conflicts by bringing them into consciousness.

8. ______________ ______________ was a humanistic psychologist who developed client-centered therapy, which uses techniques such as active listening to help clients reach their full potential.

Brief Essay Question

9. For no apparent reason, Carmen has been depressed for more than two weeks, and she wants to see a therapist. Carmen's sister, who doesn't believe therapy works, is encouraging her to get more sleep, stay busy, and use some self-discipline to feel better. Carmen has asked your opinion, knowing that you have been taking a psychology course. In two paragraphs of about three sentences each, explain to Carmen what psychologists believe about the effectiveness of psychotherapy.

Self-Test Answers

Matching Terms and Definitions

6. a. (4), b. (8), c. (1), d. (11), e. (3), f. (7), g. (10), h. (2), i. (12), j. (5)

Fill-in-the-Blank Questions

7. Sigmund Freud, 8. Carl Rogers

Brief Essay Question

9. Students should tell Carmen that she is already on the road to recovery since seeking help is often effective in making people better. Since she is experiencing certain symptoms that indicate a specific condition (depression), she will probably benefit from psychotherapy. Additionally, she needs to find a licensed practitioner so that her insurance will be more likely to cover her treatment and to ensure that she is receiving therapy based on researched techniques.

MODULE 31

Performance Standards

Standard Area: Treatment of Psychological Disorders

Content Standard 1: Treatment methods for psychological disorders

Performance Standard 1.1 Describe the various treatment techniques for those with psychological disorders.

- Explain how antipsychotic drugs work and discuss some of their negative side effects. (Student Text p. 601)
- Explore the use of antianxiety drugs. Discuss the dangers of extended use of antianxiety medications. (Student Text p. 602)
- Investigate antidepressant drugs, such as Prozac. Discuss how they affect the neurotransmitter serotonin. (Student Text pp. 602–604)
- Discuss the use of electroconvulsive therapy to treat severe depression. Investigate the mystery of how it works. (Student Text pp. 604–606)
- Examine new biomedical techniques, such as repetitive transcranial magnetic stimuation (rTMS), to treat depression. (Student Text p. 606)
- Consider the use of psychosurgery to treat psychological disorders. (Student Text pp. 606–607)

Performance Standard 1.2 Assess the effectiveness of various types of therapies and prevention.

- Discuss historical methods of treating those with psychological disorders before the development of drug therapies. (Student Text p. 599)
- Discuss deinstitutionalization and the implications for the homeless population in the United States. (Student Text pp. 599–600)
- Explain why it is so difficult to determine the effectiveness of antidepressants drugs. (Student Text pp. 602–604)
- Discuss the historic use of lobotomies. Explain why their use dropped off so rapidly after the early half of the twentieth century. (Student Text pp. 606–607)

Materials NETWORK

All of the items from the Video, Activity, and Enrichment Centers listed below come from the *Teacher's Resource Binder.* These items will help you teach and expand on concepts presented in Module 31.

trb This logo indicates when an item from the Materials Network may be used in conjunction with a specific note found in this module's *Teacher's Edition.*

Drug Therapies

V Video Center

Consult the faculty guide from *The Mind* and *The Brain* video series for descriptions of these modules.

- Videocassette: *The Mind,* Second Edition, Module 33: "Mood Disorders: Medication and Talk Therapy" (*Teacher's Resource Binder,* p. 31-1)
- Videocassette: *The Brain,* Second Edition, Module 28: "Schizophrenia: Pharmacological Treatment" (*Teacher's Resource Binder,* p. 31-1)

Activity Center

- Critical Thinking Activity: *Fact or Falsehood?* With this activity, students' preconceptions about biomedical therapies are either exposed as incorrect or reinforced as correct. (*Teacher's Resource Binder,* p. 31-1; Handout 31–1)

Enrichment Center

- Enrichment Lesson: *Fluoxetine (Prozac)* Introduced in 1987, fluoxetine (which students are more likely to recognize as Prozac) has become the world's most widely prescribed antidepressant. As of early 2000, more than 35 million people have used it. Students learn more about this popular drug in this lesson. (*Teacher's Resource Binder,* p. 31-1)
- Enrichment Lesson: *Cosmetic Psychopharmacology* Is it proper to prescribe Prozac to those who suffer no specific psychological disorder but who want to function more effectively in their personal and social lives? Is this "cosmetic psychopharmacology," akin to a psychological nose job? Students explore this question in this lesson. (*Teacher's Resource Binder,* p. 31-1)
- Enrichment Lesson: *A Pill for Stage Fright (Anxiety)* Michael Skoler reports that Inderal, a heart medication (known generically as propranolol), is the antianxiety drug for intellectuals. Unlike tranquilizers, Inderal does not cloud the mind or impair physical coordination. Professional musicians, lawyers, college students, and even physicians now take this beta-blocker before important presentations or tests. (*Teacher's Resource Binder,* p. 31-1)

Electroconvulsive Therapy

V Video Center

- Videocassette: *The Mind,* Second Edition Module 34: "Treating Depression: Electroconvulsive Therapy (ECT)" Consult the faculty guide from *The Mind* video series for a description of this module. (*Teacher's Resource Binder,* p. 31-1)

Enrichment Center

- Enrichment Lesson: *Electroconvulsive Therapy* Harold Sackeim has attempted to correct misconceptions surrounding ECT and to prove that it is a valid, even life-saving, option. (*Teacher's Resource Binder,* p. 31-1)

Psychosurgery

Enrichment Center

- Enrichment Lesson: *Lobotomies* This lesson extends the text's treatment of lobotomies, a disturbing and controversial treatment for mentally ill people. This surgery has a long and colorful history, and it took a combined force of science and public policy advocates to end its barbarous run. (*Teacher's Resource Binder,* p. 31-1)
- Enrichment Lesson: *Cingulotomy* For the most part, psychosurgery has become taboo, even though refinements targeting very limited areas in the brain are now much safer. One notable exception is a procedure known as cingulotomy, which has been performed at Massachusetts General Hospital. (*Teacher's Resource Binder,* p. 31-1)

MODULE 31

Biomedical Therapies

Introducing the Module

The Points: Module Objectives

- Explain how antipsychotic drugs work, pointing out some of their negative side effects.
- Evaluate the dangers of extended use of antianxiety medications.
- Analyze why it is difficult to determine the effectiveness of antidepressant drugs.
- Examine why electroconvulsive therapy is used, and explain how it works.
- Examine why lobotomies were performed so frequently in the first half of the twentieth century, and evaluate why their use dropped off rapidly after that.

Building Vocabulary

Have students create flashcards for the terms in this module. Students should write the term on one side of the flashcard. Where relevant, on the other side of the card, students should list the different disorders that type of drug or therapy treats in addition to the advantages and drawbacks of each.

web ■ **TEACHING TIP**

Students can learn more about the life of John Forbes Nash and the economic theory that earned him the Nobel Prize at the Web site **www.pbs.org/wgbh/amex/nash**. It extends the *American Experience* PBS television show entitled "A Brilliant Madness."

MODULE 31

Biomedical Therapies

Drug Therapies

Electroconvulsive Therapy

Psychosurgery

▶ **biomedical therapy** Treatment of psychological disorders that involves changing the brain's functioning by using prescribed drugs, electroconvulsive therapy, or surgery.

▶ **deinstitutionalization** The release of patients from mental hospitals to the community at large. The development of drug treatments led to an 80 percent decline in the number of hospitalized mental patients in the second half of the twentieth century.

Two films have won multiple Academy Awards, including Best Picture, for their examination of the **biomedical therapies** that are this module's topic. In 1975, *One Flew Over the Cuckoo's Nest* illustrated the horror of inappropriately using shock treatments and brain surgery as a way of punishing rather than treating hospitalized mental patients. In 2001, *A Beautiful Mind,* based on the true story of Nobel prize–winning mathematician John Nash's descent into and apparent recovery from paranoid schizophrenia, brought the issue of involuntary drug treatment to the forefront. These films illustrate the controversies that swirl around the biomedical therapies—controversies that are more intense than those related to the psychological therapies, which are based on changing thoughts, feelings, and behaviors through nonmedical means.

The biomedical approaches have received a lot of media attention, some portraying them accurately and some not. This has led to a degree of fear and uncertainty. Let's set the record straight concerning the three major biomedical approaches: drugs, electric shock, and surgery.

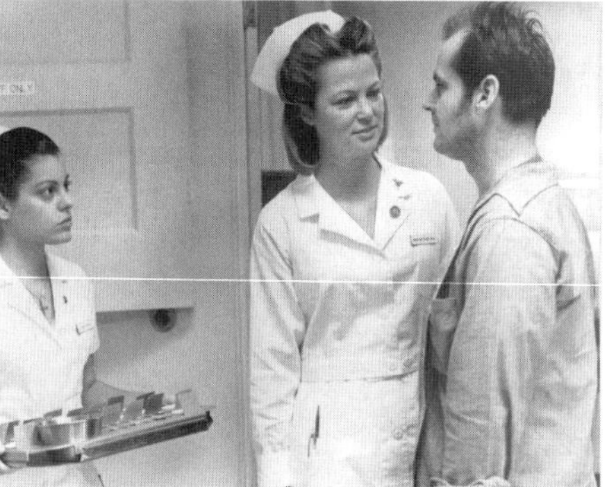

Dramatic Illustrations *One Flew Over the Cuckoo's Nest* and *A Beautiful Mind* both provide a historical perspective on how therapists have used biomedical treatments for mental disorders. They raise controversial issues related to these treatments.

Getting Started

Ask if students have seen either of the two films mentioned in this module: *One Flew Over the Cuckoo's Nest* and *A Beautiful Mind*. You might pose the following questions to students about those films:

- What were your impressions of the type of therapy used?
- What beliefs did you develop about institutionalization and being mentally ill from watching these movies?

trb You may wish to use **Critical Thinking Activity:** *Fact or Falsehood?* (*Teacher's Resource Binder*, p. 31-1; **Handout 31–1**) as a prereading strategy to evaluate what students already know about biomedical therapies. This activity will prime students to look out for information that could prove or disprove their preconceptions about these therapies.

Drug Therapies

Up into the 1950s, few options existed for treating serious psychological disorders such as schizophrenia. People with these disorders were usually hospitalized, but even in this environment the number of tools available for treatment was limited. Some hospitals were well run, with staffs who genuinely cared about the patients. Other less competent institutions served largely as warehouses, hiding away a segment of the population for whom little could be done. Patients often spent their days wiling away the hours in bare wards with no structured activities to occupy their time. Treatment—particularly in the 1800s and early 1900s—often subjected patients to mechanical devices that today strike us as little more than means of torture (Figure 31.1). Restraints, in the form of strait jackets and bed straps, vied with padded isolation rooms as techniques for preventing violent patients from harming themselves or others. It was a bleak picture of long-term hospitalization in a system that rarely produced improvement.

Figure 31.1 Treatment or Torture? Benjamin Rush developed this chair 200 years ago, believing that the restraint and restricted sensation it provided would help patients regain their self-control. Despite the look of this apparatus, Rush founded a movement to reform mental health care and treat mental patients with kindness.

That picture changed dramatically with the development of effective drug therapies in the middle of the twentieth century. Suddenly, therapists had a way to help patients overcome the most devastating symptoms of their illness and "break through" to a more stable hold on reality. Moreover, these drugs made it possible to release patients from the large warehouselike hospitals everyone agreed constituted a horrible environment in which to get well. After decades of increase, patient populations at the hospitals dropped rapidly. Releasing hospitalized mental patients to their communities is called **deinstitutionalization,** a mouthful of a word but one that accurately describes what occurred. By the end of the century, there were only one-fifth as many hospitalized patients as there were in 1950 (Figure 31.2, page 600) (Bureau of the Census, 1999).

In theory, deinstitutionalization was a wonderful advance. In practice, it did not work out quite as well as expected. If released patients lack resources and the support of family or friends, they often end up on the streets. This happened repeatedly as more and more people were treated with

Hospital or Warehouse? Before the advent of effective biomedical treatment, mental hospitals often did little more than house patients in bleak, crowded wards. How easy would it be to get well in an environment like this?

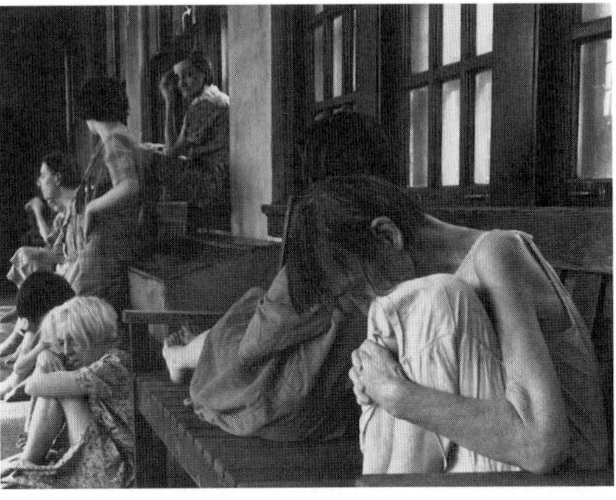

MODULE 31

Teaching the Points

web ■ TEACHING TIP

You can log on as an instructor to the book companion site for *Thinking About Psychology* at **www.worthpublishers.com/thinkingaboutpsych**. It contains teacher resources for class presentations as well as review and assessment of module concepts and terms.

F • Y • I

Until the early 1970s, people who weren't mentally ill were routinely committed involuntarily to mental hospitals. In many states, family members could commit a relative for any reason. Young women who became pregnant out of wedlock would be committed, as would wives of men who wanted a divorce. Mildly mentally retarded people would be placed in the same large, impersonal rooms as violent criminals, people with schizophrenia, and unwed mothers.

■ LOOKING AT THE ISSUES

Before a Supreme Court ruling in 1972, more than 5000 patients were housed at Bryce State Mental Hospital in Alabama. Doors in the older portions of the building, built in 1851, are short on the bottom by about a foot, which allowed caretakers at the hospital to slide food trays under the doors for the 200 or so patients to scramble to for a meal. As of 2003, Bryce housed roughly 400 patients in modern buildings. Patients are afforded private and semiprivate living quarters, and they are rarely kept there for more than six months.

Have students explore why such changes in institutions were needed. The following questions can guide research and a subsequent discussion of students' findings:

- What effect would such inhumane conditions have on a well person's mental health? Consider, then, the effect it would have on someone who suffered from paranoid schizophrenia or depression.
- What does current law in your state say about the rights of institutionalized mentally ill people?
- What do state and federal laws specify are the reasons someone can be committed?

Suggested Readings

Use the following books as teacher-preparation tools or as enrichment for advanced students:

Balter, M., & Katz, R. (1987). *Nobody's child.* Reading, MA: Addison-Wesley.

Baur, S. (1991). *The dinosaur man: Tales of madness and enchantment from the back ward.* New York: HarperCollins.

Johnson, A. B. (1990). *Out of Bedlam: The truth about deinstitutionalization.* New York: BasicBooks.

Kramer, P. (1993). *Listening to Prozac: A psychiatrist explores antidepressant drugs and the remaking of the self.* New York: Viking.

Sarason, I., & Sarason, B. (1999). *Abnormal psychology* (9th ed.). Upper Saddle River, NJ: Prentice Hall.

Szasz, T. S. (1994). *Cruel compassion: Psychiatric control of society's unwanted.* New York: Wiley.

Torrey, E. F. (1988). *Nowhere to go: The tragic odyssey of the homeless mentally ill.* New York: Harper & Row.

Winerip, M. (1994). *9 Highland Road: Sane living for the mentally ill.* New York: Vintage Books.

MODULE 31

■ APPLYING THE POINTS

Have students research the community mental health resources available in your community. Use the following questions to discuss students' findings:

- What types of services are available to the recently deinstitutionalized?
- What regulations must the patients follow to continue to receive services?
- How long can a patient receive services?
- Does insurance cover these services? If not, who pays for them?

tr A four-color transparency of Figure 31.2, Deinstitutionalization, is available in the **Overhead Transparencies Set.**

■ LOOKING AT THE ISSUES

Homelessness is very problematic for the mentally ill since these people do not have the support necessary to remain in treatment programs that address their illnesses. Have students research and discuss the following questions:

- What are the rates of homelessness for your area or for a major city in your state?
- What policies or services are offered for the mentally ill homeless?
- Are the homeless or mentally ill more likely to commit crimes?

■ TEACHING TIP

Distinguish between *main effects* and *side effects* of drug treatments:

- **Main effects** are the effects the drugs are supposed to create in patients. Antianxiety drugs and antidepressant drugs are supposed to decrease anxiety and depression in patients who take them.
- **Side effects** are unintended consequences of taking drugs. Patients may experience nausea, headaches, sexual side effects, and exacerbation of other medical conditions. Side effects can vary from person to person.

trb **tr** A black-line master of Figure 31.3, Drug Treatments, is available in the **Black-Line Masters Appendix** in the *Teacher's Resource Binder.*

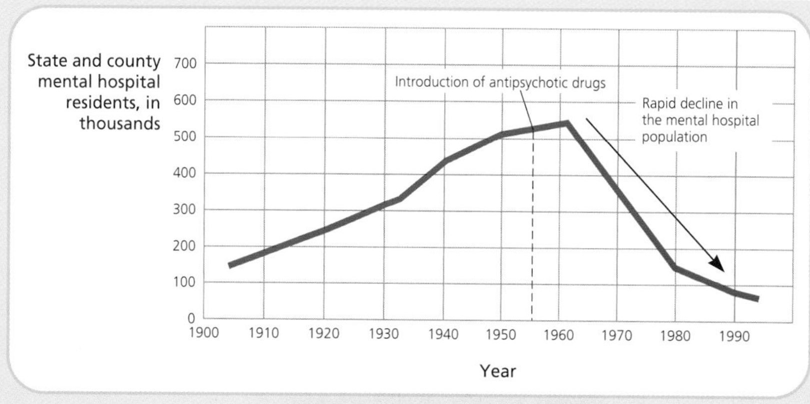

Figure 31.2
Deinstitutionalization Once medications for serious mental disorders were introduced in the 1950s, the number of people in mental hospitals dropped dramatically. Unfortunately, the homeless population has increased in the United States as the number of hospitalized mental patients has decreased. (Data from the National Institute of Mental Health and Bureau of the Census, 1999.)

drugs and released from state, county, and private mental hospitals. Our homeless population, which now numbers in the hundreds of thousands nationwide (Leshner, 1992), has increased as the population of hospitalized mental patients has decreased. Research shows that about one-third of the homeless population has a serious psychological disorder (Fischer & Breakey, 1991; McCarty & others, 1991).

The drugs that enabled deinstitutionalization fall into three broad categories (Figure 31.3): antipsychotic, antianxiety, and antidepressant. Like all drugs, they produce both main effects and side effects, some of which are undesirable. Establishing the correct dosage can be tricky because not everyone responds the same way. A decision to prescribe these drugs must therefore be made carefully, with attention to the details of the individual case.

Figure 31.3 **Drug Treatments**

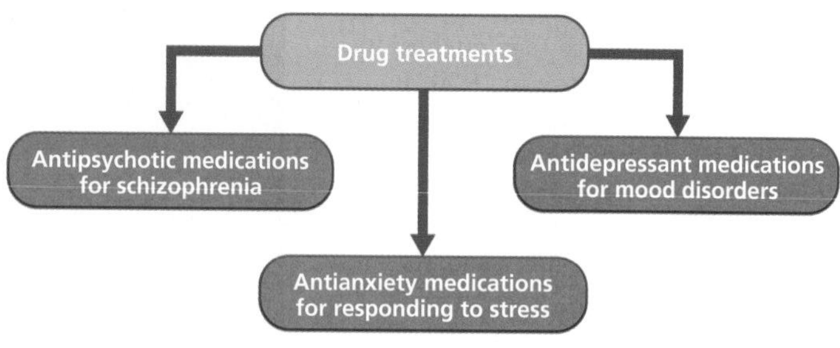

Cross-Curricular Connections

HISTORY Have students research the history of mental health care. From ancient practices, like trephining, to modern laws that outline those who can be committed and for how long, the history lesson will prove to be a rich eye-opener. Consider the following topics:

- trephining and other ancient methods of curing mental illness
- Phillipe Pinel and his pioneering work to bring humane treatment for the mentally ill to Europe
- Dorothea Dix's work to bring humane mental health treatment to the United States
- Supreme Court cases that ruled for more humane treatment of the mentally ill (including *Wyatt v. Stickney*)

For extra credit, invite students to develop and present oral reports to the class on the historical subject they researched.

Antipsychotic Drugs

What's the Point? 1. How do the antipsychotic drugs work, and what are some of their negative side effects?

▶ **antipsychotic drugs** A category of medications used primarily to treat schizophrenia.

Antipsychotic drugs are used primarily to treat *schizophrenia,* a serious psychological disorder that usually involves distorted thinking and perception in the form of delusions and hallucinations. Antipsychotic medications reduce the level of delusions and hallucinations (Lehman & others, 1998). They also help people with schizophrenia focus their attention on significant rather than irrelevant aspects of their environment, as when patients find it impossible to stop attending to the color of a wall or the sound of a clock. Many patients thus feel more connected to the real world. These drugs work by blocking the activity of the neurotransmitter *dopamine,* the brain chemical that, in high levels, is associated with schizophrenia.

The first dopamine-lowering drug, and the one most responsible for starting the move toward deinstitutionalization, was Thorazine, which is still on the market today. It has a host of negative side effects, including dry mouth, blurred vision, and constipation. Its most serious side effect is a permanent condition of muscle tremors known as *tardive dyskinesia,* which most often develops in patients who have taken large doses of the drug over a long period of time. This condition is similar to Parkinson's disease, which is associated with low levels of dopamine (Kaplan & Saddock, 1989).

One new drug with similar positive effects but fewer negative side effects is Clozaril, now considered the most effective treatment for schizophrenia (Wahlbeck & others, 1999). It is an expensive treatment, though, because those who use it must have their blood tested regularly to ensure that they aren't among the small percentage of patients who experience another serious side effect—damage to their white blood cells. An even newer drug, Risperdal, eliminates the need for such blood tests, but its use still costs the average user several thousand dollars each year. This is a rapidly evolving area, with new drugs being introduced regularly.

A Better Life Daphne Moss no longer suffers from paranoid delusions that her parents are witches thanks to the antipsychotic drug Clozapine. She is now able to hold a job and live independently.

Note that none of the antipsychotic drugs is a "feel-good" drug—these powerful substances do not produce the euphoric "high" that many people associate with drug use. In fact, the negative side effects are unpleasant enough that many people resist taking them, which contributes to the homelessness problem of deinstitutionalized patients. Individuals no longer under the supervision of hospital staff may not be motivated enough to continue their medication. Then the symptoms of their disease return, and they have even more difficulty succeeding in the outside world.

■ TEACHING TIP

Remind students that psychosis involves a break with reality. Breaks with reality can include delusions (false beliefs) and hallucinations. Researchers believe that these breaks with reality are the result of biochemical imbalances in the brain, which helps explain why antipsychotic drugs help patients who experience these problems.

■ LOOKING AT THE ISSUES

Some students may wonder why schizophrenic patients would stop taking their medications if those medicines were helpful in relieving the unpleasant psychotic symptoms they experience. People often resist taking medication because they feel like they are not their "normal" selves while on the drugs. Have students brainstorm about reasons people would be resistant to taking medication, sometimes for life, by posing the following questions:

- How might someone with paranoid schizophrenia view taking medication?
- How might someone with mania feel about taking drugs that made them less manic?
- How might someone with ADHD feel about taking drugs that made them less distracted?

(V) At this point, you may wish to show Videocassette: *The Mind,* Second Edition, Module 28: "Schizophrenia: Pharmacological Treatment" (*Teacher's Resource Binder,* p. 31-1).

■ CHECKING FOR UNDERSTANDING

Spot check students' understanding of antipsychotic drugs by having them summarize what drugs like Clozaril and Risperdal do, and to whom they are prescribed.

Enriching

Have students research the different types of drugs (mentioned in the questions below) for treatment of psychosis.

- How are Clozaril and Risperdal different from Thorazine?
- Do all bind exclusively to dopamine receptors? If not, what receptors do they bind to?
- Does insurance offer benefits for long-term use of these drugs? Why or why not?

Interested students might work in small groups to research the drugs cited above. For extra credit, each group can present an oral report of their findings to the class.

(V) At this point, you may wish to show Videocassette: *The Mind,* Second Edition, Module 28: "Schizophrenia: Pharmacological Treatment" (*Teacher's Resource Binder,* p. 31-1).

MODULE 31

F • Y • I

GABA, or gamma-aminobutyrate, is an amino acid that acts like a neurotransmitter throughout the body. GABA and its alter ego, glutamate, are more plentiful than any other neurotransmitter in the body. Although glutamate is excitatory, GABA is inhibitory, acting on the presynaptic cell to cause it to stop releasing its particular neurotransmitter into the synapse. By boosting GABA, antianxiety drugs stop the overabundance of neurotransmitters that cause tension.

■ TEACHING TIP

Link discussion of the *relief of tension* to *negative reinforcement.* Reinforcement is designed to encourage a behavior by either giving a reward or taking away something unpleasant. Negative reinforcement does the latter, taking away something that the person wants to avoid. In cases of anxiety, people are going to be more likely to take their drugs to relieve feelings of anxiety and tension because the drugs do take those feelings away. Although this is effective in the short term, the strong power of negative reinforcement encourages people to take drugs any time they feel anxious—even in situations they could handle without using drugs.

trb At this point, you may wish to use **Enrichment Lesson:** *A Pill for Stage Fright (Anxiety)* (*Teacher's Resource Binder,* p. 31-1).

■ JOURNAL WRITING

Invite students to use the following questions and writing prompts as springboards for entries in their psychology journals.

- Why might a drug/behavior therapy combination be more effective in alleviating anxiety than drugs or behavior therapy alone?
- Have you or someone you know taken prescription drugs to alleviate anxious or depressive feelings? Did they help?

V At this point, you may wish to show **Videocassette:** ***The Mind,* Second Edition, Module 33: Mood Disorders: "Medication and Talk Therapy"** (*Teacher's Resource Binder,* p. 31-1).

Unavoidable Stress The families and friends who waited more than three days for the rescue of nine miners in Pennsylvania in July of 2002 were under a great deal of stress, not knowing if their loved ones were dead or alive. In such situations, physicians sometimes prescribe antianxiety medications to help people cope with short-term stress. This story had a happy ending, with all nine miners safely rescued, but it was a very difficult time for their families.

Antianxiety Drugs

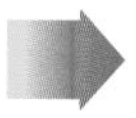

2. What are some dangers of extended use of antianxiety medications?

Antianxiety drugs are most often prescribed for people undergoing significant stress in their lives—divorce, loss of a job, the death of a loved one, and so forth. These drugs work, in part, by boosting a neurotransmitter (GABA) that helps our brain to reduce the anxiety associated with such stressful situations. This relief of tension—plus the drugs' sedative effect and ability to produce euphoria—is a powerful reinforcing influence that may keep people coming back to these drugs over and over until dependency develops. Antianxiety drugs, in and of themselves, do not solve a person's problems. Rather, they provide temporary relief. Whatever stressors led the person to take antianxiety medications are likely to still be present when the drug wears off. For all these reasons, these drugs are best used in combination with other forms of psychotherapy to help the individual learn effective coping strategies that ultimately will eliminate the need for the drug.

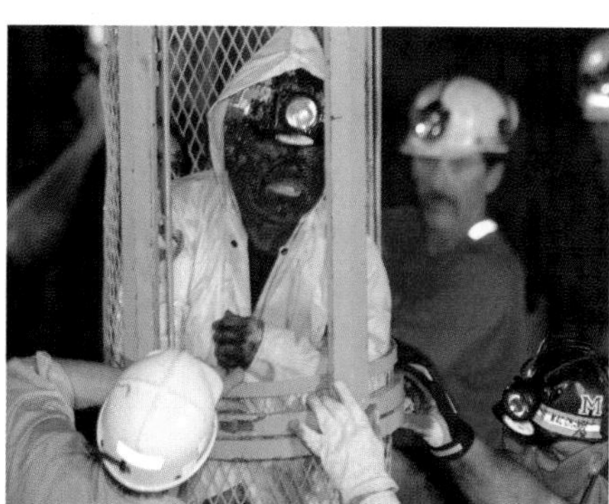

Examples of antianxiety drugs are Valium, Librium, and Xanax. They should not be taken with other central nervous system depressants such as alcohol because the interaction of the two types of substances can produce a potentially lethal overdose.

Antidepressant Drugs

3. Why is it difficult to determine the effectiveness of antidepressant drugs?

As the name so clearly indicates, **antidepressant drugs** are useful for treating major depression. There are several different groups of antidepressants, classified by the way they work, but all of them affect neurotransmitter chemicals in the brain, particularly *serotonin.* Low levels of serotonin are associated with depression, and these drugs boost the mood-lifting effect of serotonin in the brain.

This category includes Prozac, Zoloft, and Paxil, all of which are classified as *selective serotonin reuptake inhibitors.* This scary sounding phrase simply describes what the drugs do, which is to block the *reuptake,* or reabsorption, of serotonin after it has been released into the synapse—the gap separating two nerve cells (Figure 31.4). This blocking action causes the serotonin to remain active in the synapse longer than it otherwise would. The use of antidepressants has skyrocketed in recent years and

▶ **antianxiety drugs** A category of medications used to treat people with anxiety disorders or suffering stress.

▶ **antidepressant drugs** A category of medications used primarily to treat major depression.

Enriching

Have students use the following questions to research and discuss certain drugs:

- What type of receptors do drugs like Valium, Librium, and Xanax bind with?
- What are the side effects of taking these drugs?
- Are these drugs addictive? If so, how are patients monitored to prevent addiction?
- How are selective serotonin reuptake inhibitors (SSRIs) different from monamine oxidase inhibitors (MAOIs)? *(MAOIs are older types of drugs that are more dangerous when taken in overdose than SSRIs.)*
- What type of side effects do SSRIs have? How effective are these different types of drugs?

trb At this point, you may wish to use **Enrichment Lesson:** *Fluoxetine (Prozac)* (*Teacher's Resource Binder,* p. 31-1).

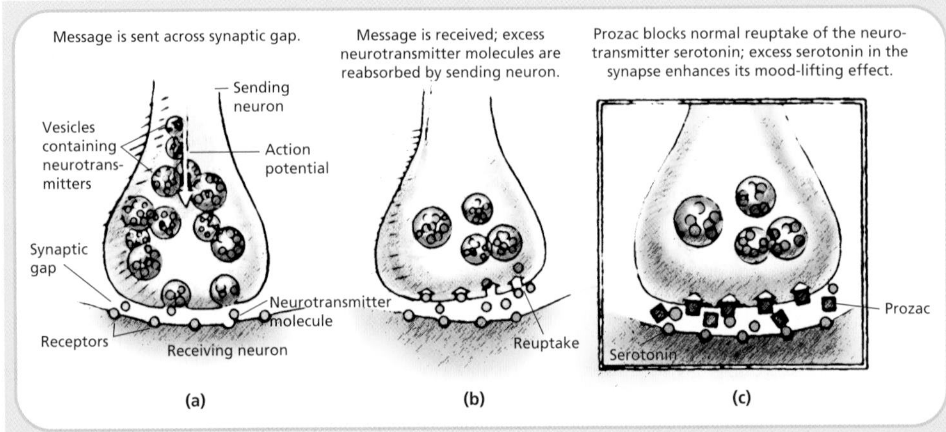

Figure 31.4 Prozac and the Brain Prozac acts to keep the neurotransmitter serotonin active longer than it otherwise would be. Higher levels of serotonin are associated with low levels of depression.

now accounts for almost $6 billion of prescriptions every year (Kaufman, 1999). Some veterinarians even prescribe Prozac for pet dogs to cure them of emotional problems perceived by their owners!

For reasons not yet fully understood, antidepressant medications must be taken for about a month before becoming fully effective. This therapeutic lag can be frustrating for the patient, especially if the first dose is too low to be effective or the first drug produces undesirable side effects. In such cases, several more weeks must elapse before the effectiveness of a different dose or a new drug can be determined. Of course, during this time, other factors can increase or decrease the patient's depression, clouding the effects of the drug. Once the proper dose of the proper drug has been determined, however, a person can usually stay on it for long periods of time with no further adjustment.

Judging the overall effectiveness of antidepressants is particularly difficult because depression is a *cyclical* disorder (Figure 31.5). This means that depression goes through cycles—just as normal moods do—lifting and deepening over time. Can you see how this cycling path makes it difficult to judge whether a medication is working? Say that a person with depression begins taking a drug like Prozac. Before any judgment can be made, the one-month therapeutic lag must pass. What if the depression lifts after that month? Can you reliably say that the drug worked? Not really, because you still don't know whether the improvement was due to the drug or to the cyclical nature of the disorder.

Other research confuses matters even further. One recent study (Kirsch & Sapirstein, 1998) combined the effects of almost two

Figure 31.5 A Mystery Researchers have yet to nail down exactly how antidepressants work. Their effect may be a combination of the factors listed here or of other factors not yet identified.

HOW DO ANTIDEPRESSANTS WORK?
1. They affect brain neurotransmitters.
2. They don't work. People's moods improve on their own because of the cyclical nature of depression.
3. They work because users expect them to work (the placebo effect).

MODULE 31

■ TEACHING TIPS

tr (1) A four-color transparency of Figure 31.4, Prozac and the Brain, is available in the **Overhead Transparencies Set.**

(2) Remind students that experiments seek to eliminate confounding variables—that is, those variables other than the independent variable that could explain the change in the dependent variable. In other words, confounding variables are any other factor that could cause the effect of the experiment to occur. In cases of research into antidepressants, the ebb-and-flow nature of the disorder could explain why symptoms are alleviated—not the drugs.

■ LOOKING AT THE ISSUES

In 2002, a "reality" television show followed model and actress Anna Nicole Smith as she tried to deal with the daily hassles of life. In one episode, she confessed that her dog had to take Prozac. The cameras showed a dog that seemed highly sedated and "spaced out." Have students research the subject of pets and psychological disorders. The following questions can guide a discussion of research findings:

- Do the drug companies that manufacture these drugs recommend their use with pets? Why or why not?
- What type of credentials does one need to have to be called a "pet psychiatrist"?
- What do veterinary medical associations say about the use of human drugs on animals?

trb At this point, you may wish to use **Enrichment Lesson:** *Fluoxetine (Prozac)* (*Teacher's Resource Binder*, p. 31-1).

Enriching

web A February 2003 study, published in the medical journal *The Lancet,* showed that long-term use of antidepressants reduced the number of relapses patients experienced. Researchers reviewed data from 31 trials involving more than 4000 depressed patients. In these trials, patients had finished the standard course of treatment (four to six months) and were offered an opportunity to continue treatment. One group of patients received a placebo while the other group took antidepressants. Since depression is a cyclic disorder, many patients suffered relapses, which longer drug therapy may have prevented.

Students may be interested in reading the full article or searching the Internet for other articles on long-term use of antidepressants.

Source: Reuters. (2003, February 21). *Longer use of antidepressants advised.* Retrieved February 22, 2003, from www.msnbc.com/news/875131.asp?0dm=C18OH.

MODULE 31

■ TEACHING TIP
Remind students that the placebo effect and the power of belief are very strong. Some studies show that simply seeking help seems to be the most influential factor in getting well. If people believe that a treatment will work, it often will—at least to the extent necessary for some people.

trb At this point, you may wish to use Enrichment Lesson: *Cosmetic Psychopharmacology* (*Teacher's Resource Binder*, p. 31-1).

■ LOOKING AT THE ISSUES
Invite interested students to investigate the evidence of the suicide-Prozac link and present their findings in a class forum.

- How many people's suicides are linked to their taking Prozac or other SSRIs?
- What evidence do opponents of the use of SSRIs use to support their contentions about these drugs' dangers?
- Is this evidence correlational or experimental? Is the government supporting any research to investigate this link?
- What might be some alternative explanations for the rate of suicide for people taking antidepressants?

trb At this point, you may wish to use Enrichment Lesson: *Fluoxetine (Prozac)* (*Teacher's Resource Binder*, p. 31-1).

■ MULTICULTURAL CONNECTIONS
Is the use of drugs to treat anxiety and depression common in all cultures? Have students research whether diverse cultures encourage the use of biomedical treatments for psychological disorders. Discuss students' findings with the following questions:

- Do countries that have a high incidence of anxiety and depression (war-torn countries, countries ravaged by disease and famine) encourage their citizens to seek help for these problems? Why or why not?
- Does the rate of drug use for treating anxiety and depression increase as gross domestic product (GDP) increases? Why or why not?

dozen carefully conducted studies. These studies compared the drug treatment results of one group given an antidepressant and another group given a *placebo*—a pill that has no chemical effect. People given the placebo reported almost as much improvement as people given the antidepressant medication. In other words, people's belief that they would feel better after being given a pill had almost as much effect on mood as did the real serotonin-enhancing drug!

Additional research will help answer the question of whether the improvement prompted by antidepressants is due more to the chemical effects of these drugs or to the expectations they produce. Such drugs sometimes have remarkably positive effects in people who might otherwise be seriously impaired, but they are not a miracle cure that instantly rids sufferers of their depression. Some of the very negative reports about the effects of the drugs—for example, that they produce suicidal behavior in a percentage of users—also require careful evaluation. Remember that users of antidepressant drugs are taking these substances precisely because they are searching for relief from depression. It should come as no surprise that a percentage of these users are suicidal—not because of the drug but because of the severity of their disorder. Carefully controlled research does not show an increased risk of suicide among users of antidepressant drugs (Tollefson & others, 1994).

One other drug deserves mention before we leave the antidepressants behind. It has been known since the 1940s that bipolar disorder, which produces wild mood swings from depression to high-energy, overly optimistic mania, responds well to compounds of *lithium*. Despite science's lack of understanding of exactly how lithium works, 70 percent of people with bipolar disorder show improvement when they take this drug (Solomon & others, 1995).

Drug therapies are changing rapidly, as new drugs are developed and older drugs are tested for multiple purposes. Our understanding of neurochemistry is growing daily, and as knowledge continues to accumulate, drug treatments should become more effective and the number of negative side effects should diminish.

Electroconvulsive Therapy

4. Why is electroconvulsive therapy used, and how does it work?

"Shock treatments." The very phrase is frightening, raising images of electrocution, pain, jerky convulsions, and Frankensteinlike laboratory experiments. Why would a doctor administer **electroconvulsive therapy (ECT)**, passing an electric current through a patient's brain until a convulsion is produced?

► **electroconvulsive therapy (ECT)** A therapy for major depression in which a brief electric current is sent through the brain of an anesthetized patient.

Cross-Curricular Connections

BIOLOGY Team-teach a lesson with your school's biology teacher on the effects of drugs on the brain and behavior. Have the biology teacher teach about the biological effects of drug use while you teach about the behavioral effects.

This form of therapy began to be used in Europe in the first half of the twentieth century. A depressed patient who also had diabetes experienced a convulsion after being given the wrong dose of insulin. Remarkably, when he recovered from the convulsion, his depression had lifted. This led to experiments in which nondiabetic depressed patients were given enough insulin to stimulate a convulsion. The results were encouraging, but the insulin was difficult to manage. Too small a dose would fail to produce a convulsion, and too large a dose would lead to death by overdose. By the late 1930s, the researchers found they could trigger convulsions far more reliably and safely with electricity than with chemicals. To do this, they placed electrodes on the patient's right and left temples and passed a current directly through the brain.

Although effective in treating depression, ECT was frightening to observe in its early days. Patients felt no pain when the shock was administered, because they instantly lost consciousness. However, the resulting convulsion caused every muscle in the body to contract, sometimes with enough force to break bones. At a minimum, patients would be very sore following the procedure. The modern version of ECT is far more humane (Figure 31.6). Medical personnel administer muscle relaxants in advance to greatly dampen the convulsion—often the only visible indication of convulsion is a minor twitch of the extremities. A sedative puts the patient to sleep, avoiding the rapid loss of consciousness that many found unpleasant.

ECT is almost always used to treat major depression, frequently when antidepressant drugs have failed. When a series of shocks is given (usually three a week for two to four weeks), 80 percent of people—even those who had not responded favorably to antidepressant drugs—show improvement (Coffey, 1993). ECT works more quickly than drugs and is effective even with deep depression, so it is sometimes used as a way to treat suicidal patients.

ECT's most serious side effect is disruption of memory, especially for the approximate time the

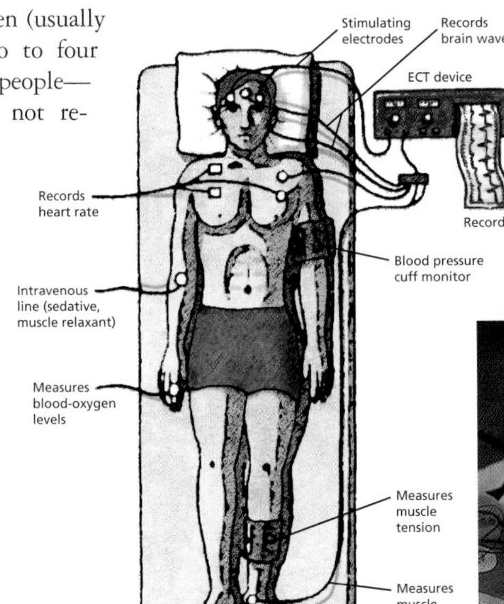

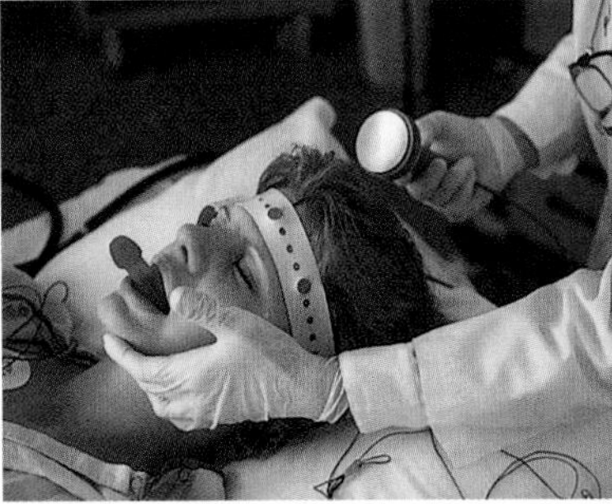

Figure 31.6
Electroconvulsive Therapy
ECT is an effective treatment for depression. Patients receiving this treatment are carefully monitored throughout the procedure. Physicians administer drugs to eliminate injuries due to convulsions and to relax the patient.

Cooperative Learning

Have students work in groups to discuss whether they would allow a loved one to use any of the therapies discussed in this module to treat a mental illness. The following questions can guide each group's discussion:

- Would you consider antianxiety, antidepressant, or antipsychotic drugs as a treatment for a mental illness? Why or why not?
- Would you allow a loved one to receive ECT to treat depression? Why or why not?
- What advice would you give a loved one if he or she were faced with these treatment options?

F•Y•I

(1) Insulin coma therapy was common in the early and middle parts of the twentieth century. John Forbes Nash, the Nobel Prize–winning mathematician featured in the Academy Award–winning motion picture *A Beautiful Mind*, endured this therapy as treatment for his paranoid schizophrenia. This type of therapy was shown to be highly effective—more than 70 percent of patients showed improvements of psychotic symptoms—but the therapy was difficult to control and not long-lasting. Other famous people subjected to insulin coma therapy were the first Secretary of Defense, James Forrestal (who eventually committed suicide), and Zelda Fitzgerald, wife of the author F. Scott Fitzgerald.

(2) The aim of electroconvulsive therapy (ECT) is to produce a seizure in the brain, similar to that which occurs spontaneously in some types of epilepsy. In fact, research suggests that without a seizure, ECT is ineffective. A small electric current passes through two electrodes placed on the patient's head. Only a portion of this current reaches the brain because most of it is deflected by the skull. Since muscle relaxants may interfere with breathing, an anesthesiologist administers oxygen. The muscle relaxants often block all outward signs of a seizure, and so the patient's brain waves must be monitored. The entire procedure takes approximately five minutes, and complications are rare.

(3) Since patients sleep through electroconvulsive therapy, it should come as no surprise that in one study 82 percent rated ECT as equally or no less upsetting than going to the dentist.

trb At this point, you may wish to use Enrichment Lesson: *Electroconvulsive Therapy* (*Teacher's Resource Binder*, p. 31-1).

V At this point, you may wish to show Videocassette: *The Mind*, Second Edition, Module 34: "Treating Depression: Electroconvulsive Therapy (ECT)" (*Teacher's Resource Binder*, p. 31-1).

MODULE 31

■ APPLYING THE POINTS

Contact a brain surgeon to discuss the use of psychosurgery in his or her practice. The following questions can guide the informal interview and presentation of your findings in class discussion:

- How often is psychosurgery performed? What patients make good candidates for psychosurgery?
- What types of psychosurgery are performed? What disorders are treated?

trb At this point, you may want to use **Enrichment Lesson:** *Cingulotomy* (*Teacher's Resource Binder*, p. 31-1).

F•Y•I

Lobotomies would have died out as a therapeutic treatment had it not been for Walter Freeman, an American physician and clinical neurologist. Freeman attended a London conference in which Moniz presented his research and became a proponent of the procedure. Freeman and his colleague, James Watts, developed the "Freeman-Watts Standard Procedure," which set strict guidelines for how to perform the surgery. Freeman eventually grew weary of the length and messiness of the Moniz-style operation, so he developed what became known as the "ice pick lobotomy." In this gruesome procedure, Freeman would insert a traditional ice pick into the eye sockets of anesthetized patients and, with a small mallet, would tap the pick through the tissue and bone into the prefrontal cortex. After insertion, he would swipe the pick back and forth like a wiper blade to sever the connections to the prefrontal cortex. This technique was much more efficient; also, it did not require a hospital stay for patients. Freeman would even have his interns time him as he performed assembly line-type operations, trying to set records for quick surgeries. But the technique was so gruesome that other neurosurgeons watching the procedure would faint at the sight. Even James Watts broke his ties with Freeman.

trb At this point, you may wish to use **Enrichment Lesson:** *Lobotomies* (*Teacher's Resource Binder*, p. 31-1).

treatment was administered, but researchers have been unable to identify any brain damage resulting from the procedure. The newest version of the procedure uses briefer electrical pulses, which seem to cause less memory loss (Fink, 1999).

If you're wondering just how administering electric shocks to the brain could alleviate depression, you're not alone. One theory says that the procedure stimulates the brain to release neurotransmitters that elevate mood, but we have no data to support this or any alternative explanation (Kapur & Mann, 1993). Our lack of understanding about how ECT works, combined with its potential for serious side effects such as memory loss, fuel continuing controversy about this treatment. To those who have been helped, however, the reason it works is less important than the fact that it does.

Research is under way to discover related, less traumatic, procedures. One promising technique, *repetitive transcranial magnetic stimulation* (rTMS), uses magnetic fields instead of electricity and usually does not produce convulsions. In one study, people who received a series of rTMS treatments showed significantly more improvement than a control group did (Klein & others, 1999).

Psychosurgery

5. Why were lobotomies performed so frequently in the early half of the twentieth century, and why did their use drop off rapidly after that?

If the specter of therapy by shocking the brain is frightening, the thought of curing by cutting is downright petrifying. The most famous example of psychosurgery was a procedure called a **lobotomy,** and it is extremely rare today. The procedure has a fascinating history, and it touched the lives of tens of thousands of patients in the United States until drug treatments replaced it in the 1950s (Valenstein, 1986). When Egas Moniz first introduced this surgery in Portugal, it was greeted with such enthusiasm that he received a Nobel prize for his work. Moniz theorized that serious disorders such as schizophrenia occurred because the brain's deep emotional centers overwhelmed the person's ability to use the rational functions of the frontal lobe. The "solution" was to disconnect the frontal lobe from the emotional centers. How? By inserting an icepicklike tool next to the eye of an unconscious patient, driving it through the thin bone of the eye socket, and swinging the pick to cut the connections at the base of the frontal lobe. This procedure could be done in minutes without even opening the skull. Two American physicians, Walter Freeman and James Watts, brought the procedure to the United States and toured from hospital to hospital performing literally thousands of lobotomies.

► **lobotomy** A now-rare form of psychosurgery once used to try to calm uncontrollably emotional or violent patients. The procedure cut the nerves that connect the frontal lobes of the brain to the deeper emotional centers.

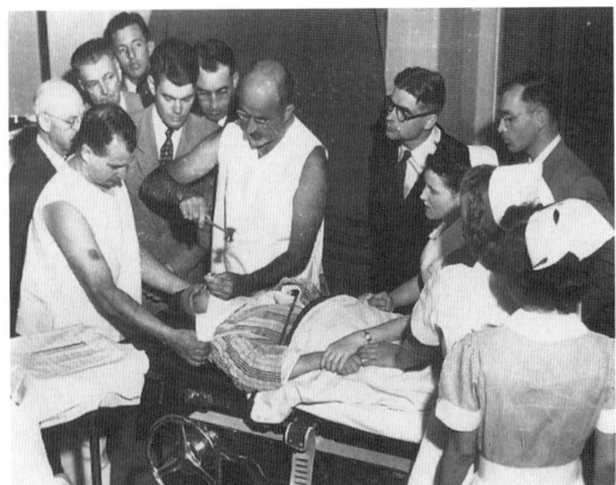

Lobotomy In this 1949 photograph, Walter Freeman demonstrates the procedure for a lobotomy. Freeman and his colleague James Watts performed thousands of such operations in the 1940s.

Moniz and his followers intended that lobotomies would be used only on uncontrollable and violent patients with schizophrenia. Remember that the procedure was developed before the antipsychotic drugs, when very few treatments were available. There were isolated cases when it worked well, but the initial rush of confidence in the procedure meant that most cases were not thoroughly evaluated for appropriateness, and few were adequately followed up after the surgery. It would be an overstatement to say that lobotomized patients were "vegetables," but much too often, the procedure reduced them to a very unmotivated and immature state in which they vacantly stared into space for long periods of time.

Public reaction to lobotomies was so negative that researchers have been reluctant to explore other, less drastic surgical procedures. In a relatively small number of cases, precisely guided surgical lesions are used to destroy very small areas of brain tissue in an effort to control seizures or disrupt severe obsessive-compulsive patterns that have not responded to other kinds of treatment (Sachdev & Sachdev, 1997). Given the permanent nature of surgery and the history of lobotomies in the United States, these new procedures are used only as a last resort.

A wide variety of therapies is available for treating psychological disorders. In this module, we have focused on biologically based medical approaches. Researchers have made tremendous strides in learning what treatments are effective and now guide patients toward the right treatment—or combination of treatments—to reduce their suffering. As former American Psychological Association president Martin Seligman says, "At least 14 disorders, previously intractable, have yielded their secrets to science and can now be either cured or considerably relieved" (Seligman & Csikszentmihalyi, 2000). We can surely say that the future is indeed much brighter than the past for the treatment of mental disorders.

■ TEACHING TIP

Remind students of the importance of the scientific method in testing a therapy's effectiveness. An overzealous physician, relying on anecdotal data, can promote a treatment that is not actually as effective as it may appear. Confirmation bias can cloud a person's ability to see evidence that contradicts what is believed to be true. Had Walter Freeman followed experimental procedures to test his belief in the effectiveness of the lobotomy, thousands of people may not have endured this inhumane treatment.

trb At this point, you may wish to use **Enrichment Lesson:** *Lobotomies* (*Teacher's Resource Binder*, p. 31-1).

Close

Today, the future is brighter for people suffering from mental disorders, but has the stigma associated with mental illness decreased with this brighter outlook? Have students discuss how they would feel if they or someone they loved were diagnosed with a mental disorder.

- Would they view it as a cognitive or biological problem? Would they seek medical treatment or psychological treatment? Why or why not?
- What type of advice and support would they give someone who was suffering from a mental disorder?

Meeting Individual Needs

trb **tr** Use any of the black-line masters from the **Black-Line Masters Appendix** in the *Teacher's Resource Binder* or four-color transparencies provided in the **Overhead Transparencies Set** to review the concepts from this module with students. Create a handout with terms blanked out for students to fill in, or cover up the terms on the transparency and have students call out the right answers as you quiz them on the relevant information.

- **Exceptional Learners** The black-line masters for this module can fill the need to provide notes for exceptional learners. These students may review terms with a student or teacher/tutor. They may refer to the black-line masters during class discussion or lecture.

MODULE 31

Checking the Points

■ TEACHING TIPS

web (1) The book companion site for *Thinking About Psychology* at www.worthpublishers.com/thinkingaboutpsych contains a module quiz, flashcards of key terms and people, and other student activities and resources for this module. You will also find PowerPoint lectures, a quiz grade book, and other teaching resources by logging on as an instructor.

trb (2) At this point, you may wish to review and confirm concepts about biomedical therapies with **Critical Thinking Activity:** *Fact or Falsehood?* (*Teacher's Resource Binder*, p. 31-1; **Handout 31–1**). If students worked with this handout earlier, have them not refer to that version. Suggest that students complete the handout in small groups, taking the time to look up information in the text to respond correctly to questions. Have all the groups meet to review the handout, again using the text to support responses.

REVIEW

Module 31: Biomedical Therapies

What's the Point?

There are three major biomedical approaches to therapy: drugs, electric shock, and surgery.

Drug Therapies

Before the advent of drug therapies in the 1950s, there were few treatment options for serious mental disorders, and most patients with these disorders were institutionalized in mental hospitals. The introduction of antipsychotic, antianxiety, and antidepressant drugs allowed more people to be treated outside of hospitals. This led to deinstitutionalization, which in theory was a good thing. However, without supervision, many patients stopped taking their medications, and as a result joined the homeless population on America's streets.

1. *How do the antipsychotic drugs work, and what are some of their negative side effects?*

   Antipsychotic drugs work by blocking the activity of brain chemicals known as neurotransmitters, particularly the neurotransmitter dopamine. These drugs are used mainly to treat schizophrenia, a serious disorder associated with high levels of dopamine. Antipsychotic drugs have negative side effects, including a permanent condition of muscle tremors and—in some cases—damage to white blood cells. The least damaging antipsychotic drugs are extremely expensive.

2. *What are some dangers of extended use of antianxiety medications?*

   By boosting the neurotransmitter GABA, antianxiety drugs reduce anxiety associated with stressful situations. Because these drugs have a sedative effect and can produce euphoria, they have a high potential for dependence and abuse. Antianxiety drugs can also interact with other central nervous system depressants, leading to death by overdose.

3. *Why is it difficult to determine the effectiveness of antidepressant drugs?*

   Antidepressant drugs relieve depression by raising levels of neurotransmitters, particularly serotonin, available in the brain. Depression is associated with low levels of serotonin. Some of these drugs block the brain cells' normal tendency to reabsorb serotonin after a certain period of time, thus prolonging the period when this substance is available. Because antidepressants need about a month to begin working, it is difficult to judge whether a decrease in depression during or after that time is a direct result of the medication or was caused by something else that happened during that period of time. Because depression is a cyclical disorder, it surges and wanes, further clouding the effects of the antianxiety drugs. And, as research has shown, people who receive any pill tend to experience a placebo effect—an expectation that something will happen, even if they have unknowingly taken only a sugar pill.

Electroconvulsive Therapy

4. *Why is electroconvulsive therapy used, and how does it work?*

   Electroconvulsive therapy (ECT) is a procedure in which medical personnel attach electrodes to a person's temples and pass an electric current through the brain to produce a convulsion. This therapy is still used, almost exclusively for major depression when all other treatments have failed, for one reason: It works. About 80 percent of people who suffer from serious depression and receive a series of ECT treatments show some improvement. No one understands why ECT works, though one theory proposes that the procedure stimulates the brain to release neurotransmitters that elevate mood. No data support this theory at this time.

Psychosurgery

5. *Why were lobotomies performed so frequently in the early half of the twentieth century, and why did their use drop off rapidly after that?*

   Lobotomies, popular in Europe and the United States in the first half of the twentieth century, were a fairly primitive form of psychosurgery in which a pick was inserted through the bone of the eye socket and twisted to cut the connections at the base of the frontal lobe. The intent was to sever the connection between the brain's emotional centers and the frontal lobe, which is the rational center. The surgery was relatively quick and easy, and it was touted as an instant cure for uncontrollable and violent patients. Many patients who had this procedure suffered serious side effects, losing motivation and staring vacantly into space. With the introduction of the antipsychotic drugs in the mid-1950s, coinciding with growing evidence of the surgery's inability to deliver on its promise, lobotomies were no longer performed.

Key Terms

biomedical therapy, p. 598
deinstitutionalization, p. 599
antipsychotic drugs, p. 601
antianxiety drugs, p. 602
antidepressant drugs, p. 602
electroconvulsive therapy (ECT), p. 604
lobotomy, p. 606

Self-Test

Multiple-Choice Questions

Choose the *best* answer for each of the following questions.

1. After observing her wild mood swings—from depression to high-energy, overly optimistic mania and then back to depression—Arleen's doctor made his diagnosis: bipolar disorder. For this condition, he will probably prescribe
   a. lithium.
   b. an antipsychotic drug.
   c. an antianxiety drug.
   d. a lobotomy.
2. Paul was one of the firefighters who participated in the 9/11 rescue efforts. Ever since that time, he has been feeling very stressed and unable to sleep. His physician may prescribe
   a. electroconvulsive therapy.
   b. an antianxiety drug.
   c. an antipsychotic drug.
   d. lithium.
3. Betty, who lives in a rural community, has suffered with major depression for years. She has had "talk" therapy, taken antidepressants, and changed her daily eating, sleeping, and exercising patterns, but nothing seems to help. Betty's physician is now recommending electroconvulsive therapy (ECT). Betty's physician

MODULE 31

Checking the Points

■ **TEACHING TIP**

If students created flashcards earlier in the module, those flashcards can now serve as a tool for review. Otherwise, have students create flashcards for the module terms. Students should write the term on one side of the flashcard. Where relevant, on the other side of the card, students should list the different disorders the type of drug or therapy treats in addition to the advantages and drawbacks of each.

tb Using the Test Bank

The *Test Bank* that accompanies this textbook offers a wide variety of questions in different formats and levels of complexity. Use the software to construct whole tests or to integrate standardized questions into teacher-made tests.

Self-Test Answers

Multiple-Choice Questions

1. a, 2. b, 3. c

MODULE 31

Self-Test Answers

Multiple-Choice Questions (continued)

4. b, 5. d

Matching Terms and Definitions

6. a. (3), b. (4), c. (2), d. (5), e. (1), f. (7)

Fill-in-the-Blank Questions

7. Antipsychotic, 8. Antianxiety, 9. Antidepressant

a. has lost touch with current practice; this treatment is no longer used because it is brutal and it does not work.
b. has lost touch with current practice; lobotomies are the treatment of choice for major depression, when other treatments have failed.
c. is making a sound recommendation; ECT often relieves major depression when other treatments cannot.
d. is making a sound recommendation, but he should have recommended ECT before trying the other forms of therapy.

4. Ronnie has delusions (he thinks he is the King of England), and he also has hallucinations (he sees and hears crowds cheering for him). Ronnie's physician has diagnosed his condition as schizophrenia, and she will probably prescribe
   a. an antidepressant drug.
   b. an antipsychotic drug.
   c. an antianxiety drug.
   d. lithium.

5. Marcus has been taking an antidepressant medication for about three weeks now, and he really doesn't feel any better than he did before he started taking the drug. Marcus is worried that he is taking the wrong medication. The best thing he could do right now is to
   a. stop taking the drug; if it isn't working, there is no use wasting the money.
   b. stop taking the drug and to ask his doctor to prescribe something else.
   c. stop taking the drug; depression is a cyclical condition, and it will probably clear up on its own.
   d. continue taking the drug for another week or two to see if the lack of effect is merely a therapeutic lag, which is normal for antidepressants.

Matching Terms and Definitions

6. For each definition, choose the *best* matching term from the list that follows:

Definition

a. Psychosurgery that severs the nerves connecting the brain's frontal lobes to the deeper emotional centers.
b. Brain chemical that, in high levels, is associated with schizophrenia; antipsychotic drugs lower the levels of this chemical.
c. Therapy for major depression in which a brief electric current is sent through the brain of an anesthetized patient.
d. Antianxiety drugs, often prescribed for people undergoing significant stress or anxiety.
e. The release of patients from mental hospitals to the community at large.
f. Brain chemical that, in low levels, is associated with depression; antidepressants increase the available levels of this chemical.

Term

(1) deinstitutionalization
(2) electroconvulsive therapy
(3) lobotomy
(4) dopamine
(5) Valium, Librium, and Xanax
(6) lithium
(7) serotonin

Fill-in-the-Blank Questions

7. ______________ drugs are used primarily to treat schizophrenia.

8. ______________ drugs are used primarily to treat people with anxiety disorders or suffering stress.

9. ______________ drugs are used primarily to treat major depression.

Brief Essay Question

10. When then-President Mikhail Gorbachev visited the United States in 1990, the media questioned him about poverty and restrictions on freedom in what was then the USSR. Gorbachev replied, with some irritation, that at least people did not have to sleep in the streets in his country. Imagine that you were appointed by the U.S. President to explain to Gorbachev how so many people with serious psychological disorders became part of the country's homeless population. Use two or three paragraphs, of two or three sentences each, to explain this situation and tell Gorbachev how this situation is related to current treatment of psychological disorders with drug therapy.

Self-Test Answers

Brief Essay Question

10. Students should discuss deinstitutionalization, a phenomenon that resulted from the effectiveness of drug therapy to alleviate symptoms of mental illness. Homelessness occurs among the mentally ill when these people do not receive the support they need after being released and when they choose not to continue their medications because of their increased freedom outside the institution.

CHAPTER 14 Social and Cultural Dimensions of Behavior

Clinical and Sociocultural Domain

Teaching with the Standards

Standard Area: Social and Cultural Dimensions of Behavior

Breakdown of Module 32: Social Thinking and Social Influence

Content Standard 1: Social thinking Module 32 introduces students to how we form our beliefs and attitudes. The author explains how we attribute behavior to personal dispositions or the situation. In addition, students are presented with research that demonstrates how our attitudes and actions interact. Foot-in-the-door phenomenon, role playing, and cognitive dissonance are all discussed as ways our actions affect our attitudes. (Student Text pp. 613–620)

Content Standard 3: Group influence Research has demonstrated that the presence of others can influence our actions. The author explains the concepts of social facilitation, social loafing, deindividuation, group polarization, and groupthink to help students understand this connection. (Student Text pp. 625–631)

Content Standard 4: Social influence Module 32 presents research on how others influence our behavior. The conditions under which we are most likely to conform and obey are investigated. The research of Solomon Asch and Stanley Milgram are considered. Groupthink is explained in the context of the 1986 shuttle disaster. (Student Text pp. 620–625, 629)

Breakdown of Module 33: Social Relations

Content Standard 1: Social thinking Module 33 investigates how physical attractiveness influences our perceptions of others. (Student Text pp. 636–637)

Content Standard 3: Group influence Module 33 examines the effects of the presence of others on individual behavior. The case of Kitty Genovese introduces students to Darley and Latané's research on bystander intervention. In addition, prejudice, stereotypes, and discrimination are defined. The concepts of ingroups, outgroups, and scapegoating are related to those concepts. Also, the author explains how categorization and the just-world phenomenon lead to the development of prejudice. Sherif's research on superordinate goals that reduce conflict among groups is discussed. (Student Text pp. 640–646, 651)

Content Standard 4: Social influence Module 33 discusses the nature of altruism in our society. Specifically the author focuses on which conditions promote altruism, such as bystander intervention, location, mood, and similarity. In addition, this module focuses on how our genetics, nervous system, biochemistry, and learning contribute to aggression. (Student Text pp. 640–642, 647–651)

Breakdown of Module 34: Cross-Cultural Psychology

Content Standard 2: Define social and cultural categories Module 34 focuses on defining culture and discussing how cultures develop. Individualistic and collectivistic cultures are compared. Universal and culture-specific behaviors and principles are defined. The author also investigates how cross-cultural research adds perspective to psychological research on personality and child development. Ethnocentrism is defined along with suggestions of how we can stay as free as possible from its influences. (Student Text pp. 656–667)

Standard Area: Life Span Development

Content Standard 3: Stage theories Module 34 investigates how culture and ethnic identity develop. Individualistic and collectivistic cultures are compared as to how such cultural differences affect development. Specifically, the author focuses on the development of self-concept, motivation, and emotion. In addition, universal and culture-specific behaviors are examined. Ethnocentrism is defined and suggestions made as to how to keep ourselves free from its influences. (Student Text pp. 656–662, 666–667)

Scope and Sequence

	Objectives	Text Reference	Standards Covered
Lesson 1	Introduce social psychology. Discuss attribution theory. Examine the relationship between our attitudes and actions.	Module 32, pp. 613–619	Standard Area: Social and Cultural Dimensions of Behavior, Content Standard 1, Performance Standards 1.2, 1.3
Lesson 2	Investigate social influence. Discuss the factors that influence conformity and obedience to authority. Discuss group influence.	Module 32, pp. 620–629	Content Standard 3, Performance Standard 3.1, Content Standard 4, Performance Standard 4.1
Lesson 3	Discuss attraction. Investigate friendship and the different types of love.	Module 33, pp. 635–639	Content Standard 1, Performance Standard 1.1
Lesson 4	Define altruism. Discuss the conditions that foster altruism in our society. Define aggression. Discuss the factors that lead to aggression.	Module 33, pp. 640-642, 647–651	Content Standard 3, Performance Standard 3.1, Content Standard 4, Performance Standards 4.2, 4.3
Lesson 5	Define prejudice, stereotypes, and discrimination. Discuss the factors that lead to prejudice. Examine how to foster cooperation among groups.	Module 33, pp. 642–646, 651	Content Standard 3, Performance Standards 3.2, 3.3
Lesson 6	Define culture. Examine how cultures develop. Compare individualistic and collectivistic cultures. Discuss how universal and culture-specific behaviors and principles differ.	Module 34, pp. 656–662	Standard Area: Social and Cultural Dimensions of Behavior, Content Standard 2, Performance Standards 2.1, 2.2, Standard Area: Life Span Development, Content Standard 3, Performance Standards 3.3, 3.4
Lesson 7	Discuss how a cross-cultural perspective influences our understanding of personality and child development. Define ethnocentrism. Explain how we can avoid ethnocentric thinking.	Module 34, pp. 662–667	Standard Area: Social and Cultural Dimensions of Behavior, Content Standard 2, Performance Standards 2.1, 2.2, Standard Area: Life Span Development, Content Standard 3, Performance Standards 3.3, 3.4
Lesson 8	Review and test		

CHAPTER 14

Sociocultural Dimensions of Behavior

Introducing the Chapter

The Points: Chapter Objectives

- Differentiate between dispositional attribution and situational attribution.
- Identify the conditions in which people are more likely to conform and obey.
- Determine how the presence of others influences actions.
- Analyze how group polarization and groupthink demonstrate the power of group influence.
- Analyze how self-fulfilling prophecies and minority influence demonstrate the power of the individual.
- Evaluate why people are attracted to some people and not to others.
- Define passionate and companionate love, differentiating between the two.
- Describe the conditions under which people are more likely to help others.
- Differentiate among the terms prejudice, stereotype, and discrimination.
- Relate the concepts of ingroups, outgroups, and scapegoats to the concepts of prejudice, stereotypes, and discrimination.
- Determine how genetics, the nervous system, and biochemistry contribute to aggression.
- Describe what helps foster cooperation among groups.
- Define culture, describing how it develops.
- Differentiate between individualism and collectivism.
- Analyze how universal behaviors and principles differ from culture-specific behaviors and principles.
- Determine the perspective cross-cultural research gives on personality theory.
- Analyze what cross-cultural psychology says about child development.
- Define ethnocentrism.

CHAPTER 14

Sociocultural Dimensions of Behavior

Many of the topics we have examined in earlier modules have focused on humans as individuals—brain processes, sensations, perceptions, motivations, emotions, and so on. But no man—or woman—is an island. Each of us is a social being, influencing and being influenced by others in our world. In these final three modules, we examine some of those influences and relationships. Finally, before leaving the world of psychology, we will consider whether our individual cultures place blinders on us, limiting our ability to understand others, and—if so—how we can improve our view of people who do not share our history and beliefs.

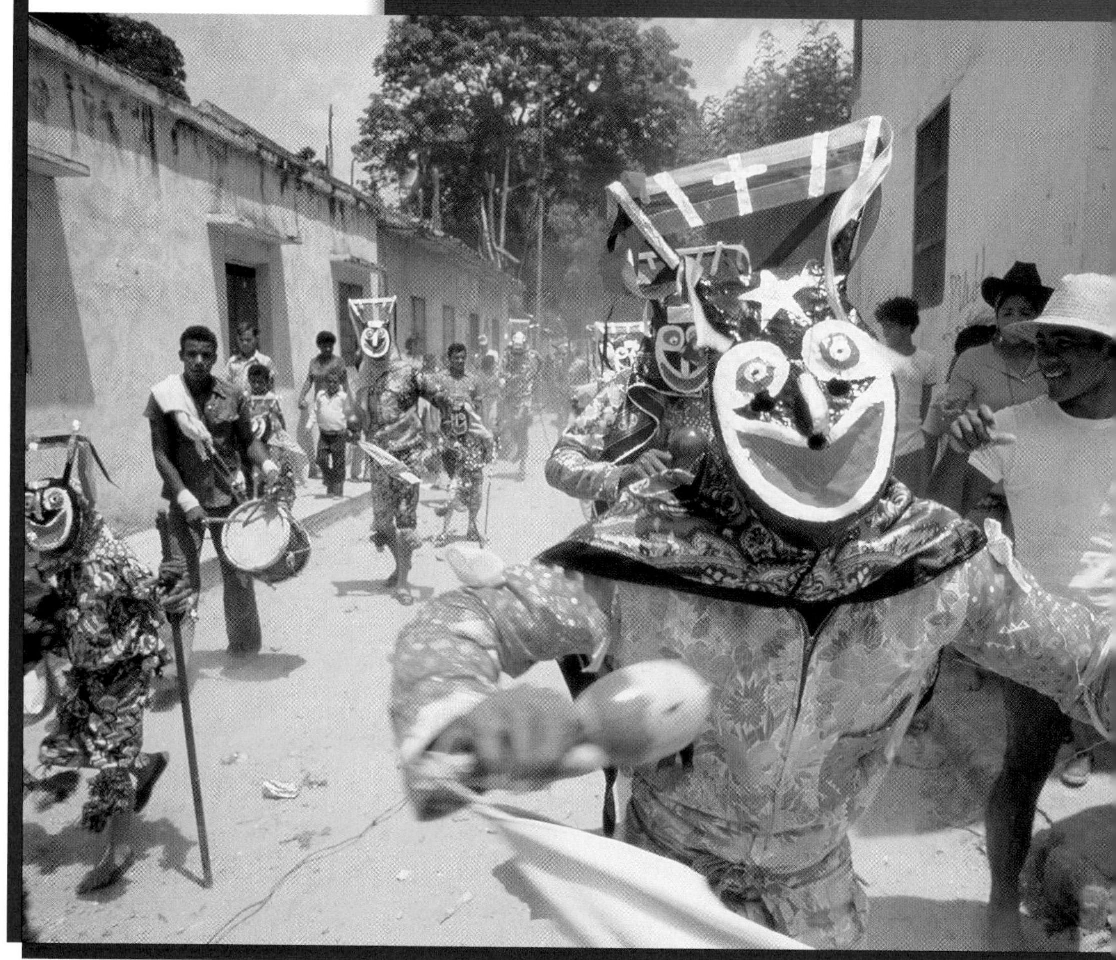

Performance Standards

Standard Area: Social and Cultural Dimensions of Behavior

Content Standard 1: Social thinking

Performance Standard 1.2 Explain how attributions affect how we explain behavior.

- Discuss attribution theory. Compare situational and dispositional attributions. Explain the fundamental attribution error. (Student Text pp. 614–616)

Performance Standard 1.3 Identify sources of attitude formation.

- Explain the effect of attitudes on our actions. (Student Text p. 617)
- Discuss the effects of actions on our attitudes. Focus on the foot-in-the-door phenomenon, role playing, and cognitive dissonance. (Student Text pp. 617–620)

Content Standard 3: Group influence

Performance Standard 3.1 Explain how the presence of others affects individual behavior.

- Discuss how the presence of others influences our actions. Focus on the concepts of social facilitation, social loafing, and deindividuation. (Student Text pp. 625–627)
- Discuss how group polarization and groupthink demonstrate the power of group influence. (Student Text pp. 628–629)

Content Standard 4: Social influence

Performance Standard 4.1 Investigate conditions under which conformity and obedience are fostered.

- Define conformity. Examine the results of Solomon Asch's research on conformity. Discuss the conditions under which we are most likely to conform. (Student Text pp. 621–623)
- Define obedience. Investigate the results of Stanley Milgram's research on obedience to authority. Discuss the conditions under which we are most likely to obey. (Student Text pp. 623–625)
- Explain the role of groupthink in contributing to the *Challenger* shuttle disaster. (Student Text p. 629)

Materials NETWORK

All of the items from the Video, Activity, and Enrichment Centers listed below come from the *Teacher's Resource Binder*. These items will help you teach and expand on concepts presented in Module 32.

trb This logo indicates when an item from the Materials Network may be used in conjunction with a specific note found in this module's *Teacher's Edition*.

Social Thinking

Activity Center

- Critical Thinking Activity: *Fact or Falsehood?* With this activity, students' preconceptions about social thinking and social influence are either exposed as incorrect or reinforced as correct. (*Teacher's Resource Binder*, p. 32-1; Handout 32–1)
- Building Vocabulary: Graphic Organizer: *Crossword Puzzle* Students can learn the concepts in this module by completing this crossword puzzle. (*Teacher's Resource Binder*, p. 32-1; Handout 32–2)
- Technology Application Activity: *Social Psychology on the Web* Students can access this Web site and participate in on-line experiments, tutorials, and activities that are designed to increase understanding of social psychology. (*Teacher's Resource Binder*, p. 32-1; Handout 32–3)
- Critical Thinking Activity: *The Fundamental Attribution Error* You can introduce this error by replicating the findings of Richard Nisbett and his colleagues. (*Teacher's Resource Binder*, p. 32-1; Handout 32–4)
- Critical Thinking Activity: *Students' Perceptions of You* If you are feeling courageous, ask students to use this activity to give their impressions of you. (*Teacher's Resource Binder*, p. 32-1; Handout 32–4)
- Critical Thinking Activity: *Introducing Cognitive Dissonance Theory* In this activity, students predict the outcomes of research on cognitive dissonance. (*Teacher's Resource Binder*, p. 32-1; Transparency Master 32–1)

Enrichment Center

- Enrichment Lesson: *Attribution and Models of Helping* This lesson presents findings by Philip Brickman and his colleagues. (*Teacher's Resource Binder*, p. 32-1)
- Enrichment Lesson: *The Looking Glass Effect* This lesson presents more on what researchers have learned about this phenomenon. (*Teacher's Resource Binder*, p. 32-1)
- Enrichment Lesson: *The Theory of Reasoned Action* Learn more about predictors of behavior. (*Teacher's Resource Binder*, p. 32-1)
- Enrichment Lesson: *Actions Influence Attitudes* This lesson highlights that action shapes attitude. (*Teacher's Resource Binder*, p. 32-1)
- Enrichment Lesson: *The Justification of Effort* Cognitive dissonance theorists discuss this concept. (*Teacher's Resource Binder*, p. 32-1)

Social Influence

V Video Center

- Videocassette: *Scientific American Frontiers,* Second Edition, Segment 29: "Superpower Ping Pong" Consult the faculty guide from the *Scientific American Frontiers* video series for a description of this segment. (*Teacher's Resource Binder*, p. 32-1)

Activity Center

- Demonstration Activity: *Suggestibility* This is a dramatic (even hilarious) classroom demonstration. (*Teacher's Resource Binder*, p. 32-1)
- Demonstration Activity: *Social Influence* This is an activity created by Robert Montgomery and Russell Enzie. (*Teacher's Resource Binder*, p. 32-1)
- Application Activity: *Violating a Social Norm* Students may feel the potency of social situations by imagining themselves violating some norms. (*Teacher's Resource Binder*, p. 32-1)
- Critical Thinking Activity: *Would You Obey?* In this activity, students make predictions about a study. (*Teacher's Resource Binder*, p. 32-1; Handout 32–5)
- Demonstration Activity: *Deindividuation* David Dodd introduces deindividuation by asking students to write down their response to a question. (*Teacher's Resource Binder*, p. 32-1)
- Cooperative Learning Activity: *Group Polarization* In this activity, students must decide how to respond. (*Teacher's Resource Binder*, p. 32-1; Handouts 32–6a and 32–6b)

Enrichment Center

- Enrichment Lesson: *The Seattle Windshield Pitting Epidemic* Among the most interesting examples of human suggestibility are cases of mass hysteria. (*Teacher's Resource Binder*, p. 32-1)
- Enrichment Lesson: *Obedience in Everyday Life* If students find Milgram's study artificial, cite some everyday situations to refute the charge. (*Teacher's Resource Binder*, p. 32-1)

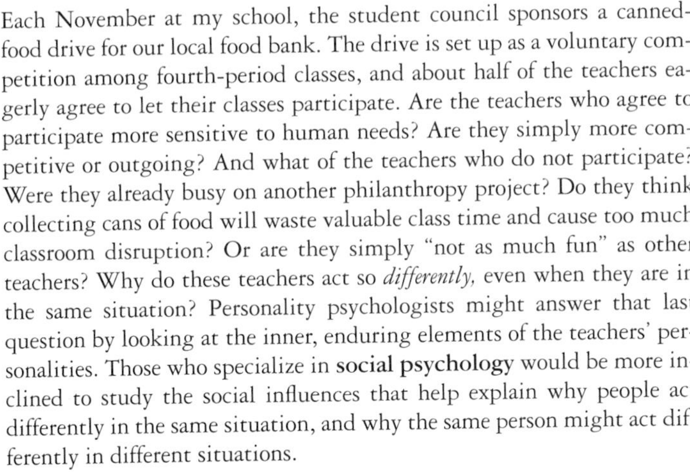

MODULE 32

Social Thinking and Social Influence

Social Thinking

Social Influence

Each November at my school, the student council sponsors a canned-food drive for our local food bank. The drive is set up as a voluntary competition among fourth-period classes, and about half of the teachers eagerly agree to let their classes participate. Are the teachers who agree to participate more sensitive to human needs? Are they simply more competitive or outgoing? And what of the teachers who do not participate? Were they already busy on another philanthropy project? Do they think collecting cans of food will waste valuable class time and cause too much classroom disruption? Or are they simply "not as much fun" as other teachers? Why do these teachers act so *differently,* even when they are in the same situation? Personality psychologists might answer that last question by looking at the inner, enduring elements of the teachers' personalities. Those who specialize in **social psychology** would be more inclined to study the social influences that help explain why people act differently in the same situation, and why the same person might act differently in different situations.

▶ **social psychology** The scientific study of how we think about, influence, and relate to one another.

Canned Food Drive Given the opportunity to donate cans of food for the food bank, some people donate and some do not. Psychologists study why people act differently in similar situations.

MODULE 32

Social Thinking and Social Influence

Introducing the Module

The Points: Module Objectives

- Differentiate between a dispositional attribution and a situational attribution.
- Analyze how our attitudes and actions interact.
- Identify the conditions under which we are most likely to conform and obey.
- Determine how the presence of others influences our actions.
- Analyze how group polarization and groupthink demonstrate the power of group influence.
- Analyze how self-fulfilling prophecies and minority influence demonstrate the power of the individual.

trb Building Vocabulary

Working individually or with partners, students can reinforce their knowledge of social thinking and social influence by completing **Building Vocabulary: Graphic Organizer:** *Crossword Puzzle* (*Teacher's Resource Binder*, p. 32-1; **Handout 32–2**). Students can learn the terms in this module and the relationship among them as they fill in the puzzle.

Getting Started

Students often underestimate the influence of society on their behavior. As teens search for their own individual identity, they may deny that peer pressure, conformity, and obedience can dictate their choices and behavior. Have students ponder the following questions:

- At school, why do you obey some rules and disobey others?
- Have you ever been convinced by friends to do something wrong? To do something right?
- Do you consider yourself a conformist? A nonconformist? Why?

trb You may wish to use **Critical Thinking Activity:** *Fact or Falsehood?* (*Teacher's Resource Binder*, p. 32-1; **Handout 32–1**) as a prereading strategy to evaluate what students already know about social thinking and social influence. This activity will prime students to look out for information that could prove or disprove their preconceptions about these topics.

MODULE 32

Teaching the Points

■ **TEACHING TIPS**

web (1) You can log on as an instructor to the book companion site for *Thinking About Psychology* at **www.worthpublishers.com/thinkingaboutpsych**. It contains teacher resources for class presentations as well as review and assessment of module concepts and terms.

web (2) Resources for the Teaching of Social Psychology may be found at **www.noctrl.edu/~ajomuel/crow**, which is part of the CROW project (Course Resources on the Web), sponsored by the Associated Colleges of Illinois. Prepared by Jon Mueller, the site includes activities and exercises, on-line studies and demonstrations, class assignments, Web projects, topic resources, on-line lectures, and student resources.

web (3) A discussion group (**LISTSERV@UGA.CC.UGA.EDU**) is available for use by instructors. It provides a forum for individuals to discuss current theory and research in social psychology as well as the teaching of social psychology. To join the list, send an e-mail message (to the above address) with the body of the message as follows: subscribe socpsy-L yourfirstname yourlastname

trb At this point, you may wish to use Technology Application Activity: *Social Psychology on the Web* (*Teacher's Resource Binder*, p. 32-1; Handout 32–3).

(4) Link discussion of *attribution* to *explanatory style* in positive psychology. We make certain attributions (or explanations) about our own behavior that are either situational or dispositional.

- Optimists are more likely to attribute good events to dispositions and bad events to situations.
- Pessimists will make dispositional attributions for bad events and situational attributions for good events.

trb At this point, you may wish to use Critical Thinking Activity: *The Fundamental Attribution Error* (*Teacher's Resource Binder*, p. 32-1; Handout 32–4).

▶ **attribution theory** The theory that we tend to give a causal explanation for someone's behavior, often by crediting either the situation or the person's disposition.

▶ **fundamental attribution error** The tendency for observers, when analyzing another's behavior, to underestimate the impact of the situation and to overestimate the impact of personal disposition.

Social Thinking

How do we form our beliefs and attitudes about the world around us? We often do this so automatically that we're not even aware of the process. Still, it is worth slowing down this process to understand how it all happens, so that we can work toward fairer, more accurate attributions and attitudes.

Attributing Behavior to Personal Disposition or the Situation

What's the Point? 1. What is the difference between a dispositional attribution and a situational attribution?

We all have a tendency to analyze and categorize the people we meet, based on the behaviors we observe. By now, you have decided whether your psychology teacher is reserved or spirited, strait-laced or easy-going, serious or light-hearted, and you have probably assigned or *attributed* those traits to your teacher's internal *disposition* rather than to the classroom *situation*. Have you ever considered how your teacher might act at a party with friends, or at home with family—in a different situation? According to **attribution theory**, we explain others' behavior as an aspect of either an internal disposition (an inner trait) or the situation (Heider, 1958). And we often make the **fundamental attribution error** by attributing behaviors to inner dispositions than to situations. Let's unpack those terms.

Say the person sitting next to you asks to borrow and copy your lecture notes from class. Almost automatically, you start to assign a cause, or a reason to your classmate's request. If you think your neighbor is lazy and didn't listen, you are making a *dispositional* attribution. If you remember your classmate was absent the day before and did not even hear the lecture, you are making a *situational* attribution.

As we try to "figure someone out," we are more likely to lean in the dispositional direction and underestimate the situation. I sometimes make the fundamental attribution error by mentally assigning the label "shy" to students who never say a word in class. I'm often surprised when I see them transformed into loudmouths at a basketball game against an archrival, insulting the other team's players and singing "Three Blind Mice" when the referee makes a call against our team. These students behave very differently when in different situations. I *underestimated* the impact of the situation and *overestimated* the impact of personal disposition. If you get cut off in traffic, are you more likely to think "Stupid driver!" or "That person must have a good reason for being in a hurry"? I don't know about you, but I'm much more likely to make the dispositional attribution. It's hard to resist attribution errors.

Suggested Readings

Use the following books as teacher-preparation tools or as enrichment for advanced students:

Aronson, E. (1995). *The social animal* (7th ed.) New York: Freeman.

Cialdini, R. B. (1998). *Influence: The psychology of persuasion.* New York: Morrow.

Jackson, S. (1992). *The lottery and other stories.* New York: Noonday Press.

Janis, I. L. (1982). *Groupthink.* Boston: Houghton Mifflin.

Milgram, S. (1974). *Obedience to authority.* New York: HarperCollins.

Myers, D. G. (1999). *Social psychology* (6th ed.). New York: McGraw-Hill.

Taylor, S., Peplau, L., & Sears, D. (2000). *Social psychology* (10th ed.). Upper Saddle River, NJ: Prentice Hall.

In one study assessing attributions, participants talked to a woman who acted *either* warm and friendly *or* distant and critical. Half of the participants, group A, heard that the woman had been told to act one way or the other. The other half, group B, heard the woman's behavior was natural. In other words, group A was given a situational explanation of the woman's behavior, and group B was given a dispositional explanation. What impact did these explanations have on the two groups' assessment of this woman? None. If the woman acted unfriendly, both group A and group B labeled her as innately unfriendly. They underestimated situational factors and overestimated dispositional factors (Napolitan & Goethals, 1979).

Actors complain of being "type-cast," meaning that after playing a certain role, perhaps a villain in a movie, for a long time, they can no longer get other kinds of parts. The problem? Directors know that viewers make attributions to actors that are hard to overcome. Mel Gibson won an Oscar for playing a heroic part in the movie *Braveheart.* We might have a hard time believing he could play a criminal, and we might therefore decide not to go see a movie where he played this part. Could you watch comic geniuses like Chris Rock and Jerry Seinfeld act the parts of serial murderers and find them believable? We judge actors as having a certain disposition, and, in so doing, we commit the fundamental attribution error.

Disposition If Chris Rock or any famous comedian was cast as a vicious criminal in a movie, we'd probably have a hard time believing in the character. Because of the fundamental attribution error, we would assume that the role the comedian plays in public reflects his own personal qualities, not the characteristics of the situation.

What about you? Are you shy or outgoing? In answering that question, you might say you are shy in class but not around your friends. You might say you talk less at a big party, but you could talk for hours at an overnighter with three of your close friends. When we explain our own behavior, we tend to include the situation as a part of our answer. But when we explain the behavior of others, we wear blinders, attributing their behavior to their permanent, personal qualities.

Every day, we try to make sense of what others do or say by making attributions. Did the person at the next locker not say "Good morning" because she is unfriendly, or because she's exhausted from staying up late studying for her history exam? Does the college admissions counselor look at your transcript and see a low grade in chemistry and think you don't care about science? Or does the same admissions person look at the rest of the semester to see if the courses you took were particularly challenging that term? Sit on a jury, and you may have to decide whether someone acted in self-defense or is aggressive by nature and should be put behind bars. The point is, these judgments or attributions matter, and whether we make the judgments based on the person or the situation also matters (Fincham & Bradbury, 1993). A wife says to her husband, "Must you always spend so much money?" In happy marriages, the husband will attribute this statement to something situational, like a bad day at the office. In an unhappy marriage, the husband is more likely to attribute the statement to disposition, perhaps thinking, "I wish she wasn't so stingy" (Fletcher & others, 1990).

Meeting Individual Needs

trb tr Help students understand how the terms in this module are related by having them complete **Building Vocabulary: Graphic Organizer:** *Crossword Puzzle* (*Teacher's Resource Binder,* p. 32-1; **Handout 32–2**).

- **Independent Learners** Students can complete the handout on their own as homework or in-class work assignment, checking the answers in class. You can use **Handout 32–2** as a transparency, inserting the correct answers and then projecting the puzzle for students to check their answers.
- **Cooperative Learners** Have students work in small groups to complete the crossword puzzle. Students can tutor each other about the concepts in the module, or you can create a competition in which students see how quickly their team can complete the puzzle correctly.

■ APPLYING THE POINTS

In 1979, rock fans were waiting to get into Riverfront Coliseum for a concert by The Who, a famous rock group. When the Coliseum doors were finally opened, people stampeded and several were trampled to death. *Time* magazine later received a letter from an outside observer and one from a participant.

- The observer: "The violently destructive message that The Who and other rock groups deliver leaves me little surprised that they attract a mob that will trample human beings to death to gain better seats. Of greater concern is a respected news magazine's adulation of this sick phenomenon."
- The participant: "While standing in the crowd at Riverfront Coliseum, I distinctly remember feeling that I was being punished for being a rock fan. My sister and I joked about this, unaware of the horror happening around us. Later, those jokes came back to us grimly as we watched the news. How many lives will be lost before the punitive and inhuman policy of festival seating at rock concerts is outlawed?"

(Participants in an event are more likely to make situational attributions, while observers are more likely to make dispositional attributions.)

■ TEACHING TIP

To get students thinking about situational versus dispositional attribution, have them consider the following questions:

- How would you explain the behavior of a friend who gets angry at you? Does something nice for you?
- If someone you have recently gotten to know walks by you in the hall but doesn't say hello (even as you try to say hello), what would you think? Why?
- Are your thoughts about your good friend's behavior different from your thoughts about someone you're only acquainted with? Why or why not?

trb At this point, you may wish to use **Enrichment Lesson:** *The Theory of Reasoned Action* (*Teacher's Resource Binder,* p. 32-1).

Are there political implications for attributions? You bet. Several researchers (Furnham, 1982; Pandey & others, 1982; Wagstaff, 1982; Zucker & Weiner, 1993) have shown that political liberals tend to explain social problems, such as poverty and unemployment, as a result of the situation. Conservatives are more likely to cite personal dispositions of the unemployed and poor. The liberal might ask, "If you could not get a good education, had to face discrimination, and lived in the same neighborhood, would you be any better off than the poorer people in your city?" The conservative's response is likely to be something like, "The poor who work hard enough will pull themselves out of poverty. People pretty much get what they deserve." Social scientists are more likely to blame present and past situations, not disposition.

Culture also affects attribution. Several banks and investment firms lost millions of dollars in the 1990s when employees made unauthorized transactions. Why did these financial institutions lose money? In the United States, we tended to blame unethical individuals—a dispositional attribution. In Japan, newspapers blamed a lack of organizational controls—a situational attribution (Menon & others, 1999).

It may be impossible to identify all the attribution errors we make in a given week or day. What is possible, though, is to realize that our attributions about others—our judgments about whether their behavior is due to situational or personal factors—carry lasting consequences (Figure 32.1).

Figure 32.1 Negative Behavior: Cutting in Line Whether you tolerate a negative behavior or respond unfavorably to it will depend in part on how you interpret the event.

Negative behavior
Someone cuts into the line in front of you.

Situational attribution
"That tired mother is so busy with her little boy, she didn't even notice the line."

Tolerant reaction

Dispositional attribution
"Who does that lady think she is? I bet she always cuts in lines."

Unfavorable reaction

MODULE 32

■ MULTICULTURAL CONNECTIONS

Have students look up foreign and domestic news reports of the corporate meltdowns of the early part of the twenty-first century (for example, Enron, Adelphia, WorldCom, and so forth). Students can find English-language reports published in foreign newspapers and compare those reports with those published in U.S. news outlets. Afterward, use the following questions to guide a class discussion:

- Do foreign reporters make more dispositional attributions or situational attributions compared to U.S. reporters?
- Are reports of corporate malfeasance in other cultures treated similarly to such reports in the United States? Why or why not?

■ TEACHING TIPS

tr (1) A four-color transparency of Figure 32.1, Negative Behavior: Cutting in Line, is available in the **Overhead Transparencies Set.**

(2) Link the discussion of *attributions* to *stereotypes* and *prejudice*. If people hold strong stereotypes or prejudices toward a particular group of people, they are likely to make a dispositional attribution for their behaviors. These people would explain similar behavior by people in their own groups by using situational attributions.

trb At this point, you may wish to use **Enrichment Lesson:** *Actions Influence Attitudes* (*Teacher's Resource Binder*, p. 32-1).

(3) *Social psychology* is different from *sociology*.

- **Social psychology** looks more to seeing how individuals interact with each other and society at large.
- **Sociologists** explore the behavior of groups and cultures as they interact internally and externally.

■ CHECKING FOR UNDERSTANDING

Ask students to give a partner an example of a dispositional and situational attribution. Visit student pairs to clarify any misconceptions.

Cross-Curricular Connections

GOVERNMENT Students can explore the differences between Republicans, who are traditionally conservative, and Democrats, who are traditionally liberal, to see if these stereotypes actually exist.

- Have students look up bills that are currently proposed for this congressional term to see if Republican-sponsored bills reflect a dispositional attitude and if Democratic-sponsored bills reflect a situational attitude toward poverty, education, and welfare.
- Students can contact local offices for the Republican and Democratic parties to ask about their views on different political issues.
- Ask students to report back on their findings and determine whether local party representatives make more dispositional or situational attributions.

Attitudes and Actions

2. How do our attitudes and our actions interact?

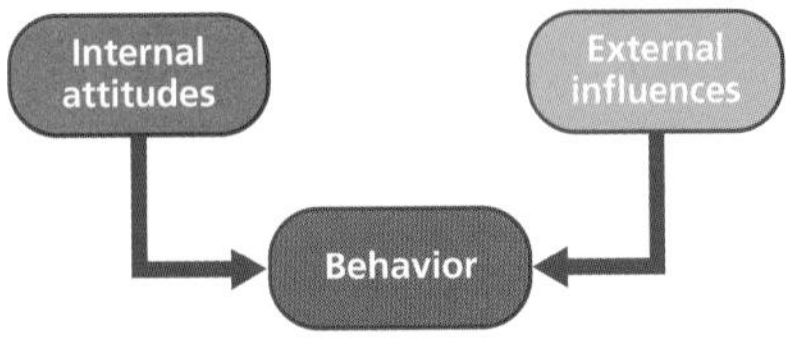

Figure 32.2 **Behavioral Influences** External influences and internal attitudes affect behavior.

A friend tells you Mr. Doane is mean and grades unfairly. Though you may never take a class with this teacher, your friend's assessment could affect your **attitude**—a belief and feeling that predisposes you to respond in a particular way to people, events, and objects. You may develop a feeling of dislike for this teacher, and perhaps even respond in an unfriendly way to one of his requests. Attitudes have a powerful effect on behavior.

The Effects of Attitudes on Actions

Several studies have shown that attitudes and behaviors are not always perfect matches (Wicker, 1971). The same students who say they're against cheating may later look at someone's paper for an answer. The people who claim to treat all people equally may behave differently toward members of another race or ethnic group. Why do we sometimes talk one way but act another? Do attitudes ever predict behavior?

Recent studies (Kraus, 1991; Wallace & others, 1996) show that our attitudes can predict behavior, if the circumstances are right (Figure 32.2). Sometimes we *do* talk the talk *and* walk the walk—but only if:

1. ***the outside influences on what we do are minimal.*** Perhaps your friend Matt swore in seventh grade that he would never smoke. Several years later, most of the members of Matt's new peer group are smokers. Giving in to this increased outside pressure, Matt starts to light up. Had the outside influences remained minimal, his attitude toward smoking would have had a better chance of remaining the same as it was in seventh grade.
2. ***we are keenly aware of our attitudes.*** When we are conscious of what we believe, our behavior is more likely to match our beliefs (Fazio, 1990). If something had made Matt fully aware of his seventh-grade attitude about smoking, he might never have started smoking.
3. ***the attitudes are relevant to the behavior.*** If you say you believe exercise is essential for good health, but you really dislike getting sweaty, you may avoid working out, even though you know it's good for you. Your attitude toward exercise will guide your physical fitness program.

The Effects of Actions on Attitudes

But behavior can also affect attitudes. Under certain conditions, behavior precedes and fosters attitudes.

▶ **attitude** A belief and feeling that predisposes one to respond in a particular way to objects, people, and events.

Enriching

To see how watching affects behavior, have students conduct an experiment. (Obtain Institutional Review Board (IRB) approval and informed consent before engaging in any research endeavor.)

- Place food in a room. A researcher tells the subject that while he or she goes to check on something, no food should be eaten. For one group, set up a video camera in an obvious location.
- For the other group, do not film. Note what food has been placed out and see if any is missing. You can also have a hidden camera if your IRB approves the use of deception.
- Another scenario that does not use deception involves eating healthy versus unhealthy food in the presence of a mirror. All participants in this scenario can be videotaped without deception.

trb At this point, you may wish to use **Enrichment Lesson:** *The Looking Glass Effect* (*Teacher's Resource Binder*, p. 32-1).

■ JOURNAL WRITING

Invite students to use the following questions and writing prompts as springboards for entries in their psychology journals:

- Has your attitude ever gotten you in trouble? What happened? Have you changed your attitude since? Why or why not?
- Do you believe that people who behave contrary to their stated attitudes are hypocritical? Why or why not?

F • Y • I

When we are keenly aware of our attitudes, they are more likely to guide our actions. Researchers have cleverly made participants self-conscious by installing mirrors in the laboratory. This is called the *looking glass effect.* Here's one example of this effect:

- Edward Diener and Mark Wallbom noted that nearly all college students say that cheating is morally wrong. So they had students work on an anagram-solving task that was presumably an IQ test. They told students to stop when a bell sounded. Left alone, 71 percent cheated by working past the bell. However, among students made self-aware by working in front of a mirror, only 7 percent cheated.

Source: Diener, E., & Wallbom, M. (1976). Effects of self-awareness on antinormative behavior. *Journal of Research in Personality, 10,* 107–111.

trb At this point, you may wish to use Enrichment Lesson: *The Looking Glass Effect* (*Teacher's Resource Binder*, p. 32-1).

■ TEACHING TIPS

trb tr (1) A black-line master for Figure 32.2, Behavioral Influences, is available in the **Black-Line Masters Appendix** in the *Teacher's Resource Binder.*

(2) Help students understand that it is easier to change attitudes than to change actions. Attitudes are internal and might not be seen or known by others. Actions, however, occur out in the open, observed by all. If an action conflicts with an attitude, we will change the attitude to fit the action instead of the other way around.

MODULE 32

■ **APPLYING THE POINTS**

Contact a local company that specializes in sales or telemarketing and ask if it has heard of the foot-in-the-door phenomenon. Report back to students the strategies this or other interviewed companies use to train their salespeople or marketing staff to maximize sales with this effect.

■ **TEACHING TIPS**

(1) Have students list situations in which they might use the foot-in-the-door phenomenon in their daily lives (in addition to the example provided on page 618). As an example, ask the following question:

- How could someone use the foot-in-the-door phenomenon to negotiate a later curfew with his or her parents?

(Explain that the person who negotiates by asking for only a slightly later curfew—say, 30 minutes—rather than a much later one—say, two hours—has a greater chance for eventual success.)

(2) Students may notice, however, that the foot-in-the-door phenomenon only works when you are trying to get someone to agree to do something—it doesn't work as well if you are trying to spend money or give bad news. Some situations must be framed in certain ways before they are successful. For example:

- What happens when a teenager asks parents or guardians to buy him or her something inexpensive before asking for something expensive? Does this strategy work? Why or why not? *(If the expensive item isn't much more in price than the inexpensive item, the parents or guardians may give in. But if the item is vastly different in price, asking for the more expensive item first—and getting compliance—would more likely result in the purchase of both items.)*
- Have students ever told their parents about a slightly bad thing they've done before dropping the bomb that they've done something they viewed as being really bad? Was the strategy successful? Why or why not? *(Sometimes telling about the really bad thing first can make the other mistake seem completely insignificant.)*

trb At this point, you may wish to use Enrichment Lesson: *Actions Influence Attitudes* (*Teacher's Resource Binder*, p. 32-1).

Foot-in-the-Door Phenomenon A student group at our school was trying to raise money for the Make-a-Wish foundation. The highest amount our school had raised in previous years was $800. In planning the fundraiser, the students made a series of requests from the administration:

If we raise $500, can we print the names of the top five donors in the daily bulletin? The answer was yes.

If we raise $1000, can we print the names of the top five donors and give them a free school lunch for a week? The answer? Yes.

Requests for rewards for increasing amounts of money continued, until the students asked, "If we raise $5000 [an unheard of amount], would you release school an hour early the last Friday of the fundraiser?" The administration approved the early dismissal and the publicity machine for this event shifted into high gear.

Posters declaring this ultimate incentive were distributed to every classroom. At the end of two weeks, our school presented a check for more than $7000 to the Make-a-Wish foundation. Everybody (except the teachers) started the weekend an hour early. It's amazing what students will do for an extra hour off, isn't it?

One of the students who made the requests of the administration later admitted to having read about the **foot-in-the-door phenomenon** in psychology class. This phenomenon is the tendency for people who have first agreed to a small request to comply later with a larger request. One researcher (Cialdini, 1993) found that if you want people to agree to something big, you should start small and work your way up. The escalating actions fuel the attitudes, and each successive act is easier to agree to. Would you put a large, ugly, poorly lettered "Drive Carefully" sign in your front yard? One study found that only 17 percent of the people in a California neighborhood would agree to post such a sign. However, when this request was made two weeks after people had agreed to display a small, 3-inch high "Be a Safe Driver" sign, a whopping 76 percent allowed the large, unsightly sign in their yards (Freedman & Fraser, 1966).

So were the students running the fund drive for the Make-a-Wish foundation smart to start with the small requests? Would the principal have agreed to the hour off from school if it had been the first request? What do you think?

► **foot-in-door phenomenon** The tendency for people who have first agreed to a small request to comply later with a larger request.

► **cognitive dissonance** The theory that we act to reduce the discomfort (dissonance) we feel when two of our thoughts (cognitions) are inconsistent. For example, when our awareness of our attitudes and of our actions clash, we can reduce the resulting dissonance by changing our attitudes.

Role Playing If you go to college, you'll be taking on a new role. At first, it may feel a little strange, as if you're "playing college" as you adjust to professors who don't take attendance and don't want to know when you use the restroom. You may at first feel strange about attending only two or three classes each day, but before long, your actions will no longer seem so artificial. You'll not only *act* like a college student, you'll *feel* like one. What we do, we eventually become. Several studies have confirmed this effect, including the Zimbardo prison study.

Demonstrating

A FOOT-IN-THE-DOOR Have students conduct a research study using surveys to test the foot-in-the-door phenomenon. (Obtain Institutional Review Board (IRB) approval and informed consent before engaging in any research endeavor.)

- Subjects can be asked either to fill out a 100-question survey first, followed by a 10-question survey or to fill out a 10-question survey first, followed by a 100-question survey.
- The survey itself is not as important as what the subjects will agree to do. For example, if the subjects agree to take the long survey after they've taken the short one, students don't have to actually make them take it.

trb At this point, you may want to use Enrichment Lesson: *Actions Influence Attitudes* (*Teacher's Resource Binder*, p. 32-1).

Psychologist Philip Zimbardo (1972) randomly assigned a group of Stanford University students to play the part of either a guard or a prisoner in a simulated prison. Though the demonstration was designed to last much longer, it ended after only six days. Why? Zimbardo called it off because the students playing guards were displaying humiliating aggressiveness and cruelty toward the students playing the prisoner role. Both guards and prisoners had adopted uncharacteristic roles, and both were becoming the characters they were playing. Behavior can shape beliefs and attitudes

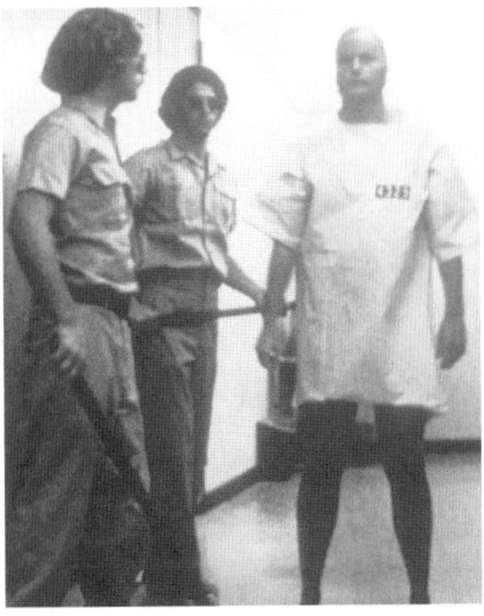

Role-Playing Prison Guards Philip Zimbardo had to call off his prison study after the role-playing got too intense.

Cognitive Dissonance A former student, J.J., who vocally supported politically liberal causes, fell head-over-heels for an officer in the Teenage Republicans club. At her request, J.J. joined the Teenage Republicans and started attending meetings. After joining, he began to feel a sort of tension between his liberal beliefs and his actions supporting the conservative club. Then J.J. noticed that his attitudes were changing from negative to positive toward the club's conservative projects. Why did J.J.'s attitude change? According to **cognitive dissonance theory,** we act to reduce the discomfort (dissonance) we feel when our thoughts (cognitions) and actions are inconsistent. When his attitudes and actions clashed, J.J. reduced the resulting dissonance by changing his attitude (Figure 32.3).

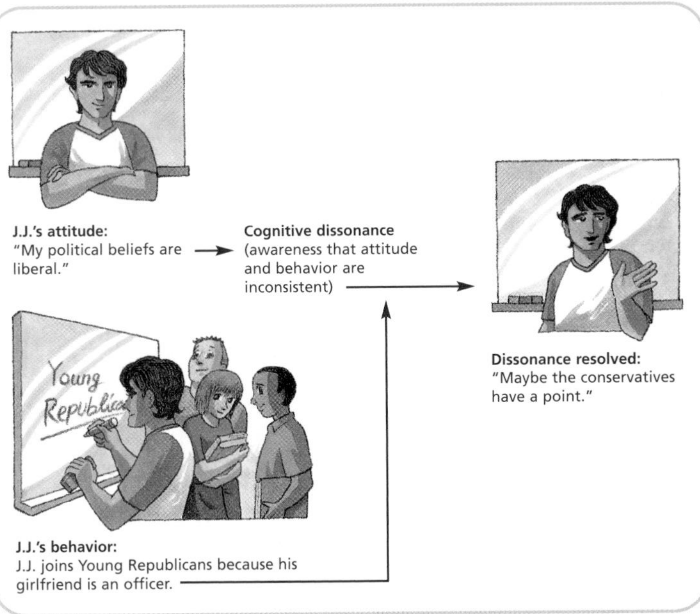

J.J.'s attitude:
"My political beliefs are liberal."
Cognitive dissonance
(awareness that attitude and behavior are inconsistent)
Dissonance resolved:
"Maybe the conservatives have a point."
Young Republicans
J.J.'s behavior:
J.J. joins Young Republicans because his girlfriend is an officer.

Figure 32.3 **Cognitive Dissonance in Action** When two thoughts are incompatible, we often reduce the discomfort (dissonance) by changing an attitude.

MODULE 32

■ TEACHING TIPS

web (1) Philip Zimbardo created a simulated prison, and then he randomly assigned college students to play the role of either guard or prisoner. A Web-based slide show at **www.prisonexp.org** provides a detailed account of this fascinating study that demonstrates how role playing can powerfully shape attitudes and even self-identity. Narrated slides show how the guards developed degrading routines and, in only six days, the prisoners broke down, rebelled, or became passively resigned. Students can provide an oral or written report on their visit to this Web site. Helpful discussion questions accompany the slide program and can be printed for classroom use.

(2) If you want someone to change an attitude, get that person to act in ways contrary to their beliefs. Like J.J. in the Student Edition, if people behave differently than they believe, they will change their beliefs first. Actions are harder to change since people have seen you behave, whereas they haven't seen your internal attitudes.

tr A four-color transparency of Figure 32.3, Cognitive Dissonance in Action, is available in the **Overhead Transparencies Set.**

trb tr At this point, you may wish to use **Critical Thinking Activity:** *Introducing Cognitive Dissonance Theory* (*Teacher's Resource Binder*, p. 32-1; **Transparency Master 32–1**).

A "LOW-BALL" EXPERIENCE Recruit a confidante for help.

- Offer a "free day" for time spent after school in a quiet study hall. Explain that you will negotiate with the principal, but students must make an offer first. Suggest 30 minutes.
- Send a confidante to the office with the offer. After a few minutes, the student will come back with the principal's "counteroffer" of two hours. The students will likely object.
- Send back another offer, going for an hour and a half. This time, the principal agrees.
- Will students take the new offer? Probably. Discuss with them how this "low-ball" technique works off the principles of foot-in-the-door and cognitive dissonance.

trb At this point, you may wish to use **Enrichment Lesson:** *Actions Influence Attitudes* (*Teacher's Resource Binder*, p. 32-1).

MODULE 32

■ TEACHING TIP
Remind students that people can learn to change their thinking patterns to become more optimistic than pessimistic. By challenging pessimistic thoughts with distancing, evidence, and alternatives, people can often begin to think optimistically—and be less depressed in the process. Most people, ordinarily, wouldn't accept pessimistic comments from others without getting upset. So why would they accept those types of thoughts from themselves?

■ APPLYING THE POINTS
Copycat crimes concern law enforcement personnel. Contact a local police station to ask about how it tries to limit the possibility of copycat crimes. Use the following questions to interview law enforcement officials and present your findings in class:

- Do law enforcement officials limit the amount of press coverage of particular crimes? Why or why not? If so, how?
- If a criminal is still at large, how can law officers tell if a crime is a copycat crime or one that is committed by the real perpetrator?
- What can schools learn from the police about limiting copycat crimes or suicides?

trb At this point, you may wish to use Enrichment Lesson: *The Seattle Windshield Pitting Epidemic* (*Teacher's Resource Binder*, p. 32-1).

■ CHECKING FOR UNDERSTANDING
In small groups, have students identify the three ways attitudes affect behavior (foot-in-the-door phenomenon, role-playing, cognitive dissonance) and give an example of each. Allow time for groups to share their examples.

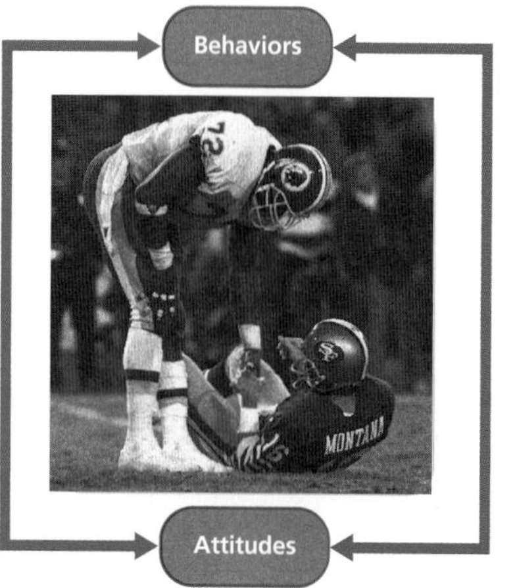

Attitudes and Behaviors Go Hand-In-Hand Helping someone, even after tackling him, promotes respect. Respect promotes positive behavior.

We can apply this principle—attitudes can follow behaviors—to our advantage. If we have an attitude we'd like to change, such as negative feelings toward people from different social groups, we can start by changing our behavior toward those individuals. In clinical settings, cognitive behavior therapists also use this principle for the benefit of their patients—for example, by encouraging patients with depression to talk more positively and to avoid self-put-downs. Therapists hope that these more positive behaviors will help change their patients' attitudes about themselves.

Social psychologists study not only the interesting ways in which we are affected by our own attitudes and actions, but also the way we are affected by the attitudes and actions of those around us.

Social Influence

Do other people influence us? You bet! Consider these very different scenarios:

- The person next to you in class yawns. Then the person in front of you yawns. Within seconds, you are fighting the urge to follow suit.
- A group of five students stands outside the front door of a building. For no good reason, they start to look up. As long as the five are out there, almost everybody approaching the building looks up as they enter, though there is nothing special to see.
- In the eight days following a murderous shooting spree in a Colorado high school, 49 states report copycat threats. Pennsylvania leads the way with 60 threats (Cooper, 1999).
- Over a brief stretch of 18 days, a school with 1500 students reports 2 suicides, 7 attempted suicides, and 23 students contemplating suicide.
- Defendants standing trial for Nazi war crimes, participants in the Holocaust that brought death to over 6 million Jews, are asked why they took part in these murders. Many, including Adolf Eichmann, the Nazi director of deportation of Jews to concentration camps, respond by saying, "I was only following orders."

There is no denying the titanic power of social influence on our actions and attitudes. Advertisers use it to sell products, and politicians use it to win votes. But in *tragic and violent* instances, such as the suicide clusters, school shootings, and genocide, what is the role of social influence? In search of answers, social psychologists have studied both conformity and obedience.

Demonstrating

COPYCATS Begin to yawn in class, and then count how many students join you in the yawning. Students can test the influence people have over each other by trying the following activities:

- After school, stand outside and look up. Have an observer count others who look up, too.
- Go to a public place and start yawning. Have an observer count the number of people who yawn as well.
- For advanced students: Set up a booth to give away some type of pamphlet or some sample items (for example, pens). See how many stop by in a certain interval of time. Then have some friends come to the booth who ask questions and take the free items. In a similar time period, count how many other people stop by. (More people should stop by if they see others doing the same.)

trb At this point, you may wish to use Demonstration Activity: *Suggestibility* (*Teacher's Resource Binder*, p. 32-1).

Conformity and Obedience

3. Under what conditions are we most likely to conform and obey?

Let's say you have a test scheduled for Friday in your psychology class. In preparation, you study very hard in the evenings leading up to the test. Then on Thursday, a classmate asks that the test be moved to Monday. You sense a wave of support for this request, as other class members voice their agreement. But you don't think it is such a good idea. You have a marching band trip planned for the weekend, and you'll arrive home very late Sunday night, exhausted from the travel and hectic schedule. A Monday morning exam is not what you need. The teacher says the test will be moved to Monday if *every* member of the class votes in favor of the move. When the vote is called for, every hand in the class goes up except yours. Your vote will make the difference. What will you do? Will you vote your own beliefs or *conform* to the class' desire to delay?

Conformity is adjusting one's behavior or thinking to coincide with a group idea or standard. Under what conditions is conformity likely to occur? Social psychologists have been asking—and answering—that question for over half a century. **Solomon Asch** (1955) conducted one of the more ingenious conformity studies, and to get a feel for how this experiment worked, you're going to have to use your imagination.

You're a college student, and you've signed up to participate in a study on perceptual judgment. Arriving at the experiment's location, you are assigned Seat 6 (out of 7), and you sit down around a large table with six others. You're told you will be shown sets of cards, and your task is to identify which of the three lines on Card B is identical to the one line on Card A (Figure 32.4). The first set is put up. Clearly, the answer is Line 2. One by one, every participant in the room agrees. The experimenter records your answers one at a time, and then puts up the second set of cards. You think to yourself, "This is easy." Again, you all agree on the same lines. Then comes the third trial, which appears to be just as easy as the first two. You're ready to say "Line 2" but to your surprise, the first person gives an answer you think is clearly wrong. Your amazement continues as all five

► **conformity** Adjusting one's behavior or thinking to coincide with a group standard.

► **Solomon Asch (1907–1996)** Social psychologist who researched the circumstances under which people conform.

Solomon Asch

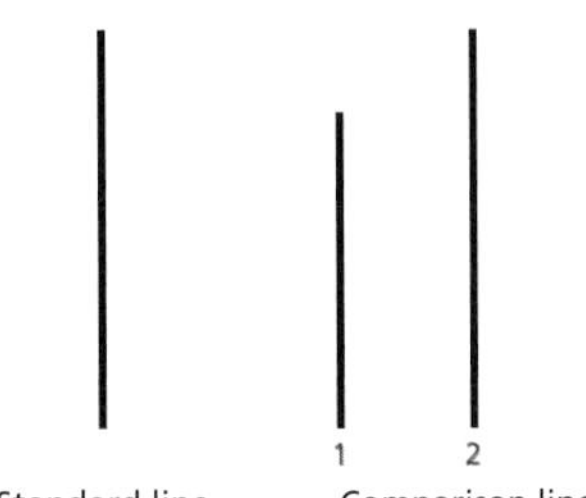

Figure 32.4 **Conformity** Which comparison line is closest in length to the standard line? What would you say if you were in a room with several others who all said line "1" was closest? Asch found that many people conformed, agreeing with the wrong answer. Not conforming led to considerable stress, as is evident herein the subject in the middle below.

CONFORMITY If students feel that conformity is not really an issue with them, ask them a question to which you will get a totally positive or negative response. (But do not ask for a show of hands.)

- How many students raise their hands?
- Who told them to raise their hands?

Although this activity demonstrates the power of conditioning, it also shows how students conform to the behavior the school demands from them—like raising hands in response to teacher requests.

Source: Adapted from **Stork, E.** (1992). Operant conditioning: Role in human behavior. In M. Sullivan, C. Blair-Broeker, T. Lindenberg, & A. Carlisle (Eds.), *Learning.* Washington, DC: American Psychological Association.

■ TEACHING TIPS

(1) Ask students what they would do in the situation the author describes about changing the test schedule. Would they vote their preference or go with the crowd? Discuss with students what personal qualities and situations would lead people to be more likely to vote their preferences.

(2) Draw students' attention to the fact that the correct answer for the student in the perceptual judgment study is quite obvious. There should be no question as to which answer to give about the lines on the card, but the power of conformity with the group led some normally confident people to choose the wrong answer instead of the right one.

■ LOOKING AT THE ISSUES

Conformity is a controversial issue among teens, who want both to fit in and to be distinct people at the same time. Suggest the following questions to help students discuss conformity in your school:

- Are the majority of students conformist or nonconformist? Why?
- Is there pressure among students at your school to dress a certain way or like certain types of music? Why or why not?
- Was there more pressure to conform in middle school versus high school? Why or why not?
- Where is the line between conformity and nonconformity? Are a group of nonconformists conforming to each other or refusing to conform with society?

trb At this point, you may wish to use **Demonstration Activity:** *Suggestibility* (*Teacher's Resource Binder*, p. 32-1).

MODULE 32

web ■ **LOOKING AT THE ISSUES**

Use the following questions to guide students in research and a discussion of the ethical issues that arise out of experiments, like Solomon Asch's conformity study:

- Does the APA Ethics Code allow for deception? Why or why not?
- Would this study be approved by an Institutional Review Board (IRB) today? Why or why not?

For more information into the APA Ethics Code, see the document online at **www.apa.org/ethics**.

■ **APPLYING THE POINTS**

Contact your local police station to talk about how the police avoid conformity when using police lineups. The following questions may be used to guide the interview as well as a class presentation of your findings:

- What procedures do the police have to follow to avoid problems with identification of suspects in a lineup?
- Are there new techniques the police use that have shown to be more effective in witnesses' identifying the right suspects? Describe them.

■ **MULTICULTURAL CONNECTIONS**

Use the questions below to help students examine which cultures are more likely to encourage conformity:

- What are the qualities of cultures that encourage conformity?
- What types of government do these cultures have? Are they communist, dictatorships, democratic, or a mixture of both?
- With whom or what do these cultures encourage conformity—government, family, adults, or all of the above?
- How do they handle people who don't conform? Do they suffer formalized punishment (jail, fines, etc.) or more informal social punishment (shunning, lack of job advancement, etc.)?

people in front of you choose the wrong line. Now it's your turn, and you must give an answer. What you don't know is that everyone else in the room *is in on* the experiment. They've all been instructed to lie during the third trial. You, the person in Seat 6, are the only participant. What will you say when it is your turn? Will you go along with the majority, or will you trust your judgment and remain true to yourself?

Asch found that if nobody else was in the room, participants made mistakes on the third trial about 1 percent of the time. However, if the five other people gave a wrong answer before the participant replied, participants gave the same wrong answer about one-third of the time. In essence, roughly one-third were willing to say that up was down.

An interesting follow-up to Asch's study assessed the role of judgment *difficulty* on conformity (Baron & others, 1996). Picking the longest line out of three is pretty easy, especially when you can stare at it for several minutes. But what about picking a stranger out of a lineup when you have had only a brief look at the person you're supposed to identify? In one study, researchers showed participants two slides. The first showed the man they were to identify, and the second showed a four-man lineup. Participants viewed Slide 1 for either five seconds (making the decision easy) or half a second (making the decision more difficult). Then they tried to select the correct person in Slide 2. Also, half the group was told their judgments were unimportant (that this was simply some preliminary testing) or important (that norms for actual police procedure were being developed, and the person making the most accurate identifications would receive $20). Researchers found that when judgments were easy and were deemed *un*important, fewer than 20 percent conformed to the judgments of the other participants. But over 50 percent conformed to others' judgment when the task was labeled important and difficult! It appears that if being correct matters, and if we're unsure of our answer, we are open to the opinions of others.

Other studies have shown that conformity tends to *increase* when

- you feel incompetent or insecure.
- you are in a group of three or more. (Groups larger than three show no additional conformity.)
- the rest of the group is unanimous.
- you are impressed by the status of the group.
- you have made no prior commitments to a response.
- you are being observed by others in the group.
- your culture strongly encourages respect for social standards.

Ultimately, our perception of whether social influence is good or bad is directly related to our beliefs. If social influence supports an ideal we oppose, we might be inclined to complain about weak-minded conformists

Cooperative Learning

When asked how they would respond in the Asch experimental situation, most predict they would resist group pressure and stick to what they know is right. Have students imagine a school situation that is a typical, but not a very serious, problem—for example, during a recital, a student in the audience claps loudly before the end of a piece of music. In small groups, have students respond to the following questions:

- How would the person in this situation most likely feel?
- What consequences would students endure for violating the norm? Is that why they conform with more typical behavior?

trb At this point, you may wish to use **Application Activity:** ***Violating a Social Norm*** (*Teacher's Resource Binder*, p. 32-1).

who can't think for themselves. But be careful of the double standard: What if social influence supports an ideal we favor? Do we suddenly think of conformists as forward thinking, responsive, and intellectual? Our view of conformity often reflects our own values.

Use your imagination one more time. This time, you're going to become a participant in what may be social psychology's most famous and most controversial study ever.

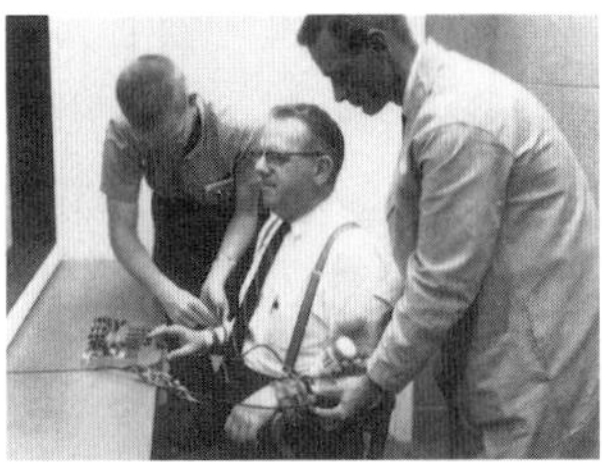

Figure 32.5 Mr. Wallace: Learner In Stanley Milgram's experiment on obedience, researchers attached electrodes to the "learner's" body. He was to be "shocked" every time he made a mistake.

What would you do in the following situation? You and another person show up to participate in a study. The experimenter, wearing a lab coat and carrying a clipboard, greets you and explains that this is a study of the effects of punishment on learning. You and the other participant, Mr. Wallace, draw slips of paper to see who will be the learner and who will be the teacher. Your slip says, "Teacher." As the teacher, you must punish Mr. Wallace with an electric shock every time he makes an error on the learning task.

You then help the experimenter strap Mr. Wallace into a chair in the learner's room and attach electrodes to his skin (Figure 32.5). The experimenter uses electrode paste, he explains, to avoid burns and blisters. The experimenter also says that the electric shocks to Mr. Wallace may cause extreme pain, but they should not result in "permanent tissue damage" (Milgram, 1974, p. 19). You are given a sample of the shock Mr. Wallace will receive if he makes a mistake, and it hurts.

Next, you take your seat in the teacher's room. You can't see Mr. Wallace, but you can hear him and talk to him. In front of you is an eerie-looking machine that will send the shocks to Mr. Wallace following an incorrect answer (Figure 32.6). The machine has 30 switches, each with a label indicating the number of volts that will be delivered for increasing levels of shock. You are told to deliver a "slight" shock (15 volts) for the first mistake and then to increase the voltage each time Mr. Wallace makes an error. Above the 150-volt switch, it says "Strong Shock." The message above the 300+ volt switches reads, "Danger: Severe Shock." Above the last switch, 450 volts, it simply says, "XXX."

You are told to begin. Mr. Wallace makes a mistake, you flip the little black switch, and a buzzing sound fills the air. But Mr. Wallace continues to make mistakes. After you throw the tenth switch, Mr. Wallace shouts, "Get me out of here! I won't be in the experiment anymore! I refuse to go on!" You look at the experimenter, who says, "Please continue." You express concern, and the experimenter says, "The experiment requires you to continue." You protest, but the experimenter says, "It is absolutely essential that you continue."

Figure 32.6 Milgram's Teaching Machine

What would you do? Would you stop? Continue? If you obey the experimenter, the learner will start yelling, obviously in agony with the increasingly painful shocks. In the experiment, the "teacher" continues, and at the 330-volt mark, the learner refuses to answer. He is now screaming in pain at the shocks he is receiving. Eventually, there is only silence from

F • Y • I

Stanley Milgram himself asked his own students to violate a minor social norm—to get on a subway (or city bus) and ask another passenger for his or her seat. Students who tried this found the task to be nearly impossible. One graduate student reported: "I just couldn't go on. It was one of the most difficult things I ever did in my life."

Unconvinced, Milgram tried it himself. He approached a seated passenger. The request "seemed lodged in my trachea and would simply not emerge. I stood there frozen, then retreated, the mission unfulfilled." After several unsuccessful attempts, Milgram finally choked out the request: "Excuse me, sir, may I have your seat?" Milgram reported, "The man immediately stood up and gave me his seat!" But the experience wasn't over. In taking the man's seat, Milgram observed, "I was overwhelmed by the need to behave in a way that would justify my request. My head sank between my knees . . . I actually felt as if I were going to perish." Not until he left the train did his tension dissipate.

Milgram concluded that this simple experiment demonstrated several social principles.

- First, enormous inhibitory anxiety usually prevents us from breaking social norms.
- Second, we have a powerful need to justify our actions after violating a norm.
- Third, the power of immediate circumstances on our feelings and behavior is immense.

trb At this point, you may want to use **Application Activity:** ***Violating a Social Norm*** (*Teacher's Resource Binder*, p. 32-1).

■ JOURNAL WRITING

Invite students to use the following questions and writing prompts as springboards for entries in their psychology journals:

- Choose one of Milgram's experiments and decide whether or not you would obey. Why or why not?
- Are you normally obedient to the rules of your parents or the school? Why or why not?

trb At this point, you may want to use **Critical Thinking Activity:** ***Would You Obey?*** (*Teacher's Resource Binder*, p. 32-1; **Handout 32–5**).

MODULE 32

tr ■ TEACHING TIP

A four-color transparency of Figure 32.7, Shocking Results, is available in the **Overhead Transparencies Set.**

F•Y•I

Although attention is naturally drawn to the majority of Milgram's participants who obeyed, we can also learn much from the minority who confronted authority. Gretchen Brandt, a 31-year-old medical technician who worked at the University Medical School, provides one fascinating example to present in class.

Gretchen emigrated from Germany five years before the obedience studies. Speaking with a thick German accent, she coolly turned to the experimenter at different points and inquired, "Shall I continue?" At the delivery of 210 volts, she announced firmly, "Well, I'm sorry, I don't think we should continue." In spite of the experimenter's prompts, she refused to go further and the study ended.

Firm and resolute throughout, Gretchen never appeared tense or nervous. She simply stated that she "did not want to be responsible for any harm to the learner." Milgram notes that her straightforward, courteous demeanor seemed to make disobedience a simple and rational deed. "Her behavior," writes Milgram, "is the very embodiment of what I had initially envisioned would be true for almost all subjects."

What made Gretchen different? Interestingly, Gretchen grew to adolescence in Nazi Germany and, for the greater part of her youth, was exposed to Hitler's propaganda. When asked about the influence of her background, she simply remarked, "Perhaps we have seen too much pain."

Source: Milgram, S. (1974). *Obedience to authority.* New York: Harper & Row.

trb At this point, you may wish to use **Critical Thinking Activity:** *Would You Obey?* (*Teacher's Resource Binder*, p. 32-1; **Handout 32–5**).

▶ **Stanley Milgram (1933–1984)** Social psychologist who researched obedience to authority.

Stanley Milgram

Mr. Wallace. The experimenter explains that silence is considered a wrong answer, and teachers should deliver the shocks all the way up to the 450-volt switch.

Perhaps you've guessed by now that this experiment had nothing to do with learning. The "learner" was an actor with a script, and he never actually received any shock. The researcher, **Stanley Milgram,** wanted to know how far the "teachers" would go—how much shock they would deliver to another person because they had been told to do so.

How far would you have gone as the teacher? Milgram asked dozens of psychiatrists and psychologists to predict the results of his experiment. They all agreed that there was only a remote possibility that anyone would go all the way to 450 volts. Only sadists, those fringe members of society who enjoy inflicting pain, would inflict such severe shocks on a learner.

All the experts were wrong. Milgram found that an incredible *63 percent* of the participants (all men) obeyed instructions, flipping all 30 switches (Figure 32.7). Follow-up studies showed that women complied at about the same rate (Blass, 1999). Had the participants figured out that the learner was not really receiving shock? No. Videotapes showed the nervous teachers, biting their lips, trembling, and drenched in sweat.

Milgram ran several different versions of this experiment and found that the likelihood of **obedience** increased when the victim could not

Figure 32.7 **Shocking Results** About two-thirds of Milgram's participants obeyed the experimenter to the fullest extent.
(Data from Milgram, 1974)

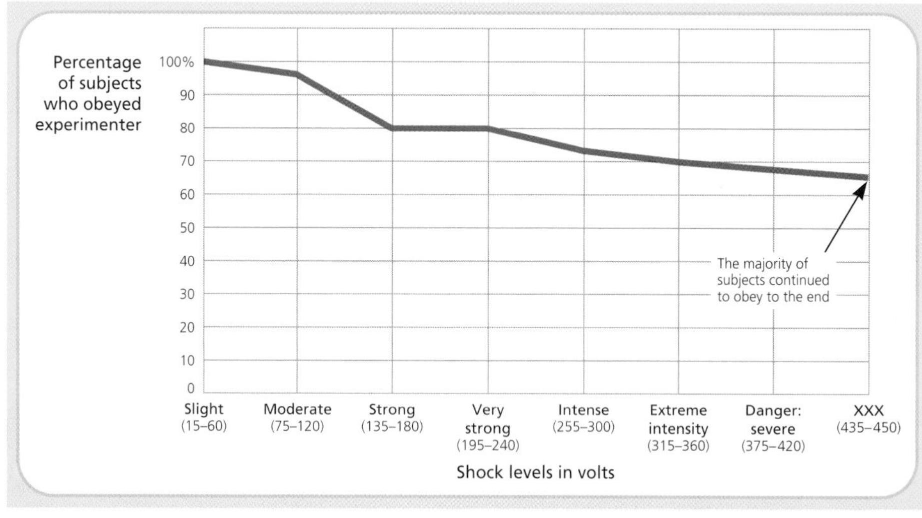

Enriching

WOLVES VERSUS SHEEP In one of Milgram's experiments, the "teacher" could select any shock level on the generator, without coercion from the experimenter. Ask students to use the scale in Figure 32.7 to make the following predictions: (1) What shock level do you think the teacher chose for the learner? (2) What percentage of teachers do you think set the shock at 450 volts? *(Milgram reported that only one subject pressed the maximum shock; in general, the shock level remained 45 to 60 volts.)*

tr A four-color transparency of Figure 32.7, Shocking Results, is available in the **Overhead Transparencies Set.**

trb Compare these results to **Critical Thinking Activity:** *Would You Obey?* (*Teacher's Resource Binder*, p. 32-1; **Handout 32–5**).

Source: Safer, M. (1980). Attributing evil to the subject, not the situation. *Personality and Social Psychology Bulletin, 6,* 205–209.

be seen, the authority figure giving the orders was close at hand, and the authority figure was part of a prestigious organization or institution. Obedience decreased if participants could observe a defiant role model.

Milgram's obedience experiment provoked a debate over research ethics. The American Psychological Association's *Code of Ethics,* developed after Milgram conducted his research, prohibits studies that stress participants as Milgram's did. Yes, the researchers debriefed the "teachers" after the experiment was over, and they all were able to see that Mr. Wallace had not been hurt. But 63 percent of those teachers had walked out of the laboratory thinking they had just shocked someone into silence. Milgram was concerned about the aftereffects on participants (Blass, 1996). He identified 40 teachers who had seemed most agonized and arranged for them to be interviewed by a psychiatrist. None of them appeared to be suffering emotionally. Experiments similar to Milgram's studies would not be allowed today.

What can we learn from Milgram's work? The lesson is not simply whether we should shock people to help them learn. Milgram, like most researchers, was not trying to re-create actual, real-life behaviors in his laboratory. Rather, he was interested in the underlying thought processes that mold behaviors.

The lesson Milgram wanted us to carry away was that ordinary people can be corrupted by an evil situation. Despite the predictions of behavior experts, normal, everyday, well-adjusted men and women were willing to follow orders and severely punish another human being for making a mistake. Soldiers also may follow orders and shoot unarmed civilians. Ordinary students who plan and carry out cruel initiation practices into clubs or other groups, using "tradition" as a lame justification, embark on a similar path. Milgram said, in summarizing his findings, "The fundamental lesson of our study is that ordinary people, simply doing their jobs, and without any particular hostility on their part, can become agents in a terrible destructive process" (1974, p. 6). This is a vivid lesson in the power of the situation. Situational factors, such as the presence of an authority figure, have far more influence on our behavior than most of us realize.

► **obedience** The tendency to comply with orders, implied or real, from someone perceived as an authority.

Group Influence

4. How does the presence of others influence our actions?

Have you ever had a friend who was very friendly when no one else was around but ignored you when other people were present? Does your behavior change when you're in a group of friends? When you're playing sports? When you're with your family? When you're around teachers or the principal? Social psychologists are interested in how we behave in small and large groups.

Cross-Curricular Connections

HISTORY Stanley Milgram conducted his experiments in the early 1960s, when people were still coming to grips with the consequences of the Holocaust. People believed that the German people were evil for being complicit in the Holocaust; Milgram, himself a Jew, wanted to demonstrate the power of social situations on people's behavior.

Have students research this particularly painful time in history, using the following questions to direct research and subsequent discussion:

- What techniques did Hitler and his propaganda officers use to convince the German people to comply with the Holocaust?
- Highlight some examples of German citizens who tried to save Jews from the genocide. Why were these people able to disobey?

MODULE 32

■ JOURNAL WRITING

Invite students to use the following questions and writing prompts as springboards for entries in their psychology journals:

- Are you surprised that women and men have similar levels of obedience? Why or why not?
- If Milgram's experiments were conducted at your school today, would he get different results? Why or why not?

trb At this point, you may wish to use Enrichment Lesson: *Obedience in Everyday Life* (*Teacher's Resource Binder,* p. 32-1).

web ■ LOOKING AT THE ISSUES

Discuss with students the ethical issues that arise out of experiments like Stanley Milgrim's obedience study.

- Does the APA Ethics Code allow for deception? Why or why not?
- Would this study be approved by an IRB today? Why or why not?
- What responsibilities do researchers have for the well-being of their subjects?

For more information about the APA Ethics Code, see the document on line at www.apa.org/ethics.

■ APPLYING THE POINTS

Colleges and universities across the country have moved to ban hazing by fraternities, sororities, and social clubs. Have students contact university student relations departments, fraternity and sorority members, and alumni of these organizations (students' parents may qualify). Use the questions below as a guide to an informal interview and subsequent discussion:

- What are current university policies regarding hazing? What sanctions will be imposed on organizations that haze?
- How did the university view hazing in the past?
- How do the fraternities' and sororities' national organizations view hazing?
- Did the alumni endure hazing? How did they view it then? Would they want their children to endure it? Why or why not?

trb At this point, you may wish to use Enrichment Lesson: *The Justification of Effort* (*Teacher's Resource Binder,* p. 32-1).

MODULE 32

■ JOURNAL WRITING

Invite students to use the following questions and writing prompts as springboards for entries in their psychology journals:

- Have you ever acted friendly toward a person when alone but not friendly when around a particular crowd that didn't like that person? Why or why not?
- Are you a different person when you play sports? If so, how? Is your performance better when you play before the home crowd or in front of a hostile away crowd? Why?
- Do you behave differently with family and friends? In different classes? Why or why not?

■ TEACHING TIPS

trb **tr** (1) A black-line master of Table 32.1, Home-Field Advantage in Major Team Sports, is available in the **Black-Line Masters Appendix** in the *Teacher's Resource Binder*.

(2) Relate *social facilitation* to *test anxiety*. Although some people feel distinct anxiety any time they take a test, most people only feel anxiety if they are not prepared. Edward Thorndike proposed the **law of readiness,** which states, in part, that if one is not ready for a performance, he or she will feel frustrated and will actively seek to avoid the performance. If one is ready, then he or she will be willing and ready to perform.

(3) The **Yerkes-Dodson law** also addresses how arousal effects performance. This law states that there needs to be an optimal level of arousal present if we want to perform our best. Too little arousal, performance is half-hearted. Too much arousal, performance is sloppy.

■ APPLYING THE POINTS

Interview your school's athletic coaches for team sports, asking them how they motivate all members of the team to do their best.

- What techniques do they use?
- What sanctions do they impose for team members who don't give their all? Is this motivating for other team members? Why or why not?

▶ **social facilitation** Improved performance of tasks in the presence of others; occurs with simple or well-learned tasks but not with tasks that are difficult or not yet learned.

Our Behavior in the Presence of Others

A track coach once told me the fastest times in both the short- and long-distance races were always turned in during the track meets with lots of fans, not during practice. Research supports the track coach's statement. Our behavior changes noticeably, and not always for the better, in the presence of others.

Social Facilitation The improved performance of tasks in the presence of others is called **social facilitation.** Some of the studies supporting social facilitation were done more than a century ago. One researcher discovered that cyclists scored faster times when racing one another than when simply racing the clock (Triplett, 1898). The same researcher asked a different set of participants to reel in a fishing line as fast as possible. These "fastest" times were bettered when the same people reeled in the same fishing line in the presence of another person reeling in line.

Both of these tasks are relatively easy. Later research has demonstrated that social facilitation is at its best with simple or well-learned tasks, but *not* with tasks that are difficult or not yet mastered. Being watched increases our arousal. Arousal strengthens our ability to perform well-learned tasks, but it diminishes our performance on tasks we have not yet mastered. This was illustrated in a study on pool players (Michaels & others, 1982). Master pool players made 71 percent of their shots when alone but upped that score to 80 percent when four people observed them play. Not-so-good pool players made 36 percent of their shots with nobody watching but only 25 percent in the presence of others. Research (Guerin, 1986; Zajonc, 1965) supports the notion that the social facilitation effect is a sword with two sides. Tasks we find difficult may seem impossible with an audience watching. But give us an audience for the things we do well—especially a supportive audience—and we're likely to do even better. Does this mean there's a home team advantage in sports? To a degree, yes (Table 32.1). Social facilitation helps explain this advantage.

TABLE 32.1 HOME-FIELD ADVANTAGE IN MAJOR TEAM SPORTS

SPORT	GAMES STUDIED	HOME TEAM WINNING PERCENTAGE
Baseball	23,034	53.5%
Football	2,592	57.3
Ice hockey	4,322	61.1
Basketball	13,596	64.4
Soccer	37,202	69.0

From Courneya & Carrron, 1992

Demonstrating

RATING PERFORMANCE Take your class to your school's gym and have some students volunteer to shoot baskets. Have them shoot baskets twice: with the class acting as a supportive home crowd and as a hostile away crowd (not too hostile— just booing and distracting). Have someone record the number of shots each volunteer gets under each of these two conditions.

- Did the person perform better under friendly or hostile conditions?
- How much experience did each person have at shooting baskets? Did a basketball team member do better than someone who had never played before? Why or why not?

Social Loafing Do we always try to do our best in the presence of others? Maybe not. Have you ever been asked by a teacher to work on a "group project"? Let's say you're put in a group of five, and your project will be given one grade. All group members will get the same grade, regardless of how much work they put in. What usually happens in this situation, where we have to perform a task as a group? If your experience is anything like mine, a couple of people usually end up doing most of the work. Social psychologists call this **social loafing,** the tendency for individuals in a group to exert themselves less when pooling their efforts toward attaining a common goal than when individually accountable. Several different studies have illustrated this tendency. In one, researchers blindfolded students, handed them a rope, and asked them to pull as hard as they possibly could (Ingham & others, 1974). When the blindfolded students thought three others were behind them pulling, their "best" pulling efforts dropped by almost 20 percent, compared with earlier measures of their individual ability.

Who's Working? In small groups, some people often do less work than others. Social loafing may happen because people feel less responsible or simply because they feel their help is not really needed.

Why does social loafing occur? Perhaps because people working in a group feel less accountable for the product. With less accountability comes less worry about what others think. Or perhaps social loafers think their efforts are simply not necessary (Harkins & Szymanski, 1989; Kerr & Bruun, 1983). Whether it's in the classroom or in some business, when group members receive an equal share of group benefits, slackers, in the form of social loafers, are likely to emerge.

Deindividuation Social facilitation increases physiological arousal. Social loafing decreases the sense of responsibility. What happens when people are in a group, and they become aroused *and* lose their sense of responsibility? Social psychologists might predict that the combination would increase the chances of **deindividuation**—the loss of self-awareness and self-restraint occurring in anonymous, arousal-fostering, group situations. Examples of deindividuation are easy to find, and they make the news when taken to an extreme. In the 2001 National Football League season, Cleveland fans covered one end of the field with beer bottles when they thought a referee's call cost them the game. Sports fans often yell things during a game that they would never yell if they were alone in the stands and easily identified. Store lootings during riots are another example of deindividuation. The less restrained and self-conscious a person feels, the more likely deindividuation is to occur. We are more responsive to group influence when we lose self-awareness.

▶ **social loafing** The tendency for people in a group to exert less effort when pooling their efforts toward attaining a common goal than when individually accountable.

▶ **deindividuation** The loss of self-awareness and self-restraint occurring in group situations that foster arousal and anonymity.

Cross-Curricular Connections

ATHLETICS Have students research your school's sports teams' statistics. Do they notice signs of social facilitation in the following statistics?

- home wins versus away wins for team sports like football, soccer, basketball, and baseball
- home wins versus away wins for individual sports like track, wrestling, and cross-country
- individual records/best games earned at home or away for all sports (For example, do basketball players hit more free throws at home or away? Do track athletes run faster at home or away? Do football players individually have higher stats for home games or away games?)

trb tr Students may want to compare their results with those in Table 32.1, Home-Field Advantage in Major Team Sports, which is available as a black-line master in the **Black-Line Masters Appendix** in the *Teacher's Resource Binder.*

■ LOOKING AT THE ISSUES

Have students brainstorm ways to minimize social loafing during group projects.

- Does assigning roles and evaluating members help minimize social loafing? Why or why not?
- How can groups motivate members to work their hardest during group work?

■ TEACHING TIP

Students may have seen news reports about sports fans rioting after both winning and losing major championship games. Have students come up with reasons why this behavior occurs and how deindividuation plays into these events.

trb At this point, you may wish to use **Demonstration Activity:** ***Deindividuation*** (*Teacher's Resource Binder,* p. 32-1).

F • Y • I

Does deindividuation always bring out hostility and aggression? Consider the following study.

The researcher ushers subjects into a chamber that is either fully lighted or totally dark, except for a tiny red light over the door. By this light, the subjects can find their way out if they want to leave the experiment. The researcher says, "You will be left in the room for no more than an hour with some other people, and there are no rules as to what you should do together. At the end you will leave the room alone and will never meet the other participants." Then, seven strangers of both sexes spend the next 60 minutes together.

In the lighted room, participants made light conversation. In the dark room, participants talked less but about more important things. Ninety percent intentionally touched someone and half hugged another. Very few disliked the experience, and most volunteered to return without pay. Anonymity had released intimacy.

Source: Gergen, K. J., Gergen, M. M., & Barton, W. H. (1979, October). Deviance in the dark. *Psychology Today,* 129–130.

MODULE 32

F•Y•I

Tell students the following true-life event to illustrate some of the results shown in Figure 32.8, Group Polarization.

Tom and John Metzger, leaders of the White Aryan Resistance (WAR) movement, appeared on *The Geraldo Rivera Show* in November of 1988, along with African-American activists. Geraldo invited both groups to the show to discuss their differences, hoping for reconciliation. But group polarization took hold of each group as racial slurs and insults began flying between the two groups. Ultimately, a brawl ensued, leaving Rivera with a broken nose. Getting two groups together to talk is not very effective in changing strongly held attitudes since group members bolster each other's commonly held beliefs, resulting in those beliefs becoming stronger.

trb At this point, you may wish to use **Cooperative Learning Activity:** *Group Polarization* (*Teacher's Resource Binder*, p. 32-1; **Handouts 32–6a** and **32–6b**).

tr A four-color transparency of Figure 32.8, Group Polarization, is available in the **Overhead Transparencies Set.**

CHECKING FOR UNDERSTANDING

In a short paper, have students explain how a group can be positively and negatively influenced. Students should be able to accurately describe social facilitation and, at times, group polarization on the positive side in addition to social loafing, deindividuation, and groupthink on the negative.

▶ **group polarization** The enhancement of a group's prevailing attitudes through discussion within the group.

Group Interaction Effects

5. How do group polarization and groupthink demonstrate the power of group influence?

The presence of others can affect us in good ways (social facilitation) or bad (deindividuation, social loafing). The same is true of group interactions. Let's take a closer look at group polarization and groupthink.

Group Polarization

When politically oriented clubs, such as the Young Democrats or Teenage Republicans (as they are called in my school), gather to discuss local and national political issues, what's most likely to happen to their attitudes? Do the liberals become more or less liberal as they talk with one another? Are the conservatives more or less likely to take more conservative stances on issues by the close of their meeting? **Group polarization,** the enhancement of a group's already existing attitudes through discussion within the group, would predict that liberals will become more liberal and conservatives will become more conservative. Evidently, our attitudes tend to migrate to an extreme, like the poles of the Earth, when we're around like-minded people. David Myers and George Bishop (1970) found just this effect. Low-prejudice groups who discussed racial issues expressed even less prejudice after their discussion than they had before (Figure 32.8). Similarly—and unfortunately—high-prejudice groups expressed higher levels of prejudice following their discussion of racial issues. Discussion among the like-minded tends to strengthen preexisting attitudes.

Figure 32.8 **Group Polarization** When like-minded people discuss issues involving prejudice, their original views on prejudice are likely to intensify. (Data from Myers & Bishop, 1970)

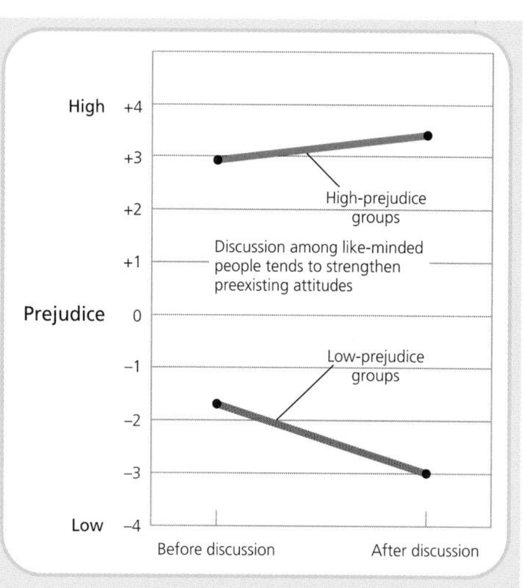

Other researchers (McCauley & Segal, 1987) studied terrorism as an example of group polarization. Terrorism does not just suddenly erupt. The terrorist mentality builds as people with the same grievances gather and become more extreme in their views. In the absence of any moderating influences, terrorism reaches the point of kidnappings, murder, and suicide bombings. Fanatics grow more fanatical as group polarization takes hold.

Groupthink

Group polarization drives us to extremes, but groupthink tends to paralyze us. I watched this happen a couple of years ago, when our Drill Team was getting ready to perform at halftime at a state boys basketball game. They decided to wear clothing, a "crop-top," that the administra-

Cooperative Learning

Choose an issue about which students can clearly argue either for or against. Ask some students to create two groups, with each group taking one side of the issue. (Group members should argue the position of their group whether, in fact, they believe in the position or not.) Give each group approximately 10 to 15 minutes to develop arguments, and then let the groups debate the issue informally in front of the class. Afterward, elicit students' feelings about these arguments.

- How did they feel about their side of the issue when they started discussion with their group?
- Did their feelings about the issue change as group members put forth convincing arguments?
- Did they become defensive about their position during the debate? Why or why not?

trb At this point, you may wish to use **Cooperative Learning Activity:** *Group Polarization* (*Teacher's Resource Binder*, p. 32-1; **Handouts 32–6a** and **32–6b**).

tion had banned. The music came up, and they danced their five-minute show in the crop-top, then left the court. When administrators later questioned the team members in an attempt to find out who was responsible for the decision to wear the banned clothing, they were amazed by the responses. Not one member of the dance group spoke up against wearing the crop-top, even though they all knew it was banned. Two had even written an advance apology to the principal, sliding it under his door after school an hour *before* the game. A senior on the squad later explained, "We didn't think anything would happen to us since it was our last performance. We had paid for the outfits and deserved to be able to wear them. And we all just wanted to get along for our last performance." What this senior did was explain that *groupthink* had taken place. **Groupthink** occurs when the desire for harmony in a decision-making group overrides a realistic appraisal of alternatives. We go along with a decision in order to get along with other people. In the case of the drill team, conformity, self-justification, overconfidence, and group polarization all fed into their groupthink decision to break the rules.

▶ **groupthink** The mode of thinking that occurs when the desire for harmony in a decision-making group overrides a realistic appraisal of the alternatives.

Groupthink seems to have played a role in several national fiascos and tragedies. Groupthink may have contributed to the 1986 explosion of the U.S. space shuttle *Challenger* (carrying social studies teacher Christa McAuliffe), for example (Esser & Lindoerfer, 1989). The NASA (National Aeronautics and Space Administration) management team had tremendous confidence in their ability to get *Challenger* into space, but they had been frustrated by numerous delays of this high-profile launch. Just before the launch was to take place, engineers voiced their opposition, citing concerns that rocket seals would not hold in the below-freezing weather. The management team demanded proof, and they did not pass on the engineers' concerns to the NASA executive in charge of the launch. The executive, thinking everybody had approved the mission, gave the order to launch, and *Challenger* flew into the history books as the biggest space disaster ever. The managers, who agreed to overlook the engineers' weather-related concerns, had given in to the lure of groupthink.

As you can see, resisting groupthink is sometimes vitally important. But *how* do you resist it? Irving Janis (1982) has three suggestions for group leaders:

1. Assign people to identify problems.
2. Be open to, and welcome, various opinions.
3. Invite experts to critique plans in various stages of development.

When it comes to making important decisions, there is strength in numbers, but only if you carefully consider your own reasons for casting your vote with the majority.

JOURNAL WRITING

Invite students to use the following questions as springboards for entries in their psychology journals:

- Have you ever gone along with a group against your better judgment? Why or why not?

APPLYING THE POINTS

Have volunteers interview your school's principal (or any teacher who has been with the school for a long time) to learn about times when students have collectively broken rules (like in the example the author offers). Suggest that volunteers use the following questions to guide their interview and a subsequent discussion of their findings:

- What rules were broken?
- What reasons did the students give for breaking those rules?
- What punishments were given to those students?
- Were any new rules or policies enacted to prevent such disobedience in the future? If so, have those been successful? Why or why not?

Cross-Curricular Connections

HISTORY Groupthink has affected several famous historical events. Using available print and online resources, have students research the following events, citing how groupthink failed to avoid or prevent dreadful consequences:

- the space shuttle *Columbia* accident
- the Bay of Pigs
- the Cuban Missile Crisis
- the Vietnam conflict

(V) At this point, you may wish to show **Videocassette: *Scientific American Frontiers*, Second Edition, Segment 29: "Superpower Ping Pong"** (*Teacher's Resource Binder*, p. 32-1).

MODULE 32

F•Y•I

The source of the quote the author attributes to his grandfather is Henry Ford, the great innovator who developed the first assembly line.

■ JOURNAL WRITING

Invite students to use the following question and writing prompt as springboards for entries in their psychology journals:

- Have you ever fallen victim to a self-fulfilling prophecy? Describe your experience.

■ LOOKING AT THE ISSUES

People who believe they are not good in school tend to do poorly, thus confirming their beliefs. Have students discuss the following questions in a class forum that addresses students' perceptions of school:

- What factors lead to someone feeling positively or negatively about school?
- Does the posting of grades lead students to feel better or worse about their performance? How?
- What can teachers do to encourage positive thinking about school?

▶ **self-fulfilling prophecy** Occurs when someone's belief about others leads one to act in ways that induce the others to appear to confirm the belief.

Our Power as Individuals

6. How do self-fulfilling prophecies and minority influence demonstrate the power of the individual?

We have talked at length about *social* thinking and social influence, or the power of the group. What about *personal control,* or the power of the individual? We can see this power in self-fulfilling prophecies and minority influence.

Self-Fulfilling Prophecies My grandfather used to say, "Whether you think you can or you can't, you're right." He didn't originate that quotation, but he was offering a perfect description of a **self-fulfilling prophecy:** We believe something to be true about others (or ourselves) and we act in ways that cause this belief to come true. In one study, researchers told men that a certain woman found them either attractive or unattractive. The researchers then recorded and analyzed conversations between the men and the woman, revealing a self-fulfilling prophecy. If the man *thought* the woman saw him as attractive, he was more charming and she was more likely to act as if she did think he was attractive (Ridge & Reber, 1998).

If self-fulfilling prophecies come true, could we foster relationships by idealizing our partners? Apparently so. Over time, people seem to accept their partner's idealized perceptions as reality (Murray & others, 1996; Murray & Holmes, 2000). So if your partner thinks of you as thoughtful and smart, you may internalize this perception and behave more thoughtfully and competently. Perhaps we can adapt grandpa's philosophy: If you think your partner is bright or dim, clever or slow, honest or untruthful, sensitive or insensitive, you may turn out to be right.

One Can Make a Difference Rosa Parks refused to sit in the back of the bus, a section reserved for African-Americans. Her refusal triggered a boycott of buses and eventually those rules changed. Rosa Parks' actions helped set the civil rights movement in motion.

Minority Influence Throughout the history of our world, individuals have had tremendous influences on groups. Rosa Parks refused to give up her seat to a white man and move to the back of a bus, and she fueled a civil rights movement. Mahatma Gandhi refused to eat as a political protest, and India won independence from Britain. Both overcame the majority's resistance to change.

Minorities can sway majorities, but only if they stand firm. Social psychologists (for example, Moscovici, 1985), found that minorities who waffle in their convictions have trouble persuading others, while those who are unwavering are

Enriching

Have students develop character studies of famous individuals who stood up against a majority to enact positive change. In these character studies, students should explore the qualities and beliefs their subjects possessed that enabled them to stand firm. Working individually or with a partner, encourage students to write their study, read it aloud to the class, and then contribute it to a collaborative student booklet that the class can then title. Encourage students to find culturally diverse examples for their subjects, in addition to those people listed below:

- Martin Luther King, Jr.
- Che Guevara
- William Wallace (of the movie *Braveheart*)
- Martin Luther
- Galileo Galilei
- Joan of Arc

far more successful in their persuasive efforts. The people steadfastly holding minority opinions may not win the popularity contests, but they may become influential. If you have the courage to voice your belief in a minority opinion, your influence on others may not be obvious at first. But by causing members of the majority to rethink their opinions, you may be planting the seeds of change.

REVIEW

Module 32: Social Thinking and Social Influence

What's the Point?

Social psychologists are interested in the way we form our beliefs and attitudes about the world around us. They also study how our behavior changes in the presence of other people.

Social Thinking

1. *What is the difference between a dispositional attribution and a situational attribution?*

   When we attribute a person's behavior, we attempt to explain it by relating it to a cause. We can attribute behaviors to a person's disposition (internal state) or to the situation (an external condition). The fundamental attribution error is the tendency when explaining other people's behavior to underestimate the effect of the situation and overestimate the effect of the person's disposition.

2. *How do our attitudes and our actions interact?*

   Attitudes are beliefs and feelings that predispose us to act in certain ways. Attitudes are not always consistent with actions. They influence our actions most when outside influences are minimal, when we are very aware of what we believe, and when our beliefs are directly related to our behaviors.

   Actions can also affect our attitudes. The foot-in-the-door phenomenon, for example, describes our tendency to grant a large request after granting a related small request. Role playing also affects our attitudes. We all play roles when we take new jobs or enter new relationships. Initially, we may feel uneasy and as though we are pretending, but after acting out the new role, we no longer feel this way. Cognitive dissonance is the action we take when we feel conflicted because our attitudes do not match our actions. If we have acted contrary to our attitudes, we tend to adjust our attitudes to match our behavior.

Social Influence

Other people's attitudes and behaviors also influence our own. Social psychologists have studied this effect in their research on conformity and obedience.

3. *Under what conditions are we most likely to conform and obey?*

   Solomon Asch is famous for his studies of conformity. He found that even in very simple judgments, people were willing to conform to the opinion of others. Other researchers demonstrated that we are most likely to conform when the task is difficult and important. We are most likely to conform when we feel incompetent or insecure; are in a group of three or more; the rest of the group shares a unanimous opinion; are impressed by the status of the group; have

MODULE 32

Close

Social influences are powerful, as this module has demonstrated. Have students consider the following questions:

- Do you feel that you are easily influenced by groups? Why or why not?
- Do you feel you are the influential one in your group? Why or why not?
- Knowing how powerful group influence can be, how can you use this knowledge to improve your life?

Checking the Points

■ **TEACHING TIPS**

web (1) The book companion site for *Thinking About Psychology* at www.worthpublishers.com/thinkingaboutpsych contains a module quiz, flashcards of key terms and people, as well as other student activities and resources for this module. You will also find PowerPoint lectures, a quiz grade book, and other teaching resources by logging on as an instructor.

trb (2) At this point, you may wish to review and confirm concepts about social thinking and social influence with **Critical Thinking Activity:** *Fact or Falsehood?* (*Teacher's Resource Binder*, p. 32-1; **Handout 32–1**). If students filled in this handout earlier in the module, ask them to set it aside. Suggest that students complete the handout in small groups, taking the time to look up information in the text in order to respond correctly to questions. Have all the groups meet to review the handout, again using the text to support their responses.

MODULE 32

trb **tr** ■ TEACHING TIP

At this point, you may wish to provide students with **Building Vocabulary: Graphic Organizer:** *Crossword Puzzle* (*Teacher's Resource Binder*, p. 32-1; **Handout 32–2**). If students completed the puzzle earlier in the module, ask them to set it aside. Have students fill out the crossword puzzle as a tool for reviewing the module concepts. You may want to show a correctly completed crossword puzzle by using the handout as a transparency and projecting it for students to check their work.

made no prior commitments to a specific response; are being observed by others in the group; and our culture strongly encourages respect for social standards.

Stanley Milgram is famous for his studies of obedience, in which "teachers" had to inflict "shocks" on "learners." Only the teachers were really participants in the experiments, and the shocks were not real. But participants did not know this, and they were willing to obey authorities and deliver what they believed to be painful shocks to others. Under the APA Code of Ethics, Milgram's studies would not be allowed today, even though no participant suffered serious psychological damage from discovering what they were willing to do. Milgram said that the lesson to be learned from the studies is that ordinary people can become agents in a destructive process.

4. *How does the presence of others influence our actions?*

   Under some conditions, the presence of others can improve our performance, an influence known as *social facilitation*. Knowing we are watched increases our arousal. Increased arousal causes us to perform better on simple or well-learned tasks, but it causes us to perform less competently on tasks we have not fully mastered. But sometimes when we work with others, we exert less effort toward a common goal. This *social loafing* may be the result of feeling less accountable for the work or believing our help is not needed. *Deindividuation*—the loss of self-awareness and self-restraint—occurs in group situations that foster arousal but also anonymity. A mob mentality results.

5. *How do group polarization and groupthink demonstrate the power of group influence?*

   Group polarization is the tendency for people's existing feelings and beliefs to intensify during discussions with like-minded people. Groupthink is the tendency to "go along to get along"—to conform to the opinions and decisions of the group, even if your own opinions would lead you to a different decision. In both cases, the presence of the group and the knowledge of their views shoves us to an extreme, or in a direction, that differs from what we might do if we were alone.

6. *How do self-fulfilling prophecies and minority influence demonstrate the power of the individual?*

   When we make a self-fulfilling prophecy, we act out our beliefs about ourselves or others. Our actions, in turn, cause others to conform to the belief we have about them, confirming our belief. Thus, if I treat you as a friend, you may behave in a friendly way toward me. Individuals can also resist the power of the group and sometimes may even change group attitudes or decisions. We are most successful in persuading others when we are consistent in our beliefs.

Key Terms

social psychology, p. 613
attribution theory, p. 614
fundamental attribution error, p. 614
attitude, p. 617
foot-in-door phenomenon, p. 618
cognitive dissonance, p. 619
conformity, p. 621
obedience, p. 624
social facilitation, p. 626
social loafing, p. 627
deindividuation, p. 627
group polarization, p. 628
groupthink, p. 629
self-fulfilling prophecy, p. 630

Key People

Solomon Asch, p. 621
Stanley Milgram, p. 624

Self-Test

Multiple-Choice Questions

Choose the *best* answer for each of the following questions.

1. Ben is a firm believer in eating healthy foods, and he exercises daily to stay in shape. Today, on the way home from the gym, he bought and quickly ate a big slice of pizza with double cheese and three kinds of meat on it. Later, Ben was feeling a little guilty about indulging himself with the high-fat food, but the more he thought about it, the healthier the pizza seemed. After all, the cheese contains calcium, the meat and the cheese contain protein, the tomato sauce has antioxidants in it, and the crust has carbohydrates for energy. Suddenly Ben realized—pizza *is* a health food. Ben is resolving his
   a. indigestion.
   b. deindividuation.
   c. social loafing.
   d. cognitive dissonance.
2. Rita recently learned to play chess. There is a chess tournament next week, and Rita's friend, Tomas, who is an expert chess player, wants her to participate. Tomas says that when he plays in front of an audience, he is always a little more skilled than when he plays with just one friend. Tomas is sure Rita's chess skills will improve when she plays in front of a crowd, too. Does research on social facilitation support Tomas' belief?
   a. No. Knowing we are watched increases our arousal, and increased arousal causes us to perform better on well-learned tasks but worse on tasks we have not fully mastered.
   b. Yes. Knowing we are watched increases our arousal, and increased arousal causes us to perform worse on well-learned tasks but better on tasks we have not fully mastered.
   c. No. Social facilitation has nothing to do with performing in front of a crowd.
   d. Yes. Social facilitation is the loss of self-awareness and self-restraint that occurs in group situations that foster anonymity.
3. Miss Seto, the librarian, always looks stern and tells everyone to be quiet and read or to leave the library. Many students were amazed to find out that Miss Seto is dating the best stand-up comedian at the local comedy club. Students have made a common mistake about Miss Seto by underestimating the effect of the situation (working in a school library) and overestimating the effect of her disposition. This is known as
   a. cognitive dissonance.
   b. the fundamental attribution error.
   c. the foot-in-the (library) door phenomenon.
   d. social facilitation.
4. Coach McGurk chose the five strongest boys in his classes to compete in the intramural tug of war contest. Each of these boys weighs at least 100 pounds, and each could easily pull his own weight 10 feet across a smooth-surfaced floor all by himself. The coach then gave the boys a practice task of pulling a 500-pound dummy 10 feet across the floor. For some reason, the boys could not perform this task. A social psychologist would suspect that the problem was
   a. social loafing.
   b. the fundamental attribution error.
   c. cognitive dissonance.
   d. groupthink.
5. Sheila is no more attractive or intelligent than other girls in her class, but she believes she is prettier and more appealing than they are. This belief causes her to be confident about her ability to make friends

tb Using the Test Bank

The *Test Bank* that accompanies this textbook offers a wide variety of questions in different formats and levels of complexity. Use the software to construct whole tests or to integrate standardized questions into teacher-made tests.

Self-Test Answers

Multiple-Choice Questions

1. d, 2. a, 3. b, 4. a, 5. c

MODULE 32

Self-Test Answers

Multiple-Choice Questions (continued)

6. a

Matching Terms and Definitions

7. a. (5), b. (8), c. (2), d. (1), e. (7), f. (4)

Fill-in-the-Blank Questions

7. Solomon Asch, 8. Stanley Milgram

Brief Essay Question

10. Adam is using groupthink to get people to follow his wishes. He knows that his senior status will likely lead people to be sympathetic to his plight. Those people will want to help him have a good senior year. People will be less likely to go against him because of his probable popularity. Getting the entire group together also encourages group polarization. The group will discuss the issue and become firm in their beliefs, further limiting dissent. Deindividuation is also present since people who are part of a big crowd are less likely to stand against the majority.

and to get dates for parties and school functions. When she talks with boys, she's quite charming and even a little bit of a flirt. Sheila is acting out a

a. form of groupthink.
b. situational attribution.
c. self-fulfilling prophecy.
d. fundamental attribution error.

6. On Halloween, groups of young teenagers in many American neighborhoods dress up in costumes and smear cars with shaving cream, throw raw eggs at houses, and try to wrap the world in toilet paper—things they would never do at noon on a bright summer day. Social psychologists would see the Halloween behavior as an example of
 a. deindividuation.
 b. obedience.
 c. group polarization.
 d. social facilitation.

Matching Terms and Definitions:

7. For each definition, choose the *best* matching term from the list that follows:

Definition

a. A belief and feeling that predisposes one to respond in a particular way to objects, people, and events.
b. The enhancement of a group's prevailing attitudes through discussion within the group.
c. The tendency to explain other people's behavior in terms of their personal qualities or internal attributes.
d. The scientific study of how we think about, influence, and relate to one another.
e. The tendency to comply with orders, implied or real, from someone we perceive as an authority.
f. The tendency for people who have first agreed to a small request to comply later with a larger request.

Term

(1) social psychology
(2) dispositional attribution
(3) situational attribution
(4) foot-in-the-door phenomenon
(5) attitude
(6) conformity
(7) obedience
(8) group polarization

Fill-in-the-Blank Questions

8. ________________ ________________ researched the circumstances under which people conform.

9. ________________ ________________ researched obedience to authority.

Brief Essay Question

10. Ted is a new eleventh-grader at Big Suburb High School. He is an exceptionally good quarterback, and he played that position on the football team at his last high school. Adam, a twelfth-grader who has been Big Suburb's star quarterback for the past two years, is worried that Ted will replace him during this final season. Adam called a meeting of the football team, the cheerleaders, the soccer team, the basketball team, and the marching band for Friday at his house. He urged all the students at that meeting to pressure Ted to drop out of football this year. Everyone agreed to try to influence Ted and to exclude him from all social gatherings if he didn't drop out. After the meeting, though, some students said that they would go along with the group decision, but they liked Ted and thought he was being treated unfairly.

 In two paragraphs of about three sentences each, describe two different forms of social influence that are at work in this situation.

Performance Standards

Standard Area: Social and Cultural Dimensions of Behavior

Content Standard 1: Social thinking

Performance Standard 1.1 Investigate person perception.

- Examine how physical attractiveness can influence our perceptions of others. (Student Text pp. 635–638)

Content Standard 3: Group influence

Performance Standard 3.1 Explain how the presence of others affects individual behavior.

- Discuss the bystander effect. Present the case of Kitty Genovese as an example. (Student Text pp. 640–642)

Performance Standard 3.2 Explain how social structures influence intergroup relationships.

- Discuss the nature of conflict. Investigate the role of superordinate goals in fostering cooperation among groups. (Student Text p. 651)

Performance Standard 3.3 Examine bias and discrimination.

- Explain how prejudice, stereotypes, and discrimination differ. (Student Text pp. 642–643)
- Explain how ingroups, outgroups, and scapegoats relate to prejudice, stereotypes, and discrimination. (Student Text pp. 644–645)
- Examine how our thought processes, such as categorization and the just-world phenomenon, foster prejudice. (Student Text pp. 645–646)

Content Standard 4: Social influence

Performance Standard 4.2 Examine the nature of altruism.

- Define altruism. Investigate the conditions that foster altruism. (Student Text pp. 640–642)

Performance Standard 4.3 Examine the nature of aggression.

- Define aggression. Examine how genetics, our nervous system, biochemistry, and learning contribute to aggression. (Student Text pp. 647–651)
- Discuss the relationship between playing violent video games and violence. (Student Text p. 650)

Materials NETWORK

All of the items from the Video, Activity, and Enrichment Centers listed below come from the *Teacher's Resource Binder.* These items will help you teach and expand on concepts presented in Module 33.

trb This logo indicates when an item from the Materials Network may be used in conjunction with a specific note found in this module's *Teacher's Edition.*

Attraction

Activity Center

- Critical Thinking Activity: *Fact or Falsehood?* With this activity, students' preconceptions about social relations are either exposed as incorrect or reinforced as correct. (*Teacher's Resource Binder*, p. 33-1; Handout 33–1)
- Building Vocabulary: Graphic Organizer: *Crossword Puzzle* Students can learn the concepts in this module by using module terms to fill in a crossword puzzle. (*Teacher's Resource Binder*, p. 33-1; Handout 33–2)
- Technology Application Activity: *Social Psychology on the Web* Students can access this site on the Web and participate in on-line experiments, tutorials, and activities designed to increase understanding of social psychology. (*Teacher's Resource Binder*, p. 33-1; Handout 33–3)
- Technology Application Activity: *PsychQuest:* "How Do We Pick Our Mates?" *PsychQuest* is an interactive CD-ROM that students can use to learn more about various topics in psychology. This activity shows how selecting a mate makes evolutionary sense. (*Teacher's Resource Binder*, p. 33-1)

Enrichment Center

- Enrichment Lesson: *What Is Beautiful Is Good* The importance of physical attractiveness is not limited to dating relationships, as this lesson explains. (*Teacher's Resource Binder*, p. 33-1)
- Enrichment Lesson: *How Do We Pick Our Mates?* People finally settle on one person to marry, after going through a series of filters to weed out people who don't meet certain qualifications. (*Teacher's Resource Binder*, p. 33-1)

Romantic Love

Activity Center

- Critical Thinking Activity: *Love Styles* Sociologist John Alan Lee and psychologists Clyde Hendrick and Susan Hendrick have described six types of love, which are assessed in this activity. (*Teacher's Resource Binder*, p. 33-1; Handout 33–4)
- Critical Thinking Activity: *The Trust Scale* Equity and self-disclosure are key ingredients of loving relationships. Introduce *trust* as a third ingredient with this activity. (*Teacher's Resource Binder*, p. 33-1; Handout 33–5)

Enrichment Center

- Enrichment Lesson: *Passionate Love* Elaine Hatfield distinguishes two types of love: *temporary passionate love* and more enduring *companionate love*. Introduce the first type with this lesson. (*Teacher's Resource Binder*, p. 33-1)

Altruism

Activity Center

- Evaluation Activity: *Why Do People Volunteer?* Not only do different volunteers pursue different goals; the same volunteer may be pursuing more than one goal. This activity will measure students' reasons for volunteering. (*Teacher's Resource Binder*, p. 33-1; Handout 33–6)
- Analysis Activity: *Pleasurable Versus Philanthropic Activities—Which Brings More Happiness?* Research on *flow* and *optimism* shows that positive affect lasts longer after a person has been engaged in rewarding yet challenging activities than in activities that bring only physical or homeostatic pleasure. Have students evaluate their own feelings about philanthropy with this lesson. (*Teacher's Resource Binder*, p. 33-1)

Enrichment Center

- Enrichment Lesson: *Case Studies in Helping* Each year, the Carnegie Hero Fund Commission reviews the stories of some 800 to 1000 rescues in the United States and Canada; then, it selects medal winners. Presenting some of these case stories in class provides a good introduction to the topic of altruism. (*Teacher's Resource Binder*, p. 33-1)
- Enrichment Lesson: *The Bystander Effect and Legislating Helping* Observers sometimes do intervene. In fact, they may actually apprehend a criminal and mete out punishment. (*Teacher's Resource Binder*, p. 33-1)
- Enrichment Lesson: *Europeans Who Helped Jews Escape* Examine Perry London's intriguing work on Europeans who risked their lives in attempting to help Jews escape Nazi-occupied Europe. (*Teacher's Resource Binder*, p. 33-1)

Prejudice

Activity Center

- Application Activity: *Measuring Stereotypes* With this lesson, demonstrate one way in which contemporary researchers measure stereotypes (a generalized belief about a group of people). (*Teacher's Resource Binder*, p. 33-1; Handout 33–7)
- Technology Application Activity: *Implicit Association Test* Invite students to visit the Web site of the Implicit Association Test (IAT). The site provides fascinating coverage of research about how our private attitudes are not always the ones that we are willing to express publicly. (*Teacher's Resource Binder*, p. 33-1; Handout 33–8)
- Technology Application Activity: *PsychQuest:* "How Do We Form Social Relationships?" *PsychQuest* is an interactive CD-ROM that students can use to learn more about various topics in psychology. This activity focuses on psychological factors that contribute to the formation of stereotypes. (*Teacher's Resource Binder*, p. 33-1)
- Cooperative Learning Activity: *Positions of Privilege and Institutional Discrimination* Sandra Lawrence provides a powerful experiential exercise that challenges white, middle-class students to see their privileged position and to question their assumptions about the less privileged. (*Teacher's Resource Binder*, p. 33-1)
- Cooperative Learning Activity: *Institutional Discrimination* Extend the text treatment of prejudice with a classroom discussion of how institutional practices as well as individuals' attitudes, perpetuate social inequality. Susan Goldstein designed this activity to facilitate student understanding of how institutional forces contribute to social oppression. (*Teacher's Resource Binder*, p. 33-1; Handout 33–9)
- Analysis Activity: *Belief in a Just World* Melvin Lerner's just-world hypothesis states that we all need to believe in a world in which people get what they deserve and conversely deserve what they get. As the text points out, this belief may contribute to prejudice by leading us to blame victims for their own fate. (*Teacher's Resource Binder*, p. 33-1; Handout 33–10)

Enrichment Center

- Enrichment Lesson: *Racial Prejudice* How has racial discrimination and prejudice changed in the United States since the 1950s? This lesson examines how researchers measure prejudice. (*Teacher's Resource Binder*, p. 33-1)

Aggression

V Video Center

- Videocassette: *The Brain,* Second Edition, Module 24: "Aggression, Violence, and the Brain" Consult the faculty guide from *The Brain* video series for a description of this module. (*Teacher's Resource Binder*, p. 33-1)

Activity Center

- Critical Thinking Activity: *Defining Aggression* Ludy Benjamin, Jr., has designed an exercise that provides an excellent introduction to the study of aggression. It demonstrates how the term *aggression* has a host of subtle meanings, making it difficult for people to agree on a definition. (*Teacher's Resource Binder*, p. 33-1; Handout 33–11)
- Technology Application Activity: *PsychSim:* "Social Decision Making" *PsychSim* is an interactive CD-ROM containing tutorials in different content areas of psychology. In this tutorial, students participate in a series of trials and games related to changing strategies based on opponents' strategies. (*Teacher's Resource Binder*, p. 33-1)
- Demonstration Activity: *Social Traps* In the October issue of *Science/84*, William Allman made a hypothetical offer to the readership. Each reader was invited to mail in a small card, asking for either $20 or $100. Each would receive what was requested, with this important stipulation: If more than 20 percent asked for $100, the deal was off and no one would get anything. Replication of the offer in class provides an excellent, simplified introduction to the concept of a social trap. (*Teacher's Resource Binder*, p. 33-1)
- Cooperative Learning Activity: *The Missiles Game* Students will come to a clear understanding of how an arms race can be viewed as a social trap by playing the "Missiles Game." (*Teacher's Resource Binder*, p. 33-1; Handouts 33–12a through 33–12d)
- Analysis Activity: *Road Rage* Psychologist Leon James of the University of Hawaii has conducted research on driving behavior since 1977. He designed this activity as a self-test of aggressive driving for persons who had volunteered to attempt to change their driving style. (*Teacher's Resource Binder*, p. 33-1; Handout 33–13)

Enrichment Center

- Enrichment Lesson: *Do We Need to Vent Our Rage?* Do we occasionally need to "blow off a little steam"? Does the expression of anger and aggression make us less violent, in the long run, and contribute to our mental health? The catharsis hypothesis suggests this to be the case. (*Teacher's Resource Binder*, p. 33-1)
- Enrichment Lesson: *Road Rage* When Scripps Howard News Service and Ohio University posed this question—"Do you think people are more likely to express anger today than they used to be?"—to 815 adults across the United States in mid-1999, 88 percent answered yes. Students learn more about this finding with this lesson. (*Teacher's Resource Binder*, p. 33-1)

Cooperation

Video Center

- Videocassette: *Scientific American Frontiers,* Second Edition, Segment 7: "Superpower Ping Pong" Consult the faculty guide from the *Scientific American Frontiers* video series for a description of this segment. (*Teacher's Resource Binder*, p. 33-1)

Enrichment Center

- Enrichment Lesson: *The Dual Concern Model of Social Conflict* Dean Pruitt, Jeffrey Rubin, and Sung Hee Kim identify five specific strategies for dealing with social conflict. Students learn more about them in this lesson. (*Teacher's Resource Binder*, p. 33-1)

MODULE 33

Social Relations

Liking, loving, helping, hating, fighting, befriending. We exhibit a wide range of behaviors in the way we *relate* to one another, all of which we will consider in this module. As with so many areas of psychology, a complex combination of biological and environmental factors affects our *social relations*.

Attraction

What's the Point? 1. Why are we attracted to some people but not to others?

Who are your friends, and how did they become your friends? Does a person have to look a certain way, dress in a certain style, or listen to the same kind of music to be your friend? *Social psychologists* consider these and other questions in their scientific study of how we think about, influence, and relate to one another. Researchers have found three key ingredients to attraction: *proximity, physical attractiveness,* and *similarity.*

Proximity

If you attend Jefferson High School in Maryland, you don't stand much of a chance of becoming friends with the Broken Bow High School students in Nebraska. A friendship can't develop if it doesn't begin. Several studies have shown the people we like, date, and even marry are typically the people living in our neighborhood, sitting next to us in class, or working in the same building. What's near becomes dear in part because of the **mere exposure effect,** in which repeated exposure to novel stimuli increases our liking of them. You can easily see how

▶ **mere exposure effect** The phenomenon that repeated exposure to novel stimuli increases liking of them.

MODULE 33

Social Relations

Introducing the Module

The Points: Module Objectives

- Evaluate why we are attracted to some people but not to others.
- Define *passionate* and *companionate love,* and differentiate between the two.
- Describe the conditions under which we are more likely to help others.
- Differentiate among prejudice, stereotype, and discrimination.
- Relate the concepts of ingroups, outgroups, and scapegoats to prejudice, stereotypes, and discrimination.
- Analyze how our thought processes foster prejudice.
- Analyze how genetics, our nervous system, and biochemistry contribute to aggression, and explain how we learn aggression.
- Describe what helps foster cooperation among groups.

trb Building Vocabulary

Students can reinforce their knowledge of social relations by completing **Building Vocabulary: Graphic Organizer:** *Crossword Puzzle* (*Teacher's Resource Binder,* p. 33-1; **Handout 33–2**). As they learn the terms in this module by filling out the puzzle, they will also better understand the relationship among these concepts.

Getting Started

Have students consider the following aphorisms:

- Birds of a feather flock together.
- Opposites attract.

Which is true? Are they both true? This module explores many of our conceptions of how people relate to others—dispelling some myths and reinforcing others.

trb You may wish to use **Critical Thinking Activity:** *Fact or Falsehood?* (*Teacher's Resource Binder,* p. 33-1; **Handout 33–1**) as a prereading strategy to evaluate what students already know about social relations. This activity will prime students to look out for information that could prove or disprove their preconceptions about these topics.

MODULE 33

Teaching the Points

web ■ TEACHING TIP

(1) You can log on as an instructor to the book companion site for *Thinking About Psychology* at www.worthpublishers.com/thinkingaboutpsych. It contains teacher resources for class presentations as well as review and assessment of module concepts and terms.

(2) Resources for the Teaching of Social Psychology at www.noctrl.edu/~ajomuel/crow is part of a CROW project, Course Resources on the Web, sponsored by the Associated Colleges of Illinois. Prepared by Jon Mueller, the site includes activities and exercises, on-line studies and demonstrations, class assignments, Web projects, topic resources, on-line lectures, and student resources.

(3) A discussion group (LISTSERV@UGA.CC.UGA.EDU) is available for use by instructors. It provides a forum for individuals to discuss current theory and research in social psychology, as well as the teaching of social psychology. To join the list, send an e-mail message to the above address, with the body of the message as follows: subscribe socpsy-L yourfirstname yourlastname

trb At this point, you may wish to use Technology Application Activity: *Social Psychology on the Web* (*Teacher's Resource Binder*, p. 33-1; Handout 33–3).

■ JOURNAL WRITING

Invite students to use the following questions and writing prompts as springboards for entries in their psychology journals:

- Have you ever dated someone? If so, what attracted you to him or her? What qualities about him or her brought you closer together?
- What physical qualities attract you to those you want to date? Why?

Love at First Listen? Ever start liking a song after listening to it several times? The mere exposure effect may explain why you like something you initially didn't care for.

this works if you think of a CD you bought because it had a hit song on track 1. Did you end up also liking the songs on tracks 2 and 3 (even though you didn't particularly like them at first) after listening to the CD several times? Did those songs even become favorites after you listened to them repeatedly? If so, you experienced the mere exposure effect.

The mere exposure effect works for human faces as well (Moreland & Zajonc, 1982; Nuttin, 1987), and promotes fondness for the people with whom we spend time (Bornstein, 1989, 1999). Two researchers (Moreland & Beach, 1992) demonstrated the mere exposure effect by enrolling four women, all of whom were judged equally attractive, in a 200-student college class. The first never attended class, the second went 5 times, the third 10 times, and the fourth attended 15 classes. After the course ended, students judged the woman who had attended most often as the most attractive.

Our ancestors benefited from the mere exposure effect. Familiar faces were less likely to be dangerous or threatening than unfamiliar faces. Some researchers believe we are born with a tendency to bond with those who are familiar to us, and to be leery of those we don't know (Zajonc, 1998).

Physical Attractiveness

What most affects our first impression of others? Is it their wit? Charm? Politeness? Intelligence? Shakespeare wrote, "Love looks not with the eyes, but with the mind." Actually, researchers have found that first impressions are based on something far shallower than brains or personality. Hundreds of studies indicate that *appearance* is the first filter we use to sort out the people we want to get to know from those we don't.

In one study, researchers matched students with blind dates for a dance. Prior to the date, all participants took a number of personality and intelligence tests, and the researchers rated them on attractiveness. After two hours of talking and dancing, all participants rated their dates. The researchers found that the only measure reliably predicting whether the two daters liked each other was attractiveness (Walster & others, 1966). Yes, women are more likely to *say* that the way a person looks does not affect them, but a woman's behavior is affected by a man's looks (Feingold, 1990; Sprecher, 1989).

We give attractive people the benefit of the doubt. We judge them as happier, healthier, and more successful than those who are less attractive, even when we know virtually nothing about these people (Eagly & others, 1991; Feingold, 1992). Your feelings about your own attractiveness predict how much you'll date and how popular you'll feel (Hatfield

Suggested Readings

Use the following books as teacher-preparation tools or as enrichment for advanced students:

Aronson, E. (1995). *The social animal* (7th ed.). New York: Freeman.

Lerner, M. (1980). *The belief in a just world.* New York: Plenum.

London, P. (1970). The rescuers: Motivational hypotheses about Christians who saved Jews from the Nazis. In J. Macaulay & L. Berkowitz (Eds.), *Altruism and helping behavior.* Orlando, FL: Academic Press.

Marsh, P. (Ed.). (1988). *Eye to eye: How people interact.* Topsfield, MA: Salem House.

Myers, D. G. (1999). *Social psychology* (6th ed.). New York: McGraw-Hill.

Oliner, S., & Oliner, P. (1988). *The altruistic personality: Rescuers of Jews in Nazi Europe.* New York: Macmillan.

Patterson, J., & Kim, P. (1991). *The day America told the truth.* New York: Prentice Hall.

Taylor, S., Peplau, L., & Sears, D. (2000). *Social psychology* (10th ed.). Upper Saddle River, NJ: Prentice Hall.

What's Attractive? Society's standards for female attractiveness change over time. Left to right: In the 1920s, thin was in. The 1950s favored a fuller figure, and today's look combines the skinny waistline of the 1920s with the buxomness of the 1950s.

& Sprecher, 1986). The attractive people in the most successful movies are often portrayed as morally superior to the unattractive actors (Smith & others, 1999). All these studies tip the scale in favor of attractiveness, but there is more to the attractiveness story.

Fortunately, few of us actually *think* of ourselves as unattractive. And in spite of what observers think, attractiveness does not seem to predict happiness or feelings of self-esteem for the person inside that handsome face (Diener & others, 1995; Major & others, 1984). Very attractive people are often suspicious of praise for their work ("Are you saying that only because I'm good-looking?"), whereas less attractive individuals are more likely to see praise as sincere (Berscheid, 1981).

We should also remember that standards for attractiveness come and go, and they vary from culture to culture. In the 1920s, ultrathin was in for women. By the 1950s, attractiveness in women reflected the full-figured voluptuousness of Marilyn Monroe. In the late 1960s, the flat-chested model Twiggy was in, and busts were out. Today, attractive women are depicted as lean and busty. Cultural standards have made breast-enlargement surgery or wearing Wonderbras a common practice in some parts of this country, but women in other cultures strap on leather clothing to give the appearance of a flat chest. I never had a student with a pierced nose until about five years ago, but women in India and Pakistan have been piercing their noses for centuries. Cultural practices that would shock Americans but that were quite ordinary methods for increasing attractiveness include neck lengthening among the Karen tribes in Thailand and Burma, and the now-outlawed Chinese practice of foot binding (to make feet look small). Beauty truly is in the eye of the culture.

Enriching

Have students conduct research in attractiveness. Ask them to collect pictures of "attractive" and "unattractive" people. These photos should be shown to various subjects, who should fill out a sheet that asks the subjects to guess the kind of job, personality, and education the people in the pictures have. Compare the types of answers for the "attractive" and "unattractive" people to determine whether there seem to be more positive predictions for the "attractive" people. (Be sure to obtain Institutional Review Board (IRB) approval and informed consent for all research endeavors.)

trb At this point, you may wish to use **Enrichment Lesson:** *What Is Beautiful Is Good* (*Teacher's Resource Binder*, p. 33-1).

■ TEACHING TIP

Students might enjoy this anecdote carried several years ago by the Associated Press:

> A mysterious student has been attending a class at Oregon State University for the past two months enveloped in a big, black bag. Only his bare feet show. Each Monday, Wednesday, and Friday at 11 o'clock in the morning, the black bag sits on a small table near the back of the classroom. Charles Goetzinger, professor of the class, knows the identity of the person inside. None of the twenty students in the class does. Goetzinger said the students' attitudes changed from hostility toward the black bag to curiosity and finally to friendship.

trb At this point, you may wish to use **Technology Application Activity:** *PsychQuest:* **"How Do We Pick Our Mates?"** (*Teacher's Resource Binder*, p. 33-1).

■ LOOKING AT THE ISSUES

Have students think about their favorite movies and television shows. Discuss with the class how heroes are portrayed as physically different from villains.

trb At this point, you may wish to use **Enrichment Lesson:** *What Is Beautiful Is Good* (*Teacher's Resource Binder*, p. 33-1).

■ APPLYING THE POINTS

Collect recent fashion magazine cover photos and photos from magazines that feature male models or famous men and compare them with photos from 30, 40, and 50 years ago. Use the following questions to discuss the comparisons:

- How were the women and men physically different in the past?
- How was women's makeup applied differently? How were hairstyles or clothes different? Are women and men more "natural" today than yesterday?

■ MULTICULTURAL CONNECTIONS

Have students obtain fashion magazines from different cultures to see how standards of beauty shown in the photos of those magazines are different from and similar to standards of beauty in the United States.

MODULE 33

■ TEACHING TIP

Students will insist that opposites do attract. They will cite examples of people who are part of their intimate circle who are vastly different from them. Use the following questions to promote a discussion of these differences to see whether the people students have mentioned really are different:

- How are you different from the person who is opposite? Is it in areas that include strongly held values and beliefs? For example, are you friends with someone who is a racist when you are strongly against racism?
- Does the friend who is opposite represent the opposite values of your parents? If so, that could represent the attraction of this friendship.

trb At this point, you may wish to use Enrichment Lesson: *How Do We Pick Our Mates?* (*Teacher's Resource Binder*, p. 33-1).

■ JOURNAL WRITING

Invite students to use the following questions and writing prompts as springboards for entries in their psychology journals:

- What qualities do you look for in a friend? Are there qualities that you would break up a friendship over? What are they?
- Have you ever been passionately in love with someone? How did you feel when you were with him or her? How did you feel when you were away? How long did the relationship last? Why?
- Have you ever been involved in a long trip, a project, or a play production and fallen for someone during the process? How long did the relationship last after the trip, project, or play was over? Why?

▶ **passionate love** An aroused state of intense positive absorption in another, usually present at the beginning of a love relationship.

Similarity

Okay, so you live close to someone and each of you thinks the other is attractive. What predicts whether you will become friends? Do opposites really attract? In the movies, we're intrigued by stories where people who are different from each other end up together. But in real life, Princess Leia does not fall for a professional smuggler like Han Solo. We are reluctant to include people *dissimilar* from us in our circle of friends (Rosenbaum, 1986). Your friends are likely to share your interests, attitudes, age, intelligence level, and economic status, as well as your beliefs on religion, smoking, and race relations. Birds of a feather do flock together. And the more alike you and your friends are, the longer you are likely to stay together (Byrne, 1971).

Similarity, physical attractiveness, and proximity all contribute to attraction, but there are other components to this feeling. One of them is our tendency to like people who like us. We respond positively and warmly to those who like us, which typically increases their affection and friendliness for us. Expressing friendship toward another increases our attractiveness. If you want a friend, be a friend.

Romantic Love

2. What do we mean by passionate love and companionate love, and how do they differ?

Another famous poet, Walt Whitman, once wrote, "I never could explain *why* I love anybody or anything." True, it may be difficult to explain why we love, but we can identify two different kinds of love: passionate and companionate (Hatfield, 1988).

Passionate Love After the highly charged passion fades and the feet get back on the ground, will there still be a loving relationship? Not likely, unless a deeper attachment has formed.

Passionate Love

At the beginning of a love relationship, we are likely to feel **passionate love**, an aroused state of intense positive absorption in another. Emotions hit us in two different ways: physical arousal and perceptions of that arousal. But what if arousal from some other source coincides with meeting a new person? How do we interpret that arousal? Psychologists decided to find out, and they discovered that men who are revved up by running in place, being frightened, or listening to something funny tend to rate a new attractive acquaintance or a girlfriend as more attractive. Those who are aroused apparently attribute some of the arousal to the presence of someone they see as attractive (Carducci & others, 1978; Dermer & Pyszczynski, 1978; White & Kight, 1984).

I've noticed that, every year, at least a few students who act together in the school plays end up going out. I know that proximity and simi-

Meeting Individual Needs

trb tr Help students understand how the terms in this module are related by having them complete Building Vocabulary: Graphic Organizer: *Crossword Puzzle* (*Teacher's Resource Binder*, p. 33-1; Handout 33–2).

- **Independent Learners** Students can complete the handout on their own as a homework or in-class assignment, checking the answers in class. You can use Handout 33–2 as a transparency by inserting the correct answers in the puzzle and projecting the completed puzzle for students to use in checking their answers.
- **Cooperative Learners** Have students work in small groups to complete the crossword puzzle. Students can tutor each other about the concepts in the module, or you can create a competition in which students see how quickly their team can complete the web correctly.

larity play a role in these relationships, but I've wondered if the arousal brought on by being in front of a large audience is sometimes transferred to another desirable person on stage.

In nearly all passionate romances, the fire inevitably goes out, and heads come out of the clouds. For a select few, a more enduring companionate love may develop.

Companionate Love

In certain countries, such as India and Pakistan, young people learn that passionate love, while thrilling and exciting, is not a good basis for marriage. They expect their families to select a partner for them—a person with similar interests and background. Interestingly, in cultures where love is not rated as important or essential for marriage, the divorce rate is lower than in our country (Levine & others, 1995). Perhaps couples in these cultures strive for a more lasting **companionate love**—a deep, affectionate attachment for those with whom our lives are intertwined. This mature, steady love fosters friendship and commitment and is based more on affection than obsession. Couples sharing companionate love stand a better chance of an enduring relationship. Couples who fail to recognize the fleeting nature of passionate love may find their relationship in trouble when passions cool down (Berscheid & others, 1984).

So, how do we develop and maintain a companionate relationship? Equity and self-disclosure are two important factors. **Equity** is a condition in which people contribute and receive at about the same rate in a relationship. In these 50-50 relationships, couples share decision-making and possessions, and they freely give and receive emotional support. In relationships where equity exists, the likelihood of a continuing companionate love is good (Gray-Little & Burks, 1983; Van Yperen & Buunk, 1990).

Self-disclosure is the revealing of intimate aspects of oneself to others. Intimate aspects of our lives include our likes, dislikes, fears, accomplishments, shameful moments, goals, and much more. Self-disclosing promotes and deepens friendship. This was demonstrated in an experiment where one group of pairs asked each other self-disclosing questions (When did you last cry in front of another?) or small-talk questions (What was your high school like?). After 45 minutes, the self-disclosing pairs reported feeling much closer to their partners than the small-talking pairs did (Aron & others, 1997). Closeness is a key ingredient in companionate love, and it is more likely to be a reality in equitable relationships where people feel they can share intimate and important details.

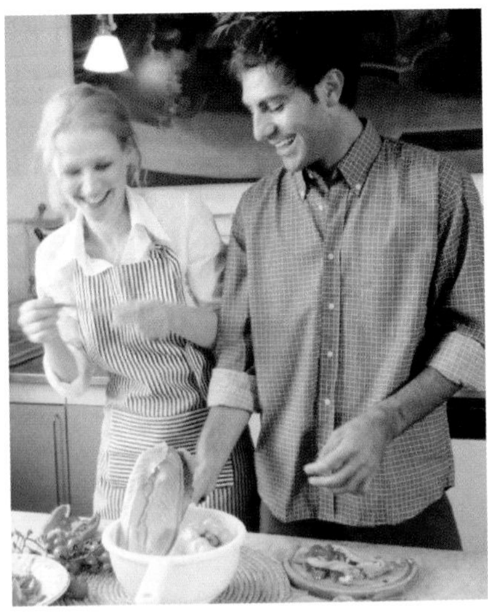

Companionate Love Loving relationships built on more than passion are more likely to endure.

► **companionate love** The deep affectionate attachment we feel for those with whom our lives are intertwined.

► **equity** A condition in which people receive from a relationship in proportion to what they give to it.

► **self-disclosure** Revealing intimate aspects of oneself to others.

■ MULTICULTURAL CONNECTIONS

Investigate the success of arranged marriages. If students in your school are from cultures where marriages are arranged, ask those who are willing to visit your class to discuss this custom. You may even want to invite the parents of these students to class if the students (and their parents) feel comfortable doing so. The following questions can help facilitate the discussion:

- How long do arranged marriages typically last?
- Do couples in arranged marriages grow to love each other? Why or why not?
- Do young people who will have marriages arranged agree with the practice? Why or why not?
- Would your students trust their parents to find a suitable mate? Why or why not?

■ LOOKING AT THE ISSUES

The divorce rate is much higher today than it was when your students' grandparents were getting married. Use the following questions to help students investigate why people get divorced:

- Are the values of society regarding divorce different today from those of a generation ago?
- What are some common reasons people cite for getting a divorce? Do these reasons point to a lack of companionship between the spouses?

trb At this point, you may wish to use **Critical Thinking Activity:** *Love Styles* (*Teacher's Resource Binder*, p. 33-1; **Handout 33–4**).

Cooperative Learning

Have students come up with a list of self-disclosing questions, like the ones the author mentions. Then have students partner with someone they don't know well and answer each other's questions. Afterward, bring the class together and ask the following questions about the experience:

- How did students feel about their partners before this exercise?
- What new things did the student partners learn about each other?
- What was the most interesting thing students learned? What things would they like to know more about their partners?

trb At this point, you may wish to use **Critical Thinking Activity:** *The Trust Scale* (*Teacher's Resource Binder*, p. 33-1; **Handout 33–5**).

MODULE 33

■ **APPLYING THE POINTS**
Have students scan local newspapers from the recent past for stories of people who acted heroically. Interested students can contact these people, if possible, and interview them. The following questions can guide the interviews and class discussion:

- How did these people feel before, during, and after the event? Why weren't they paralyzed by fear or concerned for their own safety?
- Have these people received recognition for their heroic acts? How did that recognition make them feel?

trb At this point, you may wish to use Enrichment Lesson: *Case Studies in Helping* (*Teacher's Resource Binder*, p. 33-1).

F•Y•I

web (1) Andrew Carnegie was inspired to establish the Hero Fund Commission, in 1904, after two attempted rescues from a coal-mining disaster in which both rescuers died. Carnegie set aside $5 million to compensate rescuers or their families. The commission has recognized more than 8300 acts of heroism. In addition to the medal, awardees or their survivors receive $3500 and, occasionally, a pension or scholarship. For more information, go to the commission's Web site at **www.carnegiehero.org**.

trb At this point, you may wish to use Enrichment Lesson: *Case Studies in Helping* (*Teacher's Resource Binder*, p. 33-1).

(2) *Reciprocity* is a powerful social norm. The author Robert Cialdini describes a university professor who sent Christmas cards to perfect strangers. Holiday cards came pouring back from people who had never met or heard of him. Most never inquired into his identity.

Source: Cialdini, R. (1998). *Influence: The psychology of persuasion.* New York: Morrow.

Altruistic Behavior Columbine High School teacher Dave Sanders directed students to safety, but he was fatally wounded in the process. His unselfish regard for the well-being of those students was a perfect example of altruism.

Altruism

3. Under what conditions are we more likely to help others?

Acts of courage are not reported in the media at the same rate as acts of lawlessness, but the stories we do hear are heartwarming and impressive. Dave Sanders, a science teacher, stood up on a table in a high school cafeteria, directing students to safety as two other students sprayed the room with bullets. One of the bullets took Sanders's life. New York firefighters charged to their deaths up the steps of the burning and doomed World Trade Center in search of the injured on 9/11. James Harrison, a college student, directed and helped pull others out of a burning plane after it had skidded down a runway and burst into flames. He died making one last trip into the cabin looking for survivors. All of these people showed uncommon courage, but they also exhibited **altruism,** unselfish regard for the welfare of others. Regard for the welfare of others became a major social psychology concern after a particularly hideous rape and murder took place in the early morning hours of March 13, 1964.

Bystander Intervention

Kitty Genovese, a young woman living in Queens, New York, worked a night shift that kept her up well into the early morning hours most days. Just before 3:00 A.M. on the night of her death, a stalker surprised Genovese on her way home from work. Over the course of the next hour, Genovese valiantly tried to fight off her attacker. At least 38 people in nearby apartments heard her scream, "Oh my God, he stabbed me!" and "Please help me!" Lights came on, people looked out their windows, but none of the 38 came to her rescue or called the police while she was being assaulted. Twice, her screams drove off the attacker, and twice he

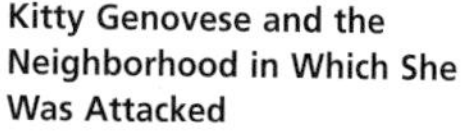

Kitty Genovese and the Neighborhood in Which She Was Attacked

Demonstrating

ACTS OF KINDNESS Ask each student to perform a random act of kindness. After performing the acts of kindness, students should write a brief paper that describes their act, the recipient's reaction, and their own reaction. Recipients' reactions, particularly when the recipient is not grateful, provide the basis for a particularly lively classroom discussion. Extend the text discussion of altruism by asking students to reflect on why some recipients might have a negative reaction to receiving help.

trb At this point, you may wish to use Analysis Activity: *Pleasurable Versus Philanthropic Activities—Which Brings More Happiness?* (*Teacher's Resource Binder*, p. 33-1).

returned. Genovese was raped twice, and she died of multiple stab wounds. The police were finally called at 3:50 A.M.

The failure of the 38 who admitted to hearing and seeing Genovese's attack and murder stirred up an international outrage. How could her neighbors hear her calls for help and not respond? Had they become desensitized to violence? Did they simply not care? How could all these bystanders be so apathetic to someone so desperately in need of help? Social psychologists sprang into action, searching for answers to these questions.

Two researchers, **John Darley** and **Bibb Latané** (1968), approached the issues surrounding Genovese's death from a unique angle. They suspected the lack of intervention was not due to cold, uncaring personalities on the part of the bystanders. Instead, they thought the answers would be found in the influence of the *situation*. That is, are there situations in which people are more or less likely to help others?

Darley and Latané decided to test this idea by setting up a number of situations in which people appeared to need help. In one study, for example, a student acted as if he were having an epileptic seizure. In another study, a person lay down on a public sidewalk with his eyes closed. In each study, the underlying questions were the same: Would others come to the aid of the person who appeared to need assistance? Would participants help someone having a seizure and call for help, or check to see if a person lying on a sidewalk was okay? After staging hundreds of false "emergencies," Darley and Latané had their answers.

In the case of the epileptic seizure, Darley and Latané found that people usually helped if they thought they were alone. That is, if participants thought they were the only ones who could help, they did. But look at Figure 33.1. Fewer people helped if they thought others were also hearing the calls for help. Those who thought others were close by were much more likely to act the way Kitty Genovese's neighbors did. This evidence provides support for the **bystander effect**, which is the tendency for any given bystander to be less likely to give aid if other bystanders are present.

A decision-making process appears to influence our likelihood of helping someone else. Would you help a stranger lying flat on his back in a public place? First, you would have to notice the situation. If you notice it, you would have to interpret it as an emergency and then assume responsibility for helping (Figure 33.2, page 642.).

▶ **altruism** Unselfish regard for the welfare of others.

▶ **John Darley** (1938–) Psychologist who, with Bibb Latané, researched the circumstances that determine when a bystander will intervene on behalf of another person.

▶ **Bibb Latané** (1937–) Psychologist who, with John Darley, researched the circumstances that determine when a bystander will intervene on behalf of another person.

▶ **bystander effect** The tendency for any given bystander to be less likely to give aid if other bystanders are present.

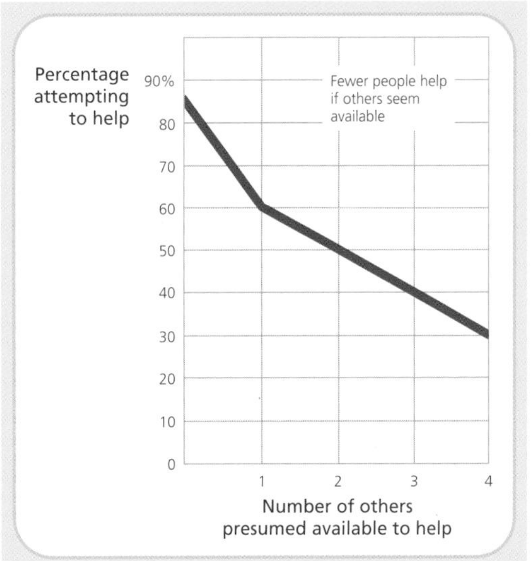

Figure 33.1 **When Do We Help?** People are less likely to help someone in need if they believe that other people are around who could also help. (Data from Darley & Latané, 1968.)

Cooperative Learning

Have student pairs go to a public area in school. The "displayer" should walk or stand about 5 feet in front of the "coder" and make eye contact with a single oncoming subject. The displayer should then signal the coder, discreetly, to observe the respondent's facial expression.

In the original study, over half the subjects responded to a smile with a smile, but few subjects responded to a frown with a frown. The reciprocity norm may explain that we should respond in kind to rewarding actions. A frown generally represents unfriendly or negative affect. Passersby seemed to respond to a frown with a look of bewilderment. Females were more likely to smile than males. People were more likely to smile at a female. Did your students find similar results? Why or why not?

Source: Hinsz, V., & Tomhave, J. (1991). Smile and (half) the world smiles with you, frown and you frown alone. *Personality and Social Psychology Bulletin, 17*, 586–592.

MODULE 33

■ LOOKING AT THE ISSUES

(1) Although the story of Kitty Genovese is tragic and horrific, there are also stories of people who didn't sit idly by.

- Many people both in and out of Nazi Germany helped Jews escape the Holocaust. Why did these people risk their own lives to help those that society had deemed unworthy of help?
- White Southerners in the Confederate South helped establish and maintain the Underground Railroad—the vehicle used by thousands of slaves to escape to the North and freedom. What caused these people to rebel against their society's norms and laws?

trb At this point, you may wish to use **Enrichment Lesson:** *Case Studies in Helping* (*Teacher's Resource Binder*, p. 33-1).

(2) Some people actually do respond to acts of violence to the point of becoming a vigilante.

- How does the law respond to vigilantism? Are vigilantes regarded as heroes or criminals?
- Should we legislate helping? Why or why not?

trb At this point, you may wish to use **Enrichment Lesson:** *The Bystander Effect and Legislating Helping* (*Teacher's Resource Binder*, p. 33-1).

■ TEACHING TIPS

trb (1) A four-color transparency of Figure 33.1, When Do We Help?, is available in the **Overhead Transparencies Set.**

(2) Link the *bystander effect* with *deindividuation* and *social loafing.*

- **Deindividuation:** When people are in a crowd, they are less likely to behave as rational individuals. Their sense of responsibility diffuses, causing them to do things like riot, loot, or vandalize.
- **Social loafing:** When people are in a group, they are less likely to exert their best effort, believing that others will take up their slack.

MODULE 33

tr ■ **TEACHING TIP**

A four-color transparency of Figure 33.2, How We Decide to Help, is available in the **Overhead Transparencies Set.**

■ **LOOKING AT THE ISSUES**

School fights happen all the time, but how many are broken up by students? Have students imagine a school fight that takes place outside their classroom. Then ask students the following questions about this scene:

- Would they go to the office to alert the principal? Why or why not?
- Would they step in to break up the fight? Why or why not? What if one person were obviously losing the fight pretty badly—would they step in then? Why or why not?
- Who do the students believe is responsible for breaking up fights at school?

trb At this point, you may wish to use **Enrichment Lesson:** *Europeans Who Helped Jews Escape* (*Teacher's Resource Binder,* p. 33-1).

■ **MULTICULTURAL CONNECTIONS**

Because bystander inaction is more typical, many European countries have "good Samaritan" laws that make it a crime not to summon aid or help someone in serious distress. In contrast, only a handful of states require people to help strangers in an emergency. Some legal experts suggest that the difference is due in part to cultural differences in values: Americans emphasize individualism, whereas Europeans focus on social solidarity.

Vermont, Minnesota, and Wisconsin are among the states that have the strongest laws, but even these laws are narrowly written, infrequently used, and (when applied) carry light punishment for violation.

Source: **Benac, N.** (1997, September 14). "Good Samaritan" laws. *Grand Rapids Press*, p. A3.

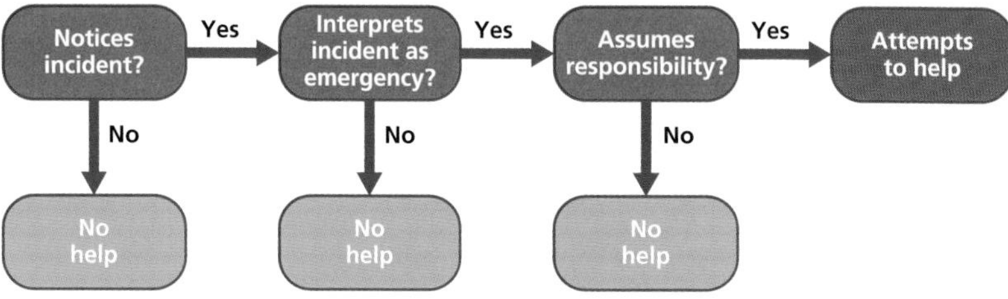

Figure 33.2 **How We Decide to Help** This flowchart shows the events and thought processes we seem to go through in deciding whether to intervene when someone needs help.

Altruism researchers have uncovered several additional situations and circumstances that increase the odds of helping someone in need. We are more likely to help if we

- are not in a hurry.
- believe the victim deserves help.
- are in a good mood.
- believe the victim is similar to us.
- are feeling guilty.
- are in a small town or rural area.
- just saw someone else being helpful.

Of all the items on that list, the most consistent finding is that happy people are helpful. No matter what it is that is making us happy, we are more eager to help and are more generous when we're in a good mood (Carlson & others, 1988).

Prejudice

4. How do prejudice, stereotype, and discrimination differ?

Prejudice is an unjustifiable (and usually negative) attitude toward a group and its members. Prejudice usually goes hand in hand with **stereotypes,** which are generalized beliefs about a group of people. Taking action against a group because of those thoughts is **discrimination.** Prejudicial beliefs may focus on people's gender, race, age, religion, body size, or numerous other characteristics.

Prejudice filters what we see and influences how we think about it. One 1970s study (Duncan, 1976) asked participants to interpret a videotape of a black man shoving a white man. Participants judged the shove to be an act of violence. However, when a different group of participants saw a white man shoving a black man, they were more likely to interpret this act as "horsing around." Our prejudices guide our perceptions.

Cooperative Learning

Have students work in pairs to create situations in which they need help. One student should do something that shows he or she needs help—like drop books. The other student should observe inconspicuously. Try several variations of this project, making sure to obtain approval from an Institutional Review Board (IRB).

- (In a crowded hall, between classes) Will people stop to help you pick up your books or carry your books to your next class? Why or why not?
- (With only one or two people around) Are one or two people more quick to help than many in the crowded hallway? Why or why not?
- (When making eye contact to specifically ask for help) Do people refuse your requests? Why or why not?

Prejudice can be blatant and obvious or subtle and hard to notice. Most people now agree that schools, athletic opportunities, and transportation should be available to all people, regardless of race or gender. This change has taken place during my lifetime. But I was reminded of how subtle prejudice still exists when I was in a large city trying to hail a cab with a psychology professor from the University of Virginia. Heading back to our hotel after a wonderful meal, my friend stood on the corner of a busy intersection with his hand raised—a signal that he needed a cab. Three empty cabs passed him by, two of which slowed down and then sped off. He looked at me and said, "You'd better try." I held up my hand, a cab stopped, and we got in.

What had just happened? A well-dressed, well-educated, middle-aged man stood on a corner and was ignored. I wasn't dressed nearly as well, but I was able to get a cab almost instantly. "Has this happened to you before?" I asked. "It happens all the time." he replied. I'm of European-American descent. He is of African-American descent.

Similar forms of subtle prejudice are not hard to find. A study of drivers on the New Jersey turnpike showed that African-Americans were only 13.5 percent of the drivers, but they made up 35 percent of those pulled over by police. A survey asked college students if they felt excluded from school activities. Around 6 percent of the European-American students felt left out. Yet, 24 percent of the Asian-Americans and 53 percent of the African-Americans felt excluded (Hurtado & others, 1994). In situations where white players are the minority, such as on NBA basketball teams, similar dynamics exist. The majority-minority make-up of these teams can lead to feelings of loneliness, exclusion, and disrespect in white team members (Schoenfeld, 1995).

Another researcher uncovered a disturbing form of prejudice when he asked participants to grade a poor essay (Harber, 1998). Half the participants were told that a white student had written the essay, and the other half that a black student had written it. Which paper do you think got the higher grade? If you guessed the one supposedly written by a white student, you guessed wrong. When participants thought a black student wrote the essay, they gave much higher grades and never handed out harsh criticism. Harber proposed that this phenomenon may be due to lower expectations for papers written by black students. If so, is this evidence of prejudice? Yes, and it's also discrimination. Less constructive criticism and inflated praise can suppress learning and achievement.

Prejudice also promotes gender inequalities. The United Nations (1991, 1993) estimates that close to 1 billion adults worldwide cannot read or write, and that two-thirds of these adults are women. In the United States, those who take care of our children (usually women) in day-care centers are typically paid much less than garbage collectors (usually men).

So, how does prejudice get started? Let's look at both social and thought processes that carry some responsibility for the development of prejudice.

▶ **prejudice** An unjustifiable (and usually negative) attitude toward a group and its members. Prejudice generally involves stereotyped beliefs, negative feelings, and a predisposition to discriminatory action.

▶ **stereotype** A generalized (sometimes accurate but often overgeneralized) belief about a group of people.

▶ **discrimination** In social relations, taking action against a group of people because of stereotyped beliefs and feelings of prejudice.

Cross-Curricular Connections

CREATIVE NONFICTION WRITING Have students write about their experiences with prejudice and discrimination. If they feel comfortable, allow some time for students to share their experiences by reading their writings and discussing the psychological impact of their experience on their lives. Have students consider the following questions:

- Have you been discriminated against? If so, how? Why?
- Have you been judged negatively on the basis of gender, race, or social status? If so, how?

F • Y • I

Psychologists have attempted to explain white people's conflicting racial attitudes in terms of two core value orientations.

- Humanitarianism-egalitarianism (HE) includes the democratic ideals of equality, justice, and concern for others. HE promotes a problack (PB) attitude because of the belief that black people have a history of being disadvantaged.
- Protestant ethic (PE) emphasizes devotion to work, achievement, and discipline. PE strengthens an antiblack (AB) attitude, viewing that blacks' problems reflect their own shortcomings.

Source: Katz, I., & Hass, R. (1988). Racial ambivalence and American value conflict: Correlational and priming studies of dual cognitive structures. *Journal of Personality and Social Psychology, 55,* 893–905.

trb At this point, you may wish to use Application Activity: *Measuring Stereotypes* (*Teacher's Resource Binder,* p. 33-1; Handout 33–7).

■ LOOKING AT THE ISSUES

Have students reflect on the following:

- Do you believe you could fall in love with a person of another race?
- How do you think friends would react if you married a person of another race?
- Do you believe that minorities are poor because they fail to take advantage of the opportunities open to them?

Research suggests that white Americans' answers reveal a subtler and more hypocritical racism. In the 1960s, many whites maintained that black people were owed compensation for the centuries of oppression. In the 1990s, white Americans held blacks responsible for their current position in U.S. society.

Source: Patterson, J., & Kim, P. (1991). *The day America told the truth.* New York: Prentice Hall.

trb At this point, you may wish to use Technology Application Activity: *Implicit Association Test* (*Teacher's Resource Binder,* p. 33-1; Handout 33–8).

web ■ **APPLYING THE POINTS**
Have students prepare a one- to two-page profile of a hate group described on the Tolerance.org Web site, which is a project of the Southern Poverty Law Center. You can find the page at **www.tolerance.org**. Invite students to use the following questions to organize their writing:

- How are the beliefs of this particular group prejudicial? What stereotypes do they hold, and against whom are they held?
- What type of discrimination do they recommend people practice against those they hate?
- Does the First Amendment protect this type of behavior? Why or why not?

trb At this point, you may wish to use Enrichment Lesson: *Racial Prejudice* (*Teacher's Resource Binder*, p. 33-1).

■ **LOOKING AT THE ISSUES**
Most schools have loosely defined cliques that separate people. Have students brainstorm about the different cliques that exist in your school, noting particular behaviors that set each group apart. Elicit students' thoughts about cliques with the following questions:

- How many different cliques are there in your school? What defines these groups?
- How do these groups differentiate themselves from other groups?
- Where do members of these groups hang out during down times at school? Where do they eat lunch? If someone from another group or a new student enters their areas, how do they react?

trb At this point, you may wish to use Technology Application Activity: *PsychQuest: "How Do We Form Social Stereotypes?"* (*Teacher's Resource Binder*, p. 33-1).

■ **TEACHING TIP**
Remind students that sometimes having a group identity is desirable. Sports teams and performing groups, like the choir or band, would be less effective if everyone didn't dress the same or bond on a personal level.

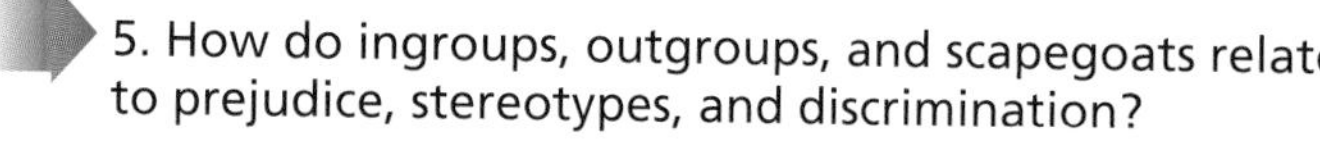

Ingroup-Outgroup: We and They

5. How do ingroups, outgroups, and scapegoats relate to prejudice, stereotypes, and discrimination?

Not long ago, a student told me he hated a high school five miles west of ours. The other school's soccer team had defeated our school's team, and this student played soccer. I asked, "You mean you hate the entire school?"

"No," he replied, "Just the kids who go there. All of them."

I was curious. "Why don't you like any of those kids?

"They aren't us," he said. "They aren't like us at all."

Like a lot of students, this young man believed his school was better than any other in town. He had drawn a mental boundary around our school, creating an **ingroup**, an "us," or people with whom he shared a common identity. Creating an ingroup simultaneously creates an **outgroup**, a group of people we perceive as different or apart from our ingroup. The outgroup becomes "them."

The desire to tell our friends from our foes and to have our group dominate or win against another programs us to be prejudiced against strangers (Whitly, 1999). We develop an **ingroup bias**, a tendency to favor members of our own group, often at the expense of those in the outgroup. In schools, students often form cliques that streamline judgment about others. Are you in a clique? The preps? Skaters? Band or drama kids? Jocks? Goths, gangsters, geeks, or freaks? How does your clique prejudge those who aren't members?

Ingroup or Outgroup? People with a common identity often form an ingroup that excludes others.

Are You in a Clique? Are you a member of an ingroup? Band kid? Drama kid? Jock? What other cliques exist in your school?

Demonstrating

INGROUP BIAS Illustrate how easy it is to fall victim to ingroup bias. Divide the class on the basis of some arbitrary characteristic (wearing sneakers or having blue eyes), making sure that at least one-third of the students are in a given group. When you have defined the groups, have them sit together. Ask one group to compile a list of reasons why those in the other group are not like them. Similarly, the other group should make up a list.

Each group usually begins by listing neutral reasons, which lead to more derogatory ones. If the groups overhear each other's less complimentary reasons, the hostility heightens. At the end of the exercise, the groups should share their lists. Students quickly learn how easily we categorize and develop ingroup bias.

Scapegoating

The soccer player who disliked students in the rival school didn't stop at the players on the other team. "The refs were terrible!" he explained, "And they never called penalties on the other team. We should have won, but we couldn't beat the refs."

When things don't go as planned, we often aim our anger at a target, someone or something we can blame for the problem. **Scapegoat theory** states that prejudice offers an outlet for anger by giving us someone to blame. Evidence for scapegoating is seen in studies where temporary frustration intensifies prejudice against another group (Koltz, 1983).

Apparently, one result of putting others down is a boost in our own self-esteem or feelings of status. In one experiment, participants were made to feel insecure after experiencing failure. Self-esteem returned after the participants belittled and criticized another person or a rival school (Cialdini & Richardson, 1980; Crocker & others, 1987). Perhaps this explains why my soccer-player student cheered when he learned that the rival school had lost at the state tournament.

▶ **ingroup** "Us"—people with whom one shares a common identity.

▶ **outgroup** "Them"—those perceived as different or apart from "us."

▶ **ingroup bias** The tendency to favor one's own group.

▶ **scapegoat theory** The theory that prejudice provides an outlet for anger by providing someone to blame.

Thought Processes and Prejudice

6. How do our thought processes foster prejudice?

Prejudice grows out of our tendency to form groups and from our urge to vent anger or blame others when times are hard. Prejudice is also a result of our mind's attempt to make the world around us easier to understand.

Categorization

It is easier for a cook to find recipes in a cookbook when they are grouped by categories, such as breakfast foods or pastas. Pharmacists keep track of the medicines they distribute by using categories such as painkillers and cough suppressants. Psychologists also categorize when they publish, with brain research likely to end up in a journal of neurology, while conformity data get printed in a social psychology journal. The cook, pharmacist, and psychologist categorize to simplify what they do. We categorize in everyday life, too, especially when we assign people to groups. When we categorize, we don't have to think as hard as when we assess each person for who they really are. Categorization simplifies.

Unfortunately, we often stereotype those we've categorized. That is, we tend to see those in a category as alike. Stereotypes may or may not contain a hint of truth, but they are likely to bias our perceptions of others. One study asked participants to listen to the radio broadcast of a basketball game, to view a photo of a particular player, and to evaluate his performance. Those who saw a photo of a black athlete assessed the player's efforts more highly than those who viewed a photo of a white athlete (Stone & others, 1997).

F • Y • I

The term *scapegoat* comes from the Hebrew tradition of Yom Kippur. According to the Torah, on Yom Kippur (the Day of Atonement for the people of Israel), the high priest would designate a goat to symbolically bear the sins of the entire nation. This goat would then be sent out into the wilderness to fend for itself, carrying away the sins of the people for another year.

■ TEACHING TIP

Link *stereotyping* to Jean Piaget's concept of *schema.* As children, we categorize the world around us into schemas. We form schemas for everything, from people to animals to plants. When we learn something new, we assimilate that information into our existing schemas. When what we learn conflicts with a schema, we need to adjust our schemas through a process called accommodation. Hopefully, prejudicial schemas are accommodated quickly when we learn positive qualities about a person or group of people!

■ CHECKING FOR UNDERSTANDING

To assess students' understanding of prejudice, have them work in small groups to create a concept web that links the following terms: *prejudice, stereotype, discrimination, ingroup, outgroup, ingroup bias,* and *scapegoat theory.* Visit with each group, asking group members to explain the links and provide definitions for the terms involved. During the visits, correct any misconceptions.

Cooperative Learning

Divide the class into homogeneous groups of students according to race, gender, or school group affiliation (band members, athletes, drama club members, and so forth). Have them write down the positive and negative stereotypes others have of their group. Facilitate a discussion of students' lists with the following questions:

- Which parts of the stereotype do you like? Which do you not like?
- Do all members of your group fit the stereotypes? Why or why not?
- How can your group communicate to others that you don't fit the stereotype?

trb At this point, you may wish to use **Cooperative Learning Activity:** *Positions of Privilege and Institutional Discrimination* (*Teacher's Resource Binder,* p. 33-1).

MODULE 33

F • Y • I

In the classic test of the *just-world hypothesis*, students come to the laboratory to participate in a study supposedly on the perception of emotional cues. By what appears to be random choice, one of the participants (actually, an accomplice of the experimenter) is selected to perform a memory task. She is to receive a painful shock for each error she makes; the other participants are to observe and note her emotional response. After watching her receive a number of painful shocks, observers are asked to evaluate her along several dimensions. How do they respond? With compassion and sympathy? No. The results indicate that when the observers are powerless to alter her fate, they tend to reject and devalue her. Subsequent research has suggested that this is particularly true of those who have a strong belief in a just world.

trb At this point, you may wish to use Analysis Activity: *Belief in a Just World* (*Teacher's Resource Binder*, p. 33-1; Handout 33–10).

■ LOOKING AT THE ISSUES

Recently, Lakshmi Raman and Gerald Winer reported that some adults believe physical illness can be a payback for bad behavior. Even victims themselves may attribute their serious illness to bad choices. Just weeks before his death from pancreatic cancer, actor Michael Landon stated, "I think I have it because for most of my life, though I was never a drunk, I drank too much. I also smoked too many cigarettes and ate a lot of wrong things. And if you do that, even if you think you are too strong to get anything, somehow you're going to pay." Elicit students' responses to the following questions:

- Do you believe that illness is payback for mistakes in life? For example, do you think that AIDS is a punishment for people who've lived a questionable or risky life? Would this apply to all people with AIDS? Why or why not?
- If you were diagnosed with a terminal illness, would you wonder what you had done to deserve such treatment? Why or why not?

▶ **just-world phenomenon** The tendency to believe that people get what they deserve and deserve what they get.

Categorization adversely affects our awareness of diversity. We know the strengths and weaknesses and even the peculiarities of people in our own groups, but we are often ignorant of, or indifferent to, diversity in those we categorize. Overestimating the similarities of those not in our group leads us to think that those we categorize think, act, and look alike. Once again, we see how categorization simplifies: By thinking others are the same, we don't have to spend time sorting one person out from another.

Just-World Phenomenon

The **just-world phenomenon** is the tendency to believe the world is just and that people therefore get what they deserve and deserve what they get. This belief reflects what many of us were taught as children, that good is rewarded and evil is punished. This kind of false assumption promotes such thoughts as, "Unsuccessful people are bad, and the poor get what they deserve." The flip-side thought is "Successful people are good, and the rich deserve their riches." By thinking the world is fair we justify our prejudices. Everything is as it should be: Just-world thinking wrongly suggests that ghettos are filled with people who are poor because they don't want to work. Therefore, the poor deserve inner-city life. Older Americans can't afford prescription drugs? Just-world thinking suggests that this is their own fault for not saving enough money for their retirement.

In our attempts to make the world seem fair, we sometimes come up with skewed thinking. We see the just-world phenomenon at work when experiments reveal a tendency to blame the victims of crimes. Researchers in one 1980s study gave participants a detailed account of a date-rape crime. Participants hearing this account viewed the victim's behavior as partially responsible for the crime. "She should have known better" than to go out with the person. However, when the same date story was presented without the rape ending, participants did not say the victims behavior invited rape (Janoff-Bulman & others, 1985). The woman's behavior was at fault only when she was a victim of a crime.

The Just-World Phenomenon?

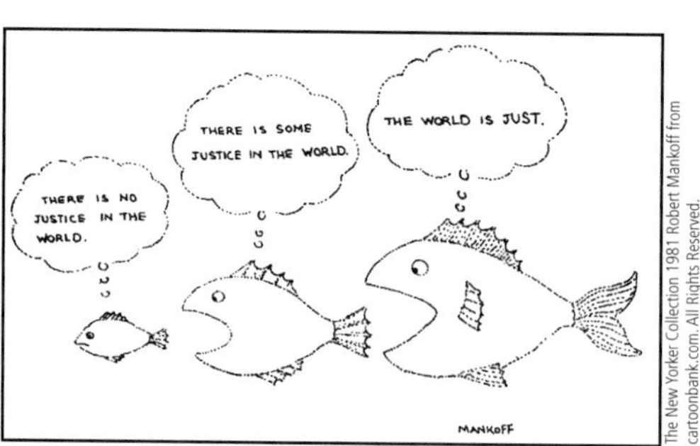

Cross-Curricular Connections

GOVERNMENT Team-teach with a government teacher about discrimination laws.

- What types of discrimination does the law allow? Why? *(preferential treatment of people with special needs in school and for affirmative action in many arenas)*
- What types of discrimination does the law not allow? Why? *(discrimination when people are voting or being hired for a job)*
- What types of discrimination does the law seem unsure about? *(areas of age discrimination, discrimination against people according to their sexual orientation, and for discrimination based on gender)*

trb At this point, you may wish to use Critical Thinking Activity: *Institutional Discrimination* (*Teacher's Resource Binder*, p. 33-1; Handout 33–9).

Aggression

7. How do genetics, our nervous system, and biochemistry contribute to aggression? How do we learn aggression?

► **aggression** Any physical or verbal behavior intended to hurt or destroy.

We hear or read about the baseball player stealing second base, the volleyball player spiking the ball over the net, or the salesperson who won't take "no" for an answer. Are these individuals behaving aggressively? Not according to psychology's definition of **aggression,** which is any physical or verbal behavior intended to hurt or destroy. Deliberately passing nasty, false rumors around school about a classmate is acting aggressively. A person who swears at you for standing in front of and blocking a locker is also acting aggressively.

Many people outside the United States see us as a country full of aggressive people. How else can one explain the fact that you are five times more likely to be murdered if you live in the United States than in Canada (United Nations, 1997)? Are these critics right? Are Americans more aggressive than people in other countries? Psychologists have not yet found the answer to that question, but they are taking a hard look at biological and environmental factors—nature and nurture—to get a better understanding of why we are aggressive.

The Biology of Aggression

What triggers aggressive behavior in bullies and thugs? Biological factors bear some of the blame. The biological influences include genes, the nervous system, and biochemistry.

Genetic and Neural Influences

Evidence for genetic aggression is apparent in certain dog breeds, which have been selectively bred to be aggressive watch dogs. Psychologists have bred genetically aggressive rats in laboratories. And in life outside the lab, studies show that genetically identical twins are more likely than nonidentical twins to report that both have violent tempers (Miles & Carey, 1997; Rowe & others, 1999).

Our nervous system is set up to make aggression possible if we are aggravated or provoked and if nothing is restraining us. Evidence suggests there is no one spot in the brain controlling violence. Rather, we have a complex neural system that either stimulates or inhibits aggressive behavior, depending on the circumstances (Moyer, 1983). A part of the brain that seems to play a prominent role in aggression is the amygdala (a-MIG-da-la). One report of this connection comes from neurosurgeons trying to diagnose a woman's disorder. When they activated an electrode implanted next to her amygdala, the woman stood up, ordered

Cooperative Learning

Have students make a chart with two columns—one labeled *Appropriate Aggression* and one labeled *Inappropriate Aggression.* Have students brainstorm about what aggressive behavior society deems appropriate and inappropriate. Then create a class list to see if everyone agrees on what is an appropriate expression of aggression. Use the following questions to discuss the lists:

- Which list is longer—appropriate or inappropriate behavior? Why?
- Does there seem to be a gender difference in the perception of aggression? Why or why not?
- Do students from different cultural backgrounds have different ideas about what is appropriate? Why or why not?

trb At this point, you may wish to use **Critical Thinking Activity:** *Defining Aggression* (*Teacher's Resource Binder,* p. 33-1; **Handout 33–11**).

■ **TEACHING TIP**

Ask your students, "Do you think people are more likely to express anger today than they used to be?" When Scripps Howard News Service and Ohio University posed this question to 815 adults across the United States in mid-1999, 88 percent answered yes. A total of 26 percent said that they themselves felt more anger than they used to feel. Clearly, public opinion can be wrong.

trb At this point, you may wish to use **Enrichment Lesson:** *Do We Need to Vent Our Rage?* (*Teacher's Resource Binder,* p. 33-1).

■ **LOOKING AT THE ISSUES**

The following is a true story of an event that took place in Birmingham, Alabama.

A woman in an SUV is driving home from work on a busy metropolitan highway. The woman in a Pontiac in front of her seems upset that the SUV is following too closely. The two cars continue for a few miles, communicating aggressively with each other. As traffic slows on the backed-up off-ramp, the woman in the Pontiac gets out of her car and starts yelling at the woman in the SUV. Moments later, a shot is fired and the yelling, irate woman is dead. Spark a discussion about aggressive behavior with the following questions:

- Have you ever felt angry or irritated with other drivers? How did you express these feelings?
- Have other drivers ever behaved aggressively toward you? If so, why? How did they behave? How did it make you feel?
- Should people be allowed to carry handguns in cars? Why or why not?
- How can people experience less road rage?

trb At this point, you may wish to use **Analysis Activity:** *Road Rage* (*Teacher's Resource Binder,* p. 33-1; **Handout 33–13**) and **Enrichment Lesson:** *Road Rage* (*Teacher's Resource Binder,* p. 33-1).

MODULE 33

■ **MULTICULTURAL CONNECTIONS**
Have students research crime rates in the United States and compare them with crime rates in other countries. Then, based on students' statistical findings, ask whether or not people living in the United States are more aggressive than people living in other countries. Challenge students to support conclusions with their findings.

■ **LOOKING AT THE ISSUES**
The main ingredients in anabolic steroids are hormones related to testosterone, the male sex hormone. People who take steroids want the benefits additional steroids offer—larger muscle mass, faster recovery from injury, improved appearance, and increased aggression. Have students discuss the following questions:

- What rules do your school and state athletic associations have about using anabolic steroids?
- Does your school test athletes to see if they are using steroids? Why or why not?
- What punishments are in store for students caught using steroids?
- What harmful side effects can adolescents experience if they use steroids?
- Not all professional athletic organizations ban the use of steroids. Why?

■ **TEACHING TIP**
Link discussion of *testosterone* and *biochemistry* to the *endocrine system*. The **endocrine system** controls different hormones secreted throughout the body. The body's master gland—the pituitary—is regulated by the hypothalamus. The hypothalamus tells the pituitary when to send signals to the other glands in the body to start secreting their respective hormones.

- **adrenal glands** (located atop the kidneys)—adrenaline and noradrenaline
- **pancreas**—insulin, which regulates body sugar levels
- **thyroid**—calcitonin, which regulates calcium and phosphorus levels in the body
- **ovaries**—estrogen and progesterone
- **testes**—testosterone

someone to take her blood pressure ("Take it now!"), and started beating her doctor. Another interesting report comes from Dorothy Lewis and her colleagues, who studied the histories of 15 death row inmates and found that all 15 had suffered brain trauma through a severe head injury (Lewis & others, 1986). Though the vast majority of neurologically impaired people are nonviolent, the research suggests that a neurological disorder may have contributed to the inmates' aggressive crimes.

Biochemistry

Alcohol, neurotransmitters, and hormones can tip the balance of your neural system's aggression control system. The primary biochemical player appears to be testosterone—the most important of the male sex hormones. Consider the following:

- Violent criminals are usually young males with lower intelligence test scores, lower levels of serotonin (a brain chemical), and higher testosterone levels (Dabbs, 1992).
- High testosterone levels have been associated with frustration, irritability, and impulsiveness, all of which can set the stage for aggression (Harris, 1994).
- Testosterone-reducing drugs suppress aggressive behavior (Pendick, 1994).
- In teenage boys, high testosterone levels are correlated with hard drug use, delinquency, and bullying responses to frustration (Berman & others, 1993; Dabbs & Morris, 1990; Olweus & others, 1988).

We should note that all of these studies represent data from correlational studies. Keep in mind that the existence of a correlation does not prove that a cause-and-effect relationship exists. Correlations tell us that certain variables *are* related, but not *why* they are related. Still, correlations are useful in helping us make predictions. If testosterone levels in young males drop, we can accurately predict their aggressiveness will decrease. In fact, both testosterone levels and the likelihood of committing a crime decrease as males age. Aggressiveness decreases with age as well.

Alcohol appears to have both a biological and a psychological impact on aggression. Frustration is more likely to produce aggression in those who have been drinking alcohol (Bushman, 1993; Ito & others, 1996; Taylor & Chermack, 1993). People under the influence of alcohol commit 40 percent of all violent crimes and 75 percent of all spouse abuse (Greenfeld, 1998). Psychologically, aggressiveness also increases in those who *think* they've been drinking, even when they haven't (White & others, 1993).

Learning Aggression

Aggression in response to a threatening event may be a natural response. But we also learn aggression through having our own aggressive behavior rewarded and by watching role models behave aggressively.

If a bully takes your lunch money today and gets away with it, she'll probably have lunch at your expense quite often in the future. When experience teaches us that being aggressive gets us what we want, the chances increase that we'll be aggressive in the future. Children can learn this by proxy: If they see another rewarded for being aggressive, they are more likely to imitate that model's behavior. Parents sometimes display the exact behavior they don't want when they discipline their children by beating them. The message children receive? One way to solve problems is through aggression (Patterson & others, 1982, 1992).

Frightening Statistics By the age of 18, most people will have seen tens of thousands of murders. The violent acts portrayed on TV rarely show the suffering and pain that accompany murder and mayhem.

So what does this mean for your generation and your younger brothers and sisters? If you're average, by the time you reach age 18, you will have spent more time watching TV than you will have spent in school. The typical grade school kid sees over 8000 murders and 100,000 violent acts even before reaching middle school or junior high (Huston & others, 1992). Most of these violent acts don't show the pain and suffering that follow the offense.

Does watching violence, on TV or at the movies, influence people to be aggressive? Correlational studies suggest that it does. Homicide rates in the United States and Canada doubled between 1956 and 1974, widely considered television's booming growth years. The same increase in homicide rates was seen in white South Africa after television was introduced in 1975 (Centerwall, 1989). After reviewing experimental data, the American Psychological Association made the following official statement; "There is absolutely no doubt that higher levels of viewing violence on television are correlated with increased acceptance of aggressive attitudes and increased aggressive behavior" (APA, 1992). Elliot Aronson (1999) provides four reasons why exposure to media violence might increase aggression:

1. *"If they can do it, so can I."* Previously learned inhibitions on being violent may be weakened by watching violent TV characters.
2. *"Oh, so that's how you do it."* Watching violent acts on TV may spur imitation.

F • Y • I

Psychologists in the late 1930s proposed that frustration was the cause of aggression. Research seems to point to several ways that frustration is linked to aggression:

- If the aggression helps to alleviate the frustration, aggression is more likely to occur.
- If a goal is almost accomplished and frustration is experienced, aggression is more likely.
- If an aggressive stimulus is seen while frustration is experienced, aggression is more likely.

Does frustration always lead to aggression? No, but environmental factors can determine when a frustrating situation will lead to someone acting aggressively.

■ **CHECKING FOR UNDERSTANDING** Quiz students on how aggression can be reinforced. Remind students that reinforcement occurs when one is rewarded or when something unpleasant is taken away when a behavior occurs. If a child is looking for attention and learns that his or her parents will pay attention when he or she is aggressive, the child will learn to be aggressive to get attention.

Enriching

Have students watch several different types of television shows to see how acts of violence are depicted. Suggest that students watch news broadcasts (both local and national), a sitcom, a police drama, a medical drama, and a nonspecific drama (family or relational shows). Be sure to operationally define "act of violence" before students begin viewing. Discuss their viewing experiences in class with the following questions:

- How many acts of violence occurred overall? How many occurred in each show?
- Does one type of program depict more violence than others? Why or why not?
- What was different about the violence depicted on the different types of shows?
- How did watching this violence affect you? Would you feel comfortable letting your children watch the acts you saw? Why or why not?

MODULE 33

■ TEACHING TIP

Link *viewing television violence* to Albert Bandura's famous *Bobo doll studies.* Bandura and his colleagues showed young children a video of adults playing with a Bobo doll (an inflated doll with sand in the bottom so it rights itself whenever it is knocked over). One group of children saw adults acting aggressively toward the doll. The other group saw the adults playing nicely. How did the children react when put in a room with a Bobo doll? Those who saw the aggressive play themselves played aggressively. Those who saw the nice behavior played nicely.

F•Y•I

Psychological research offers limited support for the **catharsis hypothesis,** which states that people experience a release (catharsis) when they vent their anger. Laboratory tests of catharsis have produced mixed results, at best. One study found that when students were allowed to counterattack someone who had provoked them, their blood pressure more quickly returned to normal. The calming effect seems to occur, however, only when the target is one's actual tormenter, the retaliation is justified, and the target is nonintimidating.

Does the viewing of aggression prove cathartic? Alfred Hitchcock once said, "One of television's great contributions is that it brought murder back into the home where it belongs. Seeing a murder on television can be good therapy. It can help work off one's antagonisms. If you have no antagonisms, the commercials will give you some." Once again, research is not supportive. Spectators at football, wrestling, and hockey matches exhibit more hostility after watching the event than before. Similarly, after a war, a nation's murder rate tends to increase, not decrease. The near-consensus in the research community is that viewing television violence increases aggression in the viewer.

Thinking Critically

Video Games and Violence

Put a dollar in the *Resident Evil 2* video game, take the video game identity of Clare Redfield, and with a little practice you can stay alive for minutes on end, firing bullets into Zombie cops and watching them slump, twitch, and bleed to death. Likewise, you can spend some more money and kick the heads off of video images that are trying to do the same thing to you. What do we learn from video games? This question was debated with great intensity after the 1999 school murders in Littleton, Colorado, and Paducah, Kentucky, when authorities revealed that the assailants were particularly good at playing games like *Mortal Kombat*, *Quake*, and *Doom*.

Video games appear to encourage aggressive thoughts and increase aggression. In one study, the most physically aggressive college males were the students who had spent the most time playing violent video games (Anderson & Dill, 2000). The same researchers found that those assigned to a nonviolent game (like *Myst*) became less hostile in follow-up tasks than those assigned to play games featuring blood, gore, and groaning victims.

There is still a lot to learn. Yes, thousands of students play violent video games and never physically harm one another. But there is little doubt that playing these games increases aggressive responses and lowers sensitivity to cruelty. Also, no data support the idea that violent games serve as valuable "release valves" for feelings of fury and anger, as some say in defense of *Mortal Kombat* and others. In fact, playing these games seems to increase feelings of hostility (Ballard & Wiest, 1998).

What Do Video Games Teach?

3. *"I think it must be aggressive feelings I'm experiencing."* The experience of watching violence on TV may make anger and aggressive responses more accessible to the viewer.
4. *"Ho-hum, another brutal beating; what's on the next channel?"* Watching violence on TV may desensitize our reactions to mayhem and reduce our sympathy for victims. Living with violence becomes easier.

Let's not forget that watching violent crimes on TV does not automatically turn a person into a villain. Likewise, lots of children grow up in oppressive situations but do not grow up to be aggressive. Having a par-

Enriching

Have students research the popularity of violent video games and survey their own video game collections.

- What are the most popular video games today? Why? Are they considered violent?
- What impact does the rating system have on the popularity of a particular video game?
- Do they have many violent video games? Why or why not?
- Do they feel violent video games affect their behavior? Why or why not?

ent who regularly uses severe physical punishment does not doom a child to the same actions. Like all behavior, aggression is an interaction between nurture (outside situational factors) and nature (inner personal factors).

Cooperation

8. What helps foster cooperation among groups?

Friendly contact between different ethnic or racial groups can decrease prejudice (Pettigrew, 1969, 1997). But contact is not usually enough to break down the barriers between two different groups. One way to break down barriers is by using **superordinate goals.** These goals override differences among people and require cooperation. **Muzafer Sherif** (1966) discovered the power behind superordinate goals in a study of 22 boys attending a summer camp.

Sherif divided the boys into two groups. He assigned each group an area of the campsite, apart from the other. The groups then competed against each other in a series of events. The winners received prizes from camp counselors and contempt from the losers. Within days, the two groups were raiding each other's cabins, engaging in food fights over dinner, and, when brought together, taunting each other.

Using superordinate goals, Sherif then turned the foes into friends. First, he created a water supply emergency. To obtain water, both groups had to pitch in and work together. A truck quit running, and all the boys had to push it to get it going. Soon, the taunting stopped, and the boys even pooled their money to pay for a recreational activity they could not otherwise afford. Whereas competition and isolation had created enemies, *cooperative contact* created friends.

Cooperation can lead people to melt the icy walls of noninclusive subgroups, creating a new, more inclusive group (Dovidio & Gaertner, 1999). An "us" and "them" mentality turns into a "we" state of mind.

Cooperative learning, where students work together on projects, promotes interracial friendships in multicultural schools (Johnson & Johnson, 1989, 1994). Cooperative learning also enhances student achievement (Slavin, 1989). These results are so positive that thousands and thousands of teachers around the country have brought interracial cooperative learning to their classrooms (Kohn, 1987). These experiences set the stage for "adult work life and for citizenship in a multicultural society" (Carnegie Council on Adolescent Development, 1989).

Perhaps there is a message on the value of cooperative contact at a time when we see more and more strife, fragmentation, and warlike activities on our planet. With increased international exchanges, maybe we'll discover that our similarities far outweigh our differences, and that we share such basic goals as having a healthy family, a safe home, and food on the table.

► **superordinate goals** Shared goals that override differences among people and require their cooperation.

► **Muzafer Sherif** (1906–1988) Psychologist who studied the impact of shared goals on cooperation.

Superordinate Goals Cooperation is necessary to meet shared goals, especially if people need to overcome differences.

■ **TEACHING TIP**

To help students understand cooperation within a group, have them sit around a shallow bowl that initially contains ten metal nuts. State that the goal is to accumulate as many nuts as possible. Each student may take as many as he or she wants, and every ten seconds the number of nuts remaining in the bowl will be doubled. What happens? Unless students are allowed some time to devise a strategy for conservation, 65 percent of the groups will never reach the first ten-second replenishment. Often they will knock the bowl off the table while grabbing for their share!

trb At this point, you may wish to use Demonstration Activity: *Social Traps* (*Teacher's Resource Binder*, p. 33-1).

Close

This module reviews the social experiences people have with each other. The spectrum of experiences covered ranges from love and aggression to cooperation. Have students discuss the wide-ranging experiences people have as they interact with each other by asking the following questions:

- Consider an average day. Are most experiences people have with each other positive or negative?
- Does the media portray people in peaceful cooperation or antagonistic competition? Why?
- What superordinate goals do you share with others in your family, school, and town?

Demonstrating

THE DOLLAR AUCTION Introduce the interplay between cooperation and competition with the dollar auction. One dollar goes to the highest bidder, but the two highest bidders must both pay their bids. Only the highest bidder gets the dollar. Many in a group begin bidding; as the bidding approaches $0.50, and the trap becomes apparent, the auction narrows to two people. The next moment of truth comes at a bid of $0.95. The lower bidder realizes that bidding more than a dollar will mean losing money. But of course failing to outbid the opponent will mean losing even more. Is cooperation or competition what's needed to beat the trap?

trb At this point, you may wish to use Cooperative Learning Activity: *The Missiles Game* (*Teacher's Resource Binder*, p. 33-1; Handouts 33–12a through 33–12d).

MODULE 33

Checking the Points

TEACHING TIPS

web (1) The book companion site for *Thinking About Psychology* at **www.worthpublishers.com/thinkingaboutpsych** contains a module quiz, flashcards of key terms and people, as well as other student activities and resources for this module. You will also find PowerPoint lectures, a quiz grade book, and other teaching resources by logging on as an instructor.

trb (2) At this point, you may wish to review and confirm concepts about social relations with **Critical Thinking Activity:** *Fact or Falsehood?* (*Teacher's Resource Binder*, p. 33-1; **Handout 33–1**). If students filled in this handout earlier in the module, ask them to set it aside. Suggest that students complete the handout, taking the time to look up information in the text in order to respond correctly to questions. Review each item with the class, allowing students to challenge each other's responses with support from text passages.

REVIEW

Module 33: Social Relations

What's the Point?

Attraction

1. *Why are we attracted to some people but not to others?*

   Proximity, physical attractiveness, and similarity are the primary influences on whether or not we are attracted to another person. Proximity is simply being near another person; if we don't meet, we can't be attracted to each other. The mere exposure effect is a term describing the tendency for repeated exposure to increase our liking of something. We may have inherited a tendency to bond with those who are familiar to us and be suspicious of those we don't know.

   We are most likely to be attracted to people whom we define as attractive. (Standards for attractiveness vary with time and place.) We see these people as happier, healthier, and more successful than their less attractive counterparts. Those who are attractive, however, do not seem to be happier or more secure than others, and they often worry that they are praised more for their appearance than for their work.

   We tend to like those who are like us—who share our interests, attitudes, age, intelligence level, economic status, and beliefs.

Romantic Love

2. *What do we mean by passionate love and companionate love, and how do they differ?*

   Passionate love is the aroused state of intense absorption we feel at the beginning of a love relationship. This kind of love does not usually endure, but it often evolves into companionate love—a more lasting, deep, and affectionate attachment for those with whom we share our lives. Equity (giving approximately what you receive) and self-disclosure (sharing intimate aspects of yourself) increase the likelihood that love will endure.

Altruism

3. *Under what conditions are we more likely to help others?*

   We are most likely to help others when we are in a good mood (this is the most important factor), not in a hurry, believe the person deserves help, believe the person is similar to us, feel guilty, are in a small town or rural area, or have just seen someone else being helpful. The bystander effect is the tendency for any one person to be less likely to help when other bystanders are present.

Prejudice

4. *How do prejudice, stereotypes, and discrimination differ?*

   Prejudice is an unjustifiable attitude toward certain groups and their members. Stereotypes are generalized beliefs about such groups. Discrimination is action based on stereotyped beliefs and prejudicial attitudes.

5. *How do ingroups, outgroups, and scapegoats relate to prejudice, stereotypes, and discrimination?*

   We define ingroups as "us" and outgroups as "them." Our prejudices, stereotypes, and discrimination are directed toward outgroups—those who are not like us. And we have an ingroup bias—we favor those who are like us. Prejudice offers an outlet for anger by giving us someone to blame—the scapegoat.

6. *How do our thought processes foster prejudice?*
   Our mind's attempt to make sense of the world around us tends to push us toward categorizing not only objects but also the people around us. Categorization is efficient because it simplifies our thinking, but it also leads to stereotypes and causes us to see people as alike because we have placed them in the same category. We readily understand that those who are in our ingroups differ from one another, but we tend to lump together all the people who are in our outgroups, losing track of their individuality and diversity. The just-world phenomenon is another thought process that leads us to stereotype people, because we tend to believe that people get what they deserve.

Aggression

7. *How do genetics, our nervous system, and biochemistry contribute to aggression? How do we learn aggression?*
   Psychologists define *aggression* as any physical or verbal behavior intended to hurt or destroy. Three primary biological factors influence aggression. Some people may have a genetic predisposition to be aggressive; laboratory experiments and dog breeding programs have produced strains of animals that are more aggressive than normal. Our complex nervous system (including the amygdala in the brain) can stimulate or inhibit aggression. And our biochemistry (neurotransmitters, effects of alcohol and other ingested drugs, and hormones—especially testosterone) can make us more aggressive.

   We learn aggression in two ways: by being rewarded for aggressive behavior, which increases the likelihood that we will repeat that behavior, and by modeling the aggression we observe in others. Violent TV programs, movies, and video games all show us behaviors from which we can learn aggression.

Cooperation

8. *What helps foster cooperation among groups?*
   Friendly contact decreases prejudice, but the best way to foster cooperation among groups is to engage them in superordinate goals—goals that override group differences. Cooperative learning, in which students work together on projects, helps promote interracial friendships and overcome group differences.

Key Terms

mere exposure effect, p. 635
passionate love, p. 638
companionate love, p. 639
equity, p. 639
self-disclosure, p. 639
altruism, p. 640
bystander effect, p. 641
prejudice, p. 643
stereotype, p. 643
discrimination, p. 643
ingroup, p. 644
outgroup, p. 644
ingroup bias, p. 644
scapegoat theory, p. 645
just-world phenomenon, p. 646
aggression, p. 647
superordinate goals, p. 651

Key People

John Darley, p. 641
Bibb Latané, p. 641
Muzafer Sherif, p. 651

trb tr ■ TEACHING TIP

At this point, you may wish to provide students with **Building Vocabulary: Graphic Organizer:** ***Crossword Puzzle*** (*Teacher's Resource Binder*, p. 33-1; **Handout 33–2**). If students worked on this puzzle earlier in the module, ask them to not refer to it. Have students fill out the answers as a tool for reviewing the concepts and terms in the module. Next, allow time for students to work in small groups to complete their handout, using the text to clarify confusing concepts. You can complete a copy of the puzzle and use it as a transparency to project for students, who can then check and confirm their own answers.

MODULE 33

Using the Test Bank

The *Test Bank* that accompanies this textbook offers a wide variety of questions in different formats and levels of complexity. Use the software to construct whole tests or to integrate standardized questions into teacher-made tests.

Self-Test Answers

Multiple-Choice Questions

1. c, 2. c, 3. d, 4. b, 5. a

Self-Test

Multiple-Choice Questions

Choose the *best* answer for each of the following questions.

1. Ten years ago, the residents of Very Snazzy Avenue were alarmed to hear that a new house being built on their street would be an ultramodern structure with lots of glass and steel in the design. They protested, but the house plan conformed to building codes and they couldn't prevent it from being constructed. This year, an equally ultramodern house is being built on a neighboring lot, and most Very Snazzy Avenue residents are not objecting. Some even say they like the design. The most likely explanation for this change in attitude is
   a. similarity.
   b. companionate feelings.
   c. the mere exposure effect.
   d. the bystander effect.

2. Serena is new in town, and she is extraordinarily beautiful. The other girls in her class are envious; they know Serena must be happier, healthier, and more successful than they are and that she will have her pick of dates for all the school events. What might a psychologist say about the assumptions Serena's classmates made about her?
   a. It is unfair to assume that Serena will be popular with boys because she is so beautiful; studies show that adolescent males value brains and personality as much as beauty.
   b. Serena's classmates are wrong to assume that because Serena is beautiful she must also excel in other areas.
   c. Since we all think of ourselves as attractive, Serena's actual beauty will not give her any advantage over the other girls.
   d. All of the above.

3. Not-a-Good-Place-to-Live has been sued for racial profiling. The police in this town routinely stop black men who drive cars through wealthy neighborhoods inhabited mainly by white people. This policy of assuming wrongdoing on the part of those caught "driving while black" is an example of
   a. a prejudice.
   b. a stereotype.
   c. discrimination.
   d. All of the above

4. On a hot July afternoon, a woman and her three young children sat in a car by the side of a small street connecting a beach parking lot and a main road. She watched in dismay as cars full of beach-goers passed by without stopping, although most of the drivers and passengers clearly had seen her car with its hood open and could hear her children crying. Social psychologists would say this is an example of
   a. the mere exposure effect.
   b. the bystander effect.
   c. aggression.
   d. equity.

5. Diana shouted, "Hurry up, you old woman," at another student who was driving slowly and making her late to class. Jamal injured an opponent's shoulder when he fell over him while running a base. Megan slapped her little brother for stealing her allowance. According to psychology's definition of *aggression*, which of these people were acting aggressively?
   a. Diana and Megan
   b. Jamal, Megan, and Megan's brother
   c. Diana, Megan, and Megan's brother
   d. Jamal and Megan

Matching Terms and Definitions

6. For each definition, choose the *best* matching term from the list that follows.

Definition

a. A sometimes accurate but often overgeneralized belief about a group of people.
b. Taking action against a group of people because of stereotyped beliefs and feelings of prejudice.
c. Psychologist who studied the impact of shared goals on cooperation.
d. An unjustifiable and usually negative attitude toward a group and its members.
e. The tendency to believe that people get what they deserve and deserve what they get.
f. The idea that prejudice provides an outlet for anger by providing someone to blame.
g. The tendency to favor one's own group.
h. Revealing intimate aspects of oneself to others.
i. Any physical or verbal behavior intended to hurt or destroy.
j. A condition in which people receive from a relationship in proportion to what they give to it.
k. Psychologist who researched the circumstances that determine when a bystander will intervene on behalf of another person.

Term or Person

(1) Muzafer Sherif
(2) just-world phenomenon
(3) aggression
(4) stereotype
(5) prejudice
(6) equity
(7) discrimination
(8) ingroup bias
(9) John Darley
(10) superordinate goals
(11) scapegoat theory
(12) self-disclosure
(13) ingroup

Fill-in-the-Blank Questions

7. Psychologists doing research on why we are attracted to some people but not to others have discovered that the three most important influences seem to be _______________, _______________ _______________, and _______________.

8. Friendly contact reduces prejudice, but engaging in goals that override group differences seems to be the best way to foster _______________ between groups.

Brief Essay Question

9. Regional High School draws students from five nearby small towns. Two of these towns have a past history of conflict and bad feelings, and students from those towns are very suspicious of each other. In two paragraphs of about three sentences each, explain what the school might do to minimize tension and foster cooperation between these two groups of students.

MODULE 33

Self-Test Answers

Matching Terms and Definitions

6. a. (4), b. (7), c. (1), d. (5), e. (2), f. (11), g. (8), h. (12), i. (3), j. (6), k. (9)

Fill-in-the-Blank Questions

7. proximity; physical attractiveness; similarity, 8. cooperation

Brief Essay Question

10. The school can establish superordinate goals, like having the two towns with a past history of conflict raise money for the same charity or work together to accomplish a common task. The school can encourage friendly contact among the towns the students come from to decrease prejudice. The school can also create cooperative learning experiences that blend students from all the towns it services, especially from the two towns with a past history of conflict.

MODULE 34

Performance Standards

Standard Area: Social and Cultural Dimensions of Behavior

Content Standard 2: Define social and cultural categories

Performance Standard 2.1 Define primary social and cultural categories.

- Define culture. Examine how culture develops. (Student Text pp. 656–658)
- Compare individualism and collectivism. Examine how different cultural perspectives influence the development of self-concept, motivation, and emotion. (Student Text pp. 658–661)
- Compare universal and culture-specific behaviors and principles. (Student Text pp. 661-662)
- Examine how a cross-cultural perspective influences our understanding of personality and child development. (Student Text pp. 662–665)

Performance Standard 2.2 Explain how social and cultural categories influence behavior.

- Compare individualism and collectivism. Examine how different cultural perspectives influence the development of self-concept, motivation, and emotion. (Student Text pp. 658–661)
- Compare universal and culture-specific behaviors and principles. (Student Text pp. 661–662)
- Examine how a cross-cultural perspective influences our understanding of personality and child development. (Student Text pp. 662–665)
- Define ethnocentrism. Explain how we can keep ourselves as free as possible from its influence. (Student Text pp. 666–667)

Standard Area: Life Span Development

Content Standard 3: Stage theories

Performance Standard 3.3 Investigate the development of ethnic identity.

- Define culture. Examine how culture develops. (Student Text pp. 656–658)
- Compare universal and culture-specific behaviors and principles. (Student Text pp. 661–662)
- Examine how a cross-cultural perspective influences our understanding of personality and child development. Focus on cognitive, moral, and social development. (Student Text pp. 662–665)
- Define ethnocentrism. Explain how we can keep ourselves as free as possible from its influence. (Student Text pp. 666–667)

Performance Standard 3.4 Examine developmental theories and their relation to cultural bias.

- Compare individualism and collectivism. Examine how different cultural perspectives influence the development of self-concept, motivation, and emotion. (Student Text pp. 658–661)

Materials NETWORK

All of the items from the Video, Activity, and Enrichment Centers listed below come from the *Teacher's Resource Binder.* These items will help you teach and expand on concepts presented in Module 34.

trb This logo indicates when an item from the Materials Network may be used in conjunction with a specific note found in this module's *Teacher's Edition.*

Culture

Activity Center

- Critical Thinking Activity: *Fact or Falsehood?* With this activity, students' preconceptions about cross-cultural psychology are either exposed as incorrect or reinforced as correct. (*Teacher's Resource Binder*, p. 34-1; Handout 34–1)
- Critical Thinking Activity: *Cross-Cultural Dialogues* Students can gain insight into the mindset of different cultural perspectives with this activity that explores cross-cultural dialogues. (*Teacher's Resource Binder*, p. 34-1; Transparency Master 34–1)

Enrichment Center

- Enrichment Lesson: *Differences in Cultural Norms* Cultural norms that are different from those followed in the United States are presented in this lesson. (*Teacher's Resource Binder*, p. 34-1)

Individualism and Collectivism

Activity Center

- Analysis Activity: *Assessing Individualism/Collectivism* Students can analyze their responses to the question "Who am I?" to learn more about their individualistic and collectivistic attitudes. (*Teacher's Resource Binder*, p. 34-1)
- Analysis Activity: *Measuring Individualism and Collectivism* Obtain a more in-depth analysis of individualism and collectivism with this measure. (*Teacher's Resource Binder*, p. 34-1; Handout 34–2)
- Analysis Activity: *Independent and Interdependent Selves* In this activity, students analyze what the text states—collectivism encourages the development of the interdependent self, whereas individualism promotes the independent self. (*Teacher's Resource Binder*, p. 34-1; Handout 34–3)

Enrichment Center

- Enrichment Lesson: *Individualism Versus Collectivism* Harry Triandis suggests that every culture emphasizes a particular combination of four behavior patterns, outlined in this lesson. (*Teacher's Resource Binder*, p. 34-1)

Cross-Cultural Research

V Video Center

- Videocassette: *The Brain,* Second Edition, Module 3: "Gender Development: Social Influences" Consult the faculty guide from *The Brain* video series for a description of this module. (*Teacher's Resource Binder*, p. 34-1)

Activity Center

- Evaluation Activity: *Gender Roles in the Home* Social learning theory, in particular, suggests that observation of adult models is crucial. (*Teacher's Resource Binder*, p. 34-1; Handout 34–4)
- Cooperative Learning Activity: *Learning Gender Roles* This activity focuses on what our society dictates as behaviors that are "male" and "female." (*Teacher's Resource Binder*, p. 34-1; Handouts 34–5a and 34–5b)
- Application Activity: *Achievement and Challenge* This activity focuses on high achievement and low achievement motivation. (*Teacher's Resource Binder*, p. 34-1)
- Analysis Activity: *Intrinsic Motivation and Achievement* This activity presents a scale for assessing three different facets of intrinsic motivation. (*Teacher's Resource Binder*, p. 34-1)

Enrichment Center

- Enrichment Lesson: *Gender Differences* Men and women, although equal, are not the same. (*Teacher's Resource Binder*, p. 34-1)
- Enrichment Lesson: *Weiner's Attributional Model of Achievement* High achievement motivation has emotional roots and cognitive roots. (*Teacher's Resource Binder*, p. 34-1)
- Enrichment Lesson: *Birth Order, Achievement, and Personality* Report the fascinating finding that birth order correlates with achievement. (*Teacher's Resource Binder*, p. 34-1)

Ethnocentrism

Activity Center

- Analysis Activity: *Intercultural Learning Activities* This activity highlights how cultural norms may be learned by outsiders. (*Teacher's Resource Binder*, p. 34-1; Handout 34–6)
- Analysis Activity: *A Matter of Context* This exercise focuses on behavior of the new person as he or she joins the group. (*Teacher's Resource Binder*, p. 34-1; Handouts 34–7a through 34–7g)

MODULE 34

Cross-Cultural Psychology

Introducing the Module

The Points: Module Objectives

- Define *culture*, and describe how it develops.
- Differentiate between individualism and collectivism.
- Analyze how universal behaviors and principles differ from culture-specific behaviors and principles.
- Discuss the perspective cross-cultural research gives on some of psychology's theories of personality.
- Analyze what cross-cultural research has to say about some of psychology's theories of child development.
- Define *ethnocentrism*, and explain how we can keep our minds as free as possible from its influences.

Building Vocabulary

Have students create flashcards of the terms in this module. One side of the flashcard should show a module term, and the other side should provide the term's definition.

MODULE 34

Cross-Cultural Psychology

Culture

1. What is culture, and how does it develop?

One of my daughters once brought home a note announcing "Multicultural Day" at her school. On the given day, she was to dress in clothes and bring food representing the country of her ancestors. Of course, the school was really advertising a *nationality* day. Nationality is not culture. Many nations, including the United States, have multiple, equally important, coexisting cultures. To say that your nation is your culture is to ignore the multiple cultures in a nation. Your passport does not always determine your culture.

Race is not culture either. First, two people of the same race can be either very different or very similar culturally. Second, the term *race* is

Race Is Not Culture Two people of the same race may have very different cultures.

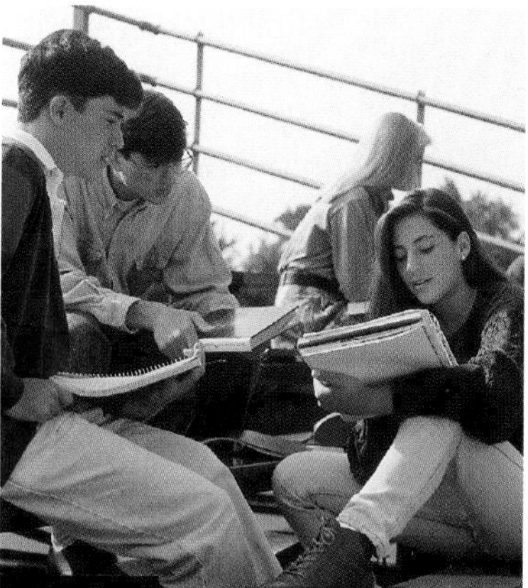

Getting Started

Ask students, "How many cultures are represented in our school?" They will probably list cultures differentiated by nationality, race, and/or ethnicity. Keep the list of cultures handy throughout the module to see how it becomes modified as students learn about what culture really is.

trb You may wish to use **Critical Thinking Activity:** *Fact or Falsehood?* (*Teacher's Resource Binder,* p. 34-1; **Handout 34–1**) as a prereading strategy to evaluate what students already know about cross-cultural psychology. This activity will prime students to look out for information that could prove or disprove their preconceptions about this area of psychology.

becoming meaningless, as researchers have discovered that the genetic differences between people *within* a race are equal to or greater than those that distinguish people of two *different* races (Keith, 2002). Your *race* is a set of characteristics programmed into your genetic code. Your *culture* is a set of behaviors and beliefs you learn from the people in your environment.

Ethnicity is a term that reflects the traits you have in common with some relatively large group of people with whom you share a history. Knowing a person's ethnicity or race does not provide meaningful information about how that person thinks and might behave. What do you know about me if I tell you that my name is Pat Dolan, I check the "black" box for race on government forms, and my ethnicity is African-American, Irish-American, and Cherokee? Could you predict my thoughts or behaviors? Surely not. What other clues might you get from knowing my culture? To answer that question, we must know more about this concept.

Psychologist **David Matsumoto** (1999) defines **culture** as a system of subtle and obvious rules established by a group to ensure its survival. These rules include the shared attitudes, beliefs, norms, and behaviors of a group that are passed from one generation to the next. Matsumoto sums up this definition by calling culture "the software of our minds."

Culture is the basis for much of our understanding of life, influencing most of the daily decisions we make. It is reflected in the food we eat, the clothes we wear, the houses we live in, and the technology we use. The effects of cultural differences are also seen in our modes of transportation, family activities, and governments. Is culture also evident in religion and science? Yes. In fact, though we never *see* culture itself, we see the manifestations of culture everywhere. How and why do so many cultural traditions develop? At least four factors influence culture development and diversity (Matsumoto, 1993):

- ***Population density*** Societies with higher population densities require more rules for maintaining social order. So, for example, there are far more traffic laws on the books in Los Angeles than there are in my hometown of Broken Bow, Nebraska. The laws in Los Angeles have become a part of the culture, reflecting a huge city's attempt to maintain order while also letting people travel as they need to.
- ***Climate*** Life-style adapts to climate. Weather affects the clothing people put on their backs and the food they put on the table. The life-style of a family living in a sparsely populated Saudi Arabian village will be very different from that of a family living in downtown Chicago. Each will need nourishment and protection from the forces of nature, but they will handle these needs in very different ways.

▶ **David Matsumoto** (1959–) Psychologist and internationally known expert on the study of cross-cultural psychology.

▶ **culture** A system of subtle and obvious rules (shared beliefs, attitudes, and behaviors) established to ensure a group's survival and passed from one generation to the next. The "software of our minds."

MODULE 34

Teaching the Points

■ TEACHING TIPS

web (1) You can log on as an instructor to the book companion site for *Thinking About Psychology* at www.worthpublishers.com/thinkingaboutpsych. It contains teacher resources for class presentations as well as review and assessment of module concepts and terms.

(2) Have students write 20 different statements in response to the simple question "Who am I?" Each statement should begin with "I am . . . ." Students should respond as if they are giving answers to themselves, not to someone else, and answers should be written in the order in which they were thought of. Tell students not to worry about importance or logic. In addition, instruct them to think and write at a fairly fast pace.

Source: Brislin, R. (1988). Increasing awareness of class, ethnicity, culture, and race by expanding on students' own experiences. In I. S. Cohen (Ed.), *The G. Stanley Hall lecture series* (Vol. 8, pp. 137–180). Washington, DC: American Psychological Association.

■ APPLYING THE POINTS

Have students meet in small groups and use the following questions to compare local laws and climate with those of cities or towns in your state or region that are larger and/or smaller:

- What are some common laws that your area has that others don't? Why don't other areas have your laws? Why don't you have some laws of other areas? What are some differences in culture between the two areas you have compared?
- How do the laws of your community affect your behavior? How does your climate affect your behavior? Would your behavior be different if you lived with different laws or in another climate? Why or why not?

Suggested Readings

Use the following books as teacher-preparation tools or as enrichment for advanced students:

Allen, L., & Santrock, J. W. (1993). *Psychology: The contexts of behavior.* Madison, WI: Brown & Benchmark.

Myers, D. G. (2000). *Exploring social psychology* (2nd ed.). New York: McGraw-Hill.

Seelye, H. N. (Ed.) (1996). *Experiential activities for intercultural learning.* Yarmouth, ME: Intercultural Press.

Storti, C. (1994). *Cross-cultural dialogues.* Yarmouth, ME:Intercultural Press.

Triandis, H. C. (1994). *Social behavior and culture.* New York: McGraw-Hill.

Weiner. B. (1992). *Human motivation: Metaphors, theories, and research.* Newbury Park, CA: Sage.

MODULE 34

■ APPLYING THE POINTS

Have students research your local government to see what resources are both plentiful and scarce in your area. Help them focus their research with the following questions:

- How does the government regulate scarce resources?
- Does this regulation affect your choices in life? Why or why not?

■ LOOKING AT THE ISSUES

Some groups worry about an "information gap" between those who have access to technology and those who don't. These groups are concerned that those who don't have access to technology will fall behind in education, socialization, and career choices. Have students consider the impact of technology on their lives. Promote class discussion with the following questions:

- How has technology affected your personal life? Do you have access to computer technology in your home? Why or why not?
- How has technology been integrated into school? What access to technology do you have at school? When do teachers use technology for instruction? How often do you use it in class?
- Should the government supply every student with a computer and Internet access? Why or why not?

■ JOURNAL WRITING

Invite students to use the following question as a springboard for an entry in their psychology journals:

- Would you want to be judged by your race, ethnicity, and/or nationality? Why or why not?

■ CHECKING FOR UNDERSTANDING

Have students write down the four factors that influence cultural development, define each one, and give an example of each.

Climate Affects Culture Lifestyle and clothing, both of which reflect culture, are affected by climate.

- ***Resources*** Working together in order to survive is essential in a land where resources are scarce. Teamwork is less likely to occur in places where resources are abundant. People in Afghanistan, where resources such as food and clothing are harder to come by, tend to experience more close-knit local societies than their counterparts in France or England.
- ***Technology*** Inventions such as the computer allow people to work alone, without any need for face-to-face interactions. The woman doing business from a personal computer in the basement of her Connecticut home will not have the face-to-face experiences of the woman selling fruits and vegetables in the streets of New Delhi.

Individualism and Collectivism

2. What's the difference between individualism and collectivism?

Do you see yourself as an independent person whose personal goals take precedence over the needs of others? Or do you see yourself connected to others, sacrificing your needs to satisfy the group? Your answer to those questions may reveal whether you were raised in a culture that values **individualism** or one that values **collectivism**. Of course, not every culture can be classified as *either* individualistic *or* collectivist. For that reason, it's more realistic to speak of an individualism-collectivism dimension, a scale on which you can indicate the degree to which your needs, wishes, and values reflect *your* individual needs or the needs of the groups to which you belong

► **individualism** Cultural style that places personal goals or needs ahead of group goals or needs.

► **collectivism** Cultural style that places group goals or needs ahead of personal goals or needs.

Cross-Curricular Connections

GOVERNMENT Invite your school's government teacher to discuss the economic systems of capitalism and communism. Ask this teacher to address the following questions in his or her presentation:

- What are the fundamental principles that underlie each of these systems?
- How are these systems similar to individualism and collectivism?
- How might living under these systems lead to people valuing individualistic or collectivistic ideals?

trb At this point, you may wish to use Enrichment Lesson: *Individualism Versus Collectivism* (*Teacher's Resource Binder*, p. 34-1) and/or Analysis Activity: *Measuring Individualism and Collectivism* (*Teacher's Resource Binder*, p. 34-1; Handout 34–2).

(Matsumoto, 1999). A teenager in Japan, a country with a tendency toward collectivism, would probably put group needs ahead of personal needs. Teens in the United States, a country with a strong tendency toward individualism, would probably place personal goals ahead of group goals.

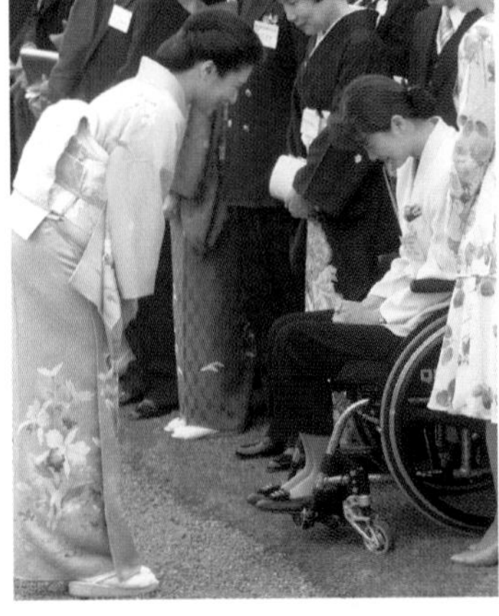

Collectivist Societies People raised in a collectivist society are more likely to value the needs of a group over needs of the individual.

One advantage of using the individualism-collectivism dimension is that we can predict and interpret cultural differences without relying on an *impression* we have about a particular cultural group that we've seen on television. In this module, we'll see how this dimension affects cultural differences in our self-concept, motivations, and emotions.

Self-Concept

Your sense of self—of who you are—is closely tied to how you understand the world and your relationships with others. The way we think about ourselves varies from culture to culture.

People raised in an individualistic culture have an *independent* understanding of self. Most Americans have this sense of self. Thus, asked to explain who you are, you are likely to discuss your personal and individual preferences, abilities, and goals. You probably have a sense that you are *separate* from people relevant to your life. Indeed, I asked my two teenage daughters to explain who they are, and they said things like, "I dance" or "I play piano," and "I like pizza." These would be considered strange and inappropriate answers from teenagers raised in a collectivist culture. Those young people probably have an *interdependent* understanding of self. They see their primary task as fitting in and helping maintain cohesiveness among individuals in their group. They also have a sense that they are *connected* to other people. And for people with this collectivist view of self, explaining who you are more likely includes a discussion of the roles you play within a group (Ernst & others, 2000).

Viewing your own abilities ("I dance," "I play the piano") as the most important information you can offer about yourself is a characteristic of individualistic cultures. We who come from this type of culture tend also to explain other people's behavior in terms of their disposition (He sure is cranky!) and to ignore the effects of the situa-

Demonstrating

ROLE WEBS Have students create concept webs about the roles they play in their lives. Have them write their names in the center circle and write the roles they play in the circles that radiate out from the center. Next to each outer circle, ask students to write the names of people in their lives who are affected by each of these different roles. Have them review the number of people affected by each role and the kinds of cultural connections attached to each.

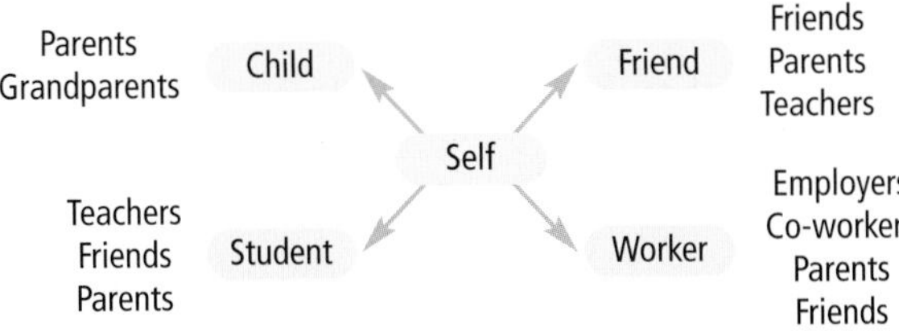

■ JOURNAL WRITING

Invite students to use the following questions and writing prompts as springboards for entries in their psychology journals:

- How do you think individualists and collectivists differ in their value systems?
- How do you think differences in individualism/collectivism affect patterns of interaction and relationships within your family, school, or classroom?
- How do you think differences in individualism/collectivism influence the judgments of other groups? Which orientation is more likely to promote ethnocentrism? Altruism?
- How do gender, religious convictions, and political attitudes influence individualism/collectivism?
- How do these two different orientations affect our personal and social well-being?

trb At this point, you may wish to use **Enrichment Lesson:** *Individualism Versus Collectivism* (*Teacher's Resource Binder*, p. 34-1) and/or **Analysis Activity:** *Independent and Interdependent Selves* (*Teacher's Resource Binder*, p. 34-1; **Handout 34–3**).

■ APPLYING THE POINTS

If a connection is possible, set up an e-mail correspondence with students at a school in a collectivist culture. As students correspond, have them report what they learn in response to the following questions:

- How is a day at a collectivist school different from a day at yours?
- What kinds of classes do students in the collectivist school take? Are the courses required or elective? Why or why not?
- For what does the collectivist school prepare its students?
- What are the likes and dislikes of the students at the collectivist school?
- In what social activities do students at the collectivist school participate?

trb At this point, you may wish to use **Analysis Activity:** *Assessing Individualism/Collectivism* (*Teacher's Resource Binder*, p. 34-1).

MODULE 34

■ **APPLYING THE POINTS**

With permission, interview students and community members from different cultural backgrounds to learn about their experience with achievement. Incorporate responses to the following questions in a lecture:

- Is getting good grades in school the most important thing to you?
- What goals do your parents have for your future?
- If you get a bad grade, how do your parents feel? How do you feel?

trb At this point, you may wish to use **Application Activity:** *Achievement and Challenge* (*Teacher's Resource Binder*, p. 34-1).

F • Y • I

To measure achievement motivation, psychologists have subjects respond to a picture by telling a story about what the person is doing in the picture. The following questions may be asked:

- What is happening? Who is in the picture?
- What has led to this situation—that is, what has happened in the past?
- What is being thought? What is wanted?
- What will happen? What will be done?

The need to achieve is indicated if the character in the story is seen as doing one or more of the following four things:

- *outperforming someone*—for example, getting a better grade on a test
- *meeting or surpassing some self-imposed standard of excellence*—for example, doing better than ever on a history test
- *doing something unique*—for example, writing a bestseller at 18 years old
- *being involved over a long term in doing something well*—for example, becoming a successful actor or athlete

trb At this point, you may wish to use **Analysis Activity:** *Intrinsic Motivation and Achievement* (*Teacher's Resource Binder*, p. 34-1).

tion (He is recovering from surgery). In contrast, members of collectivist cultures are much more likely to believe their success in fitting in with their group (I am respected by my family) is their most important characteristic and that behavior (such as responding angrily to a simple request) is guided by situational factors. Being raised in an individualist or collectivist culture influences more than our self-concepts. It also significantly impacts what motivates our behavior and our emotional reactions.

Motivation and Emotion

How many times have your family and teachers urged you to excel—to be the best you can be, or to strive to achieve your goals? *Achievement motivation* refers to this desire to excel, and it is very much a product of your cultural environment. Desire to achieve is rooted in the tangible personal rewards of achievement, which often means pulling ahead of other students. Individualistic cultures, which view motivation as an internal push and achievement as an individual triumph, like achievement motivation. Collectivist cultures have different achievement goals, and they relate to enhancing one's family's social standing. Desires to achieve emerge out of a sense of indebtedness to parents and are guided by the expectations of family members and other relevant people. Obligation to others or a sense of duty to the group drives this version of achievement (Yang, 1982). A researcher addressing, for example, why some students get much higher grades than others, despite similar levels of intelligence, would be wise to consider these cultural differences in achievement motivation as a possible factor.

But how can culture influence our emotional reactions? Consider this: How good are you at recognizing emotions? Can you tell when your friends are happy, angry, or embarrassed? Would you be able to recognize a more subtle emotion, combining compassion, love, and sadness? The Ifaluk of Micronesia can. They call this emotion *fago,* and they believe it promotes helping behavior. But a similar emotion, *ker,* combines happiness with excitement, and the Ifaluk view it as socially disruptive and dangerous (Lutz, 1988). The collectivist views of the Ifaluk have clearly colored their emotional expression and interpretation, just as our individualistic views color ours. It's impossible to identify all the emotions that people around the world recognize. But isn't it interesting to

***Fago* or *Ker*?** This person is experiencing an emotion the Ifaluk of Micronesia might call *ker,* a combination of happiness and excitement they consider socially disruptive. Culture affects our display of emotion and our perception of it.

Cooperative Learning

Assign different groups a different emotion, such as *anger, happiness, sadness,* and so forth. Have each group create a continuum that identifies the variety of the emotion, from most intensely felt to least intensely felt. Have groups present their completed continuums to the class. Afterward, encourage an analytical class discussion by posing the following questions:

- How many different emotional responses were charted?
- Are some of these emotions culturally specific? Why or why not?

trb At this point, you may wish to use **Enrichment Lesson:** *Gender Differences* (*Teacher's Resource Binder*, p. 34-1).

consider that emotions exist that we've never been exposed to? Researchers have discovered that many emotions—including anger, fear, and happiness—are found in all cultures, but others, such as *ker,* are unique and identified only in particular cultures (Russell, 1991).

▸ **cross-cultural research** Research that tests hypotheses on many groups of people to understand whether principles apply across cultures.

▸ **culture-specific** Principles that are true only for people of a certain culture; in contrast, *universal* principles are true of people in all cultures.

Cross-Cultural Research

3. How do universal behaviors and principles differ from culture-specific behaviors and principles?

We report results from hundreds of studies in this book. For example, we've explored the circumstances under which people are likely to help others, the conditions that set the stage for obedience to an authority, and the situations leading to attachment between parent and child. Nearly all of the research supporting these and other findings was conducted in the United States. Do the findings on helping, obedience, and attachment hold true in other parts of the world? **Cross-cultural research** attempts to understand principles and truths about humans across cultures. Psychologists who conduct research from this perspective travel great distances to study people in various settings, and they attempt to use participants from many different cultural backgrounds in their experiments in their own countries. They also run studies to obtain data from one cultural group and compare them with data obtained from another (Ernst & others, 2000).

Cross-cultural research often reveals that some psychological principles are *universal*, or true for people of all cultures. For example, all people everywhere use language to communicate but sometimes cross-cultural research indicates that psychological principles or behaviors are true only for people of a certain culture, making them **culture-specific** or *culture-bound.* For example, in some cultures it is customary to shake hands when greeting someone, other cultures bow as a greeting gesture. Some behav-

Cultural Universal or Culture-Specific? Which of these behaviors would you find in all cultures? Which are culture-bound?

MODULE 34

■ **APPLYING THE POINTS**

Have students contact local universities to find out if they offer studies in cross-cultural psychology or related fields. Suggest the following questions to help students in these informal interviews:

- Where can someone study cross-cultural psychology or related fields?
- How much education does one need to get a job doing work in these fields?
- What type of work can one find with a degree that has a cross-cultural emphasis?
- Are there any professional organizations that support cross-cultural fields? What type of support do these organizations offer?

■ **TEACHING TIP**

Have students explore culturally specific behaviors and customs. They can interview people from a culture, look up information about that culture on the Internet, or research different books that contain cultural information. These differences in culture that students uncover should help students better understand and appreciate diverse cultural traditions.

Enriching

Have students write a reflective paper about a cultural experience. Ask them to recall their first (or a recent) experience of cultural difference and discuss how it happened, as well as how the experience made them feel.

If applicable to students' experiences, have them also explain the importance of cultural context, in particular when ethnic and cultural stumbling blocks develop because of language, ethnocentrism, culture-related values, class-related values, nonverbal communications, racism, or stereotypes.

Source: Adapted from **Ernst, R.M.** (1997, January). *A matter of context.* Paper presented at the National Institute for the Teaching of Psychology, St. Petersburg, FL.

trb At this point, you may wish to use **Application Activity:** *Achievement and Challenge* (*Teacher's Resource Binder,* p. 34-1).

MODULE 34

■ **LOOKING AT THE ISSUES**

If you travel abroad, what kind of behaviors should you understand before you go—in the culture you're going to visit in addition to in your own? Have students research what behaviors are appropriate and inappropriate in another culture. Ask volunteers to share their findings in a class discussion. For extra credit, invite students to write guidelines that would advise American travelers of the appropriate behavior to display while visiting a particular culture.

■ **APPLYING THE POINTS**

Have students conduct an informal survey of their friends, family, and neighbors to discover what these people consider to be rude behavior in their culture. The following questions may be used to conduct the informal interviews as well as subsequent class discussion:

- What do you consider rude? Why do you consider it rude?
- What kind of politeness do you expect from others? Why?
- Do you confront people who are rude or impolite? Why or why not?

■ **TEACHING TIP**

Have students meet in small groups to consider how a person's gender can be an influential factor in determining a person's cultural perspective. Present the following questions for groups to address:

- Are there gender differences that make male and female culture different?
- Do male and female culture differ in different cultures? How?

trb At this point, you may wish to use **Evaluation Activity:** *Gender Roles in the Home* (*Teacher's Resource Binder*, p. 34-1; **Handout 34–4**) and/or **Cooperative Learning Activity:** *Learning Gender Roles* (*Teacher's Resource Binder*, p. 34-1; **Handouts 34–5a** and **34–5b**).

► **locus of control** A person's perception of the source of control over fate or what happens in life. People with an internal locus of control believe they control their fate through their behavior. People with an external locus of control believe their fate is controlled by external circumstances.

iors can be viewed as both universal and culture-specific. Let's say you are talking to a new student who has just moved to town. She looks down while you're talking to her, avoiding eye contact. Eye contact is made once or twice but is quickly broken off. Her behavior seems odd, because you are used to looking people straight in the eye when you talk, and having them look back at you. You wonder, "Is this person interested in our conversation?" or "Do I seem boring? What is up with her?" Perhaps you are so put off by this behavior that you avoid talking to this student in the future. At the same time, the other student is wondering, "Why are you staring at me? Don't you know it's rude to stare at someone while you're talking?" Obviously, the two of you come from different cultures: One culture says looking at someone while you talk is polite, while the other says not looking at someone while you talk is polite. Whether you gaze at the person while speaking is culture-specific. However, the motivation behind looking at someone else, which is the desire to be polite to another while speaking, is more likely a universal principle (Matsumoto, 1994).

Cross-cultural researchers examine everything from language development to emotions, and from child-rearing practices to psychological disorders. Let's see what they have to say about personality.

Culture and Personality

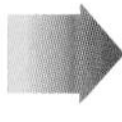

4. What perspective does cross-cultural research give us on some of psychology's theories of personality?

Many of the leading personality theorists, including Sigmund Freud, Carl Jung, Abraham Maslow, and Carl Rogers, came from Western civilizations. All four saw personality as a relatively enduring set of behaviors and thought processes, stable over time and in different situations. But some cultures take a different view of personality. Cross-cultural research suggests that the concept of personality is culture-bound, tied to the thinking of people in a particular culture (Berry & others, 1992). In some parts of Africa, for example, people use a three-layer model to explain personality, which is very different from the theories of Freud and Maslow. The three-layer model assumes that a person's personality will change according to the situation. At the core, the inner layer is spirituality. The second layer, around the core, is psychological strength. The outer layer is physical strength. Combine these layers and add a person's ancestral line, and you have another culture's take on what personality is. What's accepted as an explanation of personality in one culture may not hold true in another.

Western personality theorists also discuss the individual's **locus of control** (Rotter, 1954), noting that some people have an *external locus of control* (they believe outside forces determine what happens to them) and others have an *internal locus of control* (they believe they control their own fate). Cross-cultural research indicates that culture affects one's locus of

Reteaching

Review the basic concepts of the theories of Freud, Jung, Maslow, and Rogers.

- **Sigmund Freud** stated that memories created in childhood are buried in the unconscious, which can affect adult behavior. The personality, made up of three components, is determined by how well we navigate through the psychosexual stages of development.
- **Carl Jung**, a student of Freud's, believed that all people share a collective unconscious, which includes similar images from the literature and mythology of various cultures.
- **Abraham Maslow**, a humanistic psychologist, proposed a hierarchy of needs. This hierarchy suggests that biological needs must be met before aesthetic needs can be achieved.
- **Carl Rogers**, also a humanistic psychologist, proposed that people need unconditional positive regard to achieve their full potential.

control. Americans and people in other Western nations are far more likely to have an internal locus of control than their Asian and African counterparts are (Dyal, 1984).

How then, should we interpret the results of personality tests that are given in Tokyo or Kenya but were written by and standardized, or normed, on Americans? The results may or may not be applicable to people from all these countries. The ongoing debate about culture-bound personality tests (and other standardized tests) has resulted in special bias reviews, where groups of people from a variety of cultures look for bias in test items. Biased items are those that are easier for one culture group to answer than for another. Test developers try to eliminate these unfair advantages. Cross-cultural researchers have taught us to exercise caution when evaluating test results from a group of people whose culture is very different from that of the people who wrote the test.

Developmental Psychology

5. What does cross-cultural research have to say about some of psychology's theories of child development?

Your development from the time you were conceived until this very minute has involved physical, cognitive (ways of thinking) and social changes. Not only have you grown bigger and stronger, but you have also learned new ways of thinking, and new ways of acting around friends, neighbors, and family. These broad statements are cultural universals, true of all children in all cultures. But how does the culture in which we're raised affect our development?

From a very young age, we each learn and internalize the rules and patterns of behavior expected in our culture. Part of this process of being *socialized* includes learning what it means to be a boy or a girl. But we also learn a wealth of other things, from how to greet an older person to how to play with friends. We learn these rules from such sources as parents, relatives, friends, television, and schools, depending on where we live. Sometimes we adopt manners and ways specific to a smaller subculture. Perhaps you grew up in a culture where it is appropriate to pray before eating or to cover your head before leaving your home. Adopting these cultural rules helps us feel comfortable, knowing we are meeting the expectations of our group. These paths to comfort all disappear when we find ourselves in a situation with different cultural expectations. What if you grew up in Mexico City, then moved to Colorado at age 15 to start high school? You would have to adapt to a new situation with new cultural norms, and it would take you

Learning New Rules Moving from one part of the world to another often means adapting to a culture that is different from the one you grew up with.

Demonstrating

CLASS CULTURAL PROFILE Demonstrate the cultural diversity in your classroom by working with students to create a class cultural profile. Use the following questions to gather information:

- How many different cultures are represented in your classroom?
- How many students represent two or more cultures?
- What group dynamics are affected by these differing cultural backgrounds?

■ **MULTICULTURAL CONNECTIONS**

Many states have adopted "high-stakes tests" as requirements for graduation. In addition, the Bush administration passed the "No Child Left Behind" law, which mandated standardized testing to measure how well schools are performing. To respond to the following questions, have students conduct research about how high-stakes testing affects students from diverse cultures:

- In states with high-stakes testing, are students who immigrate to this country required to pass the same tests? Why or why not?
- Can students who don't speak English get modified tests or help on those tests? Why or why not?
- Can school systems report test results from newly immigrated students separate from the general population? Why or why not?

trb At this point, you may wish to use Application Activity: *Achievement and Challenge* (*Teacher's Resource Binder*, p. 34-1).

■ **TEACHING TIP**

Using the following questions, have students explore gender differences in other cultures:

- What are some cultural differences in gender roles? In what cultures are women the leaders of the culture (matrilineal)? In what cultures are men the leaders (patrilineal)?
- Are the cultural differences in gender roles the law of the land or just the custom of the people? Why or why not?

V At this point, you may wish to show Videocassette: *The Brain,* Second Edition, Module 3: "Gender Development: Social Influences" (*Teacher's Resource Binder*, p. 34-1).

trb At this point, you may wish to use Enrichment Lesson: *Gender Differences* (*Teacher's Resource Binder*, p. 34-1).

MODULE 34

■ APPLYING THE POINTS

Have students contact a support group for new immigrants to the United States and ask the group about its members' adjustment to U.S. culture. You can also establish a cross-cultural dialogue with students in your school who have immigrated with their families to the United States. With permission, interview those students and members of their families to see how they made the adjustment from their home culture to U.S. culture. The following questions may be used to conduct interviews, as well as subsequent class discussion of students' findings:

- How does your family continue traditions from your home culture?
- Do your parents worry that you will forget "the old ways"? Why or why not?
- How do you plan to help your own children maintain your cultural heritage?

trb At this point, you may wish to use Analysis Activity: *Intercultural Learning Activities* (*Teacher's Resource Binder*, p. 34-1: Handout 34–6).

■ LOOKING AT THE ISSUES

Present the following questions to help students explore how formal education can create a cultural bias:

- If the definition of advanced cognition is based on fundamental knowledge one acquires in school, how does that definition affect people who don't have access to formal education?
- Is a formal college education for everyone? Why or why not?
- How can definitions of *intelligence* be refined to preclude the necessity of a formal education?

a while to figure out how to fit in and regain your feelings of being comfortable. When a family moves to a new country, the parents often worry that their children will forget "the old ways" and learn new and different manners or behaviors that will not meet with their parental approval. And often their concerns are justified, because psychologists know that peer influence is very powerful.

Let's turn now to what cross-cultural research can teach us about cognition, moral development, and attachment.

Cognitive Development

Psychologists have looked to Jean Piaget's *cognitive development* theory for help in understanding how thinking in children grows and develops over time. He based his theory primarily on observations of Swiss children, noticing that at various ages, children solve problems quite differently. His theory assumed that development occurs in a fixed order of stages across cultures. Piaget thought children reaching his last stage, which he called *formal operations,* possessed scientific reasoning skills that those in lower stages had not developed. Piaget considered this last stage the endpoint, the ultimate achievement in cognitive development (Piaget, 1952).

Piaget's theory has, indeed, been very useful in helping us understand how children in Western cultures develop more complex ways of thinking about the world around them. Other developmental psychologists have revised some of Piaget's concepts and built upon his work. Cross-cultural psychologists, however, have asked a different question: Do Piaget's developmental stages occur in non-Western cultures? Western cultures (particularly American psychology teachers) value scientific reasoning. But *all* cultures do not value this kind of thinking as the ultimate cognitive development goal (Matsumoto, 1994). In addition, success on the tasks Piaget used to measure advancement appears to depend on the previous knowledge of the person taking the test. People who have not attended high school or college usually do worse on these tasks than those who have attended (Shea, 1985). So, people in cultures that do not emphasize formal education may perform poorly on Piaget's tasks. The tasks used to assess Piagetian stages may be more reflective of cultural values than cognitive skills.

Moral Development

American psychologist Lawrence Kohlberg first published his theory tracking the moral development of humans in the 1960s. He proposed three stages, with each stage showing an increasingly higher level of moral reasoning. At the lowest stage, wrote Kohlberg, we obey rules either to avoid punishment or gain reward. He believed that following

Reteaching

Review the basic concepts of the theories of Piaget and Kohlberg.

- **Jean Piaget** proposed four different stages of *cognitive development*—sensorimotor, preoperations, concrete operations, and formal operations. Piaget believed that cognitive development moved through a series of stages from reflexive investigation of the world to thinking abstractly about transcendent concepts and ideas.
- **Lawrence Kohlberg** developed a *three-stage theory of moral development,* with each stage having three substages. Kohlberg felt that moral development progressed from externalized values to internalized values.

your personal convictions, even if your convictions conflict with the law, was the highest, most desirable level of moral reasoning (Kohlberg, 1976). Kohlberg's participants were mostly white American men. However well Kohlberg's categories apply to this population, they appear to be less valid for those outside the white male culture of the 1960s, both in and out of the United States.

Our culture does seem to focus our judgments on what is and is not moral. For example, an ice skater from South Korea in the 2002 winter Olympics thought he had won a race and started skating around the rink carrying his country's flag. However, the judges ruled he had interfered with another skater, and they disqualified him. He immediately threw his flag down on the ice in disgust. Many American viewers, who grew up learning that your national flag is not supposed to touch the ground, were shocked. There are lots of other examples, but it is hard to escape the cultural biases one group holds compared to another when assessing right and wrong. Assessing moral development across cultures appears to be more challenging than Kohlberg imagined almost half a century ago.

Attachment

In this country, we typically think of *secure attachment* between infant and caregiver as the ideal bond. But not all cultures share this notion.

A survey of parents in other parts of the world show that families from countries other than the United States do not necessarily value secure attachment. German parents are more likely to see securely attached infants as "spoiled" (Grossman & others, 1985). Traditionally raised Japanese infants often show a high degree of what U.S. researchers call "anxious unsure attachment." Japanese parents tend to prefer this type of attachment, believing that it fosters family loyalty (Miyake & others, 1985). Finally, there is the case of a forest-dwelling tribe, the Efe, who live in West Africa. Efe (often incorrectly referred to as "pygmies," a name the Efe do not like) parents often spend time away from their infants. They leave the children in the care of a variety of people. Even when in the care of parents, the children can always be seen or heard by around 10 others. Efe children show no emotional deficits despite having multiple caregivers (Tronick & others, 1992).

We need to be aware of the impact of cultural differences on attachment. The attachment pattern we consider "best" in our culture, whether we were born in Japan, Africa, or the United States, may not be best for all people. Different cultures have different values and their preferred ways of raising children often reflect these values.

Cross-cultural psychology is particularly relevant to the study of development. As David Matsumoto (1994) explains, examining the socialization and development processes of other cultures helps us see who we are, and how we developed into the people we are today.

Enriching

Have students explore their relationship to the people around them by creating a spheres of influence chart like the one here. Encourage students to name particular people who have positively influenced them. Suggest that students express their appreciation by contacting those people they named.

■ **LOOKING AT THE ISSUES**

Have students explore how people from other cultures would view moral issues we take for granted, such as the following:

- *cheating*—Do other cultures view cheating on tests as dishonorable? Why or why not?
- *polygamy*—What cultures view multiple spouses to be part of their cultural fabric?
- *patriotism*—Do people in all cultures feel an affinity to a national government? Why or why not?

trb At this point, you may wish to use Analysis Activity: *Intercultural Learning Activities* (*Teacher's Resource Binder*, p. 34-1: Handout 34–6).

F•Y•I

Researchers measure secure attachment by placing children in a Strange Situation room. In this room, the child is away from the primary caregiver and subjected to a new experience. Infants who are securely attached are initially distressed, but eventually they begin to explore the new environment. Japanese children, since they spend most, if not all, of their waking moments with their mothers (even sleeping in the same bed with their parents), become greatly distressed in the Strange Situation. Does this mean that Japanese infants are not securely attached to their caregivers? It seems to be more likely that the measuring tool for secure attachment is culturally biased toward Western ideas of attachment.

■ **CHECKING FOR UNDERSTANDING**

Have students write a brief paragraph in which they explain what cross-cultural research is and why it is important.

MODULE 34

■ APPLYING THE POINTS

Collect several news articles that deal with a situation that occurred in a culture different from that of your students. Have students write a reflective paper about one of the articles, noting how people in the particular culture handled the described situation and pointing out similarities and differences in how they themselves would have handled it. The papers should include responses to the following questions:

- What responses seemed specific to that cultural perspective?
- What would your social/cultural position have been? How would your position have influenced your response?
- If you were reared in that cultural perspective, how would you have handled the situation?

trb At this point, you may wish to use Critical Thinking Activity: *A Matter of Context* (*Teacher's Resource Binder*, p. 34-1: Handouts 34–7a through 34–7g).

■ LOOKING AT THE ISSUES

The United States has been described as a "melting pot" into which people from all cultures can come and fit in, blending their experiences into the "American way." Elicit students' responses to the following questions in a full-class discussion:

- What other cultures, in addition to the United States, expect a "melting pot" mentality from immigrants?
- What cultures expect a "tossed salad" mentality, where people can maintain their cultural heritage as part of the national identity?
- Should immigrants shed their old ways and adopt new ones in their new home countries? Why or why not?
- What exactly is the "American identity"? Has it changed in recent years? If so, how? If not, why not?

Ethnocentrism

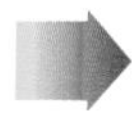

6. What is ethnocentrism, and how can we keep our minds as free as possible from its influences?

You turn on the TV and start flipping channels. On one channel, the Pope is addressing a large group of people outside the Vatican. On another a parade celebrates Columbus Day. A third channel shows actors imitating past presidents, making these famous leaders look rather foolish. How do you react to these programs? Do you stop and listen to the Pope, or skip quickly to the next channel? Do you call a brother or sister over to watch the parade, or do you comment on how celebrations of Columbus Day are an insult to the Native Americans who lived in the lands Columbus "discovered"? Are you amused or offended by the fun poked at our past presidents? **Ethnocentrism**, the tendency to view the world through our own cultural filters, will surely affect your reactions. Ethnocentrism is not necessarily a bad or a good thing—just a reflection of the way we view the world. We all look at the world through cultural filters, and we all wear these filters when we meet and have first impressions about others.

Our ethnocentrism shows up in the spoken and unspoken rules we live by and expect of others. When someone behaves in a way we do not consider socially appropriate or "normal," we react negatively. Those who do not wear black clothing every day may avoid those who do, labeling them "Goths" or perhaps even making jokes at their expense. The sophomore who parks a car in the lot designated for juniors and seniors may cause anger and frustration, especially if an older student can't find a place to park!

As you might predict, we seem to have the strongest negative reactions to people coming from cultures very different from our own. We may find refugees who have moved to the United States from war-torn parts of the world "peculiar" because of their dress or mannerisms. The United States is one of the few countries in the world where people tend to take baths or shower every day, so we may be quickly offended when someone from another country violates this cultural rule.

If people behave according to our cultural expectations, we say, "You all are good." But when others behave in ways we do not expect, or that are contrary to our beliefs, we are more likely to think of these people as bad or weird. The problem is, our ethnocentrism makes us susceptible to making snap judgments about others that may not be fair or even true.

Though we are all ethnocentric to some degree, many are *not aware* of their ethnocentric tendencies. If you are unaware of your cultural filters, you are likely to develop *inflexible ethnocentrism,* which inevitably leads to problems in our multicultural world. Your inability to see beyond your cultural filters may function as a wall between you and those who have

▶ **ethnocentrism** The tendency to view the world based on your own experiences, or through your own "cultural filters."

Cross-Curricular Connections

HISTORY Imperialism has changed the cultural landscape in each historical era as cultures have taken one another over. For extra credit, invite students to use research findings to field and respond to questions about the effects of imperialism on cultures in a class forum.

The following cultures may be interesting research topics for students:

- Chinese dynasties
- Roman Empire
- Ottoman Empire
- Spain's New World colonies
- British Empire
- U.S. interventions

different cultural viewpoints. Inflexibility discourages us from learning about other cultures in our states, cities, and schools. To counter these tendencies, Matsumoto (1999) suggests trying to establish a *flexible ethnocentrism* when interacting with others. Flexible ethnocentrism has the following goals (adapted from Ernst & others, 2000):

1. Accepting that we are all ethnocentric, and that our cultural filters vary.
2. Realizing that our cultural filters can distort reality so that we see things only in a certain way.
3. Recognizing and appreciating that people of different cultural backgrounds produce their own distortions of reality.
4. Learning to deal with our emotions and our judgments of morality and personality as a result of ethnocentrism.

Flexible Ethnocentrism Moving beyond your initial, emotional reaction is an important step in understanding people from cultures different from your own.

How do we achieve that fourth goal? First, if you believe a negative initial reaction to someone may be due to your own limiting ethnocentrism, try to put your emotional reactions on hold. Next, try to learn the other person's viewpoints. Finally, do not assume that you need to abandon your own cultural filters in order to avoid inaccurate perceptions of others. Increasing your knowledge of other cultures allows you to *add* to your own filters, helping you see things from many perspectives.

Cultural conflicts will not disappear simply because we are aware of and study them. But we are better equipped to understand cultural differences when they occur if we have studied the importance of culture. Studying culture builds respect for, and appreciation of, all the cultural differences we will encounter in our everyday lives. Psychologists today are indeed more sensitive to culture's impact on experimental results and build measures into their studies that help ensure meaningful results. Cross-cultural psychologists hope to continue their work toward discovering both universal and culture-specific results, in an ongoing effort to broaden our view of the field of psychology.

Studying Cultures Learning to appreciate cultures different from our own helps us understand and respect other people's behaviors, attitudes, and traditions.

Close

Harvard Business School professor John Kotter once said, "The tolerant are intolerant of the intolerant." Trying to have a culture-free perspective may be an impossible goal that leaves a person feeling frustrated with those who cannot help but see the world through a cultural filter. Have students consider the following questions:

- In what practical ways can you apply flexible ethnocentrism?
- How can you be an example to people who don't seem to exhibit flexible ethnocentrism?
- What activities could you plan for your peers to increase cultural awareness?

Alternative Assessment

Have students work in groups to choose a "sister city" in another culture that shares characteristics similar to those of their own community. Have them choose a city or town that has a similar size and population but that differs in other aspects of culture. Group members may find pen pals who might be willing to discuss more personal aspects of culture. Groups can create a multimedia presentation that highlights different aspects of their sister city's culture with answers to the following questions:

- How are the two cultures similar and different?
- How does each culture's access to technology differ?
- What impact do scarce resources have on the culture?
- How does climate affect activities people engage in for both work and leisure?

MODULE 34

Checking the Points

■ TEACHING TIPS

web (1) The book companion site for *Thinking About Psychology* at www.worthpublishers.com/thinkingaboutpsych contains a module quiz, flashcards of key terms and people, as well as other student activities and resources for this module. You will also find PowerPoint lectures, a quiz grade book, and other teaching resources by logging on as an instructor.

trb (2) At this point, you may wish to review and confirm concepts about cross-cultural psychology with **Critical Thinking Activity:** *Fact or Falsehood?* (*Teacher's Resource Binder*, p. 34-1; **Handout 34–1**). If students completed the handout earlier in the module, ask them not to refer to previous versions. Suggest that students complete the handout in small groups, taking the time to look up information in the text to respond correctly to questions. Have all the groups meet to review the handout, again using the text to support the responses.

REVIEW

Module 34: Cross-Cultural Psychology

What's the Point?

Culture

1. *What is culture, and how does it develop?*

   Culture is a system of subtle and obvious rules, including shared attitudes, beliefs, norms, and behaviors, established by a group and passed from one generation to the next to ensure the group's survival. Four factors—population density, climate, resources, and technology—influence culture development and diversity.

Individualism and Collectivism

2. *What's the difference between individualism and collectivism?*

   Individualism is a cultural style that places personal goals or needs ahead of group goals or needs. Collectivism is a cultural style that places group goals or needs ahead of personal goals or needs. Individualism and collectivism affect the self-concepts of individuals who are the bearers of these cultural styles. They also influence our interpretations of what will motivate us and the ways we display and read our own emotions and the emotions of those around us.

Cross-Cultural Research

3. *How do universal behaviors and principles differ from culture-specific behaviors and principles?*

   Universal principles apply to all humans, and a universal behavior is one that all people perform. Language, for example, is a universal behavior, and the statement that all people use language is a universal principle. Culture-specific (or culture-bound) behaviors and principles apply only to the people in a particular culture. Piaget's final stage of cognitive development, for example, seems to be culture-specific, and the math and science skills associated with that stage are culture-specific behaviors, according to cross-cultural psychologists.

4. *What perspective does cross-cultural research give us on some of psychology's theories of personality?*

   Cross-cultural research suggests that people in non-Western cultures may not share our view of personality as a relatively enduring set of behaviors and thought processes, stable over time and in different situations. If personality tests based on Western assumptions are given to people who do not share those assumptions, the test results may not be valid.

5. *What does cross-cultural research have to say about some of psychology's theories of child development?*

   Cross-cultural research indicates that the final stage of Piaget's theory of cognitive development may be culture-bound—that is, it may not hold up in non-Western cultures that do not value scientific method and research. Similarly, Kohlberg's theory of moral development seems too simplified to support moral views held in all cultures. And, finally, psychology's assumptions about the preferred types of attachment do not correspond to preferred attachment styles in all other cultures.

Ethnocentrism

6. *What is ethnocentrism, and how can we work to keep our minds as free as possible from its influences?*
   Ethnocentrism is our tendency to view the world based on our own experiences, through the "filters" of our own culture. In extreme doses, inflexible ethnocentrism leads us to make snap judgments about—and often reject—those who are different from us. We can work to be more flexible by accepting that everyone is ethnocentric and that cultural filters vary; realizing that cultural filters distort reality; understanding and appreciating the fact that people of different cultural backgrounds produce their own distortions of reality; and learning to deal with the emotions and judgments of morality that result from ethnocentrism.

Key Terms

culture, p. 657
individualism, p. 658
collectivism, p. 658
cross-cultural research, p. 661
culture-specific, p. 661
locus of control, p. 662
ethnocentrism, p. 666

Key People

David Matsumoto, p. 657

Self-Test

Multiple-Choice Questions

Choose the *best* answer for each of the following questions.

1. Akbar, who was attending college to become an electrical engineer, dropped out of school when his father had a serious heart attack. Akbar now lives at home and runs the family business, which manufactures small items for the tourist trade in resort areas. He regrets losing his own personal opportunity—and his dream—to work with computers, perhaps designing a new generation of hardware. Akbar nevertheless gets a lot of satisfaction from knowing he is helping his father and other family members meet their needs and goals. Akbar's views are consistent with those of
   a. an individualistic cultural style.
   b. a collectivist cultural style.
   c. a multiethnic viewpoint.
   d. inflexible ethnocentrism.
2. Kate's parents always told her that it didn't matter what she chose to be, as long as she followed her own path and excelled at whatever she did. Kate internalized this message, and she now tries very hard to be the leader and top person in every activity. She is president of her class, on the honor roll every term, and captain of the girls' soccer team. Kate's actions are consistent with the values found in
   a. an individualistic cultural style.
   b. a collectivist cultural style.
   c. flexible ethnocentrism.
   d. inflexible ethnocentrism.
3. Cross-cultural researchers are studying language in children in many different cultures. So far, they have found that Desta, a 6-month-old girl living in Ethiopia;

■ **TEACHING TIP**

If students did not create flashcards for module terms at the beginning of the module, have them do so now. Working with partners, students can use the flashcards as a review and comprehension tool. Once student pairs know the terms and their definitions, they can test their deeper understanding of these module terms. Partners can alternate asking a question and showing the correct response, which would be a module term that appears on one of the flashcards.

tb Using the Test Bank

The *Test Bank* that accompanies this textbook offers a wide variety of questions in different formats and levels of complexity. Use the software to construct whole tests or to integrate standardized questions into teacher-made tests.

Self-Test Answers

Multiple-Choice Questions

1. c, 2. a, 3. a

MODULE 34

Self-Test Answers

Multiple-Choice Questions (continued)

4. d, 5. d

Matching Terms and Definitions

6. a. (6), b. (3), c. (4), d. (8), e. (2), f. (7), g. (5)

Lolita, a 6-month-old girl living in Spain; Sergei, a 6-month-old boy living in Russia; and Billy, a 6-month-old boy living in the United States, all babble but do not speak in sentences. If the researchers discover that this pattern applies to many children living in many different places, they will have shown that babbling at 6 months of age is

a. a cultural universal.
b. a culture-specific behavior.
c. a culture-bound behavior.
d. part of everyone's locus of control.

4. In the United States, parents who had babies in the 1940s and 1950s were advised that they should maintain strict sleep schedules for children. If children did not fall asleep at the proper time, parents should put their children in cribs to let them cry themselves to sleep. In the late 1960s and the 1970s, parents were told that they should not let their babies cry alone in their cribs but should instead rock their children to sleep or try to adjust to the children's natural schedule. These two sets of apparently conflicting child-care practices are examples of
   a. collectivist cultural styles.
   b. individualistic cultural styles.
   c. cultural universals.
   d. culture-specific behaviors.

5. In the early 1900s, Lewis Terman developed intelligence tests and recommended their use as screening tests to exclude certain groups of people who wanted to emigrate from other countries and become U.S. citizens. Because of the content in these tests, they accidentally favored people of Anglo-Saxon heritage. Terman, himself a person of Anglo-Saxon heritage, was one of many who, without any real understanding of people from other cultures, wanted to restrict their access to opportunities and, sometime, even to parenthood. Terman's attitude is an example of
   a. an internal locus of control.
   b. an external locus of control.
   c. flexible ethnocentrism.
   d. inflexible ethnocentrism.

Matching Terms and Definitions:

6. For each definition, choose the *best* matching term from the list that follows.

Definition

a. Belief that outside forces are responsible for the things that happen to you.
b. Tendency to view the world based on your own experiences, through your own "cultural filters."
c. The desire to excel.
d. Belief that your own internal states are responsible for the things that happen to you.
e. Statements that apply only to the people of a certain culture.
f. Statements that apply to all people in all cultures.
g. The testing of hypotheses on many groups of people to understand whether principles apply across cultures.

Term

(1) culture
(2) culture-specific principles
(3) ethnocentrism
(4) achievement motivation
(5) cross-cultural research
(6) external locus of control
(7) universal principles
(8) internal locus of control

Fill-in-the-Blank Questions

7. ______________ ______________ is a psychologist and international expert on the study of cross-cultural psychology.

8. The four factors that influence culture development and diversity are ______________, ______________, ______________, and ______________.

9. ______________ is a cultural style that places personal goals or needs ahead of group goals or needs. ______________ is a cultural style that places group goals or needs ahead of personal goals or needs.

Brief Essay Question

10. Cross-cultural psychologists attempt to test their hypotheses on many different groups of people. In two paragraphs of about two sentences each, explain why these psychologists are interested in seeing test results from such a diverse group of human beings.

Self-Test Answers

Fill-in-the-Blank Questions

7. David Matsumoto, 8. climate; resources; technology; population density, 9. Individualism; collectivism

Brief Essay Question

9. Students should understand that getting data from different groups of people can help psychologists determine whether the constructs they are studying are universal or culture-specific. These tests results can also explore how cultures are similar and how they differ, which can lead to the development of interventions that address the particular needs of a culture.

APPENDIX

Psychology's Statistics

Statistics are more a matter of attitude than numbers. Many people (not *you,* of course) have a negative view of statistics and convince themselves that this is a topic beyond comprehension. Maybe it's the word—*statistics* is hard to pronounce! The concepts themselves are really not so hard. Lots of people enjoy the subject, and there is no denying its usefulness. Without a basic understanding of statistical processes, you are at a serious disadvantage because statistical information is all around us. TV, newspapers, magazines, and the Internet are all full of statistical data. Some people do use statistics accurately and appropriately, but others use statistics inappropriately due to lack of knowledge or in an effort to deliberately mislead. To think critically about all the information bombarding you, you'll need to sort the good stuff from the bad. Educated people need statistical literacy as much as computer literacy.

Statistical Literacy People in modern society need to understand statistics well enough to make informed decisions about data presented in the media.

Appendix

Psychology's Statistics

Introducing the Appendix

The Points: Appendix Objectives

- Explain what frequency distributions tell us.
- Identify the three measures of central tendency, and explain the advantage of each.
- Explain in what ways statistics can determine the variation of a distribution of scores.
- Identify the important characteristics of a normal distribution.
- Distinguish between percentage and percentile rank.
- Explain how a correlation coefficient indicates the strength of a relationship.
- Understand, in research, what determines whether a result is statistically significant.

Building Vocabulary

Have students use index cards to create flashcards of the terms in this appendix. One side of the card should show a key term, and the other side should provide a definition. Encourage students to work with partners to learn the terms. To test their understanding, one partner can ask a question whose answer is a term presented on a flashcard, while the other partner can choose the flashcard whose term answers the question. Partners should alternate asking questions and providing answers.

Getting Started

Have each student collect a variety of news stories—at least four—from local and national newspapers. Divide the class into small groups, and have the groups look over the sample articles of its members. To focus their analysis of these samples, ask groups to discuss the following questions:

- How many of these articles include statistical information?
- What types of statistics are used?
- Why are they used in those particular stories?
- Do you feel the use of statistics represented responsible journalism? Why or why not?

Allow time for the groups to report their findings to the rest of the class.

(Save these newspaper articles to reuse for the activity "Demonstrating: Mean, Median, and Mode," on page A-5 of this *Teacher's Edition.*)

Appendix

Teaching the Points

■ TEACHING TIPS

web (1) You can log on as an instructor to the book companion site for *Thinking About Psychology* at www.worthpublishers.com/thinkignabout psych. It contains teacher resources for class presentations, as well as review and assessment of the concepts and terms in this appendix.

(2) The authors offer the example of a grade on a test to show the meaningfulness of statistics. Create your own examples to show students that statistics, in isolation, can be misinterpreted and used to manipulate the thinking of others.

trb tr (3) A black-line master of Figure A.1, Experimental Design for Headphones Experiment, is available in the **Black-Line Masters Appendix** in the *Teacher's Resource Binder.*

F • Y • I

Statistics is a word that is both singular and plural. The plural form refers to the subject of statistics as well as to the meaning "figures."

Statistics may seem difficult at first simply because this is a new way of looking at things. Riding a bike or driving a car seem hard the first time you try, too. Think of the first time you went bowling, the first time you picked up a musical instrument, the first time you attempted a new computer game. These were all significant challenges the first time around. If you're like me, you're willing to work hard to learn something, despite the initial difficulty, if you believe in an activity's value. And statistics does have value—your efforts to understand will arm you with tools that will help you think critically about lots of choices you'll be making in life. So stick with me as we take a guided tour of this important area.

Before we begin, take note of this key concept: *The overall purpose of statistics is to make data more meaningful.* If a friend told you she got 27 right on her history test, how meaningful would that be? Wouldn't you also need to know how many items were on the test? If she got 27 right out of 30, that's great, but if she got 27 out of 100. . . . Well, you get the picture. And isn't it also important to know how other students did? Even if she did get 27 out of 30 that may have been the lowest score in the class on a very easy test. Or 27 out of 100 could be a good score if it was the highest score in the class on an exceptionally difficult test. Statistics are an important extension of critical thinking, providing a method of organizing information so we can understand what a number really means.

To illustrate the statistics we discuss, we'll rely on an example we used in Module 2 to demonstrate research strategies: How would banning the use of headphones for listening to music affect student learning in study halls? To find out, we designed an experiment (see Figure A.1) with two groups. The experimental group contained stu-

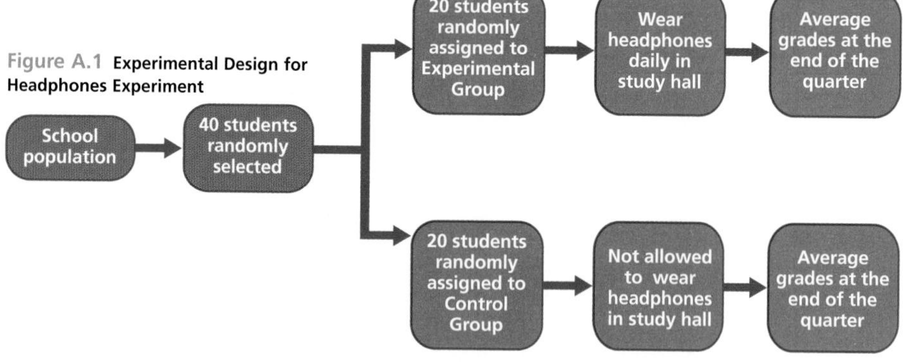

Figure A.1 Experimental Design for Headphones Experiment

dents assigned to wear headphones in study hall; the control group contained students who were not allowed to wear headphones. We decided to measure the effect of wearing headphones (our independent variable) by examining the two groups' average end-of-quarter grades (our dependent variable). We settled on a hypothesis that the headphone-wearing students in the experimental group would have higher grades at the end of the quarter than the nonheadphone-wearing control group students.

Our experiment, of course, was make-believe, which means there is no reason we can't just go ahead and make up some numbers to use as results!

► **frequency distribution** A list of scores placed in order from highest to lowest.

■ **TEACHING TIP**

Create your own data sets and have students calculate the measures of central tendency and graph the frequency distributions. You can also use real test data so students can see how their class's scores distribute for each test.

trb tr A black-line master of Figure A.2, Frequency Distributions, is available in the **Black-Line Masters Appendix** in the *Teacher's Resource Binder.*

Frequency Distributions

What's the point? 1. What do frequency distributions tell us?

A **frequency distribution** is, quite simply, an ordered list of scores. Figure A.2 shows some possible data from our hypothetical experiment, before and after being made into an ordered list. Notice how much more useful these numbers are after we arrange them in a frequency distribution from highest to lowest? At a glance, you can tell the high score for each group and the low score for each group.

The information from the frequency distribution can be easily presented as a graph, like the bar graph in Figure A.3, (page A-4). Viewing our scores this way we can discover the meaning behind the numbers even more easily.

Grades, in random order		Frequency distributions	
No headphones	Headphones	No headphones	Headphones
80	65	97	94
58	83	93	92
97	75	93	87
77	72	89	83
93	92	89	82
69	67	84	79
67	87	84	77
89	79	84	75
93	94	80	74
78	74	78	72
84	82	77	71
73	77	72	69
84	68	69	68
84	71	67	68
89	69	58	64

Figure A.2 **Frequency Distributions** Putting scores in order creates a frequency distribution and makes the raw data much more meaningful.

F • Y • I

In Figure A.3, the jagged line that appears before the first bar on the x-axis indicates the part of the graph which has been omitted because no data occur between 0 and 51. This creates a cleaner-looking graph.

trb tr A black-line master of Figure A.3, Bar Graphs, is available in the **Black-Line Masters Appendix** in the *Teacher's Resource Binder.*

■ **LOOKING AT THE ISSUES**

In a distribution the **mode** is the piece of data that is repeated most often. But the mode can be a misleading measure of central tendency because the most common score does not always fall in the middle. Have students consider and respond to the following questions, based on Figure A.4, Measure of Central Tendency:

- Imagine that the mode for the headphones group consisted of three scores of 30. If all other statistics remained the same, would the mode be a representative statistic? Why or why not?
- How many scores from a data set would you want to see to feel comfortable that the mode represented the group?

trb tr A black-line master of Figure A.4, Measure of Central Tendency, is available in the **Black-Line Masters Appendix** in the *Teacher's Resource Binder.*

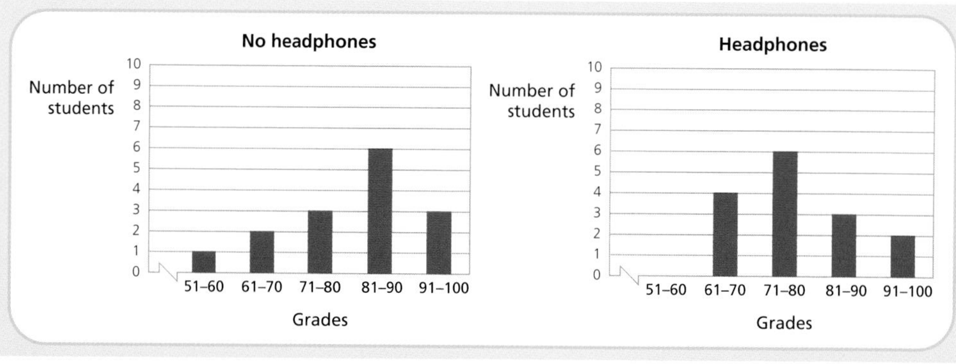

Figure A.3 **Bar Graphs** Data from a frequency distribution can easily be converted to a bar graph.

Measures of Central Tendency

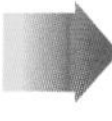

2. What are the three measures of central tendency, and what is the advantage of each?

The next thing we need to know is where the center of a distribution—the "normal" score—is. For our study hall research, we have two groups—one that wears headphones and one that does not—and we just learned how to create a frequency distribution for each. If the center of one distribution is higher than the center of the other, this may help us decide whether our hypothesis is correct. It seems as though there should be some easy and reliable way to determine the center, but unfortunately, there isn't. There are three methods, each appropriate only in certain situations. The three choices are *mode, mean,* and *median.*

Figure A.4 **Measure of Central Tendency** The three primary methods of finding the center of a distribution of scores are the mode, mean, and median. Each has its own strengths and weaknesses.

	No headphones	Headphones
Mode (Most common)	84	68
Mean (Average)	$\frac{1215}{15} = 81$	$\frac{1155}{15} = 77$
Median (Middle score)	84	75

Mode

The **mode** is the score that occurs most frequently in the distribution. Using our sample data from our frequency distributions, we can see that the mode for the headphones group is 68, and the mode for the nonheadphones group is 84 (Figure A.4). Modes are not the most ideal source of information—at least for our purposes here. It's possible for the most common score (the mode) to *not* be near the center of the distribution. (I once gave a test to my students where almost everyone did either very well or very poorly; the common scores did not represent the center of the distribution!) The mode is most useful in circumstances where the data can only be put into distinct groups. For example, if you were categorizing people as male—by assigning males the number *1*—or female *2*—it would not make any sense to say that the average sex for the group was *1.5*. Individuals can be either male or female, they cannot be somewhere in between. When the numbers represent discrete groups, the mode is the only appropriate way to establish central tendency. Here's another example: If a high school had 100 sophomores, 200 juniors, and 150 seniors, the mode would be grade 11, the group with the largest number.

▶ **mode** The most frequently occurring score in a distribution.

▶ **mean** The arithmetic average of a distribution, obtained by adding the scores and then dividing by the number of scores.

▶ **median** The middle score in a ranked distribution; half the scores are above it and half are below it.

▶ **skewed** Distorted; not evenly distributed around the mean.

Mean

The most familiar measure of central tendency is the **mean,** or average. As you know, we compute averages by adding all the scores and dividing by the total number of scores. The means for the two groups in the headphone study are presented in Figure A.4. Under most circumstances, the mean is the statistic of choice for central tendency. Many advanced statistical calculations use this measure of central tendency.

Sometimes, however, the mean can mislead us. This occurs when a few scores are either extremely high or extremely low. It's not a good idea to use the mean, for example, to report the central tendency for housing costs in a community, because most communities have a few very valuable homes. When you calculate a mean, these few expensive homes will affect the mean much more than each of the moderately priced homes will. As a result, housing will appear to be more expensive than it really is.

Median

The third measure of central tendency—the **median**—shows us the middle of a distribution (just as the median of a rural interstate highway, often a strip of grass running between the two sets of lanes, shows us the center of the highway). In any distribution where the scores have been placed in order, the median is the point where exactly half of the scores are higher and half are lower. An extreme score in the top or bottom half of the distribution will have no more impact than any other score. Figure A.4 also shows the median for the headphone- and nonheadphone-wearing students.

When the mean, median, and mode are all the same it's easy to identify central tendency. They can, however, be vastly different. Figure A.5 on page A-6 shows what can happen when a distribution is **skewed,** or distorted. To say a distribution is skewed means that the scores don't spread themselves evenly around the center. There is an unusual number of high scores or low scores.

F•Y•I

When a graph shows that students do either very well or very poorly, the graph usually looks like a two-humped camel. This type of graph is called a **bimodal distribution**. These graphs usually have two modes, showing two different most-common scores.

■ **TEACHING TIP**

Have students consider when the mean might not be a useful statistic. If two or three students did poorly on a test, then it might appear that the class overall didn't do as well. The mean, however, is a generally good statistic—that is, if outlying scores don't skew it!

Demonstrating

MEAN, MEDIAN, AND MODE If possible, have students reuse the news stories they collected for the " Getting Started" activity on page A-1 of the *Student Edition*. Working in small groups, ask students to review the articles to see if news stories use the mode, median, and/or mean in reporting statistics. Groups can focus their discussion with the following questions:

- Are these statistics responsibly reported? Why or why not?
- Do outlying statistics seem to skew these stats? Why or why not?

Have groups present their findings to the class.

Appendix

■ TEACHING TIPS

(tr) (1) A four-color transparency of Figure A.5, Central Tendency in a Skewed Distribution, is available in the **Overhead Transparencies Set.**

(trb) (tr) (2) A black-line master of Figure A.6, Variation Makes a Difference, is available in the **Black-Line Masters Appendix** of the *Teacher's Resource Binder.*

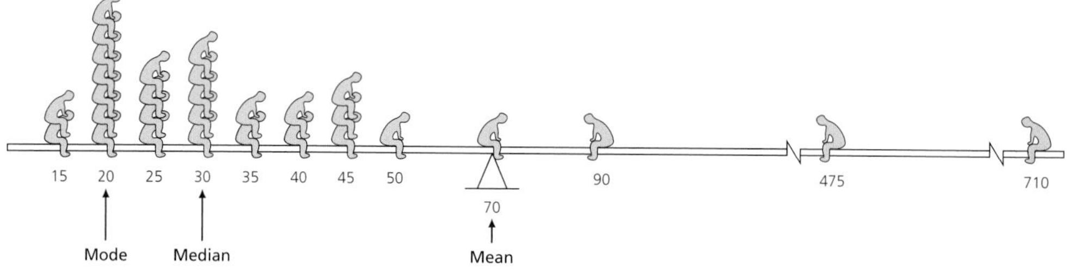

Figure A.5 **Central Tendency in a Skewed Distribution** This diagram shows the three measures of central tendency for a distribution of incomes that is skewed by a few families with very high income. Notice that, under these circumstances, the mean (which, as the average, "balances" the distribution) produces a result that is far above what most people would consider the center of this distribution. In cases like this, the median is probably a better representation of central tendency.

Measures of Variation

3. In what ways can statistics determine the variation of a distribution of scores?

It is important to have a sense of where the center of a distribution falls. To truly understand the meaning of the numbers, however, we need to add another piece of the puzzle. Two distributions can have the same center, and still be very different. Consider a school "C's-Only Club" that was open only to people who got a grade of C in every class they took. The modal grade for this club would be C. So would the mean and median grades. But you can also imagine a situation where *all* students in a school were invited to join an, "Everybody's Welcome Club," and the modal, mean, and median grades would still be a C. The B students would balance the D students, and the A students would balance the failing students. The students in the C's-Only Club are all packed in at the same point on the grade distribution. The students in the Everybody's Welcome Club are spread throughout the distribution. These differences are represented in Figure A.6. In this section, we examine some ways to measure how spread-out scores are.

Figure A.6 **Variation Makes a Difference** Both of these bar graphs represent distributions of students where the measures of central tendency are C grades. It's clear, however, that the distributions are very different. Measures of variation allow us to understand such differences.

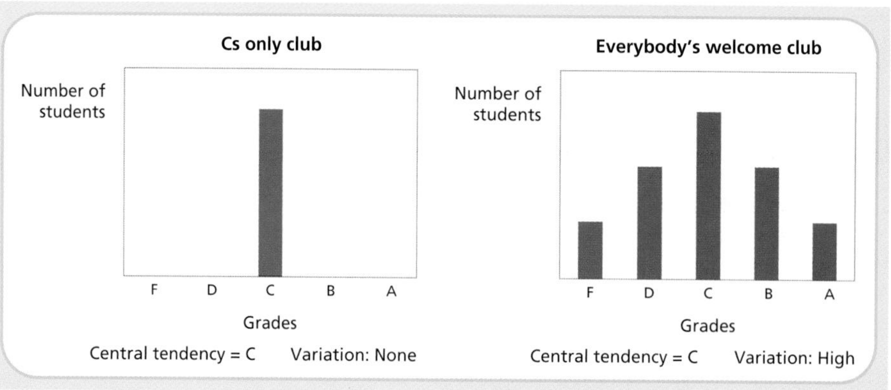

Range

The simplest measure of variation is the **range,** the spread between the high score and the low score. The range is a simple, often helpful, indicator of how much variation there is in a distribution. It's nice to know, for example, that the range of grades for the headphones group was from a high of 94 to a low of 64 points, and that the range for the no-headphones group was 97 to 58. The only problem is that a range considers only two scores: the highest and the lowest. Let's assume for a minute that the student who got a 58 in the no-headphones group missed a lot more school due to illness. This already marginal student's grade might easily have dropped to a 38 because of the absences. A change in this one student's grade could add 20 points to the range! A better statistic would consider *every* score, not just the two most extreme. That's where the standard deviation comes in.

▶ **range** The difference between the highest and lowest scores in a distribution.

▶ **standard deviation** A computed measure of how much scores vary around the mean score; the higher the standard deviation, the more spread out scores are.

Standard Deviation

Standard deviation is a measure of the overall variation of a distribution of numbers. The smaller the standard deviation, the more closely the scores are packed near the mean. In fact, if a distribution had a standard deviation of zero, it would signify that *every* score was the mean score—there would be no variation at all! This would happen in the C's-Only Club. The standard deviation would be 0 because every grade would be the average grade of C. The Everybody's Welcome Club would have a higher standard deviation because its members have a variety of grades. The more variation there is among the scores, the bigger the standard deviation grows.

Figure A.7 shows an example of how the standard deviation is calculated for a small set of scores (in this case, punting distances for a football player). It is a very logical process, and you should take a careful look to see how it is done. However, the important thing to under-

Punting distance	Deviation from mean (40 yards)	Deviation squared
36 yards	–4 yards	16 yards^2
38 yards	–2 yards	4 yards^2
41 yards	+1 yard	1 yard^2
45 yards	+5 yards	25 yards^2
Mean = $\frac{160}{4}$ = 40 yards		46 yards^2 = Sum of (deviations)^2

$$\text{Standard deviation} = \sqrt{\frac{\text{Sum of (deviations)}^2}{\text{Number of punts}}} = \sqrt{\frac{46 \text{ yards}^2}{4}} = 3.4 \text{ yards}$$

Figure A.7 Standard Deviation This figure shows the process for calculating the standard deviation. The steps in the process are as follows:

- Calculate the mean.
- Determine how far each score (punt distances, in this example) deviates (differs) from the average.
- Square the deviation scores and average them. Note that you can't just average the deviations without squaring them, because the sum of the deviation scores will always be zero.
- Take the square root of the average of the squared deviation scores. This step brings us back to the original units—yards rather than yards squared.

Appendix

■ **LOOKING AT THE ISSUES**

A lack of variation in grades has led many to charge that grades are inflated. Many colleges and universities have studied whether professors give out too many *A*s. Elicit students' responses about this controversy with the following questions:

- Are grades inflated at your school? Why or why not?
- Would you support a policy mandating that every teacher must assure that grades aren't inflated? Why or why not?

■ **TEACHING TIPS**

(1) Have students consider how they would feel differently about a test score if the following were true:

- You made an 84 on a test on which the lowest grade was an 83.
- You made a 69 on a test on which the highest score was a 72.

trb tr (2) A black-line master of Figure A.7, Standard Deviation, is available in the **Black-Line Masters Appendix** of the *Teacher's Resource Binder.*

■ TEACHING TIPS

(1) Have students investigate whether the grades in your classes represent a normal distribution by asking the following question:

- Is it desirable to have a pure normal distribution? Why or why not?

tr (2) A four-color transparency of Figure A.8, A Normal or Bell-Shaped Curve, is available in the **Overhead Transparencies Set.**

F•Y•I

If a graph does not look like a bell, then it is skewed in one of two ways:

- **Positive skew** occurs when the curve leans too heavily to the right.
- **Negative skew** occurs when the curve leans too heavily to the left.

► **normal distribution** The symmetrical, bell-shaped curve that describes the distribution of many physical and psychological variables. Most scores fall near the mean, with fewer and fewer scores at the extremes.

stand here is the meaning behind the statistic. In this case, you are coming up with a number that represents how far the scores spread away from the mean.

Calculating the standard deviation by hand would be tedious if you have more than just a few scores. Thank goodness for calculators and computer spreadsheets that will do the job with a few pushes of a button or clicks of a mouse! My computer tells me that the standard deviation for our headphone wearers is 9.1 points, and the standard deviation for the control group is 10.9 points. This means the scores for the headphone wearers are packed a little closer together.

Normal Distribution

4. What are the important characteristics of a normal distribution?

Much psychological data can be represented in a graph called a **normal distribution,** or bell-shaped curve. A normal distribution, like the one in Figure A.8, is not skewed; its left and right sides are mirror images of each other. Furthermore, the high point of a normal distribution is in the center. This high point represents all three measures of central tendency: the mode, the mean, and the median. Many collections of data produce a normal distribution. In intelligence test scores, for example, most people "pile up" at or near the middle of the distribution. The further you move above or below the mean, the fewer people are represented. This distinctive pile-up produces the bell shape of the normal distribution.

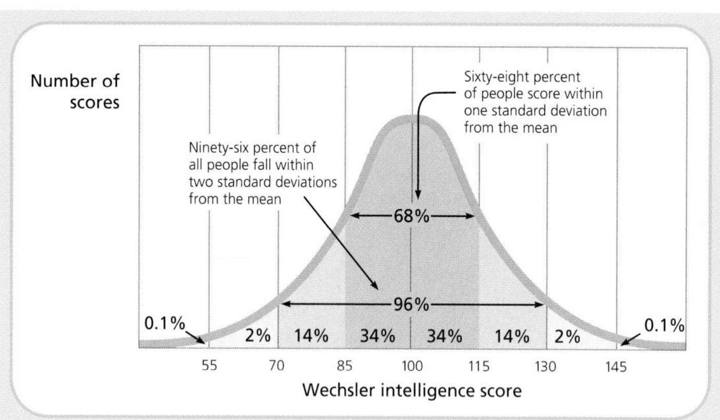

Figure A.8 **A Normal or Bell-Shaped Curve** Intelligence test scores form a normal distribution with a mean of 100 points and a standard deviation of 15 points. The percentage figures shown are true for *any* normal distribution, not just for intelligence scores.

Cross-Curricular Connections

MATHEMATICS Invite a mathematics teacher to class to demonstrate how to use a calculator to calculate statistics. Using a statistics function, students can easily input and calculate a wide range of statistics that would be tedious to compute by hand.

Data distributed in a bell-shaped curve illustrate some useful principles. Let's take a look at scores on intelligence tests. Scores on the Wechsler intelligence tests (the most widely used family of tests) produce a mean score of 100 points and a standard deviation of 15 points. This means that a person with a score of 115 is one standard deviation above average on this test. A person with a score of 80 falls about 1.33 standard deviations below average. There are some remarkable consistencies about normally distributed data. The most important things to remember, illustrated in Figure A.8, are these:

- Approximately 68 percent of the population will fall within one standard deviation of the average. In the case of the Wechsler test scores, this means that 68 percent of the population scores between 85 (one standard deviation below average) and 115 (one standard deviation above average). Roughly two-thirds of a population falls in this range.
- If you move one more standard deviation on both sides of the mean, you have now accounted for about 96 percent of the population. In other words, about 19 out of 20 people fall within two standard deviations of the mean. For the Wechsler test scores, this represents the spread from a score of 70 (two standard deviations below average) to a score of 130 (two standard deviations above average).
- By the time you've gone one more standard deviation, you've included just about everyone. Slightly more than 99.7 percent of the population fall within three standard deviations of the mean. For the Wechsler test scores, this is the range from a score of 55 to a score of 145. Statistically then, it is quite unusual for people to have Wechsler test scores below 55 or above 145. No matter what is being tested, in a normal distribution, it is equally unusual for any individual to exceed three standard deviations away from the mean in either direction.

Comparative Statistics

5. What is the difference between percentage and percentile rank?

The two major comparative statistics are percentage and percentile rank. Each of these two statistical tools gives us information about a comparison. **Percentage,** as you probably know, compares a score to an imaginary set of one hundred. If a student scores 83 percent on a test, for example, that the student would have had 83 right on a test

▸ **percentage** A comparative statistic that compares a score to a perfect score, assuming the perfect score is 100 points.

Appendix

F • Y • I

Advanced Placement exams use the bell curve to determine what the passing scores are for each year. When the tests are scored, the scores are pulled together and put into the curve. Those scores that make up 68 percent of the scores are given a 3. Those that fall within two standard deviations from the mean get either a 2 or a 4, depending on which side of the mean they fall. Those that fall in the third standard deviation from the mean get a 1 or a 5, again depending on which side of the mean they fall. So the actual passing score is different each year, depending on how the scores distribute in that given year.

■ TEACHING TIP

Students may have heard of *grading on the curve*. They may even feel that *curving the grades* is desirable and, possibly, might encourage you to grade in such a way. Help students understand that grading on the curve and curving grades are two totally different concepts:

- **Grading on the curve** is what most standardized tests do to "norm" the scores. A teacher who grades on the curve takes the scores on a test and applies the characteristics of the normal curve to the scores. In such a case, 68 percent of the scores will earn a grade of C. If your score falls above one standard deviation from the mean, you will get an A or B. If it falls below, you will get a D or F. So even if you made a 75 on your test, if everyone else made a higher grade than you, your grade would be an F.
- **Curving grades,** in theory, creates a more normal-looking graph by making the highest grade on the test an A. Many teachers who curve grades will make the highest score an automatic 100, adding the amount of points it took to make that grade a 100 to every other grade. This only serves to shift the graph to the center or left.

■ APPLYING THE POINTS

Remind students that they have seen percentile ranks on achievement test scores they have taken over the years. Have the guidance counselor or testing coordinator come to class to go over students' own standardized test scores so they can be better-informed consumers of information.

■ TEACHING TIPS

trb tr (1) A black-line master of Figure A.9, Percentage Scores and Percentile Ranks, is available in the **Black-Line Masters Appendix** of the *Teacher's Resource Binder.*

(2) Help students see that a *positive correlation* does not indicate a desirable outcome and a *negative correlation* does not indicate an undesirable outcome.

- **Positive** refers to positive coefficients and a direct relationship.
- **Negative** refers to negative coefficients and inverse relationships.

(3) Remind students that *correlation* does not mean "causation." This fundamental principle in psychological research is often misunderstood. Many media outlets will incorrectly report correlational data as indicating a cause-and-effect relationship.

Figure A.9 **Percentage Scores and Percentile Ranks** These two common comparative statistics have similar names and are calculated with similar formulas, but they have different meanings.

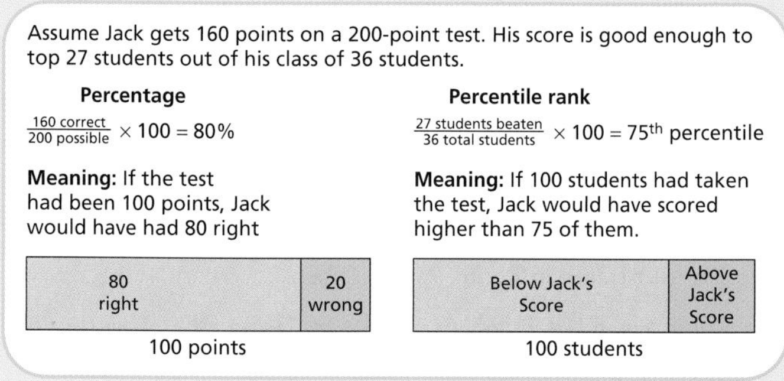

with 100 questions. The **percentile rank** compares one score with other scores in an imaginary group of 100 individuals. It tells you where a particular score stands in that group and how many people had equal or lower scores. If our student scores at the 83rd percentile, it means that score would have equaled or exceeded 83 of every 100 people who took the test. Figure A.9 shows an example of how percentages and percentiles are calculated.

Assume Jack gets 160 points on a 200-point test. His score is good enough to top 27 students out of his class of 36 students.
Percentage
$\frac{\text{160 correct}}{\text{200 possible}} \times 100 = 80\%$
Meaning: If the test had been 100 points, Jack would have had 80 right
80 right
20 wrong
100 points
Percentile rank
$\frac{\text{27 students beaten}}{\text{36 total students}} \times 100 = 75^{\text{th}}$ percentile
Meaning: If 100 students had taken the test, Jack would have scored higher than 75 of them.
Below Jack's Score
Above Jack's Score
100 students

Correlation Coefficient

6. How does a correlation coefficient indicate the strength of a relationship?

Positive Correlation The more this person trains, the stronger he will become.

Another highly useful statistic is the **correlation coefficient,** a number that represents how strong a relationship is between two variables. Things can be related in two different ways: They can travel together, or they can move away from each other. If both variables increase (or decrease) together, there is a *positive correlation.* An example of a positive correlation is the one between a weight-lifting conditioning program and strength: People who participate in a properly designed lifting program grow stronger as they lift. Strength and lifting travel together, in the same direction: Lift more, grow stronger. *Negative correlations* involve two variables that change in opposite directions. There is a negative correlation between tooth flossing and dental decay: Floss more, have fewer cavities.

The calculation of a correlation coefficient is quite complicated, so we won't go through it here. What's important to remember is that the number produced by the calculation has a value that always falls between −1 and +1. When $r = -1$ (the letter r stands for "correlation coefficient"), we have a perfect negative correlation. Every time one variable increases by a certain amount, the other variable would decrease by an equally certain amount. Graph a of Figure A.10 shows a perfect negative correlation (−1.00).

If $r = +1$, we are looking at a perfect positive correlation between two variables. Every time one variable increases by a certain amount, the other variable will also increase by an equally certain amount. Similarly, every time one variable decreases by a certain amount, the other variable will decrease by an equally certain amount (Figure A.10b).

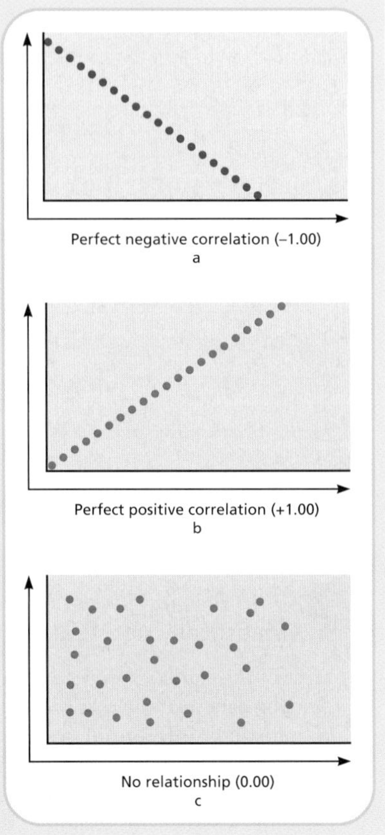

Figure A.10
Correlations

There is no correlation whatsoever between two variables if $r = 0$. Examples of this seem quite silly, like the relationship between dental flossing and the temperature in Mexico City, or the relationship between the Los Angeles Lakers' basketball scores and the number of late arrivals into London's Heathrow Airport. When the first variable changes, we know absolutely nothing about what the second variable will do. When graphed, no relationship is apparent, as you can see in Figure A.10, graph c.

We've now illustrated three situations: a perfect negative correlation, a perfect positive correlation, and no correlation at all. As you might imagine, the real world is rarely so neat and tidy. Positive correlations are usually less than $r = +1$, and negative correlations don't often get all the way to $r = -1$. Figure A.11 on page A-12 shows you what a graph called a *scatterplot* would look like in a more realistic correlation between two variables—height and temperament.

▶ **percentile rank** A comparative statistic that compares a score to other scores, assuming there are a hundred scores altogether. The percentile rank indicates how many of the hundred scores are at or below a particular score.

▶ **correlation coefficient** A statistical measure of the extent to which two things vary together.

■ **CHECKING FOR UNDERSTANDING**
Have students identify different correlational coefficients as indicating a direct or inverse relationship. Throw in numbers above and below +1 and −1 to see if students remember that correlation coefficients only range from −1 to +1.

■ **TEACHING TIPS**
trb tr (1) A black-line master of Figure A.10, Correlations, is available in the **Black-Line Masters Appendix** of the *Teacher's Resource Binder.*

(2) Have students find variables that may or may not be related and collect data on these variables. They may choose hours spent studying and GPA, frequency of tardiness to school and test scores, or library book check-outs and attendance. Have them create a scatterplot of these data to see if a relationship seems to exist.

Demonstrating

CREATING A SCATTERPLOT Have students work with partners to create a scatterplot of the data found in Figure A.2, Frequency Distributions, on page A-3 of the *Student Edition.* Review the scatterplots by asking students the following questions about their findings:

- What type of correlation does this data indicate?
- What conclusions could you draw from viewing the graph of this data?

trb tr A black-line master of Figure A.2, Frequency Distributions, is available in the **Black-Line Masters Appendix** of the *Teacher's Resource Binder.*

Appendix

■ TEACHING TIPS

 (1) A black-line master of Figure A.11, Scatterplot of a Moderately Positive Correlation, is available in the **Black-Line Masters Appendix** of the *Teacher's Resource Binder.*

(2) Help students see that although measures of central tendency and variation are useful, they should not be used to draw meaningful conclusions. People shouldn't infer intelligence from a grade on a test. Those statistics serve only to describe a group of data, not to imply meaning.

F • Y • I

Typically, if someone were taking a 100-question multiple-choice test, with each question having four choices for the answer, even if the person were to randomly select answers, he or she would have a statistical chance of getting between 20 and 25 of the answers correct. So students should realize that higher scores are not due to luck or chance—at the very least, they must actually know something about the material to make an educated guess.

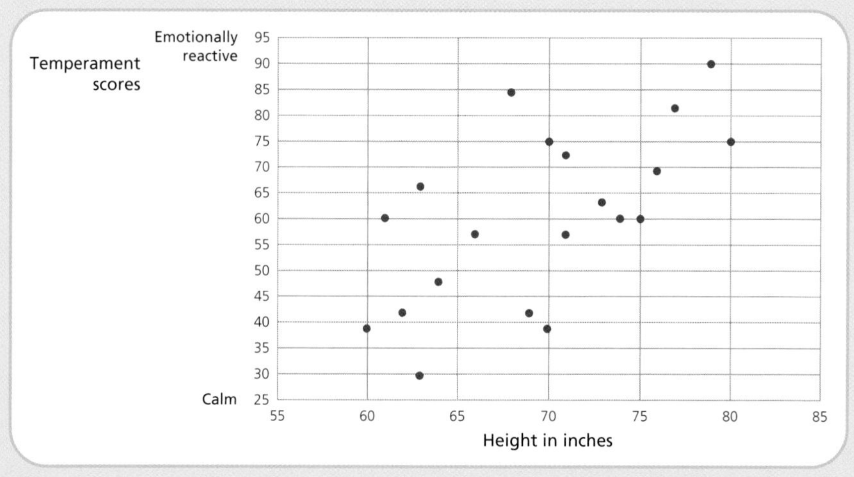

Figure A.11 Scatterplot of a Moderately Positive Correlation These sample data show that taller people are somewhat more likely to be emotionally reactive than shorter people.

Statistical Inference

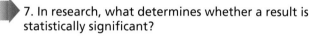

7. In research, what determines whether a result is statistically significant?

Most of the statistics we've discussed so far are *descriptive statistics.* They describe data in a way that makes them more meaningful. Another kind of statistics—**inferential statistics**—lets us make decisions or reach conclusions about a set of data. Inferential statistics are of great use to both statisticians and psychologists because they give us guidelines for deciding whether, for example, data support our hypotheses. Because inferential statistics are more complicated than descriptive statistics to calculate and interpret, we will provide only a general discussion here.

Let's return, one last time, to our headphone example. (Will you miss it?) Assume we've collected grade data from our two groups: the experimental group, whose members did wear headphones, and the control group, whose members didn't. Figure A.4 (on page A-4) presents the measures of central tendency we calculated earlier. You can see that the headphones group did not perform quite as well as the no-headphones group. By the end of the experiment, there was a 4-point difference between the means of the two groups (81 for the no-headphone group, and 77 for the headphone group). The key question is whether this difference is **statistically significant.** In other words, does it represent a *real* difference, one that would be reflected in real-world conditions? Or is it simply due to chance—a matter of "luck" that can be accounted for by some difference (say in study skills) between our two groups, despite our efforts to make them the same by using random as-

▶ **inferential statistics** Statistics that can be used to make a decision or reach a conclusion about data.

▶ **statistical significance** A statistical statement of how likely it is that a result occurred by chance alone.

signment? We will never know with 100 percent certainty, but some statistics can tell us how likely it is that this difference is real.

There is much more depth to inferential statistics than we are able to present here, but essentially, most psychologists are willing to accept up to a 5 percent likelihood that an experiment's results are due to chance. This means being at least 95 percent sure that a difference in results is due to the manipulation of the *independent variable,* which in this case was whether or not students wear headphones, and not to some other unknown variable. A series of calculations with our results in the imaginary headphones experiment would tell us that with our 4-point difference we can be only 40 percent sure that the headphones caused the difference in scores. So, this is not even close to a statistically significant result. For the difference to be statistically significant, the two groups would have to be more clearly separated, with a larger difference or less overlap between them.

There are a number of factors involved in inferential statistics. Here are the three most important:

- *The difference between the two groups' means.* If the means are far apart, the result is more likely to be significant.
- *The number of participants.* If each group has only a few people, the results are not as likely to be as significant as they would be if each group has a large number of randomly selected people in it.
- *The standard deviation of the two groups.* If the scores of both groups are mostly packed in close to the means, the means don't need to be separated by as much to produce a significant result. If the scores are widely spread (represented by high standard deviations), the two groups are likely to overlap quite a bit. Many participants will score in the same "overlap range," no matter which group they are assigned to, and the result is not likely to be significant. This is illustrated in Figure A.12.

Figure A.12 Statistical Significance When two distributions show little overlap, the difference between them is more likely to be statistically significant.

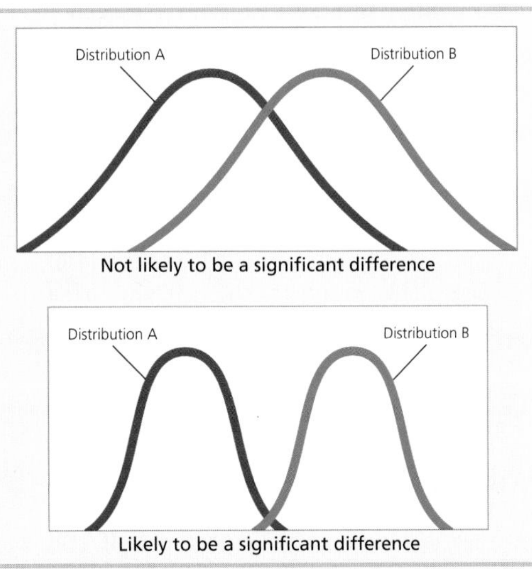

There is much to know about statistics, and much of it is beyond the scope of an introductory psychology course. This appendix has been just a brief introduction, but I hope you have learned some basic points. First, there is nothing particularly scary about statistics. Each formula is a logical application of accepted procedures that can be organized in a series of straightforward steps. Second, we use statistics to uncover meaning in numbers. The more you know about statistics, the better equipped you will be to critically evaluate information in the world around you.

■ **TEACHING TIP**

(tr) A four-color transparency of Figure A.12, Statistical Significance, is available in the **Overhead Transparencies Set.**

Close

Pose the following questions to students:

- How do statistics affect your daily life?
- How can knowing about the difference between descriptive and inferential statistics make one a better consumer of information?

Appendix

Checking the Points

web ■ TEACHING TIP

The book companion site for *Thinking About Psychology* at www.worthpublishers.com/thinkingaboutpsych contains a quiz, flashcards of key terms and people, and other student activities and resources for this appendix. You will also find PowerPoint lectures, a quiz grade book, and other teaching resources by logging on as an instructor.

REVIEW

Statistics Appendix

What's the Point?

The purpose of statistics is to make data more meaningful. Educated people need to be literate in statistics to understand the wealth of information that bombards us today.

Frequency Distributions

1. *What do frequency distributions tell us?*

   Frequency distributions arrange data in order—for example, from highest to lowest scores. This orderly arrangement gives us a broad view of data and reveals meaning we might not otherwise notice. We might, for example, locate the highest and lowest scores without too much effort, but it would be hard to see at a glance where other scores fall in between those extremes.

Measures of Central Tendency

2. *What are the three measures of central tendency, and what is the advantage of each?*

   The three measures of central tendency are the mode, mean, and median. The mode is the score that occurs most often in a group of data, and it is useful when we want to describe clumps of data. The mode would tell you, for example, who won the election for class president: the person with the most votes would also represent the mode for that collection of data. The mean is the average of a group—the total of all scores divided by the number of scores. If the junior class collected canned food for a food bank, you could figure out how many cans the average junior collected by counting all the cans and dividing by the number of juniors. But means can deceive us because they can create false impressions. If 100 students collected 1000 cans, we can't assume each student collected 10 cans. Perhaps one student collected 901, and each of the others brought in only one. The median is the middle score in any group of data: Half of the scores fall above it, and half fall below it. Median scores are useful because they are not influenced by very high or very low scores, as the mean is. When data are not evenly distributed on either side of the mean, then we say that the distribution is skewed.

Measures of Variation

3. *In what ways can statistics determine the variation of a distribution of scores?*

   Two measures of variation are the range and the standard deviation. The range describes the spread between the high score and the low score. The standard deviation is a statistical measure that tells us how much scores vary around a mean score. If scores are packed tightly around the mean, the standard deviation will be small. If scores are spread out widely on either side of the mean, the standard variation will be larger.

Normal Distribution

4. *What are the important characteristics of a normal distribution?*

   A normal distribution is one in which most scores fall near the mean and very few scores fall at the extremes. Normal distributions are not skewed. The mean, median, and mode are all the same. When represented as a graph, a normal distribution forms a bell-shaped curve: The mean, median, and mode all fall at the high point of the graph, and the left and right sides of the curve are mirror images of each other. In a normal distribution, 68 percent of the population fall within one standard deviation of the average, and 96 percent fall within two standard deviations of the mean. More than 99.7 percent fall within three standard deviations.

Comparative Statistics

5. *What is the difference between percentage and percentile rank?*

   Both percentage and percentile rank let us compare two or more things. Percentage lets us compare a score to an imaginary perfect score of 100. Percentage tells us how many points a person scored out of 100 possible points. Percentile rank lets us compare a score to other scores in an imaginary group of 100 scores. Percentile rank tells us how a particular score ranks in comparison to all 100 scores.

Correlation Coefficient

6. *How does a correlation coefficient indicate the strength of a relationship?*

   A correlation coefficient is a number that results when we apply a mathematical formula to variables to see the extent to which they vary together. Knowing this, we have some knowledge about the strength of their relationship. Correlation coefficients are represented by the letter r followed by an equal sign, either a plus or a minus sign, and a number. The plus sign indicates a positive relationship: The two things travel in the same direction. As one increases, the other increases; as one decreases, the other decreases. The minus sign indicates a negative relationship: The two things travel in opposite directions. As one increases, the other *decreases;* as one decreases, the other *increases.* The number, which can range from 0 to 1 in decimal degrees, indicates the strength of the relationship. If the number is 0, there is no relationship. If the number is +1, there is a perfect positive relationship. If the number is −1, there is a perfect negative relationship. Most correlations are not these ideal numbers. Data for correlations can be mapped as dots on a graph called a scatterplot.

Statistical Inference

7. *In research, what determines whether a result is statistically significant?*

   Inferential statistics let us make decisions or reach conclusions about a set of data. (The other statistical measures discussed in this appendix are descriptive statistics, and they describe data in meaningful ways so that we can see them more clearly.) Psychologists have agreed that a result is statistically significant if there is no more than a 5 percent chance that the result could have occurred by chance alone. The three most important factors to consider in inferential statistics are the difference between the two groups' means, the number of participants in the study, and the standard deviation of the two groups.

Key Terms

frequency distribution, p. A-3
mode, p. A-4
mean, p. A-5
median, p. A-5
skewed, p. A-5
range, p. A-7
standard deviation, p. A-7
normal distribution, p. A-8
percentage, p. A-9
percentile rank, p. A-10
correlation coefficient, p. A-10
inferential statistics, p. A-11
statistical significance, p. A-11

Checking the Points

Building Vocabulary

If students did not do so earlier, have them now create their own flashcards of the terms in this appendix by showing a term on one side of an index card and the definition on the other side. To test their understanding of key terms, have students work with partners. One partner can ask a question whose answer is a term presented on a flashcard, while the other partner can choose the flashcard whose term answers the question. Partners should alternate asking questions and providing answers.

Appendix

Checking the Points

tb Using the Test Bank

The *Test Bank* that accompanies this textbook offers a wide variety of questions in different formats and levels of complexity. Use the software to construct whole tests or to integrate standardized questions into teacher-made tests.

Self-Test Answers

Multiple-Choice Questions

1. d, 2. a, 3. d, 4. c, 5. b

Self-Test

Multiple-Choice Questions

Choose the *best* answer for each of the following questions.

1. Senator Goodguy is introducing a bill in Congress to raise the minimum wage. He's decided that he can build support by citing some income statistics for one town in his state, where most residents work full time but live at the poverty level. The town he will cite also has a small number of millionaires living along the shore in an exclusive closed community. If Senator Goodguy wants to avoid giving a distorted view of the incomes of the working poor people, he should use the town's ________________ when discussing their plight.
   a. range of incomes
   b. median income
   c. mean income
   d. modal income

2. Zelda likes Liam, and she has invited him to her birthday party. Liam wants to be Zelda's friend, but not her boyfriend. He has decided that he must choose his present for Zelda very carefully, to avoid giving the wrong impression. He has therefore talked to everyone else who will be at the party and has obtained a list stating what their gift will be and how much it will cost. Liam plans to buy a gift like the ones that most people will be giving Zelda, so that it won't appear to be special. Liam's gift will fall at the ________________ of this group of gifts.
   a. mode
   b. median
   c. second standard deviation
   d. third standard deviation

3. Daisy is looking at a graph that represents all the intelligence test scores for the students in her class. The mean, median, and mode all fall at the same point. The highest point of the graph is exactly in the center, and the left and right sides of the graph are mirror images of each other. This bell-shaped graph represents a
   a. negative correlation.
   b. positive correlation.
   c. skewed distribution.
   d. normal distribution.

4. Angel and Oscar, who live in Boston, want to schedule a day of skiing in a local park for their father's birthday on Halloween. They are doing some research to try to predict whether it will snow in Boston on October 31. After gathering their data for the past 20 years, they used a statistical formula to create a correlation coefficient, which was –0.90. After considering this number, they decided
   a. to schedule the trip for a later winter month; this positive correlation indicates that it almost never snows in Boston on October 31.
   b. to schedule the trip for October 31; because this number is close to 1.0, there is an excellent chance that it will snow in Boston on October 31.
   c. to schedule the trip for a later winter month; this negative correlation indicates that it almost never snows in Boston on October 31.
   d. to take their chances and schedule the trip for October 31; because this is a negative correlation, there is no way to predict whether it will snow in Boston on October 31.

5. Sofia and Nick were watching TV and saw an ad for a psychic named Madame Louisa.

Madame Louisa proudly announced that her findings were so reliable that a psychologist had said there was only a 75 percent likelihood they could occur by chance alone. Sofia and Nick, who have taken a psychology course, laughed out loud because they

a. were happy to finally find a reliable psychic, backed by psychologists.
b. knew that 75 percent is not a good result; psychologists consider a result statistically significant only if the likelihood of its occurring by chance alone is 5 percent or lower.
c. knew that 75 percent is not a good result; psychologists consider a result statistically significant only if the likelihood of its occurring by chance alone is 50 percent or lower.
d. knew that 75 percent is not a good result; psychologists consider a result statistically significant only if the likelihood of its occurring by chance alone is 0.5 percent or lower.

Matching Terms and Definitions:

6. For each definition, choose the *best* matching term from the list that follows.

Definition

a. The most frequently occurring score in a distribution.
b. The difference between the highest and lowest scores in a distribution.
c. Distorted; not evenly distributed around the mean.
d. Symmetrical, bell-shaped curve that describes the distribution of many variables.
e. The arithmetic average of a distribution, obtained by adding the scores and then dividing by the number of scores.
f. A computed measure of how much scores vary around the mean score.
g. Comparative statistic that compares a score to other scores, assuming there are a hundred scores altogether.
h. The middle score in a ranked distribution; half the scores are above it and half are below it.
i. A statistical measure of the extent to which two things vary together.

Term

(1) mode
(2) mean
(3) median
(4) correlation coefficient
(5) skewed
(6) range
(7) standard deviation
(8) inferential statistics
(9) percentage
(10) percentile rank
(11) normal distribution

Fill-in-the-Blank Questions

7. A ________________ ________________ is an ordered list of data (test scores, for example) that reveals meaning we might not otherwise notice.

8. ________________ statistics describe data in a way that makes them more meaningful; ________________ statistics let us make decisions or reach conclusions about a set of data.

Brief Essay Question

9. A friend of yours who is also taking psychology has complained that he's not interested in statistics and he doesn't understand why he has to learn this part of psychology. In two paragraphs of two or three sentences each, explain to your friend (1) the overall purpose of statistics and (2) why educated people need to be literate in statistics.

Appendix

Self-Test Answers

Matching Terms and Definitions

6. a. (1), b. (6), c. (5), d. (11), e. (2), f. (7), g. (9), h. (3), i. (4)

Fill-in-the-Blank Questions

7. frequency distribution, 8. Descriptive; inferential

Brief Essay Question

9. (1) Students should understand that statistics are designed to make data more meaningful. (2) Students should relate that statistical literacy is important to being a better consumer of information. Our society bombards us with statistical information on a daily basis, and knowing the difference between descriptive and inferential statistics can help one realize what data should be used for descriptive purposes and what data can be used to draw conclusions.

Glossary of Key Terms and Key People

A

absolute threshold. The minimum stimulation needed to detect a particular stimulus 50 percent of the time. (p. 158)

accommodation. Adapting one's current understandings (schemas) to incorporate new information. (p. 63)

acetylcholine [ah-seat-el-KO-leen]. A neurotransmitter that triggers muscle contraction and affects learning and memory. (p. 128)

achievement motivation. A desire for significant accomplishment: for mastery of things, people, or ideas; for attaining a high standard. (p. 214)

achievement tests. Tests that attempt to measure what the test-taker has accomplished. (p. 468)

acquisition. In classical conditioning, the process of developing a learned response. (p. 284)

action potential. A neural impulse; a brief electrical charge that travels down the axon of a neuron. (p. 123)

active listening. Empathic listening in which the listener echoes, restates, and clarifies. A feature of Rogers' client-centered therapy. (p. 578)

Adler, Alfred. (1870–1937) Neo-Freudian who thought social tensions were more important than sexual tensions in the development of personality. (p. 486)

adolescence. The transition period from childhood to adulthood, extending from puberty to independence. (p. 81)

adrenal glands. Endocrine glands that help to arouse the body in times of stress. (p. 134)

aggression. Any physical or verbal behavior intended to hurt or destroy. (p. 647)

agonist. A drug that boosts the effect of a neurotransmitter. (p. 128)

algorithm. A problem-solving strategy that guarantees the solution to the problem. (p. 433)

all-or-none principle. The principle stating that if a neuron fires, it always fires at the same intensity; all action potentials are the same strength. (p. 124)

Allport, Gordon. (1897–1967) American psychologist and trait theorist who researched the idea that individual personalities are unique. (p. 508)

altruism. Unselfish regard for the welfare of others. (p. 640)

Alzheimer's disease. A progressive and irreversible brain disorder characterized by gradual deterioration of memory, reasoning, language, and, finally, physical functioning. (p. 103)

amphetamines. Drugs that stimulate neural activity, speeding up body functions, and associated energy and mood changes. (p. 419)

amygdala [ah-MIG-dah-la]. Two almond-shaped neural clusters in the limbic system that are linked to emotions, such as fear and anger. (p. 145)

anorexia nervosa. An eating disorder in which normal-weight people (usually adolescent females) suffer delusions of being overweight, put themselves on self-starvation regimens, and become dangerously underweight (15 percent or more). (p. 220)

antagonist. A drug that blocks the effect of a neurotransmitter. (p. 128)

antianxiety drugs. A category of medications used to treat people with anxiety disorders or suffering stress. (p. 602)

antidepressant drugs. A category of medications used primarily to treat major depression. (p. 602)

antipsychotic drugs. A category of medications used primarily to treat schizophrenia. (p. 601)

antisocial behavior. Negative, destructive, unhelpful behavior. (p. 328)

antisocial personality disorder. A personality disorder in which the person (usually a man) shows a lack of conscience for wrongdoing and a lack of respect for the rights of others. (p. 567)

anxiety. A vague feeling of apprehension or nervousness. The basis of the anxiety disorders. (p. 534)

applied research. Scientific study that aims to solve practical problems. (p. 13)

G-1

aptitude tests. Tests that attempt to predict the test-taker's future performance. (p. 468)

Asch, Solomon. (1907–1996) Social psychologist who researched the circumstances under which people conform. (p. 621)

assimilation. Interpreting one's new experience in terms of one's existing schemas. (p. 63)

attachment. An emotional tie with another person; young children demonstrate attachment by seeking closeness to the caregiver and showing distress on separation. (p. 69)

attitude. A belief and feeling that predisposes one to respond in a particular way to objects, people, and events. (p. 617)

attribution theory. The theory that we tend to give a causal explanation for someone's behavior, often by crediting either the situation or the person's disposition. (p. 614)

auditory canal. The opening through which sound waves travel as they move into the ear for processing. The auditory canal ends at the tympanic membrane, or eardrum. (p. 170)

auditory nerve. The nerve that carries sound information from the ears to the temporal lobe of the brain. (p. 172)

authoritarian parenting. Style of parenting marked by imposing rules and expecting obedience. (p. 72)

authoritative parenting. A style of parenting marked by making demands on the child, being responsive, setting and enforcing rules, and discussing the reasons behind the rules. (p. 73)

automatic processing. The unconscious encoding of some information, such as space, time, and frequency, without effort. (p. 336)

autonomic [aw-tuh-NAHM-ik] nervous system. The division of the peripheral nervous system that controls the glands and muscles of the internal organs (such as the heart). Its subdivisions are the sympathetic (arousing) division and the parasympathetic (calming) division. (pp. 131, 232)

availability heuristic. Estimating the likelihood of events based on their availability in memory. We are sometimes right and sometimes wrong in assuming events available in memory are likely. (p. 438)

aversive conditioning. A type of counterconditioning that associates an unpleasant state (such as nausea) with an unwanted behavior (such as drinking alcohol). (p. 582)

axon. The extension of a neuron through which neural impulses are sent. (p. 122)

axon terminal. The endpoint of a neuron, where neurotransmitters are stored. (p. 123)

B

Bandura, Albert. (1925–) Canadian-American psychologist and major figure in the study of observational learning. Also developed the social-cognitive perspective on personality, stressing that one must consider the situation and the person's thoughts before, during, and after an event. (pp. 326, 505)

barbiturates. Drugs that depress the activity of the central nervous system, reducing anxiety but impairing memory and judgment. (p. 414)

basal metabolic rate. The body's resting rate of energy expenditure. (p. 218)

basic research. Pure science that aims to increase the scientific knowledge base. (p. 13)

behavior genetics. Within psychology, the perspective that focuses on the relative power and limits of genetic and environmental influences on behavior—the extent to which our genes and our environment influence our individual differences. (pp. 11, 39)

behaviorism. The view that psychology should restrict its efforts to studying observable behaviors, not mental processes. (p. 283)

behaviorist perspective. School of thought that focuses on how we learn observable responses. (p. 6)

belief perseverance. Clinging to one's initial beliefs even after new information discredits the basis on which they were formed. (p. 440)

benzodiazepines. Drugs (such as Valium) that depress the activity of the central nervous system without most of the side effects associated with barbiturates. (p. 415)

Binet, Alfred. (1857–1911) Developer of the first test to classify children's abilities using the concept of mental age. (p. 460)

binocular cues. Depth cues that require the use of both eyes. (p. 187)

biological perspective. School of thought that focuses on the physical structures and substances underlying a particular behavior, thought, or emotion. (p. 9)

biological rhythms. Periodic physiological fluctuations. (p. 378)

bio-psycho-social perspective. A contemporary perspective which assumes that biological, psychological, and sociocultural factors combine and interact to produce psychological disorders. (p. 522)

bipolar cells. Cells that form the middle layer in the retina. Bipolar cells gather information from the rods and cones and pass it on to the ganglion cells. (p. 166)

bipolar disorder. A mood disorder (formerly called *manic depressive disorder*) in which the person alternates between the hopelessness of depression and the overexcited and unreasonably optimistic state of mania. (p. 546)

blind spot. The point at which the optic nerve travels through the retina to exit the eye. The lack of receptor rods and cones at this point creates a small blind spot. (p. 166)

body mass index (BMI). Your weight in kilograms (pounds multiplied by .45) divided by your squared height in meters (inches divided by 39.4). U.S. government guidelines encourage a body mass index (BMI) under 25. The World Health Organization and many countries define obesity as a BMI of 30 or over. (p. 270)

bottom-up processing. Information processing that focuses on the raw material entering through our eyes, ears, and other organs of sensation. (p. 157)

brainstem. The oldest part and central core of the brain, beginning where the spinal cord swells as it enters the skull; the brainstem is responsible for automatic survival functions. (p. 140)

Broca's area. A brain area of the frontal lobe, usually in the left hemisphere, that directs the muscle movements involved in speech. (p. 148)

bulimia nervosa. An eating disorder characterized by episodes of overeating, usually of high-calorie foods, followed by vomiting, use of laxative, fasting, or excessive exercise. (p. 220)

burnout. Physical, emotional, and mental exhaustion brought on by persistent job-related stress. (p. 248)

bystander effect. The tendency for any given bystander to be less likely to give aid if other bystanders are present. (p. 641)

C

caffeine. Stimulant found in coffee, chocolate, tea, and some soft drinks. (p. 416)

Calkins, Mary Whiton. (1863–1930) First woman to complete the requirements for a Ph.D. in psychology; first woman to be elected president of the American Psychological Association. (p. 8)

Cannon, Walter. (1871–1943) American physiologist who, along with Philip Bard, concluded that physiological arousal and emotional experience occur simultaneously (*see Cannon-Bard theory*). (pp. 228, 246)

Cannon-Bard theory. The theory that an emotion-arousing stimulus simultaneously triggers (1) physiological responses, and (2) the subjective experience of emotion. (p. 228)

case study. A research technique in which one person is studied in depth in the hope of revealing universal principles. (pp. 20, 142)

Cattell, Raymond. (1905–1998) English psychologist who researched whether some traits predicted others. He proposed 16 key personality dimensions or *factors* to describe personality. (p. 500)

central nervous system (CNS). The brain and spinal cord. (pp. 131, 409)

cerebellum [sehr-uh-BELL-um]. The "little brain" attached to the rear of the brainstem; it helps coordinate voluntary movements and balance. (p. 141)

cerebral [seh-REE-bruhl] cortex. The intricate fabric of interconnected neural cells that form the cerebral hemispheres; the body's ultimate control and information-processing center. (p. 145)

Chomsky, Noam. (1928–) Linguist who argued that children have a predisposition to learn language, as though their brains were hard-wired to pick up vocabulary and rules of grammar. (p. 445)

chromosomes. Threadlike structures made of DNA molecules that contain the genes. (p. 40)

chronological age. Actual age. In Terman and Stern's intelligence quotient (IQ) formula, chronological age is abbreviated as CA. (p. 460)

chunking. Organizing information into meaningful units. (p. 342)

circadian (ser-KAY-dee-un) rhythms. Biological rhythms (for example, of temperature and wakefulness) that occur approximately every 24 hours. (p. 378)

classical conditioning. A type of learning where a stimulus gains the power to cause a response because it predicts another stimulus that already produces the response. (p. 281)

client-centered therapy. A humanistic therapy, developed by Carl Rogers, in which the therapist uses techniques such as active listening within a genuine, accepting, empathic environment to facilitate the client's growth. (Also called *person-centered therapy*.) (p. 578)

cocaine. Stimulant derived from leaves of the coca plant. (p. 418)

cochlea. The major organ of hearing, a snail-shaped, bony, fluid-filled structure in the inner ear where sound waves are changed to neural impulses. (p. 171)

cognition. Mental processes; all the mental activities associated with thinking, knowing, and remembering. (pp. 63, 283)

cognitive abilities. All the mental activities associated with thinking, knowing, and remembering. (p. 430)

cognitive-behavior therapy. An integrated therapy that combines cognitive therapy (changing self-defeating thinking) with behavior therapy (changing inappropriate behaviors). (p. 586)

cognitive dissonance. The theory that we act to reduce the discomfort (dissonance) we feel when two of our thoughts (cognitions) are inconsistent. For example, when our awareness of our attitudes and of our actions clash, we can reduce the resulting dissonance by changing our attitudes. (p. 619)

cognitive map. A mental representation of a place. (p. 316)

cognitive perspective. School of thought that focuses on how we take in, process, store, and retrieve information. (p. 9)

cognitive therapy. Therapy that teaches people new, more adaptive ways of thinking and acting; based on the assumption that thoughts intervene between events and our emotional reactions. (p. 584)

collective unconscious. Carl Jung's concept of a shared, inherited reservoir of memory traces from our ancestors' history. (p. 486)

collectivism. Cultural style that places group goals or needs ahead of personal goals or needs and defines personal identity in terms of group identification. (pp. 48, 658)

companionate love. The deep affectionate attachment we feel for those with whom our lives are intertwined. (p. 639)

computerized axial tomography (CT or CAT) scan. A series of x-ray photographs taken from different angles and combined by computer into a composite representation of a slice through the body. (p. 143)

concept. A mental grouping based on shared similarity. (p. 431)

concrete operational stage. In Piaget's theory, the stage of cognitive development (from about 6 or 7 to 11 years of age) during which children gain the mental skills that let them think logically about concrete events. (p. 67)

conditioned response (CR). In classical conditioning, the response to the conditioned stimulus. (p. 284)

conditioned stimulus (CS). In classical conditioning, a previously neutral stimulus that, through learning, has gained the power to cause a conditioned response. (p. 284)

cones. Visual receptor cells located in the retina. Cones detect sharp details and color, but they require more light than rods. (p. 165)

confirmation bias. The tendency to focus on information that supports one's preconceptions. (p. 437)

conformity. Adjusting one's behavior or thinking to coincide with a group standard. (p. 621)

confounding variable. In an experiment, a variable, other than the independent variable, that could influence the dependent variable. To draw cause-and-effect conclusions from an experiment, researchers must control for confounding variables. (p. 26)

consciousness. Awareness of yourself and your environment. (p. 378)

conservation. The principle (which Piaget believed to be a part of concrete operational reasoning) that properties such as mass, volume, and number remain the same despite changes in the forms of objects. (p. 66)

context. The setting or environment in which we interpret sensory stimuli. (p. 197)

context effect. The enhanced ability to retrieve information when you are in an environment similar to the one in which you encoded the information. (p. 351)

continuous reinforcement. In operant conditioning, a schedule of reinforcement in which a reward follows every correct response. (p. 312)

control group. The participants in an experiment who are not exposed to the independent variable. These individuals function as a comparison for the experimental group participants. (p. 26)

convergence. A binocular depth cue related to the tension in the eye muscles when the eyes track inward to focus on objects close to the viewer. (p. 188)

cornea. The clear bulge on the front of the eyeball. The curvature of the cornea begins bending the light rays, a process the lens continues to produce a focused image on the retina. (p. 164)

corpus callosum [KOR-pus kah-LOW-sum]. The large band of neural fibers that connects the two brain hemispheres and carries messages between them. (p. 146)

correlational study. A research project designed to discover the degree to which two variables are related to each other. (p. 21)

correlation coefficient. A statistical measure of the extent to which two things vary together. (p. A-10)

critical period. An optimal period shortly after birth when an organism's exposure to certain stimuli or experiences produces proper development. (p. 70)

critical thinking. Thinking that does not blindly accept arguments and conclusions. Rather, it examines assumptions, discerns hidden values, evaluates evidence, and assesses conclusions. (p. 19)

cross-cultural research. Research that tests hypotheses on many groups of people to understand whether principles apply across cultures. (p. 661)

cross-sectional study. A research technique that compares individuals from different age groups at one time. (p. 24)

crystallized intelligence. One's accumulated knowledge and verbal skills; tends to increase with age. (p. 105)

culture. The shared attitudes, beliefs, norms, and behaviors of a group communicated from one generation to the next; may function to ensure a group's survival. (pp. 48, 657)

culture-specific principles. Principles that are true only for a people of a certain culture; in contrast, *universal* principles are true of people in all cultures. (p. 661)

D

Darley, John. (1938–) Psychologist who, with Bibb Latané, researched the circumstances that determine when a bystander will intervene on behalf of another person. (p. 641)

decibel (dB). A measure of the height of a sound wave, which determines the loudness of a sound. (p. 169)

defense mechanisms. In psychoanalytic theory, the ego's protective methods of reducing anxiety by unconsciously distorting reality. (p. 483)

deindividuation. The loss of self-awareness and self-restraint occurring in group situations that foster arousal and anonymity. (p. 627)

deinstitutionalization. The release of patients from mental hospitals to the community at large. The development of drug treatments led to an 80 percent decline in the number of hospitalized mental patients in the second half of the twentieth century. (p. 599)

delta sleep. Stages 3 and 4 of N-REM sleep, characterized by large, slow delta waves; delta sleep is minimal during the last four hours of sleep. (p. 385)

delusions. False beliefs that are symptoms of schizophrenia and other serious psychological disorders. (p. 560)

Dement, William. (1928–) Sleep researcher who coined the term *REM.* (p. 380)

dendrite. The bushy, branching extensions of a neuron that receive messages and conduct impulses toward the cell body (soma). (p. 122)

dependence. A state of physiological and/or psychological need to take more of a substance after continued use. Withdrawal follows if the drug is discontinued. (p. 408)

dependent variable (DV). The research variable that is influenced by the independent variable. In psychology, the behavior or mental process where the impact of the independent variable is measured. (p. 25)

depressants. Drugs (such as alcohol and sedatives) that reduce neural activity and slow body function. (p. 412)

depth perception. The ability to see in three dimensions and judge distance. (p. 186)

difference threshold (just noticeable difference). The minimum difference that a person can detect between two stimuli 50 percent of the time. (p. 159)

discrimination. *In classical conditioning,* the ability to distinguish between two similar signals or stimuli. *In operant conditioning,* the process by which an organism produces different responses to two similar stimuli. *In social relations,* taking action against a group of people because of stereotyped beliefs and feelings of prejudice. (pp. 289, 311, 642)

display rules. The cultural rules governing how and when a person may express emotion. (p. 237)

dissociative amnesia. A dissociative disorder characterized by loss of memory in reaction to a traumatic event. (p. 556)

dissociative disorders. Disorders in which the sense of self has become separated (dissociated) from previous memories, thoughts, or feelings. (p. 555)

dissociative fugue. A dissociative disorder characterized by loss of identity and travel to a new location. (p. 556)

dissociative identity disorder. A rare and controversial dissociative disorder in which an individual experiences two or more distinct and alternating personalities. (p. 557)

distributed rehearsal. Spreading rehearsal out in several sessions separated by periods of time. (p. 339)

divided consciousness theory. The theory that during hypnosis, our consciousness—our awareness of ourselves and others—splits, so that one aspect of consciousness is not aware of the role other parts are playing. (p. 397)

DNA (deoxyribonucleic acid). A complex molecule containing the genetic information that makes up the chromosomes. (p. 40)

dopamine [DO-pa-mean]. A neurotransmitter that affects learning, attention, and emotions; excess dopamine activity is associated with schizophrenia. (p. 129)

double-blind procedure. An experimental procedure in which both the research participants and the research staff are ignorant (blind) as to the expected outcome of the research. This procedure is used to control for the effects of expectation as a confounding variable. (p. 29)

drive-reduction theory. The idea that a physiological need creates an aroused tension state (a drive) that motivates an organism to satisfy the need. (p. 208)

drives. In drive-reduction theory, aroused tension states created by imbalances that prompt an organism to restore the balance, typically by reducing the drive. (p. 208)

DSM-IV-TR. The American Psychiatric Association's *Diagnostic and Statistical Manual of Mental Disorders* (Fourth Edition, Text Revision), a widely used system for classifying psychological disorders. (p. 524)

E

eardrum (tympanic membrane). The tissue barrier at the end of the auditory canal. It transfers sound vibration from the air to the three tiny bones of the middle ear. (p. 170)

Ebbinghaus, Hermann. (1850–1909) German philosopher who conducted pioneering memory studies. (pp. 336, 361)

eclectic approach. An approach to psychotherapy that, depending on the person's problems, uses techniques from various forms of therapy. (p. 574)

ecstasy. Also called *MDMA*, this hallucinogenic drug produces lowered inhibitions, pleasant feelings, and greater acceptance of others. Even moderate use may result in permanent brain damage. (p. 420)

effortful processing. Encoding that requires attention and conscious effort. (p. 336)

ego. The largely conscious, "executive" part of personality that, according to Freud, mediates among the demands of the id, superego, and reality. The ego operates on the *reality principle,* satisfying the id's desires in ways that will realistically bring pleasure rather than pain. (p. 483)

egocentrism. In Piaget's theory, the inability of the preoperational child to take another's point of view, or to understand that symbols can represent other objects. (p. 67)

electroconvulsive therapy (ECT). A therapy for major depression in which a brief electric current is sent through the brain of an anesthetized patient. (p. 604)

electroencephalogram (EEG). An amplified recording of the waves of electrical activity that sweep across the brain's surface. These waves, measured by electrodes placed on the scalp, are helpful in evaluating brain function. (p. 143)

electroencephalograph (EEG). A machine that amplifies and records waves of electrical activity that sweep across the brain's surface. Electrodes placed on the scalp measure these waves. (p. 384)

electromagnetic energy. An energy spectrum that includes X rays, radar, and radio waves, among other things. A small portion of this spectrum includes visible light energy, which can be detected by the eye. (p. 162)

embryo. The developing human organism from about two weeks after fertilization through the end of the eighth week. (p. 58)

emotional intelligence. The ability to perceive, express, understand, and regulate emotions. (p. 458)

emotions. Whole-organism responses, involving (1) physiological arousal, (2) expressive behaviors, and (3) conscious experience. (p. 226)

encoding. The process of getting information into the memory system. The first stage of the information processing model of memory. (pp. 335, 359)

endocrine [EN-duh-krin] system. One of the body's two communication systems; a set of glands that produce hormones, chemical messengers that circulate in the blood. (p. 133)

endorphins. "Morphine within"—natural, opiatelike neurotransmitters linked to pain control and to pleasure. (p. 415)

environment. Every nongenetic influence, from prenatal nutrition to the people and things around us. (p. 39)

equity. A condition in which people receive from a relationship in proportion to what they give to it. (p. 639)

Erikson, Erik. (1902–1994) Founder of the eight-stage theory of psychosocial development. (pp. 88, 107)

ethnocentrism. The tendency to view the world based on your own experiences, through your own "cultural filters." (p. 666)

evolutionary psychology. The study of the evolution of behavior and the mind, using principles of natural selection. (p. 42)

excitatory effect. A neurotransmitter effect that makes it more likely that the receiving neuron will generate an action potential (impulse). (p. 126)

experiment. A research method in which the researcher manipulates one or more factors (independent variables) to observe the effect on another variable (dependent variable) while controlling for confounding variables. (p. 24)

experimental group. The participants in an experiment who are exposed to the treatment, that is, the independent variable. (p. 26)

explanatory style. The habits we have for thinking about the good or bad causes of events. (p. 266)

explicit memory. Memory of facts and experiences that one must consciously retrieve and declare. (p. 348)

external locus of control. The perception that chance, or forces beyond your control, controls your fate. (p. 508)

extinction. *In classical conditioning,* the diminishing of a learned response; when an unconditioned stimulus does not follow a conditioned stimulus. *In operant conditioning,* the loss of a behavior when no consequence follows it. (pp. 285, 311)

extrasensory perception (ESP). The controversial claim that perception can occur apart from sensory input. (p. 198)

extrinsic motivation. A desire to perform a behavior because of promised rewards or threats of punishment. (p. 212)

Eysenck, Hans. (1916–1997) German psychologist who researched the genetically influenced dimensions of personality, including extraversion and introversion. (p. 500)

F

family therapy. Therapy that treats the family as a system. Views an individual's unwanted behaviors as influenced by or directed at other family members; attempts to guide family members toward positive relationships and improved communication. (p. 587)

fetal alcohol syndrome (FAS). A series of physical and cognitive abnormalities that appear in children whose mothers consumed large amounts of alcohol while pregnant. Symptoms may include noticeable facial misproportions. (p. 59)

fetus. The developing human organism from nine weeks after conception to birth. (p. 58)

figure-ground. The organization of the visual field into objects (the *figures*) that stand out from their surroundings (the *ground*). (p. 184)

fixation. A mental set that hinders the solution of a problem. (p. 436)

fixed-interval reinforcement schedule. In operant conditioning, a partial reinforcement schedule that rewards only the first correct response after some defined period of time. (p. 312)

fixed-ratio reinforcement schedule. In operant conditioning, a partial reinforcement schedule that rewards a response only after some defined number of correct responses. (p. 314)

flashbulb memory. A vivid, clear memory of an emotionally significant moment or event. (p. 346)

flow. A state of optimal experience; for flow to occur, the experiences must be a challenge requiring skill, have clear goals, and provide feedback. (p. 264)

fluid intelligence. One's ability to reason speedily and abstractly; tends to decrease during late adulthood. (p. 105)

foot-in-door phenomenon. The tendency for people who have first agreed to a small request to comply later with a larger request. (p. 618)

formal operational stage. In Piaget's theory, the stage of cognitive development (normally beginning about age 12) during which people begin to think logically about abstract concepts and form strategies. (p. 67)

fovea. The central focal point of the retina, the spot where vision is best. (p. 165)

framing. The way an issue is worded or presented; framing can influence decisions and judgments. (p. 440)

fraternal twins. Twins who develop from separate eggs. They are genetically no closer than brothers and sisters, but they share a fetal environment. (p. 42)

free association. In psychoanalysis, a method of exploring the unconscious in which the person relaxes and says whatever comes to mind, no matter how trivial or embarrassing. (p. 481)

frequency distribution. An list of scores placed on order from highest to lowest. (p. A-3)

Freud, Sigmund. (1856–1939) Founder of psychoanalysis, a controversial theory about the workings of the unconscious mind and the psychosexual stages of development. (pp. 5, 107, 364, 479, 573)

frontal lobes. The portion of the cerebral cortex lying just behind the forehead; includes the motor cortex; is involved in making plans and judgments. (p. 146)

functional fixedness. The tendency to think of things only in terms of their usual functions; an impediment to problem solving. (p. 436)

functionalism. Theory that emphasized the functions of consciousness and the ways consciousness helps people adapt to their environment. (p. 5)

fundamental attribution error. The tendency for observers, when analyzing another's behavior, to underestimate the impact of the situation and to overestimate the impact of personal disposition. (p. 614)

G

ganglion cells. The top layer of cells in the retina. Ganglion cells receive information from bipolar cells and transmit it through their axons, which together form the optic nerve. (p. 166)

Garcia, John. (1917–) Identified, along with colleague Robert Koelling, the phenomenon of taste aversion, which established that classical conditioning was influenced by biological predispositions. (p. 293)

Gardner, Howard. (1943–) Author of a contemporary theory of multiple intelligences consisting of eight separate kinds of intelligence. (p. 456)

general adaptation syndrome (GAS). Selye's concept of the body's adaptive response to stress in three stages—alarm, resistance, exhaustion. (p. 246)

general intelligence (*g*). A general intelligence factor that Spearman believed underlies specific mental abilities and is therefore measured by every task on an intelligence test. (p. 459)

generalization. A process in which an organism produces the same response to two similar stimuli. (p. 289)

generalized anxiety disorder. Characterized by disruptive levels of persistent, unexplained feelings of apprehension and tenseness. (p. 534)

genes. A segment of DNA; biochemical units of heredity that make up the chromosomes and direct how cells become specialized for various functions (such as brain, lungs, heart, hair) during prenatal development. (pp. 39, 58)

genome. The complete instructions for making an organism, consisting of all the genetic material in its chromosomes. (p. 41)

gestalt. The "whole," or the organizational patterns, that we tend to perceive. The Gestalt psychologists emphasized that the whole is greater than the sum of its parts. (p. 183)

Gestalt psychology. Psychological perspective that emphasizes our tendency to integrate pieces of information into meaningful wholes. (p. 5)

grammar. A system of rules governing how we can combine morphemes and words and arrange them in sentences to communicate with others. (p. 443)

grouping. The perceptual tendency to organize stimuli into understandable groups. (p. 185)

group intelligence tests. Originally developed by the U.S. Army to efficiently assess recruits during World War I and now widely used by schools. Usually administered by teachers in their classrooms, these tests are not as reliable as individually administered tests, such as the Stanford-Binet or Wechsler tests. (p. 466)

group polarization. The enhancement of a group's prevailing attitudes through discussion within the group. (p. 628)

groupthink. The mode of thinking that occurs when the desire for harmony in a decision-making group overrides a realistic appraisal of the alternatives. (p. 629)

H

hair cells. The receptor cells for hearing, located in the cochlea and responsible for changing sound vibrations into neural impulses. (p. 171)

Hall, G. Stanley. (1844–1924) First American man to earn a Ph.D. in psychology; opened first psychology lab in the United States; founded, and was the first president, of the American Psychological Association (APA). (p. 8)

hallucinations. False perceptions that are symptoms of schizophrenia and other serious psychological disorders. (p. 561)

hallucinogens. Psychedelic ("mind-manifesting") drugs, such as LSD, that distort perceptions and evoke sensory images in the absence of sensory input. (p. 419)

Harlow, Harry. (1906–1981) Psychologist who researched the relationship of body contact and nourishment to attachment, using infant monkeys and artificial mothers. (p. 69)

health psychology. A subfield of psychology that focuses on how stress affects our well-being and our health. (p. 245)

heritability. The proportion of variation among individuals that we can attribute to genes. (p. 43)

hertz (Hz). A measure of the number of sound wave peaks per second, or frequency, of a sound wave. Hertz determine the pitch of a sound. (p. 169)

heuristic. A rule-of-thumb problem-solving strategy that makes a solution more likely and efficient but does not guarantee a solution. (p. 434)

hierarchy of needs. Maslow's pyramid of human needs, beginning at the base with physiological needs and proceeding through safety needs and then to psychological needs. Higher-level needs won't become active until lower-level needs have been satisfied. (p. 213)

Hilgard, Ernest. (1904–2001) Pioneering hypnosis researcher and an advocate of the divided consciousness theory of hypnosis. (p. 398)

hippocampus. A neural center located in the limbic system; it helps process new memories for permanent storage. (p. 145)

homeostasis. A tendency to maintain a balanced or constant internal state; the regulation of any aspect of body chemistry, such as blood glucose, around a particular level. (p. 210)

hormone. Chemical messengers produced by the endocrine glands and circulated in the blood. (p. 133)

Horney, Karen. (1885–1952) Neo-Freudian who found psychoanalysis negatively biased toward women and believed cultural variables are the foundation of personality development. (p. 487)

hue. The color of light; determined by the wavelength of light energy. (p. 162)

humanistic psychology. A perspective that focuses on the study of conscious experience, the individual's freedom to choose, and the capacity for personal growth. (pp. 6, 489)

hypnosis. A social interaction in which one person (the hypnotist) makes suggestions about perceptions, feelings, thoughts, or behaviors, and another person (the subject) follows those suggestions. (p. 396)

hypnotic induction. The process in which a hypnotist creates a state of hypnosis in a subject, generally by voicing a series of suggestions. (p. 398)

hypochondriasis. A somatoform disorder characterized by imagined symptoms of illness. (p. 558)

hypothalamus [hi-po-THAL-uh-muss]. A neural structure lying below the thalamus; it directs maintenance activities such as eating, drinking, and body temperature and is linked to emotion. (p. 144)

hypothesis. An investigator's testable prediction about the outcome of research. (p. 24)

I

id. According to Freud, the part of personality that consists of unconscious, psychic energy and strives to satisfy basic sexual and aggressive drives. The id operates on the *pleasure principle,* demanding immediate gratification. (p. 482)

identical twins. Twins who develop from a single fertilized egg that splits in two, creating two genetically identical organisms. (p. 42)

identity. One's sense of self; according to Erikson, the adolescent's task is to solidify a sense of self by testing and integrating various roles. (p. 89)

image. A mental picture. (p. 450)

implicit memory. Memory of skills and procedures, like how to walk, that are retrieved without conscious recollection. (p. 348)

imprinting. The process by which certain animals form attachments during a critical period very early in life. (p. 70)

independent variable (IV). The research variable that a researcher actively manipulates, and if the hypothesis is correct, will cause a change in the dependent variable. (p. 25)

individualism. Cultural style that places personal goals or needs ahead of group goals or needs and defines identity in terms of personal attributes rather than group identification. (pp. 48, 658)

inferential statistics. Statistics that can be used to make a decision or reach a conclusion about data. (p. A-12)

inferiority complex. According to Alfred Adler, a condition that comes from being unable to compensate for normal inferiority feelings. (p. 486)

infradian (in-FRAY-dee-un) rhythms. Biological rhythms that occur once a month or once a season. (p. 378)

ingroup. "Us"—people with whom one shares a common identity. (p. 644)

ingroup bias. The tendency to favor one's own group. (p. 644)

inhibitory effect. A neurotransmitter effect that makes it less likely that a receiving neuron will generate an action potential (impulse). (p. 126)

insight. The sudden realization (Aha!) of the solution to a problem. (p. 434)

insomnia. Recurring problems in falling asleep or staying asleep. (p. 389)

instinct. A complex, unlearned behavior that is rigidly patterned throughout a species. (p. 208)

intelligence. The ability to learn from experience, solve problems, and use knowledge to adapt to new situations. (p. 456)

intelligence quotient (IQ). The number that results from Terman and Stern's formula for computing the level of a

G-9

person's intelligence: mental age (MA) divided by chronological age (CA) multiplied by 100. (p. 461)

internal locus of control. The perception that you control your own fate. (p. 508)

interneurons. Nerve cells in the brain and spinal cord responsible for processing information related to sensory input and motor output. (p. 127)

interpretation. In psychoanalysis, the analyst's noting of supposed dream meanings, resistance's, and other significant behaviors in order to promote insight. (p. 575)

intimacy. In Erikson's theory, the ability to form close, loving, open relationships; a primary task in early adulthood. (p. 91)

intrinsic motivation. A desire to perform a behavior for its own sake and to be effective. (p. 212)

iris. A ring of muscle tissue that forms the colored portion of the eye; regulates the size of the pupil, a hole in the center of the iris, to admit the proper amount of light to the eye. (p. 164)

J

James, William. (1842–1910) First American psychologist and author of the first psychology textbook, who believed our awareness of physiological responses leads to our experience of emotion (*see James-Lange theory*). (pp. 5, 228)

James-Lange theory. The theory that our experience of emotion is our awareness of our physiological responses to an emotion-arousing stimulus. (p. 228)

Jung, Carl. (1875–1961) Neo-Freudian who believed that humans share a *collective unconscious*. (p. 486)

just-world phenomenon. The tendency to believe that people get what they deserve and deserve what they get. (p. 646)

K

Kahneman, Daniel. (1934–) Psychologist who, along with Amos Tversky, conducted research to discover factors that influence human judgment and decision making. He won the Nobel prize for this work in 2002. (p. 438)

kinesthetic sense. The system for sensing the position and movement of individual body parts. (p. 176)

Kohlberg, Lawrence. (1927–1987) Created a three-stage theory of moral development. (p. 85)

L

Lange, Carl. (1834–1900) Danish physiologist who proposed a theory of emotion similar to, and at about the same time as, William James' theory that our awareness of physiological responses leads to our experiences of emotion (*see James-Lange theory*). (p. 228)

language. Our spoken, written, or gestured words and the ways we combine them to communicate meaning. (p. 441)

Latané, Bibb. (1937–) Psychologist who, with John Darley, researched the circumstances that determine when a bystander will intervene on behalf of another person. (p. 641)

latent learning. Learning that occurs but is not apparent until the learner has an incentive to demonstrate it. (p. 316)

Lazarus, Richard. (1922–) American psychologist who concluded that some emotional responses do not require conscious thought. (p. 231)

learned helplessness. The hopelessness and passive resignation an animal or human learns when unable to avoid repeated bad events. (p. 509)

learning. A relatively permanent change in behavior due to experience. (p. 281)

lens. A transparent structure behind the pupil in the eye; the thickness of the lens changes to focus images on the retina. (p. 164)

limbic system. A ring of structures at the border of the brainstem and cerebral cortex; it helps regulate important functions such as memory, fear, aggression, hunger, and thirst. Includes the hypothalamus, hippocampus, and amygdala. (p. 144)

linguistic relativity hypothesis. Benjamin Whorf's hypothesis that language determines the way we think. (p. 449)

lobotomy. A now-rare form of psychosurgery once used to try to calm uncontrollably emotional or violent patients. The procedure cut the nerves that connect the frontal lobes of the brain to the deeper emotional centers. (p. 606)

locus of control. A person's perception of the source of control over fate or what happens in life. People with an internal locus of control believe they control their fate through their behavior. People with an external locus of control believe their fate is controlled by external circumstances. (p. 662)

Loftus, Elizabeth. (1944–) University of California, Irvine, psychologist whose research established the constructed nature of memory. (p. 367)

longitudinal fissure. The long crack running all the way from the front to the back of the cerebral cortex, separating the left and right hemispheres. (p. 145)

longitudinal study. A research technique that studies the same group of individuals over a long period of time. (p. 23)

long-term memory. The relatively permanent and limitless storehouse of the memory system. (p. 345)

long-term potentiation. An increase in a synapse's firing efficiency. Believed to be the neural basis of learning and memory. (p. 347)

Lorenz, Konrad. (1903–1989) Researcher who focused on critical attachment periods in baby birds, a concept he called *imprinting.* (p. 70)

LSD (lysergic acid diethylamide). Powerful hallucinogenic drug; also known as *acid.* (p. 420)

M

magnetic resonance imaging (MRI). A technique that uses magnetic fields and radio waves to produce computer-generated images that distinguish among different types of soft tissue; allows us to see structures within the brain. (p. 143)

major depressive disorder. A mood disorder in which a person, for no apparent reason, experiences at least two weeks of depressed moods, diminished interest in activities, and other symptoms such as feelings of worthlessness. (p. 542)

marijuana. Leaves, stems, resin, and flowers from the hemp plant that when smoked, lower inhibitions and produce feelings of relaxation and mild euphoria. (p. 421)

Maslow, Abraham. (1908–1970) Humanistic psychologist who proposed a hierarchy of needs, with self-actualization as the ultimate psychological need. (pp. 6, 213, 490)

massed rehearsal. Putting all rehearsal time together in one long session (cramming). (p. 339)

Matsumoto, David. (1959–) Psychologist and internationally known expert on the study of cross-cultural psychology. (p. 657)

maturation. Biological growth processes that enable orderly changes in behavior, relatively uninfluenced by experience. (p. 61)

mean. The arithmetic average of a distribution, obtained by adding the scores and then dividing by the number of scores. (p. A-5)

median. The middle score in a ranked distribution; half the scores are above it and half are below it. (p. A-5)

medical model. The concept that diseases have physical causes that can be diagnosed, treated, and, in most cases, cured. When applied to psychological disorders, the medical model assumes that these "mental" illnesses can be diagnosed on the basis of their symptoms and cured through therapy, which may include treatment in a psychiatric hospital. (p. 522)

medulla [muh-DUL-uh]. The base of the brainstem; controls life-support functions like heartbeat and breathing. (p. 141)

melatonin. A hormone that helps regulate daily biological rhythms. (p. 383)

menopause. The time of natural cessation of menstruation; also refers to the biological changes a woman experiences as her ability to reproduce declines. (p. 101)

mental age. The chronological age that corresponds to the difficulty level of the questions a child can answer. In Terman and Stern's intelligence quotient (IQ) formula, mental age is abbreviated as MA. (p. 460)

mental set. A tendency to approach a problem in a particular way. Mental set may or may not be helpful in solving a new problem. (p. 435)

mere exposure effect. The phenomenon that repeated exposure to novel stimuli increases liking of them. (p. 635)

method of loci. A mnemonic device in which you associate items you want to remember with imaginary places. (p. 341)

Milgram, Stanley. (1933–1984) Social psychologist who researched obedience to authority. (p. 624)

Minnesota Multiphasic Personality Inventory (MMPI). The most widely researched and clinically used of all personality tests. Originally developed to identify emotional disorders (still considered its most appropriate use), this test is now used for many other screening purposes. (p. 504)

misinformation effect. Incorporating misleading information into one's memory of an event. (p. 367)

mnemonic device. A memory trick or technique. (p. 341)

mode. The most frequently occurring score in a distribution. (p. A-4)

model. The person observed in observational learning. (p. 325)

modeling. The process of observing and imitating a specific behavior. (p. 326)

monocular cues. Depth cues that require the use of only one eye. (p. 187)

morpheme. In language, the smallest unit that carries meaning; may be a word or a part of a word. (p. 442)

morphine. Strong sedative and pain-relieving drug derived from opium. (p. 415)

motivation. A need or desire that energizes and directs behavior. (p. 207)

motor cortex. A brain area at the rear of the frontal lobes that controls voluntary movements. (p. 147)

motor nerves. Nerves that carry information to the muscles and glands from the central nervous system. (p. 127)

Murray, Henry. (1893–1988) Neo-Freudian who first established the concept of achievement motivation and also developed important personality testing tools. (p. 214)

mutation. Random errors in gene replication that lead to a change in the individual's genetic code; the source of all genetic diversity. (p. 41)

N

narcolepsy. A sleep disorder characterized by uncontrollable sleep attacks. The sufferer may lapse directly into REM sleep, often at inopportune times. (p. 390)

naturalistic observation. Observing and recording behavior in naturally occurring situations without trying to manipulate and control the situation. (p. 20)

natural selection. The principle that, among the range of inherited trait variations, those contributing to survival will most likely be passed on to succeeding generations. (p. 42)

negative reinforcement. In operant conditioning, anything that increases the likelihood of a behavior by following it with the *removal* of an undesirable event or state. (p. 303)

neuron. A nerve cell; the basic building block of the nervous system. (pp. 122, 409)

neurotransmitters. Chemical messengers that, when released by a sending neuron, travel across the synapse (the gap between two neurons) and bind to receptor sites on receiving neurons, setting up the next link in the chain of communication within the nervous system. (pp. 125, 410)

nicotine. Behavioral stimulant found in tobacco. (pp. 269, 417)

night terrors. A sleep-related problem characterized by high arousal and an appearance of being terrified; unlike nightmares, night terrors occur during Stage 4 sleep, within 2 or 3 hours of falling asleep, and are seldom remembered. (p. 391)

normal distribution. The symmetrical, bell-shaped curve that describes the distribution of many physical and psychological variables. Most scores fall near the mean, with fewer and fewer scores at the extremes. (p. A-8)

norms. Understood rules for accepted and expected behavior; norms prescribe "proper" behavior. (p. 48)

N-REM sleep (non–rapid eye movement sleep). The period of sleep in which sleep Stages 1 through 4 occur; not characterized by eye movement or vivid dreams. (p. 385)

O

obedience. The tendency to comply with orders, implied or real, from someone perceived as an authority. (p. 624)

object permanence. The awareness that things continue to exist even when you cannot see or hear them. (p. 65)

observational learning. Learning by observing others. (p. 325)

obsessive-compulsive disorder. Characterized by unwanted, repetitive thoughts and actions. (p. 535)

occipital [ahk-SIP-uh-tuhl] lobes. The portion of the cerebral cortex lying at the back of the head; includes the visual processing areas. (p. 147)

olfactory cells. The chemical receptor cells for smell, located in the nasal passages. (p. 174)

operant conditioning. A type of learning in which the frequency of a behavior depends on the consequence that follows that behavior. (p. 300)

operational definition. A specification of the exact procedures used to make a variable specific and measurable for research purposes. (p. 24)

opiates. Opium and its derivatives, such as morphine and heroin; they depress neural activity, temporarily lessening pain and anxiety. (p. 415)

opponent-process theory. Theory of color vision that says color is processed in opponent pairs (red-green, yellow-blue, and black-white). Light that stimulates one half of the pair inhibits the other half. (p. 168)

optic nerve. The nerve that carries visual information from the eye to the occipital lobes of the brain. (p. 166)

ossicles (hammer, anvil, and stirrup). Three tiny bones that transfer sound waves from the eardrum to the cochlea. (p. 171)

outgroup. "Them"—those perceived as different or apart from "us." (p. 644)

oval window. The point on the surface of the cochlea which receives sound vibrations from the three tiny bones of the middle ear. (p. 171)

overconfidence. The tendency to be more accurate than correct when estimating the accuracy of one's beliefs and judgments. (p. 439)

overjustification effect. The effect of promising a reward for doing what one already likes to do. The reward may lessen and replace the person's original, natural motivation, so that the behavior stops if the reward is eliminated. (p. 317)

overlearning. Rehearsal of information beyond the point where it has been learned. Overlearning is an effective strategy for improving memory. (p. 337)

P

panic disorder. Characterized by sudden bouts of intense, unexplained panic. (p. 535)

parasympathetic division. The part of the autonomic nervous system that calms the body. (p. 132)

parietal [puh-RYE-uh-tuhl] lobes. The portion of the cerebral cortex lying at the top of the head and toward the rear; includes the somatosensory cortex and general association areas used for processing information. (p. 146)

partial reinforcement schedule. In operant conditioning, a schedule of reinforcement follows that rewards only some correct responses. (p. 312)

participant bias. A tendency for reseach participants to respond in a certain way because they know they are being observed or they believe they know what the researcher wants. (p. 19)

passionate love. An aroused state of intense positive absorption in another, usually present at the beginning of a love relationship. (p. 638)

Pavlov, Ivan. (1849–1936) Russian physiologist famous for the discovery of classical conditioning. (pp. 6, 286)

peg-word system. A mnemonic device in which you associate items you want to remember with a list of peg words you have already memorized. (p. 341)

percentage. A comparative statistic that compares a score to a perfect score, assuming the perfect score is 100 points. (p. A-9)

percentile rank. A comparative statistic that compares a score to other scores, assuming there are a hundred scores altogether. The percentile rank indicates how many of the hundred scores are at or below a particular score. (p. A-10)

perception. The process of organizing and interpreting sensory information. (pp. 157, 183)

perceptual constancy. Perceiving the size, shape, and lightness of an object as unchanging, even as the retinal image of the object changes. (p. 194)

perceptual set. A mental predisposition to perceive something one way and not another. (p. 196)

peripheral nervous system (PNS). The sensory and motor nerves that connect the central nervous system to the rest of the body. (p. 131)

permastore memory. Long-term memories that are especially resistant to forgetting and are likely to last a lifetime. (p. 361)

permissive parenting. Style of parenting marked by submitting to children's desires, making few demands, and using little punishment. (p. 73)

personality. An individual's characteristic pattern of thinking, feeling, and acting. (pp. 479, 499)

personality disorders. Psychological disorders characterized by inflexible and lasting behavior patterns that disrupt social functioning. (p. 565)

personality inventories. Questionnaires (often with true-false or agree-disagree items) on which people respond to items designed to gauge a wide range of feelings and behaviors; used to assess selected personality traits. (p. 503)

phobia. Characterized by disruptive, irrational fears of objects or situations. (p. 535)

phoneme. In spoken language, the smallest distinctive sound unit. (p. 442)

Piaget, Jean. (1896–1890) Pioneer in the study of developmental psychology; introduced a stage theory of cognitive development that led to a better understanding of children's thought processes. (pp. 6, 63, 85)

Pinel, Philippe. (1745–1826) French physician who worked to reform the treatment of people with mental disorders. (p. 521)

pitch. A sound's highness or lowness, which depends on the frequency of the sound wave. (p. 169)

pituitary gland. The endocrine system's highly influential "master gland" that, in conjunction with the brain, controls the other endocrine glands. (p. 133)

placebo. A nonactive substance or condition that may be administered instead of a drug or active agent to see if the drug has an effect beyond the expectations produced by taking it. (p. 29)

plasticity. The brain's capacity for modification, as evident in brain reorganization following damage (especially in children). (p. 149)

polygraph. A machine, commonly used in attempts to detect lies, that measures several physiological responses (such as perspiration, heart rate, blood pressure, and breathing changes) accompanying emotion. (p. 234)

population. All the cases in a group, from which samples may be drawn for a study. (p. 23)

positive psychology. A movement in psychology that focuses on the study of optimal human functioning and the factors that allow individuals and communities to thrive. (pp. 12, 263, 510)

positive reinforcement. In operant conditioning, anything that increases the likelihood of a behavior by following it with a desirable event or state. (p. 303)

positron emission tomography (PET) scan. A visual display of brain activity that detects where a radioactive form of glucose (blood sugar) goes while the brain performs a given task. (p. 143)

posthypnotic amnesia. The supposed inability to remember what happened during hypnosis because the hypnotist suggests that the subject will have no memory of that period of time. (p. 401)

posthypnotic suggestion. A suggestion, made during a hypnosis session, that the subject will carry out when no longer hypnotized. (p. 400)

posttraumatic stress disorder. Characterized by reliving a severely upsetting event in unwanted recurring memories and dreams. (p. 535)

preconscious. According to Freud, a region of the mind holding information that is not conscious but is retrievable into conscious awareness. (p. 481)

prejudice. An unjustifiable (and usually negative) attitude toward a group and its members. Prejudice generally involves stereotyped beliefs, negative feelings, and a predisposition to discriminatory action. (p. 642)

preoperational stage. In Piaget's theory, the stage (from about 2 to 6 or 7 years of age) during which a child learns to use language but does not yet comprehend the mental operations of concrete logic. (p. 66)

primary reinforcement. Something that is naturally reinforcing, such as food (if you are hungry), warmth (if you are cold), and water (if you are thirsty). (p. 307)

primary sex characteristics. The body structures (ovaries, testes, and external genitalia) that make sexual reproduction possible. (p. 83)

proactive interference. The disruptive effect of earlier learning on the recall of recently stored information. (p. 363)

projective tests. A personality test, such as the Rorschach or TAT, that provides ambiguous stimuli to trigger projection of one's inner thoughts and feelings. (p. 487)

prosocial behavior. Positive, constructive, helpful behavior. (p. 328)

Prosser, Inez Beverly. (1897–1934) First African-American woman to receive a Ph.D. in psychology. (p. 8)

prototype. A typical best example incorporating the major features of a concept. (p. 431)

pseudoscientific claim. Any assertion that is not based on science, even though in some circumstances, attempts are made to appear scientific. (p. 378)

psychoactive drug. A chemical substance that alters perceptions, mood, or behavior. (p. 408)

psychoanalysis. Freud's theory of personality; also, a therapeutic technique that attempts to provide insight into one's thoughts and actions by exposing and interpreting the underlying unconscious motives and conflicts. (pp. 480, 574)

psychoanalytic perspective. School of thought that focuses on how behavior springs from unconscious drives and conflicts; also called *psychodynamic perspective.* (p. 5)

psychodynamic perspective. A view of personality that retains some aspects of Freudian theory (such as the importance of unconscious thought processes) but is less likely to see unresolved childhood conflicts as a source of personality development. (p. 480)

psychological disorder. A "harmful dysfunction" in which behaviors are judged maladaptive, unjustifiable, disturbing, and atypical. (p. 519)

psychological perspective. A particualr view of behavior and/or mental processes that has grown into a movement. (p. 9)

psychology. The scientific study of behavior and mental processes. (p. 4)

psychosexual stages. The childhood stages of development (oral, anal, phallic, latency, genital) during which, according to Freud, the id's pleasure-seeking energies focus on different parts of the body. (p. 485)

psychotherapy. An emotionally charged, confiding interaction between a trained therapist and someone who suffers from psychological difficulties. (p. 573)

puberty. The period of sexual maturation, during which a person becomes capable of reproducing. (p. 82)

punishment. Any consequence that *decreases* the likelihood of a behavior. (p. 302)

pupil. The adjustable opening in the center of the iris; controls the amount of light entering the eye. (p. 164)

R

random assignment. Assigning participants to experimental and control groups by chance, thus minimizing preexisting differences among those assigned to different groups. (p. 26)

random sample. A sample that fairly represents a population because each member has an equal chance of inclusion. (p. 23)

range. The difference between the highest and lowest scores in a distribution. (p. A-7)

Rayner, Rosalie. (1900–1935) Graduate student of John Watson and co-researcher for the famous Little Albert demonstration of classically conditioned emotion. (p. 290)

recall. A measure of memory in which you must retrieve information you learned earlier, as on a fill-in-the-blank test. (p. 350)

receptor cells. Cells present in every sensory system to change (transduce) some other form of energy into neural impulses that the brain can process. (pp. 126, 165)

reciprocal determinism. The interaction between personality and environmental factors. (p. 507)

recognition. A measure of memory in which you must *identify* items you learned earlier, as on a multiple-choice test. (p. 350)

refractory period. The "recharging phase" when a neuron, after firing, cannot generate another action potential. (p. 123)

rehearsal. The conscious repetition of information. (p. 336)

reinforcement. Any consequence that *increases* the likelihood of a behavior. (p. 302)

reliability. The extent to which a test yields consistent results. (pp. 468, 503)

REM sleep. Rapid eye movement sleep; a recurring sleep stage during which vivid dreams commonly occur. Also known as *paradoxical sleep,* because muscles are relaxed but other body systems are active. (p. 386)

replication. Repeating a research study to see whether the results can be reliably reproduced. Unless a study can be replicated, the results are likely to be a fluke occurrence. (p. 31)

repression. In Sigmund Freud's psychoanalytic theory, the process of moving anxiety-producing memories to the unconscious. (p. 364)

Rescorla, Robert. (1940–) Developed, along with colleague Allan Wagner, a new theory that emphasized the importance of cognitive processes in classical conditioning. (p. 293)

researcher bias. A tendency for researchers to engage in behaviors and selectively notice evidence that supports their hypotheses or expectations. (p. 19)

resistance. In psychoanalysis, the blocking from consciousness of anxiety-laden material. (p. 575)

response. Any behavior or action. (p. 282)

resting potential. The state of a neuron when it is at rest and capable of generating an action potential. (p. 123)

reticular formation. A nerve network in the brainstem that plays an important role in controlling wakefulness and arousal. (p. 141)

retina. The light-sensitive surface at the back of the eyeball; contains rod and cone cells that convert light energy to nerve impulses. (p. 165)

retinal disparity. A binocular depth cue resulting from slightly different images produced by the separation of the retinas in the left and right eyes. (p. 187)

retrieval. The process of getting information out of memory storage. The third and final stage of the information processing model of memory. (pp. 335, 359)

retroactive interference. The disruptive effect of new learning on the recall of previously stored information. (p. 363)

rods. Visual receptor cells located in the retina. Rods detect only black, white, and gray, but they respond in less light than the color-detecting cone cells. (p. 165)

Rogers, Carl. (1902–1987) Humanistic psychologist who developed client-centered therapy and stressed the importance of acceptance, genuineness, and empathy in fostering human growth. (pp. 6, 491, 578)

rooting reflex. A baby's tendency, when touched on the cheek, to open the mouth and search for the nipple; this is an automatic, unlearned response. (p. 59)

Rorschach inkblot test. The most widely used projective test, a set of 10 inkblots, designed by Hermann Rorschach; seeks to identify people's inner feelings by analyzing their interpretations of the blots. (p. 488)

S

scapegoat theory. The theory that prejudice provides an outlet for anger by providing someone to blame. (p. 645)

Schachter, Stanley. (1922–1997) American psychologist who, along with Jerome Singer, concluded that emotion requires a cognitive label of physiological arousal (*see two-factor theory*). (p. 230)

schemas. Concepts or mental frameworks that organize and interpret information. (pp. 63, 196)

schizophrenia. A group of severe disorders characterized by disorganized and delusional thinking, disturbed perceptions, and inappropriate emotions and actions. (p. 560)

G-15

scientific method. A method of learning about the world through the application of critical thinking and tools such as observation, experimentation, and statistical analysis. (p. 17)

secondary reinforcement. Something that you have learned to value, like money. (p. 307)

secondary sex characteristics. Nonreproductive sexual characteristics, such as female breasts and hips, male voice quality, and body hair. (p. 83)

selective attention. Focusing conscious awareness on a particular stimulus to the exclusion of others, like being so lost in a book that you don't notice something else happening in the room. (p. 161)

self-actualization. According to Abraham Maslow, the ultimate psychological need that arises after basic physical and psychological needs are met and self-esteem is achieved; the motivation to fulfill one's potential. (pp. 213, 490)

self-concept. All our thoughts and feelings about ourselves, in answer to the question, "Who am I?" (p. 492)

self-disclosure. Revealing intimate aspects of oneself to others. (p. 639)

self-fulfilling prophecy. Occurs when one person's belief about others leads one to act in ways that induce the others to appear to confirm the belief. (p. 630)

self-reference effect. The enhanced semantic encoding of information that is personally relevant. (p. 339)

Seligman, Martin. (1942–) American psychologist and proponent of positive psychology. (pp. 258, 509)

Selye, Hans. (1907–1982) Psychologist who researched a recurring response to stress that he called the general adaptation syndrome. (p. 246)

semantic encoding. The encoding of meaning. (p. 339)

senile dementia. The mental disintegration that accompanies alcoholism, tumor, stroke, aging, and most often, Alzheimer's disease. (p. 103)

sensation. The process by which our sensory systems (eyes, ears, and other sensory organs) and nervous system receive stimuli from our environment. (p. 157)

sensorimotor stage. In Piaget's theory, the stage (from birth to about 2 years of age) during which infants know the world mostly in terms of their sensory impressions and motor activities. (p. 64)

sensory adaptation. Diminished sensitivity as a result of constant stimulation. (p. 160)

sensory memory. The brief, initial coding of sensory information in the memory system. (p. 344)

sensory nerves. Nerves that carry information from the sense receptors to the central nervous system. (p. 127)

serial position effect. Our tendency to recall best the first and last items in a list. (p. 338)

serotonin [sare-oh-TON-in]. A neurotransmitter that affects hunger, sleep, arousal, and mood; serotonin appears in lower than normal levels in depressed persons. (p. 129)

set point. The point at which an individual's "weight thermostat" is supposedly set. When the body falls below this weight, increased hunger and a lowered metabolic rate may act to restore the lost weight. (pp. 218, 272)

sexual orientation. An enduring sexual attraction toward members of either one's own gender (homosexual orientation) or the other gender (heterosexual orientation). (p. 84)

shaping. Reinforcement of behaviors that are more and more similar to the one you want to occur. Shaping is the operant technique used to establish new behaviors. (p. 310)

Sherif, Muzafer. (1906–1988). Psychologist who studied the impact of shared goals on cooperation. (p. 651)

short-term memory. Conscious, activated memory that holds about seven chunks of information briefly before the information is stored more permanently or forgotten. Also called *working memory.* (p. 344)

signal detection theory. Set of formulas and principles that predict when we will detect the presence of a faint stimulus ("signal") amid background stimulation ("noise"). Detection depends on qualities of the stimulus, the environment, and the person who is detecting. (p. 159)

skewed. Distorted; not evenly distributed around the mean. (p. A-5)

Skinner, B. F. (1904–1990) American psychologist who studied the role of responses in learning; developed the fundamental principles and techniques of operant conditioning and devised ways to apply them in the real world. (pp. 6, 301, 445)

sleep apnea. A sleep disorder characterized by temporary cessations of breathing during sleep and consequent momentary reawakenings. (p. 390)

social clock. The culturally preferred timing of social events such as marriage, parenthood, and retirement. (p. 99)

social-cognitive perspective. Perspective stating that understanding personality involves considering situation and thoughts before, during, and after an event. (p. 499)

social-cultural perspective. School of thought that focuses on how thinking or behavior changes in different contexts or situations. (p. 9)

social facilitation. Improved performance of tasks in the presence of others; occurs with simple or well-learned tasks but not with tasks that are difficult or not yet learned. (p. 626)

social influence theory. The theory that powerful social influences can produce a state of hypnosis. (p. 397)

social leadership. Group-oriented leadership that builds teamwork, mediates conflict, and offers support. (p. 216)

social loafing. The tendency for people in a group to exert less effort when pooling their efforts toward attaining a common goal than when individually accountable. (p. 627)

social psychology. The scientific study of how we think about, influence, and relate to one another. (p. 613)

soma. The cell body of a neuron, which contains the nucleus and other parts that keep the cell healthy. (p. 122)

somatic nervous system. The division of the peripheral nervous system that controls the body's skeletal muscles. (p. 131)

somatoform disorders. Psychological disorders in which the symptoms take a somatic (bodily) form without apparent physical cause. (p. 558)

somatosensory cortex. A brain area at the front of the parietal lobes that registers and processes body sensations. (p. 148)

somnambulism. Sleepwalking, which usually starts in the deeper stages of N-REM sleep. The sleepwalker can walk and talk and is able to see but rarely has any memory of the event. (p. 391)

spacing effect. The tendency for distributed practice to yield better retention than is achieved through massed practice. (p. 339)

Spearman, Charles. (1863–1945) Theorized that a general intelligence factor, *g*, underlies other, more specific aspects of intelligence. (p. 459)

spindles. Bursts of brain-wave activity that characterize Stage 2 of N-REM sleep. (p. 385)

spontaneous recovery. The reappearance, after a rest period, of an extinguished conditioned response. (p. 285)

standard deviation. A computed measure of how much scores vary around the mean score; the higher the standard deviation, the more spread out scores are. (p. A-7)

Stanford-Binet intelligence test. The widely used American revision (by Terman at Stanford University) of Binet's original test. (p. 461)

state-dependent memory. The enhanced ability to retrieve information where you are in the same physical and emotional state you were in when you encoded the information. (p. 352)

statistical significance. A statistical statement of how likely it is that a result occurred by chance alone. (p. A-12)

stereotype. A generalized (sometimes accurate but often overgeneralized) belief about a group of people. (p. 642)

Sternberg, Robert. (1949–) Author of a contemporary theory of multiple intelligences consisting of analytical, creative, and practical intelligence. (p. 457)

stimulants. Drugs (such as caffeine, nicotine, and the more powerful amphetamines and cocaine) that excite neural activity and speed up body functions. (p. 416)

stimulus. Anything in the environment that one can respond to. (p. 281)

storage. The retention of encoded information over time. The second stage of the information processing model of memory. (pp. 335, 359)

stranger anxiety. The fear of strangers that infants commonly display, beginning by about 8 months of age. (p. 69)

stress. The process by which we perceive and respond to certain events, called *stressors,* that we appraise as threatening or challenging. (p. 245)

structuralism. Theory that analyzed the basic elements of thoughts and sensations to determine the structure of conscience experience. (p. 4)

Sumner, Francis Cecil. (1895–1954) First African-American man to receive a Ph.D. in psychology. (p. 8)

superego. The part of personality that, according to Freud, represents internalized ideals and provides standards for judgment (the conscience) and for future aspirations. (p. 482)

superordinate goals. Shared goals that override differences among people and require their cooperation. (p. 651)

survey method. A research technique designed to discover the self-reported attitudes or behaviors of a sample of people through the use of questionnaires or interviews. (p. 22)

sympathetic division. The part of the autonomic nervous system that arouses the body to deal with perceived threats. (p. 132)

synapse. The tiny, fluid-filled gap between the tip of the sending neuron and the receptor site on the receiving neuron. The tiny gap at this junction is called the synaptic *gap* or *cleft.* (pp. 125, 410)

systematic desensitization. A type of counterconditioning that associates a pleasant relaxed state with gradually increasing anxiety-triggering stimuli. Commonly used to treat phobias. (p. 580)

T

task leadership. Goal-oriented leadership that sets standards, organizes work, and focuses attention. (p. 216)

temperament. A person's characteristic emotional reactivity and intensity. (p. 60)

temporal lobes. The portion of the cerebral cortex lying roughly above the ears; includes the auditory (hearing) areas. (p. 147)

teratogens. Substances that cross the placental barrier and prevent the fetus from developing normally. (p. 58)

Terman, Lewis. (1877–1956) Adapted Binet's tests for use in the United States as the Stanford-Binet intelligence test, which reported intelligence as a calculated IQ score. (p. 461)

thalamus [THAL-uh-muss]. The brain's sensory switchboard, located on top of the brainstem; it directs messages to the sensory receiving areas in the cortex. (p. 141)

Thematic Apperception Test (TAT). A projective test in which people express their inner feelings and interests through the stories they make up about ambiguous scenes. (p. 487)

Thorndike, Edward. (1874–1949) Author of the law of effect, the basic principle that forms the basis of operant conditioning. (p. 301)

thyroid gland. Endocrine gland that helps regulate energy level in the body. (p. 134)

Titchener, E. B. (1867–1927) Founder of structuralism. (p. 4)

token economy. An operant conditioning procedure that attempts to modify behavior by giving rewards for desired behaviors. These tokens can be exchanged for various privileges or treats. (p. 583)

tolerance. Reduced responsiveness to a drug, prompting the user to increase dosage to achieve effects previously obtained by lower doses. (p. 409)

top-down processing. Information processing that focuses on our expectations and experiences in interpreting incoming sensory information. (p. 157)

trait. A characteristic pattern of behavior or a disposition to feel and act, as assessed by self-report inventories and peer reports. (p. 499)

transference. In psychoanalysis, the patient's transfer to the analyst of emotions (such as love or hatred) linked with other relationships. (p. 576)

trichromatic (three-color) theory. Theory of color vision that says cones are "tuned" to detect red, green, or blue light. Various levels of stimulation in these three kinds of cones enable us to identify millions of different color combinations. (p. 167)

Tversky, Amos. (1937–1996) Psychologist who, along with Daniel Kahneman, conducted research to discover factors that influence human judgment and decision making. (p. 438)

two-factor theory. The theory that to experience emotion one must (1) be physically aroused, and (2) cognitively label the arousal. (p. 230)

Type A. Friedman and Rosenman's term for competitive, hard-driving, impatient, verbally aggressive, and anger-prone people. (p. 252)

Type B. Friedman and Rosenman's term for easygoing, relaxed people. (p. 252)

U

ultradian (ul-TRAY-dee-un) rhythms. Biological rhythms that occur more than once each day. (p. 378)

unconditional positive regard. According to Carl Rogers, an attitude of total acceptance toward another person. (p. 491)

unconditioned response (UCR). In classical conditioning, the automatic response to the unconditioned stimulus. (p. 284)

unconditioned stimulus (UCS). In classical conditioning, a stimulus that triggers a response automatically and reflexively. (p. 283)

unconscious. According to Freud, a region of the mind that is a reservoir of mostly unacceptable thoughts, wishes, feelings, and memories. (p. 481)

V

validity. The extent to which a test measures or predicts what it is supposed to test. (pp. 469, 503)

variable-interval reinforcement schedule. In operant conditioning, a partial reinforcement schedule that rewards the first correct response after an unpredictable amount of time. (p. 314)

variable-ratio reinforcement schedule. In operant conditioning, a partial reinforcement schedule that rewards an unpredictable number of correct responses. (p. 315)

vestibular sense. The system for sensing body orientation and balance, located in the semicircular canals of the inner ear. (p. 177)

visual cliff. A laboratory device for testing depth perception in infants and young animals. (p. 186)

W

Washburn, Margaret Floy. (1871–1930) First woman to receive a Ph.D. in psychology. (p. 8)

Watson, John B. (1878–1958) Founder of behaviorism, the view that psychology should restrict its efforts to studying observable behaviors, not mental processes. (pp. 6, 283)

Wechsler, David. (1896–1981) Developer of the Wechsler intelligence scales, which have become the most widely used individual intelligence tests in the United States. These were the first tests to report scores for both verbal and performance intelligence. (p. 462)

Wechsler intelligence scales. A series of intelligence tests tailored to three different age groups (adults, children, and preschoolers); currently the most widely used individual intelligence tests in the United States. (p. 462)

wellness. The common result of a healthy lifestyle and healthy attitudes. (p. 258)

Wernicke's [ver-NIC-keys] area. A brain area involved in language comprehension and expression; usually in the left temporal lobe. (p. 149)

Whorf, Benjamin. (1897–1941) Linguist who developed the linguistic relativity hypothesis—the idea that our language structures the way we can think about the world. (p. 449)

withdrawal. The discomfort and distress that follow when a person who is dependent on a drug discontinues the use of that drug. (pp. 269, 409)

Wundt, Wilhelm. (1832–1920) Founder of modern psychology. (p. 4)

Y

Yerkes-Dodson law. The theory that a degree of psychological arousal helps performance, but only up to a certain point. (p. 210)

Z

Zajonc, Robert. (1923–) American psychologist who concluded that some emotional reactions involve no deliberate thinking and that cognition is not always necessary for emotion. (p. 230)

zygote. The fertilized egg; it enters a two-week period of rapid cell division and develops into an embryo. (p. 58)

Glosario de términos y personas clave

A

absolute threshold/umbral absoluto. Intensidad mínima requerida para detectar un estímulo la mitad de las veces. (pág. 158)

accommodation/acomodación. Acción de adaptar el entendimiento que se posee (esquemas) con el propósito de incorporar nueva información. (pág. 63)

acetylcholine [ah-seat-el-KO-leen]/acetilcolina. Neurotransmisor que produce contracción muscular e interviene en el aprendizaje y la memoria. (pág. 128).

achievement motivation/motivación de logro. Deseo de lograr algo importante, con respecto a cosas, personas o ideas; deseo de lograr un alto estándar. (pág. 214)

achievement tests/pruebas de rendimiento. Pruebas destinadas a medir los logros de la persona que las toma. (pág. 468)

acquisition/adquisición. Según el condicionamiento clásico, proceso mediante el cual se adquiere una respuesta aprendida. (pág. 284)

action potential/potencial de acción. Impulso nervioso; corriente eléctrica breve que pasa por el axón de una neurona. (pág. 123)

active listening/escuchar activamente. Escuchar compenetradamente, haciendo eco, repitiendo y clarificando lo que dice otra persona. Una de las características de la terapia centrada en el cliente, propuesta por Rogers. (pág. 578)

Adler, Alfred. (1870–1937) Neofreudiano que sostenía que las tensiones sociales son más importantes para el desarrollo de la personalidad que las tensiones sexuales. (pág. 486)

adolescence/adolescencia. Etapa de transición de la niñez a la edad adulta, que se extiende desde la pubertad hasta la independencia del individuo. (pág. 81)

adrenal glands/glándulas suprarrenales. Glándulas endocrinas que contribuyen a la estimulación del cuerpo cuando hay estrés. (pág. 134)

aggression/agresión. Comportamiento físico o verbal que tiene la intención de causar daño o destruir. (pág. 647)

agonist/agonista. Medicamento que aumenta el efecto de un neurotransmisor. (pág. 128)

algorithm/algoritmo. Estrategia de resolución de problemas que garantiza la solución correcta. (pág. 433)

all-or-none principle/principio de todo o nada. Principio que sostiene que si una neurona transmite un impulso, siempre lo hace con la misma intensidad; todos los potenciales de acción tienen la misma potencia. (pág. 124)

Allport, Gordon. (1897–1967) Psicólogo y teórico de rasgos de la personalidad, nacido en Estados Unidos, que realizó investigaciones basadas en la idea de que cada personalidad es única. (pág. 500)

altruism/altruismo. Consideración desinteresada por el bienestar de los demás. (pág. 640)

Alzheimer's disease/enfermedad de Alzheimer. Trastorno progresivo e irreversible del cerebro, que se caracteriza por el deterioro gradual de la memoria, el razonamiento, el lenguaje y, por último, el funcionamiento físico. (pág. 103)

amphetamines/anfetaminas. Medicamentos que estimulan la actividad nerviosa acelerando las funciones del organismo y los cambios de energía y estados de ánimo asociados con dichos cambios. (pág. 419)

amygdala [ah-MIG-dah-la]/amígdala. Dos conjuntos de fibras nerviosas con forma de almendra que se hallan en el sistema límbico e intervienen en emociones tales como el miedo y el enojo. (pág. 145)

anorexia nervosa/anorexia nerviosa. Trastorno alimenticio en el cual las personas de peso normal (generalmente muchachas adolescentes) padecen de delirios que les hacen pensar que pesan demasiado, se someten a dietas de hambre y llegan a la delgadez extrema y peligrosa (bajando de peso un 15 por ciento o más). (pág. 220)

antagonist/antagonista. Medicamento que bloquea el efecto de un neurotransmisor. (pág. 128)

antianxiety drugs/medicamentos antiansiedad. Categoría de medicamentos que se emplean para tratar a personas que padecen de trastornos de ansiedad o estrés. (pág. 602)

GE-1

antidepressant drugs/medicamentos antidepresivos. Categoría de medicamentos que se emplean principalmente para tratar la depresión grave. (pág. 602)

antipsychotic drugs/medicamentos antipsicóticos. Categoría de medicamentos que se emplean principalmente para tratar la esquizofrenia. (pág. 601)

antisocial behavior/comportamiento antisocial. Conducta negativa, destructiva y poco servicial. (pág. 328)

antisocial personality disorder/trastorno antisocial de la personalidad. Trastorno de personalidad en el cual un individuo (generalmente un hombre) no es consciente de que causa daño y no respeta los derechos de los demás. (pág. 567)

anxiety/ansiedad. Sensación vaga de aprensión o nerviosismo. Es la base de los trastornos de ansiedad. (pág. 534)

applied research/investigación aplicada. Estudio científico que tiene el propósito de resolver problemas prácticos. (pág. 13)

aptitude tests/pruebas de aptitud. Pruebas cuyo propósito es predecir el desempeño futuro de una persona. (pág. 468)

Asch, Solomon. (1907–1996) Psicólogo social que estudió las circunstancias bajo las cuales las personas demuestran conformismo. (pág. 621)

assimilation/asimilación. Interpretación que realiza una persona de una experiencia nueva basándose en esquemas ya existentes. (pág. 63)

attachment/apego. Lazo afectivo con otra persona; los niños pequeños demuestran apego cuando quieren mantenerse cerca de la persona que los cría y se angustian al separarse de dicha persona. (pág. 69)

attitude/actitud. Creencia y sentimiento que predispone a un individuo a responder de una manera en particular a objetos, personas y sucesos. (pág. 617)

attribution theory/teoría de atribución. Teoría según la cual tendemos a dar una explicación casual del comportamiento de una persona, generalmente atribuyéndolo a la situación o la disposición de esa persona. (pág. 614)

auditory canal/conducto auditivo. Apertura por la cual pasan las ondas sonoras para llegar al oído donde son procesadas. Acaba en la membrana timpánica. (pág. 170)

auditory nerve/nervio auditivo. Nervio que transmite la información sonora de los oídos al lóbulo temporal del cerebro. (pág. 172)

authoritarian parenting/crianza autoritaria. Estilo de crianza en el que se imponen reglas y se exige obediencia. (pág. 72)

authoritative parenting/crianza disciplinada. Estilo de crianza en el cual los padres exigen cosas al niño, son receptivos, imponen reglas y las hacen cumplir conversando con el niño acerca de las razones por las que imponen dichas reglas. (pág. 73)

automatic processing/procesamiento automático. Codificación inconsciente de cierta información, tal como el espacio, el tiempo y la frecuencia, que se lleva a cabo sin esfuerzo. (pág. 336)

autonomic [aw-tuh-NAHM-ik] nervous system/sistema nervioso autónomo. División del sistema nervioso periférico que controla las glándulas y los músculos de los órganos (tales como el corazón). Sus subdivisiones son la división simpática (estimulación) y la división parasimpática (relajación). (págs. 131, 232)

availability heuristic/heurística de la disponibilidad. Estimación de la probabilidad de que ocurra un suceso, que se basa en la disponibilidad de dicho suceso en la memoria. A veces tenemos razón y a veces no, al suponer que los sucesos disponibles en la memoria son probables. (pág. 438)

aversive conditioning/condicionamiento aversivo. Tipo de condicionamiento en el que se asocia un estado desagradable (tal como las náuseas) con un comportamiento inapropiado (tal como la ingestión de alcohol). (pág. 582)

axon/axón. Prolongación de una neurona por la que se transmiten los impulsos nerviosos. (pág. 122)

axon terminal/terminal del axón. Extremo de una neurona, en donde se almacenan los neurotransmisores. (pág. 123)

B

Bandura, Albert. (1925–) Psicólogo de origen canadiense y estadounidense; figura principal en el estudio del aprendizaje observacional. También elaboró la perspectiva social-cognitiva de la personalidad, poniendo énfasis en que se debe considerar la situación y los pensamientos del individuo antes, durante y después de ocurrido un suceso. (págs. 326, 505)

barbiturates/barbitúricos. Medicamentos que deprimen la actividad del sistema nervioso central reduciendo la ansiedad, pero que perjudican la memoria y el juicio. (pág. 414)

basal metabolic rate/índice de metabolismo basal. Índice del consumo de energía del cuerpo durante el descanso. (pág. 218)

basic research/investigación básica. Ciencia pura cuya mira es aumentar la base de los conocimientos científicos. (pág. 13)

behavior genetics/genética del comportamiento. Perspectiva dentro de la psicología, que se concentra en el poder relativo y los límites de la genética y las influencias del entorno en el comportamiento, es decir, la forma en que los genes y el entorno determinan las diferencias entre individuos. (págs. 11, 39)

behaviorism/conductismo. Perspectiva según la cual la psicología debe limitarse a estudiar la conducta observable, y no los procesos mentales. (pág. 283)

behaviorist perspective/perspectiva conductual. Corriente de pensamiento que se concentra en la manera de aprender las respuestas observables. (pág. 6)

belief perseverance/perseverancia en las creencias. Empeño en mantener creencias aun después de que un nuevo conocimiento desacredita la base en la que fueron fundadas dichas creencias. (pág. 440)

benzodiazepines/benzodiazapinas. Medicamentos (tales como el Valium) que deprimen la actividad del sistema nervioso central sin la mayoría de los efectos asociados con los barbitúricos. (pág. 415)

Binet, Alfred. (1857–1911) Creador de la primera prueba para clasificar la capacidad de los niños empleando el concepto de la edad mental. (pág. 460)

binocular cues/claves binoculares. Señales de profundidad que requieren el uso de los dos ojos. (pág. 187)

biological perspective/perspectiva biológica. Corriente de pensamiento que se concentra en las estructuras físicas y en las substancias que influencian un comportamiento, pensamiento o sentimiento en particular. (pág. 9)

biological rhythms/ritmos biológicos. Fluctuaciones fisiológicas periódicas. (pág. 378)

bio-psycho-social perspective/perspectiva biopsicosocial. Perspectiva contemporánea que supone que los trastornos psicológicos se producen por la combinación e interacción de factores biológicos, psicológicos y sociales. (pág. 522)

bipolar cells/células bipolares. Células que forman la capa intermedia de la retina. Reúnen la información transmitida por los bastoncillos y los conos y la envían a las células ganglionares. (pág. 166)

bipolar disorder/trastorno bipolar. Trastorno anímico (anteriormente se denominaba *enfermedad maníaco-depresiva*) en el que el individuo oscila entre la desesperanza de la depresión y la excitación extrema y el estado irracionalmente optimista de la manía. (pág. 546)

blind spot/punto ciego. Punto en el cual el nervio óptico pasa por la retina para salir del ojo. La falta de bastoncillos y conos receptores en este lugar produce un pequeño punto ciego. (pág. 166)

body mass index (BMI)/índice de masa corporal (IMC). Peso de una persona en kilogramos (número de libras multiplicado por .45) dividido por su altura al cuadrado en metros (número de pulgadas dividido por 39.4). La guía del gobierno de Estados Unidos recomienda un índice de masa corporal (IMC) por debajo de 25. La Organización Mundial de la Salud y muchos países definen la obesidad con un IMC de 30 o más. (pág. 270)

bottom-up processing/procesamiento del fondo hacia arriba. Procesamiento de la información en bruto que entra por los ojos, los oídos y otros órganos de los sentidos. (pág. 157)

brainstem/tronco cerebral. Parte central y más antigua del cerebro, que comienza en donde la médula espinal se ensancha para entrar en el cráneo. Controla las funciones automáticas de la sobrevivencia. (pág. 140)

Broca's area/área de Broca. Parte del lóbulo frontal del cerebro, generalmente en el hemisferio izquierdo, que dirige los movimientos musculares relacionados con el habla. (pág. 148)

bulimia nervosa/bulimia nerviosa. Trastorno de alimentación que se caracteriza por episodios de ingestión excesiva de alimentos, generalmente de alto contenido calórico, seguidos de vómito, uso de laxantes, ayuno o ejercicios físicos excesivos. (pág. 220)

burnout/agotamiento. Cansancio extremo a nivel físico, emocional y mental, causado por un continuo estrés relacionado con el trabajo. (pág. 248)

bystander effect/comportamiento de transeúnte. Tendencia de un transeúnte a ser menos capaz de prestar ayuda si están presentes otros transeúntes. (pág. 641)

C

caffeine/cafeína. Estimulante que se halla en el café, el chocolate, el té y algunas bebidas gaseosas. (pág. 416)

Calkins, Mary Whiton. (1863–1930) Primera mujer que completó los requisitos del doctorado en psicología; primera mujer elegida presidenta de la American Psychological Association (Asociación estadounidense de psicología). (pág. 8)

Cannon, Walter. (1871–1943) Psicólogo estadounidense que, junto con Philip Bard, concluyó que la estimulación fisiológica y la experiencia emocional ocurren simultáneamente (véase la *teoría de Cannon-Bard*). (págs. 228, 246)

Cannon-Bard theory/teoría de Cannon-Bard. Teoría según la cual un estímulo que evoca emociones provoca simultáneamente (1) reacciones fisiológicas y (2) la experiencia subjetiva de la emoción. (pág. 228)

case study/estudio de caso. Técnica de investigación en la cual se estudia a un individuo a fondo con la esperanza de descubrir principios universales. (págs. 20, 142)

Cattell, Raymond. (1905–1998) Psicólogo inglés que estudió la posibilidad de que unos rasgos predijeran otros. Propuso 16 dimensiones clave o *factores* para describir la personalidad. (pág. 500)

central nervous system (CNS)/sistema nervioso central. El cerebro y la médula espinal. (págs. 131, 409)

cerebellum [sehr-uh-BELL-um]/cerebelo. Es el "pequeño cerebro" y está unido a la parte posterior del tronco cerebral; permite coordinar los movimientos voluntarios y el equilibrio. (pág. 141)

cerebral [seh-REE-bruhl] cortex/corteza cerebral. Estructura compleja de células nerviosas conectadas entre sí, que forman los hemisferios cerebrales; principal centro de control y procesamiento de información del organismo. (pág. 145)

Chomsky, Noam. (1928–) Lingüista que sostuvo que los niños están predispuestos a aprender el lenguaje, como si su cerebro tuviera un sistema integrado que les permitiera absorber vocabulario y reglas gramaticales. (pág. 445)

chromosomes/cromosomas. Estructuras con forma de hilos, compuestas de moléculas de ADN portadoras de los genes. (pág. 40)

chronological age/edad cronológica. Edad verdadera. Siguiendo el cociente intelectual (CI) de Terman y Stern, la edad cronológica se representa con la abreviatura "EC". (pág. 460)

chunking/agrupamiento de pensamientos. Información ordenada en unidades coherentes. (pág. 342)

circadian (ser-KAY-dee-un) rhythms/ritmos circadianos. Ritmos biológicos (por ejemplo, de temperatura y estado de vigilia) que ocurren aproximadamente cada 24 horas. (pág. 378)

classical conditioning/condicionamiento clásico. Tipo de aprendizaje en el cual un estímulo adquiere el poder de producir una respuesta porque predice otro estímulo que ya produce dicha respuesta. (pág. 281)

client-centered therapy/terapia centrada en el cliente. Tipo de psicoterapia humanista creada por Carl Rogers, en la cual el terapeuta emplea técnicas tales como escuchar activamente dentro de un entorno genuino, con aceptación y empatía, para facilitar el crecimiento personal del cliente. (También se denomina *terapia centrada en la persona*). (pág. 578)

cocaine/cocaína. Estimulante que proviene de las hojas de la planta de coca. (pág. 418)

cochlea/cóclea. Órgano principal del oído. Estructura con forma de caracol, ósea y rellena de fluido que se halla en el oído interno en donde las ondas sonoras se convierten en impulsos nerviosos. (pág. 171)

cognition/cognición. Procesos mentales; todas las actividades mentales asociadas con el pensamiento, el saber y el recordar. (págs. 63, 283)

cognitive abilities/habilidades cognitivas. Todas las actividades mentales asociadas con el pensamiento, el conocimiento y la memoria. (pág. 430)

cognitive-behavior therapy/terapia cognitivo-conductual. Terapia integrada que combina la terapia cognitiva (que cambia los pensamientos contraproducentes) con la terapia conductual (que cambia la conducta inadecuada). (pág. 586)

cognitive dissonance/disonancia cognitiva. Teoría según la cual llevamos a cabo una acción con el propósito de reducir la incomodidad (disonancia) que sentimos cuando tenemos dos pensamientos (cogniciones) contradictorios. Por ejemplo, cuando tenemos consciencia de que nuestra actitud y nuestras acciones entran en conflicto, logramos reducir la disonancia resultante si cambiamos nuestra actitud. (pág. 619)

cognitive map/mapa cognitivo. Representación mental de un lugar. (pág. 316)

cognitive perspective/perspectiva cognitiva. Corriente de pensamiento que se concentra en la forma en que absorbemos, procesamos, almacenamos y recuperamos información. (pág. 9)

cognitive therapies/terapias cognitivas. Terapias que enseñan a las personas formas de pensar y actuar nuevas y más adaptables; se basan en la suposición de que los pensamientos intervienen en los sucesos y nuestras reacciones emocionales. (pág. 584)

collective unconscious/inconsciente colectivo. Concepto de Carl Jung de una reserva compartida y heredada proveniente de rastros de recuerdos de la historia de nuestra antepasados. (pág. 486)

collectivism/colectivismo. Estilo cultural que pone las metas o necesidades del grupo antes que las metas o necesidades personales y define la identidad personal de acuerdo con la identificación con el grupo. (págs. 48, 658)

companionate love/amor entre personas relacionadas. Apego profundo y cariñoso que sentimos por aquellos con quienes se comparte la vida. (pág. 639)

computerized axial tomography (CT or CAT) scan/tomografía axial computarizada. Serie de radiografías tomadas desde distintos ángulos y combinadas por medio de una computadora que crea una representación de una porción del cuerpo. (pág. 143)

concept/concepto. Agrupación mental basada en semejanzas compartidas. (pág. 431)

concrete operational stage/período operacional concreto. Según la teoría de Piaget, nivel del desarrollo cognitivo (desde aproximadamente los seis o siete años hasta los once años) durante el cual los niños adquieren la capacidad mental que les permite pensar lógicamente en situaciones concretas. (pág. 67)

conditioned response (CR)/respuesta condicionada. Según el condicionamiento clásico, respuesta al estímulo condicionado. (pág. 284)

conditioned stimulus (CS)/estímulo condicionado. Según el condicionamiento clásico, estímulo previamente neutral que, mediante el aprendizaje, ha adquirido el poder de provocar una respuesta condicionada. (pág. 284)

cones/conos. Células receptoras de la vista ubicadas en la retina. Los conos detectan los detalles bien definidos y el color, pero requieren más luz que los bastoncillos. (pág. 165)

confirmation bias/sesgo confirmatorio. Tendencia a concentrarse en la información que confirma las ideas preconcebidas que uno tiene. (pág. 437)

conformity/conformidad. Acomodación del comportamiento o el pensamiento para coincidir con el estándar de un grupo. (pág. 621)

confounding variable/variable de confusión. En un experimento, se dice de la variable, distinta de la variable independiente, que tendría influencia sobre la variable dependiente. Los investigadores deben controlar las variables de confusión para poder sacar conclusiones de causa y efecto durante un experimento. (pág. 26)

consciousness/consciencia. Conocimiento de uno mismo y su ambiente. (pág. 378)

conservation/conservación. Principio (que Piaget consideraba parte del razonamiento operacional concreto) que sostiene que las propiedades tales como la masa, el volumen y el número se mantienen iguales a pesar de los cambios que ocurren en la forma de los objetos. (pág. 66)

context/contexto. Marco o ambiente en el cual interpretamos los estímulos sensoriales. (pág. 197)

context effect/efecto del contexto. Capacidad de recordar información más fácilmente cuando se está en un ambiente similar al ambiente donde se estaba cuando se adquirió dicha información. (pág. 351)

continuous reinforcement/refuerzo continuo. Según el condicionamiento operante, programa de refuerzo en el cual se da una recompensa después de cada respuesta correcta. (pág. 312)

control group/grupo control. Participantes de un experimento que no están expuestos a la variable independiente. Estos individuos son comparados con los participantes del grupo experimental. (pág. 26)

convergence/convergencia. Señal de profundidad binocular relacionada con la tensión de los músculos del ojo cuando los ojos se mueven hacia adentro para enfocarse en objetos que están cerca de la cara. (pág. 188)

cornea/córnea. Bulto transparente en la parte anterior del globo ocular. La curvatura de la córnea dobla los rayos luminosos y luego el cristalino del ojo produce una imagen enfocada sobre la retina. (pág. 164)

corpus callosum [KOR-pus kah-LOW-sum]/cuerpo calloso. Franja gruesa de fibras nerviosas que conecta los dos hemisferios cerebrales y transmite mensajes entre los mismos. (pág. 146).

correlational study/estudio de correlación. Proyecto de investigación que permite descubrir hasta qué punto dos variables están relacionadas entre sí. (pág. 21)

correlation coefficient/coeficiente de correlación. Medida estadística que indica hasta qué punto dos cosas varían de la misma manera. (pág. A-10)

critical period/período crítico. Etapa óptima inmediatamente después del parto, en la cual la presencia de ciertos estímulos o experiencias produce un desarrollo apropiado del organismo. (pág. 70)

critical thinking/pensamiento crítico. Forma de pensar en la que no se aceptan razones y conclusiones ciegamente; por el contrario, se examinan las suposiciones, se distinguen los valores escondidos, se evalúa la evidencia y se calculan las conclusiones. (pág. 19)

cross-cultural research/estudio transcultural. Investigación que prueba hipótesis en varios grupos de personas para averiguar si los principios se aplican a distintas culturas. (pág. 661)

cross-sectional study/estudio transversal. Método de investigación en el cual se comparan individuos de distintas edades al mismo tiempo. (pág. 24)

crystallized intelligence/inteligencia cristalizada. Conocimiento acumulado y capacidad verbal de una persona; tiende a aumentar con la edad. (pág. 105)

culture/cultura. Actitudes, creencias, normas y comportamientos de un grupo que se comunican de generación en generación; posiblemente la cultura asegure la supervivencia del grupo. (págs. 48, 657)

culture-specific/específico de una cultura. Dícese de los principios que son válidos solamente entre las personas de una cultura en particular, a diferencia de los principios *universales,* que son válidos en todas las culturas. (pág. 661)

D

Darley, John. (1938–) Psicólogo que, junto con Bibb Latané, estudió las circunstancias que determinan cuándo un transeúnte intervendrá a favor de otra persona. (pág. 641)

decibel (dB)/decibelio (dB). Medida de la altura de una onda sonora, que determina el volumen de un sonido. (pág. 169)

defense mechanisms/mecanismos de defensa. Según la teoría psicoanalítica, estrategias de protección del ego para reducir la ansiedad, en las que se distorsiona inconscientemente la realidad. (pág. 483)

deindividuation/desindividuación. Pérdida de la consciencia de uno mismo y de las inhibiciones, que ocurre cuando se está en un grupo en el que se fomenta la excitación y el anonimato. (pág. 627)

deinstitutionalization/desinstitucionalización. Situación en la que se da de alta a pacientes de hospitales psiquiátricos permitiéndoles reingresar a la comunidad. Durante la segunda mitad del siglo XX, la creación de tratamientos con medicamentos provocó una disminución del 80 por ciento en el número de pacientes psiquiátricos internados. (pág. 599)

delta sleep/sueño delta. Etapas 3 y 4 del sueño NREM, que presentan ondas delta grandes y lentas; el sueño delta es muy breve durante las últimas cuatro horas del sueño. (pág. 385)

delusions/delirios. Creencias falsas que son síntomas de esquizofrenia y otros trastornos psicológicos graves. (pág. 560)

Dement, William. (1928–) Investigador que estudió el sueño y creó el término *REM.* (pág. 380)

dendrite/dendrita. Prolongación ramificada de la neurona que recibe mensajes y envía impulsos hacia el cuerpo neuronal (soma). (pág. 122)

dependence/dependencia. Necesidad fisiológica o psicológica de aumentar la cantidad que se toma de una substancia después después de uso prolongado. Si dicha substancia dejara de tomarse, se sufrirían síntomas de abstinencia. (pág. 408)

dependent variable (DV)/variable dependiente (VD). En un experimento, la variable sobre la que influye la variable independiente. En psicología, el comportamiento o los procesos mentales en los cuales se mide el impacto de la variable independiente. (pág. 25)

depressants/depresivos. Substancias (tales como el alcohol y los sedantes) que reducen la actividad nerviosa y hacen más lentas las funciones del organismo. (pág. 412)

depth perception/percepción de profundidad. Capacidad de ver en tres dimensiones y juzgar la distancia. (pág. 186)

difference threshold (just noticeable difference)/umbral diferencial (diferencia que apenas se nota). Diferencia mínima que una persona es capaz de detectar entre dos estímulos la mitad de las veces. (pág. 159)

discrimination/discriminación. Según el *condicionamiento clásico,* capacidad de distinguir entre dos señales o estímulos similares. Según el *condicionamiento operante,* proceso mediante el cual un organismo produce distintas respuestas a dos estímulos similares. En las *relaciones sociales,* acción en contra de un grupo de personas basándose en creencias estereotipadas y sentimientos prejuiciados. (págs. 289, 311, 642)

display rules/reglas de expresión. Reglas culturales que dictan cómo y cuándo puede una persona expresar sus emociones. (pág. 237)

dissociative amnesia/amnesia disociativa. Trastorno disociativo que se caracteriza por la pérdida de la memoria como reacción a un suceso traumático. (pág. 556)

dissociative disorders/trastornos disociativos. Trastornos en los cuales la identidad de una persona se separa (se disocia) de recuerdos, pensamientos y sentimientos previos. (pág. 555)

dissociative fugue/fuga disociativa. Trastorno disociativo en el que la persona pierde su identidad y viaja para establecerse en otro lugar. (pág. 556)

dissociative identity disorder/trastorno de identidad disociativo. Trastorno disociativo poco común y controvertido, en el cual una persona experimenta dos o más personalidades claramente definidas que se alternan entre sí. (pág. 557)

distributed rehearsal/ensayo repartido. División de un ensayo en varias sesiones separadas por períodos de tiempo. (pág. 339)

divided consciousness theory/teoría de la consciencia dividida. Teoría que sostiene que, durante la hipnosis, nuestra consciencia (o conocimiento de nosotros mismos y de los demás) se divide y una parte de ésta no tiene conocimiento del papel que cumplen las otras partes. (pág. 397)

DNA (deoxyribonucleic acid)/ADN (ácido desoxirribonucleico). Molécula compleja que contiene la información genética que forma los cromosomas. (pág. 40)

dopamine[DO-pa-mean]/dopamina. Neurotransmisor que influye en el aprendizaje, la atención y las emociones; el exceso de actividad de la dopamina se asocia con la esquizofrenia. (pág. 129)

double-blind procedure/procedimiento doble ciego. Procedimiento experimental en el cual los participantes y el personal de investigación ignoran (van a ciegas) los resultados que se esperan del experimento. Este procedimiento se emplea para evitar la influencia de las expectativas y de la variable de confusión. (pág. 29)

drive-reduction theory/teoría de reducción de impulsos. Idea de que una necesidad fisiológica produce la activación de un estado de tensión (impulso) que motiva a un organismo a satisfacer dicha necesidad. (pág. 208)

drives/impulsos. Según la teoría de reducción de impulsos, activación de estados de tensión causados por desequilibrios, que llevan al organismo a reestablecer el equilibrio, generalmente mediante la reducción del impulso. (pág. 208)

DSM-IV-TR/Manual diagnóstico y estadístico de trastornos mentales. Abreviatura en inglés del *Manual diagnóstico y estadístico de trastornos mentales* (cuarta edición, texto revisado), un sistema ampliamente usado para clasificar los trastornos psicológicos. (pág. 524)

E

eardrum (tympanic membrane)/tímpano(membrana timpánica). Tejido que funciona como barrera y se halla al final del conducto auditivo. Transfiere las vibraciones del sonido del aire a los tres huesecillos del oído medio. (pág. 170)

Ebbinghaus, Hermann. (1850–1909) Filósofo alemán que fue pionero en el estudio de la memoria. (págs. 336, 361)

eclectic approach/perspectiva ecléctica. Enfoque psicoterapéutico que se basa en que se basa en el empleo de técnicas de distintas terapias, según los problemas que presente el cliente. (pág. 524)

ecstasy/éxtasis. También llamada *MDMA*, esta droga reduce las inhibiciones, produce sensaciones agradables y hace aceptar más a los demás. Aun el consumo moderado puede resultar en daño cerebral permanente. (pág. 420)

effortful processing/procesamiento esforzado. Codificación que requiere atención y esfuerzo continuo. (pág. 336)

ego/ego. Parte "ejecutiva" de la personalidad y mayormente consciente que, según Freud, actúa como mediadora entre las exigencias del ello, el superyó y la realidad. El ego funciona a partir del *principio de la realidad* y busca satisfacer los deseos del ello (o id) de maneras que, siendo realistas, brindarán placer en vez de dolor. (pág. 483)

egocentrism/egocentrismo. Según la teoría de Piaget, incapacidad del niño preoperacional de tomar el punto de vista de otra persona, o de entender que los símbolos pueden representar otros objetos. (pág. 67)

electroconvulsive therapy (ECT)/terapia electroconvulsiva. Terapia para el tratamiento de la depresión grave. Consiste en el suministro de breves descargas eléctricas al cerebro del paciente, mientras éste está bajo anestesia. (pág. 604)

electroencephalogram (EEG)/electroencefalograma. Registro amplificado de las ondas de actividad eléctrica provenientes de la superficie del cerebro. Estas ondas se miden con electrodos colocados sobre el cuero cabelludo y permiten evaluar el funcionamiento del cerebro. (pág. 143)

electroencephalograph (EEG)/electroencefalógrafo. Instrumento que amplifica y registra las ondas de actividad eléctrica provenientes de la superficie del cerebro. Estas ondas se miden con electrodos colocados sobre el cuero cabelludo. (pág. 384)

electromagnetic energy/energía electromagnética. Espectro de energía que incluye, entre otras cosas, los rayos X y las ondas de radar y de radio. Una pequeña porción de este espectro incluye la energía de la luz visible, la cual es posible detectar a simple vista. (pág. 162)

embryo/embrión. Organismo humano en desarrollo, desde aproximadamente la segunda semana después de la fecundación hasta el final de la octava semana. (pág. 58)

emotional intelligence/inteligencia emocional. Capacidad de percibir, expresar, entender y regular las emociones. (pág. 458)

emotions/emociones. Respuestas de todo el organismo que presentan (1) estimulación fisiológica, (2) comportamientos expresivos y (3) experiencia consciente. (pág. 226)

encoding/codificación. Proceso mediante el cual se almacena información en el sistema de la memoria. Primera etapa del modelo de procesamiento de información de la memoria. (págs. 335, 359)

endocrine [EN-duh-krin] system/sistema endocrino. Uno de los dos sistemas de comunicación del cuerpo; conjunto de glándulas que producen hormonas, los mensajeros químicos que circulan en sangre. (pág. 133)

endorphins/endorfinas. Neurotransmisores naturales, similares a los opiatos, que están ligados al control del dolor y el placer. También se denominan "morfinas internas." (pág. 415)

environment/ambiente. Toda influencia que no es genética, desde la alimentación prenatal hasta las personas y las cosas que nos rodean. (pág. 39)

equity/equidad. Condición dentro de una relación en la cual las personas reciben en proporción a lo que dan. (pág. 639)

Erikson, Erik. (1902–1994) Fundador de la teoría de las ocho etapas del desarrollo psicosocial. (págs. 88, 107)

ethnocentrism/etnocentrismo. Tendencia a ver el mundo a partir de las experiencias personales y a través de los "filtros culturales" que uno tiene. (pág. 666)

evolutionary psychology/psicología evolutiva. Estudio de la evolución del comportamiento y la mente, que emplea los principios de la selección natural. (pág. 42)

excitatory effect/efecto excitador. Efecto de un neurotransmisor que aumenta la probabilidad de que la neurona receptora genere un potencial de acción (impulso). (pág. 126)

experiment/experimento. Método de investigación en el cual el investigador manipula uno o más factores (variables independientes) para observar su efecto en otra variable (variable dependiente), a la vez que excluye las variables de confusión. (pág. 24)

experimental group/grupo experimental. Sujetos de un experimento que están expuestos al tratamiento, o sea, a la variable independiente. (pág. 26)

explanatory style/estilo explicativo. Costumbres que se adquieren al pensar en las buenas o las malas causas de los sucesos. (pág. 266)

explicit memory/memoria explícita. Memoria de hechos y experiencias que uno debe recuperar y declarar conscientemente. (pág. 348)

external locus of control/locus de control externo. Impresión de que nuestro destino está controlado por el azar o por fuerzas que están más allá de nuestro control. (pág. 508)

extinction/extinción. *Según el conductismo clásico,* disminución de una respuesta aprendida, cuando un estímulo incondicionado no sigue a un estímulo condicionado. *En el conductismo operante,* pérdida de un comportamiento cuando no está seguido de una consecuencia. (págs. 285, 311)

extrasensory perception (ESP)/percepción extrasensorial. Idea polémica que propone la posibilidad de que la percepción ocurra por una vía distinta de la estimulación de los sentidos. (pág. 198)

extrinsic motivation/motivación extrínseca. Deseo de llevar a cabo un comportamiento porque promete recompensas o existe la amenaza de un castigo. (pág. 212)

Eysenck, Hans. (1916–1997) Psicólogo alemán que investigó las dimensiones de la personalidad que tienen influencia genética, incluidas la extraversión y la introversión. (pág. 500)

F

family therapy/terapia de familia. Terapia que trata a la familia como a un sistema. Considera que los comportamientos inapropiados de un individuo son influenciados por otros miembros de la familia o dirigidos hacia ellos; guía a los miembros de la familia para que logren tener relaciones positivas y mejorar la comunicación. (pág. 587)

fetal alcohol syndrome (FAS)/síndrome de alcoholismo fetal. Conjunto de anormalidades físicas y cognitivas que aparecen en los niños cuyas madres consumen grandes cantidades de alcohol durante el embarazo. Los síntomas a veces incluyen desproporción de los rasgos faciales. (pág. 59)

fetus/feto. Organismo humano en desarrollo, desde la novena semana después de la concepción hasta el nacimiento. (pág. 58)

figure-ground/figura y fondo. Disposición del campo visual en donde los objetos (las *figuras*) resaltan en su entorno (el *fondo*). (pág. 184)

fixation/fijación. Predisposición mental que dificulta la solución a un problema. (pág. 436)

fixed-interval schedule/programa de intervalo fijo. En el condicionamiento operante, programa de reforzamiento parcial en el cual se suministra una recompensa solamente para la primera respuesta correcta, después de haber transcurrido un determinado período de tiempo. (pág. 312)

fixed-ratio schedule/programa de proporción fija. En el condicionamiento operante, programa de reforzamiento parcial en el cual se suministra una recompensa solamente después de que haya ocurrido un número definido de respuestas correctas. (pág. 314)

flashbulb memory/memoria episódica. Recuerdo vívido y claro de un momento o suceso emocionalmente significativo. (pág. 346)

flow/fluidez. Estado óptimo de experiencia; para que ocurra la fluidez, las experiencias deben significar un desafío que requiera destreza, metas claras y la producción de respuestas. (pág. 264)

fluid intelligence/inteligencia fluida. Capacidad de una persona de razonar de manera rápida y abstracta; tiende a disminuir en la vejez. (pág. 105)

foot-in-door phenomenon/fenómeno del pie en la puerta. Tendencia de las personas que accedieron a un pedido menor de acceder luego a un pedido de mayores proporciones. (pág. 618)

formal operational stage/período operacional formal. Según la teoría de Piaget, etapa del desarrollo cognitivo (normalmente desde los doce años) durante la cual las personas comienzan a pensar de manera lógica en conceptos abstractos y a formar estrategias. (pág. 67)

fovea/fóvea. Parte central y focal de la retina, donde ocurre la mejor visión. (pág. 165)

framing/encuadre. Forma en que se presenta una cuestión; el encuadre puede influenciar las decisiones y las opiniones. (pág. 440)

fraternal twins/gemelos bivitelinos. Hermanos gemelos que se forman de dos óvulos distintos. En términos genéticos, su relación no es más cercana que la que existe con los demás hermanos y hermanas, excepto que comparten el ambiente fetal. (pág. 42)

free association/asociación libre. En el psicoanálisis, método para explorar el inconsciente durante el cual la persona se siente tranquila y dice todo lo que le viene a la mente, sin importarle lo trivial o incómodo que sea lo que dice. (pág. 481)

frequency distribution/distribución de frecuencias. Lista de puntajes ordenados de mayor a menor. (pág. A-3)

Freud, Sigmund. (1856–1939) Fundador del psicoanálisis, una controvertida teoría acerca del funcionamiento de la parte inconsciente de la mente y las etapas psicosexuales del desarrollo. (págs. 5, 107, 364, 479, 573)

frontal lobes/lóbulos frontales. Porción de la corteza cerebral que se halla inmediatamente detrás de la frente; incluye la corteza motora y se relaciona con la planificación y la formación de opiniones. (pág. 146)

functional fixedness/fijeza funcional. Tendencia a pensar en las cosas solamente en términos de sus funciones acostumbradas; impedimento en la resolución de problemas. (pág. 436)

functionalism/funcionalismo. Teoría que enfatizaba las funciones de la consciencia y las formas en que ésta permitía a las personas adaptarse a su ambiente. (pág. 5)

fundamental attribution error/error fundamental de la atribución. Tendencia de los observadores, cuando analizan el comportamiento ajeno, a subestimar el impacto de la situación y a sobrestimar el impacto de la disposición personal. (pág. 614)

G

ganglion cells/células ganglionares. Capa superior de las células de la retina. Reciben información de las células bipolares y la transmiten a través de sus axones, los cuales forman en conjunto el nervio óptico. (pág. 166).

Garcia, John. (1917–) Investigador que identificó, junto con su colega Robert Koelling, el fenómeno de aversión a un gusto, lo cual demostró que el condicionamiento clásico recibía influencias de las predisposiciones biológicas. (pág. 293)

Gardner, Howard. (1943–) Autor de una teoría contemporánea de inteligencias múltiples que distingue entre ocho tipos distintos de inteligencia. (pág. 456)

general adaptation syndrome (GAS)/síndrome de adaptación general. Concepto de Selye según el cual el cuerpo responde al estrés pasando por tres fases: la inquietud, la resistencia y el agotamiento. (pág. 246)

general intelligence (*g*)/inteligencia general (*g*). Según la creencia de Spearman, factor de inteligencia general que subyace tras capacidades mentales específicas y se mide, por lo tanto, con cada uno de los ejercicios de una prueba de inteligencia. (pág. 459)

generalization/generalización. Proceso en el cual un organismo genera la misma respuesta a dos estímulos similares. (pág. 289)

generalized anxiety disorder/trastorno de ansiedad generalizado. Trastorno que se caracteriza por sentimientos persistentes e inexplicables de aprensión y tensión que alcanzan niveles perjudiciales. (pág. 534)

genes/genes. Segmentos de ADN; unidades bioquímicas de la herencia que forman los cromosomas y dirigen el modo en que se especializan las células para cumplir diversas funciones (por ejemplo, las funciones cerebrales, pulmonares, cardíacas y capilares) durante el desarrollo prenatal. (págs. 39, 58)

genome/genoma. Instrucciones completas para la formación de un organismo que consisten en todo el material genético de sus cromosomas. (pág. 41)

gestalt/gestalt. Se dice del "todo" , o patrones de organización, que tendemos a percibir. Los psicólogos que ejercían la psicología Gestalt enfatizaban la idea de que el todo es más grande que la suma de las partes que lo componen. (pág. 183)

Gestalt psychology/psicología Gestalt. Perspectiva psicológica que enfatiza nuestra tendencia a integrar datos para formar un todo significativo. (pág. 5)

grammar/gramática. Sistema de reglas que dicta cómo combinar morfemas y palabras y ordenarlos en oraciones para comunicarnos con los demás. (pág. 443)

group intelligence tests/pruebas de inteligencia de grupo. Pruebas elaboradas inicialmente por el ejército de Estados Unidos para evaluar eficazmente a los reclutas durante la primera guerra mundial, y empleadas ampliamente en la actualidad en las escuelas. Generalmente son administradas por los maestros en los salones de clase. No son tan fiables como las pruebas individuales de Stanford-Binet o de Wechsler. (pág. 466)

group polarization/polarización grupal. Potenciación de las actitudes predominantes de un grupo, cuando los miembros de éste se hallan enfrascados en una conversación. (pág. 628)

grouping/agrupamiento. Tendencia de percepción que clasifica los estímulos en grupos que tienen sentido. (pág. 185)

groupthink/pensamiento grupal. Modo de pensar que ocurre en un grupo que debe tomar decisiones, cuando el deseo de mantener la armonía, anula una evaluación realista de las alternativas. (pág. 629)

H

hair cells/células ciliares. Células receptoras sensibles al sonido, que se hallan en la cóclea y se encargan de convertir las vibraciones del sonido en impulsos nerviosos. (pág. 171)

Hall, G. Stanley. (1844–1924) Primer hombre estadounidense en sacar un doctorado en psicología; abrió el primer laboratorio de psicología de Estados Unidos; fundó y fue el primer presidente de la *American Psychological Association* (APA, o Asociación estadounidense de psicología). (pág. 8)

hallucinations/alucinaciones. Percepciones falsas que son síntomas de la esquizofrenia y otros trastornos psicológicos graves. (pág. 561)

hallucinogens/alucinógenos. Drogas psicodélicas, tales como el ácido lisérgico y dietilamina, que distorsionan las percepciones y provocan imágenes sensoriales sin la presencia de estimulación sensorial, es decir, hacen que se manifiesten en la mente cosas que en condiciones normales están ocultas. (pág. 419)

Harlow, Harry. (1906–1981) Psicólogo que estudió la relación entre el contacto corporal y la alimentación y el apego, empleando en sus experimentos monos recién nacidos y madres artificiales. (pág. 69)

health psychology/psicología de la salud. Rama de la psicología que representa el aporte de la psicología dentro de la medicina conductual. (pág. 245)

heritability/heredabilidad. Proporción de la variación entre individuos que es posible atribuir a la herencia. (pág. 43)

hertz (Hz)/hercio o hertz. Medida del número de crestas de onda por segundo, o frecuencia de una onda sonora. Los hercios determinan el tono de un sonido. (pág. 169)

heuristic/heurística. Regla práctica en la estrategia de resolución de problemas que hace que una solución sea más probable y eficaz, pero que no garantiza soluciones. (pág. 434)

hierarchy of needs/jerarquía de necesidades. Pirámide de Maslow de las necesidades humanas, en cuya base están las necesidades fisiológicas, y luego siguen las necesidades de seguridad personal y, por último, las necesidades psicológicas. Las necesidades de nivel más elevado no se activan hasta que las de niveles más bajos estén satisfechas. (pág. 213)

Hilgard, Ernest. (1904–2001) Investigador pionero en el campo de la hipnosis y defensor de la teoría de la consciencia dividida. (pág. 398)

hippocampus/hipocampo. Centro nervioso ubicado en el sistema límbico; participa en el procesamiento de recuerdos nuevos para su almacenamiento permanente. (pág. 145)

homeostasis/homeóstasis. Tendencia a mantener un estado interno equilibrado y constante; regulación de cualquier proceso químico del organismo, tal como el de la glucosa en sangre, para mantener un equilibrio específico. (pág. 210)

hormones/hormonas. Mensajeros químicos producidos por las glándulas endocrinas que circulan en sangre. (pág. 133)

Horney, Karen. (1885–1952) Neofreudiana que consideraba que el psicoanálisis estaba prejuiciado en contra de la mujer y creía que las variables culturales eran la base del desarrollo de la personalidad. (pág. 487)

hue/tono. Color de la luz; está determinado por la longitud de onda de la energía luminosa. (pág. 168)

humanistic psychology/psicología humanista. Perspectiva que enfatiza el estudio de la experiencia consciente, la libertad de decisión del individuo y la capacidad de crecimiento personal. (págs. 6, 489)

hypnosis/hipnosis. Interacción social en la cual una persona (el hipnotizador) hace sugerencias relacionadas con percepciones, sentimientos, pensamientos o comportamientos, y otra persona (el sujeto) obedece a dichas sugerencias. (pág. 396)

hypnotic induction/inducción hipnótica. Proceso en el cual un hipnotizador crea un estado de hipnosis en el sujeto, generalmente al expresar una serie de sugerencias. (pág. 398)

hypochondriasis/hipocondría. Trastorno somatoforme que se caracteriza por síntomas de enfermedad imaginarios. (pág. 558)

hypothalamus [hi-po-THAL-uh-muss]/hipotálamo. Estructura nerviosa ubicada debajo del tálamo; dirige actividades de mantenimiento tales como la ingestión de alimentos y de líquidos y la temperatura del cuerpo, y está ligado a las emociones. (pág. 144)

hypothesis/hipótesis. Predicción realizada por un investigador y que debe someterse a prueba, acerca de los resultados de un experimento. (pág. 24)

I

id/ello. Según Freud, parte de la personalidad compuesta por energía psíquica e inconsciente, que busca la satisfacción de impulsos sexuales y agresivos básicos. Funciona de acuerdo con el *principio del placer,* y requiere satisfacción inmediata. (pág. 482)

identical twins/gemelos univitelinos. Gemelos que se forman de un sólo óvulo fecundado, el cual se divide en dos y crea dos organismos idénticos. (pág. 42)

identity/identidad. Sentido de uno mismo; de acuerdo con Erikson, la tarea del adolescente es solidificar el sentido de sí mismo probando e integrando una variedad de roles. (pág. 89)

image/imagen. Figura mental. (pág. 450)

implicit memory/memoria implícita. Memoria que permite recordar destrezas y formas de hacer las cosas, tal como caminar, que ocurre sin tener que hacer un esfuerzo consciente. (pág. 348)

imprinting/impronta. Proceso mediante el cual ciertos animales forman apegos durante un período crítico que ocurre a muy temprana edad. (pág. 70)

independent variable (IV)/variable independiente (VI). Variable de un experimento que el investigador manipula activamente y, si la hipótesis es correcta, producirá un cambio en la variable dependiente. (pág. 25)

individualism/individualismo. Estilo cultural que pone las metas o necesidades personales antes que las metas o necesidades del grupo y define la identidad de acuerdo con las cualidades personales en vez de la identificación con el grupo. (págs. 48, 658)

inferential statistics/estadística inferencial. Estadística que se puede emplear para tomar una decisión o llegar a una conclusión basada en los datos. (pág. A-12)

inferiority complex/complejo de inferioridad. De acuerdo con Alfred Adler, estado que resulta de la incapacidad de compensar por sentimientos normales de inferioridad. (pág. 486)

infradian (in-FRAY-dee-un) rhythms/ritmos infradianos. Ritmos biológicos que ocurren una vez al mes o una vez por estación. (pág. 378)

ingroup/grupo propio. "Nosotros", o sea, las personas con las que uno comparte una identidad en común. (pág. 644)

ingroup bias/estereotipo de grupo propio. Tendencia a favorecer al grupo al que uno pertenece. (pág. 644)

inhibitory effect/efecto inhibitorio. Efecto de un neurotransmisor que hace menos probable que la neurona receptora genere un potencial de acción (impulso). (pág. 126)

insight/agudeza. Entendimiento repentino (¡Ajá!) de cómo se resuelve un problema. (pág. 434)

insomnia/insomnio. Dificultad recurrente para conciliar el sueño o para mantenerse dormido. (pág. 389)

instinct/instinto. Comportamiento complejo y no aprendido que está rigurosamente entretejido en patrones que posee toda una especie. (pág. 208)

intelligence/inteligencia. Capacidad de aprender de la experiencia, resolver problemas y emplear conocimientos para adaptarse a situaciones nuevas. (pág. 456)

intelligence quotient (IQ))/coeficiente intelectual (CI). Número derivado de la fórmula de Terman y Stern, que se emplea para calcular el nivel de inteligencia de una persona: edad mental (EM) dividida por la edad cronológica (EC) multiplicada por 100. (pág. 461)

internal locus of control/locus de control interno. Impresión de que controlamos nuestro propio destino. (pág. 508)

interneurons/interneuronas. Células nerviosas del cerebro y la médula espinal, que se encargan de procesar información relacionada con la estimulación sensorial y las respuestas motoras. (pág. 127)

interpretation/interpretación. En el psicoanálisis, observación que hace el analista de supuestos significados de sueños, resistencias y otros comportamientos significativos, con el propósito de facilitar el entendimiento. (pág. 575)

intimacy/intimidad. Según la teoría de Erikson, capacidad de formar relaciones cercanas, afectivas y abiertas; tarea primaria del comienzo de la vida adulta. (pág. 91)

intrinsic motivation/motivación intrínseca. Deseo de llevar a cabo un comportamiento por el sólo hecho de hacerlo y de tener el resultado esperado. (pág. 212)

iris/iris. Aro de tejido muscular que forma la parte coloreada del ojo; regula el tamaño de la pupila, o agujero en el centro del iris, para que pase al ojo la cantidad correcta de luz. (pág. 164)

J

James, William. (1842–1910) Primer psicólogo estadounidense y escritor del primer libro de texto de psicología, que pensaba que nuestra consciencia de las reacciones fisiológicas nos lleva a sentir las emociones (véase *la teoría de James-Lange*). (págs. 5, 228)

GE-11

James-Lange theory/teoría de James-Lange. Teoría según la cual nuestra experiencia de una emoción es la consciencia que tenemos de nuestras reacciones fisiológicas ante un estímulo que evoca emociones. (pág. 228)

Jung, Carl. (1875–1961) Neofreudiano que pensaba que los seres humanos comparten un *inconsciente colectivo.* (pág. 486)

just-world phenomenon/fenómeno de un mundo justo. Tendencia a suponer que las personas reciben lo que merecen y merecen lo que reciben. (pág. 646)

K

Kahneman, Daniel. (1934–) Psicólogo que, junto con Amos Tversky, realizó estudios para descubrir los factores que influyen en las opiniones y la toma de decisiones de los seres humanos. Su trabajo lo llevó a obtener el premio Nobel en 2002. (pág. 438)

kinesthetic sense/sentido cinético. Sistema que permite sentir la posición y el movimiento de las partes del cuerpo. (pág. 176)

Kohlberg, Lawrence. (1927–1987) Creó una teoría que divide al desarrollo moral en tres etapas. (pág. 85)

L

Lange, Carl. (1834–1900) Fisiólogo danés que propuso, casi simultáneamente, una teoría de las emociones similar a la de William James, que propone que nuestra consciencia de las respuestas fisiológicas nos lleva a experimentar las emociones (véase *la teoría de James-Lange*). (pág. 228)

language/lenguaje. Palabras habladas, escritas o gesticuladas y las formas en las que las combinamos para comunicar significados. (pág. 441)

Latané, Bibb. (1937–) Psicólogo que, junto con John Darley, estudió las circunstancias que determinan cuándo un transeúnte intervendrá a favor de otra persona. (pág. 641)

latent learning/aprendizaje latente. Aprendizaje que ocurre pero no es aparente hasta que la persona tiene un incentivo para manifestarlo. (pág. 316)

Lazarus, Richard. (1922–) Psicólogo estadounidense que concluyó que algunas respuestas emocionales no requieren pensamientos conscientes. (pág. 231)

learned helplessness/impotencia aprendida. Desesperanza y resignación pasiva que aprende un animal o ser humano cuando es incapaz de evitar una sucesión de episodios desagradables. (pág. 509)

learning/aprendizaje. Cambio relativamente permanente del comportamiento debido a la experiencia. (pág. 281)

lens/cristalino del ojo. Estructura transparente ubicada detrás de la pupila del ojo; el grosor del cristalino cambia para enfocar las imágenes en la retina. (pág. 164)

limbic system/sistema límbico. Aro de estructuras ubicadas en el borde del tronco cerebral y la corteza cerebral; contribuye a la regulación de funciones importantes tales como la memoria, el miedo, la agresión, el hambre y la sed. Incluye el hipotálamo, el hipocampo y la amígdala. (pág. 144)

linguistic relativity hypothesis/hipótesis de relatividad linguística. Hipótesis de Benjamin Whorf según la cual el lenguaje determina la forma en que pensamos. (pág. 449)

lobotomy/lobotomía. Tipo de psicocirugía, actualmente rara, que se empleaba para calmar a pacientes emocionalmente incontrolables o violentos. El procedimiento consiste en cortar los nervios que conectan los lóbulos frontales del cerebro con los centros emocionales más profundos. (pág. 606)

locus of control/locus de control. Impresión que tiene una persona acerca de la fuente de control de las recompensas. Las personas que tienen un locus de control interno creen que controlan sus propias recompensas a través de su conducta. Las personas que tienen un locus de control externo creen que las recompensas son controladas por circunstancias externas. (pág. 662)

Loftus, Elizabeth. (1944–) Psicóloga de la Universidad de California, Irvine, cuya investigación demostró la naturaleza estructurada de la memoria. (pág. 367)

longitudinal fissure/cisura interhemisférica. Surco largo que se extiende desde la parte anterior hasta la parte posterior de la corteza cerebral y separa el hemisferio derecho del izquierdo. (pág. 145)

longitudinal study/estudio longitudinal. Técnica de investigación en la cual se estudia el mismo grupo de individuos durante un largo período de tiempo. (pág. 23)

long-term memory/memoria remota. Centro de almacenamiento relativamente permanente e ilimitado del sistema de la memoria. (pág. 345)

long-term potentiation/potenciación a largo plazo. Aumento en la eficacia de una sinapsis para transmitir impulsos. Se considera la base nerviosa del aprendizaje y la memoria. (pág. 347)

Lorenz, Konrad. (1903–1989) Investigador que estudió las etapas críticas de apego en los pichones de aves, concepto que denominó *impronta.* (pág. 70)

LSD (lysergic acid diethylamide)/ácido lisérgico y dietilamina. Poderosa droga alucinógena; también se conoce como *ácido.* (pág. 420)

M

magnetic resonance imaging (MRI)/imágenes de resonancia magnética. Técnica que emplea campos magnéticos y ondas de radio para producir imágenes generadas por una computadora en las que se distingue entre los distintos tipos de tejidos blandos; nos permite ver las estructuras cerebrales. (pág. 143)

major depressive disorder/trastorno de depresión grave. Trastorno del estado de ánimo en el que un individuo, sin razón aparente, experimenta por lo menos dos semanas de depresión, disminución de interés en actividades, y síntomas tales como la sensación de que su vida no tiene valor. (pág. 542)

marijuana/marihuana. Hojas, tallos, resina y flores de la planta de cáñamo que, al fumarse, reduce las inhibiciones y produce sensaciones de tranquilidad y euforia leve. (pág. 421)

Maslow, Abraham. (1908–1970) Psicólogo humanista que propuso una jerarquía de necesidades, en donde la realización personal es la máxima necesidad psicológica. (págs. 6, 213, 490)

massed rehearsal/ensayo concentrado. Juntar todo el tiempo de ensayo en una sola sesión (atiborrar). (pág. 349)

Matsumoto, David. (1959–) Psicólogo y experto internacional en el estudio de la psicología transcultural. (pág. 657)

maturation/maduración. Procesos de crecimiento biológico que permiten cambios ordenados en el comportamiento y son relativamente independientes de la experiencia. (pág. 61)

mean/media. Promedio aritmético de una distribución, que se obtiene sumando los puntajes y luego dividiéndolos por el número de puntajes. (pág. A-5)

median/mediana. Puntaje que está en el medio de una distribución clasificada; la mitad de los puntajes está por encima de la mediana y la otra mitad, por debajo. (pág. A-5)

medical model/modelo médico. Concepto que afirma que las enfermedades tienen causas físicas que es posible diagnosticar, tratar y, en la mayoría de los casos, curar. Cuando se aplica a los trastornos psicológicos, el modelo médico supone que estas enfermedades "mentales" se diagnostican de acuerdo con los síntomas y se curan por medio de terapia, la cual a veces incluye un tratamiento en un hospital psiquiátrico. (pág. 522)

medulla [muh-DUL-uh]/médula oblonga. Base del tronco cerebral; controla las funciones vitales, tales como el latido del corazón y la respiración. (pág. 141)

melatonin/melatonina. Hormona que contribuye a la regulación de los ritmos biológicos diarios. (pág. 383)

menopause/menopausia. Período de la vida en que cesa naturalmente la menstruación; también se refiere a los cambios biológicos que experimenta una mujer a medida que disminuye su capacidad de reproducción. (pág. 101)

mental age/edad mental. Edad cronológica que corresponde con el nivel de dificultad de las preguntas que un niño es capaz de contestar. Siguiendo el cociente intelectual de Terman y Stern, la edad cronológica se representa con la abreviatura "EC". (pág. 460)

mental set/predisposición mental. Tendencia a resolver problemas de una forma en particular. La predisposición mental a veces facilita la resolución de un problema nuevo y a veces, no. (pág. 435)

mere exposure effect/efecto de mera exposición. Fenómeno en el cual la exposición repetida a estímulos novedosos aumenta el agrado que se siente ante dichos estímulos. (pág. 635)

method of loci/método de loci. Recurso nemotécnico en el cual uno asocia los datos que quiere recordar con lugares imaginarios. (pág. 341)

Milgram, Stanley. (1933–1984) Psicólogo social que investigó la obediencia a la autoridad. (pág. 624)

Minnesota Multiphasic Personality Inventory (MMPI)/ Inventario Multifásico de la Personalidad de Minnesota. Prueba de la personalidad que es, entre todas, la más ampliamente estudiada y empleada clínicamente. Se elaboró originalmente para identificar trastornos emocionales, y aún hoy este uso se considera el más apropiado. Actualmente también se emplea para muchos otros propósitos de examinación. (pág. 504)

misinformation effect/efecto de información errónea. Acción de incorporar en la memoria de uno mismo información engañosa acerca de un suceso. (pág. 367)

mnemonic device/recurso nemotécnico. Técnica para auxiliar a la memoria. (pág. 341)

mode/moda. Puntaje que ocurre más frecuentemente en una distribución. (pág. A-4)

model/modelo. Persona que se observa en el aprendizaje por observación. (pág. 325)

modeling/modelar. Proceso de observar e imitar un comportamiento en particular. (pág. 326)

monocular cues/claves monoculares. Señales de profundidad que requieren el uso de un solo ojo. (pág. 187)

morpheme/morfema. En el lenguaje, unidad más pequeña con significado; puede ser una palabra o parte de una palabra. (pág. 442)

morphine/morfina. Sedante potente, se usa para calmar los dolores y se extrae del opio. (pág. 417)

motivation/motivación. Necesidad o deseo que vigoriza y dirige el comportamiento. (pág. 207)

motor cortex/corteza motora. Parte del cerebro en la parte posterior de los lóbulos frontales, que controla los movimientos voluntarios. (pág. 145)

motor nerves/nervios motores. Nervios que portan información del sistema nervioso central. (pág. 127)

Murray, Henry. (1893–1988) Neofreudiano, fue el primero en establecer el concepto de motivación de logro; también creó importantes mecanismos para evaluar la personalidad. (pág. 214)

mutation/mutación. Errores en la duplicación de los genes, que se producen al azar y resultan en un cambio en el código genético de un individuo; fuente de toda la diversidad genética. (pág. 41)

N

narcolepsy/narcolepsia. Trastorno caracterizado por ataques incontrolables de sueño. El individuo entra directamente en el sueño REM, generalmente en momentos inoportunos. (pág. 340)

naturalistic observation/observación naturalista. Observación y registro de comportamientos en situaciones que ocurren naturalmente, sin tratar de manipular y controlar dichas situaciones. (pág. 20)

natural selection/selección natural. Principio según el cual, entre la variedad de rasgos heredados, aquellos que contribuyen a la supervivencia tienen gran probabilidad de pasar a las generaciones futuras. (pág. 42)

negative reinforcement/reforzamiento negativo. En el condicionamiento operante, cualquier cosa que aumenta la probabilidad de que se produzca un comportamiento, causando la *desaparición* de un suceso o estado desagradable. (pág. 303)

neuron/neurona. Célula nerviosa; unidad básica del sistema nervioso. (págs. 122, 409)

neurotransmitter/neurotransmisor. Mensajero químico que, al ser liberado por una neurona, atraviesa la sinapsis (espacio entre dos neuronas) y entra en los receptores de las neuronas receptoras, formando el siguiente eslabón en la cadena de comunicación del sistema nervioso. (págs. 125, 410)

nicotine/nicotina. Estimulante del comportamiento que se halla en el tabaco. (págs. 269, 417)

night terrors/terrores nocturnos. Trastorno del sueño caracterizado por excitación fisiológica intensa y expresión de miedo extremo en la cara del sujeto; a diferencia de las pesadillas, los terrores nocturnos ocurren en la etapa 4 del sueño, durante las dos o tres primeras horas de estar dormido, y rara vez se los recuerda. (pág. 391)

normal distribution/distribución normal. Curva simétrica y en forma de campana que describe la distribución de muchas variables físicas y psicológicas. La mayoría de los puntajes están cerca de la media, con cada vez menos puntajes hacia los extremos. (pág. A-8)

norms/normas. Reglas establecidas para el comportamiento aceptado y esperado; las normas rigen el comportamiento "adecuado". (pág. 48)

N-REM sleep (non–rapid eye movement sleep)/sueño NREM (movimientos oculares no rápidos). Período del sueño en el que ocurren las etapas 1 a 4; no se caracteriza por movimientos de los ojos ni sueños vívidos. (pág. 385)

O

obedience/obediencia. Tendencia a hacer caso a las órdenes, ya sea implícitas o explícitas, de alguien a quien se percibe como autoridad. (pág. 624)

object permanence/permanencia del objeto. Consciencia de que las cosas continúan existiendo aún cuando no se las ve ni se las escucha. (pág. 65)

observational learning/aprendizaje observacional. Aprendizaje que ocurre por la observación a otras personas. (pág. 325)

obsessive-compulsive disorder/trastorno obsesivo-compulsivo. Trastorno que se caracteriza por pensamientos y acciones indeseadas y repetitivas. (pág. 535)

occipital [ahk-SIP-uh-tuhl] lobes/lóbulos occipitales. Porción de la corteza cerebral ubicada en la parte posterior de la cabeza; incluye las áreas de procesamiento de la visión. (pág. 147)

olfactory cells/células olfativas. Células receptoras del olfato que son sensibles a las sustancias químicas; se ubican en los conductos nasales. (pág. 174)

operant conditioning/condicionamiento operante. Tipo de aprendizaje en el que la frecuencia de un comportamiento depende de las consecuencias que éste provoca. (pág. 300)

operational definition/definición operacional. Especificación de los procedimientos exactos que se deben llevar a cabo para que una variable sea específica y se pueda medir durante un experimento. (pág. 24)

opiates/opiáceos. Se dice del opio y sus derivados, tales como la morfina y la heroína; deprimen la actividad nerviosa, reduciendo temporalmente el dolor y la ansiedad. (pág. 415)

opponent-process theory/teoría de los colores opuestos. Teoría de la visión del color según la cual el color se procesa en pares de opuestos (rojo-verde, amarillo-azul y negro-blanco). Cuando la luz estimula la mitad de un par, inhibe la otra mitad. (pág. 168)

optic nerve/nervio óptico. Nervio que lleva información visual desde el ojo hasta los lóbulos occipitales del cerebro. (pág. 166)

ossicles/huesecillos. Tres huesos (martillo, yunque, y estribo) muy pequeños que transmiten las ondas sonoras del tímpano a la cóclea. (pág. 171)

outgroup/grupo ajeno. "Ellos", o sea, las personas a las que percibimos como distintas o separadas de "nosotros". (pág. 644)

oval window/ventana oval. Punto de la superficie de la cóclea que recibe las vibraciones sonoras de los tres huesecillos del oído medio. (pág. 171)

overconfidence/exceso de confianza. Tendencia a ser más preciso que acertado cuando se estima lo certero de las creencias y las opiniones propias. (pág. 439)

overjustification effect/efecto de justificación excesiva. Efecto de prometer una recompensa por algo que a uno de antemano le gusta hacer. La recompensa podría disminuir y reemplazar la motivación original y natural de la persona, por lo que el comportamiento se interrumpe si la recompensa se elimina. (pág. 317)

overlearning/sobreaprender. Ensayar información después de haberla aprendido. El sobreaprendizaje es una estrategia eficiente para mejorar la memoria. (pág. 337)

P

panic disorder/trastorno del pánico. Trastorno que se caracteriza por ataques repentinos de pánico intenso e inexplicable. (pág. 535)

parasympathetic division/división parasimpática. Parte del sistema nervioso autónomo que calma el cuerpo. (pág. 132)

parietal [puh-RYE-uh-tuhl] lobes/lóbulos parietales. Porción de la corteza cerebral ubicada en la parte superior de la cabeza y hacia atrás; incluye la corteza somatosensorial y las áreas de asociación general que participan en el procesamiento de información. (pág. 146)

partial schedule/programa parcial. En el condicionamiento operante, programa de reforzamiento que premia sólo algunas respuestas correctas. (pág. 312)

participant bias/parcialidad de participante. Tendencia de los participantes de un experimento a responder de cierta manera porque saben que se los está observando o creen saber lo que tiene en mente el investigador. (pág. 19)

passionate love/amor apasionado. Estado de entusiasmo y concentración positiva e intensa en otra persona, que generalmente se presenta al comienzo de una relación amorosa. (pág. 638)

Pavlov, Ivan. (1849–1936) Fisiólogo ruso que se hizo famoso por su descubrimiento del condicionamiento clásico. (págs. 6, 286)

peg-word system/sistema de asociación por palabra clave. Recurso nemotécnico en el cual uno asocia datos que quiere recordar con una lista de palabras clave que ya ha aprendido de memoria. (pág. 341)

percentage/porcentaje. Estadística comparativa en la que se compara un puntaje con un puntaje perfecto, suponiendo que el puntaje perfecto es de 100 puntos. (pág. A-9)

percentile rank/categoría de porcentil. Estadística comparativa en la que se compara un puntaje con otros, suponiendo que hay cien puntajes en total. Indica cuántos de esos cien puntajes son iguales o están por debajo de un puntaje en particular. (pág. A-10)

perception/percepción. Proceso de organización e interpretación de información sensorial. (págs. 157, 183)

perceptual constancy/constancia perceptiva. Percepción de que el tamaño, la forma y el peso de un objeto no cambian, aún cuando cambie la imagen de dicho objeto en la retina. (pág. 194)

perceptual set/predisposición perceptiva. Predisposición mental a percibir algo de una manera y no de otra. (pág. 196)

peripheral nervous system (PNS)/sistema nervioso periférico. Nervios sensoriales y motores que conectan el sistema nervioso central con el resto del cuerpo. (pág. 131)

permastore memory/memoria permanente. Recuerdos de la memoria remota que son especialmente resistentes al olvido y se conservan generalmente toda la vida. (pág. 361)

permissive parenting/crianza permisiva. Estilo de crianza en el cual los padres se someten a los deseos de los niños, tienen pocas exigencias y emplean pocos castigos. (pág. 73)

personality/personalidad. Patrones de pensamiento, sentimiento y comportamiento característicos de un individuo. (págs. 479, 499)

personality disorders/trastorno de personalidad. Trastornos psicológicos caracterizados por patrones de comportamiento inflexibles y duraderos que perturban el funcionamiento social. (pág. 565)

personality inventories/inventarios de personalidad. Cuestionarios (que generalmente se responden con las opciones verdadero-falso o de acuerdo-en desacuerdo) en los que se responde a preguntas diseñadas para medir una amplia variedad de sentimientos y comportamientos; se emplean para evaluar rasgos de la personalidad escogidos. (pág. 503)

phobia/fobia. Miedos perjudiciales e irracionales a objetos o situaciones. (pág. 442)

phoneme/fonema. En el lenguaje hablado, unidad más pequeña en la que se distingue un sonido. (pág. 442)

Piaget, Jean. (1896–1980) Pionero en el estudio de la psicología del desarrollo; propuso una teoría de las etapas del desarrollo cognitivo que condujo a un mejor entendimiento de los procesos del pensamiento de los niños. (págs. 6, 63, 85)

Pinel, Philippe. (1745–1826) Médico francés que se dedicó a reformar el tratamiento de las personas con trastornos mentales. (pág. 521)

pitch/tono. Intensidad de un sonido, que depende de la frecuencia de una onda sonora. (pág. 169)

pituitary gland/glándula pituitaria. "Glándula maestra" del sistema endocrino. Su importancia es tal que, junto con el cerebro, controla las demás glándulas endocrinas. (pág. 133)

placebo/placebo. Substancia o condición inactiva que a veces se administra en vez de un medicamento o agente activo, para ver si dicho medicamento tiene efecto más allá de las expectativas creadas cuando una persona lo utiliza. (pág. 29)

plasticity/plasticidad. Capacidad del cerebro de modificarse, como es evidente en el reordenamiento que ocurre después de un daño cerebral (especialmente en los niños). (pág. 149)

polygraph/detector de mentiras. Máquina que se emplea comúnmente como medio para detectar mentiras. Mide las diversas respuestas fisiológicas (tales como cambios en la transpiración, el ritmo cardíaco, la presión sanguínea y la respiración) que acompañan las emociones. (pág. 234)

population/población. Todos los casos de un grupo, entre los cuales se pueden extraer muestras para un estudio. (pág. 23)

positive psychology/psicología positiva. Movimiento en la psicología que se concentra en el estudio del funcionamiento óptimo del ser humano y en los factores que permiten la prosperidad de individuos y comunidades. (págs. 12, 263, 510)

positive reinforcement/reforzamiento positivo. En el condicionamiento operante, cualquier cosa que aumenta la probabilidad de que se produzca un comportamiento cuando se proporciona un suceso o estado deseable. (pág. 303)

positron emission tomography (PET) scan/tomografía por emisión de positrones. Muestra visual de la actividad cerebral que detecta por dónde va un tipo de glucosa (azúcar en sangre) radiactiva en el momento en que el cerebro realiza una función en particular. (pág. 143)

posthypnotic amnesia/amnesia poshipnótica. Supuesta incapacidad de recordar lo que ocurre durante la hipnosis porque el hipnotizador sugiere al sujeto no recordar ese lapso de tiempo. (pág. 401)

posthypnotic suggestion/sugestión poshipnótica. Sugestión hecha durante una sesión de hipnosis, para que el sujeto la cumpla cuando ya no esté hipnotizado. (pág. 400)

posttraumatic stress disorder/trastorno de estrés postraumático. Trastorno en el que se repite la experiencia de un suceso muy perturbador en recuerdos y sueños recurrentes. (pág. 535)

preconscious/preconsciente. Según Freud, parte de la mente donde existe información que no es consciente pero que es posible recordarla conscientemente. (pág. 481)

prejudice/prejuicio. Actitud injustificable (y frecuentemente negativa) hacia un grupo y sus miembros. Generalmente incluye creencias estereotipadas, sentimientos negativos y predisposición a acciones discriminatorias. (pág. 642)

preoperational stage/etapa preoperacional. Según la teoría de Piaget, etapa (aproximadamente desde los dos hasta los siete años) durante la cual el niño aprende a emplear el lenguaje pero aún no comprende las operaciones mentales de lógica concreta. (pág. 66)

primary reinforcement/reforzamiento primario. Algo que refuerza naturalmente, tal como la comida (si se tiene hambre), el calor (si se tiene frío) y el agua (si se tiene sed). (pág. 307)

primary sex characteristics/características sexuales primarias. Estructuras del cuerpo (ovarios, testículos y órganos sexuales externos) que posibilitan la reproducción. (pág. 83)

proactive interference/interferencia proactiva. Efecto negativo que tiene algo aprendido anteriormente, en el acto de recordar información almacenada más recientemente. (pág. 363)

projective tests/pruebas de proyección. Pruebas de la personalidad, tales como la Rorschach o la prueba de apercepción temática, que proveen estímulos ambiguos para provocar la proyección de los pensamientos y los sentimientos de una persona. (pág. 487)

prosocial behavior/comportamiento prosocial. Comportamiento positivo, constructivo y útil. (pág. 328)

Prosser, Inez Beverly. (1897–1934) Primera mujer afroamericana en obtener un doctorado en psicología. (pág. 8)

prototype/prototipo. Ejemplo que incorpora más típicamente y de mejor manera las características principales de un concepto. (pág. 431)

pseudoscientific claim/planteamiento pseudocientífico. Toda afirmación que no está basada en las ciencias, aún cuando en algunas circunstancias, se intente darle una apariencia científica. (pág. 378)

psychoactive drug/droga psicoactiva. Sustancia química que altera las percepciones y el estado de ánimo. (pág. 408)

psychoanalysis/psicoanálisis. Teoría de la personalidad de Freud; también, técnica terapéutica que intenta proporcionar a un individuo un entendimiento de sus pensamientos y acciones exponiendo e interpretando los motivos y conflictos inconscientes subyacentes. (págs. 480, 574)

psychoanalytic perspective/perspectiva psicoanalítica. Corriente de pensamiento que se concentra en la forma en que el comportamiento surge de impulsos y conflictos inconscientes; también se denomina *perspectiva psicodinámica.* (pág. 5)

psychodynamic perspective/perspectiva psicodinámica. Concepto de la personalidad que retiene algunas de las características de la teoría freudiana (tales como la importancia de los procesos inconscientes del pensamiento), pero que es menos capaz de ver los conflictos irresueltos de la niñez como fuente del desarrollo de la personalidad. (pág. 480)

psychological disorder/trastorno psicológico. “Disfunción dañina” en la cual los comportamientos se juzgan como inadaptados, injustificados, perturbadores y atípicos. (pág. 519)

psychological perspective/perspectiva psicológica. Concepto particular del comportamiento y/o los procesos mentales, que se ha convertido en movimiento. (pág. 9)

psychology/psicología. Estudio científico del comportamiento y los procesos mentales. (pág. 4)

psychosexual stages/etapas psicosexuales. Etapas del desarrollo de la niñez (oral, anal, fálica, latente y genital) durante las cuales, según Freud, las energías de búsqueda de placer del ello se concentran en las distintas zonas erógenas. (pág. 485)

psychotherapy/psicoterapia. Interacción de caracter emocional y confidencial, entre un terapeuta calificado y alguien que sufre de dificultades psicológicas. (pág. 573)

puberty/pubertad. Etapa de maduración sexual durante la cual una persona se vuelve capaz de reproducirse. (pág. 82)

punishment/castigo. Todo tipo de consecuencia que *disminuye* la futura probabilidad de que se produzca un comportamiento. (pág. 302)

pupil/pupila. Apertura ajustable del centro del iris; controla la cantidad de luz que entra al ojo. (pág. 164)

R

random assignment/asignación aleatoria. Asignación al azar de participantes a grupos de control y experimentales, para minimizar diferencias preexistentes entre los asignados a distintos grupos. (pág. 26)

random sample/muestra aleatoria. Muestra que representa correctamente a una población porque cada uno de los miembros tiene igual probabilidad de ser incluido. (pág. 23)

range/intervalo. Diferencia entre el puntaje más alto y el más bajo de una distribución. (pág. A-7)

Rayner, Rosalie. (1900–1935) Alumna de postgrado de John Watson y coinvestigadora en el famoso estudio del Pequeño Albert, sobre el condicionamiento clásico de las emociones. (pág. 290)

recall/recordación. Medida de la memoria que consiste en recuperar información aprendida anteriormente, tal como en las pruebas de rellenar espacios en blanco. (pág. 350)

receptor cells/células receptoras. Células que se encuentran en todo sistema sensorial y transforman (transducen) otros tipos de engergía en impulsos que el cerebro es capaz de procesar. (págs. 126, 165)

reciprocal determinism/determinismo recíproco. Influencias de la interacción entre factores de la personalidad y del ambiente. (pág. 507)

recognition/reconocimiento. Medida de la memoria que consiste en *identificar* cosas que se aprendieron anteriormente, tal como en una prueba de escogencia múltiple. (pág. 350)

refractory period/período sin respuesta. Fase en que una neurona se recarga, después de enviar un estímulo, en la que no le es posible generar otro potencial de acción. (pág. 123)

rehearsal/ensayo. Repetición consciente de información. (pág. 336)

reinforcement/reforzamiento. Todo tipo de consecuencia que *aumenta* la probabilidad de que se produzca un comportamiento en el futuro. (pág. 302)

reliability/fiabilidad. Medida en la que una prueba produce resultados uniformes, sin importar quién la administra o dónde se la da. (págs. 468, 503)

REM sleep/sueño REM. Sueño en el que ocurren movimientos oculares rápidos; etapa recurrente del sueño en la cual generalmente ocurren sueños vívidos. También se conoce como *sueño paradójico,* porque los músculos están relajados pero los demás sistemas del cuerpo están activos. (pág. 386)

replication/duplicación. Repetición de un estudio científico, en la cual se observa si es posible reproducir los resultados. Cuando un estudio no se puede duplicar, se considera que los resultados se han dado por casualidad. (pág. 31)

repression/represión. Según la teoría psicoanalítica de Sigmund Freud, proceso en el que se pasan al inconsciente los recuerdos que producen ansiedad. (pág. 364)

Rescorla, Robert. (1940–) Investigador que desarrolló, junto con su colega Allan Wagner, una nueva teoría que enfatizaba la importancia de los procesos cognitivos en el condicionamiento clásico. (pág. 293)

researcher bias/prejuicio del investigador. Tendencia de los investigadores a ser selectivos cuando notan evidencias y a comportarse de una manera que apoya sus hipótesis o expectativas. (pág. 19)

resistance/resistencia. Según el psicoanálisis, bloqueo de la consciencia de recuerdos que producen ansiedad. (pág. 575)

response/respuesta. Todo tipo de comportamiento o acción. (pág. 282)

resting potential/potencial de reposo. Estado de descanso de una neurona cuando es capaz de generar un potencial de acción. (pág. 283)

reticular formation/formación reticular. Red de fibras nerviosas en el bulbo raquídeo, que cumple un papel importante en la regulación de la vigilia y la estimulación. (pág. 141)

retina/retina. Superficie sensible a la luz que está ubicada en la parte posterior del globo ocular; contiene bastoncillos y conos que convierten la energía luminosa en impulsos nerviosos. (pág. 165)

retinal disparity/disparidad retiniana. Clave de profundidad binocular que resulta de la producción de imágenes ligeramente distintas por la separación de las retinas del ojo izquierdo y el derecho. (pág. 182)

retrieval/recuperación. Proceso mediante el cual se recuerda información almacenada en la memoria. Tercera y última etapa del modelo de procesamiento de información de la memoria. (págs. 335, 359)

retroactive interference/interferencia retroactiva. Efecto negativo que tiene algo que se acaba de aprender en el acto de recordar información almacenada anteriormente. (pág. 363)

rods/bastoncillos. Células receptoras de la visión ubicadas en la retina. Detectan sólo el negro, el blanco y el gris, pero responden con menos luz que los conos que detectan el color. (pág. 165)

Rogers, Carl. (1902–1987) Psicólogo humanista que elaboró la terapia centrada en el cliente y enfatizó la importancia de la aceptación, la autenticidad y la empatía para fomentar el crecimiento personal del ser humano. (págs. 6, 491, 578)

rooting reflex/reflejo de búsqueda. Tendencia de los bebés, cuando se les toca la mejilla, a abrir la boca y buscar el pezón; es una respuesta automática que no ha tenido que aprenderse. (pág. 59)

Rorschach inkblot test/prueba de Rorschach. Conjunto de diez manchas de tinta diseñado por Hermann Rorschach. Es la prueba de proyección empleada con más frecuencia y tiene el propósito de identificar los sentimientos de las personas mediante el análisis de sus interpretaciones de las manchas. (pág. 488)

scapegoat theory/teoría de chivo expiatorio. Teoría según la cual el prejuicio representa una vía de escape al enojo porque proporciona a alguien a quién culpar. (pág. 645)

Schachter, Stanley. (1922–1997) Psicólogo estadounidense que, junto con Jerome Singer, concluyó que las emociones requieren una identificación cognitiva de estimulación fisiológica (véase *la teoría de las emociones de dos factores*). (pág. 230)

schemas/esquemas. Conceptos de marcos mentales que ordenan e interpretan información. (págs. 63, 196)

schizophrenia/esquizofrenia. Conjunto de trastornos graves caracterizados por pensamientos desordenados y delirantes, percepciones perturbadas y emociones y acciones inapropiadas. (pág. 560)

scientific method/método científico. Método de aprendizaje del mundo que nos rodea mediante la aplicación del pensamiento crítico y mecanismos tales como la observación, la experimentación y el análisis estadístico. (pág. 17)

secondary reinforcement/reforzamiento secundario. Se dice de algo que se ha aprendido a valorar, por ejemplo, el dinero. (pág. 307)

secondary sex characteristics/características sexuales secundarias. Características sexuales que no están directamente relacionadas con la reproducción, tales como los senos y las caderas en la mujer, el tono de voz en el hombre y el vello del cuerpo. (pág. 83)

selective attention/atención selectiva. Capacidad de enfocar la consciencia en un estímulo en particular excluyendo a los demás, como cuando se está tan compenetrado en una lectura que uno no se da cuenta de lo que ocurre a su alrededor. (pág. 161)

self-actualization/autorrealización. Según Abraham Maslow, necesidad psicológica más importante que surge después de satisfacer las necesidades físicas y psicológicas y de lograr la autoestima; motivación de realizar el potencial personal. (págs. 213, 490)

self-concept/concepto de uno mismo. Todo lo que pensamos y sentimos acerca de nosotros mismos cuando respondemos a la pregunta: "¿Quién soy?" (pág. 492)

self-disclosure/revelación de uno mismo. Revelación a los demás de cosas que uno considera íntimas. (pág. 639)

self-fulfilling prophecy/predicción que acarrea su propio cumplimiento. Predicción que ocurre cuando las opiniones de una persona acerca de los demás hacen que uno actúe de tal manera que induce a las demás personas a parecer que confirman dichas opiniones. (pág. 630)

self-reference effect/efecto de autorreferencia. Facilitación de la codificación semántica de una información que es relevante a nivel personal. (pág. 339)

Seligman, Martin. (1942–) Psicólogo estadounidense que propuso la psicología positiva. (págs. 238, 509)

Selye, Hans. (1907–1982) Psicólogo que investigó las respuestas recurrentes al estrés y que él denominó síndrome de adaptación general. (pág. 246)

semantic encoding/codificación semántica. Codificación del significado. (pág. 339)

senile dementia/demencia senil. Desintegración mental que acompaña al alcoholismo, un tumor, un derrame cerebral, la edad y, más a menudo, la enfermedad de Alzheimer. (pág. 103)

sensation/sensación. Proceso mediante el cual los sistemas sensoriales (ojos, oídos y otros órganos sensoriales) y el sistema nervioso reciben estímulos del ambiente. (pág. 157)

sensorimotor stage/etapa sensorio motriz. Según la teoría de Piaget, etapa (desde el nacimiento hasta aproximadamente los dos años) durante la cual los niños conocen el mundo mayormente en términos de sus impresiones sensoriales y sus actividades motoras. (pág. 64)

sensory adaptation/adaptación sensorial. Disminución en la sensibilidad que resulta de la estimulación constante. (pág. 160)

sensory memory/memoria sensorial. Etapa inicial y breve de codificación de información sensorial en el sistema de la memoria. (pág. 344)

sensory nerves/nervios sensoriales. Nervios que transmiten información al sistema nervioso central. (pág. 127)

serial position effect/efecto de posición serial. Tendencia a recordar los elementos del comienzo y el fin de una lista con mayor facilidad. (pág. 338)

serotonin [sare-oh-TON-in]/serotonina. Neurotransmisor asociado con el hambre, el sueño, la estimulación y el estado de ánimo; está presente en menor cantidad en las personas deprimidas. (pág. 129)

set point/punto fijo. Punto en el que se supone que está puesto el "medidor de peso" de un individuo. Cuando el cuerpo baja de ese peso, es posible que aumente el hambre y disminuya el metabolismo para recuperar el peso perdido. (págs. 218, 272)

sexual orientation/orientación sexual. Atracción sexual duradera hacia miembros del mismo sexo (orientación homosexual) o del sexo opuesto (orientación heterosexual). (pág. 84)

shaping/modelamiento. Reforzamiento de comportamientos que son cada vez más similares al que uno desea que ocurra. Es la técnica del condicionamiento operante que se emplea para establecer nuevos comportamientos. (pág. 310)

Sherif, Muzafer. (1906–1988) Psicólogo que estudió el impacto que tienen las metas compartidas en la cooperación. (pág. 651)

short-term memory/memoria inmediata. Memoria consciente y activada que retiene brevemente unos siete trozos de información antes de que ésta sea almacenada más permanentemente o se olvide. También se denomina *memoria operativa.* (pág. 344)

signal detection theory/teoría de la detección de señales. Conjunto de fórmulas y principios que predicen cuándo detectaremos la presencia de un estímulo leve ("señal") entre la estimulación de fondo ("ruido"). La detección depende de las características del estímulo, el ambiente y la persona que realiza la detección. (pág. 159)

skewed/asimétrico. Distorsionado; que no está distribuido uniformemente alrededor de la media. (pág. A-5)

Skinner, B. F. (1904–1990) Psicólogo estadounidense que estudió la función que cumplen las respuestas en el aprendizaje; elaboró los principios y las técnicas fundamentales del condicionamiento operante y creó maneras de aplicarlos en situaciones reales. (págs. 6, 301, 445)

sleep apnea/apnea del sueño. Trastorno del sueño en el que se interrumpe temporalmente la respiración, lo cual hace que la persona se despierte por momentos. (pág. 390)

social-cognitive perspective/perspectiva cognitivo-social. Perspectiva según la cual el entendimiento de la personalidad se basa en considerar la situación y los pensamientos que ocurren antes, durante y después de un suceso. (pág. 499)

social-cultural perspective/perspectiva sociocultural. Corriente de pensamiento enfocada en los cambios del pensamiento o el comportamiento en distintos contextos o situaciones. (pág. 9)

social clock/reloj social. Momento apropiado, según la preferencia cultural, para eventos sociales tales como el matrimonio, la crianza de los hijos y el retiro laboral. (pág. 99)

social facilitation/facilitación social. Mejora en el desempeño de tareas ante la presencia de otras personas; ocurre con tareas sencillas y bien aprendidas pero no con tareas difíciles o que aún no se dominan muy bien. (pág. 626)

social influence theory/teoría de influencia social. Teoría que propone que las influencias sociales de gran impacto son capaces de producir un estado hipnótico. (pág. 397)

social leadership/liderazgo social. Liderazgo dentro de un grupo cuya función es fomentar el trabajo en equipo, facilitar la mediación en los conflictos y ofrecer apoyo. (pág. 217)

social loafing/disminución de productividad en un grupo. Tendencia de las personas de un grupo a esforzarse menos cuando aportan su esfuerzo para el logro de una meta común, que cuando son responsables de manera independiente. (pág. 627)

social psychology/psicología social. Estudio científico que observa cómo nos relacionamos con los demás, los influenciamos y pensamos en ellos. (pág. 613)

soma/soma. Cuerpo celular de la neurona que contiene el núcleo y otros elementos que mantienen el funcionamiento celular. (pág. 122)

somatic nervous system/sistema nervioso somático. Subdivisión del sistema nervioso periférico que controla los músculos esqueléticos del cuerpo. (pág. 131)

somatoform disorders/trastornos somatoformes. Trastornos psicológicos cuyos síntomas se expresan de forma somática (del cuerpo) sin causa física aparente. (pág. 558)

somatosensory cortex/corteza somatosensorial. Parte cerebral ubicada delante de los lóbulos parietales que registra y procesa las sensaciones del cuerpo. (pág. 148)

somnambulism/sonambulismo. Caminar dormido, lo cual generalmente comienza en las etapas de sueño NREM más profundo. La persona sonámbula es capaz de caminar, de hablar y también de ver, pero pocas veces recuerda esos episodios. (pág. 391)

spacing effect/efecto de espaciamiento. Tendencia, durante la práctica repartida, de lograr mejor retención que durante la práctica concentrada. (pág. 339)

Spearman, Charles. (1863–1945) Investigador que propuso la teoría de que existe un factor de inteligencia general (se abrevia *g*) que tiene una función subyacente en otras características más específicas de la inteligencia. (pág. 459)

spindles/husos. Oleadas de actividad de las ondas cerebrales que caracteriza la etapa 2 del sueño NREM. (pág. 385)

spontaneous recovery/recuperación espontánea. Reaparición, después de un período de descanso, de una respuesta condicionada extinguida. (pág. 285)

standard deviation/desviación estándar. Medida calculada de cuántos puntajes varían alrededor del puntaje de la media; entre más alta sea la desviación estándar, más esparcidos están los puntajes. (pág. A-7)

Stanford-Binet intelligence test/escala de inteligencia Stanford-Binet. Revisión estadounidense (realizada por Terman en Stanford University) y de uso muy extendido, de la prueba original de Binet. (pág. 461)

state-dependent memory/memoria dependiente del estado. Capacidad potenciada de recuperar información cuando uno está en el mismo estado físico y emocional que estaba cuando se codificó esa información. (pág. 352)

statistical significance/significación estadística. Afirmación estadística que indica la probabilidad de que un resultado ocurra solamente al azar. (pág. A-12)

stereotype/estereotipo. Creencia generalizadora (a veces acertada, pero a menudo demasiado generalizadora) acerca de un grupo de personas. (pág. 642)

Sternberg, Robert. (1949–) Autor de una teoría contemporánea de inteligencias múltiples que distingue entre la inteligencia analítica, la creativa y la práctica. (pág. 457)

stimulants/estimulantes. Drogas (tales como la cafeína, la nicotina y otras más potentes como las anfetaminas y la cocaína) que estimulan la actividad nerviosa y aceleran las funciones del cuerpo. (pág. 416)

stimulus/estímulo. Cualquier cosa del ambiente a lo que uno es capaz de responder. (pág. 281)

storage/almacenamiento. Retención de información codificada a lo largo del tiempo. Segunda etapa del modelo de procesamiento de información de la memoria. (págs. 335, 359)

stranger anxiety/ansiedad ante los extraños. Miedo a personas desconocidas que se presenta comúnmente en los bebés y que comienza aproximadamente a los ocho meses de vida. (pág. 69)

stress/estrés. Proceso mediante el cual percibimos y respondemos a ciertos sucesos *estresantes,* que calificamos como amenazantes o desafiantes. (pág. 245)

structuralism/estructuralismo. Teoría que analizaba los elementos básicos de los pensamientos y las sensaciones para determinar la estructura de la experiencia consciente. (pág. 4)

Sumner, Francis Cecil. (1895–1954) Primer hombre afroamericano en obtener un doctorado en psicología. (pág. 8)

superego/superyó. Según Freud, componente de la personalidad que representa ideales internalizados y proporciona parámetros de juicio (el consciente) y de aspiraciones futuras. (pág. 482)

superordinate goals/metas superiores. Metas compartidas que anulan las diferencias entre individuos y requieren de su colaboración. (pág. 651)

survey method/método de estudio o **encuesta.** Técnica de investigación diseñada para descubrir actitudes o comportamientos. Muestras de personas ofrecen sus comunicados voluntariamente mediante cuestionarios o entrevistas. (pág. 22)

sympathetic division/división simpática. Parte del sistema nervioso autónomo que estimula el cuerpo para responder a situaciones que se perciben como amenazas. (pág. 132)

synapse/sinapsis. Intersección entre el extremo del axón de una neurona que envía un mensaje y la dendrita de la neurona receptora. El pequeño espacio lleno de fluido en esta intersección se denomina *espacio intersináptico.* (págs. 125, 410)

systematic desensitization/desensibilización sistemática. Tipo de contracondicionamiento en el cual se asocia un estado tranquilo y agradable con estímulos que provocan ansiedad y que se aplican de manera gradual y en aumento. Se emplea comúnmente para tratar fobias. (pág. 580)

T

task leadership/liderazgo de tareas. Liderazgo orientado hacia una meta, en el que se asientan parámetros, se organiza el trabajo y se enfoca la atención. (pág. 216)

temperament/temperamento. Reacción e intensidad emocional características de un individuo. (pág. 60)

temporal lobes/lóbulos temporales. Porción de la corteza cerebral ubicada más o menos encima de las orejas; incluye las áreas auditivas (del oído). (pág. 147)

teratogens/teratógenos. Sustancias que penetran la barrera placentaria e impiden el desarrollo normal del feto. (pág. 58)

Terman, Lewis. (1877–1956) Investigador que adaptó las pruebas de Binet para su uso en Estados Unidos bajo el nombre de escala de inteligencia Stanford-Binet, la cual mide la inteligencia con un puntaje de cociente intelectual calculado. (pág. 461)

thalamus [THAL-uh-muss]/tálamo. Tablero de control sensorial del cerebro, ubicado encima del tronco cerebral; dirige mensajes a las áreas de la corteza cerebral que reciben mensajes sensoriales. (pág. 141)

Thematic Apperception Test (TAT)/Prueba de apercepción temática. Prueba de proyección en la cual las personas expresan sus sentimientos e intereses a través de cuentos que inventan basándose en escenas ambiguas. (pág. 487)

Thorndike, Edward. (1874–1949) Creador de la ley del efecto, principio que forma la base del condicionamiento operante. (pág. 301)

thyroid gland/glándula tiroides. Glándula endocrina que asiste en la regulación del nivel de energía del cuerpo. (pág. 134)

Titchener, E. B. (1867–1927) Fundador del estructuralismo. (pág. 4)

token economy/economía de fichas. Procedimiento del condicionamiento operante que intenta modificar el comportamiento dando recompensas por los comportamientos deseables. Estas fichas se pueden cambiar por varios privilegios o gustos. (pág. 583)

tolerance/tolerancia. Receptividad reducida a una substancia, que da lugar a que la persona aumente la dosis para sentir los efectos que anteriormente obtenía con dosis más pequeñas. (pág. 409)

top-down processing/procesamiento de arriba hacia abajo. Procesamiento de información que enfatiza nuestras expectativas y experiencias cuando interpretamos la información sensorial que recibimos. (pág. 157)

trait/rasgo. Patrón de comportamiento característico o disposición a sentir y actuar, de la manera que se especifica en inventarios de autoinformes e informes de coetáneos. (pág. 499)

transference/transferencia. En el psicoanálisis, transferencia del paciente al analista de emociones (tales como

GE-21

amor u odio) que están ligadas a otras relaciones. (pág. 576)

trichromatic theory/teoría tricromática. Teoría de la visión del color que plantea que los conos están "calibrados" para detectar la luz roja, verde o azul. En estos tipos de conos existen varios niveles de estimulación que nos permiten identificar millones de combinaciones de colores distintas. (pág. 167)

Tversky, Amos. (1937–1996) Psicólogo que, junto con Daniel Kahneman, realizó estudios para descubrir los factores que influyen en las opiniones y la toma de decisiones de los seres humanos. (pág. 438)

two-factor theory/teoría de las emociones de dos factores. Teoría que propone que para experimentar emociones debe (1) existir estimulación física y (2) identificarse el estímulo a nivel cognitivo. (pág. 230)

Type A/tipo A. Término de Friedman y Rosenman que se refiere a los individuos competidores, luchadores, impacientes, agresivos verbalmente y propensos al enojo. (pág. 252)

Type B/tipo B. Término de Friedman y Rosenman que se refiere a los individuos de trato fácil y tranquilos. (pág. 252)

U

ultradian (ul-TRAY-dee-un) rhythms/ritmos ultradianos. Ritmos biológicos que ocurren más de una vez al día. (pág. 378)

unconditional positive regard/estima positiva incondicional. Según la teoría de Carl Rogers, actitud de aceptación total hacia otra persona. (pág. 491)

unconditioned response (UCR)/respuesta incondicionada. En el condicionamiento clásico, respuesta automática al estímulo no condicionado. (pág. 284)

unconditioned stimulus (UCS)/estímulo incondicionado. En el condicionamiento clásico, estímulo que provoca una respuesta automática y reflexivamente. (pág. 283)

unconscious/inconsciente. Según Freud, región de la mente que actúa como reserva de pensamientos, deseos, sentimientos y recuerdos mayormente inaceptables. (pág. 481)

V

validity/validez. Punto hasta el cual una prueba mide o predice lo que se espera que mida o prediga. (págs. 469, 503)

variable-interval schedule/programa de intervalos variables. En el condicionamiento operante, programa de reforzamiento parcial que administra recompensas por la primera respuesta correcta después de una cantidad de tiempo impredecible. (pág. 314)

variable-ratio schedule/programa de proporción variable. En el condicionamiento operante, programa de reforzamiento parcial que administra recompensas por un número impredecible de respuestas correctas. (pág. 315)

vestibular sense/sentido vestibular. Sistema que percibe la orientación y el equilibrio del cuerpo y está ubicado en los canales semicirculares del oído interno. (pág. 177)

visual cliff/precipicio visual. Aparato de laboratorio que examina la percepción de profundidad de los bebés recién nacidos y de los animales jóvenes. (pág. 186)

W

Washburn, Margaret Floy. (1871–1930) Primera mujer en recibir un doctorado en psicología. (pág. 8)

Watson, John B. (1878–1958) Fundador del conductismo, perspectiva según la cual la psicología debe limitarse a estudiar los comportamientos observables y no los procesos mentales. (págs. 6, 283)

Wechsler, David. (1896–1981) Creador de las escalas de inteligencia de Wechsler, que se han convertido en las pruebas individuales de inteligencia que más se administran en Estados Unidos. Fueron las primeras pruebas en tener puntajes tanto para la inteligencia verbal como para la de desempeño. (pág. 462)

Wechsler intelligence scales/escalas de inteligencia de Wechsler. Serie de pruebas de inteligencia diseñadas para tres grupos de edades distintas (adultos, niños y niños preescolares); en la actualidad, son las pruebas individuales de inteligencia que más se administran en Estados Unidos. (pág. 462)

wellness/bienestar. Resultado de un estilo de vida y actitudes saludables. (pág. 258)

Wernicke's [ver-NIC-keys] area/área de Wernicke. Parte del cerebro que participa en la comprensión y la expresión del lenguaje; generalmente está ubicada en el lóbulo temporal izquierdo. (pág. 149)

Whorf, Benjamin. (1897–1941) Lingüista que formuló la hipótesis de relatividad lingüística, según la cual nuestro lenguaje ordena la forma en que pensamos acerca del mundo que nos rodea. (pág. 449)

withdrawal/síntomas de abstinencia. Malestar y angustia que ocurren a una persona que depende de una droga adictiva cuando deja de consumirla. (págs. 269, 409)

Wundt, Wilhelm. (1832–1920) Fundador de la psicología moderna. (pág. 4)

Y

Yerkes-Dodson law/ley de Yerkes-Dodson. Teoría según la cual un grado de estimulación psicológica facilita el rendimiento, pero sólo hasta cierto punto. (pág. 210)

Z

Zajonc, Robert. (1923–) Psicólogo estadounidense que concluyó que algunas reacciones emocionales no requieren un pensamiento intencionado y que la cognición no siempre es necesaria en lo que respecta a las emociones. (pág. 230)

zygote/cigoto. Óvulo fecundado; tras un período de dos semanas de división celular rápida, se convierte en embrión. (pág. 58)

GE-23

References

Abramson, L. Y., Metalsky, G. I., & Alloy, L. B. (1989). Hopelessness depression: A theory-based subtype. *Psychological Review, 96,* 358–372.

Adelmann, P. K., Antonucci, T. C., Crohan, S. F., & Coleman, L. M. (1989). Empty nest, cohort, and employment in the well-being of midlife women. *Sex Roles, 20,* 173–189.

Ainsworth, M. D. S. (1979). Infant-mother attachment. *American Psychologist, 34,* 932–937.

Allport, G. W., & Odbert, H. S. (1936). Trait-names: A psycholexical study. *Psychological Monographs, 47*(1).

Amabile, T. M. (1996). *The context of creativity.* Boulder, CO: Westview.

American Psychiatric Association. (1994). *Diagnostic and statistical manual of mental disorders* (4th ed.). Washington, DC: American Psychiatric Press.

American Psychiatric Association. (2000). *Diagnostic and statistical manual of mental disorders* (4th ed., Text Revision). Washington, DC: American Psychiatric Press.

American Psychological Association. (1992). Ethical principles of psychologists and code of conduct. *American Psychologist, 47*, 1597–1611.

American Psychological Association Commission on Violence and Youth. (1993). *Violence & youth: Psychology's response: Vol. I: Summary report of the American Psychological Association Commission on Violence and Youth.* Washington, DC: American Psychological Association.

Anderson, C. A., & Dill, K. E. (2000). Video games and aggressive thoughts, feelings, and behavior in the laboratory and in life. *Journal of Personality and Social Psychology, 78,* 772–790.

Andreasen, N. C., Arndt, S., Swayze, V., II, Cizadlo, T., & Flaum, M. (1994). Thalamic abnormalities in schizophrenia visualized through magnetic resonance image averaging. *Science, 266,* 294–298.

Armony, J. L., Quirk, G. J., & LeDoux, J. E. (1998). Differential effects of amygdala lesions on early and late plastic components of auditory cortex spike trains during fear conditioning. *Journal of Neuroscience, 18,* 2592–2601.

Aron, A., Melinat, E., Aron, E. N., Vallone, R. D., & Bator, R. J. (1997). The experimental generation of interpersonal closeness: A procedure and some preliminary findings. *Personality and Social Psychology Bulletin, 23,* 363–377.

Aronson, E. (1999). *The social animal* (8th ed.). New York: Worth Publishers.

Asch, S. E. (1955). Opinions and social pressure. *Scientific American, 193,* 31–35.

Atkinson, R. (1988). The teenage world: Adolescent self-image in ten countries. New York: Plenum Press.

Atkinson, R. C., & Schiffrin, R. M. (1968). Human memory: A control system and its control processes. In K. Spence (Ed.), *The psychology of learning and motivation* (Vol. 2). New York: Academic Press.

Avery, R. D., & others. (1994, December 13). Mainstream science on intelligence. *Wall Street Journal*, A-18.

Baddeley, A. D. (1982). *Your memory: A user's guide.* New York: Macmillan.

Bahrick, H. P. (1984). Semantic memory content in permastore: 50 years of memory for Spanish learned in school. *Journal of Experimental Psychology: General, 111,* 1–29.

Bahrick, H. P., Bahrick, L. E., Bahrick, A. S., & Bahrick, P. E. (1993). Maintenance of foreign language vocabulary and the spacing effect. *Psychological Science, 4,* 316–321.

Bailey, J. M., Bobrow, D., Wolfe, M., & Mikach, S. (1995). Sexual orientation of adult sons of gay fathers. *Developmental Psychology, 31,* 124–129.

Ballard, M. E., & Wiest, J. R. (1998). Mortal Kombat: The effects of violent videogame play on males' hostility and cardiovascular responding. *Journal of Applied Social Psychology, 26,* 717–730.

Bandura, A. (1965). Influence of a model's reinforcement contingencies on the acquisition of imitative responses. *Journal of Personality and Social Psychology, 1,* 589–595.

Bandura, A. (1977). *Social learning theory* (original work published in 1971). Englewood Cliffs, NJ: Prentice-Hall.

Bandura, A. (1986). *Social foundations of thought and action: A social-cognitive theory.* Englewood Cliffs, NJ: Prentice-Hall.

Bandura, A., Blanchard, E. B., & Ritter, B. (1969). Relative efficacy of desensitization and modeling approaches for inducing behavioral, affective, and attitudinal changes. *Journal of Personality and Social Psychology, 13,* 173–199.

R-1

Bandura, A., Ross, D., & Ross, S. A. (1961). Transmission of aggression through imitation of aggressive models. *Journal of Abnormal and Social Psychology, 63,* 575–582.

Bard, P. (1934). On emotional experience after decortication with some remarks on theoretical views. *Psychological Review, 41,* 309–329.

Baron, R. S., Vandello, J. A., & Brunsman, B. (1996). The forgotten variable in conformity research: Impact of task importance on social influence. *Journal of Personality and Social Psychology, 71,* 915–927.

Bartoshuk, L. M., Duffy, V. B., & Miller, I. J. (1994). PTC/PROP taste: Anatomy, psychophysics, and sex effects. *Physiology & Behavior, 56,* 1165–1171.

Baruch, G. K., & Barnett, R. (1986). Role quality, multiple role involvement, and psychological well-being in midlife women. *Journal of Personality and Social Psychology, 51,* 578–585.

Bashore, T. R., & Rapp, P. E. (1993). Are there alternatives to traditional polygraph procedures? *Psychological Bulletin, 113*(1), 3–22.

Bashore, T. R., Ridderinkhof, K. R., & van der Molen, M. W. (1997). The decline of cognitive processing speed in old age. *Current Directions in Psychological Science, 6,* 163–169.

Bass, E., & Davis, L. (1988). *The courage to heal.* New York: Harper & Row.

Bates, J. P., Pettit, G., Dodge, K., & Ridge, B. (1998). Interaction of temperamental resistance to control and restrictive parenting in the development of externalizing behavior. *Developmental Psychology, 34,* 982–995.

Baumeister, R. F. (1989). The optimal margin of illusion. *Journal of Social and Clinical Psychology, 8,* 176–189.

Baumeister, R. F., Stillwell, A., & Wotman, S. R. (1990). Victim and perpetrator accounts of interpersonal conflict: Autobiographical narratives about anger. *Journal of Personality and Social Psychology, 59,* 994–1005.

Baumrind, D. (1971). Current patterns of parental authority. *Developmental Psychology Monograph, 4* (1, Part 2).

Baumrind, D. (1996). The discipline controversy revisited. *Family Relations, 45,* 405–414.

Bee, H. (1997). *The developing child* (8th ed.). New York: Longman.

Belsky, J., Lang, M., & Huston, T. L. (1986). Sex typing and division of labor as determinants of marital change across the transition to parenthood. *Journal of Personality and Social Psychology, 50,* 517–522.

Ben-Shakhar, G., & Furedy, J. J. (1990). *Theories and applications in the detection of deception: A psychophysiological and international perspective.* New York: Springer-Verlag.

Benson, J. A., Jr., & Watson, S. J., Jr. (1999). *Marijuana and medicine: Assessing the science base.* Washington, DC: National Academy Press.

Berger, K. S. (2001). *The developing person through the life span* (5th ed.). New York: Worth Publishers.

Berman, M., Gladue, B., & Taylor, S. (1993). The effects of hormones, Type A behavior pattern, and provocation on aggression in men. *Motivation and Emotion, 17,* 125–138.

Bernard, L. L. (1924). *Instinct.* New York: Holt, Rinehart & Winston.

Berry, J. W., Poorting, Y. H., Segall, M. H., & Dasen, P. R. (1992). *Cross-cultural psychology: Research and applications.* New York: Cambridge University Press.

Berscheid, E. (1981). An overview of the psychological effects of physical attractiveness and some comments upon the psychological effects of knowledge of the effects of physical attractiveness. In G. W. Lucker, K. Ribbens, & J. A. McNamara (Eds.), *Psychological aspects of facial form* (Craniofacial growth series). Ann Arbor: Center for Human Growth and Development, University of Michigan.

Berscheid, E., Gangestad, S. W., & Kulakowski, D. (1984). Emotion in close relationships: Implications for relationship counseling. In S. D. Brown & R. W. Lent (Eds.), *Handbook of counseling psychology.* New York: Wiley.

Beyerstein, B., & Beyerstein, D. (Eds.). (1992). *The write stuff: Evaluations of graphology.* Buffalo, NY: Prometheus Books.

Bickman, L. (1999). Practice makes perfect and other myths about mental health services. *American Psychologist, 54,* 965–978.

Bishop, G. D. (1991). Understanding the understanding of illness: Lay disease representations. In J. A. Skelton & R. T. Croyle (Eds.), *Mental representation in health and illness.* New York: Springer-Verlag.

Blackmore, S. J. (1997). Probability misjudgment and belief in the paranormal: A newspaper survey. *British Journal of Psychology, 88,* 683–689.

Blaikie, A. (1999). Ageing: Old visions, new times? *Lancet, 354* (Suppl. 4), 5103.

Blass, T. (1996). Stanley Milgram: A life of inventiveness and controversy. In G. A. Kimble, C. A. Boneau, & M. Wertheimer (Eds.), *Portraits of pioneers in psychology* (Vol. II). Washington, DC, and Mahwah, NJ: American Psychological Association and Lawrence Erlbaum Publishers.

Blass, T. (1999). The Milgram paradigm after 35 years: Some things we now know about obedience to authority. *Journal of Applied Social Psychology, 29,* 955–978.

Bloom, B. S. (Ed.). (1985). *Developing talent in young people.* New York: Ballantine.

Blum, D. (1998, September/October). Face it! *Psychology Today,* 32–39, 66–67.

Bock, B. C., Marcus, B. H., King, T. E., Borrelli, B., & Roberts, M. R. (1999). Exercise effects on withdrawal and mood among women attempting smoking cessation. *Addictive Behavior, 24,* 399–410.

R-2

Boring, E. G. (1930). A new ambiguous figure. *American Journal of Psychology, 42,* 444–445.

Bothwell, R. K., Deffenbacher, K. A., & Brigham, J. C. (1987). Correlation of eyewitness accuracy and confidence: Optimality hypothesis revised. *Journal of Applied Psychology, 72,* 691–695.

Botwin, M. D., Buss, D. M., & Shackelford, T. K. (1997). Personality and mate preferences: Five factors in mate selection and marital satisfaction. *Journal of Personality, 65,* 107–136.

Bouchard, T. J., Lykken, D. T., McGue, M., Segal, N. L., & Tellegren, A. (1990). Sources of human psychological differences. The Minnesota study of twins reared apart. *Science, 250,* 223–228.

Bower, G. H. (1986). Prime time in cognitive psychology. In P. Eelen (Ed.), *Cognitive research and behavior therapy: Beyond the conditioning paradigm.* Amsterdam: North Holland Publishers.

Bower, T. G. R. (1982). *Development in infancy* (2nd ed.). San Francisco: Freeman.

Bowers, K. S. (1976). *Hypnosis for the seriously curious.* New York: Norton.

Bowers, K. S. (1984). Hypnosis. In N. Endler & J. M. Hunt (Eds.), *Personality and behavioral disorders* (2nd ed.). New York: Wiley.

Bowers, K. S., & LeBaron, S. (1986). Hypnosis and hypnotizability: Implications for clinical intervention. *Hospital and Community Psychiatry, 37,* 457–467.

Boynton, R. M. (1979). *Human color vision.* New York: Holt, Rinehart & Winston.

Bradley, D. R., Dumais, S. T., & Petry, H. M. (1976). Reply to Cavonius. *Nature, 261,* 78.

Bradshaw, J. (1990). Homecoming: Reclaiming and championing your inner child. New York: Bantam Books.

Braun, S. (1996). New experiments underscore warnings on maternal drinking. *Science, 273,* 738–739.

Brems, C., Thevenin, D. M., & Routh, D. K. (1991). The history of clinical psychology. In C. E. Walker (Ed.), *Clinical psychology: Historical and research foundations* (pp. 3–35). New York: Plenum Press.

Brewer, C. L. (1998). Personal communication.

Brodzinsky, D. M., & Schechter, M. D. (Eds.). (1990). *The psychology of adoption.* New York: Oxford University Press.

Brown, E. L., & Deffenbacher, K. (1979). *Perception and the senses.* New York: Oxford University Press.

Bruck, M., & Ceci, S. J. (1999). The suggestibility of children's memory. *Annual Review of Psychology, 50,* 419–439.

Buck, R. (1984). *The communication of emotion.* New York: Guilford Press.

Buehler, R., Griffin, D., & Ross, M. (1994). Exploring the "planning fallacy": Why people underestimate their task completion times. *Journal of Personality and Social Psychology, 67,* 366–381.

Bugelski, B. R., Kidd, E., & Segmen, J. (1968). Image as a mediator in one-trial paired-associate learning. *Journal of Experimental Psychology, 76,* 69–73.

Bureau of the Census. (1998). *Statistical abstract of the United States 1998.* Washington, DC: U.S. Government Printing Office.

Bureau of the Census. (1999). *Statistical abstract of the United States 1999.* Washington DC: U.S. Government Printing Office.

Burger, J. M., & Burns, L. (1988). The illusion of unique invulnerability and the use of effective contraception. *Personality and Social Psychology Bulletin, 14,* 264–270.

Buri, J. R., Louiselle, P. A., Misukanis, T. M., & Mueller, R. A. (1988). Effects of parental authoritarianism and authoritativeness on self-esteem. *Personality and Social Psychology Bulletin, 14,* 271–282.

Busch, C. M., Zonderman, A. B., & Costa, P. T. (1994). Menopausal transition and psychological distress in a nationally representative sample: Is menopause associated with psychological distress? *Journal of Aging and Health, 6,* 209–228.

Bushman, B. J. (1993). Human aggression while under the influence of alcohol and other drugs: An integrative research review. *Current Directions in Psychological Science, 2,* 148–152.

Butler, R. N., Lewis, M., & Sunderland, T. (1991). *Aging and mental health: Positive psychosocial and biomedical holdings* (4th ed.). New York: Merrill.

Byrne, D. (1971). *The attraction paradigm.* New York: Academic Press.

Cahill, L. (1994). (Beta)-adrenergic activation and memory for emotional events. *Nature, 371,* 702–704.

Campos, J. J., Bertenthal, B. I., & Kermoian, R. (1992). Early experience and emotional development: The emergence of wariness and heights. *Psychological Science, 3,* 61–64.

Cannon, T. D., & Marco, E. (1994). Structural brain abnormalities as indicators of vulnerability to schizophrenia. *Schizophrenia Bulletin, 20,* 89–102.

Cannon, W. B. (1929). *Bodily changes in pain, hunger, fear, and rage.* New York: Branford.

Carducci, B. J., Cosby, P. C., & Ward, D. D. (1978). Sexual arousal and interpersonal evaluations. *Journal of Experimental Social Psychology, 14,* 449–457.

Carey, G. (1990). Genes, fears, phobias, and phobic disorders. *Journal of Counseling and Development, 68,* 628–632.

Carlson, M., Charlin, V., & Miller, N. (1988). Positive mood and helping behavior: A test of six hypotheses. *Journal of Personality and Social Psychology, 55,* 211–229.

Carnegie Council on Adolescent Development. (1989, June). *Turning points: Preparing American youth for the 21st*

R-3

century (The report of the Task Force on Education of Young Adolescents). New York: Carnegie Corporation.

Carson, M. (1995, August 29). Quoted in S. Blakeslee, In brain's early growth, timetable may be crucial. *New York Times*, pp. C1, C3.

Carson, S. (1985). A double-blind test of astrology. *Nature, 318,* 419–425.

Cartwright, R. D. (1978). *A primer on sleep and dreaming.* Reading, MA: Addison-Wesley.

Case, R. B., Moss, A. J., Case, N., McDermott, M., & Eberly, S. (1992). Living alone after myocardial infarction: Impact on prognosis. *Journal of the American Medical Association, 267,* 515–519.

Cassidy, J., & Shaver, P. R. (1999). *Handbook of attachment.* New York: Guilford.

Cattell, R. B. (1963). Theory of fluid and crystallized intelligence: A critical experiment. *Journal of Educational Psychology, 54,* 1–22.

Cattell, R. B., & Krug, S. E. (1986). The number of factors in the 16PF: A review of the evidence with special emphasis on methodological problems. *Educational and Psychological Measurement, 46,* 509–522.

Cavalli-Sforza, L., Menozzi, P., & Piazza, A. (1994). *The history and geography of human genes.* Princeton, NJ: Princeton University Press.

Ceci, S. J., & Bruck, M. (1993). Child witnesses: Translating research into policy. *Social Policy Report* (Society for Research in Child Development), 7(3), 1–30.

Centerwall, B. S. (1989). Exposure to television as a risk factor for violence. *American Journal of Epidemiology, 129,* 643–652.

Chambless, D. L., Baker, M. J., Baucom, D. H., Beutler, L. E., Calhoun, K. S., Crits-Christoph, P., Daiuto, A., DeRubeis, R., Detweiler, J., Haaga, D. A. F., Johnson, S. B., McCurry, S., Mueser, K. T., Pope, K. S., Sanderson, W. C., Shoham, V., Stickle, T., Williams, D. A., & Woody, S. R. (1997). Update on empirically validated therapies, II. *The Clinical Psychologist, 51*(1), 3–16.

Chance News. (1997, 25 November). More on the frequency of letters in texts. Dart.Chance@Dartmouth.edu.

Chassin, L., Presson, C. C., Sherman, S. J., & McGrew, J. (1987). The changing smoking environment for middle and high school students: 1980–1983. *Journal of Behavioral Medicine, 10,* 581–593.

Chess, S., & Thomas, A. (1987). *Know your child: An authoritative guide for today's parents.* New York: Basic Books.

Childers, S. R., & Breivogel, C. S. (1998). Cannabis and endogenous cannabinoid systems. *Drug and Alcohol Dependence, 51,* 173–187.

Chomsky, N. (1959). Review of B. F. Skinner's *Verbal behavior. Language, 35,* 26–58.

Chomsky, N. (1972). *Language and mind.* New York: Harcourt Brace Jovanovich.

Chomsky, N. (1987). *Language in psychological setting.* Sophia Linguistic Working Papers in Linguistics, No. 22, Sophia University, Tokyo.

Chu, J. A., Frey, L. M., Ganzel, B. L., & Matthews, J. A. (1999). Memories of childhood abuse: Dissociation, amnesia, and corroboration. *American Journal of Psychiatry, 156,* 749–755.

Cialdini, R. B. (1993). *Influence: Science and practice* (3rd ed.). New York: HarperCollins.

Cialdini, R. B., & Richardson, K. D. (1980). Two indirect tactics of image management: Basking and blasting. *Journal of Personality and Social Psychology, 39,* 406–415.

Clark, R., Anderson, N. B, Clark, V. R., & Williams, D. R. (1999). Racism as a stressor for African Americans: A biopsychosocial model. *American Psychologist, 54,* 805–816.

Coats, E. J., & Feldman, R. S. (1996). Gender differences in non-verbal correlates of social status. *Personality and Social Psychology Bulletin, 22,* 1014–1022.

Coffey, C. E. (Ed.). *Clinical science of electroconvulsive therapy.* Washington, DC: American Psychiatric Press.

Cohen, G., Conway, M. A., & Maylor, E. A. (1994, September). Flashbulb memories in older adults. *Psychology and Aging, 9*(3), 454–463.

Cohen, S. (1988). Psychosocial models of the role of social support in the etiology of physical disease. *Health Psychology, 7,* 269–297.

Cohen, S., Doyle, W. J., Skoner, D. P., Rabin, B. S., & Gwaltney, J. M., Jr. (1997). Social ties and susceptibility to the common cold. *Journal of the American Medical Association, 277,* 1940–1944.

Cohen, S., Frank, E., Doyle, W. J., Skoner, D. P., Rabin, B. S., & Gwaltney, J. M., Jr. (1998). Types of stressors that increase susceptibility to the common cold in healthy adults. *Health Psychology, 17,* 214–223.

Cohen, S., Tyrrell, D. A. J., & Smith, A. P. (1991). Psychological stress and susceptibility to the common cold. *New England Journal of Medicine, 325,* 606–612.

Coile, D. C., & Miller, N. E. (1984). How radical animal activists try to mislead humane people. *American Psychologist, 39,* 700–701.

Consumer Reports. (1995, November). Does therapy help? Pp. 734–739.

Conway, M. & Ross, M. (1984). Getting what you want by revising what you had. *Journal of Personality and Social Psychology, 47,* 738–748.

Cook, E. W., III, Hodes, R. L., & Lang, P. J. (1986). Preparedness and phobia: Effects of stimulus content on human visceral conditioning. *Journal of Abnormal Psychology, 95,* 195–207.

Coombs, R. H. (1991, January). Marital status and personal well-being. A literature review. *Family Relations, 40,* 97–102.

Cooper, K. J. (1999, May 1). This time, copycat wave is broader. *Washington Post.* Retrieved from http://www.washingtonpost.com

Coren, S. (1996). *Sleep thieves: An eye-opening exploration into the science and mysteries of sleep.* New York: Free Press.

Coren, S., Ward, L.M., & Enns, J.T. (1999). *Sensation and perception* (5th ed.). New York: Harcourt Brace.

Costa, P. T., Jr., Zonderman, A. B., McCrae, R. R., Cornoni-Huntley, J., Locke, B. Z., & Barbano, H. E. (1987). Longitudinal analyses of psychological well-being in a national sample: Stability of mean levels. *Journal of Gerontology, 42,* 50–55.

Courtney, J. G., Longnecker, M. P., Theorell, T., & de Verdier, M. G. (1993). Stressful life events and the risk of colorectal cancer. *Epidemiology, 4,* 407–414.

Cowan, N. (1988). Evolving conceptions of memory storage, selective attention, and their mutual constraints within the human information-processing system. *Psychological Bulletin, 104,* 163–191.

Craik, F. I. M., & Tulving, E. (1975). Depth of processing and the retention of words in episodic memory. *Journal of Experimental Psychology: General, 104,* 268–294.

Craik, F. I. M., & Watkins, M. J. (1973). The role of rehearsal in short-term memory. *Journal of Verbal Learning and Verbal Behavior, 12,* 599–607.

Crandall, C. S. (1988). Social contagion of binge eating. *Journal of Personality and Social Psychology, 55,* 588–598.

Crandall, C. S. (1994). Prejudice against fat people: Ideology and self-interest. *Journal of Personality and Social Psychology, 66,* 882–894.

Crocker, J., Thompson, L. L., McGraw, K. M., & Ingerman, C. (1987). Downward comparison, prejudice, and evaluation of others: Effects of self-esteem and threat. *Journal of Personality and Social Psychology, 52,* 907–916.

Crook, T. H., & West, R. L. (1990). Name recall performance across the adult life-span. *British Journal of Psychology, 81,* 335–340.

Csikszentmihalyi, M. (1990). *Flow: The psychology of optimal experience.* New York: Harper & Row.

Cunningham, S. (1985, May). Humanists celebrate gains, goals. *APA Monitor,* 16, 18.

Cutler, B. L., & Penrod, S. D. (1989). Forensically relevant moderators of the relation between eyewitness identification accuracy and confidence. *Journal of Applied Psychology, 74,* 650–652.

Dabbs, J. M., Jr. (1992). Testosterone measurements in social and clinical psychology. *Journal of Social and Clinical Psychology, 11,* 302–321.

Dabbs, J. M., Jr., & Morris, R. (1990). Testosterone, social class, and antisocial behavior in a sample of 4,462 men. *Psychological Science, 1,* 209–211.

Damasio, H., Grabowski, T., Frank, R., Galaburda, A. M., & Damasio, A. R. (1994). The return of Phineas Gage: Clues about the brain from the skull of a famous patient. *Science, 264,* 1102–1105.

Darley, J. M., & Latané, B. (1968). Bystander intervention in emergencies: Diffusion of responsibility. *Journal of Personality and Social Psychology, 8,* 377–383.

Darrach, B., & Norris, J. (1984, August). An American tragedy. *Life,* 58–74.

Dasen, P. R. (1994). Culture and cognitive development from a Piagetian perspective. In W. J. Lonner & R. S. Malpass (Eds.), *Psychology and culture.* Needham Heights, MA: Allyn & Bacon.

Davidson, R. J. (1999). Biological bases of personality. In V. J. Darlega, B. A. Winstead, & W. H. Jones (Eds.), *Personality: Contemporary theory and research.* Chicago: Nelson-Hall.

Davies, K. (2001, April 14). The news that shocked the world: We only have about twice as many genes as your average fruit fly. Retrieved from http://www.pbs.org/wgbh/nova/genome/debate.html

Dawes, R. M. (1994). *House of cards: Psychology and psychotherapy built on myth.* New York: Free Press.

Dean, G. A., Kelly, I. W., Saklofske, D. H., & Furnham, A. (1992). Graphology and human judgment. In B. Beyerstein & D. Beyerstein (Eds.), *The write stuff: Evaluations of graphology.* Buffalo, NY: Prometheus Books.

de Boysson-Bardies, B., Halle, P., Sagart, L., & Durand, C. (1989). A cross linguistic investigation of vowel formats in babbling. *Journal of Child Language, 16,* 1–17.

DeLoache, J. S., & Brown, A. L. (1987, October–December). Differences in the memory-based searching of delayed and normally developing young children. *Intelligence, 11*(4), 277–289.

Dement, W. C. (1978). *Some must watch while some must sleep.* New York: Norton.

Dement, W. C. (1999). *The promise of sleep.* New York: Delacorte Press.

Dempster, F. N. (1988). The spacing effect: A case study in the failure to apply the results of psychological research. *American Psychologist, 43,* 627–634.

DeNeve, K. M., & Cooper, H. (1998). The happy personality: A meta-analysis of 137 personality traits and subjective well-being. *Psychological Bulletin, 124,* 197–229.

Denton, K., & Krebs, D. (1990). From the scene to the crime: The effect of alcohol and social context on moral judgment. *Journal of Personality and Social Psychology, 59,* 242–248.

DePaulo, B. M., Blank, A. K., Swaim, G. W., & Hairfield, J. G. (1992). Expressiveness and expressive control. *Personality and Social Psychology Bulletin, 18,* 276–285.

Dermer, M., & Pyszczynski, T. A. (1978). Effects of erotica upon men's loving and liking responses for women they love. *Journal of Personality and Social Psychology, 36,* 1302–1309.

DeRubeis, R. J., & Crits-Christoph, P. (1998). Empirically supported individual and group psychological treatments for adult mental disorders. *Journal of Consulting and Clinical Psychology, 66,* 37–52.

DeValois, R. L., & DeValois, K. K. (1975). Neural coding of color. In E. C. Carterette & M. P. Friedman (Eds.), *Handbook of perception: Vol. V. Seeing.* New York: Academic Press.

Diener, E. (2000). Paper presented at Akumal II Conference, Akumal, Mexico.

Diener, E. (2002). Personal correspondence.

Diener, E., Emmons, R. A., & Sandvik, E. (1986). The dual nature of happiness: Independence of positive and negative moods. Unpublished manuscript, University of Illinois.

Diener, E., Wolsic, B., & Fujita, F. (1995). Physical attractiveness and subjective well-being. *Journal of Personality and Social Psychology, 69,* 120–129.

DiLalla, D. L., Carey, G., Gottesman, I. I., & Bouchard, T. J., Jr. (1996). Heritability of MMPI personality indicators of psychopathology in twins reared apart. *Journal of Abnormal Psychology, 105,* 491–499.

Dinges, N. G., & Hull, P. (1992). Personality, culture, and international studies. In D. Lieberman (Ed.), *Revealing the world: An interdisciplinary reader for international studies.* Dubuque, IA: Kendall-Hunt.

Discover (1996, May). A fistful of risks. 82–83.

Doherty, E. W., & Doherty, W. J. (1998). Smoke gets in your eyes: Cigarette smoking and divorce in a national sample of American adults. *Families, Systems, and Health, 16,* 393–400.

Dohrenwend, B., Pearlin, L., Clayton, P., Hamburg, B., Dohrenwend, B. P., Riley, M., & Rose, R. (1982). Report on stress and life events. In G. R. Elliott & C. Eisdorfer (Eds.), *Stress and human health: Analysis and implications of research* (A study by the Institute of Medicine/National Academy of Sciences). New York: Springer.

Dorner, G. (1976). *Hormones and brain differentiation.* Amsterdam: Elsevier Scientific.

Doty, R. L., Shaman, P., Applebaum, S. L, Giberson, R., Siksorski, L., & Rosenberg, L. (1984). Smell identification ability: Changes with age. *Science, 226,* 1441–1443.

Dovidio, J. F., & Gaertner, S. L. (1999). Reducing prejudice: Combating intergroup biases. *Current Directions in Psychological Science, 8,* 101–105.

Druckman, D., & Bjork, R. A. (Eds.). (1994). *Learning, remembering, believing: Enhancing human performance.* Washington, DC: National Academy Press.

Drummey, A. B., & Newcombe, N. (1995). Remembering versus knowing the past: Children's explicit and implicit memories for pictures. *Journal of Experimental Child Psychology, 59,* 549–565.

Drummond, T. (1998, July 27). Touch early and often. *Time, 152*(4). Retrieved from http://www.time.com/time/magazine/1998/dom/980727/health.touch_early_and_o14.html

Duke, M., & Nowicki, S., Jr. (1979). *Abnormal psychology: Perspectives on being different.* Pacific Grove, CA: Brooks/Cole.

Duncan, B. L. (1976). Differential social perception and attribution of intergroup violence: Testing the lower limits of stereotyping of blacks. *Journal of Personality and Social Psychology, 34,* 590–598.

Dyal, J. A. (1984). Cross-cultural research with the locus of control construct. In H. M. Lefcourt (Ed.), *Research with the locus of control construct* (Vol. 3). New York: Academic Press.

Eagly, A. (1994). Are people prejudiced against women? Donald Campbell Award invited address, American Psychological Association convention.

Eagly, A. H., Ashmore, R. D., Makhijani, M. G., & Kennedy, L. C. (1991). What is beautiful is good, but . . .: A meta-analytic review of research on the physical attractiveness stereotype. *Psychological Bulletin, 110,* 109–128.

Eastman, C. L., Young, M. A., Fogg, L. F., Liu, L., & Meaden, P. M. (1998). Bright light treatment of winter depression: A placebo-controlled trial. *Archives of General Psychiatry, 55,* 883–889.

Ebbinghaus, H. (1885). *Über das Gedachtnis.* Leipzig: Duncker & Humblot. Cited in R. Klatzky (1980), *Human memory: Structures and processes.* San Francisco: Freeman.

Eckensberger, L. H. (1994). Moral development and its measurement across cultures. In W. J. Lonner & R. Malpass (Eds.), *Psychology and culture.* Boston: Allyn & Bacon.

Eckert, E. D., Heston, L. L., & Bouchard, T. J., Jr. (1981). MZ twins reared apart: Preliminary findings of psychiatric disturbances and traits. In L. Gedda, P. Paris, & W. D. Nance (Eds.), *Twin research: Vol. 3. Pt. B. Intelligence, personality, and development.* New York: Alan Liss.

Edelman, S., & Kidman, A. D. (1997). Mind and cancer: Is there a relationship? A review of the evidence. *Australian Psychologist, 32,* 1–7.

Edwards, C. P. (1981). The comparative study of the development of moral judgment and reasoning. In R. H. Munroe, R. L. Munroe, & B. B. Whiting (Eds.), *Handbook of cross-cultural human development.* New York: Garland Press.

Edwards, C. P. (1982). Moral development in comparative cultural perspective. In D. A. Wagner & H. W. Stevenson (Eds.), *Cultural perspectives on child development.* San Francisco: Freeman.

Eich, E. (1995). Searching for mood dependent memory. *Psychological Science, 6,* 67–75.

Eich, J. E. (1980). The cue-dependent nature of state-dependent retrieval. *Memory and Cognition, 8,* 157–173.

Einstein, G. O., & McDaniel, M. A. (1990). Normal aging and prospective memory. *Journal of Experimental Psychology: Learning, Memory, and Cognition, 16,* 717–726.

Einstein, G. O., McDaniel, M. A., Richardson, S. L., Guynn, M. J., & Cunfer, A. R. (1995). Aging and prospective memory: Examining the influences of self-initiated retrieval processes. *Journal of Experimental Psychology: Learning, Memory, and Cognition, 21,* 996–1007.

Einstein, G. O., McDaniel, M. A., Smith, R. E., & Shaw, P. (1998). Habitual prospective memory and aging: Remembering intentions and forgetting actions. *Psychological Science, 9,* 284–288.

Ekman, P. (1994). Strong evidence for universals in facial expressions: A reply to Russell's mistaken critique. *Psychological Bulletin, 115,* 268–287.

Ekman, P., & Friesen, W. V. (1975). *Unmasking the face.* Englewood Cliffs, NJ: Prentice-Hall.

Ekman, P., Friesen, W. V., O'Sullivan, M., Chan, A., Diacoyanni-Tarlatzis, I., Heider, K., Krause, R., LeCompte, W. A., Pitcairn, T., Ricci-Bitti, P. E., Scherer, K., Tomita, M., & Tzavaras, A. (1987). Universals and cultural differences in the judgments of facial expressions of emotion. *Journal of Personality and Social Psychology, 53,* 712–717.

Elkin, I., Shea, T., Watkins, J. T., Imber, S. D., Sotsky, S. M., Collins, J. F., Glass, D. R., Pilkonis, P. A., Leber, W. R., Docherty, J. P., Fiester, S. J., & Parloff, M. B. (1989). National Institute of Mental Health treatment of depression collaborative research program. *Archives of General Psychiatry, 46,* 971–983.

Elkind, D. (1970). The origins of religion in the child. *Review of Religious Research, 12,* 35–42.

Elkind, D. (1978). *The child's reality: Three developmental themes.* Hillsdale, NJ: Erlbaum.

Elliot, A. (1996, January 18). Personal communication between Nielsen Media Research Director of Communications and David Myers, via e-mail.

Epstein, S, & Meier, P. (1989). Constructive thinking: A broad coping variable with specific components. *Journal of Personality and Social Psychology, 57,* 332–350.

Erel, O., & Burman, B. (1995). Interrelatedness of marital relations and parent-child relations: A meta-analytic review. *Psychological Bulletin, 118,* 108–132.

Erikson, E. H. (1963). *Childhood and society.* New York: Norton.

Ernsberger, P., & Koletsky, R. J. (1999). Biomedical rationale for a wellness approach to obesity: An alternative to a focus on weight loss. *Journal of Social Issues, 55,* 221–260.

Ernst, R. E., Matsumoto, D., Freeman, J., Weseley, A. (2000). *An introduction to cross-cultural psychology: A five-day unit plan prepared for teachers of psychology in secondary schools.* Washington, DC: American Psychological Association.

Esser, J. K., & Lindoerfer, J. S. (1989). Groupthink and the space shuttle *Challenger* accident: Toward a quantitative case analysis. *Journal of Behavioral Decision Making, 2,* 167–177.

Etnier, J. L., Salazar, W., Landers, D. M., Petruzzello, S. J., Han, M., & Nowell, P. (1997). The influence of physical fitness and exercise upon cognitive functioning: A meta-analysis. *Journal of Sport & Exercise Psychology, 19,* 249–277.

Everson, S. A., Goldberg, D. E., Kaplan, G. A., Cohen, R. D., Pukkala, E., Tuomilehto, J., & Salonen, J. T. (1996). Hopelessness and risk of mortality and incidence of myocardial infarction and cancer. *Psychosomatic Medicine, 58,* 113–121.

Eysenck, H. J. (1952). The effects of psychotherapy: An evaluation. *Journal of Consulting Psychology, 16,* 319–324.

Eysenck, S. B. G., & Eysenck, H. J. (1963). The validity of questionnaire and rating assessments of extraversion and neuroticism, and their factorial stability. *British Journal of Psychology, 54,* 51–62.

Fava, M., Copeland, P. M., Schweiger, U., & Herzog, D. B. (1989). Neurochemical abnormalities of anorexia nervosa and bulimia nervosa. *American Journal of Psychiatry, 146,* 963–971.

Fazio, R. H. (1990). Multiple processes by which attitudes guide behavior: The MODE model as an integrative framework. In M. P. Zanna (Ed.), *Advances in experimental social psychology* (Vol. 23). San Diego: Academic Press.

Feingold, A. (1990). Gender differences in effects of physical attractiveness on romantic attraction: A comparison across five research paradigms. *Journal of Personality and Social Psychology, 59,* 981–993.

Feingold, A. (1992). Good-looking people are not what we think. *Psychological Bulletin, 111,* 304–341.

Feldman, R. S., Meyer, J. S., & Quenzer, L. F. (1997). *Principles of neuropsychopharmacology.* Sunderland, MA: Sinauer.

Fichter, M. M., & Noegel, R. (1990). Concordance for bulimia nervosa in twins. *International Journal of Eating Disorders, 9,* 255–263.

Fincham, F. D., & Bradbury, T. N. (1993). Marital satisfaction, depression, and attributions: A longitudinal analysis. *Journal of Personality and Social Psychology, 64,* 442–452.

Fineburg, A. (2000, October). Positive psychology: A unit plan to teach positive psychology. Presented at the second annual Positive Psychology Summit, Washington, DC.

Fink, M. (1999). *Electroshock: Restoring the mind.* New York: Oxford University Press.

Fischer, P. J., & Breakey, W. R. (1991). The epidemiology of alcohol, drug, and mental disorders among homeless persons. *American Psychologist, 46,* 1115–1128.

Fischhoff, B., Slovic, P., & Lichtenstein, S. (1977). Knowing with certainty: The appropriateness of extreme confidence. *Journal of Experimental Psychology: Human Perception and Performance, 3,* 552–564.

Fiske, S. T. (1993). Controlling other people: The impact of power on stereotyping. *American Psychologist, 48,* 621–628.

Fletcher, G. J. O., Fitness, J., & Blampied, N. M. (1990). The link between attributions and happiness in close relationships: The roles of depression and explanatory style. *Journal of Social and Clinical Psychology, 9,* 243–255.

Foa, E. B., & Kozak, M. J. (1986). Emotional processing of fear: Exposure to corrective information. *Psychological Bulletin, 99,* 20–35.

Foree, D. D., & LoLordo, V. M. (1973). Attention in the pigeon: Differential effects of food-getting versus shock-avoidance procedures. *Journal of Comparative and Physiological Psychology, 85,* 551–558.

Forgas, J. P. (1998). On feeling good and getting your way: Mood effects on negotiator cognition and bargaining strategies. *Journal of Personality and Social Psychology, 74,* 565–577.

Fouts, R. S., & Rigby, R. L. (1977). Man-chimpanzee communication. In T. A. Sebeok (Ed.), *How animals communicate.* Bloomington: Indiana University Press.

Fox, B. H. (1998). Psychosocial factors in cancer incidence and prognosis. In P. M. Cinciripini & others (Eds.), *Psychological and behavioral factors in cancer risk*. New York: Oxford University Press.

Frank, J. D. (1982). Therapeutic components shared by all psychotherapies. In J. H. Harvey & M. M. Parks (Eds.), *The Master Lecture Series: Vol. 1. Psychotherapy research and behavior change*. Washington, DC: American Psychological Association.

Freedman, J. L., & Fraser, S. C. (1966). Compliance without pressure: The foot-in-the-door technique. *Journal of Personality and Social Psychology, 4,* 195–202.

Freud, S. (1933). *New introductory lectures on psychoanalysis.* New York: Carlton House.

Freud, S. (1935; reprinted 1960). *A general introduction to psychoanalysis*. New York: Washington Square Press.

Friedman, M., & Ulmer, D. (1984). *Treating Type A behavior—and your heart.* New York: Knopf.

Frieze, I. H., Parsons, J. E., Johnson, P. B., Ruble, D. N., & Zellman, G. L. (1978). *Women and sex roles: A social psychological perspective*. New York: Norton.

Fromkin, V., & Rodman, R. (1983). *An introduction to language* (3rd ed.). New York: Holt, Rinehart & Winston.

Fromm-Reichmann, F. (1948). Notes on the development of treatment of schizophrenia by psychoanalytic therapy. *Psychiatry, 11,* 263–273.

Fuller, M. J., & Downs, A. C. (1990). Spermarche is a salient biological marker in men's development. Poster presented at the American Psychological Society convention.

Funder, D. C. (1991). Global traits: A neo-Allportian approach to personality. *Psychological Science, 2,* 31–39.

Funder, D. C. (1995). On the accuracy of personality judgment: A realistic approach. *Psychological Review, 102,* 652–670.

Furnham, A. (1982). Explanations for unemployment in Britain. *European Journal of Social Psychology, 12,* 335–352.

Furnham, A. (1993). A comparison between psychology and nonpsychology students' misperceptions of the subject. *Journal of Social Behavior and Personality, 8,* 311–322.

Furnham, A., & Baguma, P. (1994). Cross-cultural differences in the evaluation of male and female body shapes. *International Journal of Eating Disorders, 15,* 81–89.

Galanter, E. (1962). Contemporary psychophysics. In R. Brown (Ed.), *New directions in psychology*. New York: Holt, Rinehart & Winston.

Gallant, S. J., Hamilton, J. A., & Popiel, D. A. (1991). Daily moods and symptoms: Effects of awareness of study focus, gender, menstrual-cycle phase, and day of the week. *Health Psychology, 10,* 180–189.

Gallup, G. H., Jr., & Newport, F. (1991, Winter). Belief in paranormal phenomena among adult Americans. *Skeptical Inquirer,* 137–146.

Gallup International Institute. (1996, February). Parents, grandparents OK with teens. *Youthviews*, 3.

Garcia, J., & Koelling, R. A. (1966). Relation of cue to consequence in avoidance learning. *Psychonomic Science, 4,* 123–124.

Gardner, H. (1983). *Frames of mind: The theory of multiple intelligences*. New York: Basic Books.

Gardner, H. (1993). *Creating minds*. New York: Basic Books.

Gardner, H. (1995). Perennial antinomies and perpetual redrawings: Is there progress in the study of mind? In R. L. Solso & D.W. Massaro (Eds.), *The science of the mind: 2001 and beyond.* New York: Oxford University Press.

Gardner, H. (1998, November 5). Do parents count? *New York Review of Books.* Retrieved from http://www.nybooks.com

Gardner, H. (1999). *Multiple views of multiple intelligence.* New York: Basic Books.

Gardner, R. A., & Gardner, B. I. (1969). Teaching sign language to a chimpanzee. *Science, 165,* 664–672.

Garnets, L., & Kimmel, D. (1990). Lesbian and gay dimensions in the psychological study of human diversity. Master lecture, American Psychological Association convention.

Garza, D. L., & Feltz, D. L. (1998). Effects of selected mental practice on performance, self-efficacy, and competition confidence of figure skaters. *The Sports Psychologist, 12,* 1–15.

Gazzaniga, M. S. (1983). Right hemisphere language following brain bisection: A 20-year perspective. *American Psychologist, 38,* 525–537.

Gazzaniga, M. S. (1988). *Mind matters: How mind and brain interact to create our conscious lives*. Boston: Houghton Mifflin.

Geen, R. G., & Quanty, M. B. (1977). The catharsis of aggression: An evaluation of a hypothesis. In L. Berkowitz (Ed.), *Advances in experimental social psychology* (Vol. 10). New York: Academic Press.

Geldard, F. A. (1972). *The human senses* (2nd ed.). New York: Wiley.

George. (1996, December). What does America believe? p. 117.

Gibson, E. J., & Walk, R. D. (1960, April). The "visual cliff." *Scientific American,* 64–71.

Gibson, H. B. (1995, April). Recovered memories. *The Psychologist,* 153–154.

Gibson, J. J. (1950). *The perception of the visual world.* Boston: Houghton Mifflin.

Gilovich, T., & Medvec, V. H. (1995). The experience of regret: What, when and why. *Psychological Review, 102,* 379–395.

Glenn, N. D. (1975). Psychological well-being in the postparental stage: Some evidence from national surveys. *Journal of Marriage and the Family, 37,* 105–110.

Godden, D. R., & Baddeley, A. D. (1975). Context-dependent memory in two natural environments: On land and underwater. *British Journal of Psychology, 66,* 325–331.

Goff, D. C., & Simms, C. A. (1993). Has multiple personality disorder remained consistent over time? *Journal of Nervous and Mental Disease, 181,* 595–600.

Goleman, D. (1995). *Emotional intelligence*. New York: Bantam.

Golombok, S., & Tasker, F. (1996). Do parents influence the sexual orientation of their children? Findings from a longitudinal study of lesbian families. *Developmental Psychology, 32,* 3–11.

Golub, S. (1992). *Periods: From menarche to menopause.* Newbury Park, CA: Sage.

Goodwin, C. J. (1991). Misportraying Pavlov's apparatus. *American Journal of Psychology, 104,* 135–141.

Gottesman, I. I. (1991). *Schizophrenia genesis: The origins of madness*. New York: Freeman.

Gottman, J., with Silver, N. (1994). *Why marriages succeed or fail*. New York: Simon & Schuster.

Gould, S. J. (1981). *The mismeasure of man*. New York: Norton.

Gove, W. R., Style, C. B., & Hughs, M. (1990). The effect of marriage on the well-being of adults: A theoretical analysis. *Journal of Family Issues, 11,* 4–35.

Grady, C. L., McIntosh, A. R., Horwitz, B., Maisog, J. M., Ungeleider, L. G., Mentis, M. J., Pietrini, P., Schapiro, M. B., & Haxby, J. V. (1995). Age-related reductions in human recognition memory due to impaired encoding. *Science, 269,* 218–221.

Graf, P. (1990) Life-span changes in implicit and explicit memory. *Bulletin of the Psychonomic Society, 28,* 353–358.

Gray-Little, B., & Burks, N. (1983). Power and satisfaction in marriage: A review and critique. *Psychological Bulletin, 93,* 513–538.

Greenfeld, L. A. (1998). *Alcohol and crime: An analysis of national data on the prevalence of alcohol involvement in crime.* Washington, DC: Document NCJ-168632, Bureau of Justice Statistics. Retrieved from http://www.ojp.usdoj.gov/bjs

Gregory, R. L. (1968, November). Visual illusions. *Scientific American,* 66–67.

Greif, E. B., & Ulman, K. J. (1982). The psychological impact of menarche on early adolescent females: A review of the literature. *Child Development, 53,* 1413–1430.

Grobstein, C. (1979, June). External human fertilization. *Scientific American,* 57–67.

Grolnick, W. S., & Ryan, R. M. (1987). Autonomy in children's learning: An experimental and individual difference investigation. *Journal of Personality and Social Psychology, 52,* 890–898.

Grossman, K., Grossman, K. E., Spangler, S., Suess, G., & Unzner, L. (1985). Maternal sensitivity and newborn attachment orientation responses as related to quality of attachment in northern Germany. In I. Bretherton & E. Waters (Eds.), *Growing points of attachment theory. Monographs of the Society of Research in Child Development, 50* (1–2 Serial No. 209).

Grossman, M., & Wood, W. (1993). Sex differences in intensity of emotional experience: A social role interpretation. *Journal of Personality and Social Psychology, 65,* 1010–1022.

Guerin, B. (1986). Mere presence effects in humans: A review. *Journal of Personality and Social Psychology, 22,* 38–77.

Guttmacher Institute. (2000). *Fulfilling the promise: Public policy and U.S. family planning clinics*. New York: Alan Guttmacher Institute.

Hackel, L. S., & Ruble, D. N. (1992). Changes in the marital relationship after the first baby is born: Predicting the impact of expectancy disconfirmation. *Journal of Personality and Social Psychology, 62,* 944–957.

Haddock, G., & Zanna, M. P. (1994). Preferring "housewives" to "feminists." *Psychology of Women Quarterly, 18,* 25–52.

Haggbloom, S. J., Warnick, R., Warnick, J. E., Jones, V. K., Yarbrough, G. L., Russell, T. M., Borecky, C. M., McGahhey, R., Powell, J. L., III, Beavers, J., & Monte, E. (2002). The 100 most eminent psychologists of the 20th century. *Review of General Psychology, 6,* 139–152.

Haimov, I., & Lavie, P. (1996). Melatonin—a soporific hormone. *Current Directions in Psychological Science, 5,* 106–111.

Halaas, J. L., Gajiwala, K. S., Maffei, M., Cohen, S. L., Chait, B. T., Rabinowitz, D., Lallone, R. L., Burley, S. K., & Friedman, J. M. (1995). Weight-reducing effects of the plasma protein encoded by the *obese* gene. *Science, 269,* 543–546.

Halberstadt, J. B., Niedenthal, P. M., & Kushner, J. (1995). Resolution of lexical ambiguity by emotional state. *Psychological Science, 6,* 278–281.

Hall, E. T., & Hall, M. R. (1990). *Understanding cultural differences.* Yarmouth, ME: Intercultural Press.

Hall, J. A. (1987). On explaining gender differences: The case of nonverbal communication. In P. Shaver & C. Hendrick (Eds.), *Review of Personality and Social Psychology, 7,* 177–200.

Halpern, D. F. (1997). Sex differences in intelligence: Implications for education. *American Psychologist, 52,* 1091–1102.

Hamida, S. B., Mineka, S., & Bailey, J. M. (1998). Sex differences in perceived controllability of mate value: An evolutionary perspective. *Journal of Personality and Social Psychology, 75,* 953–966.

Harber, K. D. (1998). Feedback to minorities: Evidence of a positive bias. *Journal of Personality and Social Psychology, 74,* 622–628.

Hardie, E. A. (1997). PMS in the workplace: Dispelling the myth of cyclic function. *Journal of Occupational and Organizational Psychology, 70,* 97–102.

Harkins, S. G., & Szymanski, K. (1989). Social loafing and group evaluation. *Journal of Personality and Social Psychology, 56,* 934–941.

Harlow, H. F., Harlow, M. K., & Suomi, S. J. (1971) From thought to therapy: Lessons from a primate laboratory. *American Scientist, 59,* 538–549.

Harris, J. R. (1998). *The nurture assumption.* New York: Free Press.

Harris, R. J. (1994). The impact of sexually explicit media. In J. Brant & D. Zillmann (Eds.), *Media effects: Advances in theory and research.* Hillsdale, NJ: Erlbaum.

Hatfield, E. (1988). Passionate and companionate love. In R. J. Sternberg & M. L. Barnes (Eds.), *The psychology of love.* New Haven: Yale University Press.

Hatfield, E., & Sprecher, S. (1986). *Mirror, mirror . . . The importance of looks in everyday life.* Albany: State University of New York Press.

Hazelrigg, M. D., Cooper, H. M., & Borduin, C. M. (1987). Evaluating the effectiveness of family therapies: An integrative review and analysis. *Psychological Bulletin, 101,* 428–442.

Hebb, D. O. (1980). *Essay on mind.* Hillsdale, NJ: Erlbaum.

Hebl, M. R., & Heatherton, T. F. (1998). The stigma of obesity in women: The difference is black and white. *Personality and Social Psychology Bulletin, 24,* 417–426.

Hedges, L. V., & Nowell, A. (1995). Sex differences in mental test scores, variability, and numbers of high-scoring individuals. *Science, 269,* 41–45.

Heider, F. (1958). *The psychology of interpersonal relations.* New York: Wiley.

Heishman, S. J., Kozlowski, L. T., & Henningfield, J. E. (1997). Nicotine addiction: Implications for public health policy. *Journal of Social Issues, 53,* 13–33.

Henley, N. M. (1989). Molehill or mountain? What we know and don't know about sex bias in language. In M. Crawford & M. Gentry (Eds.), *Gender and thought: Psychological perspectives.* New York: Springer-Verlag.

Henninger, P. (1992). Conditional handedness: Handedness changes in multiple personality disordered subject reflect shift in hemispheric dominance. *Consciousness and Cognition, 1,* 265–287.

Hershberger, S. L. (1997). A twin registry study of male and female sexual orientation. *Journal of Sex Research, 34,* 212–222.

Hilgard, E. R. (1980). Consciousness in contemporary psychology. *Annual Review of Psychology, 31,* 1–26.

Hilgard, E. R. (1986). *Divided consciousness: Multiple controls in human thought and action.* New York: Wiley.

Hilgard, E. R. (1992). Dissociation and theories of hypnosis. In E. Fromm & M. R. Nash (Eds.), *Contemporary hypnosis research.* New York: Guilford.

Hines, T. M. (1998). Comprehensive review of biorhythm theory. *Psychological Reports, 83,* 19–64.

Hinz, L. D., & Williamson, D. A. (1987). Bulimia and depression: A review of the affective variant hypothesis. *Psychological Bulletin, 102,* 150–158.

Hoffman, A. (1994). Notes and documents concerning the discovery of LSD. *Agents and Actions, 43,* 79–81.

Hoffman, D. D. (1998). *Visual intelligence: How we create what we see.* New York: Norton.

Hokanson, J. E., & Edelman, R. (1966). Effects of three social responses on vascular processes. *Journal of Personality and Social Psychology, 3,* 442–447.

Holahan, C. K., & Sears, R. R. (1995). *The gifted group in later maturity.* Stanford, CA: Stanford University Press.

Holden, C. (1980a). Identical twins reared apart. *Science, 207,* 1323–1325.

Holden, C. (1980b, November). Twins reunited. *Science, 80,* 55–59.

Holden, C. (1995, Jan. 13). The high price of freedom: Russia. *Science, 267,* 170–171.

Horn, J. L. (1982). The aging of human abilities. In J. Wolman (Ed.), *Handbook of developmental psychology.* Englewood Cliffs, NJ: Prentice-Hall.

Horne, J. A. (1989). Sleep loss and "divergent" thinking ability. *Sleep, 11,* 528–536.

Horney, K. (1950). *Neurosis and human growth: The struggle toward self-realization.* New York: Norton.

Howe, M. L. (1997). Children's memory for traumatic experiences. *Learning and Individual Differences, 9,* 153–174.

Hummer, R. A., Rogers, R. G., Nam, C. B., & Ellison, C. G. (1999). Religious involvement and U.S. adult mortality. *Demography, 36,* 273–285.

Hunsley, J., & Bailey, J. M. (1999). The clinical utility of the Rorschach: Unfulfilled promises and an uncertain future. *Psychological Assessment, 11*(3), 266–277.

Hurtado, S., Dey, E. L., & Trevino, J. G. (1994). Exclusion or self-segregation? Interaction across racial/ethnic groups on college campuses. Paper presented at the American Educational Research Association annual meeting.

Huston, A. C., Donnerstein, E., Fairchild, H., Feshbach, N. D., Katz, P. A., & Murray, J. P. (1992). *Big world, small screen: The role of television in American society*. Lincoln: University of Nebraska Press.

Hyman, R. (1981). Cold reading: How to convince strangers that you know all about them. In K. Frazier (Ed.), *Paranormal borderlands of science*. Buffalo, NY: Prometheus Books.

Ingham, A. G., Levinger, G., Graves, J., & Peckham, V. (1974). The Ringelmann effect: Studies of group size and group performance. *Journal of Experimental Social Psychology, 10,* 371–384.

Inglehart, R. (1990). *Culture shift in advanced industrial society*. Princeton, NJ: Princeton University Press.

Isen, A. M., & Means, B. (1983). The influence of positive affect on decision-making strategy. *Social Cognition, 2,* 28–31.

Ito, T. A., Miller, N., & Pollock, V. E. (1996). Alcohol and aggression: A meta-analysis on the moderating effects of inhibitory cues, triggering events, and self-focused attention. *Psychological Bulletin, 120,* 60–82.

Izard, C. E. (1977). *Human emotions.* New York: Plenum Press.

Izard, C. E. (1994). Innate and universal facial expressions: Evidence from developmental and cross-cultural research. *Psychological Bulletin, 115,* 288–299.

Jackson, J. (1986, May 16). An address to Lincoln High School students, Lincoln, Nebraska.

Jacobs, B. L. (1994). Serotonin, motor activity, and depression-related disorders. *American Scientist, 82,* 456–463.

James, W. (1890). *The principles of psychology* (Vol. 2). New York: Holt.

Jamison, K. R. (1993). *Touched with fire: Manic-depressive illness and the artistic temperament*. New York: Free Press.

Jamison, K. R. (1995, February). Manic-depressive illness and creativity. *Scientific American*, 62–67.

Jang, K. L., McCrae, R. R., & Angleitner, A. (1998). Heritability of facet-level traits in a cross-cultural twin sample: Support for a hierarchical model of personality. *Journal of Personality and Social Psychology, 74,* 1556–1565.

Janis, I. L. (1982). *Groupthink: Psychological studies of policy decisions and fiascoes.* Boston: Houghton Mifflin.

Janoff-Bulman, R., Timko, C., & Carli, L. L. (1985). Cognitive biases in blaming the victim. *Journal of Experimental Social Psychology, 21,* 161–177.

Jarvik, L. F. (1975). Thoughts on the psychobiology of aging. *American Psychologist, 30,* 576–583.

Johnson, D. (1990). Animal rights and human lives: Time for scientists to right the balance. *Psychological Science, 1,* 213–214.

Johnson, D. W., & Johnson, R. T. (1989). *Cooperation and competition: Theory and research*. Edina, MN: Interaction Book.

Johnson, D. W., & Johnson, R. T. (1994). Constructive conflict in the schools. *Journal of Social Issues, 50*(1), 117–137.

Johnson, E. J., & Tversky, A. (1983). Affect, generalization, and the perception of risk. *Journal of Personality and Social Psychology, 45,* 20–31.

Johnson, M. H. (1992). Imprinting and the development of face recognition: From chick to man. *Current Directions in Psychological Science, 1,* 52–55.

Johnson, M. H., Dziurawiec, S., Ellis, H., & Morton, J. (1991). Newborns' preferential tracking of face-like stimuli and its subsequent decline. *Cognition, 40,* 1–19.

Johnston, L. D., Backman, J. G., & O'Malley, P. M. (2002). Drug trends among American teens are mixed. Ann Arbor: News and Information Services, University of Michigan.

Jolly, A. (1985). *The evolution of primate behavior* (2nd ed.). New York: Macmillan.

Jones, M. C. (1924). A laboratory study of fear: The case of Peter. *Journal of Genetic Psychology, 31,* 308–315.

Jorm, A. F., Korten, A. E., & Henderson, A. S. (1987). The prevalence of dementia: A quantitative integration of the literature. *Acta Psychiatrica Scandinavica, 76,* 465–479.

Julien, R. M. (2001). *A primer of drug action* (9th ed.). New York: Worth Publishers.

Kagan, J., Arcus, D., Snidman, N., Feng, W. Y., Hendler, J., & Greene, S. (1994). Reactivity in infants: A cross-national comparison. *Developmental Psychology, 30,* 342–345.

Kahill, L. (1994). (Beta)-adrenergic activation and memory for emotional events. *Nature, 371,* 702–704.

Kahneman, D., & Tversky, A. (1979). Intuitive prediction: Biases and corrective procedures. *Management Science, 12,* 313–327.

Kandel, E. R., & Schwartz, J. H. (1982). Molecular biology of learning: Modulation of transmitter release. *Science, 218,* 433–443.

Kaplan, H. I., & Saddock, B. J. (Eds.). (1989). *Comprehensive textbook of psychiatry, V*. Baltimore, MD: Williams & Wilkins.

Kaprio, J., Koskenvuo, M., & Rita, H. (1987). Mortality after bereavement: A prospective study of 95,647 widowed persons. *American Journal of Public Health, 77,* 283–287.

R-11

Kapur, S., & Mann, J. J. (1993). Antidepressant action and the neurobiologic effects of ECT: Human studies. In C. E. Coffey (Ed.), *The clinical science of electroconvulsive therapy*. Washington, DC: American Psychiatric Press.

Kaufman, A. S., Reynolds, C. R., & McLean, J. E. (1989). Age and WAIS-R intelligence in a national sample of adults in the 20- to 74-year age range: A cross-sectional analysis with educational level controlled. *Intelligence, 13,* 235–253.

Kaufman, M. (1999, April 6). Newer antidepressants not better. *Washington Post*, p. Z7.

Kaye, K. L., & Bower, T. G. R. (1994). Learning and intermodal transfer of information in newborns. *Psychological Science, 5,* 286–288.

Keith, K. (2002). Personal correspondence.

Kelley, J., & De Graaf, N. D. (1997). National context, parental socialization, and religious belief: Results from 15 nations. *American Sociological Review, 62,* 639–659.

Kellogg, W. N., & Kellogg, L. (1933). *The ape and the child.* New York: McGraw-Hill.

Kelly, I. W. (1997). Modern astrology: A critique. *Psychological Reports, 81,* 1035–1066.

Kempe, R. S., & Kempe, C. C. (1978). *Child abuse.* Cambridge, MA: Harvard University Press.

Kempermann, G., & Gage, F. H. (1999, May). New nerve cells for the adult brain. *Scientific American,* 48–53.

Kerr, N. L., & Bruun, S. E. (1983). Dispensability of member effort and group motivation losses: Free-rider effects. *Journal of Personality and Social Psychology, 44,* 78–94.

Kessler, R. C., & Zhao, S. (1999). The prevalence of mental illness. In A. V. Horwitz & T. L. Scheid (Eds.), *Sociology of mental health and illness*. Cambridge: Cambridge University Press.

Kiecolt-Glaser, J. K., Page, G. G., Marucha, P. T., MacCallum, R. C., & Glaser, R. (1998). Psychological influences on surgical recovery: Perspectives from psychoneuroimmunology. *American Psychologist, 53,* 1209–1218.

Kihlstrom, J. F. (1985). Hypnosis. *Annual Review of Psychology, 36,* 385–418.

Kihlstrom, J. F. (1990). The psychological unconscious. In L. A. Pervin (Ed.), *Handbook of personality: Theory and research*. New York: Guilford Press.

Kihlstrom, J. F., & McConkey, K. M. (1990). William James and hypnosis: A centennial reflection. *Psychological Science, 1,* 174–177.

Kihlström, J. F., Tataryn, D. J., & Hoyt, I. P. (1993). Dissociative disorders. In P. B. Sucker & H. E. Adams (Eds.), *Comprehensive handbook of psychopathology* (2nd ed.). New York: Plenum Press.

Kirsch, I., & Sapirstein, G. (1998). Listening to Prozac but hearing placebo: A meta-analysis of antidepressant medication. *Prevention and Treatment, 1.* Retrieved from http://journals.apa.org/prevention/volume1/toc-jun26-98.html

Klein, E., Kreinin, I., Chistyakov, A., Koren, D., Mecz, L., Marmur, S., Ben-Shachar, D., & Feinsod, M. (1999). Therapeutic efficacy of right prefrontal slow repetitive transcranial magnetic stimulation in major depression. *Archives of General Psychiatry, 56,* 315–320.

Kleinke, C. L. (1986). Gaze and eye contact: A research review. *Psychological Bulletin, 100,* 78–100.

Kleinmuntz, B., & Szucko, J. J. (1984). A field study of the fallibility of polygraph lie detection. *Nature, 308,* 449–450.

Kochanska, G., & Thompson, R. A. (1997). The emergence and development of conscience in toddlerhood and early childhood. In J. E. Grusec & R. A. Thompson (Eds.), *Parenting and children's internalization of values*. New York: Wiley.

Koenig, H. G., Cohen, H. J., George, L. K., Hays, J. C., Larson, D. B., & Blazer, D. G. (1997). Attendance at religious services, interleukin-6, and other biological indicators of immune function in older adults. *International Journal of Psychiatry in Medicine, 23,* 233–250.

Koenig, H. G., & Larson, D. B. (1998). Use of hospital services, religious attendance, and religious affiliation. *Southern Medical Journal, 91,* 925–932.

Kohlberg, L. (1976). Moral stages and moralization: The cognitive-developmental approach. In J. Lickona (Ed.), *Moral development behavior: Theory, research and social issues.* New York: Holt, Rinehart & Winston.

Kohlberg, L. (1981). *The philosophy of moral development: Essays on moral development* (Vol. I). San Francisco: Harper & Row.

Kohlberg, L. (1984). *The psychology of moral development: Essays on moral development* (Vol. II). San Francisco: Harper & Row.

Köhler, W. (1927). *The mentality of apes*. New York: Harcourt Brace.

Kohn, A. (1987, October). It's hard to get left out of a pair. *Psychology Today,* 53–57.

Kohn, P. M., & Macdonald, J. E. (1992). The survey of recent life experiences: A decontaminated hassles scale for adults. *Journal of Behavioral Medicine, 15,* 221–236.

Kolb, B., & Whishaw, I. Q. (1998). Brain plasticity and behavior. *Annual Review of Psychology, 49,* 43–64.

Koltz, C. (1983, December). Scapegoating. *Psychology Today,* 68–69.

Kraus, S. J. (1991). Attitudes and the prediction of behavior. Doctoral dissertation, Harvard University.

Kreiger, D. (1993). *Accepting your power to heal: The personal practice of therapeutic touch.* Santa Fe, NM: Bear.

Kring, A. M., & Gordon, A. H. (1998). Sex differences in emotion: Expression, experience, and physiology. *Journal of Personality and Social Psychology, 74,* 686–703.

Kuhl, P. K., & Meltzoff, A. N. (1982). The bimodal perception of speech in infancy. *Science, 218,* 1138–1141.

R-12

Kuhn, D., Weinstock, M., & Flaton, R. (1994). How well do jurors reason? Competence dimensions of individual variation in a juror reasoning task. *Psychological Science, 5,* 289–296.

Labouvie-Vief, G., & Schell, D. A. (1982). Learning and memory in later life. In B. B. Wolman (Ed.), *Handbook of developmental psychology.* Englewood Cliffs, NJ: Prentice-Hall.

Lachman, M. E., & Weaver, S. L. (1998). The sense of control as a moderator of social class differences in health and well-being. *Journal of Personality and Social Psychology, 74,* 763–773.

Ladd, E. C. (1998, August/September). The tobacco bill and American public opinion. *The Public Perspective,* 5–19.

Landfield, P., Cadwallader, L. B., & Vinsant, S. (1988). Quantitative changes in hippocampal structure following long-term exposure to delta-9-tetrahydrocannabinol: Possible mediation by glucocorticoid systems. *Brain Research, 443,* 47–62.

Langer, E. J. (1983). *The psychology of control.* Beverly Hills, CA: Sage.

Langer, E. J., & Abelson, R. P. (1974). A patient by any other name...: Clinician group differences in labeling bias. *Journal of Consulting and Clinical Psychology, 42,* 4–9.

Langer, E. J., & Imber, L. (1980). The role of mindlessness in the perception of deviance. *Journal of Personality and Social Psychology, 39,* 360–367.

Larsen, R. J., & Diener, E. (1987). Affect intensity as an individual difference characteristic: A review. *Journal of Research in Personality, 21,* 1–39.

Laumann, E. O., Gagnon, J. H., Michael, R. T., & Michaels, S. (1994). *The social organization of sexuality: Sexual practices in the United States.* Chicago: University of Chicago Press.

Laursen, B., Coy, K. C., & Collins, W. A. (1998). Reconsidering changes in parent-child conflict across adolescence: A meta-analysis. *Child Development, 69,* 817–832.

Lazarus, R. S. (1990). Theory-based stress measurement. *Psychological Inquiry, 1,* 3–13.

Lazarus, R. S. (1991). Progress on a cognitive-motivational-relational theory of emotion. *American Psychologist, 46,* 352–367.

Lazarus, R. S. (1998). *Fifty years of the research and theory of R. S. Lazarus: An analysis of historical and perennial issues.* Mahwah, NJ: Erlbaum.

Lebow, J. (1982). Consumer satisfaction with mental health treatment. *Psychological Bulletin, 91,* 244–259.

LeDoux, J., & Armony, J. (1999). Can neurobiology tell us anything about human feelings? In D. Dahneman, E. Diener, & N. Schwartz (Eds.), *Well-being: The foundations of hedonic psychology.* New York: Sage.

Leeper, R. W. (1955). A study of a neglected portion of the field of learning. The development of sensory organization. *Pedagogical Seminary and Journal of Genetic Psychology, 46,* 41–75.

Lefcourt, H. M. (1982). *Locus of control: Current trends in theory and research.* Hillsdale, NJ: Erlbaum.

Lehman, A. F., Steinwachs, D. M., Dixon, L. B., Goldman, H. H., Osher, F., Postrado, L., Scott, J. E., Thompson, J. W., Fahey, M., Fischer, P., Kasper, J. A., Lyles, A., Skinner, E. A., Buchanan, R., Carpenter, W. T., Jr., Levine, J., McGlynn, E. A., Rosenheck, R., & Zito, J. (1998). Translating research into practice: The schizophrenia patient outcomes research team (PORT) treatment recommendations. *Schizophrenia Bulletin, 24,* 1–10.

Lehman, D. R., Wortman, C. B., & Williams, A. F. (1987). Long-term effects of losing a spouse or child in a motor vehicle crash. *Journal of Personality and Social Psychology, 52,* 218–231.

Lepper, M. R., Greene, D., & Nisbett, R. E. (1973). Undermining children's intrinsic interest with extrinsic rewards: A test of the "overjustification" hypothesis. *Journal of Personality and Social Psychology, 28,* 129–137.

Leproult, R., Van Reeth, O., & Byrne, M. M. (1997). Sleepiness, performance, and neuroendocrine function during sleep deprivation: Effects of exposure to bright light or exercise. *Journal of Biological Rhythms, 12,* 245–258.

Leshner, A. I. (1992). *Outcasts on Main Street: Report of the federal task force on homelessness and severe mental illness.* Washington, DC: Interagency Council on the Homeless, Office of the Programs for the Homeless Mentally Ill, National Institute of Mental Health.

LeVay, S. (1991). A difference in hypothalamic structure between heterosexual and homosexual men. *Science, 253,* 1034–1037.

Levin, J. S., Larson, D. B., & Puchalski, C. M. (1997). Religion and spirituality in medicine: Research and education. *Journal of the American Medical Association, 278,* 792–793.

Levine, R., Sato, S., Hashimoto, T., & Verma, J. (1995). Love and marriage in eleven cultures. *Journal of Cross-Cultural Psychology, 26,* 554–571.

Lewis, D. O., Pincus, J. H., Feldman, M., Jackson, L., & Bard, B. (1986). Psychiatric neurological, and psychoeducational characteristics of 15 death row inmates in the United States. *American Journal of Psychiatry, 143,* 838–845.

Lewis, J. J. (2002). *Women's voices: Quotations by women. Jacqueline Kennedy Onassis.* Retrieved from http://womenshistory.about.com/library/qu/blquonas.htm.

Lewontin, R. (1982). *Human diversity.* New York: Scientific American Library.

Lewy, A. J., Bauer, V. K., Cutler, N. L., Sack, R. L., Ahmed, S., Thomas, K. H., Blood, M. L., & Jackson, J. M. L. (1998). Morning vs. evening light treatment of patients with winter depression. *Archives of General Psychiatry, 55,* 890–896.

R-13

Linville, P. W., Fischer, G. W., & Fischhoff, B. (1992). AIDS risk perceptions and decision biases. In J. B. Pryor & G. D. Reeder (Eds.), *The social psychology of HIV infection.* Hillsdale, NJ: Erlbaum.

Lissner, L., Odel, P. M., D'Agostino, R. B., Stokes, J., Kreger, B. E., Belanger, A. J., & Brownell, K. D. (1991). Variability of body weight and health outcomes in the Framingham population. *New England Journal of Medicine, 324,* 1839–1844.

Locke, E. A., & Latham, G. P. (1990). Work motivation and satisfaction: Light at the end of the tunnel. *Psychological Science, 1,* 240–246.

Loehlin, J. C., McCrae, R. R., & Costa, P. T., Jr. (1998). Heritabilities of common and measure-specific components of the Big Five personality factors. *Journal of Research in Personality, 32,* 431–453.

Loftus, E. F. (1996). Memory distortion and false memory creation. *Bulletin of the American Academy of Psychiatry and the Law, 24,* 281–295.

Loftus, E. F. (2000). Remembering what never happened. In E. Tulving (Ed.), *Memory, consciousness, and the brain: The Tallinn Conference.* Philadelphia: Psychology Press/Taylor & Francis.

Loftus, E. F., Levidow, B., & Duensing, S. (1992). Who remembers best? Individual differences in memory for events that occurred in a science museum. *Applied Cognitive Psychology, 6,* 93–107.

Loftus, E. F., & Palmer, J. C. (1974, October). Reconstruction of automobile destruction: An example of the interaction between language and memory. *Journal of Verbal Learning & Verbal Behavior, 13*(5), 585–589.

Loftus, G. R. (1992). When a lie becomes memory's truth: Memory distortion after exposure to misinformation. *Current Directions in Psychological Science, 1,* 121–123.

Long, P. (1986, January). Medical mesmerism. *Psychology Today,* 28–29.

Lord, C. G., Ross, L., & Lepper, M. (1979). Biased assimilation and attitude polarization: The effects of prior theories on subsequently considered evidence. *Journal of Personality and Social Psychology, 37,* 2098–2109.

Lorenz, K. (1937). The companion in the bird's world. *Auk, 54,* 245–273.

Lovaas, O. I. (1987). Behavioral treatment and normal educational and intellectual functioning in young autistic children. *Journal of Consulting and Clinical Psychology, 55,* 3–9.

Lowe, G. (1987). Combined effects of alcohol and caffeine on human state-dependent learning. *Medical Science Research: Psychology & Psychiatry, 15,* 25–26.

Lowry, P. E. (1997). The assessment center process: New directions. *Journal of Social Behavior and Personality, 12,* 53–62.

Lu, Z.-L., Williamson, S. J., & Kaufman, L. (1992). Behavioral lifetime of human auditory sensory memory predicted by physiological measures. *Science, 258,* 1668–1670.

Lutz, C. (1988). *Unnatural emotions: Everyday sentiments on a Micronesian atoll and their challenge to Western theory.* Chicago: University of Chicago Press.

Lykken, D. (1999). *Happiness.* New York: Golden Books.

Maas, J. B. (1998). *Power sleep.* New York: Villard.

MacArthur Foundation Research Network on Successful Midlife Development (1999). *Report of latest findings.* Vero Beach, FL: MacArthur Foundation.

MacDonald, T. K., Zanna, M. P., & Fong, G. T. (1995). Decision making in altered states: Effects of alcohol on attitudes toward drinking and driving. *Journal of Personality and Social Psychology, 68,* 973–985.

Major, B., Carrington, P. I., & Carnevale, P. J. D. (1984). Physical attractiveness and self-esteem: Attribution for praise from an other-sex evaluator. *Personality and Social Psychology Bulletin, 10,* 43–50.

Malmquist, C. P. (1986). Children who witness parental murder: Post-traumatic aspects. *Journal of the American Academy of Child Psychiatry, 25,* 320–325.

Mandler, J. M., & McDonough, L. (1995). Long-term recall of event sequences in infancy. *Journal of Experimental Child Psychology, 59,* 457–474.

Marlatt, G. A. (1991). Substance abuse: Etiology, prevention, and treatment issues. Master Lecture, American Psychological Association convention.

Martin, S. (1995, January). Field's status unaltered by the influx of women. *APA Monitor,* 9.

Maslach, C. (1982). *Burnout: The cost of caring.* Englewood Cliffs, NJ: Prentice-Hall.

Maslow, A. H. (1970). *Motivation and personality* (2nd ed.). New York: Harper & Row.

Matarazzo, J. D. (1983). Computerized psychological testing. *Science, 221,* 323.

Matsumoto, D. (1993). Ethnic differences in affect intensity, emotion judgments, display rule attitudes, and self-reported emotional expression in an American sample. *Motivation and Emotion, 17*(2), 107–123.

Matsumoto, D. (1994). *Cultural influences on research methods and statistics.* Pacific Grove, CA: Brooks/Cole.

Matsumoto, D. (1996). *Culture and psychology.* Pacific Grove, CA: Brooks/Cole.

Matsumoto, D. (1997). *Culture and modern life.* Belmont, CA: Brooks/Cole.

Matsumoto, D. (1999). *People: Psychology from a cultural perspective* (2nd ed). Pacific Grove, CA: Brooks/Cole.

Matsumoto, D., & Ekman, P. (1989). American-Japanese cultural differences in intensity ratings of facial expressions of emotion. *Motivation and Emotion, 13,* 143–157.

R-14

Matthews, D. A., & Larson, D. B. (1997). *The faith factor: An annotated bibliography of clinical research on spiritual subjects* Vol. I–IV. Rockville, MD: National Institute for Healthcare Research and Georgetown University Press.

Matthews, K. A. (1992). Myths and realities of the menopause. *Psychosomatic Medicine, 54,* 1–9.

Mayer, J. D., & Salovey, P. (1993). The intelligence of emotional intelligence. *Intelligence, 17,* 433–442.

Mayne, T. J., Norcross, J. C., & Sayette, M. A. (1994). Admission requirements, acceptance rates, and financial assistance in clinical psychology programs. *American Psychologist, 49,* 806–811.

McBurney, D. H., & Gent, J. F. (1979). On the nature of taste qualities. *Psychological Bulletin, 86,* 151–167.

McCall, R. B. (1994). Academic underachievers. *Current Directions in Psychological Science, 3,* 15–19.

McCann, I. L., & Holmes, D. S. (1984). Influence of aerobic exercise on depression. *Journal of Personality and Social Psychology, 46,* 1142–1147.

McCann, U. D. (1999). Cognitive performance in 3,4-methylene-dioxymethamphetamine (MDMA, "Ecstasy") users. *Psychopharmacology, 143,* 417–425.

McCarty, D., Argeriou, M., Huebner, R. B., & Lubran, B. (1991). Alcoholism, drug abuse, and the homeless. *American Psychologist, 46,* 1139–1148.

McCauley, C. R., & Segal, M. E. (1987). Social psychology of terrorist groups. In C. Hendrick (Ed.), *Group processes and intergroup relations*. Beverly Hills, CA: Sage.

McClellend, D. C., Atkinson, J. W., Cark, R. A., & Lowell, E. L. (1953). *The achievement motive*. New York: Appleton-Century-Crofts.

McConkey, K. M. (1992). The effects of hypnotic procedures on remembering: The experimental findings and their implications for forensic hypnosis. In E. Fromm & M. R. Nash (Eds.), *Contemporary hypnosis research*. New York: Guilford Press.

McConkey, K. M. (1995). Hypnosis, memory, and the ethics of uncertainty. *Australian Psychologist, 30,* 1–10.

McCrae, R. R., Costa, P. T., Jr., de Lirna, M. P., Simoes, A., Ostendorf, F., Angleitner, A., Marusic, I., Bratko, D., Caprara, G. V., Barbaranelli, C., Chae, J-H., & Piedmont, R. L. (1999). Age differences in personality across the adult life span: Parallels in five cultures. *Developmental Psychology, 35,* 466–477.

McCrae, R. R., Costa, P. T., Jr., del Pilar, G. H., Rolland, J. P., & Parker, W. D. (1998). Cross-cultural assessment of the five-factor model: The revised NEO personality inventory. *Journal of Cross-Cultural Psychology, 29,* 171–188.

McFarland, C., Ross, M., & DeVourville, N. (1989). Women's theories of menstruation and biases in recall of menstrual symptoms. *Journal of Personality and Social Psychology, 57,* 522–31.

McFarlane, J. M., Martin, C. L., & Williams, T. M. (1988). Mood fluctuations: Women versus men and menstrual versus other cycles. *Psychology of Women Quarterly, 12,* 201–223.

McGrath, J. J., & Welham, J. L. (1999). Season of birth and schizophrenia: A systematic review and meta-analysis of data from the Southern hemisphere. *Schizophrenia Research, 35,* 237–242.

McGrath, M. J., & Cohen, D. G. (1978). REM sleep facilitation of adaptive waking behavior: A review of the literature. *Psychological Bulletin, 85,* 24–57.

McGue, M., Bouchard, T. J., Jr., Iacono, W. G., & Lykken, D. T. (1993). Behavioral genetics of cognitive ability: A life-span perspective. In R. Plomin & G. E. McClearn (Eds.), *Nature, nurture, and psychology.* Washington, DC: American Psychological Association.

McGue, M., & Lykken, D. T. (1992). Genetic influence on risk of divorce. *Psychological Science, 3,* 368–373.

McHugh, P. R. (1995). Resolved: Multiple personality disorder is an individually and socially created artifact. *Journal of the American Academy of Child and Adolescent Psychiatry, 34,* 957–959.

McKenna, M. C., Zevon, M. A., Corn, B., & Rounds, J. (1999). Psychosocial factors and the development of breast cancer: A meta-analysis. *Health Psychology, 18,* 520–531.

McKinlay, J. B., McKinlay, S. M., & Brambilla, D. J. (1987). Health status and utilization behavior associated with menopause. *American Journal of Epidemiology, 125,* 110–121.

McVeigh, C. (1999, October 1). Medical schools offering spirituality and medicine courses. Personal correspondence between David Myers and C. McVeigh, National Institute for Healthcare Research.

Mediascope. (1995). *National television violence study: Executive summary, 1994–1995*. Studio City, CA: Mediascope, Inc.

Mednick, S. A., Huttunen, M. O., & Machon, R. A. (1994). Prenatal influenza infections and adult schizophrenia. *Schizophrenia Bulletin, 20,* 263–267.

Meltzoff, A. N., & Borton, R. W. (1979). Intermodal matching by human neonates. *Nature, 282,* 403–404.

Melzack, R., & Wall, P. D. (1965). Pain mechanisms: A new theory. *Science, 150,* 971–979.

Menon, T., Morris, M. W., Chiu, C-Y., & Hong, Y-Y. (1999). Culture and the construal of agency: Attribution to individual versus group dispositions. *Journal of Personality and Social Psychology, 76,* 701–717.

Mento, A. J., Steel, R. P., & Karren, R. J. (1987). A meta-analytic study of the effects of goal setting on task performance: 1966–1984. *Organizational Behavior and Human Decision Processes, 39,* 52–83.

Michaels, J. W., Bloomel, J. M., Brocato, R. M., Linkous, R. A., & Rowe, J. S. (1982). Social facilitation and inhibition in a natural setting. *Replications in Social Psychology, 2,* 21–24.

R-15

Middlebrooks, J. C., & Green, D. M. (1991). Sound localization by human listeners. *Annual Review of Psychology, 42,* 135–159.

Miles, D. R., & Carey, G. (1997). Genetic and environmental architecture of human aggression. *Journal of Personality and Social Psychology, 72,* 207–217.

Milgram, S. (1974). *Obedience to authority*. New York: Harper & Row.

Miller, G. A. (1956). The magical number seven, plus or minus two: Some limits on our capacity for processing information. *Psychological Review, 63,* 81–97.

Miller, G. A., & Gildea, P. M. (1987, September). How children learn words. *Scientific American,* 94–99.

Miller, J. G., & Bersoff, D. M. (1992). Culture and moral judgment: How are conflicts between justice and interpersonal responsibilities resolved? *Journal of Personality and Social Psychology, 62,* 541–554.

Miller, J. G., & Bersoff, D. M. (1995). Development in the context of everyday family relationships: Culture, interpersonal morality and adaptation. In M. Killen & D. Hart (Eds.), *Morality in everyday life: A developmental perspective.* New York: Cambridge University Press.

Miller, N. E. (1995). Clinical-experimental interactions in the development of neuroscience: A primer for nonspecialists and lessons for young scientists. *American Psychologist, 50,* 901–911.

Miller, P. C., Lefcourt, H. M., Holmes, J. G., Ware, E. E., & Saleh, W. E. (1986). Marital locus of control and marital problem solving. *Journal of Personality and Social Psychology, 51,* 161–169.

Miller, T. Q., Smith, T. W., Turner, C. W., Guijarro, M. L., & Hallet, A. J. (1996). A meta-analytic review of research on hostility and physical health. *Psychological Bulletin, 119,* 322–348.

Mineka, S. (1985). The frightful complexity of the origins of fears. In F. R. Brush & J. B. Overmier (Eds.), *Affect, conditioning and cognition: Essays on the determinants of behavior.* Hillsdale, NJ: Erlbaum.

Mischel, W. (1981). Current issues and challenges in personality. In L. T. Benjamin, Jr. (Ed.), *The G. Stanley Hall Lecture Series* (Vol. 1). Washington, DC: American Psychological Association.

Mischel, W. (1993). Toward a cognitive social learning reconceptualization of personality. *Psychological Review,* 102, 252–253.

Mischel, W., Shoda, Y., & Rodriguez, M. L. (1989). Delay of gratification in children. *Science, 244,* 933–938.

Mitchell, T. R., Thompson, L., Peterson, E., & Cronk, R. (1997). Temporal adjustments in the evaluation of events: The "rosy view." *Journal of Experimental Social Psychology, 33,* 421–448.

Miyake, K., Chen, S., & Campos, J. J. (1985). Infant temperament, mother's mode of interaction, and attachment in Japan. An interim report. In I. Bretherton & E. Waters (Eds.), *Growing points of attachment theory. Monographs of the Society of Research in Child Development, 50*(1–2 Serial No. 209).

Mondloch, C. J., Lewis, T. L., Budreau, D. R., Maurer, D., Dannemiller, J. L., Stephens, B. R., & Kleiner-Gathercoal, K. A. (1999). Face perception during early infancy. *Psychological Science, 10,* 419–422.

Moreland, R. L., & Beach, S. R. (1992). Exposure effects in the classroom: The development of affinity among students. *Journal of Experimental Social Psychology, 28,* 255–276.

Moreland, R. L., & Zajonc, R. B. (1982). Exposure effects in person perception: Familiarity, similarity, and attraction. *Journal of Experimental Social Psychology, 18,* 395–415.

Morgan, M. J. (1999). Recreational use of 'Ecstasy' (MDMA) is associated with elevated impulsivity. *Neuropsychopharmacology, 19,* 252–264.

Moscovici, S. (1985). Social influence and conformity. In G. Lindzey & E. Aronson (Eds.), *The handbook of social psychology* (3rd ed.). Hillsdale, NJ: Erlbaum.

Moss, A. J., Allen, K. F., Giovino, G. A., & Mills, S. L. (1992, December 2). Recent trends in adolescent smoking, smoking-update correlates, and expectation about the future. *Advance Data* No. 221 (from Vital and Health Statistics of the Centers for Disease Control and Prevention).

Moyer, K. E. (1983). The physiology of motivation: Aggression as a model. In C. J. Scheier & A. M. Rogers (Eds.), *G. Stanley Hall Lecture Series* (Vol. 3). Washington, DC: American Psychological Association.

Mroczek, D. K., & Kolarz, D. M. (1998). The effect of age on positive and negative affect: A developmental perspective on happiness. *Journal of Personality and Social Psychology, 75,* 1333–1349.

Mueller, C. M., & Dweck, C. S. (1998). Praise for intelligence can undermine children's motivation and performance. *Journal of Personality and Social Psychology, 75,* 33–52.

Muller, J. E., & Verrier, R. L. (1996). Triggering of sudden death—Lessons from an earthquake. *New England Journal of Medicine, 334,* 460–461.

Murphy, G. E., & Wetzel, R. D. (1990). The lifetime risk of suicide in alcoholism. *Archives of General Psychiatry, 47,* 383–392.

Murray, H. (1938). *Explorations in personality*. New York: Oxford University Press.

Murray, S. L., & Holmes, J. G. (1999). The (mental) ties that bind: Cognitive structures that predict relationship resilience. *Journal of Personality and Social Psychology, 77,* 1228–1244.

Murray, S. L., Holmes, J. G., & Griffin, D. (1996). The benefits of positive illusions: Idealization and the construction of satisfaction in close relationships. *Journal of Personality and Social Psychology, 70,* 79–98.

Myers, D. G. (2000). *The American paradox: Spiritual hunger in an age of plenty.* New Haven: Yale University Press.

Myers, D. G., & Bishop, G. D. (1970). Discussion effects on racial attitudes. *Science, 169,* 778–779.

Myers, D. G., & Diener, E. (1995). Who is happy? *Psychological Science, 6,* 10–19.

Napolitan, D. A., & Goethals, G. R. (1979). The attribution of friendliness. *Journal of Experimental Social Psychology, 15,* 105–113.

National Center for Health Statistics. (1988). Advance report of final mortality statistics, 1986. *NCHS Monthly Vital Statistics Report, 37* (Suppl. 6). Washington, DC: U.S. Department of Health and Human Services.

National Center for Health Statistics. (1991). Family structure and children's health: United States, 1988. *Vital and Health Statistics, Series 10, No. 178,* DHHS Publication No. PHS 91-1506 by Deborah A. Dawson.

National Center for Health Statistics. (1992, May). *Health United States 1991.* Hyattsville, MD: Department of Health and Human Services Pub. No PHS 92-1232, Table 27.

National Institutes of Health. (1998). Clinical guidelines on the identification, evaluation, and treatment of overweight and obesity in adults. Executive summary, Obesity Evaluation Initiative, National Heart, Lung, and Blood Institute.

National Transportation Safety Board. (1995). Washington, DC: U.S. Government Printing Office.

Neisser, U., Boodoo, G., Bouchard, T. J., Jr., Boykin, A. W., Brody, N., Ceci, S. J., Halpern, D. F., Loehlin, J. C., Perloff, R., Sternberg, R. J., & Urbina, S. (1996). Intelligence: Knowns and unknowns. *American Psychologist, 51,* 77–101.

Neubauer, P. B., & Neubauer, A. (1990). *Nature's thumbprint: The new genetics of personality.* Reading, MA: Addison-Wesley.

Newcomb, M. D., & Harlow, L. L. (1986). Life events and substance use among adolescents: Mediating effects of perceived loss of control and meaninglessness in life. *Journal of Personality and Social Psychology, 51,* 564–577.

Newcombe, N., & Fox, N. A. (1994). Infantile amnesia: Through a glass darkly. *Child Development, 65,* 31–40.

Nickerson, R. S., & Adams, M. J. (1979). Long-term memory for a common object. *Cognitive Psychology, 11,* 287–307.

Nisbet, M. (1998, May/June). Psychic telephone networks profit on yearning, gullibility. *Skeptical Inquirer,* 5–6.

Nishizawa, S. (1996). The religiousness and subjective well-being of Japanese students. Paper presented at the XXVI International Congress of Psychology.

Noble, E. P. (1993). The D2 dopamine receptor gene: A review of association studies in alcoholism. *Behavior Genetics, 23,* 119–129.

Nobles, A. Y., & Sciarra, D. T. (2000). Cultural determinants in the treatment of Arab Americans: A primer for mainstream therapists. *American Journal of Orthopsychiatry, 70*(2), 182–191.

Nolen-Hoeksema, S., & Larson, J. (1999). *Coping with loss.* Mahwah, NJ: Erlbaum.

North, M. M., North, S. M., & Coble, J. R. (1998). Virtual reality therapy: An effective treatment for phobias. In G. Riva & B. K. Wiederhold (Eds.), *Virtual environments in clinical psychology and neuroscience: Methods and techniques in advanced patient-therapist interaction.* Amsterdam: IOS Press.

Nuttin, J. M., Jr. (1987). Affective consequences of mere ownership: The name letter effect in twelve European languages. *European Journal of Social Psychology, 17,* 381–402.

O'Leary, A. (1990). Stress, emotion, and human immune function. *Psychological Bulletin, 108,* 363–382.

Ofshe, R. J., & Watters, E. (1994). *Making monsters: False memory, psychotherapy, and sexual hysteria.* New York: Scribners.

Olweus, D., Mattsson, A., Schalling, D., & Low, H. (1988). Circulating testosterone levels and aggression in adolescent males: A causal analysis. *Psychosomatic Medicine, 50,* 261–272.

Opoku, K. A. (1989). African perspective in death and dying. In A. Berger, P. Badham, A. K. Kutscher, J. Berger, V. M. Petty, & J. Beloff (Eds.), *Perspectives on death and dying: Cross-cultural and multidisciplinary views.* Philadelphia: Charles Press.

Orne, M. T. (1982, April 28). Affidavit submitted to State of Pennsylvania.

Orne, M. T., & Evans, F. J. (1965). Social control in the psychological experiment: Antisocial behavior and hypnosis. *Journal of Personality and Social Psychology, 1,* 189–200.

Ouellette, J. A., & Wood, W. (1998). Habit and intention in everyday life: The multiple processes by which past behavior predicts future behavior. *Psychological Bulletin, 124,* 54–74.

Overmier, J. B., & Murison, R. (1997). Animal models reveal the "psych" in the psychosomatics of peptic ulcers. *Current Directions in Psychological Science, 6,* 180–184.

Paffenbarger, R. S., Jr., Hyde, R. T., Wing, A. L., & Hsieh, C.-C. (1986). Physical activity, all-cause mortality, and longevity of college alumni. *New England Journal of Medicine, 314,* 605–612.

Palumbo, S. R. (1978). *Dreaming and memory: A new information-processing model.* New York: Basic Books.

Pandey, J., Sinha, Y., Prakash, A., & Tripathi, R. C. (1982). Right-left political ideologies and attribution of the causes of poverty. *European Journal of Social Psychology, 12,* 327–331.

Parlee, M. B. (1994). The social construction of premenstrual syndrome: A case study of scientific discourse as cultural contestation. In M. G. Winkler & L. B. Cole (Eds.), *The good body: Asceticism in contemporary culture.* New Haven, CT: Yale University Press.

Parloff, M. B. (1987, February). Psychotherapy: An import from Japan. *Psychology Today,* 74–75.

Patterson, G. R., Chamberlain, P., & Reid, J. B. (1982). A comparative evaluation of parent training procedures. *Behavior Therapy, 13,* 638–650.

Patterson, G. R., Reid, J. B., & Dishion, T. J. (1992). *Antisocial boys.* Eugene, OR: Castalia.

Pendick, D. (1994, January/February). The mind of violence. *Brain Work: The Neuroscience Newsletter,* 1–3, 5.

Pennington, N., & Hastie, R. (1993). The story model for juror decision making. In R. Hastie (Ed.), *Inside the juror: The psychology of juror decision making.* New York: Cambridge.

Perkins, K. A., Dubbert, P. M., Martin, J. E., Faulstich, M. E., & Harris, J. K. (1986). Cardiovascular reactivity to psychological stress in aerobically trained versus untrained mild hypertensives and normotensives. *Health Psychology, 5,* 407–421.

Perlmutter, M. (1983). Learning and memory through adulthood. In M. W. Riley, B. B. Hess, & K. Bond (Eds.), *Aging in society: Selected reviews of recent research.* Hillsdale, NJ: Erlbaum.

Peterson, L. R., & Peterson, M. J. (1959). Short-term retention of individual verbal items. *Journal of Experimental Psychology, 58,* 193–198.

Peto, R. (1994). *Mortality from smoking in developed countries, 1950–2000. Indirect estimates from national vital statistics.* New York: Oxford University Press.

Pettigrew, T. F. (1969). Racially separate or together? *Journal of Social Issues, 25,* 43–69.

Pettigrew, T. F. (1997). Generalized intergroup contact effects on prejudice. *Personality and Social Psychology Bulletin, 23,* 173–185.

Pfeiffer, E. (1977). Sexual behavior in old age. In E. W. Busse & E. Pfeiffer (Eds.), *Behavior and adaptation in late life* (2nd ed.). Boston: Little, Brown.

Piaget, J. (1952). *The origins of intelligence in children.* New York: International Universities Press.

Pike, K. M., & Rodin, J. (1991). Mothers, daughters, and disordered eating. *Journal of Abnormal Psychology, 100,* 198–204.

Pillemer, D. (1998). *Momentous events, vivid memories.* Cambridge, MA: Harvard University Press.

Pingitore, R., Dugoni, B. L., Tindale, R. S., & Spring, B. (1994). Bias against overweight job applicants in a simulated employment interview. *Journal of Applied Psychology, 79,* 909–917.

Pipe, M-E. (1996). Children's eyewitness memory. *New Zealand Journal of Psychology, 25,* 36–43.

Pliner, P. (1982). The effects of mere exposure on liking for edible substances. *Appetite: Journal for Intake Research, 3,* 283–290.

Pliner, P., Pelchat, M., & Grabski, M. (1993). Reduction of neophobia in humans by exposure to novel foods. *Appetite, 20,* 111–123.

Plomin, R., & Crabbe, J. (2000). DNA. *Psychological Bulletin, 126,* 806–828.

Plomin, R., & Daniels, D. (1987). Why are children in the same family so different from one another? *Behavioral and Brain Sciences, 10,* 1–60.

Plomin, R., Fulker, D. W., Corley, R., & DeFries, J. C. (1997). Nature, nurture and cognitive development from 1 to 16 years: A parent-offspring adoption study. *Psychological Science, 8,* 442–447.

Pope, H. G., Jr., & Hudson, J. I. (1992). Is childhood sexual abuse a risk factor for bulimia nervosa? *American Journal of Psychiatry, 149,* 455–463.

Pope, H. G., & Yurgelun-Todd, D. (1996). The residual cognitive effects of heavy marijuana use in college students. *Journal of the American Medical Association, 275,* 521–527.

Powell, K. E., Thompson, P. D., Caspersen, C. J., & Kendrick, J. S. (1987). Physical activity and the incidence of coronary heart disease. *Annual Review of Public Health, 8,* 253–287.

Powell, R. A., & Boer, D. P. (1994). Did Freud mislead patients to confabulate memories of abuse? *Psychological Reports, 74,* 1283–1298.

Presson, P. K., & Benassi, V. A. (1996). Locus of control orientation and depressive symptomatology: A meta-analysis. *Journal of Social Behavior and Personality, 11,* 201–212.

Public Opinion. (1987, May/June). Teen angels (report of University of Michigan survey). P. 32.

Putnam, F. W. (1991). Recent research on multiple personality disorder. *Psychiatric Clinics of North America, 14,* 489–502.

Rabin, A. S., Kaslow, N. J., & Rehm, L. P. (1986). Aggregate outcome and follow-up results following self-control therapy for depression. Paper presented at the American Psychological Association convention.

Raine, A. (1999). Murderous minds: Can we see the mark of Cain? *Cerebrum: The Dana Forum on Brain Science, 1*(1), 15–29.

Ramey, S. L., & Ramey, C. T. (1992). Early educational intervention with disadvantaged children—To what effect? *Applied and Preventive Psychology, 1,* 131–140.

Rauch, S. L., & Jenike, M. A. (1993). Neurobiological models of obsessive-compulsive disorder. *Psychomatics, 34,* 20–32.

Rescorla, R. A., & Wagner, A. R. (1972). A theory of Pavlovian conditioning: Variations in the effectiveness of reinforcement and nonreinforcement. In A. H. Black & W. F. Perokasy (Eds.), *Classical conditioning II: Current theory.* New York: Appleton-Century-Crofts.

Resnick, S. M. (1992). Positron emission tomography in psychiatric illness. *Current Directions in Psychological Science, 1,* 92–98.

Richardson, J. T. E. (1993). The premenstrual syndrome: A brief history. Paper presented to the Annual Conference of the British Psychological Society.

Ridge, R. D., & Reber, J. S. (1998). Women's responses to men's flirtations in a professional setting: Implications for sexual harassment. Paper presented at the annual meeting of the American Psychological Society, Washington, DC.

Robins, L., & Regier, D. (Eds.). (1991). *Psychiatric disorders in America*. New York: Free Press.

Rock, I., & Palmer, S. (1990, December). The legacy of Gestalt psychology. *Scientific American*, 84–90.

Rodin, J. (1984, December). A sense of control [interview]. *Psychology Today,* 38–45.

Rodin, J. (1986). Aging and health: Effects of the sense of control. *Science, 223,* 1271–1276.

Roehling, M. V. (2000). Weight-based discrimination in employment: Psychological and legal aspects. *Personnel Psychology, 52*(4), 969–1016.

Rogers, C. R. (1980). *A way of being*. Boston: Houghton Mifflin.

Rohan, M. J., & Zanna, M. P. (1996). Value transmission in families. In C. Seligman, J. M. Olson, & M. P. Zanna (Eds.), *The psychology of values: The Ontario Symposium* (Vol. 8). Malwah, NJ: Erlbaum.

Rohner, R. P. (1994). Patterns of parenting: The warmth dimension in worldwide perspective. In W. J. Lonner & R. Malpass (Eds.), *Psychology and culture*. Boston: Allyn & Bacon.

Rosa, L., Rosa, E., Sarner, L., & Barrett, S. (1998). A close look at therapeutic touch. *Journal of the American Medical Association, 279,* 1005–1010.

Rosch, E. (1978). Principles of categorization. In E. Rosch & B. L. Lloyd (Eds.), *Cognition and categorization*. Hillsdale, NJ: Erlbaum.

Rose, J. S., Chassin, L., Presson, C. C., & Sherman, S. J. (1999). Peer influences on adolescent cigarette smoking: A prospective sibling analysis. *Merrill-Palmer Quarterly, 45,* 62–84.

Rosenbaum, M. (1986). The repulsion hypothesis: On the nondevelopment of relationships. *Journal of Personality and Social Psychology, 51,* 1156–1166.

Rothbaum, B. O., Hodges, L. F., Kooper, R., Opdyke, D., Williford, J., & North M. M. (1995). Effectiveness of computer-generated (virtual reality) graded exposure in the treatment of acrophobia. *American Journal of Psychiatry, 152,* 626–628.

Rothbaum, B. O., Hodges, L., & Kooper, R. (1997). Virtual reality exposure therapy. *Journal of Psychotherapy Practice and Research, 6,* 219–226.

Rothstein, W. G. (1980). The significance of occupations in work careers: An empirical and theoretical review. *Journal of Vocational Behavior, 17,* 328–343.

Rotter, J. B. (1954). *Social learning and clinical psychology*. Englewood Cliffs, NJ: Prentice-Hall.

Rowe, D. C., Almeida, D. M., & Jacobson, K. C. (1999). School context and genetic influences on aggression in adolescence. *Psychological Science, 10,* 277–280.

Ruback, R. B., Carr, T. S., & Hopper, C. H. (1986). Perceived control in prison: Its relation to reported crowding, stress, and symptoms. *Journal of Applied Social Psychology, 16,* 375–386.

Rubin, K. H., Coplan, R. J., Nelson, L. J., Cheah, C. S. L., & Lagrace-Seguin, D. G. (1999). Peer relationships in childhood. In M. H. Bornstein & M. E. Lamb (Eds.), *Developmental psychology: An advanced textbook* (4th ed.). Mahwah, NJ: Erlbaum.

Rubonis, A. V., & Bickman, L. (1991). Psychological impairment in the wake of disaster: The disaster-psychopathology relationship. *Psychological Bulletin, 109,* 384–399.

Ruffin, C. L. (1993). Stress and health—little hassles vs. major life events. *Australian Psychologist, 28,* 201–208.

Russell, J. A. (1991). Culture and the categorization of emotions. *Psychological Bulletin, 110,* 426–450.

Ryckman, R. M., Robbins, M. A., Kaczor, L. M., & Gold, J. A. (1989). Male and female raters' stereotyping of male and female physiques. *Personality and Social Psychology Bulletin, 15,* 244–251.

Sachdev, P., & Sachdev, J. (1997). Sixty years of psychosurgery: Its present status and its future. *Australian and New Zealand Journal of Psychiatry, 31,* 457–464.

Sanz, C., Blicher, A., Dalke, K., Gratton-Farbi, L., McClure-Richards, T. & Fouts, R. (1998, Winter-Spring). Enrichment object use. *Friends of Washoe, 19* (1, 2), 9–14.

Sapolsky, B. S., & Tabarlet, J. O. (1991). Sex in primetime television: 1979 versus 1989. *Journal of Broadcasting and Electronic Media, 35,* 505–516.

Sapolsky, R. (1999, March). Stress and your shrinking brain. *Discover,* 116–120.

Savoy, C., & Beitel, P. (1996). Mental imagery for basketball. *International Journal of Sport Psychology, 27,* 454–462.

Sax, L. J., Astin, A. W., Korn, W. S., & Mahoney, K. M. (1999). *The American freshman: National norms for fall 1999*. Los Angeles: Higher Education Research Institute, UCLA.

Scarr, S. (1993, May/June). Quoted in *Psychology Today,* Nature's thumbprint: So long, superparents. 16.

Schachter, S., & Singer, J. E. (1962). Cognitive, social and physiological determinants of emotional state. *Psychological Review, 69,* 379–399.

Schacter, D. L. (1996). *Searching for memory: The brain, the mind, and the past.* New York: Basic Books.

Schaie, K. W., & Willis, S. L. (1996). *Adult development and aging.* New York: HarperCollins.

Scheiber, B., & Selby, C. (1997, May–June). UAB final report of therapeutic touch—An appraisal. *Skeptical Inquirer, 21,* 53–54.

Schmidt, F. L., & Hunter, J. E. (1998). The validity and utility of selection methods in personnel psychology: Practical and theoretical implications of 85 years of research findings. *Psychological Bulletin, 124,* 262–274.

Schoenfeld, B. (1995, May 14). The loneliness of being white. *New York Times Magazine,* 34–37.

Schonfield, D., & Robertson, B. A. (1966). Memory storage and aging. *Canadian Journal of Psychology, 20,* 228–236.

Schulenberg, J., Bachman, J. G., O'Malley, P. M., & Johnston, L. D. (March, 1994). High school educational success and subsequent substance use: A panel analysis following adolescents into young adulthood. *Journal of Health and Social Behavior, 35*(1), 45–62.

Schultz, D., & Schultz, S. (1996). *A history of modern psychology* (6th ed.). Fort Worth: Harcourt Brace & Company.

Schuman, H., & Scott, J. (1989, June). Generations and collective memories. *American Sociological Review, 54*(3), 359–381.

Schwartz, J. E., Friedman, H. S., Tucker, J. S., Tomlinson-Keasey, C., Wingard, D. L., & Criqui, M. H. (1995). Sociodemographic and psychosocial factors in childhood as predictors of adult mortality. *American Journal of Public Health, 85,* 1237–1245.

Sechrest, L., Stickle, T. R., & Stewart, M. (1998). The role of assessment in clinical psychology. In A. Bellack, M. Hersen (Series eds.), & C. R. Reynolds (Vol. ed.), *Comprehensive clinical psychology: Vol. 4 Assessment.* New York: Pergamon.

Seeman, P., Guan, H-C., & Van Tol, H. H. M. (1993). Dopamine D4 receptors elevated in schizophrenia. *Nature, 365,* 441–445.

Segal, N. L. (1999). *Entwined lives: Twins and what they tell us about human behavior*. New York: Dutton.

Segerstrom, S. C., Taylor, S. E., Kemeny, M. E., & Fahey, J. L. (1998). Optimism is associated with mood, coping, and immune change in response to stress. *Journal of Personality and Social Psychology, 74,* 1646–1655.

Seligman, M. E. P. (1975). *Helplessness: On depression, development and death.* San Francisco: Freeman.

Seligman, M. E. P. (1991). *Learned optimism*. New York: Knopf.

Seligman, M. E. P. (1994). *What you can change and what you can't.* New York: Knopf.

Seligman, M. E. P. (1995). The effectiveness of psychotherapy: The *Consumer Reports* study. *American Psychologist, 50,* 945–974.

Seligman, M. E. P. (1998, January). Building human strength: Psychology's forgotten mission. *APA Monitor.* Retrieved from http://www.apa.org

Seligman, M. E. P., & Csikszentmihalyi, M. (2000). Positive psychology: An introduction. *American Psychologist, 55,* 5–14.

Selye, H. (1976). *The stress of life*. New York: McGraw-Hill.

Shadish, W. R., Montgomery, L. M., Wilson, P., Wilson, M. R., Bright, I., & Okwumabua, T. (1993). Effects of family and marital psychotherapies: A meta-analysis. *Journal of Consulting and Clinical Psychology, 61,* 992–1002.

Sharma, A. R., McGue, M. K., & Benson, P. L. (1998). The psychological adjustment of United States adopted adolescents and their nonadopted siblings. *Child Development, 69,* 791–802.

Shea, J. D. (1985). Studies of cognitive development in Papua New Guinea. *International Journal of Psychology, 20,* 33–61.

Sheldon, W. H. (1954). *Atlas of man: A guide for somatotyping the adult male of all ages*. New York: Harper & Rowe.

Shepard, R. N. (1990). *Mind sights*. New York: Freeman.

Sherif, M. (1966). *In common predicament: Social psychology of intergroup conflict and cooperation.* Boston: Houghton Mifflin.

Shettleworth, S. J. (1993). Where is the comparison in comparative cognition? Alternative research programs. *Psychological Science, 4,* 179–184.

Siegel, R. K. (1990). *Intoxication*. New York: Pocket Books.

Simonton, D. K. (1988). Age and outstanding achievement: What do we know after a century of research? *Psychological Bulletin, 104,* 251–267.

Simonton, D. K. (1990). Creativity in the later years: Optimistic prospects for achievement. *The Gerontologist, 30,* 626–631.

Singer, J. L. (1981). Clinical intervention: New developments in methods and evaluation. In L. T. Benjamin, Jr. (Ed.), *The G. Stanley Hall Lecture Series* (Vol. 1). Washington, DC: American Psychological Association.

Sjostrom, L. (1980). Fat cells and body weight. In A. J. Stunkard (Ed.), *Obesity*. Philadelphia: Saunders.

Skinner, B. F. (1953). *Science and human behavior*. New York: Free Press.

Skinner, B. F. (1961, November). Teaching machines. *Scientific American,* 91–102.

Skinner, B. F. (1990). Address to the American Psychological Association convention.

Slade, P. (1984). Premenstrual emotional changes in normal women: Fact or fiction? *Journal of Psychosomatic Research, 28,* 1–7.

Slotkin, T. A. (1998). Fetal nicotine or cocaine exposure: Which one is worse? *Journal of Pharmacological and Experimental Therapeutics, 285,* 931–945.

Smith, M. L., Glass, G. V., & Miller, R. L. (1980). *The benefits of psychotherapy.* Baltimore: Johns Hopkins University Press.

Smith, P. F., (1995). Cannabis and the brain. *New Zealand Journal of Psychology, 24,* 5–12.

Smith, S. B. (1999). *Diana in search of herself: Portrait of a troubled princess*. New York: Times Books.

Smith, S. M., McIntosh, W. D., & Bazzini, D. G. (1999). Are the beautiful good in Hollywood? An investigation of the beauty-and-goodness stereotype on film. *Basic and Applied Social Psychology, 21,* 69–80.

Smith, T. W. (1998, December). American sexual behavior: Trends, socio-demographic differences, and risk behavior. National Opinion Research Center GSS Topical Report No. 25.

Snarey, J. (1987, June). A question of morality. *Psychology Today,* 6–7.

Snarey, J. R. (1985). Cross-cultural universality of social-moral development: A critical review of Kohlbergian research. *Psychological Bulletin, 97,* 202–233.

Snodgrass, S. E. (1992). Further effects of role versus gender on interpersonal sensitivity. *Journal of Personality and Social Psychology, 62,* 154–158.

Snyder, C. R. (1994). *The psychology of hope.* New York: Free Press.

Snyder, R., & Scott, J. (1972). The psychophysiology of sleep. In N. S. Greenfield & R. A. Sterbach (Eds.), *Handbook of psychophysiology.* New York: Holt, Rinehart & Winston.

Solomon, D. A., Keitner, G. I., Miller, I. W., Shea, M. T., & Keller, M. B. (1995). Course of illness and maintenance treatments for patients with bipolar disorder. *Journal of Clinical Psychiatry, 56,* 5–13.

Spanos, N. P. (1991). Hypnosis, hypnotizability, and hypnotherapy. In C. R. Snyder & D. R. Forsyth (Eds.), *Handbook of social and clinical psychology: The health perspective.* New York: Pergamon Press.

Spanos, N. P., & Coe, W. C. (1992). A social-psychological approach to hypnosis. In E. Fromm & M. R. Nash (Eds.), *Contemporary hypnosis research.* New York: Guilford.

Spence, J. T., & Helmreich, R. L. (1983). *Achievement and achievement motives: Psychological and sociological approaches.* New York: Freeman.

Sperling, G. (1960). The information available in brief visual presentations. *Psychological Monographs, 74* (Whole No. 498).

Spiegel, K., Leproult, R., & Van Cauter, E. (1999). Impact of sleep debt on metabolic and endocrine function. *Lancet, 354,* 1435–1439.

Spielberger, C., & London, P. (1982). Rage boomerangs. *American Health, 1,* 52–56.

Spitzer, R. L., Gibbon, M., Skodol, A. E., Williams, J. B. W., & First, M. B. (1989). *DSM-III-R Casebook.* Washington, DC: American Psychiatric Press.

Sprecher, S. (1989). The importance to males and females of physical attractiveness, earning potential, and expressiveness in initial attraction. *Sex Roles, 21,* 591–607.

Sroufe, L. A., Fox, N. E., & Pancake, V. R. (1983). Attachment and dependency in developmental perspective. *Child Development, 54,* 1615–1627.

Statistics Canada. (1999). *Statistical report on the health of Canadians.* Prepared by the Federal, Provincial and Territorial Advisory Committee on Population Health for the meeting of Ministers of Health, Charlottetown, PEI, September 16–17, 1999.

Stavin, R. E. (1989). Cooperative learning and student achievement. In R. E. Slavin (Ed.), *School and classroom organization.* Hillsdale, NJ: Erlbaum.

Stephens, T. (1988). Physical activity and mental health in the United States and Canada: Evidence from four population surveys. *Preventive Medicine, 17,* 35–47.

Stepp, L. S. (1996, July 2). Universal goals: Family, achievement and dreams. *International Herald Tribune,* p. 2.

Sternberg, R. J. (1985). *Beyond IQ: A triarchic theory of human intelligence.* New York: Cambridge University Press.

Sternberg, R. J. (1997). *Successful intelligence.* New York: Plume.

Sternberg, R. J. (1999). The theory of successful intelligence. *Review of General Psychology, 3,* 292–316.

Sternberg, R. J., & Wagner, R. K. (1993). The *g*-ocentric view of intelligence and job performance is wrong. *Current Directions in Psychological Science, 2,* 1–5.

Sternberg, R. J., Wagner, R. K., Williams, W. M., & Horvath, J. A. (1995). Testing common sense. *American Psychologist, 50,* 912–927.

Stone, J., Perry, Z. W., & Darley, J. M. (1997). "White men can't jump": Evidence for the perceptual confirmation of racial stereotypes following a basketball game. *Basic and Applied Social Psychology, 19*(3), 291–306.

Storms, M. D. (1983). *Development of sexual orientation.* Washington, DC: Office of Social and Ethical Responsibility, American Psychological Association.

Straus, M. A., & Gelles, R. J. (1980). *Behind closed doors: Violence in the American family.* New York: Anchor/Doubleday.

Suddath, R. L., Christison, G. W., Torrey, E. F., Casanova, M. F., & Weinberger, D. R. (1990). Anatomical abnormalities in the brains of monozygotic twins discordant for schizophrenia. *New England Journal of Medicine, 322,* 789–794.

Suomi, S. J. (1986). Anxiety-like disorders in young nonhuman primates. In R. Gettleman (Ed.), *Anxiety disorders of childhood.* New York: Guilford Press.

Suppes, P. (1982). Quoted in R. H. Ennis, Children's ability to handle Piaget's propositional logic: A conceptual critique. In S. Modgil & C. Modgil (Eds.), *Jean Piaget: Consensus and controversy.* New York: Praeger.

Swartz, J. M., Stoessel, P. W., Baxter, L. R., Jr., Martin, K. M., & Phelps, M. E. (1996). Systematic changes in cerebral glucose metabolic rate after successful behavior modification treatment of obsessive-compulsive disorder. *Archives of General Psychiatry, 53,* 109–113.

Swim, J K. (1994). Perceived versus meta-analytic effect sizes: An assessment of the accuracy of gender stereotypes. *Journal of Personality and Social Psychology, 66,* 21–36.

Symons, C. S., & Johnson, B. T. (1997). The self-reference effect in memory: A meta-analysis. *Psychological Bulletin, 121*(3), 371–394.

R-21

Tanner, J. M. (1978). *Fetus into man: Physical growth from conception to maturity*. Cambridge, MA: Harvard University Press.

Taylor, S. E. (1989). *Positive illusions*. New York: Basic Books.

Taylor, S. P., & Chermack, S. T. (1993). Alcohol, drugs and human physical aggression. *Journal of Studies on Alcohol,* Suppl. 11, 78–88.

Temoshok, L. (1992). *The Type C connection: The behavioral links to cancer and your health*. New York: Random House.

Terman, L. M. (1916). *The measurement of intelligence*. Boston: Houghton Mifflin.

Tesser, A., Forehand, R., Brody, G., & Long, N. (1989). Conflict: The role of calm and angry parent-child discussion in adolescent development. *Journal of Social and Clinical Psychology, 8,* 317–330.

Thayer, R. E. (1987). Energy, tiredness, and tension effects of a sugar snack versus moderate exercise. *Journal of Personality and Social Psychology, 52,* 119–125.

Thayer, R. E. (1993). Mood and behavior (smoking and sugar snacking) following moderate exercise: A partial test of self-regulation theory. *Personality and Individual Differences, 14,* 97–104.

Tollefson, G. D., Rampey, A. H., Beasley, C. M., & Enas, G. G. (1994). Absence of a relationship between adverse events and suicidality during pharmacotherapy for depression. *Journal of Clinical Psychopharmacology, 14*, 163–169.

Tolman, E. C., & Honzik, C. H. (1930). Introduction and removal of reward, and maze performance in rats. *University of California Publications in Psychology, 4,* 257–275.

Torrey, E. F., Miller, J., Rawlings, R., & Yolken, R. H. (1997). Seasonality of births in schizophrenia and bipolar disorder: A review of the literature. *Schizophrenia Research, 28,* 1–38.

Travis, J. (1994). Glia: The brain's other cells. *Science, 266,* 970–972.

Triandis, H. C. (1994). *Culture and social behavior*. New York: McGraw-Hill.

Triplett, N. (1898). The dynamogenic factors in pacemaking and competition. *American Journal of Psychology, 9,* 507–533.

Tronick, E. Z., Morelli, G. A., & Ivey, P. K. (1992). The Efe forager infant and toddlers pattern of social relationships: Multiple and simultaneous. *Developmental Psychology, 28,* 568–577.

True, R. M. (1949). Experimental control in hypnotic age regression states. *Science, 110,* 583–584.

Tsuang, M. T., & Faraone, S. V. (1990). *The genetics of mood disorders*. Baltimore, MD: Johns Hopkins University Press.

Tubbs, M. E. (1986). Goal setting: A meta-analytic examination of the empirical evidence. *Journal of Applied Psychology, 71,* 474–483.

Tversky, A., & Kahneman, D. (1974). Judgment under uncertainty: Heuristics and biases. *Science, 185,* 1124–1131.

United Nations. (1991). *The world's women 1970–1990: Trends and statistics*. New York: United Nations.

United Nations. (1992). *1991 demographic yearbook*. New York: United Nations.

United Nations. (1997). *Infonation*. United Nations Statistic Division. Retrieved from http://srch.un.org

Valenstein, E. S. (1986). *Great and desperate cures: The rise and decline of psychosurgery*. New York: Basic Books.

van den Boom, D. (1990). Preventive intervention and the quality of mother-infant interaction and infant exploration in irritable infants. In W. Koops, H. J. G. Soppe, J. L. van der Linden, P. C. M. Molenaar, & J. J. F. Schroots (Eds.), *Developmental psychology behind the dikes: An outline of developmental psychology research in The Netherlands*. The Netherlands: Uitgeverij Eburon. Cited in C. Hazan & P. R. Shaver (1994). Deeper into attachment theory. *Psychological Inquiry, 5,* 68–79.

Van der Hart, O., Brown, P., & Graafland, M. (1999). Trauma-induced dissociative amnesia in World War I combat soldiers. *Australian and New Zealand Journal of Psychiatry, 33,* 37–46.

Van Yperen, N. W., & Buunk, B. P. (1990). A longitudinal study of equity and satisfaction in intimate relationships. *European Journal of Social Psychology, 20,* 287–309.

Vemer, E., Coleman, M., Ganong, L. H., & Cooper, H. (1989). Marital satisfaction in remarriage: A meta-analysis. *Journal of Marriage and the Family, 51,* 713–725.

Verhaeghen, P., & Salthouse, T. A. (1997). Meta-analyses of age-cognition relations in adulthood: Estimates of linear and nonlinear age effects and structural models. *Psychological Bulletin, 122,* 231–249.

Vincelli, F., & Molinari, E. (1998). Virtual reality and imaginative techniques in clinical psychology. In G. Riva, B. K. Wiederhold, & E.Molinari (Eds.), *Virtual environments in clinical psychology and neuroscience: Methods and techniques in advanced patient-therapist interaction*. Amsterdam: IOS Press.

Vita, A. J., Terry, R. B., Hubert, H. B., & Fries, J. F. (1998). Aging, health risks, and cumulative disability. *New England Journal of Medicine, 338,* 1035–1041.

Wachs, T. D. (1999). Celebrating complexity: Conceptualization and assessment of the environment. In S. Friedman & T. D. Wachs (Eds.), *Measuring environment across the life-span: Emerging methods and concepts*. Washington, DC: American Psychological Association.

Waddington, J. L. (1993). Neurodynamics of abnormalities in cerebral metabolism and structure in schizophrenia. *Schizophrenia Bulletin, 19*, 55–69.

Wade, N. (1999, September 23). Largest chromosome has 250 million nucleotides while the smallest has 50 million. *New York Times.* Retrieved from http://www.nytimes.com

Wagstaff, G. (1982). Attitudes to rape: The "just world" strikes again? *Bulletin of the British Psychological Society, 13,* 275–283.

R-22

Wahlbeck, K., Cheine, M., Essali, A., & Adams, C. (1999). Evidence of clozapine's effectiveness in schizophrenia: A systematic review and meta-analysis of randomized trials. *American Journal of Psychiatry, 156,* 990–999.

Wallace, D. S., Lord, C. G., & Bond, C. F., Jr. (1996). Which behaviors do attitudes predict? Review and meta-analysis of 60 years' research. Unpublished manuscript, Ohio University.

Walster (Hatfield), E., Aronson, V., Abrahams, D., & Rottman, L. (1966). Importance of physical attractiveness in dating behavior. *Journal of Personality and Social Psychology, 4,* 508–516.

Warr, P., & Payne, R. (1982). Experiences of strain and pleasure among British adults. *Social Science and Medicine, 16,* 1691–1697.

Watson, J. B. (1913). Psychology as the behaviorist views it. *Psychological Review, 20,* 158–177.

Watson, J. B., & Rayner, R. (1920). Conditioned emotional reactions. *Journal of Experimental Psychology, 3,* 1–14.

Wayment, H. A., & Peplau, L. A. (1995). Social support and well-being among lesbian and heterosexual women: A structural modeling approach. *Personality and Social Psychology Bulletin, 21,* 1189–1199.

Webb, W. B. (1982). Some theories about sleep and their clinical applications. *Psychiatric Annals, 11,* 415–422.

Webb, W. B. (1992). *Sleep: The gentle tyrant.* Bolton, MA: Ankler Publishing.

Weingartner, H., Rudorfer, M. V., Buchsbaum, M. S., & Linnoila, M. (1983). Effects of serotonin on memory impairments produced by ethanol. *Science, 221,* 472–473.

Weinstein, N. D. (1980). Unrealistic optimism about future life events. *Journal of Personality and Social Psychology, 39,* 806–820.

Weinstein, N. D. (1982). Unrealistic optimism about susceptibility to health problems. *Journal of Behavioral Medicine, 5,* 441–460.

Weinstein, N. D. (1996, October 4). 1996 optimistic bias bibliography (weinstein_c@aesop.rutgers.edu).

Weiss, J. M. (1977). Psychological and behavioral influences on gastrointestinal lesions in animal models. In J. D. Maser & M. E. P. Seligman (Eds.), *Psychopathology: Experimental models.* San Francisco: Freeman.

Weissman, M. M. (1999). Interpersonal psychotherapy and the health care scene. In D. S. Janowsky (Ed.), *Psychotherapy indications and outcomes.* Washington, DC: American Psychiatric Press.

Westen, D. (1996). Is Freud really dead? Teaching psychodynamic theory to introductory psychology. Presentation to the Annual Institute on the Teaching of Psychology, St. Petersburg Beach, Florida.

Wetter, D. W., Fiore, M. C., Gritz, E. R., Lando, H. A., Stitzer, M. L., Hasselblad, V., & Baker, T. B. (1998). The Agency for Health Care Policy and Research. Smoking cessation clinical practice guideline: Findings and implications for psychologists. *American Psychologist, 53,* 657–669.

Whitam, F. L., Diamond, M., & Martin, J. (1993). Homosexual orientation in twins: A report on 61 pairs and three triplet sets. *Archives of Sexual Behavior, 22,* 187–206.

White, G. L., & Kight, T. D. (1984). Misattribution of arousal and attraction: Effects of salience of explanations for arousal. *Journal of Experimental Social Psychology, 20,* 55–64.

White, H. R., Brick, J., & Hansell, S. (1993). A longitudinal investigation of alcohol use and aggression in adolescence. *Journal of Studies on Alcohol,* Suppl. 11, 62–77.

White, L., & Edwards, J. (1990). Emptying the nest and parental well-being: An analysis of national panel data. *American Sociological Review, 55,* 235–242.

Whitley, B. E., Jr. (1999). Right-wing authoritarianism, social dominance orientation, and prejudice. *Journal of Personality and Social Psychology, 77,* 126–134.

Whorf, B. L. (1956). Science and linguistics. In J. B. Carroll (Ed.), *Language, thought, and reality: Selected writings of Benjamin Lee Whorf.* Cambridge, MA: MIT Press.

Wicker, A. W. (1971). An examination of the "other variables" explanation of attitude-behavior inconsistency. *Journal of Personality and Social Psychology, 19,* 18–30.

Wiens, A. N., & Menustik, C. E. (1983). Treatment outcome and patient characteristics in an aversion therapy program for alcoholism. *American Psychologist, 38,* 1089–1096.

Wiggins, J. S. (1984). Cattell's system from the perspective of mainstream personality theory. *Multivariate Behavioral Research, 19,* 176–190.

Wiggins, J. S. (1996). *The five-factor model of personality: Theoretical perspectives.* New York: Guilford Press.

Williams, L. M. (June, 1995). Recall of childhood trauma: A prospective study of women's memories of child sexual abuse: Correction. *Journal of Consulting and Clinical Psychology, 63* (3).

Williams, R. (1989). *The trusting heart: Great news about Type A behavior.* New York: Random House.

Williams, R. (1993). *Anger kills.* New York: Times Books.

Williams, S. L. (1987). Self-efficacy and mastery-oriented treatment for severe phobias. Paper presented to the American Psychological Association convention.

Wolpe, J. (1958). *Psychotherapy by reciprocal inhibition.* Stanford, CA: Stanford University Press.

Wolpe, J., & Plaud, J. J. (1997). Pavlov's contribution to behavior therapy: The obvious and the not so obvious. *American Psychologist, 52,* 966–972.

Wood, W., Rhodes, N., & Whelan, M. (1989). Sex differences in positive well-being: A consideration of emotional style and marital status. *Psychological Bulletin, 106,* 249–264.

Woods, N. F., Dery, G. K., & Most, A. (1983). Recollections of menarche, current menstrual attitudes, and premenstrual

R-23

symptoms. In S. Golub (Ed.), *Menarche: The transition from girl to woman*. Lexington, MA: Lexington Books.

Wooley, S., & Wooley, O. (1983). Should obesity be treated at all? *Psychiatric Annals, 13*(11), 884–885, 888.

Worthington, E. L., Jr. (1989). Religious faith across the life span: Implications for counseling and research. *The Counseling Psychologist, 17,* 555–612.

Wortman, C. B., & Silver, R. C. (1989). The myths of coping with loss. *Journal of Consulting and Clinical Psychology, 57,* 349–357.

Wright, W. (1998). *Born that way: Genes, behavior, personality*. New York: Knopf.

Wu, T-C., Tashkin, D. P., Djahed, B., & Rose, J. E. (1988). Pulmonary hazards of smoking marijuana as compared with tobacco. *New England Journal of Medicine, 318,* 347–351.

Wulsin, L. R., Vaillant, G. E., & Wells, V. E. (1999). A systematic review of the mortality of depression. *Psychosomatic Medicine, 61,* 6–17.

Wynn, K. (1992). Addition and subtraction by human infants. *Nature, 358,* 749–759.

Wynn, K. (1998). Psychological foundations of number: Numerical competence in human infants. *Trends in Cognitive Science, 2,* 296–303.

Yalom, I. D. (1985). *The theory and practice of group psychotherapy* (3rd ed.). New York: Basic Books.

Yang, K. S. (1982). Causal attributions of academic success and failure and their affective consequences. *Chinese Journal of Psychology* [Taiwan], *24,* 65–83. (Only the abstract is in English.)

Yarnell, P. R., & Lynch, S. (1970). Retrograde memory immediately after concussion. *Lancet, 1,* 863–864.

Yarrow, L. J., Goodwin, M. S., Manheimer, H., & Milowe, I. D. (1973). Infancy experience and cognitive and personality development at ten years. In L. J. Stone, H. T. Smith, & L. B. Murphy (Eds.), *The competent infant*. New York: Basic Books.

Zajonc, R. B. (1965). Social facilitation. *Science, 149,* 269–274.

Zajonc, R. B. (1980). Feeling and thinking: Preferences need no interferences. *American Psychologist, 35,* 151–175.

Zajonc, R. B. (1984). On the primacy of affect. *American Psychologist, 39,* 117–123.

Zajonc, R. B. (1998). Emotions. In D. Gilbert, S. T. Fiske, & G. Lindzey (Eds.), *Handbook of social psychology* (4th ed). New York: McGraw-Hill.

Zeidner, M. (1990). Perceptions of ethnic group modal intelligence: Reflections of cultural stereotypes or intelligence test scores? *Journal of Cross-Cultural Psychology, 21,* 214–231.

Zimbardo, P. G. (1972, April). Pathology of imprisonment. *Transaction/Society,* 4–8.

Zucker, G. S., & Weiner, B. (1993). Conservatism and perceptions of poverty: An attributional analysis. *Journal of Applied Social Psychology, 23,* 925–943.

R-24

Illustration Credits

Domain Opener Images

p. xxvi Anonymous (15th Century) drawing illustrating pre-Cartesian brain theories: Bayerische Staatsbibliothek, Munich; **p. 54** Detail from Leonardo da Vinci, "The Babe in the Womb," c. 1510–1512: The Royal Collection © 2003, Her Majesty Queen Elizabeth II; **p. 118** From René Descartes, "Vision and Visual Perception," 1677: Courtesy of the National Library of Medicine; **p. 278** Leonardo da Vinci, "Head of a Woman," c. 1472–75: Scala/Art Resource, NY; **p. 476** Oval World Map, 1570: Corbis.

Chapter Opener Photos

Chapter 1 (pp. viii, 1, 2) Tim Matsui/IPN/Aurora; **Chapter 2 (pp. ix, 55, 56)**, Francisco Cruz/SuperStock; **Chapter 3 (pp. ix, 119, 120)** Adam Smith/SuperStock; **Chapter 4 (pp. x, 119, 156)** Tom Stewart/Corbis; **Chapter 5 (pp. x, 119, 206)** Reuters NewMedia Inc./Corbis; **Chapter 6 (pp. xi, 119, 243)** Steve Casimiro/Getty Images; **Chapter 7 (pp. xi, 279, 280)** David Zickl/SuperStock; **Chapter 8 (pp. xii, 279, 333)** Soriano/Bilderberg/Aurora; **Chapter 9 (pp. xii, 279, 376)** David McLain/Aurora; **Chapter 10 (pp. xiii, 279, 429)** Zigy Kaluzny/Getty Images; **Chapter 11 (pp. xiii, 477, 478)** LWA-Dann Tardif/Corbis; **Chapter 12 (pp. xiv, 477, 517)** Laurent/Yakou/BSIP/Science Source/Photo Researchers, Inc.; **Chapter 13 (pp. xiv, 477, 572)** Alvis Upitis/Brand X Pictures/PictureQuest; **Chapter 14 (pp. xv, 477, 612)** Jacques Jangoux/Getty Images.

Module 1

p. 4 *(top left)* Kevin Radford/SuperStock; *(top right)* Esbin-Anderson/The Image Works; *(bottom left)* Ellen Senisi; *(bottom right)* V.C.L./Getty Images; **p. 7** Left to right by row: *(row 1)* Corbis; Corbis; Archives of the History of American Psychology, The University of Akron; Corbis; *(row 2)* Stock Montage; Wellesley College Archives; National Library of Medicine; Sovfoto; *(row 3)* Archives of the History of American Psychology, The University of Akron; Archives of the History of American Psychology, The University of Akron; Archives of the History of American Psychology, The University of Akron; Yves Debraine/Stockphoto.com; *(row 4)* Archives of the History of American Psychology, The University of Akron; Yvonne Hemsey/The Gamma Liaison Network/Getty News Images; Archives of the History of American Psychology, The University of Akron; Corbis; *(row 5)* Courtesy of Brandeis University; Archives of the History of American Psychology, The University of Akron; Courtesy of Albert Bandura, Stanford University; Corbis; *(row 6)* Courtesy of the Archives, California Institute of Technology; Russell Fernald, Courtesy of the Stanford University News Service; Courtesy of Sandra Bem; Chet Snedden/American Airlines Corporate Communications; **p. 14** Michael Newman/PhotoEdit Inc.

Module 2

p. 17 *(top left)* Jeff Greenberg/PhotoEdit Inc.; *(top right)* Alex Farnsworth/The Image Works; *(bottom)* Richard T. Nowitz/Photo Researchers, Inc.; **pp. 18, 19, 20** Charles Blair-Broeker.

Module 3

p. 39 Nick Clements/FPG/Getty Images; **p. 42** Pat Miller/Stockphoto.com; **p. 43** Mary Kate Denny/PhotoEdit, Inc.; **p. 44** David Young-Wolff/PhotoEdit, Inc.; **p. 46** Lawrence Migdale/Stock Boston; **p. 47** Bob Daemmrich/The Image Works; **p. 49** Lester Sloan/Woodfin Camp & Associates.

Module 4

p. 58 *(top)* Kwame Zikomo/SuperStock; *(bottom)* Petit Format/Science Source/Photo Researchers, Inc.; **p. 59** David Young-Wolff/PhotoEdit, Inc.; **p. 60** *(left)* Petit Format/Photo Researchers, Inc.; *(right)* Flash! Light!/Stock, Boston; **p. 61** Adapted from Conel, J. L. (1939–1963). *The postnatal development of the human cerebral cortex* (Vols. I–VI). Reprinted by permission. **p. 65** Bill Anderson/Photo Researchers, Inc.; **p. 69** Kathy McLaughlin/The Image Works; **p. 70** Harlow Primate Laboratory, University of Wisconsin.

Module 5

p. 81 Ariel Skelley/Corbis; **p. 82** *(left)* Elizabeth Holmes/Omni-Photo Communications; *(middle)* Monika Graff/The Image Works; *(right)* Andrew Garn/TimePix; **p. 83** J. Gerard Smith; **p. 85** David Young-Wolff/PhotoEdit; **p. 89** *(top)* David Young-Wolff/PhotoEdit, Inc.; *(bottom)* Andre Gallant/Getty Images; **p. 90** *(left)* David Vance/ The Image Bank; **p. 90** *(right)* David Delossy/The Image Bank; **p. 91** Jeff Greenberg/PhotoEdit, Inc.

Module 6

p. 99 *(left)* Mark Scott/Taxi/Getty Images; **p. 103** *(left)* David Young-Wolff/PhotoEdit, Inc.; *(right)* Tom McCarthy/Picture Cube; **p. 106** *(both)* Ken and Mary Pargett; **p. 108** Scott Barrow/International Stock/ImageState, Inc.; **p. 109** Blair Seltz/Photo Researchers, Inc.; **p. 111** Ken and Mary Pargett; **p. 112** C. Ampanie/The Image Works.

Module 7

p. 122 David Young-Wolff/PhotoEdit, Inc.

Module 8

p. 139 Kes Gilhome/AP/Wide World Photos; **p. 144** Christophe Ena/AP/Wide World Photos; **p. 145** Pix*ELATION from Fran Heyl Associates; **p. 146** Martin M. Rotker; **p. 148** Rob van Nostrand; **p. 150** Hanna Damasio, M.D. University of Iowa and

I-1

Science; p. 151 *(top row, left to right)* Mark Thomas/SPL/Photo Researchers, Inc.; Stephen McBrady/PhotoEdit, Inc.; Michael Rosenfeld/Stone/Getty Images; CC Studio/Science Photo Library/ Photo Researchers, Inc.; *(bottom row, left to right)* Alfred Pasieka/ Science Photo Library/Photo Researchers, Inc.; Pix*ELATION from Fran Heyl Associates; Science Photo Library/Photo Researchers, Inc.; Wellcome Department of Cognitive Neurology/ Science Photo Library/Photo Researchers, Inc.

Module 9
p. 158 *(top)* Adapted from Stanley Coren, Lawrence M. Ward, & James T. Enns. *Sensation and perception,* 5th ed. Copyright © 1999 by Harcourt, Brace, and Company. Reprinted by permission. *(bottom)* Michel Viard/Peter Arnold, Inc.; p. 159 Carol Lee/Stone/ Getty Images; p. 160 John Berry/The Image Works; p. 167 Fritz Goro, LIFE Magazine ©1971 Time Warner, Inc.; p. 168 David Young-Wolff/PhotoEdit, Inc.; p. 172 Robert Preston & Joseph E. Hawkins, Kresge Hearing Research Institute, University of Michigan; p. 174 Bob Krist/Corbis; p. 176 *(both)* David Willey; p. 177 Brian Bahr/Getty Images.

Module 10
p. 185 From Roger Shepard, *Mindsights.* Copyright © 1990 by W. H. Freeman. Used by permission of Henry Holt. p. 187 *(top)* Enrico Ferorelli; *(bottom)* Elizabeth Crews; p. 189 Rudi Von Briel/PhotoEdit, Inc.; p. 190 Mitch Wojnarowicz/The Image Works; p. 191 Jean-Marc Giboux/Getty Images; p. 192 *(top)* Jean-Marc Giboux/Getty Images; *(bottom)* Rainer Grosskopf/ Stone/Getty Images; p. 194 Pete Turner/The Image Bank/Getty Images; p. 196 *(top)* Kjell B. Sandved/Photo Researchers, Inc.; *(bottom)* Marc Carter/Stone/Getty Images; p. 197 Andrew Brilliant; p. 200 *(top photos)* Richard T. Nowitz/Photo Researchers, Inc.; *(bottom)*Adapted from G. Kanizsa (1955), Margini quasi-percettivi in campi con stimolazione omogenea in *Revista di Psychologia, 49,* 7–30. p. 201 *(top)* From Hoffman, D. & Richards, W. (1984). Parts of recognition. *Cognition,* 63, 29–78. Reprinted by permission of Elsevier Science-NL, Sara Burgerhartstraat 25, 1055 KV Amsterdam, The Netherlands. *(middle)* From Ramachandran, V. S. (1988). Perceiving shape from shading. *Scientific American.* Copyright © 1988 by Scientific American Inc. Photo © George V. Kelvin. All rights reserved.

Module 11
p. 207 Mark Ludak/The Image Works; p. 208 *(left)* Frank Siteman/ PhotoEdit, Inc.; *(right)* C/B Productions/Corbis; p. 212 Mary Kate Denny/PhotoEdit, Inc.; p. 213 Ann Kaplan/Corbis; p. 214 From McClelland, D. C., et al. (1953). *The achievement motive.* New York: Appleton-Century Crofts. Reprinted by permission of Irvington Publishers, New York; p. 217 *(left)* David Young-Wolff/ PhotoEdit, Inc.; *(middle)* Tony Anderson/Taxi/Getty Images; *(right)* David Young-Wolff/PhotoEdit, Inc.; p. 218 Pix*ELATION from Fran Heyl Associates; p. 219 Richard Howard; p. 220 Lara Jo Regan/The Gamma Liaison Network/Getty News Images; p. 221 Bill Aron/PhotoEdit, Inc.

Module 12
p. 226 Spencer Grant/PhotoEdit, Inc.; p. 228 *(left)* Science Photo Library/ Photo Researchers, Inc.; *(right)* The Royal Library, Denmark; p. 230 Courtesy of Columbia University, Office of Public Affairs; p. 234 John Boykin/Stock Connection/ PictureQuest; p. 236 Richard Lord/PhotoEdit, Inc.; p. 238 *(all)* Ekman & Matsumoto, Japanese and Caucasian Facial Expressions of Emotions.

Module 13
p. 245 *(top)* Michael Siluk/Index Stock Imagery/PictureQuest; *(bottom)* Lon C. Diehl/PhotoEdit, Inc.; p. 247 Sergei Grits/AP/ Wide World Photos; p. 249 Jack Kurtz/The Image Works; p. 251 Lennart Nilsson/Boehringer Ingelheim International GmbH.

Module 14
p. 259 Jeff Greenberg/The Image Works; p. 260 Larry Dale Gordon/The Image Bank/Getty Images; p. 262 Todd Bigelow/ Aurora; p. 264 Peter Hvizdak/The Image Works; p. 269 Paul J. Milette/Palm Beach Post; p. 271 *(left)* Felicia Martinez/ PhotoEdit, Inc.; *(right)* SuperStock; p. 272 Science Photo Library/Photo Researchers, Inc.

Module 15
p. 286 Sovfoto; p. 290 *(top)* Mike Agliolo/SuperStock; *(bottom)* Brown Brothers; p. 292 Ron Chapple/Thinkstock/PictureQuest; p. 293 Courtesy of John Garcia; p. 294 Dean Conger/Corbis.

Module 16
p. 302 Charlotte van Oyen Witvliet; p. 304 *(top)* Richard Wood/ The Picture Cube; *(bottom)* Sam Falk; p. 305 Bernard Hoffman/ TimePix; p. 309 Bob Daemmrich/Stock, Boston; p. 310 Marc Romanelli/The Image Bank/Getty Images; p. 311 Jeff Greenberg/ Stock, Boston; p. 315 Bob Daemmrich/Stock, Boston; p. 316 Will and Deni McIntyre/Photo Researchers; p. 318 *(top)* Lionel Cironneau/AP/Wide World Photos; *(bottom)* David Young-Wolff/ PhotoEdit, Inc.

Module 17
p. 326 *(top)* Margot Granitsas/The Image Works; *(bottom)* Courtesy of Albert Bandura, Stanford University; p. 327 Courtesy of Albert Bandura, Stanford University; p. 328 Suzanne Plunkett/AP/Wide World Photos; p. 329 *(top)* George P. Widman/AP/Wide World Photos; *(bottom)* Bob Daemmrich/The Image Works.

Module 18
p. 337 *(left)* Mug Shots/Corbis; p. 338 Frank Siteman/Stock, Boston p. 340 Robert Clark/Aurora; p. 346 R. J. Erwin/Photo Researchers, Inc.; p. 347 From: N. Toni et al., *Nature,* Volume 402, November 25, 1999. Courtesy of Dominique Muller; p. 348 Rhoda Sidney/Stock, Boston; p. 350 *(left)* Courtesy Randal Ernst; *(right)* Courtesy Charles Blair-Broeker.

Module 19
p. 362 Charles Gupton/Corbis; p. 367 Courtesy of Elizabeth Loftus, University of California, Irvine; p. 369 Laura Dwight/ PhotoEdit, Inc.; p. 370 Sean Roberts/The Everett Collection.

Module 20
p. 377 Ellen Senisi/The Image Works; p. 383 Pix*ELATION from Fran Heyl Associates; p. 384 Hank Morgan/ Rainbow; p. 388 *(top)* Marc Chagall, "I and the Village." 1911. Oil on canvas, 6' 3 ⅝" × 59 ⅝" (192.1 × 151.4 cm). The Museum of Modern Art, New York. Mrs. Simon Guggenheim Fund. Photograph ©1997 The Museum of Modern Art, New York; *(bottom photos)* David Falconer/Folio, Inc.; p. 390 Ann and Rob Simpson.

I-2

Module 21
p. 396 *(left)* AP/Wide World Photos; p. 398 Courtesy of the late Ernest Hilgard, Photo News and Publications Service, Stanford University; p. 400 Rachel Epstein/PhotoEdit, Inc.; p. 401 AP/Wide World Photos; p. 402 AP/Wide World Photos; p. 403 AP/Wide World Photos.

Module 22
p. 413 George Hipple/AP/Wide World Photos; p. 414 Table 22.1 from the National Institute on Alcohol Abuse and Alcoholism; p. 416 Peter Cade/Stone/Getty Images; p. 417 Charles Blair-Broeker; p. 418 A. Glauberman/Science Source/ Photo Researchers, Inc.; p. 420 Greg Smith/AP/Wide World Photos.

Module 23
p. 431 The Everett Collection p. 432 *(left)* Rob Melnychuk/Taxi/ Getty Images; *(right)* Monica Lau/PhotoDisc/Getty Images; p. 434 Bruce Forster/Stone/Getty Images; p. 435 © Tribune Media Services, Inc. All rights reserved. Reprinted with permission; p. 437 Bob Daemmrich/The Image Works; p. 439 Tami Chappell/Reuters/TimePix; p. 441 *(left)* Pete Saloutos/Corbis; *(right)* Paul Conklin/PhotoEdit, Inc.; p. 448 Archives of the History of American Psychology, Winthrop N. Kellogg Collection; p. 449 Rachel Epstein/PhotoEdit, Inc.

Module 24
p. 455 Mary Kate Denny/PhotoEdit, Inc.; p. 458 *(left)* Courtesy of Dr. Robert Sternberg; *(right)* John Chase/Harvard News Office, © 2001 President and Fellows of Harvard College; p. 459 *(left)* National Library of Medicine; *(middle)* News Service, Stanford University; *(right)* Archives of the History of American Psychology, David Wechsler Collection; p. 460 Omni Photo Communications, Inc./Index Stock Imagery; p. 463 Lew Merrim; p. 464 AP/Wide World Photos; p. 465 AP/Wide World Photos; p. 466 *(top)* Spencer Grant/PhotoEdit, Inc.; *(bottom left)* Spencer Grant/PhotoEdit, Inc.; *(bottom right)* Ariel Skelley/Corbis; p. 470 Jeff Greenberg/The Image Works.

Module 25
p. 479 Bettmann/Corbis; p. 480 Mary Evans/Sigmund Freud Copyrights; p. 486 *(top)* Bettmann/Corbis; *(bottom)* Dmitri Kessel/TimePix; p. 487 (top) Bettmann/Corbis; *(bottom)* Lewis J. Merrim/Photo Researchers, Inc.; p. 488 Palmer and Brilliant/ Index Stock Imagery; p. 490 Bettmann/Corbis; p. 491 Bettmann/Corbis; p. 492 Hazel Hankin/Stock, Boston.

Module 26
p. 500 *(top left)* Frank Siteman/PhotoEdit, Inc.; *(top right)* V.C.L./ Taxi/Getty Images; *(middle left)* Corbis; *(middle right)* Walter Smith/Corbis; *(bottom)* Bettmann/Corbis; p. 505 Jon Brenneis/ TimePix; p. 507 Robin Sachs/PhotoEdit, Inc.; p. 509 Michael Wickes/The Image Works; p. 510 Courtesy of Dr. Martin Seligman, University of Pennsylvania.

Module 27
p. 520 Hans Deryk/AP/Wide World Photos; p. 521 Bettmann/Corbis; p. 524 Reprinted with permission from *Diagnostic and Statistical Manual of Mental Disorders,* Fourth Edition, Text Revision. Copyright © 2000 by the American Psychiatric Association. p. 525 Owen Franken/Stock, Boston.

Module 28
p. 534 Bob Daemmrich/The Image Works; p. 538 The Everett Collection; p. 540 Norbert Schafer/Corbis; p. 541 *(top left)* From Baxter, L. R., et al. (1987). Local cerebral glucose metabolic rates in obsessive-compulsive disorder. *Archives of General Psychology,* 44(3), 211–218. Copyright © 1987 American Medical Association; *(top right)* NIH/SPL/Custom Medical Stock Photo; p. 541 *(bottom right)* Owen Franken/Corbis; p. 542 AFP/Corbis; p. 544 Cleve Bryant/ PhotoEdit, Inc.; p. 546 Burstein Collection/Corbis; p. 547 *(all)* Courtesy of Drs. Lewis Baxter and Michael E. Phelps, UCLA School of Medicine; p. 548 Jaime Puebla/AP/Wide World Photos.

Module 29
p. 556 Scott Nelson/Getty Images; p. 557 *(top)* John Springer Collection/Corbis; *(bottom)* The Everett Collection; p. 559 Bill Varie/Corbis; p. 561 Universal Studios/Dreamworks/Topham/The Image Works; p. 564 *(top)* Courtesy of Genain family; *(bottom left and right)* From Suddath, Richard L., et al. (1990). Anatomical abnormalities in the brains of monozygotic twins discordant for schizophrenia. *The New England Journal of Medicine,* 322, 12. © 1990 by the Massachusetts Medical Society. Photo courtesy of Daniel R. Weinberger, M.D., NIH-NIMH/NSC; p. 567 Courtesy of Adrian Raine, University of Southern California.

Module 30
p. 573 Keystone/The Image Works; p. 576 Richard Nowitz/ Photo Researchers, Inc.; p. 578 Michael Rougier/TimePix; p. 581 *(both)* Bob Mahoney/The Image Works; p. 587 Bob Daemmrich/ Stock, Boston/PictureQuest; p. 592 Robert F. Bukaty/AP/Wide World Photos.

Module 31
p. 598 *(both)* The Everett Collection; p. 599 *(top)* The Bettmann Archive; *(bottom)* Jerry Cooke/Photo Researchers, Inc.; p. 600 Lee Snider/The Image Works; p. 601 Lynn Johnson/Stockphoto.com; p. 602 Guy Wathen, POOL/AP/Wide World Photos; p. 605 Will McIntyre/Photo Researchers, Inc.; p. 607 Bettmann/Corbis.

Module 32
p. 613 Michael Newman/PhotoEdit, Inc.; p. 615 Reuters NewMedia/Corbis; p. 619 Philip G. Zimbardo, Ph.D., Stanford University; p. 620 Bettmann/Corbis; p. 621 *(top)* Archives of the History of American Psychology, The University of Akron; *(bottom)* William Vandivert/*Scientific American;* p. 623 *(both)* © 1965 by Stanley Milgram. From the film *Obedience,* distributed by Penn State Media Sales; p. 624 Courtesy of CUNY Graduate School and University Center; p. 627 Rhoda Sidney/Stock Boston; p. 630 Bettmann/Corbis.

Module 33
p. 636 David Young-Wolff/PhotoEdit, Inc.; p. 637 *(left)* Hulton-Deutsch Collection/Corbis; *(middle)* Bettmann/Corbis; *(right)* AFP/Corbis; p. 638 Michael Newman/PhotoEdit, Inc.; p. 639 SIE Productions/Corbis; p. 640 *(top)* AP/Wide World Photos; *(bottom left)* The New York Times; *(bottom right)* Edward Hausner/The New York Times; p. 644 *(top)* Vicky Kasala/Getty Images; *(middle)* A. Ramey/PhotoEdit, Inc.; *(bottom left)* Tony Freeman/PhotoEdit, Inc.; *(bottom middle)* Bob Mitchell/Corbis; *(bottom right)* John Boykin/PhotoEdit, Inc.; p. 649 David Young-Wolff/PhotoEdit, Inc.; p. 650 Phil Martin/PhotoEdit, Inc.; p. 651 Al Campanie/Syracuse Newspapers/The Image Works.

I-3

Module 34

p. 656 *(left)* Syracuse Newspapers/The Image Works; *(right)* Phil Cantor/Index Stock Imagery; p. 658 *(left)* Robert Caputo/IPN/Aurora; *(middle)* B & C Alexander/Photo Researchers, Inc.; *(right)* B.S.P.I./Corbis; p. 659 B.S.P.I./Corbis; p. 660 Brian Yarvin/The Image Works; p. 661 *(left)* David Pollack/Corbis; *(middle left)* Bill Lai/Index Stock Imagery; *(middle right)* Jose Luis Pelaez, Inc./Corbis; *(right)* Ron Edmonds/AP/Wide World Photos; p. 663 Ed Kashi/Corbis; p. 667 *(top)* Spencer Grant/PhotoEdit, Inc.; *(bottom)* Michael Newman/PhotoEdit, Inc.

Appendix

p. A-1 Ronnen Eshel/Corbis; p. A-10 Bob Daemmrich/Stock, Boston.

I-4

Name Index

NI-1

D

E

F

G

H

I

J

K

L

M

N

O

P

Q

R

S

T

U

V

W

NI-6

Y

Z

NI-7

Subject Index

References followed by italic *t* indicate material in tables.

A

SI-1

B

C

D

E

F

G

H

I

J

K

L

SI-9

M

O

P

Q

R

S

SI-15

U

V

W

Y

Z